World Band Radio

W9-DJC-626

International Broadcasting Services, Ltd.

ISSN 0897-0157

OUR READER IS THE MOST IMPORTANT PERSON IN THE WORLD!

Editorial

Editor-in-Chief	Lawrence Magne
Editor	Tony Jones
Contributing Editors	Jock Elliott (U.S.), Craig Tyson (Australia), George Zeller (U.S.)
Consulting Editor	John Campbell (England)
Founder Emeritus	Don Jensen (U.S.)
WorldScan® Contributors	Gabriel Iván Barrera (Argentina), James Conrad (U.S.), Alok Dasgupta (India), Graeme Dixon (New Zealand), Nicolás Eramo (Argentina), Manosij Guha (India), *Jembatan DX*/Juichi Yamada (Japan), Anatoly Klepov (Russia), Marie Lamb (U.S.), *Número Uno*/Jerry Berg (U.S.), Toshimichi Ohtake (Japan), *Radio Nuevo Mundo* (Japan), *Relámpago DX*/Takayuki Inoue Nozaki (Japan), Henrik Klemetz (Colombia), Nikolai Rudnev (Russia), Don Swampo (Uruguay), David Walcutt (U.S.)
WorldScan® Software	Richard Mayell
Laboratory	Sherwood Engineering Inc.
Artwork	Gahan Wilson, cover
Graphic Arts	Bad Cat Design; Mike Wright, layout
Printing	World Color Press

Administration

Publisher	Lawrence Magne
Associate Publisher	Jane Brinker
Advertising & Distribution	Mary Kroszner, MWK
Offices	IBS North America, Box 300, Penn's Park PA 18943, USA; www.passport.com
	Advertising & Distribution: Phone +1 (215) 794-3410; Fax +1 (215) 794 3396; mwk@passport.com
	Editorial: Fax +1 (215) 598 3794
	Orders (24 hours): Phone +1 (215) 794-8252; Fax +1 (215) 794 3396; mwk@passport.com; www.passport.com
Media Communications	Jock Elliott, Lightkeeper Communications, 29 Pickering Lane, Troy NY 12180, USA; Fax +1 (518) 271 6131; media@passport.com

Bureaus

IBS Latin America	Tony Jones, Casilla 1844, Asunción, Paraguay; schedules@passport.com; Fax +1 (215) 598 3794
IBS Australia	Craig Tyson, Box 2145, Malaga WA 6062; Fax +61 (8) 9342 9158; addresses@passport.com
IBS Japan	Toshimichi Ohtake, 5-31-6 Tamanawa, Kamakura 247; Fax +81 (467) 43 2167; ibsjapan@passport.com

Library of Congress Cataloging-in-Publication Data

Passport to World Band Radio.
1. Radio Stations, Shortwave—Directories. I. Magne, Lawrence
TK9956.P27 1998 384.54'5 98-22739
ISBN 0-914941-48-8

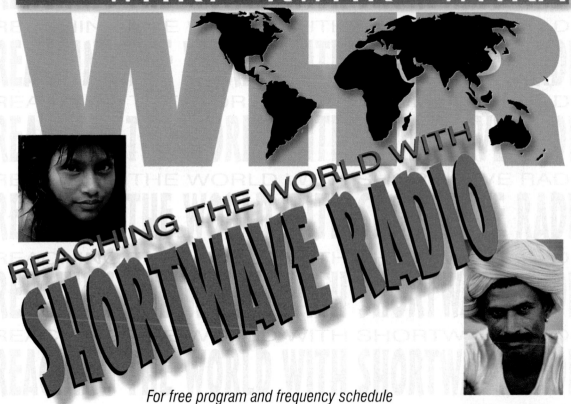

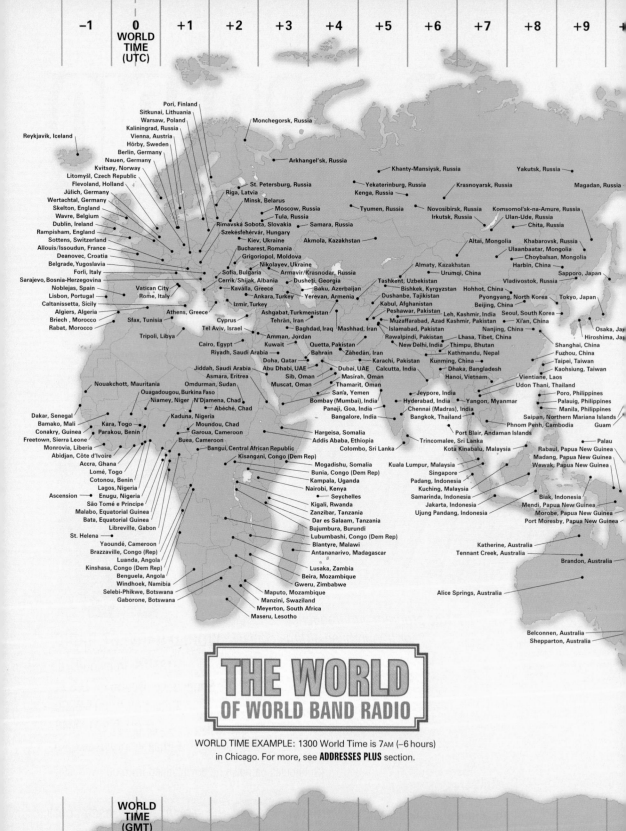

THE WORLD
OF WORLD BAND RADIO

WORLD TIME EXAMPLE: 1300 World Time is 7AM (–6 hours) in Chicago. For more, see **ADDRESSES PLUS** section.

−11 | +12 | −11 | −10 | −9 | −8 | −7 | −6 | −5 | −4 | −3 | −2

Anchor Point, Alaska, USA
Palana, Russia
Petropavlovsk-Kamchatskiy, Russia

Calgary AB, Canada
Vancouver BC, Canada

Toronto ON, Canada
Montréal PQ, Canada
Monticello ME, USA
Greenbush ME, USA
Sackville NB, Canada
St. John's NF, Canada
Halifax NS, Canada
Noblesville IN, USA
Bethel PA, USA
Red Lion PA, USA

Salt Lake City UT, USA
Boulder CO, USA
Delano CA, USA
Rancho Simi CA, USA
Dallas TX, USA
Mesquite NM, USA

Upton KY, USA
Nashville TN, USA
McCaysville GA, USA
Greenville NC, USA
Cypress Creek SC, USA
Macon GA, USA
Birmingham AL, USA
New Orleans LA, USA
Okeechobee FL, USA
Miami FL, USA
Havana, Cuba

Hermosillo, Mexico

Santo Domingo, Dominican Republic
Anguilla
Antigua

ekaha, Kauai Island, Hawai'i, USA

Naalehu, "Big Island," Hawai'i, USA

Linares, Mexico
Mérida, Mexico
México City, Mexico
Veracruz, Mexico
Puerto Cabezas, Nicaragua
Guatemala City, Guatemala
Tegucigalpa, Honduras
San José, Costa Rica
Santa Fé de Bogotá, Colombia
Villavicencio, Colombia
Florencia, Colombia
Quito, Ecuador
Tena, Ecuador

Bonaire, Netherlands Antilles
Caracas, Venezuela
Puerto Ayacucho, Venezuela
Georgetown, Guyana
Paramaribo, Surinam
Montsinéry, French Guiana

Cayenne, French Guiana

Tarawa, Kiribati

Loja, Ecuador
Iquitos, Peru
Cajamarca, Peru
Pucallpa, Peru

Belem, Brazil
Manaus, Brazil

Honiara, Solomon Islands

Guayaramerín, Bolivia
Cobija, Bolivia
Lima, Peru
Cusco, Peru
Arequipa, Peru
La Paz, Bolivia
Santa Cruz, Bolivia
Sucre, Bolivia

Porto Velho, Brazil
Salvador, Brazil
Cuiabá, Brazil
Brasília, Brazil
Goiânia, Brazil

Port-Vila, Vanuatu

Tahiti, French Polynesia

Asunción, Paraguay
Villarrica, Paraguay
Encarnación, Paraguay

Belo Horizonte, Brazil
Rio de Janeiro, Brazil
São Paulo, Brazil
Curitiba, Brazil
Foz do Iguaçu, Brazil
Florianópolis, Brazil
Porto Alegre, Brazil
Artigas, Uruguay
Montevideo, Uruguay
Buenos Aires, Argentina

Santiago, Chile
Malargüe, Argentina

Temuco, Chile

Rangitaiki, New Zealand
Levin, New Zealand

Coyhaique, Chile

Base Esperanza, Antarctica (−3)

−11 | +12 | −11 | −10 | −9 | −8 | −7 | −6 | −5 | −4 | −3 | −2

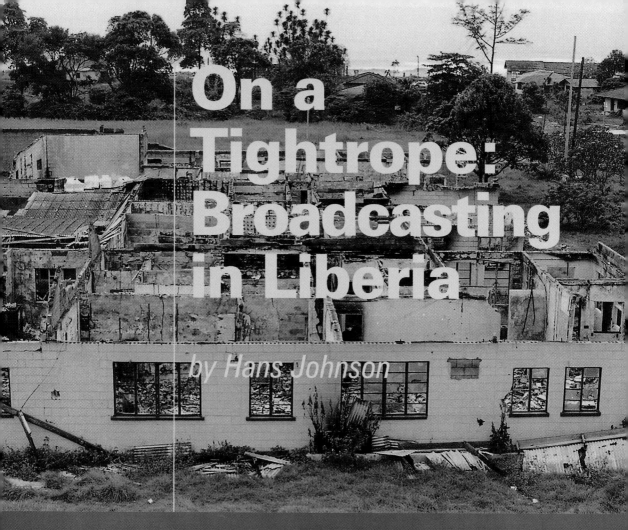

On a Tightrope: Broadcasting in Liberia

by Hans Johnson

World band has had a wild ride in Liberia. As this West African nation has seesawed between peace and bloodshed, world band radio has often been Liberia's best on-scene reporter—and at times a key player in unfolding events.

It began in the early 1950s, when youthful dreamers set out to inaugurate Liberian shortwave broadcasting. All under 25, they made up in enthusiasm what they lacked in experience.

The idea was to establish a non-colonial Christian radio presence in Africa at a time when European colonies still were the rule in Africa. They narrowed the field to two independent nations: Ethiopia, where the Coptic Church opposed any such operation, and Liberia, the nation established in 1847 by freed

American slaves and resident West Africans. Liberia, fully independent, won out by default.

President Tubman Gives Okay to Station

The resulting organization, the West African Broadcasting Association (WABA), secured an audience with then-Liberian president William Tubman. WABA, longer on hopes than funds, exhausted its last dime to send member Bill Watkins to confer with President Tubman.

Raised in Africa and wise beyond his years in the ways of the continent, Watkins persistently and patiently pursued his goal. It paid off. He returned with a station license and call letters, ELWA: EL, the official prefix for Liberian radio stations, and WA for West Africa.

WABA's persistence had carried it far, but the penniless young group needed money, contacts and experience. A merger with the Sudan Interior Mission (SIM) in 1952 provided all three. Things finally began to fall into place.

Watkins and SIM personnel found a site for ELWA some 11 miles— 18 kilometers—south of the Liberian capital of Monrovia. Working together with native laborers, SIM literally carved the site out of the jungle. "It was beautiful, with crashing surf and palm trees—it looked like Hawai'i," recalls Ray de la Haye, then ELWA's field superintendent.

But natural beauty concealed a problem which in future years would have unforseen consequences: theft. "This was in the days before air

> "One visitor took my pants. We got quite a laugh out of this, as my pants were much too large for any Liberian."

The best of times, ELWA during its heyday. SIM

conditioning, so we slept with all the windows opened," remembers Dick Reed, former station manager. "We would have 'visitors' at night, and items would be missing. One night, a 'visitor' took my pants that were hanging on a peg in our bedroom. We got quite a laugh out of this, as my pants were much too large for any Liberian. We finally hired a night watchman, and the nighttime visits stopped."

Other adjustments had to be made. "Teaching our local help to housekeep and cook proved to be a real experience," recalls Reed's spouse, Jane, "but we got over sweeping dirt into cracks in the floor and making sandwiches separate from the side items, rather than as just one big 'stew'."

Salt Spray Prompts Sarnoff Comment

The ocean presented another challenge—its salt spray corroded everything from guy wires to refrigerators. "That salt spray at ELWA was murder," explains Walt Konestco, Systems Supervisor for the Voice of America. "The housewives had to Simonize their refrigerators, but they still rusted out within a year and a half."

David Sarnoff, president of RCA, issued a characteristically blunt opinion on the corrosion problem when he visited the station years later. "You are doing good work here, but we wouldn't choose such a location," declared the legendary broadcasting pioneer.

For the most part, though, good fortune followed ELWA at its inception. Proceeds from an American amusement park, of all places, paid for the station's first shortwave transmitter. The park's owner, infected by ELWA's enthusiasm, enjoyed a great summer and donated $25,000—serious money in those days—for the purchase of a 10 kW unit, which began serving rural Liberia from late 1954.

A verdict from on high was not long in coming. A beaming President Tubman tuned into the station and declared, "I find the broadcasts of ELWA convincing, convicting and converting." The station was off and running with full official blessing.

A Liberian family follows the national news over ELWA. SIM

Add MORE World To Your World Radio

ICOM Wide-Band Receivers Catch MORE of the Action

Performers from Talking Drum Studio, Manjo Bolay, Isabelle Wreh, and Ten Cent Johnson, entertain and educate a market crowd in Monrovia about BayGen radios (*see* page 106).

Common Ground Productions

ELWA Gains Grass-Roots Support

ELWA excelled by being a surrogate national broadcaster for Liberia, complementing the official Liberian Broadcasting Company's 1 kW world band operation on 6022 kHz. Liberians listened to the station because it spoke to them in their own languages. It also gained grass-roots support by hiring native speakers as announcers, and visiting villages to record local music for later broadcast to appreciative audiences.

Electrical power was touch and go at the outset. "In the early years, there was an electrical crane operating in the port of Monrovia," reminisces Cork Loken, former chief engineer at the station. "When that crane would go to take a scoop, our voltage at ELWA would drop."

"There is a voice under every palm tree. All you need is a box to catch it."

"There is a voice under every palm tree. All you need is a box to catch it," Reed recalls a Gio preacher telling him. The station provided the "boxes" by loaning to listeners radios which could only tune to ELWA. (Liberian customs regulations prevented the station from selling or giving away sets).

Station Diminishes Tribalism

ELWA also served as a catalyst for Liberian nationalism. After listening to the broadcasts, people who once thought of themselves only in tribal terms now saw themselves as Liberians. "You have done much to unite my country," expressed a grateful President Tubman.

The station involved its public even in small ways. For example, in 1958 it held a contest to determine what "ELWA" should stand for.

RCSS™ REMOTE

RCSS™ Remote pictured with optional wideband receiver internally installed.

Simultaneous High Speed Data and Full Duplex Audio Over a Single Phone Line.

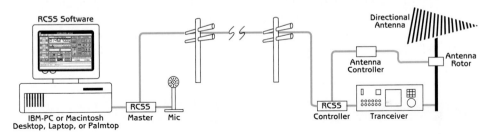

RCSS™ Remote provides a unique solution to remote systems control. It enables high speed data and full duplex wideband audio over any standard or cellular phone line. Audio and data are transferred simultaneously, not time sliced, providing true real time control.

Remote operation can be fully automated with RCSS™ software. A simple point and click graphical user interface via Microsoft Win-

dows™ provides quick learning and easy operation. RCSS™ software is also available separately to provide automated control of AOR and ICOM receivers, among others.

The RCSS™ master unit can be used with any serial terminal including desktops, laptops, and the new palmtops. RCSS™ Remote is housed in a rugged aluminum case for military style dependability. It is constructed using several processors and the latest DSP technology

available. All RCSS™ components are fully shielded from RF leakage. Power is supplied from either AC or DC sources for portability.

The RCSS™ modular design allows the configuration to be modified as user needs expand. Special user developed programs can be uploaded for custom applications.

For more information call, write, fax, or e-mail today. Or, via computer, visit our web page at http://www.sasiltd.com/sasi

Systems & Software
INTERNATIONAL·LTD

Systems & Software International is in its 10th year, and manufactures all equipment in the USA. Please contact us at:
4639 Timber Ridge Drive, Dumfries, Virginia, 22026-1059, USA; **(703) 680-3559**; Fax (703) 878-1460; E-mail 74065.1140@compuserve.com

"Elephants Love West Africa" proved to be the funniest, but the winner was "Eternal Love Winning Africa," recounts former ELWA field superintendent de la Haye. Many an old-time radio enthusiast still has early ELWA correspondence with this slogan.

Voice of America Moves to Liberia

The Voice of America (VOA) needed a site for its broadcasts to sub-Saharan Africa, so it joined ELWA in Liberia in 1959. "Liberia was acceptable politically and offered good propagation," explains Bill Harmon, former resident engineer.

A VOA team picked a site at Careysburg, a 1,300-acre (525-hectare) location away from the ocean, yet an easy drive from Monrovia. "The value of the land the VOA leased was determined by how many rubber trees there were per acre," recounts Jim Alley, former resident engineer. The VOA quickly installed a transportable station consisting of three 50 kW transmitters in trailers containing generators. Italian and American construction firms

built the permanent site, which opened five years later.

"The new relay station had no fence around it, and villagers walked right through it as they went about their business," relates Fred Wulff, former chief of VOA's Analysis and Planning Division and co-author of *The Technical History of VOA*. A separate receiving site picked up VOA broadcasts from other locations and passed them on to be aired from the Liberian site.

Golda Meir Visits "Christian Kibbutz"

ELWA did not stand still while this was going on, but continued to grow, eventually airing over 30 vernaculars for Liberia alone. A fringe benefit was that its world band signal brought in a distant audience, sometimes in unexpected places.

This became apparent in the late 1960s, when the station had a most unusual visitor. To this day, very few are aware that Golda Meir, then prime minister of Israel, claimed to be an ELWA listener. During a

GHOST STATIONS

These stations are flirting with world band broadcasts and are worth keeping an ear on.

• Hope Radio from Monrovia used world band during and after the election campaign. Senator Kekura Kpoto owns a Yaesu transceiver hooked up to a linear amplifier that has been used on 3955 kHz around 20:30 World Time and 6180 kHz at 05:00. Kpoto lost interest in the station after his election to the Senate in 1997. Off the air for the moment, it could easily return—particularly if Kpoto wants to expand his power base.

• Radio Liberty is an FM station run by George Boley, who led an organization called the Liberian Peace Council. He also ran for president in 1997 and lost. Boley's girlfriend once worked at Radio Veritas, so there is a good chance that they will move into world band broadcasting with an equipment setup similar to Hope Radio. Check 5675 kHz at 20:00 World Time and 6144 kHz around 05:00.

• Since the Nigerians took back their transmitter, ELBC has been without a world band outlet. James Wolo of ELBC explains that they hope to get a transmitter from the European Community and return to ELBC's pre-war frequency of 7275 kHz.

state visit to Liberia, she toured the ELWA village. "I'd like to call your place a Christian kibbutz," is how she described what she saw.

Troubles Begin with 1980 Coup

ELWA and the VOA continued to operate quietly and effectively during the 1970s, but that changed in the next decade. In 1980, army Master Sergeant Samuel Doe overthrew the elected government of Liberia in a coup. The once-close relations between the United States and Liberia deteriorated, which affected the VOA's relay station. The United States government refused to invest in the station, and its infrastructure suffered as a result. The only improvement was the installation of an Intelsat facility for receiving VOA program feeds for rebroadcast.

The situation continued to crumble until civil war eventually broke out in 1989. Previous political trouble had always been confined to Monrovia, and the ELWA and VOA sites were just far enough outside the city to avoid entanglement. But Charles Taylor's National Patriotic Front didn't start out from Monrovia; rather, his forces approached the country from abroad.

This had unfortunate consequences for both ELWA and the VOA. Taylor's advancing army reached the outskirts of the ELWA village in 1990, so terror-stricken refugees flocked to both ELWA and the VOA, which they saw as safe havens. But it didn't last.

Taylor's men captured ELWA and, at gunpoint, forced some of the staff to broadcast a false message that the government had been overthrown. The government was outraged and retaliated by shelling ELWA. What artillery didn't destroy, looters did. It was a tragic chapter for a station which had been serving the country and region so peacefully for over 35 years.

New Station Appears in 1990 . . .

With Liberians accustomed to listening to world band for news and inspiration, Taylor quickly filled the vacuum by starting up his own station. "We started broadcasts in 1990 from Gbarnga with a homemade shortwave transmitter," explains Sylvester Jah, special assistant to the chief executive officer of the Liberian Communications Network. "It was really just a community station for Gbarnga," he adds. With ELWA

ELWA's American staff and other Americans were forced to evacuate when fighting flared up in May 1996. SIM

An Easter Service shortly before fighting engulfed the ELWA compound in 1990.　Cork Loken, SIM

destroyed, it was the best Taylor could do on world band for the moment.

. . . but VOA Forced Out

Just like ELWA, the VOA also got caught up in the war. As the situation grew worse, the VOA reacted. They "hardened" the Voice's facility by evacuating dependents, boarding up windows and moving the once-separate receiving site to the transmitter location. In 1990 the American embassy evacuated remaining U.S. personnel from the relay station to the embassy compound. "When things would settle down a little, they would go out to the site," explains Konestco. This continued until the station was behind Taylor's lines.

The embassy then forbade visits to the transmitter site, so all remaining American staff were forced to leave the country.

Liberian personnel stayed behind and operated the station for six months, communicating with the VOA on a 24-hour radiotelephone link to the VOA's facility in Greenville, North Carolina. When Taylor's men would approach the station, the VOA's head Liberian would warn the soldiers that the site was VOA property, and therefore they should leave.

But the site wasn't American property and the ruse eventually ran out. Taylor's men arrived one day in September and dragooned the remaining staff. With no one left to protect it, Taylor's men looted and destroyed the VOA station.

This was the only time the VOA lost a world band site as a result of war.

The VOA attempted to make up for the loss of the station. It purchased time on radio station "Afrique Numéro Un" in Gabon, but at $800 per transmitter-hour

this was not a long-term solution. So in 1992 the VOA rushed equipment to its station in Botswana, partially filling the gap at a more reasonable cost.

So ended the VOA's role in Liberia. Even given recent political stability in Liberia, returning would be an expensive and difficult proposition. Refugees now occupy the site, favoring the concrete reinforced buildings, and anything of value that could be sold has been removed.

Two Stations Constructed, then Destroyed

The VOA wasn't the only one scrambling to find world band outlets—so was Charles Taylor. In 1992, he purchased two 10 kW transmitters and set up an antenna field for them at his alternative capital in the town of Gbarnga. "We called the station the 'Liberian Broadcasting Corporation,' the same as the government station in Monrovia," explains Sylvester Jah.

This station lasted only a few years before it suffered what was becoming an all too common fate in Liberia—it was destroyed during fighting in 1994. Taylor immediately started working on a new station, but this time he would choose the site much more carefully.

New Stations Fill Vacuum

The fighting in the early 1990s resulted in the government holding on to Monrovia and not much else. From there, an intervention force of troops from various west African countries, ECOMOG, kept the government in power. It also gave the government's ELBC a world band voice in 1990, using an old Nigerian transmitter operating from the ECOMOG compound in Monrovia.

ELWA cautiously reentered the scene in 1993. "We used a new 10 kW [transmitter] for English, but we never ran it at more than 5 kW," explains Loken. Generators were the only way to power the station, as all the aluminum electrical transmission lines had been melted down to make cooking pots.

The station also planned to resume a service to West Africa. So, it obtained a vintage transmitter from the former KGEI in California, and started to set it up in Monrovia when the station was again destroyed during a flare up in fighting in May of 1996. Having been literally burned out of Liberia twice in the 1990s, ELWA gave up on plans to resume world band transmissions from Liberia. Although there have been published reports about ELWA's eventually resuming operation using a

WORLD BAND AS A TOOL FOR PEACE

Common Ground Productions is an international nonprofit organization that set up the Monrovia-based Talking Drum Studio in May of 1997. Talking Drum Studio uses radio to promote reconciliation and peace by finding common ground between conflicting parties.

News and talk shows are part of the fare. Radio dramas are also used, with themes such as Forgiveness and Tribalism. Radio stations in the country are free to air the programs, and most do.

"Three-quarters of Monrovians are familiar with our central message of peace and reconciliation," explains John Langlois, director of Common Ground Productions in Liberia. "We now expect our improving exposure on Liberian world band stations to help establish rural listenership and familiarity," he adds.

donated 10 kW world band transmitter, informed sources remain skeptical.

Taylor found a site for his station at a spot in Tubman's Farm in Totota, northeast of Monrovia. Hoping to protect it from Nigerian Alpha jets, the new station, Radio Liberia International, started broadcasting in 1996 from a new American transmitter squirreled away at a small site hacked out of the bush.

Peace and elections in July 1997 opened up the field for world band. Charles Taylor, now running for president, soapboxed from his Radio Liberia International.

Other politicians saw the power of world band, too. With ELWA gone, new shortwave stations filled the vacuum in educational and developmental programs. As part of the peace accord prior to the elections, ELBC was operated by Alhaji Kromah, one of Taylor's rivals.

ELBC left world band after the election. "The Nigerians took back their transmitter," explains Francis Blamu, a technician for the station. Although technically a government station, ELBC has suffered from a lack of funding.

The future will be interesting for all world band stations in Liberia. With Taylor's election to president, his station, Radio Liberia International, became the de facto government station. It plans to transfer its world band operation from Totota to Monrovia sometime in the future.

Another station, Star Radio, began broadcasts on FM just before the elections, adding world band transmissions several months later. The Fondation Hirondelle, a Swiss-based private organization, runs the station. Star Radio considers itself to be an independent voice for all Liberians, many of whom tune in for news and information. Star also takes its role of education very seriously, airing programs from other non-governmental organizations like UNICEF and Save The Children.

The Catholic Church has also stepped into the void left by the absence of ELWA. "Radio Veritas, a longtime FM broadcaster, expanded into world band radio with a transmitter donated by the European Union," explains Steve Kennah, station manager. Like Star Radio, it airs plenty of educational and developmental programming.

President Taylor is having problems with the Nigerian-led ECOMOG forces that remain in Liberia. Nigeria has not hesitated to use its jets to bomb stations in both Liberia and Sierra Leone. Until there are better relations between Liberia and ECOMOG, Radio Liberia International will have a precarious future.

Other world band stations in Liberia will also be walking a tightrope. The Taylor government continues to tinker with media laws in the country as a way of putting stations on notice. It has threatened to shut down Radio Veritas, and used a ploy to force Star Radio off the air for a month in early 1998.

Liberia needs the educational, developmental, and information programs these stations provide, but Veritas and Star will be able to do so only with the continuing approval of Charles Taylor.

It is tragic that stations have come and gone as a result of civil war in Liberia. World band stations convey an image of power with their ability to send messages around the earth. Yet, the Liberian experience has shown that the ability to broadcast can be fragile and vulnerable—when the wrong circumstances prevail.

Hans Johnson has been enjoying broadcasts from Liberia and other parts of the world for over 20 years. He is also founder of the Cumbre DX *electronic DX newsletter, and makes his home in Conroe, Texas.*

A New Awakening: Latino Stations Go Spiritual

by Henrik Klemetz

Until recently many domestic world band stations in Latin America would offer the good stuff—live performances of regional folk music and local drama, *radionovelas*. As the sun would awaken at rural stations throughout South and Central America, local musicians would gather around what was often a station's only microphone for such programs as *Amanecer Andino* (Andean Dawn), *Alegre Despertar* (Joyful Awakening) and *Buenos días, Bolivia* (Good morning, Bolivia). After dark, audiences would be treated to even more of the same. With guitars strumming and flutes piping, these homegrown artists acted as electronic cocks' crows and musical sandmen.

Not just for Latino listeners, either. World band DXers in North America and Europe relished the opportunity to tweak their receivers to savor some of the most entertaining programming to be heard anywhere.

Change Comes to Latino Scene

Alas, with the spread of television and Western rock music, this happens much less often now except during local fiestas and other special events. Yes, Latino radio has been undergoing real change. Recorded music, public affairs, sports, advertising, witchcraft and gospel: This is the reality of today's world band radio throughout much of Latin America.

There are many reasons for this. To begin with, world band radio is not quite the presence it once was in some countries, while in others it is actually growing.

> Something must be terribly wrong with the antenna or transmitter, he reasoned, so he shut the whole thing off.

World Band Faces Hurdles

Especially in those parts of Latin America where rural populations are migrating to metropolitan settings, financial odds do not favor world band radio. Running a vintage or homebrew shortwave

Colombian pirate station Radio Católica Nacional, 3580 kHz, was run by Indian nature headler and botanist José Celio Díaz from his house on an Indian reservation in southwestern Colombia. R. Klemetz

Radio Centinela del Sur ("Sentinel of the South") in Loja, Ecuador operates each evening on 4770 kHz. It celebrates its 43rd anniversary on November 18, 1999.   H. Klemetz

transmitter in a little village is actually a costly—and chancy—proposition as compared to the economics of a solid-state transmitter on FM or mediumwave AM in a metropolitan area.

Too, spare parts for a shortwave transmitter can be expensive and hard to come by, and advertising revenue in the forlorn countryside doesn't begin to approach the figures that can be obtained in an urban radio market.

World band's relatively low visibility in the telecommunication industry also hampers it, sometimes in unexpected ways. For example, nowadays the properties of shortwave propagation are not necessarily understood by key decision makers reared on FM and personal computers.

Take Radio Mundial in Caracas, Venezuela. When it decided to go onto world band (5050 kHz) in the mid-eighties, the general manager was astounded by reception reports the station was receiving from Japan. Something must be terribly wrong with the antenna or transmitter, he reasoned, so he shut the whole thing off.

In a number of Latin American countries, domestic world band operations have been virtually eclipsed by other media. Yet, at least 20 or 30 new domestic Latin American shortwave stations make their debut every year—mostly in Peru. Some of these new Peruvian stations disappear for unknown reasons within a matter of weeks. Many of the remainder wind up switching to FM or mediumwave AM as soon as they obtain the appropriate license.

For other Peruvian newcomers, world band radio is a training spot for announcers, technicians and other broadcasting staff. At least one new station, Radio Cristal on 7746 kHz, carries ads inviting trainees for regular courses at the station.

Radio Messages: Poor Man's Cell Phone

Radio is a marketplace for all sorts of opinion and messages. "If your organization has a message . . . for Latin America, we can get it there for you," boasts a promo over WRMI, transmitting to the Americas from powerful shortwave facilities in Miami.

Domestic world band stations in Latin America are in the same game: "you pay, we play." In many of the less-developed areas of the continent, radio continues its vital role in getting through to people who cannot reach one another by phone. For example, a number of stations in the Andes region regularly air personal messages like this, from a Peruvian

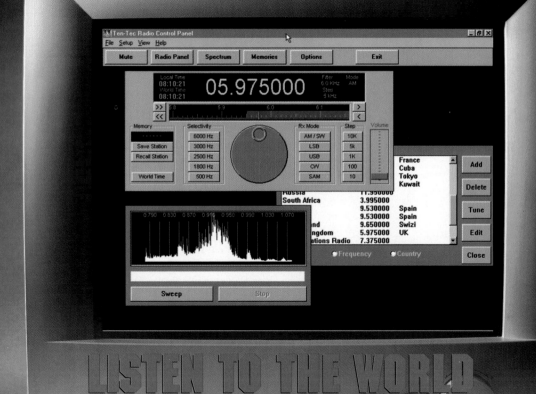

LISTEN TO THE WORLD ON YOUR PC

Worldwide shortwave listening is now only a mouse click away with **PC RADIO**. Designed for both the PC user who has never listened to shortwave and the experienced SWL who appreciates the powerful marriage of PC and shortwave listening.

Local AM broadcasting offers in-depth news, sports, and talk radio. Most countries broadcast around the globe on nearly a dozen international shortwave bands. Catch both world and local news from their viewpoint and a wealth of culture, politics, and music. Hams are spread out across nine bands, talking across town or half way around the world. You will also hear military operations, commercial airlines, and CB. The manual includes a phenomenal beginner's guide written by respected author and columnist, Joe Carr.

Launch the PC RADIO, tune in an interesting station, and then put it in the background while you do other PC tasks. In fact, you could surf the Web and listen to shortwave at the same time!

Unlike conventional receivers, this is a revolutionary Digital Signal Processing, or "DSP", based design. This cutting edge, software-based technology dramatically reduces the number of individual electronic components inside. It's possible to provide features only dreamed of in previous receivers in this price class. Even the most experienced enthusiasts will marvel at the performance.

- tunes 100 kHz to 30 MHz
- needs only a serial port and one 1 meg of hard drive space
- runs on either Windows® 3.1 or 95
- no need to go inside your PC
- built-in, telescoping whip antenna

Call **1-800-833-7373** to request literature, or visit our web site at www.tentec.com.

$295*
factory-assembled only

- No-Risk 30-day Money-Back Guarantee**
- We accept VISA, Mastercard, and Discover
- Visit our home page at www.tentec.com
*Plus shipping and handling
**Customer pays shipping both ways.

CALL TODAY 1-800-833-7373
Monday - Friday
9:00 a.m. - 5:30 p.m. EST

You can reach us at:
1185 Dolly Parton Parkway
Sevierville, TN 37862
Office: (423) 453-7172
FAX: (423) 428-4483
e-mail: sales@tentec.com
Repair Dept.: (423) 428-0364 (8a - 4p EST)

TEN-TEC
MADE IN TENNESSEE

For those who like to build, we offer two other receivers in kit form. Request our T-KIT catalog covering these and many more budget-priced projects.

9-BAND SWL RECEIVER

"First radio kit" classic. Five transistor, 3 IC design. Tune both AM broadcast and SSB/CW from 1.8 - 22 MHz. Has Main and Fine tuning, Regen, RF gain, Volume. Use built-in speaker, your own, or stereo phones. Use 8 C cells or ext. 12 VDC. **1253**..**$59***

(Build in 8 hrs)

PORTABLE SWL RECEIVER

Enjoy quality shortwave listening comparable to factory built portables. Listen to AM broadcast as well as SSB/CW.
- 100 kHz - 30 MHz   • 15 memories
- 2.5 kHz and 100 kHz tuning steps • Dual conversion, superheterodyne
- 13.8 VDC operation; AC wall transformer included

(Build in 25 hrs)

1254..**$195***

Old-timer Emisoras Gran Colombia, in Ecuador, left world band for FM some years back. The station still possess the original shortwave transmitter, but for now there doesn't appear to be the necessary funds to get it back on the air.   H. Klemetz

broadcaster: "Meet me with a pair of donkeys at the road junction on Thursday morning. Please acknowledge receipt of this message in the Estación C message slot on Wednesday morning."

Messages are paid for like any other commercial advertising. If snippets aren't adequate, on numerous stations anyone can also hire airtime for more elaborate messages.

Spiritual Programming Gains Ground

As evangelical and other religious movements gain ground in countries where the Catholic Church once held sway, new and sometimes exotic types of religious programming are sprouting up.

For example, over many Peruvian and Ecuadorian world band stations there is a constant flow of nature healers, shamans and witch doctors buying airtime on stations in towns they are scheduled to visit, like tent revivalists, on their continuous journey from one place to another.

These nature healers are now being outpaced by spiritual healers, notably from evangelical churches like the Brazilian-based Pentecostal "Deus é Amor" ("God Is Love," or *Dios es Amor* in Spanish). In Peru, this organization has purchased what was formerly the state-owned Radio Victoria on 6020 and 9721.7 kHz. It now carries a 24-hour-a-day mixture of sermons and testimonials for faith healing, all topped with a dressing of gospel hymns in the Brazilian *sertaneja* style.

There are more than sixty local "Dios es Amor" churches in Peru. Many carry leased airtime for locally produced "La Voz de la Liberación" programs, which can be heard on 20-plus tropical band outlets below 5.1 MHz.

At least one shortwave transmitter has been reactivated for the sole purpose of airing this ubiquitous program: Radio JSV in the town of Huánuco, Peru. Their transmitter operates on and around the frequency of 6060 kHz, curiously enough interfering with Rádio Universo, also on 6060 kHz—one of the Brazilian stations that carries the very same "A Voz da Libertação" around the clock.

In Brazil, many other stations carry that program—Rádio Gazeta in São Paulo on 5955, 9685 and 15325 kHz; and Rádio IPB AM in Campo Grande on 4895 kHz among them.

Sometimes a whole network of stations outside Brazil, notably in Peru, Colombia and Venezuela, will take the satellite-fed signal emanating from the church's Brazilian headquarters in São Paulo.

Not surprisingly, and tending to confirm this recent trend in programming, as of mid-1998 two out of four new Latin-American world band stations are spiritual, including one which airs gospel music. They are Voz Cristiana in Chile broadcasting on several channels between 6070 and 21550 kHz, and Sistema LBV Mundial in Brazil on 6160 kHz and irregularly on 11895 kHz.

The remaining two—Radio 88 Estereo in Costa Rica on 6075 kHz, and Radio La Voz de Bolívar in Peru on 5460 kHz—are traditional broadcasters devoted to musical entertainment and sports.

So, yes, traditional programming is still alive and kicking over Latin American world band stations. But as Chuck Berry put it in "Roll Over, Beethoven," this fare now has to share the airwaves with a new breed of religious broadcasters—broadcasters with attitude.

Author Klemetz poses with station pennants.

Henrik Klemetz started DXing in his native Sweden in the 1950s. As a linguist and freelance journalist, he travels widely in Latin America and has been stationed in Colombia since 1992. He follows the broadcasting scene for Passport to World Band Radio, *as well as the Latin American edition of* Radio World *magazine.*

La Voz de Saquisilí returned to the air in August, 1998, operating from 1100-1300 and 2230-0030 World Time on 4899.6 kHz. Shown, the grandson of owner Arturo Mena.   H. Klemetz

Voice of Shangri-La

by Manosij Guha

Nestled along the wuthering heights of the Himalayas is Nepal, a land of sublime beauty and diversity. Known as the fabled homeland Shangri-La, its richness in scenic splendor and kaleidoscope of cultures helps make up for the material poverty of its people. With a tangle of vaulted pagodas, ancient temples, decaying palaces and domed stupas, it is where time stands still.

The size of Michigan, little Nepal's topography rises from about 300 feet or 100 meters above sea level in the lowlands of the Terai, to the 29,000 foot (8,848 meter) behemoth of Mount Everest, the "Roof of the World." It is not only home to the world's tallest mountains, but also vast plains, fertile valleys and dense jungles. It also boasts an astounding diversity of animal life, most of which are protected within vast national parks and reserves.

Birthplace of Buddha Becomes Hindu Nation

The diversity found in the landscape is also reflected in the Nepalese people. With an estimated 23 million people, it is a mosaic of Aryan and Mongoloid races. It has about 30 ethnic groups and as many languages, although Nepali is the official tongue.

It is the birthplace of Buddha, even though Nepal has long been a Hindu nation. Today, the religious scene is dominated by a heady mixture of Hindu and Buddhist beliefs, with a pantheon of Tantric deities tagged on. Those who aren't Buddhist or Hindu are either Muslim, Christian or shaman.

Little is known about Nepal's earliest recorded history, except that the first to arrive, from the east, were Kiratis in the seventh or eighth century BC. It was during this period that Buddhism first came to the country when, it is claimed, Buddha visited the Kathmandu Valley. By 200 AD, Buddhism had waned, replaced by Hinduism brought in by the Licchavis. These invaders swept in from northern India and overthrew the last Kirati king, ushering in a classical age of Nepalese art and architecture.

By 879, the Licchavi era had petered out and was succeeded by the Thakuri dynasty. A grim period of instability and invasion followed, but the Kathmandu Valley's strategic location ensured the kingdom's survival and growth.

Several centuries later the Thakuri king, Arideva, founded the Malla dynasty, jump-starting another renaissance of Nepali culture. Despite intermittent earthquakes, the occasional invasion and feuding among independent city-states, the dynasty flourished, reaching its zenith during the 15th century under Yaksha Malla.

Little Buddha. Buddhism first came to Nepal several hundred years BC, when Buddha is said to have visited the Kathmandu Valley. M. Guha

The rulers of Gorkha, the most easterly region, under the inspired leadership of Prithvi Narayan Shah, launched a campaign to conquer the valley. They triumphed in 1768 after a 27-year campaign, then moved the capital to Kathmandu. From this new base the kingdom's power expanded, borne by a seemingly unstoppable army, until progress was halted in 1792 by a brief and chastening war with Tibet.

Peace reigned until a territorial dispute with the British in 1814. After two years of skirmishes, the Nepalese were eventually brought to heel and compelled to sign the 1816 Sugauli Treaty, which ceded some territory to British India. After this costly setback, Nepal remained largely neutral during India's fight for independence from the British.

The Shah dynasty continued at the helm until the Kot Massacre of 1846. At that

Patan, Durbar Square, attracts worshipers and tourists from all over. Its architecture is breathtaking, thanks in part to ongoing maintenance and restoration.
M. Guha

point a courtier, Jung Bahadur, wrested control from the king, proclaiming himself prime minister for life, later making the office hereditary. What followed was tyranny. Rana rulers luxuriated in huge palaces, while their subjects eked out a pitiful hand-to-mouth existence.

End of War Ushers in Democracy

The end of World War II and subsequent withdrawal of British support, hastened by a host of insurrections, sounded the death knell in 1948 for the Rana regime. In 1951, when sporadic fighting spilled onto the streets, the Ranas were compelled to abdicate, at the behest of India, in favor of King Tribhuvan.

A constitutional monarchy was hastily established. But this dabbling with democracy was short-lived as King Mahendra, Tribhuvan's son and successor, hit upon a party-less system where the king selected the prime minister and the cabinet—besides appointing a large proportion of the national assembly, which conveniently rubber-stamped his policies.

Matters came to a head in 1989, when the Nepalese, fed up with years of exploitation and suffering, revolted, leaving several hundred dead. When the next king, Birendra, assumed the throne in 1972, he inherited a sorry mess. He decided to give his impoverished kingdom a taste of democracy in the real sense. In the elections of May 1991, a 205-seat parliament was formed, with the Nepali Congress Party and the Communist Party of Nepal sharing most of the votes.

Since then Nepal has had the ominous task of establishing a workable democracy—no mean feat when the numbers required to maintain a parliamentary majority simply do not add up. The situation has been further exacerbated by a wafer-thin economy overly dependent upon foreign aid and tourist revenue. The nation is faced with massive unemployment, illiteracy, and an ethnically and religiously fragmented population that continues to grow at an alarming rate. In the meantime, rural Shangri-La wannabes are attempting to attract low-volume, high-demographic Western ecotourism to boost their rudimentary local economies.

Get It Firsthand
With Drake World Band
The Finest Line of Products For
The Shortwave Enthusiast.

R8B Communications Receiver

SW8 Worldband Receiver

SW2 Shortwave Receiver

SW1 Shortwave Receiver

Drake's current line of world band communication receivers continues its history of excellence. Drake has something for everyone - regardless of skill or interest level.

For the avid enthusiast, the top of the line R8B offers serious performance with Selectable Sideband Synchronous Detection and five built-in filters. For the listener on the go, the SW8 provides all the advanced features of a tabletop unit, but is completely portable. Expensive taste with a small budget? The SW2 fits the bill. The SW2 boasts expensive features like Selectable Sideband Synchronous Detection, 100 programmable memories and an optional infrared remote control - all at a moderate price. Just getting started? The SW1 is perfect for the beginning hobbyist. User friendly operation lets you pull in AM broadcasts from the far corners of the world.

Whatever your level of interest, you'll appreciate the craftsmanship, quality and performance that is built into every Drake communications receiver.

R.L. Drake Company
phone 513-746-4556

230 Industrial Dr.
fax 513-743-4510

Franklin, OH 45005 U.S.A.
on-line www.rldrake.com

(Left) Newscaster reads national Nepali news. (Right) Raur Karki, director, Radio Nepal, at work with Passport.

M. Guha

Fleapowered Transmitter Brings Radio to Nepal

Broadcasting came relatively late to Nepal. But with the advent of democracy there was an immediate need to reach out to people, for which radio was ideal. Thus, Nepal Radio, now Radio Nepal, was established on April 1, 1951, with three daily transmissions totaling three hours and 15 minutes via a 250 Watt shortwave communications transmitter modified for broadcast use on 7100 kHz.

The studio-cum-transmitting base was a quaint building in the palatial compound of Singha Durbar, in the heart of Kathmandu, which was actually part of a school for the children of the servants of the royal family. This building still exists and is presently used as an office for the engineers, while the room from which the broadcasts emanated is now the office of the director of engineering.

> The first Nepalese world band station was in a quaint building which was actually a school for the children of the servants of the royal family.

Foreign Aid Upgrades Broadcast Facilities

In 1960 Australian aid arrived in the form of a five kilowatt AWA shortwave transmitter on which a national service was carried in the 31, 41 and 90 meter tropical band segments. This was enhanced by a British grant in 1968, which underwrote the construction of the first modern broadcasting house, with six professional studios to produce programming in a national format. These studios are still in use, mostly for production of programs for the FM service.

To put in a strong signal to the largely rural masses in their mountainous habitat, a powerful 100 kilowatt Marconi shortwave transmitter was installed at a new transmitting base in Khumaltar, near the suburb of Lalitpur and towards the western fringe of Kathmandu. A further boost came when the Nepal government chipped in for a 100 kW Harris shortwave transmitter in 1970, followed by another identical transmitter in 1979.

All transmitters are located in the spacious transmitter hall at the Khumaltar site. Signals from the energy-efficient Harris transmitters are radiated via dipole-curtain arrays across the road at a new antenna farm, which is now engulfed by the concrete morass of a housing estate where construction goes on unabated.

These transmitters were a welcome addition to the aging Marconi unit, which was well past its prime, being kept alive largely due to the untiring efforts of the station's engineer and a dwindling supply of spare parts. The Marconi still labors for 16 hours a day—more on weekends— airing the national service on the mainstay channel of 5005 kHz. It overheats badly, while the solid-state Harris plays it cool by churning out the same programming on 7165 kHz summers, 3230 kHz winters.

There is not enough power from the Nepal Electricity Authority to run all three transmitters at a time, so one of the Harris units is always on standby. But during the equinoctial months, when the electricity gods are willing, the three transmitters can be heard operating simultaneously on a trio of designated channels.

In 1980 Nepalese broadcasting benefitted from a generous Japanese overseas development program, this time resulting in one of the most modern and comprehensive regional broadcasting infrastructures in South Asia. A second ultra-modern studio complex has been constructed adjacent to the old broadcasting house.

Global Reach on World Band and Web Radio

Radio Nepal broadcasts for 15 hours daily, including two hours of regional programming, extended by an additional two hours on public holidays. Forty percent of the programs are informative and educational— the rest are commercial.

Programs are mostly in Nepali, but there are also segments in 11 minority languages spoken by about 90 percent of the population. Ten-minute news bulletins in English are also broadcast three times daily at 02:15, 07:20 and 14:15 hours World Time. However, an external service aimed at foreigners and diplomats, with updates on news and events for 15 minutes daily, was discontinued in 1989.

Although Radio Nepal is now a regional world band powerhouse, for listeners farther afield it represents a proud DX catch. Web surfers can also hear it at www.catmando.com/news/radio-nepal.

Singha Durbar, formerly the king's palace, now houses the facilities of Radio Nepal. M. Guha

From Jungle Radio to International Voice

by Manosij Guha

Hiding behind a media image of cyclones, floods and entrenched misery is a lush and beautiful territory woven with rich history. This land, Bangladesh, embraces a variety of cultures and landscapes you don't expect from a country only the size of Illinois.

It is one of the few nations that can be explored almost entirely by Mississippi-type paddle boat. Visitors can check out the world's longest natural beach and largest littoral mangrove forest, or explore archaeological ruins from Biblical times and the decaying 19th century mansions of maharajas. Despite being the world's most crowded country and one of the poorest, friendly people welcome visitors with a ready smile and a cup of tea.

Bangladesh is often described as Asia's backwater, with grinding poverty and rising unemployment. Thanks to that depressing image painted by the world's media, this impoverished country has been touted as a disaster zone rather than as a travel destination. But vision and hard work have done wonders. With more than $150 billion in exports of garments and jute, even in today's economy it is emerging as an Asian success story.

This low-lying nation is nestled in the crook of the Bay of Bengal, almost enveloped by India, but also sharing a small southeastern border with Myanmar (Burma), fronting onto the bay. It is flat, and dominated by the intricate riverine network of the Ganges-Brahmaputra-Jamuna delta. Where land ends and the sea begins is a murky zone of shifting sediments, watercourses, flood waters and silt. Most of the country is composed of alluvial plains less than 33 feet or 10 meters above sea level, making it an inviting proposition to flood-prone rivers and tidal waves—besides making it the most arable land.

Bangladesh is home to a myriad of wild animals, especially the Royal Bengal tiger found in the mangrove depths of the Sunderbans, where crocodiles and a variety of poisonous snakes also roam free.

The Royal Bengal tiger is found in the mangrove depths of the Sunderbans, where crocodiles and a variety of poisonous snakes also roam free.

Centuries of Bengali Heritage

The Bengal region has a multifaceted folk heritage, enriched by its ancient animist, Buddhist, Hindu and Muslim roots. Weaving, pottery and terra-cotta sculpture are some of the earliest forms of artistic expression. Although 94 percent of the population is Muslim, they live with their Hindu neighbors in relative harmony.

Musicians gather at the studios of Radio Bangladesh for a recording session. M. Guha

Cattle grazing undisturbed amid antennas at Radio Bangladesh's Kalyanpur transmitting station. M. Guha

The area's early history featured a succession of Indian empires, internal squabbling, and a tussle between Hinduism and Buddhism for dominance. All of this was just a prelude to the unstoppable tide of Islam, which washed over northern India at the end of the 12th century.

Under the ruling Mughal *nawabs*, art and literature flourished, overland trade expanded and Islamic Bengal became a center for maritime trade—which attracted the Europeans to establish themselves in the region. The Portuguese arrived as early as the 15th century, but were ousted in 1633 by local opposition. The British arrived initially as traders in 1690, which was the beginning of two and a half centuries of dominance as the region became part of the burgeoning British Indian Empire.

Secedes from Pakistan

At the close of the second World War, when European colonialism had run its course, Bengal chose to join with Pakistan and East Bengal to form the state of East Pakistan. It was administered unfavorably from West Pakistan, with which it shared few similarities apart from the Muslim faith. Inequalities between the two regions soon stirred up a sense of Bengali nationalism that had not been reckoned with during the push for Muslim independence. After a war of attrition with West Pakistan, which was one of the shortest and bloodiest of modern times, with Indian help it finally became independent in 1971.

Since then, governance in Bangladesh has faced trying times. In 1973-4, after the euphoria of nationalism died down, the newly independent nation was ravaged by famine. This was followed by martial law, successive military coups and political assassinations, interspersed with short-lived experiments in democracy.

Since 1991 democracy has been reestablished, but a political standoff between the two major parties has become the new norm. Repeated strikes, protest marches, rallies and street arson are now the ultimate means of political expression.

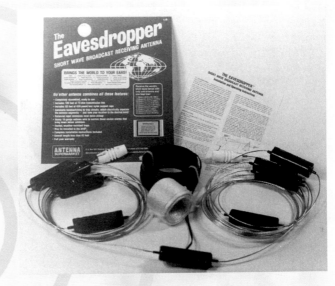

Radio Bangladesh's veteran Marconi transmitter continues to function reliably, thanks to its conservative design, solid construction and careful maintenance.

M. Guha

World Band Starts after Pakistani Independence

For a small country, Bangladesh has had a checkered history of radio broadcasting. The first station in what today is Bangladesh was set up in 1939 in the capital, Dhaka. Its purpose was to provide a complement to All India Radio's station in Calcutta, which covered the Bengali populace. To accomplish this, a 5 kW Marconi mediumwave AM transmitter was installed at Kalyanpur. Until 1948 the studios were in a rented building on Nizamuddin Road, which has since been converted into Burhanuddin College.

> **Broadcasts played a major role in boosting the morale of the Bengali freedom fighters.**

The Kalyanpur site still exists as a graveyard of old transmitters lying disused and unkempt as relics; it also houses a sophisticated 10 kW NEC mediumwave AM transmitter which carries the Dhaka "C" service. The adjacent land has been converted into a housing colony for Radio Bangladesh employees, and old antenna masts can still be seen through the trees where cattle graze overgrown grounds.

With the formation of Pakistan on August 14, 1947, All India Radio Dhaka became "Radio Pakistan Dhaka." When maintaining a radio link between the geographically separated peoples of East and West Pakistan became a priority, a Marconi 7.5 kW shortwave transmitter was installed at Kalyanpur. There was also a rudimentary receiving center in Boubazar, in the Gazipur district, to rebroadcast Radio Pakistan from Karachi.

A year later a new broadcasting house in Shahabag in the heart of Dhaka was constructed. This building now houses the administrative offices, while the old studios are still in use by the commercial and FM services.

In 1968 a 100 kW Continental "Ampliphase" shortwave transmitter was installed in the outskirts of the capital among the rural surroundings of Savar, yet another transmitting site. This transmitter continues to carry a mix of domestic and external world band services on 15520v kHz during local evenings.

Freedom Aided by Clandestine Jungle Radio

One of the most intriguing chapters of Bangladesh's broadcasting history was its clandestine operation during its war of independence. On March 26, 1971, on the eve of the liberation war, Swadhin Bangla Betar Kendra, or Radio Free Bangladesh, began irregular transmission via a "liberated" 10 kW mediumwave AM transmitter at Kalurghat, near Chittagong.

A day later, the fledgling nation's declaration of independence was announced via this transmitter—which the Pakistan Army proceeded to bomb out of existence three days later. But the station was quickly back on air with a smaller one-kilowatt Collins mediumwave AM transmitter installed in the jungles of Ramgarh. Later, a 0.1 kW shortwave communications transmitter was lent by the Indian Border Security Force to bolster the efforts of the fledgling station. This flea-powered world band station broadcast on 60 meters from the security of the Ramgarh cantonment.

When fighting intensified, the mediumwave AM and shortwave transmitters were relocated to Bogata near the Indian border with Agartala. Later, they were moved once again, this time to transmitters of All India Radio in Calcutta, where Indian staffers saw this as their contribution to the pan-Bengali movement. These Radio Free Bangladesh broadcasts played a major role in boosting the morale of Bengali freedom fighters and the citizenry at large, and helped gain support from the West Bengali community with whom they shared a common culture and language.

Just before the final surrender on December 16, 1971, the retreating Pakistan Army managed to disable many broadcasting installations by removing key components. The broadcasting apparatus that was inherited thus was in shambles. This led to a delay in restarting those stations after liberation, especially as supply warehouses were in Karachi. But thanks to the dedicated staff, old transmitters were repaired and new ones installed with the assistance of foreign aid and barter agreements.

World Band Now World Class

An example of the latter was a shortwave transmitter installed with Russian help in 1976. To this day, it continues to carry the domestic world band service on 4880v kHz at anywhere from 30 to 100 kW.

In 1983 Japanese aid led to construction of a national broadcasting center at Sher-e-Bangla Nagar in Dhaka with new state-of-the-art studios. All national and external services programs are now produced here and fed by VHF link to various transmitter sites.

With French aid in 1984, Radio Bangladesh's latest and most modern transmitting station was created. As a result, down the highway from Savar, among paddy fields, is the station's Kabirpur site. Here are housed two powerful 250 kW Thomson-CSF shortwave transmitters with massive directional curtain antennas.

This world-class facility radiates almost six hours of programming in seven languages, putting in a sizeable signal to external audiences and expatriates in south and southeast Asia, the Middle East and Europe. Even listeners in the Americas can hear the station when conditions are right.

It's a far cry from the lone local station that started it all in 1939—or the tiny jungle transmitter which helped bring about national independence. Bangladesh radio has come a long way, baby!

Radio from a Troubled Eden

by Manosij Guha

Serendib, Taprobane, Ceylon, Resplendent Isle, Island of Dharma, Pearl of the Orient—just some of the names which reveal the richness and beauty of what is today called Sri Lanka. Rubies and sapphires deep in the earth, orchids dangling from trees, elephants roaming dense jungles. Cinnamon, cardamom and saffron-robed Buddhist monks with parasols. Mountains. Exquisite beaches.

A strong whiff of this paradise translates into legend. At Adam's Peak, one of the island's tallest mountains, is said to be the footprint of Adam when he came to earth—Sri Lanka thus became the original Eden.

For centuries it seduced travelers, who returned home with enchanting images of a languorous tropical isle of deep spirituality and serenity, a Tahiti of the East. But the most wilful exoticism has been perforated by an unending ethno-religious conflict that has turned this island nation into a veritable Northern Ireland of the Indian Ocean.

Indeed, Sri Lanka is itself about the size of Ireland. Given its unique shape, Sri Lanka can be likened to a giant teardrop falling from the southern tip of the vast Indian peninsula, separated only by the 50-kilometer, or 31-mile, Palk Strait. A series of stepping-stone coral islets, known as Adam's Bridge, almost form just that—a land bridge between the two countries.

Sri Lanka's 19 million people are three-quarters Sinhala, with Tamils and Muslims forming sizable minorities. Its classical architecture, sculpture and painting are predominantly Buddhist. Stupas sprinkle the countryside, and there are several extravagantly large sculptures of Buddha. Colonial remnants include Dutch forts, churches and a canal; as well as British residences, clubs and courthouses.

Galle is the finest colonial city on the island, while Ratnapura is the center of Sri Lanka's gem trade. Colombo, the island's largest city, is noisy and frenetic—the breakdowns, snarled traffic and power cuts are received with a shrug and a smile. Trincomalee, once a naval town, has one of the finest and biggest natural harbors in the world. Batticaloa, a few miles to the south, has an expansive pretty lagoon with fish that "sing"—particularly on moonlit nights.

> **The original inhabitants were nomadic people of almost pygmy stature. Some still survive with their unique lifestyle.**

Elephants decked out for a festival procession.

Lionel Pinto, SLBC's Director General of Engineering, in his Colombo office.   M. Guha

Veddah Pioneers Followed by Waves of Invaders

The early history of this island nation seems to fade into the mists of legend, having only a frail basis in reality. The original inhabitants were the Veddahs— nomadic people of dark, slight and almost pygmy stature, a few of whom still survive with their unique lifestyle. Folklore has it that they were pushed from the plains to the central jungles around the fifth or sixth century B.C. by Aryan invaders from northern India, who would become the indigenous stock forming the Sinhala race.

Buddhism was introduced in the third century B.C. by Mahinda, son of the Indian Mauryan emperor Ashoka, and it quickly became the established religion and the focus of a strong and positive nationalism. A number of Sinhala kingdoms mush-roomed across the island during the fourth century B.C., with Anuradhapura, in the northern plains, emerging as the strongest.

Lured by spice and cinnamon, the Portu-guese arrived in Colombo in 1505 and gained a monopoly on the invaluable trade. By 1597, the Portuguese colonizers had taken formal control of the island.

However, they failed to dislodge the powerful Sinhala kingdom in Kandy which, in 1658, enlisted Dutch help to expel them.

When the British arrived in 1796, the Dutch put up only a half-hearted resis-tance. The British succeeded in whittling away at Kandy's sovereignty, and in 1815 became the first European power to rule the entire island. Empire building moved inexorably forward as roads were con-structed and English was introduced as the national language. Simultaneously, coffee, tea, cinnamon and coconut plantations sprang up—worked by legions of Tamil laborers imported from southern India.

Disenfranchised Tamil Minority Rebels

Sri Lanka, or Ceylon as it was still known, achieved full independence as a dominion within the British Commonwealth on February 4, 1948. The first government adopted socialist policies, strengthening social services and maintaining a strong economy, but also disenfranchising 800,000 Tamil plantation workers in the hill country. The pro-Sinhala policies of the nationalist government elected in 1956 further disenchanted the ethnic Tamil minority.

The alienated Tamil Hindu minority, spearheaded by the Liberation Tigers of Tamil Eelam (LTTE), began pressing for greater autonomy in the main Tamil areas in the north and east. This was to become the start of a long period of bloody communal strife, giving ethnic cleansing a new meaning: an estimated 90,000 people have perished, although over the last few years government forces have made rapid gains.

While Sri Lanka celebrates 50 years of independence from colonial rule, its war-torn economy is suffering from high inflation, steep unemployment, poor infrastructure and corruption. Spending on

Entrance to the offices and studios of the Sri Lanka Broadcasting Corporation, Colombo.

M. Guha

defense saps almost 20 percent of government expenditure, and the domestic economy is propped up by the $1.5 billion sent home every year by Sri Lankans working abroad, mainly in the Gulf States. A resolution of the conflict and renewed economic growth remain inextricably linked.

First Station Built from Captured Submarine Radio

State-of-the-art Kokusai transmitters carry the domestic national and commercial services.

The earliest indication of organized broadcasting came with the formation of the Ceylon Amateur Radio Society in 1922 in Colombo. By 1923 the Ceylon Telegraph Department was broadcasting gramophone music on around 700 kHz in the mediumwave AM band from a small transmitter built from a captured German submarine's radio. So successful were these that the government commenced regular broadcasting using a reconditioned marine communications transmitter made available by the Coastal Wireless Station in Colombo on 375 kHz longwave. The first public demonstration of radio occurred on July 27, 1924 with the broadcast of the governor's speech. On December 16, 1925, the Government Broadcasting Station, later Radio Ceylon, was formed.

The transmitter and studio continued to be in a small room in the Central Telegraph Office. A year later, when this cramped facility became inadequate, it was transferred to a government building in Torrington Square from where it operates to this day. A separate transmitter was built in June, 1930 at the new site of Welikada on the outskirts of Colombo, followed by a receiving station. These worked in conjunction to pick up and rebroadcast the BBC Empire Service, precursor to today's BBC World Service.

Shortwave Inaugurated 1934, Reactivated 1945

Local experimentation in shortwave broadcasting began in 1934 around 6 MHz to provide a better signal to the outlying provinces. However, these shortwave services were discontinued in June, 1938, as they were not economically viable.

With the start of the second World War and the resulting new communication needs of the British Empire, Radio SEAC (South East Asia Command) was established. By March, 1945, a new transmitting station had been constructed in Ekala, about 13 miles from downtown Colombo. Initially it had a 7.5 kilowatt RCA shortwave unit, but a mammoth 100 kilowatt Marconi, two more 7.5 kilowatt RCAs and a smaller one-kilowatt unit were added over the next few years. It continued to serve as a BBC relay base until 1951.

Yankee Doodle Comes to Town

On May 14, 1951, an agreement was signed between the United States and Ceylonese governments which gave a fillip to shortwave broadcasting on the island. Three new 35 kilowatt Collins shortwave transmitters were installed by the Voice of America at its own expense, with Radio Ceylon being given secondary use of the equipment.

During 1950 the commercial service of Radio Ceylon started on shortwave, beamed towards India via the old SEAC transmitters. Thanks to the apathy shown by the Indian government towards the need for commercial broadcasting on the Subcontinent, there was a mass exodus of programmers and advertisers to Colombo. This made Radio Ceylon the most listened-to station on the Subcontinent for years to come. On September 7, 1978, thanks to a new democratic governmental structure, Radio Ceylon became part of the Sri Lanka Broadcasting Corporation.

Facilities a Mix of Modern and Vintage

Today, the SLBC, besides running national and commercial services in Sinhala and Tamil, also airs English, local, sports and regional services, along with the External and All Asia Services. Its modern studios are located in a white-stucco building on

Torrington—or rather, Independence Square—in the heart of Colombo. To maintain historic continuity, some of the old oak-paneled studios from which the pioneering broadcasts took place are still in use as audio mixing rooms.

The shortwave transmitting station is located at Ekala, about 35 kilometers or 22 miles downtown from Colombo towards the international airport, in a secluded hamlet where antenna masts and palm trees coexist in serenity. The gatehouse leads to a driveway, which is surrounded by three transmitter halls. The first hall to the left houses the decaying 100 kilowatt Marconi transmitter, a remnant of SEAC days, which actually radiates only about 75 kilowatt. Its tube becomes red hot when revved up, so it is cooled by water—enough to heat a swimming pool. It is well past its retirement age, and spare parts are difficult to come by. Yet, it still faithfully churns out the All Asia English Service eight hours a day on 9730 kHz.

On the other side of the same hall are four Phillips ten-kilowatt transmitters which were installed through British aid. Of these only one is operational, being used to transmit the All Asia Hindi Service on 7190 kHz, along with evangelical programs to southern India from Trans World Radio.

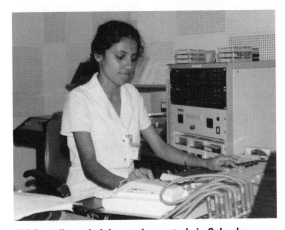

SLBC studio technician at the controls in Colombo.

M. Guha

Author Guha listens to SLBC commentary in the deepest jungles of the Wanni region of northern Sri Lanka.

Located at the far end of the hall are four Kokusai Electric shortwave transmitters donated by Japan for domestic broadcasting. These state-of-the-art units are variously used to carry the domestic national and commercial services in Sinhala, Tamil and English, although they are increasingly being replaced by FM and mediumwave AM.

The second but smaller transmitter hall houses the transmitters of the Voice of America, whose equipment is operated and maintained mainly by SLBC staff, along with visiting VOA personnel. It contains three aging 35 kilowatt Collins transmitters and two ten-kilowatt Phillips transmitters. For the time being, VOA technicians have taken care of the problem of spare parts by cannibalizing two Collins transmitters imported from their relay base in the Philippines. The transmitters radiate VOA English programs to India, as well as the SLBC's external service in English and Hindi. They are fed by speech-grade landlines from the studios in Colombo.

VOA Switches Antennas with Long Stick

The last and the most modern transmitter hall is that of Radio Japan, which is in stark contrast to the antediluvian equipment that otherwise abounds. The hall has a fully automated control room and a transmitter room containing two diminutive 300 kilowatt Kokusai Electric transmitters. These transmitters are almost maintenance-free, and are also operated by trained SLBC engineers. They broadcast nine-and-a-half hours of programs to the Indian subcontinent, and are fed by satellite from Radio Japan studios in Tokyo to the SLBC's master control room in Colombo, then by microwave to Ekala.

The mile-wide antenna farm consists of nine antennas, of which four each are used by the SLBC and Radio Japan, while a single array is used by the VOA. The antennas range from state-of-the-art curtain arrays for Radio Japan to simple dipoles for the VOA, which have to be switched manually with a long stick.

Deutsche Welle Relay Overcomes Attacks

Deutsche Welle also has a world band relay station, near the picturesque beach resort and naval town of Trincomalee. This station is also a converted SEAC base, and houses three powerful 250 kilowatt shortwave transmitters and a 400-kilowatt mediumwave AM transmitter to relay Deutsche Welle's programs to South Asia and the Middle East.

This facility was for some time the target of numerous attacks from Tamil Tiger guerillas, who on occasion managed to overrun and trash the place. Most organizations would have thrown in the towel after making one costly repair after another, but Deutsche Welle stayed the course and is now reaping its reward with powerful,

> **The Deutsche Welle facility was for some time a target of attacks from Tamil Tiger guerillas.**

Sri Lanka Broadcasting Corporation's antenna farm and transmitter hall, located at Ekala.

M. Guha

clearly heard signals for its large Asian listening audience.

New VOA Station to Fire Up in Mid-1999

The VOA, currently making do at its Ekala facilities, is now building a massive world band relay station at Iranawila, near the town of Chilaw. Construction of the station started in earnest in 1993, and is in full swing at the fortified complex. Because of unexpected delays, including a transmitter fire in November, 1996, broadcasting is not expected to begin until mid-1999.

The new station's vast fenced-in compound includes a gatehouse, a transmitter complex, maintenance and storage buildings, and a generator shed. The transmitter complex houses offices, a training room and the broadcast operations area. The operations area includes the control room, transmitters, electrical switching gear and a dummy-load test antenna.

This new facility will be fed by the local utility, Ceylon Electricity Board, to an on-site substation. Additionally, the radio station will have a large 1.6 Megawatt generator capable of powering up to two transmitters at reduced power. A second, smaller, generator will handle the control

systems, emergency transmitter, communications equipment and selected air conditioning units during power outages.

The shortwave transmitters are already in place—three energy-efficient Marconis, each capable of delivering either 500 or 250 kilowatts. The station's sixteen electrically slewable curtain antennas are already up, and can be seen from miles away.

Programming will be received from the VOA's Washington headquarters via satellite. When the facility is fully operational, it will be maintained by five American and 60 Sri Lankan engineering and administrative staff, a number of whom have already been recruited and are being trained.

So it is that a charming island is, and long has been, host to a wide range of shortwave broadcasting activities. Sri Lanka's world band stations can be heard at many times of the day in a number of countries, with best reception in North America being around sunrise and early morning.

Veteran contributor Manosij Guha, who prepared this edition's three articles on Asian broadcasting, is the widely traveled news producer for the ARD _German television network's India bureau in New Delhi._

Ten of the Best: 1999's Top Shows

Variety—it's just one of the many reasons why 600 million people feed their minds with world band radio. PASSPORT's comprehensive guide to hundreds of world band shows is "What's On Tonight," farther back in this book. That *TV Guide*-type section takes you, hour-by-hour, through the full range of choices of what's being aired in English.

But, like mousetraps, some shows are better than others, so here is a sampling of programs that have well earned the right to your time. Schedules are in World Time, with "winter" and "summer" referring to seasons in the Northern Hemisphere.

"Everywoman"
BBC World Service

When the BBC's program planners discovered that most of their listeners were men, they set out to court women.

One of the first offerings was a much ballyhooed soap called "Westway," complete with foreign accents that made audibility a hit-and-miss affair by the time the ionosphere had finished bouncing the signal back and forth.

Fortunately, the planners had something else in the schedule—a weekly show promoted as "a program for and about women around the world." Doubting Thomases, suspecting an onslaught of Me, Woman programming, breathed easier once they discovered that topics like "women taking revenge" made good listening for men and women, alike.

The show covers just about anything, from women in a Muslim society to medical questions sent in by listeners—and, sometimes, husbands. Social, political, environmental, health and domestic issues are just some of the ingredients, and all from a woman's perspective.

There's humor, too, not to mention surprise. How many are aware that the physiotherapist of the Jamaican national soccer team, the Reggae Boys, is—you guessed it!—a woman?

Presenters Anna Umbina and Jane Garvey of BBC's "Everywoman."

BBC World Service

Listeners in *North America* have just one opportunity, at 1530 Wednesday on 9515, 9590 (or 11865), 15220 and 17840 kHz.

Timings for *Europe* are 0830 Wednesday on 7325 (winter), 9410, 12095, 15565 and 17640 kHz; and seven hours later, at 1530, on 6195 (winter), 9410, 12095, 15575 and (summer) 17640 kHz.

In the *Middle East*, the 0830 broadcast is available year-round on 15565 kHz, and winters also on 11760 kHz. At 1530, tune to 12095 or 15575 kHz.

Southern Africa gets two bites: 0830 Saturday on 6190, 11940 and 15400 kHz; with a repeat at 1030 Monday on 6190 and 11940 kHz.

In *East Asia*, there's just the one slot, 0830 Friday on 9740, 15360, 17760 and 21660 kHz. Listeners in *Southeast Asia* can hear the same broadcast on 9740, 11955, 15310 (winter) and 15360 kHz. In winter, 9740 kHz is also available at 1830 Tuesday, when the program is nominally beamed to Australasia, but is also audible farther afield.

For *Australasia*, it's a choice between that 1830 Tuesday slot on 9740 kHz, and 0830 Friday on 11955 and 15360 kHz (9740 kHz is also available during summer in the Southern Hemisphere).

"Hard Country"
Country Music Radio/Merlin Network One

World band is not renowned for its audio quality. So it's not surprising that in recent years a number of high-fidelity alternatives, such as Web radio, have been promoted as 'the way of the future.'

Interestingly, 1998 saw the first signs of a move in the opposite direction, with stations already on satellite, cable or the Internet choosing shortwave as an additional vehicle to deliver their signals to the world.

The first of these was a hybrid arrangement between Merlin Communications—which currently oversees and maintains all shortwave transmission facilities formerly belonging to the BBC World Service—and a number of niche broadcasters beaming their programs to European audiences via satellite and cable networks. Among these is Country Music Radio, CMR.

American country music to European audiences? You bet! Traditional American country music has a strong following in Central Europe, according to veteran performer Johnny Western upon his return to Wichita, Kansas, from a 1998 tour in Germany and Austria. "Over there, they want traditional country much more than the newer styles," explains Western, who points out that there are some American country musicians who spend more time performing in Europe than they do in the United States.

If your appreciation of country music is limited to just one or two particular styles,

"Hard Country" is unlikely to satisfy your appetite. On the other hand, if your interest in the genre is all-embracing, this show should fit you like a glove.

For two hours each week, expect to hear the best of country music from the past 60 years or so. Rockabilly from the early fifties rubs shoulders with a Johnny Horton classic or Dolly Parton's latest release, while Hank Williams, Sr. shares the stage with the Texas Polka Band, Country Joe and the Fish or Doc and Earl Watson. And if it's nostalgia you want, how about a country swing favorite from the forties: "Red River Valley," courtesy of the inimitable Bob Wills and his Texas Playboys.

Better yet, go back even farther and listen to some classic slide guitar from Cliff Carlisle's 1936 recording of "Shanghai Rooster Yodel." They just don't play like that any more.

Whatever your taste in country music, you'll find it here—country rock, ballads, 12-string, Cajun, talking blues, boogie, rockabilly and more. There's also music from Canada, Australia, the United Kingdom and even Germany.

But if you're one of those who believes this kind of music belongs exclusively in the United States, lend an ear to the fabulous sound of the Tequila Sisters, and their unique combination of guitar and Welsh harp.

"Hard Country" is eclectic country, and it's great listening.

The show is aired at 2200-2400 Wednesday, one hour earlier in summer. The winter channel for North America is 7325 kHz; in summer, choose between 11985 and 13690 kHz, with 9780 kHz also available during the second hour.

For Europe, try 3985 kHz in winter. Summer frequencies are 9645 (from 2200) and 11915 kHz.

"The World Today," presented by Anna Korycinska and Julian Keane. Although meant as a breakfast show for Europe, it is easily heard in much of North America.

BBC World Service.

"The World Today"
BBC World Service

In 1998, the BBC World Service and the Voice of America—two world band giants—launched a "rolling news" format. While the Voice of America's "News Now" generated more negative than positive feedback, the BBC's "The World Today" got off to a flying start.

"The World Today" is a new show with an old name, the original version now being known as "Insight." For the time being, it exists solely as a breakfast show for Europe, though it's also easily heard in parts of eastern North America and beyond. Another program along similar lines is scheduled for Asia and the Pacific sometime in 1999, and will probably replace the shows currently heard from 2200 onwards. Other regional editions may follow.

"The World Today" is everything the VOA's "News Now" should have been, but isn't.

Broadcast for 150 minutes Monday through Friday, the program gives priority to important international and European news, with bulletins on the hour and half-hour, plus updates and summaries in between. A team of two hosts switches seamlessly back and forth between the latest news, background reports, sports updates, business news and international press reviews—and there's still time for the occasional offbeat story.

"The World Today" is everything the VOA's "News Now" should have been, but isn't.

Winters, the show is heard at 0430-0700 on 3955, 6180, 6195 and 9410 kHz; summers, one hour earlier on 6180, 6195, 9410 and (from 0400) 12095 kHz. Reception outside Europe and Eastern North America is likely to be limited to nearby places.

"Música del Ecuador"
HCJB—Voice of the Andes

Some shows never lose their appeal, no matter how long they've been on the air, and "Música del Ecuador" has been a source of enjoyment to world band listeners for many a year.

It is one of only a handful of secular or near-secular offerings from friendly inspirational station HCJB—The Voice of the Andes—which has been broadcasting its religious message from Quito to the world for several decades.

Ecuadorian music tends to lack the emotional impact of some other forms of Andean music, notably the Peruvian *huayno*, but it is uncommonly pleasant to listen to. African, Andean and Amazonian influences reflect the diverse ethnic and cultural character of the country.

The Andean region is home to a rich variety of indigenous musical instruments.

J. Zambrano, HCJB

"Música del Ecuador" is not a showpiece of the best in Ecuadorian music, nor is it intended to be. What it does is reflect the country's many different musical styles, using recordings of local singers and musicians. There's an authentic feel to the music which is often absent from similar recordings available internationally.

The melancholic and sentimental *pasillo* can be heard alongside other popular rhythms like the *pasacalle*, *tonada* and *carnaval*, and the ubiquitous local orchestras are never far away from HCJB's microphones.

In *North America*, there are two opportunities each Saturday (Friday evening, locally): 0130 and 0430 on 9745 kHz (12015 kHz may also be available). The 0430 airing is better out west.

Jorge Zambrano, Producer of "Música del Ecuador," is seen here in HCJB's multi-track recording studio.

J. Zambrano, HCJB

Robyn Williams presents "Ockham's Razor," Radio Australia's hard-nosed look at science, technology and medicine.   ABC

Europe has three available slots: 0730 Friday, winters on 5865 kHz, and summers on 11960 kHz; plus 2100 Monday and 1930 Friday on (winter) 12015 or (summer) 17735 kHz.

For *Australasia*, it's 0930 Friday on 9640 kHz.

"Ockham's Razor" Radio Australia

The international airwaves are not short of programs dealing with scientific topics, but most tend to be on the technical side. Few delve into the ethical considerations of the latest advances in science and technology.

There is one notable exception— "Ockham's Razor," Radio Australia's critical look at the world of science, medicine and technology. There's no alchemy here—the sharp, incisive comments fully justify the program's title.

It is not all negative criticism, though; nor are the subjects necessarily current. Indeed, some of the topics might be considered downright unscientific. Doomsday predictions and the rights of rabbits and brush-tailed possums would seem to have little to do with science . . . until you hear the show.

But not all is arcane. There is also news you and your family can use: interesting and informative talks on chronic diseases, for example, and it's all easily understandable.

If what you're looking for is scientific straight talking, they don't come much straighter than this.

Radio Australia's broadcasting capability has been drastically curtailed since losing its Darwin transmitting site due to budget cuts, so reception outside Australasia and the Pacific may not be optimum.

In *East* and *Southeast Asia*, try 1530 Friday on 9500 and 11660 kHz; 0205 Saturday on 15240, 15415, 17750 and 21725 kHz; 1905 Saturday on 6080 and 9500 kHz; and 0605 Sunday on 15240, 15415, 17750 and 21725 kHz.

For *Australasia* and the *Pacific*, take your pick from the following: 1530 Friday on 5995 and 9580 kHz; 0205 Saturday and 0605 Sunday on 9660, 12080, 15240, 15510, 17715 and 21725 kHz; and 1905 Saturday on 6080, 7240, 9580, 9660 and 11880 kHz.

There are no specific broadcasts to *North America*, but reception is often adequate in the western United States and Canada. Best bets are 1530 Friday on 5995 and 9580 kHz; plus 0205 Saturday (Friday evening, North American date) and 0605 Sunday (Saturday night, North American date) on 17715 kHz. In Eastern North America, the 1530 airing is best during the winter, whereas the 0205 transmission is the better bet summer.

"The Jazz Place"
Radio Habana Cuba

If you are lucky enough to live within range of a good jazz FM station, you may think there's not much point in listening else-where. Or you might choose one of the several Web radio jazz sites. Trouble is, you'd still be missing out on some excellent and highly unusual offerings, a number of which you can't find in record stores or catalogs.

Some of the hottest lips and coolest cats can be found in Havana. Not Havana, Florida, nor the ones in Illinois or Kansas, but the real article. Where great cigars and Arturo Sandoval come from.

"The Jazz Place" has been part of Radio Habana Cuba's program lineup for many a year, and is treasured by aficionados. The show features musicians who live and play in Cuba, as well as recordings of overseas artists who have performed on the island.

African influences come through strongly in some of the local bands, and give the music an added injection of excitement and pace. But it's not all drums and bongos by any means—cool jazz also has its place. Some of the music completely defies description . . . how do you define what sounds like a barbershop quartet in Spanish, sung to the sound of a clarinet in the New Orleans tradition?

Sadly, the program is only available in the service for North America. Worse, is now only broadcast once every two weeks because of budget limitations. But, as the saying goes, good things come in small quantities.

There are three opportunities to drop in at the "The Jazz Place"—0131, 0331 and 0531 Monday (Sunday evening, North American date) on 6000 and 9820 kHz. Listeners in Europe can try 9830 kHz, but there's a catch. The transmitter operates only in the upper-sideband mode, audible with

Radio Netherlands' modern headquarters. "Roughly Speaking" is but one of several one-of-a-kind offerings from this creative station.   RNW

difficulty only on certain receivers, and even then operation can be erratic.

"Roughly Speaking"
Radio Netherlands

Self-denominated as "The Voice of Young Holland," this comparatively recent addition to the Radio Netherlands lineup is one of the top youth programs on the world's airwaves, and has prestigious international awards to prove it. This is all the more surprising when taking into account that "Roughly Speaking" is basically a project to stimulate new talent at the station.

As one might expect, the show reflects the liberal values associated with both Holland and today's youth. Not surprisingly, themes like fashion, music and personal relation-ships feature prominently. Interviews with female motorcycle mechanics share airtime with tips on body decoration and Dutch hip-hop music. A feature on sky diving gives way to a report from Amsterdam's Gay Games.

The young crew of Radio Netherlands' European youth lifestyle program, "Roughly Speaking." From left: Max Ohlenschlager, Maike van Pelt and Reza Kartosen.

RNW

"Roughly Speaking" is targeted at a specific age group, and makes no concessions to the rest of the listenership. But what it does, it does well.

In *North America*, tune in at 2354 Saturday on 6020, 6165 and (summer) 9845 kHz. The timings for *Europe* are a little more complicated: winters, it's 1254 Saturday on 5975 and 6045 kHz; and summers, two hours earlier (1054) on 6045 and 9860 kHz.

In *Southern Africa,* expect a solid signal year round at 1854 Saturday on 6020 kHz.

Best for *East* and *Southeast Asia* is 1054 Saturday, winters on 7260 and 9810 kHz; and summers on 12065 and 13710 kHz. In *Australasia*, shoot for 0854 Saturday on 5965, 9830 and 13700 kHz, replaced midyear by 9720 and 9820 kHz. In western parts of the continent, the 1054 slot for Asia should also provide adequate reception.

"One Planet"
BBC World Service

Successor to the former BBC environmental show "Global Concerns," the aptly named "One Planet" maintains its predecessor's strong appeal for listeners interested in environmental and development issues.

Not surprisingly, themes like toxic waste and global warming get high priority. However, equal attention is given to both small-scale development projects and major global issues.

The show is not confined to scientific and political debate—every once in a while a major legal question raises its ugly head. One of the most interesting has been the argument about how to avoid cross-pollenation when genetically altered crops are within "bee range" of organically grown produce. And what legal action, if any, can be taken to protect the interests of farmers and gardeners.

"One Planet" is a half-hour package of discussions, interviews and correspondent reports. There is a summary of the latest environmental news about halfway through the program. Workmanlike, informative and highly topical.

In *North America*, best bet is 0530 Wednesday (Tuesday evening, locally) on 5975 and 6175 kHz. There is a year-round slot at 1030 Wednesday on 6195 kHz (best in areas bordering the Caribbean), with 5965 kHz also available in summer. In winter, look for an additional opportunity at 1830 Tuesday on 17840 kHz. This last timing is mainly for central and western parts of the United States.

For *Europe*, the choices are 1830 Tuesday on 3955 (winter), 6180, 6195, 12095 and (summer) 15575 kHz; and 1030 Wednesday on 9410, 12095, 15565 and 17640 kHz.

Listeners in the *Middle East* have three opportunities: 1830 Tuesday on 9410 (summer only) and 12095 kHz; 0530 Wednesday on 11760 and 15575 kHz; and 1030 the same day on 11765, 15565 and 15575 kHz.

In *Southern Africa*, choose between two Wednesday slots: 0915 on 6190, 11940 and 15400 kHz; and 1930 on 3255, 6190 and 15400 or (midyear) 11835 kHz.

East Asia is well served, with four Wednesday timings: 0230 on 15280 and 15360 kHz; 0730 on 9740, 15360, 17760 and 21660 kHz; 1030 on 9740 and (winter) 11765 kHz; and 2130 on 5965 and (winter) 6120 or (summer) 11945 kHz.

BBC's "One Planet" is presented by Sheena Harold and Rahul Sarnaik.   BBC World Service

Southeast Asia gets the same good deal as East Asia, but with even more channels to choose from: 0230 on 9410 (winter only) and 15360 kHz; 0730 on 9740, 11955, 15310 (winter) and 15360 kHz; 1030 on 6195, 9740, 11765 and 15310 kHz; and 2130 on 3915, 5975 (winter), 6195 and 9740 kHz.

In *Australasia*, the first broadcast can be heard at 0730 Wednesday on 7145, 11955 and 15360 kHz; with two repeats later in the day: at 1030 on 9740 (or 11765) kHz, and 2130 on 5975 and 9740 kHz.

"Mystery Project"
CBC/Radio Canada International

The detective story makes a perfect half-hour play, especially if it is in the form of a serial. This was demonstrated to good effect during the "good old days" of the

BBC's "Thirty-Minute Drama," before the series was dropped and eventually replaced by a soap opera.

Canada to the rescue. Aficionados of radio theater, and especially of detective plays, now have a chance to hear the domestic Canadian Broadcasting Corporation's excellent series, "The Mystery Project," relayed via Radio Canada International.

Classic mystery fiction from the likes of Raymond Chandler and Arthur Conan Doyle are complemented by works from Canadian authors of the caliber of James W. Nichol and Alf Silver. This is theater of the mind at its most entertaining.

That's the good news. Not so good is that "The Mystery Project" is broadcast only to the United States and the Caribbean, and not to other parts of the world. Why this should be is probably the greatest mystery of all.

Winters, the sleuthing begins at 2330 Saturday on 5960, 6040, 9535, 9755 and 11865 kHz; summers, it's one hour earlier on 5960, 9755 and 13670 kHz.

"Short Story"
BBC World Service

A good short story, like a good play, evokes many images. It can be just as entertaining, moving or disturbing as its stage or television cousin. It is also a centuries-old genre which can be found in virtually all parts of the world.

Once upon a time, some bright soul at the BBC World Service came up with a simple but effective idea to unearth the wealth of untapped writing talent among the station's listeners—invite them to contribute short stories of around 2,000 words, with a cash payment if they are broadcast over the air.

The rest is history. Today, the 15-minute "Short Story" is an institution, with millions of regular listeners worldwide.

There is no apparent limit to the subject matter which inspires the authors: mysteries, the supernatural, personal experience, the whole gamut of human emotions, aboriginal tales, life in the big city—almost as many themes as contributors. What often gives the stories an extra edge is the local flavor, be it of a Pakistani village, a Chinese mountain or the Pacific coast of California.

The first broadcast for *North America* is at 0145 Saturday (Friday evening local American date) on 5975, 6175 and 9590 kHz; and is repeated 11 hours later (at 1245) on 5965 (winter), 6195 and 15220 kHz.

Europe has two airings: 1245 Saturday on 9410, 12095, 15565 and 17640 kHz; and 0815 Sunday on the same channels (7325 kHz is also available in winter). These broadcasts can also heard in the *Middle East* on 15565 and 15575 kHz, with 11760 kHz additionally available at 0815, winters.

For *Southern Africa*, there are two Sunday slots: 0715 on 6190, 9600 and 11940 kHz; and 2145 on 3255, 6005 and 6190 kHz.

The first opportunity for *East Asia* is at 0915 Sunday on 6065, 9580, 9740, 11765 (winter), 11955, 15280, 15360, 17760 (summer) and 21660 kHz. Repeats can be heard at 2115 Monday on 5965 and 6120 (or 11945) kHz; and 0030 Friday on 15360 kHz.

These same slots are also available to *Southeast Asia*: 0915 Sunday on 6195, 9740, 11765 and 15360 kHz; 2115 Monday on 3915, 5975 (winter), 6195 and 9740 kHz; and 0030 Friday on 6195, 9410 and 15360 kHz.

First shot for *Australasia* is at 0915 Sunday on 9740 and 15360 kHz, replaced midyear by the single channel of 11765 kHz. A repeat is aired at 2115 Monday on 5975 and 9740 kHz.

———————————

Prepared by Don Swampo and the staff of Passport to World Band Radio.

Cool Radio.

Grundig, together with the F.A. Porsche Design Group, has developed a revolutionary new product in every sense. With an aluminum paint finish, leather cover, and stylish details, Grundig scores again with this amazingly compact and impressive digital direct-frequency-entry radio!

Compleat Idiot's Guide to Getting Started

Four "Must" Tips to Catch the World

World band radio is information and entertainment, on the spot—your unfiltered connection to what's going on all over. But it's not as easy to receive as conventional radio, so here are four "must" tips to get started.

"Must" #1: Set Clock for World Time

World band schedules use a single worldwide time, *World Time*. After all, world band radio is global, with nations broadcasting around-the-clock from virtually every time zone.

Imagine the chaos if each broadcaster used its own local time for scheduling. In England, 9 PM is different from nine in the evening in Japan or Canada. How would anybody know when to tune in?

World Time, or Coordinated Universal Time (UTC), was formerly and in some circles still is known as Greenwich Mean Time (GMT). It is keyed to the Greenwich meridian in England and is announced in 24-hour format, like military time. So 2 PM, say, is 1400 ("fourteen hundred") hours.

There are four easy ways to know World Time. First, you can tune to one of the standard time stations, such as WWV in Colorado and WWVH in Hawaii in the United States, or CHU in Ottawa, Canada. WWV and WWVH are on 5000, 10000 and 15000 kHz around-the-clock, with WWV also on 2500 and 20000 kHz; CHU is on 3330, 7335 and 14670 kHz. There, you will hear time "pips" every second, followed just before the beginning of each minute by an announcement of the exact World Time. Boring, yes, but very handy when you need it.

> **World Time is used by most stations.**

Second, you can tune to one of the major international broadcasters, such as London's BBC World Service or Washington's Voice of America. Most announce World Time at the top of the hour.

Third, you can access the Internet Web site tycho.usno.navy.mil/what.html.

Fourth, here are some quick calculations.

If you live on the East Coast of the United States, *add* five hours winter (four hours summer) to your local time to get World Time. So, if it is 8 PM EST (the 20th hour of the day) in New York, it is 0100 hours World Time.

On the U.S. West Coast, add eight hours winter (seven hours summer).

In Britain, it's easy—World Time (oops, Greenwich Mean Time) is the same as local winter time. However, you'll have to subtract one hour from local summer time to get World Time.

Elsewhere in Western Europe, subtract one hour winter (two hours summer) from local time.

PASSPORT'S FIVE-MINUTE START

In a hurry? Here's how to get to get going with the most fire and least smoke:

1. Wait until evening, when signals are strongest. If you live in a concrete-and-steel building, put your radio by a window or sit on the balcony.

2. Make sure the radio is plugged in or has fresh batteries. Extend the telescopic antenna fully and vertically. Set the DX/local switch (if there is one) to "DX," but otherwise leave the controls the way they came from the factory.

3. Turn on your radio. Set it to 5900 kHz and begin tuning slowly toward 6200 kHz. You will now begin to encounter a number of stations from around the world. Adjust the volume to a level that is comfortable for you. *Voilà!* You are now an initiate of world band radio.

Other times? Read on, especially "Best Times and Frequencies for 1999."

Live elsewhere? Flip through the next few pages until you come to "Setting Your World Time Clock."

Once you know the correct World Time, adjust the settings on your radio's clock so you'll have the time handy whenever you want to listen. No 24-hour clock? Pick up the phone and order one (world band specialty firms sell them for as little as $10, see box). Unless you enjoy doing weird computations in your head (it's 6:00 PM here, so add five hours to make it 11:00 PM, which on a 24-hour clock converts to 23:00 World Time—but, whoops, I forgot that it's summer and I should have added four hours instead of five . . .), it'll be the best dime you ever spent.

"Must" #2: Wind Your Calendar

What happens at midnight, World Time? A new World Day arrives as well. This can trip up even experienced listeners—sometimes radio stations, too.

Remember: Midnight World Time means a new day. So if it is 9 PM EST Wednesday in New York, it is 0200 hours World Time *Thursday*. Don't forget to "wind your calendar"!

"Must" #3: Know How to Find Stations

Passport provides station schedules three ways: by country, by time of day and by frequency. By-country is best to hear a given station. "What's On Tonight," the time-of-day section, is like *TV Guide* and includes program details. The by-frequency Blue Pages are for when you're dialing around the bands.

Frequencies may be given either in kilohertz (kHz) or Megahertz (MHz). The only difference is three decimal places, so

WORLD TIME CLOCKS

Bargain Models

For the relatively unfamiliar 24-hour World Time, digital clocks are much easier to read than timepieces with hands. Here are four value-priced choices that work well and are easy to find.

MFJ-24-107B, $9.95. Despite its paucity of features, this battery-powered "Volksclock" does the trick.

NI8F LCD, $14.95. Same as the MFJ, above, but with a handsome walnut frame instead of aluminum. It is less likely than MFJ models to scratch surfaces. From Universal Radio.

MFJ-24 HOUR LCD CLOCK
MODEL MFJ-107B

MFJ's battery-powered "Volksclock" does the trick.

MFJ 114, $39.95. If you want your World Time *VISIBLE*, here's a bold alternative. MFJ's 114 uses tall (2 1/4 inches or 60 mm) bright-red LEDs instead of the small, low-contrast LCD screens used by most other digital timepieces. Unlike LCD clocks, which are battery powered, the 114 plugs into the wall, using a battery only for backup.

MFJ-108B, $19.95. For those who also want local time. Two battery-powered LCD clocks—24-hour format for World Time, separate 12-hour display for local time—side-by-side.

Sophisticated Timepieces

If you want to go for the gold, there are sophisticated 24-hour World Time clocks ranging from under $100 to over $2,000.

Backwoods cabins are ultimate hideaways for world band under the stars. A small roll of insulated antenna wire helps bring in exotic stations.

Simo Soininen

6175 kHz is the same as 6.175 MHz. But forget all the technobabble. All you need to know is that 6175, with or without decimals, refers to a certain spot on your radio's dial.

Here are the main sectors where you'll find world band stations and when they're most active. Except for the 4750-5075 kHz segment, which has mainly low-powered Latin American and African stations, you'll discover a huge variety of stations.

4750-5075 kHz	Night and twilight, mainly during winter
5730-6205 kHz	Night and twilight; sometimes day, too
7100-7595 kHz	Night, early morning and late afternoon
9350-10000 kHz	Night, early morning and late afternoon
11550-12160 kHz	Night and day, especially dusk
13570-13870 kHz	Day and, to some degree, night
15000-15710 kHz	Day and, to some degree, night
17500-17900 kHz	Day and, to a limited degree, night
21450-21850 kHz	Day and, rarely, night

> **There are several sectors where stations cluster. Some perform better at night, others by day.**

You're already used to hearing mediumwave AM and FM stations at the same place on the dial, day and night, or Web radio stations at the same Websites. But things are a lot different when you roam the international airwaves.

World band radio is like a global bazaar where a variety of merchants come and go at different times. Similarly, stations enter and leave a given spot on the dial throughout the day and night. Where you once tuned in, say, a French station, hours later you might find a Russian or Chinese broadcaster roosting on that same spot.

Or on a nearby perch. If you suddenly hear interference from a station on an adjacent channel, it doesn't mean something is wrong with your radio; it probably means another station has begun broadcasting on a nearby frequency. There are more stations on the air than there is space for them, so sometimes they try to outshout each other.

BEST TIMES AND FREQUENCIES FOR 1999

With world band, if you dial around randomly, you're almost as likely to get dead air as you are a favorite program. For one thing, a number of world band segments are alive and kicking by day, while others are nocturnal. Too, some fare better at specific times of the year.

"Neighborhoods" Where to Tune

Official "neighborhoods," or segments, of the shortwave spectrum are set aside for world band radio by the International Telecommunication Union. However, the ITU countenances some broadcasting outside these parameters, so the "real world" situation is actually more generous. This is what's shown below.

This guide is most accurate if you're listening from north of Africa or South America. Even then, what you'll actually hear will vary—depending upon such variables as your precise location, where the station transmits from, the time of year and your radio (e.g., *see* Propagation in the glossary). Although world band is active 24 hours a day, signals are usually best from an hour or two before sunset until sometime after midnight. Too, try a couple of hours on either side of dawn.

Here, then, are the most attractive times and frequencies for world band listening, based on reception conditions forecast for the coming year. Unless otherwise indicated, frequency ranges are occupied mainly by international broadcasters, but also include some domestic stations or overseas relays of domestic stations. In the Americas, 3900-4000 kHz and 7100-7300 kHz are reserved for use by amateur radio ("hams"), even though world band transmissions from other parts of the world manage to be heard there. **Nights** refers to your local hours of darkness, plus dawn and dusk.

Possible Reception during Nights except Summer

2 MHz (120 meters) **2300-2500 kHz** (overwhelmingly domestic stations)

Limited Reception during Nights

3 MHz (90 meters) **3200-3400 kHz** (mostly domestic stations)

Good-to-Fair except Summer Nights in Europe and Asia; Limited Reception during Nights Elsewhere

4 MHz (75 meters) **3900-4080 kHz** (international and domestic stations, primarily not in or beamed to the Americas—3900-3950 mainly Asian and Pacific transmitters; 3950-4000 also includes European and African transmitters)

Some Reception during Nights; Regional Reception Daytime

5 MHz (60 meters) **4700-5100 kHz** (mostly domestic stations)

Excellent during Nights; Regional Reception Daytime

6 MHz (49 meters) **5730-6250 kHz**

To cope with this, purchase a radio with superior adjacent-channel rejection, also known as selectivity. The lab measurements and listening tests in PASSPORT REPORTS, a major section of this book, tell you how successfully the various radios leap this hurdle.

One of the most pleasant things about world band radio is cruising up and down the airwaves. Daytime, you'll find most stations above 11500 kHz; night, below 16000 kHz.

Tune slowly, savor the sound of foreign tongues sprinkled alongside English shows. Enjoy the music, weigh the opinions of other peoples and the events that shape their lives.

If a station fades out, there is probably nothing wrong with your radio. The atmosphere's *ionosphere* bounces world band signals earthward, like a dribbled basketball, and it changes constantly. The result is that broadcasters operate in different parts of the world band spectrum, depending upon the time of day and season of the year.

That same changeability can also work in your favor, especially if you like to eavesdrop on signals not intended for your part of the world. Sometimes stations from exotic locales—places you would not ordinarily hear—become surprise arrivals at your radio, thanks to the shifting characteristics of the ionosphere.

"Must" #4: Get A Radio That Really Works

Choose carefully, but you shouldn't need a costly set. Cheap radios should be avoided—they suffer from one or more

---

Good during Nights; Regional Reception Daytime

7 MHz (41 meters) **7100-7600 kHz (also 6890-6995 kHz)** (7100-7300 kHz, no American-based transmitters and few transmissions targeted to the Americas)

9 MHz (31 meters) **9250-10000 kHz (also 9020-9080 kHz)**

Good during Nights except Mid-Winter; Some Reception Daytime and Winter Nights; Good Asian and Pacific Reception Mornings in America

11 MHz (25 meters) **11500-12160 kHz**

Good during Daytime; Good during Summer Nights

13 MHz (22 meters) **13570-13870 kHz**

15 MHz (19 meters) **15000-15800 kHz**

Good during Daytime; Variable, Limited Reception Summer Nights

17 MHz (16 meters) **17480-17900 kHz**

19 MHz (15 meters) **18900-19020 kHz**

21 MHz (13 meters) **21450-21850 kHz**

Inactive at Present

25 MHz (11 meters) **25670-26100 kHz**

> Daytime, you'll hear most stations above 11500 kHz; night, below 16000 kHz.

major defects. But with one of the better-rated portables, usually less than the price of a VCR, you'll be able to hear much of what world band has to offer.

You won't need an exotic outside antenna, either, unless you're using a tabletop model. All portables, and to some extent portatops, are designed to well work off the built-in telescopic antenna—solo or, better, with several yards or meters of insulated wire clipped on. But try to purchase a radio with digital frequency display. Its accuracy will make tuning far easier than with out-moded slide-rule tuning.

Does that mean you should avoid a tabletop or portatop model? Hardly, especially if you listen during the day, when signals are weaker, or to hard-to-hear stations. The

SETTING YOUR WORLD TIME CLOCK

PASSPORT's "Addresses PLUS" lets you arrive at the local time in another country by adding or subtracting from World Time. Use that section to determine the time within a country you are listening to.

This box, however, gives it from the other direction—that is, what to add or subtract from your local time to determine World Time at your location. Use this to set your World Time clock.

Where You Are	To Determine World Time
North America	
Newfoundland St. John's NF, St. Anthony NF	Add 3½ hours winter, 2½ hours summer
Atlantic St. John NB, Battle Harbour NF	Add 4 hours winter, 3 hours summer
Eastern New York, Atlanta, Toronto	Add 5 hours winter, 4 hours summer
Central Chicago, Nashville, Winnipeg	Add 6 hours winter, 5 hours summer
Mountain Denver, Salt Lake City, Calgary	Add 7 hours winter, 6 hours summer
Pacific San Francisco, Vancouver	Add 8 hours winter, 7 hours summer
Alaska Anchorage, Fairbanks	Add 9 hours winter, 8 hours summer
Hawaii Honolulu, Hilo	Add 10 hours year round
Europe	
United Kingdom, Ireland and Portugal London, Dublin, Lisbon	Same time as World Time winter, subtract 1 hour summer

best-rated tabletop, and even portatop, models can bring more faint and difficult signals to life—especially when they're connected to a good external antenna. But if you just want to hear the big stations, you'll do fine with a moderately priced portable. PASSPORT REPORTS rates virtually all available models.

Radio in hand, read or at least glance over your owner's manual—yes, it *is* worth it.

You'll find that, despite a few unfamiliar controls, your new world band receiver isn't all that much different from radios you have used all your life. Experiment with those controls so you'll become comfortable with them. After all, you can't harm your radio by twiddling switches and knobs.

Prepared by Jock Elliott, Tony Jones and Lawrence Magne.

Continental Western Europe; parts of Central and Eastern Continental Europe Paris, Berlin, Stockholm, Prague, Rome, Madrid	Subtract 1 hour winter, 2 hours summer
Elsewhere in Continental Europe; Cyprus Belarus, Bulgaria, Cyprus, Estonia, Finland, Greece, Latvia, Lithuania, Moldova, Romania, Russia (Kaliningradskaya Oblast), Turkey and Ukraine	Subtract 2 hours winter, 3 hours summer
Mideast & Southern Africa	
Egypt, Israel, Lebanon and Syria	Subtract 2 hours winter, 3 hours summer
South Africa, Zambia and Zimbabwe	Subtract 2 hours year round
East Asia & Australasia	
China, including Taiwan	Subtract 8 hours year round
Japan	Subtract 9 hours year round
Australia: *Victoria, New South Wales, Tasmania*	Subtract 11 hours local summer, 10 local winter (midyear)
Australia: *South Australia*	Subtract 10½ hours local summer, 9½ hours local winter (midyear)
Australia: *Queensland*	Subtract 10 hours year round
Australia: *Northern Territory*	Subtract 9½ hours year round
Australia: *Western Australia*	Subtract 8 hours year round
New Zealand	Subtract 13 hours local summer, 12 hours local winter (midyear)

First Tries: Ten Easy Catches

Want to listen to something right away? Here are ten stations in English that are easy to hear—wherever you are.

All times and days of the week are in World Time, explained elsewhere in this book.

EUROPE
France

Despite the size of the French government deficit, **Radio France** **Internationale** continues to enjoy a level of funding that is enviable compared to that of most other international broadcasters. Because much of the station's mandate has to do with promoting the French language, little programming is in English. Yet, RFI's English shows are worth hearing, if only for their peerless coverage of African events. Alas, they are aired to North America only at offbeat times.

North America: 1200-1300 on 13625 (winter), 15530 (summer) and 17575 kHz. Nominally targeted at Central America, but still a powerhouse in much of North America. If reception is unsatisfactory, try 15540 kHz via the relay in Gabon. Though targeted at West Africa, the signal is audible in parts of eastern North America and the Caribbean. The 1600 broadcast to Africa is also sometimes audible in eastern North America.

Europe: 1200-1300 on 9805, 15155 and 15195 kHz.

Middle East: 1400-1500 on 17560 kHz; plus 1600-1730 on 9485, 11615 or 15460 kHz (intended mainly for Africa).

Asia: 1200-1300 on 11600 kHz, and 1400-1500 on 7110 (or 11910) and 12030 (or 15405) kHz. Some of these should also be audible in *Australia* (better to the west).

Michael Behrens is Head of English Programs for Deutsche Welle. DW

Africa: RFI's broadcasts for Africa are one of the best sources of news about that continent, and can often be heard well outside the intended target area. Audible at 1600-1700 on 9485, 11615, 11700/ 11705, 12015, 15210, 15460 and 15530 kHz (some of which are seasonal); and at 1700-1730 on two of these channels: 9485, 11615, 15210 and 15460 kHz. The 1200 transmission for Europe and North America also goes out to West Africa on 15540 kHz.

Germany

Deutsche Welle, now a shining example of German efficiency, has few doubts about where it is headed. Despite some rethinking about where its priorities lie, the station continues its firm commitment to a strong news-based service in English, concentrating its efforts on regional coverage of world affairs. An exceptional source of European news, the station also provides excellent reports on events in Africa and the Asia-Pacific region.

> Deutsche Welle is a shining example of German efficiency and an exceptional source for European news.

North and Central America: 0100-0150 winters on 5960, 6040, 6085, 6145 and 9640 kHz; summers on 6040, 6085, 6145, 9640 and 11810 kHz. The next edition is at 0300-0350: winters on 6045, 6085, 6185, 9535 and 9640 kHz; summers on 6085, 6145, 6185, 9535 and 9640 kHz. The third and final broadcast goes out at 0500-0550, winters on 5960, 6100, 6120 and 6185 kHz; and summers on 6045, 6185, 9615 and 11810 kHz. This last slot is best for western North America.

Europe: 2000-2050 winters on 7285 kHz, summers on 9615 kHz.

Middle East: 0600-0650 winters on 21705 kHz, summers on 21680 kHz.

Southern Africa: 0400-0450 winters (summer in the Southern Hemisphere) on 6015, 6065, 7225, 7265 and 9565 kHz; summers on 5990, 6015, 7225, 9565 and 11765 kHz. The second slot is at 0900-0950 on 9565, 15145 (winter), 15205 (summer), 15410, 17800 and 21600 kHz; and the third and final broadcast goes out at 1600-1650, winter on

Deutsche Welle's "COOL" duo Erica Gingerich and Anke Rasper. DW

7120, 9735, 11810, 13750 and 15145 kHz; and summer on 7130, 9735, 11810 and 21695 kHz.

Asia and the Pacific: 0900-0950 winters on 6160, 7380, 11715, 12055 and 17820 kHz; summers on 6160, 12055, 17560 and 21680 kHz. A second broadcast airs at 2100-2150 on 7115 (summer), 9670, 9765 and 11785 kHz. There's also an additional transmission for South and Southeast Asia at 2300-2350, winters on 6045, 6130 and 7235 kHz; summers on 5975, 6090, 7235 and 9815 kHz.

Holland

Radio Nederland—or **Radio Netherlands**—is a popular station with a strong following, despite the occasional controversy. It exemplifies the best of what world band is about: providing an abundance of programs for the intellectually curious. Easily audible in most parts of the world.

North America: Good reception throughout much of North America at 2330-0125 on 6020, 6165 and (summer) 9845 kHz. Out west, try 0430-0525 on 6165 and 9590 kHz. Too, the broadcasts for Africa at 1830-2025 on 15315 kHz are often well heard in parts of the United States.

Europe: 1130-1325 winters on 6045 and 7190 kHz (5975 kHz may replace 7190 kHz

from 1230); 1030-1225 summers on 6045 and 9860 kHz.

Middle East: There is nothing specifically targeted to this area, but try the winter frequency of 13700 kHz at 1330-1525.

Southern Africa: 1730-1925 on 6020 kHz.

East Asia: 0930-1125 winters on 7260 and 9810 kHz, and summers on 12065 and 13710 kHz.

Australia and the Pacific: 0730-0825 winters (summer in Australasia) on 9830 and 11895 kHz, and midyear on 9720 and 9820 kHz; 0830-0925 winters on 5965, 9830 and 13700 kHz; midyear on 9720 and 9820 kHz. Too, the 0930-1125 broadcasts for East Asia are often well received in parts of Australasia.

Russia

For the **Voice of Russia**, 1998 was the worst year in its long history. It received two draconian budget cuts, and also has had to cope with various internal "adjustments." What was for decades the world's mightiest broadcaster has now slumped to almost 20th position in the world band standings.

Although hours of transmission are now greatly reduced, the station's most popular shows remain intact. What happens next depends to a great extent on whether the Russian government can resolve the worst of its financial and economic problems.

To make the best of a difficult situation, the Voice of Russia has chosen to limit the number of transmitters it uses in order to step up the power of those left at its disposal. As a result the station's broadcasts can still be heard in many areas, albeit for shorter periods and on fewer channels.

Eastern North America was by far the worst hit of all areas. Winters, try 7100/7105 kHz at 0200-0600 (5940 kHz may also be available at 0300-0400), and 7125 kHz at 0400-0600; best summer bets are 7125 kHz (0300-0500) and 9665 kHz (0200-0500). In addition, especially during winter afternoons, try frequencies beamed to Europe—some of these make it to eastern North America. If you don't find anything on these channels, dial around nearby. The Voice of Russia is not renowned for sticking to its frequencies, but it often stays within the same segments of the world band spectrum.

Western North America: In winter, try the following: 0200-0300 on 9580, 12045 and 13665 kHz; 0300-0500 on 5930, 7175, 9580 and 12045 kHz; and 0500-0600 on 5930, 6065 and 7175 kHz. For summer, choose from 15180 (0300-0500), 15425 (0100-0500) and 15595 (0300-0500). Reception in western parts is more reliable than farther east, and channel usage tends to be more predictable.

Dutch listener S. Van Zoest uses a vintage receiver to tune in China Radio International's programs. CRI

Europe: 1800-2200 (one hour earlier in summer). Best winter choices are in the 6, 7 and 9 MHz segments. At 1800-2000, try 6130, 7210, 7440 and 9890 kHz; for 2000-2200, look to 5940, 5965, 6130, 6145, 7205 (from 2100), 7355, 7390 and 9890 kHz. For summer, dial around the 9 and 11MHz ranges. Worth a look are 9765 and 9775 kHz which should be available throughout the 1700-2100 period.

Middle East: 1600-1800 (1500-1700 in summer). Try the likes of 4730, 4940 and 4975 kHz during the first hour; too, take a look at the 7 and 9 MHz bands for winter frequencies; 11 and 15 MHz in summer.

Southern Africa: 1800-2000, although some channels may be audible till 2100. One hour earlier in summer. Try dialing around the 7 and 9 MHz segments, with the 9 and 11 MHz bands a better bet in summer.

Southeast Asia: 1400-1600 winter on a limited number of channels in the 7 and 9 MHz segments. In summer, try 17570 and

21760 kHz at 1300-1400, and 12025 and 17570 kHz an hour later. Probably better is to try some of the frequencies for Australasia, earlier in the day.

Australasia: 0600-1000 winter (summer in OZ) on 9825, 15460, 15470, 17495, 17570, 17860 and 21790 kHz; midyear, 0500-0900 on 9450, 15490, 17495, 17665, 21760 and 21790. Dial around nearby if there's nothing on these channels—usage tends to vary. Not all frequencies are available for the full period.

Switzerland

In Spring 1998, **Swiss Radio International** lost its longest-serving transmitting site. Local environmentalists finally achieved their goal, and Schwarzenburg was shut down for good. As a result, most of the station's broadcasts now go out over leased transmitters in other countries.

In spite of these changes, the program lineup has changed little from that of

The new General Manager of Swiss Radio International, Carla Ferrari. SRI

recent years. SRI continues to provide some of the best reporting on humanitarian issues and events in less-developed countries, and the rest of the programming has a strong Swiss flavor. This is especially true weekends.

North America: 0100-0130 and 0400-0500 on 9885 and 9905 kHz.

Europe: (everything one hour earlier in summer) 0500-0530 and 0630-0700 on 5840 and 6165 kHz; 1100-1130 and 1300-1330 on 6165 and 9535 kHz; and 2000-2030 on 7410 (9885 in summer) and 6165 kHz.

Southern Africa: 0730-0800 on 9885, 11860 and 13635 kHz; and 2000-2030 on 9840 (summer), 9885 and (winter) 9905 kHz.

East and Southeast Asia: 1100-1200 winter on any two channels from 9810, 9885, 12075 and 13635 kHz; and summers on 9810 and 17515 kHz. The broadcast is repeated at 1300-1400 on 7230 and 7480 kHz.

Australasia: 0830-0900 on 9885 and 13685 kHz.

United Kingdom

Listeners may complain about some of the program changes, but the **BBC World Service** is still the world band quality champ. With the introduction of a breakfast show for Europe, and another planned for Asia and the Pacific, the Beeb continues to consolidate its position as the world's most respected news source. While some consider all that current-events output to be excessive, especially to the Americas, there are still plenty of features and entertainment to keep everybody happy.

> The BBC World Service is the world's most respected news source. Great features and entertainment, too.

North America: Winter mornings, easterners can listen at 1100-1200 on 5965, 6195 and 15220 kHz (6195 and 15220 kHz carry alternative programs for the Caribbean at 1100-1130 on weekdays); 1200-1400 on 5965, 6195, 9515 and 15220 kHz; 1400-1615 on 9515 and 17840 kHz; and 1615-1700 on 17840 kHz (also available Saturdays on 9515 kHz). The summer schedule is 1000-1100 on 5965 and 6195 kHz; 1100-1200 on 5965, 6195 and 15220 kHz; 1200-1400 on 9515 and 15220 kHz; and 1400-1700 on 9515 (till 1615, Sunday through Friday) and 17840 kHz. Listeners in or near the Caribbean area can tune in at 1000-1100 on 6195 kHz; 1100-1400 on 6195 and 15220 kHz; and 1400-1700 on 17840 kHz.

For winter reception in western North America, try 1200-1400 on 6195, 9515, 9590 (from 1300), 9740 and 15220 kHz; 1400-1600 on 9515, 9590, 9740, 15220 and 17840 kHz; and 1600-1900 on 17840 kHz (9515 kHz is also available until 1615, extended to 1700 on Saturdays). In summer, it's 1200-1300 on 9515, 9740 and 15220 kHz; 1300-1400 on 9515, 9740, 11865 and 15220 kHz; 1400-1600 on 9515, 9740, 11865, 15220 and 17840 kHz; and 1600-1800 on 17840 kHz (also on 9515 till 1700 Saturday; 1615 on other days). Note that 9740

Bush House in London, home to the BBC World Service. Despite cutbacks and some privatization, the BBC's international news, analysis and entertainment continue to be awesome. BBC World Service

kHz carries programs for Asia and the Pacific, which are often different from those targeted at North America.

Early evenings in eastern North America, go for 5975 kHz at 2100-2200. This slot contains the informative "Caribbean Report," aired at 2115-2130 Monday through Friday, also carried on 15390 and 17715 kHz.

Throughout the evening, most North Americans can listen in at 2200-0700 (0800 in winter) on a number of frequencies. Times vary, but workhorse channels are 5975, 6175 and 9590 kHz.

Europe: A powerhouse 0300-2330 (one hour earlier in summer) on 3955, 6180, 6195, 7325, 9410, 12095, 15565, 15575 and 17640 kHz (times vary for each channel).

Middle East: 0200-2100 year round. Key frequencies (times vary according to

whether it is winter or summer) are 9410, 11760, 12095, 15565 and 15575 kHz.

Southern Africa: 0300-2200 on (among others) 3255, 6005, 6190, 9600, 11835 (midyear), 11940, 15400, 21470 and 21660 kHz (times vary for each channel).

East and Southeast Asia: 0000-0300 on 6195 (till 0200), 15280 (except 0030-0100) and 15360 kHz; 0300-0330 on 15360 and 21660 kHz; 0330-0500 on 11955, 15280, 15310 (winter) and 21660 kHz; 0500-0945 on 6195 (from 0900), 9740, 11955, 15280 (0500-0530 and 0900-0945), 15310 (winter, to 0915), 15360, 17760 and 21660 kHz; 0945-1100 on 6195, 9740, 11765, 15310, 15360 (till 1030) and 21660 kHz; 1100-1300 on 6195, 7235 (winter), 9580, 9740, 11955 and (summer) 15280 kHz; 1300-1615 on 5990, 6195 and 9740 kHz; and 1615-1745 (to Southeast Asia) on 3915 and

Staff from CRI's English Service after the flag-raising cermony for CRI's new office building. CRI

7135 (or 7160) kHz. For morning reception, try 2100-2200 on 3915, 5965, 5975 (winter), 6120 (11945 in summer) and 6195 kHz; 2200-2300 on 5905 (9890 in summer), 5965, 6195, 7110 and 11955 kHz; and 2300-2400 on 5965, 6035, 6195, 7110, 9580, 11945 and 11955 kHz. In winter, 9740 kHz (1830-2200) is also available for Southeast Asia.

Australasia: 0500-0900 on 7145 (0600-0815), 9740 (not midyear), 11955 and 15360 kHz; 0900-1100 on 9740 and (till 1030) 15360 kHz, replaced midyear by the single frequency of 11765 kHz; 1100-1615 and 1830-2000 on 9740 kHz; 2000-2200 on 5975 and 9740 kHz; and 2200-2400 on 11955 kHz. At 2200-2300, 9660 and 12080 kHz are also available for some parts of the region.

ASIA
China

For **China Radio International**, 1998 was a great year. The staff moved to an impressive new building, program production went digital, and two major transmitting sites—Urümqi and Kunming—became fully operational.

The audio quality from some transmitters, especially those at Xi'an, is still sub-optimum, but signals from the new transmitting centers at Urümqi and Kunming are as clear as any on the world bands.

Tian Wei is designer, writer and producer of CRI's "Voices from Other Lands." CRI

Eastern North America: 0300-0400 on 9690 kHz; 0400-0500 on 9730 kHz; and 0500-0600 (0400-0500 in summer) on 9560 kHz.

Western North America: As for eastern parts, plus 1400-1600 (one hour earlier in summer) on 7405 kHz.

Europe: 2000-2200 on 6950 and 9920 kHz.

Middle East: There are no specific broadcasts for this area, but try the transmission to Europe at 2000-2200; also 1900-2000 on 6955 (11515 in summer) and 9440 kHz.

Southern Africa: 1600-1700 on 9565 and 9620 kHz; 1700-1800 on 7150, 7405 and 9570 kHz; and 2000-2100 on 7160 and 7170 kHz; and 2100-2130 on 7170, 7180 and 9535 kHz.

Asia: 1200-1300 on 9715 and 11660 kHz; 1300-1400 on 11660 and 11980 kHz; 1400-1500 on 7260, 9535, 9700 and 11825 kHz; and 1500-1600 on 7160 and 9785 kHz.

Australasia: 0900-1100 on 9785 and 11755 kHz; 1200-1300 on 6950 and 7385 kHz; and 1300-1400 on 7385 kHz.

Japan

Radio Japan, another powerful Asian voice, can be heard just about anywhere in the world. News—especially from the Asia-Pacific rim—continues to be an important part of the station's programming, and some recently added music shows have livened up formerly staid format.

Shoko Fukui presents "Japan This Week." RHK

Jim Craig, host of RCI's weekday magazine program, "Spectrum."

RCI

Eastern North America: Best bet is 1100-1200 (winters, to 1300) on 6120 kHz. There is also a summers-only broadcast at 0000 on 11705 kHz.

Western North America: 0100 (winter only) on 11790 and 13630 kHz; 0500 on 6110 and (summer) 9835 and 15230 kHz; 0600 winter on 6190 and 9505 kHz, summer on 15230 kHz, and year round on 9835 kHz; 1400 summer on 9505 kHz; 1500 and 1700 on 9505 or 9535 kHz; and 2100 on 13630 kHz.

Europe: 0500 on 6150 (winter) and 7230 kHz; 0600 on 5975 (winter) and 7230 kHz; 0700 winter on 7230 kHz; 1700 on 7110 kHz; 2100 summer on 9725 kHz; and 0000 on 6155 and 6180 kHz..

Middle East: 0700 winter on 15230 kHz; 1400 summer on 11880 kHz; and 1700 winter on 11880 kHz.

Southern Africa: 1500 winter and 1700 summer on 15355 kHz.

Asia: 0100 on 11860, 11890 (winter), 15570, 15590 (summer) and 17810 kHz; 0300 summer on 17855 kHz; 0500 year-round on 11715 and 11840 kHz, and summer on 11760 and 17810 kHz; 0600 on 11740, 11840, 11910, 15550 (winter), 15570 (winter) and 17810 kHz; 0700 winter on 11740, 11840, 15570 and 17810 kHz; 1000 summer on 9695 and 11730 kHz; 1100-1300 winter on 7125 and 11815 kHz, replaced summer by 9695 and 11730 kHz; 1400 winter on 7200 kHz, and summer on 11730 kHz; 1500 on 7200, 7240 (winter), 9750 and (summer) 11730 kHz; 1700 winter on 6035, 7200, 7225 and 11730 kHz; and summer on 6090 and 9825 kHz; and 2100 winter on 6035 kHz. Transmissions to Asia are often heard in other parts of the world, as well.

Australasia: 0100 on 21610 kHz; 0300 on 17685 kHz; 0500-0700 on 11850 or 11920 kHz; 0700 winter (summer Down Under) on 11850 and 11920 kHz; 1000 midyear on 11850 kHz; and 2100 midyear on 6035 and 11850 kHz.

David Blair hosts "Venture Canada," a weekend program in English that looks at Canadian business interests in Canada and around the world. RCI

NORTH AMERICA
Canada

For the first time in years, **Radio Canada International** is not facing a budget crisis—or worse, imminent closure. At least in the short term, the station's funding is assured.

What the future holds is anyone's guess, but domestic politics notwithstanding, the future looks brighter than it has in a long time. For the present, RCI still relies heavily on the domestic Canadian Broadcasting Corporation for program material. Although CBC programs are mainly of interest to Canadians abroad, much of RCI's output still appeals to non-Canadian listeners.

North America: Morning reception is better in eastern North America than farther west, but the evening broadcasts are reasonably audible in virtually the whole of the United States. Winters, the first daytime slot is at 1300-1400 (weekdays till 1500) on 9640 and 11855 kHz. There is also a three-hour Sunday broadcast at 1400-1700 on the same frequencies. In summer the same broadcasts go out one hour earlier on 9640 (except for 1300-1600 Sunday), 11855 and 13650 kHz. During winter, evening broadcasts air at 2300-0100 on 5960 and 9755 kHz (6040, 9535 and 11865 kHz are also available part of the time); 0200-0300 on 6155, 9535, 9755, 9780 and 11865 kHz; and 0300-0330 (0400, weekends) on 6155, 9755 and 9780 kHz. The summer schedule is 2200-2400 on 5960, 9755 and 13670 kHz; 0100-0200 on 5960, 9535, 9755, 11715 and 13670 kHz (only 5960 and 9755 kHz is available 0130-0200 weekday evenings); and 0200-0230 (0300, weekends) on 9535, 9755, 11715 and 13670 kHz.

The evening transmission for Africa is also audible in parts of North America; winters at 2100-2230 on 11945, 13690, 15150 and 17820 kHz; and summers one hour earlier on 13670, 15150 and 17820 kHz.

Europe: Winters at 1430-1500 on 9555, 11915, 11935 and 15325 kHz; 2100-2200 on 5925, 5995, 7235, 9805 and 13650 kHz; and 2200-2230 on 5995, 7235 and 9805 kHz. Summer broadcasts are one hour earlier: 1330-1400 Monday through Saturday on 17820 kHz, and daily on 11935 and 15325 kHz; and 2000-2130 on 5995 (until 2100), 7235, 11690, 13650, 15325 and (until 2100) 17870 kHz.

Europe, Middle East and Africa: 0600-0630 winter weekdays on 6050, 6150, 9740, 9760 and 11905 kHz. Summers, it goes out one hour earlier on 7295, 9595, 11835 and 15430 kHz.

Middle East: Winters, at 0400-0430 on 6150, 9505 and 9645 kHz; 1430-1500 on 9555, 11935 and 15325 kHz; and 2000-2100 on 5995 kHz. In summer, try 0400-0430 on 9715, 11835 and 11975 kHz;

1330-1400 on 15325 kHz; and 2000-2130 on 5995 (till 2100) and 7235 kHz.

Southern Africa: 2100-2230 winter (summer in Southern Hemisphere) on 13690, 15150 and (to 2200) 17820 kHz; and 2000-2130 summer on 13670, 15150 and 17820 kHz.

Asia: To East Asia at 1200-1230, winter on 6150 and 11730 kHz, and summer on 9660 and 15195 kHz; 1330-1400 on 6150 (summers on 11795) and 9535 kHz; to South Asia at 1630-1700 on 6140 and 7150 kHz; and to Southeast Asia at 2200-2230 on 11705 kHz.

United States

With its former Cold War mission gone, the venerable **Voice of America** is under real threat from political interference and incompetence in high places. An increase in surrogate broadcasting has added fuel to the argument about who within American officialdom broadcasts when and to where.

To make matters worse, a major change in the format of the station's English-language broadcast has caused considerable disenchantment among listeners. Gone are some of the VOA's best feature programs, replaced by a "rolling news" format that has been compared unflatteringly to a "round-the-clock breakfast show."

North America: The two best times to listen are at 0000-0200 Monday through Friday (Tuesday through Saturday local weekday evenings in North America) on 5995, 6130, 7405, 9455, 9775 and 13740 kHz (with 11695 kHz also available at 0000-0100); and 1000-1100 daily on 6165, 7405 and 9590 kHz. This is when the VOA broadcasts to South America and the Caribbean. The African Service can also be heard in much of North America—try part of the morning broadcast on 6035 (0500-0700); 1600-1800 on 13710, 15445 and 17895

VOA staff (top left to right) anchor Tony Riggs, anchor Erin Brummett, correspondent Michael Leland, anchor Victor Beattie; (bottom left to right) correspondent Pamela Taylor, anchor Charlene Porter, correspondent Art Chimes, and correspondent Michele Kelemen. VOA

kHz; and 1800-2200 (Saturday to 2130) on 15410, 15580 and (from 2000) 17725 kHz.

Europe lost its VOA channels to the financial axe in September 1995, and has been left to rely on broadcasts beamed to other areas. Try 0400-0700 on 7170 kHz, 1500-1800 on 15205 kHz and 1700-2200 on 9760 kHz.

Middle East: 0400-0500 summer on 15205 kHz; 0500-0700 on 11825 (winter) and 15205 kHz (11965 kHz is also available summers at 0400-0600); 1400-1500 (winter) on 15205 kHz; 1500-1800 on 9700 and 15205 kHz; 1700-1900 (winter) on 6040 kHz; and 1800-2200 on 9760 kHz.

Southern Africa: 0300-0500 on 6080, 7280 (summer), 7340 (to 0430), and 9575 kHz; 0400-0600 (winter) on 9775 kHz; 0500-0700 on 6035 kHz; 1600-2200 (to 2130 Saturday) on 7415, 11920 (winter), 12040

(winter), 13710, 15410, 15445, 15580 and 17895 kHz (not all available for the full broadcast).

Australasia: 1000-1200 on 5985, 9645 (from 1100), 11720 and 15425 kHz; 1200-1330 on 11715 and 15425 kHz, 1330-1500 on 9645 (till 1400) and 15425 kHz; 1900-2000 on 9525, 11870 and 15180 kHz; 2100-2200 on 11870, 15185 and 17735 kHz; 2200-2400 on 15185, 15305 and 17735 kHz; and 0000-0100 on 15185 and 17735 kHz.

East and Southeast Asia: 1100-1200 on 9760, 11720 and 15160 kHz; 1200-1330 on 9760, 11715 and 15160 kHz; 1330-1500 on 9760 and 15160 kHz; 2200-2400 on 15290, 15305, 17735 and 17820 kHz; and 0000-0100 on 15290, 17735 and 17820 kHz.

Prepared by Don Swampo and the staff of Passport to World Band Radio.

How to Choose a World Band Radio

Some electronic goodies, like VCRs, have evolved into commodity products. With a little common sense you can pretty much get what you want without fuss or bother.

Not so world band receivers, which vary greatly from model to model. As usual, money talks—but even that's a fickle barometer. Some models use old technology, or mis-apply new technology, so they're unhandy or function poorly. But others can perform nicely, indeed.

Crammed with Stations

World band radio is a jungle: *1,100 channels*, with stations scrunched cheek-by-jowl. This crowding is much greater than on FM or mediumwave AM. To make matters worse, the international voyage

Some folks get their jollies by using restored old-time tabletop receivers. Shown, Radio Canada International veteran Ian McFarland with colleague on vintage yacht. L. Magne

often causes signals to be weak and quivery. To cope, a radio has to perform some exceptional electronic gymnastics. Some succeed, others don't.

This is why PASSPORT REPORTS was created. Since 1977 we've tested hundreds of world band products—the good, the bad and the ugly.

PASSPORT STANDARDS: OUR THIRD DECADE

Our reviewers, and no one else, have written everything in PASSPORT REPORTS. These include our laboratory findings, all of which are done independently for us by a specialized contract laboratory that is recognized as the world's leader in this field. (For more on this, please see the Radio Database International White Paper, *How to Interpret Receiver Lab Tests and Measurements*.)

Our review process is completely separate from any advertising, and our team members may not accept review fees from manufacturers or "permanently borrow" radios. Neither International Broadcasting Services nor any of its editors owns any stake in, or is employed by, firms which manufacture, sell or distribute world band radios, antennas or related hardware.

PASSPORT recognizes superior products regardless of when they first happen to appear on the market. So we don't bestow annual awards, which recognize only models released during a given year. Some years, many worthy models are introduced, whereas in other years virtually none appear. Thus, a "best" receiver for one year may be markedly inferior to a "non-best" receiver from another year.

Instead, we designate each exceptional model, regardless of its year of introduction, as *Passport's Choice*.

This edition marks the 21st year we have been adhering to these standards. We hope to be doing more of the same for you in the years to come.

Can't decide between a portable and a tabletop model? Consider a portatop, such as the Drake SW8. These are too bulky for air travel or backpacking, but are ideal for the backyard or RV.   R.L. Drake

These evaluations include rigorous hands-on use by veteran listeners and newcomers alike, plus specialized lab tests we've developed over the years. These form the basis of this PASSPORT REPORTS, and for premium models are detailed to the nth degree in our acclaimed series of Radio Database International White Papers®.

Five Things to Check for

Before you pore over which radio does what, here's a basic checklist to get oriented.

What to spend? Don't be fooled by the word "radio"—able world band radios are sophisticated devices. Yet, for all they do, they cost only about as much as a VCR.

If you're just starting out, figure the equivalent of what sells in the United States for $75-200, or which sells for

£50-130 in the United Kingdom, in a model with two-and-a-half stars or more. If you're looking for top performance, shoot for a portable with three-and-a-half stars— at least $330 or £360—or look into one of the sophisticated portatop or tabletop models that cost somewhat more.

If price isn't a reliable guide, why not go for the cheapest? Research shows that once the novelty wears thin, most people quit using cheap radios, especially those under $70 or £50. It's like driving a lawn tractor instead of a car on a highway—it's cheaper, all right, but not up to the task. On most stations low-cost radios sound terrible, and they're clumsy to tune.

What do you want to hear? Just the big stations? Or do you also hanker for soft voices from exotic lands? Decide, then choose a model that surpasses your expected needs by a good notch or so—

this helps ensure against disappointment without wasting money. After all, you don't need a Ferrari to go to the mall, but you also don't want a golf cart for the autobahn.

Keep in mind that, except to some extent for the Sony ICF-2010, portables don't do brilliantly with tough signals—those that are weak, or hemmed in by interference from other stations. If it's important to you to ferret out as much as possible, think four stars—perhaps five—in a portatop or tabletop. The rub is that these cost much more, usually several hundred dollars or a few hundred pounds, or more.

Where are you located? Signals are strongest in and around Europe, second-best in eastern North America. If you live in either place, you might get by with any of a number of reasonably rated models.

Elsewhere in the Americas, or in Hawaii or Australasia, choose with more care. You'll need a receiver that's unusually sensitive to weak signals—some sort of accessory antenna will help, too.

If you're an urban listener in a high-rise building, you may find an ordinary portable radio to be insufficient—try to hedge your bet by buying one on a money-back basis. Sometimes the best choice is a tabletop or portatop model fed by a simple outboard antenna mounted at or just outside a window or balcony. For more on this, see the introduction to the tabletop section of this PASSPORT REPORTS.

What features make sense? Separate features into those which affect performance and those that don't (see sidebars). Don't rely on performance features alone, though. As PASSPORT REPORTS demonstrates, much more besides features goes into performance.

> Location helps determine which radio is right for you. Californians need radios with high weak-signal performance, for example, whereas Europeans profit from radios with superior dynamic range.

Compact portables are popular for traveling. They are even small enough for backpacking, even though tinier models are also available. Lextronix

FEATURES FOR SUPERIOR PERFORMANCE

The bottom line is that a signal should not just come in, but also sound pleasant. There are several features that help bring this about—some are concerned with keeping out unwanted sounds, others with enhancing the audio quality of the station you're trying to hear.

For example, *multiple conversion* (also called *double conversion*, *up conversion*, *dual conversion* or *two IFs*) is important to rejecting spurious "image" signals—unwanted growls, whistles, dih-dah sounds and the like. Few models under $100 or £70 have it; nearly all over $150 or £100 do. This borders on a "must" for all but casual listening.

Also look for two or more *bandwidths* for superior rejection of stations on adjacent channels. Bandwidths are measured at -6 dB, and in a radio with multiple bandwidths one should measure between 4 kHz and 7 kHz, another between 2 kHz and 3 kHz. Most portables come with only one bandwidth, which to perform properly should measure between 4 kHz and 6 kHz.

Another alternative is to look for properly functioning *synchronous selectable sideband* (synchronous detection with selectable sideband), a superb high-tech feature for enhanced adjacent-channel rejection and reduced fading. Some models incorporate this *and* multiple bandwidths—a killer combination for minimizing adjacent-channel interference.

Large speakers are another aural plus, as are *tone controls*—preferably continuously tunable with separate bass and treble adjustments.

For world band reception, *single-sideband* (SSB) reception capability is irrelevant, but it's essential if you want to eavesdrop on utility or "ham" signals. On costlier models you'll get it whether you want it or not.

Heavy-hitting tabletop models and their portatop cousins are designed to flush out virtually the most stubborn signal. Look for a tunable *notch filter* to zap howls; *passband offset*, also known as *passband tuning* and *IF shift*, for superior adjacent-channel rejection and audio contouring, especially in conjunction with synchronous selectable sideband; and multiple *AGC* decay rates (e.g., *AGC slow*, *AGC fast)*, ideally with selectable *AGC off*. Rarely, a given model will also allow for adjustment of the AGC attack and hang times; some will appreciate this refinement, but for many the resulting n^{th}-degree of tweaking is more trouble than it's worth.

A *noise blanker* sounds like a better idea than it really is, given the received-frequency technology in use. But at some electrically noisy locations it is essential. Some models are noticeably better than others in this regard.

Digital signal processing (DSP) is the latest high-tech attempt to enhance mediocre signal quality. Until recently it has been much smoke, little fire, but the technology is finally beginning to click. Watch for more DSP receivers in the years to come.

With portables, an *AC adaptor* not only reduces operating costs, it may also improve weak-signal performance. However, with tabletop models an *inboard AC power supply* is marginally handier than an outboard AC adaptor, and supposedly is less likely to cause a fire.

Looking ahead, *digital shortwave transmission* is more a question of if and how, rather than when. If it is compatible with analog receivers—this approach is known as *in-band, on-channel* (IBOC)—it could supplement and gradually replace the current analog-only mode over the years to come. This should result in much-improved reception quality for listeners, with reduced transmission costs for broadcasters.

However, the strongest push to date has been for incompatible systems which, perhaps naively, require replacing existing receivers with new, digital-technology models. Either way, don't expect to hear world band broadcasts in digital mode anytime soon—they don't exist yet.

FEATURES FOR HANDY OPERATION

The single most desirable operating feature for a world band radio is *digital frequency readout*—this is a virtual "must" to find stations quickly. A *24-hour clock* for World Time is another "must," and it is best if you can see it whether the radio is on or off. However, standalone 24-hour clocks and watches are available if the radio you want doesn't come with a World Time clock.

Other important features to look for are direct-access tuning via *keypad* and *presets* ("memories"); and any combination of a *tuning knob*, up/down *slewing controls* or *"signal-seek" scanning* to hunt around for stations.

Sets with digital frequency readout virtually always have presets, and *vice versa*. These two features are especially important. First, there are many channels; if you can't see the frequencies displayed digitally, you'll have to resort to hit-and-miss tuning by ear. Second, world band stations, unlike local stations, don't stay on the same frequency all the time. Being able to store the various frequencies of a favorite broadcaster into presets makes it much handier to tune it in regularly. With sophisticated tabletop receivers, presets should be able to store not only frequency, but also such other parameters as bandwidth, chosen sideband and AGC decay.

Useful, but less important, is an *on/off timer*, especially if it can control a separate tape recorder—better, some timer-controlled models come with built-in cassette recorders. Also look for an *illuminated display*; *single-keystroke call up* (separate button for each preset, rather than having to use the 1-0 keypad); *numerically displayed seconds* on the 24-hour clock; and a good *signal-strength indicator*. Travelers should stick to portables with power-lock switches that keep the radio from going on accidentally. However, on many Chinese portables the power lock doesn't keep the display illumination from coming on accidentally, a drawback.

The bottom line is that handiness of operation—ergonomics—is a subjective and complex issue. When ergonomics stand out, positively or negatively, this is noted in the individual receiver's evaluation. In general, though, receivers with comparable levels of performance that have many controls are easier to operate than like receivers with few controls. Yes, all those complicated-looking knobs and buttons can actually make operation less complicated.

But technology isn't standing still. If a complex PC can be operated by a mouse, world band receivers with excellent ergonomics and a minimum of controls can't be far off.

South Asian fisherman uses an inexpensive compact radio to keep in touch with the world.   M. Guha

Where to buy? Unlike TVs and ordinary radios, world band sets don't test well in stores other than the handful of world band specialty showrooms which have proper outdoor antennas. Even there, given the fluctuations over time in world band reception, long-term satisfaction is hard to gauge from a single spot test, so repeated visits are advisable.

Nevertheless, to some extent you can evaluate audio quality and ergonomics in a store. Even if a radio can't pick up much world band in the building, you can get a good idea of how you relate to its ergonomics, or "operating handiness," by diddling with it. Too, you can get a thumbnail idea of fidelity by listening to some mediumwave AM stations. But because mediumwave AM channels are 9 kHz or 10 kHz apart, what you hear may be deceptive, inasmuch as world band operates under more stringent 5 kHz channel spacing.

If you're not familiar with a store you're trying, a good way to judge it is to use the old *Guide Michelin* trick. Visibly bring along or mention your PASSPORT. Reputable dealers—reader feedback suggests most are—welcome it as a sign you are serious and knowledgeable. The rest react accordingly.

Otherwise, whether you buy in a mall, through the mail or on the Web makes little difference. Use the same street smarts you employ when buying anything sophisticated.

Are repairs important? Judging from our experience and reports from readers, the quality and availability of repairs tends to correlate with price. At one extreme, some off-brand portables from China are essentially unserviceable, although most outlets will exchange a defective unit within warranty. On the other hand, superb service is available for most tabletop and portatop models.

Better portables are almost always serviced or replaced within warranty. If you can possibly swing it, insist upon a replacement. Repairs to portables, even from the most respected of manufacturers, can be a nightmare.

After warranty expiration, nearly all factory-authorized service for portables tends to fall woefully short, sometimes even making a radio perform worse instead of better. Grundig worldwide—and, in the United States, Radio Shack and Sangean—spring to mind as exceptions to some extent. However, note that Sangean offices service only Sangean-brand products, not those made by Sangean for other firms and sold under other names.

On the other hand, for tabletop and portatop models factory-authorized service is usually available to keep them purring for many years to come. Drake, Watkins-Johnson and AOR are legendary in this regard. Lowe was, too, when it made its own receivers, but in 1998 the Lowe receiver operation was sold to another firm, which hopefully will maintain the tradition. Drake and Watkins-Johnson are especially valued because they have a decades-long track record of maintaining a healthy parts inventory, even for older models.

> **Tabletops and portatops can usually be repaired properly, but not most portables.**

Of course, nothing quite equals service at the factory itself. So if repair is especially important to you, bend a little toward the home team: Drake and Watkins-Johnson in the United States, Grundig and Kneisner + Doering in Germany, Lowe and AOR in the United Kingdom, Japan Radio and AOR in Japan, and so on.

Radio Bangladesh engineer tunes elder Sony (top), Drake (middle) and Racal (bottom) receivers.

M. Guha

ACCESSORY ANTENNAS: WHO NEEDS THEM?

If you're wondering what accessory antenna you'll need for your new radio, the answer for portables and portatops is usually simple: none—almost—as all come with built-in telescopic antennas. Indeed, for evening use in Europe or eastern North America most portables will perform *less* well with sophisticated outboard antennas than with their built-in ones or a simpler external antenna.

"Volksantenna" Best for Portables

But especially if you listen during the day, or live in such places as the North American Midwest or West, your portable will probably benefit from a touch more oomph. The best solution in the United States is also the cheapest: ten bucks or so for Radio Shack's 75-foot (23-meter or 25-yard) "SW Antenna Kit," which comes with insulators and other goodies, plus $2 for a claw clip. This sort of "inverted-L" antenna itself may be a bit too long for your circumstances, but you can always trim it.

By how much? Experimentation is the best way to find out for sure, but as a rough rule of thumb the less costly the portable, the shorter the antenna should be. A crude guide when using a 75-foot simple antenna is to use the entire length if you have a model which sells for over $300 . . . or if you live in such weak-signal parts of the world as central and western North America, Latin America or Australasia.

For cheaper portables used in other parts of the world, divide 1,500 by the price in U.S. dollars as cited in PASSPORT REPORTS; the resulting figure is the (very!) approximate minimum amount, in yards or meters, which should be trimmed from that antenna. A $200 radio would thus call for an inverted-L antenna length of no more than roughly 17.5 yards or meters, for example.

Alternatively, many electronics and world band specialty firms sell the necessary parts and wire for you to make your own inverted-L antenna. An appendix in the Radio Database International White Paper® *Evaluation of Popular Outdoor Antennas* gives minutely detailed step-by-step instructions for making and erecting such an antenna.

Basically, you attach the antenna to your radio using a claw clip, which is clamped onto your radio's collapsed telescopic antenna—this is sometimes better than the set's external antenna input socket, which may have a desensitizing circuit. Then run the antenna out a window, as high as is safe and practical, to some tall point, like a tree. Unless you want to become Crispy the Cadaver, *keep your antenna clear of any hazardous wiring—the electrical service to your house, in particular—and respect heights.* If you live in an apartment, run it to your balcony or window—as close to the fresh outdoor air as possible.

This "volksantenna"—best disconnected when you're not listening, and especially when thunder, snow or sand storms are nearby—will probably help with most signals. But if it occasionally makes a station sound worse, just disconnect the claw clip and use your radio's extended telescopic antenna.

New Antenna Helps with Portables

Apartment dwellers and travelers are unlikely to find an external wire antenna to be an attractive alternative. For them, the new Sony AN-LP1 is one of those rare offerings: an active antenna that actually works properly with portables.

Sony offers it separately or bundled with certain Sony portables. It's no barnburner, but it can help bring some weaker stations out of the mud.

Specialized Antennas for Tabletop Models

It's a different story with tabletop receivers. They require an external antenna, either passive or electrically amplified ("active"). Although portatop models don't require an outboard antenna, they invariably work better with one.

Most active antennas use short wire or rod elements, but beef up incoming signals with high-gain electronic circuitry. For apartment dwellers and some others, they can be a godsend—provided they work right. Choosing a suitable active antenna for your tabletop or portatop receiver takes some care, as some are pretty awful. Yet, certain models—notably, Britain's Datong AD 370—work relatively well with tabletop and portatop receivers, even if they are generally inappropriate for portables.

If you have space outdoors, a passive outdoor wire antenna is much better, especially when it's designed for world band frequencies. Besides not needing problematic electronic circuits, a good passive antenna also tends to reduce interference from the likes of fluorescent lights and electric shavers—noises which amplified antennas boost, right along with the signal. As the cognoscenti put it, the "signal-to-noise ratio" tends to be better with passive antennas.

Eavesdropper wire antennas not only come completely assembled, but are also usually equipped with built-in lightning protectors. For other makes of antennas, you can purchase a modestly priced lightning protector. Or, if you have deep pockets, there's the Ten-Tec Model 100 protector, which automatically shuts out your antenna and power cord when lightning appears nearby. Still, with any outdoor antenna, especially if it is high out in the open, it is best to disconnect it and affix it to something like an outdoor ground rod if there is lightning nearby. Otherwise, sooner or later, you may be facing a costly repair bill.

A surge protector on the radio's power cord is good insurance, too. These are available at any computer store, and cheap MOV-based units are usually good enough. But you can also go for the whole hog, as we do, with an innovative Zero Surge device (800/996-6696, 908/996-7700 or www.ZeroSurge.com).

Many firms—some large, some tiny—manufacture world band antennas. Among the best passive models—all under $100 or £60—are those made by Antenna Supermarket ("Eavesdropper") and Alpha Delta Communications, both available from world band stores. A detailed report on these is in the same Radio Database International White Paper® mentioned above, *Evaluation of Popular Outdoor Antennas*.

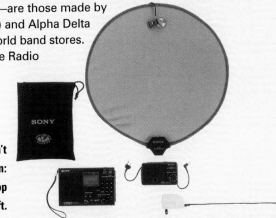

In general, active (amplified) antennas don't work properly with portables. One exception: Sony's AN-LP1. Its "tennis racket" loop compresses to fit into bag on the left.

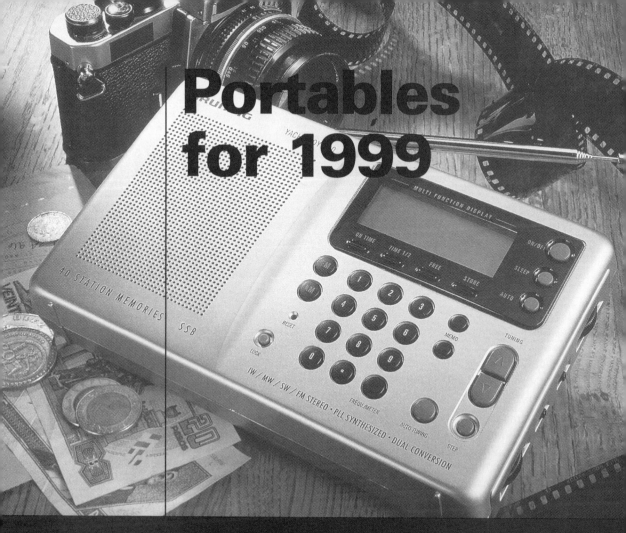

Portables for 1999

Interested in hearing major world band stations? If so, a good portable provides real value. Unless you live in a high-rise, the best digitally tuned portables will almost certainly meet your needs—especially evenings, when signals are strongest.

That's singularly true in Europe and the Near East, or even along the east coast of North America. Signals tend to come in well in these places, where virtually any highly rated portable should be all you need.

Weak Signals?

But signals are weaker in places like central and western North America, Australasia, and the Caribbean or Pacific islands. There, focus on models PASSPORT has found to be unusually sensitive to weak signals.

Yet, even in Europe and eastern North America daytime signals tend to be weaker than at night. If you listen then—some programs are heard in North America only during the day—weak-signal performance should be a priority.

Longwave Useful for Some

The longwave band is still used for some domestic broadcasts in Europe, North Africa and Russia. If you live in or travel to these parts of the world, longwave coverage is a slight plus for daytime listening to regional radio stations, especially in the hinterland. Otherwise, forget it.

Keep in mind, though, that when a low-cost analog model is available with longwave, that band may be included at the expense of some world band coverage.

Sick Radio?

If you wind up purchasing a genuinely defective world band portable, insist upon an exchange. Many vendors and virtually all world band specialty outlets will be cooperative if a just-sold radio turns out to be defective or "DOA"; others even have 30-day or similar return policies.

That's because manufacturers' repair facilities have an atrocious record when it comes to fixing world band portables. (Grundig is a commendable exception during the warranty; after-warranty service is performed by designated independent agents, which reportedly are of high quality but slow). In North America, Sangean-*branded* models, not those manufactured for other companies by Sangean, also tend to be treated better for service. Of course, the longer you own a radio, the less likely it is you'll be able to have it exchanged, so check it out carefully after you purchase it.

Shelling Out

Only observed approximate selling, or "street," prices (including VAT, where applicable) are cited in PASSPORT. Of course, street prices vary plus or minus, so take them as the general guide they are meant to be.

In the United States, shortwave specialty outlets often have the best prices worldwide. Canadian outlets are becoming highly competitive, too; ditto to an increasing extent dealers within the United Kingdom and Germany. Duty-free shopping is usually no bargain, though, especially if you have to declare the radio at your destination.

Certain countries, such as Singapore, offer some genuine bargains. However, don't look for anything comparable in Beijing, where even Chinese-made radios are overpriced. Japan, too, where the go-go days of bargain hunting in Tokyo's famous Akihabara are over, although currency fluctuation sometimes results in attractive buys for foreigners. World band radios are no longer widely available, with only a few outlets, such as X-One and T-Zone, having much selection.

☞ If you're bringing in or ordering a radio from outside your country, check beforehand to see how this may affect warranty coverage. In many cases the warranty requires you to return the radio to the country of purchase for repair.

Naturally, all prices are as we go to press and may fluctuate. Recently, though, prices have been remarkably stable—even dropping slightly—so the prices in PASSPORT should be fairly accurate throughout 1999.

We try to stick to plain English, but some specialized terms have to be used. If you come across something that's not clear, check it out in the A-Z glossary farther back in this edition.

MAKE YOUR PORTABLE "HEAR" BETTER

Regardless of which portable you own, you can give it at least some additional sensitivity on the cheap.

How cheap? Nothing, for starters.

Find Your Room's "Sweet Spots"

Sony's AN-LP1 is a surprisingly good antenna for portables.

Just wander around the room looking for "sweet spots." Stations may improve if the radio is placed in one of these endowed locations than if you simply plop it down. Try near windows, appliances, telephones and the like; although at times these locations make things worse by introducing electrical noise. Just keep experimenting.

If your portable has an AC adaptor, try that, then batteries; usually the AC adaptor does a better job. Best is the adaptor designed for your radio by the manufacturer and certified by the appropriate safety authorities, such as Underwriters Laboratories. If you travel abroad, look for a multivoltage version—standard on a few models.

Outdoor Antenna Best

An outdoor antenna can help. With portable receivers, simplest is best. Use an alligator or claw clip to connect several meters or yards of insulated wire, elevated outdoors above the ground, to your set's telescopic antenna. It's fast and cheap, yet effective.

☞ Nearby thunder, sand and snow storms can generate static electricity that fries semiconductors faster than you can say "Colonel Sanders." Use outdoor antennas only when needed, disconnecting them during stormy conditions and when the radio is off. And try to avoid touching the antenna during dry weather, as you may discharge static electricity from your body right into the radio.

☞ Outboard antennas can sometimes cause "overloading," usually at certain times of the night or day on one or more frequency segments with lots of strong signals. You'll know this when you tune around and most of what you hear sounds like murmuring in a TV courtroom scene. Remedy: Disconnect the wire antenna and just use the radio's telescopic rod.

Fancy $50+ outdoor wire antennas? These are designed for tabletop and portatop models. For portables, a length of ordinary insulated wire works better and costs nearly nothing.

If you are in a weak-signal part of the world, such as the North American Midwest or West, and want something with more oomph, best is to erect an inverted-L (so-called "longwire") antenna. This is available as a kit through Radio Shack (278-758, $9.99) and some other radio specialty outlets, or may be easily constructed from detailed instructions found in the RDI White Paper, *Popular Outdoor Antennas*.

Indoor Solutions

Antennas, like football players, almost always do best outdoors. But if your supplementary antenna simply must be indoors, place it along the middle of a window with Velcro or tape. Another solution, if you're listening in a reinforced-concrete building which absorbs radio signals, is to use the longest telescopic car antenna you can find. Affix it outdoors, almost horizontally, onto a windowsill or balcony rail.

Amplified, or "active," antennas often do more harm than good with portables. Inexpensive electronic signal-booster devices also tend to fare poorly, although anecdotal evidence suggests that some can help in given listening situations. Purchase these on a money-back basis so you can experiment with little risk.

Sony Antenna Worthy Performer

Sony has come up with a surprisingly good active antenna for portables, the AN-LP1, sold separately for $79.95. It also comes bundled with the widely sold Sony ICF-SW7600GS ($249.95) and ICF-SW1000TS radio/timer/recorder ($499.95).

The AN-LP1 uses a small amplifier module powered by two "AA" cells, along with a separate collapsible loop antenna that looks like the head of an oversized tennis racket (see photo, p. 89). These are joined together by over a dozen feet—four meters—of cable which can be reeled back into the amplifier module, like a tape measure. The amplifier, in turn, connects to almost any world band portable through its external-antenna socket or by being clipped onto the smallest element of its telescopic antenna. A variety of adapters for this purpose comes with the antenna when it is sold as a separate device, but not when it comes bundled with the ICF-SW7600G or ICF-SW1000TS.

The AN-LP1 performs nicely, usually boosting signal strength enough to make a real difference with weaker signals. It has a nine-position preselector which not only improves front-end selectivity, it also helps allow for maximum gain. When needed with low-quality receivers, it can even do the opposite by allowing you to use a contiguous setting, like an upscale attenuator, to eliminate overloading from in-band powerhouse signals. Thanks to this sophisticated circuitry, antenna-induced overloading occurs only with the lowest quality of portables, and the antenna circuitry itself is thankfully free from cross-modulation and the like.

However, with some radios the antenna's powerful circuitry picks up traces of digital hash being emitted by the receiver itself—fundamentally the result of imperfect receiver shielding, but which wouldn't be a problem if the antenna's non-element components were fully shielded. Perhaps for this reason, the AN-LP1 is not supposed be used with the Sony ICF-SW77. With the top-rated Sony ICF-2010, though, only a bit of digital hash comes through.

In all, Sony's new AN-LP1 is a welcome active antenna for portables in need of a modest improvement in weak-signal performance.

☞ Sony makes several models of active antennas for portables. All are decent performers, but the AN-LP1 is best.

Virtually All Available Models Included

We've scoured the earth to evaluate nearly every digital portable currently produced that at least meets minimum standards of performance. Here, then, are the results of our hands-on and laboratory tests.

What PASSPORT's Ratings Mean

Star ratings: ✪✪✪✪✪ is best, ✪ is a dog. We award stars solely for overall performance and meaningful features, plus to some extent ergonomics and build quality. Price, appearance, country of manufacture and the like are not taken into account. To facilitate comparison, the same rating system is used for portable and portatop models, reviewed elsewhere in this PASSPORT. Whether a radio is portable, a portatop or a tabletop model, a given rating—three stars, say—means pretty much the same thing.

A rating of three or more stars should please most who listen to major stations regularly during the evening. However, for a throw-away on trips, a small portable with as little as one-and-a-half stars may suffice.

If you are listening from a weak-signal part of the world, such as central and western North America or Australasia, lean strongly towards models that have weak-signal sensitivity among the listed advantages. Too, check out the portatop and tabletop sections of this PASSPORT REPORTS.

Passport's Choice. La crème de la crème. Our test team's personal picks of the litter—digital portables we would buy or have bought for our personal use.

☝: denotes a price-for-performance value. A designated model may or may not be truly inexpensive, but it *will* provide exceptional performance for the relatively reasonable amount of money spent.

How Models Are Listed

Models are listed by size; and, within size, in order of world band listening suitability. Street, or typical selling, prices are given. Models designed for sale in Saudi Arabia do not receive single-sideband signals and may have reduced tuning ranges. Unless otherwise indicated, each digital model includes:

- Tuning by keypad, up/down slewing, presets and scanning.
- Digital frequency readout.
- Coverage of the world band shortwave spectrum from at least 3200-26100 kHz.
- Coverage of the usual 87.5-108 MHz FM band.
- Coverage of the AM (mediumwave) band in selectable 9 and 10 kHz channel increments from about 513-1705 kHz.

POCKET/BACKPACK PORTABLES

Handy for Travel, Poor for Home

Pocket/backpack portables weigh under a pound, or half-kilogram, and are somewhere between the size of an audio cassette box and one of the larger hand-held calculators. They operate off two to four ordinary small "AA" (UM-3 penlite) batteries. These diminutive models do one job well: provide news and entertainment when you're backpacking or biking—or flying abroad (they're easily stashed on your person, where snoopy officials seldom look).

Don't expect much more, once the novelty has worn off. Listening to tiny speakers can be tiring, so most pocket/backpack portables aren't suitable for hour-after-hour listening except through good headphones. This isn't an attractive option, given that none has the full array of Walkman-type features, such as a hidden antenna.

Too, none of the available digitally tuned pocket/backpack portables are as sensitive to weak signals as they could be, although some come close. Outboard antennas,

They don't come much snazzier than the Sony ICF-SW100, used by David Letterman when traveling. This lilliputian offering comes with almost everything, including synchronous selectable sideband.

sometimes supplied, help—but they defeat the point of having a pocket/backpack model: hassle-free portability.

Best bet? If price and sound quality through the speaker are paramount, try Sangean's relatively affordable ATS 606A or ATS 606p, also available as the Roberts R617. Or look at the inexpensive Grundig Traveller II Digital—also sold as the Grundig TR II Digital and Grundig Yacht Boy 320. Otherwise, check out Sony's innovative but pricey ICF-SW100S and ICF-SW100E.

Don't forget to look over the large selection of compact models, just after the pocket/backpack portables reviewed in this section. They're not much larger, so they also travel well. But, unlike their smaller cousins, compacts usually sound better because they have larger speakers and stronger audio amplification.

✪✪✪
Sony ICF-SW100S

Price: $359.95 in the United States. CAN$499.00-599.00 in Canada. £239.95 in the United Kingdom.

Pro: Extremely small. Superior overall world band performance for size. Excellent synchronous detection with selectable sideband. Good audio when earpieces (supplied) are used. FM stereo through earpieces. Exceptional number of helpful tuning features, including "page" storage with presets. Tunes in precise 100 Hz increments. Worthy ergonomics for size and features. Illuminated display. Clock for many world cities, which can be made to work as a *de facto* World Time clock. Timer/snooze features. Travel power lock. Receives longwave and Japanese FM bands. Amplified outboard antenna (supplied), in addition to usual built-in antenna, enhances weak-signal reception. High-quality travel case for radio. *Except for North America:* Self-regulating AC adaptor, with American and European

plugs, adjusts automatically to all local voltages worldwide.

Con: Tiny speaker, although an innovative design, has mediocre sound and limited loudness. Weak-signal sensitivity could be better, although outboard active antenna (supplied) helps. Expensive. No tuning knob. Clock not readable when station frequency displayed. As "London Time" is used by the clock for World Time, the summertime clock adjustment cannot be used if World Time is to be displayed accurately. Rejection of certain spurious signals ("images"), and 10 kHz "repeats" when synchronous selectable sideband off, could be better. In some urban locations, FM signals from 87.5 to 108 MHz can break through into world band segments with distorted sound, e.g. between 3200 and 3300 kHz. Synchronous selectable sideband tends to lose lock if batteries not fresh, or if NiCd cells are used. Batteries run down faster than usual when radio off. "Signal-seek" scanner sometimes stops 5 kHz before a strong "real" signal. No meaningful signal-strength indicator. Mediumwave AM reception only fair. Mediumwave AM channel spacing adjusts peculiarly. Flimsy battery cover. In early production samples, the cable connecting the two halves of the "clamshell" case tended to lose continuity with extended or rough use; this appears to have been resolved in production starting around early 1996. *North America:* AC adaptor 120 Volts only.

Note: Although Sony's factory alignment procedures now seem to be commendably precise, with any compact or pocket Sony portable having synchronous selectable sideband it doesn't hurt to check in the store, or immediately after purchase, to ensure it was aligned properly at the factory: 1) put fresh batteries into the radio, 2) tune in a local mediumwave AM station, and 3) adjust the "sync" function back and forth between LSB and USB. If all is well, the audio will sound similar in both

cases—*similar*, not identical, as there will always be at least some difference. However, if one choice sounds significantly muddier and bassier than the other, the unit is probably out of alignment and you should select another sample.

Verdict: An engineering *tour de force.* Speaker and, to a lesser extent, weak-signal sensitivity keep it from being all it could have been. Yet, it still is the handiest pocket/backpack portable around, and one of the niftiest gift ideas in years.

✪✪✪
Sony ICF-SW100E

Price: £149.95 in the United Kingdom. AUS$649.00 in Australia. Not distributed by Sony within North America.

Verdict: This version, available in Europe but not North America, nominally includes a case, tape-reel-type passive antenna and earbuds. Otherwise, it is identical to the Sony ICF-SW100S, above.

✪✪✪
Roberts R617, Sangean ATS 606A, Roberts R876, Sangean ATS 606p

Price: *R617:* £114.95 in the United Kingdom. *ATS 606A:* $149.95 in the United States. CAN$239.00 in Canada. AUS$229.00 in Australia. *Roberts R876:* £119.95 in the United Kingdom. *ATS 606p:* $179.95 in the United States. CAN$279.00 in Canada.

Pro: Exceptional simplicity of operation for technology class. Speaker audio quality superior for size class, improves with (usually supplied) earpieces. Various helpful tuning features. Keypad has exceptional feel and tactile response. Longwave. World Time clock, displayed separately from frequency, and local clock. Alarm/snooze features. Travel power lock. Clear warning when batteries weak. Stereo FM via earpieces. Superior FM reception. Superior quality of construction. *R876 and ATS*

606p: Reel-in passive wire antenna. Self-regulating AC adaptor, with American and European plugs, adjusts automatically to most local voltages worldwide.

Con: No tuning knob. World Time clock readable only when radio is switched off. Keypad not in telephone format. No meaningful signal-strength indicator. No carrying strap or handle. *R617 and ATS 606A:* AC adaptor extra.

Verdict: A sensible choice, thanks to superior sound through the speaker. If the regular version seems Spartan, there's the "876/p" version with handy goodies.

Grundig Traveller II Digital, Grundig TR II Digital, Grundig Yacht Boy 320

Price: *Traveller II Digital and TR II Digital:* $99.95 in the United States. CAN$129.95 in Canada. *Yacht Boy 320:* £59.95 in the United Kingdom.

Pro: Price. Superior audio quality for pocket size. 24-hour clock with alarm feature and clock-radio capability. Up/down slew tuning with "signal-seek" scanning. Illuminated LCD. Travel power lock (*see* Con). FM in stereo through earpieces, not included.

Con: Poor rejection of certain spurious signals ("images"). Doesn't cover 7400-9400 kHz world band range, although like other single-conversion sets it can be tricked into receiving the lower part of this range at reduced strength by tuning the 6505-6700 kHz "image" frequencies. Lacks keypad and tuning knob. Few presets (e.g., only five for 2300-7400 kHz range). Tunes world band only in coarse 5 kHz steps. Even-numbered frequencies displayed with final zero omitted; e.g., 5.73 rather than conventional 5.730 or 5730. Poor spurious-signal ("image") rejection. So-so adjacent-channel rejection (selectivity). Unhandy "SW1/SW2" switch to go between

For thrifty backpackers and globetrotters, Sangean's diminutive ATS 606—sold in the U.K. as the Roberts R617 and R876—is hard to beat.

2300-7400 kHz and 9400-26100 kHz ranges. World Time clock not displayed independent of frequency. Nigh-useless signal-strength and battery-dead indicators. LCD illumination not disabled when travel power lock activated. No carrying strap or handle. AC adaptor extra. No longwave.

Verdict: Warts and all, a decent offering at an attractive price, with audio quality superior to that of most pocket/backpack models.

The small Grundig Yacht Boy Traveller II Digital, sold in Europe as the Yacht Boy 320, goes for under $100 or £60.

COMPACT PORTABLES

Good for Travel, Fair for Home

Compact portables are the most popular category because of their intersection of price, performance, size and speaker quality. Several worthy models are found between $90 and $200 in the United States, a bit more elsewhere.

Compacts tip in at one to two pounds, under a kilogram, and are typically sized 8 x 5 x 1.5 inches, or 20 x 13 x 4 cm. Like pocket/backpack models, they feed off "AA" (UM-3 penlite) batteries—but, usually, more of them. They travel almost as well as smaller models, but sound better and usually receive better, too. For some travelers, they also suffice as home sets—something pocket/backpack units can't really do. However, if you don't travel abroad often, you may find better value and performance in a lap portable.

Which stand out? Three, in particular, provide an unusually favorable intersection of price and performance. Grundig's Yacht Boy 400PE has generally superior audio quality and two bandwidths, and it's straightforward to operate. For hearing signals hemmed in by interference, the Sony ICF-SW7600G brings real affordability to synchronous selectable sideband, and

its build quality now appears to be superior. Both are great buys, especially if you don't live where signals are relatively weak.

If you live in a weak-signal area, consider the larger and better Sony ICF-2010, or even a portatop or tabletop model. But between the similarly priced YB 400 and ICF-SW7600G, the latter has a slight edge in such weak-signal parts of the world as central and western North America.

"Bells and whistles"? Among three-star models, the Sony ICF-SW55 and the Sangean ATS 909 are laden with snazzy operating features and accessories that come standard. However, neither has the one feature that really counts: synchronous selectable sideband.

Bargains? Sony's advanced ICF-7600G, which ties for top compact, is a steal at its current $169.95 American street price, and at $119.95 the Sangean ATS-808A is no slouch, either—both clearly outperform cheaper alternatives. The best under-$100 performer is the Sony ICF-SW30, but its tuning abilities are seriously challenged. Otherwise, go for the new Sangean ATS 404 with superior weak-signal sensitivity, or the Radio Shack DX-375, although both suffer from mediocre spurious-signal ("image") rejection.

Altered for 1999

✪✪✪¼ ⓒ *Passport's Choice*
Grundig Yacht Boy 400PE

Price: $199.95 in the United States. CAN$229.95 in Canada. £119.95 in the United Kingdom. £119.95 in the United Kingdom. AUS$399.00 in Australia.

Pro: Unusually good value. Audio quality tops in size category for those with sharp hearing. Two bandwidths, both well-chosen. Ergonomically superior for advanced-technology radio. A number of helpful tuning features, including keypad, up/down slewing, 40 station presets,

Given a new coat of paint and free AC adaptor for 1999, the Grundig Yacht Boy 400PE is one of the most popular world band radios on the market.

"signal seek" frequency scanning and scanning of station presets. Signal-strength indicator. World Time clock with second time zone, any one of which is shown at all times; however, clock displays seconds only when radio is off. Single-voltage AC adaptor comes standard. Illuminated display. Alarm/snooze features. Demodulates single-sideband signals, used by hams and utility stations, with unusual precision for a portable. Fishing-reel-type outboard passive antenna to supplement telescopic antenna. Generally superior FM performance. FM in stereo through headphones. Longwave.

Sony's advanced-technology ICF-SW7600G, already a bargain at $200, is 15 percent cheaper in some countries for 1999.

Con: Circuit noise ("hiss") can be slightly intrusive with weak signals. No tuning knob. At some locations, there can be breakthrough of powerful AM or FM stations. Keypad not in telephone format. No LSB/USB switch.

Changes for 1999: Single-voltage AC adaptor now comes standard. The new so-called Professional Edition can also be distinguished from the earlier "non-PE" version by its aluminum-colored finish.

Verdict: An excellent choice made even better for 1999 by the inclusion of an AC adaptor. The Grundig Yacht Boy 400PE's audio quality is what sets this model apart, even though circuit noise with weak signals could be lower. (It helps if you clip on several yards or meters of strung-out doorbell wire to the built-in antenna).

★★★¼ ☺ *Passport's Choice*
Sony ICF-SW7600G, Sony ICF-SW7600GS

Price: *ICF-SW7600G:* $169.95 in the United States. CAN$299.00 in Canada. £124.95 in the United Kingdom. AUS$499.00 in Australia. ¥2,700 in China. *ICF-SW7600GS:* $249.95 in the United States.

Pro: Exceptionally good value. Far and away the least-costly model available with high-tech synchronous detection coupled to selectable sideband; this generally performs very well, reducing adjacent-channel interference and fading distortion on world band, longwave and mediumwave AM signals (*see* Con). Single bandwidth, especially when the synchronous-detection feature is used, exceptionally effective at adjacent-channel rejection. Numerous helpful tuning features, including keypad, two-speed up/down slewing, 20 presets (ten for world band) and "signal-seek, then resume" scanning. Demodulates single-sideband signals, used by hams and utility stations, with unusual precision for a portable. For those with limited hearing of high-frequency sounds, such as some men over the half-century mark, audio quality may be preferable to that of Grundig Yacht Boy 400PE. World Time clock, easy to set. Tape-reel-type outboard passive antenna accessory comes standard. Snooze/timer features. Illuminated display. Travel power lock. FM stereo through earpieces or headphones. Receives longwave and Japanese FM bands. Dead-battery indicator. Comes standard with vinyl carrying case. *ICF-SW7600GS:* Comes with AN-LP1 active antenna system.

Con: Certain controls, notably for synchronous selectable sideband, located unhandily at the side of the cabinet. No tuning knob. Clock not readable when radio is switched on. No meaningful signal-strength indicator. No AC adaptor comes standard, and polarity difference disallows use of customary Sony adaptors. No earphones/earpieces come standard. Although the "GS" bundled version costs the same as the radio and antenna purchased separately, and separately the antenna comes with more connectors.

Note: Although Sony's factory alignment procedures now appear to be commendably precise, with any compact or pocket Sony portable having synchronous selectable sideband it doesn't hurt to check in the store, or immediately after purchase, to ensure it was aligned properly at the factory: 1) put fresh batteries into the radio, 2) tune in a local mediumwave AM station, and 3) adjust the "sync" function back and forth between LSB and USB. If all is well, the audio will sound similar in both cases—*similar*, not identical, as there will always be at least some difference. However, if one choice sounds significantly muddier and bassier than the other, the unit is probably out of alignment and you should select another sample.

Verdict: What a deal! The '7600G is the

TIPS FOR GLOBETROTTING

Airport security and customs personnel at major gateways are accustomed to world band portables, which have become a staple among world travelers. Yet, a few simple practices will help in avoiding hassles:

- Take along a pocket or compact model, nothing larger. Portable radios are a favorite of terrorists for stashing explosives, but for their misdeeds to succeed they need a radio of reasonable proportions.

- Models with built-in recorders (see next chapter), especially if they're not small, may attract unfavorable attention. With these, give yourself a few extra minutes to clear security.

- Stow your radio in a carry-on bag, not in checked luggage or on your person.

- Take along fresh batteries so you can demonstrate that the radio actually works, as gutted radios can be used to carry illegal material. To ensure batteries haven't run down by accident in your carry-on, be sure to activate your radio's power lock, if it has one; if it doesn't, remove at least one power battery from the radio.

- If asked what the radio is for, state that it is for your personal use.

- If traveling in zones of war or civil unrest, or off the beaten path in much of Africa or parts of South America, take along a radio you can afford to lose, and which fits inconspicuously on your person in a pocket.

- If traveling to Bahrain, avoid taking a radio which has the word "receiver" on its case, as security personnel have been known to mistakenly believe that "receiver" connotes a device used for espionage. If this is impractical, use creative, but not amateurish or obvious, means to disguise or eliminate the offending term.

Theft? Remember that radios, cameras, binoculars, laptop computers and the like are almost always stolen to be resold. The more worn the item looks—affixing scuffed stickers helps—the less likely it is to be confiscated by corrupt inspectors or stolen by thieves.

best compact model available for rejecting adjacent-channel interference and selective fading distortion—a major plus—although audio quality otherwise is *ordinaire*. Superior quality control and build quality.

✪✪✪
Sony ICF-SW55, Sony ICF-SW55E

Price: $349.95 in the United States. CAN$499.00-599.00 in Canada. £249.95 in the United Kingdom. AUS$819.00 in Australia.

Pro: Although sound emerges through a small port, rather than the usual speaker grille, audio quality is better than most in its size class. Dual bandwidths. Tunes in precise 0.1 kHz increments (displays only in 1 kHz increments). Controls neatly and logically laid out. Innovative tuning system, including factory pre-stored station presets and displayed alphabetic identifiers for groups ("pages") of stations. Weak-signal sensitivity a bit better than most. Good single-sideband reception, although reader reports continue to complain of some BFO "pulling" or "wobbling" (not found in our unit). Comes complete with carrying case containing reel-in wire antenna, AC adaptor, DC power cord and in-the-ear earpieces. Signal/battery strength indicator. Local and World Time clocks, either (but not both) of which is displayed separately from frequency. Summer time adjustment for local time clock. Snooze/alarm features. Five-event (daily only) timer nominally can automatically turn on/off certain cassette recorders—a plus for VCR-type multiple-event recording. Illuminated display. Receives longwave and Japanese FM bands.

Con: "Page" tuning system difficult for some to grasp. Operation sometimes unnecessarily complicated by any yard-stick, but especially for listeners in the Americas. Spurious-signal rejection, notably in higher world band segments, not fully commensurate with price class.

The Sony ICF-SW55 uses a sophisticated operating system. Tapes automatically, too, like a VCR.

Wide bandwidth somewhat broad for world band reception. Display illumination dim and uneven. Costly to operate from batteries. Cabinet keeps antenna from tilting fully, a slight disadvantage for reception of some FM signals.

Verdict: If the ICF-SW55's operating scheme meets with your approval—for example, if you are comfortable utilizing the more sophisticated features of a typical VCR or computer—and you're looking for a small portable with good audio, this radio is a superior performer in its size class. It can also tape like a VCR, provided you have a suitable recorder to connect to it.

✪✪✪
Radio Shack DX-398, Roberts R861, Sangean ATS 909

Price: *Radio Shack:* $249.99 in the United States. *Roberts:* £169.95 in United Kingdom. *Sangean:* $249.95 in the United States. CAN$469.00 in Canada. AUS$399 in Australia. CAN$429.00 in Canada.

Pro: Exceptionally wide range of tuning facilities and hundreds of presets, including one which works with a single touch. Alphanumeric station descriptors (*see* Con). Two voice bandwidths, well-chosen.

The ATS 909 is Sangean's best seller in North America. It is also sold in the U.K. as the Roberts R861 and worldwide as the Radio Shack DX-398.

Tunes single sideband in unusually precise 0.04 kHz increments. Sensitivity to weak signals slightly above average. Superb multivoltage AC adaptor with North American and European plugs. Travel power lock. 24-hour clock shows at all times, and can display local time in various cities of the world (*see* Con). 1-10 digital signal-strength indicator. Clock radio function offers three "on" times for three discrete frequencies. Snooze feature. FM performs well overall, has RDS feature (*see* Con), and is in stereo through earpieces, included. Superior quality of construction.

Con: Tuning knob tends to mute stations during bandscanning; remediable by modification via at least one American dealer (C. Crane). Large for a compact. Signal-seek scanner tends to stop on few active shortwave signals. Although scanner can operate out-of-band, reverts to default (in-band) parameters after one pass. Two-second wait between when preset is keyed and station becomes audible. Under certain conditions, alphanumeric station descriptor stays on full time, regardless of when designated station is active; as a result, the LCD can repeat, incorrectly, the same displayed single station ID throughout all channels in the world band spectrum; the solution, commanding the set to revert to

page 29 every time this happens, adds to tuning complexity. "Page" tuning system difficult for some to grasp, even aside from the preceding difficulty. No carrying handle or strap. 24-hour clock set up to display home time, not World Time, although this is easily overcome by not using world-cities-time feature. Clock does not compensate for daylight (summer) time in each displayed city. RDS, which can automatically display FM-station IDs and update clock, is of limited use, as on this model it requires a stronger signal than it should to activate. Heterodyne interference, possibly related to the digital display, sometimes interferes with reception of strong mediumwave AM signals. AC adaptor lacks UL approval.

Verdict: Not tops in its class, but a pleasant offering even with software and other shortcomings. Appropriate for those seeking a wide range of operating features or superior tuning of single-sideband signals.

✪✪✪
Grundig Yacht Boy 500

Price: £139.95 in the United Kingdom. AUS$599.00 in Australia. Also available in the Middle East and Africa, but not the Americas.

Pro: Attractive layout. Audio-boost circuitry for superior volume. 40 presets. Displays operator-assigned alphanumeric names for stations in presets. RDS circuitry for FM. ROM with 90 factory-preassigned world band channels for nine international broadcasters. Two 24-hour clocks, either one of which displays full time. Battery-low indicator. FM in stereo via headphones. Travel power lock. Three-increment signal-strength indicator. Elevation panel. Single-sideband reception via LSB/USB key. Illuminated display. Timer/snooze features. Comes with worldwide dual-voltage AC adaptor and two types of plugs. Audio quality pretty good. Longwave.

Con: Circuit noise relatively high. Lacks tuning knob. Telescopic antenna tends to get in the way of right-handed users. Volume slider fussy to adjust. Keypad not in telephone format. Key design and layout increase likelihood of wrong key being pushed. Owner's manual, although thorough, poor for quick answers. Twenty-four hour clocks display without leading zeroes. Elevation panel flimsy. Socket for AC adaptor appears to be flimsy. Factory-preassigned channels, of use mainly to beginners, relatively complex for beginners to select. AC adaptor lacks UL seal of approval. Relatively high number of spurious "birdie" signals.

Verdict: Attractive design, good performance, with powerful audio and a number of interesting features. Withal, for most users, slightly better performance can be had in other models for the same price or less.

The Grundig Yacht Boy 500 sometimes puts styling ahead of operating convenience. Yet, it is a solid performer.

Roberts R809, Sangean ATS-808A

Price: *Roberts:* £89.95 in the United Kingdom. *Sangean:* $119.95 in the United States. CAN$249.95 in Canada. AUS$269.00 in Australia.

Pro: A solid value. Relatively simple to operate for technology class. Dual bandwidths, unusual in this size radio (*see* Con). Various helpful tuning features. Weak-signal sensitivity a bit better than most. Keypad has exceptional feel and tactile response. Longwave. World Time clock, displayed separately from frequency, and local clock. Alarm/snooze features. Signal strength indicator. Travel power lock. Stereo FM via earpieces, included. Superior FM reception. Superior quality of construction.

Con: Fast tuning mutes receiver when tuning knob is turned quickly. Narrow bandwidth performance only fair. Spurious-signal ("image") rejection very slightly substandard for class. Pedestrian audio. Display not illuminated. Keypad not in telephone format. No carrying strap or handle. AC adaptor extra.

Verdict: With more presets, the revised version of this classic Sangean offering continues to be a good value, with relative simplicity of operation and good overall performance. However, mediocre for bandscanning.

The Sangean ATS-808A, sold in the U.K. as the Roberts R809, is the best bet among compacts between $100 and the Sony ICF-SW7600G.

The best performer in the under-$100 category is the Sony ICF-SW30, but it is clunky to tune.

★★½ ⊘
Sony ICF-SW30

Price: $89.95 in the United States. CAN$179.95 in Canada. £69.95 in the United Kingdom. AUS$299.00 in Australia.

Pro: Excellent value. Superior reception quality, with excellent adjacent-channel rejection (selectivity) and spurious-signal rejection. Weak-signal sensitivity a bit better than most. World Time and local time clock. Audio, although lacking in bass, unusually intelligible. Alarm/snooze features. Travel power lock. FM stereo through headphones, not supplied. Battery-life indicator. Receives Japanese FM band.

Con: No keypad or tuning knob. Synthesizer chugging and poky slewing degrade bandscanning. Only seven world band station presets. Does not cover two minor world band segments (2 and 3 MHz), the new 19 MHz segment and a scattering of other world band channels. Clock not displayed independent of frequency. Radio suddenly goes dead when batteries get weak. No longwave. AC adaptor, much-needed, is extra.

Verdict: The best-performing radio in the "economy" category and simple to operate, but tuning convenience is pedestrian. An excellent buy if you listen to only a limited number of stations.

WORLD BAND FOR CRANKS

If you want a radio that doesn't depend upon batteries or house current to do its job, the popular BayGen Freeplay radio may be your answer. It is powered by a spring which takes 20 seconds to wind up for over half an hour of listening pleasure.

A number of dealers offer it throughout the world, usually for around $100 (under CAN$150 in Canada, around £70 in the United Kingdom), and Coca-Cola even offers a razzleberry-red version. That's a bit steep for what it is, but profits from sales in developed countries are used to help subsidize sales within poorer parts of Africa.

For your money, you get a three-band receiver with FM, mediumwave AM and world band: Model FPR1 version "A" tunes 3.2-12.1 MHz, whereas version "B" covers 5.8-18 MHz. (Model FPR2 and the "see-through" model lack world band coverage.) The FPR1 is analog-tuned and has limited fidelity, but is adequate for hearing major international stations.

BayGen Freeplay: portability through perspiration.

⭐⭐½
Sony ICF-SW40

Price: $119.95 in the United States. £89.95 in the United Kingdom.

Pro: Relatively affordable. Technologically unintimidating, using advanced digital circuitry in a radio disguised as slide-rule, or analog, tuned. 24-hour clock. Double-conversion circuitry, unusual in price class, reduces likelihood of reception of spurious "image" signals. Two "on" timers and snooze facility. Travel power lock. Illuminated LCD. Covers Japanese FM band.

Con: Single bandwidth is relatively wide, reducing adjacent-channel rejection. No keypad. Lacks coverage of 1625-1705 kHz portion of North American mediumwave AM band. No single sideband or synchronous selectable sideband.

Verdict: If you're turned off by things digital and complex, Sony's ICF-SW40 will feel like an old friend in your hands. Otherwise, look elsewhere.

New for 1999
⭐⭐½ ✍
Sangean ATS 404

Price: $99.95 in the United States. Too new at presstime for prices to be established elsewhere.

Pro: Excellent value. Superior weak-signal sensitivity. Several handy tuning features. Stereo FM through earpieces (supplied). Two 24-hour clocks display seconds numerically. Alarm/snooze facilities. Travel power lock. Illuminated LCD. Battery indicator.

Con: Poor image rejection. No tuning knob. Overloading, controllable by shortening telescopic antenna on world band and collapsing it on mediumwave AM band. Picks up some internal digital hash. Tunes only in relatively coarse 5 kHz increments. No signal-strength indicator. Frequency and time cannot be displayed

Sony's ICF-SW40, technology for technophobes.

simultaneously. No single sideband or synchronous selectable sideband. Power lock does not disable LCD illumination. No single sideband. No longwave. No handle or carrying strap. AC adaptor extra.

Verdict: A welcome new offering in the under-$100 category, especially with the discontinuation of the popular Grundig Yacht Boy 305.

Evaluation of New Model: Taiwan's Sangean was once the *wunderkind* among world band manufacturers. For years it turned out more world band radios than any other firm on earth, although most of these radios were sold under such non-Sangean names as Roberts and Radio

The new Sangean ATS 404 is arguably the best model, overall, in the under-$100 category.

IMPORTANT THINGS TO LOOK FOR

Helpful tuning features. Digitally tuned models are by now so superior and cost-effective that they are virtual "musts." Most come with such handy tuning aids as direct-frequency access via keypad, presets (programmable channel memories), up-down tuning via tuning knob and/or slew keys, band/segment selection, and signal-seek or other scanning. In general, the more such features a radio has, the easier it is to tune—no small point, given that a hundred or more channels may be audible at any one time. However, there is the occasional model, identified in PASSPORT REPORTS under "Con," with features that can make tuning excessively complicated for some users.

Worthy audio quality. Few models, especially among portables, have rich, full audio—for mellow sound. But some are distinctly better than others. If you listen regularly and have either exacting ears or difficulty in hearing, focus on those models with superior audio quality—and try to buy on a money-back or exchange basis.

Effective adjacent-channel rejection ("selectivity"). World band stations are packed together about twice as closely as ordinary mediumwave AM stations, so they tend to interfere with each other. Radios with superior selectivity are better at rejecting this. However, enhanced selectivity also means less high-end ("treble") audio response, so having more than one "bandwidth" allows you to choose between superior selectivity ("narrow bandwidth") when it is warranted, and more realistic audio ("wide bandwidth") when it is not.

Synchronous selectable sideband. When it is designed and manufactured correctly, this advanced feature further improves audio quality and selectivity. First, it virtually eliminates distortion resulting from fading. Second, because each world band signal consists of two identical "halves," in a number of situations it can simultaneously reduce adjacent-channel interference by selecting the "better half."

☞ On some portables with this feature that have only one bandwidth, you can usually increase high-end ("treble") audio response by detuning the radio one or two kilohertz with the synchronous selectable sideband feature activated. (Of course, you can detune *any* radio, but if it doesn't have this feature distortion will tend to increase the more you detune.)

Sensitivity to weak signals. How a radio sounds doesn't mean much if the radio can't cough up the station in the first place. Most models have adequate sensitivity for listening to major stations if you're in such parts of the world as Europe, North Africa or the Near East. However, in places like Australia or North America west of the east coast, received signals tend to be weak. There, sensitivity to weak signals is a crucial factor.

Superior ergonomics or ease of use. Certain radios are easier to use than others. In some cases, that's because they don't have features which complicate operation. For example, a radio without single-sideband reception (for hearing hams and other non-world-band signals) is inherently more foolproof to use for world band than one with this feature. However, even models with complex features can be designed to operate relatively intuitively.

World Time clock. Unless you listen to nothing more than the same one or two stations, a World Time clock (24-hour format) borders on a "must." You can buy these separately

Shack. Then the market slipped with the downturn in the sunspot cycle, which coincided with increased competition from Chinese manufacturers and a series of forgettable new models from Sangean.

Now, things may be moving in the right direction once again. The sunspot cycle has turned about, but more important is that the ATS 404, Sangean's newest world band portable, represents a major step forward. Indeed, this model, made in China, ranks right up at the top among economy digital portables—and is a pleasant eyeful, to boot.

Its easy-to-read LCD shows frequency, as well as World Time and local time, although the leading time zero is unaccountably suppressed. The time can't show while the frequency is being displayed, but the time does display exact seconds numerically. There are the usual alarm and snooze-timer facilities.

Tuning is by keypad in telephone format, as well as up/down slewing in 5 kHz increments for shortwave, "signal-seek" scanning, world band segment selector and 45 presets—but no tuning knob. There is some muting when tuning from one channel to another, but it is brief.

Useful features not always found at this price point include an illuminated LCD, a power lock (which fails to disable the LCD lighting), a flip-out elevation panel to cock the radio at a handy listening angle and a soft travel case.

Performance is quite pleasing for its class. Sensitivity to weak shortwave signals is superior, with any resulting overloading being overcome by shortening the telescopic antenna. Indeed, if you don't fully collapse the telescopic antenna when tuning the mediumwave AM band, you may encounter wall-to-wall overloading.

The radio's high sensitivity also helps cause it to pick up traces of digital hash from its own circuitry within the mediumwave AM band and lower shortwave bands. Most shortwave signals aren't affected, though.

Selectivity is decent, nothing more. On our unit, the filter was asymmetrical, being broader on the upper sideband than the lower. Image rejection is poor, as with all economy portables except the Sony ICF-SW30. Audio quality is reasonable for the radio's size, with a three-level treble-cut control and limited low-frequency repro-duction.

Although the Sangean ATS 404 doesn't perform quite so well as the Sony ICF-SW30, it is much more flexible to tune and has a nicer roster of features. For many the '404 is the best choice under $100.

for as little as $10, but many radios come with them built in. The best built-ins always display World Time; worst is a radio that has to be switched off for the clock to display, or which has a 12-hour-format clock. As a compromise, some models have a button that allows you to display the time briefly while the radio is on.

AC adaptor. Back when portables were larger, they sometimes had built-in AC power supplies and could be plugged right into the wall, as well as run off batteries. Now, an outboard AC adaptor ("wall wart") is needed. An AC adaptor that comes standard with the radio is best, as it is designed to work with that particular radio, and a multivoltage adaptor is ideal if you spend a lot of time traveling abroad. It's a sad commentary that $60 telephone answering machines and the like come standard with an AC adaptor, but not most world band portables costing far more.

Radio Shack's DX-375 is a bargain when it is on sale.
Even at the normal price it offers decent value.

★★½ ◎
Radio Shack DX-375

Price: Usually $99.99, but as low as
$69.99 during special sales in the United
States. Not available in Australia.

Pro: Excellent value at $100, rises to an
outstanding value when on sale. Several
handy tuning features. Weak-signal
sensitivity a bit above average. Stereo FM
through headphones, not supplied. Travel
power lock. Timer. 30-day money-back
trial period in the United States.

Con: Mediocre spurious-signal ("image")
rejection. Unusually long pause of silence
when tuning from channel to channel. Lacks

For sheer visual pizzazz, nothing comes close to
the Grundig G2000A "Porsche Design."

tuning knob. Doesn't tune 6251-7099 kHz.
Tunes only in relatively coarse 5 kHz
increments. Antenna swivel sometimes
needs tightening. AC adaptor plug easy to
insert accidentally into headphone socket.
Build quality, although adequate, appears
to be slightly below average. Static
discharges sometimes disable microprocessor (usually remediable if batteries are
removed for a time, then replaced). No
World Time clock. Signal-strength indicator
only a single LED. No single sideband. AC
adaptor extra. No longwave.

Verdict: A great buy when on sale for
around $70.

★★
Grundig G2000A "Porsche Design"

Price: $149.95 in the United States,
CAN$199.95 in Canada.

Pro: Arguably the most functionally
attractive world band radio on the market,
with generally superior ergonomics that
include an effective and handy lambskin
protective case. Superior adjacent-channel
rejection—selectivity—for price and size
class. Keypad (in proper telephone format),
handy meter-band carousel control,
"signal-seek" scanning and up/down slew
tuning. Twenty station presets, of which
ten are for world band and the rest for FM
and mediumwave AM stations. World Time
clock. Timer/snooze/alarm. Illuminated
display. Travel power lock. Microprocessor
reset control.

Con: Sensitivity mediocre between 9400-
26100 kHz, improving slightly between
2300-7400 kHz. Poor spurious-signal
("image") rejection. Does not tune such
important world band ranges as 7405-7550
and 9350-9395 kHz. Tunes world band
only in coarse 5 kHz steps and displays in
nonstandard XX.XX MHz/XX.XX5 MHz
format characteristic of low-cost Chinese
radios. No tuning knob. Annoying one-
second pause when tuning from one

channel to the next. Old-technology SW1/SW2 switch complicates tuning. Protruding power button can get in the way of nearby slew-tuning and meter-carousel keys. Leather case makes it difficult to retrieve folded telescopic antenna. Magnetic catches weak on leather case. No carrying strap. No longwave. Signal-strength indicator nigh useless. Clock not displayed separately from frequency. AC adaptor extra.

Comment: Strong signals within the 7405-7595 kHz range can be tuned, at reduced strength, via the "image" signal 900 kHz down; e.g., 7425 kHz may be heard on 6525 kHz.

Verdict: Five stars for design, two for performance.

✪✪
Grundig Traveller III

Price: $129.95 in the United States, CAN$149.95 in Canada.

Pro: Superior adjacent-channel rejection—selectivity—for price and size class. Keypad

The Grundig Traveller III is virtually the same as Grundig's platinum-blonde Porsche model, but don't try to show it off in Las Vegas.

(in proper telephone format), handy meter-band carousel control, "signal-seek" scanning and up/down slew tuning. Twenty station presets, of which ten are for world band and the rest for FM and mediumwave AM stations. World Time clock. Timer/snooze/alarm. Travel power lock. Microprocessor reset control.

Con: Sensitivity mediocre between 9400-26100 kHz, improving slightly between

GRUNDIG TO REVIVE SATELLIT SERIES

For years, Grundig's top-of-the-line Satellit models had a faithful following among fussy listeners in Central Europe and beyond. Indeed, to this day the last of its beefy "suitcase specials," the Satellit 650/600, is considered to have the best audio quality of any portable made in recent times.

So you can imagine the excitement when in 1995 Grundig announced its new Satellit 900. Glossy ads appeared, announcements were made, dealers smacked their lips. But there was one problem—the receiver never materialized.

Now, it seems as if this one-time vaporware is about to appear, after all. Sometime soon Grundig plans to release a Satellit receiver with an as-yet-secret designation, followed in due course by the full-blown Satellit 900. Both are expected to have different circuitry from the originally conceived 900, and manufacturing will be at a special facility in China. Prices are not yet set, but the first one could be tagged around $700.

With no photos, it is impossible to say how either radio will look except that F.A. Porsche Design probably is not involved. However, the buzz at Grundig is that they want to give their world band radios as much styling panache as radio performance. So, Porsche or no Porsche, look for something visually whammo to separate Grundig products from everybody else's offerings.

2300-7400 kHz. Poor spurious-signal ("image") rejection. Does not tune such important world band ranges as 7405-7550 and 9350-9395 kHz. Tunes world band only in coarse 5 kHz steps and displays in nonstandard XX.XX MHz/XX.XX5 MHz format characteristic of cheap Chinese radios. No tuning knob. Annoying one-second pause when tuning from one channel to the next. Old-technology SW1/SW2 switch complicates tuning. No carrying strap. No longwave. Signal-strength indicator nigh useless. Clock not displayed separately from frequency. Display not illuminated. AC adaptor extra.

Comment: Strong signals within the 7405-7595 kHz range can be tuned, at reduced strength, via the "image" signal 900 kHz down; e.g., 7425 kHz may be heard on 6525 kHz.

Verdict: Virtually identical to the Grundig G2000A, preceding, but cheaper and without the Porsche pizzazz and illuminated dial. Not the most appropriate choice for use in western North America and Australasia.

★★ ∅
Electro Brand SW-3000, Tesonic R-3000

Price: *SW-3000:* $49.99 in the United States. *R-3000:* ¥620 in China.

Pro: Relatively inexpensive for a model with digital frequency display, keypad and

The Electro Brand SW-3000, also sold under other names, has occasionally been offered with a tunable outboard active antenna.

station presets (18 for world band, 18 for FM and mediumwave AM). Up/down slew tuning with "signal-seek" scanning. Slightly better adjacent-channel rejection (selectivity) than usual for price category. World Time and local clocks (*see* Con). Alarm/snooze timer. Illuminated display. FM stereo via optional headphones. *Some versions:* AC adaptor included.

Con: Mediocre build quality, with one sample having poor sensitivity, another having skewed bandwidth filtering. Inferior dynamic range and spurious-signal rejection. Does not tune 5800-5815, 9300-9495, 11500-11575, 13570-13870, 15000-15095, 18900-19020 kHz and some other useful portions of the world band spectrum. No tuning knob. Tunes world band only in coarse 5 kHz steps. No longwave. No signal-strength indicator. No travel power lock (lock provided serves another function), but power switch not easy to turn on accidentally. Clocks do not display independent of frequency. Static discharges occasionally disable microprocessor in high-static environments (usually remediable if batteries are removed for a time, then replaced). *Some versions:* No AC adaptor.

Verdict: Made by the Disheng Electronic Cooperative, Ltd., in Guangzhou, China, this bargain-priced model has excellent features, but lacks complete frequency coverage and appears to have unusually high sample-to-sample variations in performance.

★★
Sangean ATS 303

Price: $64.95 in the United States.

Pro: LCD has large digits and excellent contrast at all viewing angles. Weak-signal sensitivity better than most. Five station preset buttons retrieve up to ten world band and ten AM/FM stations. Easy-to-set World Time clock. Timer/snooze/alarm. Travel power lock. Stereo FM via earpieces.

Con: Intolerably slow tuning by single-speed up/down slew buttons—no tuning knob or other remedy beyond presets and scanning. Mediocre spurious-signal ("image") rejection and adjacent-channel rejection (selectivity), plus some distorted spurious FM broadcast signals may intrude within the world band spectrum. Does not tune such important world band ranges as 7305-7600 and 9300-9495 kHz. Tunes world band only in coarse 5 kHz steps. Old-technology SW1/SW2 switch complicates tuning. No longwave. Signal-strength indicator nigh useless. No display illumination. Clock not displayed separately from frequency. No carrying strap or handle. AC adaptor extra.

Comment: Strong signals within the 7305-7595 kHz range can be tuned, at reduced strength, via the "image" signal 900 kHz down; e.g., 7425 kHz may be heard on 6525 kHz.

Verdict: Somewhat superior sensitivity to weak signals and excellent LCD notwithstanding, tortoise-slow tuning, missed frequencies and mediocre performance make this a model to avoid.

Bolong HS-490

Price: ¥360 in China.

Pro: Inexpensive for a model with digital frequency display, ten world band station presets, and ten station presets for mediumwave AM and FM. World Time clock (*see* Con). Tape-reel-type outboard passive antenna accessory comes standard. AC adaptor. Illuminated display. Alarm/snooze features. FM stereo (*see* Con) via earbuds, included.

Con: Requires patience to get a station, as it tunes world band only via 10 station presets and multi-speed up/down slewing/scanning. Tunes world band only in coarse 5 kHz steps. Even-numbered frequencies

Sangean makes several worthy radios, but the **ATS 303** is not one of them.

displayed with final zero omitted; e.g., 5.75 rather than conventional 5.750 or 5750. Poor spurious-signal ("image") rejection. So-so adjacent-channel rejection (selectivity). World Time clock not displayed independent of frequency. Does not receive relatively unimportant 6200-7100 kHz portion of world band spectrum. Does not receive 1615-1705 kHz portion of expanded AM band in the Americas. No signal-strength indicator. No travel power lock. Mediumwave AM tuning increments not switchable, which may make for inexact tuning in some parts of the world other than where the radio was purchased. FM

The Bolong HS-490 is no prize, but it reportedly is the best-selling shortwave radio in China.

WORLD BAND ON THE ROAD

Becker, the German firm which provides gilt-edged radios for Mercedes-Benz, offers the Mexico 2340 world band car radio, $449.95 in the United States. It is available throughout much of Europe and North America, and comes with the usual stereo features, including an inboard cassette drive and optional outboard CD changer.

Unlike most world band radios, those in cars have to overcome electrical noise from ignitions, microprocessor chips, wiper motors and the like. Diesels generate no ignition noise, but even they are a poor substitute for the relative quiet of a home environment.

There's not much you can do about electrical noise, but it's generally not serious enough to dampen listening to major world band stations. The Becker is sensitive enough for this and more, and you can improve weak-signal sensitivity by replacing your car's telescopic antenna with one that's longer, or the one offered by some Becker dealers.

Ergonomics for Safe Driving

When you're driving along crowded roads, you can't devote much attention to the nuances of tuning stations. Ergonomics thus are not a luxury, but an important safety issue, just as with cellular car phones. Fortunately, the Becker has reasonable ergonomics, albeit with a learning curve, weird keypad and no tuning knob. There are ten one-push buttons to call up presets—ten presets for world band, 30 for FM—as well as for direct-frequency entry. An even bigger plus is that its "signal-seek" scan circuit works well.

There's only one bandwidth, an ergonomic virtue even if normally two bandwidths would be better. It is well chosen, being narrow enough to keep most interference at bay, yet wide enough to let through surprisingly pleasant audio.

Indeed, the Becker sounds magnificent for listening to world band programs, better than virtually any regular tabletop or portable model. If your ears crave rich, full audio, then the 2340 may have you looking forward to driving just to hear how pleasant world band can really sound. And not just world band—FM and mediumwave AM also perform commendably, and the FM comes with an RDS system for automatic identification of stations.

Limited Frequency Coverage

However, frequency coverage is only between 5900 and 15700 kHz. Daytime, that means you miss the 17, 19, 21 and 26 MHz segments, although of these only the first and third really count. Evenings, you can't tune in the growing roster of stations between 5730-5895 kHz, much less Latin American and other stations found between 4750-5100 kHz.

Ditto the mediumwave AM band, which covers only 531-1600 kHz. That's a hundred kilohertz—ten channels—lower than the upper limit of AM in North America, and one silly kilohertz higher than the 530 kHz occupied by a couple of Canadian stations.

Birdies, Images, Chugging and Pauses

There are spurious "images" from signals 900 kHz higher, as well as a few silent-carrier "birdies," including one covering time stations on 10000 kHz. Tuning can annoy, too. There's chugging during bandscanning, and the radio has to stop to "think" in silence for a second or two when coming onto a new station.

selectivity and capture ratio mediocre. FM stereo did not trigger on our unit.

Verdict: Made by a joint venture between Xin Hui Electronics and Shanghai Huaxin Electronic Instruments. No prize, but as good you'll find among the truly cheap, which probably accounts for its being the #1 seller among digital world band radios in China.

✪✪
Lowe SRX-50, Amsonic AS-908, Galaxis G 1380/4, Morphy Richards R191, Yorx AS-908

Price: *Lowe:* £39.95 in the United Kingdom. *Galaxis:* About the equivalent of US$33 in the European Union. *Morphy Richards:* £37.00 in the United Kingdom. *Yorx:* CAN$56 in Canada.

Pro: Inexpensive for a model with digital frequency display, five world band station presets (ten on the Yorx), plus ten station presets for mediumwave AM and FM. Relatively simple to operate for technology class. Illuminated display. Alarm/snooze features. FM stereo via headphones. *Except Yorx:* World Time clock. Longwave. *Yorx:* Ten, rather than five, world band station presets. AC adaptor and stereo earpieces come standard. *Galaxis and Lowe:* Headphones included.

Con: Substandard build quality. No tuning knob; tunes only via station presets and multi-speed up/down slewing/scanning. Tunes world band only in coarse 5 kHz steps. Even-numbered frequencies displayed with final zero omitted; e.g., 5.75 rather than conventional 5.750 or 5750. Poor spurious-signal ("image") rejection.

"World on Wheels" Works Well

Fortunately—after all, outside of Singapore and some other Asian locales it's the only serious act in town—the great-sounding Becker Mexico 2340 generally checks out well. And, unlike most other car radios that seem to be made like Dixie cups, it is manufactured to perform dependably over the passage of time.

The 2340 is not widely offered. Best bet for North Americans is to contact Erie Aviation at (800) 395-8934 or hansb@erieaviation.com, or Becker's North American office at (888) 423-3537. Elsewhere, Becker headquarters is at Postfach 742260, D-76303 Karlsbad, Germany. Of course, if you own a Mercedes you can try out your local authorized M-B dealer.

The Becker Mexico 2340 sounds great on the road. Its price has come down to earth, too.

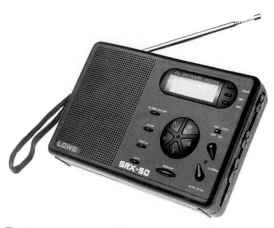

The low-cost Amsonic AS-908 is sold under many designations, including the Lowe SRX-50.

Mediocre selectivity. Does not receive 1605-1705 kHz portion of expanded AM band in the Americas. No signal-strength indicator. No travel power lock. Clock not displayed independent of frequency display. Mediumwave AM tuning increments not switchable, which may make for inexact tuning in some parts of the world other than where the radio was purchased. Power switch has no position labeled "off," although "auto radio" power-switch position performs a comparable role. *Except Yorx:* Does not tune important 5800-5895, 17500-17900 and 21750-21850 kHz segments; 15505-15695 kHz tunable only to limited extent (*see* Comment). No AC adaptor. *Yorx:* Does not receive 7300-9499 and 21750-21850 kHz portions of the world band spectrum. Clock in 12-hour format.

Comment: Strong signals within the 15505-15800 kHz range can be tuned via the "image" signal 900 kHz down; e.g., 15685 kHz may be heard on 14785 kHz.

Verdict: Outclassed by newer models.

✪✪
Elektro AC 101

Price: $49.95 plus $4 shipping by mail order in the United States. About the equivalent of US$50 in China.

Pro: One of the least costly portables with digital frequency display and presets (ten for world band, ten for AM/FM) and "signal-seek" scan tuning. Slightly more selective than usual for price category. Relatively simple to operate for technology class. World Time clock. Alarm/snooze features. Illuminated display. FM stereo via optional headphones.

Con: Mediocre build quality. Relatively lacking in weak-signal sensitivity. No tuning knob; tunes only via presets and multi-speed up/down slewing. Tunes world band only in coarse 5 kHz steps. Mediumwave AM tuning steps do not conform to channel spacing in much of the world outside the Americas. Frequency display in confusing XX.XX/XX.XX$_5$ MHz format. Poor spurious-signal ("image") rejection. Mediocre dynamic range. Does not tune relatively unimportant 6200-7100 and 25600-26100 kHz world band segments. Does not receive longwave band or 1615-1705 kHz portion of expanded AM band in the Americas. No signal-strength indicator. No travel power lock switch. No AC adaptor. Antenna swivels, but does not rotate; swivel breaks relatively easily. Limited dealer network.

Verdict: Audi cockpit, moped engine.

✪✪
Amsonic AS-138, Scotcade 65B 119 UCY Digital World Band, Shimasu PLL Digital, World Wide 4 Band Digital Receiver

Price: *Rodelvox and Rodelsonic:* $99.95 plus $6.95 shipping in United States.

Amsonic: ¥265 in China. *Scotcade:* £29.99 plus shipping in the United Kingdom.

Pro: Relatively inexpensive for a model with digital frequency display and 20 station presets (ten for world band, ten for mediumwave AM and FM). Relatively simple to operate for technology class. Alarm/snooze features with World Time clock. Illuminated display. FM stereo via optional headphones.

Con: Poor build quality. Modest weak-signal sensitivity. No tuning knob; tuned only by station presets and multi-speed up/down slewing/scanning. Tunes world band only in coarse 5 kHz steps. Even-numbered frequencies displayed with final zero omitted; e.g., 5.75 rather than conventional 5.750. Poor spurious-signal ("image") rejection. Mediocre dynamic range. Does not receive 1635-1705 kHz portion of expanded AM band in the Americas. No signal-strength indicator. Clock in 12-hour format, not displayed independent of frequency. No travel power lock. No AC adaptor. Quality of construction appears to be below average. Mediumwave AM tuning increments not switchable, which may make for inexact tuning in some parts of the world other than where the radio was purchased. *Except Scotcade:* Does not tune important 7305-9495 and 21755-21850 kHz segments. No longwave.

Note: The Amsonic is available in at least five versions: AS-138 for China, AS-138-0 for Europe, AS-138-3 for USA/Canada, AS-138-4 for Japan, and AS-138-6 for other countries and Europe. Each version has FM and mediumwave AM ranges and channel spacing appropriate to the market region, plus the Japanese version replaces coverage of the 21 MHz band with TV audio.

Comment: Strong signals within the 7305-7595 kHz range can be tuned via the "image" signal 900 kHz down; e.g., 7435 kHz may be heard on 6535 kHz.

Verdict: Poorly made, no bargain.

★★
Jäger PL-440, Omega

Price: *Jäger:* $79.95 plus $6.00 shipping in the United States. *Omega:* 1,500 francs in Belgium.

Pro: Relatively inexpensive for a model with digital frequency display. Tuning aids include up/down slewing buttons with "signal-seek" scanning, and 20 station presets (five each for world band, FM, longwave and mediumwave AM). Relatively simple to operate for technology class. World Time clock. Snooze/timer features. Longwave. Antenna rotates and tilts, unusual in price class. Travel power lock.

Con: Mediocre build quality. Limited coverage of world band spectrum omits important 5800-5945, 15605-15695, 17500-17900 and 21450-21850 kHz ranges, among others. No tuning knob; tunes only via station presets and multi-speed up/down slewing/scanning. Tunes world band only in coarse 5 kHz steps. Tortoise-slow band-to-band tuning, remediable by using station presets as band selectors. Slow one-channel-at-a-time slewing is the only means for bandscanning between world band

The Jäger PL-440 may still be available as an Omega offering. Either way, this radio doesn't begin to equal a number of other models in the under-$100 price class.

segments. Slightly insensitive to weak signals. Poor adjacent-channel rejection (selectivity). Even-numbered frequencies displayed with final zero omitted; e.g., 5.75 rather than conventional 5.750 or 5750. No signal-strength indicator. Clock not displayed independent of frequency display. Display not illuminated. Not offered with AC adaptor. Does not receive 1605-1705 kHz portion of expanded AM band in the Americas. Lacks selector for 9/10 kHz mediumwave AM steps.

Verdict: An Omega not to watch out for.

✪½ **Aroma SEG SED-ECL88C** and **Giros R918.** Avoid.

LAP PORTABLES

Good for Home, Fair for Travel

If you're looking for a home set, yet one that also can be taken out in the backyard and on the occasional trip, a lap portable is probably your best bet. These are large enough to perform well and can sound pretty good, yet are compact enough to tote in your suitcase now and then. Most take 3-4 "D" (UM-1) or "C" (UM-2) cells, plus they may also use a couple of "AA" (UM-3) cells for their fancy computer circuits.

How large? Typically just under a foot wide—that's 30 cm—and weighing in around 3-4 pounds, or 1.3-1.8 kg. For air travel, that's okay if you are a dedicated listener, but a bit much otherwise. Too, larger sets with snazzy controls occasionally attract unwanted attention from suspicious customs and airport-security personnel in some parts of the world.

One model stands out for most listeners: the high-tech Sony ICF-2010. The Sangean ATS-818 is hardly in the same league, but at its current American pricing it is an outstanding buy.

✪✪✪½ 📖 *Passport's Choice*
Sony ICF-2010

Price: $349.95 in the United States. CAN$599.00 in Canada. ¥4,500 in China. Not distributed at retail in several parts of the world, but is available worldwide by mail order from U.S. and Canadian world band specialty firms.

Pro: High-tech synchronous detection with selectable sideband, thanks to a Sony proprietary chip with sideband phase canceling; on the '2010, this feature performs very well, indeed, reducing adjacent-channel interference and fading distortion on world band, longwave and mediumwave AM signals. This is further aided by two bandwidths which offer superior tradeoff between audio fidelity and adjacent-channel rejection (selectivity). Use of 32 separate station preset buttons in rows and columns is ergonomically the best to be found on any model, portable or tabletop, at any price—simply pushing one button one time brings in your station, a major convenience. Numerous other helpful tuning features. Weak-signal sensitivity better than most. Tunes and displays in precise 0.1 kHz increments. Separately displayed World Time clock. Alarm/snooze features, with four-event timer. Illuminated LCD. Travel power lock. Signal-strength indicator. Covers longwave and the Japanese FM band. FM unusually sensitive to weak signals, making it appropriate for fringe reception in some areas (*see* Con). Superior overall reception of fringe and distant (DX) mediumwave AM signals. Some passable reception of air band signals (most versions). AC adaptor.

Con: Audio quality only average, with mediocre tone control. Because there are so many controls and high-tech features, they may initially intimidate or confuse, although thereafter this model tends to be straightforward to use. Station presets and clock/timer features immediately erase whenever computer batteries are replaced, and also sometimes when set is jostled (changing to a different brand of battery sometimes helps); this erasing also sometimes happens irregularly with no apparent cause on aging units. At 9.4 kHz, the wide bandwidth tends to be broad for world band reception; yet, narrower aftermarket replacement filters, notably the 4 kHz filter from Kiwa Electronics, reportedly cause sound to be too muffled for some ears, although others find the 6 kHz replacement filter to be worthwhile. "Signal-seek" scanning works poorly. Telescopic antenna swivel gets slack with use, requiring periodic adjustment of tension screw. Synchronous selectable sideband alignment can drift slightly with temperature and battery voltage, causing synchronous selectable sideband reception to be more muffled in one sideband than the other, particularly with the narrow bandwidth. Synchronous selectable sideband does not switch off automatically during tuning. Lacks up/down slewing. Keypad not in telephone format. LCD clearly readable only when radio viewed from below. Chugs slightly when tuned. 100 Hz tuning resolution means that non-synchronous single-sideband reception can be mis-tuned by up to 50 Hz. In urban areas, FM band can overload badly, causing false "repeat" signals to appear (see Pro). Air band insensitive to weak signals. Recently, some Sony of America repair facilities appear to have assumed that any model introduced more than a few years ago must have been discontinued, and have refused to provide service for the '2010; this problem has been addressed by Sony, but should you encounter it, anyway, contact Sony headquarters in Park Ridge, New Jersey and press the matter with vigor.

Verdict: Our panelists, like opinionated Supreme Court justices, usually issue split decisions, but not with this model. Since its

There is only one best portable, and this is it—the Sony ICF-2010.

introduction, it has always been, and very much still is, our unanimous favorite among portables. It is among the best for rejection of one of world band's major bugaboos, adjacent-channel interference, and yet it is able to retain a relatively wide audio bandwidth for listening pleasure. Alone among sophisticated receivers, it allows dozens of stations to be brought up literally at the single touch of a button. Except for everyday audio quality and urban FM, Sony's high-tech offering is the best performing portable—regardless of where you live—and is the only portable to approach portatop and tabletop performance.

🗎 An *RDI WHITE PAPER* is available for this model.

★★★½
Sony ICF-SW77, Sony ICF-SW77E

Price: $469.95 in the United States. CAN$699.00 in Canada. £359.95 in the United Kingdom. AUS$1,249.00 in Australia. ¥8,000 in China.

Pro: A rich variety of tuning features, including innovative computer-type graphical interface not found on other world band models. Synchronous selectable sideband, which in most samples performs as it should, is exceptionally handy to operate; it significantly reduces fading distortion and

Sony's priciest portable, the ICF-SW77, isn't its best— but comes close. Its main characteristic is a page-oriented operating system.

adjacent-channel interference on world band, longwave and mediumwave AM signals. Two well-chosen bandwidths provide superior adjacent-channel rejection. Tunes in exacting 50 Hz increments; displays in precise 100 Hz increments. Two illuminated multi-function liquid crystal displays. Pre-set world band segments. Keypad tuning. Tuning "knob" with two speeds. 162 station presets, including 96 frequencies stored by country or station name. "Signal-seek" scanning. Separately displayed World Time and local time clocks. Station name appears on LCD when station presets used. Signal-strength indicator. Flip-up chart for calculating time differences. VCR-type five-event timer

controls radio and optional outboard recorder alike. Continuous bass and treble tone controls. Superior FM audio quality. Stereo FM through headphones. Receives longwave and Japanese FM. AC adaptor.

Con: Excruciatingly complex for many, but by no means all, to operate. Station presets can't be accessed simply, as they can on most models. Synthesizer chugging, as bad as we've encountered in our tests, degrades the quality of tuning by knob. Dynamic range only fair. Synchronous selectable sideband subject to imperfect alignment, both from factory and from seeming drift after purchase, causing synchronous selectable sideband reception to be more muffled in one sideband than the other, particularly with the narrow bandwidth. Flimsy telescopic antenna. Display illumination does not stay on with AC power. On mediumwave AM band, relatively insensitive, sometimes with spurious sounds during single-sideband reception; this doesn't apply to world band reception, however. Mundane reception of difficult FM signals. Signal-strength indicator over-reads.

Verdict: The '77, a generally superior performer since it was improved some years back, uses innovative high technology in an attempt to make listening easier. Results, however, are a mixed bag: What is gained in convenience in some areas is lost in others. The upshot is that whether using the '77 is enjoyable or a hair-pulling exercise comes down to personal taste. In our survey some relish it, most don't. Best bet: If you're interested, try it out first.

✪✪½ ∅
Roberts R827, Sangean ATS-818

Price: *Roberts:* £139.95 in the United Kingdom. *Sangean:* $139.95 in the United States. CAN$289.00 in Canada. £129.95 in the United Kingdom. AUS$349.00 in Australia.

You can buy three Sangean ATS-818 radios for the price of one Sony ICF-SW77, with change left over.

Pro: Outstandingly priced in the United States. Superior overall world band performance. Numerous tuning features, including 18 world band station presets. Two bandwidths for good fidelity/interference tradeoff. Superior spurious-signal ("image") rejection. Illuminated display. Signal-strength indicator. Two 24-hour clocks, one for World Time, with either displayed separately from frequency. Alarm/snooze/timer features. Travel power lock. FM stereo through headphones. Longwave. Superior quality of construction. *Sangean:* AC adaptor.

Con: Mutes when tuning knob turned quickly, making bandscanning difficult (*see* Note, below). Wide bandwidth a bit broad

ANALOG PORTABLES

With digitally tuned portables now commonplace and affordable, there's little reason to purchase an analog, or slide-rule-tuned, model. They lack every tuning aid except a knob, and their coarse indicators make it almost impossible to tell the frequency.

Yet, for the money—nearly all sell for under the equivalent of US$100 or £70—these models sometimes have better weak-signal sensitivity and battery consumption than some of their digital counterparts.

Coming Up: Radio Shack is shortly to introduce a new basic analog model, the DX-397.

Pocket/Backpack Analog Portables

✪✪ **Sony ICF-SW22.** Tiny, with superior spurious signal ("image") rejection, but tinny sound and limited frequency coverage.

✪½ **Grundig Yacht Boy 207, Grundig Yacht Boy 217, InterNational WR-689, Panasonic RF-B11, Roberts R101, Sangean MS-101, Sangean MS-103, Sangean MS-103L, Sangean SG-789A, Sangean SG-789L, Grundig Mini World, Sharper Image VA100, Sony ICF-SW12.**

✪ **International R-110**

Compact Analog Portables

✪½ **Amsonic AS-912, Cougar H-116, Cougar H-123, Elektro AC 100, International AC 100, Kchibo KK-168, Kchibo KK-210B, MCE-7760, Pace, Roberts R621, Sangean SG 621, Sangean SG 631, Sangean SG-700L, SEG Precision World SED 110, Sony ICF-SW10, Sony ICF-SW12, SoundTronic Multiband Receiver, TEC 235TR.**

✪ **Apex 2138, Cougar H-88, Cougar RC210, Garrard Shortwave Radio 217, Grundig Traveller II (analog version), International MT-718, Opal OP-35, Panashiba FX-928, Precision World SED 901, Shiba Electronics FX-928, Silver International MT-798, Windsor 2138.**

Analog Lap Portables

✪✪ ⊘ **Sony ICF-SW600.** Superior audio and built-in AC power supply. No longer available new within United States, although still being sold inexpensively in Canada.

✪ **Alconic Series 2959, Dick Smith D-2832, Electro Brand 2971, Electro Brand SW-2000, Rhapsody Multiband, Shimasu Multiband, Steepletone MBR-7, Steepletone MBR-8, Venturer Multiband.**

WORLD BAND CASSETTE RECORDERS

What happens if your favorite show comes on at an inconvenient time? Why, tape it, of course, with a world band cassette recorder—just like on your VCR.

Two models are offered, and there's no question which is better: the Sony. It's a lot smaller, too, so it is less likely to raise eyebrows among airport security personnel. But its price difference over the Sangean—a nice, serviceable model—is considerable. Wrestle with your conscience, then decide.

Keep in mind that a few ordinary portables can be programmed to switch not only themselves on and off, but also a cassette recorder. Less handy, but it can be cheaper.

✪✪✪¼ *Passport's Choice*
Sony ICF-SW1000T, Sony ICF-SW1000TS

Price: *ICF-SW1000T:* $449.95 in the United States. CAN$779.00 in Canada. £369.95 in the United Kingdom. *ICF-SW1000TS:* $499.95 in the United States.

Pro: Built-in recorder has two user-programmable on/off events. Relatively small, important for airport security. Synchronous selectable sideband reduces adjacent-channel interference and fading distortion on world band, longwave and mediumwave AM signals (*see* Con). Single bandwidth, especially when the sync feature is used, exceptionally effective at adjacent-channel rejection. Numerous helpful tuning features, including keypad, two-speed up/down slewing, 32 presets and "signal-seek" scanning. Effectively demodulates single-sideband signals, used by hams and utility stations. World Time clock, easy to set. Snooze/timer features. Illuminated display. Travel power lock. Easy on batteries. FM stereo through earpieces (supplied). Receives longwave and Japanese FM bands. Tape-reel-type outboard passive antenna accessory included. Dead-battery indicator. Comes standard with lapel mic and vinyl carrying case. *ICF-SW1000TS:* Comes with AN-LP1 active antenna system.

Con: Costly. Incredibly at this price, only one bandwidth, and no AC adaptor comes standard. Synchronous selectable sideband tends to lose lock if batteries not fresh, or if NiCd cells are used. No tuning knob. Clock not readable when radio switched on except for ten-seconds when button is pushed. No meaningful signal-strength indicator. No recording-level indicator. Lacks built-in mic and stereo mic facility. Lacks flip-out elevation panel; uses less-handy plug-in elevation tab, instead. FM sometimes overloads. Telescopic antenna exits from the side, which limits tilting choices for FM.

Note: With any compact or pocket Sony portable having synchronous selectable sideband, it's a good idea to check in the store, or immediately after purchase, to ensure it was aligned properly at the factory: 1) put fresh batteries into the radio, 2) tune in a local mediumwave AM station, and 3) adjust the "sync" function back and forth between LSB and USB. If all is well, the audio will sound similar in both cases—*similar*, not identical, as there will always be at least some difference. However, if one choice sounds significantly muddier and bassier than the other, the unit is probably out of alignment and you should select another sample.

Verdict: An innovative, neat little package—but it doesn't come cheap. *Tip:* Best buy is the "TS" package; the AN-LP1 antenna that's normally $80 is thrown in for only $50 extra.

for world band reception. Keypad not in telephone format. For single-sideband reception, relies on a touchy variable control instead of separate LSB/USB switch positions. Does not come with tape-recorder jack.

Verdict: With a price in some places that's hard to resist, this is a decent, predictable radio—performance and features, alike—although it is mediocre for bandscanning.

———————————

The PASSPORT *portable-radio review team includes Lawrence Magne and Tony Jones, with laboratory measurements performed independently by Sherwood Engineering. Additional research by Robert Raimo and Craig Tyson.*

✪✪½ ⊘
Radio Shack DX-392, Roberts RC828, Sangean ATS-818CS

Price: *Radio Shack:* Usually $259.99 in the United States, but as low as $199.99 during special sales. *Roberts:* £199.95 in the United Kingdom. *Sangean:* $199.95 in the United States. CAN$359.00 in Canada. AUS$399.95 in Australia.

Pro: Built-in cassette recorder. Price low relative to competition. Superior overall world band performance. Numerous tuning features, including 18 world band station presets. Two bandwidths for good fidelity/interference tradeoff. Superior spurious-signal ("image") rejection. Illuminated display. Signal-strength indicator. Two 24-hour clocks, one for World Time, with either displayed separately from frequency. Alarm/snooze/timer features. Travel power lock. Stereo through headphones. Longwave. Built-in condenser mic. Superior quality of construction, including tape deck. *Sangean:* Supplied with AC adaptor. *Radio Shack:* 30-day money-back trial period (in United States).

Con: Recorder has no multiple recording events, just one "on" time only (quits when tape runs out). Mutes when tuning knob turned quickly, making bandscanning difficult (*see* Note under review of regular Sangean ATS-818 portable). Wide bandwidth a bit broad for world band reception. Keypad not in telephone format. For single-sideband reception, relies on a touchy variable control instead of separate LSB/USB switch positions. Recorder has no level indicator and no counter. Fast-forward and rewind controls installed facing backwards. *Radio Shack:* AC adaptor, which some readers complain causes hum and buzz, is extra.

Verdict: Great value, but only single-event.

The champ, Sony's ICF-SW1000T.

Sangean's ATS-818CS is priced to move.

Portatop Receivers for 1999

Superior Performance for Home, RV or Outdoors

Most of us buy a world band radio not for just one room, but to be used throughout the house—maybe outdoors, too. That's why portables sell so well. Yet, even the very best portables don't sound as good as some tabletop models. Nor can they cut the mustard with really tough signals, although the Sony ICF-2010 comes close.

Solution: Combine the most desirable characteristics of portables and tabletops into one single receiver, a portatop. For years, now, manufacturers have been nibbling at the edges of this idea. Finally, they're getting it right.

What PASSPORT's Ratings Mean

Star ratings: ✪✪✪✪✪ is best. PASSPORT awards stars solely for overall performance and meaningful features, plus to some extent ergonomics and build quality. Price, appearance, country of manufacture and the like are not taken into account. With portatop models there is roughly equal emphasis on the ability to flush out tough, hard-to-hear signals, and program-listening quality with stronger broadcasts.

Passport's Choice. La crème de la crème. Our test team's personal picks of the litter—models we would buy or have bought for our personal use.

☞: A bargain.

Prices: Approximate selling, or "street," prices (including VAT, where applicable). Prices vary plus or minus, so take them as the general guide they are meant to be.

✪✪✪✪½ 📄 *Passport's Choice*
Drake SW8

Price: $779.95 in the United States. CAN$1,129.00 in Canada. £699.00 in the United Kingdom. AUS$1,599.00 in Australia.

Pro: Portatop design approaches tabletop performance with many of the conveniences of a portable; portability made easier by optional carrying case. Above-average audio quality with internal speaker or headphones. High-tech synchronous selectable sideband feature reduces adjacent-channel interference and fading distortion on world band, longwave and mediumwave AM signals. Three bandwidths provide worthy adjacent-channel rejection. Continuous tone control. Numerous helpful tuning aids, including 70 presets. Helpful signal-strength indicator, digital. Single-sideband reception well above the portable norm. Weak-signal sensitivity excellent with external antenna.

Superior blocking performance aids usable sensitivity. Two timers and 24-hour clocks (*see* Con). Display illuminated. FM, in mono through speaker but stereo through headphones, performs well. Covers longwave down to 100 kHz and VHF aeronautical band. Superior factory service. Fifteen-day money-back trial period if ordered from the factory or certain dealers.

Con: Sounds "hissy" when used with built-in antenna; clipping on a length of wire to the built-in antenna helps greatly. Bereft of certain features—among them notch filter, adjustable noise blanker and passband tuning—found on premium-priced tabletop models. Ergonomics mediocre, including pushbuttons that rock on their centers. Key pushes must each be done within three seconds, lest receiver wind up being mis-tuned or placed into an unwanted operating mode. Wide bandwidth—nominally 6 kHz, actually 7.8 kHz—a bit broader than it should be. Drake's 120 VAC power supply, via a separate outboard adaptor. Telescopic antenna doesn't swivel fully for best FM

Drake's SW8 is almost as good as a top-notch tabletop model, but less costly and more flexible. FM, too.

reception. Clocks don't display when frequency is shown. Carrying/elevation handle clunky to adjust, with adjustment stops that can break if handle forced. Optional MS8 outboard speaker not equal to receiver's fidelity potential.

Verdict: The current version of the Drake SW8 is very nearly everything a top-notch portatop should be: performance only a skootch below that of the fanciest tabletop supersets, yet at a price that's lower, with portability and FM thrown in. A superior all-around receiver for use both indoors and out, but hiss with built-in antenna continues to be a drawback (carry around a $3 roll of insulated hookup wire to create an instant booster antenna).

An *RDI WHITE PAPER* is available for this model.

✪✪✪✪ 📄
Lowe HF-150, (Lowe HF-150E)

Price, without keypad or other options: *HF-150:* $599.95 in the United States. CAN$899.00 in Canada. £399.95 in the United Kingdom . AUS$1,150.00 in Australia. *HF-150E:* $699.95 in the United States. £499.95 in the United Kingdom.

The Lowe HF-150, whether barefoot or in its "Europa" incarnation, has excellent audio quality when used with a good external speaker.

HF-150M: $639.95 in the United States. £419.95 in the United Kingdom. *Keypad:* $79.95 in the United States. £39.95 in the United Kingdom.

Pro: *HF-150:* Attractive price for level of performance. Top-notch world band and mediumwave AM audio quality—a treat for the ears—provided a good external speaker or simple headphones are used. High-tech synchronous detection reduces fading distortion on world band, longwave and mediumwave AM signals. Synchronous detection circuit, which holds lock unusually well, allows for either selectable-sideband or double-sideband reception. Synchronous detector switches out automatically during tuning, which aids in bandscanning. Exceptionally rugged cast-aluminum housing of a class normally associated with professional-grade equipment. Mouse keypad, virtually foolproof and a *de rigeur* option, performs superbly for tuning and presets. Sixty presets store frequency and mode. Tunes, but does not display, in exacting 8 Hz increments, the most precise found in any model with portable characteristics. Single-sideband reception well above the portable norm. Small footprint saves space and adds to portability. Excellent operating manual. Available with IF-150 optional computer interface and cable.

Con: *HF-150:* Grossly inferior front-end selectivity can result in creation of spurious signals if the radio is connected to a significant external antenna or used near mediumwave AM transmitters; depending upon several variables, this may be a couple of kilometers or miles, or it may be several. (Lowe's excellent optional PR-150 preselector eliminates this disadvantage, albeit at a hefty cost in treasure, bulk and simplicity of operation. Also, Kiwa Electronics's BCB Rejection Filter accomplishes much the same thing more simply and at lower cost. However, neither solution is practical during portable operation.) Clumsy to use as a portable. Lacks FM broadcast reception, normally found on portables. Built-in speaker produces only okay audio quality as compared to simple earphones or a good external speaker. No tone control. Frequency displays no finer than 1 kHz resolution. Lacks lock indicator or similar aid (e.g., finer frequency-display resolution) for proper use of synchronous detector, which can result in less-than-optimum detector performance. Keypad overpriced, should come standard. Bereft of certain features—among them notch filter, adjustable noise blanker and passband tuning—found on premium-priced tabletop models. Lacks signal-strength indicator. Operation of some front-panel button functions tends to be confusing until you get the hang of it. Light weight allows radio to slide on table during operation more than do heavier models. Lacks much-needed elevation feet. Erratic contact on outboard-speaker socket. Display not illuminated. AC power supply via a separate outboard adaptor, rather than inboard.

☞ Lowe's receiver manufacturing operation was sold in 1998 to South Midlands Communications Ltd. Our attempts to communicate with this firm have not been rewarding. However, an unconfirmed published report indicates they plan to focus on the African market, such as it is, for shortwave receivers.

☞ The HF-150E "Europa" version has improved bandwidth filters, front-end bandpass filtering, screened RF coils, high-quality diodes and LCD illumination, according to the former manufacturer. Unfortunately, our test unit was neither receiving properly nor could we confirm LCD illumination, and there was no time remaining to replace or repair it.

☞ An improved keypad, "KPAD-2," is supposed to be made available shortly. According to the manufacturer, it will allow for input of data on mode settings and presets (memories).

Verdict: The shortcomings of the pioneering HF-150 portatop are by now beginning to loom large, although the "Europa" version nominally helps resolve a number of these, such as front-end selectivity—this version certainly is worth trying. The regular HF-150 sorely needs to be upgraded with some sort of workable front end, a better speaker, dial illumination, FM broadcast reception and true portability, among other improvements. Yet, at under $600 in the United States it remains a tough and affordable little radio. Its outstanding synchronous selectable/double sideband provides superb fidelity on world band, longwave and mediumwave AM—*if* you don't live near any longwave or mediumwave AM transmitters. If audio quality is your overriding passion, with other factors being relatively unimportant, this is the portatop model to get—indeed, for audiophiles this is arguably the *tabletop* model to get, provided you use a high-quality outboard passive or amplified speaker or headphones. But beware the possible need at your location for an outboard preselector or high-pass filter, as front end selectivity on this radio is as bad as we've ever encountered.

> **The Lowe HF-150 is smaller than the Drake SW8, yet less portable.**

📄 An *RDI WHITE PAPER* is available for this model.

The PASSPORT *portatop review team includes Jock Elliott, along with Lawrence Magne, Tony Jones and Craig Tyson, with John Wagner. Laboratory measurements by Robert Sherwood.*

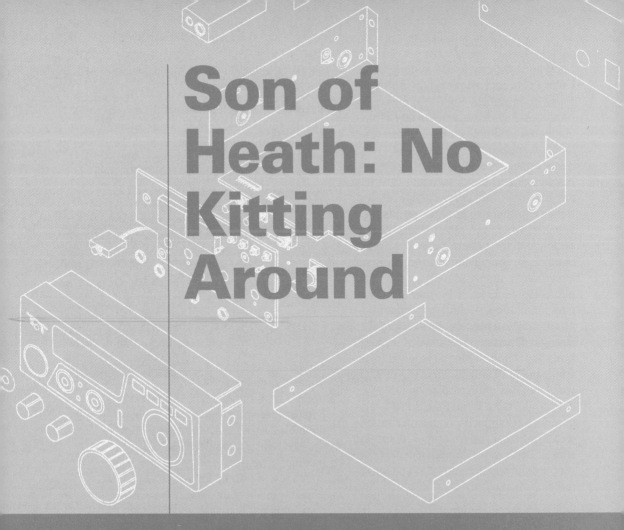

Son of Heath: No Kitting Around

Go to any gathering of world band veterans, and you'll find that many were introduced to shortwave listening by way of radio kits, usually gifts from their fathers. Something as simple as assembling a radio became a turning point in their lives.

During the golden era of kits—the fifties and early sixties—most were turned out by the Heath Company of Benton Harbor, Michigan, but there were others: EICO of Flushing, New York . . . Lafayette of Long Island . . . Knight of Chicago. Some, such as H.H. Scott and Dynakit, didn't make world band radios, but did produce serious high-fidelity gear in kit form. One outfit, Schober, even offered an electronic organ kit for the then-hefty price of $495—including bench and rhythm-section kits!

The key to the success of these great kit manufacturers was customer support. Heath's engineering talent may have been of modest proportions, but legions of bright bulbs labored to design foolproof assembly manuals. Customer support by mail and phone was a refined art at Heath, polished off with Midwestern friendliness. If all else failed, patient technicians would take back your nonperforming assembled kit and bring it to full vigor—with a smile and for free, except shipping.

Back then, the only chips associated with radio kits were those eaten while you hunched over a high-wattage soldering gun. Capacitors looked like weenies-in-a-blanket, and some even dripped wax. There were resistors bigger than a baby's pinkie, and real room-warming tubes. The only thing solid state in those kits was the beefy chassis, and circuit board meant you were bored with circuits.

Today, chips, surface-mounted devices and lilliputian layouts have overhauled electronic assembly. Factories have become home to tireless robots and patient Asian women squinting at parts through magnifying glasses. No wonder that kit building went the way of bowling alleys and dial phones!

> **Like so many other "lost arts," old-fashioned radio kit building is undergoing something of a revival.**

Lost Art Being Revived

But like so many other "lost arts," old-fashioned radio kit building is undergoing something of a revival. So, three cheers for Ten-Tec for bringing out the first superheterodyne shortwave radio kit since Heathkit's forgettable SW-7800, discontinued in 1991. This is no regenerative novelty or toy—it is a real radio designed by serious engineers at one of America's leading manufacturers of shortwave gear.

Ten-Tec's Model 1254 kit is unpretentious, yet good at what it does.

Yet, there are potential pitfalls with reviving a lost art form. Back before the Civil War, wood-burning fireplaces faded from popularity as they were replaced by more efficient coal stoves, furnaces and the like. It wasn't until the turn of the century that the Adirondack crowd brought back the fireplace—not so much for warmth as for charm. But by then all the old fireplace craftsmen were gone, so fireplace construction had to be reinvented. The result was the low, deep fireplace we find in modern homes . . . cutesy cubicles that take out more heat then they create.

Fortunately, the gap between the demise of kit making and its recent revival is shorter, and it shows in Ten-Tec's retention of much of the old kit-manufacturer's heritage. By and large, the 1254's weighty assembly manual is well-written, and the parts are appropriate and go together properly. Still, there are some hiccups that would never have occurred with a Heathkit, so to succeed you'll need a certain degree of neatness, organization, care, patience and, on occasion, creative problem solving—along with the usual small tools, a low-wattage soldering iron, and an everyday VOM ($32.95 from Ten-Tec, or $15 and up at Radio Shack). Above all, take no shortcuts.

If you have a problem, Ten-Tec provides helpful customer support by phone or email. If this fails and you have to return the receiver, there is an hourly charge to get it working properly or to explain how to fix it yourself. However, if the fault lies in a defective part the charge is waived. In today's economic environment this grasping for dollars is probably inevitable, but it certainly isn't in the Heathkit tradition.

Another lapse from the old days is the lack of foolproof soldering instructions. Heath used to be religious about this, back when most of its customers probably already knew how to solder. But now, when hand soldering is about as common as under-water basket weaving, Ten-Tec largely brushes this off in two basic paragraphs that include such pithy advice as, "If you are inexperienced, ask any electronics technician how it's done." (Noticed how many electronic techs, especially in PC repair, *don't* know how to solder?)

So while this isn't your grandfather's idiot-proofed Heathkit, Ten-Tec has done a decent job of making assembly a fun way to spend a week's worth of evenings—figure 24 hours, 27 max. Our interaction with them couldn't have been more helpful, and customers who have had to call upon Ten-Tec's customer support have had nothing but praise. Anyone who has had to wrestle with what passes for customer "support" at most PC outfits knows how rare and valuable good support like this can be.

Affordable Price, Worthy Quality

The 1254 is a straightforward tabletop receiver that is actually smaller than some portables, tuning 100 kilohertz through 30 Megahertz. Including shipping, it goes for $204 throughout the continental United States, and US$210 from the factory to Hawai'i, Alaska and Canada. In the United Kingdom, dealers carry it for £189.95, and it is available locally in a number of other countries, as well.

Parts and cabinet quality seem to be excellent, and on the surface this would appear to be a robust receiver—certainly more so than any plastic portable. Additionally, its relative lack of features means that there is less to go wrong and, as the owner is also the assembler, homebrew repairs are more likely to succeed.

The 1254 has precious little in the way of features: no keypad, for example, and no signal-strength indicator. No synchronous selectable sideband or tilt bail, either, or LSB/USB settings for single-sideband—much less adjustable AGC or any of the other goodies found on pricey tabletop supersets. It is powered by a simple outboard AC adaptor, and won't accept inboard batteries.

Digitally synthesized tuning is in increments as small as 2.5 kHz for single sideband and 5 kHz for AM-mode reception, such as world band. The bright red LEDs read out to the nearest 2.5 kHz in the single-sideband mode, the nearest 5 kHz in the AM mode. There is also a fast-tuning rate for the knob, which helps greatly in going from one part of the radio spectrum to another. (Remember, there is no keypad.) For adjustment between synthesizer tuning increments, there is an analog clarifier which works in all modes but doesn't change the displayed frequency.

Rounding out the minimalist roster of features are 15 presets. Because of the lack of a keypad or much else in the way of tuning facilities, these presets can be made to serve as handy bandswitches set to frequencies midway within each of the 15 band segments: 200 kHz longwave; 1100 kHz mediumwave AM; and world band 2400, 3300, 4900, 6000, 7300, 9700, 11800, 13700, 15400, 17700, 18960, 21650 and 25900 kHz.

Performance Generally Good

There is but one bandwidth, 5.6 kHz. It is effective and well-chosen for AM-mode reception, but is too wide for single-sideband. Its ultimate rejection is a worthy 70 dB—better than some $1,000+ receivers we have tested. Also showing up well in our lab are image rejection (although first IF rejection is only fair), shortwave sensitivity to weak signals, blocking (related to sensitivity), AGC threshold and frequency stability. Dynamic range is fair, yet comparable to that of some highly regarded receivers costing over $1,000.

However, phase noise is poor, reflecting economies taken in the synthesizer's design. Front-end selectivity is little better, which is especially noticeable by the presence of false signals within the longwave spectrum. Sensitivity on longwave and mediumwave AM is poor, and the set's digital circuitry radiates hash aplenty. This is clearly not a DX receiver for the longwave or mediumwave AM bands.

Although overall distortion runs the gamut from poor at 100 Hz AF in the AM mode to superb at 2,000 Hz AF in the single-sideband mode, it averages out as good. The radio generally sounds surprisingly good, too . . . provided a good external speaker or headphones is used. With its internal speaker the receiver sounds little better than an everyday compact portable.

Is there a fly in the ointment? You bet. All this fine sound is audibly compromised by the combination of an excessively fast AGC decay time, which allows noise to be brought up during pauses in speech, and no synchronous detection to clean up selective fading distortion during fades. Synchronous selectable sideband is complicated and expensive, but lengthening the AGC decay rate would be a no-brainer for Ten-Tec to incorporate.

Nice Radio, Fun Project

Bottom line is that Ten-Tec's sturdy little Model 1254 kit is no serious DX receiver, but it is darned nice for listening to world band and makes a fun project. It is honestly simple, has no great faults and does a yeoman's job in bringing world band programs to satisfied kit constructors.

This little rig should be a tempting gift for Father's Day, or for that shrinking contingent of youngsters who still enjoy putting something together, switching it on, and basking in the satisfaction that it actually works.

Prepared by George Zeller and Larry Magne, with historical feedback from Don Jensen. Laboratory measurements by J. Robert Sherwood.

Tabletop Receivers for 1999

Tabletop receivers exist to flush out tough game—faint stations, often swamped by competing signals. That's why they are prized by serious radio aficionados known as "DXers," a term derived from telegraph code meaning long distance.

But these tabletop models aren't for everybody. If all you want to hear are non-DX stations and a portable can't quite hack it, you can also get excellent results with a portatop model or the Sony ICF-2010 portable.

Too, if at your listening location you have audible electrical noise that already interferes with radio signals on a portable even if an outdoor antenna is used, then you'll get fewer of the benefits of a tabletop rig.

Big Guns for American West— Aussies, too

Tabletop supersets, like portatops, are the heavy artillery needed where signals are weak, but folks are strong. Places like the North American Midwest and West, or Australia and New Zealand. Even elsewhere there can be a problem when world band signals have to follow paths over or near the geomagnetic North Pole. To check, place a string on a globe—a map won't do—between you and where signals come from. If the string passes near or above latitude 60° N, beware.

Hear More Daytime Signals

With the end of the Cold War, some stations have compressed their hours of transmission. The result is that some excellent English-language programs are heard only during the day.

Daytime signals are weaker, especially when they are not beamed to your part of the world. However, thanks to the scattering properties of shortwave, you can still eavesdrop on many of these "off-beam" signals. But it's harder, and that's where a well-rated tabletop's longer reach comes in.

Good High-Rise Listening, but No FM

In high-rise buildings—especially in urban areas—portables can disappoint. Reinforced buildings soak up signals from afar, and local broadcast and cellular/PCS transmitters can interfere.

Here, your best bet for bringing in tough stations is to connect a good tabletop or portatop model to a homebrew insulated-wire antenna that runs along, or protrudes just outside, a window or balcony. Also try an ordinary telescopic car antenna sticking out from a window or balcony ledge, flagpole-style. If your radio has a built-in preamplifier, all the better. With portatop

models, the built-in preamplifier can be accessed by connecting your antenna to the receiver's whip-antenna input.

You can also try amplified ("active") antennas that have reception elements and amplifiers in separate modules, not together as part of the same cabinet. Properly made active antennas are found only at world band specialty outlets, but even these sometimes produce false signals—although Datong models have traditionally been superior in this regard. The quality of performance of active antennas is very location-specific, so try to purchase these on a returnable basis.

Most tabletop receivers are pricier than portables. For that extra money you tend to get not only better performance, but also a better-made device. However, what you rarely find in a tabletop is reception of the everyday 87.5-108 MHz FM band. It is an omission based on the evolution of shortwave receivers along a non-consumer-electronics path—specifically, most tabletop receiver manufacturers have roots in, or also still manufacture, equipment for the "ham" radio community.

External Antenna a "Must"

Nearly all tabletop models require an outboard world band antenna. Even those that have a built-in antenna should have a first-rate outboard antenna to perform to full advantage.

Tabletop performance is greatly determined by antenna quality and placement. A first-rate world band outdoor wire antenna, such as those made by Antenna Supermarket and Alpha Delta, usually sells for under $100—a bargain, given all they do. If you don't live in an apartment, this is the way to go. Check with the PASSPORT Radio Database International White Paper, *Popular Outdoor Antennas*, for the full scoop.

Virtually Every Model Tested

Every tabletop receiver evaluated, regardless of its introduction year, has been put through stringent testing hurdles we have honed since 1977, when we first started reviewing world band equipment.

First, receivers are thoroughly tested in the laboratory, using techniques we developed specially for the strenuous and specific requirements of world band reception. Each receiver then undergoes extensive hands-on evaluation, usually for months, before we begin preparing our detailed internal report. That report, in turn, forms the basis for this PASSPORT REPORTS.

Unabridged Reports Available

These unabridged laboratory and hands-on test results are too exhaustive to reproduce here. However, for selected serious tabletop models they are available as PASSPORT's Radio Database International White Papers—details on availability are elsewhere in this book.

Tips for Using this Section

Receivers are listed in order of suitability for listening to difficult-to-hear world band stations. Important secondary consideration is given to audio fidelity and ergonomics. We cite street—actual selling—prices, which are as of when we go to press. Of course, these prices vary plus or minus, so take them as the general guide they are meant to be.

Unless otherwise stated, all tabletop models have:

- Digital frequency synthesis and display.
- Full coverage of at least the 155-29999 kHz longwave, mediumwave AM and shortwave spectra—including all world band frequencies—but no coverage of the FM broadcast band (87.5-108 MHz). Models designed for sale in Saudi Arabia have reduced tuning ranges.

- A wide variety of helpful tuning features.
- Synchronous selectable sideband, which reduces interference and fading distortion.
- Proper demodulation of non-world-band shortwave signals, except for models designed to be sold in Saudi Arabia. These include single-sideband and CW (Morse code); also, with suitable ancillary devices, radioteletype and radio fax.
- Meaningful signal-strength indication.
- Illuminated display.

What PASSPORT's Rating Symbols Mean

Star ratings: ✪✪✪✪✪ is best. We award stars mainly for overall performance and meaningful features, plus to some extent ergonomics and construction quality. Price, appearance, country of manufacture and the like are not taken into account. With tabletop models there is a slightly greater emphasis than with portables or portatops on the ability to flush out tough, hard-to-hear signals, as this is one of the main reasons these sets are chosen.

Passport's Choice. La crème de la crème. Our test team's personal picks of the litter—models we would buy or have bought for our personal use.

🛇: No, this doesn't mean cheap—none of these models is cheap. Rather, it denotes a model that costs appreciably less than usual for the satisfying level of performance provided.

✪✪✪✪✪ *Passport's Choice*
Watkins-Johnson HF-1000

Price: *HF-1000:* $3,799.00 in the United States. CAN$5,400 in Canada. £4,495.00 in the United Kingdom. AUS$7,900 in Australia. *Sherwood SE-3 MK III accessory:* $495.00 plus shipping worldwide.

Pro: Unsurpassed reception of weak world band DX signals. Exceptional reception of "utility" stations. Generally superior audio quality (*see* Con), especially when used with the Sherwood SE-3 fidelity-enhancing accessory and a worthy external speaker (*see* below). Unparalleled bandwidth flexibility, with no less than 58 outstandingly high-quality bandwidths. Digital signal processing (DSP). Tunes and displays in extremely precise .001 kHz increments. Extraordinary operational flexibility—virtually every receiver parameter is adjustable. One hundred station presets. Synchronous detection reduces distortion with world band, mediumwave AM and longwave signals (*see* Con). Built-in preamplifier. Tunable notch filter. Highly adjustable scanning of both frequency ranges and channel presets. Easy-to-read displays. Large tuning knob. Can be fully and effectively computer and remotely controlled. Passband tuning (*see* Con). Built-in test equipment (BITE) diagnostics. Built-in 455 kHz IF output makes for instant installation of Sherwood SE-3 accessory (*see* below). Superior factory service.

Con: Very expensive. Static and modulation splash sound harsher than with most other models, although this has been improved somewhat in the latest version of the receiver's operating software. Complex to operate to full advantage. Synchronous detection not sideband-selectable, so it does not aid in reduction of adjacent-channel interference. Requires coaxial antenna feed line to avoid receiver-generated digital noise emanating from audio output connector; however, thanks to a connector design change this problem is now less serious than it was with early production units (indeed, early production units also emanated digital noise from the headphone socket, but this was quickly resolved with a new, no-noise socket). Passband tuning operates only in CW mode. Jekyll-and-Hyde ergonomics: sometimes wonderful, sometimes awful. No traditional cabinet, and front-panel rack "ears" protrude. In principle, mediocre front-end selectivity; however, problems were not apparent during listening tests;

After several years of improvements and use on DXpeditions, the Watkins-Johnson HF-1000 reigns as the king of kings for snaring the toughest world band catches. Other models do better for more typical listening, though—and at far cheaper cost.

and, if needed (say, if you live very close to a mediumwave AM station), a sub-octave preselector option can be added or installed at factory. Cumbersome operating manual.

☞ Within the Americas and many other parts of the world, the $599.95 optional sub-octave preselector offered by Watkins-Johnson is rarely necessary. However, within Europe and other strong-signal parts of the world, the preselector may improve spurious-signal rejection.

Improved Performance with Accessory: George Zeller, one of our panelists, has been using his personal HF-1000 in combination with a Sherwood SE-3 outboard accessory for some time, now, to enhance performance at home and on DX-peditions. George reports emphatically that, yes, even this top-rated $3,800 receiver is noticeably better with the SE-3, and installation takes about one minute and no tools. For starters, the receiver has only double-sideband synchronous detection, whereas the SE-3 allows it to have synchronous selectable sideband, a major improvement. The receiver's passband tuning operates only in the CW mode, but the SE-3 allows for passband tuning in all modes. Too, with the SE-3 in use no receiver-generated digital noise is present, as the receiver's audio output no longer needs to be used. Finally, with the SE-3 the receiver's audio quality improves noticeably.

Verdict: In its latest incarnation, the HF-1000 is, by a hair, the ultimate machine for down-and-dirty DXing where money is no object. With a final solution to the digital hash problem—and the addition of a tone control, passband tuning and synchronous selectable sideband—the '1000 would have been even better, especially for program listening. Fortunately, the Sherwood SE-3 accessory remedies all these problems, and improves audio fidelity, to boot. For those who don't wish to go the SE-3 route, the Alpha-Delta "DX-Ultra" antenna eliminates nearly all the hash problem. Thus, the HF-1000 now is exceptionally well-suited to demanding aficionados with suitable financial wherewithal—provided they want a high degree of manual receiver control.

Retested for 1999

⭐⭐⭐⭐⭐ 📖 *Passport's Choice*
Drake R8B

Price: $1,199.00 in the United States. CAN$1,759.00 in Canada. £995.00 in the United Kingdom. For the time being, not available from Drake's Australian outlet.

Pro: Superior all-round performance for listening to world band programs and hunting DX catches, as well as utility, amateur and mediumwave AM signals. Mellow, above-average audio quality, especially with suitable outboard speaker or headphones. Selectable-sideband

The Drake R8B is the world's best-selling tabletop receiver, and no wonder. It does nearly everything well and is not overpriced.

synchronous detector excels at reducing distortion caused by fading, as well as at diminishing or eliminating adjacent-channel interference; also has synchronous double sideband. Five well-chosen bandwidths, four suitable for world band. Highly flexible operating controls, including a powerful tunable AF notch filter (tunes to 5,100 Hz AF and is now easier to adjust, but *see* Con) and an excellent passband offset control. Best ergonomics of any five-star model, plus LCD unusually easy to read. Tunes and displays in precise 0.01 MHz increments. Slow/fast/off AGC with superior performance characteristics. Exceptionally effective noise blanker. Helpful tuning features include 1,000 presets and sophisticated scanning functions; presets can be quickly accessed via tuning knob and slew buttons. Built-in preamplifier. Accepts two antennas, selectable via front panel. Two 24-hour clocks, with seconds displayed numerically and two-event timer (*see* Con). Helpful operating manual. Superior factory service. Fifteen-day money-back trial period if ordered from the factory or certain dealers.

Con: Virtually requires a good outboard speaker for non-headphone listening, but optional Drake MS8 outboard speaker not equal to the receiver's audio potential; try a good amplified computer speaker or high-efficiency passive speaker instead. Neither clock shows when frequency displayed. Lightweight tuning knob lacks flywheel effect. No IF output. Otherwise-excellent tilt bail difficult to open. Notch filter does not tune below 500 Hz (AF).

Verdict: Yes, the Watkins-Johnson HF-1000 is better as a serious DX receiver. And yes, the AOR AR7030 and Kneisner + Doering KWZ 30 have even better dynamic range and audio quality. And yes, the Japan Radio NRD-545 has the best ergonomics. And, yes, any of the foregoing are more ruggedly constructed. But the Drake

R8B is the only receiver we have ever tested—portable, portatop or tabletop—that gets *everything* right, where there isn't something important missing or sputtering, or ergonomics are wanting.

📄 An *RDI WHITE PAPER* is available for this model.

✪✪✪✪✪ *Passport's Choice*
AOR AR7030, AOR AR7030 "PLUS"

Price: *AR7030:* $999.00 in the United States. CAN$1,899.00 in Canada. £695.00 in the United Kingdom. AUS$2,150.00 in Australia. *AR7030 PLUS:* $1,249.00 in the United States. £949.00 in the United Kingdom.

Decades back, the Morgan—an English sports car—was so ornery that owners used to quip that it had no springs. Yet, the Morgan legend thrives, like it does with the British AOR AR7030. Hostile to operate, but what a performer!

Pro: In terms of sheer performance for program listening, as good a radio as we've ever tested. Except for sensitivity to weak signals (*see* Con), easily overcome, the same comment applies to DX reception. Exceptionally quiet circuitry. Superior audio quality. Synchronous selectable sideband performs quite well for reduced fading and easier rejection of interference. Synchronous detection circuit allows for either selectable-sideband or double-sideband reception. Best dynamic range of any consumer-grade radio we've ever tested. Nearly all other lab measurements are top-drawer. Four voice bandwidths (2.3, 7.0, 8.2 and 10.3 kHz), with cascaded ceramic filters, come standard; up to six, either ceramic or mechanical, upon request (*see* Con). Superior audio quality, so well suited to listening to programs hour after hour. Advanced tuning and operating features aplenty, including passband tuning. Tunable AF notch and noise blanker now available, but as an option. Notch filter extremely effective, with little loss of audio fidelity. Built-in preamplifier (*see* Con). Automatically self-aligns all bandwidths for optimum performance, then displays the measured bandwidth of each. Remote keypad (*see* Con). Accepts two antennas. IF output. Optional improved processor unit now has 400 memories, including 14-character alphanumeric readout for station names. World Time clock, which displays seconds, calendar and timer/snooze features. Superior mediumwave AM performance. Superior factory service.

Con: Unusually hostile ergonomics, especially in PLUS version. Remote control unit, which has to be aimed carefully at either the front or the back of the receiver, is required to use certain features, such as direct frequency entry; not all panelists were enthusiastic about this arrangement, wishing that a mouse-type umbilical cable had been used instead. Although remote keypad can operate from across a room, the LCD characters are too small and lack sufficient intensity to be seen from such a distance. LCD omits certain important information, such as signal strength, when radio in various status modes. Sensitivity to weak signals good, as are related noise-floor measurements, but could be a bit better; a first-rate antenna overcomes this. Because of peculiar built-in preamplifier/

attenuator design in which the two are linked, receiver noise rises slightly when preamplifier used in +10 dB position, or attenuator used in –10 dB setting; however, PLUS version remedies this. When six bandwidths used (four standard ceramics, two optional mechanicals), ultimate rejection, although superb with widest three bandwidths, cannot be measured beyond –80/–85 dB on narrowest three bandwidths because of phase noise; still, ultimate rejection is excellent even with these three narrow bandwidths. Lacks, and would profit from, a bandwidth of around 4 or 5 kHz; a Collins mechanical bandwidth filter of 3.5 kHz (nominal at -3db, measures 4.17 kHz at –6 dB) is an option. Such Collins filters, in the two optional bandwidth slots, measure as having poorer shape factors (1:1.8 to 1:2) than the standard-slot MuRata ceramic filters (1:1.5 to 1:1.6). LCD emits some digital electrical noise, potentially a problem if an amplified (active) antenna is used with its pickup element (e.g. tele-scopic rod) placed near the receiver. Minor microphonics (audio feedback), typically when internal speaker is used, noted in laboratory; in actual listening, however, this is not noticeable. Uses outboard AC adapter instead of built-in power supply.

☞ The features of the PLUS version can be incorporated into existing regular models by skilled electronic technicians. Contact the manufacturer or its agents for specifics.

Verdict: AOR's sterling AR7030 is now even better in its PLUS incarnation. But operation, already peculiar and cumber-some in the "barefoot" version, is even more complex in this advanced unit. Ergonomics and slightly limited sensitivity to weak signals aside, the '7030 is the best DX choice available on the sweet side of a Watkins-Johnson HF-1000. This is a radio you'll really need to get your hands on for a few days before you'll know whether it's love or hate—or something in between.

New for 1999

✪✪✪✪¾

Kneisner + Doering KWZ 30

Price: *KWZ 30 receiver:* DM3,005 in Germany. *KWZ-TT remote keypad:* DM232 in Germany.

Pro: Exceptional quality of construction. Exceptional audio quality with powerful amp (*see* Con). Superb skirt selectivity (*see* Con). Tunes and displays in ultra-precise 1 Hz increments. Precision four-level adjustment of AGC (decay, attack, hang and digital gain). Circuitry audibly very quiet. Large, easy-to-read illuminated LCD. Superior shielding. Innovative AM detector superior to ordinary detector, although inferior to synchronous detector, for reducing selective fading. DSP noise reduction sometimes aids in weak-signal comprehension. Wide range of tuning aids includes 250 presets. Superb wide (20 kHz separation) dynamic range (*see* Con). Superior reception of world band and utility DX signals. Signal-strength indica-tor, digital, the most accurate we have encountered—and arguably the most agreeable to read. Superior tuning knob. Automatic notch filter (*see* Con). Passband offset (*see* Con). Excellent if brief operating manual, also available in English.

Con: Relatively few dedicated controls. Phase noise and effects of blocking limit measurement of ultimate rejection and skirt selectivity. Poor narrow (5 kHz separation) dynamic range. Slight artifici-ality to sound. Runs off external AC adaptor rather than internal power supply. No World Time clock, timer or related facilities. Notch filter performance not all it could be, and no option for manual tuning of notch. Passband offset does not function in AM mode. No IF output.

Verdict: In many ways the new Kneisner + Doering receiver is the best available, but it falls short in certain respects.

Evaluation of New Model: Kneisner + Doering, a new German manufacturer of tabletop shortwave receivers, has come up with the KWZ 30, a receiver built like the Pyramids. Although black, the case is made of stainless steel, while the front panel is two-millimeter laser milled. Inside is a large metal shield that successfully prevents most digital hash from being radiated from the receiver. As a result there is but a trace of digital hash, emanating no further than a few inches from the LCD. This receiver is physically of professional caliber.

The KWZ 30, like the new Japan Radio NRD-545 and the more established Watkins-Johnson HF-1000, is also a true digital signal processing (DSP) receiver. However, it uses two microprocessors instead of the one used by the '545. Although microprocessors clearly differ in performance—2 × "A" is not necessarily twice as powerful as 1 × "B"—this "two-banger" approach may well account for the more impressive performance of the KWZ 30 relative to the NRD-545.

Operationally, the KWZ 30 is akin to the highly rated AOR AR7030 in that there are few discrete controls. Instead, operation is by multilingual software commands that have more in common with DOS than any of today's GUI favorites, such as Windows 98. Yet, while the AR7030 requires the zeal of a Sherlock Holmes to manipulate to full advantage, the KWZ 30 is much kinder. This results from a combination of a larger display, the inclusion of four function keys and more intuitive software. Taken together, these allow the KWZ 30 to cross the Rubicon which has heretofore kept receivers of this sort from becoming popular among DXers.

In practice, we found the operating system to be satisfactory, although still not the equal of a front panel laid out with dedicated operating controls. The well-written owner's manual helps, and

The Kneisner + Doering KWZ 30 is a real eyebrow-raiser. Designed by German amateur radio enthusiast-engineers as a ham receiver, this rig has flopped in its intended market but shows great potential as a world band receiver.

thankfully it is also available in English. While it is true that something as complicated as a PC can be operated using a solitary mouse, this approach also requires a full-sized display with foolproof icons. Absent something so elegant on a humble radio, the best we could hope for with the KWZ 30 is that in the future the receiver incorporate more function keys—a total of ten, say—assuming the manufacturer is uninterested in the alternative of using enough discrete controls to bring smiles to our faces.

Among the radio's few controls is a terrific tuning knob that gets high marks for its feel, as well as its versatility in tuning speed. It is large, with a rubber perimeter and flywheel—you'll love it!

The keys are more a question of taste, being plastic tabs which click when pushed. Hopefully they are as rugged as the rest of the receiver, as if the keypad ever acts up the radio would be as useless as a rudderless ship.

The KWZ 30 tunes and displays in ultra-precise one Hertz increments from 6 kHz through 30 MHz, with reduced sensitivity below 50 kHz. Its large backlit liquid-crystal display is easy to read under a wide variety of conditions.

Disappointingly, the receiver is powered by an outboard AC adaptor, rather than a multivoltage inboard AC power supply. The manufacturer provides only a 220 VAC adaptor, so for Europeans the radio is ready-to-go. But dealers and direct-mail customers in countries with other voltages need to procure a suitable adaptor locally and affix it to the ready-to-solder male plug provided by K+D.

Within the Americas we've been using a $40 three-amp 120 VAC power supply from Radio Shack (catalog #22-504), which works fine but runs hot. The adaptor's banana plugs need to be affixed to K+D's male plug, a procedure which requires minimal soldering and a short length of cable or wire.

The receiver is fused internally; unfortunately, replacement requires cabinet disassembly, which in turn requires a special type of screwdriver. The 1.6 amp fusing may be conservative, as on our unit the fuse blew on one occasion for no apparent reason. A two-amp fuse resolved the problem.

Except for a clock, which it doesn't have, the KWZ 30 includes many features any serious DXer would want. The notch filter is designed to zap offending heterodynes automatically, although it doesn't work anywhere as well as the one on the Watkins-Johnson HF-1000. (A manually tunable notch as a switchable option would be a plus.) There is also passband offset, but unfortunately it doesn't function in the AM mode. The DSP noise reduction, however, actually works in helping bring station IDs out of the static, provided you adjust it carefully. There are also 250 presets that store a wide range of useful data, but not alphanumeric station names.

Additionally, there are two characteristics which put the KWZ 30 in a class unto itself. First, there is no synchronous selectable (or double) sideband. Instead,

K+D has come up with a type of AM detection in which the AM decoder uses both sidebands and precisely calculates the envelope curve of the audio. This obviates the detector's need for a carrier, so in principle the receiver is immune to selective fading distortion, which occurs when the fade acts by selectively attenuating the carrier more than the sidebands.

In principle, as we found that so long as both sidebands have identical characteristics all goes according to theory. However, with shortwave most fades roll through the signal piece by piece, first affecting one sideband, then the carrier, and finally the other sideband. Between that for shortwave and the sideband characteristics for mediumwave AM-stereo, in practice the audible result of the KWZ 30's novel detection system doesn't equal what synchronous detection can accomplish; yet, it does go about half the distance. Whether K+D will try to improve upon their new technique or offer synchronous selectable sideband remains to be seen, but they are constructively aware that their innovative detection scheme is not yet quite the equal of a synchronous detector.

Second, the automatic gain control (AGC) time constants can be minutely controlled. No, not just the decay rate, but also the attack and hang times, as well as the digital gain, which is similar to an IF gain—all these are individually adjustable. This incredible degree of control is not only useful for practitioners of extreme DX, it is especially helpful with a DSP receiver, where nuances of AGC timing can make a material difference in audio quality. Even with all that the AGC could be better, but the manufacturer is aware of this and hopes to upgrade it in due course.

So, even with the tendency for DSP technology to produce "funny" sound—plus an imperfect AM detection scheme and no tone control—with a good outboard speaker the audio quality of this receiver is nothing short of outstanding both for program listening and critical DXing. Overall distortion, which ranges from three to ten percent, wasn't really noticed by panelists, although in principle it could contribute to listening fatigue over long listening periods. There is some selective fading distortion, but it sounds to the ear like only about half that encountered with a normal AM detector. Bottom line is that once all the controls are adjusted properly this radio sounds great, and its audio is mighty powerful, too.

Unfortunately, there is no IF output, nor can one be retrofitted, so a Sherwood SE-3 accessory synchronous detector can't be added. However, there is a reasonable chance that the KWZ 30, perhaps in a special version, will eventually be upgraded to include a 455 kHz IF output to satisfy the requirements of commercial and military clients.

Overall, the KWZ 30's performance is worthy, but not yet fully equal to the promise this unusual new receiver holds. Further to promise, we found certain of the manufacturer's published measurements of performance to be optimistic.

Phase noise and the effects of blocking makes measurements of ultimate rejection meaningless beyond 50 dB. In turn, the same applies to the bandwidth shape factors, which require a minimum of 60 dB ultimate rejection in order for a measurement to be made. Our adjusted measurement norm to allow shape factors to be measured, in a fashion, for the nine available voice bandwidths show them to range from 1:1.3 to 1:1.8. This is a superb showing, but in reality they should be and clearly are better than this—we just can't know precisely by how much.

A surprising disappointment is close-in dynamic range. At the wide 20 kHz signal separation points, both dynamic range (100 dB) and the even-more-telling third-order intercept point (+20 dBm) were superb, even if not quite in the same exalted league as the AOR AR7030. So far, so good, but at the more critical 5 kHz separation points, corresponding to the 5 kHz channel separation on world band, dynamic range plummets to a poor 60 dB, and the third-order at –40 dBm fares only marginally better. This is a design shortcoming that used to crop up on such otherwise interesting receivers as the Drake R-4C from the mid-seventies, but which is unexpected today.

Otherwise, the KWZ 30 acquits itself well in the lab, with a roster of measurements ranging from good (e.g., frequency stability) to superb (image rejection). Sensitivity, fair, is worse than the noise floor, which is good, because the AGC comes on unusually early. This can be adjusted, but the more you turn down the gain, the less the sensitivity. Regardless, the receiver is audibly very quiet, even more so than the Watkins-Johnson HF-1000.

Hands-on use was even more positive. Program listening, world band DXing and utility DXing were all handled with aplomb by this new German rig. Even the digital signal-strength indicator drew rave comments for its readability and unmatched accuracy.

Overall, although the Kneisner + Doering KWZ 30 is arguably something of a work in progress, it is already an extremely interesting receiver. In some respects, such as construction and audio quality, it is magnificent. In others, such as close-in dynamic range, it flunks. Our talks with the manufacturer were encouraging in that they appear to have the needed combination of engineering expertise and open minds to make a wide range of improvements over time. If they can muster the resources of time and treasure to accomplish these upgrades, the KWZ 30 should evolve into an even more exceptional receiver.

As of when we go to press, the only way the KWZ 30 is being made available is through the factory in Germany (+49 531/61-03-52 or kud@compuserve.com). However, talks reportedly are underway with Universal Radio for possible distribution within North America. If this comes to pass, the radio would be sold to the American public with the correct 120 VAC power supply.

New for 1999
✪✪✪✪½
Japan Radio NRD-545 ("B/B" Version)

Price: $1,799.95 in the United States. £1,595.00 in the United Kingdom. AUS$3,499.95 in Australia. ¥178,000 in Japan.

Pro: Fully 998 bandwidths provide unprecedented flexibility. Razor-sharp skirt selectivity, especially with voice bandwidths. Outstanding array of tuning aids, including 1,000 presets. Wide array of reception aids, including passband offset, tunable notch and synchronous selectable sideband having good lock. Highly adjustable AGC in all modes requiring BFO. Tunes in unusually precise 1 Hz increments; displays in 10 Hz increments. Superior ergonomics, among the best to be found. Some audio shaping. Virtually no spurious radiation of digital "hash." Superior reception of utility signals. Easily upgraded by changing software ROMs.

The new Japan Radio NRD-545 has not lived up to expectations, but is currently only in the "B/B" version. JRC enthusiasts hope for more improvements as time goes by.

Con: Ultimate rejection, although improved, is still substandard. Audio quality, upgraded after initial version, continues to be tough sledding in the unvarnished AM mode (the synchronous-AM detector helps clear things up). No AGC adjustment in AM mode or with synchronous selectable sideband, and lone AGC decay rate too fast. Dynamic range only fair. Selectable sideband feature of synchronous selectable sideband did not work in our unit with "B/B" ROMs, presumably an anomaly that will not show up regularly. Notch filter tunes no higher than 2,500 Hz AF. Signal-strength indicator overreads at higher levels. Frequency display misreads by up to 30 Hz. No IF output, nor can one be retrofitted. World Time clock doesn't show when frequency displayed.

Verdict: In many ways Japan Radio's new NRD-545 is a remarkable performer—and with its first-class ergonomics it is always a pleasure to operate. The latest "B/B" version represents a definite improvement over the short-lived initial two versions, but more is needed to make this the ultimate receiver it could and should be. Given the manufacturer's demonstrated willingness to keep improving this model, and if the microprocessor isn't maxed out, more upgrades may be in the offing.

Evaluation of New Model: It was years ago that one of our reviewers first heard about Japan Radio—in an excited call from his old friend Perry Ferrell, late head of what was then Gilfer Shortwave. At that time, Gilfer was "it" in shortwave retailing, and Perry Ferrell was already a legend for, among other things, his many years as editor of Ziff-Davis' Popular Electronics.

Perry was a pro's pro, but that day he was like a kid who had just gotten his first bicycle. The cause for his excitement was the Japan Radio NRD-505, the first JRC receiver to be targeted to a non-professional market. Japan Radio had been making bulletproof receivers for the maritime industry for decades, but these were so expensive that few individuals could afford them. Now, this was all changing.

He had good cause to be aroused, as the '505 was built like a panzer and had performance to match. The price was steep for a consumer product, but in short order Japan Radio went back to the drawing board and came up with an even better model at lower cost: the NRD-515, revered by radio cognoscenti to this day. This was followed by the disappointing NRD-525, the excellent NRD-535, the value-priced NRD-345 and, now, the new NRD-545.

Alas, the results of our lab and hands-on tests of the original version of the '545 were extremely disappointing. Assuming there must be something wrong with our unit, we reported these disturbing findings to JRC, which confirmed that they were inherent in the set's design. As a result they modified the receiver, making it in effect the second version. Although improved, that had problems, as well, so shortly thereafter the manufacturer released a new set of ROMs to create the third version, with both chip designators ending in "B"; *viz.*, 7DEDN006B and 7DEDN005B. It is that "B/B" version that we report on here.

The Japan Radio NRD-545 is a fully synthesized digital-signal processing (DSP) receiver. It uses a single Analog Devices SHARC DSP (*see* www.analog.com) and tunes from 0.01-30 MHz with reduced performance below 0.1 MHz. An optional converter, where legally available, brings the tuning range up to 2,000 MHz. Modes are straight AM, AM with synchronous selectable sideband, AM-stereo (via audio jacks on the rear panel), LSB, USB, CW, RTTY and narrowband FM.

The digital frequency display is to the nearest 10 Hz and tuning is in hairsplitting 1 Hz steps. The frequency display can be off by up to 30 Hz within the higher reaches of the shortwave spectrum, but this can be cured to some extent by an internal adjustment so that exact readings fall within the part of the radio spectrum you choose. The World Time clock has large digits and displays seconds numerically, which is helpful if you're waiting for an ID on the hour. Unfortunately, the clock shares the display with the frequency, so you can see one or the other, but not both at the same time.

Tuning aids include 1,000 presets, a handy system for scanning those presets, frequency scanning, a keypad and a tuning knob. Each preset can store frequency, mode, bandwidth, AGC decay timing, attenuator status and tuning step. Listening aids include passband offset that is fussy to adjust, automated notch filtering, modestly performing DSP audio shaping, and a peculiar tone control. There is a digital signal-strength indicator, along with a timer, but no alphanumeric station-name display.

Unlike most other tabletop receivers, which come with anywhere from two to several bandwidths, the '545 is tunable in 10 Hz steps from 0.01 to 9.99 kHz bandwidths or, if you prefer, 100 Hz steps from 0.1-9.9 kHz. That's an unprecedented 998 bandwidths (98 with the coarser option), effectively a continuously tuned bandwidth throughout the entire range used by SWLs, DXers, hams and utility aficionados. In practice, the "coarser" setting is more convenient and fully adequate.

The ergonomics reflect the design concepts originally brought to Japan Radio by Paul Lannuier, who took over the now-defunct Gilfer from the Ferrell family. Operation is excellent in terms of layout, logic and feel, even though the "fast" tuning speed is uncomfortably rapid. This receiver is simply a joy to operate.

Image rejection, IF rejection, front-end selectivity, frequency stability, blocking and shortwave sensitivity/noise floor are all excellent or better, even though there is no preamplifier; sensitivity drops slightly on mediumwave AM and more on longwave. Phase noise and notch depth are both good, as is noise-blanker performance in the "narrow" setting. There is virtually no spurious radiation of digital "hash" into nearby antennas, which is good news for mediumwave AM DXers who use loop antennas.

Overall distortion is more complicated. In the initial version distortion ran as high as 12 percent. Now, with version B/B, it varies from an outstanding 0.1 percent at certain higher audio frequencies to five percent or slightly higher at 100 Hertz AF. By and large, though, overall distortion is now very low—under one percent. Dynamic range and the third-order intercept point, however, remain only fair, like on the predecessor NRD-535.

In the first two versions the synchronous selectable sideband circuit did as you would expect by attenuating adjacent-channel interference. All versions have held lock well, too. However, with our "B/B" ROMs the selectable sideband feature didn't work. Presumably this was a fluke that shouldn't be appearing regularly in production.

Bandwidth skirt selectivity is breathtaking, ranging from 1:1.06 for the 6 kHz bandwidth to 1:1.13 for the 2.4 kHz bandwidth. This coupled to the huge number of available bandwidths is one of the key virtues of the '545, and to the extent it works it is superb. This is selectivity like DXers have been dreaming of.

The catch is that deep-skirt selectivity, known as ultimate rejection, is only 50 dB, measured conservatively, to 65 dB, measured generously—call it roughly 60 dB. The fly in the ointment is that the receiver generates numerous spurious tones which add a subjective variable to what normally is an objective measurement.

What this means in practice is that if you are listening to a weak station on a channel adjacent to a very powerful signal, the adjacent signal may "creep in under the skirts" to cause interference to the station you're hearing. That is why deep ultimate selectivity—80 dB or more—is important for serious world band and mediumwave AM band DXing. Virtually all other supersets have this, but not the '545.

Still, 60 dB or so is a major improvement over the original version, which had ultimate rejection of no more than about 45 dB.

Japan Radio receivers rarely have been characterized by excellence in audio quality, and the initial version of the '545 was mediocre even by this feeble tradition. However, although audio quality in the "B/B" version is hardly inspiring and there is some "static emphasis," it is certainly acceptable, just as it was in the second version.

In principle, audio quality could be upgraded with a Sherwood SE-3 audio-enhancing device, which couples to a receiver's IF output. However, the '545 has no IF output, nor can one be retrofitted, so there is no getting around the '545's lack of audio excellence except patience, tolerant ears and a good outboard speaker.

The AGC decay rate is exceptionally adjustable—from 0.4 to 5.1 seconds in 0.02 second increments—and the decay time is shown on the display. However, it is not adjustable whatsoever in the AM mode— with or without the synchronous detector in use. Not only is this a drawback of exceptional proportions for a receiver in this class, the sole AGC decay rate that is offered is too fast, making listening even more tiring.

There are lesser shortcomings, all of which pale compared to those already described. For example, the audio notch only tunes to 2.5 kHz, which greatly limits its use with shortwave broadcasts which are 5 kHz apart and thus tend to produce a five kilohertz heterodyne. And the signal-strength meter overreads.

Fortunately, Japan Radio has shown its commitment to making continuing improvements by releasing two versions during the short period following the introduction of the original version. This is encouraging, as there is no reason the '545 shouldn't be a stellar performer unless its lone DSP has been taxed to its limit. With improved ultimate rejection, AGC adjustments functional in the AM and synchronous modes, notch coverage to 5.1 kHz, better audio quality and an IF output the '545 could be turned into the Lamborghini of tabletops. How much of this will actually come to pass remains to be seen.

⭐⭐⭐⭐½
Japan Radio "NRD-345SE"

Price: $1,195.00 plus shipping worldwide.

Evaluation of Enhanced Model: Sherwood Engineering is introducing the Japan Radio "NRD-345SE," the unofficial moniker for its version of the '345 when sold by Sherwood equipped with the Sherwood SE-3 fidelity-enhancing accessory and requisite IF output. The outboard SE-3 allows for first-rate synchronous selectable sideband and superior audio quality.

We tested a pre-production sample of this version, and it sounded very good, indeed—a major improvement in audio quality and interference rejection over the barefoot '345. The downside is that this version costs $400 more and complicates operation.

The "SE" version resolves most of the '345's shortcomings with aplomb, notably if you're listening within North America. However, Europeans should note that it does nothing to improve the '345's pedestrian dynamic range.

For other details, *see* Japan Radio NRD-345, farther below.

The Japan Radio NRD-345 is no barnburner, but is greatly improved in its unofficial "SE" incarnation.

⭐⭐⭐⭐ 🗎
Icom IC-R9000

Price: $6,199.00 to authorized purchasers in the United States, or for export. CAN$8,999.00 in Canada or for export. £4,080.00 in the United Kingdom. AUS$10,050 in Australia.

Pro: Exceptional tough-signal performance (*see* Note, below). Flexible, above-average audio for a tabletop model when used with suitable outboard speaker. Three AM-mode bandwidths (*see* Note, below). Tunes and displays frequency in precise 0.01 kHz increments. Video display of radio spectrum occupancy, a rarely found feature. Sophisticated scanner/timer. Extraordinarily broad coverage of radio spectrum, including portions forbidden to be listened to by the general public in the United States. Exceptional assortment of flexible operating controls and sockets. Good ergonomics. Superb

The ICOM IC-R9000 is available nearly everywhere in the world except the United States, where Federal regulations prohibit it.

reception of utility and ham signals. Two 24-hour clocks.

Con: In the United States, the Federal government bans sales to the public of receivers, such as the '9000, which can hear cellular frequencies. Dreadfully expensive. No synchronous selectable sideband. Power supply runs hot, although over the years this does not appear to have caused premature component failure. Both AM-mode bandwidths too broad for most world band applications. Both single-sideband bandwidths almost identical. Dynamic range merely adequate. Reliability, especially when roughly handled, may be wanting. Front-panel controls of only average construction quality.

☞ The above star rating can be viewed as conservative *if*, at a minimum, the barn-wide 11.3 kHz AM-mode bandwidth filter is changed to something in the vicinity of 4.5-5.5 kHz. Too, when suitably enhanced by Sherwood Engineering to have such a filter and an SE-3 synchronous detector, the R9000 is an outstanding receiver.

Verdict: The Icom IC-R9000, with at least one changed AM-mode bandwidth filter—

available from some world band specialty firms—is pretty much right up there with the best-performing models for DX reception of faint, tough signals. That is, of course, if you're allowed to buy one in the first place; best bet for Americans is to order one by mail from Canada. Where it shines is if you want a visual indication of spectrum occupancy and certain other characteristics of stations within a designated segment of the radio spectrum. Nevertheless, this model has been around for several years, and other models now offer virtually the same level, or even better, construction quality and performance, plus synchronous selectable sideband—sadly lacking on the 'R9000 unless the Sherwood SE-3 is added—for far less money.

📄 An *RDI WHITE PAPER* is available for this model.

✪✪✪✪
Japan Radio NRD-345, NRD-345G

Price: $799.95 in the United States. £699.00 in the United Kingdom. AUS$1,430.00 in Australia.

Pro: Superior construction quality by any yardstick, but especially for price. Excellent ergonomics, including superb tuning knob. Tunes in very precise 0.005 kHz increments with four manually selectable tuning speeds; displays to nearest 0.01 kHz. Superior weak-signal sensitivity and spurious-signal rejection. Two switchable antenna inputs, one low-impedance and the other high-impedance. Clock/timer functions. Tone control helps shape audio which, although lacking in treble, is already reasonably good and has minimal distortion. Slow/fast/off AGC (*see* Con). Memory scanning. Signal-strength indicator is analog. Double-fused for safety and protection. Worthy owner's manual.

Con: No tunable notch filter. Lacks passband tuning. Synchronous detector not sideband-selectable and provides little improvement even in double-sideband. Mediocre dynamic range limits strong-signal handling. Uses AC adaptor instead of built-in power supply. World Time clock does not show when frequency displayed. AGC "off" virtually useless because of no RF gain control. Mediumwave AM performance suffers from reduced sensitivity and limited dynamic range.

Verdict: First rate ergonomics and construction quality, along with good performance, make the '345 an attractive value.

Among "DC-to-daylight" receivers, the ICOM IC-R8500 comes out on top by a squeak.

✪✪✪✪
Icom IC-R8500

Price: $1,869.00 in the United States. CAN$2,849.00 in Canada. £1,549.00 in the United Kingdom. AUS$2,790.00 in Australia.

Pro: Wide-spectrum multimode coverage from 0.1-2000 MHz includes longwave, mediumwave AM, shortwave and scanner frequencies all in one receiver. Physically very rugged, with professional-grade cast-aluminum chassis and impressive computer-type innards. Generally superior ergonomics, with generous-sized front panel having large and well-spaced controls, plus outstanding tuning knob with numerous tuning steps. 1,000 presets and 100 auto-write presets have handy naming function. Superb weak-signal sensitivity. Pleasant, low-distortion audio aided by audio peak filter. Passband tuning ("IF shift"). Unusually readable LCD. Tunes and displays in precise 0.01 kHz increments. Three antenna connections. Clock-timer, combined with record output and recorder-activation jack, make for superior hands-off recording of favorite programs.

Con: No synchronous selectable sideband. Bandwidth choices for world band and other AM-mode signals leap from a very narrow 2.7 kHz to a broad 7.1 kHz with nothing between, where something is most needed; third bandwidth is 13.7 kHz, too wide for world band, and no provision is made for a fourth bandwidth filter. Only one single-sideband bandwidth. Unhandy carousel-style bandwidth selection with no permanent indication of which bandwidth is in use. Poor dynamic range, surprising at this price point. Passband tuning ("IF shift") does not work in the AM mode, used by world band and mediumwave AM-band stations. No tunable notch filter. Built-in speaker mediocre. Uses outboard AC adaptor instead of customary inboard power supply.

Versions Available: The Icom IC-R8500 is available in two similarly priced versions, "02" and "03." The "02" incarnation, sold to the public in the United States, is the same as the "03" version, but does not receive the *verboten* 824-849 and 869-894 MHz cellular bands. In the U.S., the "03" version is available legally only to government-approved organizations, although others reportedly have been bootlegging the "03" version by mail order from Canada. Outside the United States, the "03" version is usually the only one sold.

Sherwood SE-3: Also tested with Sherwood SE-3 non-factory accessory, which was outstanding at adding selectable synchronous sideband and provides passband tuning in the AM mode used, among other things, by world band stations. This and replacing the widest bandwidth with a 4 to 5 kHz bandwidth dramatically improve performance on shortwave, mediumwave AM and longwave.

Verdict: The large Icom IC-R8500 is really a scanner that happens to cover world band, rather than *vice versa*. As a standalone world band receiver, it makes little sense, but it is well worth considering if you want worthy scanner and shortwave performance all in one rig.

New for 1999 is the AOR AR5000+3. It aims to excel with world band reception, but results are mixed.

New for 1999
✪✪✪✪
AOR AR5000+3

Price: *AR5000+3 receiver:* $2,695.00 in the United States. CAN$3,999.00 in Canada. £1,574.00 in the United Kingdom. AUS$3,799.95 in Australia. *Collins 6 kHz mechanical filter (recommended):* $149.95 in the United States. £69.95 in the United Kingdom.

Pro: Ultra-wide-spectrum multimode coverage from 0.1-2,600 MHz includes longwave, mediumwave AM, shortwave and scanner frequencies all in one receiver. Helpful tuning features include fully 2,000 presets. Narrow bandwidth filter and optional Collins wide filter both have superb skirt selectivity (standard wide filter's skirt selectivity unmeasurable because of limited ultimate rejection). Synchronous selectable and double sideband (*see* Con). Front-end selectivity, image rejection, IF rejection, weak-signal sensitivity, AGC threshold and frequency stability all superior. Exceptionally precise frequency readout to nearest Hertz. Most accurate displayed frequency measurement of any receiver tested to date. Superb circuit shielding results in virtually zero radiated digital "hash." IF output (*see* Con). Automatic Frequency Control (AFC) works on AM-mode, as well as FM, signals. Owner's manual, important because of operating system, unusually helpful.

Con: Synchronous detector loses lock easily, especially if selectable sideband feature in use, greatly detracting from the utility of this high-tech feature. Substandard rejection of unwanted sideband with selectable synchronous sideband. Overall distortion rises when synchronous detector used. Ultimate rejection of "narrow" 2.7 kHz bandwidth filter only 60 dB. Ultimate rejection mediocre (50 dB) with standard 7.6 kHz "wide" bandwidth filter, improves to an uninspiring 60 dB when replaced by optional 6 kHz "wide" Collins mechanical filter. Installation of optional Collins filter requires expertise, patience and special equipment. Poor dynamic range. Cumbersome ergonomics. No passband offset. No tunable notch filter. Needs good external speaker for good audio quality. World Time clock does not show when frequency displayed. IF output frequency 10.7 MHz instead of standard 455 kHz.

Verdict: Unbeatable in some respects, inferior in others—it comes down to what use you will be putting the radio to. The optional 6 kHz Collins filter is strongly recommended, but it should be installed by dealer at time of purchase.

Evaluation of New Model: AOR's new AR5000+3 ("Plus 3") is, unlike its sibling AR500, designed and manufactured in Japan. A genuinely wideband receiver, it covers fully 10 kHz through 2,600 MHz, with coverage "holes" in the version sold in the United States, where Federal law prohibits the public from tuning to certain frequencies.

There are—count 'em!—2,000 presets that store all kinds of useful data. There is also knob tuning, a small keypad that's not in telephone format, and full scanning facilities. There is no passband offset control, nor is there a tunable notch for heterodyne rejection. There is, however, a World Time clock, although it doesn't display while the frequency is being read out.

The "+3" version includes features not found on the regular AR5000: synchronous AM reception, automatic frequency control (AFC) and a noise blanker. Interestingly, that AFC works not just on FM signals, but also on AM-mode signals, including world band.

The synchronous detector acts both ways: selectable sideband and double sideband. However, rejection of the unwanted sideband is not equal to that of many other models. Worse, it noisily loses lock so often that we gave up on this feature altogether.

For shortwave listening and DXing, two voice bandwidths are offered: 2.7 kHz (nominally 3 kHz) and 7.6 kHz (nominally 6 kHz), both using ceramic filters. We installed the optional 6 kHz Collins mechanical filter, but not before measuring performance of the standard "6 kHz" ceramic. Installation of the optional filter requires considerable electronic expertise and specialized equipment; we strongly recommend that you have this installed by your dealer at the time of purchase.

The standard "wide" filters measure 7.6 kHz, whereas the optional Collins replacement filter measures a much-better 6.0 kHz. The Collins filter and standard 2.7 kHz filter both have superb skirt selectivity, as well. However, the ultimate rejection of the standard 7.6 kHz filter is only 50 dB, making it impossible to measure skirt

PASSPORT'S CHOICE

Only three models have earned this distinction—the Watkins-Johnson HF-1000, Drake R8B and AOR AR7030. Of these, the Drake has far and away the widest appeal because of operating convenience and, in some countries, price. Yet, the current version of the Watkins-Johnson is the ultimate in world band DX machines, albeit by only a slight amount, and for less money the unusual AOR comes quite close.

Honorable mention goes to the Kneisner + Doering KWZ 30. Although this just-introduced model from a new manufacturer is not quite "there" yet, it is lovingly crafted and holds much promise.

selectivity. Fortunately, this improves to 60 dB with the Collins filter installed. Ultimate selectivity for the 2.7 kHz filter is 60 dB.

While 60 dB is acceptable, it is clearly substandard for a serious communications receiver; 80 dB or greater is the norm.

Because of excessive phase noise, dynamic range is unmeasurable at the customary 5 kHz and 20 kHz separation points. At 50 kHz separation, where phase noise is less of a problem, dynamic range and the third-order intercept point are both poor. In much of North America, this is not likely to result in overloading, but it could in such places as Europe.

Otherwise, the shortwave performance of the AR5000+3 is commendable. Its front-end selectivity and image rejection are both excellent, and second IF rejection is superb. Sensitivity with the preamp on is excellent, and almost as good with the preamp off. The related measurement of blocking is good.

AGC threshold and stability are also of a high caliber, although the noise blanker is only fair and is complex to operate. Overall distortion in the AM mode is almost minimal, slightly higher but still decent in the single-sideband mode, and good but higher yet with the synchronous detector in use. Overall audio quality with the internal speaker is pedestrian, but improves noticeably with a good external speaker.

Unlike with virtually every other receiver we have tested over the past 21 years, the frequency readout is unfailingly accurate to the nearest Hertz. This should make the AR5000+3 of exceptional interest to broadcast engineers.

Broadcast engineers doing field work, as well as mediumwave AM enthusiasts, will also be pleased to find that the '5000+3 emits no detectable noise from its complex digital circuitry. This is the lowest emission among digital receivers we have ever tested, and means, for example, that longwave and mediumwave loop antennas won't pick up a peep of digital hash from this receiver.

The AR5000+3's ergonomics are generally cumbersome; even though most functions of the receiver are adjustable, there are few conventional controls. Instead, most receiver functions are adjusted from software menus which usually act upon instructions from the keypad. Added to this are default settings and other software specifics that are unhandy, inappropriate or both. The unusually thorough operating manual helps overcome this, even though it lacks an index.

Serious shortwave DXers rarely purchase "DC-to-daylight" receivers because they can't equal the performance of the best HF-and-below models, such as AOR's own outstanding AR7030. However, radio dealers indicate there is a consistent traffic in radios which are very good, even if not great, in covering the bulk of the radio spectrum . For these enthusiasts with broad interests, the AR5000+3 provides an interesting alternative to the similarly rated broadband Icom IC-R8500.

✪✪✪✪
Lowe HF-250E

Price (including remote control): CAN$1,999.00 in Canada. £719.00 in the United Kingdom. AUS$2,500.00 in Australia. £676.00 plus shipping elsewhere.

Pro: Top-notch world band and mediumwave AM audio quality, aided by effective tone control, so it's well suited to listening to world band programs hour after hour. Clean, simple panel keeps operating controls to a minimum. Synchronous detection circuit allows for either selectable-sideband for reduced fading and easier rejection of interference, or double-sideband reception for reduced fading (*see* Con). Four worthy voice bandwidths. Exceptionally rugged cast-aluminum housing of a class normally associated with professional-grade equipment. Relatively small footprint. Digital display unusually easy to read. World Time clock shows seconds numerically (*see* Con). Superior factory service.

Con: Synchronous detector only okay in holding lock with signals suffering from flutter fading. Operation of some front-panel button functions tends to be confusing until you get the hang of it. Nonstandard keypad layout. Bereft of certain features—among them notch filter, adjustable AGC and passband tuning—found on some premium-priced models. Occasional minor hum from AC adaptor unless antenna uses coaxial-cable feedline. Signal-strength indicator has small numbers, hard to read. Clock not displayed when frequency is showing. Minor "braap" chugging within some frequency ranges.

Verdict: Think of the Lowe HF-250E as a cleaned-up HF-150 that while generally moving forward, also took a couple of steps backward with the offbeat keypad and "on-during-bandscanning" synchronous detector that could be better at holding lock. It's a hardy, advanced-fidelity receiver for the dedicated listener to world band programs.

The Lowe HF-250E is pricey for what it does. It is no longer sold in the United States.

timers, 52 tunable station presets that store frequency and mode data, a variety of scanning schemes and an all-mode squelch. A communications-FM module, 500 Hz CW bandwidth and high-stability crystal are optional.

Con: No keypad for direct frequency entry (remediable, *see* Note, below). No synchronous selectable sideband. Lacks features found in "top-gun" receivers: passband tuning, notch filter, adjustable RF gain. Simple controls and display, combined with complex functions, can make certain operations confusing. Dynamic range only fair. Uses AC adaptor instead of built-in power supply.

☞ An outboard accessory keypad is virtually a "must" for the FRG-100, and is a no-brainer to attach. Brodier E.E.I. (3 Place de la Fontaine, F-57420 Curvy, France)

✪✪✪✪ ⊘ 🗋
Yaesu FRG-100B

Price: $599.95 in the United States. CAN$899.00 in Canada. £459.00 in the United Kingdom. AUS$999.00 in Australia.

Pro: Excellent performance in many respects. Relatively low price. Covers 50 Hz to 30 MHz in the LSB, USB, AM and CW modes. Includes three bandwidths, a noise blanker, selectable AGC, two attenuators, the ability to select 16 pre-programmed world band segments, two clocks, on-off

The Yaesu FRG-100B is a pleasant receiver, but by the time a keypad is added it is overshadowed by the similarly priced Drake SW8 portatop.

makes the best keypad, sold direct and for $59.95 through Universal Radio in the United States; also, Martin Lynch in England and Charly Hardt in Remscheid, Germany. Reasonably similar is the costlier QSYer—SWL Version, available from Stone Mountain Engineering Company in Stone Mountain GA 30086 USA.

Verdict: While sparse on features, in many respects the Yaesu FRG-100B succeeds in delivering worthy performance within its price class. Its lack of a keypad for direct frequency entry is now easily remediable (*see* Note, above).

📄 An *RDI WHITE PAPER* is available for this model.

✪✪✪½
Drake SW2

Price: *Receiver:* $499.00 in the United States. CAN$699.00 in Canada. £499.00 in the United Kingdom. AUS$1,050.00 in Australia. *Infrared remote control:* $49.00 in the United States. CAN$75.00 in Canada. £49.95 in the United Kingdom.

Pro: Synchronous selectable sideband performs unusually well for reduced fading and easier rejection of interference; also, synchronous detector works in double-sideband mode. Several useful tuning features, including keypad, slewing and 100 presets. Superb dynamic range puts most other receivers to shame, regardless of price. This, combined with generally superior weak-signal sensitivity, make for generally good mediumwave DX performance. Pleasant audio with minimal distortion. Worthy ergonomics, including outstandingly easy-to-read frequency display with dimmer. Superior factory service. Fifteen-day money-back trial period if ordered from the factory or certain dealers.

Con: Only one (7 kHz) of two voice bandwidths usable in AM mode—the mode used *inter alia* for world band reception. Tunes in relatively coarse 50 Hz steps with some minor chugging. No notch filter, passband tuning, manually selectable AGC or noise blanker. No clock or timer. "Wall wart" AC adaptor instead of internal power supply. Optional remote control, which doesn't control volume, not worth the money for most, although its utility is aided by the receiver's bright LEDs, which can be read easily across a room.

Verdict: Close, but no cigar. Imagine a V-8 engine with a double-barrel carburetor where the manufacturer has plugged up

The Drake SW2 is neither fish nor fowl, being priced at $500 but not performing accordingly. The wide bandwidth is so useless—fixing it would cost Drake nothing—that the question arises whether Drake is more concerned about cross-competition with its own SW8 than in turning out a strong contender.

one of the barrels, then think of radio. The Drake SW2 is a fine all-round performer, but even though it has two voice bandwidths—one narrow, one wide—only the wide is accessible for world band.

New Version for 1999
✪✪✪ ✐
Lowe SRX100, Target HF3, Target HF3M, (Target HF3S), (Target HF3E)

Target receivers, now available in a number of versions, target the low end of the tabletop market.

Price: *SRX100:* £129.00 in the United Kingdom. *HF3:* £159.95 in the United Kingdom. AUS$439.00 in Australia. *HF3M:* $289.95 in the United States. £209.95 in the United Kingdom. *HF3S (not tested):* £159.95 in the United Kingdom. *HF3E (not tested):* £299.00 in the United Kingdom.

Pro: *SRX100, HF3 and HF3M:* Low price. Superior rejection of spurious "image" signals. Third-order intercept point indicates superior strong-signal handling capability. Bandwidths have superb ultimate rejection. *HF3M:* Equipped for weatherfax ("WEFAX") reception.

Con: *SRX100, HF3 and HF3M:* No keypad and variable-rate tuning knob is difficult to control. When switched on, goes not to the last-tuned frequency and mode, but rather to the frequency and mode in the lone preset. Volume control fussy to adjust. Bandwidths not selectable independent of mode. The only AM-mode bandwidth, used for world band reception, is somewhat wide because of broad skirt selectivity. Single-sideband bandwidth too great. Synthesizer tunes in relatively coarse 1 kHz increments, supplemented by an analog fine-tuning "clarifier" control. Single sideband requires both tuning controls to be adjusted. No synchronous selectable sideband, notch filter or passband tuning. Frequency readout off by 2 kHz in single-sideband mode. Uses AC adaptor instead of built-in power supply. No clock, timer or snooze feature. LCD not illuminated. *SRX100 and HF3:* Only one preset. No elevation feet or

tilt bail. *HF3S and HF3M:* Only ten presets. *U.K. only:* Two year warranty.

☞ According to the manufacturer, the HF3S is identical to the HF3 but with ten presets, whereas the HF3E is comparable to the HF3M, but with a "quasi-synchronous" detector and illuminated LCD.

Verdict: Surprisingly good world band performance for the price, but frustrating to operate. If you want this receiver, go for the new "M" version; the new "E" version, not tested, appears to be relatively pricey for what is offered.

✪✪½ ✐
Radio Shack DX-394

Price: £149.95 in the United Kingdom. AUS$599.95 in Australia. No longer available within North America.

Pro: Super-low price for 1999 in those parts of the world where the '394 is still sold. Advanced tuning features include 160 tunable presets (*see* Con). Tunes and displays in precise 0.01 kHz. Modest size, light weight and built-in telescopic antenna provide some portable capability. Bandwidths have superior shape factors and ultimate rejection. Two 24-hour clocks, one of which shows independent of frequency display. Five programmable timers. 30/60 minute snooze feature. Noise blanker. 30-day money-back trial period in the United States.

Radio Shack has had tough slogging with tabletop receivers since it discontinued the Realistic DX-160 receiver decades back. The DX-394 also appears to be headed to an unmourned extinction.

Con: What appear to be four bandwidths turn out to be virtually one bandwidth, and it is too wide for optimum reception of many signals. Bandwidths, such as they are, not selectable independent of mode. No synchronous selectable sideband. Presets cumbersome to use. Poor dynamic range for a tabletop, a potential problem in Europe and other strong-signal parts of the world if an external antenna is used. Overall distortion, although acceptable, higher than desirable.

Verdict: Modest dimensions and equally modest performance, but you can't beat the U.K. price. Get 'em while you can!

The Drake SW1 is a tough but simple hombre that costs less than some portables. Excellent factory service, too.

★★½ ☺
Drake SW1

Price: $249.95 in the United States. CAN$399.00 in Canada. AUS$620.00 in Australia.

Pro: Exceptionally low price, especially for high level of construction quality. Dynamic range, sensitivity to weak signals and certain other performance variables above average for price class. Pleasant audio. Large, bright digital display using LEDs much easier to read indoors than most. Easiest and simplest to use of any tabletop tested, with quality ergonomics. Superior factory service. 15-day money-back trial period if ordered from the factory or certain dealers.

Con: Mediocre adjacent-channel rejection (selectivity) from the single bandwidth. No features—*nada*, not even a signal-strength indicator—except for tuning. No single sideband. No synchronous selectable sideband. Increments for tuning and frequency display are relatively coarse. Annoying chugging during bandscanning. Uses AC adaptor instead of built-in power supply.

Verdict: A nice value as far as it goes, but where are the features? And why such mediocre selectivity and loud chugging? Still, in many respects, such as quality of construction and service, Drake's SW1 offers solid value at a bargain-basement price. Because of construction quality and service, no other model of world band radio of any type under $400 comes as close to being a "friend for life."

The PASSPORT tabletop-model review team consists of Lawrence Magne and George Zeller, with Jock Elliott and Tony Jones; also, George Heidelman and Craig Tyson. Laboratory measurements by J. Robert Sherwood.

WHERE TO FIND IT: INDEX TO DIGITAL RADIOS

PASSPORT TO WORLD BAND RADIO tests nearly every model on the market. This index lists all digital models reviewed, with those that are new, changed or retested for 1999 being in **bold**. Additionally, *75 analog portables* are rated on page 121 and the windup *BayGen* analog portable is on page 106. The *Sony AN-LP1 active antenna* for portables is reviewed on page 93.

Comprehensive PASSPORT® Radio Database International White Papers® are available for the most popular premium receivers and antennas. Each RDI White Paper®—$6.95 in North America, $9.95 airmail to Europe and Australasia—contains virtually all our panel's findings and comments during hands-on testing, as well as laboratory measurements and what these mean to you. These unabridged reports are available from key world band dealers, or you can contact our 24-hour automated VISA/MC order channels (www.passport.com, autovoice +1 215/794-8252, fax +1 215/794 3396), or write us at PASSPORT RDI White Papers, Box 300, Penn's Park, PA 18943 USA.

🗐 *Radio Database International White Paper*® available.

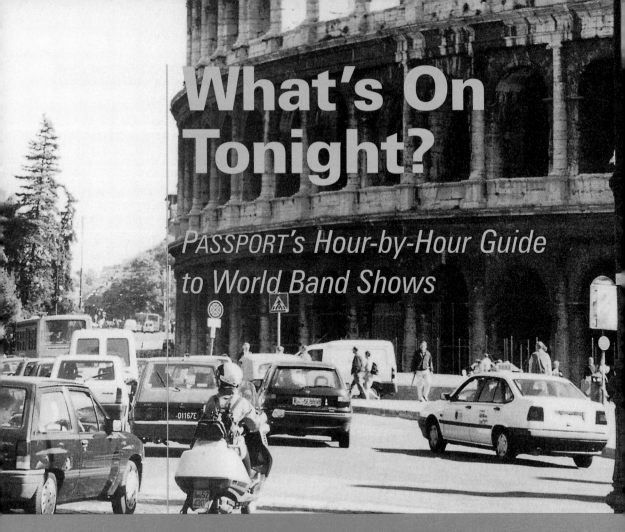

What's On Tonight?

PASSPORT's Hour-by-Hour Guide to World Band Shows

World band's unequaled news output, plus loads of music, make for great listening. But there's a catch: So much is on the air that it is nigh impossible to keep track of it all.

Passport to the rescue! Here, hour by hour, is a rundown of what's available. To help you separate the thoroughbreds from the rest of the pack, here are some handy symbols:

■ Station with programs that are almost always superior

● Top-notch show

To be as helpful as possible throughout the year, PASSPORT's schedules consist not just of observed activity, but also that which we have creatively opined will take place during the forthcoming year. This predictive material is original from us, and although of real value, is inherently not so exact as real-time data.

Key frequencies are given for North America, Western Europe, East Asia and Australasia, plus general coverage of the Mideast, Southern Africa and Southeast Asia. Information on secondary and seasonal channels, as well as frequencies for other parts of the world, are in "Worldwide Broadcasts in English" and the Blue Pages.

All times are World Time, days as World Day, both explained in the Glossary and "Compleat Idiot's Guide to Getting Started." (Many stations announce World Time at the beginning of each broadcast or on the hour.)

"Summer" and "winter"? These refer to seasons in the Northern Hemisphere, regardless of where the station is located. Many stations supplement their programs with newsletters, tourist brochures, magazines, books, souvenirs and other goodies—often free. See Addresses PLUS for the complete breakdown.

All times are World Time, days as World Day.

Adventist World Radio's station at Forlì, Italy. This station broadcasts to Europe in English, Arabic, French, German and Italian. AWR

0000-0559
North America—Evening Prime Time
Europe & Mideast—Early Morning
Australasia & East Asia—Midday and Afternoon

00:00

■**BBC World Service for the Americas.** Starts the hour with ●*Newsdesk*, which is then followed by a 15-minute feature and ●*Britain Today*. Pick of the features are Wednesday's ●*The Farming World* (Tuesday evening, local American date), Thursday's ●*From Our Own Correspondent*, Saturday's *From the Weeklies* and Sunday's ●*Letter from America*. Continuous programming to North America and the Caribbean on 5975, 6175 and 9590 kHz.

■**BBC World Service for Asia.** Similar to the service for the Americas, except for some of the features at 0030. Among the more interesting offerings are ●*From Our Own Correspondent* (Thursday), ●*Short Story* (Friday) and Saturday's *From the Weeklies*. Audible in East Asia (till 0030) on 9580 (winter), 11945, 15280 and (summer)

17790 kHz; and a full hour on 15360 kHz. In Southeast Asia, tune to 3915 (till 0030), 6195, 7110 (till 0030), 9410 or 15360 kHz.

Radio Bulgaria. Winters only at this time. *News*, then Tuesday through Friday there's 15 minutes of current events in *Today*, replaced Saturday by *Weekly Spotlight*. The remainder of the broadcast is given over to features dealing with Bulgarian life and culture, and includes some lively Balkan folk music. Sixty minutes to eastern North America and Central America on 7375 and 9485 kHz. One hour earlier in summer.

Radio Exterior de España ("Spanish National Radio"). *News*, then Tuesday through Saturday (local weekday evenings in the Americas) it's *Panorama*, which features a recording of popular Spanish

Star Radio counteracts African stations which fan the flames of tribal hatred.

Foundation Hirondelle

music, a commentary or a report, a review of the Spanish press, and weather. The remainder of the program is a mixture of literature, science, music and general programming. Tuesday (Monday evening in North America), there's *Sports Spotlight* and *Cultural Encounters*; Wednesday features *People of Today* and *Entertainment in Spain*; Thursday brings *As Others See Us* and, biweekly, *The Natural World* or *Science Desk*; Friday has *Economic Report* and *Cultural Clippings*; and Saturday offers *Window on Spain* and *Review of the Arts*. The final slot is give over to a language course, *Spanish by Radio*. On the remaining days, you can listen to Sunday's *Hall of Fame*, *Distance Unknown* (for radio enthusiasts) and *Gallery of Spanish Voices*; and Monday's *Visitors' Book*, *Great Figures in Flamenco* and *Radio Club*. Sixty minutes to eastern North America on 6055 kHz.

Radio Canada International. Winters only at this time. Tuesday through Saturday (weekday evenings in North America), it's the final hour of the CBC domestic service news program ●*As It Happens*, which features international stories, Canadian news and general human interest features. Sundays feature ●*Quirks and Quarks* (science), replaced Monday by *Sound Advice*, both from the CBC's domestic output. To North America on 5960 and 9755 kHz, with the first half hour also available on 6040, 9535 and 11865 kHz. One hour earlier in summer.

Radio Yugoslavia. Monday through Saturday (Sunday through Friday, local American evenings) and summers only at this time. *News* and information with a strong local flavor, and worth a listen if you are interested in the area. Thirty minutes to Eastern and Central North America on 9580 and 11870 kHz. One hour later in winter.

Radio Pyongyang, North Korea. Strictly of curiosity value only, this station is a broadcasting dinosaur, almost totally

removed from reality. The "Great Leader" and "Beloved Comrade" continue to feature prominently, as does choral adulation of the country's leader. An hour of old-style communist programming to Southeast Asia and the Americas on 11845, 13650 and 15230 kHz.

Radio Ukraine International. Summers only at this time. An hour's ample coverage of just about everything Ukrainian, including news, sports, politics and culture. Well worth a listen is ●*Music from Ukraine*, which fills most of the Monday (Sunday evening in the Americas) broadcast. Sixty minutes to Europe and eastern North America on 5905, 5915, 7180, 7240, 9550 and 12040 kHz. One hour later in winter.

Radio Australia. Part of a 24-hour service to Asia and the Pacific, but which can also be heard at this time in parts of North America (better to the west). Begins with world *news*, then Tuesday through Friday there's *Asia Pacific*, replaced Saturday by *Feedback* (a listener-response program), Sunday by *Oz Sounds* and Monday by *Correspondents' Report*. On the half-hour, look for a bit of variety, depending on the day of the week. Monday's *Innovations* deals with the invented and innovative; Tuesday's cultural spot is *Arts Australia*; Wednesday, take a trip up country in *Rural Reporter*; Thursday, it's *Book Talk*; Friday spotlights the environment in *Earthbeat*; and weekends there's Saturday's *Asia Pacific* and Sunday's *Correspondents' Report*. Targeted at Asia and the Pacific on 9660, 12080, 15240, 17715, 17750, 17795 and 21740 kHz. In North America (best during summer) try 17715, 17795 and 21740 kHz; and in East Asia go for 15240 and 17750 kHz. Best bet for Southeast Asia is 17750 kHz.

Radio Prague, Czech Republic. *News*, then Tuesday through Saturday (weekday evenings in the Americas), there's *Current Affairs*. These are followed by one or more

ABC's Art Bell regularly focuses on world band topics. Here, he reports from Egypt via satellite phone. R. Crane

features. Tuesday's offering is *Magazine '99*; Wednesday, it's *Talking Point* and *Media Czech*; Thursday brings *The Arts* and *History Czech*; Friday's lineup is *Economic Report* and *I'd Like You to Meet...*; and Saturday there's *Between You and Us*. The Sunday slot is an excellent musical feature, and Monday there's *The Week in Politics*, *From the Weeklies* and *Media Czech*. Thirty minutes to eastern North America on 5930 and 7345 kHz.

Voice of America. The first 60 minutes of a two-hour broadcast to the Caribbean and Latin America which is aired Tuesday through Saturday (weekday evenings in the Americas). *News Now*, a rolling news format covering political, business and other developments. On 5995, 6130, 7405, 9455, 9775, 11695 and 13740 kHz. The final hour of a separate service to East and Southeast Asia and Australasia (see 2200) can be heard on 7215, 9770, 11760, 15185, 15290, 17735 and 17820 kHz.

Radio Thailand. *Newshour*. Not as dry as it used to be, but a little added vitality would not be amiss. Thirty minutes to eastern and southern parts of Africa (who listens at this hour?), winters on 9680 kHz and summers on 9690 kHz. An extra half hour is available for listeners in Asia on 9655 and 11905 kHz.

All India Radio. The final 45 minutes of a much larger block of programming targeted at Southeast Asia, and heard well beyond. On 7150, 9705, 9950 and 11620 kHz.

Radio Cairo, Egypt. The final half-hour of a 90-minute broadcast to eastern North America on 9900 kHz. See 2300 for specifics.

Radio New Zealand International. A friendly package of *news* and features sometimes replaced by live sports commentary. Part of a much longer broadcast for the South Pacific, but also heard in parts of North America (especially during summer) on 17675 kHz.

FEBC Radio International, Philippines. *Good Morning from Manila*, a potpourri of secular and religious programming targeted at South and Southeast Asia, but heard well beyond. The first 60 minutes of a two-hour broadcast on 15450 kHz.

WWCR, Nashville, Tennessee. Carries a variety of disestablishmentarian programs at this hour, depending on the day of the week. Winters on 5065 kHz, there's "The Voice of Liberty" and "The Hour of Courage"; in summer it's "Protecting your Wealth," "World of Prophecy" and "Full Disclosure Live." On 7435 kHz, look for yet more of the same.

WJCR, Upton, Kentucky. Twenty-four hours of gospel music targeted at North America on 7490 and (at this hour) 13595 kHz. Also heard elsewhere, mainly during darkness hours. For more religious broadcasting at this hour, try **WYFR—Family Radio** on 6085 kHz, and **KTBN** on (winters) 7510 or (summers) 15590 kHz. For something a little more controversial, tune to Dr. Gene Scott's University Network, via **WWCR** on 13845 kHz or **KAIJ** on 13815 kHz. Traditional Catholic programming can be heard via **WEWN** on 7425 kHz.

00:30

■**Radio Netherlands.** *News*, then Tuesday through Sunday (Monday through Saturday evenings in North America) there's ●*Newsline*, a current affairs program. These are followed by a different feature each day, including the well-produced ●*Research File* (science, Tuesday); *Music 52-15* (eclectic, Wednesday); the excellent award-winning ●*Documentary* (Thursday); *Media Network* (Friday); ●*A Good Life* (Saturday); and Sunday's ●*Weekend*. Monday's features are a listener-response program and *Sounds Interesting*. Fifty-five minutes to North America on 6020, 6165 and (summers) 9845 kHz; and a full hour to South Asia (also widely heard in other parts of the continent, as well as Australasia), winters on 5905, 7305, 9860 and 11660 kHz; and summers on 9855, 11655 and 12090 kHz.

Radio Austria International. Summers only at this time. ●*Report from Austria*, which includes a brief bulletin of *news*, followed by a series of current events and human interest stories. Ample coverage of national and regional issues, and an excellent source for news of Central Europe. Thirty minutes to eastern North America on 9655 kHz.

Radio Vilnius, Lithuania. A half hour that's heavily geared to *news* and background reports about events in Lithuania.

World band expert Sue Crane in an old fortress archway on a hilltop in Greece. R. Crane

Of broader appeal is *Mailbag*, aired every other Sunday (Saturday evenings local American date). For a little Lithuanian music, try the next evening, following the news. To eastern North America winters on 5890 kHz, and summers on 9855 kHz.

Voice of the Islamic Republic of Iran. One hour of *news*, commentary and features with a strong Islamic slant. Targeted at North and Central America. Try 6015, 6150, 6175, 7180, 9022 and 9670 kHz. Apart from 9022 kHz, channel usage tends to be variable.

Radio Thailand. *Newshour*. Thirty minutes to North America winters on 11905 kHz, and summers on 15395 kHz.

HCJB—Voice of the Andes, Ecuador. Tuesday through Saturday (weekday

MFJ's high performance *tuned* active antenna rivals long wires hundreds of feet long!

MFJ-1020B $69⁹⁵

Receive strong clear signals from all over the world with this indoor tuned active antenna that rivals the reception of long wires hundreds of feet long!

"World Radio TV Handbook" says MFJ-1020B is a "fine value . . . fair price . . . performs very well indeed!" Set it on your desktop and listen to the world!

No need to go through the hassle of putting up an outside antenna you have to disconnect when it storms.

Covers 300 kHz to 30 MHz so you can pick up all of your favorite stations. And discover new ones you couldn't get before. Tuned circuitry minimizes intermodulation, improves selectivity and reduces noise from phantom signals, images and out-of-band signals.

Adjustable telescoping whip gives you maximum signal with minimum noise. Full set of controls for tuning, band selection, gain and On-Off/Bypass. 5x2x6 in.

Also, doubles as preselector with external antenna . Use 9 volt battery or 110 VAC with MFJ-1312, $12.95.

MFJ tunable DSP filter

MFJ-784B $249⁹⁵ **Super** filter uses state-of-the-art *Digital Signal Processing* technology!

It *automatically* searches for and eliminates *multiple* heterodynes.

Tunable, pre-set and programmable "brick wall" filters with 60 dB *attenuation just 75 Hz away from cutoff frequency* literally knocks out interference signals.

Adaptive noise reduction reduces random background noise up to 20 dB.

Works with all signals including all voice, CW and data signals. Plugs between radio and speaker or phones.

Dual Tunable Audio Filter

MFJ-752C $99⁹⁵ **Two** separately tunable filters let you peak desired signals and notch out interference at the same time. You can peak, notch, low or high pass signals to eliminate heterodynes and interference. Plugs between radio and speaker or phones. 10x2x6 in.

Super Active Antenna

"World Radio TV Handbook" says MFJ-1024 is a "first rate easy-to-operate active antenna . . . quiet . . . excellent dynamic range . . . good gain . . . low noise . . . broad frequency coverage."

Mount it outdoors away from electrical noise for maximum signal, minimum noise. Covers 50 KHz to 30 MHz.

Receives strong, clear signals from all over the world. 20dB attenuator, gain control, ON LED. Switch two receivers and aux. or active antenna. 6x3x5 in. remote has 54 inch whip, 50 ft. coax. 3x2x4 in. 12 VDC or 110 VAC with MFJ-1312, $12.95.

MFJ-1024 $129⁹⁵

Eliminate noise and interference

MFJ-1026 **Completely** $169⁹⁵ cancel interference, power line noise and lightning crashes *before they get into your receiver!* Works on all modes -- SSB, AM, CW, FM -- and on all shortwave bands. Plugs between your external antenna and receiver. Use built-in active antenna or external antenna to pick up noise and interference for cancellation. Also use as an active antenna. Use 12 VDC or 110 VAC with MFJ-1312B, $12.95.

MFJ Antenna Matcher

MFJ-959B $99⁹⁵

Matches your antenna to your receiver so you get maximum signal and minimum loss.

Preamp with gain control boosts weak stations 10 times. 20 dB attenuator prevents overload. Pushbuttons let you select 2 antennas and 2 receivers. Covers 1.6-30 MHz. 9x2x6 inches.

SWL's Guide for Apartments

World renowned MFJ-36 SWL expert Ed $9⁹⁵ Noll's book tells you what shortwave bands to listen to, the best times to tune in, how to DX and QSL, how to send for schedules and construct indoor antennas plus more!

Easy-Up Antennas Book

How to build and put up inexpensive, fully tested wire antennas using readily available parts that'll bring signals in like you've never heard before. Antennas MFJ-38 from 100 KHz to 1000 MHz. $16⁹⁵

High-Q Passive Preselector

High-Q passive LC preselector that lets you boost your favorite stations while rejecting images, intermod and other phantom signals. 1.5-30 MHz. MFJ-956 $39⁹⁵

MFJ *Lightning Surge Protector* for 50 ohm coax

MFJ-270 **MFJ** *Lightning* $29⁹⁵ *Surge Protector* safeguards your expensive shortwave receiving equipment from damaging static electricity and lightning induced surges. Ultra-fast gas discharge tube safely shunts up to 5,000 amps of peak impulse current harmlessly to independent ground. Plugs between antenna and receiver. Does not protect against a direct lightning hit.

High-Gain Preselector

MFJ-1045C $69⁹⁵

High-gain, high-Q receiver preselector covers 1.8-54 MHz. Boost weak signals 10 times with low noise dual gate MOSFET. Reject out-of-band signals and images with high-Q tuned circuits. Pushbuttons let you select 2 antennas and 2 receivers. Dual coax and phono connectors. Use 9-18 VDC or 110 VAC with MFJ-1312, $12.95.

MFJ Communications Speaker

NEW! MFJ-281 $9⁹⁵ **Top** grade Mylar speaker in speech-enhancing baffle. AM, SSB, FM, CW never sounded so crystal-clear! Swivel mount. Handles 8 watts. 8 ohms. 6 foot cord, 3.5 mm mono plug.

Super *Passive* Preselector

NEW! MFJ-1046 $99⁹⁵ **Greatly** suppresses strong out-of-band signals that cause intermod, blocking, cross modulation and phantom signals. MFJ's exclusive Hi-Q *series tuned* preselector adds super sharp front-end selectivity -- gives you narrow bandwidth, excellent stopband attenuation, very low passband loss. An *air* variable capacitor and vernier drive gives you smooth precision tuning 1.6-33 MHz. Plugs between antenna and receiver.

Tap into *secret* Shortwave Signals

Turn mysterious signals into exciting text messages with this new MFJ MultiReader™

MFJ-462B

$179⁹⁵

Plug this *MFJ MultiReader™* into your shortwave receiver's earphone jack.

Then *watch* mysterious chirps, whistles and buzzing sounds of RTTY, ASCII, AMTOR FEC and CW turn into exciting text messages as they scroll across your easy-to-read LCD display.

You'll *read* fascinating commerical, military, diplomatic, weather, aeronautical, maritime and amateur traffic from all over the world . . . traffic your friends can't read -- unless they have a decoder.

Eavesdrop on the World

Eavesdrop on the world's press agencies transmitting *unedited* late breaking news in English -- China News in Taiwan, Tanjug Press in Serbia, Iraqui News in Iraq.

Printer monitors 24 hours a day

MFJ's exclusive *TelePrinterPort™* lets you monitor any station 24 hours a day by printing their transmissions on your Epson compatible printer. Printer cable, **MFJ-5412**, $9.95.

MFJ *MessageSaver™*

You can save several pages of text in 8K of memory for re-reading or later review using MFJ's exclusive *MessageSaver™*.

Easy to use, tune and read

It's easy to use -- just push a button to select modes and features from a menu.

It's easy to tune -- a precision tuning indicator makes tuning your receiver fast and easy for best copy.

It's easy to read -- the 2 line 16 character LCD display is mounted on a sloped front panel for easy reading.

Copies most standard shifts and speeds. Has *MFJ AutoTrak™* Morse code speed tracking.

Use 12 VDC or use 110 VAC with MFJ-1312B AC adapter, $12.95. 5¼x2½x5¼ inches.

Compact Active Antenna

Plug this new *compact* MFJ all band active antenna into your general coverage receiver and you'll hear strong clear signals from all over the world from 300 KHz to 200 MHz.

MFJ-1022
$39⁹⁵

Detachable 20 inch telescoping antenna. 9 volt battery or 110 VAC with MFJ-1312B, $12.95. 3⅛x1¼x4 in.

MFJ Antenna Switches

MFJ-1704
$59⁹⁵

MFJ-1702C
$21⁹⁵

MFJ-1704 heavy duty antenna switch lets you select 4 antennas or ground them for static and lightning protection. Unused antennas automatically grounded. Replaceable lightning surge protection device. Good to over 500 MHz. 60 db isolation at 30 MHz.
MFJ-1702C,$21.95, for 2 antennas.

MFJ 12/24 Hour Clocks

MFJ-107B
$9⁹⁵

MFJ-105C
$19⁹⁵

MFJ-108B
$19⁹⁵

MFJ-112
$24⁹⁵

MFJ-108B, *dual* clock displays 24 UTC and 12 hour local time.
MFJ-107B, single clock shows you 24 hour UTC time. *3 star rated* by *Passport to World Band Radio!*
MFJ-105C, accurate 24 hour UTC *quartz wall clock* with huge 10 in. face.
MFJ-112, accurate 24/12 hour world map clock. Push buttons let you move a flashing time zone east/west on map to a major city in every time zone. Gold and brown trim. 4½x3⅜x2¼ inches.

World Band Radio Kit

MFJ-8100K
$59⁹⁵ *kit*
MFJ-8100W
$79⁹⁵ *wired*

Build this *regenerative* shortwave receiver *kit* and listen to shortwave signals from all over the world. With just a 10 foot wire antenna.

Has RF stage, vernier reduction drive, smooth regeneration, five bands.

Enjoy *World Bands* in your car

Add
World Band shortwave

MFJ-306
$79⁹⁵

reception to your AM car radio and hear late breaking news as it happens from all over the world! Covers 19, 25, 31, 49 Meters. Plugs between radio and antenna.

Pocket Size Morse Tutor™

See code as it's sent with big LCD! Learn

MFJ-418
$79⁹⁵

Morse code anywhere with MFJ's pocket size Morse Code Tutor™!

This pocket size tutor takes you from zero code speed with a beginner's course to Extra Class with customized code practice. Follows ARRL/VEC format. Speed sets from 3-55 wpm.

Select letters, numbers, punctuations or prosigns or any combination or words or QSOs with normal or Farnsworth spacing. Use earphones or built-in speaker.
MFJ-281, $9.95. *ClearTone™* speaker plugs into MFJ-418 for *extra-loud* sound.

MFJ High Pass TVI Filter

MFJ-711
$19⁹⁵

Suppress annoying TV interference

with the MFJ-711 High Pass Filter for 75 Ohm TV input impedance. Use between cable and VCR and VCR or TV set. Reduces signals operating below 30 MHz.

Code Practice Oscillator

MFJ-557
$24⁹⁵

Have fun learning Morse code! Morse key, oscillator and speaker mounted on a heavy steel base so it stays put on table. Earphone jack, tone, volume controls, adjustable key.

FAX, WeFAX, RTTY, ASCII, CW!

Use your PC computer and radio to receive and display brilliant *full color* FAX news photos and incredible 16 gray level WeFAX weather maps.Also receives RTTY, ASCII and Morse code.

MFJ-1214PC
$149⁹⁵

Animate weather maps. Display 10 global pictures *simultaneously*. Zoom any part of picture or map. Freq. Manager lists over 900 FAX stations. Auto picture capture.

Includes interface, software, cables, power supply, manual, Jump-Start™ guide. Requires 286 or better computer with VGA monitor.

All Band Shortwave Antenna

Super shortwave antenna covers all shortwave bands 75 thru 11 Meters. 102 feet heavy duty #14 gauge stranded copper wire, 32½ feet of 450 ohm ladder line matching section. Add coax to your receiver for super shortwave reception.

MFJ-1778
$49⁹⁵

Entrance to Radio
Bangladesh's Savar
transmitting station. Its
100 kW transmitter is
heard on 15520 kHz.

M. Guha

evenings in North America), there's the popular *Focus on the Family*, hosted by James Dobson. This is replaced weekends by Sunday's *Musical Mailbag* and Monday's *Mountain Meditations*. To eastern North America on 9745 kHz.

00:45

Radio Tirana, Albania. Summers only at this time. Approximately 15 minutes of *news* and commentary from this Balkan country. To North America on 6115 and 7160 kHz. One hour later in winter.

RAI International—Radio Roma, Italy. Actually starts at 0050. *News* and Italian music make up this 20-minute broadcast to North America on 6010, 9675 and 11800 kHz.

01:00

■**BBC World Service for the Americas.** The 30-minute ●*Newsdesk*, then one or more features. Regular shows include ●*Sports Roundup* at 0145 Sunday (Saturday evening in the Americas), *Seven Days* (0130 Tuesday), ●*Discovery* (science, 0130 Wednesday), ●*Omnibus* (same time Thursday) and ●*Short Story* (0145 Saturday). There is also an excellent classical music feature at 0130 Friday. Continuous programming to North America and the Caribbean on 5975, 6175 and 9590 kHz.

■**BBC World Service for Asia.** Ten minutes of *World News*, then five more of the religious *Pause for Thought*. Tuesday through

Saturday, these are followed by ●*Insight* (current events), replaced Sunday by ●*Health Matters* and Monday by *The Farming World*. The second half hour is evenly split between another bulletin of *World News* and ●*Sports Roundup*. Continuous to East Asia on 15280 and 15360 kHz, and to Southeast Asia on 6195, 9410 and 15360 kHz.

Radio Canada International. Summers only. *News*, followed Tuesday through Saturday (weekday evenings local American date) by *Spectrum* (topics in the news), which in turn is replaced Sunday by *Venture Canada* (business and economics) and the interesting ●*Earth Watch*. On Monday (Sunday evening in North America), *Arts in Canada* is followed by a listener-response program. Sixty minutes to North America on 5960 and 9755 kHz. You can also try 9535, 11715 and 13670 kHz, but they are only available for the first 30 minutes, except at weekends. One hour later in winter.

■**Deutsche Welle,** Germany. *News*, followed Tuesday through Saturday (weekday evenings in the Americas) by the comprehensive ●*NewsLink*—commentary, interviews, background reports and analysis. This is followed by ●*Man and Environment* (ecology, Tuesday), ●*Insight* (analysis, Wednesday), *Living in Germany* (Thursday), *Spotlight on Sport* (Friday), or Saturday's *German by Radio*. Sunday fare is *Saturday Review* and *Inside Europe*, replaced Monday by *Mailbag* and *Arts on the Air*. Fifty minutes of very good reception in North America and the Caribbean, winters on 5960, 6040, 6085, 6145 and 9640 kHz; and summers on 6040, 6085, 6145, 9640 and 11810 kHz.

Radio Slovakia International. *Slovakia Today*, a 30-minute window on Slovak life and culture. Tuesday (Monday evening in the Americas), there's a variety of short features; Wednesday puts the spotlight on tourism and Slovak personalities;

Thursday's slot is devoted to business and economy; and Friday is given over to a mix of politics, education and science. Saturday offerings include cultural features, *Slovak Kitchen* and the off-beat *Back Page News*; while Sunday brings the *"Best of"* series. Monday's fare is very much a mixed bag, and includes *Listeners' Tribune* and some enjoyable Slovak music. A friendly half hour to eastern North America and the Caribbean on 5930 kHz; to South America on 9440 kHz; and for African night owls on 7300 kHz.

Radio Norway International. Mondays (Sunday evenings, local American date) only. *Norway Now*. Thirty minutes of *news* and chat from and about Norway. To North and Central America winters on 7465 kHz, and summers on 9560 kHz.

Radio Budapest, Hungary. Summers only at this time. *News* and features, some of which are broadcast on a regular basis. These include Monday's *Bookshelf* (local Sunday evening in North America), a press review (Tuesday, Wednesday, Friday and Saturday), *Profiles* (Wednesday), and *Focus on Business* (Thursday). Thirty minutes to North America on 9580 and 11685 kHz. One hour later in winter.

Radio Prague, Czech Republic. Repeat of the 0000 broadcast; see there for specifics. Thirty minutes to North America, better to the East, on 6200 and 7345 kHz.

Swiss Radio International. *Newsnet*. A workmanlike compilation of news and background reports on world and Swiss events. Somewhat lighter fare on Sunday (Saturday evening in North America), when the biweekly *Capital Letters* (a listener-response program) alternates with *Name Game* and *Sounds Good*. A half hour to North America and the Caribbean on 9885 and 9905 kHz.

Radio Japan. *News*, then Tuesday through Saturday (weekday evenings local American date) there's 10 minutes of *Asian*

Top News followed by a half-hour feature. Take your pick from *Profile* (Tuesday), *Enjoy Japanese* (Wednesday and Friday), *Town and Around* (Thursday) and Saturday's *Music and Book Beat*. On the remaining days, look for *Asia Weekly* (Sunday) or Monday's *Let's Learn Japanese*, *Media Roundup* and *Viewpoint*. The broadcasts end with the daily *Tokyo Pop-in*. One hour to eastern North America summers only on 5960 kHz via the powerful relay facilities of Radio Canada International in Sackville, New Brunswick. Also year-round to western North America on 11885, 9605 (winter) and (summer) 11790 kHz. Also available to Asia on 11840, 11860, 11890/11900, 11910, 17810 and 17845 kHz.

Radio Exterior de España ("Spanish National Radio"). Repeat of the 0000 transmission. To eastern North America on 6055 kHz.

Radio For Peace International, Costa Rica. The first hour in English (the initial 60 minutes are in French or Spanish) of an eight-hour cyclical block of social-conscience and counterculture programming audible in Europe and the Americas on 6975 and (summers) 21460 kHz.

Voice of Vietnam. A relay via the facilities of the Voice of Russia. Begins with *news*, then there's *Commentary* or *Weekly Review*, followed by short features and some pleasant Vietnamese music (especially at weekends). Repeated at 0230 on the same channel. Thirty minutes to eastern North America; winters on 5940 kHz, and summers on 7250 kHz. Repeated at 0230 on the same channels.

Voice of Russia World Service. Summers only at this hour. *News*, then Tuesday through Saturday (weekday evenings in North America), there's ●*Commonwealth Update*. The second half-hour contains some interesting fare, with just about everyone's favorite being

Tuesday's ●*Folk Box*. For listeners who like classical music, don't miss Friday's ●*Music at Your Request* or the excellent ●*Music and Musicians* (from 0111, Sunday and Monday). Pick of the remaining fare is Saturday's ●*Moscow Yesterday and Today*, although Wednesday's *Jazz Show* also has a sizable following. Where to tune? There's not much choice at this hour—15425 kHz is the only available channel, and it's mainly for western North America. The former English channels have mostly given way to Russian broadcasts, so there's little you can do except be patient and hope the Russian economy improves.

Radio Habana Cuba. The start of a two-hour cyclical broadcast to eastern North America, and made up of *news* and features such as *Latin America Newsline*, *DXers Unlimited*, *The Mailbag Show* and ●*The Jazz Place*, interspersed with some lively Cuban music (though not as much as there used to be). To eastern North America on 6000 and 9820 kHz. Also available on 9830 kHz upper sideband, though not all radios, unfortunately, can process such signals.

Radio Australia. *World News*, then a feature. Monday's offering—unusual, to say the least—is *Awaye*, a program dealing with indigenous affairs. This is replaced Tuesday by *Science Show* and Wednesday by *Natural Interest* (topical events). Thursday's presentation is *Background Briefing* (news analysis); Friday brings *Hindsight*; Saturday is given over to *Oz Sounds* and *Arts Australia*; and the Sunday slot belongs to *The Europeans*. Continuous programming to Asia and the Pacific on 9660, 12080, 15240, 15415, 17715, 17750, 17795 and 21740 kHz. In North America (best during summer), try 17715, 17795 and 21740 kHz. Best bets for East Asia are 15240, 15415 and 17750 kHz; in southeastern parts, shoot for 17750 kHz. Some channels carry a separate sports service on winter Saturdays.

Reporter Manosij Guha on assignment in rural Bangladesh. M. Guha

Radio Yugoslavia. Monday through Saturday (Sunday through Friday, local American evenings) and winters only at this time. *News* and short reports, dealing almost exclusively with local and regional topics. Professionally done, and worth a listen. Thirty minutes to eastern and central North America on 6195 and 7115 kHz. One hour earlier in summer.

HCJB—Voice of the Andes, Ecuador. Tuesday through Saturday (weekday evenings in North America) it's *Studio 9*, featuring nine minutes of world and Latin American *news*, followed by 20 minutes of in-depth reporting on Latin America. The final portion of *Studio 9* is given over to one of a variety of 30-minute features— including *You Should Know* (issues and ethics, Tuesday), *El Mundo Futuro* (science, Wednesday), *Ham Radio Today* (Thursday), *Woman to Woman* (Friday), and the unique and enjoyable ●*Música del Ecuador* (Saturday). On Sunday (Saturday evening in the Americas), the news is followed by *DX Partyline*, which in turn is replaced Monday by *Saludos Amigos*—HCJB's

international friendship program. Continuous programming to eastern North America on 9745 kHz.

Voice of America. The second and final hour of a two-hour broadcast to the Caribbean and Latin America which is aired Tuesday through Saturday (weekday evenings in the Americas). *News Now*, a rolling news format covering political, business and other developments. On the half-hour, a program in "Special" (slow-speed) English is carried on 7405, 9775 and 13740 kHz; with mainstream programming continuing on 5995, 6130 and 9455 kHz.

WRMI—Radio Miami International, Miami, Florida. Tuesday through Saturday only (local weekday evenings in the Americas). Part of a much longer multilingual transmission to the Caribbean. Thirty minutes of *Viva Miami!*—a potpourri of information, music and entertainment. Also includes regular weather updates during the hurricane season (June-November). Heard in much of the Americas on 9955 kHz. Repeated one hour later during winter.

Radio Ukraine International. Winters only at this time; see 0000 for program details. Sixty minutes of informative programming targeted at eastern North America and European night owls. Try 5905, 5940, 6020, 6050, 6080, 7150, 7205, 7420 and 9560 kHz. One hour earlier in summer.

Radio New Zealand International. A package of *news* and features sometimes replaced by live sports commentary. Part of a much longer broadcast for the South Pacific, but also heard in parts of North America (especially during summer) on 17675 kHz.

Radio Tashkent, Uzbekistan. *News* and features with a strong Uzbek flavor; some exotic music, too. A half hour to West and South Asia and the Mideast, occasionally heard in North America; winters on 5040, 5955, 5975, 7205 and 9540 kHz; summers on 7190, 9375, 9530 and 9715 kHz.

FEBC Radio International, Philippines. The final 30 minutes of *Good Morning from Manila* (see 0000 for specifics), followed by a half hour of religious fare. Targeted at South and Southeast Asia on 15450 kHz, but heard well beyond.

"American Dissident Voices," WRNO. This time summers only. Neo-Nazi anti-Israel program, hosted by Kevin Alfred Strom. Only of interest to those with similar beliefs. Thirty minutes Sunday (Saturday evening local American date) on 7355 kHz; try four hours later on 7395 kHz if preempted by live sports. Targeted at North America, but reaches beyond. Is followed by "Herald of Truth," another disestablishmentarian program in a similar vein.

WWCR, Nashville, Tennessee. Carries a variety of disestablishmentarian programs at this hour, depending on the day of the week. Winters, there's "Protecting your Wealth," "World of Prophecy" and "Full Disclosure Live" on 5065 kHz; while 7435 kHz carries a similar bunch of programs.

WJCR, Upton, Kentucky. Continues with country gospel music for North American listeners on 7490 and 13595 kHz. Also with religious programs to North America at this hour are **WYFR—Family Radio** on 6065 and 9505 kHz, **WWCR** on 13845 kHz and **KTBN** on 7510 kHz. For traditional Catholic programming, tune to **WEWN** on 7425 kHz.

01:30

Radio Austria International. Winters only at this time. ●*Report from Austria*, which includes a brief bulletin of *news* followed by a series of current events and human interest stories. Tends to spotlight national and regional issues, and is an excellent source of news about Central Europe. Thirty minutes to the Americas on 9655 (or 7325), 9495 (or 13730) and 9870 kHz. One hour later in summer.

Radio Sweden. Tuesday through Saturday, it's *news* and features in *Sixty Degrees North*, concentrating heavily on Scandinavian topics. Tuesday's accent is on sports; Wednesday has electronic media news; Thursday brings *Money Matters*; Friday features ecology or science and technology; and Saturday offers a review of the week's news. Sunday, there's *Spectrum* (arts) or *Sweden Today* (current events), while Monday's offering is *In Touch with Stockholm* (a listener-response program) or the musical *Sounds Nordic*. Thirty minutes to Asia and Australasia, winters on 7265 kHz and summers on 9435 and 11985 kHz.

■**Radio Netherlands.** *News*, followed Tuesday through Saturday by ●*Newsline*, a current affairs program. Then there's a different feature each day, including *Aural*

Tapestry (Tuesday);●*A Good Life* (Wednesday); *Sounds Interesting* (Thursday); ●*Research File* (science, Friday) and the excellent (sometimes superb) ●*Documentary* (Saturday). Making up the week are Sunday's award-winning youth show, ●*Roughly Speaking*, and Monday's *Wide Angle* and *Siren Song*. One hour to South Asia (also widely heard in other parts of the continent, as well as Australasia); winters on 9860 and 11655 kHz; and summers on 9855 and 11655 kHz.

Radio Tirana, Albania. Summers only at this time. Thirty minutes of Balkan news and music to North America on 6220 and 7160 kHz. One hour later during winter.

Voice of Greece. Preceded and followed by programming in Greek. Approximately 10 minutes of English *news*, then Greek music, a short feature about the country, and more music. Resumes programming in Greek at 0200. To North America on any three frequencies from 6260, 7450, 9420, 9935 and 11645 kHz.

01:45

Radio Tirana, Albania. Winters only at this time. Approximately 15 minutes of *news* and commentary from one of Europe's smallest and least known countries. To North America on 6115 and 7160 kHz. One hour earlier in summer.

02:00

■BBC World Service for Europe and the Americas. Thirty minutes of ●*Newsday*, then Monday through Thursday (Sunday through Wednesday evenings in the Americas) it's a look at the arts, in *Meridian*. At 0230 Friday there's ●*Focus on Faith*, replaced Saturday by ●*People and Politics*, and Sunday by a feature on classical music. Continuous programming to North America and the Caribbean on

5975, 6175, 9590 (till 0230) and (from 0230) 9895 kHz; and available summers to Eastern Europe on 9410 kHz.

■BBC World Service for Asia. ●*Newsday* and a 30-minute feature (except Sunday, when there are two shorter shows). Take your pick from an interesting pack: ●*Letter from America* (Sunday), *The Works* (technology, Monday), ●*Discovery* (science, Tuesday), ●*One Planet* (the environment, Wednesday) ●*Assignment* (Friday), and Saturday's ●*People and Politics*. Continuous to East Asia on 15280 and 15360 kHz, and to Southeast Asia on 9410 and 15360 kHz.

Radio Cairo, Egypt. Repeat of the 2300 broadcast, and the first hour of a 90-minute potpourri of *news* and features about Egypt and the Arab world. Fair reception, but often mediocre audio quality, to North America on 9475 kHz.

Radio Argentina al Exterior—R.A.E. Tuesday through Saturday only. *News* and short features dealing with multiple aspects of Argentinian life, and interspersed with samples of the country's various musical styles. Whether you tap your feet to the heavy beat of a tango, or listen to a chamamé or zamba from the provinces, there's some fine music to be enjoyed. Fifty-five minutes to North America on 11710 kHz. Sometimes preempted by live soccer commentary in Spanish.

Radio Budapest, Hungary. This time winters only; see 0100 for specifics. Thirty minutes to North America on 6030 and 9580 kHz. One hour earlier in summer.

Radio Canada International. Starts off with *News*, then Tuesday through Saturday (weekday evenings local American date) it's the topical *Spectrum*. Winter Sundays, there's *Venture Canada* (business and economics) and the environmental ●*Earth Watch*, replaced Monday by *The Arts in*

In Sri Lanka, coconut palms make great antenna masts.

M. Guha

Canada and *Mailbag*. Summer substitutes are *The Vestibules* and *The Muckraker* (Sunday), with the cultural *Tapestry* filling the Monday slot. One hour winters to North America on 6155, 9535, 9755, 9780 and 11865 kHz. Summers, it's just 30 minutes Tuesday through Saturday, with a full hour on the remaining days. Choose from 9535, 9755, 11715 and 13670 kHz.

Radio Yugoslavia. Winters only at this time. *News* and reports with a strong local flavor. An informative half hour to western North America on 6100 and 7130 kHz.

■**Deutsche Welle,** Germany. *News,* followed Tuesday through Saturday by the excellent ●*NewsLink*—commentary, interviews, background reports and analysis. The final part of the broadcast consists of a feature. Take your pick from ●*Man and Environment* (ecology, Tuesday),

●*Insight* (analysis, Wednesday), *Living in Germany* (Thursday), *Spotlight on Sport* (Friday), or Saturday's *German by Radio*. Sunday's offerings are *Saturday Review* and *Mailbag,* replaced Monday by *Sunday Review* and *Marks and Markets*. Fifty minutes nominally targeted at South Asia, but widely heard elsewhere. Winters on 6035, 7265, 7285, 7355, 9515, 9615 and 9815 kHz; and summers on 7285, 9615, 9690, 11945, 11965 and 12045 kHz.

Radio Bulgaria. Summers only at this time. Starts with 15 minutes of *news,* followed Tuesday through Friday by *Today* (current events), and Saturday by *Weekly Spotlight,* a summary of the major political events of the week. At other times, there are features dealing with multiple aspects of Bulgarian life and culture, including some lively Balkan folk music. To eastern North America and Central America on 9485 and 11720 kHz. One hour later in winter.

HCJB—Voice of the Andes, Ecuador. A mixed bag of religious and secular programming, depending on the day of the week. Tuesday (Monday evening in North America) is given over to *Master Control* and *Classical Favorites;* Wednesday airs *Unshackled* and *SHOUT!;* and Thursday brings *The Latest Catch* (a feature for radio enthusiasts), *The Book Nook* and *Sounds of Joy.* On Friday, you can hear the Australian-produced *Pacific Currents* and *Inspirational Classics;* Saturday has the Europe-oriented *On-Line* followed by *On Track* (contemporary Christian music); Sunday features *Sounds of Joy* and *Solstice* (a youth program); and Monday is devoted to *Radio Reading Room* and *Dr. Francis Schaeffer.* Continuous to North America on 9745 kHz.

Radio Taipei International, Taiwan. The broadcast opens with 15 minutes of *News,* and closes with a quarter-hour of *Let's Learn Chinese,* which has a series of segments for beginning, intermediate and advanced learners. In between, there are either one or two features. Take your pick from *Jade Bells and Bamboo Pipes* (Monday), *People* and *Trends* (Tuesday), *Taiwan Today* and *Miss Mook's Big Countdown* (Wednesday), *Treasures of the Orient* and *Hot Spots* (Thursday), *Taipei Magazine* and *Life on the Outside* (Friday), *Kaleidoscope* and *Reflections* (Saturday) and *Food, Poetry and Others* followed by *Mailbag Time* on Sunday. Radio Taipei International is almost unrecognizable from its former incarnation as the "Voice of Free China"— the old stuffiness and formality have given way to a more lively presentation, and gone is much of the old propaganda against the Mainland. When you hear reports of Chinese delegations visiting Taiwan, and interviews with Taiwanese who live in Beijing, there's no doubting the magnitude of the changes. One hour to North and Central America on 5950, 9680 and 11740 kHz; and to Southeast Asia on 11825 and 15345 kHz.

Voice of Russia World Service. Winters, the start of a four-hour block of programming to North America; summers, it's the beginning of the second hour. *News*, features and music to suit all tastes. Winter fare includes ●*Commonwealth Update* (0211 Tuesday through Saturday), ●*Music and Musicians* (same time Sunday and Monday), and after 0230, ●*Folk Box* (Tuesday), ●*Music at Your Request* (Friday) and Russian jazz on Wednesday. Best in summer are ●*Moscow Yesterday and Today* (0231 Thursday) and ●*Audio Book Club* (same time Saturday); though some listeners may prefer *Science and Engineering* (0211 Tuesday and Friday), the business-oriented *Newmarket* (0211 Wednesday and Saturday) or the many-faceted *Kaleidoscope* (0231 Tuesday). A listener-response program is aired at 0211 Monday, Thursday and Sunday. Note that these days are World Time; locally in North America it will be the previous evening. There's little for eastern North America at

this hour, but try 7100/7105 kHz in winter, and 9665 kHz in summer. Listeners farther west should try 9580, 12045 and 13665 kHz in winter; and 15425 kHz in summer.

Radio Habana Cuba. The second half of a two-hour broadcast to eastern North America; see 0100 for program details. On 6000 and 9820 kHz. Also available on 9830 kHz upper sideband.

Radio Australia. Continuous programming to Asia and the Pacific, but well heard in parts of North America (especially to the west). Begins with *World News*, then Monday through Friday it's *The World Today* (comprehensive coverage of world events). At 0205 Saturday, look for some incisive scientific commentary in ●*Ockham's Razor*, which is then followed by *Health Report*. These are replaced Sunday by the more sedate *Fine Music Australia* and *Religion Report*. Targeted at Asia and the Pacific on 9660, 12080, 15240, 15415, 15510, 17715, 17750 and 21725 kHz. Best heard in North America (especially during summer) on 17715 kHz. For East and Southeast Asia, choose from 15240, 15415, 17750 and 21725 kHz. Some of these channels carry a separate sports service on summer (midyear) weekends and winter Saturdays.

YLE Radio Finland. Summers only at this time. Most days it's *Compass North* and a press review. Exceptions are Saturday's *Starting Finnish* (a language lesson), Sunday's *Capital Café* and Monday's *Nordic Update*. Thirty minutes to North America on 9780 and 11900 kHz.

Radio For Peace International, Costa Rica. The second hour in English of an eight-hour cyclical block of social-conscience and counterculture programming audible in Europe and the Americas on 6975 kHz.

Radio Korea International, South Korea. Opens with *news* and commentary, followed Tuesday through Thursday

(Monday through Wednesday evenings in the Americas) by *Seoul Calling*. Weekly features include *Echoes of Korean Music* and *Shortwave Feedback* (Monday), *Tales from Korea's Past* (Tuesday), *Korean Cultural Trails* (Wednesday), *Pulse of Korea* (Thursday), *From Us to You* (a listener-response program) and *Let's Learn Korean* (Friday), *Let's Sing Together* and *Korea Through Foreigners' Eyes* (Saturday), and Sunday's *Discovering Korea*, *Korean Literary Corner* and *Weekly News*. Sixty minutes to the Americas on 11725, 11810 and 15575 kHz; and to East Asia on 7275 kHz.

Radio Romania International. *News*, commentary, press review and features on Romania. Regular spots include Wednesday's *Youth Club* (Tuesday evening, local American date), Thursday's *Romanian Musicians*, and Friday's *Listeners' Letterbox* and ●*Skylark* (Romanian folk music). Fifty-five minutes to North America on 5990, 6155, 9510, 9570 and 11940 kHz.

"American Dissident Voices," WRNO. Winter Sundays only (Saturday evenings, local American date) at this time. See 0100 for program details. Thirty minutes to North America and beyond on 7355 kHz; try four hours later on 7395 kHz if preempted by live sports.

WWCR, Nashville, Tennessee. Carries a variety of disestablishmentarian programs at this hour, depending on the day of the week, and whether it is summer or winter. These include "Protecting Your Wealth," "World of Prophecy" and "Radio Free America"; choose between 5065 and 2390 (or 7435) kHz.

WJCR, Upton, Kentucky. Continues with country gospel music for North American listeners on 7490 kHz. Also with religious broadcasts to North America at this hour are **WYFR—Family Radio** on 6065 and 9505 kHz, **WWCR** on 5935 kHz, **KAIJ on** 5810 kHz, and **KTBN** on 7510 kHz.

Traditional Catholic programming can be heard via **WEWN** on 7425 kHz.

02:30

Radio Austria International. Summers only at this time. ●*Report from Austria*, a popular compilation of news, current events and human interest stories. Good coverage of national and regional issues. Thirty minutes to the Americas on 9655, 9870 and 13730 kHz. One hour earlier in winter.

Radio Sweden. Tuesday through Saturday (weekday evenings in North America), it's *news* and features in *Sixty Degrees North*, with the accent heavily on Scandinavian topics. Tuesday's theme is sports; Wednesday has news of the electronic media; Thursday brings *Money Matters*; Friday features ecology or science and technology; and Saturday offers a review of the week's news. Sunday, there's *Spectrum* (arts) or *Sweden Today* (current events), while Monday's offering is *In Touch with Stockholm* (a listener-response program) or the musical *Sounds Nordic*. Thirty minutes to North America, winters on 7280 kHz and summers on 7135 or 9495 kHz.

Radyo Pilipinas, Philippines. Monday through Saturday, the broadcast opens with *Voice of Democracy* and closes with *World News*. These are separated by a daily feature: *Save the Earth* (Monday), *The Philippines Today* (Tuesday), *Changing World* (Wednesday), *Business Updates* (Thursday), *Brotherhood of Men* (Friday), and Saturday's *Listeners and Friends*. Sunday fare consists of *Asean Connection*, *Sports Focus* and *News Roundup*. Approximately one hour to South and East Asia on 17760, 17865 and 21580 kHz.

Radio Budapest, Hungary. Summers only at this time. *News* and features, some of which are broadcast on a regular basis.

The Voice of America's transmitter hall in Sri Lanka. In 1999 the VOA plans to fire up powerful new transmitters from near Chilaw. M. Guha

These include Tuesday's *Musica Hungarica* (local Monday evening in North America), *Focus on Business* and *The Weeklies* (Thursday), *Letter Home* (Friday) and *Profiles* (Sunday). Thirty minutes to North America on 9840 and 11910 kHz. One hour later in winter.

Voice of Vietnam. Repeat of the 0100 broadcast; see there for specifics. A relay to eastern North America via the facilities of the Voice of Russia, winters on 5940 kHz, and summers on 7250 kHz.

■Radio Netherlands. Repeat of the 0030 transmission. Fifty-five minutes to South Asia, but heard well beyond, on 9855 (or 9860) and 11655 kHz.

Radio Tirana, Albania. Winters only at this time. The programs now have more variety than in the past, and still include some lively Albanian music. A half hour to North America on 6140 and 7160 kHz. One hour earlier in summer.

02:50

Vatican Radio. Concentrates heavily, but not exclusively, on issues affecting Catholics around the world. Twenty minutes to eastern North America, winters on 6095 and 7305 kHz, and summers on 7305 and 9605 kHz.

03:00

■BBC World Service for the Americas and the Mideast. Five minutes of *World News*, followed Tuesday through Saturday (weekday evenings in the Americas) by 10 minutes of incomparable business and financial reporting in ●*World Business Report*. This is replaced Sunday by the equally informative ●*World Business Review*, and Monday by *Write On* (a listener-response program). The next quarter-hour is devoted to the highly informative ●*Sports Roundup*. These are followed Tuesday through Saturday by ●*Insight* (analysis of current events) and ●*Off the Shelf* (book readings). Weekend replacements are Sunday's ●*From Our Own Correspondent* and Monday's compilation of the previous week's episodes of *Westway* (strictly for those who like soap operas). Continuous programming to North America and the Caribbean on 5975, 6175 and 9895 kHz. The last frequency is only available until 0330 in summer. To the Mideast on 9410 (summers till 0330), 9605 (winter) and 11760 kHz.

■BBC World Service for Europe.

Winters and the first half hour in summer, the same programming as to the Americas. Summer weekdays at 0330, there's an excellent breakfast news show, ●*The World Today*. This is replaced Saturday by ●*Weekend* and Sunday by ●*From Our Own Correspondent*. Winters to Eastern Europe on 6195 and 9410 kHz, and summers to most of the continent on 6180, 6195 and 9410 kHz.

■BBC World Service for Africa.

Identical to the service for the Americas until 0330, then Monday through Friday it's *Network Africa*, a fast-moving breakfast show. The Saturday substitute is ●*Focus on Faith*, replaced Sunday by *African Quiz* or *Postmark Africa*. If you are interested in what's going on in the continent, tune to 3255, 6005, 6190 and 9600 kHz.

■BBC World Service for Asia. *World News* and ●*Sports Roundup*, followed on the half-hour by the weekday ●*Off the Shelf* (readings from world literature). The weekend slots are occupied by *The Vintage Chart Show* (Saturday) and *Global Business* (Sunday). Monday through Friday, the final 15 minutes are taken up by a feature, the best of which is undoubtedly Friday's ●*The*

Learning World (replaced by *Waveguide* on either the first or last Friday of the month). Audible in East Asia till 0330 on 15360 and 21660 kHz, and thereafter on 11955, 15280 and 21660 kHz. For Southeast Asia there's only 15360 kHz until 0330, but you might also try 15310 kHz for the full hour in winter.

Radio Canada International. Winters only at this time. Starts off with *News*, then Tuesday through Saturday (weekday evenings local American date) you can hear *Spectrum* (current events). Weekends, there's a full hour of programs from the domestic service of RCI's parent organization, the Canadian Broadcasting Corporation. Sunday, expect some comedy during the first 30 minutes, while Monday's *Tapestry* is a more serious cultural offering. To eastern North America and the Caribbean on 6155, 9755 and 9780 kHz. One hour earlier in summer.

Radio Taipei International, Taiwan. Similar to the 0200 transmission, but with the same programs broadcast one day later. To North and Central America on 5950 and 9680 kHz; to East Asia on 11745 kHz; and to Southeast Asia on 11825 and 15345 kHz.

China Radio International. *News* and commentary, followed Wednesday through Saturday (Tuesday through Friday evenings in the Americas) by *Current Affairs*. These are followed by various feature programs, such as *Focus* and *Cultural Spectrum* (Friday); *Cultural Information*, *Snapshots*, *Report from Developing Countries*, *Song of the Week* and *Listeners' Letterbox* (Monday); *Open Windows* (Tuesday); *Orient Arena* and *Voices from Other Lands* (Wednesday); *Profile* (Thursday); *Learn to Speak Chinese* (Tuesday and Thursday); and *Life in China* and *Global Review* (Saturday). Arguably, the most interesting offerings are left till Sunday, when you can hear *Asia-Pacific News*, *Chinese Folk Tales*, *Cooking Show*, *China*

Scrapbook and ●*Music from China*. One hour to North America on 9690 kHz.

■**Deutsche Welle,** Germany. *News*, then Tuesday through Saturday (weekday evenings in North America) it's ●*NewsLink*—a comprehensive package of commentary, interviews, background reports and analysis. The remainder of the transmission is taken up by a feature: ●*Man and Environment* (Tuesday), ●*Insight* (Wednesday), *Living in Germany* (Thursday), *Spotlight on Sport* (Friday) and *German by Radio* on Saturday. The Sunday offerings are *Saturday Review* and *Spectrum*; while Monday brings *Religion and Society* and *Arts on the Air*. Fifty minutes to North America and the Caribbean on 6045 (winter), 6085, 6145 (summer), 6185, 9535 and 9640 kHz.

Voice of America. Three and a half hours (four at weekends) of continuous programming aimed at an African audience. Monday through Friday, there's the informative and entertaining ●*Daybreak Africa*, with the remaining airtime taken up by *News Now*—a mixed bag of sports, science, business and other news and features. Although beamed to Africa, this service is widely heard elsewhere, including parts of the United States. Try 6035 (winter), 6080, 6115 (summer), 7105, 7275 (summer), 7290, 7415 (winter), 9575 (winter) and 9885 kHz.

Voice of Russia World Service. Continues to North America. *News*, then winters it's a listener-response program (Monday, Thursday and Sunday), the business-oriented *Newmarket* (Tuesday and Saturday), or *Science and Engineering* (Tuesday). At 0331, there's ●*Audio Book Club* (Saturday), *Kaleidoscope* (Tuesday), *This is Russia* (Wednesday), ●*Moscow Yesterday and Today* (Thursday), *Russian by Radio* (Friday), and mostly music on the remaining days. Note that these days are World Time, so locally in North America it will be the previous evening. In summer,

look for *News and Views* at 0311 Tuesday through Sunday, replaced Monday by *Science and Engineering*. Apart from ●*Christian Message from Moscow* (Sunday) and ●*Audio Book Club* (Monday), the 0330 summer slot is allocated to "alternative programs." These can be quality shows from the station's archives, mind-numbing religious paid programming, or anything in between. For eastern North America there's little on offer, but try 7100/7105 kHz in winter and 7125 and 9665 kHz in summer. In western North America, the situation is a little better—good winter bets are 5920 (or 5930), 7175, 9580 and 12045 kHz; in summer, go for 15180, 15425 and 15595 kHz.

XERMX—Radio México Internacional. Summers only at this time. Tuesday through Saturday (weekday evenings in North America), there's a summary of the Spanish-language *Antena Radio*, replaced Sunday by *Universal Forum*. Monday's programming is in Spanish. On the half-hour, look for 30 minutes of music. To North America on 9705 kHz. One hour later in winter.

Radio Australia. *World News*, then Monday through Friday it's *Australia Talks Back* (discussion of topical issues). Weekends, look for a novel experience in Saturday's *Book Reading*, which is followed by the out-of-town *Rural Reporter*. The Sunday offerings are *Feedback* (listener-response) and *Correspondents' Reports*. Continuous to Asia and the Pacific on 9660, 12080, 15240, 15415, 15510, 17715, 17750 and 21725 kHz. Also heard in western North America, best on 17715 kHz. In East and Southeast Asia, pick from 15240, 15415, 17750 and 21725 kHz. Some of these channels carry a separate sports service at weekends.

Radio Habana Cuba. Repeat of the 0100 broadcast. To eastern North America on 6000 and 9820 kHz, and also available on 9830 kHz upper sideband.

Radio Norway International. Winter Mondays (Sunday evenings, local American date) only. *Norway Now. News* and features from one of the friendliest stations on the international airwaves. Thirty minutes to western North America on 7465 kHz.

Radio Thailand. *Newshour.* Thirty minutes to western North America winters on 11890 kHz, and summers on 15395 kHz. Also available to Asia on 9655 and 11905 kHz.

Radio Ukraine International. Summers only at this time. Repeat of the 0000 broadcast (see there for specifics). One hour to Europe and eastern North America on 5905, 6020, 6080, 7410, 9550, 12040 and 13590 kHz. One hour later in winter.

HCJB—Voice of the Andes, Ecuador. Predominantly religious programming at this hour. Try *Joy International*, a selection of Christian music favorites, at 0330 Monday (local Sunday in North America). Continuous to the United States and Canada on 9745 kHz.

Radio Prague, Czech Republic. Repeat of the 0000 broadcast; see there for specifics. A half hour to North America on 5930 (winter), 7345 and (summer) 9435 kHz. This is by far the best opportunity for listeners in western parts.

Radio Cairo, Egypt. The final half-hour of a 90-minute broadcast to North America on 9475 kHz.

Radio Bulgaria. Winters only at this time; see 0200 for specifics. A distinctly Bulgarian potpourri of news, commentary, interviews and features, plus a fair amount of music. Sixty minutes to eastern North America and Central America on 7375 and 9485 kHz. One hour earlier in summer.

Radio Japan. *News*, followed by the weekday *Radio Japan Magazine Hour*. This consists of *News Commentary*, *Japan Diary*, *Close Up*, a feature (two on Tuesday) and a

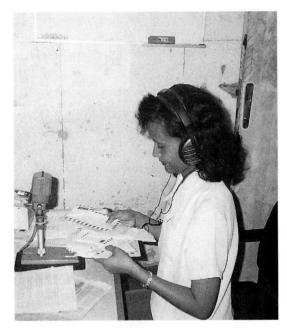

Ms. Anif of Indonesia's RRI Semerang answers audience mail over the air. The station hears mainly from listeners in Indonesia, Japan, Australia and Europe. N. Grace

final news bulletin. Monday (Sunday evening in North America), you can hear *Sports Column*, Tuesday features *Japanese Culture* and *Today*, Wednesday has *Asian Report*, Thursday brings *Crosscurrents*, and Friday's offering is *Business Focus*. Weekend fare is made up of Saturday's *This Week* and Sunday's *Hello from Tokyo*. Sixty minutes to western North America winters on 9605 and 11960 kHz, and summers on 11790 and 15230 kHz. Available to East and Southeast Asia on 11840 and 17810 kHz. Winters only, can also be heard in eastern North America on 5960 kHz.

Channel Africa, South Africa. Thirty minutes of mostly news-oriented fare. To East Africa on 5955 kHz, but often heard much farther afield.

Radio New Zealand International. A friendly broadcasting package targeted at a regional audience. Part of a much longer transmission for the South Pacific, but also heard in parts of North America (especially during summer) on 17675 kHz. Often carries commentaries of local sporting events.

Voice of Turkey. Summers only at this time. *News*, followed by *Review of the Turkish Press* and features (some of them arcane) with a strong local flavor. Selections of Turkish popular and classical music complete the program. Fifty minutes to eastern North America on 9655 kHz, and to the Mideast on 7270 kHz. One hour later during winter.

WJCR, Upton, Kentucky. Continues with country gospel music for North American listeners on 7490 kHz. Also with religious programs to North America at this hour are **WYFR—Family Radio** on 6065 and 9505 kHz, **WWCR** on 5935 kHz, **KAIJ** on 5810 kHz and **KTBN** on 7510 kHz. For traditional Catholic fare, try **WEWN** on 7425 kHz.

"For the People," WHRI, Noblesville, Indiana. A two-hour edited repeat of the 1900 (1800 in summer) broadcast. Promotes classic populism—an American political tradition going back to 1891. Suspicious of concentrated wealth and power, *For the People* promotes economic nationalism ("buying foreign amounts to treason"), little-reported health concepts and a sharply progressive income tax, while opposing the "New World Order" and international banking. This two-hour talk show, hosted by former deejay Chuck Harder, can be heard Tuesday-Saturday (Monday through Friday local days) on 5745 kHz. Targeted at North America, but heard beyond.

Radio For Peace International, Costa Rica. Continues with a variety of counter-culture and social-conscience features. There is also a listener-response program at 0330 Wednesday (Tuesday evening in the Americas). Audible in Europe and the Americas on 6975 kHz.

WWCR, Nashville, Tennessee. "Radio Free America," a populist show hosted by Tom Valentine for two hours Tuesday through Saturday (Monday through Friday evenings, local American date). Winters, starts at this time; summers, it is already at its halfway point. Well heard in North America on 5065 kHz.

03:30

United Arab Emirates Radio, Dubai. *News*, then a feature devoted to Arab and Islamic history or culture. Twenty minutes to North America on 12005, 13675 and 15400 kHz; heard best during the warm-weather months.

Radio Sweden. Repeat of the 0230 transmission; see there for program specifics. Thirty minutes to North America, winters on 7115 kHz and summers on 9475 or 11665 kHz.

Radio Prague, Czech Republic. *News*, then Tuesday through Saturday, there's *Current Affairs*. These are followed by one or more features. Tuesday's offering is *Magazine '99*; Wednesday, it's *Talking Point* and *Media Czech*; Thursday brings *The Arts* and *History Czech*; Friday's lineup is *Economic Report* and *I'd Like You to Meet...*; and Saturday there's *Between You and Us*. The Sunday slot is an excellent musical feature; and Monday there's *The Week in Politics*, *From the Weeklies* and *Media Czech*. A half hour to the Mideast and beyond on 9480 (or 7350) and 11600 kHz.

Radio Budapest, Hungary. This time winters only; see 0230 for specifics. Thirty minutes to North America on 6010 and 9840 kHz. One hour earlier in summer.

Voice of Greece. Actual start time subject to slight variation. Ten to fifteen minutes of English *news*, preceded by long periods of Greek music and programming. To North America on any three frequencies from 6260, 7448, 9420, 9935 and 11645 kHz.

04:00

■**BBC World Service for the Americas and the Mideast.** The first half hour is given over to part of Europe's ●*The World Today* (Monday through Friday, summer only) or ●*Newsdesk*. Tuesday through Saturday (local weekday evenings in the Americas), there's the eclectic and entertaining ●*Outlook*—a listeners' favorite for more than three decades, and still going strong. The hour is rounded off with a five-minute mini-feature. These are replaced Sunday by *Global Business*, and Monday by a half-hour feature. A full hour of top-notch programming to North America on 5975 and 6175 kHz, and audible in the Mideast on 11760 and 15575 kHz.

■**BBC World Service for Europe.** Winters, there's ●*Newsdesk*, followed Monday through Friday by the first half hour of ●*The World Today*. Summer weekdays, it's a continuation of the same breakfast news show. The Saturday and Sunday slots are the same as for the Americas. Continuous programming to Europe on 3955, 6180, 6195, 9410 and (summer) 12095 kHz.

■**BBC World Service for Africa.** Monday through Friday, it's ●*The World Today*, then *Network Africa*. Weekends, look for ●*Newsdesk* followed by Saturday's *African Quiz* or *This Week and Africa*, and Sunday's *Art Beat*. Targeted at African listeners, but also heard elsewhere, on 3255, 6005, 6190, 7160 and 9600 kHz.

Vani, a noted Liberian wood artist, listens to a fixed-frequency radio once given out by missionary station ELWA.

SIM

■**BBC World Service for Asia.** Weekdays, starts with ●*The World Today*, replaced weekends by ●*Newsdesk*. The second half hour is aimed mostly at a youthful audience—*Multitrack* (Monday, Tuesday, Thursday and Saturday), *Megamix* (Wednesday) and ●*John Peel* on Friday. The only change of pace is Sunday, when ●*From Our Own Correspondent* takes to the air. Continuous to East Asia on 11955, 15280 and 21660 kHz. Winters, listeners in Southeast Asia can try 15310 kHz, but there's nothing for them in summer.

Radio Habana Cuba. Continuous programming to eastern North America and the Caribbean on 6000, 6180 and 9820 kHz. Also available on 9830 kHz upper sideband.

Swiss Radio International. Repeat of the 0100 broadcast to North America plus an additional 30 minutes. On 9885 and 9905 kHz.

XERMX—Radio México Internacional. Tuesday through Saturday winters (weekday evenings in North America), there's a summary of the Spanish-language *Antena Radio*, replaced Sunday by *Universal Forum*. Monday's programming is in Spanish. The summer lineup consists of *Eternally Mexico* (Tuesday), *Mirror of Mexico* (Thursday), *The Sounds of Mexico* (Friday) and Saturday's *Mailbox*. Wednesday's broadcast is in French, and there are no programs on Sunday or Monday. On the half-hour, look for 30 minutes of music. To North America on 9705 kHz.

HCJB—Voice of the Andes, Ecuador. Sixty minutes of religious programming. *Songs in the Night* (0400 Monday), *Afterglow* (0430 Sunday and Monday) and *Nightsounds* (0430 Tuesday through Saturday) probably offer the most appeal. Continuous to eastern North America on 9745 kHz.

Radio Australia. *World News*, then Monday through Friday it's *The World Today* (in-depth coverage of current events). The weekend fare is also news-oriented, with *Pacific Focus* followed by Saturday's *Asia Pacific* or Sunday's *Week's End*. Continuous to Asia and the Pacific on 9660, 12080, 15240, 15415, 15510, 17715, 17750 and 21725 kHz. Should also be audible in western North America (best during summer) on 17715 kHz. For East and Southeast Asia, choose from 15240, 15415, 17750 and 21725 kHz. Some channels carry separate sports programming at weekends.

■**Deutsche Welle, Germany.** *News*, followed Tuesday through Saturday by ●*NewsLink* and *Good Morning Africa* (replaced Saturdays by *German by Radio*). The Sunday slots are *Saturday Review* and *Inside Europe*, substituted Monday by *Sunday Review* and *Marks and Markets*. A 50-minute broadcast aimed primarily at East and Southern Africa, but also heard in parts of the Mideast and eastern North America. Winters on 6015, 6065, 7225, 7265 and 9565 kHz; and summers on 5990, 6015, 7225, 9565 and 11765 kHz.

> Radio México Internacional is heard throughout much of North America in English, French and Spanish.

Religious celebration near the Western Wall in Jerusalem. Kol Israel airs the Reshet Bet domestic service on world band.

R. Crane

Radio Canada International. *News*, then Tuesday through Saturday it's the topical *Spectrum*. This is replaced Sunday by *Venture Canada* (business and economics), and Monday by a listener-response program. Thirty minutes to the Mideast, winters on 6150, 9505 and 9645 kHz; summers on 9715, 11835 and 11975 kHz.

Radio Norway International. Summer Mondays (Sunday evenings in the target area) only. *Norway Now*. A half hour of *news* and human-interest stories targeted at western North America on 7465 (or 7520) kHz.

Swiss Radio International. Summers only at this hour. *Newsnet*. A workmanlike compilation of news and background reports on world and Swiss events. Somewhat lighter fare on Sunday (Saturday evening in North America), when the biweekly *Capital Letters* (a listener-response program) alternates with *Name Game* and *Sounds Good*. A half hour to Europe on 5840 and 6165 kHz. One hour later in winter.

Voice of America. Directed to Africa and the Mideast, but widely heard elsewhere. *News Now*—a mixed bag of sports, science, business and other news and features. Weekdays on the half-hour, the African service leaves the mainstream programming and carries its own ●*Daybreak Africa*. To North Africa year round on 7170 kHz, and to the Mideast summer on 11965 kHz. The African service is available on 6035 (winter), 6080, 7265 and 7275 (summer), 7415 (winter), 9575, 9775 (winter) and 9885 kHz. Some of these are only available until 0430. Reception of some of these channels is also possible in North America.

Channel Africa, South Africa. Thirty minutes of predominantly news-oriented programming to Central and Southern Africa on 5955 kHz.

Radio Romania International. Similar to the 0200 transmission (see there for specifics). Fifty-five minutes to North America on 5990, 6155, 9510, 9570 and 11940 kHz.

Radio Ukraine International. Winters only at this time. Repeat of the 0100 broadcast (see 0000 for specifics). Sixty minutes to Europe and North America on 6020, 7150 and 7205 kHz. One hour earlier in summer.

Voice of Turkey. Winters only at this time. See 0300 for specifics. Fifty minutes to Europe and eastern North America on 7300 kHz, to the Mideast on 9685 kHz, and to Southeast Asia and Australasia on 17705 kHz. One hour earlier in summer.

WJCR, Upton, Kentucky. Continues with country gospel music for North American listeners on 7490 kHz. Also with religious programs to North America at this hour are **WYFR—Family Radio** on 6065 and 9505 kHz, **WWCR** on 5935 kHz, **KAIJ** on 5810 kHz and **KTBN** on 7510 kHz. Traditional Catholic programming is available via **WEWN** on 7425 kHz

Kol Israel. Summers only at this time. *News* for 15 minutes from Israel Radio's domestic network. To Europe and eastern North America on 9435 and 11605 kHz, and to Australasia on 17535 kHz. One hour later in winter.

China Radio International. Repeat of the 0300 broadcast; one hour to North America on 9730 and (summers only) 9560 kHz.

Radio New Zealand International. Continues with regional programming for the South Pacific. Part of a much longer broadcast, which is also heard in parts of North America (especially during summer)

on 17675 kHz. Sometimes carries commentaries of local sporting events.

Radio For Peace International, Costa Rica. Part of an eight-hour cyclical block of predominantly social-conscience and counterculture programming. Some of the offerings at this hour include a women's news-gathering service, *WINGS,* (0430 Friday); a listener-response program (same time Saturday); and *The Far Right Radio Review* (0400 Sunday). Audible in Europe and the Americas on 6975 kHz.

Voice of Russia World Service. Continuous to North America at this hour. Tuesday through Sunday winters, it's *News and Views,* replaced Monday by *Science and Engineering.* During the second half hour, the Sunday slot is filled by ●*Christian Message from Moscow,* replaced Monday by ●*Audio Book Club.* The remaining days feature "alternative programs"—religious paid programming or a show from the Voice of Russia's archives or transcription department. The summer lineup has plenty of variety, and includes *Jazz Show* (0431 Monday), ●*Music at Your Request* (same time Wednesday), the business-oriented *Newmarket* (0411 Thursday), *Science and Engineering* (same time Wednesday and Saturday), ●*Folk Box* (0431 Thursday), *Moscow Mailbag* (0411 Tuesday and Friday) and Sunday's retrospective ●*Moscow Yesterday and Today* (0431 Sunday). In eastern North America, try 7100/7105 and 7125 kHz. Reception is a bit iffy, but you may be lucky. Farther west, best winter bets are 5920 (or 5930), 7175, 9580 and 12045 kHz; in summer, try 15180, 15425 and 15595 kHz.

"For the People," WHRI, Noblesville, Indiana. See 0300 for specifics. The second half of a two-hour broadcast targeted week-nights to North America on 5745 kHz.

Radio Pyongyang, North Korea. Fifty soporific minutes of old-fashioned com-

Radio Nepal's original studio is still in use, upgraded to meet today's needs.   Radio Nepal

munist propaganda. To Southeast Asia on 15180, 15230 and 17765 kHz.

WWCR, Nashville, Tennessee. Carries a variety of disestablishmentarian programs at this hour, depending on the day of the week, and whether it is summer or winter. These include "America First Radio," "Hour of the Time," "Duncan Long Show" and "Radio Free America"; choose between 5065 and 2390 (or 7435) kHz.

04:30

Radio Yugoslavia. Summers only at this time. *News* and short background reports heavily geared to local issues. Worth a listen if you are interested in the region. Thirty minutes to western North America on 9580 and 11870 kHz.

■**Radio Netherlands.** Repeat of the 0030 transmission (see there for specifics). Fifty-five minutes to western North America on 6165 and 9590 kHz.

Radio Austria International. Summers only at this time. ●*Report from Austria*, which includes a brief bulletin of *news*, followed by a series of current events and human interest stories. A popular source of news about Central Europe. Thirty minutes to Europe on 6155 and 13730 kHz. One hour later in winter.

05:00

■**BBC World Service for the Americas and the Mideast.** Thirty minutes of ●*The World Today* (except Saturday and Sunday, when it is replaced by ●*Newsday*). followed by some of the BBC's best output. Take your choice from *The Works* (technology, Monday), ●*Discovery* (science, Tuesday), ●*One Planet* (the environment, Wednesday), ●*The Learning World* (education, 0545 Thursday), ●*Assignment* (Friday), ●*Science in Action* (Saturday) and Sunday's ●*Play of the Week* (Americas only—in the Mideast, you'll hear *In Praise* *of God*). Audible in North America (better to the west) on 5975 and 6175 kHz, and in the Mideast on 11760 and 15575 kHz.

■**BBC World Service for Europe.**
Weekdays, it's a full hour of the excellent ●*The World Today*. This is replaced weekends by ■*Newsday* and Saturday's ●*Science in Action* or Sunday's *In Praise of God*. Continuous to Europe on 3955, 6180, 6195, 9410 and 12095 kHz. Some of these channels may carry the Americas service during summer.

■**BBC World Service for Africa.**
Monday through Friday, it's ●*The World Today*, then *Network Africa*. Weekends, look for ●*Newsday* followed by Saturday's *Talkabout Africa* and Sunday's *Postmark Africa*. Continuous programming on 3255, 6005, 6190, 7160, 9600, 15420 and 17885 kHz.

■**BBC World Service for Asia and the Pacific.** Starts with 30 minutes of ●*The World Today* (Monday through Friday) or ●*Newsday* (weekends). Thereafter, it's a mixed bag of features. Best of the regular shows are Wednesday's *Sports International* and Friday's ●*Focus on Faith*. Continuous to East Asia on 9740, 15360, 17760 and 21660 kHz; and to Southeast Asia on 9740, 11955, 15310 (winter) and 15360 kHz. In Australasia, choose from 9740 (winter), 11955 and 15360 kHz.

■**Deutsche Welle,** Germany. Repeat of the 50-minute 0100 transmission to North America, except that Sunday's *Inside Europe* is replaced by *Marks and Markets*; and *Arts on the Air* gives way to *Cool*. Winters on 5960, 6100, 6120 and 6185 kHz; and summers on 6045, 6185, 9615 and 11810 kHz. This slot is by far the best for western North America.

Radio Exterior de España ("Spanish National Radio"). Repeat of the 0000 and 0100 transmissions to North America, on 6055 kHz.

Radio Canada International. Summer weekdays only. See 0600 for program details. To Europe, Africa and the Mideast on 7295, 9595, 11835 and 15430 kHz. One hour later during winter.

Vatican Radio. Summers only at this time. Twenty minutes of programming oriented to Catholics. To Europe on 5880 and 7250 kHz. Frequencies may vary slightly. One hour later in winter.

Channel Africa, South Africa. A half hour of news-oriented programming for West Africa, and sometimes heard in Europe and eastern North America. On 9525 or 9675 kHz.

XERMX—Radio México Internacional. Winters only at this time. Starts with a feature: *Eternally Mexico* (Tuesday), *Mirror of Mexico* (Thursday), *The Sounds of Mexico* (Friday) and Saturday's *Mailbox*. Wednesday's broadcast is in French, and there are no programs on Sunday or Monday. On the half-hour, there's 30 minutes of music. To North America on 9705 kHz.

China Radio International. This time winters only. Repeat of the 0300 broadcast; one hour to North America on 9560 kHz.

HCJB—Voice of the Andes, Ecuador. Repeat of the 0100 transmission. To western North America on 9745 kHz.

Voice of America. Continues with the morning broadcast to Africa and the Mideast. *News Now*—a mixed bag of sports, science, business and other news and features. To North Africa on 7170 and (winters only) 5995 and 11805 kHz; to the Mideast on 11825 (winter) or (summer) 11965 kHz; and to the rest of Africa on 5970, 6035, 6080, 7195 (summer), 7295 (winter), 9630(summer) and 12080 kHz. Some of these channels are audible in parts of North America.

Radio Bangladesh got its start before independence, in 1939, at this modest mediumwave facility at Kalyanpur.   M. Guha

Radio Habana Cuba. Repeat of the 0100 transmission. To western North America winter on 6000 (or 9505) kHz, and summer on 9820 kHz. Also available to Europe on 9830 kHz upper sideband.

Voice of Nigeria. Targeted mainly at West Africa, but also audible in parts of Europe and North America, especially during winter. Monday through Friday, opens with the lively *Wave Train* followed by *VON Scope*, a half hour of *news* and press comment. Pick of the weekend programs is ●*African Safari*, a musical journey around the African continent, which can be heard Saturdays at 0500. This is replaced Sunday by five minutes of *Reflections* and 25 minutes of music in *VON Link-Up*, with the second half-hour taken up by *News*. The first 60 minutes of a daily two-hour broadcast on 7255 and 15120 kHz.

Swiss Radio International. Winters only at this hour. *Newsnet*. A workmanlike compilation of news and background reports on world and Swiss events. Somewhat lighter fare on Sunday (Saturday evening in North America), when the biweekly *Capital Letters* (a listener-response program) alternates with *Name Game* and *Sounds Good*. A half hour to Europe on 5840 and 6165 kHz. One hour earlier in summer.

Radio New Zealand International. Continues with regional programming for the South Pacific. Part of a much longer broadcast, which is also heard in parts of North America (especially during summer) on 11690 or 11905 kHz.

Radio Australia. *World News*, then Monday through Friday there's *Pacific Beat* (background reporting on events in the Pacific)—look for a sports bulletin at 0530. Weekends, the news is followed by *Oz Sounds*; then, on the half-hour, it's either Saturday's *Sports Factor* or Sunday's *Media Report*. Continuous to Asia and the Pacific on 9660, 12080, 15240, 15510, 17715, 17750 and 21725 kHz. In North America (best during summer) try 17715 kHz. For East Asia, best options are 15240 and 21725 kHz. Some channels carry alternative sports programming at weekends.

Voice of Russia World Service. Winters, the *news* is followed by a wide variety of programs. These include *Jazz Show* (0531 Monday), ●*Music at Your Request* (same time Wednesday), the business-oriented *Newmarket* (0511 Thursday), *Science and Engineering* (same time Wednesday and Saturday), ●*Folk Box* (0531 Thursday), *Moscow Mailbag* (0511 Tuesday and Friday) and Sunday's retrospective ●*Moscow Yesterday and Today* (0531 Sunday). Tuesday through Saturday summers, there's *Focus on Asia and the Pacific*, replaced Sunday by *Science and Engineering* and Monday by *Moscow Mailbag*. On the half-hour, look for *This is*

Russia (Monday and Friday), ●*Audio Book Club* (Sunday), ●*Music at Your Request* (Tuesday), ●*Moscow Yesterday and Today* (Thursday), ●*Christian Message from Moscow* (Saturday) and *Russian by Radio* on Wednesday. Winters only to eastern North America on 7100/7105 and 7125 kHz, and to western parts on 5920 (or 5930), 6065 and 7175 kHz. Also available summers to Australasia on 9450, 15490, 17495, 17665, 21760 and 21790 kHz. If these channels are empty, dial around nearby—the Voice of Russia is not re-nowned for sticking to its frequencies, but it does tend to use the same world band segments.

Radio For Peace International, Costa Rica. Continues at this hour with a pot-pourri of United Nations, counterculture and other programs. These include *WINGS* (news for and of women, 0530 Wednes-day) and *Vietnam Veterans Radio Network* (0530 Thursday). Audible in Europe and the Americas on 6975 kHz.

Kol Israel. Winters only at this time. *News* for 15 minutes from Israel Radio's domestic network. To Europe and eastern North America on 7465 and 9435 kHz, and to Australasia on 17545 kHz. One hour earlier in summer.

Radio Japan. Repeat of the 0300 broad-cast, except that Sunday's *Hello from Tokyo* is replaced by *Let's Learn Japanese*, *Media Roundup* and *Viewpoint*; and the daily end-of-broadcast news gives way to *Tokyo Pop-in*. Sixty minutes to Europe winters on 5975 and 6150 kHz, and summers on 7230 kHz; to East and Southeast Asia on 11725, 11740 and 17810 kHz; to Australasia on 11920 kHz; and to western North America on 6110 kHz. There is also a 30-minute broadcast to West North America and Central America on 11885, 11895, 11960 (winter) and (summer) 15230 kHz.

WWCR, Nashville, Tennessee. Carries a variety of disestablishmentarian programs at this hour, depending on the day of the week, and whether it is summer or winter. These include winter's "America First Radio" and "Hour of the Time"; and summer's "Herald of Truth," "The Hour of Courage" and "Seventieth Week Maga-zine." On 5065 and 2390 (or 7435) kHz.

WJCR, Upton, Kentucky. Continues with country gospel music for North American listeners on 7490 kHz. Also with religious programs to North America at this hour are **WYFR—Family Radio** on 5985 kHz, **WWCR** on 5935 kHz, **KAIJ** on 5810 kHz and **KTBN** on 7510 kHz. For traditional Catholic programming (some of which may be in Spanish), tune to **WEWN** on 7425 kHz.

05:30

Radio Austria International. ●*Report from Austria*; see 0430 for more details. Thirty minutes year-round to North America on 6015 kHz; and winters only to Europe on 6155 and 13730 kHz, and to the Mideast on 15410 and 17870 kHz.

Swiss Radio International. Summers only at this time. Repeat of the 0400 broadcast; see there for specifics. A half hour to Europe on 5840 and 6165 kHz. One hour later in winter.

United Arab Emirates Radio, Dubai. See 0330 for program details. To East Asia and Australasia on 15435, 17830 and 21700 kHz.

Radio Thailand. Thirty minutes of *news* and short features. To Europe on 15115 kHz. Also available to Asia on 9655 and 11905 kHz.

Radio Romania International. *News*, commentary, a press review, and one or more short features. Thirty minutes to southern Africa (and heard elsewhere) on 11810 (or 11740), 11940, 15250 (or 15270), 15340 (or 15365), 17745 (winter) and 17790 kHz.

0600-1159
Australasia & East Asia—Evening Prime Time
Western North America—Late Evening
Europe & Mideast—Morning and Midday

06:00

■**BBC World Service for the Americas and the Mideast.** Except for Sunday, starts with 15 minutes of *World News*. Tuesday through Saturday, this is followed by ●*Insight* (current events), replaced Monday by a feature. At 0630, regular spots include ●*Omnibus* (Monday), ●*Sports International* (Wednesday) and *Meridian* (Thursday and Saturday). Sunday (Americas only), it's a continuation of ●*Play of the Week*, which can run to either 0630 or 0700. If it's the former, you also get 30 minutes of popular music and zany humor in *A Jolly Good Show*. In the Mideast, you can hear the Sunday programs for Europe at this hour. Continuous to North America (better to the west) on 5975 and 6175 kHz, and to the Mideast on 11760, 15565 and 15575 kHz.

■**BBC World Service for Europe.** Summers and winter weekends, identical to the service for the Americas, except Sunday, when you can hear 15 minutes of *World News* followed by ●*Letter from America* and *A Jolly Good Show*. Winter weekdays, it's the final hour of ●*The World Today*. Continuous programming on 3955 (winter), 6180, 6195, 7325, 9410, 12095 and 15565 kHz. Some of these channels may carry the service for the Americas.

■**BBC World Service for Africa.** Opens with 15 minutes of *World News*, then Monday through Friday it's ●*Sports Roundup* and the breakfast show *Network Africa*. Saturday has ●*Letter from America* and *African Quiz* or *This Week and Africa*; Sunday, there's a quarter-hour feature followed by *African Perspective*. Continuous

to most parts of the continent on 6005, 6190, 7160, 9600, 11940 and 15400 kHz.

■**BBC World Service for Asia and the Pacific.** *World News*, followed Tuesday through Saturday by ●*Insight* (current events), replaced Sunday by ●*Letter from America* and Monday by *Seven Days*. Offerings on the half-hour include the arts show *Meridian* (Sunday, Thursday and Saturday), *Jazzmatazz* (Monday), ●*Composer of the Month* (classical music, Tuesday) and *On Screen* (cinema, Wednesday). Continuous to East Asia on 9740, 15360, 17760 and 21660 kHz; to Southeast Asia on 9740, 11955, 15310 (winter) and 15360 kHz; and to Australasia on 7145, 9740 (winter), 11955 and 15360 kHz.

■**Deutsche Welle, Germany.** Repeat of the 0400 broadcast. Fifty minutes to the Mideast, winters on 21705 kHz, and summers on 21680 kHz. Also to West Africa (and sometimes heard well in Europe), winters on 6045, 7225, 9565 and 11765 kHz; and summers on 11915, 13790, 15185 and 17860 kHz. May also be available to East Asia on 17820 kHz.

Radio Habana Cuba. Repeat of the 0200 transmission. To western North America winter on 6000 (or 9505) kHz, and summer on 9820 kHz. Also available to Europe on 9830 kHz upper sideband.

Radio Norway International. Summer Sundays only. *Norway Now*. Thirty minutes of *news* and human-interest stories. To Europe on 7180 kHz, and to Australasia on 7295 and 9590 kHz.

Radio Canada International. Winter weekdays only. Monday's *Vinyl Café* is

A Radio Bangladesh monitoring engineer operates from the outback, where radio signals aren't disrupted by local electrical noises.

M. Guha

replaced by *Spectrum* (current events) from Tuesday to Friday. Thirty minutes to Europe, Africa and the Mideast on 6050, 6150, 9740, 9760 and 11905 kHz. One hour earlier in summer.

Voice of America. Final segment of the transmission to Africa and the Mideast. Monday through Friday, the mainstream African service carries just 30 minutes of ●*Daybreak Africa*, with other channels carrying a full hour of *News Now*—a mixed bag of sports, science, business and other news and features. Weekend programming is the same to all areas—60 minutes of *News Now*. To North Africa on 5995 (winter), 7170, 9680 (summer) and 11805 kHz; to the Mideast on 11825 (winter) or (summer) 11965 kHz; and to mainstream Africa on 5970, 6035, 6080, 7195 (summer), 7285 (winter), 9630 (summer), 11950 (winter), 11995 (summer), 12080 and (winter) 15600 kHz. Some of these channels are audible in North America.

Radio Australia. Ten minutes of *News* (five at weekends), then a couple of features. Weekdays, these are separated by a 10-minute sports bulletin on the half-hour. Monday through Friday, the accent is heavily on music, and you get two bites at the same cherry. Each 20-minute show airing at 0610 is repeated at 0640 the following day (except for the Friday slot which is repeated on Monday). The lineup starts with Monday's *Australian Music Show*, then it's *At Your Request* (Tuesday), *Blacktracker* (Australian aboriginal music, Wednesday), *Australian Country Style* (Thursday), and Friday's *Music Deli*. Weekends bring Saturday's *Feedback* (a listener-response program) and *Arts Australia*, replaced Sunday by the sharp ●*Ockham's Razor* (science talk) and *Correspondents' Report*. Continuous to Asia and the Pacific on 9660, 12080, 15240, 15415, 15510, 17715, 17750 and 21725 kHz. Listeners in western North America should try 17715 kHz. For East and Southeast Asia, best bets are 15240, 15415 and 21725 kHz. Some channels carry an alternative sports program until 0700 on weekends (0800 midyear).

Voice of Nigeria. The second (and final) hour of a daily broadcast mainly intended for listeners in West Africa, but also heard in parts of Europe and North America (especially during winter). Features vary from day to day, but are predominantly concerned with Nigerian and West African affairs. There is a listener-response program at 0600 Friday and 0615 Sunday, and other slots include *Across the Ages* and *Nigeria and Politics* (Monday), *Southern Connection* and *Nigerian Scene* (Tuesday), *West African Scene* (0600 Thursday) and *Images of Nigeria* (0615 Friday). There is a weekday 25-minute program of *news* and commentary on the half-hour, replaced weekends by the more in-depth *Weekly Analysis*. To 0657 on 7255 and 15120 kHz.

Channel Africa, South Africa. A 30-minute news-oriented package for West Africa, and sometimes heard in Europe and eastern North America. On 11900 kHz.

Radio New Zealand International. Continues with regional programming for the South Pacific. Part of a much longer broadcast, which is also heard in parts of North America (especially during summer) on 11690 or 11905 kHz.

Voice of Russia World Service. *News*, then winters it's *Focus on Asia and the Pacific* (Tuesday through Saturday), *Science and Engineering* (Sunday), and *Mailbag* (Monday). On the half-hour, look for *This is Russia* (Monday and Friday), ●*Audio Book Club* (Sunday), ●*Music at Your Request* (Tuesday), ●*Moscow Yesterday and Today* (Thursday), ●*Christian Message from Moscow* (Saturday) and *Russian by Radio* on Wednesday. In summer, the news is followed by *Science and Engineering* (Monday and Friday), the business-oriented *Newmarket* (Wednesday and Saturday), and a listener-response program on the remaining days. The lineup for the second half hour includes ●*Moscow Yesterday and Today* (Wednesday), ●*Audio Book Club* (Thursday), *Russian by Radio*

(Sunday and Monday); the eclectic *Kaleidoscope* (Tuesday and Friday) and *This is Russia* on Saturday. Continuous programming to Australasia (and also audible in Southeast Asia). In winter (local summer in Australasia), try 9825, 15460, 15470, 17495, 17570, 17860 and 21790 kHz; midyear, go for 9825, 15490, 17495, 17665, 21760 and 21790 kHz. If there's nothing on these channels, dial around nearby—frequency usage tends to vary.

Radio For Peace International, Costa Rica. Continues with counterculture and social-conscience programs—try Monday's *The Far Right Radio Review*. Audible in Europe and the Americas on 6975 kHz.

Radio Pyongyang, North Korea. See 1100 for specifics. Fifty minutes to Southeast Asia on 15180 and 15230 kHz.

Vatican Radio. Winters only at this time. Twenty minutes with a heavy Catholic slant. To Europe on 4005 and 5882 kHz. One hour earlier in summer. Frequencies may vary slightly.

WJCR, Upton, Kentucky. Continues with country gospel music to North America on 7490 kHz. Also with religious programs for North American listeners at this hour are **WYFR—Family Radio** on 5985 kHz, **WWCR** on 5935 kHz, **KAIJ** on 5810 kHz, **KTBN** on 7510 kHz, and **WHRI—World Harvest Radio** on 5760 and 7315 kHz. Traditional Catholic fare (some of it may be in Spanish) is available on 7425 kHz.

Voice of Malaysia. Actually starts at 0555 with opening announcements and program summary, followed by *News*. Then comes *This is the Voice of Malaysia*, a potpourri of news, interviews, reports and music. The hour is rounded off with *Personality Column*. Part of a 150-minute broadcast to Southeast Asia and Australia on 6175, 9750 and 15295 kHz.

Radio Japan. Repeat of the 0300 transmission, except that the end-of-broadcast

Audio from Wayang Kulit shadow puppet shows is aired live by RRI Semarang. N. Grace

news is replaced by *Tokyo Pop-in*. Sixty minutes to East and Southeast Asia on 11725, 11860 and 17810 kHz; and to Australasia on 11850 kHz.

HCJB—Voice of the Andes, Ecuador. Tuesday through Saturday, a repeat of the 0200 broadcast. Pick of the remaining fare is *Musical Mailbag* (0630 Sunday) and *Radio Reading Room* (0600 Monday). One hour of predominantly religious programming. To western North America on 9745 kHz.

06:30

Radio Austria International. Winters only at this time. ●*Report from Austria* (see 0430). A half hour via the Canadian relay, aimed primarily at western North America on 6015 kHz.

Swiss Radio International. Winters only at this hour. Repeat of the 0500 broadcast; see there for specifics. A half hour to Europe on 5840 and 6165 kHz. One hour earlier in summer.

YLE Radio Finland. Summers only at this time. Most days it's *Compass North*

and a press review. Exceptions are Saturday's *Capital Café*; Sunday's world band curiosity, *Nuntii Latini* (news in Latin), heard at 0653; and Monday's *Nordic Update*. Thirty minutes to Asia and Australasia on 11945 and 17830 kHz.

Radio Romania International. Actually starts at 0631. A nine-minute news broadcast to Europe winters on 7105, 9510, 9570, 9665 and 11745 kHz; and summers on 9550, 9665 and 11810 kHz.

06:45

Radio Romania International. *News*, commentary, a press review and short features, with interludes of lively Romanian folk music. Fifty-five minutes to East Asia and Australasia on 11740, 11840, 15250, 15270, 15405, 17720 and 17805 kHz, some of which are seasonal.

07:00

■BBC World Service for the Americas, Europe and the Mideast. Fifteen minutes of *World News*, then it's a mixed bag. Best of the pack are ●*Off the Shelf*

(0715 Monday through Friday), *The Vintage Chart Show* (0730 Monday), ●*Composer of the Month* (classical music, 0730 Tuesday), ●*From the Weeklies* (0715 Saturday) and ●*Health Matters* (same time Sunday). Winters only to North America (and better to the west) on 5975 and 6175 kHz. Year round to Europe on 7325, 9410, 12095, 15565 and 17640 kHz; and to the Mideast on 11760, 15565 and 15575 kHz.

■**BBC World Service for Asia and the Pacific.** *World News*, then Monday through Friday there's ●*Off the Shelf* (readings from world literature). Best of the remaining offerings (all at 0730) are *A Jolly Good Show* (Sunday), ●*John Peel* (Tuesday), ●*One Planet* (the environment, Wednesday), ●*The Learning World* (Thursday, and replaced by *Waveguide* on either the first or last Thursday of the month), ●*World of Music* (Friday) and Saturday's ●*People and Politics*. Plenty of good listening, and something for everyone. Continuous to East Asia on 9740, 15360, 17760 and 21660 kHz; to Southeast Asia on 9740, 11955, 15310 (winter) and 15360 kHz; and to Australasia on 7145, 9740 (winter), 11955 and 15360 kHz.

Voice of Malaysia. First, there is a daily feature with a Malaysian theme (except for Thursday, when *Talk on Islam* is aired), then comes a half hour of *This is the Voice of Malaysia* (see 0600), followed by 15 minutes of *Beautiful Malaysia*. Not much doubt about where the broadcast originates! Continuous to Southeast Asia and Australia on 6175, 9750 and 15295 kHz.

Radio Prague, Czech Republic. Summers only at this time. See 0800 for specifics. Thirty minutes to Europe on 7345 and 9505 kHz. One hour later in winter.

Radio Slovakia International. Summers only at this time. *Slovakia Today*, a 30-minute review of Slovak life and culture. Monday, there's a potpourri of short features; Tuesday spotlights tourism and Slovak personalities; Wednesday is devoted to business and economy; and Thursday brings a mix of politics, education and science. Friday offerings include cultural items, cooking recipes and the off-beat *Back Page News*; and Saturday has the *"Best of"* series. Sunday's show is a melange of this and that, and includes *Listeners' Tribune* and some enjoyable Slovak music. A friendly half hour to Australasia on 9440, 15460 and 17550 kHz.

Radio Australia. *World News*, then Monday through Friday it's *Pacific Beat*, news and features for listeners in the Pacific, with a 10-minute sports bulletin on the half-hour. Weekends, the news is followed by *Pacific Focus* and either Saturday's *Week's End* or Sunday's *Rural Reporter*. Continuous to Asia and the Pacific on 9660, 12080, 15240, 15415, 15510, 17715, 17750 and 21725 kHz. Listeners in western North America can try 17715 kHz (best during summer), while East Asia is served by 15240, 15415, 17750 and 21725 kHz. For Southeast Asia, take your pick from 15415 and 17750 kHz.

> The Voice of Malaysia airs one of the few English shows on Islam. Later, there's "Beautiful Malaysia."

King Birendra of Nepal (center) speaks with the first director of Radio Nepal. M. Guha

Radio For Peace International, Costa Rica. Continues with counterculture and social-conscience programming. Audible in Europe and the Americas on 6975 kHz.

Voice of Russia World Service. *News,* then a variety of features. The winter lineup includes *Science and Engineering* (Monday and Friday), the business-oriented *Newmarket* (Wednesday and Saturday), and a listener-response program on the remaining days. During the second half hour, choose from ●*Moscow Yesterday and Today* (Wednesday), ●*Audio Book Club* (Thursday), *Russian by Radio* (Sunday and Monday), the multifaceted *Kaleidoscope* (Tuesday and Friday) and *This is Russia* on Saturday. Summers, the news is followed by the informative ●*Commonwealth Update* which airs on Tuesday, Thursday and Saturday. Other offerings include *Science and Engineering* (Wednesday), *Moscow Mailbag* (Friday) and

Monday's thoroughly enjoyable ●*Music and Musicians.* On the half-hour, there's some of the Voice of Russia's best—●*Audio Book Club* (Wednesday), ●*Moscow Yesterday and Today* (Friday), ●*Folk Box* (Tuesday) and *This is Russia* on Thursday. Sundays, it's a continuation of ●*Music and Musicians.* Continuous programming to Australasia (also audible in Southeast Asia). In winter (local summer in Australasia), try 9825, 15460, 15470, 17495, 17570, 17860 and 21790 kHz; midyear, go for 9825, 15490, 17495, 17665, 21760 and 21790 kHz. If there's nothing on these channels, dial around nearby— frequency usage tends to be volatile.

WJCR, Upton, Kentucky. Continues with country gospel music for North American listeners on 7490 kHz. Also with religious programs to North America at this hour are **WWCR** on 5935 kHz, **KAIJ** on 5810 kHz, **KTBN** on 7510 kHz, and **WHRI—**

World Harvest Radio on 5745 and 9495 kHz. For traditional Catholic programming, tune **WEWN** on 7425 kHz.

Radio Pyongyang, North Korea. See 1100 for specifics. Fifty minutes from the last of the old-time communist stations. To Southeast Asia on 15340 and 17765 kHz.

Radio Norway International. Winter Sundays only. *Norway Now*. A half hour of *news* and human-interest stories targeted at Australasia on 7180 kHz.

Radio New Zealand International. Continues with regional programming for the South Pacific. Part of a much longer broadcast, which is also heard in parts of North America (especially during summer) on 6100 or 9700 kHz.

Radio Taipei International, Taiwan. Repeat of the 0200 transmission. Best heard in southern and western parts of the United States on 5950 kHz.

Radio Japan. Monday through Friday, it's *Radio Japan News Round* followed by *Radio Japan Magazine Hour*, which consists of *Close Up* and a feature (two on Tuesday). On Monday you can hear *Sports Column*, Tuesday has *Japanese Culture* and *Today*, Wednesday features *Asian Report*, Thursday brings *Crosscurrents*, and Friday's offering is *Business Focus*. Weekend fare is made up of a bulletin of *news*, followed by Saturday's *This Week* or Sunday's *Let's Learn Japanese*, *Media Roundup* and *Viewpoint*. The broadcast ends with a daily *news* summary. Sixty minutes to Europe on 5975 (winter), 7230 and 15165 kHz; to the Mideast on 15165 kHz; to Africa on 15165 and 17815 kHz; to East and Southeast Asia on 11725, 11740, 17810 and 21610 kHz; and to Australasia on 11850 and 11920 kHz.

HCJB—Voice of the Andes, Ecuador. Opens with 30 minutes of syndicated religious programming—except for *The Latest Catch* and *The Book Nook* (Wednes-day), *On Line* (Friday) and *Musical Mailbag* (Saturday). Then comes the weekday *Studio 9* (see 0030 for more details, except that all features are one day earlier), replaced Saturday by *DX Partyline*, and Sunday by *Saludos Amigos*—the HCJB international friendship program. To Europe winters on 5865 or 11960 kHz. A separate block of religious programming is broadcast to Australasia on 9640 kHz.

07:30

■**Radio Netherlands.** *News*, then Monday through Saturday it's ●*Newsline* followed by a feature. Pick of the pack are ●*Research File* (science, Monday); ●*A Good Life* (Friday); ●*Weekend* (Saturday) and Wednesday's award-winning ●*Documentary*. On the remaining days, you can hear *Music 52-15* (Tuesday) and *Media Network* (Thursday). Sunday fare consists of *Sincerely Yours* (a listener-response program) and *Sounds Interesting*. To Australasia winters on 9830 and 11895 kHz, and midyear on 9720 and 9820 kHz. Quality programming.

Swiss Radio International. *Newsnet*—news and background reports on world and Swiss events. Some lighter fare on Saturdays, when the biweekly *Capital Letters* (a listener-response program) alternates with *Name Game* and *Sounds Good*. A half hour to West and southern Africa on 9885, 11860 and 13635 kHz.

Radio Austria International. Summers only at this time. ●*Report from Austria*, which includes a short bulletin of *news* followed by a series of current events and human interest stories. Good coverage of national and regional issues. Thirty minutes to Europe on 6155 and 13730 kHz, and to the Mideast on 15410 and 17870 kHz. Winters, it's one hour later to Europe, and two hours earlier to the Mideast.

Radio Vlaanderen Internationaal,
Belgium. Summers only at this time. *News*,
then *Press Review* (except Sunday),
followed Monday through Friday by
Belgium Today (various topics) and
features like *The Arts* (Monday and
Thursday, *Tourism* (Monday), *Focus on
Europe* (Tuesday), *Living in Belgium* and
Green Society (Wednesday), *Around Town*
(Thursday), and *Economics* and *International
Report*(Friday). Weekend features
consist of Saturday's *Music from Flanders*
and Sunday's *P.O. Box 26* (a listener-
response program) and *Radio World*.
Twenty-five minutes to Europe on 7290
and 9940 kHz; and to Australasia on 9940
kHz. One hour later in winter.

07:45

KTWR—Trans World Radio, Guam.
Actually starts at 0740. Ninety-five minutes
of evangelical programming targeted at
Southeast Asia on 15200 kHz.

Voice of Greece. Actual start time varies
slightly. Ten minutes of English news from
and about Greece. Part of a longer broadcast of predominantly Greek programming. To Europe and Australasia on two or
more channels from 7450, 9425 and 11645
kHz.

08:00

**■BBC World Service for Europe and
the Mideast.** *News*, then the religious
Pause for Thought, followed by a wide
variety of programming, depending on the
day of the week. Select offerings include
●*Short Story* and ●*The Greenfield Collection*
(Sunday), ●*Anything Goes* (0830 Tuesday),
●*Everywoman* (0830 Wednesday), ●*John
Peel* (0830 Friday) and ●*World of Music*
(same time Saturday). Continuous to
Europe on 7325 (winter), 9410, 12095,
15565 and 17640 kHz; and to the Mideast
on 11760 (winter), 15565 and (weekends)
15575 kHz.

**■BBC World Service for Asia and the
Pacific.** Starts with *World News* and the
religious *Pause for Thought*. The next 45
minutes are a mixed bag of features.
Aficionados of classical music should try
●*The Greenfield Collection* (0830 Sunday)
and ●*Concert Hall* (or its substitute) at
0815 Tuesday. For other tastes, there's *The
Vintage Chart Show* (0830 Wednesday),
●*From Our Own Correspondent* (0815
Thursday) and ●*Everywoman* (0830
Friday). Continuous to East Asia on 9740,
15360, 17760 and 21660 kHz; to Southeast
Asia on 9740, 11955, 15310 (winter) and
15360 kHz; and to Australasia on 9740
(winter), 11955 and 15360 kHz.

HCJB—Voice of the Andes, Ecuador.
Continuous programming to Europe and
Australasia. For Europe there's the final 30
minutes of *Studio 9* (or weekend variations), while Australasia gets a full hour's
serving of predominantly religious fare. To
Europe winters on 5865 or 11960 kHz; and
to Australasia on 9640 kHz.

Voice of Malaysia. *News* and commentary, followed Monday through Friday by
Instrumentalia, which is replaced weekends by *This is the Voice of Malaysia* (see
0600). The final 25 minutes of a much
longer transmission targeted at Southeast
Asia and Australia on 6175, 9750 and
15295 kHz.

Radio Norway International. Summer
Sundays only. *Norway Now*. A pleasant half
hour of *news* and human-interest stories
from and about Norway. To Australasia on
17860 kHz.

Radio Prague, Czech Republic. Winters
only at this time. *News*, then Monday
through Friday there's *Current Affairs*,
followed by one or more features.
Monday's lineup is *Magazine '99*; Tuesday,
it's *Talking Point* and *Media Czech*;
Wednesday features *The Arts* and *History
Czech*; Thursday brings *Economic Report*
and *I'd Like You to Meet...*; and Friday

there's *Between You and Us*. Saturday's offering is a thoroughly enjoyable musical feature, replaced Sunday by *The Week in Politics*, *From the Weeklies* and *Media Czech*. Thirty minutes to Europe on 9505 and 11600 kHz. One hour earlier in summer.

Radio Australia. Part of a 24-hour service to Asia and the Pacific, but which can also be heard at this time throughout much of North America. Begins with a bulletin of *World News*, then Monday through Friday there's an in-depth look at current events in *PM*. Weekends, the news is followed by *Grandstand Wrap*, a roundup of the latest Australian sports action, which gives way to a feature on the half-hour. Saturday, it's *Asia Pacific*, replaced Sunday by *Innovations*. To Asia and the Pacific on 5995, 9580, 9710, 9770, 12080, 15415, 15510, 17750 and 21725 kHz. Audible in North America on 9580 kHz. Best bets for East and Southeast Asia are 9770, 15415, 17750 and 21725 kHz.

WJCR, Upton, Kentucky. Continues with country gospel music to North America on 7490 kHz. Other U.S. religious broadcasters operating at this hour include **WWCR** on 5935 kHz, **KAIJ** on 5810 kHz, **KTBN** on 7510 kHz, and **WHRI—World Harvest Radio** on 5745 and 9495 kHz. Traditional Catholic programming can be heard via **WEWN** on 7425 kHz.

Radio Pyongyang, North Korea. See 1100 for specifics. Fifty minutes of mediocrity to Southeast Asia on 15180 and 15230 kHz.

Voice of Russia World Service. Winters, *News* is followed by ●*Commonwealth Update* on Tuesday, Thursday and Saturday. Other features include *Science and Engineering* (Wednesday), *Moscow Mailbag* (Friday) and Monday's thoroughly enjoyable ●*Music and Musicians*. On the half-hour, there's some of the Voice of Russia's best—●*Audio*

Book Club (Wednesday), ●*Moscow Yesterday and Today* (Friday), ●*Folk Box* (Tuesday) and *This is Russia* on Thursday. In summer, ●*Commonwealth Update* is only available on Wednesday and Friday. It is replaced Monday by *Science and Engineering*, Tuesday by *Focus on Asia*, Thursday by *Newmarket* and Saturday by *Moscow Mailbag*. Sunday's offering is the 45-minute ●*Music and Musicians*—a jewel among classical music shows. Choice pickings from the second half hour include ●*Moscow Yesterday and Today* (Monday), ●*Folk Box* (Thursday) and Saturday's ●*Christian Message from Moscow*. Other slots include *Moscow Mailbag* (Tuesday), *This is Russia* (Wednesday) and Friday's *Jazz Show*. Continuous programming to Australasia (and also audible in Southeast Asia). In winter (local Oz summer), try 9825, 15460, 15470, 17495, 17570, 17860 and 21790 kHz; midyear, go for 9825, 15490, 17495, 17665, 21760 and 21790 kHz. If there's nothing on these channels, dial around nearby—Moscow's frequencies tend to change more than most.

KTWR—Trans World Radio, Guam. Continuation of evangelical programming to Southeast Asia on 15200 kHz, and the start of another ninety-minute block to Australasia on 15330 kHz.

Radio New Zealand International. Continues with regional programming for the South Pacific. Part of a much longer broadcast, which is also heard in parts of North America (especially during summer) on 6100 or 9700 kHz.

Radio Korea International, South Korea. Opens with *news* and commentary, followed Monday through Wednesday by *Seoul Calling*. Weekly features include *Echoes of Korean Music* and *Shortwave Feedback* (Sunday), *Tales from Korea's Past* (Monday), *Korean Cultural Trails* (Tuesday), *Pulse of Korea* (Wednesday), *From Us to You* (a listener-response program) and

Let's Learn Korean (Thursday), *Let's Sing Together* and *Korea Through Foreigners' Eyes* (Friday), and Saturday's *Discovering Korea*, *Korean Literary Corner* and *Weekly News Focus*. Sixty minutes to Europe on 13670 kHz, and to Australasia on 9570 kHz.

08:30

Radio Austria International. Winters only at this time. The comprehensive ●*Report from Austria*; see 0430 for more details. A half hour to Europe on 6155 and 13730 kHz, and to Australasia on 17870 kHz. Midyear, it's one hour earlier to Europe, and one hour later to Australasia.

Radio Slovakia International. Winters only at this time. *Slovakia Today*—30 minutes of *news*, reports and features, all with a distinct Slovak flavor. Tuesday, there's a potpourri of short features; Wednesday puts the accent on tourism and Slovak personalities; Wednesday has a historical feature; Thursday's slot is devoted to business and economy; and Friday brings a mix of politics, education and science. Saturday has a strong cultural content; Sunday features the *"Best of"* series; and Monday brings *Listeners' Tribune* and some enjoyable Slovak music. To Australasia on 11990, 17485 and 21705 kHz.

■**Radio Netherlands.** The second of two hours aimed at Australasia. *News*, followed Monday through Saturday by ●*Newsline*, then a feature. Choice pickings include ●*A Good Life* (Tuesday), ●*Research File* (Thursday), ●*Roughly Speaking* (Saturday) and Friday's ●*Documentary*. Other offerings include *Aural Tapestry* (Monday), *Sounds Interesting* (Wednesday) and Sunday's *Siren Song*. Winters on 5965, 9830 and 13700 kHz; and midyear on 9720 and 9820 kHz.

Swiss Radio International. Thirty minutes of *news* and background reports on world and Swiss events. Look for some lighter fare on Saturdays, when *Capital Letters* (a biweekly listener-response program) alternates with *Name Game* and *Sounds Good*. To Australasia on 9885 and 13685 kHz.

Radio Vlaanderen Internationaal, Belgium. Winters only at this time. *News*, then *Press Review* (except Sunday), followed Monday through Friday by *Belgium Today* (various topics) and features like *The Arts* (Monday and Thursday, *Tourism* (Monday), *Focus on Europe* (Tuesday), *Living in Belgium* and *Green Society* (Wednesday), *Around Town* (Thursday), and *Economics* and *International Report*(Friday). Weekend features consist of Saturday's *Music from Flanders* and Sunday's *P.O. Box 26* (a listener-response program) and *Radio World*. Twenty-five minutes to Europe on 6130 and 13795 kHz; and to Australasia on 13795 kHz. One hour earlier in summer.

Radio Vilnius, Lithuania. Summers only at this time; see 0930 for program specifics. Thirty minutes to Europe on 9710 kHz. One hour later in winter.

Voice of Armenia. Summer Sundays only. Mainly of interest to Armenians abroad. Thirty minutes of Armenian *news* and culture. To Europe on 15270 (or 15170) kHz. One hour later in winter.

09:00

■**BBC World Service for Europe and the Mideast.** Starts with *News* followed by ●*World Business Report/Review* (not Sunday), and ends with *Sports Roundup*. The remaining time is taken up by a number of features, the best of which are *The Farming World* (0915 Wednesday), ●*The Learning World* (same time Friday, and replaced by *Waveguide* on either the first or last Friday of the month) and ●*From Our Own Correspondent* (0915 Sunday). Continuous to Europe on 9410,

ELWA used local musicians to appeal to its African audience. SIM

12095, 15565 and 17640 kHz; and to the Mideast on 11760 (summer), 15565 and 15575 kHz.

■**BBC World Service for Asia and the Pacific.** Starts and ends like the service for Europe, but the features are different. Monday through Friday at 0915 there's a series of educational programs. These are replaced Saturday by ●*Omnibus*, and Sunday by ●*Short Story* and a 15-minute feature. To East Asia on 6065, 9580, 9740, 11765, 11955, 15360 and 21660 kHz; to Southeast Asia on 6195, 9740, 11765, 15310 (summer) and 15360 kHz; and to Australasia winters on 9740 and 15360 kHz, and midyear on 11765 kHz.

■**Deutsche Welle,** Germany. *News*, followed Monday through Friday by ●*NewsLink*, and then a feature. Monday, it's *Development Forum* or *Women on the Move*; Tuesday has the interesting ●*Man and Environment*; Wednesday brings

●*Insight*; Thursday, there's *Living in Germany*; and Friday's slot is *Spotlight on Sport*. Weekend fare consists of Saturday's *Talking Point* and *African Kaleidoscope*; and Sunday's *Religion and Society* and *Cool*. Fifty minutes to East and Southern Africa on 9565, 15145 (winter), 15205 (summer), 15410, 17800 and 21600 kHz. For a separate service to Asia and the Pacific, see the next item.

■**Deutsche Welle,** Germany. *News*, then Monday through Friday it's ●*NewsLink* and *Asia Pacific Report*. These are replaced Saturday by *Talking Point* and *Marks and Markets*; and Sunday by *Religion and Society* and *Cool*. Fifty minutes to Asia and Australasia winters on 6160, 7380, 11715, 12055 and 17820 kHz; and summers on 6160, 12055, 17560 and 21680 kHz.

HCJB—Voice of the Andes, Ecuador. Monday through Friday it's *Studio 9*, featuring nine minutes of world and Latin

American *news*, followed by 20 minutes of in-depth reporting on Latin America. The final portion of *Studio 9* is given over to one of a variety of 30-minute features—including *You Should Know* (issues and ethics, Monday), *El Mundo Futuro* (science, Tuesday), *Ham Radio Today* (Wednesday), *What's Cooking in the Andes* (Thursday) and Friday's thoroughly enjoyable ●*Música del Ecuador*. On Saturday, the news is followed by *DX Partyline*, which in turn is replaced Sunday by *Saludos Amigos*—HCJB's international friendship program. Continuous to Australasia on 9640 kHz.

China Radio International. *News* and commentary, followed Tuesday through Friday by *Current Affairs*. These are followed by various feature programs. Sunday's lineup includes *Cultural Information*, *Snapshots*, *Report from Developing Countries*, *Song of the Week* and *Listeners' Letterbox*; Monday's offerings are *Open Windows* and *Let's Learn Chinese*; Tuesdays, it's *Orient Arena* and *Voices from Other Lands*; Wednesday, there's *Profile* and another chance to *Learn to Speak Chinese*; Thursday's presentations are *Focus* and *Cultural Spectrum*; while Friday's features are *Life in China* and *Global Review*. To round off the week, there's an eclectic Saturday menu consisting of *Asia-Pacific News*, *Chinese Folk Tales*, *Cooking Show*, *China Scrapbook* and ●*Music from China*. One hour to Australasia on 9785 and 11755 kHz. May also be available on 9890 kHz or another test frequency.

Radio New Zealand International. Continuous programming for the islands of the South Pacific, where the broadcasts are targeted. Summers on 6100 kHz, and winters on 9700 kHz. Audible in much of North America.

Voice of Russia World Service. Winters only at this time. *News*, followed by ●*Commonwealth Update* on Wednesday and Friday. This is replaced Monday by *Science and Engineering*, Tuesday by *Focus* on Asia, Thursday by *Newmarket* and Saturday by *Moscow Mailbag*. Sunday's offering is the 45-minute ●*Music and Musicians*—not to be missed if you are a fan of classical music. Choice pickings from the second half hour include ●*Moscow Yesterday and Today* (Monday), ●*Folk Box* (Thursday) and Saturday's ●*Christian Message from Moscow*. Other slots include *Moscow Mailbag* (Tuesday), *This is Russia* (Wednesday) and Friday's *Jazz Show*. Continuous programming to Australasia (and also audible in Southeast Asia). In winter, try 9825, 15460, 15470, 17495, 17570, 17860 and 21790 kHz; midyear, go for 9825, 15490, 17495, 17665, 21760 and 21790 kHz. If there's nothing on these channels, dial around nearby—frequency usage can be volatile.

Radio Prague, Czech Republic. This time summers only. *News*, then Monday through Friday there's *Current Affairs*, followed by one or more features. Monday's lineup is *Magazine '99*, replaced Tuesday by *Talking Point* and *Media Czech*; Wednesday offers *The Arts* and *History Czech*; Thursday brings *Economic Report* and *I'd Like You to Meet...*; and Friday there's *Between You and Us*. Saturday's offering is a thoroughly enjoyable musical feature, replaced Sunday by *The Week in Politics*, *From the Weeklies* and *Media Czech*. Thirty minutes to the Mideast and beyond on 21745 kHz, and to West Africa on 17485 kHz.

Radio Australia. *World News*, followed Monday through Friday by *Countrywide* and a five-minute sports bulletin at 0935. The final 20 minutes are devoted to a feature. Monday, it's *Australian Music Show*, replaced Tuesday by *At Your Request*, and Wednesday by *Blacktracker* (Australian aboriginal music). Thursday's *Australian Country Style* shows that country music is alive and well a long way from Nashville, while Friday's *Music Deli* spotlights music from a variety of cultures. These are

replaced weekends by Saturday's *Science Show* and Sunday's *Hindsight* (a look at past events). Continuous to Asia and the Pacific on 6080, 9580, 9770, 11880 and 17750 kHz; and heard in North America on 9580 kHz. Listeners in East Asia can choose from 6080, 9770, 11880 and 17750 kHz; with the last two channels also audible in much of Southeast Asia.

KTWR—Trans World Radio, Guam. Final thirty minutes of evangelical programming to Australasia on 15330 kHz.

WJCR, Upton, Kentucky. Continues with country gospel music to North America on 7490 kHz. Other U.S. religious broadcasters operating at this hour include **WWCR** on 5935, **KAIJ** on 5810, **KTBN** on 7510 kHz, and **WHRI—World Harvest Radio** on 5745 and 9495 kHz. Traditional Catholic programming is aired via **WEWN** on 7425 kHz.

Radio Japan. Repeat of the 0300 broadcast; see there for specifics. Up-to-the-minute news from and about the Far East. Sixty minutes to East and Southeast Asia on 6090 (winter), 9610 (summer) and 15190 kHz; and to Australasia on 11850 kHz.

09:30

Radio Austria International. ●*Report from Austria*, which consists of a short bulletin of *news* followed by a series of current events and human interest stories. Tends to focus on national and regional issues. To East Asia on 15455 kHz, and to Australasia on 17870 kHz. Daily in winter, but only Monday through Saturday in summer.

■**Radio Netherlands.** *News*, then Monday through Saturday it's ●*Newsline* followed by a feature. Well worth your attention are ●*Research File* (science, Monday); ●*A Good Life* (Friday); ●*Weekend* (Saturday) and Wednesday's well produced

●*Documentary*. On the remaining days, you can hear *Music 52-15* (Tuesday) and *Media Network* (Thursday). The Sunday slots are filled by *Sincerely Yours* (a listener-response program) and *Sounds Interesting*. One hour to East and Southeast Asia, winters on 7260 and 9810 kHz, and summers on 12065 and 13710 kHz. Recommended listening.

Radio Vilnius, Lithuania. Winters only at this time. A half hour that's mostly *news* and background reports about events in Lithuania. Of broader appeal is *Mailbag*, aired every other Sunday. For a little Lithuanian music, try the second half of Monday's broadcast. To Europe on 9710 kHz. One hour earlier in summer.

FEBC Radio International, Philippines. Opens with *World News Update*, then it's mostly religious features. For something with a more general appeal, try Thursday's *Mailbag* or Sunday's *DX Dial* (a show for radio enthusiasts). The first half-hour of a 90-minute predominantly religious broadcast targeted at East and Southeast Asia on 11635 kHz.

Voice of Armenia. Winter Sundays only. Mainly of interest to Armenians abroad. Thirty minutes of Armenian *news* and culture. To Europe on 15270 kHz. One hour earlier in summer.

10:00

■**BBC World Service for the Americas, Europe and the Mideast.** Thirty minutes of ●*Newsdesk* followed by some excellent features. These include ●*Omnibus* (Monday), *On Screen* (cinema, Tuesday), ●*One Planet* (the environment, Wednesday), ●*Discovery* (science, Thursday) and *Global Business* (Sunday). To eastern North America and the Caribbean on 5965 (summer) and 6195 kHz; to Europe on 9410, 12095, 15565 and 17640 kHz; and to the Mideast on 11760, 15565 and 15575 kHz.

RKPD Blitar station personnel Pristiwanto and Jukarni in their Indonesian studio.

N. Grace

■**BBC World Service for Asia and the Pacific.** Thirty minutes of ●*Newsdesk*, then features. The weekday lineup has plenty to offer: *The Works* (technology, Monday); *Jazzmatazz* (Tuesday); ●*One Planet* (the environment, Wednesday); ●*World of Music* (Thursday); and Friday's all-embracing ●*Focus on Faith*. Weekends, there's Saturday's ●*Anything Goes* and Sunday's *In Praise of God*. Continuous to East Asia on 9740, 11765 (winter), 15360 (till 1030) and 21660 kHz; to Southeast Asia on 6195, 9740, 11965, 15310 and (till 1030) 15360 kHz; and to Australasia on 9740 (winter) or (midyear) 11765 kHz.

Radio Australia. *World News*, then weekdays it's *Asia Pacific* and a feature on the half-hour. Monday's slot is given over to *Innovations*, replaced Tuesday by *Arts Australia*, and Wednesday by *Rural Reporter*. Recommendations for a good read can be found in Thursday's *Book Talk*, with Friday spotlighting environmental topics in *Earthbeat*. The weekend lineup consists of Saturday's *Jazz Notes* and *Asia Pacific*, plus Sunday's *Oz Sounds* and *Correspondents' Report*. Continuous to Asia and the Pacific on 6080, 9580, 9770, 11880 and 17750 kHz; and well heard in North America on 9580 kHz. Listeners in East and

Southeast Asia can choose from 6080 (East Asia only), 9770, 11880 and 17750 kHz.

Swiss Radio International. Summers only at this time. *Newsnet*—news and background reports on world and Swiss events. Look for some lighter fare on Saturdays, when the biweekly *Capital Letters* (a listener-response program) alternates with *Name Game* and *Sounds Good*. Thirty minutes to Europe on 6165 and 9535 kHz. One hour later in winter.

Radio Prague, Czech Republic. This time winters only. Repeat of the 0800 broadcast (see there for specifics). Thirty minutes to West Africa on 17485 kHz, and to the Mideast and beyond on 21705 kHz.

Voice of Vietnam. Begins with *news*, then there's *Commentary* or *Weekly Review*, followed by short features and some pleasant Vietnamese music (especially at weekends). Heard extensively on 9840 and 12020 (or 15010) kHz. Targeted to Asia at this hour.

Voice of America. The start of the VOA's daily broadcasts to the Caribbean. *News Now*—a mixed bag of sports, science, business and other news and features. On 6165, 7405 and 9590 kHz. For a separate service to Australasia, see the next item.

Voice of America. The ubiquitous *News Now*, but unlike the service to the Caribbean, this is part of a much longer broadcast. To Australasia on 5985, 11720, and 15425 kHz.

China Radio International. Repeat of the 0900 broadcast, but with news updates. One hour to Australasia on 9785 and 11755 kHz. May also be available on 9890 kHz or another test frequency.

FEBC Radio International, Philippines. The final hour of a 90-minute mix of religious and secular programming for East and Southeast Asia. Monday through Friday, it's *Focus on the Family*, then a 15-minute religious feature, *Asian News Update* (on the half-hour) and *In Touch*. All weekend offerings are religious in nature. On 11635 kHz.

All India Radio. *News*, then a composite program of commentary, press review and features, interspersed with ample servings of enjoyable Indian music. To East Asia on 11585 and 17840 kHz; and to Australasia on 13700, 15050 and 17387 kHz.

WJCR, Upton, Kentucky. Continues with country gospel music to North America on 7490 kHz. Other U.S. religious broadcasters operating at this hour include **WWCR** on 5935 kHz, **KTBN** on 7510 kHz, **WYFR—Family Radio** on 5950 kHz, and **WHRI—World Harvest Radio** on 6040 and 9495 kHz. For traditional Catholic programming, try **WEWN** on 7425 kHz.

HCJB—Voice of the Andes, Ecuador. Sixty minutes of religious and secular programming to Australasia. See 0200 for program specifics, except that features are one day earlier, and not necessarily in the same order. On 9640 kHz.

10:30

Radio Korea International, South Korea. Summers only at this time. Starts off with *News*, followed Monday through Wednesday by *Economic News Briefs*. The remainder of the 30-minute broadcast is taken up by a feature: *Shortwave Feedback* (Sunday), *Seoul Calling* (Monday and Tuesday), *Pulse of Korea* (Wednesday), *From Us to You* (Thursday), *Let's Sing Together* (Friday) and *Weekly News Focus* (Saturday). On 11715 kHz via their Canadian relay, so this is the best chance for North Americans to hear the station. One hour later in winter.

Radio Prague, Czech Republic. This time summers only. Repeat of the 0700 broadcast; see 1130 for program specifics. A half hour to Europe on 7345 and 11640 kHz. One hour later during winter.

■**Radio Netherlands.** The second of two hours targeted at East and Southeast Asia. *News*, followed Monday through Saturday by ●*Newsline*, then a feature. Quality offerings include ●*A Good Life* (Tuesday), ●*Research File* (Thursday), ●*Roughly Speaking* (Saturday) and Friday's excellent ●*Documentary*. Other offerings include *Aural Tapestry* (Monday), *Sounds Interesting* (Wednesday) and Sunday's *Siren Song*. Fifty-five minutes to East and Southeast Asia, winters on 7260 and 9810 kHz, and summers on 12065 and 13710 kHz (also audible in parts of Australasia). A full hour summers to Western Europe on 6045 and 9860 kHz.

Radio Vlaanderen Internationaal, Belgium. Summers only at this time. *News*, then *Press Review* (except Sunday), followed Monday through Friday by *Belgium Today* (various topics) and features like *The Arts* (Monday and Thursday, *Tourism* (Monday), *Focus on Europe* (Tuesday), *Living in Belgium* and *Green Society* (Wednesday), *Around Town* (Thursday), and *Economics* and *International Report*(Friday). Weekend features consist of Saturday's *Music from Flanders* and Sunday's *P.O. Box 26* (a listener-response program) and *Radio World*. Twenty-five minutes to Europe on 9925 and 15535 kHz.

United Arab Emirates Radio, Dubai. *News*, then a feature dealing with one or more aspects of Arab life and culture. Weekends, there are replies to listeners' letters. To Europe on 13675, 15395, 17630 and 21605 kHz.

11:00

■**BBC World Service for the Americas, Europe and the Mideast.** ●*Newsdesk*, followed on the half-hour by a variety of features, depending on the day of the week. Try *Jazzmatazz* (Monday), *Sports International* (Wednesday), ●*The*

Learning World and ●*From Our Own Correspondent* (Thursday), ●*Focus on Faith* (Friday), ●*People and Politics* (Saturday) and last but not least, Sunday's eclectic ●*Anything Goes*. Continuous programming to eastern North America and the Caribbean on 5965, 6195 and 15220 kHz. Weekdays, for the first half hour, 6195 and 15220 kHz carry alternative programming for the Caribbean. Also to Europe on 9410, 12095, 15565 and 17640 kHz; and to the Mideast on 11760, 15565 and 15575 kHz.

■**BBC World Service for Asia and the Pacific.** Starts with ●*Newsdesk*, and then there's a 30-minute feature. *Meridian* (the arts) is aired on Monday, Wednesday and Friday; Tuesday has *On Screen* (cinema); Saturday, there's the classical *Music Review*; and Sunday features popular music. Continuous to East Asia on 7235 (winter), 9580, 9740, 11955 and (summer) 15280 kHz; to Southeast Asia on 6195, 9740 and (winter) 15310 kHz; and to Australasia on 9740 kHz.

Voice of Asia, Taiwan. A broadcast divided into four 15-minute blocks, the first of which is *News*. This is followed by two quarter-hour features, except for Monday's *Floating Air* which occupies a full 30-minute slot. Tuesday's offerings are *People* and *Trends*; Wednesday brings *Taiwan Today* and *Miss Mook's Big Countdown*; Thursday's themes are *Treasures of the Orient* and *Hot Spots*; Friday features *Taipei Magazine* and *Life on the Outside*; Saturday, there's *Kaleidoscope* and *Amanda's Café*; and Sunday it's *Mailbag Time* and *Music Box*. Saturday's broadcast ends with *Reflections*; otherwise it's *English 101* (Sunday and Wednesday) or *Let's Learn Chinese* on the remaining days. One hour to Southeast Asia on 7445 kHz. Some of these programs are also carried by Radio Taipei International.

Radio Australia. *World News*, then weekdays it's *Asia Pacific*, a sports bulletin on the half-hour, and *Countrywide* five minutes later. Weekends, the news is followed by Saturday's *Fine Music Australia* and *Book Reading*, or Sunday's *Jazz Notes* and *Week's End*. Continuous to East Asia and the Pacific on 6080, 9580 and 9770 kHz; and easily heard in much of North America on 9580 kHz.

Radio Bulgaria. Summers only at this time. *News*, then Monday through Thursday there's 15 minutes of current events in *Today*. This is replaced Friday by *Weekly Spotlight*, a summary of the week's major political events. The remainder of the broadcast is given over to features dealing with Bulgaria and its people, plus some lively folk music. Sixty minutes to Europe on 15175 and 17585 kHz. One hour later during winter.

HCJB—Voice of the Andes, Ecuador. First 60 minutes of a five-hour block of religious programming to the Americas on 12005 and 15115 kHz.

Voice of America. A mixed bag of sports, science, business and other news and features. To East Asia on 6110 (or 6160), 9760, 11705 (winter) and 15160 kHz, and to Australasia on 5985 (or 9770), 9645, 11720 and 15425 kHz.

Radio Jordan. Summers only at this time. A 60-minute partial relay of the station's domestic broadcasts, beamed to Europe and eastern North America on 11970 kHz. One hour later in winter.

Voice of Vietnam. Repeat of the 1000 broadcast. A half hour to Asia on 7285 and 9730 kHz. Both frequencies vary somewhat.

Radio Singapore International. A three-hour package for Southeast Asia, and widely heard beyond. Starts with nine minutes of *news* (five at weekends), then Monday through Friday there's *Business and Market Report*, replaced Saturday by *Asia Below the Headlines*, and Sunday by *The Film Programme*. These are followed on the quarter-hour by *Arts Arena* (Mon-

day), *Profile* (Tuesday), and *Star Trax* (Wednesday). A self-denominated lifestyle magazine—*Living*—pairs up with *Afterthought* on Thursday, and the eclectic and informative *Frontiers* fills the Friday slot. Weekends, look for *Regional Press Review* (1120 Saturday) and *Business World* (1115 Sunday). There's a daily 5-minute news bulletin on the half-hour, then one or more short features. Weekdays, take your pick from *Wired Up* (Internet, Monday), *Vox Box* (a radio soapbox, Tuesday), *Reflections* (musings, Wednesday), *The Film Programme* (Thursday), and *The Written Word* (Friday). The hour is rounded off with the 15-minute *Newsline*. Saturday fare consists of *Eco-Watch*, *Comment* and *Business World*; Sunday, there's *Frontiers* and *Regional Press Review*. On 6015 and 6150 kHz.

CBC North-Québec, Canada. Summers only at this time; see 1200 for specifics. Intended for a domestic audience, but also heard in the northeastern United States on 9625 kHz.

Swiss Radio International. Thirty minutes of *news* and background reports on world and Swiss events. Look for some lighter fare on Saturdays, when *Capital Letters* (a biweekly listener-response program) alternates with *Name Game* and *Sounds Good*. To Europe winters on 6165 and 9535 kHz, and year round to East and Southeast Asia on any two channels from 9810, 9885, 12075 and 13635 kHz.

Radio Japan. On weekdays, opens with *Radio Japan News Round*, with news oriented to Japanese and Asian affairs. This is followed by *Radio Japan Magazine Hour*, which includes features like *Sports Column* (Monday), *Japanese Culture* and *Today* (Tuesday), *Asian Report* (Wednesday), *Crosscurrents* (Thursday) and *Business Focus* (Friday). *Commentary* and *News* round off the hour. These are replaced Saturday by *This Week*, and Sunday by *Hello from Tokyo*. One hour to North

America on 6120 kHz, and to East and Southeast Asia on 6090 (winter), 9610 (summer) and 15350 kHz.

Radio Pyongyang, North Korea. One of the last of the old-time communist stations, with quaint terms like "Great Leader" and "Unrivaled Great Man" being the order of the day. Starts with *"news,"* with much of the remainder of the broadcast devoted to revering the late Kim Il Sung. Abominably bad programs, but worth the occasional listen just to hear how awful they are. Fifty minutes to North America on 6575, 9975 and 11335 kHz.

WJCR, Upton, Kentucky. Continues with country gospel music to North America on 7490 kHz. Other U.S. religious broadcasters operating at this hour include **WWCR** on 5935 (or 15685) kHz, **KTBN** on 7510 kHz, **WYFR—Family Radio** on 5950 and 7355 (or 11830) kHz, and **WHRI—World Harvest Radio** on 6040 and 9495 kHz. Traditional Catholic programming (some of which may be in Spanish) can be found on **WEWN** on 7425 kHz.

11:30

Radio Korea International, South Korea. Winters only at this time. See 1030 for program details. A half hour on 9650 kHz via their Canadian relay, so a good chance for North Americans to hear the station. One hour earlier in summer.

■Radio Netherlands. *News,* then Monday through Saturday it's ●*Newsline* followed by a feature. Pick of the pack are ●*Research File* (science, Monday); ●*A Good Life* (Friday); ●*Weekend* (Saturday) and Wednesday's award-winning ●*Documentary.* On the remaining days, you can hear *Music 52-15* (Tuesday) and *Media Network* (Thursday). Sunday fare consists of *Sincerely Yours* (a listener-response program) and *Sounds Interesting.* One hour to western Europe, winters on

Little monk in Nepal.   M. Guha

5975 (or 7190) and 6045 kHz, and summers on 6045 and 9860 kHz.

Radio Prague, Czech Republic. Winters only at this time. *News,* then Monday through Friday there's *Current Affairs,* followed by one or more features. Early in the week, take your pick from Monday's *Magazine '99*; Tuesday's *Talking Point* and *Media Czech*; and Wednesday's *The Arts* and *History Czech.* The Thursday lineup is *Economic Report* and *I'd Like You to Meet...*; and Friday's slot is *Between You and Us.* Saturday's offering is a thoroughly enjoyable musical feature, replaced Sunday by *The Week in Politics*, *From the Weeklies* and *Media Czech.* A half hour to Europe on 7345 and 9505 kHz. One hour earlier in summer.

Radio Sweden. Summers only at this time; see 1230 for program details. To North America on 15235 (or 15240) and 17870 kHz.

Voice of the Islamic Republic of Iran. Sixty minutes of *news*, commentary and features, much of it reflecting the Islamic point of view. Targeted at the Mideast and South and Southeast Asia on 11745, 11790, 11875 (summer), 11930, 15260 and 11930 kHz.

1200-1759
Western Australia & East Asia—Evening Prime Time
North America—Morning
Europe & Mideast—Afternoon and Early Evening

12:00

■**BBC World Service for the Americas, Europe and the Mideast.** *World News*, then Monday through Saturday there's 10 minutes of specialized business and financial reporting. Weekdays at 1215, you can hear the informative ●*Britain Today*, replaced Saturday by *A Jolly Good Show*, and Sunday by *In Praise of God*. Most tempting of the features on the half-hour are Monday's *Seven Days* and Tuesday's ●*Health Matters*. ●*Sports Roundup* follows at 45 minutes past the hour, except for Saturday, when it is replaced by ●*Short Story*. Continuous to North America and the Caribbean on 5965 (winter), 6195, 9515 and 15220 kHz. Weekdays, for the first 15 minutes, 6195 and 15220 kHz carry alternative programming for the Caribbean. In Europe, tune to 9410, 12095, 15565 or 17640 kHz; and in the Mideast, 11760, 15565 or 15575 kHz.

■**BBC World Service for Asia and the Pacific.** Monday through Saturday, opens with *World News* and ●*World Business Report/Review*. Weekdays, these are followed by ●*Britain Today*, ●*Off the Shelf* (readings of world literature) and ●*Sports Roundup*. At 1230 Saturday, from September to December, there's ●*Brain of Britain*, arguably one of the best quizzes anywhere. Continuous to East Asia on 7235 (winter), 9580, 9740, 11955 and (summer) 15280 kHz; to Southeast Asia on 6195, 9740 and (winter) 11955 and 15310 kHz; and to Australasia on 9740 kHz. Also audible in western North America on 9740 kHz.

Radio Canada International. Summer weekdays only. Monday through Friday, there's two hours of the Canadian Broadcasting Corporation's domestic news program *This Morning*, which is replaced Saturday by *The House* (current events), and Sunday by ●*Quirks and Quarks* (science). To North America and the Caribbean on 9640, 11855 and 13650 kHz. One hour later in winter.

Radio Tashkent, Uzbekistan. *News* and commentary, followed by features such as *Life in the Village* (Wednesday), a listeners' request program (Monday), and local music (Thursday). Heard better in Asia, Australasia and Europe than in North America. Thirty minutes winters on 5060, 5975, 6025 and 9715 kHz; and summers on 7285, 9715, 15295 and 17775 kHz.

■**Radio France Internationale.** The first 30 minutes are made up of *news* and correspondents' reports, with a review of the French press rounding off the half hour. The next 25 minutes are given over to a series of short features, including Sunday's *Paris Promenade* and *Club 9516* (a listener-response program); the weekday *RFI Europe*; sports (Monday and Thursday); *Arts in France*, *Books* and *Science Probe* (Tuesday); *Bottom Line* (business and finance) and *Land of France* (Wednesday); the biweekly *North/South* (or *Planet Earth*) and *The Americas* (Thursday); *Film Reel* and *Made in France* (Friday); and Saturday's *Focus on France*, *Spotlight on Africa* and *Counterpoint* (human rights) or *Echoes from Africa*. A fast-moving information-packed 55 minutes to Europe on 9805, 15155 and 15195 kHz; and to North America on 13625 (15530 in summer) and 17575 kHz. In eastern North America you can also try 15540 kHz, targeted at West

Africa. Also available to Southeast Asia and parts of Australasia on 11600 kHz.

Radio Bulgaria. This time winters only; see 1100 for specifics. Sixty minutes to Europe on 15130 and 15290 kHz. One hour earlier in summer.

Polish Radio Warsaw, Poland. This time summers only. Fifty-five minutes of news, commentary, features and music—all with a Polish accent. Monday through Friday, it's *News from Poland*—a potpourri of news, reports and interviews. This is followed by *Jazz, Folk, Rock and Pop from Poland* (Monday), *Request Concert* and *A Day in the Life of...* (Tuesday), classical music and the historical *Flashback* (Wednesday), a communications feature and *Letter from Poland* (Thursday), and a Friday feature followed by *Business Week*. The Saturday broadcast begins with a bulletin of *news*, then there's *Weekend Papers* (a press review), *What We Said* (a summary of the station's output during the previous week) and an arts magazine, *Focus*. Sundays, you can hear *Weekend Commentary*, *Panorama* (a window on day-to-day life in Poland) and *Postbag*, a listener-response program. To Europe on 6095, 7145, 7270, 9525 and 11815 kHz. This last frequency can be heard weekends in the northeastern United States and southeastern Canada, when the broadcast is not subject to co-channel interference from the Radio Exterior de España relay in Costa Rica. One hour later in winter.

Poland's economy has soared since the fall of communism. Its progress is followed on Polish Radio Warsaw's "Business Week."

Radio Australia. *World News*, then Monday through Thursday it's *Late Night Live* (round-table discussion). On the remaining days you can listen to a relay of the domestic Radio National service. Continuous to the Pacific on 5995, 6020 and 9580 kHz; and well heard in much of North America on 5995 and 9580 kHz.

Radio Canada International. *News*, followed Monday through Friday by *Spectrum* (topical events). Saturday features the environmental *Earth Watch*, and *The Mailbag* occupies the Sunday slot. Thirty minutes to East and Southeast Asia, winters on 6150 and 11730 kHz, and summers on 9660 and 15195 kHz.

Radio Jordan. Winters only at this time. A 60-minute partial relay of the station's domestic broadcasts, beamed to Europe and eastern North America on 11970 (or 11940) kHz. One hour earlier in summer.

Swiss Radio International. Summers only at this time. Repeat of the 1000 broadcast; see there for specifics. To Europe on 6165 and 9535 kHz. One hour later in winter.

Radio Korea International, South Korea. Opens with *news* and commentary, followed Monday through Wednesday by *Seoul Calling*. Weekly features include *Echoes of Korean Music* and *Shortwave Feedback* (Sunday), *Tales from Korea's Past* (Monday), *Korean Cultural Trails* (Tuesday), *Pulse of Korea* (Wednesday), *From Us to You* (a listener-response program) and *Let's Learn Korean* (Thursday), *Let's Sing Together* and *Korea Through Foreigners' Eyes* (Friday), and Saturday's *Discovering Korea*, *Korean Literary Corner* and *Weekly News Focus*. Sixty minutes to East Asia on 7285 kHz.

CBC North-Québec, Canada. Part of an 18-hour multilingual broadcast for a domestic audience, but which is also heard in the northeastern United States. Weekend programming at this hour is in English, and features *news* followed by the enjoyably eclectic ●*Good Morning Québec* (Saturday) or *Fresh Air* (Sunday). Starts at this time winters, but summers it is already into the second hour. On 9625 kHz.

HCJB—Voice of the Andes, Ecuador. Continuous religious programming to North America on 12005 and 15115 kHz. Monday through Friday, there's the live— and lively—*Morning in the Mountains*.

Radio Norway International. Summer Sundays only. *Norway Now*, a friendly 30-minute package of *news* and features aimed at Europe on 9590 kHz, and East Asia on 13800 and 15305 kHz.

Radio Singapore International. Continuous programming to Southeast Asia and beyond. Starts with five minutes of *news*, a weather report, and either the weekday *Front Page* (headlines from local and regional dailies) or instrumental music (Saturday and Sunday). Weekdays, the next 20 minutes are devoted to music. Take your pick from *E-Z Beat* (Monday and Tuesday), *Classic Gold* (Wednesday and Friday) and *Love Songs* on Thursday. There are two Saturday slots, *Star Trax* and *Currencies*, replaced Sunday by *Comment* and *Profile*. On the half-hour, it's either the weekday *Business and Market Report* or a five-minute news bulletin. The next 25 minutes are given over to features. Monday, it's *The Written Word* and *Business World*; Tuesday, there's *Living* and *Asia Below the Headlines*; and Wednesday's

pairing is *Wired Up* and *Frontiers*. Thursday's offerings are *Vox Box* and *Arts Arena*; and Friday brings *Reflections* and *Profile*. Weekends are devoted to repeats of shows aired earlier in the week— Saturday's features are *Arts Arena* and *Wired Up*; and Sunday's lineup is *Living*, *Snapshots*, *Afterthought* and *Currencies*. On 6015 and 6150 kHz.

Radio Taipei International, Taiwan. The broadcast opens with 15 minutes of *News*, and closes with a quarter-hour of *Let's Learn Chinese*, which has a series of segments for beginning, intermediate and advanced learners. In between, you can take your pick from *Jade Bells and Bamboo Pipes* (Monday), *People* and *Trends* (Tuesday), *Taiwan Today* and *Miss Mook's Big Countdown* (Wednesday), *Treasures of the Orient* and *Hot Spots* (Thursday), *Taipei Magazine* and *Life on the Outside* (Friday), *Kaleidoscope* and *Reflections* (Saturday) and *Food, Poetry and Others* followed by *Mailbag Time* on Sunday. Formerly the "Voice of Free China," this station has gone through a metamorphosis few would have dared to predict. One hour to East Asia on 7130 kHz, and to Australasia on 9610 kHz.

Voice of America. A mixed bag of current events, sports, science, business and other news and features. To East Asia on 6110 (or 6160), 9760, 11715, 11705 (winter) and 15160 kHz; and to Australasia on 9645, 11715 and 15425 kHz.

China Radio International. *News* and a variety of features—see 0900 for specifics. One hour to Southeast Asia on 9715 and 11660 kHz; and to Australasia on 6950 and 7385 kHz. May also be available on 9945, 11675 and 11980 kHz or other test frequencies.

Radio Nacional do Brasil (Radiobras), Brazil. Monday through Saturday, you can hear *Life in Brazil* or *Brazilian Panorama*, a potpourri of news, facts and figures about this South American giant, garnished with samples of some of the country's many musical styles. The *Sunday Special*, on the other hand, is devoted to one particular theme, and often contains lots of exotic Brazilian music. In recent months, the station's audio quality has tended to deteriorate and some of the shows are reruns from earlier years. Eighty minutes to North America on 15445 kHz.

WJCR, Upton, Kentucky. Continues with country gospel music to North America on 7490 kHz. Other U.S. religious broadcasters operating at this hour include **WWCR** on 5935 (or 13845) and 15685 kHz, **KTBN** on 7510 kHz, **WYFR—Family Radio** on 5950, 6015 (or 7355), 11830 and 11970 (or 17750) kHz, and **WHRI—World Harvest Radio** on 6040 and 9495 kHz. For traditional Catholic programming, tune **WEWN** on 7425 kHz.

12:15

Voice of Mongolia. Actually starts at 1210. Most days, it's *news*, reports and short features, all with a local flavor. The programs provide an interesting insight into the life and culture of a nation largely unknown to the rest of the world. The entire Sunday broadcast is devoted to exotic Mongolian music. Thirty minutes to Australasia on 12085 kHz.

Radio Cairo, Egypt. The start of a 75-minute package of news, religion, culture and entertainment, much of it devoted to Arab and Islamic themes. The initial quarter hour consists of virtually anything, from quizzes to Islamic religious talks, then there's *news* and commentary, which in turn give way to political and cultural items. To Asia on 17595 kHz.

12:30

Radio Austria International. Summers only at this time. ●*Report from Austria*, a compilation of national and regional news,

current events and human interest stories. Thirty minutes to Europe on 6155 and 13730 kHz, with the latter frequency also available for eastern North America. One hour later in winter.

Radio Bangladesh. *News*, followed by Islamic and general interest features and pleasant Bengali music. Thirty minutes to Southeast Asia, also heard in Europe, on 7185 and 9550 kHz. Frequencies may vary slightly.

■**Radio Netherlands.** Winters only at this time. The second of two hours for European listeners. *News*, followed Monday through Saturday by ●*Newsline*, then a feature. Highly recommended listening, with the best being ●*A Good Life* (Tuesday), ●*Research File* (science, Thursday), ●*Roughly Speaking* (a youth program, Saturday) and Friday's ●*Documentary*. Other offerings include *Aural Tapestry* (Monday), *Sounds Interesting* (Wednesday) and Sunday's *Siren Song*. On 6045 and 5975 (or 7190) kHz.

Radio Vlaanderen Internationaal, Belgium. Summers only at this time. *News*, then *Press Review* (except Sunday), followed Monday through Friday by *Belgium Today* (various topics) and features like *The Arts* (Monday and Thursday, *Tourism* (Monday), *Focus on Europe* (Tuesday), *Living in Belgium* and *Green Society* (Wednesday), *Around Town* (Thursday), and *Economics* and *International Report*(Friday). Weekend features consist of Saturday's *Music from Flanders* and Sunday's *P.O. Box 26* (a listener-response program) and *Radio World*. Twenty-five minutes to North America on 15545 kHz.

YLE Radio Finland. Summer Sundays only at this hour. *Compass North* and *Capital Café*—Finnish news and general interest stories. Thirty minutes to North America on 11900 and 15400 kHz. One hour later in winter.

Voice of Vietnam. Repeat of the 1000 transmission. A half hour to Asia on 9840 and 12020 (or 15010) kHz. Frequencies may vary slightly.

Radio Thailand. Thirty minutes of *news* and short features. To Southeast Asia and Australasia, winters on 9810 kHz, and summers on 9885 kHz.

Voice of Turkey. This time summers only. Fifty minutes of *news*, features and Turkish music beamed to Europe on 15290 kHz. One hour later in winter.

Radio Sweden. Monday through Friday, it's *news* and features in *Sixty Degrees North*, concentrating heavily on Scandinavian topics. Monday's accent is on sports; Tuesday has electronic media news; Wednesday, there's *Money Matters*; Thursday features ecology or science and technology; and Friday offers a review of the week's news. Saturday's slot is filled by *Spectrum* (arts) or *Sweden Today*, and Sunday fare consists of *In Touch with Stockholm* (a listener-response program) or the musical *Sounds Nordic*. A half hour winters to North America on 11650 (or 13740) and 15240 kHz; and summers to Asia and Australasia on 13740 and 15240 kHz.

Radio Korea International, South Korea. Starts off with *news*, followed Monday through Wednesday by *Economic News Briefs*. The remainder of the broadcast is taken up by a feature: *Shortwave Feedback* (Sunday), *Seoul Calling* (Monday and Tuesday), *Pulse of Korea* (Wednesday), *From Us to You* (Thursday), *Let's Sing Together* (Friday) and *Weekly News Focus* (Saturday). Thirty minutes to East and Southeast Asia on 6055, 9570, 9640 and 13670 kHz.

Voice of Greece. Summers only at this time, and actually starts around 1235. Several minutes of English news surrounded by a lengthy period of Greek music and programming. To North America on 15175 and 15650 kHz. One hour later during winter.

13:00

■BBC World Service for the Americas, Europe and the Mideast.
●*Newshour*—there are none better! Sixty minutes to North America and the Caribbean on 5965 (winter), 6195, 9515, 9590 (winter), 11865 (summer) and 15220 kHz; to Europe on 9410, 12095, 15565 and 17640 kHz; and to the Mideast on 11760, 15565 and 15575 kHz.

■BBC World Service for Asia and the Pacific. Same as for Europe and the Americas. Broadcast worldwide at this hour, it's too good to miss. To East Asia on 5990 and 9740 kHz; to Southeast Asia on 6195, 9740 and (winter) 11955 and 15310 kHz; and to Australasia on 9740 kHz. Also audible in western North America on 9740 kHz.

Radio Canada International. Tuesday through Saturday winters, there's news and current events. This is replaced Sunday by ●*Quirks and Quarks*, and Monday by comedy and *The Inside Track*. In summer, it's news-related fare, and weekdays only. Sixty minutes to North America and the Caribbean on 9640, 11855 and (summer) 13650 kHz. For an additional service, see the next item.

Radio Canada International. Summers only at this time; see 1400 for program details. Sunday only to North America and the Caribbean on 11855 and 13650 kHz.

Radio Pyongyang, North Korea. Repeat of the 1100 transmission. Fifty minutes to Europe on 9345 and 11740 kHz, to North America on 13760 and 15230 kHz, and to South and Southeast Asia on 9640 and 15230 kHz.

Swiss Radio International. Repeat of the 1100 broadcast. *Newsnet*—a workmanlike compilation of news and background reports on world and Swiss events. Somewhat lighter fare on Saturday, when the biweekly *Capital Letters* (a listener-response program) alternates with *Name Game* and *Sounds Good*. Thirty winter minutes to Europe on 6165 and 9535 kHz, and one hour earlier in summer. This and an additional half hour of programming can be heard year round in East and Southeast Asia on 7230 and 7480 kHz.

Radio Norway International. Sundays only. *Norway Now*. A friendly half hour of *news* and human-interest stories, winters to Europe on 9590 kHz, to East Asia on 7315 (or 11850) kHz, and to Southeast Asia and Western Australia on 15605 kHz; in summer, the broadcast is aimed at eastern North America on 15340 kHz, and at Southeast Asia and Western Australia on 13800 kHz.

Radio Nacional do Brasil (Radiobras), Brazil. The final 20 minutes of the broadcast beamed to North America on 15445 kHz.

Radio Vlaanderen Internationaal, Belgium. Winters only at this time. *News*, then *Press Review* (except Sunday), followed Monday through Friday by *Belgium Today* (various topics) and features like *The Arts* (Monday and Thursday, *Tourism* (Monday), *Focus on Europe* (Tuesday), *Living in Belgium* and *Green Society* (Wednesday), *Around Town* (Thursday), and *Economics* and *International Report*(Friday). Weekend features consist of Saturday's *Music from Flanders* and Sunday's *P.O. Box 26* (a listener-response program) and *Radio World*. Twenty-five minutes to North America on 13680 kHz.

China Radio International. See 0900 for specifics. One hour to western North America summers on 7405 kHz; and year-round to Southeast Asia on 11660 and 11980 kHz; also available to Australasia on 7385, 9945 and 11675 kHz. Except for 7385, 7405 and 11660 kHz, these are test frequencies and may be subject to change.

Polish Radio Warsaw, Poland. This time winters only. *News*, commentary, music and a variety of features. See 1200 for specifics. Fifty-five minutes to Europe on 6095, 7145, 7270, 9525 and 11815 kHz. Listeners in southeastern Canada and the northeastern United States can also try 11815 kHz, especially weekends, when co-channel Radio Exterior de España is off the air. One hour earlier during summer.

Radio Prague, Czech Republic. Summers only at this time. *News*, then Monday through Friday there's *Current Affairs*. These are followed by one or more features. Monday's offering is *Magazine '99*; Tuesday, it's *Talking Point* and *Media Czech*; Wednesday's pairing is *The Arts* and *History Czech*; Thursday brings *Economic Report* and *I'd Like You to Meet...*; and Friday's slot is *Between You and Us*. On Saturday, make the most of a thoroughly enjoyable musical feature, which alternates between classical, folk and jazz. The Sunday lineup consists of *The Week in Politics*, *From the Weeklies* and *Media Czech*. Thirty minutes to East Africa and the Mideast on 21745 kHz, and to South and Southeast Asia on 13580 kHz.

Radio Cairo, Egypt. The final half-hour of the 1215 broadcast, consisting of listener participation programs, Arabic language lessons and a summary of the latest news. To Asia on 17595 kHz.

CBC North-Québec, Canada. Continues with multilingual programming for a domestic audience. *News*, then winter Saturdays it's the second hour of ●*Good Morning Québec*, replaced Sunday by *Fresh Air*. In summer, the news is followed by *The House* (Canadian politics, Saturday) or the highly professional ●*Sunday Morning*. Weekday programs are mainly in languages other than English. Audible in the northeastern United States on 9625 kHz.

Radio Romania International. First afternoon broadcast for European listen-

World band expert Simo Soininen visits Finland's Yleisradio.   S. Soininen

ers. *News*, commentary, press review, and features about Romanian life and culture, interspersed with some lively Romanian folk music. Fifty-five minutes winters on 11940, 15390 and 17745 kHz; summers on 9690, 11940, 15365 and 17720 kHz.

Radio Australia. Monday through Friday, there's a quarter-hour of *news* followed by 45 minutes of World Music in ●*The Planet*. Weekends, after five minutes of *news*, look for a relay of the domestic ABC Radio National service. Continuous programming to the Pacific on 5995, 6020 and 9580 kHz; and easily audible in much of North America on the last two frequencies.

Radio Singapore International. The third and final hour of a daily broadcasting package to Southeast Asia and beyond. Starts with a five-minute bulletin of the latest *news*, then most days it's music: *Singapop* (local talent, Monday and Thursday); *Music and Memories* (nostalgia,

Tuesday); *Spin the Globe* (world music, Wednesday and Saturday); and *Hot Trax* (new releases, Saturday). *Friends of the Airwaves*, a listener-participation show, occupies the Sunday slot. There's more news on the half-hour, then a short feature. Monday's offering is *Snapshots*, replaced Tuesday by *Afterthought*. Wednesday and Thursday feature *Eco-Watch*, with the Thursday edition repeated the following Wednesday. The rest of the lineup consists of *Comment* (Friday), *The Written Word* (Saturday) and Sunday's *Reflections*. Weekdays, these are followed by *Newsline*, replaced Saturday by *Regional Press Review*, and Sunday by *Vox Box*. The broadcast ends with yet another five-minute news update. On 6015 and 6150 kHz.

WJCR, Upton, Kentucky. Continues with country gospel music to North America on 7490 kHz. Other U.S. religious broadcasters operating at this hour include **WWCR** on 5935 (or 13845) and 15685 kHz, **KTBN** 7510 kHz, **WYFR—Family Radio** on 5950, 6015 (or 9705), 11830 and 11970 (or 17750) kHz, and **WHRI—World Harvest Radio** on 6040 and 15105 kHz. Traditional Catholic programming is available via **WEWN** on 7425 kHz.

HCJB—Voice of the Andes, Ecuador. Sixty minutes of religious broadcasting. Look for the live *Morning in the Mountains* at 1330 weekends. Continuous to the Americas on 12005 and 15115 kHz.

Channel Africa, South Africa. Weekends only at this time. The first half of a two-hour broadcast to Africa which is widely heard outside the continent. To southern Africa on 9445 kHz; to West Africa on 17675 kHz; and to East Africa on 17870 kHz. Best for distant listeners are 17675 and 17870 kHz.

FEBC Radio International, Philippines. The first 60 minutes of a three-hour (mostly religious) package to South and Southeast Asia. Weekdays, starts with *Good Evening Asia,* which includes *News Insight* and a number of five-minute features (world band enthusiasts should look for Wednesday's *DX Dial*). Other offerings include *World News Update* (1330 Monday through Saturday) and *News from the Philippines* (1335 weekdays). Most of the remaining features are religious in nature. On 11995 kHz.

Voice of America. A mix of current events and sports, science, business and other news and features. To East Asia on 6110 (or 6160), 9760, 11705 (winter) and 15160 kHz; and to Australasia on 9645 and 15425 kHz. Both areas are also served by 11715 kHz until 1330.

> Listeners in Europe and beyond can try Channel Africa weekdays on 17675 and 17870 kHz.

13:30

United Arab Emirates Radio, Dubai. *News,* then a feature devoted to Arab and Islamic history and culture. Twenty minutes to Europe (also audible in eastern North America) on 13675, 15395, 17630 and 21605 kHz.

Radio Austria International. Winters only at this time. ●*Report from Austria* (see 1230 for more details). Thirty minutes to Europe on 6155 and 13730 kHz, and to eastern North America on 13730 kHz. One hour earlier in summer.

Voice of Turkey. This time winters only. *News,* followed by *Review of the Turkish Press* and features (some of them arcane) with a strong local flavor. Selections of Turkish popular and classical music complete the program. Fifty minutes to Europe on 15290 kHz, and to the Mideast, Southeast Asia and Australasia on 9630 kHz. One hour earlier in summer.

Radio Yugoslavia. Winters only at this time. *News* and short background reports with a strong local flavor. Worth a listen if you are interested in the region. Thirty minutes to Australasia on 11835 kHz.

YLE Radio Finland. Winter Sundays only at this hour; see 1230 for program specifics. Thirty minutes to North America on 11735 and 15400 kHz. One hour earlier in summer.

Radio Canada International. *News*, followed Monday through Friday by *Spectrum* (topical events), Saturday by *Venture Canada*, and Sunday by a listener-response program. To East Asia on 6150 (winter), 9535, and (summer) 11795 kHz. Also to Europe, the Mideast and Africa, summers only, on 11935, 15325, 17820 and 21455 kHz. The frequency of 17820 kHz is not available on Sundays.

■**Radio Netherlands.** *News*, then Monday through Saturday it's ●*Newsline* and a feature. Pick of an excellent pack are ●*Research File* (science, Monday); ●*A Good Life* (Friday); ●*Weekend* (Saturday) and Wednesday's award-winning ●*Documentary*. *Music 52-15* (Tuesday) and *Media Network* (Thursday) complete the lineup. Sunday fare consists of *Sincerely Yours* (a listener-response program) and *Sounds Interesting*. Aimed at South Asia, winters on 9895, 13700 (also well heard in the Mideast) and 15585 kHz; and summers on 9890 and 15585 kHz.

Radio Sweden. See 1230 for program details. Thirty minutes to North America summers on 15240 kHz, and winters to Asia and Australasia on 9705 and 13740 kHz.

Voice of Vietnam. Begins with *news*, then there's *Commentary* or *Weekly Review*, followed by short features and some pleasant Vietnamese music (especially at weekends). A half hour to East Asia on 9840 and 12020 (or 15010) kHz. Also audible in parts of North America, especially during summer.

Voice of Greece. Winters only at this time, and actually starts around 1335.

Several minutes of English news, surrounded by lots of Greek music and programming. To North America on 9420 and 15650 kHz. One hour earlier during summer.

All India Radio. The first half-hour of a 90-minute package of exotic Indian music, regional and international *news*, commentary, and a variety of talks and features of general interest. To Southeast Asia and beyond on 9545, 11620 and 13710 kHz.

Radio Tashkent, Uzbekistan. *News* and commentary, then features. Look for an information and music program on Tuesdays, with more music on Sundays. Apart from Wednesday's *Business Club*, most other features are broadcast on a non-weekly basis. Heard in Asia, Australasia, Europe and occasionally in North America; winters on 5060, 5975, 6025 and 9715 kHz; and summers on 7285, 9715, 15295 and 17775 kHz.

13:45

Vatican Radio. Twenty minutes of religious and secular programming to Southeast Asia and Australasia on 9500, 11625 and 13765 (or 15585) kHz.

14:00

■**BBC World Service for the Americas, Europe and the Mideast.** *World News*, then Monday through Friday it's ●*Outlook*—still a favorite with listeners after more than three decades. The second half hour is devoted to a youth-oriented audience, with *Megamix* occupying the Wednesday slot, and *Multitrack* on Tuesday, Thursday and Friday. Weekend programming consists of Saturday's *Sportsworld* and a Sunday feature. Continuous to North America and the Caribbean on 9515, 9590 (winter), 11865 (summer), 15220 and 17840 kHz; to Europe on 9410, 12095, 15565 and 17640 kHz; and to the Mideast on 12095 (winter), 15565 and 15575 kHz.

■BBC World Service for Asia and the Pacific. Similar to the service for Europe and the Americas, but with different features on the half-hour, Monday through Friday. Regular shows include ●*Discovery* (Tuesday), ●*Sports International* (Wednesday), ●*Assignment* (Thursday) and Friday's ●*Science in Action*. Continuous to East Asia on 5990 and 9740 kHz; to Southeast Asia on 6195, 9740 and (summer) 15310 kHz; and to Australasia on 9740 kHz. Also audible in western North America on 9740 kHz.

Radio Japan. Repeat of the 0600 broadcast; see there for specifics. One hour to western North America on 9535 and 11705 kHz, and to Asia on 6090 (winter), 9610 (summer), 9695 (winter), 11895 and (summer) 11915 kHz.

■Radio France Internationale. *News*, press reviews and correspondents' reports, with emphasis on events in Asia and the Mideast. These are followed, on the half-hour, by two or more short features (see the 1200 broadcast for specifics, although there may be one or two minor alterations). Fifty-five minutes of interesting and well-produced programming to the Mideast and beyond on 17560 kHz, and to South and Southeast Asia winters on 7110 and 12030 kHz, replaced summers by 11910 and 15405 kHz. Listeners in western parts of Australia should also get reasonable reception on 12030/15405 kHz.

Voice of Russia World Service. Summers only at this time. Eleven minutes of *News*, followed Monday through Saturday by much of the same in *News and Views*. Making up the list is *Sunday Panorama*. On the half-hour, the lineup includes some of the station's better entertainment features. Try Monday's ●*Folk Box*, Tuesday's ●*Music at Your Request* and Friday's retrospective

●*Moscow Yesterday and Today*, all of which should please. For different tastes, there's *Jazz Show* (Wednesday), *Kaleidoscope* (Sunday) and Thursday's *Yours for the Asking*. Mainly to the Mideast and West Asia at this hour. Try 4730, 4940 and 4975 kHz, plus frequencies in the 11 and 15 MHz world band segments.

Radio Australia. Begins some days with *World News*, and the rest of the time it's a relay of domestic ABC Radio National programming. Continuous to the Pacific on 5995 and 9580 kHz (both channels are also widely heard in North America, especially to the west). Additionally available to East and Southeast Asia from 1430 on 9500 and 11660 kHz (may also be heard in Europe).

Radio Prague, Czech Republic. Winters only at this time. See 1300 for program specifics. A half hour to eastern North America, South Asia and Australasia on 13580 kHz, and to East Africa and beyond on 21700 kHz.

Voice of America. This time winters only. The first of several hours of continuous programming to the Mideast. *News*, current events and short features covering sports, science, business, entertainment and other topics. On 15205 kHz.

XERMX—Radio México Internacional. Summers only at this time. Monday through Friday, there's a summary of the Spanish-language *Antena Radio*, replaced Saturday by *The Sounds of Mexico*, and Sunday by *Mirror of Mexico*. On the half-hour, look for 30 minutes of musical programming. Best heard in western and southern parts of the United States on 5985 and 9705 kHz. One hour later in winter.

Kol Israel. Summers only at this time. A 30-minute relay from Israel Radio's domestic network. To Europe and eastern North America on 15650 and 17535 kHz. One hour later in winter.

China Radio International. *News* and commentary, followed Tuesday through Friday by *Current Affairs.* These are followed by various feature programs. Sundays, look for *Cultural Information, Snapshots, Report from Developing Countries, Song of the Week* and *Listeners' Letterbox*; Mondays, you can hear *Open Windows* and *Let's Learn Chinese*; Tuesdays, there's *Orient Arena* and *Voices from Other Lands*; Wednesday, it's *Profile* and another chance to *Learn to Speak Chinese*; Thursday brings *Focus* and *Cultural Spectrum*; while Friday's features are *Life in China* and *Global Review.* To round off the week, the Saturday menu consists of *Asia-Pacific News, Chinese Folk Tales, Cooking Show, China Scrapbook* and ●*Music from China.* One hour to North America on 7405 kHz. Also available to South Asia and beyond on 7260, 9535, 9700 and 11825 kHz (some of which are test frequencies and subject to change).

All India Radio. The final hour of a 90-minute package of regional and international *news*, commentary, features and exotic Subcontinental music. To Southeast Asia and beyond on 9545, 11620 and 13710 kHz.

Radio Canada International. *News* and the Canadian Broadcasting Corporation's popular ●*Sunday Morning.* A three-hour broadcast starting at 1400 winters, and 1300 summers. Sunday only to North America and the Caribbean on 9640 (winter), 11855 and (summer) 13650 kHz.

HCJB—Voice of the Andes, Ecuador. Another hour of religious fare to the Americas on 12005 and 15115 kHz.

CBC North-Québec, Canada. Continues with multilingual programming for a domestic audience. *News*, followed winter Saturdays by *The House* (Canadian politics). In summer, it's *The Great Eastern*, a magazine for Newfoundlanders. Sundays, there's the excellent ●*Sunday Morning.*

Weekday programs are in languages other than English. Audible in the northeastern United States on 9625 kHz.

Radio Jordan. Summers only at this time. A partial relay of the station's domestic broadcasts, beamed to Europe on 11970 kHz. Continuous till 1630, and one hour later in winter.

Channel Africa, South Africa. The final 55 minutes of a weekends-only broadcast to Africa which is widely heard outside that continent. To southern Africa on 9445 kHz; to West Africa on 17675 kHz; and to East Africa on 17870 kHz. Best for distant listeners are 17675 and 17870 kHz.

Voice of America. *News* and reports on a variety of topics. To East Asia on 6110 (or 6160), 9760, 11705 (winter) and 15160 kHz; and to Australasia on 15425 kHz.

FEBC Radio International, Philippines. Continues with mostly religious programming for South and Southeast Asia. For some secular fare, try *World News Update* (1430 Monday through Saturday) and *DX Dial* (for radio enthusiasts, 1440 Saturday). On 11995 kHz, and widely heard beyond the target areas.

Radio Thailand. Thirty minutes of *news* and short features for Southeast Asia and Australasia; winters on 9530 kHz, and summers on 9830 kHz.

WJCR, Upton, Kentucky. Continues with country gospel music to North America on 7490 kHz. Other U.S. religious broadcasters operating at this hour include **WWCR** on 13845 and 15685 kHz, **KTBN** on 7510 kHz, **WYFR—Family Radio** on 5950, 9705 (winter), 11830 and 17750 kHz, and **WHRI—World Harvest Radio** on 6040 and 15105 kHz. For traditional Catholic fare, try **WEWN** on 7425 kHz.

CFRX-CFRB, Toronto, Canada. Audible throughout much of the northeastern United States and southeastern Canada during the hours of daylight with a modest, but clear, signal on 6070 kHz. This pleasant, friendly station carries news, sports, weather and traffic reports—most of it intended for a local audience. Call in if you'd like at +1 (514) 790-0600—comments from outside Ontario are welcomed. Weekdays at this hour, you can hear *The Charles Adler Show*.

14:30

■**Radio Netherlands.** The second of two hours aimed at South Asia, but heard well beyond. *News*, followed Monday through Saturday by ●*Newsline*, then a feature. Choice selections include ●*A Good Life* (Tuesday), ●*Research File* (science, Thursday), ●*Roughly Speaking* (an award-winning youth program, Saturday) and Friday's ●*Documentary* (winner of several prestigious awards). Other offerings include *Aural Tapestry* (Monday), *Sounds Interesting* (Wednesday) and Sunday's *Siren Song*. Winters on 9895, 13700 and 15585 kHz; and summers on 9890 and 15585 kHz.

Radio Canada International. This time winters only. *News,* followed Monday through Friday by *Spectrum* (current events), Saturday by *Venture Canada* (business), and Sunday by *The Mailbag* (a listener-response program). Thirty minutes to Europe, the Mideast and Africa on 9555, 11915, 11935 and 15325 kHz. One hour earlier in summer.

Voice of Mongolia. *News*, reports and short features, with Sunday featuring lots of exotic Mongolian music. Thirty minutes to South and Southeast Asia on 9720 and 12085 kHz. Frequencies may vary slightly.

Radio Romania International. Fifty-five minutes of *news*, commentary, features and some enjoyable Romanian folk music. Targeted at the Mideast and South Asia winters on 11740, 11810 and 15335 kHz; an summers on 11775 and 15335 kHz.

Radio Sweden. Winters only at this time. Repeat of the 1330 broadcast; see 1230 for program specifics. *News* and features (sometimes on controversial subjects not often discussed on radio), with the accent strongly on Scandinavia. Thirty minutes to North America on 11650 and 15240 kHz, and to Asia and Australasia on 11880 kHz.

15:00

■**BBC World Service for the Americas, Europe and the Mideast.** *News*, followed Monday through Thursday by 10 minutes of ●*Sports Roundup* (replaced Friday by *Football Extra*). The remainder is a thoroughly mixed bag of programs—some of them forgettable—depending on the day of the week. Try the following, all on the half-hour: ●*The Greenfield Collection* (classical music, Tuesday), ●*Everywoman* (Wednesday), *The Vintage Chart Show* (Thursday) and ●*Science in Action* (Friday). Aficionados of classical music will not want to miss ●*Concert Hall* (or its substitute) at 1515 Sunday, while sports fans can tune in to the second hour of Saturday's live extravaganza, *Sportsworld*. Continuous to North America on 9515, 9590 (winter), 11865 (summer), 15220 and 17840 kHz; to Europe on 9410, 12095 and 15575 kHz; and to the Mideast on 12095 and 15575 kHz.

■**BBC World Service for South Asia.** A Sunday opportunity to hear the best in world theater—●*Play of the Week*. On other days, this frequency carries mainstream programming for Asia and the Pacific. On 6195 kHz.

■**BBC World Service for Asia and the Pacific.** Monday through Friday, it's a half hour of ●*East Asia Today* followed by 25 minutes of the long-running ●*Outlook* (three decades, and still going strong). The hour ends with a five-minute mini-feature. Weekends, look for Saturday's *Sportsworld*, replaced Sunday by a couple of music

The Royal School for employees of the king became Radio Nepal's first studio. It's now also used as the station's canteen and engineering office. M. Guha

features. Be warned—the music is sometimes pre-empted by live sports. Continuous to East Asia on 5990 and 9740 kHz; to Southeast Asia on 6195 and 9740 kHz; and to Australasia on 9740 kHz. The ubiquitous 9740 kHz can also be heard in western North America.

China Radio International. See 1400 for program details. One hour to western North America winters on 7405 kHz. One hour earlier during summer. Also available year-round to South Asia and beyond on 7160 and 9785 kHz.

Radio Australia. Continuous programming to Asia and the Pacific. At this hour there's a relay of the domestic ABC Radio National service. To the Pacific on 5995 and 9580 kHz (also well heard in western North America). Additionally available to East and Southeast Asia on 9500 and 11660 kHz (may also be heard in Europe).

Radio Pyongyang, North Korea. See 1100 for program details. Fifty minutes to Europe, the Mideast and beyond on 9325, 9640, 9975 and 13785 kHz.

Voice of America. Continues with programming to the Mideast. A mixed bag of current events and sports, science,

business and other news and features. Winters on 9575 and 15205 kHz, and summers on 9700 and 15205 kHz. Also heard in much of Europe.

Kol Israel. Winters only at this time. A 30-minute relay from Israel Radio's domestic network. To Europe and eastern North America on 9365 and 12080 kHz. One hour earlier in summer.

Radio Norway International. Winter Sundays only. *Norway Now. News* and features from and about Norway. A pleasant thirty minutes to the Mideast on 9520 and 11730 kHz.

Channel Africa, South Africa. Thirty minutes of news-related fare for East Africa on 9440 or 9445 kHz. Audible in parts of the Mideast.

Radio Canada International. Continuation of the CBC domestic program ●*Sunday Morning.* Sunday only to North America and the Caribbean on 9640 (winter), 11855 and (summer) 13650 kHz.

XERMX—Radio México Internacional. Winter weekdays, there's an English summary of the Spanish-language *Antena Radio*, replaced Saturday by *The Sounds of Mexico*, and Sunday by *Mirror of Mexico*. Summers, the lineup consists of *Universal Forum* (Monday and Friday), *Eternally Mexico* (Tuesday and Sunday) and *Mailbox* (Wednesday and Saturday). On Thursday, the English program is replaced by one in French. On the half-hour, look for 30 minutes of musical programming. Best heard in western and southern parts of the United States on 5985 and 9705 kHz.

Radio Japan. *News*, then weekdays there's 10 minutes of *Asian Top News* followed by a half-hour feature. Take your pick from *Profile* (Monday), *Enjoy Japanese* (Tuesday, repeated Thursday), *Town and Around* (Wednesday) and Friday's *Music and Book Beat*. Weekends, look for *Asia Weekly* (Saturday) or Sunday's *Hello from Tokyo*. The broadcasts end with the daily *Pop-in* (Sunday excepted) and a summary of *news*. To western North America on 9535 kHz; to Southern Africa on 15355 kHz; and to South and Southeast Asia winters on 7240 and 9695 kHz, and summers on 11880/11930 and 11915 kHz.

> **FEBC Radio International, Philippines, airs "World News Update" Monday through Saturday.**

Voice of Russia World Service. Predominantly news-related fare for the first half-hour, then a mixed bag, depending on the day and season. At 1531 winter, look for ●*Folk Box* (Monday), *Jazz Show* (Wednesday), *Yours for the Asking* (Thursday), ●*Music at Your Request* (Tuesday), the multifaceted *Kaleidoscope* (Sunday) and Friday's retrospective ●*Moscow Yesterday and Today*. Summers at this time, look for some listener favorites. Take your pick from *This is Russia* (Monday), ●*Moscow Yesterday and Today* (Tuesday's long look into history), ●*Audio Book Club* (dramatized reading, Wednesday) and Thursday's ●*Folk Box*. Weekend fare is split between Saturday's *Kaleidoscope* and Sunday's *Russian by Radio*. Continuous to the Mideast and West Asia on 4730, 4940 and 4975 kHz, as well as frequencies in other world band segments. Winters, dial around the 7 and 9 MHz ranges; in summer, 11 and 15 MHz should give better results.

FEBC Radio International, Philippines. The final 60 minutes of a three-hour (mostly religious) broadcast to South and Southeast Asia. For secular programming, try the five-minute *World News Update* at 1530 Monday through Saturday, and a listener-response feature at 1540 Saturday. On 11995 kHz, and often heard outside the target area.

WJCR, Upton, Kentucky. Continues with country gospel music to North America on 7490 and 13595 kHz. Other U.S. religious broadcasters operating at this hour include **WWCR** on 13845 and 15685 kHz, **KTBN** on 7510 (or 15590) kHz, and **WYFR—Family Radio** on 11830 and (winter) 15215 kHz. Traditional Catholic programming is available from **WEWN** on 7425 kHz.

Radio Jordan. A partial relay of the station's domestic broadcasts, beamed to Europe on 11690 kHz. Continuous till 1730, and one hour earlier in summer.

CFRX-CFRB, Toronto, Canada. See 1400. Monday through Friday, it's a continuation of *The Charles Adler Show*. Look for *News and Commentary* summers at 1550. Weekend fare consists of *The CFRB Gardening Show* (Saturday) replaced the following day by *CFRB Sunday*. On 6070 kHz.

15:30

Voice of the Islamic Republic of Iran. Sixty minutes of *news*, commentary and features, most of it reflecting the Islamic point of view. To South and Southeast Asia (and also heard elsewhere) on 9575 (winter), 11790 (winter), 11875 (summer), 15260 and 17750 kHz.

15:45

Radio Tirana, Albania. Summers only at this time. Approximately 15 minutes of *news* and commentary from and about Albania. To Europe on 11735 and 12085 kHz.

16:00

■**BBC World Service for the Americas, Europe and the Mideast.** Winter weekdays, a quarter hour of *World News* is followed by ●*Insight* (current events), a 15-minute feature and ●*Sports Roundup*. Pick of the features is Wednesday's ●*From Our Own Correspondent*. In summer, the accent is strongly on Europe. The hour starts with ●*Europe Today*, which is followed by 15 minutes of unmatched financial reporting in ●*World Business Report*. The final slot is ●*Britain Today*. Weekends, a five-minute bulletin of *World News* is followed by *Sportsworld*. Continuous to North America on 9515 (till 1615 Sunday through Friday, and a full hour on Saturday) and 17840 kHz. Also to Europe on 6195, 9410, 12095 and 17640 kHz; and to the Mideast on 12095 and 15575 kHz.

■**BBC World Service for Asia and the Pacific.** *World News*, then weekdays it's a series of shows (mainly rock or popular music) geared to a youthful audience. *Multitrack* airs on Monday, Wednesday and Friday, *Megamix* on Tuesday, and a couple of 15-minute features on Thursday. Weekends are given over to *Sportsworld*. Continuous to Southeast Asia on 3915 and 7135 (or 7160) kHz; and to Australasia (till 1615) on 9740 kHz.

■**Radio France Internationale.** *News*, press reviews and correspondents' reports, with particular attention paid to events in Africa. These are followed by two or more short features (basically a repeat of the 1200 broadcast, except for weekends when there is more emphasis on African themes). A fast-moving fifty-five minutes to Africa on 9485, 11615, 11700/11705, 12015, 15210, 15460, 15530 and 17850 kHz (some of which are seasonal). Formerly available to Europe on 6175 kHz, but was dropped, much to the chagrin of listeners in that part of the world. Audible in the Mideast on 9485, 11615 or 15460 kHz (one of the three, depending on the time of year). Some of these frequencies are also audible, to a varying degree, in eastern North America.

United Arab Emirates Radio, Dubai. Starts with a feature on Arab history or culture, then music, and a bulletin of *news* at 1630. Answers listeners' letters at weekends. Forty minutes to Europe (also heard in eastern North America) on 13675, 15395, 17630 and 21605 kHz.

■**Deutsche Welle,** Germany. *News*, then Monday through Friday it's ●*NewsLink* followed by *Africa Report*. Weekends, the Saturday news is followed by *Talking Point* and *Spectrum*, with *Religion and Society* and *Arts on the Air* filling the Sunday slots. Fifty minutes aimed primarily at Africa, but also audible in the Mideast. Winters on 7120, 9735, 11810, 13750 and 15145 kHz;

and summers on 7130, 9735, 11810 and 21695 kHz.

Radio Korea International, South Korea. Opens with *news* and commentary, followed Monday through Wednesday by *Seoul Calling*. Weekly features include *Echoes of Korean Music* and *Shortwave Feedback* (Sunday), *Tales from Korea's Past* (Monday), *Korean Cultural Trails* (Tuesday), *Pulse of Korea* (Wednesday), *From Us to You* (a listener-response program) and *Let's Learn Korean* (Thursday), *Let's Sing Together* and *Korea Through Foreigners' Eyes* (Friday), and Saturday's *Discovering Korea*, *Korean Literary Corner* and *Weekly News Focus*. One hour to East Asia on 5975 kHz, and to the Mideast and much of Africa on 9515 and 9870 kHz.

Radio Norway International. Summer Sundays only. *Norway Now*. A half hour of *news* and human-interest stories targeted at western North America on 11840 kHz, East Africa on 13805 kHz, and South Asia and beyond on 11860 kHz.

Radio Pakistan. Fifteen minutes of *news* from the Pakistan Broadcasting Corporation's domestic service, followed by a similar period at dictation speed. Intended for the Mideast and Africa, but heard well beyond on several channels. Try 9650, 11570, 15170, 15375, 15570 and 17720 kHz, some of which are seasonal.

Radio Prague, Czech Republic. Summers only at this time. *News*, then Monday through Friday there's *Current Affairs*. This is followed by *Magazine '99* (Monday), *Talking Point* and *Media Czech* (Tuesday), *The Arts* and *History Czech* (Wednesday), *Economic Report* and *I'd Like You to Meet...* (Thursday), and *Between You and Us* (Friday). Weekend fare consists of a Saturday musical feature (well worth hearing), and Sunday's *The Week in Politics*, *From the Weeklies* and *Media Czech*. A half hour to Europe on 5930 kHz, and to East Africa on 17485 kHz. One hour later in winter.

Channel Africa, South Africa. Thirty minutes of *news*, reports and interviews for southern Africa on 5995 or 6000 kHz.

Voice of Vietnam. *News*, followed by *Commentary* or *Weekly Review*, then some short features and pleasant Vietnamese music (especially at weekends). A half hour to Africa (and heard well beyond) on 9840 and 12020 (or 15010) kHz.

Radio Australia. Continuous to Asia and the Pacific. At this hour there's a relay of domestic ABC Radio National programs. Beamed to the Pacific on 5995 and 9580 kHz (also well heard in western North America). Additionally available to East and Southeast Asia on 9500 and 11660 kHz (may also be heard in Europe).

Radio Ethiopia. An hour-long broadcast divided into two parts by the 1630 *news* bulletin. Regular weekday features include *Kaleidoscope* and *Women's Forum* (Monday), *Press Review* and *Africa in Focus* (Tuesday), *Guest of the Week* and *Ethiopia Today* (Wednesday), *Ethiopian Music* and *Spotlight* (Thursday) and *Press Review* and *Introducing Ethiopia* on Friday. For weekend listening, try *Contact* and *Ethiopia This Week* (Saturday), or Sunday's *Listeners' Choice* and *Commentary*. Best heard in parts of Africa and the Mideast, but sometimes audible in Europe. On 7165, 9560 and 11800 kHz.

Radio Jordan. A partial relay of the station's domestic broadcasts, beamed to Europe on 11970 kHz. Continuous till 1730 (1630 during winter).

Voice of Russia World Service. *News*, then very much a mixed bag, depending on the day and season. Winter weekdays, there's *Focus on Asia and the Pacific*, with Saturday's *Newmarket* and Sunday's program preview making up the week. On the half-hour, choose from *This is Russia* (Monday), ●*Moscow Yesterday and Today* (Tuesday), ●*Audio Book Club* (dramatized reading, Wednesday) and Thursday's ●*Folk

Box. Weekend fare is split between Saturday's *Kaleidoscope* and Sunday's *Russian by Radio*. Summers, the news is followed by the business-oriented *Newmarket* (Monday and Thursday), *Science and Engineering* (Tuesday and Sunday), *Moscow Mailbag* (Wednesday and Friday) and last—but certainly not least—Saturday's ●*Music and Musicians*. Weekdays on the half-hour, you can hear "alternative programs"—religious paid programming or a show from the Voice of Russia's archives or transcription department. Continuous to the Mideast and West Asia on 4730, 4940 and 4975 kHz, as well as frequencies in other world band segments. Winters, dial around the 7 and 9 MHz ranges; in summer, 11 and 15 MHz should give better results.

Radio Canada International. Winters only. Final hour of CBC's ●*Sunday Morning*. Sunday only to North America and the Caribbean on 9640 and 11855 kHz.

"Rush Limbaugh Show," WRNO, New Orleans, Louisiana. Summer weekdays only at this time. The first sixty minutes of a three-hour live package. Arguably of little interest to most listeners outside North America, but popular and controversial within the United States. To North America and Caribbean on 7355 (or 15420) kHz.

XERMX—Radio México Internacional. Winters only at this time. Starts with a feature: *Universal Forum* (Monday and Friday), *Eternally Mexico* (Tuesday and Sunday) and *Mailbox* (Wednesday and Saturday). Thursdays, the English program is replaced by one in French. On the half-hour, there's 30 minutes of music. Best heard in western and southern parts of the United States on 5985 and 9705 kHz.

China Radio International. *News* and commentary, then Tuesday through Friday there's *Current Affairs*. These are followed by various feature programs such as Sunday's *Cultural Information*, *Snapshots*, *Report from Developing Countries*, *Song of the Week* and *Listeners' Letterbox*; Monday's *Open Windows* and *Let's Learn Chinese*; and Tuesday's *Orient Arena* and *Voices from Other Lands*. Wednesday brings *Profile* and another chance to *Learn to Speak Chinese*; Thursday's offerings are *Focus* and *Cultural Spectrum*; and Friday's features are *Life in China* and *Global Review*. To round off the week, there's a Saturday menu consisting of *Asia-Pacific News*, *Chinese Folk Tales*, *Cooking Show*, *China Scrapbook* and ●*Music from China*. One hour to Southern Africa on 9565 and 9620 kHz.

Voice of America. Several hours of continuous programming aimed at an African audience. At this hour, there's a split between mainstream programming and news and features in "Special" (slow-speed) English. The former can be heard on 6035, 13710, 15225 and 15410 kHz, and the "Special" programs on 13600, 15445 and (summer) 17895 kHz. For a separate service to the Mideast, see the next item.

Voice of America. *News Now*—a mixed bag of news and reports on current events, sports, science, business and more. To the Mideast winters on 9575 and 15205 kHz, and summers on 9700 and 15205 kHz. Also heard in much of Europe.

WJCR, Upton, Kentucky. Continues with country gospel music to North America on 7490 and 13595 kHz. Other U.S. religious broadcasters operating at this hour include **WWCR** on 13845 and 15685 kHz, **KTBN** on 15590 kHz, and **WYFR—Family Radio** on 11705 (or 15215) and 11830 kHz. Traditional Catholic programming can be heard via **WEWN** on 7425 kHz.

CFRX-CFRB, Toronto, Canada. See 1400. Winter weekdays, it's the final part of *The Charles Adler Show*, with *The CFRB Gardening Show* and *CFRB Sunday* the weekend offerings. Summers, look for *The Motts*

Monday through Friday, and ●*The World at Noon* on weekends.

16:30

Radio Slovakia International. Summers only at this time; see 1730 for specifics. Thirty minutes of friendly programming to Western Europe on 5920, 6055 and 7345 kHz. One hour later in winter.

Radio Vlaanderen Internationaal, Belgium. Summers only at this time. Weekdays, there's *News*, *Press Review* and *Belgium Today*, followed by features like *Focus on Europe* (Monday), *Living in Belgium* and *Green Society* (Tuesday), *The Arts* (Wednesday and Friday), *Around Town* (Wednesday), *Economics* and *International Report* (Thursday), and *Tourism* (Friday). Weekend features include *Music from Flanders* (Saturday) and Sunday's *P.O. Box 26* (a listener-response program) and *Radio World*. Twenty-five minutes to Europe on 5910 and 7290 kHz. One hour later in winter.

Radio Canada International. *News*, then Monday through Friday it's *Spectrum* (current events). *Innovation Canada* airs on Saturday, and a listener-response program occupies Sunday's slot. A half hour to Asia on 6140 (or 9550) and 7150 kHz.

Radio Austria International. Summers only at this time. See 1730 for more details. An informative half-hour of ●*Report from Austria*. Available to Europe on 6155 and 13730 kHz, to the Mideast on 11855 kHz, and to South and Southeast Asia on 13710 kHz. One hour later in winter.

Radio Cairo, Egypt. The first 30 minutes of a two-hour package of Arab music and features reflecting Egyptian life and culture, with *news* and commentary about events in Egypt and the Arab world. There are also quizzes, mailbag shows, and answers to listeners' questions. To southern Africa on 15255 kHz.

Radio Almaty, Kazakhstan. Summers only at this time. See 1730 for further details. Thirty minutes to Asia on 9505 kHz. One hour later during winter.

17:00

■**BBC World Service for the Americas, Europe and the Mideast.** Winter weekdays, the accent is firmly on Europe. Starts with ●*Europe Today*, which is followed by 15 minutes of specialized financial reporting in ●*World Business Report*. The final slot is ●*Britain Today*. In summer, *World News* is followed by ●*Insight* (current events), a 15-minute feature and ●*Sports Roundup*. Best of the features are *Seven Days* (Monday) and Wednesday's ●*From Our Own Correspondent*. Weekends, a five-minute bulletin of *World News* is followed by *Sportsworld*. To North America on 17840 kHz; to Europe on 6180, 6195, 9410, 12095 and (summer) 15575 kHz; and to the Mideast on 6095 and 12095 kHz.

■**BBC World Service for Africa.** *World News*, *Focus on Africa*, *African News* and ●*Sports Roundup*. Part of a 20-hour daily service to the African continent on a variety of channels, including 6190, 15400 and 17830 kHz. The last two channels are widely heard outside Africa, including parts of North America.

Radio Prague, Czech Republic. See 1600 for program specifics. A half hour of *news* and features beamed to Europe on 5930 kHz; also winters to East Africa on 9430 kHz, and summers to central and southern Africa on 17485 kHz.

Radio Australia. Continuous programming to Asia and the Pacific. At this hour there's a relay of the domestic ABC Radio National service. Beamed to the Pacific on 5995, 9580 and 11880 kHz (and also heard in western North America). Additionally available to East and Southeast Asia on 9500 kHz (may also be heard in Europe).

Polish Radio Warsaw, Poland. This time summers only. Monday through Friday, it's *News from Poland*—a compendium of news, reports and interviews. This is followed by *Request Concert* and *A Day in the Life of...* (Monday), classical music and the historical *Flashback* (Tuesday), a communications feature and *Letter from Poland* (Wednesday), a feature and a talk or special report (Thursday), and Friday's *Focus* (the arts in Poland) followed by *Business Week*. The Saturday broadcast begins with a bulletin of *news*, then there's *Weekend Papers* (a press review), *Panorama* (a window on day-to-day life in Poland) and a listener-response program, *Postbag*. Sundays, you can hear *What We Said* (a summary of the station's output during the previous week) and *Jazz, Folk, Rock and Pop from Poland*. Fifty-five minutes to Europe on 6095, 7270 and 7285 kHz. One hour later during winter.

Radio Jordan. Winters only at this time. The last 30 minutes of a partial relay of the station's domestic broadcasts, beamed to Europe on 11970 kHz.

Voice of Russia World Service. *News*, then it's a mixed bag, depending on the day and season. Winters, the news is followed by the business-oriented *Newmarket* (Monday and Thursday), *Science and Engineering* (Tuesday and Sunday), *Moscow Mailbag* (Wednesday and Friday) and Saturday's 45-minute ●*Music and Musicians*. Weekdays on the half-hour, you can hear "alternative programs"— religious paid programming or a show from the Voice of Russia's archives or transcription department. In summer, the news is followed Monday through Saturday by *News and Views*, with *Sunday Panorama* making up the week. On the half-hour, the lineup includes *This is Russia* (Sunday), *Kaleidoscope* (Monday), ●*Moscow Yesterday and Today* (Wednesday), ●*Music at Your Request* (Thursday) and Friday's ●*Folk Box*. To Europe sum-

mers on channels in the 9 and 11 MHz segments (9765 and 9775 kHz are reasonable bets). Also to the Mideast winters— look for suitable frequencies in the 7 and 9 MHz ranges. In southern Africa, dial around the 7, 9 and 11 MHz bands to find the best signal.

Radio Japan. Repeat of the 1500 broadcast, except that Sunday's *Hello from Tokyo* is replaced by *Let's Learn Japanese*, *Media Roundup* and *Viewpoint*. One hour to the Mideast on 11930 kHz; to western North America on 9535 kHz; and to Asia on 6035/6150 (East), 7280/11880 (South) and (Southeast) 9580 kHz.

Channel Africa, South Africa. Thirty minutes of *news*, reports and interviews. To West Africa on 15240 kHz, and often heard in parts of Europe and eastern North America.

Radio Pyongyang, North Korea. Repeat of the 1100 transmission. Fifty minutes to Europe, the Mideast and beyond on 9325, 9640, 9975 and 13785 kHz.

China Radio International. Repeat of the 1600 transmission. One hour to eastern and southern parts of Africa on 7150 (winter), 7405, 9570, 9745 and (midyear) 11910 kHz.

Voice of America. Continuous programming to the Mideast and North Africa. *News*, then Monday through Friday it's the interactive *Talk to America*. Weekends, there's the ubiquitous *News Now*. Winters on 6040, 9760 and 15205 kHz; and summers on 9760, 15135 and 15255 kHz. Also heard in much of Europe. For a separate service to Africa, see the next item.

Voice of America. Programs for Africa. Monday through Saturday, identical to the service for Europe and the Mideast (see previous item). Sunday on the half-hour, look for the entertaining ●*Music Time in Africa*. Audible well beyond where it is targeted. On 6035, 7415, 11920, 11975,

12040, 13710, 15410, 15445 and 17895 kHz, some of which are seasonal. For yet another service (to East Asia and the Pacific), see the next item.

Voice of America. Monday through Friday only. *News*, followed by the interactive *Talk to America*. Sixty minutes to Asia on 5990, 6045, 6110/6160, 7125, 7215, 9525, 9645, 9670, 9770, 11945, 12005 and 15255 kHz, some of which are seasonal. For Australasia, try 9525 and 15255 kHz in winter, and 7150 and 7170 kHz in summer.

■**Radio France Internationale.** An additional half-hour (see 1600) of predominantly African fare. To East Africa on any two frequencies from 9485, 11615, 15210 and 15460 kHz. Also audible in parts of the Mideast, and occasionally heard in eastern North America.

Radio Cairo, Egypt. See 1630 for specifics. Continues with a broadcast to southern Africa on 15255 kHz.

"Rush Limbaugh Show," WRNO, New Orleans, Louisiana. Monday through Friday only; see 1600 for specifics. Starts at this time winters; summers, it's already into the second hour. Continuous to North America and the Caribbean on 7355 (or 15420) kHz.

WJCR, Upton, Kentucky. Continues with country gospel music to North America on 7490 and 13595 kHz. Other U.S. religious broadcasters operating at this hour include **WWCR** on 13845 and 15685 kHz, **KTBN** on 15590 kHz, and **WHRI—World Harvest Radio** on 13760 and 15105 kHz.

CFRX-CFRB, Toronto, Canada. See 1400. Winter weekends at this time, there's ●*The World at Noon*; summers, it's *The Mike Stafford Show*. Monday through Friday, look for *The Motts*. On 6070 kHz.

17:30

■**Radio Netherlands.** Targeted at Africa, but heard well beyond. *News*, then Monday through Saturday there's *Newsline* and a feature. Choice plums include ●*Research File* (Monday), ●*Documentary* (Wednesday), ●*A Good Life* (Friday), and Saturday's ●*Weekend*. For another interesting

Panataran Temple, East Java's finest example of its ancient Hindu roots, dates to the 13th century. N. Grace

offering, try the eclectic *Music 52-15* aired each Tuesday. Other programs include Thursday's *Media Network* and Sunday's *Sincerely Yours* and *Sounds Interesting*. Monday through Friday there is also a *Press Review*. Sixty minutes on 6020 (best for southern Africa), 7120 (summer), 9605 (winter) and 11655 kHz.

Radio Austria International. Winters only at this time. ●*Report from Austria*, a half hour of news and human interest stories. Ample coverage of national and regional issues. To Europe on 6155 and 13730 kHz; to the Mideast on 9655 kHz; and to South and Southeast Asia on 13710 kHz. One hour earlier in summer

Radio Slovakia International. Winters only at this time. *Slovakia Today*, a 30-minute look at Slovak life and culture. Tuesday, there's a mixed bag of short features; Wednesday puts the accent on tourism and Slovak personalities; Thursday's slot is devoted to business and economy; and Friday brings a mix of politics, education and science. Saturday offerings include cultural items, *Slovak Kitchen* and the off-beat *Back Page News*; and Sunday brings the *"Best of"* series. Monday's show is more relaxed, and includes *Listeners' Tribune* and some enjoyable Slovak music. A friendly half hour to Western Europe on 5915, 6055 and 7345 kHz. One hour earlier in summer.

Radio Sweden. Summers only at this hour; see 1830 for program specifics. Thirty minutes of Scandinavian fare for Europe, the Mideast and Africa on 6065 (Monday through Saturday), 13855 (Sunday) and 15735 kHz. One hour later during winter.

Radio Vlaanderen Internationaal, Belgium. Weekdays, there's *News*, *Press Review* and *Belgium Today*, followed by features like *Focus on Europe* (Monday), *Living in Belgium* and *Green Society*

(Tuesday), *The Arts* (Wednesday and Friday), *Around Town* (Wednesday), *Economics* and *International Report* (Thursday), and *Tourism* (Friday). Weekend features include *Music from Flanders* (Saturday) and Sunday's *P.O. Box 26* (a listener-response program) and *Radio World*. Twenty-five minutes to Europe winters on 5910 and 9925 kHz; also to Africa summers on 17655 kHz; and year round to the Mideast on 11680 (winter) or (summer) 11810 kHz.

Radio Romania International. *News*, commentary, a press review, and one or more short features. Thirty minutes to Eastern and Southern Africa (also audible in parts of the Mideast). Winters on 9750, 11740 and 11940 kHz; and summers on 9550, 9750, 11830 and 11940 kHz.

Radio Almaty, Kazakhstan. Winters only at this time. Due to financial constraints, news and features have largely been replaced by recordings of exotic Kazakh music. If you like world music, this is definitely a station to try for. Heard in much of Asia on 9505 kHz. One hour earlier in summer.

17:45

All India Radio. The first 15 minutes of a two-hour broadcast to Europe and Africa, consisting of regional and international *news*, commentary, a variety of talks and features, press review and exotic Indian music. Continuous till 1945. To Europe on 7410, 9950 and 11620 kHz; and to Africa on 11935, 13780 and 15075 kHz. Easily audible in the Mideast, but dial around to find the best frequency for your location.

Voice of Armenia. Summers only at this time. Mainly of interest to Armenians abroad. Fifteen minutes of *news* from and about Armenia. To Eastern Europe and the Mideast on 4810, 4990 and 7480 kHz. One hour later in winter.

1800-2359
Europe & Mideast—Evening Prime Time
East Asia—Early Morning
Australasia—Morning
Eastern North America—Afternoon
Western North America—Midday

18:00

■**BBC World Service for the Americas, Europe and the Mideast.** Thirty minutes of ●*Newsdesk*, with the next half hour containing some of the BBC's finest shows. Sunday, there's ●*Play of the Week* (world theater), replaced Monday (September through December) by the immensely popular ●*Brain of Britain*, and Tuesday by ●*One Planet* (the environment). Then it's *The Works* (technology, Wednesday). ●*Assignment* (Thursday), ●*Focus on Faith* (Friday) and ●*Science in Action* (Saturday). To North America winters on 17840 kHz; year round to Europe on 3955 (winter), 6180, 6195, 9410 and 12095 kHz; and to the Mideast on 9410 (winter) and 12095 kHz.

■**BBC World Service for Africa.** ●*Newsdesk*, then Monday through Friday it's *Focus on Africa*. Weekends, look for Saturday's ●*World of Music* and *A Jolly Good Show* on Sunday. Continuous programming to the African continent (and heard well beyond) on 3255, 6005 (from 1830), 6190, 9630 (from 1830), 15400 and 17830 kHz. The last two channels are audible in parts of North America.

■**BBC World Service for the Pacific.** Identical to the service for Europe at this hour, but only available from 1830 onwards. To Australasia on 9740 kHz.

Radio Kuwait. The start of a three-hour package of *news*, Islamic-oriented features and western popular music. Some interesting features, even if you don't particu-

larly like the music. There is a full program summary at the beginning of each transmission, to enable you to pick and choose. To Europe and eastern North America on 11990 kHz.

Voice of Vietnam. Begins with *news*, then there's *Commentary* or *Weekly Review*, followed by short features and some pleasant Vietnamese music (especially at weekends). A half hour to Europe on 9840 and 12020 (or 15010) kHz.

Radio For Peace International, Costa Rica. Part of a continuous eight-hour cyclical block of predominantly social-conscience and counterculture programming. To Europe and North America on 15050 and 21460 kHz.

All India Radio. Continuation of the transmission to Europe, Africa and the Mideast (see 1745). *News* and commentary, followed by programming of a more general nature. To Europe on 7410, 9950 and 11620 kHz; and to Africa on 11935, 13780 and 15075 kHz. In the Mideast, choose the channel best suited to your location.

Radio Prague, Czech Republic. Winters only at this time. Repeat of the 1700 broadcast (see 1600 for program details). A half hour to Europe on 5930 kHz, and to Australasia on 9430 kHz.

Radio Norway International. Summer Sundays only. *Norway Now*. Repeat of the 1200 transmission. Thirty minutes of friendly programming from and about

Norway. To Europe on 7485 kHz, to the Mideast on 9590 kHz, and to Africa on 13805 and 15220 kHz.

Radio Australia. Friday and Saturday, you can hear a relay of the domestic ABC Radio National service. On the remaining days there's a ten-minute bulletin of world *news*, followed by regional news in *Asia Pacific*. Part of a continuous 24-hour service, and at this hour beamed to the Pacific on 6080, 7240, 9580, 9660 and 11880 kHz. Additionally available to East and Southeast Asia on 9500 kHz (may also be heard in Europe). In western North America, try 9580 and 11880 kHz.

Radio Nacional do Brasil (Radiobras), Brazil. Monday through Saturday, you can hear *Life in Brazil* or *Brazilian Panorama*, a potpourri of news, facts and figures about the country, interspersed with examples of the country's unique musical styles. The *Sunday Special*, on the other hand, is devoted to one particular theme, and often contains lots of exotic Brazilian music. Eighty minutes to Europe on 15265 kHz. Unfortunately, the station sometimes uses tapes of old programs, and the audio quality may not be all it should be.

Channel Africa, South Africa. Thirty minutes of *news*, reports and interviews. To West Africa on 15240 kHz, and often heard in parts of Europe and eastern North America.

Polish Radio Warsaw, Poland. This time winters only. See 1700 for program specifics. *News*, music and features, covering multiple aspects of Polish life and culture. Fifty-five minutes to Europe on 6095, 7270 and 7285 kHz. One hour earlier in summer.

Voice of Russia World Service. Predominantly news-related fare during the initial half hour, with *News and Views* available Monday through Saturday winter, and ●*Commonwealth Update* on

summer weekdays. At 1830, the winter lineup includes *This is Russia* (Sunday), *Kaleidoscope* (Monday), ●*Moscow Yesterday and Today* (Wednesday), ●*Music at Your Request* (Thursday) and Friday's pulsating ●*Folk Box*. Summer weekdays, there are "alternative programs"—regular shows, transcription programs or religious paid programming. The Saturday slot is occupied by *This is Russia*, replaced Sunday by ●*Christian Message from Moscow* (a fascinating look at Russian Orthodoxy). Continuous to Europe and southern Africa. Winters, Europe is best served by 9890 kHz and frequencies in the 6 and 7 MHz segments; best summer channels are in the 9 and 11 MHz ranges (try 9765 and 9775 kHz). In southern Africa, dial around the 7 and 9 MHz bands in winter, and 9 and 11 MHz midyear.

Voice of America. Continuous programming to the Mideast and North Africa. *News Now*—reports and features on a variety of topics. On 6040 (winter) and 9760 kHz. For a separate service to Africa, see the next item.

Voice of America. Monday through Friday, it's *News Now* and *Africa World Tonight*. Weekends, there's a full hour of the former. To Africa—but heard well beyond—on 7275, 11920, 11975, 12040, 13710, 15410, 15580 and 17895 kHz, some of which are seasonal.

Radio Algiers, Algeria. *News*, then western and Arab popular music, with an occasional feature thrown in. One hour of so-so reception in Europe, and occasionally heard in eastern North America. Try 11715, 11750 or 15160 kHz. Sometimes heard irregularly on 17745 kHz.

Radio Cairo, Egypt. See 1630 for specifics. The final 30 minutes of a two-hour broadcast to southern Africa on 15255 kHz.

Radio Omdurman, Sudan. A one-hour package of *news* and features (often from a pro-government viewpoint), plus a little ethnic Sudanese music. Better heard in Europe than in North America, but occasionally audible in the eastern United States. On 9024 kHz.

"Rush Limbaugh Show," WRNO, New Orleans, Louisiana. Monday through Friday only; see 1600 for specifics. Continuous to North America and the Caribbean on 7355 (or 15420) kHz.

"For the People," WHRI, Noblesville, Indiana. Summers only at this time; see 0300 for specifics. Three hours of live populist programming targeted at North America on 9495 kHz. One hour later in winter.

WJCR, Upton, Kentucky. Continues with country gospel music to North America on 7490 and 13595 kHz. Other U.S. religious broadcasters operating at this time include **WWCR** on 13845 and 15685 kHz, **KTBN** on 15590 kHz, and **WHRI—World Harvest Radio** on 13760 and 15105 kHz. For traditional Catholic programming, tune **WEWN** on 7425 kHz.

CFRX-CFRB, Toronto, Canada. Audible throughout much of the northeastern United States and southeastern Canada during the hours of daylight with a modest, but clear, signal on 6070 kHz. This pleasant, friendly station carries news, sports, weather and traffic reports—most of it intended for a local audience. Winter weekdays at this hour, it's *The Motts*; summers, look for *The John Oakley Show*. Weekends feature *The Mike Stafford Show*.

18:15

Radio Bangladesh. *News*, followed by Islamic and general interest features; some nice Bengali music, too. Thirty minutes to Europe on 7190 and 9550 kHz, and irregularly on 15520 kHz. Frequencies may be slightly variable.

18:30

■Radio Netherlands. Part of a three-hour block of programming for Africa, but also well heard in parts of North America at this hour. *News*, followed Monday through Saturday by *Newsline* and a feature. Some excellent shows, including ●*A Good Life* (Tuesday), ●*Research File* (science, Thursday), ●*Roughly Speaking* (an award-winning youth program, Saturday) and Friday's ●*Documentary*. Other offerings include *Aural Tapestry* (Monday), *Sounds Interesting* (Wednesday) and Sunday's *Siren Song*. Sixty minutes on 6020, 7120 (summer), 9605 (winter), 9895, 11655, 15315 and (summer) 17605 kHz. The last two frequencies, via the relay in the Netherlands Antilles, are best for North American listeners. In southern Africa, tune to 6020 kHz.

Radio Slovakia International. Summers only at this time; see 1930 for specifics. Thirty minutes of *news* and features with a strong Slovak flavor. To Western Europe on 5920, 6055 and 7345 kHz. One hour later in winter.

Radio Vlaanderen Internationaal, Belgium. Winters only at this time. Weekdays, there's *News*, *Press Review* and *Belgium Today*, followed by features like *Focus on Europe* (Monday), *Living in Belgium* and *Green Society* (Tuesday), *The Arts* (Wednesday and Friday), *Around Town* (Wednesday), *Economics* and *International Report* (Thursday), and *Tourism* (Friday). Weekend features include *Music from Flanders* (Saturday) and Sunday's *P.O. Box 26* (a listener-response program) and *Radio World*. Twenty-five minutes to Africa (and heard well beyond) on 9925 and 13745 kHz. One hour earlier in summer.

Voice of Turkey. This time summers only. *News*, followed by *Review of the Turkish Press*, then features on Turkish history, culture and international relations, interspersed with enjoyable selections of the country's popular and classical music. Fifty minutes to Western Europe on 9445 and 11765 kHz. One hour later in winter.

Voice of Mongolia. *News*, reports and short features with the accent on local topics. Some exotic Mongolian music, too, especially on Sundays. Thirty minutes to Europe on 9720 and 12085 kHz. Frequencies may vary slightly.

Radio Sweden. Winters only at this time. Monday through Friday, it's *news* and features in *Sixty Degrees North*, concentrating heavily on Scandinavian topics. Monday's accent is on sports; Tuesday spotlights electronic media news; Wednesday has *Money Matters*; Thursday features ecology or science and technology; and Friday offers a review of the week's news. Saturday's slot is filled by *Spectrum* (arts) or *Sweden Today*, and Sunday fare consists of *In Touch with Stockholm* (a listener-response program) or the musical *Sounds Nordic*. Thirty minutes to Europe, the Mideast and Africa on 6065 (not Sunday) and 9645 kHz. One hour earlier in summer.

Radio Yugoslavia. Summers only at this time. *News* and background reports with a strong local flavor. Thirty minutes to Europe on 6100 kHz, and to Southern Africa on 9720 kHz. One hour later during winter.

18:45

Voice of Armenia. Monday through Friday, winters only at this time. Mainly of interest to Armenians abroad. Fifteen minutes of *news* from and about Armenia. To Eastern Europe and the Mideast on 4810, 4990 and 7480 kHz. One hour earlier in summer.

19:00

■BBC World Service for Europe and the Mideast. Starts with a brief summary

of the latest *news*, then Monday through Friday it's the popular and long-running ●*Outlook*, followed by five minutes of the religious *Pause for Thought*. On the half-hour, the programs are geared to younger listeners: *Multitrack* (Monday, Wednesday and Friday), *Megamix* (Tuesday) and ●*John Peel* (Thursday). Best of the Saturday fare is ●*From Our Own Correspondent* at 1930. Sunday brings continuation of ●*Play of the Week* and, if the play doesn't overrun, the popular ●*Anything Goes*. Continuous to Europe on 3955 (winters), 6180, 6195, 9410 and 12095 kHz; and to the Mideast on 5975, 9410 and (summer) 12095 kHz. Some of these channels are also heard in eastern North America.

■BBC World Service for the Pacific. ●*Newshour*. The best. To Australasia on 9740 and 11955 kHz.

■BBC World Service for Africa. A series of features aimed at the African continent, but worth a listen even if you live farther afield. The list includes *Fast Track* and *On Screen* (Monday), *Art Beat* (Tuesday), *Talkabout Africa* and ●*One Planet* (Wednesday), ●*Assignment* and *The Works* (Thursday), *Fast Track* and ●*Science in Action* (Friday), ●*Omnibus* and *Meridian* (Saturday) and Sunday's *African Perspective*. Continuous programming to the African continent (and heard well beyond) on 6005, 6190, 9630, 15400 and 17830 kHz. The last two channels are audible in parts of North America.

Radio Nacional do Brasil (Radiobras), Brazil. Final 20 minutes of the 1800 broadcast to Europe on 15265 kHz.

Radio Yugoslavia. Summers only at this time. *News* and short background reports heavily geared to local issues. Worth a listen if you are interested in the region. Thirty minutes to Australasia on 7230 kHz.

Radio Australia. Begins with *World News*, then Sunday through Thursday it's

Pacific Beat (in-depth reporting on the region). Friday's slots go to ●*Pacific Focus* and *Media Report*, replaced Saturday by the aptly named *Ockham's Razor* (science talk at its sharpest) and *The Sports Factor*. Continuous to Asia and the Pacific on 6080, 7240, 9500, 9580, 9660 and 11880 kHz. Listeners in western North America can try 9580 and 11880 kHz. Best bet for East and Southeast Asia is 9500 kHz (may also be audible in Europe).

Radio Norway International. Winter Sundays only. *Norway Now*. News and features from and about Norway. Thirty minutes to Europe on 5960 kHz, to Australasia on 7115 kHz; and to Africa on 7485 and 9590 kHz.

Radio Kuwait. See 1800; continuous to Europe and eastern North America on 11990 kHz.

Kol Israel. Summers only at this time. ●*Israel News Magazine*. Thirty minutes of even-handed and comprehensive news reporting from and about Israel. To Europe and North America on 9435, 11605 and 15650 kHz; and to Africa and South America on 15640 kHz. One hour later in winter.

All India Radio. The final 45 minutes of a two-hour broadcast to Europe, Africa and the Mideast (see 1745). Starts off with *news*, then continues with a mixed bag of features and Indian music. To Europe on 7410, 9950 and 11620 kHz; and to Africa on 11935, 13780 and 15075 kHz. In the Mideast, choose the channel best suited to your location.

Radio Bulgaria. Summers only at this time. *News*, then Monday through Thursday there's 15 minutes of current events in *Today*, replaced Friday by *Weekly Spotlight*, a summary of the week's major political stories. The remainder of the broadcast is given over to features dealing with Bulgaria and Bulgarians, and includes some lively ethnic music. Sixty minutes to

Europe on 9700 and 11720 kHz. One hour later during winter.

HCJB—Voice of the Andes, Ecuador. The first of three hours of religious and secular programming targeted at Europe. Monday through Friday it's *Studio 9*, featuring nine minutes of world and Latin American *news*, followed by 20 minutes of in-depth reporting on Latin America. The final portion is given over to one of a variety of 30-minute features—including *You Should Know* (issues and ethics, Monday), *El Mundo Futuro* (science, Tuesday), *Ham Radio Today* (Wednesday), *Woman to Woman* (Thursday) and Friday's exotic and enjoyable ●*Música del Ecuador*. On Saturday, the news is followed by *DX Partyline*, which in turn is replaced Sunday by *Saludos Amigos*—HCJB's international friendship program. Winter on 12015 kHz, and summer on 17735 kHz.

Radio Budapest, Hungary. Summers only at this time. *News* and features, some of which are broadcast on a regular basis. These include Sunday's *Bookshelf* a press review (Monday, Tuesday, Thursday and Friday), *Profiles* (Tuesday), and *Focus on Business* (Wednesday). Thirty minutes to Europe on 3975 and 7170 kHz. One hour later in winter.

■**Deutsche Welle,** Germany. *News*, then Monday through Friday it's ●*NewsLink* followed by *Africa Report*. Weekends, the Saturday news is followed by *Talking Point* and *Spectrum*; Sunday, by *Religion and Society* and *Arts on the Air*. Fifty minutes to Africa, but also heard in Europe and beyond. Winters, try 9640, 9765, 11785, 11810, 13690, 15135 and 15425 kHz; in summer, go for 9640, 9670, 11785, 11810, 13790, 15245 and 15390 kHz.

Radio Romania International. *News*, commentary, press review and features. Regular spots include *Youth Club* (Tuesday), *Romanian Musicians* (Wednesday), and Thursday's *Listeners' Letterbox* and

●*Skylark* (Romanian folk music). Fifty-five minutes to Europe; winters on 6105, 7105, 7195 and 9510 kHz; and summers on 9550, 9690, 11810 and 11940 kHz. Also audible in eastern North America.

XERMX—Radio México Internacional. Summers only at this time. Monday through Friday, there's a summary of the Spanish-language *Antena Radio*, replaced Saturday by *Mirror of Mexico*, and Sunday by *Universal Forum*. On the half-hour, look for 30 minutes of musical programming. Best heard in western and southern parts of the United States on 5985 and 9705 kHz. One hour later in winter.

Radio Japan. Repeat of the 1500 transmission; see there for specifics. One hour to East and Southeast Asia on 6035/6150 and 9580 kHz; to Australasia on 6035, 7140 and 11850 kHz; and to western North America on 9535 kHz.

Voice of Russia World Service. *News*, followed winter weekdays by ●*Commonwealth Update*. Summers, choose from *Science and Engineering* (Wednesday and Saturday), *Newmarket* (Tuesday and Friday), *Moscow Mailbag* (Monday and Thursday) and Sunday's classical showpiece, ●*Music and Musicians*. Winter weekends at 1930, the Saturday slot is filled by *This is Russia*, replaced Sunday by ●*Christian Message from Moscow*. The remaining days feature "alternative programs"—religious paid programming or a show from the Voice of Russia's archives or transcription department. The summer lineup includes ●*Moscow Yesterday and Today* (Monday), *This is Russia* (Tuesday), *Kaleidoscope* (Wednesday), ●*Audio Book Club* (Thursday), *Russian by Radio* (Friday) and Saturday's ●*Christian Message from Moscow*. Winters, Europe is best served by 9890 kHz and frequencies in the 6 and 7 MHz segments; best summer channels are in the 9 and 11 MHz ranges (try 9765 and

9775 kHz). In southern Africa, dial around the 7 and 9 MHz bands in winter, and 9 and 11 MHz midyear.

China Radio International. Repeat of the 1600 transmission. One hour to Africa on 6955 (winter), 9440 and (midyear) 11515 kHz. Also audible in the Mideast.

Voice of Greece. Winters only at this time, and actually starts about three minutes into the broadcast, following some Greek announcements. Approximately ten minutes of *news* from and about Greece. To Europe on 9375 or 9380 kHz.

Radio Thailand. A 60-minute package of *news*, features and (if you're lucky) enjoyable Thai music. To Northern Europe winters on 7295 kHz, and summers on 7210 kHz. Also available to Asia on 9655 and 11905 kHz.

Radio For Peace International, Costa Rica. Continues with a variety of counterculture and social-conscience features. There is also a listener-response program at 1930 Tuesday. Audible in Europe and North America on 15050 and 21460 kHz.

Swiss Radio International. This time summers only. World and Swiss *news* and background reports, with some lighter and more general features on Saturdays. Thirty minutes to Europe on 6165 and 9885 kHz. One hour later during winter.

Voice of Vietnam. Repeat of the 1800 transmission (see there for specifics). A half hour to Europe on 9840 and 12020 (or 15010) kHz.

Voice of America. Continuous programming to the Mideast and North Africa. *News Now*—news and reports on a wide variety of topics. On 9760 and (summer) 9770 kHz. Also heard in Europe. For a separate service to Africa, see the next item.

Voice of America. *News Now*, then Monday through Friday it's *World of Music*.

Best of the weekend programs is ●*Music Time in Africa* at 1930 Sunday. Continuous to most of Africa on 6035, 7375, 7415, 11920, 11975, 12040, 15410, 15445 and 15580 kHz, some of which are seasonal. For yet another service, to Australasia, see the following item.

Voice of America. Sixty minutes of news and reports covering a variety of topics. One hour to Australasia on 9525, 11870 and 15180 kHz.

"Rush Limbaugh Show," WRNO, New Orleans, Louisiana. See 1600 for specifics. Winters only at this time. The final sixty minutes of a three-hour presentation. Popular and controversial within the United States, but of little interest to most other listeners. To North America and the Caribbean on 7355 (or 15420) kHz.

Radio Korea International, South Korea. Opens with *news* and commentary, followed Monday through Wednesday by *Seoul Calling*. Weekly features include *Echoes of Korean Music* and *Shortwave Feedback* (Sunday), *Tales from Korea's Past* (Monday), *Korean Cultural Trails* (Tuesday), *Pulse of Korea* (Wednesday), *From Us to You* (a listener-response program) and *Let's Learn Korean* (Thursday), *Let's Sing Together* and *Korea Through Foreigners' Eyes* (Friday), and Saturday's *Discovering Korea*, *Korean Literary Corner* and *Weekly News Focus*. Sixty minutes to East Asia on 5975 and 7275 kHz.

Radio Argentina al Exterior—R.A.E. Monday through Friday only. *News* and short features dealing with Argentinian life and culture, interspersed with fine examples of the country's various musical styles, from chamamé to zamba. Fifty-five minutes to Europe on 15345 kHz.

"For the People," WHRI, Noblesville, Indiana. See 0300 for specifics. Monday through Friday only. A three-hour populist package broadcast live to North America on 9495 kHz.

WJCR, Upton, Kentucky. Continues with country gospel music to North America on 7490 and 13595 kHz. Other U.S. religious broadcasters operating at this time include **WWCR** on 13845 and 15685 kHz, **KTBN** on 15590 kHz, and **WHRI—World Harvest Radio** on 13760 kHz. For traditional Catholic programming, try **WEWN** on 7425 kHz.

CFRX-CFRB, Toronto, Canada. See 1800. Weekdays at this time, you can hear *The John Oakley Show*; weekends, it's replaced by *The Mike Stafford Show*. On 6070 kHz.

19:15

Radio Tirana, Albania. Winters only at this time. Approximately 15 minutes of *news* and commentary from and about Albania. To Europe on 6025 and 7135 kHz.

19:30

Polish Radio Warsaw, Poland. Summers only at this time. Weekdays, it's *News from Poland*—news, reports and interviews on the latest events in the country. This is followed by classical music and the historical *Flashback* (Monday), *DX-Club* and *Letter from Poland* (Tuesday), a feature and a talk or special report (Wednesday), *Focus* (the arts in Poland) and *A Day in the Life of...* (Thursday), and *Postbag* (a listener-response program) followed by *Business Week* (Friday). The Saturday transmission begins with a bulletin of *news*, then there's *Weekend Papers* (a press review) and, later in the broadcast, *Jazz, Folk, Rock and Pop from Poland*. Sundays, you can hear *Panorama* (a window on day-to-day life in Poland) and *Request Concert*. Fifty-five minutes to Europe on 6035, 6095 and 7285 kHz. One hour later during winter.

Radio Slovakia International. Winters only at this time. *Slovakia Today*, a 30-minute review of Slovak life and culture.

Monday, there's a potpourri of short features; Tuesday spotlights tourism and Slovak personalities; Wednesday is devoted to business and economy; and Thursday brings a mix of politics, education and science. Friday offerings include cultural items, cooking recipes and the offbeat *Back Page News*; and Saturday has the "*Best of*" series. Sunday's show is a melange of this and that, and includes *Listeners' Tribune* and some enjoyable Slovak music. A friendly half hour to Western Europe on 5915, 6055 and 7345 kHz. One hour earlier in summer.

Voice of Turkey. Winters only at this time. See 1830 for program details. Some unusual programming and friendly presentation make this station worth a listen. Fifty minutes to Europe on 5960 and 6175 kHz. One hour earlier in summer.

Voice of the Islamic Republic of Iran. Sixty minutes of *news*, commentary and features with a strong Islamic slant. Not the lightest of programming fare, but reflects a point of view not often heard in western countries. To Europe on 7260 and 9022 kHz.

Radio Yugoslavia. Winters only at this time; see 1830 for specifics. Thirty minutes to Europe on 6100 kHz, and to Southern Africa on 9720 kHz. One hour earlier in summer.

Radio Sweden. Summers only at this time, and a repeat of the 1730 broadcast. See 1830 for program details. Thirty minutes to Europe on 6065 kHz.

■**Radio Netherlands.** Repeat of the 1730 transmission; see there for specifics. Fifty-five minutes to Africa on 6020 (best for southern parts), 7120 (summer), 9605 (winter), 9895, 11655, 15315 and (summer) 17605 kHz. The last two frequencies are heard well in many parts of North America.

RAI International—Radio Roma, Italy. Actually starts at 1935. Approximately 12 minutes of *news*, then some Italian music. Twenty minutes to western Europe winters on 6015 and 7225 kHz, and summers on 5970, 7145 and 9670 kHz.

19:50

Vatican Radio. Summers only at this time. Twenty minutes of programming oriented to Catholics. To Europe on 4005, 5880 and 7250 kHz. One hour later in winter.

20:00

■**BBC World Service for Europe and the Mideast.** ●*Newshour*, the standard for all in-depth news shows from international broadcasters. There's nothing quite like it. One hour to Europe on 3955 (winter), 6180, 6195, 7325 and 9410 kHz; and to the Mideast on 9410 kHz. Some of these channels are also audible in eastern North America.

■**BBC World Service for Asia and the Pacific.** Identical to the service for Europe at this hour. Winters only to Southeast Asia on 5975 and 9740 kHz, and year round to Australasia on 9740 kHz (5975 kHz also available midyear).

■**BBC World Service for Africa.** The incomparable ●*Newshour*. Continuous programming to the African continent (and heard well beyond) on 6005, 6190, 9630, 15400 and 17830 kHz. The last two channels are audible in parts of North America.

■**Deutsche Welle,** Germany. *News*, then Monday through Friday it's the in-depth ●*NewsLink* followed a feature. Monday, it's *German by Radio*; Tuesday has the interesting ●*Man and Environment*; Wednesday brings ●*Insight*; Thursday, there's *Living in Germany*; and Friday's slot is *Spotlight on Sport. Saturday Review* and ●*Weekend* can be heard on—you guessed it!—Saturday, and are replaced the next day by *Sunday*

Graham J. Barclay of KIWI Radio, New Zealand's infamous "Free Radio" operator. KIWI Radio

Review and *Arts on the Air.* Fifty minutes to Europe winters on 7285 kHz, and summers on 9615 kHz.

Radio Canada International. Summers only at this time. The first hour of a 90-minute broadcast to Europe and beyond. *News,* followed Monday through Friday by *Spectrum* (current events), which is replaced Saturday by *Venture Canada* and ●*Earth Watch,* and Sunday by *Arts in Canada* and *The Mailbag.* To Europe and Africa on 5995 (also available in the Mideast), 7235, 11690, 13650, 13670, 15150, 15325, 17820 and 17870 kHz. Some of these are audible in parts of North America. One hour later during winter.

Radio Damascus, Syria. Actually starts at 2005. *News,* a daily press review, and different features for each day of the week. These can be heard at approximately 2030

and 2045, and include *Arab Profile* and *Palestine Talk* (Monday), *Syria and the World* and *Listeners Overseas* (Tuesday), *Around the World* and *Selected Readings* (Wednesday), *From the World Press* and *Reflections* (Thursday), *Arab Newsweek* and *Cultural Magazine* (Friday), *Welcome to Syria* and *Arab Civilization* (Saturday), and *From Our Literature* and *Music from the Orient* (Sunday). Most of the transmission, however, is given over to Syrian and some western popular music. One hour to Europe, often audible in eastern North America, on 12085 and 13610 (or 15095) kHz.

Radio Norway International. Summer Sundays only. *Norway Now.* Thirty friendly minutes to Australasia on 9590 kHz.

Swiss Radio International. Thirty minutes of *Newsnet*—news and background reports on world and Swiss events. Somewhat lighter fare on Saturday, when the biweekly *Capital Letters* (a listener-response program) alternates with *Name Game* and *Sounds Good.* To Europe winters on 7410 and 6165 kHz (one hour earlier in summer), and year-round to Africa (also audible in eastern North America) on 9840 (summer), 9885 and (winter) 9905 kHz.

XERMX—Radio México Internacional. Winter weekdays, there's an English summary of the Spanish-language *Antena Radio,* replaced Saturday by *Mirror of Mexico,* and Sunday by *Universal Forum.* Summers, the lineup consists of Monday's *The Sounds of Mexico,* replaced Tuesday and Sunday by *Mailbox,* Thursday by *Eternally Mexico* and Friday by *Mirror of Mexico.* Wednesdays and Saturdays, the English program gives way to one in French. On the half-hour, look for 30 minutes of music. Best heard in western and southern parts of the United States on 5985 and 9705 kHz.

Radio Australia. Starts with *World News,* then Sunday through Thursday there's

Pacific Beat (in-depth reporting). Friday fare consists of *Oz Sounds* and *Health Report*, and Saturday it's the first of four hours of *Australia All Over*. Continuous programming to the Pacific on 9580, 9660, 11880 and 12080 kHz; and to East and Southeast Asia on 9500 kHz (may also be audible in Europe). In western North America, try 9580 and 11880 kHz.

Voice of Russia World Service. *News*, then a variety of features, depending on the day and season. Monday through Saturday, the same three shows—*Science and Engineering*, *Newmarket* and *Moscow Mailbag*—are broadcast twice each week, but the winter timings are different from those in summer. Winters on the half-hour, the lineup includes ●*Moscow Yesterday and Today* (Monday), *This is Russia* (Tuesday), *Kaleidoscope* (Wednesday), ●*Audio Book Club* (Thursday), *Russian by Radio* (Friday) and Saturday's ●*Christian Message from Moscow*. Best of the summer offerings at this time are Thursday's ●*Folk Box* and Friday's *Jazz Show*. There's also classical music on Wednesday. Continuous to Europe winters on 9890 kHz and frequencies in the 6 and 7 MHz segments; best summer channels are in the 9 and 11 MHz ranges (try 9765 and 9775 kHz). Some of these channels are audible in eastern North America.

Radio Kuwait. The final sixty minutes of a three-hour broadcast to Europe and eastern North America (see 1800). Regular features at this time include *Theater in Kuwait* (2000), *Saheeh Muslim* (2030) and *News in Brief* at 2057. On 11990 kHz.

Radio Bulgaria. This time winters only. *News*, then Monday through Thursday there's 15 minutes of current events in *Today*, replaced Friday by *Weekly Spotlight*, a summary of the week's major political stories. The remainder of the broadcast is given over to features dealing with Bulgaria and Bulgarians, and includes some lively ethnic music. To Europe, also audible in eastern North America, on 7530 and 9700 kHz. One hour earlier during summer.

Voice of Greece. Summers only at this time and actually starts about three minutes into the broadcast, after a little bit of Greek. Approximately ten minutes of *news* from and about Greece. To Europe on 7430 or 9420 kHz.

Radio Budapest, Hungary. Winters only at this time; see 2100 for specifics. Thirty minutes to Europe on 3975 and 9835 kHz. One hour earlier in summer.

China Radio International. *News* and commentary, followed Tuesday through Friday by *Current Affairs*. These, in turn, are followed by various feature programs. Sunday's lineup includes *Cultural Information*, *Snapshots*, *Report from Developing Countries*, *Song of the Week* and *Listeners' Letterbox*; Monday's offerings are *Open Windows* and *Let's Learn Chinese*; Tuesdays, it's *Orient Arena* and *Voices from Other Lands*; Wednesday, there's *Profile* and another chance to *Learn to Speak Chinese*; Thursday's presentations are *Focus* and *Cultural Spectrum*; while Friday's features are *Life in China* and *Global Review*. To round off the week, there's an eclectic Saturday menu consisting of *Asia-Pacific News*, *Chinese Folk Tales*, *Cooking Show*, *China Scrapbook* and ●*Music from China*. One hour to Europe on 6950 and 9920 kHz, and to Africa on 7160, 7170, 7175 and 9440 kHz. May also be available on 11840 or 11975 kHz. In the Mideast, try 7175 and 9440 kHz.

Radio Nacional de Angola ("Angolan National Radio"). The first 30 minutes or so consist of a mix of music and short features, then there's *news* near the half-hour. The remainder of the broadcast is given over to some thoroughly enjoyable Angolan music. Sixty minutes to Southern Africa on 3354 and (when active) 9535 kHz, with the second frequency also audible in parts of Europe and eastern North America, especially during winter.

Radio Pyongyang, North Korea. Repeat of the 1100 broadcast. To Europe, the Mideast and beyond on 6575, 9345, 9640 and 9975 kHz.

"For the People," WHRI, Noblesville, Indiana. Monday through Friday only; see 0300 for specifics. Part of a three-hour populist package broadcast live to North America on 9495 kHz.

Kol Israel. Winters only at this time. Thirty minutes of *news* and in-depth reporting from and about Israel. To Europe and North America on 7465, 9365 and 9435 kHz; and to Australasia on 15640 kHz. One hour earlier in summer.

YLE Radio Finland. Summers only at this time; see 2100 for specifics. A half hour to Europe on 6135 kHz. One hour later in winter.

HCJB—Voice of the Andes, Ecuador. Continues with a three-hour block of religious and secular programming to Europe. Monday through Friday it's the same features as 0200 (see there for specifics), but one day earlier. Weekends, look for *Solstice* and *Sports Spectrum* on Saturday, replaced Sunday by *Radio Reading Room* and *Joy International*. Winter on 12015 kHz, and summer on 17735 kHz.

Voice of America. Continuous programming to the Mideast and North Africa. *News*, reports and capsulated features covering everything from politics to entertainment. On 6095 (winter), 9760, and (summer) 9770 kHz. For African listeners there's the weekday *Africa World Tonight*, replaced weekends by *Nightline Africa*, on 6035, 7275, 7375, 7415, 11715, 11855, 15410, 15445, 15580, 17725 and 17755 kHz, some of which are seasonal. Both transmissions are heard well beyond their target areas, including parts of North America.

Radio For Peace International, Costa Rica. Part of an eight-hour cyclical block of predominantly social-conscience and counterculture programming. Some of the offerings at this hour include a women's news-gathering service, *WINGS*, (2030 Thursday) and a listener-response program (same time Friday). Audible in Europe and North America on 15050 and 21460 kHz.

WJCR, Upton, Kentucky. Continues with country gospel music to North America on 7490 and 13595 kHz. Other U.S. religious broadcasters which operate at this time include **WWCR** on 13845 and 15685 kHz, **KTBN** on 15590 kHz, and **WHRI—World Harvest Radio** on 13760 kHz. For traditional Catholic programming, tune **WEWN** on 7425 kHz.

Radio Prague, Czech Republic. Summers only at this time. *News*, then Monday through Friday there's *Current Affairs*. These are followed by one or more features. Monday has *Magazine '99*; Tuesday, it's *Talking Point* and *Media Czech*; Wednesday's offerings are *The Arts* and *History Czech*; Thursday brings *Economic Report* and *I'd Like You to Meet...*; and Friday there's *Between You and Us*. Look for some excellent entertainment in Saturday's musical feature, replaced Sunday by *The Week in Politics*, *From the Weeklies* and *Media Czech*. Thirty minutes to Europe on 5930 kHz, and to Southeast Asia and Australasia on 11600 kHz.

CFRX-CFRB, Toronto, Canada. See 1800. Summer weekdays at this time, you can hear ●*The World Today*, three hours of news, interviews, sports and commentary. On 6070 kHz.

20:15

Voice of Armenia. Summers only at this time. Mainly of interest to Armenians abroad. Thirty minutes of Armenian *news*

Allen Graham is HCJB's Interim Director of English Language Service and Producer of "DX Paryline" and "El Mundo Futuro." HCJB

and culture. To Europe on 9965 kHz. Sometimes audible in eastern North America. One hour later in winter.

20:30

Radio Sweden. Daily in winter, but weekends only in summer. See 1830 for program details. Thirty minutes year round to Europe on 6065 kHz, and summers to Africa on 13830 kHz.

Voice of Vietnam. *News*, followed by *Commentary* or *Weekly Review*, then some short features and pleasant Vietnamese music (especially at weekends). A half hour to Europe on 9840 and 12020 (or 15010) kHz.

Radio Thailand. Fifteen minutes of *news* targeted at Europe. Winters on 9535 (or 11805) kHz, and summers on 9680 kHz. Also available to Asia on 9655 and 11905 kHz.

Voice of Turkey. This time summers only. *News*, followed by *Review of the Turkish Press* and features (some of them arcane) with a strong local flavor. Selections of Turkish popular and classical music complete the program. Fifty minutes

to Southeast Asia and Australasia on 7210 kHz. One hour later during winter.

Radio Tashkent, Uzbekistan. Thirty minutes of *news*, commentary and features, with some exotic Uzbek music. To Europe winters on 7105 and 9540 kHz, and summer on 9540 and 9545 kHz.

RAI International—Radio Roma, Italy. Actually starts at 2025. Twenty minutes of *news* and music targeted at the Mideast, winters on 7125, 9685 and 11840 kHz; and summers on 7120, 9710 and 11880 kHz.

20:45

All India Radio. The first 15 minutes of a much longer broadcast, consisting of a press review, Indian music, regional and international *news*, commentary, and a variety of talks and features of general interest. Continuous till 2230. To Western Europe on 7410, 9950 and 11620 kHz; and to Australasia on 7150, 9910, 11620 and 11715 kHz. Early risers in Southeast Asia can try the Australasian channels.

Vatican Radio. Winters only at this time, and actually starts at 2050. Twenty minutes of predominantly Catholic fare. To

Europe on 4015 and 5882 kHz. Frequencies may vary slightly. One hour earlier in summer.

21:00

■BBC World Service for Europe and the Americas. *World News*, then 10 minutes of specialized business and financial reporting—except Sunday, when *Write On*, a listener-response show is aired. These are followed at 2115 by ●*Britain Today* or (on 5975 kHz) ●*Caribbean Report*. On the half-hour, regular spots include *Meridian* (Tuesday, Thursday and Saturday), *On Screen* (Wednesday), ●*People and Politics* (Friday) and the classical *Music Review* on Sunday. To eastern North America and the Caribbean on 5975 kHz. If you prefer *Britain Today* to the Caribbean alternative, try 11750 or 12095 kHz, targeted at South America. For Europe, choose from 3955 (winter), 6180, 6195, 7325 and 9410 kHz.

■BBC World Service for Asia and the Pacific. *World News*, a business report and a wide variety of features. Pick of the litter are ●*Short Story* (2115 Monday), ●*Discovery* (2130 Tuesday), ●*From Our Own Correspondent* and ●*One Planet* (Wednesday), ●*The Learning World* and ●*Assignment* (Thursday), and Friday's more specialized offerings—*The Farming World* and *The Works* (technology). Saturday, there's 45 minutes of some of the best in classical music. To East Asia on 5965, 6120 (winter) and (summer) 11945 kHz; to Southeast Asia on 3915, 5975 (winter), 6195 and 9740 kHz; and to Australasia on 5975 and 9740 kHz.

> Radio Exterior de España presents "Great Figures in Flamenco" each Sunday, followed by "Radio Club."

Radio Exterior de España ("Spanish National Radio"). *News*, followed Monday through Friday by *Panorama* (Spanish popular music, commentary, press review and weather), then a couple of features: *Sports Spotlight* and *Cultural Encounters* (Monday); *People of Today* and *Entertainment in Spain* (Tuesday); *As Others See Us* and, biweekly, *The Natural World* or *Science Desk* (Wednesday); *Economic Report* and *Cultural Clippings* (Thursday); and *Window on Spain* and *Review of the Arts* (Friday). The broadcast ends with a language course, *Spanish by Radio*. On weekends, there's Saturday's *Hall of Fame*, *Distance Unknown* (for radio enthusiasts) and *Gallery of Spanish Voices*; replaced Sunday by *Visitors' Book*, *Great Figures in Flamenco* and *Radio Club*. One hour to Europe on 6125 kHz, and to Africa on 11775 kHz.

Radio Ukraine International. Summers only at this time. *News*, commentary, reports and interviews, covering multiple aspects of Ukrainian life. Saturdays feature a listener-response program, and most of Sunday's broadcast is a showpiece for Ukrainian music. Sixty minutes to Europe on 5905, 6020, 6080, 7180, 7240, 7410, 9550, 9560, 12040 and 13590 kHz; and to Australasia on 7380 kHz. Also audible in parts of eastern North America. One hour later in winter.

Radio Canada International. Winters, the first hour of a 90-minute broadcast; summers, the last half-hour of the same. Winters, there's *News*, followed Monday through Friday by *Spectrum* (current events), which is replaced Saturday by *Venture Canada* and ●*Earth Watch*, and Sunday by *Arts in Canada* and a listener-response program. Summer weekdays, it's the CBC domestic service's ●*The World at Six*, with weekend fare consisting of *The World This Weekend*. To Europe and Africa winters on 5925, 5995, 7235, 9805, 11945, 13670, 13690, 15150 and 17820 kHz; and summers on 5995 (also for the Mideast), 7235, 11690, 13650, 13670, 15150, 15325 and 17820 kHz. Some of these are also audible in parts of North America.

Radio Prague, Czech Republic. Winters only at this time; see 2000 for program details. *News* and features dealing with Czech life and culture. A half hour to western Europe and eastern North America on 5930 kHz, and to West Africa on 7345 kHz.

Radio Bulgaria. This time summers only; see 1900 for specifics. *News*, features and some entertaining folk music. To Europe and eastern North America on 9700 and 11720 kHz. One hour later during winter.

China Radio International. Repeat of the 2000 transmission. One hour to Europe on 6950 and 9920 kHz. A 30-minute shortened version is also available to Africa on 7170, 7180 and 9535 kHz.

Voice of Russia World Service. Winters only at this time. *News*, then *Science and Engineering* (Monday and Thursday), the business-oriented *Newmarket* (Wednesday and Saturday), *Moscow Mailbag* (Tuesday and Friday) or *Sunday Panorama*. Best offerings on the half-hour are Thursday's ●*Folk Box* and Friday's *Jazz Show*. There's also classical music on Wednesday. Continuous to Europe winters on 9890 kHz and frequencies in the 6 and 7 MHz segments; best summer channels are in the 9 and 11 MHz ranges (try 9765 and 9775 kHz). Some of these channels are audible in eastern North America.

Radio Budapest, Hungary. Summers only at this time. *News* and features, some of which are broadcast on a regular basis. These include Monday's *Musica Hungarica*, *Focus on Business* and *The Weeklies* (Wednesday), *Letter Home* (Thursday) and *Profiles* (Saturday). Thirty minutes to Europe on 3975 and 11700 kHz. One hour later in winter.

Radio Australia. *World News*, then Sunday through Thursday it's current events in *AM* (replaced Friday by a listener-response program, *Feedback*). Next, on the half-hour, there's a daily feature. Take your pick from *Earthbeat* (environment, Sunday); *Innovations* (the invented and innovative, Monday and Friday); *Arts Australia* (culture, Tuesday) *Rural Reporter* (regional Australia, Wednesday); and *Book Talk* (new books, Thursday). The Saturday slot is filled by the second hour of *Australia All Over*. Continuous to the Pacific on 7240, 9660, 11880, 12080, 17715 and 21740 kHz; and to East and Southeast Asia (till 2130) on 9500 kHz. Listeners in western North America can try 11880 and 17715 kHz.

■**Deutsche Welle,** Germany. *News*, then weekdays (Tuesday through Saturday in the target areas) it's ●*NewsLink* followed by a feature. Monday, it's either *Development Forum* or *Women on the Move*; Tuesday, there's a look at ●*Man and Environment*; Wednesday's slot is ●*Insight*; Thursday, there's *Living in Germany*; and Friday's slot is *Spotlight on Sport*. The weekend starts with *Saturday Review* and *Mailbag*, and ends with *Sunday Review* and *Arts on the Air*. Fifty minutes to Asia and Australasia on 7115 (summer), 9670, 9765 and 11785 kHz. An almost identical broadcast (except that Saturday's *Mailbag* is replaced by *African Kaleidoscope*) goes out simultaneously to West Africa, and is audible in much of eastern North America. Winters on 9615, 9690, 11865 and 15275 kHz; and summers on 9735, 11865 and 15135 kHz.

Radio Japan. Repeat of the 1700 transmission; see there for specifics. One hour to East and Southeast Asia winters on 6035, 7125 and 7140 kHz; and summers on 6035, 9535 and 9560 kHz. Also to Australasia on 11850 kHz. There is also a separate 10-minute *news* broadcast to Southeast Asia on 7190 or 11685 kHz.

Radio Yugoslavia. Summers only at this time. *News* and short background reports, mostly about local issues. An informative half hour to Europe on 6100 and 6185 kHz. One hour later in winter.

Radio Romania International. *News*, commentary and features (see 1900), interspersed with some thoroughly enjoyable Romanian folk music. One hour to Europe winters on 5955, 5990, 7105 and 7195 kHz; summers on 5990, 7105, 7195 and 9690 kHz. Also audible in eastern North America.

Radio Habana Cuba. A 60-minute package of *news* (predominantly about Cuba and Latin America), features about the island and its people, and some thoroughly enjoyable Cuban music. To Europe on (winter) 9550 kHz and (summer) 11705 or 13715 kHz.

Radio Korea International, South Korea. Starts with *news*, followed Monday through Wednesday by *Economic News Briefs*. The remainder of the broadcast is taken up by a feature: *Shortwave Feedback* (Sunday), *Seoul Calling* (Monday and Tuesday), *Pulse of Korea* (Wednesday), *From Us to You* (Thursday), *Let's Sing Together* (Friday) and *Weekly News Focus* (Saturday). Thirty minutes to Europe summers on 3970 kHz, and one hour later in winter. Also at this time, a repeat of the 1900 one-hour

broadcast to East Asia is beamed to Europe year round on 6480 and 15575 kHz.

Radio For Peace International, Costa Rica. Continues at this hour with a potpourri of United Nations, counterculture and other programs. These include *WINGS* (news for and of women, 2130 Tuesday) and *Vietnam Veterans Radio Network* (same time Wednesday). Audible in Europe and North America on 15050 and 21460 kHz.

YLE Radio Finland. Winters only at this time. Most days it's *Compass North* and a press review. Exceptions are Saturday's *Capital Café* and Sunday's world band curiosity, *Nuntii Latini* (news in Latin), heard at 2123. Thirty minutes to Europe on 6135 kHz. One hour earlier in summer.

HCJB—Voice of the Andes, Ecuador. The final sixty minutes of a three-hour block of predominantly religious programming to Europe, winter on 12015 kHz, and summer on 17735 kHz.

Voice of America. For Africa and Australasia, it's *News Now*—a series of reports and features covering a multitude of topics. Also available to the Mideast and North Africa on 6040, 9535 (summer) and 9760 kHz. In Africa, tune to 6035, 7375, 7415, 11715, 11975, 13710, 15410, 15445, 15580 and 17725 kHz (some of which are seasonal); and in Southeast Asia and the Pacific to 11870, 15185 and 17735 kHz.

XERMX—Radio México Internacional. Winters only at this time. Starts with a feature. Monday, it's *The Sounds of Mexico*, replaced Tuesday and Sunday by *Mailbox*, Thursday by *Eternally Mexico* and Friday by *Mirror of Mexico*. Wednesdays and Saturdays, the English program gives way to one in French. On the half-hour, there's 30 minutes of music. Best heard in western and southern parts of the United States on 5985 and 9705 kHz.

All India Radio. Continues to Western Europe on 7410, 9950 and 11620 kHz; and to Australasia on 7150, 9910, 11620 and 11715 kHz. Look for some authentic Indian music from 2115 onwards. The European frequencies are audible in parts of eastern North America, while those for Australasia are also heard in Southeast Asia.

"For the People," WHRI, Noblesville, Indiana. winters only at this time. Monday through Friday only; see 0300 for specifics. The final hour of a three-hour populist package broadcast live to North America on 9495 kHz. One hour earlier in summer.

CFRX-CFRB, Toronto, Canada. If you live in the northeastern United States or southeastern Canada, try this pleasant little local station, usually audible for hundreds of miles/kilometers during daylight hours on 6070 kHz. Winter weekdays at this time, you can hear ●*The World Today* (summers, starts at 2000)— three hours of news, sport and interviews.

be clearly heard throughout much of eastern North America. This brief, 15-minute program provides comprehensive coverage of Caribbean economic and political affairs, both within and outside the region. Monday through Friday only, on 6110, 15390 and 17715 kHz.

Radio Cairo, Egypt. The start of a 90-minute broadcast devoted to Arab and Egyptian life and culture. The initial quarter-hour of general programming is followed by *news,* commentary and political items. This in turn is followed by a cultural program until 2215, when the station again reverts to more general fare. A Middle Eastern melange, including exotic Arab music, beamed to Europe on 9900 kHz.

WJCR, Upton, Kentucky. Continuous gospel music to North America on 7490 and 13595 kHz. Other U.S. religious

21:15

Radio Damascus, Syria. Actually starts at 2110. *News,* a daily press review, and a variety of features (depending on the day of the week) at approximately 2130 and 2145. These include *Arab Profile* and *Economic Affairs* (Sunday), *Camera and Masks* and *Selected Readings* (Monday), *Reflections* and *Back on the Stage* (Tuesday), *Listeners Overseas* and *Palestine Talking* (Wednesday), *From the World Press* and *Arab Women in Focus* (Thursday), *Arab Newsweek* and *From Our Literature* (Friday), and *Human Rights* and *Syria and the World* (Saturday). The transmission also contains Syrian and some western popular music. Sixty minutes to North America and Australasia on 12085 and 13610 (or 15095) kHz.

■**BBC World Service for the Caribbean.** ●*Caribbean Report*, although intended for listeners in the area, can also

broadcasters operating at this hour include **WWCR** on 13845 and 15685 and kHz, **KTBN** on 15590 kHz, and **WHRI—World Harvest Radio** on 13760 kHz. Traditional Catholic programming is available from **WEWN** on 7425 kHz.

21:15

Voice of Armenia. Winters only at this time. Mainly of interest to Armenians abroad. Thirty minutes of Armenian *news* and culture. To Europe on 9965 kHz, and sometimes audible in eastern North America. One hour earlier in summer.

21:30

BBC World Service for the Falkland Islands. *Calling the Falklands* has long been one of the curiosities of international broadcasting, and consists of news and features for this small community in the South Atlantic. Topics are often unusual, and range from news about isolated islands to Argentinian politics. Fifteen minutes Tuesdays and Fridays on 11680 kHz—easily heard in eastern North America.

Radio Austria International. Summers only at this time. Thirty minutes of news and human-interest stories in ●*Report from Austria*. A worthy source of national and regional news. To Europe on 5945 and 6155 kHz; and to southern Africa on 13730 kHz. One hour later during winter.

Radio Tashkent, Uzbekistan. Thirty minutes of *news*, commentary and features, plus some exotic Uzbek music. To Europe winters on 7105 and 9540 kHz, and summer on 9540 and 9545 kHz.

Radio Tirana, Albania. Summers only at this time. *News*, reports and some lively Albanian music. Thirty minutes to Europe on 6025 and 7165 kHz.

Voice of the Islamic Republic of Iran. Sixty minutes of *news*, commentary and features with a strong Islamic slant. On 6175 and 9670 kHz, but may be subject to change.

Voice of Turkey. This time winters only. *News*, followed by *Review of the Turkish Press* and features (some of them arcane) with a strong local flavor. Selections of Turkish popular and classical music complete the program. Fifty minutes to Southeast Asia and Australasia on 7200 kHz. One hour earlier in summer.

Radio Sweden. Daily in summer, but winter weekends only. Thirty minutes of predominantly Scandinavian fare (see 2230 for specifics). Year-round to Europe and the Mideast on 6065 kHz; and to Africa on 9655 (winter) or (summer) 9430 kHz.

22:00

■**BBC World Service for Europe and the Americas.** Thirty minutes of ●*Newsdesk*, followed by ●*Insight* (current events, Monday through Friday), ●*Play of the Week* (world theater, Saturday) or Sunday's ●*Health Matters*. The final quarter hour Sunday through Friday is devoted to ●*Sports Roundup*. Continuous programming to North America and the Caribbean on 5975, 6175 and 9590 kHz; and to Europe on 3955 (winter), 6195 and (till 2230) 7325 and 9410 kHz. In summer, transmissions to Europe end at 2230.

■**BBC World Service for Asia and the Pacific.** Starts with 30 minutes of ●*Newsdesk*, and ends with a quarter hour of ●*Sports Roundup*. In between, it's the weekday ●*World Business Report* (Tuesday through Saturday local Asian days), Saturday's *From the Weeklies*, or Sunday's ●*Letter from America*. Continuous to East Asia on 5905 (winter), 5965, 9890 (summer) and 11955 kHz; to Southeast Asia on 6195, 7110, 9660 and 11955 kHz; and to Australasia on 9660, 11955 and 12080 kHz.

John Beck, station manager and producer of "Ham Radio Today" from powerful HCJB in Quito, Ecuador. HCJB

Radio Bulgaria. This time winters only. *News*, then Monday through Thursday there's 15 minutes of current events in *Today*, replaced Friday by *Weekly Spotlight*, a summary of the week's major political stories. The remainder of the broadcast is given over to features dealing with Bulgaria and Bulgarians, and includes some lively ethnic music. To Europe and eastern North America on 7530 and 9700 kHz. One hour earlier in summer.

Radio Cairo, Egypt. The second half of a 90-minute broadcast to Europe on 9900 kHz; see 2115 for program details.

Voice of America. The beginning of a three-hour block of programs to East and Southeast Asia and the Pacific. The ubiquitous *News Now*—news and reports on current events, sports, science, business, entertainment and more. To East and Southeast Asia on 7215, 9705, 9770, 11760, 15185, 15290, 15305, 17735 and 17820 kHz; and to Australasia on 15185, 15305 and 17735 kHz. The first half hour is also available weekday evenings to Africa on 7340, 7375 and 7415 kHz.

Radio Australia. *News*, followed Sunday through Thursday by *AM* (current events). The hour is rounded off with a 20-minute music feature. The lineup starts with Sunday's samples from different cultures, *Music Deli*, and ends with Thursday's *Australian Country Style*. In-between, choose from *Australian Music Show* (Monday); *At Your Request* (Tuesday); and *Blacktracker* (aboriginal music, Wednesday). Friday's features are *Jazz Notes* and a later-than-usual edition of *AM*; Saturday, it's the third hour of *Australia All Over*. Continuous programming to the Pacific on 17715, 17795 and 21725 kHz. Also audible in parts of western North America.

Radio Taipei International, Taiwan. *News*, then features. The last is *Let's Learn Chinese*, which has a series of segments for beginning, intermediate and advanced learners. Other features include *Jade Bells and Bamboo Pipes* (Monday), *People and Trends* (Tuesday), *Taiwan Today* and *Miss Mook's Big Countdown* (Wednesday), *Treasures of the Orient* and *Hot Spots* (Thursday), *Taipei Magazine* and *Life on the Outside* (Friday), *Kaleidoscope* and *Reflections* (Saturday) and *Food, Poetry and Others* followed by *Mailbag Time* on Sunday. Sixty minutes to western Europe, winters on 5810 and 9985 kHz, and summers on 15600 and 17750 kHz.

Radio Tirana, Albania. Winters only at this time. Thirty minutes of Balkan news and music. To Europe on 6025 and 7135 kHz.

Radio Habana Cuba. Sixty minutes of *news* (mainly about Cuba and Latin America), features about the island and its inhabitants, and some thoroughly enjoyable Cuban music. To the Caribbean and southern United States on 6180 kHz, and to eastern North America and Europe on (winter) 9505 and (summer) 13720 kHz upper sideband.

Radio Budapest, Hungary. Winters only at this time; see 2100 for specifics. Thirty minutes to Europe on 3975 and 9840 kHz. One hour earlier in summer.

Voice of Turkey. Summers only at this time. *News*, followed by *Review of the Turkish Press* and features with a strong local flavor. Selections of Turkish popular and classical music complete the program. Fifty minutes to Europe on 7190 and 9655 kHz, and to eastern North America on 9655 kHz. One hour later during winter.

Radio Yugoslavia. Winters only at this time. Repeat of the 1930 broadcast. Thirty minutes to Europe on 6100 and 6185 kHz. One hour earlier in summer.

Radio Canada International. This time winters only. The final half-hour of a 90-minute broadcast. Monday through Friday, it's the CBC domestic service's ●*The World at Six*, with weekend fare consisting of Saturday's *Madly Off in All Directions* and Sunday's *The Inside Track*. To Europe and Africa on 5995, 7235, 9805, 11945, 13690 and 15150 kHz. For a separate summer service, see the following item.

Radio Canada International. Summers only; a relay of CBC domestic programming, except for the final 30 minutes weekends. Monday through Friday, there's ● *The World at Six*; Saturday and Sunday, *The World This Weekend*. On the half-hour, the weekday ●*As It Happens* is replaced Saturday by ●*The Mystery Project* and Sunday by *Sound Advice*. Sixty minutes to North America on 5960, 9755 and 13670 kHz. One hour later in winter. For a separate year-round service to Asia, see the next item.

Radio Canada International. Monday through Friday, it's ●*The World At Six*; Saturday and Sunday summer, *The World This Weekend*. Winter weekends, look for Saturday's comedy spot and Sunday's *The Inside Track*. Thirty minutes to Southeast Asia on 11705 kHz.

Radio Norway International. Sundays only. *Norway Now*. Thirty minutes of *news* and human-interest stories from and about Norway. Winters to East Asia on 7115 kHz, and to eastern North America on 6200 kHz; in summer, to Australasia on 9485 kHz.

RAI International—Radio Roma, Italy. Approximately ten minutes of *news* followed by a quarter-hour feature (usually music). Twenty-five minutes to East Asia on 6150, 9675 and 11900 kHz.

Radio Korea International, South Korea. Winters only at this hour. Starts with *news*, followed Monday through Wednesday by *Economic News Briefs*. The remainder of the broadcast is taken up by a feature: *Shortwave Feedback* (Sunday), *Seoul Calling* (Monday and Tuesday), *Pulse of Korea* (Wednesday), *From Us to You* (Thursday), *Let's Sing Together* (Friday) and *Weekly News Focus* (Saturday). Thirty minutes to Europe on 3970 kHz, and one hour earlier in summer.

Radio Ukraine International. Winters only at this time. A potpourri of all things Ukrainian, with the Sunday broadcast often featuring some excellent music. Sixty minutes to Europe and beyond on 5905, 5940, 6010, 6020, 6080, 7205 and 7420 kHz. Often audible in eastern North America.

Radio For Peace International, Costa Rica. Continues with counterculture and social-conscience programs. Audible in Europe and North America on 15050 and 21460 kHz.

All India Radio. The final half-hour of a transmission to Western Europe and Australasia, consisting mainly of news-related fare. To Europe on 7410, 9950 and 11620 kHz; and to Australasia on 7150, 9910, 11620 and 11715 kHz. Frequencies for Europe are audible in parts of eastern North America, while those for Australasia are also heard in Southeast Asia.

WJCR, Upton, Kentucky. Continues with country gospel music to North America on 7490 and 13595 kHz. Other U.S. religious broadcasters heard at this hour include **WWCR** on 13845 kHz, **KAIJ** on 13815 kHz, **KTBN** on 15590 kHz, and **WHRI—World Harvest Radio** on 5745 (or 13760) kHz. For traditional Catholic programming, try **WEWN** on 7425 kHz.

CFRX-CFRB, Toronto, Canada. See 2100.

22:30

Radio Sweden. Winters only at this time. Monday through Friday, it's *news* and features in *Sixty Degrees North*, concentrating heavily on Scandinavian topics. Monday's accent is on sports; Tuesday brings the latest in electronic media news; Wednesday, there's *Money Matters*; Thursday features ecology or science and technology; and Friday offers a review of the week's news. Saturday's slot is filled by *Spectrum* (arts) or *Sweden Today*, and Sunday fare consists of *In Touch with Stockholm* (a listener-response program) or the musical *Sounds Nordic*. Thirty minutes to Europe on 6065 kHz. One hour earlier in summer.

Radio Austria International. Winters only at this time. The informative and well-presented ●*Report from Austria*. Ample coverage of national and regional issues. Thirty minutes to Europe on 5945 and 6155 kHz, and to southern Africa on 13730 kHz. One hour earlier in summer.

Radio Prague, Czech Republic. *News*, then Monday through Friday there's *Current Affairs*, followed by one or more features. Early in the week, take your pick from Monday's *Magazine '99*; Tuesday's *Talking Point* and *Media Czech*; and Wednesday's *The Arts* and *History Czech*. The Thursday lineup is *Economic Report* and *I'd Like You to Meet...*; and Friday's slot is *Between You and Us*. Saturday's offering is a thoroughly enjoyable musical feature, replaced Sunday by *The Week in Politics*, *From the Weeklies* and *Media Czech*. A half hour to eastern North America, winters on 5930 and 7345 kHz, and summers on 9435 and 11600 kHz.

Voice of Greece. Actually starts around 2235. Fifteen minutes of English news from and about Greece. Part of a much longer, predominantly Greek, broadcast. To Australasia on 9425 kHz.

22:45

All India Radio. The first 15 minutes of a much longer broadcast, consisting of Indian music, regional and international *news*, commentary, and a variety of talks and features of general interest. Continuous till 0045. To Southeast Asia (and beyond) on 7150, 9705, 9950 and 11620 kHz.

Vatican Radio. Twenty minutes of religious and secular programming to East and Southeast Asia and Australasia on 6065, 7305, 9600 and 11830 kHz, some of them seasonal.

23:00

■**BBC World Service for the Americas.** Sunday through Friday, opens with *World News*. This is followed weekday evenings by the popular and long-running

●*Outlook*, replaced Sunday by short features. Saturday, it's a continuation of ●*Play of the Week*. During the week, the second half hour is geared to a younger audience—*Multitrack* (Monday, Wednesday and Friday), *Megamix* (Tuesday) and ●*John Peel* (Thursday). If Saturday's play doesn't overrun, you can hear ●*World of Music* at 2230, replaced Sunday by the more sedate *In Praise of God*. Continuous to North America and the Caribbean on 5975, 6175 and 9590 kHz. Winters, the initial 30 minutes is also available to Europe on 3955 and 6195 kHz.

■BBC World Service for Asia and the Pacific. *World News*, then Sunday through Friday (Monday through Saturday local Asian days) there's ●*East Asia Today*. This, in turn, is followed Monday through Friday by 15 minutes of ●*Insight* (current events). The remainder of the schedule is mostly made up of short features, the best of which is Thursday's ●*Health Matters*. The exceptions are ●*From Our Own Correspondent* and ●*Science in Action* (Saturday), and the eclectic ●*Anything Goes* (2330 Sunday), all of which last 30 minutes. Continuous to East Asia on 5965, 6035, 9580 (winter), 11945, 11955 and (summer) 15280 and 17790 kHz; to Southeast Asia on 6195, 7110 and 11955 kHz; and to Australasia on 11955 kHz.

Voice of Turkey. Winters only at this hour. See 2200 for program details. Fifty minutes to Europe on 6135 and 9655 kHz, and to eastern North America on 9655 kHz. One hour earlier in summer.

■Deutsche Welle, Germany. Repeat of the 2100 broadcast. Fifty minutes to South and Southeast Asia, winter on 6045, 6130 and 7235 kHz; and summer on 5975, 6090, 7235 and 9815 kHz.

Radio Japan. Very similar to the 1500 transmission (see there for specifics), except that Monday through Friday the news is extended at the expense of *Tokyo Pop-in*.

Sixty minutes to Europe on one or more channels from 5965, 6055 and 6155 kHz; to East and Southeast Asia winter on 7125 and 7140 kHz, and summer on 9535 and 9560 kHz; and to Australasia on 11850 kHz.

Radio Australia. *World News*, followed Monday through Thursday by *Asia Pacific* (replaced Friday by *Book Reading*, and Sunday by *Correspondents' Reports*). On the half-hour, look for a feature. *Media Report* occupies the Sunday slot, and is replaced Monday by *The Sports Factor*. Then come Tuesday's *Health Report*, Wednesday's *Law Report*, Thursday's *Religion Report*, and Friday's *Week's End*. Not very original, but you know what you're getting. Saturday, there's the fourth and final hour of *Australia All Over*. Continuous to the Pacific on 9660, 12080, 17715, 17795 and 21740 kHz. Listeners in western North America should try the last three channels, especially in summer.

Radio Canada International. Summer weekdays, the final hour of ●*As It Happens*; winters, the first 30 minutes of the same, preceded by the up-to-the-minute *news* program ●*World at Six*. Summer weekends, look for ●*Quirks and Quarks* (Saturday, science) and *Sound Advice* (Sunday, culture). These are replaced winter by *The World This Weekend* (both days), ●*Mystery Project* (Saturday) and *Sound Advice* (Sunday). To eastern North America on 5960 and 9755 kHz, with 13670 kHz also available in summer.

Radio Pyongyang, North Korea. Fifty minutes of old-time communist propaganda to the Americas on 11700 and 13650 kHz.

Radio For Peace International, Costa Rica. The final 60 minutes of a continuous eight-hour cyclical block of United Nations, counterculture, social-conscience and New Age programming. Audible in Europe and the Americas on 15050 and 21460 kHz.

Radio Cairo, Egypt. The first hour of a 90-minute potpourri of exotic Arab music and features reflecting Egyptian life and culture, with *news* and commentary about events in Egypt and the Arab world. There are also quizzes, mailbag shows, and answers to listeners' questions. Fair reception and mediocre audio quality to North America on 9900 kHz.

Radio Romania International. A recently introduced broadcast. *News*, commentary and features, interspersed with some thoroughly enjoyable Romanian folk music. Fifty-five minutes to Northern Europe and eastern North America. Try 7135, 9570, 9625 and 11940 kHz.

WRMI—Radio Miami International, Miami, Florida. Part of a much longer multilingual transmission to the Caribbean. Summer weekdays at this time, you can hear 30 minutes of *Viva Miami!*—a potpourri of information, music and entertainment. Also includes regular weather updates during the hurricane season (June-November). Heard in much of the Americas on 9955 kHz. One hour later in winter.

Radio Bulgaria. Summers only at this time; see 1900 for specifics. A potpourri of *news* and features with a strong Bulgarian flavor. Sixty minutes to eastern North America on 9485 and 11720 kHz. One hour later during winter.

Voice of America. Continues with programs aimed at East Asia and the Pacific on the same frequencies as at 2200.

WWCR, Nashville, Tennessee. Carries a variety of disestablishmentarian programs at this hour, depending on the day of the week, and whether it is summer or winter. These include winter's "Norman Resnick Show" and summer's "The Hour of Courage" and "The Voice of Liberty." On 5065 kHz.

WJCR, Upton, Kentucky. Continuous country gospel music to North America on 7490 and 13595 kHz. Other U.S. religious broadcasters heard at this time include **WWCR** on 13845 kHz, **KAIJ** on 13815 kHz, **KTBN** on 15590 kHz, and **WHRI—World Harvest Radio** on 5745 kHz. For traditional Catholic programming, tune **WEWN** on 7425 kHz.

23:30

■**Radio Netherlands.** *News*, followed Monday through Saturday by ●*Newsline*, then a feature program. Select offerings include ●*A Good Life* (Tuesday), ●*Research File* (Thursday), ●*Roughly Speaking* (Saturday) and Friday's ●*Documentary*. The remaining lineup consists of *Aural Tapestry* (Monday), *Sounds Interesting* (Wednesday) and Sunday's *Wide Angle* and *Siren Song*. One hour to North America on 6020, 6165 and (summers) 9845 kHz.

All India Radio. Continuous programming to Southeast Asia. A potpourri of *news*, commentary, features and exotic Indian music. On 7150, 9705, 9950 and 11620 kHz.

Voice of Vietnam. *News*, then it's *Commentary* or *Weekly Review*. These are followed by short features and some pleasant Vietnamese music (especially at weekends). A half hour to Asia (also heard in Europe) on 9840 and 12020 (or 15010) kHz.

Voice of Greece. Actually starts around 2335. Ten minutes of English news from and about Greece. Part of a much longer multilingual broadcast. To Central America (and well heard in eastern North America) on any two (sometimes three) frequencies from 9395, 9425. 9935, 11595 and 11640 kHz.

Prepared by Don Swampo and the staff of Passport to World Band Radio.

Addresses
PLUS—1999

E-Mail and Postal Addresses . . .
PLUS World Wide Websites,
Phones and Faxes, Contact
Personnel, Bureaus, Future Plans,
Items for Sale, Free Gifts . . .
PLUS Summer and Winter Times
in Each Country!

Other sections of PASSPORT tell how stations' signals reach you, but this section is different: It spins the bottle the other way by showing how you can reach the stations. It also reveals other ways that stations can inform and entertain you.

"Applause" Replies

When radio was new, listeners sent in "applause" cards not only to let stations know about reception qual-ity, but also how much their shows were—or were not—being appre-ciated. By way of saying "thanks," stations would reply with a letter or attractive card verifying ("QSLing" in radio lingo) that the station the listener reported hearing was, in fact, theirs. While they were at it, some would also throw in a free souvenir of their station—a calendar, perhaps, or a pennant or sticker.

This is still being done today. You can see how by looking under Verification in the glossary farther back in this book, then making use of Addresses PLUS for contact specifics.

Electronic Bazaar

Stations sell offbeat items, too. Besides the obvious, such as world band radios, some stations peddle native recordings, books, magazines, station T-shirts, ties, tote bags, aprons, caps, watches, clocks, pens, knives, letter openers, lighters, refrigerator magnets, keyrings and other collectables. One Miami-based station will even sell you airtime for a dollar a minute!

Paying Postfolk

Most stations prefer to reply to listener correspondence—even e-mail—via the postal system. That way, they can send out printed schedules, verification cards and other "hands-on" souvenirs. Big stations usually do so for free, but smaller ones often want to be reimbursed for postage costs.

Most effective, especially for Latin American and Indonesian stations, is to enclose some unused (mint) stamps from the station's country. These are available from Plum's Airmail Postage, 12 Glenn Road, Flemington NJ 08822 USA, phone +1 (908) 788-1020, fax +1 (908) 782 2612. Too, you can try DX Stamp Service, 6137 Patriot Drive, Apt. 13, Ontario NY 14519-8606 USA, phone +1 (315) 524-8806; or DX-QSL Associates, 434 Blair Road NW, Vienna VA 22180 USA. One way to help ensure your return-postage stamps will be put to your intended use is to stick them onto a pre-addressed return airmail envelope (self-addressed stamped envelope, or SASE).

You can also prompt reluctant stations by donating one or more U.S. dollars, preferably hidden from prying eyes by a piece of foil-covered carbon paper or the like. Registration helps, too, as cash tends to get stolen. Additionally, International Reply Coupons (IRCs), which recipients may exchange locally for air or surface stamps, are available at many post offices worldwide. Thing is, they're relatively costly, are not fully effective, and aren't accepted by postal authorities in all countries.

Girls sing on their way to school in Jerusalem. Kol Israel reaches out to listeners worldwide in a variety of languages, including English. R. Crane

ELWA's "Aunt Clara," when she used to read stories to youngsters in Liberia. SIM

Stamp Out Crime

Yes, even in 1999 mail theft is a problem in several countries. We identify these, and for each one offer proven ways to avoid theft.

Remember that some postal employees are stamp collectors, and in certain countries they freely steal mail with unusual stamps. When in doubt, use everyday stamps or, even better, a postal meter. Another option is to use an aerogram.

¿Que Hora Es?

World Time, explained elsewhere in this book, is essential if you want to find out when your favorite station is on. But if you want to know what time it is in any given country, World Time and Addresses PLUS work together to give you the most accurate local times within each country.

How accurate? The United States' official expert on international local times tells us that her organization finds PASSPORT's local times to be the most accurate available from any source, anywhere.

So that you don't have to wrestle with seasonal changes in your own local time, we give local times for each country in terms of hours' difference from World Time, which stays the same year-round. For example, if you look below under "Algeria," you'll see that country is World Time +1; that is, one hour ahead of World Time. So, if World Time is 1200, the local time in Algeria is 1300 (1:00 PM). On the other hand, México City is World Time –6; that is, six hours behind World Time. If World Time is 1200, in México City it's 6:00 AM. And so it goes for each country in this section. Times shown in parentheses are for the middle of the year—roughly April-October; specific dates of seasonal-time changeovers for individual countries can be obtained (U.S. callers only) by dialing toll-free 1 (800) 342-5624.

Spotted Something New?

Has something changed since we went to press? A missing detail? Please let us know! Your update information, especially photocopies of material received from stations, is highly valued. Contact the IBS Editorial Office, Box 300, Penn's Park, PA 18943 USA, fax +1 (215) 598 3794, e-mail addresses@passport.com.

Many thanks to the kindly folks and helpful organizations mentioned at the end of this chapter for their cooperation in the preparation of this section. Without you, none of this would have been possible.

Using PASSPORT's Addresses PLUS Section

Stations included: All stations known to reply, however erratically, or new stations which possibly may reply, to correspondence from listeners.

Leased-time programs: Private non-political organizations that lease air time, but which possess no world band transmitters of their own, are not necessarily listed. However, they may be reached via the stations over which they are heard.

Postal addresses. Communications addresses are given. These sometimes differ from the physical locations given in the Blue Pages.

E-mail addresses and URLs. Given in Internet format. Periods, commas and semicolons at the end of an address are normal sentence punctuation, *not* part of that address.

Fax numbers. To help avoid confusion, fax numbers are given *without* hyphens, telephone numbers with hyphens, and are configured for international dialing once you add your country's international access code (011 in the United States and Canada, 010 in the United Kingdom, and so on). For domestic dialing within countries outside the United States, Canada and the Caribbean, replace the country code (1-3 digits preceded by a "+") by a zero.

Giveaways. If you want freebies, say so politely in your correspondence. These are usually available until supplies run out.

Web radio. World band stations which also have RealAudio, NetShow or comparable Web audio programming are indicated by ☞. Full coverage of the 1,550 or so FM, mediumwave AM and world band stations simulcasting via Web radio are in PASSPORT TO WEB RADIO (www.passport.com).

Unless otherwise indicated, stations:

- Reply regularly within six months to most listeners' correspondence in English.

- Provide, upon request, free station schedules and verification ("QSL") postcards or letters (see "Verification" in the glossary for further information). We specify when other items are available for free or for purchase.

- Do not require compensation for postage costs incurred in replying to you. Where compensation is required, details are provided.

Local times. These are given in difference from World Time. For example, "World Time –5" means that if you subtract five hours from World Time, you'll get the local time in that country; so if it were 1100 World Time, it would be 0600 local time in that country. Times in (parentheses) are for the middle of the year—roughly April-October.

AFGHANISTAN   World Time +4:30

NOTE: Postal service to this country is occasionally suspended.
Radio Voice of Shari'ah, Afghan Radio TV, P.O. Box 544, Kabul, Afghanistan. Phone: +93 25241. Contact: A. Rahaman Nasseri, President of Planning and Foreign Relations. Replies occasionally.

ALBANIA   World Time +1 (+2 midyear)

Radio Tirana, External Service, Rruga Ismail Qemali, Tirana, Albania. Phone: (general) +355 (42) 23-239. Fax: (External Service) +355 (42) 23 650; (General Directorate) +355 (42) 26 203; (Technical Directorate) +355 (42) 27 745. Contact: Bardhyl Pollo, Director of External Services; Adriana Bislea, English Department; or Diana Koci; (Technical Directorate) Irfan Mandija, Chief of Radio Broadcasting, Technical Directorate; Hector Karanxha; or Rifat Kryeziu, Director of Technical Directorate. Replies from the station are again forthcoming, but it is advisable to include return postage ($1 should be enough).
Trans World Radio—*see* Monaco.

ALGERIA   World Time +1 (+2 midyear)

Radio Algiers International—same details as "Radio Algérienne," below.
Radio Algérienne (ENRS)
NONTECHNICAL AND GENERAL TECHNICAL: 21 Boulevard des Martyrs, Algiers 16000, Algeria. Phone: (general) +213 (2) 590-700; (head of international relations) +213 (2) 594-266; (head of technical direction) +213 (2) 692-867. Fax: +213 (2) 605 814. Contact: (nontechnical) L. Zaghlami; Chaabane Lounakil, Head of International Arabic Section; Mrs. Zehira Yahi, Head of International Relations; or Relations Extérieures; (technical) M. Lakhdar Mahdi, Head of Technical Direction. Replies irregularly. French or Arabic preferred, but English accepted.
FREQUENCY MANAGEMENT OFFICE: Télédiffusion d'Algérie, route de Bainem, B.P. 50, Bouzareah, Algeria. Fax: +213 (2) 797 390 or +213 (2) 941 390. Contact: Mouloud Lahlou, Director General.

ANGOLA   World Time +1

Emissora Provincial de Benguela (if reactivated), C.P. 19, Benguela, Angola. Contact: Simão Martíns Cuto, Responsável Administrativo; Carlos A. A. Gregório, Diretor; or José Cabral Sande. $1 or return postage required. Replies irregularly.
Emissora Provincial de Bié (if reactivated), C.P. 33, Kuito, Bié, Angola. Contact: José Cordeiro Chimo, Diretor. Replies occasionally to correspondence in Portuguese.
Emissora Provincial de Moxico (if reactivated), C.P. 74, Luena, Angola. Contact: Paulo Cahilo, Diretor. $1 or return postage required. Replies to correspondence in Portuguese.
Other **Emissora Provincial** stations (if reactivated)—same address, etc., as Rádio Nacional, below.
Rádio Nacional de Angola, C.P. 1329, Luanda, Angola. Fax: +244 (2) 391 234. Contact: Bernardino Costa, Public Opinion Office; Sra. Luiza Fancony, Diretora de Programas; Lourdes de Almeida, Chefe de Secção; or César A.B. da Silva, Diretor Geral. Formerly replied occasionally to correspondence, preferably in Portuguese, but replies have been more difficult recently. $1, return postage or 2 IRCs most helpful.

ANTARCTICA   World Time –3 Base Antárctica Esperanza

Radio Nacional Arcángel San Gabriel—LRA36, Base Esperanza, Tierra del Fuego, Antártida e Islas del Atlántico Sur, 9411 Argentina. Contact: Luis Dupuis; Tte. Cnel. Hugo Casela, Jefe Base Esperanza; or Sra. Adriana Figueroa. Return postage required. Replies to correspondence in Spanish, and sometimes to correspondence in English and French, depending upon who is at the station. If no reply, try sending your correspondence (but don't write the station's name on your envelope) and 2 IRCs via the helpful Gabriel Iván Barrera, Casilla 2868, 1000 Buenos Aires, Argentina; fax +54 (1) 322 3351.

ANGUILLA   World Time –4

Caribbean Beacon, Box 690, Anguilla, British West Indies. Phone: +1 (809) 497-4340. Fax: +1 (809) 497 4311. Contact: Monsell Hazell, Chief Engineer. $2 or return postage helpful. Relays Dr. Gene Scott's University Network—*see* USA.

ANTIGUA   World Time –4

BBC World Service—Caribbean Relay Station, P.O. Box 1203, St. John's, Antigua. Phone: +1 (809) 462-0994. Fax: +1 (809) 462 0436. Contact: (technical) G. Hoef, Manager; Roy Fleet; or R. Pratt, Company Engineer. Nontechnical correspondence should be sent to the BBC World Service in London (*see*).
Deutsche Welle—Relay Station Antigua—same address and contact as BBC World Service, above. Nontechnical correspondence should be sent to Deutsche Welle in Germany (*see*).

ARGENTINA   World Time –3

"De Colección," Casilla 96, 1900 La Plata, Argentina. Phone: +54 (21) 270-507; or +54 (21) 216-607. Contact: Jorge Bourdet, Editor. Program aired on shortwave from a local medium wave station from La Plata city. Beamed to Antarctica on Sundays only in the SSB mode. Include 2 IRCs when writing.
Radio América Internacional, Intendente Abel Costa 289, 1708 Morón, Argentina. Phone: +54 (1) 629-5730; or (USA) +1 (650) 347-1587). Fax: +54 (1) 347 6320. Contact: José Holowaty. Tested during October 1997, and hopes to begin regular tranmissions in 1999.
Radiodifusión Argentina al Exterior—RAE, C.C. 555 Correo Central, 1000 Buenos Aires, Argentina. Phone: +54 (1) 325-6368 or +54 (1) 343-1736. Fax: +54 (1) 325 9433. Contact: (general) Paul F. Allen, Announcer, English Team; John Anthony Middleton, Head of the English Team; María Dolores López; Rodrigo Calderón, English Department; or Sandro Cenci, Chief, Italian Section; (administration) Señorita Perla Damuri, Directora; (technical) Gabriel Iván Barrera, DX Editor; or Patricia Menéndez. Free paper pennant and tourist literature. Return postage or $1 appreciated.
Radio La Colifata—LT22, Casilla 17, 1640 - Martínez (B.A.), Argentina. E-mail: colifata@interactive.com.ar. Contact: Alfredo Olivera, Director General; or Norberto Pugliese, Producción onda corta. Verifies reception reports and replies to correspondence in Spanish. Return postage (2 IRCs) required. Normally transmits only on FM, from its location in the Dr. J. T. Borda Municipal Neuropsychiatric Hospital, but occasionally has special programs broadcast via stations like WRMI, USA. Programs are produced by residents of the hospital.

Radio Malargüe (if reactivated), Esq. Aldao 350, 5613 Malargüe, Argentina. Contact: Eduardo Vicente Lucero, Jefe Técnico; Nolasco H. Barrera, Interventor; or José Pandolfo, Departamento Administración. Free pennants. Return postage necessary. Prefers correspondence in Spanish.

Radio Nacional Buenos Aires, Maipú 555, 1006 Buenos Aires, Argentina. Phone: +54 (1) 325-9100. Fax: (general) +54 (1) 325 9433; (technical) +54 (1) 325 5742. Contact: Patricia Ivone Barral, Directora Nacional; Patricia Claudia Dinale de Jantus, Directora Administrativa; or María Eugenia Baya Casal, Directora Operativa. $1 helpful. Prefers correspondence in Spanish, and usually replies via RAE (*see* above). If no reply, try sending your correspondence (but don't write the station's name on your envelope) and 1 IRC via the helpful Gabriel Iván Barrera, Casilla 2868, 1000 Buenos Aires, Argentina; fax +54 (1) 322 3351.

Radio Nacional Mendoza (if reactivated), Av. Emilio Civit 460, 5500 Mendoza, Argentina. Phone: (administrative) +54 (61) 38-15-27. Phone/fax: (general) +54 (61) 25-79-31. Fax: +54 (61) 38 05 96. Contact: (general/administrative) Lic. Jorge Horacio Parvanoff, Director; (technical) Juan Carlos Fernández, Jefe del Departamento Técnico. Free pamphlets and stickers. Replies to correspondence, preferably in Spanish, but English also accepted.

Radio Pasteur, Casilla 1852 Correo Central, 1000 Buenos Aires, Argentina. E-mail: morales.arg@ sicoar.com. Contact: Claudio Morales. A radio production carried out by students of a journalism workshop in Buenos Aires. Features Sports, Arts, Culture and Entertainment. Also looks at Ecology and the Environment, Customs and Traditions plus Social and Human Rights in Argentina. Letters and reception reports welcome. Return postage helpful.

Radio Rivadavia (when operating to Antarctica), Arenales 2467, 1124 Buenos Aires, Argentina. Fax: +54 (1) 824 6927.

ARMENIA   World Time +3 (+4 midyear)

Armenian Radio—*see* Voice of Armenia for details.

Lutherische Stunde (religious program aired over Radio Intercontinental), Postfach 1162, D-27363 Sottrum, Germany.

Mitternachtsruf (religious program aired via Radio Intercontinental), Postfach 62, D-79807 Lottstetten, Germany; Postfach 290, Eicholzstrasse 38, CH-8330 Pfaffikon, Switzerland; or P.O. Box 4389, W. Columbia, SC 29171 USA. Contact: Jonathan Malgo or Paul Richter. Free stickers and promotional material.

Radio Intercontinental
MAIN ADDRESS: Vardanants 28, No. 34, Yerevan 70 Armenia.
GERMAN ADDRESS: D-51702 Bergneustad, Germany.
SWITZERLAND ADDRESS: (Mitternachtsruf) Postfach 8051, Zurich, Switzerland.

Voice of Armenia, Radio Agency, Alek Manoukyan Street 5, 375025 Yerevan, Armenia. Phone: +374 (2) 558-010. Fax: +374 (2) 551 513. Contact: V. Voskanian, Deputy Editor-in-Chief; R. Abalian, Editor-in-Chief; Armenag Sansaryan, International Relations Bureau; Laura Baghdassarian, Deputy Manager, Radioagency; or Dr. Levon V. Ananikian, Director. Free postcards and stamps. Replies slowly. At present telephone, fax and mail services in and out of Armenia are very erratic.

ASCENSION   World Time exactly

BBC World Service—Atlantic Relay Station, English Bay, Ascension (South Atlantic Ocean). Fax: +247 6117. Contact: (technical) Jeff Cant, Staff Manager; M.R. Watkins, A/Assis-

tant Resident Engineer; or Mrs. Nicola Nicholls, Transmitter Engineer. Nontechnical correspondence should be sent to the BBC World Service in London (*see*).

Radio Japan, Radio Roma and Voice of America via BBC Ascension Relay Station—All correspondence should be directed to the regular addresses in Japan, Italy and USA (*see*).

AUSTRALIA   World Time +11 (+10 midyear) Victoria (VIC), New South Wales (NSW), Australian Capital Territory (ACT) and Tasmania (TAS); +10:30 (+9:30 midyear) South Australia (SA); +10 Queensland (QLD); +9:30 Northern Territory (NT); +8 Western Australia (WA)

Australian Broadcasting Corporation Northern Territory HF Service—ABC Darwin, Administrative Center for the Northern Territory Shortwave Service, ABC Box 9994, GPO Darwin NT 0820, Australia. Phone: +61 (8) 8943-3222, +61 (8) 8943-3229, or +61 (8) 8943-3231; (engineering) +61 (8) 8943-3210. Fax: +61 (8) 8943 3235 or +61 (8) 8943 3208. Contact: (general) Sue Camilleri, Broadcaster and Community Liaison Officer; Yvonne Corby; Christine Kakakios; or Fred McCue, Producer, "Mornings with Michael Mackenzie"; (technical) Peter Camilleri, Production Manager. Free stickers. Free "Traveller's Guide to ABC Radio." T-shirts US$20. Three IRCs or return postage helpful.

Australian Defence Forces Radio, Department of Defence, EMU (Electronic Media Unit) ANZAC Park West, APW 1-B-07, Reid, Canberra, ACT 2601, Australia. Phone: +61 (2) 6266-6669. Fax: +61 (2) 6266 6565. Contact: (general) Adam Iffland, Presenter; (technical) Hugh Mackenzie, Managing Presenter; or Brian Langshaw. SAE and 2 IRCs needed for a reply. Station replies to verification inquiries only. At last check, transmissions were emanating from a 10 kW single-sideband transmitter in Belconnen (Canberra) at HMAS Harman.

BBC World Service via Radio Australia—For verification direct from the Australian transmitters, contact John Westland, Director of English Programs at Radio Australia (*see*). Nontechnical correspondence should be sent to the BBC World Service in London (*see*).

CAAMA Radio—ABC, Central Australian Aboriginal Media Association, Bush Radio Service, P.O. Box 2924, Alice Springs NT 0871, Australia. Phone: +61 (8) 8952-9204. Fax: +61 (8) 8952 9214. Contact: Merridie Satoar, Department Manager; Mark Lillyman, News Director; Nova Mack, Receptionist; or Owen Cole, CAAMA General Manager; (administration) Graham Archer, Station Manager; (technical) Warren Huck, Technician. Free stickers. Two IRCs or return postage helpful.

📻**Radio Australia—ABC**
STUDIOS AND MAIN OFFICES: GPO Box 428G, Melbourne VIC 3001, Australia. Phone: ("Openline" voice mail for listeners' messages and requests) +61 (3) 9626-1825; (switchboard) +61 (3) 9626-1500 or +61 (3) 9626-1800; (English programs) +61 (3) 9626-1922. Fax & Faxpoll: (general) +61 (3) 9626 1899; (engineering) +61 (3) 9626 1917. E-mail: (Radio Australia transmissions & programs) raelp@radioaus.abc.net.au; (Pacific Services) rapac@ radioaus.abc.net.au; (Internet and World Wide Web Coordinator) naughton.russell@a2.abc.net.au. URL: (includes RealAudio) www.abc.net.au/ra/ (RealAudio in English also at www.wrn.org/stations/abc.html). Contact: (general) John Westland, Head, English Language Programming; Roger Broadbent, Producer "Feedback"; Tony Hastings, Director of Programs; or Jean-Gabriel Manguy, General Manager; (technical) Nigel Holmes, Transmission Manager, Transmission Management Unit. Free stickers and sometimes

pennants and souvenirs available. As from the 1st of July 1997, Radio Australia has been operating at a greatly reduced capacity. Budget cuts of more than 50% in 1997 and continuing over the next 3 years, will reduce this station's ability to broadcast successfully on shortwave. Despite this situation, Radio Australia will attempt to answer listener's letters even though this will largely depend on the availability of resources and a reply may no longer be possible in all cases. All reception reports received by Radio Australia will now be forwarded to the Australian Radio DX Club for assessment and checking. ARDXC will forward completed QSLs to Radio Australia for mailing. For further information, contact John Westland, Director of English Programs at Radio Australia (E-mail: westland.john@ a2.abc.net.au); or John Wright, Secretary/Editor, ARDXC (E-mail: dxer@fl.net.au). Plans to add new aerials and re-locate 250 kW transmitters.

NEW YORK BUREAU, NONTECHNICAL: Room 2260, 630 Fifth Avenue, New York NY 10020 USA. Phone: (representative) +1 (212) 332-2540; or (correspondent) +1 (212) 332-2545. Fax: +1 (212) 332 2546. Contact: Maggie Jones, North American Representative.

LONDON BUREAU, NONTECHNICAL: 54 Portland Place, London W1N 4DY, United Kingdom. Phone: +44 (171) 631-4456. Fax: (administration) +44 (171) 323 0059, (news) +44 (171) 323 1125. Contact: Robert Bolton, Manager.

BANGKOK BUREAU, NONTECHNICAL: 209 Soi Hutayana off Soi Suanplu, South Sathorn Road, Bangkok 10120, Thailand. Fax: +66 (2) 287 2040. Contact: Nicholas Stuart.

SAN FRANCISCO OFFICE, SCHEDULES: 2654 17th Avenue, San Francisco CA 94116 USA. Phone: +1 (415) 564-9968. Contact: George Poppin. This address, a volunteer office, only provides Radio Australia schedules to listeners. All other correspondence should be sent directly to the main office in Melbourne.

Radio Rum Jungle—ABC (program studios), Top Aboriginal Bush Association, Corner Speed Street & Gap Road, Batchelor NT 0870, Australia. Phone: +61 (8) 8952-3433. Fax: +61 (8) 8952 2093. Contact: Mae-Mae Morrison, Announcer; Andrew Joshua, Chairman; or George Butler. Three IRCs or return postage helpful. May send free posters.

Radio VNG (official time station)

PRIMARY ADDRESS: National Standards Commission, P.O. Box 282, North Ryde, NSW 2113, Australia. Toll-free telephone number (Australia only) (008) 251-942. Phone: +61 (2) 9888-3922. Fax: +61 (2) 9888 3033. E-mail: richardb@ozemail.com.au. Contact: Dr. Richard Brittain, Secretary, National Time Committee. Station offers a free 16-page booklet about VNG and free promotional material. Free stickers and postcards. Three IRCs helpful. May be forced to close down if sufficient funding is not found.

ALTERNATIVE ADDRESS: VNG Users Consortium, GPO Box 1090, Canberra ACT 2601, Australia. Fax: +61 (2) 6249 9969. Contact: Dr. Marion Leiba, Honorary Secretary. Three IRCs appreciated.

AUSTRIA   World Time +1 (+2 midyear)

📻**Radio Austria International**

MAIN OFFICE: Würzburggasse 30, A-1136 Vienna, Austria. Phone: (general) +43 (1) 87878-2130; (voice mail) +43 (1) 87878-3636; (technical) +43 (1) 87878-2629. Fax: (general) +43 (1) 87878 4404; (technical) +43 (1) 87878 2773. E-mail: (frequency plans, reception reports) roi.service@orf.at; (intermedia/special programmes) roi@orf.at; (technical) hfbc@orf.at. URLs: (general) www.orf.at/roi/; (RealAudio in

English and German) www.wrn.org/stations/orf.html. Contact: (general) Vera Bock, Listener's Service; "Postbox"/ "Hörerbriefkasten" listeners' letters shows; ("Kurzwellen Panorama") Wolf Harranth, Editor; or Michaela Gangl, Listener's Service; (administration) Prof. Paul Lendvai, Director; Dr. Edgar Sterbenz, Deputy Director; (English Department) David Ward; (German Department) Helmut Blechner; (French Department) Robert Denis; (Spanish Department Jacobo Naar-Carbonell; (Internet Service) Marianne Veit or Oswald Klotz; (technical) Ing. Ernst Vranka, Frequency Manager; or Ing. Klaus Hollndonner, Technical Director. Free stickers and program schedule twice a year, as well as quiz prizes. Mr. Harranth seeks collections of old verification cards and letters for the highly organized historical archives he is maintaining.

WASHINGTON NEWS BUREAU: 1206 Eaton Ct. NW, Washington DC 20007 USA. Phone: +1 (202) 822-9570. Contact: Eugen Freund.

AZERBAIJAN   World Time +3 (+4 midyear)

Azerbaijani Radio—*see* Radio Dada Gorgud for details.
Radio Dada Gorgud (Voice of Azerbaijan), Medhi Hüseyin küçäsi 1, 370011 Baku, Azerbaijan. Phone: +7 (8922) 398-585. Fax: +7 (8922) 395 452. Contact: Mrs. Tamam Bayatli-Öner, Director. Free postcards. $1 or return postage helpful. Replies occasionally to correspondence in English.

BAHRAIN   World Time +3

Radio Bahrain (if reactivated), Broadcasting & Television, Ministry of Information, P.O. Box 702, Al Manāmah, Bahrain. Phone: (Arabic Service) +973 781-888; (English Service) +973 629-085. Fax: (Arabic Service) +973 681 544; (English Service) +973 780 911. URL: www.gna.gov.bh/e-brtc-5.htm. Contact: A. Suliman (for Director of Broadcasting). $1 or IRC required. Replies irregularly.

BANGLADESH   World Time +6

📻**Bangladesh Betar**

NONTECHNICAL CORRESPONDENCE: External Services, Bangladesh Betar, Shahbagh Post Box No. 2204, Dhaka 1000, Bangladesh; (physical address) Betar Bhaban Sher-e-Bangla Nagar, Agargaon Road, Dhaka 1207, Bangladesh. Phone: (general) +880 (2) 865-294; (Rahman Khan) +880 (2) 863-949; (external services) +880 (2) 868-119. Fax: +880 (2) 862 021. URL: (RealAudio only) www.banglaradio.com/. Contact: Mrs. Dilruba Begum, Director, External Services; Ashfaque-ur Rahman Khan, Director - Programmes; or (technical) Muhammed Nazrul Islam, Station Engineer. For further technical contacts, *see* below.

TECHNICAL CORRESPONDENCE: National Broadcasting Authority, NBA Bhaban, 121 Kazi Nazrul Islam Avenue, Shahabagh, Dhaka 1000, Bangladesh. Phone: +880 (2) 500-143/7, +880 (2) 500-490, +880 (2) 500-810, +880 (2) 505-113 or +880 (2) 507-269; (Shakir) +880 (2) 818-734; (Das) +880 (2) 500-810. Fax: +880 (2) 817 850; (Shakir) +880 (2) 817 850. E-mail: dgradio@drik.bgd.toolnet.org. Contact: Syed Abdus Shakir, Chief Engineer; (reception reports) Manoranjan Das, Station Engineer, Dhaka; or Muhammed Romizuddin Bhuiya, Senior Engineer (Research Wing). Verifications not common from this office.

Once part of Radio Pakistan, the Kalyanpur station is now a bone yard for old transmission hardware, as well as a mediumwave station for Dhaka. M. Guha

BELARUS World Time +2 (+3 midyear)

Belarussian Radio—*see* Radio Belarus for details.
Grodno Radio—*see* Radio Belarus for details.
Mogilev Radio—*see* Radio Belarus for details.
Radio Belarus/Radio Minsk, vul. Chyrvonaya 4 [or ul. Krasnaja 4], 220807 Minsk, Belarus. Phone: +375 (172) 395-831; +375 (172) 395-875. Fax: +375 (172) 366 643. URL: www.nestor.minsk.by/radiorod/indexen.htm. Contact: Irina Polozhentseva, English Program Editor; Jürgen Eberhardt, Editor German Service. Free Belarus stamps.
Voice of Orthodoxy (program)
MINSK OFFICE: V. Pristavko, P.O. Box 17, 220012 Minsk, Belarus. Aired via transmission facilities of Radio Trans Europe, Portugal; the Voice of Hope, Lebanon; and Deutsche Telekom, Germany. Correspondence and reception reports welcomed.
PARIS OFFICE: B.P. 416-08, F-75366 Paris Cedex 08, France. Contact: Valentin Korelsky, General Secretary.

BELGIUM World Time +1 (+2 midyear)

▣ Radio Vlaanderen Internationaal
NONTECHNICAL AND GENERAL TECHNICAL: P.O. Box 26, B-1000 Brussels, Belgium. Phone: +32 (2) 741-5611, +32 (2) 741-3807 or +32 (2) 741-3802. Fax: (administration and Dutch Service) +32 (2) 732 6295; (other language services) +32 (2) 732 8336. BBS: +32 (3) 825-3613. E-mail: info@rvi.be. URLs: (general) www.rvi.be/; (RealAudio in English and Dutch) www.wrn.org/stations/rvi.html. Contact (general) Deanne Lehman, Producer, "P.O. Box 26" letterbox program; Liz Sanderson, Head, English Service; Maryse Jacob, Head, French Service; Martina Luxen, Head, German Service; (general technical) Frans Vossen, Producer, "Radio World." Sells RVI T-shirts (large/extra large) for 400 Belgian francs. Remarks and reception reports can also be sent c/o the following diplomatic addresses:
NIGERIA EMBASSY: Embassy of Belgium, 1A, Bak Road, Ikoyi-Island, Lagos, Nigeria.
ARGENTINA EMBASSY: Embajada de Bélgica, Defensa 113 - 8° Piso, 1065 Buenos Aires, Argentina.

FREQUENCY MANAGEMENT OFFICE: BRTN, Ave. Reyerslaan 52, B-1043 Brussels, Belgium. Phone: +32 (2) 741-5571. Fax: +32 (2) 741 5567. E-mail: (Gauderis) hugo.gauderis@brtn.be; (Devos) willy.devos@brtn.be. Contact: Hugo Gauderis or Willy Devos, Frequency Manager.

BENIN World Time +1

Office de Radiodiffusion et Télévision du Benin, La Voix de la Révolution, B.P. 366, Cotonou, Bénin; this address is for Cotonou and Parakou stations, alike. Contact: (Cotonou) Damien Zinsou Ala Hassa; Emile Desire Ologoudou, Directeur Generale; or Leonce Goohouede; (technical) Anastase Adjoko, Chef de Service Technique; (Radio Parakou, general) J. de Matha, Le Chef de la Station, or (Radio Parakou, technical) Léon Donou, Le Chef des Services Techniques. Return postage, $1 or IRC required. Replies irregularly and slowly to correspondence in French.

BHUTAN World Time +7

Bhutan Broadcasting Service
STATION: Department of Information and Broadcasting, Ministry of Communications, P.O. Box 101, Thimphu, Bhutan. Phone: +975 223-070. Fax: +975 223 073. Contact: (general) Ashi Renchen Chhoden, News and Current Affairs; Narda Gautam; or Sonam Tshong, Executive Director; (technical) Sonam Tobgyal, Station Engineer; or Technical Head. Two IRCs, return postage or $1 required. Replies extremely irregularly; correspondence to the U.N. Mission (*see* following) may be more fruitful.
UNITED NATIONS MISSION: Permanent Mission of the Kingdom of Bhutan to the United Nations, Two United Nations Plaza, 27th Floor, New York NY 10017 USA. Fax: +1 (212) 826 2998. Contact: Mrs. Kunzang C. Namgyel, Third Secretary; Mrs. Sonam Yangchen, Attaché; Ms. Leki Wangmo, Second Secretary; Thinley Dorrji, Second Secretary; or Hari K. Chhetri, Second Secretary. Free newspapers and booklet on the history of Bhutan.

BOLIVIA World Time –4

NOTE ON STATION IDENTIFICATIONS: Many Bolivian stations listed as "Radio . . ." may also announce as "Radio Emisora . . ." or "Radiodifusora . . ."

Galaxia Radiodifusión—*see* Radio Galaxia, below.

Hitachi Radiodifusión—*see* Radio Hitachi, below.

Paitití Radiodifusión—*see* Radio Paitití, below.

Radio Abaroa, Calle Nicanor Gonzalo Salvatierra 249, Riberalta, Beni, Bolivia. Contact: René Arias Pacheco, Director. Return postage or $1 required. Replies rarely to correspondence in Spanish.

Radio A.N.D.E.S., Casilla No. 16, Uyuni, Provincia Antonio Quijarro, Departamento de Potosí, Bolivia. Phone: +591 (69) 32-145. Owners: La Federación Unica de Trabajadores Campesinos del Altiplano Sud. Contact: Francisco Quisbert Salinas, Secretario Permanente del Consejo de Administración; Audo Ramos Colque; Rita Salvatierra Bautista; or César Gerónimo Alí Flores, Reporteros. Spanish preferred. Return postage in the form of two U.S. dollars appreciated, as the station depends on donations for its existence.

Radio Animas, Chocaya, Animas, Potosí, Bolivia. Contact: Julio Acosta Campos, Director. Return postage or $1 required. Replies irregularly to correspondence in Spanish.

Radio Camargo—*see* Radio Emisoras Camargo, below.

Radio Carlos Palenque, Casilla de Correo 8704, La Paz, Bolivia. Phone: +591 (2) 354-418, +591 (2) 375-953, +595 (2) 324-394 or +595 (2) 361-176. Fax: +591 (2) 356 785. Contact: Rodolfo Beltrán Rosales, Jefe de Prensa de "El Metropolicial." Free postcards and pennants. $1 or return postage necessary.

Radio Centenario "La Nueva"
MAIN OFFICE: Casilla 818, Santa Cruz de la Sierra, Bolivia. Phone: +591 (3) 529-265. Fax: +591 (3) 524 747. E-mail: mision.eplabol@mail.sobbs-bo.com. Contact: Julio Acosta

---

TIPS FOR EFFECTIVE CORRESPONDENCE

Write to be read. Winning correspondence, on paper or by e-mail, is interesting and helpful from the recipient's point of view, yet friendly without being chummy. Comments on specific programs are almost always appreciated.

They don't know English? No problem. A basic form of translation service, performed by computer, is available for free via Globalink over the World Wide Web at www.globalink.com/xlate.html. That same organization—and many more, including some university language departments—will do translations by human beings, usually for a modest fee.

Incorporate language courtesies. Writing in the broadcaster's tongue is always a plus—this section of PASSPORT indicates when it is a requirement—but English is usually the next-best bet. In addition, when writing in any language to Spanish-speaking countries, remember that what gringos think of as the "last name" is actually written as the penultimate name. Thus, Juan Antonio Vargas García, which can also be written as Juan Antonio Vargas G., refers to Sr. Vargas; so your salutation should read, *Estimado Sr. Vargas*.

What's that "García" doing there, then? That's *mamita's* father's family name. Latinos more or less solved the problem of gender fairness in names long before the Anglos.

But, wait—what about Portuguese, used by all those lovely stations in Brazil? Same concept, but in reverse. *Mamá's* father's family name is penultimate, and the "real" last name is where English-speakers are used to it, at the end.

In Chinese, the "last" name comes first. However, when writing in English, Chinese names are sometimes reversed for the benefit of *weiguoren*—foreigners. Use your judgement. For example, "Li" is a common Chinese last name, so if you see "Li Dan," it's "Mr. Li." But if it's "Dan Li," and certainly if it's been anglicized into "Dan Lee," he's already one step ahead of you, and it's still "Mr. Li" (or Lee). Less widely known is that the same can also occur in Hungarian. For example, "Bartók Béla" for Béla Bartók.

If in doubt, fall back on the ever-safe "Dear Sir" or "Dear Madam," or use e-mail, where salutations are not expected. And be patient—replies by post usually take weeks, sometimes months. Slow responders, those that tend to take six months or more to reply, are cited in this section, as are erratic repliers.

Campos, Director. May send a calendar. Free stickers. Return postage or $1 required. Audio cassettes of contemporary Christian music and Bolivian folk music $10, including postage; CDs of Christian folk music $15, including postage. Replies to correspondence in English and Spanish.

U.S. BRANCH OFFICE: LATCOM, 1218 Croton Avenue, New Castle PA 16101 USA. Phone: +1 (412) 652-0101. Fax: +1 (412) 652 4654. Contact: Hope Cummins.

Radiodifusoras Integración—*see* Radio Integración, below.

Radiodifusoras Minería, Casilla de Correo 247, Oruro, Bolivia. Phone: +591 (52) 77-736. Contact: Dr. José Carlos Gómez Espinoza, Gerente y Director General; or Srta. Costa Colque Flores, Responsable del programa "Minería Cultural." Free pennants. Replies to correspondence in Spanish.

Radiodifusoras Trópico, Casilla 60, Trinidad, Beni, Bolivia. Contact: Eduardo Avila Alberdi, Director. Replies slowly to correspondence in Spanish. Return postage required for reply.

Radio Eco

MAIN ADDRESS: Correo Central, Reyes, Ballivián, Beni, Bolivia. Contact: Gonzalo Espinoza Cortés, Director. Free station literature. $1 or return postage required. Replies to correspondence in Spanish.

ALTERNATIVE ADDRESS: Rolmán Medina Méndez, Correo Central, Reyes, Ballivián, Bolivia.

Radio Eco San Borja (San Borja la Radio), Correo Central, San Borja, Ballivián, Beni, Bolivia. Contact: Gonzalo Espinoza Cortés, Director. Free station poster promised to correspondents. Return postage appreciated. Replies slowly to correspondence in Spanish.

Radio El Mundo, Casilla 1984, Santa Cruz de la Sierra, Bolivia. Phone: +591 (3) 464-646. Fax: +591 (3) 465 057. Contact: Freddy Banegas Carrasco, Gerente; Lic. José Luis Vélez Ocampo C., Director; or Lic. Juan Pablo Sainz, Gerente General. Free stickers and pennants. $1 or return postage required. Replies irregularly to correspondence in Spanish.

Radio Emisora Dos de Febrero (when operating), Calle Vaca Diez 400, Rurrenabaque, Beni, Bolivia. Contact: John Arze von Boeck. Free pennant, which is especially attractive. Replies occasionally to correspondence in Spanish.

Radio Emisora Galaxia—*see* Radio Galaxia, below.

Radio Emisora Padilla—*see* Radio Padilla, below.

Radio Emisora San Ignacio, Calle Ballivián s/n, San Ignacio de Moxos, Beni, Bolivia. Contact: Carlos Salvatierra Rivero, Gerente y Director. $1 or return postage necessary.

Radio Emisora Villamontes—*see* Radio Villamontes, below.

Radio Emisoras Camargo, Casilla 09, Camargo, Provincia Nor-Cinti, Bolivia. Contact: Pablo García B., Gerente Propietario. Return postage or $1 required. Replies slowly to correspondence in Spanish.

Radio Emisoras Minería—*see* Radiodifusoras Minería.

Radio Estación Frontera—*see* Radio Frontera, below.

Radio Fides, Casilla 9143, La Paz, Bolivia. Fax: +591 (2) 379 030. E-mail: rafides@wara.bolnet.bo. Contact: Pedro Eduardo Pérez Iribarne, Director; Felicia de Rojas, Secretaria; Roberto Carrasco Guzmán, Gerente de Ventas y RRHH; or Roxana Beltrán C. Replies occasionally to correspondence in Spanish.

Radio Frontera, Casilla 179, Cobija, Pando, Bolivia. Contact: Lino Miahuchi von Ancken, CP9AR. Free pennants. $1 or return postage necessary. Replies to correspondence in Spanish.

Radio Galaxia (when operating), Calle Beni s/n casi esquina Udarico Rosales, Guayaramerín, Beni, Bolivia. Contact: Dorián Arias, Gerente; Héber Hitachi Banegas, Director; or Carlos Arteaga Tacaná, Director-Dueño. Return postage or $1 required. Replies to correspondence in Spanish.

Radio Grigotá (if reactivated), Casilla 203, Santa Cruz de la Sierra, Bolivia. Phone/fax: +591 (3) 326-443. Fax: +591 (3) 362 795. Contact: (general) Víctor Hugo Arteaga B., Director General; (technical) Tania Martins de Arteaga, Gerente Administrativo. Free stickers, pins, pennants, key rings and posters. $1 or return postage required. Replies occasionally to correspondence in English, French, Portuguese and Spanish. May replace old Philips transmitter.

Radio Hitachi (Hitachi Radiodifusión) (when operating), Calle Sucre 20, Guayaramerín, Beni, Bolivia. Contact: Héber Hitachi Banegas, Director. Return postage of $1 required.

Radio Illimani, Casilla 1042, La Paz, Bolivia. Phone: +591 (2) 376-364. Fax: +591 (2) 359 275. Contact: Rubén D. Choque, Director; or Lic. Manuel Liendo Rázuri, Gerente General. $1 required, and your letter should be registered and include a tourist brochure or postcard from where you live. Replies irregularly to friendly correspondence in Spanish.

Radio Integración (if reactivated), Casilla 7902, La Paz, Bolivia. Contact: Lic. Manuel Liendo Rázuri, Gerente General; Benjamín Juan Carlos Blanco Q., Director Ejecutivo; or Carmelo de la Cruz Huanca, Comunicador Social. Free pennants. Return postage required.

Radio Juan XXIII [Veintitrés], Avenida Santa Cruz al frente de la plaza principal, San Ignacio de Velasco, Santa Cruz, Bolivia. Phone: +591 (962) 2188. Contact: Fernando Manuel Picazo Torres, Director; or Pbro. Elías Cortezón, Director. Return postage or $1 required. Replies occasionally to correspondence in Spanish.

Radio La Cruz del Sur, Casilla 1759, La Paz, Bolivia. Contact: Hazen Parent, General Director; or José Luis Chávez Zambrana, Director Gerente. Pennant $1 or return postage. Replies slowly to correspondence in Spanish.

Radio La Palabra, Parroquia de Santa Ana de Yacuma, Beni, Bolivia. Phone: +591 (848) 2117. Contact: Padre Yosu Arketa, Director. Return postage necessary. Replies to correspondence in Spanish.

Radio La Plata (when operating), Casilla 276, Sucre, Bolivia. Phone: +591 (64) 31-616. Fax: +591 (64) 41 400. Contact: Freddy Donoso Bleichner.

Radio Libertad (if reactivated), Casilla 5324, La Paz, Bolivia. Phone: +591 (2) 365-154. Fax: +591 (2) 363 069. Contact: (general) Oscar Violetta Barrios; (technical) Lic. Teresa Sanjinés Lora, Gerente General. Depending upon what's on hand, pamphlets, stickers, pins, pennants, purses, pencil sharpeners, key rings and calendars. If blank cassette and $2 is sent, they will be happy to dub recording of local music. Sells T-shirts for $10. Return postage or $1 required for reply. Upon request, they will record for listeners any type of Bolivian music they have on hand, and send it to that listener for the cost of the cassette and postage; or, if the listener sends a cassette, for the cost of postage. Replies fairly regularly to correspondence in English and Spanish.

Radio Loyola, Casilla 40, Sucre, Bolivia. Phone: +591 (64) 30-222. Fax: +591 (64) 42 555. URL: (experimental RealAudio) www.nch.bolnet.bo/loyola.ram. Contact: (general) Lic. José Weimar León G., Director; (technical) Tec. Norberto Rosales. Free stickers and pennants. Replies occasionally to correspondence in English, Italian and Spanish. Considering replacing 19-year old transmitter.

Radio Mauro Núñez (if reactivated), Centro de Estudios para el Desarrollo de Chuquisaca (CEDEC), Casilla 196, Sucre, Bolivia. Phone: +591 (64) 25-008. Fax: +591 (64) 32 628. Contact: Jorge A. Peñaranda Llanos; Ing. Raúl Ledezma, Director Residente "CEDEC"; José Peneranda; or Jesús Urioste. Replies to correspondence in Spanish.

Radio Minería—*see* Radiodifusoras Minería.

Radio Movima, Calle Baptista No. 24, Santa Ana de Yacuma, Beni, Bolivia. Contact: Rubén Serrano López, Director; Javier Roca Díaz, Director Gerente; or Mavis Serrano, Directora. Return postage or $1 required. Replies irregularly to correspondence in Spanish.

Radio Nacional de Huanuni, Casilla 681, Oruro, Bolivia. Contact: Rafael Linneo Morales, Director General; or Alfredo Murillo, Director. Return postage or $1 required. Replies irregularly to correspondence in Spanish.

Radio Norte, Calle Warnes 195, 2do piso del Cine Escorpio, Montero, Santa Cruz, Bolivia. Phone: +591 (92) 20-970. Contact: Leonardo Arteaga Ríos, Director.

Radio Padilla (if reactivated), Padilla, Chuquisaca, Bolivia. Contact: Moisés Palma Salazar, Director. Return postage or $1 required. Replies to correspondence in Spanish.

Radio Paitití, Casilla 172, Guayaramerín, Beni, Bolivia. Contact: Armando Mollinedo Bacarreza, Director; Luis Carlos Santa Cruz Cuéllar, Director Gerente; or Ancir Vaca Cuéllar, Gerente-Propietario. Free pennants. Return postage or $3 required. Replies irregularly to correspondence in Spanish.

Radio Panamericana, Casilla 5263, La Paz, Bolivia (physical address: Av. 16 de Julio, Edif. 16 de Julio, Of. 902, El Prado, La Paz, Bolivia). Contact: Daniel Sánchez Rocha, Director. Replies irregularly, with correspondence in Spanish preferred. $1 or 2 IRCs helpful.

Radio Perla del Acre, Casilla 7, Cobija, Departamento de Pando, Bolivia. Return postage or $1 required. Replies irregularly to correspondence in Spanish.

Radio Pío XII [Doce], Siglo Veinte, Potosí, Bolivia. Phone: +591 (58) 20-250. Contact: Pbro. Roberto Durette, OMI, Director General; or René Paco, presenter of "Los Pikichakis" program (aired Saturdays at 2300-0100 World Time). Return postage necessary. As mail delivery to Siglo Veinte is erratic, latters may be sent instead to: Casilla 434, Oruro, Bolivia; to the attention of Adenor Alfaro, periodista de Radio Pío XX (phone: +591 (52) 76-163).

Radio San Gabriel, Casilla 4792, La Paz, Bolivia. Phone: +591 (2) 355-371. Phone/fax: +591 (2) 321 174. Contact: Hno. José Canut Saurat, Director General; or Sra. Martha Portugal, Dpto. de Publicidad. $1 or return postage helpful. Free book on station, Aymara calendars and *La Voz del Pueblo Aymara* magazine. Replies fairly regularly to correspondence in Spanish. Station of the Hermanos de la Salle Catholic religious order.

Radio San Miguel, Casilla 102, Riberalta, Beni, Bolivia. Phone: +591 (852) 8268. Contact: Félix Alberto Rada Q., Director; or Gerin Pardo Molina, Director. Free stickers and pennants; has a different pennant each year. Return postage or $1 required. Replies irregularly to correspondence in Spanish. Feedback on program "Bolivia al Mundo" (aired 0200-0300 World Time) especially appreciated.

Radio Santa Ana, Calle Sucre No. 250, Santa Ana de Yacuma, Beni, Bolivia. Contact: Mario Roberto Suárez, Director; or Mariano Verdugo. Return postage or $1 required. Replies irregularly to correspondence in Spanish.

Radio Santa Cruz, Emisora del Instituto Radiofónico Fé y Alegría (IRFA), Casilla 672 (or 3213), Santa Cruz, Bolivia. Phone: +591 (3) 531-817. Fax: +591 (3) 532 257. Contact: Padre Francisco Flores, S.J., Director General; Srta. María Yolanda Marco E., Secretaria; Señora Mirian Suárez, Productor, "Protagonista Ud.", Director General; or Lic. Silvia Nava S.

Free pamphlets, stickers and pennants. Return postage required. Replies to correspondence in English, French and Spanish.

Radio Sararenda, Casilla 7, Camiri, Santa Cruz, Bolivia. Phone: +595 (952) 2121. Contact: Freddy Lara Aguilar, Director; or Kathy Arenas, Administradora. Free stickers and photos of Camiri. Replies to correspondence in Spanish.

Radio Televisión Colonia (if reactivated), Correo Central, Yapacani, Santa Cruz de la Sierra, Bolivia. Phone/fax: +591 (933) 61-64. Fax: +591 (933) 60 00. Contact: (general) Yrey Fausto Montaño Ustárez, Gerente Propietario; (technical) Ing. Rene Zambrana. Replies to correspondence in English, French, Italian, Japanese, Portuguese and Spanish. Free pamphlets, stickers, pins, pennants and small handicrafts made by local artisans. Return postage required for reply.

Radio Villamontes, Avenida Méndez Arcos No. 156, Villamontes, Departamento de Tarija, Bolivia. Contact: Gerardo Rocabado Galarza, Director. $1 or return postage required.

BOSNIA-HERCEGOVINA   World Time +1 (+2 midyear)

Radio & Television of Bosnia-Hercegovina, Bulevar Mese Selimovica 4, BH-71000 Sarajevo, Bosnia-Hercegovina. Phone: +387 (71) 646-014, +387 (71) 462-886 or +387 (71) 455-124. Fax: +387 (71) 645 142, +387 (71) 464 061 or +387 (71) 455 104. Contact: Milenko Vockic, Director; Mr. N. Dizdarevic; or Rodzic Nerin.

BOTSWANA   World Time +2

Radio Botswana, Private Bag 0060, Gaborone, Botswana. Phone: +267 352-541. Fax: +267 357 138. Contact: (general) Ted Makgekgenene, Director; or Monica Mphusu, Producer, "Maokaneng/Pleasure Mix"; (technical) Kingsley Reebang. Free stickers, pennants and pins. Return postage, $1 or 2 IRCs required. Replies slowly and irregularly.

Voice of America—Botswana Relay Station

TRANSMITTER SITE: Voice of America, Botswana Relay Station, Moepeng Hill, Selebi-Phikwe, Botswana. Phone: +267 810-932. Fax: +267 810 252. Contact: Dennis G. Brewer, Station Manager. This address for specialized technical correspondence only. All other correspondence should be directed to the regular VOA address (*see* USA).

BRAZIL   World Time –1 (–2 midyear) Atlantic Islands; –2 (–3 midyear) Eastern, including Brasília and Rio de Janeiro, plus the town of Barra do Garças; –3 (–4 midyear) Western; –5 Acre. Most, if not all, northern states keep midyear time year round.

NOTE: Postal authorities recommend that, because of the level of theft in the Brazilian postal system, correspondence to Brazil be sent only via registered mail.

Emissora Rural A Voz do São Francisco, C.P. 8, 56300-000 Petrolina PE, Brazil. Contact: Maria Letecia de Andrade Nunes. Return postage necessary. Replies to correspondence in Portuguese.

Rádio Alvorada (Londrina), Rua Senador Souza Naves 9, 9 Andar, 86010-921 Londrina PR, Brazil. Contact: Padre José Guidoreni, Diretor; or Padre Manuel Joaquim. Pennants $1 or return postage. Replies to correspondence in Portuguese.

Rádio Alvorada (Parintins), Travessa Leopoldo Neves 503, 69150-000 Parintins AM, Brazil. Contact: Raimunda Ribeira da Motta, Diretora. Return postage required. Replies occasionally to correspondence in Portuguese.

Rádio Alvorada (Rio Branco), Avenida Ceará 2150—Altos de Gráfica Globo, 69900-470 Rio Branco AC, Brazil. Occasionally replies to correspondence in Portuguese.

Rádio Anhanguera, C.P. 13, 74823-000 Goiânia GO, Brazil. URL: (RealAudio only) www2.opopular.com.br/hpmain.htm. Contact: Rossana F. da Silva; or Eng. Domingos Vicente Tinoco. Return postage required. Replies to correspondence in Portuguese.

Rádio Aparecida, Avenida Getulio Vargas 185, 12570-000 Aparecida SP, Brazil; or C.P. 14547, 03698-970 Aparecida SP, Brazil. Phone: +55 (12) 565-1133. Fax: +55 (12) 565 1138. Contact: Padre C. Cabral; Savio Trevisan, Departamento Técnico; Cassiano Macedo, Producer, "Encontro DX"; Padre Cesar Moreira; or João Climaco, Diretor Geral. Return postage or $1 required. Replies occasionally to correspondence in Portuguese.

Rádio Bandeirantes, C.P. 372, Rua Radiantes 13, Morumbí, 01059-970 São Paulo SP, Brazil. Fax: +55 (11) 843 5391. E-mail: rbradio@uol.com.br. URL: (includes RealAudio) www.uol.com.br/bandeirantes/. Contact: Samir Razuk, Diretor Geral; Carlos Newton; or Salomão Esper, Superintendente. Free stickers, pennants and canceled Brazilian stamps. $1 or return postage required.

Rádio Baré, Avenida Santa Cruz Machado 170 A, 69010-070 Manaus AM, Brazil. Contact: Fernando A.B. Andrade, Diretor Programação e Produção. The Diretor is looking for radio catalogs.

Radiobrás—see Rádio Nacional da Amazônia and Rádio Nacional do Brasil.

Rádio Brasil, C.P. 625, 13000-000 Campinas, São Paulo SP, Brazil. Contact: Wilson Roberto Correa Viana, Gerente. Return postage required. Replies to correspondence in Portuguese.

Rádio Brasil Central, C.P. 330, 74001-970 Goiânia GO, Brazil. Contact: Ney Raymundo Fernández, Coordinador Executivo; Sergio Runens da Silva; or Arizio Pedro Soarez, Diretor Gerente. Free stickers. $1 or return postage required. Replies to correspondence in Portuguese.

Rádio Brasil Tropical, C.P. 405, 78005-970 Cuiabá MT, Brazil (physical address: Rua Joaquim Murtinho 1456, 78020-830 Cuiabá MT, Brazil). Phone: +55 (65) 321-6882 or +55 (65) 321-6226. Fax: +55 (65) 624 3455. E-mail: rcultura@nutecnet.com.br. URL: www.solunet.com.br/rcultura/. Contact: Klécius Antonio dos Santos, Diretor Comercial. Free stickers. $1 required. Replies to correspondence in Portuguese.

Rádio Caiari, C.P. 104, 78900-000 Porto Velho RO, Brazil. Contact: Carlos Alberto Diniz Martins, Diretor Geral. Free stickers. Return postage helpful. Replies irregularly to correspondence in Portuguese.

Rádio Canção Nova, C.P. 15, 12630-000 Cachoeira Paulista SP, Brazil (physical address: Rua João Paulo II s/n, Alto da Bela Vista, 12630-000 Cachoeira Paulista SP, Brazil). Phone: +55 (12) 561-2400. Fax: +55 (12) 561 2074. E-mail: cancao.nova@fastnet.com.br. URL: (includes RealAudio) www.fastnet.com.br/tvcn/. Contact: Benedita Luiza Rodrigues; Ana Claudia de Santana; or Valera Guimarães Massafera, Secretária. Free stickers, pennants and station brochure sometimes given upon request. May send magazines. $1 helpful.

Rádio Capixaba, C.P. 509, 29000-000 Vitória ES, Brazil. Contact: Jairo Gouvea Maia, Diretor; or Sofrage do Benil. Replies occasionally to correspondence in Portuguese.

Rádio Carajá (if reactivated), C.P. 520, 75001-970 Anápolis GO, Brazil. Contact: Nilson Silva Rosa, Diretor Geral. Return

postage helpful. Replies to correspondence in Portuguese.

Rádio Clube do Pará, C.P. 533, 66000-000 Belém PA, Brazil. Contact: Edyr Paiva Proença, Diretor Geral; or José Almeida Lima de Sousa. Return postage required. Replies irregularly to correspondence in Portuguese.

Rádio Clube de Ribeirao Preto, Ribeirao Preto SP, Brazil. Phone/fax: +55 (16) 610-3511. E-mail: scc@clube.com.br. URL: (includes RealAudio) www.clube.com.br.

Rádio Clube de Rondonópolis, C.P. 190, 78700-000 Rondonópolis MT, Brazil. Contact: Canário Silva, Departamento Comercial; or Saúl Feliz, Gerente-Geral. Return postage helpful. Replies to correspondence in Portuguese.

Radio Clube Paranaense, Rua Rockefeller 1311, Prado Velho, CEP 80230-130 Curitiba, Brazil. Phone: +55 (41) 332-4255 or +55 (41) 332-6644. Contact: Vicente Mickosz, Superintendente.

Rádio Clube Varginha, C.P. 102, 37000-000 Varginha MG, Brazil. Contact: Juraci Viana. Return postage necessary. Replies slowly to correspondence in Portuguese.

Rádio Coari—see Rádio Educação Rural-Coari.

Rádio Cultura Araraquara, Avenida Feijó 583 (Centro), 14801-140 Araraquara SP, Brazil. Phone: +55 (16) 232-3790. Fax: +55 (16) 232 3475. E-mail: cultura@techs.com.br. URL: www.techs.com.br/cultura/. Contact: Antonio Carlos Rodrigues dos Santos. Return postage required. Replies slowly to correspondence in Portuguese.

Quito, Ecuador, with Mt. Cotopaxi in the background. Although Quito is modern and urban, much of the Ecuadorian population consists of rural descendants of Inca and other Indian tribes.
HCJB

Rádio Cultura de Campos, C.P. 79, 28100-970 Campos RJ, Brazil. $1 or return postage necessary. Replies to correspondence in Portuguese.

Rádio Cultura de Foz do Iguaçu (Onda Corta), C.P. 84, 85852-520 Foz do Iguaçu PR, Brazil. Phone: +55 (45) 574-3010. Contact: Francisco Pires dos Santos, Gerente-Geral; or Sandro Souza. Return postage necessary. Replies to correspondence in Portuguese.

Rádio Cultura do Pará, Avenida Almirante Barroso 735, 66090-000 Belém PA, Brazil. Phone: +55 (91) 228-1000. Fax: +55 (91) 226 3989. Contact: Ronald Pastor; or Augusto Proença, Diretor. Return postage required. Replies irregularly to correspondence in Portuguese.

Rádio Cultura Ondas Tropicais, Rua Barcelos s/n Praça 14, 69020-060 Manaus AM, Brazil. Phone: +55 (92) 633-3857/2030. Fax: +55 (92) 633 3332. Contact: Luíz Fernando de Souza Ferreira; or Maria Jerusalem dos Santos, Chefe da Divisão de Rádio. Replies to correspondence in Portuguese. Return postage appreciated. Station is part of the FUNTEC, Fundação Televisão e Rádio Cultura do Amazonas network.

Rádio Cultura São Paulo, Rua Cenno Sbrighi 378, 05099-900 São Paulo SP, Brazil. Phone: +55 (11) 861-2140, +55 (11) 874-3080, +55 (11) 874-3086. Fax: +55 (11) 861 1914. E-mail: (general) radio@tvcultura.com.br; (Cultura AM, relayed on 9615 and 17815 kHz) radioam@tvcultura.com.br; (Cultura FM, relayed on 6170 kHz) radiofm@tvcultura.com.br; (technical) tecnica@tvcultura.com.br. URL: Contact: Thais de Almeida Dias, Chefe de Produção e Programação; Sra. Maria Luíza Amaral Kfouri, Chefe de Produção; or Valvenio Martins de Almeida, Coordenador de Produção. $1 or return postage required. Replies slowly to postal correspondence in Portuguese. May respond to English messages sent to the "radio" and "tecnica" e-mail addresses, above.

Rádio Difusora Cáceres, C.P. 297, 78200-000 Cáceres MT, Brazil. Contact: Sra. Maridalva Amaral Vignardi. $1 or return postage required. Replies occasionally to correspondence in Portuguese.

Rádio Difusora de Aquidauana, C.P. 18, 79200-000 Aquidauana MS, Brazil. Phone: +55 (67) 241-3956 or +55 (67) 241-3957. Contact: Primaz Aldo Bertoni, Diretor. Free tourist literature and used Brazilian stamps. $1 or return postage required. This station sometimes identifies during the program day as "Nova Difusora," but its sign-off announcement gives the official name as "Rádio Difusora, Aquidauana."

Rádio Difusora de Londrina, C.P. 1870, 86000-000 Londrina PR, Brazil. Contact: Walter Roberto Manganoti, Gerente. Free tourist brochure, which sometimes seconds as a verification. $1 or return postage helpful. Replies irregularly to correspondence in Portuguese.

Rádio Difusora do Amazonas, C.P. 311, 69000-000 Manaus AM, Brazil. Contact: J. Joaquim Marinho, Diretor. Joaquim Marinho is a keen stamp collector and especially interested in Duck Hunting Permit Stamps. Will reply to correspondence in Portuguese or English. $1 or return postage helpful.

Rádio Difusora do Maranhão (when active), C.P. 152, 65000-000 São Luís MA, Brazil. Contact: Alonso Augusto Duque, BA, Presidente; José de Arimatéa Araújo, Diretor; or Fernando Souza, Gerente. Free tourist literature. Return postage required. Replies occasionally to correspondence in Portuguese.

Rádio Difusora Jataí, C.P. 33 (or Rua de José Carvalhos Bastos 542), 75800-000 Jataí GO, Brazil. Contact: Zacarías Faleiros, Diretor Gerente.

Rádio Difusora Macapá (when active), C.P. 2929, 68900-000 Macapá AP, Brazil. Contact: Francisco de Paulo Silva Santos; Rui Lobato; or Eng. Arquit. Benedito Rostan Costa Martins, Diretor. $1 or return postage required. Replies irregularly to correspondence in Portuguese.

Rádio Difusora Poços de Caldas, C.P. 937, 37701-970 Poços de Caldas MG, Brazil. Phone/fax: +55 (35) 722-1530. URL: www.pocos-net.com.br/difusora/. Contact: Marco Aurelio C. Mendoça, Diretor; or W. Paulo de Mello. $1 or return postage required. Replies to correspondence in Portuguese.

Rádio Difusora Roraima, Avenida Capitão Ene Garcez 830, 69304-000 Boa Vista RR, Brazil. Contact: Francisco G. França, Diretor Gerente; Marcia Seixas, Diretora Geral; Benjamin Monteiro, Locutor; or Francisco Alves Vieira. Return postage required. Replies occasionally to correspondence in Portuguese.

Rádio Difusora "6 de Agosto," Rua Pio Nazário 31, 69930-000 Xapuri AC, Brazil. Contact: Francisco Evangelista de Abreu. Replies to correspondence in Portuguese.

Rádio Difusora Taubaté (when active), Rua Dr. Sousa Alves 960, 12020-030 Taubaté SP, Brazil. No contact details available at press time.

Rádio Educação Rural—Campo Grande, C.P. 261, 79002-233 Campo Grande MS, Brazil. Phone: +55 (67) 384-3164, +55 (67) 382-2238 or +55 (67) 384-3345. Contact: Ailton Guerra, Gerente-Geral; Angelo Venturelli, Diretor; or Diácono Tomás Schwamborn. $1 or return postage required. Replies to correspondence in Portuguese.

Rádio Educação Rural—Coari, Praça São Sebastião 228, 69460-000 Coari AM, Brazil. Contact: Lino Rodrigues Pessoa, Diretor Comercial; Joaquim Florencio Coelho, Diretor Administrador da Comunidade Salgueiro; or Elijane Martins Correa. $1 or return postage helpful. Replies irregularly to correspondence in Portuguese.

Rádio Educadora Cariri, C.P. 57, 63100-000 Crato CE, Brazil. Contact: Padre Gonçalo Farias Filho, Diretor Gerente. Return postage or $1 helpful. Replies irregularly to correspondence in Portuguese.

Rádio Educadora da Bahia, Centro de Rádio, Rua Pedro Gama 413/E, Alto Sobradinho Federação, 40230-291 Salvador BA, Brazil. Phone: +55 (71) 339-1180. Fax: +55 (71) 339 1170. URL: (includes RealAudio) www.svn.com.br/irdeb/re.htm. Contact: Elza Correa Ramos; or Walter Sequieros R. Tanure. $1 or return postage required. May send local music CD. Replies to correspondence in Portuguese.

Rádio Educadora de Bragança (when active), Rua Barão do Rio Branco 1151, 68600-000 Bragança PA, Brazil. Contact: José Rosendo de S. Neto or Zelina Cardoso Gonçalves. $1 or return postage required. Replies to correspondence in Portuguese.

Rádio Educadora de Guajará Mirim, Praça Mario Correa No.90, 78957-000 Guajará Mirim RO, Brazil. Contact: Padre Isidoro José Moro. Return postage helpful. Replies to correspondence in Portuguese.

Rádio Gaúcha, Avenida Ipiranga 1075 2do andar, Azenha, 90169-900 Porto Alegre RS, Brazil. Phone: +55 (51) 223-6600. E-mail: (general) gaucha@rdgaucha.com.br; (technical) gilberto.kussler@rdgaucha.com.br. URL: (includes RealAudio) www.rdgaucha.com.br:8080/index2.htm. Contact: Marco Antônio Baggio, Gerente de Jornalismo/Programação; Armindo Antônio Ranzolin, Diretor Gerente; Gilberto Kussler, Gerente Tecnico; Geraldo Canali. Replies occasionally to correspondence, preferably in Portuguese.

Rádio Gazeta, Avenida Paulista 900, 01310-940 São Paulo SP, Brazil. Fax: +55 (11) 285 4895. Contact: Shakespeare Ettinger, Superv. Geral de Operação; Bernardo Leite da Costa; José Roberto Mignone Cheibub, Gerente Geral; or Ing. Aníbal Horta Figueiredo. Free stickers. $1 or return postage necessary. Replies to correspondence in Portuguese. Currently leasing all its airtime to the "Deus é Amor" Pentecostal church, but has been observed in the past to sometimes carry its own programming on at least one of its three shortwave channels.

Rádio Globo, Rua do Russel 434-Glória, 22213-900 Rio de Janeiro RJ, Brazil. URL: (Real Audio) www.radioglobo.com.br/.

Contact: Marcos Libretti, Diretor Geral. Replies irregularly to correspondence in Portuguese. Return postage helpful.

Rádio Globo, Rua das Palmeiras 315, 01288-900 São Paulo SP, Brazil. URL: (RealAudio) www.radioglobo.com.br/. Contact: Ademar Dutra, Locutor, "Programa Ademar Dutra"; Guilherme Viterbo; or José Marques. Replies to correspondence, preferably in Portuguese.

Rádio Guaíba, Rua Caldas Junior 219, 90019-900 Porto Alegre RS, Brazil. Phone: +55 (51) 224-3755 or +55 (51) 224-4555. E-mail: guaiba@cpovo.net. URL: (includes RealAudio) www.cpovo.net/radio/. Return postage may be helpful.

Rádio Guarani, Avenida Assis Chateaubriand 499, Floresta, 30150-101 Belo Horizonte MG, Brazil. URL: (includes RealAudio) www.guarani.com.br/index.html. Contact: Junara Belo, Setor de Comunicações. Replies slowly to correspondence in Portuguese. Return postage helpful.

Rádio Guarujá

STATION: C.P. 45, 88000-000 Florianópolis SC, Brazil. Contact: Acy Cabral Tieve, Diretor; Joana Sempre Bom Braz, Assessora de Marketing e Comunicação; or Rosa Michels de Souza. Return postage required. Replies irregularly to correspondence in Portuguese.

NEW YORK OFFICE: 45 West 46 Street, 5th Floor, Manhattan, NY 10036 USA.

Rádio Inconfidência, C.P. 1027, 30650-540 Belo Horizonte MG, Brazil. Fax: +55 (31) 296 3070. E-mail: inconfidencia@plugway.com.br. URL: (includes RealAudio) www.plugway.com.br/inconfidencia/. Contact: Isaias Lansky, Diretor; Manuel Emilio de Lima Torres, Diretor Superintendente; Jairo Antolio Lima, Diretor Artístico; or Eugenio Silva. Free stickers and postcards. May send CD of Brazilian music. $1 or return postage helpful.

Rádio Integração (when active), Rua Alagoas 270, 69980-000 Cruzeiro do Sul AC, Brazil. Contact: Oscar Alves Bandeira, Gerente. Return postage helpful.

Rádio IPB AM, Rua Itajaí 473, Bairro Antonio Vendas, 79041-270 Campo Grande MS, Brazil. Contact: Iván Páez Barboza, Diretor Geral (hence, the station's name, "IPB"); Pastor Laercio Paula das Neves, Dirigente Estadual; Agenor Patrocinio S., Locutor; Pastor José Adão Hames; or Kelly Cristina Rodrigues da Silva, Secretária. Return postage required. Replies to correspondence in Portuguese. Most of the airtime is leased to the "Deus é Amor" Pentecostal church.

Rádio Itatiaia, Rua Itatiaia 117, 31210-170 Belo Horizonte MG, Brazil. Fax: +55 (31) 446 2900. E-mail: itatiaia@itatiaia.com.br. URL: (includes RealAudio) www.itatiaia.com.br/. Contact: Lúcia Araújo Bessa, Assistente da Diretória; or Claudio Carneiro.

Rádio Jornal "A Crítica," C.P. 2250, 69061-970 Manaus AM, Brazil. Contact: Sr. Cotrere, Gerente.

Rádio Liberal, C.P 498, 66017-970 Belém PA, Brazil. Phone: +55 (91) 241-1330. E-mail: radamjlm@libnet.com.br. URL: www.radioliberal.com.br. Contact: Flavia Vasconcellos.

Rádio Marajoara (if reactivated), Travessa Campos Sales 370, Centro, 66019-904 Belém PA, Brazil. Contact: Elizete Maria dos Santos Pamplona, Diretora Geral; or Sra. Neide Carvalho, Secretária da Diretoria Executiva. Return postage required. Replies irregularly to correspondence in Portuguese.

Rádio Marumby, C.P. 62 (C.P. 296 is the alternative box), 88010-970 Florianópolis SC, Brazil; or (missionary parent organization) Gideões Missionários da Última Hora—GMUH, Ministério Evangélico Mundial, Rua Joaquim Nunes 244, C.P. 4, 88340-000 Camboriú SC, Brazil. Contact: Davi Campos, Diretor Artístico; Dr. Cesario Bernardino, Presidente, GMUH;

Pb. Claudiney Nunes, Diretor; Dr. Nildair Santos, Coordinador; or Jair Albano, Diretor. $1 or return postage required. Free diploma and stickers. Replies to correspondence in Portuguese.

Rádio Marumby, Curitiba—*see* Rádio Novas de Paz, Curitiba, below.

Rádio Meteorologia Paulista, C.P. 91, 14940-970 Ibitinga, São Paulo SP, Brazil. Contact: Roque de Rosa, Diretora. Replies to correspondence in Portuguese. $1 or return postage required.

Rádio Missões da Amazônia, Travessa Ruy Barbosa 142, 68250-000 Obidos PA, Brazil. Contact: Max Hamoy; Edérgio de Moras Pinto; or Maristela Hamoy. Return postage required. Replies occasionally to correspondence in Portuguese.

Rádio Mundial, Rua da Consolação 2608, 1º Andar, CJ. 11, 01416-000 Consolação, São Paulo SP, Brazil. Fax: +55 (11) 258 5838 or +55 (11) 258 0152.

Rádio Nacional da Amazônia, Radiobrás, SCRN 702/3 Bloco B Lote 16/18, Ed. Radiobrás, 70323-900 Brasília DF, Brazil. Fax: +55 (61) 321 7602. URL: http:www.radiobras.gov.br/radioamz.htm. Contact: (general) Luíz Otavio de Castro Souza, Diretor; Fernando Gómez da Camara, Gerente de Escritório; or Januario Procopio Toledo, Diretor. Free stickers, but no verifications.

Rádio Nacional do Brasil—Radiobrás, External Service, C.P. 08840, 70912-790, Brasília DF, Brazil. Phone: +55 (61) 321-3949. Fax: +55 (61) 321 7602. E-mail: maurilio@webserver.radiobras.gov.br or ana.felicia@webserver.radiobras.gov.br. URL: www.radiobras.gov.br/. Contact: Otavio Bonfim, Gerente do Serviço Internacional; Michael Brown, Announcer; or Gabriela Barga. Free stickers. Correspondence welcomed in English and other languages. Unlike Radiobrás' domestic service (preceding entry), Radiobrás' External Service verifies regularly.

Rádio Nacional São Gabriel da Cachoeira, Avenida Alvaro Maia 850, 69750-000 São Gabriel da Cachoeira AM, Brazil. Contact: Luíz dos Santos França, Gerente; or Valdir de Souza Marques. Return postage necessary. Replies to correspondence in Portuguese.

Rádio Novas de Paz, Avenida Paraná 1896, 82510-000 Curitiba PR, Brazil; or C.P. 22, 80000-000 Curitiba PR, Brazil. Phone: +55 (41) 257-4109. Contact: João Falavinha Ienzen, Gerente. $1 or return postage required. Replies irregularly to correspondence in Portuguese.

Rádio Nova Visão
STUDIOS: Rua do Manifesto 1373, 04209-001 São Paulo SP, Brazil. Contact: José Eduardo Dias, Diretor Executivo; Rev. Iván Nunes; Cesino Bernardino, Presidente GMUH; Claudiney Nunes, Gerente Geral; Nildair Santos, Coordenador; or Marlene P. Nunes, Secretária. Return postage required. Replies to correspondence in Portuguese. Free stickers. Relays Rádio Trans Mundial fulltime.
TRANSMITTER: C.P. 551, 97000-000 Santa Maria RS, Brazil; or C.P. 6084, 90000-000 Porto Alegre RS, Brazil. Reportedly issues full-data verifications for reports in Portuguese or German, upon request, from this location. If no luck, try contacting, in English or Dutch, Tom van Ewijck, via e-mail at egiaroll@mail.iss.lcca.usp.br.

Rádio Oito de Setembro, C.P. 8, 13690-000 Descalvado SP, Brazil. Contact: Adonias Gomes. Replies to corrrespondence in Portuguese.

Rádio Pioneira de Teresina, Rua 24 de Janeiro 150 sul/centro, 64001-230 Teresina PI, Brazil. Contact: Luíz Eduardo Bastos; or Padre Tony Batista, Diretor. $1 or return postage required. Replies slowly to correspondence in Portuguese.

Rádio Poti (if reactivated), C.P. 145, 59001-970 Natal RN, Brazil. Contact: Cid Lobo. Return postage helpful. Replies slowly to correspondence in Portuguese.

Rádio Progresso (when operating), Estrada do Belmont s/n, Bº Nacional, 78903-400 Porto Velho RO, Brazil. Return postage required. Replies occasionally to correspondence in Portuguese.

Rádio Record
STATION: C.P. 7920, 04084-002 São Paulo SP, Brazil. Contact: Mário Luíz Catto, Diretor Geral. Free stickers. Return postage or $1 required. Replies occasionally to correspondence in Portuguese.
NEW YORK OFFICE: 630 Fifth Avenue, Room 2607, New York NY 10111 USA.

Rádio Ribeirão Preto, C.P. 1252, 14025-000 Ribeirão Preto SP, Brazil (physical address: Av. 9 de Julho 600, 14025-000 Ribeirão Preto SP, Brazil). Phone/fax: +55 (16) 610-3511. E-mail: scc@clube.com.br. URL: (includes RealAudio) www.clube.com.br. Contact: Lucinda de Oliveira, Secretária; Luis Schiavone Junior; or Paulo Henríque Rocha da Silva. Replies to correspondence in Portuguese.

Rádio Rio Mar, Rua José Clemente 500, 69010-070 Manaus AM, Brazil. Replies to correspondence in Portuguese. $1 or return postage necessary.

Rádio Rural Santarém, Rua Floriano Peixoto 632, 68005-060 Santarém PA, Brazil. Contact: João Elias B. Bentes, Gerente Geral; or Edsergio de Moraes Pinto. Replies slowly to correspondence in Portuguese. Free stickers. Return postage or $1 required.

Rádio Timbira (if reactivated), Rua do Correio s/n, Bairro de Fátima, 65030-340 São Luís MA, Brazil. Contact: Sandoval Pimentel Silva, Diretor Geral. Free picture postcards. $1 helpful. Replies occasionally to correspondence in Portuguese; persist.

Rádio Trans Mundial, Caixa Postal 18300 (Aeroporto), 04699-970 São Paulo SP, Brazil. E-mail: transmun@uol.com.br; or transmun@sp.dglnet.com.br. URL: www.transmundial.com.br/. Program aired via Rádio Nova Visão—*see* above.

Rádio Tropical (if reactivated), C.P. 23, 78600-000 Barra do Garças MT, Brazil. Contact: Alacir Viera Cándido, Diretor e Presidente; or Walter Francisco Dorados, Diretor Artístico. $1 or return postage required. Replies slowly and rarely to correspondence in Portuguese.

Rádio Tupi, Avenida Nadir Dias Figueiredo 1329, 02110-901 São Paulo SP, Brazil. Contact: Alfredo Raymundo Filho, Diretor Geral; Montival da Silva Santos; or Elia Soares. Free stickers. Return postage required. Replies occasionally to correspondence in Portuguese.

Rádio Universo/Rádio Tupi, C.P. 7133, 80000-000 Curitiba PR, Brazil. Contact: Luíz Andreu Rúbio, Diretor. Replies occasionally to correspondence in Portuguese. Rádio Universo's program time is rented by the "Deus é Amor" Pentecostal church, and is from the Rádio Tupi network. Identifies on the air as "Radio Tupi, Sistema Universo de Comunicação" or, more often, just as "Radio Tupi."

Rádio Verdes Florestas, C.P. 53, 69981-970 Cruzeiro do Sul AC, Brazil. Contact: Marlene Valente de Andrade. Return postage required. Replies occasionally to correspondence in Portuguese.

Sistema LBV Mundial (when operating), Legião da Boa Vontade, Rua Sérgio Tomás 740, Bom Retiro, 01131-010 São Paulo SP, Brazil. URL: (includes RealAudio) www.lbv.org/radio/index.html. Contact: André Tiago. Replies very irregularly.

BULGARIA   World Time +2 (+3 midyear)

Radio Bulgaria

NONTECHNICAL AND TECHNICAL: P.O. Box 900, BG-1000, Sofia, Bulgaria. Phone: +359 (2) 661-954 or +359 (2) 854-633. Fax: (general, usually weekdays only) +359 (2) 871 060, +359 (2) 871 061 or +359 (2) 650 560; (Managing Director) +359 (2) 662 215; (Frequency Manager) +359 (2) 963 4464. E-mail: rcorresp1@fon15.bnr.acad.bg. Contact: (general) Mrs. Iva Delcheva, English Section; Kristina Mihailova, In Charge of Listeners' Letters, English Section; Christina Pechevska, Listeners' Letters, English Section; Svilen Stoicheff, Head of English Section; or Sta. Katia Tomor, Sección Española; (administration and technical) Anguel H. Nedyalkov, Managing Director; (technical) Atanas Tzenov, Director. Free tourist literature, postcards, stickers, T-shirts, bookmarks and pennants. Gold, silver and bronze diplomas for correspondents meeting certain requirements. Free sample copies of *Bulgaria* magazine. Replies regularly, but sometimes slowly. Return postage helpful, as the station is financially overstretched due to the economic situation in the country. For concerns about frequency usage, contact BTC, below, with copies to Messrs. Nedyalkov and Tzenov of Radio Bulgaria.

FREQUENCY MANAGEMENT AND TRANSMISSION OPERATIONS: Bulgarian Telecommunications Company (BTC), Ltd., 8 Totleben Blvd., 1606 Sofia, Bulgaria. Phone: +359 (2) 88-00-75. Fax: +359 (2) 87 58 85 or +359 (2) 80 25 80. Contact: Roumen Petkov, Frequency Manager; or Mrs. Margarita Krasteva, Radio Regulatory Department.

Radio Horizont (when active), Bulgarian Radio, 4 Dragan Tsankov Blvd., 1040 Sofia, Bulgaria. Phone: +359 (2) 652-871. Fax: (weekdays) +359 (2) 657 230. Contact: Borislav Djamdjiev, Director; Iassen Indjev, Executive Director; or Martin Minkov, Editor-in-Chief.

Radio Varna, 22 blv. Primorski, 9000 Varna, Bulgaria. Replies irregularly. Return postage required.

BURKINA FASO   World Time exactly

Radiodiffusion-Télévision Burkina, B.P. 7029, Ouagadougou, Burkina Faso. Phone: +226 310-441. Contact: (general) Raphael L. Onadia or M. Pierre Tassembedo; (technical) Marcel Teho, Head of Transmitting Centre. Replies irregularly to correspondence in French. IRC or return postage helpful.

BURMA—*see* MYANMAR.

BURUNDI   World Time +2

La Voix de la Révolution, B.P. 1900, Bujumbura, Burundi. Phone: +257 22-37-42. Fax: +257 22 65 47 or +257 22 66 13. Contact: (general) Grégoire Barampumba, Head of News Section; or Frederic Havugiyaremye, Journaliste; (administration) Gérard Mfuranzima, Le Directeur de la Radio; or Didace Baranderetse, Directeur Général de la Radio; (technical) Abraham Makuza, Le Directeur Technique. $1 required.

CAMBODIA   World Time +7

National Radio of Cambodia

STATION ADDRESS: 106 Preah Kossamak Street, Monivong Boulevard, Phnom Penh, Cambodia. Phone: +855 (23) 23-369 or +855 (23) 22-869. Fax: + 855 (23) 27 319. Contact: (general) Miss Hem Bory, English Announcer; Kem Yan, Chief of External Relations; or Touch Chhatha, Producer, Art Department; (administration) In Chhay, Chief of Overseas Service; Som Sarun, Chief of Home Service; Van Sunheng, Deputy Director General, Cambodian National Radio and Television; or Ieng Muli, Minister of Information; (technical) Oum Phin, Chief of Technical Department. Free program schedule. Replies irregularly and slowly. Do not include stamps, currency, IRCs or dutiable items in envelope. Registered letters stand a much better chance of getting through.

CAMEROON   World Time +1

NOTE: Any CRTV outlet is likely to be verified by contacting via registered mail, in English or French with $2 enclosed, James Achanyi-Fontem, Head of Programming, CRTV, B.P. 986, Douala, Cameroon.

Cameroon Radio Television Corporation (CRTV)—Bafoussam (when active), B.P. 970, Bafoussam (Ouest), Cameroon. Contact: (general) Boten Celestin; (technical) Ndam Seidou, Chef Service Technique. IRC or return postage required. Replies irregularly in French to correspondence in English or French.

Cameroon Radio Television Corporation (CRTV)—Bertoua (when active), B.P. 230, Bertoua (Eastern), Cameroon. Rarely replies to correspondence, preferably in French. $1 required.

Cameroon Radio Television Corporation (CRTV)—Buea, P.M.B., Buea (Sud-Ouest), Cameroon. Contact: Ononino Oli Isidore, Chef Service Technique. Three IRCs, $1 or return postage required.

Cameroon Radio Television Corporation (CRTV)—Douala (when active), B.P. 986, Douala (Littoral), Cameroon. Contact: (technical) Emmanual Ekite, Technicien. Free pennants. Three IRCs or $1 required.

Cameroon Radio Television Corporation (CRTV)—Garoua, B.P. 103, Garoua (Nord/Adamawa), Cameroon. Contact: Kadeche Manguele. Free cloth pennants. Three IRCs or return postage required. Replies irregularly and slowly to correspondence in French.

Cameroon Radio Television Corporation (CRTV)—Yaoundé, B.P. 1634, Yaoundé (Centre-Sud), Cameroon. Phone: +237 214-077 or +237 214-088. Fax: +237 204 340. Contact: (technical or nontechnical) Gervais Mendo Ze, Directeur-Général; (technical) Eyebe Tanga, Directeur Technique. $1 required. Replies slowly (sometimes extremely slowly) to correspondence in French.

CANADA   World Time –3:30 (–2:30 midyear) Newfoundland; –4 (–3 midyear) Atlantic; –5 (–4 midyear) Eastern, including Quebec and Ontario; –6 (–5 midyear) Central; except Saskatchewan; –6 Saskatchewan; –7 (–6 midyear) Mountain; –8 (–7 midyear) Pacific, including Yukon

BBC World Service via RCI/CBC—For verification direct from RCI's CBC shortwave transmitters, contact Radio Canada International (*see* below). Nontechnical correspondence should be sent to the BBC World Service in London (*see*).

Canadian Broadcasting Corporation (CBC)—English Programs, P.O. Box 500, Station A, Toronto, Ontario, M5W 1E6, Canada. Phone: +1 (416) 975-3311. URLs: (general, including RealAudio) www.cbc.ca/; (CBC Websites and e-mail

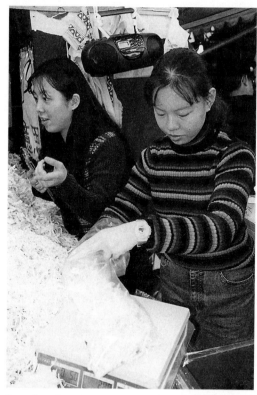

Bargains abound on Di Hwa Street in Taipei, Taiwan.
R. Crane

addresses) www.cbc.ca./aboutcbc/address/address.html. CBC prepares some of the programs heard over Radio Canada International (see).

Canadian Broadcasting Corporation (CBC)—French Programs—see Radio Canada International, below, for mailing address. E-mail (comments on programs): auditoire@montreal.src.ca. Welcomes correspondence sent to this address but cannot reply due to shortage of staff. URL: (includes RealAudio) www.radio-canada.com/index.htm. CBC prepares some of the programs heard over Radio Canada International (see).

CBC Northern Quebec Shortwave Service—see Radio Canada International, below.

CFCX-CIQC/CKOI (when operating)

TRANSMITTER (CFCX); ALSO, STUDIOS FOR CIQC ENGLISH-LANGUAGE PROGRAMS: CFCX-CIQC, 211 Gordon Avenue, 3rd Floor, Verdun, Quebec, H3G 2R2, Canada. Phone: +1 (514) 767-9250. Fax: +1 (514) 766 9569. E-mail: am600@ciqc.com. URL: (includes RealAudio) www.ciqc.com. Currently off shortwave due to transmitter problems.

FRENCH-LANGUAGE PROGRAM STUDIOS: CKOI, Metromedia CMR, Inc., 211 Gordon Avenue, Verdun, Quebec, H4G 2R2,

Canada. Fax: (CKOI—Programming Dept.) +1 (514) 766 2474; (sister station CKVL) +1 (514) 761 0136. URL: (includes RealAudio) www.ckoi.com/. Free stickers and possibly T-shirts. Correspondence in French preferred, but English and Spanish accepted.

CFRX-CFRB

MAIN ADDRESS: 2 St. Clair Avenue West, Toronto, Ontario, M4V 1L6, Canada. Phone:(main switchboard) +1 (416) 924-5711; (access line) +1 (416) 872-CFRB; (news centre) +1 (416) 924-6717; (talk shows) +1 (416) 872-1010. Fax: +1 (416) 323 6830. E-mail: comments@cfrb.com. URL: (includes RealAudio) http://cfrb.istar.ca/. Contact: (nontechnical) Bob Macowycz, Operations Manager; or Gary Slaight, President; (technical) Ian Sharp. Reception reports should be sent to verification address, below.

VERIFICATION ADDRESS: Ontario DX Association, P.O. Box 161, Station 'A', Willowdale, Ontario, M2N 5S8, Canada. Phone: +1 (416) 293-8919. Fax: +1 (416) 293 6603. E-mail: 70400.2660@compuserve.com. URL: www.durhamradio.ca/odxa. Contact: Steve Canney. Free CFRB/CFRX information sheet and ODXA brochure enclosed with verification. Reception reports are processed quickly if sent to this address, rather than to the station itself.

CFVP-CKMX, AM 1060, Standard Broadcasting, P.O. Box 2750, Stn. "M", Calgary, Alberta, T2P 4P8, Canada. Phone: (general) +1 (403) 240-5800; (news) +1 (403) 240-5844; (technical) +1 (403) 240-5867. Fax: (general and technical) +1 (403) 240 5801; (news) +1 (403) 246 7099. Contact: (general) Gary Russell, General Manager; or Beverley Van Tighem, Exec. Ass't.; (technical) Ken Pasolli, Technical Director.

CHNX-CHNS, P.O. Box 400, Halifax, Nova Scotia, B3J 2R2, Canada. Phone: +1 (902) 422-1651. Fax: +1 (902) 422 5330. E-mail: chns@ns.sympatico.ca. Contact: Garry Barker, General Manager; (programs) Troy Michaels, Operations Manager; (technical) Wayne Harvey, Chief Engineer. Program schedules, stickers and small souvenirs sometimes available. Return postage or $1 helpful. Replies irregularly.

CHU-Canada (official time and frequency station), Time and Frequency Standards, Bldg. M-36, National Research Council, Ottawa, Ontario, K1A 0R6, Canada. Phone: (general) +1 (613) 993-5186; (administration) +1 (613) 993-1003 or +1 (613) 993-2704. Fax: +1 (613) 993 1394. E-mail: radio.chu@nrc.ca. URL: www.ems.nrc.ca/inms. Contact: Dr. J.S. Boulanger, Programme Leader; or R. Pelletier, Technical Officer. Official standard frequency and World Time station for Canada on 3330, 7335 and 14670 kHz. Brochure available upon request. Those with a personal computer, Bell 103 standard modem and appropriate software can get the exact time, via CHU's cesium clock, off the air from their computer; details available upon request.

CKZN-CBN, CBC, P.O. Box 12010, Station "A", St. John's, Newfoundland, A1B 3T8, Canada. Phone: +1 (709) 576-5155. Fax: +1 (709) 576 5099. URL: www.radio.cbc.ca. Contact: (general) Heather Elliott, Communications Officer; (technical) Shawn R. Williams, Manager, Transmission & Distribution; or Jerry Brett, Transmitter Department. Free CBC sticker and verification card with the history of Newfoundland included. Don't enclose money, stamps or IRCs with correspondence, as they will only have to be returned.

CKZU-CBU, CBC, P.O. Box 4600, Vancouver, British Columbia, V6B 4A2, Canada. Toll-free telephone (U.S & Canada only) 1-800-961-6161. Phone: (general) +1 (604) 662-6000; (engineering) +1 (604) 662-6064. Fax: (general) +1 (604) 662 6350; (engineering) +1 (604) 662 6350. URL: www.cbc.ca. Contact:

(general) Public Relations; (technical) Dave Newbury, Transmission Engineer.

▣Radio Voice of Canada (formerly Radio Asia Canada International), 680 Progress Avenue Unit #1, Toronto, Ontario M1H 3A5, Canada. Phone: +1 (416) 289-1522. Fax: +1 (416) 289 1840. E-mail: general@radioasiacanada.ca; (reception reports) tech@radioasiacanada.ca. URL: (includes RealAudio) www.radioasiacanada.ca/. Contact: Phillip Pradeep Koneswaran, Vice President. Transmits via facilities of Deutsche Telekom, Germany (see).

▣Radio Canada International

NOTE: (CBC Northern Quebec Service): The following RCI address, fax and e-mail information for the Main Office and Transmission Office is also valid for the CBC Northern Quebec Shortwave Service, provided you make your communication to the attention of the particular service you seek to contact.

MAIN OFFICE: P.O. Box 6000, Montréal, Quebec, H3C 3A8, Canada. Phone: (general) +1 (514) 597-7500; (Audience Relations) +1 (514) 597-7555; (English and French programming) +1 (514) 597-7551; (Russian programming) +1 (514) 597-6866; (CBC's "As It Happens' Talkback Machine") +1 (416) 205-3331. Fax: (RCI) +1 (514) 284 0891 or +1 (514) 284 9550; (English and French Programming) +1 (514) 597 7617. E-mail: (general) rci@montreal.src.ca; (Audience Relations) rci@cam.org. URL: (includes RealAudio) www.rcinet.ca/en/index.htm. Contact: (general) Maggy Akerblom, Director of Audience Relations; or Mark Montgomery, Producer/Host, the "Mailbag"; (administration) Bob O'Reilly, Executive Director; (technical— verifications) Bill Westenhaver, CIDX. Free stickers and other small station souvenirs. 50th Anniversary T-shirts, sweatshirts, watches, lapel pins and tote bags available for sale; write to the above address for a free illustrated flyer giving prices and ordering information.

TRANMISSION OFFICE: 1055 Boul. Rene Levesque East, Montréal, H2L, 4S5 Canada. Phone: +1 (514) 597-7616/17/18/19/20. Fax: +1 (514) 284 2052. E-mail: (Théorêt) gtheoret@montreal.src.ca; (Bouliane) jbouliane@montreal.src.ca. Contact: (general) Gérald Théorêt, Frequency Manager; or Nicole Vincent; (administration) Jacques Bouliane, Director of Engineering. This office only for informing about transmitter-related problems (interference, modulation quality, etc.), especially by fax. Verifications not given out at this office; requests for verification should be sent to the main office, above.

TRANSMITTER SITE: CBC, P.O. Box 1200, Sackville New Brunswick, E0A 3CO, Canada. Phone: +1 (506) 536-2690/1. Fax: +1 (506) 536 2342. Contact: Marc Leblanc, Plant Manager. All correspondence not concerned with transmitting equipment should be directed to the appropriate address in Montréal, above. Free tours given during normal working hours.

RCI MONITORING STATION: P.O. Box 322, Station C, Ottawa, Ontario, K1Y 1E4, Canada. Phone: +1 (613) 831-2801. Fax: +1 (613) 831 0342. Contact: Derek Williams, Plant Manager.

LABOR REPRESENTATION AND RCI BOOSTERS' ORGANIZATION: Coalition to Restore Full RCI Funding, SCFP Local 675, 1250 de la Visitation, Montréal, Quebec, H2L 3B4, Canada. Phone: +1 (514) 844-2262. Fax: +1 (514) 521 3082. E-mail: rci@cam.org. Contact: Wojtek Gwiazda. Local 675 is active in maintaining RCI as an active force in international broadcasting, and welcomes correspondence from like-minded individuals and organizations.

WASHINGTON NEWS BUREAU: CBC, National Press Building, Suite 500, 529 14th Street NW, Washington DC 20045 USA. Phone: +1 (202) 638-3286. Fax: +1 (202) 783 9321. Contact: Jean-Louis Arcand, David Hall or Susan Murray.

LONDON NEWS BUREAU: CBC, 43-51 Great Titchfield Street, London W1P 8DD, England. Phone: +44 (171) 412-9200. Fax: +44 (171) 631 3095.

PARIS NEWS BUREAU: CBC, 17 avenue Matignon, F-75008 Paris, France. Phone: +33 (1) 43-59-11-85. Fax: +33 (1) 44 21 15 14.

Radio Monte-Carlo Middle East (via Radio Canada International)—*see* Cyprus.

Shortwave Classroom, G.L. Comba Public School, P.O. Box 580, Almonte, Ontario, K0A 1A0, Canada. Phone: +1 (613) 256-2735. Fax: +1 (613) 256 3107. E-mail: 713861@ican.net. Contact: Neil Carleton, Organizer. *The Shortwave Classroom* newsletter, three times per year, for "$10 and an accompanying feature to share with teachers in the newsletter." Ongoing nonprofit volunteer project of teachers and others to use shortwave listening in the classroom to teach about global perspectives, media studies, world geography, languages, social studies and other subjects. Interested teachers and parents worldwide are invited to make contact.

CENTRAL AFRICAN REPUBLIC World Time +1

Radio Centrafrique, Radiodiffusion-Télévision Centrafricaine, B.P. 940, Bangui, Central African Republic. Contact: (technical) Jacques Mbilo, Le Directeur des Services Techniques; or Michèl Bata, Services Techniques. Replies on rare occasions to correspondence in French; return postage required.

CHAD World Time +1

Radiodiffusion Nationale Tchadienne—N'djamena, B.P. 892, N'Djamena, Chad. Contact: Djimadoum Ngoka Kilamian. Two IRCs or return postage required. Replies slowly to correspondence in French.

Radio Diffusion Nationale Tchadienne—Radio Abéché, B.P. 105, Abéché, Ouaddai, Chad. Return postage helpful. Replies rarely to correspondence in French.

Radiodiffusion Nationale Tchadienne—Radio Moundou, B.P. 122, Moundou, Logone, Chad. Contact: Dingantoudji N'Gana Esaie.

CHILE World Time –3 (–4 midyear)

Radio Esperanza

OFFICE: Casilla 830, Temuco, Chile. Phone/fax: +56 (45) 240-161. Contact: (general) Juanita Cárcamo, Departmento de Programación; Eleazar Jara, Dpto. de Programación; Ramón P. Woerner K., Publicidad; or Alberto Higueras Martínez, Locutor; (verifications) Juanita Carmaco M., Dpto. de Programación; (technical) Juan Luis Puentes, Dpto. Técnico. Free pennants, stickers, bookmarks and tourist information. Two IRCs, $1 or 2 U.S. stamps appreciated. Replies, usually quite slowly, to correspondence in Spanish or English.

STUDIO: Calle Luis Durand 03057, Temuco, Chile. Phone/fax: +56 (45) 240-161.

Radio Santa María, Apartado 1, Coyhaique, Chile. Phone: +56 (67) 23-23-98, +56 (67) 23-20-25 or +56 (67) 23-18-17. Fax: +56 (67) 23 13 06. Contact: Pedro Andrade Vera, Coordinador. $1 or return postage required. May send free tourist cards. Replies to correspondence in Spanish and Italian.

Radio Triunfal Evangélica, Calle Las Araucarias 2757, Villa Monseñor Larrain, Talagante, Chile. Phone: +56 (1) 815-4765. Contact: Fernando González Segura, Obispo de la Misión Pentecostal Fundamentalista. Two IRCs required. Replies to correspondence in Spanish.

Voz Cristiana, Casilla 490, Santiago 3, Chile. Phone: +56 (2) 855-7046. Fax: +56 (2) 855 7053. E-mail: (engineering) vozing@interaccess.cl; (administration) vozcrist@ interaccess.cl. URL: www.christianvision.org/christian-vision/chile.htm. Contact: Andrew Flynn, Chief Engineer.

CHINA

World Time +8; still nominally +6 ("Urümqi Time") in the Xinjiang Uighur Autonomous Region, but in practice +8 is observed there, as well.

NOTE: China Radio International, the Central People's Broadcasting Station and certain regional outlets reply regularly to listeners' letters in a variety of languages. If a Chinese regional station does not respond to your correspondence within four months—and many will not, unless your letter is in Chinese or the regional dialect—try writing them c/o China Radio International.

Central People's Broadcasting Station (CPBS)—China National Radio, Zhongyang Renmin Guangbo Diantai, P.O. Box 4501, CN-100866 Beijing, China. Phone: +86 (10) 6851-2435 or +86 (10) 6851-5522. Fax: +86 (10) 6851 6630. Contact: Wang Changquan, Audience Department, China National Radio. Tape recordings of music and news $5 plus postage. CPBS T-shirts $10 plus postage; also sells ties and other items with CPBS logo. No credit cards. Free stickers, pennants and other small souvenirs. Return postage helpful. Responds regularly to correspondence in English and Standard Chinese (Mandarin). Although in recent years this station has officially been called "China National Radio" in English-language documents, all on-air identifications in Standard Chinese continue to be "Zhongyang Renmin Guangbo Dientai" (Central People's Broadcasting Station). CPBS-1 also airs Chinese-language programs co-produced by CPBS and Radio Canada International.

China Huayi Broadcasting Company, P.O. Box 251, Fuzhou City, 35001 Fujian, China. Contact: Lin Hai Chun, Announcer. Replies to correspondence in English and Chinese.

China National Radio—see Central People's Broadcasting Station/CPBS, above.

China Radio International

MAIN OFFICE, NON-CHINESE LANGUAGES SERVICE: 16A Shijingshan Street, 100040 Beijing, China. Phone: (director's office) +86 (10) 6889-1676; (Audience Relations.) +86 (10) 6889-1617 or +86 (10) 6889-1652; (English Newsroom) +86 (10) 6889-1619; (current affairs) +86 (10) 6889-1588; (technical director) +86 (10) 6609-2577. Fax: (director's office) +86 (10) 6889 1582; (English Service) +86 (10) 6889 1378 or +86 (10) 6889 1379; (Audience Relations) +86 (10) 6851 3175; or (administration) +86 (10) 6851 3174. E-mail: (English Service) crieng@bta.net.cn; or (audience relations) crieng@ mail.cri.cngb.com. URLs: (official) www.cri.cngb.com/; (unofficial, but regularly updated) http://pw2.netcom.com/~jleq/ cri.htm. Contact: Ms. Qi Guilin, Director of Audience Relations, English Service; Shang Chunyan, "Listener's Letterbox"; Xu Ming, Editor; or Xia Jixuan, Director of English Service; (technical) Wang Guoqing, Technical Director; (administration) Zhang Zhenhua, Director General, China Radio International; Wang Guoqing, Cong Yingmin and Wong Rufeng, Deputy Directors, China Radio International. Free bi-monthly

Messenger newsletter for loyal listeners, pennants, stickers, desk calendars, pins and handmade papercuts. Sometimes China Radio International will hold contests or quizzes. All those participating will get a prize, but the overall prize winner will win a free trip to China. T-shirts for $8. Two-volume, 820-page set of Day-to-Day Chinese language-lesson books $15, including postage worldwide; a new 155 page book Learn to Speak Chinese: Sentence by Sentence, plus two cassettes for $15. Two chinese music tapes for $15. Various other Chinese books (on arts, medicine, etc.) in English available from Yinglian, Audience Relations Department, English Service, China Radio International, 100040 Beijing China. Every year, the Audience Relations Department will renew the mailing list of the Messenger newsletter. CRI is also relayed via shortwave transmitters in Brazil, Canada, France, French Guiana, Mali, Russia, Spain and Switzerland.

MAIN OFFICE, CHINESE LANGUAGES SERVICE: China Radio International, 100040 Beijing, China. Prefers correspondence in Chinese (Mandarin), Cantonese, Hakka, Chaozhou or Amoy.

ARLINGTON NEWS BUREAU: 2000 South Eads Street APT#712, Arlington VA 22202 USA. Phone: +1 (703) 521-8689. Contact: Mr. Zhenbang Dong.

CHINA (HONG KONG) NEWS BUREAU: 387 Queen's Road East, Room 1503, Hong Kong, China. Phone: +852 2834-0384. Contact: Ms. Zhang Jiaping.

JERUSALEM NEWS BUREAU: Flat 16, Hagdud, Ha'ivri 12, Jerusalem 92345, Israel. Phone: +972 (2) 566-6084. Contact: Mr. H. Yi.

LONDON NEWS BUREAU: 13B Clifton Gardens, Golders Green, London NW11 7ER, United Kingdom. Phone: +44 (181) 458-6943. Contact: Ms. Xu Huazhen.

NEW YORK NEWS BUREAU: 630 First Avenue #35K, New York NY 10016 USA. Fax: +1 (212) 889 2076. Contact: Mr. Qian Yurun.

SYDNEY NEWS BUREAU: Unit 53, Block A15 Herbert Street, St. Leonards NSW 2065, Australia. Phone: +61 (2) 9436-1493. Contact: Mr. Shi Chungyong.

Fujian People's Broadcasting Station, Fuzhou, Fujian, China. $1 helpful. Replies occasionally and usually slowly.

Gansu People's Broadcasting Station, Lanzhou, China. Contact: Li Mei. IRC helpful.

Guangxi People's Broadcasting Station, No. 12 Min Zu Avenue, Nanning, 530022 Guangxi, China. Contact: Song Yue, Staffer; Yuan Ri Qin; or Li Hai Li, Staffer. Free stickers and handmade papercuts. IRC helpful. Replies irregularly.

Guizhou People's Broadcasting Station, 259 Qingyun Lu, 550002 Guiyang, Guizhou, China.

Heilongjiang People's Broadcasting Station, No. 115 Zhongshan Road, Harbin City, Heilongjiang, China. $1 or return postage helpful.

Honghe People's Broadcasting Station, Jianshe Donglu 32, 661400 Geji City, Yunnan, China. Contact: Shen De-chun, Head of Station; or Mrs. Cheng Lin, Editor-in-Chief. Free travel brochures.

Hubei People's Broadcasting Station, No. 563 Jiefang Dadao, Wuhan, 430022 Hubei, China.

Hunan People's Broadcasting Station, 27 Yuhua Lu, Changsha, 410007 Hunan, China.

Jiangxi People's Broadcasting Station, Nanchang, Jiangxi, China. Contact: Tang Ji Sheng, Editor, Chief Editor's Office. Free gold/red pins. Replies irregularly. Mr. Tang enjoys music, literature and stamps, so enclosing a small memento along these lines should help assure a speedy reply.

Nei Menggu (Inner Mongolia) People's Broadcasting

Station, 19 Xinhua Darjie, Hohhot, 010058 Nei Menggu, China. Contact: Zhang Xiang-Quen, Secretary; or Liang Yan. Replies irregularly.

Qinghai People's Broadcasting Station, 96 Kunlun Lu, Xining, 810001 Qinghai, China. Contact: Liqing Fangfang; or Ghou Guo Liang, Director, Technical Department. $1 helpful.

Sichuan People's Broadcasting Station, Chengdu, Sichuan, China. Replies occasionally.

Voice of Jinling, P.O. Box 268, Nanjing, 210002 Jiangsu, China; or (physical address) 1376 Hongqiao Road, Shanghai, China. Phone: +86 (21) 6208-2797. Fax: +86 (25) 413 235 or +86 (21) 6208 2850. Contact: Strong Lee, Producer/Host, "Window of Taiwan." Free stickers and calendars, plus Chinese-language color station brochure and information on the Nanjing Technology Import & Export Corporation. Replies to correspondence in Chinese and to simple correspondence in English. $1, IRC or 1 yuan Chinese stamp required for return postage.

Voice of Pujiang, 1376 Hongqiao Road, Shanghai, China; or P.O. Box 3064, 200002 Shanghai, China. Phone: +86 (21) 6208-2797. Fax: +86 (21) 6208 2850. Contact: Jiang Bimiao, Editor & Reporter.

Voice of the Strait, People's Liberation Army Broadcasting Centre, P.O. Box 187, Fuzhou, 350012 Fujian, China. Replies irregularly.

Wenzhou People's Broadcasting Station, Wenzhou, China.

Xilingol People's Broadcasting Station, Xilinhot, Xilingol, China.

Xinjiang People's Broadcasting Station, No. 84 Tuanjie Lu (United Road), Urümqi, 830044 Xinjiang, China. Contact: Zhao Ji-shu. Free tourist booklet, postcards and used Chinese stamps. Replies to correspondence in Chinese and to simple correspondence in English.

Xizang People's Broadcasting Station, Lhasa, Xizang (Tibet), China. Contact: Lobsang Chonphel, Announcer. Free stickers and brochures. Enclosing an English-language magazine may help with a reply.

Yunnan People's Broadcasting Station, No 73 Renmin Road (W), Central Building of Broadcasting & TV, Kunming, 650031 Yunnan, China. Contact: Sheng Hongpeng or F.K. Fan. Free Chinese-language brochure on Yunnan Province, but no QSL cards. $1 or return postage helpful. Replies occasionally.

Zhejiang People's Broadcasting Station, 11 Wulin Xiang, Moganshan Lu, Hangzhou, 310005 Zhejiang, China.

CHINA (TAIWAN) World Time +8

Central Broadcasting System (CBS), 55 Pei'an Road, Tachih, Taipei 104, Taiwan, Republic of China. Phone: +886 (2) 591-8161. URL: www.cbs.org.tw/. Contact: Lee Ming, Deputy Director. Free stickers.

Radio Taipei International, P.O. Box 24-38, Taipei 106, Taiwan, Republic of China. Phone: +886 (2) 752-2825 or +886 (2) 771-0151. Fax: +886 (2) 751 9277. URL: www.cbs.org.tw/eng/engb.html. Contact: (general) Daniel Dong, Chief, Listeners' Service Section; Paula Chao, Producer, "Mailbag Time";Yea-Wen Wang; or Phillip Wong, "Perspectives"; (administration) John C.T. Feng, Director; or Dong Yu-Ching, Deputy Director; (technical) Wen-Bin Tsai, Engineer, Engineering Department; Tai-Lau Ying, Engineering Department; Tien-Shen Kao; or Huang Shuh-shyun, Director, Engineering Department. Free stickers, caps, shopping bags, annual diary, "Let's Learn Chinese" language-learning course materi-

als, booklets and other publications, and Taiwanese stamps. T-shirts $5. The station's programs are relayed to the Americas via WYFR's transmitters in Okeechobee, Florida, USA (see).
OSAKA NEWS BUREAU: C.P.O. Box 180, Osaka Central Post Office, Osaka 530-091, Japan.
TOKYO NEWS BUREAU: P.O Box 21, Azubu Post Office, Tokyo 106, Japan.
SAN FRANCISCO NEWS BUREAU: P.O. Box 192793, San Francisco CA 94119-2793 USA.

Voice of Asia, P.O. Box 24-777, Taipei, Taiwan, Republic of China. Phone:+886 (2) 771-0151, X-2431. Fax: +886 (2) 751 9277. URL: same as for Radio Taipei International, above (select from menu). Contact: (general) Vivian Pu, Co-Producer, with Isaac Guo of "Letterbox"; or Ms. Chao Mei-Yi, Deputy Chief; (technical) Engineering Department. Free shopping bags, inflatable globes, coasters, calendars, stickers and booklets. T-shirts $5.

CLANDESTINE—*see* DISESTABLISHMENTARIAN.

COLOMBIA World Time –5

NOTE: Colombia, the country, is always spelled with two o's. It is never written as "Columbia."

Armonías del Caquetá, Apartado Aéreo 71, Florencia, Caquetá, Colombia. Phone: +57 (88) 352-080. Contact: Padre Alvaro Serna Alzate, Director. Replies occasionally and slowly to correspondence in Spanish. Return postage required.

Caracol Arauca—see La Voz del Cinaruco.

Caracol Colombia
MAIN OFFICE: Apartado Aéreo 9291, Santafé de Bogotá, D.C., Colombia. Phone: +57 (1) 337-8866. Fax: +57 (1) 337 7126. URL: (RealAudio in Spanish; news in Spanish & correspondence) www.caracol.com.co. Contact: Hernán Peláez Restrepo, Jefe Cadena Básica; or Efraín Jiménez, Director de Operaciones. Free stickers. Replies to correspondence in Spanish and English.
MIAMI OFFICE: 2100 Coral Way, Miami FL 33145 USA. Phone: +1 (305) 285-2477 or +1 (305) 285-1260. Fax: +1 (305) 858 5907.

Caracol Florencia (when active), Apartado Aéreo 465, Florencia, Caquetá, Colombia. Phone: +57 (88) 352-199. Contact: Guillermo Rodríguez Herrera, Gerente; or Vicente Delgado, Operador. Replies occasionally to correspondence in Spanish.

Caracol Villavicencio—*see* La Voz de los Centauros.

Colmundo Bogotá, Diagonal 58 No. 26A-29, Santafé de Bogotá, Colombia; or Apartado Aéreo 36.750, Santafé de Bogotá, Colombia. Contact: María Teresa Gutiérrez, Directora Gerente; Marcela Aristizábal, Presidente; Jorge Eliecer Hernández, Gerente Nacional de Programacion; Carlos Arturo Echeverry, Chief Engineer; or Néstor Chamorro, Presidente de la Red Colmundo. E-mail: colradio@latino.net.co.Actively seeks reception reports from abroad, preferably in Spanish. Free stickers and program schedule.

Ecos del Atrato, Apartado Aéreo 196, Quibdó, Chocó, Colombia. Phone: +57 (49) 711-450. Contact: Absalón Palacios Agualimpia, Administrador. Free pennants. Replies to correspondence in Spanish.

Ecos del Orinoco (when active), Gobernación del Vichada, Puerto Carreño, Vichada, Colombia.

La Voz de la Selva—*see* Caracol Florencia.

La Voz de los Centauros (Caracol Villavicencio), Cra.

31 No. 37-71 Of. 1001, Villavicencio, Meta, Colombia. Phone: +57 (86) 214-995. Fax: +57 (86) 623 954. Contact: Carlos Torres Leyva, Gerencia; or Olga Arenas, Administradora. Replies to correspondence in Spanish.

La Voz del Cinaruco (when active), Calle 19 No. 19-62, Arauca, Colombia. Contact: Efrahim Valera, Director. Pennants for return postage. Replies rarely to correspondence in Spanish; return postage required.

La Voz del Guaviare, Carrera 22 con Calle 9, San José del Guaviare, Colombia. Phone: +57 (986) 840-153/4. Fax: +57 (986) 840 102. Contact: Luis Fernando Román Robayo, Director General. Replies slowly to correspondence in Spanish.

La Voz del Llano, Calle 38 No. 30A-106, Villavicencio, Meta, Colombia. Phone: +57 (86) 624-102. Fax: +57 (86) 625 045. Contact: Alcides Antonio Jáuregui B., Director; or Edgar Valenzuela Romero. Replies occasionally to correspondence in Spanish. $1 or return postage necessary.

La Voz del Río Arauca
STATION: Carrera 20 No. 19-09, Arauca, Colombia. Phone: +57 (818) 52-910. Contact: Jorge Flórez Rojas, Gerente; Luis Alfonso Riaño, Locutor; or Mario Falla, Periodista. $1 or return postage required. Replies occasionally to correspondence in Spanish; persist.
BOGOTÁ OFFICE: Cra. 10 No. 14-56, Of. 309/310, Santafé de Bogotá, D.C., Colombia.

La Voz del Yopal (when active), Calle 9 No. 22-63, Yopal, Casanare, Colombia. Phone: +57 (87) 558-382. Fax: +57 (87) 557 054. Contact: Pedro Antonio Socha Pérez, Gerente; or Marta Cecilia Socha Pérez, Subgerente. Return postage necessary. Replies to correspondence in Spanish.

Ondas del Meta (when active), Calle 38 No. 30A-106, Villavicencio, Meta, Colombia. Phone: +57 (86) 626-783. Fax: +57 (86) 625 045. Contact: Yolanda Plazas Agredo, Administradora. Free tourist literature. Return postage required. Replies irregularly and slowly to correspondence in Spanish. Plans to reactivate from a new antenna site.

Ondas del Orteguaza, Calle 16, No. 12-48, piso 2, Florencia, Caquetá, Colombia. Phone: +57 (88) 352-558. Contact: Sandra Liliana Vásquez, Secretaria; or Señora Elisa Viuda de Santos; or Henry Valencia Vásquez. Free stickers. IRC, return postage or $1 required. Replies occasionally to correspondence in Spanish.

Radiodifusora Nacional de Colombia
MAIN ADDRESS: Edificio Inravisión, CAN, Av. Eldorado, Santafé de Bogotá, D.C., Colombia. Phone: +57 (1) 222-0415. Fax: +57 (1) 222 0409 or +57 (1) 222 8000. Contact: Rubén Darío Acero, Jefe Sistemas AM y Onda Corta; or Dra. Athala Morris, Directora. Free lapel badges, membership in Listeners' Club and monthly program booklet.
CANAL INTERNACIONAL: Apartado Aéreo 93994, Santafé de Bogotá, D.C., Colombia. Contact: Jesús Valencia Sánchez.

RCN (Radio Cadena Nacional)
MAIN OFFICE: Apartado Aéreo 4984, Santafé de Bogotá, D.C., Colombia. URL: (RealAudio, news & correspondence) http://rcn.com.co. Contact: Antonio Pardo García, Gerente de Producción y Programación. Will verify all correct reports for stations in the RCN network. Spanish preferred and return postage necessary.

Radio Macarena (when active), Calle 38 No. 32-41, piso 7, Edif. Santander, Villavicencio, Meta, Colombia. Phone: +57 (986) 626-780. Phone/fax: +57 (986) 624-507. Contact: (general) Pedro Rojas Velásquez; or Carlos Alberto Pimienta, Gerente; (technical) Sra. Alba Nelly González de Rojas, Administradora. Sells religious audio cassettes for 3,000 pe-

sos. Return postage required. Replies slowly to correspondence in Spanish. Considering installing a more powerful transmitter and Audimax audio processor.

Radio Melodía (Cadena Melodía) (when active), Apartado Aéreo 58721, Santafé de Bogotá, D.C., Colombia; or Apartado Aéreo 19823, Santafé de Bogotá, D.C., Colombia. Phone: +57 (1) 217-0423, +57 (1) 217-0720, +57 (1) 217-1334 or +57 (1) 217-1452. Fax: +57 (1) 248 8772. Contact: Gerardo Páez Mejía, Vicepresidente; Elvira Mejía de Pérez, Gerente General; or Gracilla Rodríguez, Asistente Gerencia. Stickers and pennants. $1 or return postage.

Radio Mira, Apartado Aéreo 165, Tumaco, Nariño, Colombia. Phone: +57 (27) 272-452. Contact: Padre Jairo Arturo Ochoa Zea. Return postage required.

Radio Super (Ibagué) (when active), Parque Murillo Toro 3-31, P. 3, Ibagué, Tolima, Colombia. Phone: +57 (82) 611-381. Fax: +57 (82) 611 471. Contact: Fidelina Caycedo Hernández; or Germán Acosta Ramos, Locutor Control. Free stickers. Return postage or $1 helpful. Replies irregularly to correspondence in Spanish.

COMOROS   World Time +4

Radio Comoro (if reactivated), B.P. 250, Moroni, Grande Comore, Comoros. Phone: +269 732-531. Contact: Ali Hamdi Hissani; or Antufi Mohamed Bacar, Le Directeur de Programme. Return postage required. Replies very rarely to correspondence in French. Currently off the air due to a technical problem with their shortwave transmitter but hope to be back on the air sometime in the future.

CONGO (DEMOCRATIC REPUBLIC) (formerly Zaïre)   World Time +1 Western, including Kinshasa; +2 Eastern

Radio Bukavu (when active), B.P. 475, Bukavu, Democratic Republic of the Congo. Contact: Jacques Nyembo-Kibeya; Kalume Kavue Katumbi; or Baruti Lusongela, Directeur. $1 or return postage required. Replies slowly. Correspondence in French preferred.

Radio CANDIP Bunia (formerly La Voix du Peuple, and prior to that, Radio CANDIP), B.P. 373, Bunia, Democratic Republic of Congo. Letters should preferably be sent via registered mail. $1 or return postage required. Correspondence in French preferred.

Radio Kisangani (when active), B.P. 1745, Kisangani, Democratic Republic of the Congo. Contact: (general) Lumeto lue Lumeto, Directeur Regional; or Lumbutu Kalome, Directeur Inspecteur; (technical) Lukusa Kowumayi Branly, Technicien. $1 or 2 IRCs required. Correspondence in French preferred. Mail to this station may be interfered with by certain staff members. Try sending letters to Lumbutu Kalome at his private address: 10e Avenue 34, Zone de la Tshopo, Kisangani, Democratic Republic of the Congo. Registering letters may also help. Replies to North American listeners sometimes are mailed via the Oakland, California, post office.

Radio Lubumbashi (when active), B.P. 7296, Lubumbashi, Democratic Republic of the Congo. Contact: Senga Lokavu, Chef du Service de l'Audiovisuel; Bébé Beshelemu, Directeur; or Mulenga Kanso, Chef du Service Logistique. Letters should be sent via registered mail. $1 or 3 IRCs helpful. Correspondence in French preferred.

Radio-Télévision Nationale Congolaise, B.P. 3171, Kinshasa-Gombe, Democratic Republic of the Congo. Contact: Faustin Mbula, Ingenieur Technicien. Letters should be sent via registered mail. $1 or 3 IRCs helpful. Correspondence in French preferred

CONGO (REPUBLIC)   World Time +1

Radio Liberté, Radiodiffusion-Télévision Congolaise, B.P. 2241, Brazzaville, Congo. Contact: (general) Antoine Ngongo, Rédacteur en chef; (administration) Albert Fayette Mikano, Directeur; or Zaou Mouanda. $1 required. Replies irregularly to letters in French sent via registered mail.

COSTA RICA   World Time –6

Adventist World Radio, the Voice of Hope, AWR-PanAmerica, Apartado 1177, 4050 Alajuela, Costa Rica. Phone: +506 483-0550/551. Fax +506 483 0555. E-mail: rmadvent@racsa.sol.cr. URL: www.awr.org/awr-panamerica/. Contact: Victor Shepherd, General Manager; David Gregory, Program Director; Miss Miriam Pottinger; or Rosaura Barrantes B., Secretaria; (technical) Karl Thompson, Chief Engineer. Free stickers, calendars, Costa Rican stamps and religious printed matter. IRCs accepted but currency notes in a major world currency preferred, or return postage stamps appreciated. Also, *see* AWR listings under Guam, Guatemala, Italy, Kenya, Russia and USA.

Faro del Caribe Internacional y Misionera—TIFC
MAIN OFFICE: Apartado 2710, 1000 San José, Costa Rica. Phone: +506 (226) 2573 or +506 (226) 2618. Fax: +506 (227) 1725. E-mail: al@casa-pres.go.cr. Contact: Carlos A. Rozotto Piedrasanta, Director Administrativo; or Mauricio Ramires; (technical) Minor Enrique, Station Engineer.Free stickers, pennants, books and bibles. $1 or IRCs helpful.
U.S. OFFICE, NONTECHNICAL: Misión Latinoamericana, P.O. Box 620485, Orlando FL 32862 USA.

▣**Radio 88 Estéreo**, Apartado 827-8000, Péréz Zeledón, Costa Rica. Phone: +506 257-8585, +506 771-6094 or (phone/fax) +506 771-6093. Fax: +506 771 5539. Contact: Juan Vega, Director.

Radio Casino, Apartado 287, 7301 Puerto Limón, Costa Rica. Phone: +506 758-0029. Fax: +506 758 3029. Contact: Edwin Zamora, Departamento de Notícias; or Luis Grau Villalobos, Gerente; (technical) Ing. Jorge Pardo, Director Técnico; or Luis Muir, Técnico.

Radio Exterior de España—Cariari Relay Station, Cariari de Pococí, Costa Rica. Phone: +506 767-7308, +506 767-7311. Fax: +506 225 2938.

Radio For Peace International (RFPI)
MAIN OFFICE: Apartado 88, Santa Ana, Costa Rica. Phone: +506 249-1821. Fax: +506 249 1095. E-mail: rfpicr@sol.racsa.co.cr. URLs: (general) www.clark.net/pub/cwilkins/rfpi/rfpi.html; (Far Right Radio Review) www.clark.net/pub/cwilkins/rfpi/frwr.html. Contact: (general) Debra Latham, General Manager of RFPI, Editor of *VISTA* and co-host of "RFPI Mailbag"; (programming) Joe Bernard, Program Coordinator; Willie Barrantes, Director, Spanish Department; or James Latham, host, "Far Right Radio Review"; (nontechnical or technical) James L. Latham, Station Manager. Replies sometimes slow in coming because of the mail. Quarterly *VISTA* newsletter, which includes schedules and program information, $40 annual membership ($50 family/organization) in "Friends of Radio for Peace International"; station commemorative T-shirts and rainforest T-shirts $20; thermo mugs $10 (VISA/MC). Actively solicits listener contributions—directly, as well as indirectly through well-wishers signing up with PeaceCOM's long distance telephone service (+1 541/345-3326), or making designated world band purchases from Grove Enterprises (1-800-438-8155). $1 or 3 IRCs appreciated. Limited number of places available for volunteer broadcasting and journalism interns; those interested should send résumé. If funding can be worked out, hopes to add a world band transmission facility in Salmon Arm, British Columbia, Canada. RFPI was created by United Nations Resolution 35/55 on December 5, 1980.
U.S. OFFICE, NONTECHNICAL: P.O. Box 20728, Portland OR 97294 USA. Phone: +1 (503) 252-3639. Fax: +1 (503) 255 5216. Contact: Dr. Richard Schneider, Chancellor CEO, University of Global Education (formerly World Peace University). Newsletter, T-shirts and so forth, as above. University of the Air courses (such as "Earth Mother Speaks" and "History of the U.N.") $25 each, or on audio cassette $75 each (VISA/MC).

Radio Reloj, Sistema Radiofónico H.B., Apartado 341, 1000 San José, Costa Rica. URL: (includes RealAudio) www.rpreloj.co.cr/. Contact: Roger Barahona, Gerente; or Francisco Barahona Gómez. Can be very slow in replying. $1 required.

Radio Universidad de Costa Rica, San Pedro de Montes de Oca, 1000 San José, Costa Rica. Phone: +506 225-3936. Contact: Marco González Muñoz; Henry Jones, Locutor de Planta; or Nora Garita B., Directora. Free postcards, station brochure and stickers. Replies slowly to correspondence in Spanish or English. $1 or return postage required.

CÔTE D'IVOIRE   World Time exactly

Radiodiffusion Télévision Ivoirienne, B.P. 191, Abidjan 1, Côte d'Ivoire. Phone: +225 32-4800.

CROATIA   World Time +1 (+2 midyear)

▣**Croatian Radio**
MAIN OFFICE: Hrvatska Radio-Televizija (HRT), Prisavlje 3, HR-41000 Zagreb, Croatia. Phone: (technical) +385 (1) 616-3355. Fax: (general) +385 (1) 616 3285; (technical) +385 (1) 616 3347. E-mail: (International Relations Department) ird@hrt.hr; (technical) zelimir.klasan@hrt.com.hr. URLs:(general) www.hrt.hr/; (program guide) www.hrt.hr/hr/program/; (RealAudio) www.hrt.hr/hr/audio/. Contact: (general) Vladimir Lusic, Head of International Relations; Darko Kragovic; or Bozidar Tomanek; (technical) Zelimir Klasan. Free Croatian stamps. Subscriptions to *Croatian Voice*. $1 helpful. Replies irregularly and slowly.
WASHINGTON NEWS BUREAU: Croatian-American Association, 1912 Sunderland Place NW, Washington DC 20036 USA. Phone: +1 (202) 429-5543. Fax: +1 (202) 429 5545. URL: www.hrnet.org/CAA/. Contact: Bob Schneider, Director.

CUBA   World Time –5 (–4 midyear)

Radio Habana Cuba, P.O. Box 6240, Havana, Cuba 10600. Phone: (general) +53 (7) 784-954 or +53 (7) 334-272; (English and Spanish Departments) +53 (7) 791-053; (French Department) +53 (7) 785-444; (Coro) +53 (7) 814-243 or (home) +53 (7) 301-794. Fax: (general) +53 (7) 783 518; (English and Spanish Departments) +53 (7) 795 007; (French Department) +53 (7) 705 810. E-mail: (general) cartas@radiohc.org; rhc@radiohc.org; (engineering, technical, and "Dxers Unlimited") arnie@radiohc.org. URL: www.radiohc.org/. Contact:

(general) Lourdes López, Head of Correspondence Dept.; Jorge Miyares, English Service; or Mike La Guardia, Senior Editor; (administration) Ms. Milagro Hernández Cuba, General Director; (technical) Arnaldo Coro Antich, ("Arnie Coro"), Producer, "DXers Unlimited"; or Luis Pruna Amer, Director Técnico. Free wallet and wall calendars, pennants, stickers, keychains and pins. DX Listeners' Club. Free sample *Granma International* newspaper. Contests with various prizes, including trips to Cuba.

Radio Rebelde, Departamento de Relaciones Públicas, Apartado 6277, Havana 10600, Cuba. Contact: Noemí Cairo Marín, Secretaria, Relaciones Públicas; Iberlise González Padua, Relaciones Públicas; Marisel Ramos Soca, Relaciones Públicas; or Jorge Luis Más Zabala, Director, Relaciones Públicas. Replies very slowly, with correspondence in Spanish preferred.

CYPRUS   World Time +2 (+3 midyear)

Bayrak Radio—BRT International (when operating), BRTK Campus, Dr. Fazil Küçük Boulevard, P.O. Box 417, Lefkosa - T.R.N.C., via Mersin 10, Turkey. Phone: (general) +90 (392) 225-5555; (public relations office) +90 (392) 228-0577. Fax: (general) +90 (392) 225 2918; (news dept.) +90 (392) 225 4991. E-mail: (general) brt@cc.emu.edu.tr; (technical, including reception reports) tosun@cc.emu.edu.tr. URL: (includes RealAudio) www.emu.edu.tr/~brt/. Contact: Mustafa Tosun, Head of Transmission Department.

BBC World Service—East Mediterranean Relay Station, P.O. Box 4912, Limassol, Cyprus. Contact: Steve Welch. This address for technical matters only. Reception reports and nontechnical correspondence should be sent to the BBC World Service in London (*see*).

Cyprus Broadcasting Corporation, Broadcasting House, P.O. Box 4824, 1397 Nicosia, Cyprus; or (physical address) RIK Street, Athalassa, Nicosia, Cyprus. Phone: +357 (2) 422-231. Fax: +357 (2) 314 050. E-mail: rik@cybc.com.cy. URL: (includes RealAudio) www.cybc.com.cy/. Contact: (general) Pavlos Soteriades, Director General; (technical) Andreas Michaelides, Director of Technical Services. Free stickers. Replies occasionally, sometimes slowly. IRC or $1 helpful.

Radio Monte-Carlo Middle East, P.O. Box 2026, Nicosia, Cyprus. Contact: M. Pavlides, Chef de Station. This address for listeners to the RMC Arabic Service, which prepares its world band programs in Cyprus, but transmits them via facilities of Radio Canada International in Canada. For details of Radio Monte-Carlo's headquarters and other branch offices, *see* Monaco.

CZECH REPUBLIC   World Time +1 (+2 midyear)

Radio Prague, Czech Radio, Vinohradská 12, 12099 Prague, Czech Republic. Phone: (general) +420 (2) 2409-4608; (Czech Department) +420 (2) 2422-2236; (English Department) +420 (2) 2421-8349; (Internet) +420 (2) 2421 5456. Fax: (nontechnical and technical) +420 (2) 2421 8239; +420 (2) 2422 2236. E-mail: (general) cr@radio.cz; (English Department) english@radio.cz; (reception reports, Nora Mikes) nora@werich.radio.cz; (free news texts) robot@radio.cz, writing "Subscribe English" (or other desired language) within the subject line; (technical, chief engineer) cip@radio.cz. URLs: (text and RealAudio in English, German, Spanish and French) www.radio.cz; www.prague.org; (RealAudio in English and

Czech) www.wrn.org/stations/prague.html; (text) ftp://ftp.radio.cz; gopher://gopher.radio.cz. Contact: (general) Markéta Albrechtová; Lenka Adamová, "Mailbag"; Zdenek Dohnal; Nora Mikes, Listener Relations; L. Kubik; or Jan Valeška, Head of English Section; (administration) Dr. Richard Seeman, Director, Foreign Broadcasts; (technical, all programs) Oldrich Čip, Chief Engineer. Free stickers, key chains, and calendars; free Radio Prague Monitor Club "DX Diploma" for regular correspondents. Free books available for Czech-language course called "Check out Czech." Samples of *Welcome to the Czech Republic* and *Czech Life* available upon request from Orbis, Vinohradská 46, 120 41 Prague, Czech Republic.

RFE-RL—*see* USA.

DENMARK   World Time +1 (+2 midyear)

Radio Danmark

MAIN OFFICE: Rosenørns Allé 22, DK-1999 Frederiksberg C, Denmark. Phone: (office, including voice mail, voice schedules in Danish and schedule by return fax). Fax: + 45 3520 57 81. E-mail: (schedule and program matters) rdk@dr.dk; (technical matters and reception reports) rdk.ek@login.dknet.dk. URL: (includes RealAudio) www.dr.dk/rdk. Contact: (general) Kate Sand, Audience Communications; or Bjorn Schionning; (technical) Erik Køie, Technical Adviser; or Dan Helto, Head of Section. Replies to correspondence in English or Danish. Will verify all correct reception reports; return postage ($1 or one IRC) appreciated. Uses transmitting facilities of Radio Norway International. All broadcasts are in Danish. "Tune In" letterbox program aired last Saturday/Sunday of the month, hourly 24 times from 16.37 UTC (summer; winter 17.37 UTC).
PRODUCTION OFFICE, ENGLISH PROGRAM: Box 666, DK-1506 Copenhagen, Denmark. E-mail: jui@dr.dk. Contact: Julian Isherwood, Producer, "Tune In" twice monthly (Saturday) letterbox program.
TRANSMISSION MANAGEMENT AUTHORITY: Tele Denmark, NIA-Broadcast, Telegade 2, DK-2630 Taastrup, Denmark. Phone: +45 4334-5746. Fax: +45 4371 1143. Contact: Ib H. Lavrsen, Senior Engineer.
NORWEGIAN OFFICE, TECHNICAL: Details of reception quality may also be sent to the Engineering Department of Radio Norway International (*see*), which operates the transmitters currently used for Radio Danmark.

DISESTABLISHMENTARIAN

NOTE ON STATIONS WITHIN THE UNITED STATES AND COSTA RICA: In the United States and Costa Rica, disestablishmentarian programs are aired within the provisions of national law, and thus usually welcome correspondence and requests for free or paid materials. Virtually all such programs in the United States are aired over a variety of private stations—WGTG in McCaysville, Georgia; WWCR in Nashville; WRNO near New Orleans; WHRI in Noblesville, Indiana; WRMI in Miami; and, arguably, KVOH in Los Angeles.

These programs usually refer to themselves as "patriotic," and include such traditional and relatively benign ideologies as populism and politically conservative evangelism. Among these categories, some go out of their way to disassociate themselves from bigotry. However, other programs, with tiny but dedicated audiences, are survivalist, antisemitic, neo-fascist, ultra-nationalist or otherwise on the fringes of the political "right," including the much-publicized militia movement.

Perhaps surprisingly, few are overtly racist, although racism is often implied.

These programs reflect the American climate of unfettered freedom of speech, as well as, in some cases, the more cynical American tradition of profiting from proselytization. ("Our society is about to be conquered by alien or internationalist forces. To cope with this, you'll need certain things, which we sell.") Thus, American disestablishmentarian programs often differ greatly from the sorts of broadcasting discourse allowed within the laws and traditions of most other countries.

Well removed from this genre is the relatively low-powered voice of Radio For Peace International (see), a largely American-staffed station in Costa Rica. RFPI airs disestablishmentarian-cum-social-conscience programs from the relatively internationalist perspective of the political "new left" that grew into prominence in North America and Europe during the late Sixties. It also regularly follows and reports on the aforementioned disestablishmentarian programs aired over stations within the United States.

NOTE ON STATIONS OUTSIDE THE UNITED STATES AND COSTA RICA: Outside the United States and Costa Rica, disestablishmentarian broadcasting activities, some of which are actually clandestine, are unusually subject to abrupt change or termination. Being operated by anti-establishment political and/or military organizations, these groups tend to be suspicious of outsiders' motives. Thus, they are most likely to reply to contacts from those who communicate in the station's native tongue, and who are perceived to be at least somewhat favorably disposed to their cause. Most will provide, upon request, printed matter in their native tongue on their cause.

For more detailed information on clandestine (but not disestablishmentarian) stations, refer to the annual publication, Clandestine Stations List, about $10 or 10 IRCs postpaid by air, published by the Danish Shortwave Clubs International, Tavleager 31, DK-2670 Greve, Denmark; phone (Denmark) +45 4290-2900; fax (via Germany) +49 6371 71790; e-mail 100413.2375@compuserve.com; its expert editor, Finn Krone of Denmark, may be reached at e-mail Krone@dk-online.dk. For CIA media contact information, see USA. Also now available on the internet The Clandestine Radio Intel Webpage, specialising in background information on these stations and organised by region and target country. The page can be accessed via: www.qsl.net/yb0rmi/cland.htm. Another informative webpage specialising in Clandestine Radio information and containing a biweekly report on the latest news and developments affecting the study of clandestine radio is Clandestine Radio Watch and it can be found at: www.geocities.com/capecanaveral/2594/geo-cla.htm.

"Agenda Cuba" (when operating), 7175 SW 8 Street, Suite 217, Miami FL 33144 USA. Contact: Pedro Solares. Program of the Agenda Cuba organization. Via WRMI, USA.

"Along the Color Line," Department of History, Columbia University, 611 Fayerweather Hall, New York NY 10027 USA. Phone: +1 (212) 854-7080. Fax: +1 (212) 854 7060. Contact: Dr. Manning Marable, Professor of History & Director of the Institute for Research in African-American Studies. Critiques a wide variety of domestic and international issues relevant to African-Americans. Via RFPI, Costa Rica.

"Alternativa", 7105 SW 8th Street, Suite 207, Miami FL 33144. Contact: Orlando Gutiérrez. Anti-Castro program of the Directorio Revolucionario Democrático Cubano. Via WRMI, USA.

"Alternative Radio," P.O. Box 551, Boulder CO 80306 USA. Phone: +1 (303) 444-8788. Contact: David Barsamian. Critiques such issues as multiculturalism, the environment, racism, American foreign policy, the media and the rights of indigenous peoples. Via RFPI, Costa Rica.

"American Dissident Voices," P.O. Box 90, Hillsboro WV 24946 USA (or P.O. Box 596, Boring OR 97009 USA). E-mail: (general) crusader@national.alliance; or triton@abszolute.org; (Strom) ka_strom@ix.netcom. URLs: (general) www.natall.com/SCHEDULE/ sched.html; (TrueSpeech/WAV audio archives) www.natall.com/radio/radio.html; (usenet) alt.politics.nationalism.white. Contact: Kevin Alfred Strom, WB4AIO, Producer. $12 for audio cassette of any given program. $55 for latest book from Canadian neonazi Ernst Zündel. Free Speech publication $40 per year. $2 for catalog of books and tapes. Free bumper stickers, "Who Rules America?" pamphlet and sample copies of Patriot Review newsletter. Program of the National Alliance, the most prominent neonazi organization in the United States. In its publicity, it claims to support "ordinary straight White America"; according to The New York Times, the National Alliance also states, "We must have a racially clean area of the earth." The show sometimes features William Pierce, chairman and founder of the American Nazi Party. Pierce, under the pen name "Andrew Macdonald," is the author of The Turner Diaries, which is felt may have given accused bomber Timothy McVeigh the idea and pyrotechnic knowledge for the Oklahoma City bombing. Via WRNO, and before that believed to be behind the U.S. clandestine station, "Voice of To-morrow," which became inactive not long before "American Dissident Voices" came on the air.

Dick Reed, left, with local announcer during ELWA's heyday in Liberia. SIM

"A Voz da Resistencia do Galo Negro" ("Voice of the Resistence of the Black Cockerel")—*see* Angola.

☞**"Baker Report,"** 2083 Springwood Road #300, York PA 17403 USA. Phone: (show, toll-free in United States) 1-800-482-5560; (orders, toll-free in United States) 1-800-782-4843; (general number/voice mail) +1 (717) 244-1110. E-mail: baker@universalweb.com. URL: (includes RealAudio) www.universalweb.com/amerinet/baker/index.htm. Contact: Dr. Jeffrey "Jeff" Baker. Three months of *The Baker Report* periodical $24.95; also sells audio tapes of programs and other items. Anti-"New World Order," Freemasonry and the Illuminati, and distrustful of official versions of various events, including the Oklahoma City bombing. Via WGTG and WRMI, USA.

"Battle Cry Sounding"

HEADQUARTERS: Command Post, ACMTC, P.O. Box 90, Berino NM 88024 USA. Fax: +1 (505) 882 7325. E-mail: prophet@cibola.net. URL: www-user.cibola.net/~prophet/. Contact: General James M. Green. Voice of the Aggressive Christianity Missions Training Corps, which seeks to eliminate churches, synagogues, mosques and central governments, thence to replace them with fundamentalist "warrior tribes"; also, operates Women's International Mobilization Movement. Publishes *Wisdom's Cry, Words of the Spirit, Tribal Call* and *Battle Cry Sounding* periodicals, and offers various other publications, as well as video and audio tapes. Via facilities of WWCR and WRMI, USA.

AFRICA OFFICE: P.O. Box 2686, Jos North, Plateau State, Nigeria. Contact: Colonel Simon Agwale, Adjutant.

"British Israel World Federation (Canada)," 313 Sherbourne Street, Toronto ON, M5A 2S3 Canada. Phone: (office, weekdays) +1 (416) 921-5996; (Nesbitt) +1 (705) 435-5044; (McConkey) +1 (705) 485-3486. Fax: +1 (416) 921 9511. Contact: Douglas Nesbitt or John McConkey. Offers *The Prophetic* magazine and 90-minute audio cassettes of past programs. Although located in Canada, this is the only British Israel office in North America, and thus serves the United States, as well. According to Kenneth Stern in *A Force upon the Plain*, "Christian Identity [*see* "Herald of Truth" and "Scriptures for America"] began as British Israelism, which traced its roots to mid-nineteenth-century claims that white Christians were the 'true Israelites,' that Jews were offspring of Satan, and that blacks and other minorities were . . . subhuman." Via WWCR, USA.

"CounterSpin," Fairness and Accuracy in Reporting, 130 W. 25th Street, New York NY 10001 USA. Phone: +1 (212) 633-6700. E-mail: fair@igc.org. URL: www.fair.org/fair/; (RealAudio) www.webactive.com/webactive/content/cspin.html. Contact: Patrice O'Neil, Co-Producer. Media watchdog organization that reports on what it feels are propaganda, disinformation and other abuses of the media, as well as citing instances of "hard-hitting, independent reporting that cuts against the prevailing media grain." Via RFPI, Costa Rica.

☞**"Democratic Voice of Burma"** ("Democratic Myanmar a-Than")

STATION: DVB Radio, P.O. Box 6720, St. Olavs Plass, N-0130 Oslo, Norway. Phone: +47 (22) 20-0021. Phone/fax: +47 (22) 36-2525. E-mail: dvb@sn.no. URL: (includes RealAudio) www.communique.no/dvb/. Contact: (general) Dr. Anng Kin, Listener Liaison; Aye Chan Naing, Daily Editor; or Thida, host for "Songs Request Program"; (administration) Harn Yawnghwe, Director; or Daw Khin Pyone, Manager; (technical) Technical Dept. Free stickers and booklets to be offered in the near future. Norwegian kroner requested for a reply, but presumably Norwegian mint stamps would also suffice. Programs produced by Burmese democratic movements, as well as professional and independent radio journalists, to provide informational and educational services for the democracy movement inside and outside Burma. Opposes the current Myanmar government. Transmits via the facilities of Radio Norway International and Deutsche Telekom, Germany.

AFFINITY GROUPS URLs:

BURMA NET. E-mail: (BurmaNet News editor, Free Burma Coalition, USA) strider@igc.apc.org; (Web coordinator, Free Burma

Coalition, USA) freeburma@pobox.com. URL: (BurmaNet News, USA) http://sunsite.unc.edu/freeburma/listservers.html. *FREE BURMA COALITION.* E-mail: justfree@ix.netcom.com. URL: http://danenet.wicip.org/fbc/.

"Democratic Voice of Iran" ("Seda-ye Azadi-khahan-e Iran"), BCM Box 5842, London, WC1N 3XX, United Kingdom; or Box 555, SE-114 79 Stockholm, Sweden. Fax: (France) +33 (1) 43 99 95 65; (Sweden) +46 (1) 831 4148; or (UK) +44 (541) 525 051. E-mail: mail@dvi.org. URL: (includes RealAudio) www.dvi.org/engdvi.html. Contact: Shahriar Azari, Chief Editor; or H.Hojabr. If corresponding with this station do not mention the name of the station or even the word "radio" on the envelope. Opposes current Iranian government. Broadcasts via transmitters in the former Soviet Union

"Executive Intelligence Review Talks," EIR News Service, P.O. Box 17390, Washington DC 20041 USA. Phone: (Executive Intelligence Review) +1 (202) 544-7010; (Schiller Institute) +1 (202) 544-7018; (21st Century Institute, general information) +1 (202) 639-6821; (21st Century Institute, subscription information) +1 (703) 777-9451; (Ben Franklin Bookstore for LaRouche publications) toll-free daytimes only within United States 1-800-453-4108, elswhere +1 (703) 777-3661. Fax: +1 (202) 544 7105. E-mail: (technical) ralphgib@aol.com. URLs: (EIR Home Page) www.larouchepub.com/index.html; (LaRouche Associates) www.erols.com/larouche/. Contact: (general) Mel Kanovsky, Frank Bell; or, asking correspondence to be forwarded, Lyndon LaRouche; (technical) Ralph Gibbons. Publishes *Executive Intelligence Review* newsletter, $896/year, and a wide variety of other periodicals and books. Supports former U.S. presidential candidate Lyndon LaRouche's populist political organization worldwide, including the Schiller Institute and 21st Century Institute of Political Action. Via WWCR, USA.

"Food Not Bombs Radio Network"

PRODUCTION FACILITY: 350 7th Avenue #35, San Francisco CA 94118 USA. Phone: +1 (415) 330-5030. Contact: Richard Edmondson, Producer. Via RFPI, Costa Rica.

ORGANIZATIONAL ADDRESS: Food Not Bombs, 3145 Gary Blvd. #12, San Francisco CA 94118 USA; also, temporarily can be reached at 25 Taylor Avenue, San Francisco CA 94118 USA. Phone: (toll-free in the U.S.) 1-800-884-1136; (elsewhere) +1 (415) 351-1672. URL: www.webcom.com/~peace. $10 for starter kit and 128-page book for starting a food recovery program; NTSC video $15. Food Not Bombs is a political activist group concerned with American homeless people, with the radio program focusing on what it views as "oppressive local, state and federal policies." The producer is a former homeless person.

"For the People", P.O. Box 150, Tampa FL 33601-0150 USA. Phone: (general) +1 (904) 719-6933; (talk show, toll-free within the United States, 1400-1700 Eastern Time only) 1-888-822-8255. Fax: +1 (904) 397 4484 or +1 (904) 397 4491. E-mail: doug@forthepeople.org; cpa14782@gte.net; or hostmail@tstradio.com. URL: www.forthepeople.org. Contact: Chuck Harder, Host; or Brice Warnick, Producer. Free monthly *Station Listing & Program Guide* Flyer. Annual FTP membership $20 ($35 outside U.S.). Sells bi-weekly *News Reporter* newspaper, NTSC videos of past FTP broadcasts, T-shirts and golf shirts; also a wide variety of books from its "For the People Bookstore"; free catalog upon request. VISA/MC. Publications and audio cassettes also available from "Eighth Day Books" (order line, toll-free within United States, 1-800-841-2541). Sells U.S.-made tabletop radio similar to Drake SW1 reviewed in Passport Reports *(see)*. The "For The People" talk show

espouses American populism, a philosophy going back to 1891. FTP's governing non-profit organization supports trade restrictions, freedom of health-care choice and progressive taxes on high incomes, while opposing racism and antisemitism. Live afternoons (local time) via WHRI, USA, and on tape evenings via WHRI and WWCR, USA; also in RealAudio (URL: www.whri.com/realaudio.htm; "Angel 1").

"Foro Militar Cubano," P.O. Box 140305, Coral Gables FL 33144-0305 USA. URL: www.cava.org. Contact: Frank Hernández Trujillo, Producer. Anti-Castro, anti-communist, privately supported by Cuban exiles and the Cuban American Veterans Association. Via WRMI, USA.

"Freedom's Call"—*see* WWCR, USA, for postal address. E-mail: bogritz@valint.net; or bo@talkamerica.com. URLs: www.bogritz.com/; www.talkamerica.com/bogritz.html; (StreamWorks audio) www.talkamerica.com/. Contact: James "Bo" Gritz. Opposes gun control, the Federal income tax, the "New World Order," Zionism, alleged Jewish "control" of such institutions as the Federal Reserve System, and the United Nations. Disputes official accounts of such events as the Oklahoma City bombing. Gritz, a retired U.S. Green Beret lieutenant colonel, America's most-decorated Vietnam veteran and former presidential candidate of the Populist Party (see "Radio Free America"), is the character upon whom the movie character "Rambo" is understood to have been based. Gritz is also credited, along with Jack McLamb (see "Officer Jack McLamb Show"), with being the key individual to persuade Randy Weaver to end the Ruby Ridge standoff. He leads two paramilitary/militia training organizations: Specially Prepared Individuals for Key Events (SPIKE), and the Idaho-based Constitutionalist Covenant Community. Via WWCR, USA.

"Full Disclosure Radio Show" (when operating), The Superior Broadcasting Company, P.O. Box 1533, Oil City PA 16301 USA. Phone: +1 (814) 676-2345. E-mail: glr@glr.com. URL: www.glr.com/net.html. Contact: Glen L. Roberts, Host. Sample newsletter $5. Offers a variety of electronics and related publications. Conservative talk show concerning such topics as political broadcasts and related communications, and eavesdropping. Via WGTG, USA.

"Global Community Forum/Far Right Radio Review"—*see* RFPI, Costa Rica, for contact information. "The Global Community Forum" and its subsection "The Far Right Radio Review," critiques populist and politically rightist programs emanating from various privately owned world band stations in the United States.

"Herald of Truth," P.O. Box 1021, Harrison AK 72602 USA. Phone: +1 (501) 741-1119. Contact: Pastor Bob Hallstrom. Free packet of information and copies of broadcast transcripts, also available from Gospel Ministries, P.O. Box 9411, Boise ID 83707 USA; or via URL: www.melvig.org/gmo.html. Program of the Kingdom Identity Ministries, a Christian Identity organization believed to be associated with "Scriptures for America" (*see*), and reportedly descended from British Israelism (see "British Israel World Federation"). Vehemently opposes to what it calls "Jews, queers, aliens and minorities," and supports "white Christians," specifically those "Aryan Jacob Israel people" originating from Western Europe. Yet, also opposes a seemingly endless roster of conservative white Christian political leaders, including Rush Limbaugh and U.S. House Speaker Newt Gingrich, and claims the late U.S. President Franklin Roosevelt was a Jewish communist. Sells various books and audio cassettes, as well as the *Patriot Report* newsletter. Via WWCR and WRMI, USA; Christian Identity programs are also aired over other American world band stations, such as WRNO.

"Hightower Radio," Saddle Burr Productions, P.O. Box 13516, Austin TX 78711 USA. Phone: +1 (512) 477-5588. Fax: +1 (512) 478 8536. E-mail: hightower@essential.org. URL: www.essential.org/hightower/; (RealAudio) www-2.realaudio.com/webactive/content/hightower.html. Contact: Jim Hightower. The term "maverick" comes from the contrarian way Texas pioneer Samuel Maverick and certain of his descendants handled cattle and other matters. Hightower Radio is considered to be heir to that spirit, featuring former Texas Agriculture Commissioner Jim Hightower, something of an establishment Texas disestablishmentarian and a gen-yew-wine Lone Star liberal. Via RFPI, Costa Rica.

"Hour of Courage," International Commerce Corporation, 135 S. Main Street, 7th Floor, Greenville SC 29601 USA. Phone: (toll-free within United States) 1-800-327-8606. Fax: +1 (803) 232 9309. Contact: Ron Wilson. *Creatures from Jeckyll Island* book $25. Forsees a conspiracy to take over the United States, opposes gun control, and is distrustful of official versions of various events, such as Waco. Also predicts the coming of a "greatest financial catastrophe in the world," and suggests that to protect against its consequences, listeners purchase precious metals from its sponsoring organization, Atlantic Bullion and Coin. Theme song: "Dixie." Via WWCR and WHRI, USA.

"Hour of the Time," The Harvest Trust, P.O. Box 1970, Eagar AZ 85925 USA. Phone/fax: +1 (520) 333-4578. E-mail: caji@pobox.com. URL: www.telepath.com/believer/page6.htm (broadcast transcripts downloadable as pkzip files from www.telepath.com/believer/page14.htm). Contact: William Cooper. Sells a variety of books, audio and video tapes. Newspaper *Veritas* available for prices ranging from $20 for six issues to $55 for 24 issues. Opposes "New World Order," the United Nations and the Federal Reserve; favors militias to resist potentially oppressive government. *Behold a Pale Horse* (Light Technology Publishing), a 1991 book by Cooper, covers his many claims, including about alien space invaders: "1 in 40 humans have been implanted with devices...aliens are building an army of implanted humans who can be activated and turned on us." Via WWCR, USA.

"Insight," The Progressive, 409 East Main Street, Madison WI 53703 USA. Phone: +1 (608) 257-4626. Fax: +1 (608) 257 3373. E-mail: editorial@progressive.org. URL: www.progressive.org/insight.htm. Contact: Matthew Rothschild, Editor. Radio outlet for *The Progressive* magazine, a disestablishmentarian publication founded in 1909. Via RFPI, Costa Rica.

"Intelligence Report," Wolverine Productions, P.O. Box 281, Augusta MI 49012 USA. Phone: +1 (616) 966-3002. Fax: +1 (616) 966 0742. Contact: (programs) John Stadtmiller. Sells various tapes and publications. Opposes the "New World Order" and supports the militia and survivalist movements. Aired via WWCR, USA.

"La Voz de Alpha 66," 1714 W. Flagler Street, Miami FL 33135 USA. Contact: Dr. Diego Medina, Producer. Anti-Castro, anti-communist; privately supported by the Alpha 66 organization. Via WHRI, USA.

"La Voz de la Fundación," 7300 NE 35th Terrace, Miami FL 33122 USA; or P.O. Box 440069, Miami FL 33122 USA. Phone: (general) +1 (305) 592-7768; (Pérez-Castellón) +1 (305) 599-3019. Fax: +1 (305) 592 7889. URLs: (Cuban American National Foundation parent organization) www.canfnet.org/; (La Voz de la Fundación) www.canfnet.org/english/prgvoz.htm. Contact: Ninoska Pérez-Castellón, Executive Producer; (technical) Mariela Ferretti. Free stickers. Anti-Castro,

anti-communist; privately supported by the Cuban American National Foundation. Via WHRI and WRMI, USA.

"La Voz de la Junta Patriótica Cubana," 4600 NW 7 Street, Miami FL 33126 USA; or P.O. Box 7799, Washington DC 20044 USA. Anti-Castro, anti-communist, privately supported by the Cuban Patriotic Council. E-mail: cabenedi@vais.net. URL: www.vais.net/~cabenedi/. Contact: Dr. Roberto Rodríguez de Aragón, Presidente de la Junta Patriótica Cubana; or Dr. Claudio F. Benedi-Beruff, Secretario de Relaciones Exteriores. Via WRMI, USA.

"La Voz del Puente de Jóvenes Profesionales Cubanos en el Exilio," P.O. Box 112453, Miami FL 33111-2453 USA. Contact: Rafael Sánchez-Aballi, Producer. Anti-Castro, supported by a group of Cuban professionals living in exile in Miami. Via WRMI, USA.

"Mujer Cubana," 747 Ponce de Leon Blvd., Suite 409, Coral Gables FL 33134 USA. Program of a group of Cuban women exiles in Miami. Via WRMI, USA.

"National Radio of the Saharan Arab Democratic Republic," (when operating)—*see* "Voice of the Free Sahara," below, which is operated by the same group, the Frente Polisario.

"Norman Resnick Show," American Freedom Network, P.O. Box 430, Johnstown CO 80534 USA. Phone: (talk show, toll-free within U.S.) 1-800-607-8255; (elsewhere) +1 (970) 587-5171; (order line, toll-free within U.S.) 1-800-205-6245. Fax: +1 (970) 587 5450. URL: (RealAudio, via WHRI) www.whri.com/realaudio.htm ("Angel 2"); (StreamWorks, via American Freedom Network) www.amerifree.com/stream.htm. Contact: Norman "Dr. Norm" Resnick, Host. Free sample of *USA Patriot News* monthly newspaper/catalog. Sells survival gear, night-vision goggles, Taiwanese shortwave radios, books and NTSC videos. VISA/MC/AX. Former professor Resnick states that he is "an observant, kosher Jew." He describes his program as discussing "educational, social, political and economic issues from a Constitutional perspective," with emphasis on the activities on the U.S. Bureau of Alcohol, Tobacco and Firearms. Opposed *inter alia* to the "New World Order" and gun control. Via WWCR and WHRI, USA.

"Officer Jack McLamb Show," P.O. Box 8712, Phoenix AZ 85066 USA. Phone: (McLamb) +1 (602) 237-2533. URLs: (general) www.police-against-nwo.com/; (RealAudio) www.whri.com/realaudio.htm ("Angel 1"). Program and sister organization, Police Against the New World Order, are headed by former Phoenix police officer Jack McLamb. Supports activities to convert American police officers and military personnel over to view and act favorably towards militias, as well as similar groups and armed individuals. Sells audio and video tapes, posters, *The Waco Whitewash*, *Vampire Killer 2000* and other publications. In *Vampire Killer 2000*, written by McLamb, he opposes, among many others, CBS News, financial interests of the Rothschild family, and gun control. McLamb is credited, along with "Bo" Gritz (*see* "Freedom's Call") with being a key individual in persuading Randy Weaver to end the Ruby Ridge standoff. Via WHRI, USA.

"Ogene Ndigbo Radio," P.O. Box 91425, Washington DC 20059 USA. E-mail: bakpa@yahoo.com/soc.culture.nigeria. Contact: Ben Akpa. Program of the Eastern Mandate Union-Abroad and the World Igbo Council of Nigeria. Via WHRA, USA.

"Overcomer Ministry" ("Voice of the Last Day Prophet of God"), P.O. Box 691, Walterboro SC 29488 USA. Phone: (0900-1700 local time, Sunday through Friday) +1 (803) 538-3892. E-mail: rgstair@odys.com. URL: www.wwcr.com/stair.htm.

Contact: Brother R.G. Stair. Sample "Overcomer" newsletter and various pamphlets free upon request. Sells a Sangean shortwave radio for $50, plus other items of equipment and various publications at appropriate prices. Primarily a fundamentalist Christian program from an exceptionally pleasant Southern town, but disestablishmentarian in such things as its characterizations of homosexuals in general, as well as the supposed homosexual and heterosexual activities of priests and nuns within the Roman Catholic Church. Also opposes Freemasonry, U.S. aid to Israel and reported abuses of powers of U.S. Federal authorities. Invites listeners to write in, giving the name of the station over which "The Overcomer" was heard and the quality of reception. Via Deutsche Telekom, Germany; and WRNO and WWCR, USA.

"Preparedness Hour," American Freedom Network, P.O. Box 430, Johnstown CO 80534 USA. Phone: (talk show, toll-free within U.S.) 1-800-607-8255; (elsewhere) +1 (970) 587-5171; (order line, toll-free within U.S.) 1-800-205-6245. Fax: +1 (970) 587 5450. Contact: (general) Bob Speer, Host; or "Don W.", Network Manager; (sponsor) Jim Cedarstrom. Free sample of *USA Patriot News* monthly newspaper/catalog. Sells survival gear, night-vision goggles, Taiwanese shortwave radios, books and NTSC videos. VISA/MC/AX. Program concentrates on such survivalist skills as growing food, making soap and cheese, home childbirth and how to obtain and train mules or donkeys. Speer is described by his associates as a "SPIKE trainer" (Specially Prepared Individuals for Key Events) for retired U.S. Green Beret lieutenant colonel James "Bo" Gritz. Sponsored by Discount Gold, which urges listeners to invest in precious metals as an alternative to holding paper money or investments. Via WWCR, USA.

"Prophecy Club," P.O. Box 750234, Topeka KS 66675 USA. Phone/fax: (club) +1 (913) 478-1112; (sponsor, toll-free in U.S. only) 1-800-525-9556. Contact: Stan Johnson, Director. Club, which takes no cards or phone orders, offers free sample newsletter and catalog; also sells newsletter subscriptions, as well as videos in NTSC format for $28.75 within the United States and $30 elsewhere, including shipping. Also offers audio cassettes for $5.75 (U.S.) or $6 (elsewhere). Sponsor accepts cards and sells similar items. Organization states that it is devoted to study and research on Bible prophecy. Programs oppose, *i.a.*, the "New World Order" and Freemasonry. Via WWCR and WHRI, USA, as well as various AM, FM and television stations.

"Protecting Your Wealth," 9188 E. San Salvador Drive #203, Scottsdale AZ 85258 USA. Phone: (program, toll-free within United States) 1-800-598-1500; (sponsoring organization, toll-free within the United States) 1-800-451-4452; (elsewhere) +1 (602) 451-0575. Fax: +1 (602) 451 4394. Contact: Mike Callahan or Eric Ceadarstrom. Opposed to the "New World Order" and groups involved in paper-based financial markets. Supports rural-based survivalism, and claims that the purpose of anti-terrorism and related American legislation is to extend government control over people so as to strip them of their assets. Alleges that paper money, bonds and securities are controlled by an elite that is about to create a second Great Depression, rendering those assets worthless. As an alternative, urges people to invest in the precious metals sold by their sponsoring organization, Viking International Trading, as well as to move to the countryside with their shortwave radios and to purchase hoardable foods sold by a sister firm. Via WRMI and WWCR, USA.

"Radio Free America"
NETWORK: Orbit 7 Radio Network. Phone: +1 (888) 467-2487;

(Valentine) +1 (941) 353-9688. E-mail: orbit7@e-z.net. URLs: (general) http://orbit7.com/val.htm; (RealAudio) http://orbit7.com; or www.whri.com/realaudio.htm ("Angel 1"). Contact: Tom Valentine, Host. Via WHRI, USA.

"Radio Free Bougainville"
MAIN ADDRESS: 2 Griffith Avenue, Roseville NSW 2069, Australia. Phone/fax: +61 (2) 9417-1001. E-mail: (Bougainville Freedom Movement) sashab@magna.com.au. URL: (Bougainville Freedom Movement) www.magna.com.au/~sashab/BFM.htm. Contact: Sam Voron, Australian Director. $5, AUS$5 or 5 IRCs required. Station's continued operation is totally dependent on the availability of local coconuts for power generation, currently the only form of power available for those living in the blockaded areas of the island of Bougainville. Station is opposed to the Papua New Guinea government, and supports armed struggle for complete independence and the "Bougainville Interim Government." With the recent signing of a peace agreement between Papua New Guinea authorities and the separatist movement of Bougainville, this station may soon stop broadcasting.
ALTERNATIVE ADDRESS: P.O. Box 1203, Honiara, Solomon Islands. Contact: Martin R. Miriori, Humanitarian Aid Coordinator. $1, AUS$2 or 3 IRCs required. No verification data issued from this address.

"Radio Free Somalia," 2 Griffith Avenue, Roseville NSW 2069, Australia. Phone/fax: +61 (2) 9417-1001. Contact: Sam Voron, Australian Director. $5, AUS$5 or 5 IRCs required. Station is operated from Gaalkacyo in the Mudug region of north-

eastern Somalia by the Somali International Amateur Radio Club. Seeks volunteers and donations of radio equipment and airline tickets.

"Radio Kudirat," NALICON U.K, P.O. Box 9663, London SE1 3LZ, United Kingdom; or NALICON U.S.A, P.O. Box 175, Boston MA 02131 USA. Phone: (Boston) +1 (617) 364-4455. Fax: (London) +44 (171) 403 6985; (Boston) +1 (617) 364 7362. E-mail: (London) rkn@postlin.demon.co.uk; (Boston) nalicon@nalicon.com; (contributions to Radio Kudirat) radio@udfn.com. URL: www.udfn.com/uradio.htm. Contact: Kayode Fayemi, Director of Communications, NALICON. Station set up to disseminate information concerning democracy, human rights and the environment in Nigeria. Anti-Nigerian government. Created by London-based Nigerian exile group, NALICON (National Liberation Council of Nigeria). Requests broadcast material and funds to maintain a regular broadcasting schedule. Welcomes scripts, and recordings from listeners and supporters. Transmits via the South African facilities of Sentech.

"Radio Kurdistan," ("Aira ezgay kurdistana, dangi hizbi socialisti democrati kurdistan"). E-mail: kurdish6065@aol.com. URL: www.members.aol.com/kurdis6065/psk.htm. Station is run by the Kurdistan Socialist Democratic Party, a member of the Democratic Alliance of Kurdistan which is a made up of five parties under the leadership of the Patriotic Union of Kurdistan (PUK).

"Radio of the Voice of Liberty & Renewal," ("idha'at sawt al-hurriyah wa al-tajdid, sawt quwwat al-tahaluf al-sudaniyyah, sawt al-intifadah al-sha'biyyah al-musallahah"). URL: (Sudan Alliance Forces) www.safsudan.com. The Sudan Alliance Forces are an opposition guerrilla army of ex-government northern soldiers, affiliated to the Asmara, Eritrea-based National Democratic Alliance (NDA). Opposes the current Sudanese government. Also identifies as "Voice of the Sudan Alliance Forces & Voice of the Popular Armed Uprising."

"Radio Patria Libre," Colombia Popular, c/o Tommy Weissbeckerhaus, Wilhelmstr.9, D-10963 Berlin, Germany.

"Radio Revista Lux," P.O. Box 451132, Miami FL 33245-1132 USA; or (physical address) 75 NW 22 Avenue, Miami FL 33125 USA. Phone: +1 (305) 643-0467. Fax: +1 (305) 643 1037. Contact: René L. Díaz. Anti-Castro program of the Union of Electrical Plant and Gas Workers of Cuba in Exile (Sindicato de Trabajadores Eléctricos, Gas y Agua de Cuba en el Exilio). Via WRMI, USA.

"Radio Roquero," P.O. Box 18005 Fairfield OH 45018 USA; or contact WRMI (see, below). Contact: Víctor García Rivera, Producer. Anti-Castro program aired via WRMI, USA.

"Radio Voice of the Mojahed"—see "Voice of the Mojahed," below.

📻**"Radio Voice of United and Free Ethiopia"** ("Yih ye andit netsa Ethiopia dimtse radio agelgilot new"), Ethiopian National Congress, P.O. Box 547, Swathmore, PA 19081 USA. E-mail: unite@ethiopia.org. URL: (RealAudio) www.ethiopia.org. Also known as "Voice of One Free Ethiopia." Opposes Ethiopian government and believed to be transmitting from a site in Central Asia. Operated by the United Front of Ethiopians formed by the Ethiopian National Congress.

"Radio Rainbow" ("Kestedamena rediyo ye selamena yewendimamach dimtse"), c/o RAPEHGA, P.O. Box 140104, D-53056 Bonn, Germany. Supposedly operated by an Ethiopian opposition group called Research and Action Group for Peace in Ethiopia and the Horn of Africa. Broadcasts via hired shortwave transmitters in Germany.

"Republic of Iraq Radio, Voice of the Iraqi People" ("Idha'at al-Jamahiriya al-Iraqiya, Saut al-Sha'b al-Iraqi"), Broadcasting Service of the Kingdom of Saudi Arabia, P.O. Box 61718, Riyadh 11575, Saudi Arabia. Phone: +966 (1) 442-5170. Fax: +966 (1) 402 8177. Contact: Suliman A. Al-Samnan, Director of Frequency Management. Anti-Saddam Hussein "black" clandestine supported by CIA, British intelligence, the Gulf Cooperation Council and Saudi Arabia. The name of this station has changed periodically since its inception during the Gulf crisis. Via transmitters in Saudi Arabia.

Sponsoring Organization: The National Accord/Iraqi National Congress, 9 Pall Mall Deposit, 124-128 Barlby Road, London W10 6BL, United Kingdom.

"Rush Limbaugh Show," EIB World Band, WABC, #2 Pennsylvania Avenue, New York NY 10121 USA; telephone (toll-free, USA only) 1-800-282-2882, (elsewhere) +1 (212) 613-3800; fax (during working hours) +1 (212) 563 9166. E-mail 70277.2502@compuserve.com. Via WRNO, USA. Reception reports concerning this program can also be sent with 2 IRCs or an SASE directly to WRNO.

"Scriptures for America," P.O. Box 766-c, Laporte CO 80535 USA. Phone: +1 (307) 745-5914. Fax: +1 (307) 745 5914. URLs: (general) www.logoplex.com/resources/sfa/; (FTP site) ftp://ftp.netcom.com/pub/SF/SFA/. Contact: Pastor Peter J. "Pete" Peters. A leader within the Christian Identity movement (also *see* "Herald of Truth" and "British Israel World Federation"). Peters vehemently opposes, *inter alia*, homosexuals, the Anti-Defamation League of the B'nai B'rith and other Jews and Jewish organizations, nonwhites, and international banking institutions. Also expresses suspicion of official and media responses to such events as the Oklahoma City bombing, and is supportive of militia activities. Like the relatively visible (e.g., advertising in *U.S. World News & Report*) Pastor Karl Schott of Christ's Gospel Fellowship/*The Pathfinder* in Spokane, Peters alleges that Christians whose ancestry is from selected parts of Europe are the true chosen people of Biblical prophecy. Free *Scriptures for America Newsletter*, brochures and catalog of publications and recordings. Via WWCR and WRNO, USA.

"Seventieth Week Magazine," P.O. Box 771, Gladewater TX 75647 USA. Contact: Ben McKnight. Free "Flash Bulletins" booklets. Opposes "New World Order," believes United Nations and UFOs are plotting to take over the United States and commit genocide against Christians and patriots, and distrusts official versions of various events, such as the Oklahoma City bombing. Via WWCR, USA.

"This Way Out," Overnight Productions, P.O. Box 38327, Los Angeles CA 90038 USA. Phone: +1 (213) 874-0874. E-mail: tworadio@aol.com. URL: http://abacus.oxy.edu/QRD/www/media/radio/thiswayout/index.html or www.qrd.org/qrd/www/media/radio/thiswayout/. News, music, interviews and features from and about lesbians and gays, mainly but not exclusively within the United States. Via RFPI.

"Treinta Minutos con el CID" (successor to "La Voz del CID"), 10020 SW 37th Terrace, Miami FL 33165 USA. Phone: (U.S.) +1 (305) 551-8484. Fax: (U.S.) +1 (305) 559 9365. E-mail: elcid@gate.net; or jurassic@sol.racsa.co.cr. URL: (parent organization) www.cubacid.com/. Contact: Alfredo Aspitia, Asistente de Prensa e Información; or Francisco Fernández. Anti-Castro, anti-communist; privately supported by Cuba Independiente y Democrática. Free political literature. Formerly transmitted from its own transmitter in El Salvador, but now via WRMI, USA.

"Vietnam Veterans Radio Network," 7807 N. Avalon,

Kansas City MO 64152 USA. Contact: John ("Doc") Upton. This radio voice of the Vietnam Veterans Against the War mixes music, commentaries and sound bites concerning some of the more difficult aspects of the Vietnam War experience. Via RFPI.

"Voice of China" ("Zhongguo Zhi Yin Guangbo Diantai"), Democratization of China, P.O. Box 11663, Berkeley CA 94701 USA; Foundation for China in the 21st Century, P.O. Box 11696, Berkeley CA 94701 USA. Phone: +1 (510) 2843-5025. Fax: +1 (510) 2843 4370. Contact: Bang Tai Xu, Director. Mainly "overseas Chinese students" interested in the democratization of China. Financial support from the Foundation for China in the 21st Century. Have "picked up the mission" of the earlier Voice of June 4th, but have no organizational relationship with it. Transmits via facilities of the Central Broadcasting System, Taiwan (see).

"Voice of Iranian Kurdistan," KDPI, c/o AFK, Boite Postale 102, F-75623 Paris Cedex, France. Anti-Iranian government.

"Voice of Iraqi Kurdistan" ("Aira dangi Kurdestana Iraqa") (when active), P.O. Box 2443, Merrifield VA 22116 USA; P.O. Box 1504, London W7 3LX, United Kingdom; KDP Press Office, P.O. Box 4912, London SE15 4EW, United Kingdom; Kurdiska Riksförbundet, Hornsgatan 80, SE-117 21 Stockholm, Sweden; or Kurdistan Press, Örnsvägen 6C, SE-172 Sundbyberg, Sweden. Phone: (KDP Press Office, London) +44 (171) 931-7764; (Stockholm) +46 (8) 668-6060 or +46 (8) 668-66088; (Sundbyberg) +46 (8) 298-332. E-mail: 101564.3336@compuserve.com; (KDP Press Office, London): 101701.153@compuserve.com. Fax: (KDP Press Office, London) +44 (171) 931 7765. URLs: (station) http://ourworld.compuserve.com/homepages/gara/; (Kurdistan Democratic Party-Iraq parent organization) www.kdp.pp.se/; or http://home1.swipnet.se/~w-11534/. Contact: (United States) Namat Sharif, Kurdistan Democratic Party. Sponsored by the Kurdistan Democratic Party, led by Masoud Barzani, and the National Democratic Iraqi Front. From its own transmitting facilities, reportedly located in the Kurdish section of Iraq.

"Voice of Kashmir Freedom" ("Sada-i Hurriyat-i Kashmir"), P.O. Box 102, Muzaffarabad, Azad Kashmir, via Pakistan. Favors Azad Kashmiri independence from India; pro-Moslem, sponsored by the Kashmiri Mojahedin organization. From transmission facilities believed to be in Pakistan.

"Voice of Liberty," Box 1776, Liberty KY 42539 USA; or Box 3987, Rex GA 32073 USA. Phone: (call-in) toll-free in United States 1-800-526-1776, or elsewhere +1 (404) 968-8865; (voice mail) +1 (404) 968-0330. Contact: Paul Parsons or Rick Tyler. Sells various audio cassettes, $50 starter kit and *News Front* newspaper. Supports the Voice of Liberty Patriots organization, and reportedly is affiliated with the Church of the Remnant and the "Intelligence Report" program (see). Opposed to certain practices of the Bureau of Alcohol, Tobacco and Firearms and various other law-enforcement organizations in the United States, abortion, and restrictions on firearms and Christian prayer. Via WWCR, USA.

"Voice of National Salvation" ("Gugugui Sori Pangsong"), Grenier Osawa 107, 40 Nando-cho, Shinjuku-ku, Tokyo, Japan. Phone: + 81 (3) 5261-0331. Fax: +81 (3) 5261 0332. URL: www.alles.or.jp/~kuguk. Contact: Kuguk Chonson. Pro-North Korea, pro-Korean unification; supported by North Korean government. On the air since 1967, but not always under the same name. Via North Korean transmitters located in Pyongyang, Haeju and Wongsan.

"Voice of Oduduwa" ("Ijinle Ohun Oduduwa"), Yoruba House, 7600 Georgia Avenue NW, Suite 405, Washington DC 20012 USA. Phone: +1 (202) 291-9471. Fax: +1 (202) 291 2973. E-mail: info@yorubanation.org. URL: www.yorubanation.org. Believed to be operated by Egbe Omo Yoruba. (Association of Yoruba Descendents Worldwide). Hires airtime via WHRA, USA.

"Voice of One Free Ethiopia"—see Radio Voice of United And Free Ethiopia, above.

"Voice of Oromo Liberation" ("Kun Segalee Bilisumma Oromooti"), Postfach 510610, D-13366 Berlin, Germany; SBO, Prinzenallee 81, D-13357 Berlin, Germany; or SBO, P.O. Box 73247, Washington DC 20056 USA. Phone: (Germany) +49 (30) 494-1036. Fax: (Germany) +49 (30) 494 3372. Contact: Taye Teferah, European Coordinator. Station of the Oromo Liberation Front of Ethiopia, an Oromo nationalist organization transmitting via facilities in Germany and Ukraine. Occasionally replies to correspondence in English or German. Return postage required.

"Voice of Palestine, Voice of the Palestinian Islamic Revolution" ("Saut al-Filistin, Saut al-Thowrah al-Islamiyah al-Filistiniyah")—see Voice of the Islamic Republic of Iran, over whose transmitters this program is clandestinely aired, for potential contact information. Supports the Islamic Resistance Movement, Hamas, which is anti-Arafat and anti-Israel.

"Voice of Peace," Inter-Africa Group, P.O. Box 1631, Addis Ababa, Ethiopia. Humanitarian organization, partially funded by UNICEF, seeking peace and reconciliation among warring factions in central and eastern Africa. Via Radio Ethiopia (see).

"Voice of Peace and Brotherhood,"—see "Rainbow Radio," above.

"Voice of Rebellious Iraq" ("Sawt al-Iraq al-Tha'ir"), P.O. Box 11365/738, Tehran, Iran; P.O. Box 37155/146, Qom, Iran; or P.O. Box 36802, Damascus, Syria. Anti-Iraqi regime, supported by the Shi'ite-oriented Supreme Assembly of the Islamic Revolution of Iraq, led by Mohammed Baqir al-Hakim. Supported by the Iranian government and transmitted from Iranian soil. Hostile to the Iraqi government.

Sponsoring Organization: Shii Supreme Council of Islamic Revolution of Iraq (SCIRI), 27a Glouster St, London WC1N 3XX, United Kingdom. Phone: +44 (171) 371-6815. Fax: +44 (171) 371 2886. E-mail: 101642.1150@compuserve.com. URL: ourworld.compuserve.com/homepages/sciri/.

"Voice of Southern Azerbaijan" ("Bura Janubi Azerbaijan Sasi"), Vosa Ltd., Postfach 108, A-1193 Vienna, Austria. Phone: (Holland) +31 (70) 319-2189. This Azeri-language station is operated by the National and Independent Front of Southern Azerbaijan, which is opposed to Iranian and Armenian influence in Azerbaijan. Transmitter located in Israel.

"Voice of Sudan," NDA, 16 Camaret Court, Lorne Gardens, London W11 4XX, United Kingdom. E-mail: sudanvoice@umma.org. Broadcasts on behalf of the National Democratic Alliance (NDA), which is opposed to the present Sudanese government. Believed to be broadcasting from studios and transmitters located in Asmara, Eritrea.

"Voice of the Communist Party of Iran" ("Seda-ye Hezb-e Komunist-e Iran"), B.M. Box 2123, London WC1N 3XX, United Kingdom; or O.I.S., Box 50050, SE-104 05 Stockholm, Sweden. E-mail: wpi@wpiran.org. URL: www.wpiran.org/. Sponsored by the Communist Party of Iran (KOMALA, formerly Tudeh).

"Voice of the Crusader"—see "Voice of the Mojahed," below.

"Voice of the Free Sahara" ("La Voz del Sahara Libre, La Voz del Pueblo Sahel") (when operating), Sahara Libre, Frente Polisario, B.P. 10, El-Mouradia, 16000 Algiers, Algeria; Sahara

Libre, Ambassade de la République Arabe Saharaui Démocratique, 1 Av. Franklin Roosevelt, 16000 Algiers, Algeria; or B.P. 10, Al-Mouradia, Algiers, Algeria. Phone (Algeria): +213 (2) 747-907. Fax, when operating (Algeria): +213 (2) 747 984. Contact: Mohamed Lamin Abdesalem; Mahafud Zein; or Sneiba Lehbib. Free stickers, booklets, cards, maps, paper flags and calendars. Two IRCs helpful. Pro-Polisario Front; supported by Algerian government and aired via the facilities of Radiodiffusion-Télévision Algerienne.

"Voice of the Iranian Revolution" ("Aira Dangi Shurashi Irana")—*see* "Voice of the Communist Party of Iran," above, for details.

"Voice of the Iraqi People"—*see* "Radio of the Iraqi Republic from Baghdad, Voice of the Iraqi People," above.

"Voice of the Islamic Revolution in Iraq"—*see* "Voice of Rebellious Iraq," above, for contact information. Affiliated with the Shi'ite-oriented Supreme Assembly of the Islamic Revolution of Iraq, led by Mohammed Baqir al-Hakim.

"Voice of the Martyrs" ("Radioemission der Hilfsaktion Martyrerkirche"), Postfach 5540, D-78434 Konstanz, Germany. Possibly linked with Internationale Radioarbeits-Gemeinschaft fur die Martyrerkirche, which previously broadcast via Radio Trans-Europe, Portugal, as Radio Stephanusbotschaft. Sometimes uses facilities of Radio Intercontinental, Armenia.

"Voice of the Mojahed" ("Seda-ye Mojahed ast")
PARIS BUREAU: Mojahedines de Peuple d'Iran, 17 rue des Gords, F-95430 Auvers-sur-Oise, France. E-mail: (National Council of Resistence of Iran umbrella organization) mardom@iran-e-azad.org. URL: (People's Mojahedin Organization of Iran parent organization) www.iran-e-azad.org/english/pmoi.html. Contact: Majid Taleghani. Station replies very irregularly and slowly. Pre-prepared verification cards and SASE helpful, with correspondence in French or Persian almost certainly preferable. Sponsored by the People's Mojahedin Organization of Iran (OMPI) and the National Liberation Army of Iran.
OTHER BUREAUS: Voice of the Mojahed, c/o Heibatollahi, Postfach 502107, 50981 Köln, Germany; M.I.S.S., B.M. Box 9720, London WC1N 3XX, United Kingdom; P.O. Box 951, London NW11 9EL, United Kingdom; or P.O. Box 3133, Baghdad, Iraq. Contact: B. Moradi, Public Relations.

"Voice of the Popular Armed Uprising,"—*see* "Voice of Liberty & Renewal," above.

"Voice of the Sudan Alliance Forces,"—*see* "Voice of Liberty & Renewal," above.

"Voice of the Tigray Revolution," P.O. Box 450, Mekelle, Tigray, Ethiopia. Contact: Fre Tesfamichael, Director. $1 helpful.

"Voice of the Worker"—same contact details as "Voice of the Communist Party of Iran" (*see* above).

"Voice of Tibet," Welhavensgate 1, N-0166 Oslo, Norway. Phone: +47 2211-4980. Fax: +47 2211 4988. E-mail: mail@vot.org or voti@online.no. URL: (includes RealAudio) www.vot.org/. Contact: Svein Wilhelmsen, Project Manager; Oystein Alme, Coordinator; or Kalsang Phuljung. Joint venture of the Norwegian Human Rights House, Norwegian Tibet Committee and World-View International. Programs, which are produced in Oslo, Norway, and elsewhere, focuses on Tibetan culture, education, human rights and news from Tibet. Anti-Chinese control of Tibet. Those seeking a verification for this program should enclose a prepared card or letter. Return postage helpful. Broadcasts via transmitters in Lithuania and Central Asia.

"Voz de la Ortodoxia," P.O. Box 35-1811, José Martí Station, Miami FL 33152 USA. Contact: Mario Jiménez. Program of the Partido Ortodoxo Cubano. Via WRMI, USA.

"Voz de la Resistencia," E-mail: (unconfirmed) farcep@comision.internal.org or elbarcino@laneta.apc.org. Program of the Fuerzas Armadas de Colombia.

"WINGS," P.O. Box 33220, Austin TX 78764 USA. Phone/fax: +1 (512) 416-9000. E-mail: wings@igc.apc.org. URL: www.wings.org. Contact: Frieda Werden, Producer. News program of the Women's International News Gathering Service, covering such issues as women's rights, women activists and movements for sociopolitical change. Via RFPI, Costa Rica.

"World of Prophecy," 1708 Patterson Road, Austin TX 78733 USA. Contact: Texe Marrs. Conservative Christian program opposing various forms of government regulation and control, such as of the environment. Via WWCR and WHRI, USA.

DOMINICAN REPUBLIC   World Time –4

Emisora Onda Musical (when active), Palo Hincado 204 Altos, Apartado Postal 860, Santo Domingo, Dominican Republic. Contact: Mario Báez Asunción, Director. Replies occasionally to correspondence in Spanish. $1 helpful.

La N-103/Radio Norte (when active), Apartado Postal 320, Santiago, Dominican Republic. Contact: José Darío Pérez Díaz, Director; or Héctor Castillo, Gerente.

Radio Amanecer Internacional, Apartado Postal 4680, Santo Domingo, Dominican Republic. Phone: +1 (809) 688-5600, +1 (809) 688-5609, +1 (809) 688-8067. Fax: +1 (809) 227 1869. E-mail: amanecer@tricom.net. URL: www.tricom.net/amanecer/. Contact: (general) Señora Ramona C. de Subervi, Directora; (technical) Ing. Sócrates Domínguez. $1 or return postage required. Replies slowly to correspondence in Spanish.

Radio Barahona (when active), Apartado 201, Barahona, Dominican Republic; or Gustavo Mejía Ricart No. 293, Apto. 2-B, Ens. Quisqueya, Santo Domingo, Dominican Republic. Contact: (general) Rodolfo Z. Lama Jaar, Administrador; (technical) Ing. Roberto Lama Sajour, Administrador General. Free stickers. Letters should be sent via registered mail. $1 or return postage helpful. Replies to correspondence in Spanish.

Radio Cima, Apartado 804, Santo Domingo, Dominican Republic. Fax: +1 (809) 541 1088. Contact: Roberto Vargas, Director. Free pennants, postcards, coins and taped music. Roberto likes collecting stamps and coins.

Radio Cristal Internacional, Apartado Postal 894, Santo Domingo, Dominican Republic. Phone: +1 (809) 565-1460 or +1 (809) 566-5411. Fax: +1 (809) 567 9107. URL: www.dominicana.com. Contact: (general) Fernando Hermón Gross, Director de Programas; or Margarita Reyes; (administration) Darío Badía, Director General; or Héctor Badía, Director de Administración. Seeks reception reports. Return postage of $2 appreciated.

Radio Quisqueya (when active), Apartado Postal 363, Puerto Plata, Dominican Republic; or Apartado Postal 135-2, Santo Domingo, Dominican Republic. Contact: Lic. Gregory Castellanos Ruano, Director. Replies occasionally to correspondence in Spanish and English.

Radio Santiago (when active), Apartado 282, Santiago, Dominican Republic.
Contact: Luis Felipe Moscos Finke, Gerente; Luis Felipe Moscos Cordero, Jefe Ingeniero; or Carlos Benoit, Announcer & Program Manager.

ECUADOR
World Time –5 (–4 sometimes, in times of drought); –6 Galapagos

NOTE: According to HCJB's "DX Party Line," during periods of drought, such as caused by "El Niño," electricity rationing causes periods in which transmitters cannot operate because of inadequate hydroelectric power, as well as spikes which occasionally damage transmitters. Accordingly, many Ecuadorian stations tend to be irregular, or even entirely off the air, during drought conditions.

NOTE: According to veteran Dxer Harald Kuhl in Hard-Core-DX of Kotanet Communications Ltd., IRCs are exchangeable only in the cities of Quito and Guayaquil. Too, overseas airmail postage is very expensive now in Ecuador; so when in doubt, enclosing $2 for return postage is appropriate.

Ecos del Oriente (when active), Sucre y 12 de Febrero, Lago Agrio, Sucumbíos, Ecuador. Phone: +593 (6) 830-141. Contact: Elsa Irene Velástegui, Secretaria. Sometimes includes free 20 sucre note (Ecuadorian currency) with reply. $2 or return postage required. Replies, often slowly, to correspondence in Spanish.

Emisoras Gran Colombia (if reactivated), Casilla 17-01-2246, Quito, Ecuador (new physical address: Vasco de Contreras 689 y Pasaje "A", Quito, Ecuador). Phone: +593 (2) 443-147. Phone/fax: +593 (2) 442-951. Contact: Nancy Cevallos Castro, Gerente General. Return postage required. Replies to correspondence in Spanish. Their shortwave transmitter is out of order. While they would like to repair or replace it, for the time being they don't have the funds to do so.

Emisoras Jesús del Gran Poder (if reactivated), Casilla 17-01-133, Quito, Ecuador. Phone: +593 (2) 513-077. Contact: Mariela Villarreal; Padre Angel Falconí, Gerente; or Hno. Segundo Cuenca OFM.

Emisoras Luz y Vida, Casilla 11-01-222, Loja, Ecuador. Phone: +593 (7) 570-426. Contact: Hermana (Sister) Ana Maza Reyes, Directora; or Lic. Guida Carrión H., Directora de Programas. Return postage required. Replies irregularly to correspondence in Spanish.

Escuelas Radiofónicas Populares del Ecuador, Casilla 06-01-693, Riobamba, Ecuador. Fax: +593 (3) 961 625. URL: www.exploringecuador.com/erpe/erpe.htm. Contact: Juan Pérez Sarmiento, Director Ejecutivo; or María Ercilia López, Secretaria. Free pennants and key rings. "Chimborazo" cassette of Ecuadorian music for 10,000 sucres plus postage; T-shirts for 12,000 sucres plus postage; and caps with station logo for 8,000 sucres plus postage. Return postage helpful. Replies to correspondence in Spanish.

Estéreo Carrizal (when active), Avenida Estudiantil, Quinta Velásquez, Calceta, Ecuador. Phone: +593 (5) 685-5470. Contact: Ovidio Velásquez Alcundia, Gerente General. Free book of Spanish-language poetry by owner. Replies to correspondence in Spanish.

HCJB World Radio, The Voice of the Andes

STATION: Casilla 17-17-691, Quito, Ecuador. Phone: +593 (2) 266-808 (X-4441, 1300-2200 World Time Monday through Friday, for the English Dept.). Fax: +593 (2) 447 263. E-mail: (English Dept.) english@hcjb.org.ec; (Spanish Dept.) spanish@hcjb.org.ec; (Japanese Dept.) japanese@hcjb.org.ec; (Frequency Management) irops@hcjb.org.ec or dlewis@hcjb.org.ec. URLs: www.hcjb.org/; www.hcjb.org.ec. Contact: (general) English [or other language] Department; "Saludos Amigos"—letterbox program; (administration) Glen Volkhardt, Director of Broadcasting; John Beck, Director of International Radio; or Curt Cole, Director, English Language

Service; (technical) David Lewis, Frequency Manager. Free religious brochures, calendars, stickers and pennants; free e-mail *The Andean Herald* newsletter. *Catch the Vision* book $8, postpaid. IRC or unused U.S. or Canadian stamps appreciated for airmail reply.

INTERNATIONAL HEADQUARTERS: HCJB World Radio, Inc., P.O. Box 39800, Colorado Springs CO 80949-9800 USA. Phone: +1 (719) 590-9800. Fax: +1 (719) 590 9801. E-mail: info@hcjb.org. Contact: Andrew Braio, Public Information; (administration) Richard D. Jacquin, Director, International Operations. Various items sold via U.S. address—catalog available. This address is not a mail drop, so listeners' correspondence, except those concerned with purchasing HCJB items, should be directed to the usual Quito address.

ENGINEERING CENTER: 2830 South 17th Street, Elkhart IN 46517-4008 USA. Phone: +1 (219) 294-8201. Fax: +1 (219) 294 8391. E-mail: webmaster@hcjbeng.org. URL: www.hcjbeng.org/. Contact: Dave Pasechnik, Project Manager; or Bob Moore, Engineering. This address only for those professionally concerned with the design and manufacture of transmitter and antenna equipment. Listeners' correspondence should be directed to the usual Quito address.

REGIONAL OFFICES: Although HCJB has over 20 regional offices throughout the world, the station wishes that all listener correspondence be directed to the station in Quito, as the regional offices do not serve as mail drops for the station.

La Voz de los Caras (if reactivated), Casilla 608, Calle Montúfar 1012, Bahía de Caráquez, Manabí, Ecuador. Fax: +593 (4) 690 305. Contact: Ing. Marcelo A. Nevárez Faggioni, Director-General. Free 50th anniversary pennants, while they last. $2 or return postage required. Replies occasionally and slowly to correspondence in English and Spanish.

La Voz de Saquisilí—Radio Libertador, Calle 24 de Mayo, Saquisilí, Cotopaxi, Ecuador. Phone: +593 (3) 721-035. Contact: Arturo Mena Herrera, Gerente-Propietario, who may also be contacted via his son-in-law, Eddy Roger Velástegui Mena, who is studying in Quito (E-mail: eddyv@uio.uio.satnet.net). The shortwave ferequency was reactivated in August 1998, after four years of silence. Reception reports actively solicited, and will be confirmed with a special commemorative QSL card. Return postage, in the form of $2 or mint Ecuadorian stamps, appreciated; IRCs difficult to exchange. Spanish strongly preferred.

La Voz del Napo, Misión Josefina, Tena, Napo, Ecuador. Phone: +593 (6) 886-422. Contact: Ramiro Cabrera, Director. Free pennants and stickers. $2 or return postage required. Replies occasionally to correspondence in Spanish.

La Voz del Río Tarqui (when operating), Manuel Vega 653 y Presidente Córdova, Cuenca, Ecuador. Phone: +593 (7) 822-132. Contact: Sra. Alicia Pulla Célleri, Administración; or Sra. Rosa María Pulla. Replies irregularly to correspondence in Spanish. Has ties with station WKDM in New York.

La Voz del Upano

STATION: Vicariato Apostólico de Méndez, Misión Salesiana, 10 de Agosto s/n, Macas, Ecuador; or Casilla 602, Quito, Ecuador. Phone: +593 (7) 700-186. Contact: P. Domingo Barrueco C., Director. Free pennants and calendars. On one occasion, not necessarily to be repeated, sent tape of Ecuadorian folk music for $2. Otherwise, $2 required. Replies to correspondence in Spanish.

QUITO OFFICE: Procura Salesiana, Equinoccio 623 y Queseras del Medio, Quito, Ecuador. Phone: +593 (2) 551-012.

Radio Bahá'í, "La Emisora de la Familia," Casilla 10-02-1464, Otavalo, Imbabura, Ecuador. Phone: +593 (6) 920-245. Fax:

+593 (6) 922 504. Contact: (general) William Rodríguez Barreiro, Coordinador; or Juan Antonio Reascos, Locutor; (technical) Ing. Tom Dopps. Free information about the Bahá'í faith, which teaches the unity of all the races, nations and religions, and that the Earth is one country and mankind its citizens. Free pennants. Return postage appreciated. Replies regularly to correspondence in English or Spanish. Enclosing a family photo may help getting a reply. Station is property of the Instituto Nacional de Enseñanza de la Fe Bahá'í (National Spiritual Assembly of the Bahá'ís of Ecuador). Although there are many Bahá'í radio stations around the world, Radio Bahá'í in Ecuador is the only one on shortwave.

Radio Buen Pastor—*see* Radio "El Buen Pastor."

Radio Católica Nacional del Ecuador (when active), Av. América 1830 y Mercadillo (Apartado 540A), Quito, Ecuador. Phone: +593 (2) 545-770. Contact: John Sigüenza, Director; or Sra. Yolanda de Suquitana, Secretaria; (technical) Sra. Gloria Cardozo, Technical Director. Free stickers. Return postage required. Replies to correspondence in Spanish.

Radio Centro, Casilla 18-01-574, Ambato, Ecuador. Phone: +593 (3) 822-240 or +593 (3) 841-126. Fax: +593 (3) 829 824. Contact: Luis Alberto Gamboa Tello, Director Gerente; or Lic. María Elena de López. Free stickers. Return postage appreciated. Replies to correspondence in Spanish.

Radio Centinela del Sur (C.D.S. Internacional), Casilla 11-01-106, Loja, Ecuador. Fax: +593 (7) 562 270. Contact: (general) Marcos G. Coronel V., Director de Programas; or José A. Coronel V., Director del programa "Ovación";(technical) José A. Coronel I., Director Propietario. Return postage required. Replies occasionally to correspondence in Spanish.

Radiodifusora Cultural Católica La Voz del Upano—*see* La Voz del Upano, above.

Radiodifusora Cultural, La Voz del Napo—*see* La Voz del Napo, above.

Radio "El Buen Pastor," Asociación Cristiana de Indígenas Saraguros (ACIS), Reino de Quito y Azuay, Correo Central, Saraguro, Loja, Ecuador. Phone: +593 (2) 00-146. Contact: (general) Dean Pablo Davis, Sub-director; Segundo Poma, Director; Mark Vogan, OMS Missionary; Mike Schrode, OMS Ecuador Field Director; Juana Guamán, Secretaria; or Zoila Vacacela, Secretaria; (technical) Miguel Kelly. $2 or return postage in the form of mint Ecuadorian stamps required, as IRCs are difficult to exchange in Ecuador. Station is keen to receive reception reports; may respond to English, but correspondence in Spanish preferred. $10 required for QSL card and pennant.

Radio Federación Shuar (Shuara Tuntuiri), Casilla 17-01-1422, Quito, Ecuador. Phone/fax: +593 (2) 504-264. Contact: Manuel Jesús Vinza Chacucuy, Director; Yurank Tsapak Rubén Gerardo, Director; or Prof. Albino M. Utitiaj P., Director de Medios. Return postage or $2 required. Replies irregularly to correspondence in Spanish.

Radio Interoceánica, Santa Rosa de Quijos, Cantón El Chaco, Provincia de Napo, Ecuador. Contact: Byron Medina, Gerente; or Ing. Olaf Hegmuir. $2 or return postage required, and donations appreciated (station owned by Swedish Covenant Church). Replies slowly to correspondence in Spanish or Swedish.

Radio Jesús del Gran Poder—*see* Emisoras Jesús del Gran Poder, above.

Radio La Voz del Río Tarqui—*see* La Voz del Río Tarqui.

Radio Luciérnaga del Cóndor, Yansatza, Zamora-Chinchipe, Ecuador. Contact: Arturo Paladínez, Director, who is looking for donations to purchase an FM transmitter.

Radio Luz y Vida—*see* Emisoras Luz y Vida, above.

Radio Municipal (if activated on shortwave), Alcaldía Municipal de Quito, García Moreno 887 y Espejo, Quito, Ecuador. Contact: Miguel Arízaga Q., Director. Currently not on shortwave, but hopes to activate a 2 kW shortwave transmitter—its old mediumwave AM transmitter modified for world band—on 4750 kHz once the legalities are completed. If this station ever materializes, which is looking increasingly doubtful, it is expected to welcome correspondence from abroad, especially in Spanish.

Radio Nacional Espejo, Casilla 17-01-352, Quito, Ecuador. Phone: +593 (2) 21-366. E-mail: mcaicedo@hoy.net. Contact: Marco Caceido, Gerente; Steve Caceido; or Mercedes B. de Caceido, Secretaria. Replies irregularly to correspondence in English and Spanish.

Radio Nacional Progreso, Casilla V, Loja, Ecuador. Contact: José A. Guamán Guajala, Director del programa "Círculo Dominical." Replies irregularly to correspondence in Spanish, particularly for feedback on "Círculo Dominical" program aired Sundays from 1100 to 1300. Return postage required.

Radio Oriental, Casilla 260, Tena, Napo, Ecuador. Phone: +593 (6) 886-033 or +593 (6) 886-388. Contact: Luis Enrique Espín Espinosa, Gerente General. $2 or return postage helpful. Reception reports welcome.

Radio Popular de Cuenca (when active), Av. Loja 2408, Cuenca, Ecuador. Phone: +593 (7) 810-131. Contact: Sra. Manena Escondón Vda. de Villavicencio, Directora y Propietaria. Return postage or $2 required. Replies very rarely to correspondence in Spanish.

Radio Quito, Casilla 17-21-1971, Quito, Ecuador. Phone/fax: +593 (2) 508-301. Contact: Xavier Almeida, Gerente General; or José Almeida, Subgerente. Free stickers. Return postage required. Replies slowly, but regularly.

Sistema de Emisoras Progreso—*see* Radio Nacional Progreso, above.

EGYPT   World Time +2 (+3 midyear)

WARNING: MAIL THEFT. Feedback from PASSPORT readership indicates that money is sometimes stolen from envelopes sent to Radio Cairo.

Egyptian Radio, P.O. Box 11511, 1186 Cairo, Egypt. URL: (RealAudio) www.sis.gov.eg/realpg/html/adfront9.htm. For additional details, *see* Radio Cairo, below.

Radio Cairo

NONTECHNICAL: P.O. Box 566, Cairo, Egypt. Contact: Mrs. Sahar Kalil, Director of English Service to North America & Producer, "Questions and Answers"; or Mrs. Magda Hamman, Secretary. Free stickers, postcards, stamps, maps, papyrus souvenirs, calendars and *External Services of Radio Cairo* book. Free booklet and individually tutored Arabic-language lessons with loaned textbooks from Kamila Abdullah, Director General, Arabic by Radio, Radio Cairo, P.O. Box 325, Cairo, Egypt. Arabic-language religious, cultural and language-learning audio and video tapes from the Egyptian Radio and Television Union sold via Sono Cairo Audio-Video, P.O. Box 2017, Cairo, Egypt; when ordering video tapes, inquire to ensure they function on the television standard (NTSC, PAL or SECAM) in your country. Once replied regularly, if slowly, but recently replies have been increasingly scarce. Comments welcomed about audio quality—*see TECHNICAL,* below. Avoid enclosing money (*see WARNING,* above). A new 500 kW shortwave transmitter is to be brought into service in the near future to improve reception.

NONTECHNICAL, HOLY KORAN RADIO: P.O. Box 1186, Cairo,

Radio Cairo covers tourist activities in Egypt. Here, an Egyptian stonemason works in the scorching desert heat much as did his ancestors when building the Pyramids. R. Crane

Egypt. Contact: Abd al-Samad al Disuqi, Director. Operates only on 9755 kHz.

TECHNICAL: Broadcast Engineering Department, 24th Floor— TV Building (Maspiro), Egyptian Radio and Television Union, P.O. Box 1186/11151, Cairo, Egypt. Phone: +20 (2) 575-7155. Phone/fax: (propagation and monitoring office, set to automatically receive faxes outside normal working hours; otherwise, be prepared to request a switchover from voice to fax) +20 (2) 578-9491. Fax: +20 (2) 772 432; (ERTU projects) +20 (2) 766 909. E-mail: to be inaugurated shortly. Contact: Dr. Eng. Abdoh Fayoumi, Head of Propagation and Monitoring; or Nivene W. Laurence, Engineer. Comments and suggestions on audio quality and level especially welcomed.

ENGLAND—*see* UNITED KINGDOM.

EQUATORIAL GUINEA   World Time +1

Radio Africa

TRANSMISSION OFFICE: Apartado 851, Malabo, Isla Bioko, Equatorial Guinea.

U.S. OFFICE FOR CORRESPONDENCE AND VERIFICATIONS: Pan American Broadcasting, 20410 Town Center Lane #200, Cupertino CA 95014 USA. Phone: +1 (408) 996-2033. Fax: +1 (408) 252 6855. E-mail: pabcomain@aol.com. Contact: (listener correspondence) Terry Kraemer; (general) Carmen Jung,

Office & Sales Administrator; or James Manero. $1 in cash or unused U.S. stamps, or 2 IRCs, required for reply.

Radio East Africa—same details as "Radio Africa," above.

Radio Nacional de Guinea Ecuatorial—Bata (Radio Bata), Apartado 749, Bata, Río Muni, Equatorial Guinea. Phone: +240 08-382. Contact: José Mba Obama, Director. If no response try sending your letter c/o Spanish Embassy, Bata, enclosing $1 for return postage. Spanish preferred.

Radio Nacional de Guinea Ecuatorial—Malabo (Radio Malabo), Apartado 195, Malabo, Isla Bioko, Equatorial Guinea. Phone: +240 92-260. Fax: +240 92 097. Contact: (general) Román Manuel Mané-Abaga, Jefe de Programación; Ciprano Somon Suakin; or Manuel Chema Lobede; (technical) Hermenegildo Moliko Chele, Jefe Servicios Técnicos de Radio y Televisión. $1 or return postage required. Replies irregularly to correspondence in Spanish.

ERITREA   World Time +3

Voice of the Broad Masses of Eritrea (Dimisi Hafash), EPLF National Guidance, Information Department, Radio Branch, P.O. Box 872, Asmara, Eritrea; Ministry of Information and Culture, Technical Branch, P.O. Box 243, Asmara, Eritrea; EPLF National Guidance, Information Department, Radio Branch, P.O. Box 2571, Addis Ababa, Ethiopia; EPLF National Guidance, Information Department, Radio Branch, Sahel Eritrea, P.O. Box 891, Port Sudan, Sudan. Phone: +291

(1) 119-100. Fax: +291 (1) 127 115. Contact: (Eritrea) Ghebreab Ghebremedhin; (Ethiopia and Sudan) Mehreteab Tesfa Giorgis. Return postage or $1 helpful. Free information on history of station, Ethiopian People's Liberation Front and Eritrea.

ETHIOPIA World Time +3

Radio Ethiopia: (external service) P.O. Box 654; (domestic service) P.O. Box 1020—both in Addis Ababa, Ethiopia. Phone: (main office) +251 (1) 116-427 or +251 (1) 551-011; (engineering) +251 (1) 200-948. Fax: +251 (1) 552 263. Contact: (external service, general) Kahsai Tewoldemedhin, Program Director; Ms. Woinshet Woldeyes, Secretary, Audience Relations; Ms. Ellene Mocria, Head of Audience Relations; or Yohaness Ruphael, Producer, "Contact"; (administration) Kasa Miliko, Head of Station; (technical) Terefe Ghebre Medhin or Zegeye Solomon. Free stickers. Very poor replier.

Radio Fana (Radio Torch), P.O. Box 30702, Addis Ababa, Ethiopia. Contact: Hameimat Tekle Haimanot, General Manager; Mesfin Alemayehu, Head, External Relations; or Girma Lema, Head, Planning and Research Department. Station is autonomous and receives its income from non-governmental educational sponsorship. Seeks help with obtaining vehicles, recording equipment and training materials.

"Voice of Peace"—see Disestablishmentarian listing earlier in this section.

FINLAND World Time +2 (+3 midyear)

📺 YLE Radio Finland

MAIN OFFICE: Box 78, FIN-00024 Helsinki, Finland. Phone: (general, 24-hour English speaking switchboard for both Radio Finland and Yleisradio Oy) +358 (9) 14801; (international information) +358 (9) 1480-3729; (administration) +358 (9) 1480-4320 or +358 (9) 1480-4316; (Technical Customer Service) +358 (9) 1480-3213. Fax: (general) +358 (9) 148 1169; (international information) +358 (9) 1480 3391; (Technical Affairs) +358 (9) 1480 3588. E-mail: rfinland@yle.fi; (Yleisradio Oy parent organization) fbc@yle.fi. URLs: (includes RealAudio in Finnish, Swedish, English, German, French, Russian and Classic Latin) www.yle.fi/fbc/radiofin.html; or (stored news audio in Finnish, Swedish, English, German, French and Russian) www.wrn.org/audio.html. Contact—Radio Finland: (English) Eddy Hawkins; (Finnish & Swedish) Pertti Seppä; (German & French) Dr. Stefan Tschirpke; (Russian) Timo Uotila and Mrs. Eija Laitinen; (administration) Juhani Niinistö, Head of External Broadcasting. Contact—Yleisradio Oy parent organization: (general) Marja Salusjärvi, Head of International PR; (administration) Arne Wessberg, Managing Director; or Tapio Siikala, Director for Domestic & International Radio. Sometimes provides free stickers and small souvenirs, as well as tourist and other magazines. Replies to correspondence. Radio Finland will verify reception reports directly if sent to: Radio Finland, Attention: Raimo Makela, PL 113, 28101 Pori, Finland (E-mail: raimo.makela@pp.inet.fi). Also, see Transmission Facility, below.

NUNTII LATINI (Program in Latin): P.O. Box 99, FIN-00024 Helsinki, Finland. Fax: +358 (9) 1480 3391. E-mail: nuntii.latini@yle.fi. URL: www.yle.fi/fbc/nuntii.html. Six years of Nuntii Latini now available in books I to III at US$30 each from: Bookstore Tiedekirja, Kirkkokatu 14, FIN-00170 Helsinki, Finland; fax: +358 (9) 635 017. VISA/MC/EURO.

FREQUENCY PLANNING: Bureau of Network Planning, Pl 20, FIN-00024 Helsinki, Finland. Phone: +358 (9) 1480-2787. Fax:

+358 (9) 148 5260. E-mail: esko.huuhka@yle.yle.mailnet.fi. Contact: Esko Huuhka, Head of Network Planning.

MEASURING STATION: Yleisradio, FIN-05400 Jokela, Finland. Phone: +358 (9) 282-005/6. Fax: +358 (9) 417 2410. Contact: Urpo Kormano, Frequency Manager; or Kari Hautala, Monitoring Engineer.

TRANSMISSION FACILITY: Yleisradio Oy, Shortwave Centre, Preiviiki, Makholmantie 79, FIN-28660 Pori, Finland. Contact: Ms. Marjatta Jokinen. Issues full-data verification cards for good reception reports, and provides free illustrated booklets about the transmitting station.

NORTH AMERICAN OFFICE—LISTENER & MEDIA LIAISON: P.O. Box 462, Windsor CT 06095 USA. Phone: +1 (860) 688-5540 or +1 (860) 688-5098. Phone/fax: (24-hour toll-free within U.S. and Canada for recorded schedule and voice mail) 1-800-221-9539. Fax: +1 (860) 688 0113. E-mail: yleus@aol.com. Contact: John Berky, YLE Finland Transcriptions. Free *YLE North America* newsletter.

FRANCE World Time +1

📺 Radio France Internationale (RFI)

MAIN OFFICE: B.P. 9516, F-75016 Paris Cedex 16, France. Phone: (general) +33 (1) 42-30-22-22; (International Affairs and Program Placement) +33 (1) 44-30-89-31 or +33 (1) 44-30-89-49; (Service de la communication) +33 (1) 42-30-29-51; (Audience Relations) +33 (1) 44-30-89-69/70/71; (Media Relations) +33 (1) 42-30-29-85; (Développement et de la communication) +33 (1) 44-30-89-21; (*Fréquence* **Monde**) +33 (1) 42-30-10-86; (English Department) +33 (1) 42-30-30-62; (Spanish Department) +33 (1) 42-30-30-48. Fax: (general) +33 (1) 42 30 30 71; (International Affairs and Program Placement) +33 (1) 44 30 89 20; (Audience Relations) +33 (1) 44 30 89 99; (other nontechnical) +33 (1) 42 30 44 81; (English Department) +33 (1) 42 30 26 74; (Spanish Department) +33 (1) 42 30 46 69. URLs: (general) www.rfi.fr/; (RealAudio and StreamWorks in French, English, Spanish & Portuguese) www.francelink.com/radio_stations/rfi/. Contact: Simson Najovits, Chief, English Department; J.P. Charbonnier, Producer, "Lettres des Auditeurs"; Joël Amar, International Affairs/Program Placement Department; Arnaud Littardi, Directeur du développement et de la communication; Nicolas Levkov, Rédactions en Langues Etrangères; Daniel Franco, Rédaction en français; Mme. Anne Toulouse, Rédacteur en chef du Service Mondiale en français; Christine Berbudeau, Rédacteur en chef, *Fréquence* **Monde**; or Marc Verney, Attaché de Presse; (administration) Jean-Paul Cluzel, Président-Directeur Général; (technical) M. Raymond Pincon, Producer, "Le Courrier Technique." Free *Fréquence* **Monde** bi-monthly magazine in French upon request. Free souvenir keychains, pins, lighters, pencils, T-shirts and stickers have been received by some—especially when visiting the headquarters at 116 avenue du Président Kennedy, in the chichi 16th Arrondissement. Can provide supplementary materials for "Dites-moi tout" French-language course; write to the attention of Mme. Chantal de Grandpre, "Dites-moi tout." "Le Club des Auditeurs" French-language listener's club ("Club 9516" for English-language listeners); applicants must provide name, address and two passport-type photos, whereupon they will receive a membership card and the club bulletin. RFI hopes to install a shortwave broadcasting center in Djibouti, which if approved could be operational in the not-too-distant future. Plans to stop shortwave broadcasting to Europe and North America. RFI exists primarily to defend and promote

Francophone culture, but also provides meaningful information and cultural perspectives in non-French languages. The French government under both socialist and conservative leadership has given RFI consistent and substantial support, and with that support RFI has grown and continues to grow into a leading position in International broadcasting.

TRANSMISSION OFFICE, TECHNICAL: TéléDiffusion de France, Direction de la Production et des Méthodes, Shortwave service, 10 rue d'Oradour sur Glane, 75732 Paris Cedex 15, France. Phone: +33 (1) 5595-1369. Fax: +33 (1) 5595 2137. E-mail: 101317.2431@compuserve.com; or danielbochent@compuserve.com. Contact: Daniel Bochent, Head of short wave service; Alain Meunier, Mme Annick Daronian or Mme Sylvie Greuillet (short wave service). This office for informing about transmitter-related problems (interference, modulation quality), and also for reception reports and verifications.

UNITED STATES PROMOTIONAL, SCHOOL LIAISON, PROGRAM PLACEMENT AND CULTURAL EXCHANGE OFFICES:

NEW ORLEANS: Services Culturels, Suite 2105, Ambassade de France, 300 Poydras Street, New Orleans LA 70130 USA. Phone: +1 (504) 523-5394. Phone/fax: +1 (504) 529-7502. Contact: Adam-Anthony Steg, Attaché Audiovisuel. This office promotes RFI, especially to language teachers and others in the educational community within the southern United States, and arranges for bi-national cultural exchanges. It also sets up RFI feeds to local radio stations within the southern United States.

NEW YORK: Audiovisual Bureau, Radio France Internationale, 972 Fifth Avenue, New York NY 10021 USA. Phone: +1 (212) 439-1452. Fax: +1 (212) 439 1455. Contact: Gérard Blondel or Julien Vin. This office promotes RFI, especially to language teachers and others within the educational community outside the southern United States, and arranges for bi-national cultural exchanges. It also sets up RFI feeds to local radio stations within much of the United States.

NEW YORK NEWS BUREAU: 1290 Avenue of the Americas, New York NY 10019 USA. Phone: +1 (212) 581-1771. Fax: +1 (212) 541 4309. Contact: Ms. Auberi Edler, Reporter; or Bruno Albin, Reporter.

WASHINGTON NEWS BUREAU: 529 14th Street NW, Suite 1126, Washington DC 20045 USA. Phone: +1 (202) 879-6706. Contact: Pierre J. Cayrol.

SAN FRANCISCO OFFICE, SCHEDULES: 2654 17th Avenue, San Francisco CA 94116 USA. Phone: +1 (415) 564-9968. Contact: George Poppin. This address, a volunteer office, only provides RFI schedules to listeners. All other correspondence should be sent directly to the main office in Paris.

Voice of Orthodoxy—*see* Belarus.

FRENCH GUIANA   World Time –3

Radio France Internationale/Swiss Radio International—Guyane Relay Station, TDF, Montsinéry, French Guiana. Contact: (technical) Chef des Services Techniques, RFI Guyane. All correspondence concerning non-technical matters should be sent directly to the main addresses (*see*) for Radio France International in France and Swiss Radio International in Berne. Can consider replies only to technical correspondence in French.

RFO Guyane, 43 bis, rue du Docteur-Gabriel-Devez, BP 7013 - Cayenne Cedex, French Guiana. Phone: +595 299-900 or +594 299-907. Fax: +594 299 958. URL: www.rfo.fr/html/pres/guy.html. Free stickers. Replies occasionally and sometimes slowly; correspondence in French preferred, but English okay.

FRENCH POLYNESIA   World Time –10 Tahiti

RFO Polynésie Française, Centre Pamatai, BP 125, Papeete, Tahiti, 98 702 French Polynesia. Phone: +689 861-616 or +689 861-650. Fax: +689 861 651. E-mail: rfopofr@mail.pf. URLs: (text) www.rfo.fr/html/pres/tah.html; (RealAudio) www.rfo.fr/html/info/bulletins.html. Contact: (general) Claude Ruben, Directeur; Patrick Durand Gaillard, Rédacteur en Chef; Jean-Raymond Bodin, Directeur des Programmes; (technical) Léon Siquin, Services Techniques. Free stickers, tourist brochures and broadcast-coverage map. Three IRCs, return postage, 5 francs or $1 helpful, but not mandatory. M. Siquin and his sons Xavier and Philippe, all friendly and fluent in English, collect pins from radio/TV stations, memorabilia from the Chicago Bulls basketball team and other souvenirs of American pop culture; these make more appropriate enclosures than the usual postage-reimbursement items.

GABON   World Time +1

Afrique Numéro Un, B.P. 1, Libreville, Gabon. Fax: +241 742 133. E-mail: africagc@club-internet.fr. URL: www.africa1.com/. Contact: (general) Gaston Didace Singangoye; or A. Letamba, Le Directeur des Programmes; (technical) Mme. Marguerite Bayimbi, Le Directeur [sic] Technique. Free calendars and bumper stickers. $1, 2 IRCs or return postage helpful. Replies very slowly.

RTV Gabonaise, B.P. 10150, Libreville, Gabon. Contact: André Ranaud-Renombo, Le Directeur Technique, Adjoint Radio. Free stickers. $1 required. Replies occasionally, but slowly, to correspondence in French.

GEORGIA   World Time +4

Georgian Radio, TV-Radio Tbilisi, ul. M. Kostava 68, Tbilisi 380071, Republic of Georgia. Phone: (domestic service) +995 (32) 368-362; (external service) +995 (32) 368-885, +995 (32) 360-063. Fax: +995 (32) 368 665. Contact: (external service) Helena Apkhadze, Foreign Editor; Tamar Shengelia; Mrs. Natia Datuaschwili, Secretary; or Maya Chihradze; (domestic service) Lia Uumlaelsa, Manager; or V. Khundadze, Acting Director of Television and Radio Department. Replies erratically and slowly, in part due to financial difficulties. Return postage or $1 helpful.

High Adventure Radio (Voice of Hope)—via Georgian Radio Relay—All correspondence should be directed to the office in the United Kingdom; *see* KVOH—High Adventure Radio, USA.

Republic of Abkhazia Radio, Abkhaz State Radio & TV Co., Aidgylara Street 34, Sukhum 384900, Republic of Abkhazia; however, as of press time, according to the station there is a total embargo on mail to the Republic of Abkhazia. Phone: +995 (32) 24-867 or +995 (32) 25-321. Fax: +995 (32) 21 144. Contact: G. Amkuab, General Director; or Yury Kutarba, Deputy General Director. A 1992 uprising in northwestern Georgia drove the majority of ethnic Georgians from the region. This area remains virtually autonomous from Georgia.

GERMANY   World Time +1 (+2 midyear)

Adventist World Radio, the Voice of Hope—*see* USA and Italy.

Bayerischer Rundfunk, Rundfunkplatz 1, D-80300 München, Germany. Phone: +49 (89) 5900-01. Fax: +49 (89)

RRI Semarang has sophisticated facilities for mobile live broadcasts from Jawa Tengah, Indonesia.

N. Grace

5900 2375. E-mail: info@br-online.de. URLs: (general) www.br-online.de/; (RealAudio) www.br-online.de/. Contact: Dr. Gualtiero Guidi; or Jutta Paue, Engineering Adviser. Free stickers and 250-page program schedule book.

BBC World Service—*see* UNITED KINGDOM

Deutsche Telekom AG

JÜLICH ADDRESS: Rundfunksendstelle, Merscher Höhe D-52428 Jülich, Germany. Phone: +49 (2461) 697-310. Fax: +49 (2461) 697 372. E-mail: hirte@04.drn.telekom400.dbp.de. Contact: Gunter Hirte, Technical Advisor for High Frequency Broadcasting. This office should only be contacted for urgent technical matters and not for general reception reports.

KÖLN ADDRESS: Niederlassung 2 Köln, Service Centre Rundfunk, D-50482 Köln Germany. Phone: (Kraus) +49 (221) 575-4000; (Hufschlag) +49 (221) 575-4011. Fax: +49 (221) 575 4090. Contact: Egon Kraus, Head of Broadcasting Service Centre; or Josef Hufschlag, Customer Advisor for High Frequency Broadcasting.

This organization operates the transmitters used by Deutsche Welle, and also leased to various non-German world band stations.

Deutsche Welle, Radio and TV International

MAIN OFFICE: Raderbergguertel 50, D-50968 Cologne, Germany. Phone: (general) +49 (221) 389-2001/2; (listeners' mail) +49 (221) 389-2500; (Program Distribution) +49 (221) 389-2731; (technical) +49 (221) 389-3221 or +49 (221) 389-3208; (Public Relations) +49 (221) 2041. Fax: (general) +49 (221) 389 4155, +49 (221) 389 2080 or +49 (221) 389 3000; (listeners' mail) +49 (221) 389 2510; (English Service, general) +49 (221) 389 4599; (English Service, Current Affairs) +49 (221) 389 4554; (Public Relations) +49 (221) 389 2047; (Program Distribution) +49 (221) 389 2777; (technical) +49 (221) 389 3200 or +49 (221) 389 3240. E-mail: (general) online@dwelle.de; (specific individuals or programs) format is firstname.lastname@dw.gmd.de, so to reach, say, Harald Schuetz, it would be harald.schuetz@dw.gmd.de (if this fails, try the format firstname@dwelle.de); (Program Distribution) 100302.2003@

compuserve.com; (technical) (Pischalka) 100565.1010@compuserve.com; (Scholz) 100536.2173@compuserve.com. URLs: (general) www.dwelle.de/; (German program, including RealAudio) www.dwelle.de/dpradio/Welcome.html; (non-German languages, including RealAudio) www.dwelle.de/language.html. Contact: (general) Ursula Fleck-Jerwin, Audience Mail Department; Dr. Ralf Siepmann, Director of Public Relations; Michael Behrens, Head of English Service; or Dr. Burkhard Nowotny, Director of Media Department; Harald Schuetz; ("German by Radio" language course) Herrad Meese; (administration) Dieter Weirich, Director General; (technical—head of engineering) Peter Senger, Chief Engineer; (technical—Radio Frequency Department) Peter Pischalka; Frequency Manager; or Horst Scholz, Head of Transmission; (technical—Transmission Management/Technical Advisory Service) Mrs. Silke Bröker; or B. Klaumann, Transmission Management. Free pennants, stickers, key chains, pens, *Deutsch—warum nicht?* language-course book, *Germany—A European Country and its People* book. Local Deutsche Welle Listeners' Clubs in selected countries. Operates via world band transmitters in Germany, Antigua, Canada, Madagascar, Portugal, Russia, Rwanda and Sri Lanka. Deutsche Welle is sheduled to move from Cologne to Bonn in the near future.

ELECTRONIC TRANSMISSION OFFICE FOR PROGRAM PREVIEWS: Infomedia, 25 rue du Lac, L-8808 Arsdorf, Luxembourg. Phone: +352 649-270. Fax: +352 649 271. This office will electronically transmit Deutsche Welle program previews to you upon request; be sure to provide either a dedicated fax number or an e-mail address so they can reply to you.

BRUSSELS NEWS BUREAU: International Press Center, 1 Boulevard Charlemagne, B-1040 Brussels, Belgium.

U.S./CANADIAN LISTENER CONTACT OFFICE: 2800 South Shirlington Road, Suite 901, Arlington VA 22206-3601 USA. Phone: +1 (703) 931-6644.

RUSSIAN LISTENER CONTACT OFFICE: Nemezkaja Wolna, Abonentnyj jaschtschik 596, Glawpotschtamt, 190000 St. Petersburg, Russia.

TOKYO NEWS BUREAU: C.P.O. Box 132, Tokyo 100-91, Japan.

WASHINGTON NEWS BUREAU: P.O. Box 14163, Washington DC 20004 USA. Fax: +1 (202) 526 2255. Contact: Adnan Al-Katib, Correspondent.

DeutschlandRadio-Berlin, Hans-Rosenthal-Platz, D-10825 Berlin Schönberg, Germany. Phone: +49 (30) 8503-0. Fax: +49 (30) 8503 9009. E-mail: dlrb@dlf.de. URL (shared with Deutschlandfunk): www.d-radio.de/. Contact: Dr. Karl-Heinz Stamm; or Ulrich Reuter.

Missionwerk Werner Heukelbach, D-51702 Bergneustadt 2, Germany. Contact: Manfred Paul. Transmits via the Voice of Russia. Replies to correspondence in English and German.

Radio Bremen, Betriebsdirektion, Postfach 330 320, D-28353 Bremen, Germany. Fax: +49 (421) 246 1010 or +49 (421) 246 2020. URL: www.radiobremen.de/. Contact: Jim Senberg. Free stickers and shortwave guidebook. Currently off shortwave due to cost saving measures which may, or may not, be permanent.

Radio Marabu, Box 1166, 49187 Belm, Germany. Phone: +49 (5406) 899 484. Fax: +49 (5406) 899 485. URL: www.mediaDD.de/radiomarabu/. Program heard via IRRS, Milano *see* Italy.

Südwestrundfunk—This station is the result of a merger between Süddeutscher Rundfunk and Südwestfunk. Based in Stuttgart, transmissions under the new banner commenced in September 1998. E-mail: info@swr3.de. URL: (includes RealAudio) www.swr3.de/.

Universelles Leben (Universal Life)
HEADQUARTERS: Postfach 5643, D-97006 Würzburg, Germany. Phone: +49 (931) 3903-0. Fax: (general) +49 (931) 3903 233; (engineering) +49 (931) 3903 299. E-mail: info@universelles-leben.org. URL: www.universelles-leben.org. Contact: Janet Wood, English Dept; "Living in the Spirit of God" listeners' letters program; or Johanna Limley. Free stickers, publications and occasional small souvenirs. Transmits "The Word, The Cosmic Wave" (Das Wort, die kosmische Welle) via the Voice of Russia, WWCR (USA) and various other world band stations, as well as "Vida Universal" via Radio Miami Internacional and WHRI in the United States. Replies to correspondence in English, German or Spanish.
SALES OFFICE: Das WORT GmbH, Im Universelles Leben, Max-Braun-Str.2, D-97828 Marktheidenfeld/Altfeld, Germany. Phone: +49 (9391) 504-135. Fax: +49 (9391) 504 133. E-mail: info@das-wort.com. URL: www.das-wort.com/. Sells books, audio cassettes and videos related to broadcast material.
NORTH AMERICAN BUREAU: The Inner Religion, P.O. Box 3549, Woodbridge CT 06525 USA. Phone: +1 (203) 281-7771. Fax: +1 (203) 230 2703.

GHANA   World Time exactly

WARNING—CONFIDENCE ARTISTS: Attempted correspondence with Radio Ghana may result in requests, perhaps resulting from mail theft, from skilled confidence artists for money, free electronic or other products, publications or immigration sponsorship. To help avoid this, correspondence to Radio Ghana should be sent via registered mail.
Ghana Broadcasting Corporation, Broadcasting House, P.O. Box 1633, Accra, Ghana. Phone: +233 (21) 221-161. Fax: +233 (21) 221 153 or +233 (21) 773 227. Contact: (general) Mrs. Maud Blankson-Mills, Acting Director of Corporate Affairs; (administration) B.A. Apenteng, Director of Radio; (technical) E. Heneath, Propagation Department. Mr. Markin states that he is interested in reception reports, as well as feedback on the program he produces, "Health Update," so directing your correspondence to him may be the best bet. Otherwise, replies are increasingly scarce, but whomever you send your correspondence to, you should register it, and enclose an IRC, return postage or $1.

GREECE   World Time +2 (+3 midyear)

Foni tis Helladas (Voice of Greece)
NONTECHNICAL: ERA-5, "The Voice of Greece", 432 Messogion Av., 153 42 Athens, Greece. Phone: +30 (1) 606-6308 or +30 (1) 606-6297. Fax: +30 (1) 606 6309. E-mail (program reports): fonel@hol.gr. URL: www.greeknews.ariadne-t.gr/Docs/Era5_1.html. Contact: Kosta Valetas, Director, Programs for Abroad. Free tourist literature.
TECHNICAL: Elliniki Radiophonia—ERA-5, General Directorate of Technical Services, 402 Messogion Av., 153 42 Athens, Greece. Phone: +30 (1) 639 7108 or +30 (1) 601-4700. Fax: +30 (1) 600 9608; or Elliniki Radiophonia Tilerasi S.A., Direction of Engineering and Development, P.O. Box 600 19, 153 10 Aghia Paraskevi Attikis, Athens, Greece. Phone: +30 (1) 601-4700 or +30 (1) 639-6762. Fax: +30 (1) 639 0652 or +30 (1) 600 9608. E-mail: skalai@leon.nrcps.ariadne-t.gr. Contact: (general) Ing. Dionysios Angelogiannis, Planning Engineer; (administration) Th. Kokossis, General Director; or Nicolas Yannakakis, Director. Technical reception reports may be sent via mail, fax or E-mail. Taped reports not accepted.

Radiophonikos Stathmos Makedonias—ERT-3, Angelaki 2, 546 21 Thessaloniki, Greece. Phone: +30 (31) 244-979. Fax: +30 (31) 236 370. E-mail: charter3@compulink.gr. Contact: (general) Mrs. Tatiana Tsioli, Program Director; or Lefty Kongalides, Head of International Relations; (technical) Dimitrios Keramidas, Engineer. Free booklets and other small souvenirs.
Voice of America/IBB—Kaválla Relay Station. Phone: +30 (5) 912-2855. Fax: +30 (5) 913 1310. Contact: Michael Nardi, Relay Station Manager. These numbers for urgent technical matters only. Otherwise, does not welcome direct correspondence; *see* USA for acceptable VOA Washington address and related information.

GUAM   World Time +10

Adventist World Radio, the Voice of Hope—KSDA
AWR-Asia, P.O. Box 8990, Agat, Guam 96928 USA. Phone: +1 (671) 565-2000. Fax: +1 (671) 565 2983. E-mail: 70673.2552@compuserve.com; or (Benton) 74617.2361@compuserve.com. URLs: (limited RealAudio, plus text) http://ourworld.compuserve.com/homepages/awr_asia/; (general information) www.awr.org/awr-asia/index.html. Contact: (general) Lolita Colegado, Listener Mail Services; (technical) Elvin Vence, Chief Engineer; Gary Benton, Assistant Engineer. Free stickers, quarterly *AWR Current*, program schedule and religious printed matter. If enclosing return postage please use currency notes in a major world currency or return postage stamps. IRCs still accepted. Also, *see* AWR listings under Costa Rica, Guatemala, Italy, Kenya, Russia and USA.

Trans World Radio—KTWR
MAIN OFFICE, NONTECHNICAL: P.O. Box CC, Agana, Guam 96910 USA. Phone: (main office) +1 (671) 477-9701; (engineering) +1 (671) 828-8637. Fax: (main office) +1 (671) 477 2838; (engineering) +1 (671) 828-8636. E-mail: (administration) estortro@twr.hafa.net.gu; (programming) wfrost@twr.hafa.net.gu; (technical) cwhite@twr.hafa.net.gu. URLs: www.guam.net/pub/twr/; or (RealAudio) www.guam.net/pub/twr/audio2.htm. Contact: (general) Karen Zeck, Listener Correspondence; Byron Tyler, Producer, "Friends in Focus" listeners' questions program; Wayne T. Frost, Program Director & Producer, "Pacific DX Report"; Janette McSurk; or Kathy Gregowski; (administration) Edward Stortro, Station Director; (programmes) Shelly Frost; (technical) Chuck White, Chief Engineer. Station plans to install a new 100kW shortwave transmitter and construct a new 41 meter band antenna. Also, *see* USA. Free small publications.
"PACIFIC DX REPORT" PROGRAM: E-mail: (reports) bpadula@compuserve.com. URL: www.wp.com/edxp/. Program compiled by EDXP and aired via KTWR. Special EDXP QSLs. Reports to: Bob Padula, 404 Mont Albert Road, Surrey Hills 3127, Victoria, Australia. Return postage necessary. E-mail reports accepted and will be confirmed by return e-mail, to bpadula@compuserve.com.
FREQUENCY COORDINATION OFFICE: 1868 Halsey Drive, Asan, Guam 96922-1505 USA. Phone: +671 828-8637. Fax: +1 (671) 828 8636. E-mail: ktwrfreq@twr.hafa.net.gu. Contact: George Zensen, Chief Engineer.
AUSTRALIAN OFFICE: Trans World Radio ANZ, 2-6 Albert Street, Blackburn, Victoria 3130, Australia. Phone: +61 (3) 9878-5922. Fax: +61 (3) 9878 5944. E-mail: 100251.1646@compuserve.com. Contact: John Reeder, National Director.
CHINA (HONG KONG) OFFICE: TWR-CMI, P.O. Box 98697, Tsimshatsui Post Office, Kowloon, Hong Kong. Phone: +852

The Greek navy is as old as the Hellenic people. I Foni tis Helladas, the Voice of Greece, airs daily programs to homesick Greek mariners, as well as to Greeks and non-Greeks worldwide.   R. Crane

2780-8336. Fax: +852 2385 5045. E-mail: (Ko) simon_ko@compuserve.com; (Lok) joycelok@compuserve.com. Contact: Simon Ko, Acting Area Director; or Joyce Lok, Programming/Follow -up Director.
INDIA OFFICE: P.O. Box 4310, New Delhi-110 019, India. Contact: N. Emil Jebasingh, Vishwa Vani; or S. Stanley.
SINGAPORE OFFICE: Trans World Radio Asia Pacific Office, 2A Martaban Road, Singapore 328627. Phone: +65 251-1887. Fax: +65 251 1846. E-mail: (Spieker) 76573.1147@compuserve.com; (Flaming) vflaming@mbox3.singnet.com.sg. Contact: Edmund Spieker, Acting Regional Director; or Vic Flaming, Regional Services Director.
TOKYO OFFICE: Pacific Broadcasting Association, C.P.O. Box 1000, Tokyo 100-91, Japan. Phone +81 (3) 3295-4921. Fax: +81 (3) 3233 2650. E-mail: pba@path.ne.jp. Contact: (administration) Nobuyoshi Nakagawa.

GUATEMALA   World Time –6

Adventist World Radio, the Voice of Hope—Unión Radio, Apartado de Correo 51-C, Guatemala City, Guatemala. Phone: +502 365-2509, +502 365-9067 or +502 365-9072. Fax:+502 365 9076. E-mail: mundi@guate.net. Contact: D. Rolando García P., Gerente General. Free tourist and religious literature and Guatemalan stamps. Return postage, 3 IRCs or $1 appreciated. Correspondence in Spanish preferred. Also, see AWR listings under Costa Rica, Guam, Italy, Kenya, Russia and USA.

La Voz de Atitlán—TGDS, Santiago Atitlán, Guatemala. Contact: Juan Ajtzip Alvarado, Director; José Miguel Pop Tziná, Director; or Esteban Ajtzip Tziná, Director Ejecutivo. Return postage required. Replies to correspondence in Spanish.
La Voz de Guatemala—TGW (if reactivated), 18 Calle 6-70 2do piso, Zona 1, Guatemala City, Guatemala.
La Voz de Nahualá, Nahualá, Sololá, Guatemala. Contact: (technical) Juan Fidel Lepe Juárez, Técnico Auxiliar; or F. Manuel Esquipulas Carrillo Tzep. Return postage required. Correspondence in Spanish preferred.
Radio Buenas Nuevas, 13020 San Sebastián, Huehuetenango, Guatemala. Contact: Israel G. Rodas Mérida, Gerente. $1 or return postage helpful. Free religious and station information in Spanish. Sometimes includes a small pennant. Replies to correspondence in Spanish.
Radio Coatán, San Sebástian Coatán, Huehuetenango, Guatemala. Contact: Domingo Hernández, Director; or Virgilio José, Locutor.
Radio Chortís, Centro Social, 20004 Jocotán, Chiquimula, Guatemala. Contact: Padre Juan María Boxus, Director. $1 or return postage required. Replies irregularly to correspondence in Spanish.
Radio Cultural—TGNA, Apartado de Correo 601, Guatemala City, Guatemala. Phone: +502 (2) 427-45 or +502 (2) 443-78. Contact: Mariela Posadas, QSL Secretary; or Wayne Berger, Chief Engineer. Free religious printed matter. Return postage or $1 appreciated.
Radio K'ekchi—TGVC, 3ra Calle 7-15, Zona 1, 16015 Fray Bartolomé de las Casas, Alta Verapaz, Guatemala; (Media Con-

sultant) David Daniell, Asesor de Comunicaciones, Apartado Postal 25, Bulevares MX, 53140 Mexico. Phone: (station) +502 950-0299; (Daniell, phone/fax) +52 (5) 572-9633. Fax: +502 950 0398. E-mail: (Daniell) DPDaniell@aol.com. Contact: (general) Gilberto Sun Xicol, Gerente; Ancelmo Cuc Chub, Director; or Mateo Botzoc, Director de Programas; (technical) Larry Baysinger, Ingeniero Jefe. Free paper pennant. $1 or return postage required. Replies to correspondence in Spanish.

Radio Mam, Acu'Mam, Cabricán, Quetzaltenango, Guatemala. Contact: Porfirio Pérez, Director. Free stickers and pennants. $1 or return postage required. Replies irregularly to correspondence in Spanish. Donations permitting (the station is religious), they would like to get a new transmitter to replace the current unit, which is failing.

Radio Maya de Barillas—TGBA, 13026 Villa de Barillas, Huehuetenango, Guatemala. Contact: José Castañeda, Pastor Evangélico y Gerente. Free pennants and pins. Station is very interested in receiving reception reports. $1 or return postage required. Replies occasionally to correspondence in Spanish and Indian languages.

Radio Tezulutlán—TGTZ, Apartado de Correo 19, 16901 Cobán, Guatemala. Contact: Sergio W. Godoy, Director; or Hno. Antonio Jacobs, Director Ejecutivo. Pennant for donation to specific bank account. $1 or return postage required. Replies to correspondence in Spanish.

GUINEA   World Time exactly

Radiodiffusion-Télévision Guinéenne, B.P. 391, Conakry, Guinea. Contact: (general) Yaoussou Diaby, Journaliste Sportif; or Seny Camara; (administration) Momo Toure, Chef Services Administratifs; or Alpha Sylla, Directeur, Sofoniya I Centre de Transmission; (technical, studio) Mbaye Gagne, Chef de Studio; (technical, overall) Direction des Services Techniques. Return postage or $1 required. Replies very irregularly to correspondence in French.

GUYANA   World Time –3

Voice of Guyana, Guyana Broadcasting Corporation, P.O. Box 10760, Georgetown, Guyana. Phone: +592 (2) 58734; +592 (2) 58083 or +592 (2) 62691. Fax: +592 (2) 58756, but persist as fax machine appears to be switched off much of the time. Contact: (general) Indira Anandjit, Personnel Assistant; or M. Phillips; (technical) Roy Marshall, Senior Technician; or Shiroxley Goodman, Chief Engineer. $1 or IRC helpful. Sending a spare sticker from another station helps assure a reply.

HOLLAND (THE NETHERLANDS)   World Time +1
(+2 midyear)

▣**Radio Nederland Wereldomroep (Radio Netherlands)**
MAIN OFFICE: P.O. Box 222, 1200 JG Hilversum, The Netherlands. Phone: (general) +31 (35) 672-4211; (English Language Service) +31 (35) 672-4242; (24-hour listener Answerline) +31 (35) 672-4222. Fax: (general) +31 (35) 672 4207, but indicate destination department on fax cover sheet; (English Language Service) +31 (35) 672 4239; (Programme Distribution & Frequency Planning Department) +31 (35) 672 4429. E-mail: (English Language Service) letters@rnw.nl. ("Media Network") media@rnw.nl. URLs: (general) www.rnw.nl (online publications are listed in the section "Real Radio"); (RealAudio and MP3 files) www.wrn.org/stations/rnw.html. Contact: (management) Lodewijk Bouwens, Director General; Jonathan Marks, Director of Programmes; Jan Hoek, Director of Finance

and Logistics; Diana Janssen, Head of Strategy and RN Interactive; Mike Shaw, Head of English Language Service; Ginger da Silva, Network Manager English; (listener correspondence) Iris Walstra, English Correspondence; or Howard Shannon, Host of listener-contact programme: "Sincerely Yours" (include your telephone number or e-mail address). Full-data verification card for reception reports, following guidelines in the RNW folder, "Writing Useful Reception Reports," available free and on the Internet. Semi-annual *On Target* newsletter also free upon request, as are stickers and booklets. Other language departments have their own newsletters. New for 1999: a regular online magazine about broadcasting, and dossiers that complement RNW's award-winning documentaries. The Radio Netherlands Music Department produces concerts heard on many NPR stations in North America, as well as a line of CDs, mainly of classical, jazz and world music. Most of the productions are only for rebroadcasting on other stations, but recordings on the NM Classics label are for sale. More details are available at the RNW website. Visitors welcome, but must call in advance.
NORTH AMERICAN OPERATION: 316 Eisenhower Parkway, Livingston, NJ 07039 USA. Phone: toll-free in the USA 1-800-797-1670; or +1 (973) 533-6761. Fax: +1 (973) 533 6762. E-mail: lee.martin@rnw.nl. Contact: Lee Martin, Manager of Client Services. This bureau markets Radio Netherlands radio and television productions in English and Spanish for the North American market. These programs are available on satellite and CD to stations.
NEW DELHI OFFICE: (local correspondence only) P.O. Box 5257, Chanakya Puri Post Office, New Delhi, 110 021, India. Forwards mail from Indian listeners to Holland every three weeks.

HONDURAS   World Time –6

La Voz de la Mosquitia (when operating)
STATION: Puerto Lempira, Dpto. Gracias a Dios, Honduras. Contact: Sammy Simpson, Director; or Larry Sexton. Free pennants.
U.S. OFFICE: Global Outreach, Box 1, Tupelo MS 38802 USA. Phone: +1 (601) 842-4615. Another U.S. contact is Larry Hooker, who can be reached at +1 (334) 694-7976.

La Voz Evangélica—HRVC
MAIN OFFICE: Apartado Postal 3252, Tegucigalpa, M.D.C., Honduras. Phone: +504 34-3468/69/70. Fax: +504 33 3933. Contact: (general) Srta. Orfa Esther Durón Mendoza, Secretaria; Tereso Ramos, Director de Programación; Alan Maradiaga; or Modesto Paluca, Jefe, Depto. Tráfico; (technical) Carlos Paguada, Director del Dpto. Técnico; (administration) Venancio Mejía, Gerente; or Nelson Perdomo, Director. Free calendars. Three IRCs or $1 required. Replies to correspondence in English, Spanish, Portuguese and German.
REGIONAL OFFICE, SAN PEDRO SULA: Apartado 2336, San Pedro Sula, Honduras. Phone: +504 57-5030. Contact: Hernán Miranda, Director.
REGIONAL OFFICE, LA CEIBA: Apartado 164, La Ceiba, Honduras. Phone: +504 43-2390. Contact: José Banegas, Director.

Radio HRET
STATION: Primera Iglesia Bautista, Domicilio Conocido, Puerto Lempira, Gracias a Dios 33101, Honduras. Fax: +504 980 018. Contact: Leonardo Alvarez López, Locutor y Operador; or Desiderio Williams, Locutor y Operador. Return postage necessary. Replies, sometimes slowly, to correspondence in Spanish.
NONTECHNICAL ENGLISH CORRESPONDENCE: David Daniell,

Asesor de Comunicaciones, Apartado Postal 25, Bulevares, MX-53140, Mexico. Replies to correspondence in English and Spanish.

TECHNICAL ENGLISH CORRESPONDENCE: Ing. Larry Baysinger, 8000 Casualwood Ct., Louisville KY 40291 USA. Replies to correspondence in English and Spanish, but calls not accepted.

Radio HRMI, La Voz de Misiones Internacionales
STATION: Apartado Postal 20583, Comayaguela, M.D.C., Honduras. Phone: +504 339-029. Contact: Wayne Downs, Director. $1 or return postage helpful.

US OFFICE: IMF World Missions, P.O. Box 6321, San Bernardino CA 92412, USA. Phone +1 (909) 370-4515. Fax: +1 (909) 370 4862. E-mail: JKPIMF@msn.com. Contact: Dr. James K. Planck, President; or Gustavo Roa, Coordinator.

Radio Internacional, Apartado 1473, San Pedro Sula, Honduras. Phone: +504 528-181. Fax: +504 581 070. Contact: Víctor Antonio ("Tito") Handal, Gerente y Propietario; or Hugo Hernández y Claudia Susana Prieto, Locutores del "Desfile de Estrellas," aired Sunday at 0200-0500 World Time. Free stickers, stamps, postcards and one-lempira banknote. $1 helpful. Appears to reply regularly to correspondence in Spanish.

Radio Luz y Vida—HRPC, Apartado 303, San Pedro Sula, Honduras. Fax: +504 57 0394. Contact: C. Paul Easley, Director; Chris Fleck; or, to have your letter read over the air, "English Friendship Program." Return postage or $1 appreciated.

HUNGARY   World Time +1 (+2 midyear)

Radio Budapest
STATION OFFICES: Bródy Sándor utca 5-7, H-1800 Budapest, Hungary. Phone: (general) +36 (1) 138-7339, +36 (1) 138-8328, +36 (1) 138-7357 +36 (1) 138-8588, +36 (1) 138-7710 or +36 (1) 138-7723; (voice mail, English) +36 (1) 138-8320; (voice mail, German) +36 (1) 138-7325; (administration) +36 (1) 138-7503 or +36 (1) 138-8415; (technical) +36 (1) 138-7226 or +36 (1) 138-8923. Fax: (general) +36 (1) 138 8517; (administration) +36 (1) 138 8838; (technical) +36 (1) 138 7105. E-mail: (Radio Budapest, English) ango11@kaf.radio.hu; (Radio Budapest, German) nemetl@kaf.radio.hu; (Hungarian Information Resources) avadasz@bluemoon.sma.com; (technical) (Füszlás) Fuszfasla@muszak.radio.hu. URLs: (RealAudio in English and Hungarian) www.wrn.org/stations/hungary.html; (general) www.eunet.hu/radio; (shortwave program) www.glue.umd.edu/~gotthard/hir/entertainment/radio/; (North American Service via Hungarian Information Resources) http://mineral.umd.edu/hir/Entertainment/Radio/Shortwave. Contact: (English Language Service) Ágnes Kevi, Correspondence; Charles Taylor Coutts, Producer, "Gatepost" (listeners' letters' program) & Head of English Language Service; Louis Horváth, DX Editor; or Sándor Laczkó, Editor; (administration) Antal Réger, Director, Foreign Broadcasting; Dr. Zsuzsa Mészáros, Vice-Director, Foreign Broadcasting; János Szirányi, President, Magyar Rádió; or János Simkó, Vice President, Magyar Rádió; (technical) László Füszfás, Deputy Technical Director, Magyar Rádió; Külföldi Adások Főszerkesztősége; or Lajos Horváth, Műszaki Igazgatósá; (Hungarian Information Resources) Andrew Vadasz. Free *Budapest International* periodical, stickers, pennants, stamps and printed tourist and other material. Also, for those whose comments or program proposals are used over the air, T-shirts, baseball-style caps and ballpoint pens. *RBSWC DX News* bul-

letin free to all Radio Budapest Shortwave Club members. Advertisements considered.

TRANSMISSION AUTHORITY: Ministry of Transport, Communications & Water Management, P.O. Box 87, H-1400 Budapest, Hungary. Phone/fax: +36 (1) 156-3493. Fax: +36 (1) 461 3392. E-mail: horvathf@cms.khvm.hu. Contact: Ferenc Horváth, Frequency Manager, Radio Communications Engineering Services.

ICELAND   World Time exactly

Radio Alpha & Omega, Omega Television, P.O. Box 3340, IS-123 Reykjavík, Iceland. Phone: +354 567-6111. Fax: +354 568 3741. Contact: Eirikur Sigurbjoernson. This Christian station, which currently operates via leased-time transmission facilities in Jülich, Germany, sells tape recordings for $20.

Ríkisútvarpid, International Relations Department, Efstaleiti 1, IS-150 Reykjavík, Iceland. Phone: +354 515-3000. Fax: +354 515 3010. E-mail: isradio@ruv.is. URLs: www.ruv.is; (RealAudio) http://this.is/ruv. Contact: Dóra Ingvadóttir, Head of International Relations; or Markús Öern Antonsson, Director.

INDIA   World Time +5:30

All India Radio
NOTE: The facility "New Broadcasting House" is being built to supplement the existing Broadcasting House on Parliament Street. It is to be used by the domestic and external services, alike, and is scheduled to be in full operation before 2001.

ADMINISTRATION: Directorate General of All India Radio, Akashvani Bhawan, 1 Sansad Marg, New Delhi-110 001, India. Phone: (general) +91 (11) 371-0006; (Engineer-in-Chief) +91 (11) 371-0058; (Frequency Management) +91 (11) 371-0145 or +91 (11) 371-4062; (Director General) +91 (11) 371-0300 or +91 (11) 371-4061. Fax: +91 (11) 371 1956. E-mail: faair@giasdl01.vsnl.net.in. Contact: (general) Shashi Kant Kapoor, Director General; (technical) H.M. Joshi, Engineer-in-Chief; or A.K. Bhatnagar, Director - Frequency Assignments; (programming) +91 (11) 371 5411, (voice mail, English) +91 (11) 376-1166, (Hindi) +91 (11) 376-1144.

AUDIENCE RESEARCH: Audience Research Unit, All India Radio, Press Trust of India Building, 2nd floor, Sansad Marg, New Delhi-110 001, India. Phone: +91 (11) 371-0033. Contact: S.K. Khatri, Director.

CENTRAL MONITORING SERVICES: Central Monitoring Services, All India Radio, Ayanagar, New Delhi-100 047, India. Phone: (Director) +91 (11) 680-1763 or +91 (11) 680-2955; (Control Room) +91 (11) 680-2362. Fax: +91 (11) 680 2679, +91 (11) 680 2362 or +91 (11) 680 2955. Contact: V.K. Arora, Director.

INTERNATIONAL MONITORING STATION—MAIN OFFICE: International Monitoring Station, All India Radio, Dr. K.S. Krishnan Road, Todapur, New Delhi-110 012, India. Phone: (general) +91 (11) 581-461;(administration) +91 (11) 680-2306; (Frequency Planning) +91 (11) 573-5936 (Chhabra) or +91 (11) 573-5937 (Malviya). Contact: D.P. Chhabra or R.K. Malviya, Assistant Research Engineers—Frequency Planning.

NEWS SERVICES DIVISION: News Services Division, Broadcasting House, 1 Sansad Marg, New Delhi-110 001, India. Phone: +91 (11) 371-0084 or +91 (11) 373-1510. Contact: D.C. Bhaumik, Director General—News.

RESEARCH & DEVELOPMENT: Office of the Chief Engineer R&D, All India Radio, 14-B Ring Road, Indraprastha Estate,

New Delhi-110 002, India. Phone: (general) +91 (11) 331-1711, +91 (11) 331-1762, +91 (11) 331-3532 or +91 (11) 331-3574; (Chief Engineer) +91 (11) 331 8329. Fax: +91 (11) 331 8329 or +91 (11) 331 6674. E-mail: rdair@giasdl01.vsnl.net.in. URL: www.air.kode.net. Contact: K.M. Paul, Chief Engineer.

TRANSCRIPTION & PROGRAM EXCHANGE SERVICES: Akashvani Bhawan, 1 Sansad Marg, New Delhi-110 001, India. Phone: +91 (11) 371-7927. Contact: D.P. Jatav, Director; or A.V. Bhavan, Chief Engineer.

All India Radio—Aizawl, Radio Tila, Tuikhuahtlang, Aizawl-796 001, Mizoram, India. Phone: +91 (3652) 2415. Contact: (technical) D.K. Sharma, Station Engineer; or T.R. Rabha, Station Engineer.

All India Radio—Bangalore

HEADQUARTERS: see All India Radio—External Services Division.

AIR OFFICE NEAR TRANSMITTER: P.O. Box 5096, Bangalore-560 001, Karnataka, India. Phone: +91 (80) 261-243. Contact: (technical) C. Iyengar, Supervising Engineer.

All India Radio—Bhopal, Akashvani Bhawan, Shamla Hills, Bhopal-462 002, Madhya Pradesh, India. Phone: +91 (755) 540-041. Contact: (technical) C. Lal, Station Engineer.

All India Radio—Calcutta, G.P.O. Box 696, Calcutta—700 001, West Bengal, India. Phone: +91 (33) 281-705. Contact: (technical) R.N. Dam, Supervising Engineer.

All India Radio—Chennai

EXTERNAL SERVICES: see All India Radio—External Services Division.

DOMESTIC SERVICE: Kamrajar Salai, Mylapore, Chennai-600 004, Tamil Nadu, India. Phone: +91 (44) 845-975. Contact: (technical) S. Bhatia, Supervising Engineer.

All India Radio—Delhi—*see* All India Radio—New Delhi.

All India Radio—External Services Division

MAIN ADDRESS: Broadcasting House, 1 Sansad Marg, P.O. Box 500, New Delhi-110 001, India. Phone: (general) +91 (11) 371-5411; (Director) +91 (11) 371-0057. Contact: (general) P.P. Setia, Director of External Services; or S.C. Panda, Audience Relations Officer; (technical) S.A.S. Abidi, Assistant Director Engineering (F.A.). E-mail (Research Dept.): rdair@giasdl01.vsnl.net.in; (comments on programs) air@kode.net. URL: (includes RealAudio in English and other languages) www.allindiaradio.org. Free monthly *India Calling* magazine and stickers. Replies erratic. Except for stations listed below, correspondence to domestic stations is more likely to be responded to if it is sent via the External Services Division; request that your letter be forwarded to the appropriate domestic station.

VERIFICATION ADDRESS: Prasar Bharati Corporation of India, Akashvani Bhawan, Room 204, Sansad Marg, New Delhi-110 001, India; or P.O. Box 500, New Delhi-110 001, India. Fax: +91 (11) 372 5212 or +91 (11) 371 4697. E-mail: faair@giasdl01.vsnl.net.in. Contact: R.K. Bhatnagar, Director, Frequency Assignments.

All India Radio—Gangtok, Old MLA Hostel, Gangtok—737 101, Sikkim, India. Phone: +91 (359) 22636. Contact: (general) Y.P. Yolmo, Station Director; (technical) Deepak Kumar, Station Engineer.

All India Radio—Gorakhpur

NEPALESE EXTERNAL SERVICE: see All India Radio—External Services Division.

DOMESTIC SERVICE: Post Bag 26, Gorakhpur-273 001, Uttar Pradesh, India. Phone: +91 (551) 337-401. Contact: (technical) Dr. S.M. Pradhan, Supervising Engineer.

All India Radio—Guwahati, P.O. Box 28, Chandmari, Guwahati-781 003, Assam, India. Phone: +91 (361) 540-135. Contact: (technical) P.C. Sanghi, Superindent Engineer.

All India Radio—Hyderabad, Rocklands, Saifabad, Hyderabad-500 004, Andhra Pradesh, India. Phone: +91 (40) 234-904. Contact: (technical) N. Srinivasan, Supervising Engineer.

All India Radio—Imphal, Palau Road, Imphal-795 001, Manipur, India. Phone: +91 (385) 20-534. Contact: (technical) M. Jayaraman, Supervising Engineer.

All India Radio—Itanagar, Naharlagun, Itanagar-791 110, Arunachal Pradesh, India. Phone: +91 (3781) 4485. Contact: J.T. Jirdoh, Station Director; or Suresh Naik, Superintending Engineer. Verifications direct from station are difficult, as engineering is done by staff visiting from the Regional Engineering Headquarters at AIR—Guwahati (*see*); that address might be worth contacting if all else fails.

All India Radio—Jaipur, 5 Park House, Mirza Ismail Road, Jaipur-302 001, Rajasthan, India. Phone: +91 (141) 366-623. Contact: (technical) S.C. Sharma, Station Engineer.

All India Radio—Jammu—*see* Radio Kashmir—Jammu.

All India Radio—Jeypore, Jeypore-764 005 Orissa, India. Phone: +91 (685) 422-524. Contact: P. Subramanium, Assistant Station Engineer; or A.C. Subuddhi, Assistant Engineer.

All India Radio—Kohima, Kohima-797 001, Nagaland, India. Phone: +91 (3866) 2121. Contact: (technical) K.G. Talwar, Superintending Engineer; K.K Jose, Assistant Engineer; or K. Morang, Assistant Station Engineer. Return postage, $1 or IRC helpful.

All India Radio—Kurseong, Mehta Club Building, Kurseong-734 203, Darjeeling District, West Bengal, India. Phone: +91 (3554) 350. Contact: (general) George Kuruvilla, Assistant Director; (technical) A.S. Guin, Chief Engineer; or R.K. Shina, Station Engineer.

All India Radio—Leh—*see* Radio Kashmir—Leh.

All India Radio—Lucknow, 18 Vidhan Sabha Marg, Lucknow-226 001, Uttar Pradesh, India. Phone: +91 (522) 244-130. Contact: R.K. Singh, Supervising Engineer. This station now appears to be replying via the External Services Division, New Delhi.

All India Radio—Mumbai

EXTERNAL SERVICES: see All India Radio—External Services Division.

COMMERCIAL SERVICE (VIVIDH BHARATI): All India Radio, P.O. Box 11497, 101 M K Road, Mumbai-400 0020, Maharashtra, India. Phone: (general) +91 (22) 203-1341 or +91 (22) 203-594; (director) +91 (22) 203-7702. Fax: +91 (22) 287 6040. Contact: Vijayalakshmi Sinha, Director.

DOMESTIC SERVICE: P.O. Box 13034, Mumbai-400 020, Maharashtra, India. Phone: +91 (22) 202-9853. Contact: S. Sundaram, Supervising Engineer; or Lak Bhatnagar, Supervisor, Frequency Assignments. Return postage helpful.

All India Radio—New Delhi, P.O. Box 70, New Delhi-110 011, India. Phone: (general) +91 (11) 371-0113. Contact: (technical) G.C. Tyagi, Supervising Engineer. $1 helpful.

All India Radio—Panaji

HEADQUARTERS: see All India Radio—External Services Division, above.

AIR OFFICE NEAR TRANSMITTER: P.O. Box 220, Altinho, Panaji-403 001, Goa, India. Phone: +91 (832) 5563. Contact: (technical) V.K. Singhla, Station Engineer; or G.N. Shetti, Assistant Engineer.

All India Radio—Port Blair, Dilanipur, Port Blair-744 102, South Andaman, Andaman & Nicobar Islands, Union Territory, India. Phone: +91 (3192) 20-682. Contact: (technical)

Yuvraj Bajaj, Station Engineer. Registering letter appears to be useful. Don't send any cash with your correspondence as it appears to be a violation of their foreign currency regulations.

All India Radio—Ranchi, 6 Ratu Road, Ranchi-834 001, Bihar, India. Phone: +91 (651) 302-358. Contact: (technical) H.N. Agarwal, Supervising Engineer.

All India Radio—Shillong, P.O. Box 14, Shillong-793 001, Meghalaya, India. Phone: +91 (364) 224-443 or +91 (364) 222-781. Contact: (general) C. Lalsaronga, Director NEIS; (technical) H.K. Agarwal, Supervising Engineer. Free booklet on station's history.

All India Radio—Simla, Choura Maidan, Simla-171 004, Himachal Pradesh, India. Phone: +91 (177) 4809. Contact: (technical) B.K. Upadhayay, Supervising Engineer; or P.K. Sood, Assistant Station Engineer. Return postage helpful.

All India Radio—Srinagar—*see* Radio Kashmir—Srinagar.

All India Radio—Thiruvananthapuram, P.O. Box 403, Bhakti Vilas, Vazuthacaud, Thiruvananthapuram-695 014, Kerala, India. Phone: +91 (471) 65-009. Contact: (technical) K.M. Georgekutty, Station Engineer.

Ministry of Information & Broadcasting, Main Secretariat, A-Wing, Shastri Bhawan, New Delhi-110 001, India. Phone: (general) +91 (11) 338-4340, +91 (11) 338-4782 or +91 (11) 379-338; (Information & Broadcasting Secretary) +91 (11) 338-2639. Fax: +91 (11) 338 3513, +91 (11) 338 7823, +91 (11) 338 4785, +91 (11) 338 7617 or +91 (11) 338 1043. Contact: (general) N.P. Nawani, Information & Broadcasting Secretary; (administration) C.M. Ibrahim, Minister for Information & Broadcasting.

Radio Kashmir—Jammu, Begum Haveli, Old Palace Road, Jammu-180 001, Jammu & Kashmir, India. Phone: +91 (191) 544-411. Fax: +91 (191) 546 658. Contact: (technical) S.K. Sharma, Station Engineer.

Radio Kashmir—Leh, Leh-194 101, Ladakh District, Jammu & Kashmir, India. Phone: +91 (1982) 2263. Contact: (technical) L.K. Gandotar, Station Engineer.

Radio Kashmir—Srinagar, Sherwani Road, Srinagar—190 001, Jammu & Kashmir, India. Phone: +91 (194) 71-460. Contact: L. Rehman, Station Director.

Radio Tila—*see* All India Radio—Aizawl.

Trans World Radio
STUDIO: P.O. Box 4407, L-15, Green Park, New Delhi-110 016, India. Phone: +91 (11) 662-058. Fax: +91 (11) 686 8049. Contact: N. Emil Jebasingh, Director. This office is used for program production and answering listeners' correspondence, and does not have its own transmission facilities.
ON-AIR ADDRESS: P.O. Box 5, Andhra Pradesh, India.

INDONESIA   World Time +7 Western: Waktu Indonesia Bagian Barat (Jawa, Sumatera); +8 Central: Waktu Indonesia Bagian Tengal (Bali, Kalimantan, Sulawesi, Nusa Tenggara); +9 Eastern: Waktu Indonesia Bagian Timur (Irian Jaya, Maluku)

NOTE: Except where otherwise indicated, Indonesian stations, especially those of the Radio Republik Indonesia (RRI) network, will reply to at least some correspondence in English. However, correspondence in Indonesian is more likely to ensure a reply.

Kang Guru II Radio English, Indonesia Australia Language Foundation, Kotak Pos 6756 JKSRB, Jakarta 12067, Indonesia. E-mail: kangguru@server.indo.net.id. URL: www.indo.net.id/ commercial/waterfall/kangguru.html. Contact: Greg Clough,

Kang Guru Project Manager. This program is aired over various RRI outlets, including Jakarta and Sorong. Continuation of this project, currently sponsored by Australia's AusAID, will depend upon whether adequate supplementary funding can be made available.

Radio Pemerintah Daerah TK II—RPD Poso, Jalan Jenderal Sudirman 7, Poso, Sulawesi Tengah, Indonesia. Contact: Joseph Tinagari, Kepala Stasiun. Return postage necessary. Replies occasionally to correspondence in Indonesian.

Radio Pemerintah Daerah Kabupaten TK II—RPDK Berau, Jalan SA Maulana, Tanjungredeb 77311, Kalimantan Timur, Indonesia. Contact: Kus Syariman or M. Auzi, Kepala Stasiun. Return postage necessary.

Radio Pemerintah Daerah Kabupaten—RPDK Bolaang Mongondow, Jalan S. Parman 192, Kotamobagu, Sulawesi Utara, Indonesia. Replies occasionally to correspondence in Indonesian.

Radio Pemerintah Daerah Kabupaten TK II—RPDK Buol-Tolitoli, Jalan Mohamed Ismail Bantilan No. 4, Tolitoli 94511, Sulawesi Tengah, Indonesia. Contact: Said Rasjid, Kepala Studio; Wiraswasta, Operator/Penyiar; or Muh. Yasin, SM. Return postage required. Replies extremely irregularly to correspondence in Indonesian.

Radio Pemerintah Daerah Kabupaten TK II—RPDK Ende, Jalan Panglima Sudirman, Ende, Flores, Nusa Tenggara Timor, Indonesia. Contact: (technical) Thomas Keropong, YC9LHD. Return postage required.

Radio Pemerintah Daerah Kabupaten TK II—RPDK Manggarai, Ruteng, Flores, Nusa Tenggara Timur, Indonesia. Contact: Simon Saleh, B.A. Return postage required.

Radio Pemerintah Daerah Kabupaten TK II—RPDK Tapanuli Selatan, Kotak Pos No. 9, Padang-Sidempuan, Sumatera Utara, Indonesia. Return postage required.

Radio Republik Indonesia—RRI Ambon, Jalan Jenderal Akhmad Yani 1, Ambon, Maluku, Indonesia. Contact: Drs. H. Ali Amran or Pirla C. Noija, Kepala Seksi Siaran. A very poor replier to correspondence in recent years. Correspondence in Indonesian and return postage essential.

Radio Republik Indonesia—RRI Banda Aceh (when operating), Kotak Pos No. 112, Banda Aceh, Aceh, Indonesia. Contact: S.H. Rosa Kim. Return postage helpful.

Radio Republik Indonesia—RRI Bandar Lampung, Kotak Pos No. 24, Bandar Lampung 35213, Indonesia. Phone: +62 (721) 52-280. Fax: +62 (721) 62 767. Contact: M. Nasir Agun, Kepala Stasiun; Hi Hanafie Umar; Djarot Nursinggih, Tech. Transmission; Drs. Zulhaqqi Hafiz, Kepala Sub Seksi Periklanan; or Asmara Haidar Manaf. Return postage helpful. Replies in Indonesian to correspondence in English or Indonesian.

Radio Republik Indonesia—RRI Bandung, Stasiun Regional 1, Kotak Pos No. 1055, Bandung 40010, Jawa Barat, Indonesia. Contact: Drs. Idrus Alkaf, Kepala Stasiun; Mrs. Ati Kusmiati; or Eem Suhaemi, Kepala Seksi Siaran. Return postage or IRC helpful.

Radio Republik Indonesia—RRI Banjarmasin, Stasiun Nusantara 111, Kotak Pos No. 117, Banjarmasin 70234, Kalimantan Selatan, Indonesia. Contact: Jul Chaidir, Stasiun Kepala; or Harmyn Husein. Free stickers. Return postage or IRCs helpful.

Radio Republik Indonesia—RRI Bengkulu, Stasiun Regional 1, Kotak Pos No. 13 Kawat, Kotamadya Bengkulu, Indonesia. Contact: Drs. Drs. Jasran Abubakar, Kepala Stasiun. Free picture postcards, decals and tourist literature. Return postage or 2 IRCs helpful.

Adventist World Radio broadcasts to Asia in 29 languages from the beautiful Pacific island of Guam. AWR

Radio Republik Indonesia—RRI Biak (when operating), Kotak Pos No. 505, Biak, Irian Jaya, Indonesia. Contact: D. Latuperissa, Head of Station.

Radio Republik Indonesia—RRI Bukittinggi (when operating), Stasiun Regional 1 Bukittinggi, Jalan Prof. Muhammad Yamin No. 199, Aurkuning, Bukittinggi 26131, Propinsi Sumatera Barat, Indonesia. Fax: +62 (752) 367 132. Contact: Mr. Effendi, Sekretaris; Zul Arifin Mukhtar, SH; or Samirwan Sarjana Hukum, Producer, "Phone in Program." Replies to correspondence in Indonesian or English. Return postage helpful.

Radio Republik Indonesia—RRI Denpasar (when operating), P.O. Box 31, Denpasar, Bali, Indonesia. Replies slowly to correspondence in Indonesian. Return postage or IRCs helpful.

Radio Republik Indonesia—RRI Dili (when operating), Stasiun Regional 1 Dili, Jalan Kaikoli, Kotak Pos 103, Dili 88000, Timor-Timur, Indonesia. Contact: Harry A. Silalahi, Kepala Stasiun; Arnoldus Klau; or Paul J. Amalo, BA. Return postage or $1 helpful. Replies occasionally to correspondence in Indonesian.

Radio Republik Indonesia—RRI Fak Fak, Jalan Kapten P. Tendean, Kotak Pos No. 54, Fak-Fak 98601, Irian Jaya, Indonesia. Contact: Bahrun Siregar, Kepala Stasiun; Aloys Ngotra, Kepala Seksi Siaran; or Richart Tan, Kepala Sub Seksi Siaran Kata. Station plans to upgrade its transmitting facilities with the help of the Japanese government. Return postage required. Replies occasionally.

Radio Republik Indonesia—RRI Gorontalo, Jalan Jenderal Sudirman, Gorontalo, Sulawesi Utara, Indonesia. Contact: Emod. Iskander, Kepala; or Saleh S. Thalib, Technical Manager. Return postage helpful. Replies occasionally, preferably to correspondence in Indonesian.

🖻 **Radio Republik Indonesia—RRI Jakarta**

STATION: Stasiun Nasional Jakarta, Kotak Pos No. 356, Jakarta, Jawa Barat, Indonesia. URL: (RealAudio via cyberstation Syahreza Radio) www.hway.net/syahreza/rri.htm. Contact: Drs.R. Baskara, Stasiun Kepala; or Drs. Syamsul Muin Harahap, Kepala Stasiun. Return postage helpful. Replies irregularly.

"DATELINE" ENGLISH PROGRAM: see Kang Guru II Radio English.

"U.N. CALLING ASIA" ENGLISH PROGRAM: Program via RRI Jakarta Programa Ibukota Satu, every Sunday. Contact address same as United Nations Radio *(see).*

Radio Republik Indonesia—RRI Jambi

STATION: Jalan Jenderal A. Yani No. 5, Telanaipura, Jambi 36122, Propinsi Jambi, Indonesia. Contact: M. Yazid, Kepala Siaran; or Buchari Muhammad, Kepala Stasiun. Return postage helpful.

Radio Republik Indonesia—RRI Jayapura, P.O. Box 1077, Jayapura 99222, Irian Jaya, Indonesia. Contact: Harry Liborang, Direktorat Radio; or Dr. David Alex Siahainenia, Kepala. Return postage helpful.

Radio Republik Indonesia—RRI Kendari, Kotak Pos No. 7, Kendari 93111, Sulawesi Tenggara, Indonesia. Contact: H. Sjahbuddin, BA; Muniruddin Amin, Programmer; or Drs. Supandi. Return postage required. Replies slowly to correspondence in Indonesian.

Radio Republik Indonesia—RRI Kupang (Regional I), Jalan Tompello No. 8, Kupang, Timor, Indonesia. Contact: Drs. P.M. Tisera, Kepala Stasiun; Qustigap Bagang, Kepala Seksi Siaran; or Said Rasyid, Kepala Studio. Return postage helpful. Correspondence in Indonesian preferred. Replies occasionally.

Radio Republik Indonesia—RRI Madiun (when operating), Jalan Mayor Jenderal Panjaitan No. 10, Madiun, Jawa Timur, Indonesia. Fax: +62 (351) 4964. Contact: Imam Soeprapto, Kepala Seksi Siaran. Replies to correspondence in English or Indonesian. Return postage helpful.

Radio Republik Indonesia—RRI Malang (when operating), Kotak Pos No. 78, Malang 65112, Jawa Timur, Indonesia; or Jalan Candi Panggung No. 58, Mojolangu, Malang 65142, Indonesia. Contact: Drs.Tjutju Tjuar Na Adikorya, Kepala Stasiun; Ml. Mawahib, Kepala Seksi Siaran; or Dra Hartati Soekemi, Mengetahui. Return postage required. Free history and other booklets. Replies irregularly to correspondence in Indonesian.

Radio Republik Indonesia—RRI Manado, Kotak Pos No. 1110, Manado 95124 Propinsi Sulawesi Utara, Indonesia. Fax: +62 (431) 63 492. Contact: Costher H. Gulton, Kepala Stasiun. Free stickers and postcards. Return postage or $1 required. Replies occasionally to correspondence in Indonesian.

Radio Republik Indonesia—RRI Manokwari, Regional II, Jalan Merdeka No. 68, Manokwari, Irian Jaya, Indonesia. Contact: Nurdin Mokogintu. Return postage helpful.

Radio Republik Indonesia—RRI Mataram, Stasiun Regional I Mataram, Jalan Langko No. 83 Ampenan, Mataram 83114, Nusa Tenggara Barat, Indonesia. Phone: +62 (364) 33-713 or +62 (364) 21-355. Contact: Drs. Hamid Djasman, Kepala; or Bochri Rachman, Ketua Dewan Pimpinan Harian. Free stickers. Return postage required. With sufficient return postage or small token gift, sometimes sends tourist information and Batik print. Replies to correspondence in Indonesian.

Radio Republik Indonesia—RRI Medan, Jalan Letkol Martinus Lubis No. 5, Medan 20232, Sumatera, Indonesia. Phone: +62 (61) 324-222/441. Fax: +62 (61) 512 161. Contact: Kepala Stasiun, Ujamalul Abidin Ass; Drs. S. Parlin Tobing, SH, Produsennya, "Kontak Pendengar"; Drs. H. Suryanta Saleh; or Suprato. Free stickers. Return postage required. Replies to correspondence in Indonesian.

Radio Republik Indonesia—RRI Merauke, Stasiun Regional 1, Kotak Pos No. 11, Merauke, Irian Jaya, Indonesia. Contact: (general) Drs. Buang Akhir, Direktor; Achmad Ruskaya B.A., Kepala Stasiun, Drs.Tuanakotta Semuel, Kepala Seksi Siaran; or John Manuputty, Kepala Subseksi Pemancar; (technical) Daf'an Kubangun, Kepala Seksi Tehnik. Return postage helpful.

Radio Republik Indonesia—RRI Nabire, Kotak Pos No. 110, Jalan Merdeka 74 Nabire 98801, Irian Jaya, Indonesia. Contact: Muchtar Yushaputra, Kepala Stasiun. Free stickers and occasional free picture postcards. Return postage or IRCs helpful.

Radio Republik Indonesia—RRI Padang, Kotak Pos No. 77, Padang 25121, Sumatera Barat, Indonesia. Phone: +61 (751) 28-363. Contact: H. Hutabarat, Kepala Stasiun; or Amir Hasan, Kepala Seksi Siaran. Return postage helpful.

Radio Republik Indonesia—RRI Palangkaraya, Jalan M. Husni Thamrin No. 1, Palangkaraya 73111, Kalimantan Tengah, Indonesia. Phone: +62 (514) 21-779. Fax: +62 (514) 21 778. Contact: Drs.Amiruddin; S. Polin; A.F. Herry Purwanto; Meyiwati SH; Supardal Djojosubrojo, Sarjana Hukum; Gumer Kamis; or Ricky D. Wader, Kepala Stasiun. Return postage helpful. Will respond to correspondence in Indonesian or English.

Radio Republik Indonesia—RRI Palembang, Jalan Radio No. 2, Km. 4, Palembang, Sumatera Selatan, Indonesia. Contact: Drs. H. Mursjid Noor, Kepala Stasiun; H.A. Syukri Ahkab, Kepala Seksi Siaran; or H.Iskandar Suradilaga. Return postage helpful. Replies slowly and occasionally.

Radio Republik Indonesia—RRI Palu, Jalan R.A. Kartini No. 39, 94112 Palu, Sulawesi Tengah, Indonesia. Phone: +62 (451) 21-621. Contact: Akson Boole; Nyonyah Netty Ch. Soriton, Kepala Seksi Siaran; Gugun Santoso; Untung Santoso, Kepala Bidang, Teknik Chief Engineer; or M. Hasjim, Head of Programming. Return postage required. Replies slowly to correspondence in Indonesian.

Radio Republik Indonesia—RRI Pekanbaru, Jalan Jenderal Sudirman No. 440, Kotak Pos 51, Pekanbaru, Riau, Indonesia. Phone: +62 (761) 22-081. Fax: +62 (761) 23 605.

Contact: (general) Drs. Mukidi, Kepala Stasiun; Arisun Agus, Kepala Seksi Siaran; Drs. H. Syamsidi, Kepala Supag Tata Usaha; or Zainal Abbas. Return postage helpful.

Radio Republik Indonesia—RRI Pontianak, Kotak Pos No. 6, Pontianak 78111, Kalimantan Barat, Indonesia. Contact: Daud Hamzah, Kepala Seksi Siaran; Achmad Ruskaya, BA; Drs. Effendi Afati, Producer, "Dalam Acara Kantong Surat"; Subagio, Kepala Sub Bagian Tata Usaha; Suryadharma, Kepala Sub Seksi Programa; or Muchlis Marzuki B.A. Return postage or $1 helpful. Replies some of the time to correspondence in Indonesian (preferred) or English.

Radio Republik Indonesia—RRI Samarinda, Kotak Pos No. 45, Samarinda, Kalimantan Timur 75001, Indonesia. Phone: +62 (541) 43-495. Fax: +62 (541) 41 693. Contact: Siti Thomah, Kepala Seksi Siaran; Tyranus Lenjau, English Announcer; S. Yati; Marthin Tapparan; or Sunendra, Kepala Stasiun. May send tourist brochures and maps. Return postage helpful. Replies to correspondence in Indonesian.

Radio Republik Indonesia—RRI Semarang, Kotak Pos No. 1073, Semarang Jateng, Jawa Tengah, Indonesia. Phone: +62 (24) 316 501. Contact: Djarwanto, SH; Drs. Sabeni, Doktorandus; Drs. Purwadi, Program Director; Dra. Endang Widiastuti, Kepala Sub Seksi Periklanan Jasa dan Hak Cipta; Bagus Giarto, Kepala Stasiun; or Mardanon, Kepala Teknik. Return postage helpful.

Radio Republik Indonesia—RRI Serui, Jalan Pattimura Kotak Pos 19, Serui 98211, Irian Jaya, Indonesia. Contact: Agus Raunsai, Kepala Stasiun; J. Lolouan, BA, Kepala Studio; Ketua Tim Pimpinan Harian, Kepala Seksi Siaran; Natalis Edowai; Albertus Corputty; or Drs. Jasran Abubakar. Replies occasionally to correspondence in Indonesian. IRC or return postage helpful.

Radio Republik Indonesia—RRI Sibolga (when operating), Jalan Ade Irma Suryani, Nasution No. 5, Sibolga, Sumatera Utara, Indonesia. Contact: Mrs. Laiya, Mrs. S. Sitoupul or B.A. Tanjung. Return postage required. Replies occasionally to correspondence in Indonesian.

Radio Republik Indonesia—RRI Sorong
STATION: Jalan Jenderal Achmad Yani No. 44, Klademak II, Kotak Pos 146, Sorong 98414, Irian Jaya, Indonesia. Phone: +62 (951) 21-003, +62 (951) 22-111, or +62 (951) 22-611. Contact: Drs. Sallomo Hamid; Tetty Rumbay S., Kasubsi Siaran Kata; Mrs. Tien Widarsanto, Resa Kasi Siaran; Ressa Molle; or Linda Rumbay. Return postage helpful.
"DATELINE" ENGLISH PROGRAM: See Kang Guru II Radio English.

Radio Republik Indonesia—RRI Sumenep, Jalan Urip Sumoharjo No. 26, Sumenep, Madura, Jawa Timur, Indonesia. Contact: Dian Irianto, Kepala Stasiun. Return postage helpful.

Radio Republik Indonesia—RRI Surabaya, Stasiun Regional 1, Kotak Pos No. 239, Surabaya 60271, Jawa Timur, Indonesia. Phone: +62 (31) 41-327. Fax: +62 (31) 42 351. Contact: Zainal Abbas, Kepala Stasiun; Usmany Johozua, Kepala Seksi Siaran; Drs. E. Agus Widjaja, MM, Kasi Siaran; or Ny Koen Tarjadi. Return postage or IRCs helpful.

Radio Republik Indonesia—RRI Surakarta, Kotak Pos No. 40, Surakarta 57133, Jawa Tengah, Indonesia. Contact: H. Tomo, B.A., Head of Broadcasting. Return postage helpful.

Radio Republik Indonesia—RRI Tanjungpinang, Stasiun RRI Regional II Tanjungpinang, Kotak Pos No. 8, Tanjungpinang 29123, Riau, Indonesia. Contact: M. Yazid, Kepala Stasiun; Wan Suhardi, Produsennya, "Siaran Bahasa Melayu"; or Rosakim, Sarjana Hukum. Return postage helpful. Replies occasionally to correspondence in Indonesian or English.

Radio Republik Indonesia—RRI Ternate, Jalan Kedaton, Ternate (Ternate), Maluku, Indonesia. Contact: (general) Abd. Latief Kamarudin, Kepala Stasiun; (technical) Rusdy Bachmid, Head of Engineering; or Abubakar Alhadar. Return postage helpful.

Radio Republik Indonesia Tual, Tual, Kepulauan Kai, Maluku, Indonesia.

Radio Republik Indonesia—RRI Ujung Pandang, RRI Nusantara IV, Kotak Pos No. 103, Ujung Pandang, Sulawesi Selatan, Indonesia. Contact: H. Kamaruddin Alkaf Yasin, Head of Broadcasting Department; Beni Koesbani, Kepala Stasiun; L.A. Rachim Ganie; Ashan Muhammad, Kepala Bidang Teknik; or Drs. Bambang Pudjono. Return postage, $1 or IRCs helpful. Replies irregularly and sometimes slowly.

Radio Republik Indonesia—RRI Wamena, RRI Regional II, Kotak Pos No. 10, Wamena, Irian Jaya 99501, Indonesia. Contact: Yoswa Kumurawak, Penjab Subseksi Pemancar. Return postage helpful.

Radio Republik Indonesia—RRI Yogyakarta, Jalan Amat Jazuli 4, Kotak Pos 18, Yogyakarta 55224, Jawa Tengah, Indonesia. Fax: +62 (274) 2784. Contact: Phoenix Sudomo Sudaryo; Tris Mulyanti, Seksi Programa Siaran; Martono, ub. Kabid Penyelenggaraan Siaran; Mr. Kadis, Technical Department; or Drs. H. Hamdan Sjahbeni, Kepala Stasiun. IRC, return postage or $1 helpful. Replies occasionally to correspondence in Indonesian or English.

Radio Siaran Pemerintah Daerah TK II—RSPD Halmahera Tengah, Soasio, Jalan A. Malawat, Soasio, Maluku Tengah 97812, Indonesia. Contact: Drs. S. Chalid A. Latif, Kepala Badan Pengelola.

Radio Siaran Pemerintah Daerah TK II—RSPD Sumba Timur, Jalan Gajah Mada No. 10 Hambala, Waingapu, Nusa Tenggara Timur 87112, Indonesia. Contact: Simon Petrus, Penanggung Jawab Operasional. Replies slowly and rarely to correspondence in Indonesian.

Radio Siaran Pemerintah Daerah Kabupaten TK II— RSPDK Maluku Tengah, Jalan Pattimura, Masohi, Seram, Maluku Tengah, Indonesia. Contact: Toto Pramurahardja, BA, Kepala Stasiun; Pak Is. Rumalutur; or John Soumokil. Replies slowly to correspondence in Indonesian.

Radio Siaran Pemerintah Daerah Kabupaten Daerah TK II—RSPDKD Ngada, Jalan Soekarno-Hatta, Bjawa, Flores, Nusa Tenggara Tengah, Indonesia. Phone: +62 (384) 21-142. Contact: Drs. Petrus Tena, Kepala Studio.

Voice of Indonesia, Kotak Pos No. 1157, Jakarta 10001, Indonesia. Phone: +62 (21) 720-3467, +62 (21) 355-381 or +62 (21) 349-091. Fax: +62 (21) 345 7132. Contact: Anastasia Yasmine, Head of Foreign Affairs Section. Free stickers and calendars. Very slow in replying.

IRAN   World Time +3:30 (+4:30 midyear)

Voice of the Islamic Republic of Iran
MAIN OFFICE: IRIB External Services, P.O. Box 19395-6767, Tehran, Iran; or P.O. Box 19395-3333, Tehran, Iran. Phone: (IRIB Public Relations) +98 (21) 204-001/2/3 and +98 (21) 204-6894/5. Fax: (external services) +98 (21) 205 1635, +98 (21) 204 1097 or +98 (21) 291 095; (IRIB Public Relations) +98 (21) 205 3305/7; (IRIB Central Administration) +98 (21) 204 1051; (technical) +98 (21) 654 841. E-mail: (general) webmaster@ irib.com; irib@dci.iran.com; (technical, Mohsen Amiri) rezairib@dci.iran.com; (Research Centre) iribrec@dci.iran.com.

URL: (includes RealAudio) www.irib.com/. Contact: (general) Hamid Yasamin, Public Affairs; Ali Larijani, Head; or Hameed Barimani, Producer, "Listeners Special"; (administration) J. Ghanbari, Director General; or J. Sarafraz, Deputy Managing Director; (technical) M. Ebrahim Vassigh, Frequency Manageri. Free seven-volume set of books on Islam, magazines, calendars, book markers, tourist literature and postcards. Verifications require a minimum of two days' reception data, plus return postage. Station is currently asking their listeners to send in their telephone numbers so that they can call and talk to them directly. Upon request they will even broadcast your conversation on air. You can send your phone number to the postal address above or you can fax it to: + 98 (21) 205 1635. If English Service doesn't reply, then try writing the French Service in French.
ENGINEERING ACTIVITIES, TEHRAN: IRIB, P.O. Box 15875-4344, Tehran, Iran. Phone: +98 (21) 2196-6127. Fax: +98 (21) 204 1051, +98 (21) 2196 6268 or +98 (21) 172 924. Contact: Mrs. Niloufar Parviz.
ENGINEERING ACTIVITIES, HESSARAK/KARAJ: IRIB, P.O. Box 155, Hessarak/Karaj, Iran. Phone: +98 (21) 204-0008. Fax: +98 (21) 2617 4926. E-mail: rezairib@dci.iran.com. Contact: Mohsen Amiri.
BONN BUREAU, NONTECHNICAL: Puetzsir 34, 53129 Bonn, Postfach 150 140, D-53040 Bonn, Germany. Phone: +49 (228) 231-001. Fax: +49 (228) 231 002.
LONDON BUREAU, NONTECHNICAL: c/o WTN, IRIB, The Interchange Oval Road, Camden Lock, London NWI, United Kingdom. Phone: +44 (171) 284-3668. Fax: + 44 (171) 284 3669.
PARIS BUREAU, NONTECHNICAL: 27 rue de Liège, escalier B, 1e étage, porte D, F-75008 Paris, France. Phone: + 33 (1) 42-93-12-73. Fax: +33 (1) 42 93 05 13.
Mashhad Regional Radio, P.O. Box 555, Mashhad Center, Jomhoriye Eslame, Iran. Contact: J. Ghanbari, General Director.

IRAQ   World Time +3 (+4 midyear)

Radio Iraq International (Idha'at al-Iraq al-Duwaliyah)
MAIN OFFICE: P.O. Box 8145 CN.12222, Baghdad, Iraq; if no reply try, P.O. Box 8125, Baghdad, Iraq; or P.O. Box 7728, Baghdad, Iraq. Contact: M. el Wettar. All broadcasting facilities in Iraq are currently suffering from operational difficulties.
INDIA ADDRESS: P.O. Box 3044, New Delhi 110003, India.

IRELAND   World Time exactly (+1 midyear)

Radio Telefis Eireann (Irish Overseas Broadcasting), P.O. Box 4950, Dublin 1, Ireland. Phone, offices: (general) +353 (1) 208-3111; (Broadcasting Development) +353 (1) 208-2350. Phone, concise news bulletins: (United States, special charges apply) +1 (900) 420-2411; (United Kingdom) +44 (891) 871-116; (Australia) +61 (3) 552-1140. Phone, concise sports bulletins: (United States, special charges apply) +1 (900) 420-2412; (United Kingdom) +44 (891) 871-117; (Australia) +61 (3) 552-1141. Fax: (general) +353 (1) 208 3082; (Broadcasting Development) +353 (1) 208 3031. E-mail: (Boyd) boydw@rte.ie. URLs: (general, includes RealAudio) www.rte.ie/radio/; (RealAudio, some programs) www.wrn.org/stations/rte.html. Contact: Wesley Boyd, Director of Broadcast Development; Julie Hayde; or Bernie Pope, Reception. IRC appreciated. Offers a variety of video tapes (mostly PAL, but a few "American Standard"), CDs and audio cassettes for sale from RTE Commercial Enterprises Ltd, Box 1947, Donnybrook, Dublin 4, Ireland; (phone) +353 (1) 208-

3453; (fax) +353 (1) 208 2620. A full list of what's on offer can be viewed at www.rte.ie/lib/store.html#music. Regular transmissions via Singapore and WWCR (USA)—*see* next item—and irregularly via other countries for sports or election coverage.

RTE Radio—a half-hour information bulletin from RTE's (*see*, above) domestic Radio 1, relayed on shortwave. Mailing address: Broadcasting Developments, RTE, Dublin 4, Ireland. Phone: +353 (1) 208-2350. Fax: +353 (1) 208 3031. E-mail: boydw@rte.ie. URL: www.rte.ie/radio/worldwide.html. Contact: Wesley Boyd, Director of Broadcast Development.

UCB Europe, P.O. Box 255, Stoke on Trent ST4 8YY, United Kingdom. Phone: (main office) +44 (1782) 642-000. Fax: +44 (1782) 641 121. E-mail: ucb@ucb.co.uk. URL: http://www.ucb.co.uk/. Contact: (general) administration; or Gareth Littler, Managing Director; (technical) Graeme Wilson, Technical Manager.

ISRAEL   World Time +2 (+3 midyear)

Bezeq, The Israel Telecommunication Corp Ltd, Engineering & Planning Division, Radio & T.V. Broadcasting Section, P.O. Box 29555, Tel-Aviv 61294, Israel. Phone: +972 (3) 519-4490. Fax: +972 (3) 519 4614. E-mail: (Taicher) ariet@mail.vod.co.il; (Shamir) rafi_sh@mail.vod.co.il. URL: www.bezeq.co.il/. Contact: Arie Taicher, Frequency Manager;

A bird's-eye view of Adventist World Radio's facility at Forlì, Italy. Its transmissions are heard throughout the Mediterranean basin and beyond. AWR

Rafael Shamir; or Marian Kaminski, Head of AM Radio Broadcasting. Bezeq is responsible for transmitting the programs of the Israel Broadcasting Authority (IBA), which *inter alia* parents Kol Israel. This address only for pointing out transmitter-related problems (interference, modulation quality, network mixups, etc.), especially by fax, of transmitters based in Israel. Verifications not given out at this office; requests for verification should be sent to English Department of Kol Israel (*see* below).

Galei Zahal, Zahal, Military Mail No. 01005, Israel. Phone: +972 (3) 512-6666. Fax: +972 (3) 512 6760. Contact: Yitshak Pasternak, Director. Israeli law allows the Galei Zahal, as well as the Israel Broadcasting Authority, to air broadcasts beamed to outside Israel.

⚑Kol Israel (Israel Radio, the Voice of Israel)
STUDIOS: Israel Broadcasting Authority, P.O. Box 1082, Jerusalem 91010, Israel. Phone: (general) +972 (2) 302-222; (Engineering Dept.) +972 (2) 535-051; (administration) +972 (2) 248-715. Fax: (English Service) +972 (2) 253 282; (Engineering Dept.) +972 (2) 388 821; (other) +972 (2) 248 392 or +972 (2) 302 327. E-mail: ask@israel-info.gov.il. URLs: (media and communications) gopher://israel-info.gov.il:70/00/cul/media/950900.med; (Foreign Ministry, general information on Israeli broadcasting) www.israel-mfa.gov.il; (RealAudio in Hebrew and English) www.virtual.co.il/city_services/news/kol.html. Contact: (general) Sara Manobla, Head of English Service; Edmond Sehayeq, Head of Programming, Arabic, Persian & Yemenite broadcasts; Yishai Eldar, Senior Editor, English Service; (administration) Shmuel Ben-Zvi, Director; (technical, frequency management) Raphael Kochanowski, Director of Liaison & Coordination, Engineering Dept. Various political, religious, tourist, immigration and language publications. IRC required for reply.
SAN FRANCISCO OFFICE, SCHEDULES: 2654 17th Avenue, San Francisco CA 94116 USA. Phone: +1 (415) 564-9968. Contact: George Poppin. This address, a volunteer office, only provides Kol Israel schedules. All other correspondence should be sent directly to the main office in Jerusalem.

ITALY   World Time +1 (+2 midyear)

Adventist World Radio, the Voice of Hope, AWR-Europe, Casella Postale 383, 47100 Forlì, Italy. Phone: +39 (0543) 766-655. Fax: +39 (0543) 768 198. E-mail: awritaly@mbox.queen.it. Contact: Erika Gysin, Listener Mail Services; or Sylva Kesheshian, Listener Mail Secretary. This office will verify reports for AWR broadcasts from Italy, Russia and Slovakia. Free religious printed matter, quarterly *AWR Current* newsletter, stickers, program schedules and other small souvenirs. Return postage, IRCs or $1 appreciated. The Italian government has awarded a shortwave license to AWR for its existing station at Forlì and for a new facility near Argenta scheduled for completion in 1999. AWR is currently considering proposals from manufacturers for this project. Also, *see* AWR listings under Costa Rica, Guam, Guatemala, Kenya, Russia and USA. *DX PROGRAM:* "Radio Magazine," produced by Dario Villani.

European Christian Radio, Postfach 500, A-2345 Brunn, Austria. Fax: +39 (2) 29 51 74 63. Contact: John Adams, Director; or C.R. Coleman, Station Manager. $1 or 2 IRCs required.

⚑Italian Radio Relay Service, IRRS-Shortwave, Nexus IBA, C.P. 10980, 20100 Milano, Italy; or alternatively to expedite cassette deliveries only, mail to: NEXUS-IBA, Attn. Anna Boschetti, Via F. D'Ovidio 6, 20131 Milano, Italy. Phone: (try first) +39 (335) 214-614 or +39 (02) 266-6971. Fax: +39 (02)

7063 8151. E-mail: (general) info@nexus.org; ("Hello There" program, broadcast on special occasions only) ht@nexus.org; (reception reports of test transmissions) test@nexus.org; (other reception reports) reports@nexus.org; (International Public Access Radio, a joint venture of IRRS and WRMI, USA) IPAR@nexus.org; (Cotroneo) alfredo@nexus.org; (Norton) ron@nexus.org. URLs: (general) www.nexus.org; (RealAudio) www.nexus.org/IRN/index.html; (schedules) www.nexus.org/NEXUS-IBA/Schedules; (International Public Access Radio) www.nexus.org/IPAR. Contact: (general) Ms. Anna S. Boschetti, Verification Manager; Alfredo E. Cotroneo, President & Producer of "Hello There"; (technical) Ron Norton. Due to recent cuts in funds this station cannot assure a reply to all listener's mail. E-mail correspondence and reception reports by e-mail are answered promptly and at no charge. A number of booklets and sometimes stickers and small souvenirs are available for sale, but check their website for further details. Two IRCs or $1 helpful.

Radio Europa International, via Gerardi 6, 25124 Brescia, Italy. Contact: Mariarosa Zahella. Replies irregularly, but return postage helpful.

Radio Europe, via Davanzati 8, 20158 Milan MI, Italy. Phone: +39 (02) 3931-0347. Fax: +39 (02) 8645 0149. E-mail: 100135.54@compuserve.com. Contact: Dario Monferini, Foreign Relations Director; or Alex Bertini, General Manager. Pennants $5 and T-shirts $25. $30 for a lifetime membership to Radio Europe's Listeners' Club. Membership includes T-shirt, poster, stickers, flags, gadgets, and so forth, with a monthly drawing for prizes. Application forms available from station. Sells airtime for $20 per hour. Two IRCs or $1 return postage appreciated.

Radio Maria Network Europe, relay Spoleto, Via Turati 7, 22036 Erba, Italy. Fax: +39 (031) 611 288. URL: www.cta.it/aziende/r_maria/info.htm.

Radiorama Radio, C.P. 873, 34100 Trieste, Italy. Contact: Valerio G. Cavallo. Program over the Italian Radio Relay Service (*see*). Verifies directly.

📻**Radio Roma-RAI International** (external services)
MAIN OFFICE: External/Foreign Service, Centro RAI, Saxa Rubra, 00188 Rome, Italy; or P.O. Box 320, Correspondence Sector, 00100 Rome, Italy. Phone: +39 (06) 33-17-2360. Fax: +39 (06) 33 17 18 95 or +39 (06) 322 6070. URLs: www.mix.it/rai; or www.mix.it/raiinternational/. Contact: (general) Rosaria Vassallo, Correspondence Sector; or Augusto Milana, Editor-in-Chief, Shortwave Programs in Foreign Languages; Esther Casas, Servicio Español; (administration) Angela Buttiglione, Managing Director; or Gabriella Tambroni, Assistant Director. Free stickers, banners, calendars and *RAI Calling from Rome* magazine. Can provide supplementary materials, including on VHS and CD-ROM, for Italian-language video course, "Viva l' italiano," with an audio equivalent soon to be offered, as well. Is constructing "a new, more powerful and sophisticated shortwave transmitting center" in Tuscany; when this is activated, RAI International plans to expand news, cultural items and music in Italian and various other language services—including Spanish, Portuguese, Italian, plus new services in Chinese and Japanese. Responses can be very slow.
SHORTWAVE FREQUENCY MONITORING OFFICE: RAI Monitoring Station, Centro di Controllo, Via Mirabellino 1, 20052 Monza (MI), Italy. Phone: +39 (039) 388-389. Phone/fax (ask for fax): +39 (039) 386-222. E-mail: cqmonza@rai.it. Contact: Signora Giuseppina Moretti, Frequency Management; or Mario Ballabio.
ENGINEERING OFFICE, ROME: Via Teulada 66, 00195 Rome,

Italy. Phone: +39 (06) 331-70721. Fax: +39 (06) 331 75142 or +39 (06) 372 3376. E-mail: isola@rai.it. Contact: Clara Isola.
ENGINEERING OFFICE, TURIN: Via Cernaia 33, 10121 Turin, Italy. Phone: +39 (011) 810-2293. Fax: +39 (011) 575 9610. E-mail: allamano@rai.it. Contact: Giuseppe Allamano.
NEW YORK OFFICE, NONTECHNICAL: 1350 Avenue of the Americas —21st floor, New York NY 10019 USA. Phone: +1 (212) 468-2500. Fax: +1 (212) 765 1956. Contact: Umberto Bonetti, Deputy Director of Radio Division. RAI caps, aprons and tote bags for sale at Boutique RAI, c/o the aforementioned New York address.
SAN FRANCISCO OFFICE, SCHEDULES: 2654 17th Avenue, San Francisco CA 94116 USA. Phone: +1 (415) 564-9968. Contact: George Poppin. This address, a volunteer office, only provides RAI schedules to listeners. All other correspondence should be sent directly to the main office in Rome.

Radio Speranza, Modena (when active), Largo San Giorgio 91, 41100 Modena, Italy. Phone/fax: +39 (059) 230-373. Contact: Padre Cordioli Luigi, Missionario Redentorista. Free Italian-language newsletter. Replies enthusiastically to correspondence in Italian. Return postage appreciated.

Radio Strike, Palermo, c/o R. Scaglione, P.O. Box 119, Succ. 34, 90144 Palermo, Italy.

RTV Italiana-RAI (domestic services)
CALTANISSETTA: Radio Uno, Via Cerda 19, 90139 Palermo, Sicily, Italy. Contact: Gestione Risorse, Transmission Quality Control. $1 required.
ROME: Centro RAI, Saxa Rubra, 00188 Rome, Italy. Fax: +39 (06) 322 6070. E-mail: grr@rai.it. URLs (experimental): (general) http:www.rai.it/; (RealAudio) www.rai.it/grr.

Tele Radio Stereo, Roma, Via Bitossi 18, 00136 Roma, Italy. Fax: + 39 (06) 353 48300.

IVORY COAST—*see* CÔTE D'IVOIRE.

JAPAN   World Time +9

NHK Fukuoka, 1-1-10 Ropponmatsu, Chuo-ku, Fukuoka-shi, Fukuoka 810-77, Japan.

NHK Osaka, 3-43 Bamba-cho, Chuo-ku, Osaka 540-01, Japan. Fax: +81 (6) 941 0612. Contact: (technical) Technical Bureau. IRC or $1 helpful.

NHK Sapporo, 1-1-1 Ohdori Nishai, Chuo-ku, Sapporo 060, Japan. Fax: +81 (11) 232 5951.

NHK Tokyo/Shobu-Kuki, JOAK, 3047-1 Oaza-Sanga, Shoubu-cho, Minami Saitamagun, Saitama 346-01, Japan. Fax: +81 (3) 3481 4985 or +81 (480) 85 1508. IRC or $1 helpful. Replies occasionally. Letters should be sent via registered mail.

Radio Japan/NHK (external service)
MAIN OFFICE: 2-2-1 Jinnan, Shibuya-ku, Tokyo 150-8001, Japan. Phone: +81 (3) 3465-1111. Fax: (general) +81 (3) 3481 1350; ("Hello from Tokyo" and Production Center) +81 (3) 3465 0966. E-mail: info@intl.nhk.or.jp. URLs: www.nhk.or.jp/rjnet. Contact: Chief Producer, "Hello from Tokyo"; Director of Public Relations; Isao Kitamoto, Deputy Director General; Hisashi Okawa, Senior Director International Planning; Director of Programming; Director of News Department; or Director of Production Center. Free *Radio Japan News* publication, sundry other small souvenirs and "Let's Learn/Practice Japanese" language-course materials.

Radio Tampa/NSB
MAIN OFFICE: Nihon Shortwave Broadcasting, 9-15 Akasaka 1-chome, Minato-ku, Tokyo 107, Japan. Fax: +81 (3) 3583 9062. E-mail: web@tampa.co.jp. URL: www.tampa.co.jp/. Contact: H. Nagao, Public Relations; M. Teshima; Ms. Terumi Onoda; or H. Ono. Sending a reception report may help with a reply. Free stickers and Japanese stamps. $1 or 2 IRCs helpful.
NEW YORK NEWS BUREAU: 1325 Avenue of the Americas #2403, New York NY 10019 USA. Fax: +1 (212) 261 6449. Contact: Noboru Fukui, reporter.

JORDAN   World Time +2 (+3 midyear)

Radio Jordan, P.O. Box 909, Amman, Jordan; or P.O. Box 1041, Amman, Jordan. Phone: (general) +962 (6) 774-111; (International Relations) +962 (6) 778-578; (English Service) +962 (6) 757-410 or +962 (6) 773-111; (Arabic Service) +962 (6) 636-454; (Saleh) +962 (6) 748-048; (Al-Areeny) +962 (6) 757-404. Fax: +962 (6) 788 115. E-mail: (general) general@jrtv.gov.jo; (programs) rj@jrtv.gov.jo; (technical) eng@jrtv.gov.jo. URL: www.jrtv.com/redio.htm. Contact: (general) Jawad Zada, Director of English Service & Producer of "Mailbag"; Mrs. Firyal Zamakhshari, Director of Arabic Programs; or Qasral Mushatta; (administrative) Hashem Khresat, Director of Radio; Mrs. Fatima Massri, Director of International Relations; or Muwaffaq al-Rahayifah, Director of Shortwave Services; (technical) Fawzi Saleh, Director of Engineering; or Yousef Al-Areeny, Director of Radio Engineering. Free stickers. Replies irregularly and slowly. Enclosing $1 helps.

KAZAKHSTAN   World Time +6 (+7 midyear)

Kazakh Radio, Kazakh Broadcasting Company, 175A Zheltoksan Street, 480013 Almaty, Kazakhstan. Phone: +7 (3272) 630-763, +7 (3272) 630-763 or +7 (3272) 635-629. Fax: +7 (3272) 631 207. Contact: B. Shalakhmentov, Chairman; or S.D. Primbetov, Deputy Chairman.

Radio Almaty ("Radio Alma-Ata" and "Radio Almaty" in English Service, "Radio Kazakhstan" in Russian and some other services), 175A Zheltoksan Street, 480013 Almaty, Kazakhstan. Phone: (head of foreign language broadcasts) +7 (3272) 637-694 or +7 (3272) 633-716. Fax: +7 (3272) 631 207. Contact: Mr. Gulnar. Correspondence welcomed in English, German, Russian, Korean and Kazakh. Station hopes to start up services in Chinese and Japanese, but not in the near future.

KENYA   World Time +3

Adventist World Radio, The Voice of Hope, AWR Africa, P.O. Box 10114, Nairobi, Kenya. Phone: +254 (2) 713-961. Fax: +254 (2) 713 907. E-mail: 74532.1575@compuserve.com. URL: www.awr.org/awr-africa/. Contact: Samuel Misiani, AWR Africa Region Director. Free home Bible study guides, program schedule and other small items. $1 preferred although IRCs still appreciated. Also, *see* AWR listings under Costa Rica, Guam, Guatemala, Italy, Russia and USA.

Kenya Broadcasting Corporation, P.O. Box 30456, Harry Thuku Road, Nairobi, Kenya. Phone: +254 (2) 334-567. Fax: +254 (2) 220 675. URL: (RealAudio only) www.africaonline.co.ke/ AfricaOnline/netradio.html. Contact: (general) Henry Makokha, Liaison Office; (administration) Philip Okundi, Managing Director; (technical) Nathan Lamu, Senior Principal Technical Officer; Augustine Kenyanjier Gochui; Lawrence Holnati, Engineering Division; or D. Githua, Assistant Manager Technical Services (Radio). IRC required. Replies irregularly.
MARALAL TRANSMITTING STATION: KBC, P.O. Box 38, Maralal, Kenya. Contact: Ouma Ojwach, Engineer in Charge. Return postage helpful.

KIRIBATI   World Time +12

Radio Kiribati, P.O. Box 78, Bairiki, Tarawa, Republic of Kiribati. Phone: +686 21187. Fax: +686 21096. Contact: (general) Atiota Bauro, Programme Organiser; Mrs. Otiri Laboia; Batiri Bataua, News Editor; or Moia Tetoa, Producer, "Kaoti Ami Iango," a program devoted to listeners views; (administration) Bill Reiher, Manager; (technical) Tooto Kabwebwenibeia, Broadcast Engineer; Martin Ouma Ojwach, Senior Superintendent of Electronics; or T. Fakaofo, Technical Staff. Cassettes of local songs available for purchase. $1 or return postage required for a reply (IRCs not accepted).

KOREA (DPR)   World Time +9

Radio Pyongyang, External Service, Korean Central Broadcasting Station, Pyongyang, Democratic People's Republic of Korea (*not* "North Korea"). Phone: +850 (2) 812-301 or +850 (2) 36-344. Fax: +850 (2) 381 410. Phone and fax numbers valid only in those countries with direct telephone service to North Korea. Free book for German speakers to learn Korean, sundry other publications, pennants, calendars, newspapers, artistic prints and pins. Do not include dutiable items in your envelope. Replies are irregular, as mail from countries not having diplomatic relations with North Korea is sent via circuitous routes and apparently does not always arrive. Indeed, some PASSPORT readers continue to report that mail to Radio Pyongyang in North Korea results in their receiving anti-communist literature from *South* Korea, which indicates that mail interdiction has not ceased. One way around the problem is to add "VIA BEIJING, CHINA" to the address, but replies via this route tend to be slow in coming. Another gambit is to send your correspondence to an associate in a country—such as China, Ukraine or India—having reasonable relations with North Korea, and ask that it be forwarded. If you don't know anyone in these countries, try using the good offices of the following person: Willi Passman, Oberhausener Str. 100, D-45476, Mülheim, Germany. Include 3 IRCs to cover the cost of forwarding.
Regional Korean Central Broadcasting Stations—Not known to

reply, but a long-shot possibility is to try corresponding in Korean to: Korean Central Broadcasting Station, Ministry of Posts and Telecommunications, Chongsung-dong (Moranbong), Pyongyang, Democratic People's Republic of Korea. Fax: +850 (2) 812 301 (valid only in those countries with direct telephone service to North Korea). Contact: Chong Ha-chol, Chairman, Radio and Television Broadcasting Committee.

KOREA (REPUBLIC)   World Time +9

⊡Korean Broadcasting System (KBS), 18 Yoido-dong, Youngdungpo-gu, Seoul, Republic of Korea 150-790. Phone: +82 (2) 781-2410. Fax: +82 (2) 761 2499. E-mail: webmaster@kbsnt.kbs.co.kr. URLs: www.kbs.co.kr/; (RealAudio) www.kbs.co.kr/radiofm/sound1.html.

⊡Radio Korea International
MAIN OFFICE: Overseas Service, Korean Broadcasting System, 18 Yoido-dong, Youngdungpo-gu, Seoul, Republic of Korea 150-790. Phone: (general) +82 (2) 781-3710 or +82 (2) 781-3721; (English Service) +82 (2) 781-3728/29/35; (Russian Service) +82 (2) 781-3714. Fax: +82 (2) 781 3799 or (toll-free fax lines now available for overseas listeners) (United States) 1-888-229-2312; (United Kingdom) 0800-89-5995; (Canada) 1-888-211-5865; (Australia) 1-800-142-644. URLs: www.kbs.co.kr/rki/rki.html; (RealAudio) www.kbs.co.kr/rki/rki.ram. Contact: (general) Chae Hong-Pyo, Director of English Service; Robert Gutnikov, English Service; Ms. Han Hee-joo, Producer/Host, "Shortwave Feedback"; Jong Kyong-Tae, Producer, Russian Service; H.A. Staiger, Deputy Head of German Service; Ms. Lee Hae-Ok, Japanese Service; or Ms. Kim Hae-Young, Producer, Japanese Service; (administration) Kim Sang-Soo, Executive Director; or Choi Jang-Hoon, Director. Free stickers, calendars, *Let's Learn Korean* book and a wide variety of other small souvenirs. *History of Korea* now available via Internet (*see* URL, above) and on CD-ROM (inquire). *WASHINGTON NEWS BUREAU:* National Press Building, Suite 1076, 529 14th Street NW, Washington DC 20045 USA. Phone: +1 (202) 662-7345. Fax: +1 (202) 662 7347.

KUWAIT   World Time +3

Ministry of Information, P.O. Box 193, 13002 Safat, Kuwait. Phone: +965 241-5301. Fax: +965 243 4511. Contact: Sheik Nasir Al-Sabah, Minister of Information.

⊡Radio Kuwait, P.O. Box 397, 13004 Safat, Kuwait. Phone: +965 241-0301 or +965 242-3774. URL: (RealAudio) www.radiokuwait.org/. E-mail: kwtfreq@ncc.moc.kw; or radiokuwait@radiokuwait.org. Fax: +965 241 5498, +965 245 6660 or +965 241 5946. Contact: (general) Manager, External Service; (technical) Nasser M. Al-Saffar, Controller, Frequency Management. Sometimes gives away stickers, calendars, pens or key chains.

KYRGYZSTAN   World Time +5 (+6 midyear)

Kyrgyz Radio, Kyrgyz TV and Radio Center, Prospekt Moloday Gvardil 63, 720 300 Bishkek, Kyrgyzstan. Phone: +7 (3312) 253-404. Fax: +7 (3312) 257 930. Contact: A.I. Vitshkov or E.M. Abdukarimov. Include your e-mail address (if you have one) when writing to the station; although the station is not online, at least one member of the staff, Natalya Moskvina, has access to an e-mail facility and has been known to reply via that route.

LAOS   World Time +7

Lao National Radio, Luang Prabang ("Sathani Withayu Kachaisiang Khueng Luang Prabang"), Luang Prabang, Laos; or B.P. 310, Vientiane, Laos. Return postage required (IRCs not accepted). Replies slowly and very rarely. Best bet is to write in Laotian or French directly to Luang Prabang, where the transmitter is located.

Lao National Radio, Vientiane, Laotian National Radio and Television, B.P. 310, Vientiane, Laos. Contact: Khoun Sounantha, Manager-in-Charge; Bounthan Inthasai, Director General; Mrs. Vinachine, English/French Sections; Ms. Mativarn Simanithone, Deputy Head, English Section; or Miss Chanthery Vichitsavanh, Announcer, English Section who says, "It would be good if you send your letter unregistered, because I find it difficult to get all letters by myself at the post. Please use my name, and 'Lao National Radio, P.O. Box 310, Vientiane, Laos P.D.R.' It will go directly to me." Sometimes includes a program schedule and Laotian stamps when replying. The external service of this station tends to be erratic.

LATVIA   World Time +2 (+3 midyear)

⊡Latvijas Radio, 8 Doma laukums, LV-1505 Riga, Latvia. Phone: (general) +371 720-6722; (Director General) +371 720-6747; (Program Director) +371 720-6750; (International Relations) +371 720-6757. Fax: (general) +371 720 6709; (International Relations) +371 782 0216; (Director General) +371 720 6709. E-mail: radio@radio.org.lv. URL: (includes RealAudio) www.radio.org.lv/. Contact: (general) Aivars Ginters, International Relations; or Mrs. Dârija Ju´keviêa, Deputy General Director & Program Manager; (administration) Dzintris Kolâts, Director General; (technical) Aigars Semevics, Technical Director. Replies to nontechnical correspondence in Latvian. Does not issue verification replies.

Radio Latvia, P.O. Box 266, LV-1098 Riga, Latvia. Contact: (general) Ms. Fogita Cimcus, Chief Editor, English. Free stickers and pennants. Unlike Latvijas Radio, preceding, Radio Latvia verifies regularly via the Chief Editor.

LEBANON   World Time +2 (+3 midyear)

High Adventure Radio (Voice of Hope), P.O. Box 3379, Limassol, Cyprus. E-mail: voh@zenon.logos.cy.net; voh@broadcast.net. URL: www.highadventure.org/voh_midd.html. Contact: Gary Hull, Station Manager; or Isaac Gronberg, Director. Free stickers. IRC requested.May send 214 page book *Voice of Hope* via USA headquarters (*see*). Due to soaring electricity bills, station has reduced transmitter powers. Also, *see* KVOH—Voice of Hope/High Adventure Ministries, USA.

⊡Voice of Charity, Rue Fouad Chéhab, B.P. 850, Jounieh, Lebanon. Phone: +961 (9) 914-901 or +961 (9) 918-090. E-mail: radiocharity@opuslibani.org.lb. URL: (includes RealAudio) www.radiocharity.org.lb/. Contact: Frère Elie Nakhoul, Managing Director. Program aired via Vatican Radio and founded by the Order of the Lebanese Missionaries. Basically, a Lebanese Christian educational radio program.

Voice of Lebanon, La Voix du Liban, B.P. 165271, Al-Ashrafiyah, Beirut, Lebanon. Phone: +961 (1) 423-189 or Phone/fax: +961 (1) 323-458. Fax: +961 (1) 347 489. Contact: M. Fuad Hamdan, Directeur. $1 required. Replies occasionally to correspondence in French or Arabic. Operated by the Phalangist organization.

Voice of Orthodoxy—*see* Belarus.

Former ELWA staff at the studios in Monrovia, Liberia. For more on ELWA's status, see the feature article on page eight. SIM

LESOTHO   World Time +2

Radio Lesotho, P.O. Box 552, Maseru 100, Lesotho. Phone: +266 323-561. Fax: +266 310 003. Contact: (general) Mrs. Florence Lesenya, Controller of Programmes; or Sekhonyana Motlohi, Producer, "What Do Listeners Say?"; (head of administration) Ms. Mpine Tente, Director; (technical) L. Monnapula, Acting Chief Engineer; or Peter L. Moepi, Studio Engineer. Return postage necessary.

LIBERIA   World Time exactly

NOTE: Mail sent to Liberia may be returned as undeliverable.
ELBC, Liberian Broadcasting System, P.O. Box 10-594, 1000 Monrovia 10, Liberia. Phone: +231 22-4984 or +231 22-2758. Contact: Jesse B. Karnley, Director General, Broadcasting; or James Morlu, Deputy Director, Broadcasting. Operates on behalf of the Economic Community of West African States' peacekeeping force, ECOMOG.
Radio Liberia International, Liberian Communications Network/KISS, P.O. Box 1103, 1000 Monrovia 10, Liberia. Phone: +231 22-6963 or +231 22-7593. Fax: (during working hours) +231 22 6003. Contact: Issac P. Davis, Engineer-in-Charge/QSL Coordinator. $5 required for QSL card.
Star Radio, Sekou Toure Avenue, Mamba Point, Monrovia, Liberia. Phone: +231 226-820, +231 226-176 or +231 227-390. Fax: +231 227 360. E-mail: libe@atge.automail.com. URL: (Star Radio Daily News) www.hirondelle.org/. Contact: George Bennett, Chief. Star radio is staffed by Liberian journalists and managed by the Swiss NGO, Fondation Hirondelle, with financing from the U.S. Agency for International Developement through the International Foundation for Election Systems. Fondation Hirondelle can be contacted at: 3 Rue Traversière, CH 1018-Lausanne, Switzerland; (phone) +41 (21) 647-2805; (fax) +41 (21) 647 4469; (e-mail) info@hirondelle.org.

LIBYA   World Time +1 (+2 midyear)

Radio Jamahiriya
MAIN OFFICE, EXTERNAL: P.O. Box 4677 (or P.O. Box 4396), Tripoli, Libya. Contact: R. Cachia. Arabic preferred.
MALTA OFFICE: European Branch Office, P.O. Box 17, Hamrun, Malta. This office, which is still be in operation, has historically replied more consistently than has the main office.
Libyan Jamahiriyah Broadcasting (domestic service), Box 9333, Soug al Jama, Tripoli, Libya. Phone: +218 (21) 603-191/5.

LITHUANIA   World Time +2 (+3 midyear)

Lietuvos Radijo ir Televizijos Centras (LRTC), Sausio 13-osios 10, LT-2044 Vilnius, Lithuania. Phone: +370 (2) 459-397. Fax: +370 (2) 451 738.
This organization operates the transmitters used by Lithuanian Radio.
⊡ Lithuanian Radio
STATION: Lietuvos Radijas, Konarskio 49, LT-2674 Vilnius, Lithuania. Phone: (general) +370 (2) 633-182; (Grumadiene) +370 (2) 634-471; (Vilciauskas) +370 (2) 233-503. Fax: +370 (2) 263 282. E-mail: format is initial.lastname@rtv.lrtv.ot.lt, so to contact, say, Juozas Algirdas Vilciauskas, it would be jvilciauskas@rtv.lrtv.ot.lt. URLs: (RealAudio, including Radio Vilnius) www.lrtv.lt/lr.htm; www3.omnitel.net/virtual/lrtv.lt/lr.htm. Contact: (general) Mrs. Laima Grumadiene, Managing Director; or Mrs. Kazimiera Mazgeliene, Programme Director; (technical) Juozas Algirdas Vilciauskas, Technical Director.
ADMINISTRATION: Lietuvos Nacionalinis Radijas ir Televizija (LNRT), Konarskio 49, LT-2674 Vilnius, Lithuania. Phone: +370 (2) 263-383. Fax: +370 (2) 263 282. E-mail: (Ilginis) ailginis@rtv.lrtv.ot.lt. URLs: www.lrtv.lt/lrtv.htm; www3.omnitel.net/virtual/lrtv.lt.lrtv.htm. Contact: Arvydas Ilginis, Director General.

Radio Vilnius, Lietuvos Radijas, Konarskio 49, LT-2674 Vilnius, Lithuania. Phone: +370 (2) 633-182. Fax: +370 (2) 263 282. E-mail: ravil@rtv.lrtv.ot.lt. URL: see Lithuanian Radio, above. Contact: Ms. Rasa Lukaite, "Letterbox"; Audrius Braukyla, Editor-in-Chief; or Ilonia Rukiene, Head of English Department. Free stickers, pennants, Lithuanian stamps and other souvenirs. Transmissions to North America are via the facilities of Deutsche Telekom in Germany (see).

MADAGASCAR   World Time +3

Adventist World Radio, the Voice of Hope—see USA and Italy. Reception reports are best sent to the Italian office.
Radio Madagasikara, B.P. 442, Antananarivo 101, Madagascar. Contact: Mlle. Rakotonirina Soa Herimanitia, Secrétaire de Direction, a young lady who collects stamps; Mamy Rafenomanantsoa, Directeur; or J.J. Rakotonirina. $1 required, and enclosing used stamps from various countries may help. Tape recordings accepted. Replies very rarely and slowly, preferably to friendly philatelist gentlemen who correspond in French.
Radio Nederland Wereldomroep—Madagascar Relay, B.P. 404, Antananarivo, Madagascar. Contact: (technical) Rahamefy Eddy, Technische Dienst.; or J.A. Ratobimiarana, Chief Engineer. Nontechnical correspondence should be sent to Radio Nederland Wereldomreop in Holland (see).

MALAWI   World Time +2

Malawi Broadcasting Corporation, P.O. Box 30133, Chichiri, Blantyre 3, Malawi. Phone: +265 671-222. Fax: +265 671 353 or +265 671 257. Contact: (general) Sam Gunde, Acting Director General; Joseph Mndeke, Director of Programmes; E.K. Lungu; P. Chinseu, Engineering Consultant; J.O. Mndeke; or T.J. Sineta; (technical) Joseph Chikagwa, Director of Engineering. Return postage or $1 helpful.

MALAYSIA   World Time +8

Asia-Pacific Broadcasting Union, P.O. Box 1164, Pejabat Pos Jalan Pantai Bahru, 59700 Kuala Lumpur, Malaysia; or (street address) 2nd Floor, Bangunan IPTAR, Angkasapuri, 50614 Kuala Lumpur, Malaysia. Phone: +60 (3) 282-3592, +60 (3) 282-2480 or +60 (3) 282-3108. Fax: +60 (3) 282 5292. E-mail: sg@abu.org.my. URL: www.abu.org.my/abu/. Contact: Dato' Jaafar Kamin, President; or Hugh Leonard, Secretary-General.
Radio Malaysia, Kuala Lumpur
MAIN OFFICE: RTM, Angkasapuri, Bukit Putra, 50614 Kuala Lumpur, Peninsular Malaysia, Malaysia. Phone: +60 (3) 282-5333 or +60 (3) 282-4976. Fax: +60 (3) 282 4735, +60 (3) 282 5103 or +60 (3) 282 5859. E-mail: sabariah@rtm.net.my. URL: (general) www.asiaconnect.com.my/rtm-net/; (RealAudio, live) www.asiaconnect.com.my/rtm-net/live/; (RealAudio, archives) www.asiaconnect.com.my/rtm-net/online/index.html. Contact (general) Madzhi Johari, Director of Radio; (technical) Ms. Aminah Din, Deputy Director Engineering; Abdullah Bin Shahadan, Engineer, Transmission & Monitoring; or Ong Poh, Chief Engineer. May sell T-shirts and key chains. Return postage required.
TRANSMISSION OFFICE: Controller of Engineering, Department of Broadcasting (RTM), 43009 Kajang, Selangor Darul Ehsan, Malaysia. Contact: Jeffrey Looi.
Radio Malaysia Kota Kinabalu, RTM, 88614 Kota Kinabalu,

Sabah, Malaysia. Contact: Benedict Janil, Director of Broadcasting; Hasbullah Latiff; or Mrs. Angrick Saguman. Registering your letter may help. $1 or return postage required.
Radio Malaysia Sarawak (Kuching), RTM, Broadcasting House, Jalan P. Ramlee, 93614 Kuching, Sarawak, Malaysia. Phone: +60 (82) 248-422. Fax: +60 (82) 241 914. Contact: (general) Tuan Haji Ahmad Shafiee Haji Yaman, Director of Broadcasting; or Human Resources Development; (technical, but also nontechnical) Colin A. Minoi, Technical Correspondence; (technical) Kho Kwang Khoon, Deputy Director of Engineering. Return postage helpful.
Radio Malaysia Sarawak (Miri), RTM, Miri, Sarawak, Malaysia. Contact: Clement Stia. $1 or return postage helpful.
Radio Malaysia Sarawak (Sibu), RTM, Jabatan Penyiaran, Bangunan Penyiaran, 96009 Sibu, Sarawak, Malaysia. Contact: Clement Stia, Divisional Controller, Broadcasting Department. $1 or return postage required. Replies irregularly and slowly.
Voice of Islam—Program of the Voice of Malaysia (see), below.
Voice of Malaysia, Suara Malaysia, Wisma Radio, P.O. Box 11272-KL, 50740 Angkasapuri, Kuala Lumpur, Malaysia. Phone: +60 (3) 282-5333. Fax: +60 (3) 282 5859. Contact: (general) Mrs. Mahani bte Ujang, Supervisor, English Service; Hajjah Wan Chuk Othman, English Service; (administration) Santokh Singh Gill, Director; or Mrs. Adilan bte Omar, Assistant Director; (technical) Lin Chew, Director of Engineering. Free calendars and stickers. Two IRCs or return postage helpful. Replies slowly and irregularly.

MALDIVES   World Time +5

Voice of Maldives (when reactivated), Ministry of Information, Arts & Culture, Moonlight Higun, Malé 20-06, Republic of Maldives. Phone: (administration & secretaries) +960 321-642; (Director General) +960 322-577; (Director of Programs) +960 322-746; (Duty Officer) +960 322-841; (programme section) +960 322-842; (studio 1) +960 325-151; (studio 2) +960 323-416; (newsroom) +960 322-253, +960 324-506 or + 960 324-507; (office assistant/budget secretary) +960 320-508; (FM Studio) +960 314-217; (technical, office) +960 322-444 or +960 320-941; (residence) +960 323-211. Fax: +960 328 357 or +960 325 371. E-mail: informat@dhivehinet.net.mv. Contact: Maizan Ahmed Manik, Director General-Engineering. Long inactive on the world bands, this station is expected to resume shortwave broadcasts in the near future with a newly installed 10 kilowatt transmitter on the island of Mafushi.

MALI   World Time exactly

Radiodiffusion Télévision Malienne, B.P. 171, Bamako, Mali. Phone: +223 22-47-27. Fax: +223 22 42 05. Contact: Karamoko Issiaka Daman, Directeur des Programmes; (administration) Abdoulaye Sidibe, Directeur General. $1 or IRC helpful. Replies slowly and irregularly to correspondence in French. English is accepted.

MALTA   World Time +1 (+2 midyear)

Voice of the Mediterranean (Radio Melita), St Francis Ravelin, Floriana, VLT 15, Malta; or P.O. Box 143, Valetta, CMR 01, Malta. Phone: +356 220-950, +356 240-421 or +356 248-080. Fax: +356 241 501. E-mail: vomradio@dream.vol.net.mt. URL: http://vol.net.mt/com/vom/. Contact: (administration)

Richard Vella Laurenti, Managing Director; (German Service and listener contact) Ingrid Huettmann. Letters and reception reports welcomed in English, French, German or Arabic.

MAURITANIA World Time exactly

Office de Radiodiffusion-Télévision de Mauritanie, B.P. 200, Nouakchott, Mauritania. Fax: +222 (2) 51264. Contact: Madame Amir Feu; Lemrabott Boukhary; Madame Fatimetou Fall Dite Ami, Secretaire de Direction; or Mr. Hane Abou. Return postage or $1 required. Rarely replies.

MAURITIUS World Time +4

Mauritius Broadcasting Corporation (if reactivated), P.O. Box 48, Curepipe, Mauritius; (physical location) 1, Louis Pasteur Street, Forest Side, Mauritius. Phone: +230 675-5001. Fax: +230 675 7332. E-mail: (general) mbc@bow.intnet.mu; (engineering) mbceng@bow.intnet.mu. URL: www.mbc-tv.com/. Contact: (general) Trilock Dwarka, Director General; or Mrs. Marie Michele Etienne, Officer in Charge of Programmes; (technical) Armoodalingum Pather, Chief Engineer; or Ashok Kariman, Deputy Chief Engineer. Currently inactive on world band, but hopes to reactivate transmissions eventually on 4855 and 9710 kHz.

MEXICO World Time –6 (–5 midyear) Central, including D.F.; –7 (–6 midyear) Mountain; –8 (–7 midyear) Pacific

Candela FM—XEQM (when operating), Apartado Postal 217, 97001-Mérida, YUC, Mexico. Phone: +52 (99) 236-155. Fax: +52 (99) 280 680. Contact: Lic. Bernardo Laris Rodríguez, Director General del Grupo RASA Mérida. Replies irregularly to correspondence in Spanish.

La Hora Exacta—XEQK (when operating), Real de Mayorazgo 83, Barrio de Xoco, 03330-México 13, D.F., Mexico. Phone: +52 (5) 628-1731, +52 (5) 628-1700 Ext. 1648 or 1659. Fax: +52 (5) 604-8292. URL: www.telecommex.com/imer/xeqk.html. Contact: Lic. Santiago Ibarra Ferrer, Gerente.

La Jarocha—XEFT (when operating), Apartado Postal 21, 91701-Veracruz, VER., Mexico. Phone: +52 (29) 322-250. Contact: C.P. Miguel Rodríguez Sáez, Sub-Director; or Lic. Juan de Dios Rodríguez Díaz, Director. Free tourist guide to Veracruz. Return postage, IRC or $1 probably helpful. Likely to reply to correspondence in Spanish.

Radio Educación—XEPPM, Apartado Postal 21-940, 04021-México 21, D.F., Mexico. Phone: (general) +52 (5) 559-6169. Fax: +52 (5) 575 6566. Contact: (general) Lic. Susana E. Mejía Vázquez, Jefe del Dept. de Audiencia y Evaluación; or María Teresa Moya Malfavón, Directora de Producción y Planeación; (administration) Luis Ernesto Pi Orozco, Director General; (technical) Ing. Gustavo Carreño López, Subdirector, Dpto. Técnico. Free stickers, calendars, station photo and a copy of a local publication, *Audio Tinta Boletín Informativo*. Return postage or $1 required. Replies, sometimes slowly, to correspondence in English, Spanish, Italian or French.

Radio Huayacocotla—XEJN
STATION ADDRESS: "Radio Huaya," Dom. Gutiérrez Najera s/n, Apartado Postal 13, 92600-Huayacocotla, VER, Mexico. Phone: +52 (775) 80067. Fax: +52 (775) 80178. E-mail: framos@uibero.uia.mx. URLs: http://mixcoac.uia.mx/Radio/huarad.html; http://148.201.1.19/sjmex/ap/huarad.html. Contact: Antonio Vázquez Quezada, Coordinador. Return

postage or $1 helpful. Replies irregularly to correspondence in Spanish.

Radio Linares—XEUJ (if reactivated), Apartado Postal 62, 67001-Linares, N.L., Mexico. Contact: (general) Marcelo Becerra González, Director General; or Joel Becerra Pecina; (technical) Ing. Gustavo Martínez de la Cruz. Free stickers, pennants and Mexican tourist cards. Replies irregularly to correspondence in Spanish, English or French.

Radio México Internacional—XERMX, Instituto Méxicano de la Radio, Apartado Postal 21-300, 04021-México 21, D.F., Mexico. Phone: +52 (5) 604-7846, +52 (5) 628-1720. Fax: +52 (5) 604 8292. E-mail: imerte04@telecommex.com. URL: www.telecommex.com/imer/rmi.html. Contact: Lic. Martín Rizo Gavira, Gerente; or Julián Santiago, Host, "Mailbag." Free stickers, post cards and stamps. Welcomes correspondence, including inquiries about Mexico, in Spanish, English, French and Italian. $1 helpful. A bilingual reception report form can be downloaded and printed from the Website.
SAN FRANCISCO OFFICE, SCHEDULES: 2654 17th Avenue, San Francisco CA 94116 USA. Phone: +1 (415) 564-9968. Contact: George Poppin. This address, a volunteer office, only provides Radio México International schedules to listeners. All other correspondence should be sent directly to the main office in México City.

Radio Mil—XEOI, NRM, Avda. Insurgentes Sur 1870, Col. Florida, 01030-México 20 D.F., Mexico; or Apartado Postal 21-1000, 04021-México 21, D.F., Mexico (this address for reception reports on the station's shortwave broadcasts). Phone: (station) +52 (5) 662-1000 or +52 (5) 662-1100; (Núcleo Radio Mil network) +52 (5) 662-6060, +52 (5) 663-0739 or +52 (5) 663 0590. Fax: (station) +52 (5) 662 0974; (Núcleo Radio Mil network) +52 (5) 662 0979. E-mail: info@nrm.com.mx. URL: www.nrm.com.mx/radiomil.html. Contact: Lic. Guillermo D. Salas Vargas, Vicepresidente Ejecutivo del Núcleo Radio Mil; Srta. Cristina Stivalet, Gerente; or Zoila Quintanar Flores. Free stickers. $1 or return postage required.

Radio Transcontinental de América—XERTA, Apartado Postal 653, 06002 México 1, D.F., Mexico; or Torre "Latinoamericana" (Desp. 3706), 06007-México 1, D.F., Mexico. Phone: +52 (5) 510-9896. Fax: +52 (5) 510 3326. Contact: Roberto Najera Martínez, Presidente de Radio Transcontinental de América.

Radio Universidad Autónoma de México (UNAM)—XEYU, Adolfo Prieto 133, Col. del Valle, 03100-México 12, D.F., Mexico. Phone: +52 (5) 523-2633. E-mail: radiounam@www.unam.mx. URL: (includes RealAudio) www.unam.mx/radiounam/. Contact: Lic. Malena Mijares Fernández, Directora General de Radio UNAM. Free tourist literature and stickers. $1 or return postage required. Replies irregularly to correspondence in Spanish.

Radio Universidad de Sonora—XEUDS (if reactivated), Apartado Postal 1817, 83002-Hermosillo, SON, Mexico. Phone: +52 (62) 133-597. E-mail: pgonzalz@guaymas.uson.mx. Contact: Lic. Patricia González Lozano, Directora de Comunicación Social.

Radio XEWW, La Voz de la América Latina (on the rare occasions when operating), Czda. De Tlalpan 3000, Col. Espartaco, 04870-México 22, D.F., Mexico. Phone: +52 (5) 327-2000. URL: www.televisa.com.mx/radio/. Contact: (general) Lic. Ricardo Rocha Reynaga, Presidente del Grupo Radiópolis; Sra. Martha Sandoval; (technical) Ing. Miguel Angel Barrientos, Director Técnico de Plantas Transmisoras. Free pennants. $1, IRC or return postage required. When operating, replies fairly regularly to correspondence in Spanish.

MOLDOVA   World Time +2 (+3 midyear)

Radio Moldova International
NOTE: As direct mail service to Moldova is often nonexistent, the best way to contact Radio Moldova International is via Rumen Pankov, P.O. Box 199, 1000 Sofia-C, Bulgaria, enclosing 5 IRCs or $2.
GENERAL CORRESPONDENCE: If direct mail service is available from your location, try Maison de la Radio, Miorița str. 1, 277028 Chişinău, Moldova. Phone: +373 (2) 721-792, + (373) (2) 723-369, +373 (2) 723-379 or +373 (2) 723-385. Fax: +373 (2) 723 329 or +373 (2) 723 307. Contact: Constantin Marin, International Editor-in-Chief; Alexandru Dorogan, General Director of Radio Broadcasting; Constantin Rotaru, Director General; Daniel Lacky, Editor, English Service; Veleriu Vasilica, Head of English Department; or Raisa Gonciar. Transmits via facilities of Radio România International. Free stickers and calendars.
RECEPTION REPORTS: Should direct mail service be available from your location, try RMI-Monitoring Action, P.O. Box 9972, 277070 Chişinău-70, Moldova.

MONACO   World Time +1 (+2 midyear)

Radio Monte-Carlo
MAIN OFFICE: 16 Boulevard Princesse Charlotte, MC-98080 Monaco Cedex, Monaco. Phone: +377 (93) 15-16-17. Fax: +377 (93) 15 16 30 or +377 (93) 15 94 48. E-mail: via URL. URL: www.twr.org/monte.htm. Contact: Jacques Louret; Bernard Poizat, Service Diffusion; or Caroline Wilson, Director of Communication. Free stickers. This station is on world band only with its Arabic Service.
MAIN PARIS OFFICE, NONTECHNICAL: 12 rue Magellan, F-75008 Paris, France. Phone: +33 (1) 40-69-88-00. Fax: +33 (1) 40 69 88 55 or +33 (1) 45 00 92 45.
PARIS OFFICE (ARABIC SERVICE): 78 Avenue Raymond Poincairé, F-75008 Paris, France. Phone: +33 (1) 45-01-53-30.
CYPRUS OFFICE (ARABIC SERVICE)—see Cyprus.

Trans World Radio
STATION: B.P. 349, MC-98007 Monte-Carlo, Monaco-Cedex. Phone: +377 (92) 16-56-00. Fax: +377 (92) 16 56 01. URL (transmission schedule): (Monte-Carlo) www.gospelcom.net/twr/t_europe.htm. Contact: (general) Mrs. Jeanne Olson; (administration) Richard Olson, Station Manager; (technical) Bernhard Schraut, Frequency Coordinator. Free paper pennant. IRC or $1 helpful. Also, *see* USA.
GERMAN OFFICE: Evangeliums-Rundfunk, Postfach 1444, D-35573 Wetzlar, Germany. Phone: +49 (6441) 957-0. Fax: +49 (6441) 957-120. E-mail: erf@erf.de; or siemens@arf.de. URL: (includes RealAudio) www.erf.de. Contact: Jürgen Werth, Direktor.
HOLLAND OFFICE, NONTECHNICAL: Postbus 176, NL-3780 BD Voorthuizen, Holland. Phone: +31 (0) 34-29-27-27. Fax: +31 (0) 34 29 67 27. Contact: Beate Kiebel, Manager Broadcast Department; or Felix Widmer.
VIENNA OFFICE, TECHNICAL: Postfach 141, A-1235 Vienna, Austria. Phone: +43 (1) 863-1233 or +43 (1) 863-1247. Fax: +43 (1) 863 1220. E-mail: (Menzel) 100615.1511@compuserve.com; (Schraut) eurofreq@twr.org; bschraut@twr.org; or 101513.2330@compuserve.com; (Roswell) eurofreq@twr.org; or croswell@twr.org. Contact: Helmut Menzel, Director of Engineering; Bernhard Schraut, Frequency Coordinator; or Charles K. Roswell, Frequency Coordinator.

SWISS OFFICE: Evangelium in Radio und Fernsehen, Witzbergstrasse 23, CH-8330 Pfäffikon ZH, Switzerland. Phone: +41 (951) 0500. Fax: +41 (951) 0540. E-mail: erf@erf.ch. URL: www.erf.ch/.

MONGOLIA   World Time +8

Mongolian Radio (Mailing address same as Voice of Mongolia, *see* below). Phone: (administration) +976 (1) 23520 or +976 (1) 28978; (correspondence) +976 (1) 29766. E-mail: radiomongolia@magicnet.mn.
Voice of Mongolia, C.P.O. Box 365, Ulaanbaatar 13, Mongolia. Phone: +976 (1) 321-624 or (English Section) +976 (1) 327-900. Fax: +976 (1) 323 096 or (English Section) +976 (1) 327 234. E-mail: (general) radiomongolia@magicnet.mn; or (International Relations Office) mrtv@magicnet.mn. URL: www.mol.mn/mrtv/. Contact: (general) Mrs. Narantuya, Chief of Foreign Service; D. Batbayar, Mail Editor, English Department; N. Tuya, Head of English Department; Dr. Mark Ostrowski, Consultant, MRTV International Relations Department; or Ms. Tsegmid Burmaa, Japanese Department; (administration) Ch. Surenjav, Director; (technical) Ing. Ganhuu, Chief of Technical Department. Correpondence should be directed to the relevant language section and 2 IRCs or 1$ appreciated. Free pennants, postcards, newspapers and Mongolian stamps. Expects to add audio to its website sometime in 1999.

MOROCCO   World Time exactly

▣Radio Medi Un
MAIN OFFICE: B.P. 2055, Tanger, Morocco (physical location: 3, rue Emsallah, 90000 Tanger, Morocco). Phone/fax: +212 (9) 936-363 or +212 (9) 935-755. E-mail: med1@medi1.com. URL: (includes RealAudio) www.medi1.com. Contact: J. Dryk, Responsable Haute Fréquence. Two IRCs helpful. Free stickers. Correspondence in French preferred.
PARIS BUREAU, NONTECHNICAL: 78 Avenue Raymond Poincaré, F-75016 Paris, France. Phone: +33 (1) 45-01-53-30. Correspondence in French preferred.
RTV Marocaine, RTM, 1 rue al-Brihi, Rabat, Morocco. Phone: +212 (7) 70-17-40. Fax +212 (7) 70 32 08. Contact: (nontechnical and technical) Mrs. Naaman Khadija, Ingénieur d'Etat en Télécommunication; (technical) Tanone Mohammed Jamaledine, Technical Director; Hammouda Mohamed, Engineer; or N. Read. Correspondence welcomed in English, French, Arabic or Berber.
Voice of America/IBB—Morocco Relay Station, Briech. Phone: (office) +212 (9) 93-24-81; (transmitter) +212 (9) 93-22-00. Fax: +212 (9) 93 55 71. Contact: Wilfred Cooper, Manager. These numbers for urgent technical matters only. Otherwise, does not welcome direct correspondence; *see* USA for acceptable VOA Washington address and related information.

MOZAMBIQUE   World Time +2

Rádio Maputo (when active)—*see* Radio Moçambique, below.
Rádio Moçambique (if operating), C.P. 2000, Maputo, Mozambique. Phone: +258 (1) 421-814, +258 (1) 429-826 or +258 (1) 429-836. Fax: +258 (1) 421 816. E-mail: (Iain Christie) christie@christie.uem.mz. Contact: (general) João B. de Sousa,

Administrador e Diretor Comercial; Daude Amade, Diretor de Programas; Iain Patrick Christie, Director of External Service; Orlanda Mendes, Produtor, "Linha Direta"; (technical) Eduardo Rufino de Matos, Diretor Técnico. Free medallions and pens. Cassettes featuring local music $15. Return postage, $1 or 2 IRCs required. Replies to correspondence in Portuguese or English. Means are being studied by which Rádio Moçambique, which the Mozambique prime minister says "is going through difficult times," may be properly financed and thus remain on the air. However, the station has recently reported a loss of its shortwave transmitting capabilities. Thieves have continually stolen copper wire at the transmitter station. It is quite unlikely the wire will be replaced due to the high cost involved. Another problem is that the shortwave transmitters are very old and finding spare parts for them is becoming increasingly difficult. Thus, this station appears to be planning a major transformation of its foreign broadcasting policy. It plans to target South Africa only, via medium wave and FM.

MYANMAR (BURMA)   World Time +6:30

Radio Myanmar
STATION: GPO Box 1432, Yangon-11181, Myanmar; or Pyay Road, Yangon-11041, Myanmar. Phone: +95 (1) 31-355. Fax: +95 (1) 30 211. Contact: Ko Ko Htway, Director of Radio.

NAMIBIA   World Time +2 (+1 midyear)

Radio Namibia/Namibian Broadcasting Corporation, P.O. Box 321, Windhoek 9000, Namibia. Phone: +264 (61) 291-3111. Fax: +264 (61) 217 760. URL: www.oneworld.org/cba/nbc.htm. Contact: P. Schachtschneider, Manager, Transmitter Maintenance; Joe Duwe, Chief Technician. Free stickers.

Old monk in Nepal. Nepal is the birthplace of Buddhism, as told starting on page 26.   M. Guha

NEPAL   World Time +5:45

Radio Nepal, P.O. Box 634, Singha Durbar, Kathmandu, Nepal. Phone: (general) +977 (1) 223-910; (engineering) +977 (1) 225-467. Fax: +977 (1) 221 952. E-mail: rne@rne.wlink.com.np; radio@rne.wlink.com.np; (engineering) radio@engg.wlink.com.np. URLs: (include RealAudio in English and Nepali) www.catmando.com/news/radio-nepal/; www.catmando.com/radio-nepal/. Contact: (general) M.P. Acharya, Executive Director; M.P. Adhikari, Deputy Executive Director; Jayanti Rajbhandari, Director - Programming; or S.K. Pant, Producer, "Listener's Mail"; (technical) Ram Sharan Kharki, Director - Engineering. 3 IRCs necessary, but station urges that neither mint stamps nor cash be enclosed, as this invites theft by Nepalese postal employees.

NETHERLANDS ANTILLES   World Time –4

Radio Nederland Wereldomroep—Bonaire Relay, P.O. Box 45, Kralendijk, Netherlands Antilles. Nontechnical correspondence should be sent to Radio Nederland Wereldomreop in Holland (see).

NEW ZEALAND   World Time +13 (+12 midyear)

Radio New Zealand International (Te Reo Irirangi O Aotearoa, O Te Moana-nui-a-kiwa), P.O. Box 123, Wellington, New Zealand. Phone: +64 (4) 474-1437. Fax: +64 (4) 474 1433 or +64 (4) 474 1886. E-mail: (general) info@rnzi.com; (technical, Adrian Sainsbury) adrian@actrix.gen.nz. URLs: (general) www.rnzi.com; (RealAudio) www.wrn.org/stations/rnzi.html; www.audionet.co.nz/ranz.html. Contact: Florence de Ruiter, Listener Mail; Myra Oh, Producer, "Mailbox"; or Walter Zweifel, News Editor; (administration) Ms. Linden Clark, Manager; (technical) Adrian Sainsbury, Frequency Manager. Free stickers, schedule/flyer about station, map of New Zealand and tourist literature available. English/Maori T-shirts for US$20; Sweatshirts $40; interesting variety of CDs, as well as music cassettes and spoken programs, in Domestic "Replay Radio" catalog (VISA/MC). Three IRCs for verification, one IRC for schedule/catalog. As of August 1998, Radio New Zealand International has been subject to reduced funding from the New Zealand Ministry of Foreign Affairs. This has resulted in staff and programming reductions.
Radio Reading Service—ZLXA, P.O. Box 360, Levin 5500, New Zealand. Phone: +64 (6) 368-2229. Fax: +64 (6) 368 7290. E-mail: nzrpd@xtra.co.nz; or alittle@xtra.co.nz. Contact: (general) Ash Bell, Manager/Station Director; (administration) Allen J. Little, Executive President. Operated by volunteers 24 hours a day, seven days a week. Station is owned by the "New Zealand Radio for the Print Disabled Inc." Free brochure, postcards and stickers. $1, return postage or 3 IRCs appreciated.

NICARAGUA   World Time –6

Radio Miskut, Barrio Pancasan, Puerto Cabezas, R.A.A.N., Nicaragua. Phone: +505 (282) 2443. Fax: +505 (267) 3032. Contact: Evaristo Mercado Pérez, Director de Operación y de Programas; or Abigail Zuniga Fagoth. T-shirts $10, and *Resumen Mensual del Gobierno y Consejo Regional* and *Revista Informativa Detallada de las Gestiones y Logros* $10 per copy. Station has upgraded to a new shortwave transmitter and is currently improving its shortwave antenna. Replies slowly and irregularly to correspondence in English and Spanish. $2 helpful, as is registering your letter.

NIGER World Time +1

La Voix du Sahel, O.R.T.N., B.P. 361, Niamey, Niger. Fax: +227 72 35 48. Contact: (general) Adamou Oumarou; Issaka Mamadou; Zakari Saley; Souley Boubacou; or Mounkaïla Inazadan, Producer, "Inter-Jeunes Variétés"; (administration) Oumar Tiello, Directeur; (technical) Afo Sourou Victor. $1 helpful. Correspondence in French preferred. Correspondence by males with this station may result in requests for certain unusual types of magazines and photographs.

NIGERIA World Time +1

WARNING—MAIL THEFT: For the time being, correspondence from abroad to Nigerian addresses has a relatively high probability of being stolen.

WARNING—CONFIDENCE ARTISTS: For years, now, correspondence with Nigerian stations has sometimes resulted in letters from highly skilled "pen pal" confidence artists. These typically offer to send you large sums of money, if you will provide details of your bank account or similar information (after which they clean out your account). Other scams are disguised as tempting business proposals; or requests for money, free electronic or other products, publications or immigration sponsorship. Persons thus approached should contact their country's diplomatic offices. For example, Americans should contact the Diplomatic Security Section of the Department of State [phone +1 (202) 647-4000], or an American embassy or consulate.

Radio Nigeria—Enugu, P.M.B. 1051, Enugu (Anambra), Nigeria. Contact: Louis Nnamuchi, Assistant Director Technical Services. Two IRCs, return postage or $1 required. Replies slowly.

Radio Nigeria—Ibadan, Broadcasting House, P.M.B. 5003, Ibadan, Oyo State, Nigeria. Fax: +234 (22) 413 930. Contact: V.A. Kalejaiye, Technical Services Department; Rev. Olukunle Ajani, Executive Director; Nike Adegoke, Executive Director; or Dare Folarin, Principal Public Affairs Officer. $1 or return postage required. Replies slowly.

Radio Nigeria—Kaduna, P.O. Box 250, Kaduna (Kaduna), Nigeria. Contact: Yusuf Garba, Ahmed Abdullahi, or Johnson D. Allen. $1 or return postage required. Replies slowly.

Radio Nigeria—Lagos, P.M.B. 12504, Ikoyi, Lagos, Nigeria. Contact: Willie Egbe, Assistant Director for Programmes; Babatunde Olalekan Raji, Monitoring Unit. Two IRCs or return postage helpful. Replies slowly and irregularly.

Voice of Nigeria, P.M.B. 40003 Falomo Post Office, Ikoyi, Lagos, Nigeria. Phone: +234 (1) 269-3078/3245/3075/. Fax: +234 (1) 269 1944. Contact: (general) Alhaji Lawal Yusef Saulawa, Director of Programming; Mrs. Stella Bassey, Deputy Director Programmes; Alhaji Mohammed Okorejior, Acting Director News; or Livy Iwok, Editor; (administration) Alhaji Mallam Yaya Abubakar, Director General; Abubakar Jijiwa, Chairman; or Dr. Walter Ofonagoro, Minister of Information; (technical) J.O. Kurunmi, Deputy Director Engineering Services; O.I. Odumsi, Acting Director, Engineering; or G.C. Ugwa, Director Engineering. Replies from station tend to be erratic, but continue to generate unsolicited correspondence from supposed "pen pals" *(see WARNING—CONFIDENCE ARTISTS,* above); faxes, which are much less likely to be intercepted, may be more fruitful. Two IRCs or return postage helpful.

NORTHERN MARIANA ISLANDS World Time +10

Far East Broadcasting Company—Radio Station KFBS Saipan
MAIN OFFICE: FEBC, P.O. Box 209, Saipan, Mariana Islands MP 96950 USA. Phone: (main office) +1 (670) 322-3481. Fax: +1 (670) 322 3060. E-mail: febc@itecnmi.com. URL: www.febc.org. Contact: Chris Slabaugh, Field Director; Irene Gabbie, QSL Secretary; Mike Adams; or Robert Springer, Director. Replies sometimes take months. Also, *see* FEBC Radio International, USA.

Herald Broadcasting Syndicate Northern Mariana Islands—KHBI Saipan, P.O. Box 1387, Saipan, Mariana Islands CM 96950-1387 USA; or write to Boston address *(see* USA). Phone: +1 (670) 234-6515. Fax: +1 (670) 234 5452. E-mail: (station manager) doming@khbi.com; (engineer) jess@khbi.com. URL: www.tfccs.com. Contact: (nontechnical) Alexander U. Igisaiar; or D.F. Villar, Station Manager; (technical) Jess Emmanuel Domingo, Engineer. Return postage is appreciated if writing to Saipan; no return postage necessary when writing to Boston. Visitors are welcome, preferably from 9:00 AM to 4:00 PM Monday through Friday, but contact the transmitter site before arrival in Saipan to make arrangements. In the course of 1998, KHBI was sold to Radio Free Asia *(see* USA) but the purchase agreement allows the Herald Broadcasting Syndicate to continue broadcasting some religious programming after the new owners take over. RFA management hopes that all current KHBI employees will remain at the station.

NORWAY World Time +1 (+2 midyear)

📻Radio Norway International
MAIN OFFICE, NONTECHNICAL: Utenlandssendingen, NRK, N-0340 Oslo, Norway. Phone: (general) +47 (23) 048-444; (Norwegian-language 24-hour recording of schedule information +47 (23) 048-008 (Americas, Europe, Africa), +47 (23) 048-009 (elsewhere). Fax: (general) +47 (23) 047 134 or +47 (22) 605 719. E-mail: radionorway@nrk.no. URL: (includes RealAudio) www.nrk.no/radionyheter/radionorway/. Contact: (general) Kirsten Ruud Salomonsen, Head of External Broadcasting; (technical) Gundel Krauss Dahl, Head of Radio Projects. Free stickers and flags.
WASHINGTON NEWS BUREAU: Norwegian Broadcasting, 2030 M Street NW, Suite 700, Washington DC 20036 USA. Phone: +1 (202) 785-1481 or +1 (202) 785-1460. Contact: Bjorn Hansen or Gunnar Myklebust.
SINGAPORE NEWS BUREAU: NRK, 325 River Valley Road #01-04, Singapore.
FREQUENCY MANAGEMENT OFFICE: Statens Teleforvaltning, Dept. TF/OMG, Revierstredet 2, P.O. Box 447 Sentrum, N-0104 Oslo, Norway. Phone: +47 (22) 824-889. Fax: +47 (22) 824 891. E-mail: olavmo@online.no. Contact: Olav Mo Grimdalen, Frequency Manager.

OMAN World Time +4

BBC World Service—Eastern Relay Station, P.O. Box 6898 (or 3716), Ruwi Post Office, Muscat, Oman. Contact: Chris Dolman, Senior Transmitter Engineer; or Dave Plater, Senior Transmitter Engineer. Technical correspondence should be sent to "Senior Transmitter Engineer"; nontechnical goes to the BBC World Service in London *(see* United Kingdom).

📻Radio Sultanate of Oman, Ministry of Information, P.O. Box 600, Muscat, Post Code 113, Sultanate of Oman. URL: (RealAudio only) www.oman-tv.gov.om/. Fax: (general) +968 602 055 or +968 602 831; (technical) +968 604 629. Contact: (Directorate General of Technical Affairs) Abdallah Bin Saif Al Nabhani, Acting Chief Engineer; Rashid Haroon Al Jabry,

Head of Radio Maintenance; or Ahmed Mohamed Al Balushi, Head of Studio's Engineering. Replies regularly, and responses are from one to two weeks. $1, return postage or 3 IRCs helpful.

PAKISTAN   World Time +5

Azad Kashmir Radio, Muzaffarabad, Azad Kashmir, Pakistan. Contact: (technical) M. Sajjad Ali Siddiqui, Director of Engineering; or Liaquatullah Khan, Engineering Manager. Registered mail helpful. Rarely replies to correspondence.

Pakistan Broadcasting Corporation—same address, fax and contact as "Radio Pakistan," below.

Radio Pakistan, P.O. Box 1393, Islamabad 44000, Pakistan. Phone: +92 (51) 813-802, +91 (51) 829-022 or +91 (51) 921-4947. Fax: +92 (51) 216 657 or +92 (51) 811 861. E-mail: cnoradio@ isb.comsats.net.pk. URL: (RealAudio) www.radio.gov.pk/. Contact: (technical) Ahmed Nawaz, Senior Broadcast Engineer, Room No. 324, Frequency Management Cell; Syed Abrar Hussain, Controller of Frequency Management; Syed Asmat Ali Shah, Senior Broadcasting Engineer; or Nasirahmad Bajwa, Frequency Management. Free stickers, pennants and *Pakistan Calling* magazine. May also send pocket calendar. Very poor replier. Plans to replace two 50 kW transmitters with 500 kW units if and when funding is forthcoming.

PALAU   World Time +9

KHBN—Voice of Hope, P.O. Box 66, Koror, Palau 96940, Pacific Islands. Phone: +680 488-2162. Fax: (main office) +680 488 2163; or (engineering) +680 544 1008. E-mail: (general) hamadmin@palaunet.com; or (engineering) khbntx@ palaunet.com. Contact: (general) Regina Subris, Station Manager; (technical) Ernie Fontanilla, Engineer. Free stickers and publications. IRC requested. Also, *see* KVOH—Voice of Hope/ High Adventure Ministries, USA.

PAPUA NEW GUINEA   World Time +10

NOTE: A number of Papua New Guinea stations are currently off air due to financial problems. It is unclear if or when they will return.

National Broadcasting Corporation of Papua New Guinea, P.O. Box 1359, Boroko, Papua New Guinea. Phone: + 675 325-5233 or +675 325-7175. Fax: +675 325 0796 or +675 325 6296. Contact: (general) Renagi R. Lohia, CBE, Managing Director and C.E.O.; or Francesca Maredei, Planning Officer; (technical) Bob Kabewa, Sr. Technical Officer; or F. Maredey, Chief Engineer. Two IRCs or return postage helpful. Replies irregularly.

Radio Bougainville, P.O. Box 35, Buka, North Solomons Province (NSP), Papua New Guinea. Contact: A.L. Rumina, Provincial Programme Manager; Ms. Christine Talei, Assistant Provincial Manager; or Aloysius Laukai, Senior Programme Officer. Replies irregularly.

Radio Central (when operating), P.O. Box 1359, Boroko, NCD, Papua New Guinea. Contact: Steven Gamini, Station Manager; or Amos Langit, Technician. $1, 2 IRCs or return postage helpful. Replies irregularly.

Radio Eastern Highlands (when operating), P.O. Box 311, Goroka, EHP, Papua New Guinea. Contact: Ignas Yanam, Technical Officer; or Kiri Nige, Engineering Division. $1 or return postage required. Replies irregularly.

Radio East New Britain (when operating), P.O. Box 393, Rabaul, ENBP, Papua New Guinea. Contact: Esekia Mael, Station Manager; or Otto Malatane, Provincial Program Manager. Return postage required. Replies slowly.

Radio East Sepik, P.O. Box 65, Wewak, E.S.P., Papua New Guinea. Contact: Elias Albert, Assistant Provincial Program Manager; or Luke Umbo, Station Manager.

Radio Enga, P.O. Box 300, Wabag, Enga Province, Papua New Guinea. Contact: (general) John Lyein Kur, Station Manager; or Robert Papuvo, (technical) Gabriel Paiao, Station Technician.

Radio Gulf (when operating), P.O. Box 36, Kerema, Gulf, Papua New Guinea. Contact: Robin Wainetta, Station Manager; or Timothy Akia, Provincial Program Manager.

Radio Madang, P.O. Box 2138, Madang, Papua New Guinea. Phone: +675 852-2415. Fax: +675 852 2360. Contact: (general) Damien Boaging, Senior Programme Officer; Geo Gedabing, Provincial Programme Manager; Peter Charlie Yannum, Assistant Provincial Programme Manager; or James Steve Valakvi, Senior Programme Officer; (technical) Lloyd Guvil, Technician.

Radio Manus, P.O. Box 505, Lorengau, Manus, Papua New Guinea. Phone: +675 470-9029. Fax: +675 470 9079. Contact: (technical and nontechnical) John P. Mandrakamu, Provincial Program Manager. Station is seeking the help of DXers and broadcasting professionals in obtaining a second hand, but still usable broadcasting quality CD player that could be donated to Radio Manus. Replies regularly. Return postage appreciated.

Radio Milne Bay(when operating), P.O. Box 111, Alotau, Milne Bay, Papua New Guinea. Contact: (general) Trevor Webumo, Assistant Manager; Simon Muraga, Station Manager; or Raka Petuely, Program Officer; (technical) Philip Maik, Technician. Return postage in the form of mint stamps helpful.

Radio Morobe, P.O. Box 1262, Lae, Morobe, Papua New Guinea. Fax: +675 472 6423. Contact: Ken L. Tropu, Assistant Program Manager; Peter W. Manua, Program Manager; Kekalem M. Meruk, Assistant Provincial Program Manager; or Aloysius R. Nase, Station Manager.

Radio New Ireland, P.O. Box 140, Kavieng, New Ireland, Papua New Guinea. Contact: Otto A. Malatana, Station Manager; or Ruben Bale, Provincial Program Manager. Return postage or $1 helpful.

Radio Northern (when operating), Voice of Oro, P.O. Box 137, Popondetta, Oro, Papua New Guinea. Contact: Roma Tererembo, Assistant Provincial Programme Manager; or Misael Pendaia, Station Manager. Return postage required.

Radio Sandaun, P.O. Box 37, Vanimo, Sandaun Province, Papua New Guinea. Contact: (nontechnical) Gabriel Deckwalen, Station Manager; Elias Rathley, Provincial Programme Manager; Mrs. Maria Nauot, Secretary; (technical) Paia Ottawa, Technician. $1 helpful.

Radio Simbu, P.O. Box 228, Kundiawa, Chimbu, Papua New Guinea. Phone: +675 735-1038 or +675 735-1082. Fax: +675 735 1012. Contact: (general) Tony Mill Waine, Provincial Programme Manager; Felix Tsiki; or Thomas Ghiyandiule, Producer, "Pasikam Long ol Pipel." Cassette recordings $5. Free two-Kina banknotes.

Radio Southern Highlands (when operating), P.O. Box 104, Mendi, SHP, Papua New Guinea. Contact: (general) Andrew Meles, Programme Manager; Miriam Piapo, Programme Officer; Benard Kagaro, Programme Officer; Lucy Aluy, Programme Officer; or Nicholas Sambu, Producer, "Questions & Answers"; (technical) Ronald Helori, Station Technician. $1 or return postage helpful; or donate a wall poster of a rock band, singer or American landscape.

Radio United Bougainville, Public Awareness Campaign Unit, P.O. Box 268, Buka, Papua New Guinea. Reportedly funded by the Bougainville Transitional Government, this essentially official station has been established to counter the rebel station, "Radio Free Bougainville" (*see* under Disestablishmentarian).

Radio Western, P.O. Box 23, Daru, Western Province, Papua New Guinea. Contact: (technical) Samson Tobel, Technician. $1 or return postage required. Replies irregularly.

Radio Western Highlands (when operating), P.O. Box 311, Mount Hagen, WHP, Papua New Guinea. Contact: (technical) Esau Okole, Technician. $1 or return postage helpful. Replies occasionally.

Radio West New Britain, P.O. Box 412, Kimbe, WNBP, Papua New Guinea. Fax: +675 983 5600. Contact: Valuka Lowa, Provincial Station Manager; Lemeck Kuam, Producer, "Questions and Answers"; or Esekial Mael. Return postage required.

PARAGUAY   World Time –3 (–4 midyear)

La Voz del Chaco Paraguayo, Filadelfia, Dpto. de Boquerón, Chaco, Paraguay. This station, currently only on mediumwave AM, hopes to add a world band transmitter within the 60-meter (5 MHz) band. However, to date nothing concrete has come of this.

Radio Encarnación, Gral. Artigas casi Gral. B. Caballero, Encarnación, Paraguay. Phone: (general) +595 (71) 4376 or +595 (71) 3345; (press) +595 (71) 4120. Fax: +595 (71) 4099. $1 or return postage helpful.

Radio Guairá (when operating), Alejo García y Presidente Franco, Villarrica, Paraguay. Phone: +595 (541) 2385 or +595 (541) 3411. Fax: +595 (541) 2130. Contact: (general) Lídice Rodríguez Vda. de Traversi, Propietaria; (technical) Enrique Traversi. Welcomes correspondence in Spanish. $1 or return postage helpful.

Radio Nacional, Blas Garay 241 entre Yegros e Iturbe, Asunción, Paraguay. Phone: +595 (21) 449-213. Fax: +595 (21) 332 750. Contact: Efraín Martínez Cuevas, Director. Free tourist brochure. $1 or return postage required. Replies, sometimes slowly, to correspondence in Spanish.

PERU   World Time –5 year-round in Loreto, Cusco and Puno. Other departments sometimes move to World Time –4 for a few weeks of the year.

NOTE: Obtaining replies from Peruvian stations calls for creativity, tact, patience—and the proper use of Spanish, not form letters and the like. There are nearly 150 world band stations operating from Perú on any given day. While virtually all of these may be reached simply by using as the address the station's city, as given in the Blue Pages, the following are the only stations known to be replying—even if only occasionally—to correspondence from abroad.

Emisoras JSV—*see* Radio JSV.

Estación C, Casilla de Correo 210, Moyobamba, San Martín, Peru.

Estación Tarapoto (if reactivated), Jirón Federico Sánchez 720, Tarapoto, Peru. Phone: +51 (94) 522-709. Contact: Luis Humberto Hidalgo Sánchez, Gerente General; or José Luna Paima, Announcer. Replies occasionally to correspondence in Spanish.

Estación Wari, Calle Nazareno 108, Ayacucho, Peru. Phone: +51 (64) 813-039. Contact: Walter Muñoz Ynga I., Gerente.

Estación X (Equis) (when operating), Plaza de Armas No. 106, Yurimaguas, Provincia de Alto Amazonas, Loreto, Peru. Contact: Franklin Coral Sousa, Director Propietario, who may also be contacted at his home address: Jirón Mariscal Castilla No. 104, Yurimaguas, Provincia de Alto Amazonas, Loreto, Peru.

Frecuencia Líder (Radio Bambamarca), Jirón Jorge Chávez 416, Bambamarca, Hualgayoc, Cajamarca, Peru. Phone: (office) +51 (74) 713-260; (studio) +51 (74) 713-249. Contact: (general) Valentín Peralta Díaz, Gerente; Irma Peralta Rojas; or Carlos Antonio Peralta Rojas; (technical) Oscar Lino Peralta Rojas. Free station photos. *La Historia de Bambamarca* book for 5 Soles; cassettes of Peruvian and Latin American folk music for 4 Soles each; T-shirts for 10 Soles each (sending US$1 per Sol should suffice and cover foreign postage costs, as well). Replies occasionally to correspondence in Spanish. Considering replacing their transmitter to improve reception.

Frecuencia San Ignacio, Jirón Villanueva Pinillos 330, San Ignacio, Cajamarca, Peru. Contact: Franklin R. Hoyos Cóndor, Director Gerente; or Ignacio Gómez Torres, Técnico de Sonido. Replies to correspondence in Spanish. $1 or return postage necessary.

Frecuencia VH—*see* Radio Frecuencia VH.

La Super Radio San Ignacio (when operating), Avenida Víctor Larco 104, a un costado del campo deportivo, San Ignacio, Distrito de Sinsicap, Provincia de Otuzco, La Libertad, Peru.

La Voz de Anta, Distrito de Anta, Provincia de Acobamba, Departamento de Huancavelica. Phone: +51 (64) 750-201.

La Voz de la Selva—*see* Radio La Voz de la Selva.

La Voz de San Juan—*see* Radio La Voz de San Juan.

La Voz del Campesino—*see* Radio La Voz del Campesino.

La Voz del Marañon—*see* Radio La Voz del Marañon.

Ondas del Suroriente—*see* Radio Ondas del Suroriente, below.

Radio Adventista Mundial—La Voz de la Esperanza, Jirón Dos de Mayo No. 218, Celendín, Cajamarca, Peru. Contact: Francisco Goicochea Ortiz, Director; or Lucas Solano Oyarce, Director de Ventas.

Radio Altura (Cerro de Pasco), Casilla de Correo 140, Cerro de Pasco, Pasco, Peru. Phone: +51 (64) 721-875, +51 (64) 722-398. Contact: Oswaldo de la Cruz Vásquez, Gerente General. Replies to correspondence in Spanish.

Radio Altura (Huarmaca), Antonio Raymondi 3ra Cuadra, Distrito de Huarmaca, Provincia de Huancabamba, Piura, Peru.

Radio Amauta del Perú, (when operating), Jirón Manuel Iglesias s/n, a pocos pasos de la Plazuela San Juan, San Pablo, Cajamarca, Nor Oriental del Marañón, Peru.

Radio América (when active), Montero Rosas 1099, Santa Beatriz, Lima, Peru. Phone: +51 (1) 265-3841/2/3. Fax: +51 (1) 265 3844. Contact: Liliana Sugobono F., Directora; or Jorge Arriola Viván, Promociones y Marketing.

Radio Ancash, Casilla de Correo 221, Huaraz, Peru. Phone: +51 (44) 721-381, +51 (44) 721-359, +51 (44) 721-487, +51 (44) 722-512. Fax: +51 (44) 722 992. Contact: Armando Moreno Romero, Gerente General. Replies to correspondence in Spanish.

Radio Andahuaylas, Jr. Ayacucho No. 248, Andahuaylas, Apurímac, Peru. Contact: Sr. Daniel Andréu C., Gerente. $1 required. Replies irregularly to correspondence in Spanish.

Radio Andina, Real 175, Huancayo, Junín, Peru. Phone: +51 (64) 231-123. Replies infrequently to correspondence in Spanish.

Radio Apurímac (when operating), Jirón Cusco 206 (or Ovalo

The AWR news staff in Peru gathers up-to-the-minute information via world band radio. AWR

El Olivo No. 23), Abancay, Apurímac, Peru. Contact: Antero Quispe Allca, Director General.

Radio Arcángel San Miguel—*see* Radio San Miguel Arcángel.

Radio Atlántida
STATION: Jirón Arica 441, Iquitos, Loreto, Peru. Phone: +51 (94) 234-452, +51 (94) 234-962. Contact: Pablo Rojas Bardales. *LISTENER CORRESPONDENCE:* Sra. Carmela López Paredes, Directora del prgrama "Trocha Turística," Jirón Arica 1083, Iquitos, Loreto, Peru. Free pennants and tourist information. $1 or return postage required. Replies to most correspondence in Spanish, the preferred language, and some correspondence in English. "Trocha Turística" is a bilingual (Spanish and English) tourist program aired weekdays 2300-2330.

Radio Ayabaca, Jirón Comercio 437, Ayabaca, Huancabamba, Peru.

Radio Ayaviri (La Voz de Melgar) (when active), Apartado 8, Ayaviri, Puno, Peru. Fax: +51 (54) 320 207, specify on fax "Anexo 127." Contact: (general) Sra. Corina Llaiqui Ochoa, Administradora; (technical) José Aristo Solórzano Mendoza, Director. Free pennants. Sells audio cassettes of local folk music for $5 plus postage; also exchanges music cassettes. Correspondence accepted in English, but Spanish preferred.

Radio Bahía, Jirón Alfonso Ugarte 309, Chimbote, Ancash, Peru. Phone: +51 (44) 322-391. Contact: Margarita Rossel Soria, Administradora; or Miruna Cruz Rossel, Administradora.

Radio Bambamarca—*see* Frecuencia Líder, above.

Radio Cajamarca, Jirón La Mar 675, Cajamarca, Peru. Phone: +51 (44) 921-014. Contact: Porfirio Cruz Potosí.

Radio Chanchamayo, Jirón Tarma 551, La Merced, Junín, Peru.

Radio Chaski, Baptist Mid-Missions, Apartado 368, Cusco, Peru; or Alameda Pachacútec s/n B-5, Cusco, Peru. Phone: +51 (84) 225-052. Contact: Andrés Tuttle H., Gerente.

Radio Chincheros, Jirón Apurímac s/n, Chincheros, Departamento de Apurímac, Peru.

Radio Chota, Jirón Anaximandro Vega 690, Apartado Postal 3, Chota, Cajamarca, Peru. Phone: +51 (44) 771-240. Contact: Aladino Gavidia Huamán, Administrador. $1 or return post-

age required. Replies slowly to correspondence in Spanish.

Radio Comas Televisión, Avenida Estados Unidos 327, Urbanización Huaquillay, km 10 de la Avenida Tupac Amaru, Distrito de Comas, Lima, Peru. Phone: +51 (1) 525-0859. Fax: +51 (1) 525 0094. Contact: Edgar Saldaña R.; or Gamaniel Francisco Chahua, Productor-Programador.

Radio Concordia (if reactived), Av. La Paz 512-A, Arequipa, Peru. If a reply is not forthcoming, try: Miguel Grau s/n Mz.2 Lt. 1, Arequipa, Peru. Phone: +51 (54) 446-053. Contact: Pedro Pablo Acosta Fernández. Free stickers. Return postage required.

Radio Continental (when operating), Av. Independencia 56, Arequipa, Peru. Phone: +51 (54) 213-253. Contact: J. Antonio Umbert D., Director General; or Leonor Núñez Melgar. Free stickers. Replies slowly to correspondence in Spanish.

🖀**Radio CORA**, Compañía Radiofónica Lima, S.A., Paseo de la República 144, Centro Cívico, Oficina 5, Lima 1, Peru. Phone: +51 (1) 433-5005, +51 (1) 433-1188, +51 (1) 433-0848. Fax: +51 (1) 433 6134. E-mail: cora@lima.business.com.pe; cora@peru.itete.com.pe. URL: (includes RealAudio) www.radiocora.com.pe/. Contact: (general) Juan Ramírez Lazo, Director Gerente; Dra. Lylian Ramírez M., Directora de Prensa y Programación; Juan Ramírez Lazo, Director Gerente; or Ms. Angelina María Abie; (technical) Srta. Sylvia Ramírez M., Directora Técnica. Free station sticky-label pads, bumper stickers and may send large certificate suitable for framing. Audio cassettes with extracts from their programs $20 plus $2 postage; women's hair bands $2 plus $1 postage. Two IRCs or $1 required. Replies slowly to correspondence in English, Spanish, French, Italian and Portuguese.

Radio Cristal, Jirón Ucayali s/n, a un costado de la Carretera Marginal de la Selva, San Hilarión, Provincia de Picota, Región San Martín, Peru. Contact: Señora Marina Gaona, Gerente; or Lucho García Gaona.

Radio Cultural Amauta (Bambamarca) (when operating), Jirón Jaime de Martínez 645, Bambamarca, Cajamarca, Peru. Contact: Valentín Mejía Vásquez, Presidente de la Central Unica Provincial de Rondas Campesinas (also via his home address: Jirón Mariscal Sucre 644, Bambamarca, Cajamarca,

Peru); Wilmer Vásquez Campos, Encargado Administración; Mauricio Rodríguez R.; or Walter Hugo Bautista. Radio Cultural Amauta is a new name for the former Radio La Voz de San Antonio.

Radio Cultural Amauta (Huanta), Cahuide 278, Apartado Postal 24, Huanta, Ayacucho, Peru. Phone: +51 (64) 832-153. Contact: Vicente Saico Tinco.

Radio Cusco, Apartado 251, Cusco, Peru. Phone: (general)+51 (84) 225-851; (management) +51 (84) 232-457. Fax: +51 (84) 223 308. Contact: Sra. Juana Huamán Yépez, Administradora; or Raúl Siú Almonte, Gerente General; (technical) Benjamín Yábar Alvarez. Free pennants, postcards and key rings. Audio cassettes of Peruvian music $10 plus postage. $1 or return postage required. Replies irregularly to correspondence in English or Spanish. Station is looking for folk music recordings from around the world to use in their programs.

Radio del Pacífico, Apartado 4236, Lima 1, Peru. Phone: +51 (1) 433-3275. Fax: +51 (1) 433 3276. Contact: J. Petronio Allauca, Secretario, Departamento de Relaciones Públicas; or P.G. Ferreyra. $1 or return postage required. Replies occasionally to correspondence in Spanish.

Radiodifusoras Huancabamba, Calle Unión 409, Huancabamba, Piura, Peru. Phone: +51 (74) 473-233. Contact: Federico Ibáñez M., Director.

Radiodifusoras Paratón, Jirón Alfonso Ugarte 1090, contiguo al Parque Leoncio Prado, Huarmaca, Huancabamba, Piura, Peru. Contact: Prof. Hernando Huancas Huancas, Gerente General; or Prof. Rómulo Chincay Huamán, Gerente Administrativo.

Radio El Sol (Lima) (when active), Avenida Uruguay 355, 7°, Lima Peru. Phone: +51 (1) 330-0713, +51 (1) 424-6107. Rarely replies, and only to correspondence in Spanish.

Radio El Sol (Pucará), Avenida Jaén s/n, Distrito de Pucará, Jaén, Cajamarca, Peru.

Radio El Sol de los Andes, Jirón 2 de Mayo 257, Juliaca, Peru. Phone: +51 (54) 321-115. Fax: +51 (54) 322-981. Contact: Armando Alarcón Velarde.

Radio Estación Uno, Barrio Altos, Distrito de Pucará, Provincia Jaén, Nor Oriental del Marañón, Peru.

Radio Frecuencia VH ("La Voz de Celendín"; "RVC"), Jirón José Gálvez 1030, Celendín, Cajamarca, Peru. Contact: Fernando Vásquez Castro, Propietario.

Radio Frecuencia San Ignacio—*see* Frecuencia San Ignacio.

Radio Horizonte (Chachapoyas), Apartado 69 (or Jirón Amazonas 1177), Chachapoyas, Amazonas, Peru. Phone: +51 (74) 757-793. Fax: +51 (74) 757 004. Contact: Sra. Rocío García Rubio, Ing. Electrónico, Directora; or Percy Chuquizuta Alvarado, Locutor; María Montaldo Echaiz, Locutora; Marcelo Mozambite Chavarry, Locutor; Juan Nancy Ruiz de Valdez, Secretaria; Yoel Toro Morales, Transmitter Technician; María Soledad Sánchez Castro, Administradora. Replies to correspondence in English, French, German and Spanish. $1 required.

Radio Horizonte (Chiclayo), Jirón Incanato 387 Altos, Distrito José Leonardo Ortiz, Chiclayo, Lambayeque, Peru. Phone: +51 (74) 252-917. Contact: Enrique Becerra Rojas, Owner and General Manager. Return postage required.

Radio Hualgayoc, Jirón San Martín s/n, Hualgayoc, Cajamarca, Peru. Contact: Máximo Zamora Medina, Director Propietario.

Radio Huamachuco (if reactivated), Jirón Bolívar 937, Huamachuco, La Libertad, Peru. Contact: Manuel D. Gil Gil, Director Propietario.

Radio Huancabamba (when operating), Calle Unión 610-Barrio Chalaco, Huancabamba, Piura, Peru. Fax: +51 (74) 320 229, specifying "Radio Huancabamba" on fax. Contact: (general) Fredy Alberca, General Manager; (administration) Edwin Arrieta. Free picture postcards. Replies occasionally to correspondence in English, French, Italian, Portuguese and Spanish. Hopes to replace transmitter. Off the air since 1996 when manager César Colunche Bustamante moved to San Ignacio where he operated Radio Melodia (now off the air) and Radio San Ignacio (*see*).

Radio Huanta 2000, Jirón Gervacio Santillana 455, Huanta, Peru. Phone: +51 (64) 932-105. Fax: +51 (64) 832 105. Contact: Ronaldo Sapaico Maravi, Departamento Técnico; or Sra. Lucila Orellana de Paz, Administradora. Free photo of staff. Return postage or $1 appreciated. Replies to correspondence in Spanish.

Radio Huarmaca, Av. Grau 454 (detrás de Inversiones La Loretana), Distrito de Huarmaca, Provincia de Huancabamba, Región Grau, Peru. Contact: Simón Zavaleta Pérez. Return postage helpful.

Radio Ilucán, Jirón Lima 290, Cutervo, Región Nororiental del Marañón, Peru. Phone: +51 (44) 737-010, +51 (44) 737-231. Contact: José Gálvez Salazar, Gerente Administrativo. $1 required. Replies occasionally to correspondence in Spanish.

Radio Imagen, Casilla de Correo 42, Tarapoto, San Martín, Peru; Jirón San Martín 328, Tarapoto, San Martín, Peru; or Apartado 254, Tarapoto, San Martín, Peru. Phone: +51 (94) 522-696. Contact: Adith Chumbe Vásquez, Secretaria; or Jaime Ríos Tapullima, Gerente General. Replies irregularly to correspondence in Spanish. $1 or return postage helpful.

Radio Integración, Av. Seoane 200, Apartado Postal 57, Abancay, Departamento de Apurímac, Peru. Contact: Zenón Hernán Farfán Cruzado, Propietario.

Radio Internacional del Perú (when operating), Jirón Bolognesi 532, San Pablo, Cajamarca, Peru.

Radio Interoceánica (if reactivated), Provincia de Azángaro, Departamento de Puno, Peru.

Radio Jaén (La Voz de la Frontera), Calle Mariscal Castilla 439, Jaén, Cajamarca, Peru.

Radio JSV, Jirón Aguilar 742-744, Huánuco, Peru. Phone: +51 (64) 512-930. Return postage required.

Radio Juliaca (La Decana), Ramón Castilla 949, Apartado Postal 67, Juliaca, San Román, Puno, Peru. Phone: +51 (54) 332-386. Fax: +51 (54) 321-372. Contact: Alberto Quintanilla Ch., Director.

Radio JVL, Jirón Túpac Amaru 105, Consuelo, Distrito de San Pablo, Provincia de Bellavista, Departamento de San Martín, Peru. Contact: John Wiley Villanueva Lara—a student of electronic engineering—who currently runs the station, and whose initials make up the station name. Replies to correspondence in Spanish. Return Postage required.

Radio La Hora, Av. Garcilaso 180, Cusco, Peru. Phone: +51 (84) 225-615, +51 (84) 231-371. Contact: Carlos Gamarra M, Gerente General. Free stickers, pins, pennants and postcards of Cusco. Return postage required. Replies occasionally to correspondence in Spanish. Hopes to increase transmitter power if and when the economic situation improves.

Radio La Inmaculada, Parroquia La Inmaculada Concepción, Frente de la Plaza de Armas, Santa Cruz, Provincia de Santa Cruz, Departamento de Cajamarca, Peru. Phone: +51 (74) 714-051. Contact: Reverendo Padre Angel Jorge Carrasco, Gerente; or Gabino González Vera, Locutor.

Radio Lajas, Jirón Rosendo Mendívil 589, Lajas, Chota,

Cajamarca, Nor Oriental del Marañón, Peru. Contact: Alfonso Medina Burga, Gerente Propietario.

Radio La Merced, Junín 163, La Merced, Junín, Peru. Phone: +51 (64) 531-199. Occasionally replies to correspondence in Spanish.

Radio La Oroya, Calle Lima 190, Tercer Piso Of. 3, Apartado Postal 88, La Oroya, Provincia de Yauli, Departamento de Junín, Peru. Phone: +51 (64) 391-401. Fax: +51 (64) 391 440. E-mail: rlofigu@net.cosapidata.com.pe. URL: www.cosapidata.com.pe/empresa/rlofigu/rlofigu.htm. Contact: Jacinto Manuel Figueroa Yauri, Gerente-Propietario. Free pennants. $1 or return postage necessary. Replies to correspondence in Spanish.

Radio La Voz, Andahuaylas, Apurímac, Peru. Contact: Lucio Fuentes, Director Gerente.

Radio La Voz de Bolívar. Provincia de Bolívar, Departamento de La Libertad, Peru.

Radio La Voz de Cutervo (if reactivated), Jirón María Elena Medina 644-650, Cutervo, Cajamarca, Peru.

Radio La Voz de Huamanga (if reactivated), Calle El Nazareno, 2do Pasaje No. 161, Ayacucho, Peru. Phone: +51 (64) 812-366. Contact: Sra. Aguida A. Valverde Gonzales. Free pennants and postcards.

Radio La Voz de la Selva, Abtao 255, Casilla de Correo 207, Iquitos, Loreto, Peru. Phone: +51 (94) 265-244/5, +51 (94) 267-890. Fax: +51 (94) 239 360. Contact: Julia Jauregui Rengifo, Directora; Marcelino Esteban Benito, Director; Pedro Sandoval Guzmán, Announcer; or Mery Blas Rojas. Replies to correspondence in Spanish.

Radio La Voz de las Huarinjas, Barrio El Altillo, Huancabamba, Piura, Peru. Phone: +51 (74) 473-126. Contact: Alfonso García Silva, Gerente Director; or Bill Yeltsin, Administrador. Replies to correspondence in Spanish.

Radio La Voz de Oxapampa, Av. Mullenbruck 469, Oxapampa, Pasco, Peru. Contact: Pascual Villafranca Guzmán, Director Propietario.

Radio La Voz de San Juan, 28 de Julio 420, Lonya Grande, Provincia de Utcubamba, Región Nororiental del Marañón, Peru. Contact: Prof. Víctor Hugo Hidrovo; or Edilberto Ortiz Chávez, Locutor. Formerly known as Radio San Juan.

Radio La Voz de Santa Cruz (if reactivated), Av. Zarumilla 190, Santa Cruz, Cajamarca, Peru.

Radio La Voz del Campesino, Av. Piura 1015, Pampa Alegre, San Miguel de El Faique, Provincia de Huancabamba, Peru. Contact: Alberto Soto Santos, Director Propietario; Gonzalo Castillo Chanta, Locutor; or Araceli Bruno L. and Gloria Huamán Flórez, Locutoras.

Radio La Voz del Marañón (if reactivated), Jirón Bolognesi 130, Barrio La Alameda, Cajamarca, Nor Oriental del Marañón, Peru. Contact: Eduardo Díaz Coronado.

Radio Libertad de Junín, Cerro de Pasco 528, Apartado Postal 2, Junín, Peru. Phone: +51 (64) 344-026. Contact: Mauro Chaccha G., Director Gerente. Replies slowly to correspondence in Spanish. Return postage necessary.

Radio Líder, Portal Belén 115, 2do piso, Cusco, Peru. Contact: Mauro Calvo Acurio, Propietario.

Radio Lircay (when operating), Barrio Maravillas, Lircay, Provincia de Angaraes, Huancavelica, Peru.

Radio Los Andes (Huamachuco) (if reactivated), Pasaje Damián Nicolau 108-110, 2do piso, Huamachuco, La Libertad, Peru. Phone: +51 (44) 441-240.

Radio Los Andes (Huarmaca), Huarmaca, Provincia de Huancabamba, Región Grau, Peru. Contact: William Cerro Calderón.

Radio LTC (if reactivated), Jirón Unión 242, Juliaca, Puno,

Peru. Phone: +51 (54) 322-452, +51 (54) 322-560. Fax: +51 (54) 322 570. Contact: Mario Leonidas Torres, Gerente Ejecutivo; Leoncio Z. Torres C. (whose initials make up the station name), Gerente General; or María Figueroa, Administradora.

Radio Luz y Sonido

STATION: Jirón Dos de Mayo 1286, Oficina 310, Apartado 280, Huánuco, Peru. Phone: +51 (64) 512-394 or +51 (64) 518-500. Fax: +51 (64) 511 985. E-mail: luz.sonido@hys.com.pe. Contact: (technical) Jorge Benavides Moreno; (nontechnical) Lic. Orlando Bravo Jesús. Return postage or $1 required. Replies to correspondence in Spanish, Italian and Portuguese. Sells video cassettes of local folk dances and religious and tourist themes.

Radio Madre de Dios, D.A. Carrión 387, Apartado Postal 37, Puerto Maldonado, Madre de Dios, Peru. Phone: +51 (84) 571-050. Contact: Alcides Arguedas Márquez, Director del programa "Un Festival de Música Internacional," heard Mondays 0100 to 0200 World Time. Sr. Arguedas is interested in feedback for this letterbox program. Replies to correspondence in Spanish. $1 or return postage appreciated.

Radio Majestad, Calle Real 1033, Oficina 302, Huancayo, Junín, Peru.

Radio Marañón (if reactivated), Apartado 50, Jaén, Cajamarca, Peru. Phone: +51 (44) 731-579, +51 (44) 733-464. Phone/fax: +51 (74) 731-147. Contact: Padre Luis Távara Martín, S.J., Director. Return postage necessary. May send free pennant. Replies slowly to correspondence in Spanish.

Radio Marginal, San Martín 257, Tocache, San Martín, Peru. Phone: +51 (94) 551-031. Rarely replies.

Radio Máster, Jirón 20 de Abril 308, Moyobamba, Departamento de San Martín, Peru. Contact: Américo Vásquez Hurtado, Director

Radio Melodía, San Camilo 501, Arequipa, Peru. Phone: +51 (54) 232-071, +51 (54) 232-327, +51 (54) 285-152. Fax: +51 (54) 237 312. Contact: Hermogenes Delgado Torres, Director; or Señora Elba Alvarez de Delgado. Replies to correspondence in Spanish.

Radio Mi Frontera, Calle San Ignacio 520, Distrito de Chirinos, Provincia de San Ignacio, Región Nor Oriental del Marañón, Peru.

Radio Mundial Adventista, Colegio Adventista de Titicaca, Casilla 4, Juliaca, Peru. Currently on mediumwave only, but is expected to add shortwave sometime in the future.

Radio Mundo, Calle Tecte 245, Cusco, Peru. Phone: + 51 (84) 232-076. Fax: +51 (84) 233 076. Contact: Valentín Olivera Puelles, Gerente. Free postcards and stickers. Return postage necessary. Replies slowly to correspondence in Spanish.

Radio Municipal de Cangallo (when active), Concejo Provincial de Cangallo, Plaza Principal No. 02, Cangallo, Ayacucho, Peru. Contact: Nivardo Barbarán Agüero, Encargado Relaciones Públicas.

Radio Nacional del Perú

ADMINISTRATIVE OFFICE: Avenida José Gálvez 1040 Santa Beatriz, Lima, Peru. Fax: +51 (14) 726 799. Contact: Henry Aragón Ibarra, Gerente; or Rafael Mego Carrascal, Jefatura de la Administración. Replies occasionally, by letter or listener-prepared verification card, to correspondence in Spanish. Return postage required.

STUDIO ADDRESS: Av. Petit Thouars 447, Lima, Peru.

Radio Naylamp, Avenida Huamachuco 1080, 2do piso, Lambayeque, Peru. Phone: +51 (74) 283-353. Contact: Dr. Juan José Grández Vargas, Director Gerente; or Delicia Coronel Muñoz, who is interested in receiving postcards and the like.

Feedback for Dr. J.J.'s weeknightly program "Buenas Tardes, Ecuador," from 0000 to 0100 World Time, appreciated. Free stickers, pennants and calendars. Return postage necessary.

Radio Nor Andina, Jirón José Gálvez 602, Celendín, Cajamarca, Peru. Contact: Misael Alcántara Guevara, Gerente; or Víctor B. Vargas C., Departamento de Prensa. Free calendar. $1 required. Donations (registered mail best) sought for the Committee for Good Health for Children, headed by Sr. Alcántara, which is active in saving the lives of hungry youngsters in poverty-stricken Cajamarca Province. Replies irregularly to casual or technical correspondence in Spanish, but regularly to Children's Committee donors and helpful correspondence in Spanish.

Radio Nor Peruana, Emisora Municipal, Jirón Ortiz Arrieta 588, 1er. piso del Concejo Provincial de Chachapoyas, Chachapoyas, Amazonas, Peru. Contact: Carlos Poema, Administrador; or Edgar Villegas, program host for "La Voz de Chachapoyas," (Sundays, 1100-1300).

Radio Nueva Sensación, Cadena Radial Nuevo Siglo, Panamericana Norte km. 361, Urbanización Ricardo Palma, Chiclayo, Peru.

Radio Onda Imperial, Calle Sacsayhuamán K-10, Urbanización Manuel Prado, Cusco, Peru. Phone: +51 (84) 232-521, +51 (84) 233-032.

Radio Ondas del Huallaga, Jirón Leoncio Prado 723, Apartado Postal 343, Huánuco, Peru. Phone: +51 (64) 511-525, +51 (64) 512-428. Contact: Flaviano Llanos Malpartida, Representante Legal. $1 or return postage required. Replies to correspondence in Spanish.

Radio Ondas del [Río] Marañón, Jirón Amazonas 315, Distrito de Aramango, Provincia de Bagua, Departamento de Amazonas, Región Nororiental del Marañón, Peru. Contact: Agustín Tongod, Director Propietario. "Rio"—river—is sometimes, but not always, used in on-air identification.

Radio Ondas del Río Mayo, Jirón Huallaga 348, Nueva Cajamarca, San Martín, Peru. Phone: +51 (94) 556-006. Contact: Edilberto Lucío Peralta Lozada, Gerente; or Víctor Huaras Rojas, Locutor. Free pennants. Return postage helpful. Replies slowly to correspondence in Spanish.

Radio Ondas del Suroriente, Jirón Ricardo Palma 510, Quillabamba, La Convención, Cusco, Peru.

Radio Oriente, Vicariato Apostólico, Calle Progreso 114, Yurimaguas, Loreto, Peru. Phone: +51 (94) 352-156. Phone/fax (ask to switch over to fax): +51 (94) 352-566. Contact: (general) Sra. Elisa Cancino Hidalgo; or Juan Antonio López-Manzanares M., Director; (technical) Pedro Capo Moragues, Gerente Técnico. $1 or return postage required. Replies occasionally to correspondence in English, French, Spanish and Catalan.

Radio Origen, Acobamba, Departamento de Huancavelica, Peru.

Radio Paccha (if reactivated), Calle Mariscal Castilla 52, Paccha, Provincia de Chota, Departamento de Cajamarca, Peru.

Radio Paucartambo, Emisora Municipal (if reactivated) *STATION ADDRESS:* Paucartambo, Cusco, Peru.
STAFFER ADDRESS: Manuel H. Loaiza Canal, Correo Central, Paucartambo, Cusco, Peru. Return postage or $1 required.

Radio Perú ("Perú, la Radio")
STUDIO ADDRESS: Jirón Atahualpa 191, San Ignacio, Región Nororiental del Marañón, Peru.
ADMINISTRATION: Avenida San Ignacio 493, San Ignacio, Región Nororiental del Marañón, Peru. Contact: Oscar Vásquez Chacón, Director General; or Idelfo Vásquez Chacón, Director Propietario. Sometimes relays the FM outlet, "Estudio 97."

Radio Power, Jirón 20 de Abril 467, Moyobamba, San Martín, Peru. Contact: Ricky Centurión Tapia, Propietario.

Radio Quillabamba, Apartado 76, Quillabamba, La Convención, Cusco, Peru. Phone: +51 (84) 281-002. Contact: Padre Francisco Panera, Director. Replies very irregularly to correspondence in Spanish.

Radio Regional, Jirón Grau s/n frente al Colegio Nuestra Señora del Carmen, Celendín, Cajamarca, Peru.

Radio Reina de la Selva, Jirón Ayacucho 944, Plaza de Armas, Chachapoyas, Región Nor Oriental del Marañón, Peru. Phone: +51 (74) 757-203. Contact: José David Reina Noriega, Gerente General; or Jorge Oscar Reina Noriega, Director General. Replies irregularly to correspondence in Spanish. Return postage necessary.

Radio San Francisco Solano, Parroquia de Sóndor, Calle San Miguel No. 207, Distrito de Sóndor, Huancabamba, Piura, Peru. Contact: Reverendo Padre Manuel José Rosas Castillo, Vicario Parroquial. Station operated by the Franciscan Fathers. Replies to correspondence in Spanish. $1 helpful.

Radio San Ignacio, Jirón Victoria 277, San Ignacio, Región Nororiental del Marañón, Peru. Contact: César Colunche Bustamante, Director Propietario; or his son, Fredy Colunche, Director de Programación.

Radio San Juan, Distrito de Aramango, Provincia de Bagua, Departamento de Amazonas, Región Nororiental del Marañón, Peru.

Radio San Juan, 28 de Julio 420, Lonya Grande, Provincia de Utcubamba, Región Nororiental del Marañón, Peru. Contact: Prof. Víctor Hugo Díaz Hidrovo; or Edilberto Ortiz Chávez, Locutor.

Radio San Miguel, Av. Huayna Cápac 146, Huánchac, Cusco, Peru. Contact: Sra. Catalina Pérez de Alencastre, Gerente General; or Margarita Mercado. Replies to correspondence in Spanish.

Radio San Miguel Arcángel, Jirón Bolívar 356, a media cuadra de la Plaza de Armas, Provincia de San Miguel, Cajamarca, Peru.

Radio San Miguel de El Faique, Distrito de El Faique, Provincia de Huancabamba, Departamento de Piura, Peru.

Radio San Nicolás, Jirón Amazonas 114, Rodríguez de Mendoza, Peru. Contact: Juan José Grández Santillán, Gerente; or Violeta Grández Vargas, Administradora. Return postage necessary.

Radio Santa Rosa, Jirón Camaná 170, Casilla 4451, Lima 1, Peru. Phone: +51 (1) 427-7488. Fax: +51 (1) 426-9219. E-mail: santarosa@protelsa.com.pe. Contact: Padre Juan Sokolich Alvarado; or Lucy Palma Barreda. Free stickers and pennants. $1 or return postage necessary. 180-page book commemorating station's 35th anniversary $10. Replies to correspondence in Spanish.

Radio Santiago, Municipalidad Distrital de Río Santiago, Puerto Galilea, Provincia de Condorcanqui, Amazonas, Peru. Contact: Juan Tuchía Oscate, Alcalde Distrital; Sara Sánchez Cubas, Locutora Comercial; or Guillermo Gómez García, Director. Free pennants and postcards. Return postage necessary. Replies to correspondence in Spanish.

Radio Satélite, Jirón Cutervo No. 543, Provincia de Santa Cruz, Cajamarca, Peru. Phone: +51 (74) 714-074, +51 (74) 714-169. Contact: Sabino Llamo Chávez, Gerente. Free tourist brochure. $1 or return postage required. Replies to correspondence in Spanish.

Radio Selecciones, Chuquibamba, Provincia de Condesuyos, Arequipa, Peru.

Radio Sicuani, Jirón 2 de Mayo 206, Sicuani, Canchis, Cusco,

Peru; or P.O. Box 45, Sicuani, Peru. Phone: +51 (84) 351-136. Contact: Mario Ochoa Vargas, Director.

Radio Soledad, Centro Minero de Retama, Distrito de Parcoy, Provincia de Pataz, La Libertad, Peru. Contact: Vicente Valdivieso, Locutor. Return postage necessary.

Radio Sudamérica, Jirón Ramón Castilla 491, tercer nivel, Plaza de Armas, Cutervo, Cajamarca, Peru. Phone: +51 (74) 736-090 or +51 (74) 737-443. Contact: Jorge Paredes Guerra, Administrador; or Amadeo Mario Muñoz Guivar, Propietario.

Radio Tacna, Aniceto Ibarra 436, Casilla de Correo 370, Tacna, Peru. Phone: +51 (54) 714-871. Fax: +51 (54) 723 745. E-mail: radiotac@principal.unjbg.edu.pe.   URL: http://principal.unjbg.edu.pe/radio/radta.html. Contact: (nontechnical and technical) Ing. Alfonso Cáceres Contreras, Sub-Gerente/Jefe Técnico; (administration) Yolanda Vda. de Cáceres C., Directora Gerente. Free stickers and samples of *Correo* local newspaper. $1 or return postage helpful. Audio cassettes of Peruvian and other music $2 plus postage. Replies irregularly to correspondence in English and Spanish.

Radio Tawantinsuyo, Av. Sol 806, Cusco, Peru. Phone: +51 (84) 226-955, +51 (84) 228-411. Has a very attractive QSL card, but only replies occasionally to correspondence, which should be in Spanish.

Radio Tarma, Jirón Molino del Amo 167, Apartado Postal 167, Tarma, Peru. Phone/fax: +51 (64) 321 167 or +51 (64) 321 510. Contact: Mario Monteverde Pomareda, Gerente General. Sometimes sends 100 Inti banknote in return when $1 enclosed. Free stickers. $1 or return postage required. Replies irregularly to correspondence in Spanish.

Radio Tayacaja, Correo Central, Distrito de Pampas, Tayacaja, Huancavelica, Peru. Phone: +51 (64) 22-02-17, Anexo 238. Contact: (general) J. Jorge Flores Cárdenas; (technical) Ing. Larry Guido Flores Lezama. Free stickers and pennants. Replies to correspondence in Spanish. Hopes to replace transmitter.

Radio Tingo María, Jirón Callao 115 (or Av. Raimondi No. 592), Casilla de Correo 25, Tingo María, Leoncio Prado, Departamento de Huánuco, Peru. Contact: Gina A. de la Cruz Ricalde, Administradora; or Ricardo Abad Vásquez, Gerente. Free brochures. $1 required. Replies slowly to correspondence in Spanish.

Radio Tropical, Casilla de Correo 31, Tarapoto, Peru. Phone: +51 (94) 522-083, +51 (94) 524-689. Fax: +51 (94) 522 155. Contact: Mery A. Rengifo Tenazoa, Secretaria; or Luis F. Mori Reátegui, Gerente. Free stickers, occasionally free pennants, and station history booklet. $1 or return postage required. Replies occasionally to correspondence in Spanish.

Radio Unión, Apartado 833, Lima 27, Peru. Phone: +51 (1) 440-2093. Fax: +51 (1) 440 7594. E-mail: runion@amauta.rcp.net.pe. Contact: Juan Zubiaga Santiváñez,

Gerente; or Juan Carlos Sologuren, Dpto. de Administración, who collects stamps. Free satin pennants and stickers. IRC required, and enclosing used or new stamps from various countries is especially appreciated. Replies irregularly to correspondence and tape recordings, especially from young women, with Spanish preferred.
Radio Uno, Av. Balta 1480, 3er piso, frente al Mercado Modelo, Chiclayo, Peru. Phone: +51 (74) 224-967. Contact: Luz Angela Romero, Directora del noticiero "Encuentros"; Plutarco Chamba Febres, Director Propietario; Juan Vargas, Administrador; or Filomena Saldívar Alarcón, Pauta Comercial. Return postage required.
Radio Victoria, Reynel 320, Mirones Bajo, Lima 1, Peru. Phone: +51 (1) 336-5448. Fax: +51 (1) 427 1195. Contact: Marta Flores Ushinahua. This station is owned by the Brazilian-run Pentecostal Church "Dios Es Amor," with local headquarters at Av. Arica 248, Lima; phone: +51 (1) (330-8023). Their program "La Voz de la Liberación" is produced locally and aired over numerous Peruvian shortwave stations.
Radio Virgen del Carmen ("RVC"), Jirón Virrey Toledo 544, Huancavelica, Peru. Phone: +51 (64) 752-740. Contact: Rvdo. Samuel Morán Cárdenas, Gerente.

PHILIPPINES   World Time +8

NOTE: Philippine stations sometimes send publications with lists of Philippine young ladies seeking "pen pal" courtships.
DZRM—Philippine Broadcasting Service (when operating), Bureau of Broadcasting Services, Media Center, Bohol Avenue, Quezon City, Philippines.
Far East Broadcasting Company—FEBC Radio International (External Service)
MAIN OFFICE: P.O. Box 1, Valenzuela, Metro Manila, Philippines 0560. Phone: +63 (2) 292-5603, or +63 (2) 292-9403. Fax: +63 (2) 292 9430, but lacks funds to provide faxed replies. E-mail: febcomphil@febc.jmf.org.ph; or ieoffice@febc.org.ph; (English Department) english@febc.jmf.org.ph; (Peter McIntyre, Host "DX Dial") dx@febc.jmf.org.ph or pm@febc.jfm.org.ph; (Jane Colley) jane@febc.jmf.org.ph; (Roger Foyle) foyle@febc.jmf.org.ph; (Mrs. Fay Olympia) alvarez@febc.jmf.org.ph; (Christine Johnson) cjohnson@febc.jmf.org.ph; (Larry Podmore) lpodmore@febc.jmf.org.ph. URL: www.febc.org/. (For some really exotic musical clips, visit the station's RealAudio page: www.febc.org/music.html.) Contact: (general) Peter McIntyre, Manager, International Operations Division & Producer, "DX Dial"; Jane Colley, Head, Audience Relations; Roger P. Foyle, Audience Relations Counsellor & Acting DX Secretary; Ella McIntyre, Producer, "Mailbag" and " Let's Hear from You"; Fay Olympia, English Programme Supervisor; Ms. Madini Tluanga, Producer, "Good Morning from Manila"; Christine D. Johnson, Head, Overseas English Service; or David Miller, Chief News Editor, FEB-News Bureau; (administration) Carlos Peña, Managing Director; (engineering) Ing. Renato Valentin, Frequency Manager; Larry Podmore, IBG Chief Engineer. Free stickers, calendar cards and DX Club Registration. Three IRCs appreciated for airmail reply. Plans to add a new 100 kW shortwave transmitter.
NEW DELHI BUREAU, NONTECHNICAL: c/o FEBA, Box 6, New Delhi-110 001, India.
Far East Broadcasting Company (Domestic Service), Bgy. Bayanan Baco Radyo DZB2, c/o ONF Calapan, Orr. Mindoro, Philippines 5200. Contact: (general) Dangio Onday, Program Supervisor/OIC; (technical) Danilo Flores, Broadcast Technician.

Radyo Pilipinas, the Voice of Democracy, Philippine Broadcasting Service, 4th Floor, PIA Building, Visayas Avenue, Quezon City 1100, Metro Manila, Philippines. Phone: (general) +63 (2) 924-2620; +63 (2) 920-3963; or +63 (2) 924-2548; (engineering) +63 (2) 924-2268. Fax: +63 (2) 924 2745. Contact: (nontechnical) Evelyn Salvador Agato, Officer-in-Charge; Mercy Lumba; Leo Romano, Producer, "Listeners and Friends"; or Richard G. Lorenzo, Production Coordinator; (technical) Danilo Alberto, Supervisor; or Mike Pangilinan, Engineer. Free postcards & stickers.
Radio Veritas Asia
STUDIOS AND ADMINISTRATIVE HEADQUARTERS: P.O. Box 2642, Quezon City, 1166 Philippines. Phone: +63 (2) 939-0011 to14, +63 (2) 939-4465 or +63 (2) 939-4692. Fax: (general) +63 (2) 938 1940; (Frequency and Monitoring) +63 (2) 939 7556. E-mail: (Program Dept.) veritas@mnl.sequel.net; (technical) info@radio-veritas.org.ph; or fmrva@pworld.net.ph. URLs: www.radio-veritas.org.ph; www.pworld.net.ph/user/fmrva/. Contact: (administration) Ms. Erlinda G. So, Manager; (general) Ms. Cleofe R. Labindao, Audience Relations Supervisor; Mrs. Regie de Juan Galindez; or Msgr. Pietro Nguyen Van Tai, Program Director; (technical) Ing. Floremundo L. Kiguchi, Technical Director; Ing. Honorio L. Llavore, Assistant Technical Director; or Frequency and Monitoring Department. Free caps, T-shirts, stickers, pennants, rulers, pens, postcards and calendars. Return postage appreciated.
TRANSMITTER SITE: Radio Veritas Asia, Palauig, Zambales, Philippines. Contact: Fr. Hugo Delbaere, CICM, Technical Consultant.
BRUSSELS BUREAUS AND MAIL DROPS: Catholic Radio and Television Network, 32-34 Rue de l' Association, B-1000 Brussels, Belgium; or UNDA, 12 Rue de l'Orme, B-1040 Brussels, Belgium.
Voice of America/IBB—Poro and Tinang Relay Stations. Phone: +63 (2) 813-0470/1/2. Fax: +63 (2) 813 0469. Contact: Frank Smith, Manager; or David Strawman, Deputy Manager. These numbers for urgent technical matters only. Otherwise, does not welcome direct correspondence; *see* USA for acceptable VOA Washington address and related information.

PIRATE

Pirate radio stations are usually one-person operations airing home-brew entertainment and/or iconoclastic viewpoints. In order to avoid detection by the authorities, they tend to appear irregularly, with little concern for the niceties of conventional program scheduling. Most are found in Europe chiefly on weekends, and mainly during evenings in North America, often just above 6200 kHz, just below 7000 kHz and just above 7375 kHz. These *sub rosa* stations and their addresses are subject to unusually abrupt change or termination, sometimes as a result of forays by radio authorities.

Two worthy sources of current addresses and other information on American pirate radio activity are: *The Pirate Radio Directory*, by Andrew Yoder and George Zeller [Tiare Publications, P.O. Box 493, Lake Geneva WI 53147 USA, U.S. toll-free phone 1-800-420-0579; or for specific inquiries, contact author Zeller directly: (fax) +1 (216) 696 0770; (e-mail) George.Zeller@acclink.com], an excellent annual reference; and A*C*E, P.O. Box 12112, Norfolk VA 23541 USA (e-mail: pradio@erols.com; URL: www.frn.net/ace/), a club which publishes a periodical ($20/year U.S., US$21 Canada, $27 elsewhere) for serious pirate radio enthusiasts.

A show on a specialized form of American pirate activity—low-powered local (usually FM) stations—is "Micro-Power Radio in the U.S.," aired over Radio for Peace International, Costa Rica, some Mondays at 2130 and some Thursdays at 2200 World Time on 6200 or 7385 kHz, plus 15050 kHz. For further information, send an e-mail message to: sues@ricochet.net; or paul_w_griffin@bmug.org.

For Europirate DX news, try:

SRSNEWS, Swedish Report Service, Ostra Porten 29, SE-442 54 Ytterby, Sweden. E-mail: srs@ice.warp.slink.se. URL: www-pp.kdt.net/jonny/index.html.

Pirate Connection, P.O. Box 4580, SE-203 20 Malmoe, Sweden; or P.O. Box 7085, Kansas City, Missouri 64113, USA. Phone: (home, Sweden) +46 (40) 611-1775; (mobile, Sweden) +46 (70) 581-5047. E-mail: etoxspz@eto.ericsson.se, xtdspz@lmd.ericsson.se or spz@exallon.se. URL: www-pp.hogia.net/jonny/pc. Six issues annually for about $23. Related to SRSNEWS, above.

Pirate Chat, 21 Green Park, Bath, Avon, BA1 1HZ, United Kingdom.

FRS Goes DX, P.O. Box 2727, NL-6049 ZG Herten, Holland. E-mail: FRSH@pi.net; or peter.verbruggen@tip.nl. URL: http://home.pi.net/~freak55/home.htm.

Free-DX, 3 Greenway, Harold Park, Romford, Essex, RM3 OHH, United Kingdom.

FRC-Finland, P.O. Box 82, FIN-40101 Jyvaskyla, Finland.

Pirate Express, Postfach 220342, Wuppertal, Germany.

A regularly updated list of addresses for European "Free Radio" stations can be found at the URL: www.club.innet.be/~ind1570/freerad.htm.

For up-to-date listener discussions and other pirate-radio information on the Internet, the usenet URLs are: alt.radio.pirate and rec.radio.pirate.

POLAND   World Time +1 (+2 midyear)

Radio Maryja, ul. Żwirki i Wigury 80, PL-87-100 Toruń, Poland. Phone: (general) +48 (56) 655-2361; (studio) +48 (56) 655-2333, +48 (56) 655-2366. Fax: +48 (56) 655 2362. E-mail: RadioMaryja@man.torun.pl. URL: www.man.torun.pl/RadioMaryja/. Contact: Father Tadeusz Rydzk, Dyrektor; or Father Jacek Cydzik. Polish preferred, but also replies to correspondence in English. Transmits via the facilities of the Voice of Russia.

Polish Radio Warsaw

STATION: External Service, P.O. Box 46, PL-00-977 Warsaw, Poland. Phone: (general) +48 (22) 645-9305 or +48 (22) 444-123; (English Section) +48 (22) 645-9262; (German Section) +48 (22) 645-9333; (placement liaison) +48 (2) 645-9002. Fax: (general and administration) +48 (22) 645 5917 or +48 (22) 645 5919; (placement liaison) +48 (2) 645 5906. E-mail (general): piatka@radio.com.pl; (English Section) rafalk@radio.com.pl; (Polskie Radio parent organization) polskie.radio@radio.com.pl. URLs: (RealAudio in English and Polish) www.wrn.org/stations/poland.html; (text in Polish) http://apollo.radio.com.pl/piatka/program5_bpl.html; (text in English) http://apollo.radio.com.pl/piatka/english/program5_ang.html. Contact: (general) Rafał Kiepuszewski, Head, English Section & Producer, "Postbag"; Peter Gentle, Presenter, "Postbag"; or Ann Flapan, Corresponding Secretary; (administration) Jerzy M. Nowakowski, Managing Director; Wanda Samborska, Managing Director; Bogumiła Berdychowska, Deputy Managing Director; or Maciej Lętowski, Executive Manager. On-air Polish language course with free printed material. Free stickers, pens, key rings and possibly T-shirts depending on financial cutbacks. DX Listeners' Club. *TRANSMISSION AUTHORITY:* PAR (National Radio-

Adventist World Radio's ever-cheerful Lolita Colegado answers mail from listeners.   AWR

communication Agency), ul. Kasprzaka 18/20, PL-01-211 Warsaw, Poland. Phone: +48 (22) 608-8140. Fax: +48 (22) 608 8195. E-mail: (Grodzicka) z.wizimirski@par.gov.pl; (Trzos) l.trzos@par.gov.pl. Contact: Mrs. Filomena Grodzicka, Head of BC Section; Lukasz Trzos; Ms. Urszula Rzepa or Jan Kondej.

PORTUGAL   World Time exactly (+1 midyear); Azores World Time −1 (World Time midyear)

📻**RDP Internacional—Rádio Portugal**, Box 1011, P-1001 Lisbon, Portugal. Phone: (main office) +351 (1) 347-5065/8; (engineering) +351 (1) 387-1109. Fax: (main office) +351 (1) 347 4475; (engineering) +351 (1) 387 1381. E-mail: rdpinternacional@rdp.pt. URL: (includes RealAudio) www.rdp.pt/internacional/. Contact: (administration) José Manuel Nunes, Chairman; or Jaime Marques Almeida, Director; (technical) Eng. Francisco Mascarenhas; or Rui de Jesús, Frequency Manager. Free stickers, paper pennants and calendars. May send literature from the Portuguese National Tourist Office.

Rádio Renascença (when operating), Rua Ivens 14, P-1294 Lisbon Codex, Portugal. Phone: +351 (1) 347-5270. Fax: +351 (1) 342 2658. Contact: C. Pabil, Director-Manager.

Radio Trans Europe (transmission facilities), 6º esq., Rua Braamcamp 84, P-1200 Lisbon, Portugal. Transmitter located at Sines.

Voice of Orthodoxy—*see* Belarus.

QATAR   World Time +3

Qatar Broadcasting Service, P.O. Box 3939, Doha, Qatar. Phone: (director) +974 86-48-05; (under secretary) +974 86-48-23; (engineering) +974 86-45-18; (main Arabic service audio feed) +974 895-895. Fax: +974 82 28 88 or +974 83 14 47. Contact: Jassim Mohamed Al-Qattan, Head of Public Relations. May send booklet on Qatar Broadcasting Service. Occasionally replies, and return postage helpful.

ROMANIA   World Time +2 (+3 midyear)

📻**Radio România International**
STATION: 60-62 Berthelot St., 70747 Bucharest, Romania; P.O. Box 111, R-70756 Bucharest, Romania; or Romanian embassies worldwide. Phone: (general) +40 (1) 222-2556, +40 (1) 303-1172, +40 (1) 303-1488 or +40 (1) 312-3645; (English Department) +40 (1) 617-2856; (engineering) +40 (1) 312-1057. Fax: (general) +40 (1) 223 2613 [if no connection, try via office of the Director General of Radio România, but mark fax "Pentru RRI"; that fax is +40 (1) 222 5641]; (Engineering Services) +40 (1) 312 1056/7 or +40 (1) 615 6992. E-mail: rri@radio.ror.ro; (Nisipeanu) emisie@radio.ror.ro. URL: (general) http://indis.ici.ro/romania/news/rri.html; (RealAudio in English) www.wrn.org/stations/romania/html. Contact: (communications in English, Romanian or German) Frederica Dochinoiu; or Dan Balamat, "Listeners' Letterbox"; (radio enthusiasts' issues, English only) "DX Mailbag," English Department; (communications in French or Romanian) Doru Vasile Ionescu, Deputy General Director; (listeners' letters) Giorgiana Zachia; (technical) Ms. Sorin Floricu; Radu Ianculescu, Frequency Monitoring Engineer; or Marius Nisipeanu, Engineering Services. Free stickers, pennants, posters, pins and assorted other items. Can provide supplementary materials for "Romanian by Radio" course on audio cassettes. Listeners' Club. Annual contests. Replies slowly but regularly. Con-

cerns about frequency management should be directed to the PTT (*see* below), with copies to the Romanian Autonomous Company (*see* farther below) and to a suitable official at RRI. *TRANSMISSION AND FREQUENCY MANAGEMENT, PTT:* General Directorate of Regulations, Ministry of Communications, 14a Al. Libertatii, R-70060 Bucharest, Romania. Phone: +40 (1) 400-1312. Fax: +40 (1) 400 1230. Contact: Mrs. Elena Danila, Head of Frequency Management Department.
TRANSMISSION AND FREQUENCY MANAGEMENT, AUTONOMOUS COMPANY: Romanian Autonomous Company for Radio Communications, 14a Al. Libertatii, R-70060 Bucharest, Romania. Phone: +40 (1) 400-1072. Fax: +40 (1) 400 1228. Contact: Mr. Marian Ionita.

RUSSIA   (Times given for republics, oblasts and krays):
- World Time +2 (+3 midyear) Kaliningradskaya;
- World Time +3 (+4 midyear) Arkhangel'skaya (incl. Nenetskiy), Astrakhanskaya, Belgorodskaya, Bryanskaya, Ivanovskaya, Kaluzhskaya, Karelia, Kirovskaya, Komi, Kostromskaya, Kurskaya, Lipetskaya, Moscovskaya, Murmanskaya, Nizhegorodskaya, Novgorodskaya, Orlovskaya, Penzenskaya, Pskovskaya, Riazanskaya, Samarskaya, Sankt-Peterburgskaya, Smolenskaya, Tambovskaya, Tulskaya, Tverskaya, Vladimirskaya, Vologodskaya, Volgogradskaya, Voronezhskaya, Yaroslavskaya;
- World Time +4 (+5 midyear) Checheno-Ingushia, Chuvashia, Dagestan, Kabardino-Balkaria, Kalmykia, Krasnodarskiy, Mari-Yel, Mordovia, Severnaya Osetia, Stavropolskiy, Tatarstan, Udmurtia;
- World Time +5 (+6 midyear) Bashkortostan, Chelyabinskaya, Kurganskaya, Orenburgskaya, Permskaya, Yekaterinburgskaya, Tyumenskaya;
- World Time +6 (+7 midyear) Altayskiy, Omskaya;
- World Time +7 (+8 midyear) Kemerovskaya, Krasnoyarskiy (incl. Evenkiyskiy), Novosibirskaya, Tomskaya, Tuva;
- World Time +8 (+9 midyear) Buryatia, Irkutskaya;
- World Time +9 (+10 midyear) Amurskaya, Chitinskaya, Sakha (West);
- World Time +10 (+11 midyear) Khabarovskiy, Primorskiy, Sakha (Center), Yevreyskaya;
- World Time +11 (+12 midyear) Magadanskaya (exc. Chukotskiy), Sakha (East), Sakhalinskaya;
- World Time +12 (+13 midyear) Chukotskiy, Kamchatskaya, Koryakskiy;
- World Time +13 (+14 midyear) all points east of longtitude 172.30 E.

WARNING—MAIL THEFT: Airmail correspondence containing funds or IRCs from North America and Japan may not arrive safely even if sent by registered air mail, as such mail enters via Moscow Airport. However, funds sent from Europe, North America and Japan via surface mail enter via St. Petersburg, and thus stand a better chance of arriving safely. Airmail service is otherwise now almost on a par with that of other advanced countries.
VERIFICATION OF STATIONS USING TRANSMITTERS IN ST. PETERSBURG AND KALININGRAD: Transmissions of certain world band stations—such as the Voice of Russia, Mayak and China Radio International—when emanating from transmitters located in St. Petersburg and Kaliningrad, may be verified directly from: World Band Verification QSL Service, The State Enterprise for Broadcasting and Radio Communications No. 2

(GPR-2), ul. Akademika Pavlova 13A, 197376 St. Petersburg, Russia. Fax: +7 (812) 234 2971 during working hours. Contact: Mikhail V. Sergeyev, Chief Engineer; or Mikhail Timofeyev, verifier. Free stickers. Two IRCs required for a reply, which upon request includes a copy of "Broadcast Schedule," which gives transmission details (excluding powers) for all transmissions emanating from three distinct transmitter locations: Kaliningrad-Bolshakovo, St. Petersburg and St. Petersburg-Popovka. This organization—which has 26 shortwave, three longwave, 15 mediumwave AM and nine FM transmitters—relays broadcasts for clients for the equivalent of about $0.70-1.00 per kW/hour.

Government Radio Agencies

C.I.S. FREQUENCY MANAGEMENT ENGINEERING OFFICE: The Main Centre for Control of Broadcasting Networks, 7 Nikolskaya Str., 103012 Moscow, Russia. Phone: +7 (095) 298-3302. Fax: +7 (095) 956 7546 or +7 (095) 921 1624. E-mail: (Titov) titov@mccbn.ru. Contact: (general) Mrs. Antonia Ostakhova Mrs. Nina Bykova; or Ms. Margarita Ovetchkina; (administration) Anatoliy T. Titov, Chief Director. This office plans the frequency usage for transmitters throughout much of the C.I.S. Correspondence should be concerned only with significant technical observations or engineering suggestions concerning frequency management improvement—not regular requests for verifications. Correspondence in Russian preferred, but English accepted.

STATE ENTERPRISE FOR BROADCASTING AND RADIO COMMUNICATIONS NO. 2 (GPR-2)—see VERIFICATION OF STATIONS USING TRANSMITTERS IN ST. PETERSBURG AND KALININGRAD, above.

STATE RADIO COMPANY: AS Radioagency Co., Pyatnitskaya 25, 113326 Moscow, Russia. Phone: (Khlebnikov and Petrunicheva) +7 (095) 233-6474; (Komissarova) +7 (095) 233-6660; (Staviskaia) +7 (095) 233-7003. Fax: (Khlebnikov, Petrunicheva and Komissarova) +7 (095) 233 1342; (Staviskaia) +7 (095) 230 2828 or +7 (095) 233 7648. Contact: Valentin Khlebnikov, Mrs. Maris Petrunicheva, Mrs. Lyudmila Komissarova or Mrs. Rachel Staviskaia.

STATE TRANSMISSION AUTHORITY: Russian Ministry of Telecommunication, ul. Tverskaya 7, 103375 Moscow, Russia. Phone: +7 (095) 201-6568. Fax: +7 (095) 292 7086 or +7 (095) 292 7128. Contact: Anatoly C. Batiouchkine.

STATE TV AND RADIO COMPANY: Russian State TV & Radio Company, ul. Yamskogo 5, Polya 19/21, 125124 Moscow, Russia. Phone: +7 (095) 213-1054, +7 (095) 213-1054 or +7 (095) 250-0511. Fax: +7 (095) 250 0105. Contact: Ivan Sitilenlov.

Adventist World Radio, the Voice of Hope, AWR-Russia, The Voice of Hope Media Center, P.O. Box 170, 300 000 Tula-Centre, Russia. Fax: +7 (087) 233 1218. E-mail: (Kulakov) 74532.2000@compuserve.com. URL: www.awr.org/awr-russia/. Contact: Peter Kulakov, Manager. Free home study Bible guides and other religious material, some small souvenirs. AWR terminated its external shortwave transmissions from Russia in October 1996, but still brodcasts via Russian domestic medium wave (AM), shortwave and FM channels. Often reception reports sent here are redirected to the AWR Europe office (*see* under Italy)—*see* also AWR listings under Costa Rica, Guam, Guatemala, Kenya and USA).

Adygey Radio (Radio Maykop), ul. Zhukovskogo 24, 352700 Maykop, Republic of Adygeya, Russia. Contact: A.T. Kerashev, Chairman. English accepted but Russian preferred. Return postage helpful.

Arkhangel'sk Radio, Dom Radio, ul. Popova 2, 163000 Arkhangel'sk, Arkhangel'skaya Oblast, Russia; or U1PR, Valentin G. Kalasnikov, ul. Suvorov 2, kv. 16, Arkhangel'sk, Arkhangel'skaya Oblast, Russia. Replies irregularly to correspondence in Russian.

Bashkir Radio, ul. Gafuri 9, 450076 Ufa, Bashkortostan, Russia.

Buryat Radio, Dom Radio, ul. Erbanova 7, 670000 Ulan-Ude, Republic of Buryatia, Russia. Contact: Z.A. Telin or L.S. Shikhanova.

Chita Radio, ul. Kostushko-Grigorovicha 27, 672090 Chita, Chitinskaya Oblast, Russia. Contact: (technical) V.A. Klimov, Chief Engineer; V.A. Moorzin, Head of Broadcasting; or A.A. Anufriyev.

Evenkiyskaya Radio, ul. 50 let Oktyabrya 28, 663370 Tura, Evenkiyskiy Avt. Okrug, Russia. Contact: B. Yuryev, Engineer. Replies to correspondence in Russian.

FEBC Russia, P.O. Box 2128, Khabarovsk 680020, Russia.

GTRK Amur, per Svyatitelya Innokentiya 15, 675000 Blagoveschensk, Russia. Contact: V.I. Kal'chenko, Chief Engineer.

Islamskaya Volna (Islamic Wave), Islamic Center of Moscow Region, Moscow Jami Mosque, Vypolzov per. 7, 129090 Moscow, Russia; or Pyatnitskaya ulitsa 25, 133326 Moscow, Russia. Phone: +7 (095) 233-6423/6, +7 (095) 233-6629 or +7 (095) 281-4904. Contact: Sheikh Ravil Gainutdin. Return postage necessary.

Kabardino-Balkar Radio (Radio Nalchik), ul. Nogmova 38, 360000 Nalchik, Republic of Kabardino-Balkariya, Russia. Contact: Kamal Makitov, Vice-Chairman. Replies to correspondence in Russian.

Kamchatka Radio, RTV Center, Dom Radio, ul. Sovietskaya 62-G, 683000 Petropavlovsk-Kamchatskiy, Kamchatskaya Oblast, Russia. Contact: A. Borodin, Chief OTK; or V.I. Aibabin. $1 required. Replies in Russian to correspondence in Russian or English.

Khabarovsk Radio, RTV Center, ul. Lenina 71, 680013 Khabarovsk, Khabarovskiy Kray, Russia; or Dom Radio, pl. Slavy, 682632 Khabarovsk, Khabarovskiy Kray, Russia. Contact: (technical) V.N. Kononov, Glavnyy Inzhener.

Khanty-Mansiysk Radio, Dom Radio, ul. Mira 7, 626200 Khanty-Mansiysk, Khanty-Mansiyskiy Avt. Okrug, Tyumenskaya Oblast, Russia. Contact: (technical) Vladimir Sokolov, Engineer.

Koryak Radio, ul. Obukhova 4, 684620 Palana, Koryakskiy Khrebet, Russia.

Krasnoyarsk Radio, RTV Center, Sovietskaya 128, 660017 Krasnoyarsk, Krasnoyarskiy Kray, Russia. Contact: Valeriy Korotchenko; or Anatoliy A. Potehin, RAØAKE. Free local information booklets in English/Russian. Replies in Russian to correspondence in English or Russian. Return postage helpful.

Magadan Radio, RTV Center, ul. Kommuny 8/12, 685013 Magadan, Magadanskaya Oblast, Russia. Contact: Viktor Loktionov or V.G. Kuznetsov. Return postage helpful. May reply to correspondence in Russian.

Mariy Radio, Mari Yel, ul. Osipenko 50, 424014 Yoshkar-Ola, Russia.

Mayak—*see* Radiostantsiya Mayak.

Murmansk Radio, sopka Varnichnaya, 183042 Murmansk, Murmanskaya Oblast, Russia; or RTV Center, Sopka Varnichaya, 183042 Murmansk, Murmanskaya Oblast, Russia.

Northern European Radio Relay Service (NERRS) (when inaugurated), World Band Verification QSL Service, The State Enterprise for Broadcasting and Radio Communications

Adventist World Radio broadcasts from Senetech's Meyerton station in South Africa to Southern and East Africa in English, French, Kiswahili and Somali.
AWR

No. 2 (GPR-2), ul. Akademika Pavlova 13A, 197376 St. Petersburg, Russia. Fax: +7 (812) 234 2971. This planned operation hopes to air non-controversial commercial world band programs to Europe.

Perm Radio, Permskaya Gosudarstvennaya Telekinoradiokompaniya, ul. Technicheskaya 21, 614600 Perm, Permskaya Oblast, Russia; or ul. Krupskoy 26, 614060 Perm, Permskaya Oblast, Russia. Contact: M. Levin, Senior Editor; or A. Losev, Acting Chief Editor.

Qala Atouraya (Voice of Assyria), ul.Pyatnitskaya 25, 113326 Moscow. Contact: Marona Arsanis, Chief Editor; or Roland T. Bidjamov, Editor. Return postage helpful. Replies irregularly.

Radio Maykop—*see* Adygey Radio, above.

Radio Nalchik—*see* Radio Kabardino-Balkar, above.

Radio Rossii (Russia's Radio), Room 121, ul. Yamskogo 5-R, Polya 19/21, 125124 Moscow, Russia. Phone: +7 (095) 213-1054 or +7 (095) 250-0511. Fax: +7 (095) 250 0105 or +7 (095) 233 6449. Contact: Sergei Yerofeyev, Director of International Operations [sic]; or Sergei Davidov, Director. Free English-language information sheet. For verification of reception from transmitters located in St. Petersburg and Kaliningrad, *see* NOTE, above, shortly after the country heading, "RUSSIA."

Radio Samorodinka, P.O. Box 898, Center, 101000 Moscow, Russia. Contact: L.S. Shiskin, Editor. This station may be licensed as other than a regular broadcaster.

Radio Seven, ul. Gagarina 6-A, 443079 Samara, Samaraskaya Oblast, Russia. Contact: A.P. Nenashjev; or Mrs. A.S. Shamsutdinova, Editor.

Radio Tatarstan, ul. Maksima Gor'kogo 15, 420015 Kazan, Tatarstan, Russia. Phone: (editorial) +8432 36-74-93. Contact: Hania Hazipovna Galimova.

Radiostantsiya Mayak, ul. Akademika Koroleva 12, 127427 Moscow, Russia. Phone: (general) +7 (095) 217-9340; (English) +7 (095) 233-6578; (administration) +7 (095) 217-7888. Fax: +7 (095) 215 0847. URL: www.radiomayak.ru/. Contact: (administration) Vladimir Povolyayev, Director. Correspondence in Russian preferred, but English increasingly accepted. For verification of reception from transmitters located in St. Petersburg and Kaliningrad, *see* NOTE, above, shortly after the country heading, "RUSSIA."

Radiostantsiya Tikhiy Okean (program of Primorsk Radio, also aired via Voice of Russia transmitters), RTV Center, ul. Uborevieha 20A, 690000 Vladivostok, Primorskiy Kray, Russia.

Radio Vladivostok (when active), RTV Center, ul. Uborevitsa 20A, 690000 Vladivostok, Primorskiy Kray, Russia. E-mail: rv1098@mail.primorye.ru. Contact: A.G. Giryuk. Return postage helpful.

Sakha Radio, Dom Radio, ul. Ordzhonikidze 48, 677007 Yakutsk, Sakha (Yakutia) Republic, Russia. Fax: +7 (095) 230 2919. Contact: (general) Alexandra Borisova; Lia Sharoborina, Advertising Editor; or Albina Danilova, Producer, "Your Letters"; (technical) Sergei Bobnev, Technical Director. Russian books $15; audio cassettes $10. Free station stickers and original Yakutian souvenirs. Replies to correspondence in English.

Sakhalin Radio, Dom Radio, ul. Komsomolskaya 209, 693000 Yuzhno-Sakhalinsk, Sakhalin Is., Sakhalinskaya Oblast, Russia. Contact: V. Belyaev, Chairman of Sakhalinsk RTV Committee.

Tyumen' Radio, RTV Center, ul. Permyakova 6, 625013 Tyumen', Tyumenskaya Oblast, Russia. Contact: (technical) V.D. Kizerov, Engineer, Technical Center. Sometimes replies to correspondence in Russian. Return postage helpful.

Voice of Russia, ul. Pyatnitskaya 25, Moscow 113326, Russia. Phone: (International Relations Department) +7 (095) 233-7801; (Deputy Editor-in-Chief) +7 (095) 950-6980 or +7 (095) 950-6586; (Programmes Directorate) +7 (095) 233-6793; (Commercial Dept.) +7 (095) 233-7934; (Audience Research) +7 (095) 233-6278; (Chairman's Secretariat) +7 (095) 233-6331; (News Directorate) +7 (095) 233-6513. Fax: (Chairman's Secretariat) +7 (095) 230 2828; (Editor-in-Chief) +7 (095) 950 5693; (World Service) +7 (095) 233 7693; (International Relations Department) +7 (095) 233 7648; (News Directorate) +7 (095) 233 7567; (technical) +7 (095) 233 1342. E-mail: (general) letters@vor.ru; (administrative) chairman@vor.ru; (backup e-mail address) root@avrora.msk.ru. URL: www.vor.ru/. Listeners with a computer equipped with a sound card can send a voice mail to the station via the Internet (for detailed instructions, *see* the Voice of Russia website). Contact: (English Service—listeners' questions to be answered over the air) Joe Adamov; (English Service—all other general correspondence) Ms. Olga

Radio Nepal's first transmitter facility, inaugurated in 1951. This quaint building was originally a school for children of the royal family's servants.

R.S. Karki, Radio Nepal

Troshina, Tanya Stukova; Elena Prolovskaya; or Elena Osipova, World Service, Letters Department; (general correspondence, all languages) Victor Kopytin, Director of International Relations Department; Vladimir Zhamkin, Editor-in-Chief; Yevgeny Nilov, Deputy Editor-in-Chief; Anatoly Morozov, Deputy Editor-in-Chief; (Japanese) Yelena Sopova, Japanese Department; (verifications, all services) Mrs. Eugenia Stepanova, c/o English Service; (administration) Yuri Minayev, First Deputy Chairman, Voice of Russia; Armen Oganesyan, Chairman, World Service, Voice of Russia; (technical) Valentin Khleknikov, Frequency Coordinator; Leonid Maevski, Engineering Services; or Maria Petrunicheva, Engineering Services. To contact other language services please contact the International Relations Department. For verification of reception from transmitters located in St. Petersburg and Kaliningrad, see NOTE, above, shortly after the country heading, "RUSSIA." For verification from transmitters in Khabarovsk, you can also write directly to the Voice of Russia, Dom Radio, Lenina 4, Khabarovsk 680020, Russia. For engineering correspondence concerning frequency management problems, besides "technical," preceding, see NOTE on C.I.S. Frequency Management towards the beginning of this "Russia" listing. Free stickers, booklets and sundry other souvenirs occasionally available upon request. Sells audio cassettes of Russian folk and classical music, as well as a Russian language-learning course. Although not officially a part of the Voice of Russia, an organization selling Russian art and handcrafts that sprung from contacts made with the Voice of Russia is "Cheiypouka," Box 266, Main St., Stonington ME 04681 USA; phone +1 (207) 367-5021.

Voice of Assyria—see Qala Atouraya, above.

RWANDA   World Time +2

Deutsche Welle—Relay Station Kigali—Correspondence should be directed to the main offices in Cologne, Germany (see).

Radio Rwanda, B.P. 404, Kigali, Rwanda. Fax: +250 (7) 6185. Contact: Marcel Singirankabo. $1 required. Rarely replies, with correspondence in French preferred.

ST. HELENA   World Time exactly

Radio St. Helena (when operating once each year), Broadway House, Main Street, Jamestown, St. Helena, South Atlantic Ocean. Phone: +290 4669. Fax: +290 4542. E-mail: tony@sthelena.se; or (Radio St. Helena Day Coordinator, Sweden) sthelena.coordinator@sthelena.se. URL: www.sthelena.se. Contact: (general) Tony Leo, Station Manager; (listeners' questions) Ralph Peters, Presenter, "Evening Shuttle." $1, required. Replies regularly but slowly; verifications can take several months or even a year. Radio St. Helena Day T-shirts (small/medium/large/XL/XXL) available for $25 airmail from: South Atlantic Travel & Trade, Box 6014, SE-600 06 Norrköping, Sweden. Is on the air on world band only once each year—"Radio St Helena Day"—usually late October on 11092.5 kHz in the upper-sideband (USB) mode.

SAO TOME E PRINCIPE   World Time exactly

Voice of America/IBB—São Tomé Relay Station, P.O. Box 522, São Tomé, São Tomé e Príncipe. Phone: +23 912 22-800. Fax: +23 912 22 435. These numbers are for timely and significant technical matters only. Contact: Manuel Neves, Transmitter Plant Technician. Replies direct if $1 included with correspondence, otherwise all communications should be directed to the usual VOA address in Washington (see USA).

SAUDI ARABIA   World Time +3

Broadcasting Service of The Kingdom of Saudi Arabia, P.O. Box 61718, Riyadh-11575, Saudi Arabia. Phone: (general) +966 (1) 404-2795; (administration) +966 (1) 442-5493; (technical) +966 (1) 442-5170. Fax: (general) +966 (1) 402 8177;

(Frequency Management) +966 (1) 404 1692. URL: (RealAudio only) http://radio.kacst.edu.sa/ithaa.ram. Contact: (general) Mutlaq A. Albegami, European Service Manager; (technical) Sulaiman Samnan, Director of Frequency Management; or A. Shah, Department of Frequency Management. Free travel information and book on Saudi history.

SENEGAL   World Time exactly

◼ **Radiodiffusion Télévision Sénégalaise**, B.P. 1765, Dakar, Senegal. Phone: +221 23-63-49. Fax: + 221 22 34 90. E-mail: rts@primature.sn. URL: (includes live NetShow audio) www.primature.sn/rts/. Contact: (technical) Joseph Nesseim, Directeur des Services Techniques; or Mme Elisabeth Ndiaye. Free stickers and Senegalese stamps. Return postage, $1 or 2 IRCs required; as Mr. Nesseim collects stamps, unusual stamps may be even more appreciated. Replies to correspondence in French.

SEYCHELLES   World Time +4

BBC World Service—Indian Ocean Relay Station, P.O. Box 448, Victoria, Mahé, Seychelles; or Grand Anse, Mahé, Seychelles. Phone: +248 78-269. Fax: +248 78 500. Contact: (administration) Peter J. Loveday, Station Manager; (technical) Peter Lee, Resident Engineer; Nigel Bird, Resident Engineer; or Steve Welch, Assistant Resident Engineer. Nontechnical correspondence should be sent to the BBC World Service in London (see).

Far East Broadcasting Association—FEBA Radio
MAIN OFFICE: P.O. Box 234, Mahé, Seychelles, Indian Ocean. Phone: (main office) +248 241-215; (engineering) +248 241-353. E-mail: spepper@febaradio.org.uk. URL: www.feba.org.uk. Contact: Station Director; or Richard Whittington, Schedule Engineer. Free stickers, pennants and station information sheet. $1 or one IRC helpful. Also, see FEBC Radio International—USA and United Kingdom.
CANADIAN OFFICE: 6850 Antrim Avenue, Burnaby BC, V5J 4M4 Canada. Fax: +1 (604) 430 5272. E-mail: dpatter@axionet.com. INDIA OFFICE: FEBA India, P.O. Box 2526, 7 Commissariat Road, Bangalore-560 025, India. Fax: +91 (80) 584 701. E-mail: 6186706@mcimail.com. Contact: Peter Muthl Raj.

SIERRA LEONE   World Time exactly

Sierra Leone Broadcasting Service, New England, Freetown, Sierra Leone. Phone: +232 (22) 240-123; +232 (22) 240-173; +232 (22) 240-497 or 232 (22) 241-919. Fax: +232 (22) 240 922. Contact: (general) Denis Smith, Acting Head of Programmes; (technical) B.D.H. Taylor, Acting Chief Engineer; or Steve Conteh, Project Engineer.

SINGAPORE   World Time +8

BBC World Service—Far Eastern Relay Station, 26 Olive Road, Singapore. Phone: + 65 260-1511. Fax: +65 253 8131. Contact: (technical) Far East Resident Engineer. Nontechnical correspondence should be sent to the BBC World Service in London (see).
◼ **Radio Corporation of Singapore**, Farrer Road, P.O. Box 968, Singapore 912899; or (physical location) Caldecott Broadcast Centre, Caldecott Hill, Andrew Road, Singapore 299939. Phone: +65 251-8622 or +65 359-7340. Fax: +65 254 8062, +65 256 9533, +65 256 9556 or +65 256 9338. E-mail: (general)

info@rcs.com.sg; (Engineering Dept.) engineering@rcs.com.sg. URLs: (general) http://rcs.com.sg/; (RealAudio) http://rcslive.singnet.com.sg/. Contact: (general) Lillian Tan, Public Relations Division; Lim Heng Tow, Manager, International & Community Relations; Tan Eng Lai, Promotion Executive; Hui Wong, Producer/Presenter; or Lucy Leong; (administration) Anthony Chia, Director General; (technical) Asaad Sameer Bagharib, V.P. Engineering; or Lee Wai Meng. Free regular and Post-It stickers, pens, umbrellas, mugs, towels, wallets and lapel pins. Do not include currency in envelope.

Radio Nederland via Singapore—For verification direct from the Singaporean transmitters, contact the BBC World Service—Far Eastern Relay Station (see above). Nontechnical correspondence should be sent to Radio Nederland in Holland (see).

Radio Japan via Singapore—For verification direct from the Singaporean transmitters, contact the BBC World Service—Far Eastern Relay Station (see above). Nontechnical correspondence should be sent to Radio Japan in Tokyo (see).

◼ **Radio Singapore International**, Farrer Road, P.O. Box 5300, Singapore 912899, Singapore; or (physical address) Caldecott Broadcast Centre, Annex Building Level 1, Andrew Road, Singapore 299939. Phone: (general) + 65 359-7662; (programme listings) +65 353-5300; (publicity) +65 350-3708 or +65 256-0401. Fax: +65 259 1357 or +65 259 1380. E-mail: rsieng@pacific.net.sg; or RSI@mediacity.com.sg. URL: http://rsi.com.sg/. Contact: (general) Anushia Kanagabasai, Producer, "You Asked For It"; Belinda Yeo, Producer, "Dateline RSI"; or Mrs. Sakuntala Gupta, Programme Manager, English Service; (administration) S. Chandra Mohan, Station Director; (technical) Selena Kaw, Office of the Administrative Executive; or Yong Wui Pin, Engineer. Free souvenir T-shirts and key chains to selected listeners. Do not include currency in envelope.

SLOVAKIA   World Time +1 (+2 midyear)

Radio Slovakia International, Mýtna 1, P.O. Box 55, SK-810 05 Bratislava, Slovakia. Phone: (Chief Editor) +421 (7) 49-62-81; (Deputy Chief Editor) +421 (7) 49-62-82; (English Service) +421 (7) 49-80-75; (Russian Service) +421 (7) 49-82-76; (Slovak Service) +421 (7) 49-82-47; (French Service) +421 (7) 49-82-67; (German Service) +421 (7) 49-62-83. Phone/fax: (technical) +421 (7) 49-76-59. Fax: (French and English Services) +421 (7) 49 82 67; (English Service) +421 (7) 49 62 82; (other language services) +421 (7) 49 82 47; (technical) +421 (7) 39 89 23. E-mail: slrozv@ba-cvt.sanet.sk. URL: www.slovakradio.sk/rsi.html. Contact: Helga Dingová, Director of English Broadcasting; Alan Jones, Producer "Listeners' Tribune"; (administration) PhDr. Karol Palkovič, Head of External Broadcasting; or Dr. Slavomira Kubickova, Head of International Relations; (technical) Edita Chocholatá, Frequency Coordinator; Jozef Krátky, Ing. "Slovak Lesson" course, but no accompanying printed materials. Free stickers, pennants, pocket calendars and other small souvenirs and publications. Reader feedback suggests station may not always receive mail addressed to it; so, if you get no reply, keep trying.

SOLOMON ISLANDS   World Time +11

Solomon Islands Broadcasting Corporation, P.O. Box 654, Honiara, Solomon Islands. Phone: +677 20051. Fax: +677 23159. Contact: (general) Julian Maka'a, Producer, "Listeners From Far Away"; Cornelius Teasi; or Silas Hule; (administration) James T. Kilua, General Manager; (technical) John Babera, Chief Engineer. IRC or $1 helpful. Problems with the domestic mail system may cause delays.

SOMALIA   World Time +3

Radio Mogadishu—Currently, there are three stations operating under the rubric Radio Mogadishu. None is known to reply to listener correspondence.

SOMALILAND   World Time +3

NOTE: "Somaliland," claimed as an independent nation, is diplomatically recognized only as part of Somalia.
Radio Hargeisa, P.O. Box 14, Hargeisa, Somaliland, Somalia. Contact: Sulayman Abdel-Rahman, announcer. Most likely to respond to correspondence in Somali or Arabic.

SOUTH AFRICA   World Time +2

BBC World Service via South Africa—For verification direct from the South African transmitters, contact Sentech (*see* below). Nontechnical correspondence should be sent to the BBC World Service in London (*see*).
Channel Africa, P.O. Box 91313, Auckland Park 2006, South Africa. Phone: (executive editor) +27 (11) 714-2255; +27 (11) 714-2551 or +27 (11) 714-3942; (technical) +27 (11) 714-3409. Fax: (executive editor) +27 (11) 482 3506; +27 (11) 714 2546, +27 (11) 714 4956 or +27 (11) 714 6377; (technical) +27 (11) 714 5812. E-mail: (general) africancan@sabc.co.za; (English News) vorstern@sabc.co.za. URL: (includes RealAudio) www.channelafrica.org/; (RealAudio in English) www.wrn.org/stations/africa/html; (technical) *see* Sentech, below. Contact: (general) Tony Machilika, Head of English Service; Robert Michel, Head of Research and Strategic Planning; or Noeleen Vorster, Corporate Communications Manager; (technical) Mrs. H. Meyer, Supervisor Operations; or Lucienne Libotte, Technology Operations. T-shirts $11 and watches $25. Prices do not include shipping and handling. Free *Share* newsletter from the Department of Foreign Affairs, stickers and calendars. Reception reports are best directed to Sentech (*see* below), which operates the transmission facilities.
Radiosondergrense (Radio Without Boundaries), Posbus 91312, Auckland Park 2006, South Africa. Phone: (general) +27 (89) 110-2525; (live studio on-air line) +27 (89) 110-4553; (management) +27 (11) 714-2702; (administration) +27 (11) 714-4406. Fax: +27 (11) 714 6445. E-mail: (Shaikh) shaikhm@sabc.co.za. URL: www.sabc.co.za/radio/afrst/1index.htm. Contact: (general) Mohamed Shaikh, Manager; (administration) Sarel Myburgh. Reception reports are best directed to Sentech (*see* below), which operates the shortwave transmission facilities. A domestic service of the South African Broadcasting Corporation (*see* below), and formerly known as Afrikaans Stereo.
Sentech (Pty) Ltd, Shortwave Services, Private Bag X06, Honeydew 2040, South Africa. Phone: (shortwave) +27 (11) 475-1596 or (Otto) +27 (11) 471-4658; (general) +27 (11) 475-5600. Fax: +27 (11) 475 5112 or (Otto) +27 (11) 471 4605. E-mail: (Otto) ottok@sentech.co.za; (Smuts) smutsn@sentech.co.za. URL: (shortwave) www.sentech.co.za/meyerton.html; (general, homepage) www.sentech.co.za/. Contact: Mr. N. Smuts, Managing Director; Rodgers Gamuti, Client Manager; or Kathy Otto. Sentech is currently issuing its own verification cards, and is the best place to direct re-

ception reports for all South African world band stations. Four additional 100 kW Brown Boveri transmitters are expected to be on the air shortly for use to such nearby targets as Mozambique, Zambia and Zimbabwe.
South African Broadcasting Corporation
ADMINISTRATION AND GENERAL TECHNICAL MATTERS: Private Bag X1, Auckland Park 2006, South Africa. Phone: (Reddy) +27 (11) 714-2306; (technical) +27 (11) 714-3409. Fax: (general) +27 (11) 714 5055; (Reddy) +27 (11) 726 2914; (technical) +27 (11) 714 3106 or +27 (11) 714 5812. E-mail: format is lastnameinitial@sabc.co.za. URL: www.sabc.co.za. Contact: Govin Reddy, Chief Executive Broadcasting Strategy. Free stickers and ballpoint pens. Reception reports are best directed to Sentech (*see* above), which operates the transmission facilities.
RADIO PROGRAMME SALES: Private Bag X1, Auckland Park 2006, South Africa. Phone: (general enquiries) +27 (11) 714-5681, +27 (11) 714-6039 or +27 (11) 714-4044; (actuality programs) +27 (11) 714-4709; (music) +27 (11) 714-4315. Fax: +27 (11) 714 3671. E-mail: botham@sabc.co.za; snymane@sabc.co.za; or corbinm@sabc.co.za. Offers a wide range of music, book readings, radio drama, comedy and other types of programs.
Trans World Radio Africa
NONTECHNICAL CORRESPONDENCE: Trans World Radio—South Africa, Private Bag 987, Pretoria 0001, South Africa. Phone: +27 (12) 807-0053. Fax: +27 (12) 807 1266. URL: www.icon.co.za/~ttatlow/Welcome.htm.
TECHNICAL CORRESPONDENCE: Reception reports and other technical correspondence are best directed to Sentech (*see* above) or to TWR's Swaziland office (*see*). Also, *see* USA.

SPAIN   World Time +1 (+2 midyear)

Radio Exterior de España (Spanish National Radio)
MAIN OFFICE: Apartado de Correos 156.202, E-28080 Madrid, Spain. Phone: (general) +34 (91) 346-1081/1083; (Audience Relations) +34 (91) 346-1149. Fax: +34 (91) 346 1815. E-mail: audiencia_ree.rne@rtve.es. URL: www.rtve.es/rne/ree/. Contact: Pilar Salvador M., Relaciones con la Audiencia; Nuria Alonso Veiga, Head of Information Service; Alejo Garcia, Director; Ricardo H. Calvo, Webmaster; or Penelope Eades, Foreign Language Programmer. Free stickers, calendars, pennants and tourist information. Reception reports can be sent to: Radio Exterior de España, Relaciones con la Audiencia, Sección DX, Apartado de Correos 156.202, E-28080 Madrid, Spain.
NOBLEJAS TRANSMITTER SITE: Centro Emisor de RNE en Onda Corta, Ctra. Dos Barrios s/n, E-45350 Noblejas-Toledo, Spain.
RUSSIAN OFFICE: P.O Box 88, 109044 Moscow, Russia.
Costa Rican Relay Facility—see Costa Rica.
TRANSCRIPTION SERVICE: Radio Nacional de España, Servicio de Transcripciones, Apartado 156.200, Casa de la Radio (Prado del Rey), E-28223 Madrid, Spain.
WASHINGTON NEWS BUREAU: National Press Building, 529 14th Street NW, Suite 1288, Washington DC 20045 USA. Phone: +1 (202) 783-0768. Contact: Luz María Rodríguez.

SRI LANKA   World Time +6:00

Deutsche Welle—Relay Station Sri Lanka, 92/2 D.S. Senanayake Mawatha, Colombo 08, Sri Lanka. Phone: +94 (1) 699-449. Fax: +94 (1) 699 450. Contact: R. Groschkus, Resi-

**Directors line up
their programs at the
Sri Lanka Broadcasting
Corporation's studios.**
M. Guha

dent Engineer. Nontechnical correspondence should be sent to Deutsche Welle in Germany (*see*).

Radio Japan/NHK, c/o SLBC, P.O. Box 574, Torrington Square, Colombo 7, Sri Lanka. This address for technical correspondence only. General nontechnical listener correspondence should be sent to the usual Radio Japan address in Japan. News-oriented correspondence may also be sent to the NHK Bangkok Bureau (*see* Radio Japan, Japan).

Sri Lanka Broadcasting Corporation (also announces as "Radio Sri Lanka" in the external service), P.O. Box 574, Independence (Torrington) Square, Colombo 7, Sri Lanka. Phone: (general) +94 (1) 697-491 or +94 (1) 697-493; (Director General) +94 (1) 696-140. Fax: (general) +94 (1) 697 150 or +94 (1) 698 576; (Director General) +94 (1) 695 488; (Sooriya, phone/fax) +94 (1) 696 1311. E-mail: slbc@sri.lanka.net; slbcweb@lanka.net. URLs: www.infolanka.com/people/sisira/slbc.html; (occasionally carries live cricket commentary in Real Audio) www.lanka.net/slbc/. Contact: (general) N. Jayhweera, Director - Audience Research; or Icumar Ratnayake, Controller, "Mailbag Program"; (SLBC administration) Eric Fernando, Director General; Newton Gunaratne, Deputy Director-General; (technical) H.M.N.R. Jayawardena, Engineer - Training & Frequency Management;Wimala Sooriya, Deputy Director - Engineering; or A.M.W. Gunaratne, Station Engineer, Ekala.

Voice of America/IBB—Sri Lanka Relay—A new shortwave relay facility is currently under construction in Sri Lanka.

SUDAN   World Time +2

Sudan National Radio Corporation, P.O. Box 572, Omdurman, Sudan. Phone: +249 (11) 53-151 or +249 (11) 52-100. Contact: (general) Mohammed Elfatih El Sumoal; (technical) Abbas Sidig, Director General, Engineering and Technical Affairs; Mohammed Elmahdi Khalil, Administrator, Engineering and Technical Affairs; or Adil Didahammed, Engineering Department. Replies irregularly. Return postage necessary.

SURINAME   World Time –3

Radio Apintie, Postbus 595, Paramaribo, Suriname. Phone: +597 40-05-00. Fax: +597 40 06 84. Contact: Ch. E. Vervuurt, Director. Free pennant. Return postage or $1 required.

SWAZILAND   World Time +2

Swaziland Commercial Radio

NONTECHNICAL CORRESPONDENCE: P.O. Box 5569, Rivonia 2128, Transvaal, South Africa. Phone: +27 (11) 884-8400. Fax: +27 (11) 883 1982. Contact: Fernando Vaz-Osiori; Rob Vickers, Manager—Religion. IRC helpful. Replies irregularly.
TECHNICAL CORRESPONDENCE: P.O. Box 99,Amsterdam 2375, South Africa. Contact: Guy Doult, Chief Engineer.
SOUTH AFRICA BUREAU: P.O. Box 1586,Alberton 1450, Republic of South Africa. Phone: +27 (11) 434-4333. Fax: +27 (11) 434 4777.

Trans World Radio—Swaziland

MAIN OFFICE: P.O. Box 64, Manzini, Swaziland. Phone: +268 52-781/2/3. Fax: +268 55 333. E-mail: (James Burnett, Regional Engineer & Frequency Manager) jburnett.twr.org; (Chief Engineer) sstavrop@twr.org; (L. Stavropoulos, DX Secretary) lstavrop@twr.org; (Greg Shaw, Follow-up Department) gshaw@twr.org. URL (transmission schedule): www.icon.co.za/~ttatlow/schedule.htm. Contact: (general) Dawn-Lynn Prediger, DX Secretary; Greg Shaw, Follow-up Department; Peter A. Prediger, Station Director; or Joseph Ndzinisa, Program Manager; (technical) Mrs. L. Stavropoulos, DX Secretary; Chief Engineer; or James Burnett, Regional Engineer. Free stickers, postcards and calendars. A free Bible Study course is available. May swap canceled stamps. $1, return postage or 3 IRCs required. Hopes to upgrade its very old 25 kW shortwave transmitter with a new 100 kW transmitter. Also, *see* USA.
AFRICA REGIONAL OFFICE: P.O. Box 4232,Kempton Park 1610, South Africa. Contact: Stephen Boakye-Yiadom, African Regional Director.

CÔTE D'IVOIRE OFFICE: B.P. 2131, Abidjan 06, Côte d'Ivoire.
KENYA OFFICE: P.O. Box 21514 Nairobi, Kenya.
MALAWI OFFICE: P. O. Box 52 Lilongwe, Malawi.
SOUTH AFRICA OFFICE: P.O. Box 36000, Menlo Park 0102, South Africa.
ZIMBABWE OFFICE: P.O. Box H-74, Hatfield, Harare, Zimbabwe.

SWEDEN   World Time +1 (+2 midyear)

IBRA Radio (program)
MAIN OFFICE: International Broadcasting Association, Box 396, SE-105 36 Stockholm, Sweden. Phone: +46 (8) 619-2540; Fax: +46 (8) 619 2539. E-mail: hq@ibra.se; or ibra@ibra.se. URLs: www.ibra.se/; www.ibra.org/. Contact: Mikael Stjernberg, Public Relations Manager. Free pennants and stickers. IBRA Radio is heard as a program over various world band radio stations, including the Voice of Hope, Lebanon, Trans World Radio, Monaco, and the Voice of Russia.
CANADA OFFICE: P.O. Box 444, Niagara Falls ON, L2E 6T8 Canada.
CYPRUS OFFICE: P.O. Box 7420, 3315 Limassol, Cyprus. Contact: Rashad Saleem. Free schedules, calendars and stickers.

Radio Sweden
MAIN OFFICE: SE-105 10 Stockholm, Sweden. Phone: (general) +46 (8) 784-7200, +46 (8) 784-7207 or +46 (8) 784-5000; (listener voice mail) +46 (8) 784-7287; (technical department) +46 (8) 784-7286. Fax: (general) +46 (8) 667 6283; (polling to receive schedule) +46 8 660 2990. E-mail: info@rs.sr.se; (schedule on demand) english@rs.sr.se; (Beckman, Technical Manager) rolf-b@stab.sr.se. URL: (RealAudio in Swedish, and text): www.sr.se/rs/index.htm; (RealAudio in English) www.sr.se/rs; or radiosweden.com; (MediaScan page) www.sr.se/english/media/media.htm; (George Wood) www.abc.se/~m8914; (English Service page) www.sr.se/rs/english/. Contact: (general) Nidia Hagstroem, Host, "In Touch with Stockholm" [include your telephone number]; Sarah Roxström, Head, English Service; Greta Grandin, Program Assistant, English Service; George Wood, Producer, MediaScan; Olimpia Seldon, Assistant to the Director; or Charlotte Adler, Public Relations & Information; (administration) Finn Norgren, Director General; (technical) Rolf Erik Beckman, Head, Technical Department. T-shirts (two sizes) $12 or £8. Payment for T-shirts may be made by international money order, Swedish postal giro account No. 43 36 56-6 or internationally negotiable bank check.
NEW YORK NEWS BUREAU: Swedish Broadcasting, 825 Third Avenue, New York NY 10022 USA. Phone: +1 (212) 688-6872 or +1 (212) 643-8855. Fax: +1 (212) 594 6413. Contact: Elizabeth Johansson.
WASHINGTON NEWS BUREAU: Swedish Broadcasting, 2030 M Street NW, Suite 700, Washington DC 20036 USA. Phone: +1 (202) 785-1727. Contact: Folke Rydén, Lisa Carlsson or Steffan Ekendahl.
TRANSMISSION AUTHORITY: TERACOM, Svensk Rundradio AB, P.O. Box 17666, SE-118 92 Stockholm, Sweden. Phone: (general) +46 (8) 671-2000; (Nilsson) +46 (8) 671-2066. Fax: (Nilsson) +46 (8) 671 2060 or +46 (8) 671 2080. E-mail: mni@teracom.se. URL: www.teracom.se. Contact: (Frequency Planning Dept.—head office): Magnus Nilsson. Free stickers; sometimes free T-shirts to those monitoring during special test transmissions. Seeks monitoring feedback for new frequency usages.

SWITZERLAND   World Time +1 (+2 midyear)

European Broadcasting Union, Case Postal 67, CH-1218 Grand-Saconnex, Geneva, Switzerland. Phone: +41 (22) 717-2111. Fax: +41 (22) 798 5897. URL: www.ebu.ch. Contact: Jean-Bernard Munch, Secretary-General.
International Telecommunication Union, Place des Nations, CH-1211 Geneva 20, Switzerland. Phone: +41 (22) 730-5111. Fax: +41 (22) 733 7256. URL: www.itu.ch/. The ITU is the world's official regulatory body for all telecommunication activities, including world band radio. Offers a wide range of official multilingual telecommunication publications in print and/or digital formats.
Swiss Radio International
MAIN OFFICE: Giacomettistrasse 1, CH-3000 Berne 15, Switzerland. Phone: (general) +41 (31) 350-9222; (English Department) +41 (31) 350-9790; (French Department) +41 (31) 350-9555; (German Department) +41 (31) 350-9535; (Italian Department) +41 (31) 350-9531). Fax: (general) +41 (31) 350 9569; (administration) +41 (31) 350 9744 or +41 (31) 350 9581; (Communication and Marketing) +41 (31) 350 9544; (Programme Department) +41 (31) 350 9569; (English Department) +41 (31) 350 9580; (French Department) +41 (31) 350 9664; (German Department) +41 (31) 350 9562; (Italian Department) +41 (31) 350 9678. E-mail: language@sri.srg-ssr.ch (e.g. english@sri.srg-ssr.ch). URLs: (general) www.srg-ssr.ch/SRI/; (RealAudio in English and Portuguese) http://srgtserver.tech-srg-ssr.ch/sri/index.html. Contact: (general) Diana Zanotti, English Department; Marlies Schmutz, Listeners' Letters, German Programmes; Thérèse Schafter, Listeners' Letters, French Programmes; Esther Niedhammer, Listeners' Letters, Italian Programmes; Beatrice Lombard, Promotion; Giovanni D'Amico, Audience Officer; (administration) Ulrich Kündig, General Manager; Nicolas Lombard, Deputy General Manager; Walter Fankhauser, Head, Communication & Marketing Services; Rose-Marie Malinverni, Head, Editorial Co-ordination Unit; Ron Grünig, Head, English Programmes; James Jeanneret, Head, German Programmes; Philippe Zahne, Head, French Programmes; Fabio Mariani, Head, Italian Programmes; (technical) Paul Badertscher, Head, Engineering Services; Bob Zanotti. Free station flyers, posters, stickers and pennants. Sells CDs of Swiss music, plus audio and video (PAL/NTSC) cassettes; also, Swiss watches and clocks, microphone lighters, letter openers, books, T-shirts, sweatshirts and Swiss Army knives. VISA/EURO/AX or cash, but no personal checks. For catalog, write Nicolas D. Lombard, Head, SRI Enterprises, c/o the above address, fax +41 (31) 350 9581, or e-mail shopping@sri.srg-ssr.ch.
TRANSMISSION AUTHORITY: Swisscom, Network Operations, HF Broadcasting / NWO-513, Speichergaße 6, CH-3050 Berne, Switzerland. Phone: +41 (31) 342-3490. Fax: +41 (31) 342 6554. E-mail: (Wegmueller) ulrich.wegmueller@swisscom.com. Contact: Ulrich Wegmüller, Frequency Manager; (administration) Dr. Walter G. Tiedweg, Head Radio Division.
WASHINGTON NEWS BUREAU: 2030 M Street NW, Washington DC 20554 USA. Phone: (general) +1 (202) 775-0894 or +1 (202) 429-9668; (French-language radio) +1 (202) 296-0277; (German-language radio) +1 (202) 7477. Fax: +1 (202) 833 2777. Contact: Christophe Erbeck, reporter.
United Nations Radio, Room G209, Palais des Nations, CH-1211 Geneva 10, Switzerland. Phone: +41 (22) 917-4222. Fax: +41 (22) 917 0123. E-mail: audio-visual@un.org. URLs: (RealAudio) www.wrn.org/stations/un.html; www.internetbroadcast.com/un/.

SYRIA World Time +2 (+3 midyear)

Radio Damascus, Syrian Radio & Television, Ommayad Square, Damascus, Syria. Phone: +963 (11) 720-700. Contact: Mr. Afaf, Director General; Lisa Arslanian; or Mrs. Wafa Ghawi. Free stickers, paper pennants and *The Syria Times* newspaper. Replies can be highly erratic, but as of late have been more regular, if sometimes slow.

TAHITI—*see* FRENCH POLYNESIA.

TAJIKISTAN World Time +5

Radio Tajikistan, ul Chapayeva 31, Dushanbe 734025, Tajikistan; or English Service, International Service, Radio Tajikistan, P.O. Box 108, Dushanbe 734025, Tajikistan. E-mail: liton@td.silk.org. Contact: Gulom Makhmudovich, Deputy Chairman; Raisamuhtan Dinova Vuncha, English Service; Gulnaz Abdullaeva, English Service Editor; Parvez Satter; or Mrs. Raisa Muhutdinova, Editor-in-Chief, English Department. Correspondence in Russian, Farsi, Dari, Tajik or Uzbek preferred, and correspondence in English is best directed to the English service. Mr Abdullaeva collects maps of different countries, so enclosing a map may help in getting a reply.Used Russian stamps appreciated, for whatever reason. Return postage (IRCs or 1$) appreciated, but enclosing currency notes is risky due to the high level of postal theft in the country.
Radio Pay-i 'Ajam-*see* Tajik Radio for details.
Tajik Radio, ul Chapayeva 31, Dushanbe 735025, Tajikistan. Contact: Mirbobo Mirrakhimov, Chairman of State Television and Radio Corporation. Correspondence in Russian, Tajik or Uzbek preferred.

TANZANIA World Time +3

📻**Radio Tanzania**, P.O. Box 9191, Dar es Salaam, Tanzania. Phone: +255 (51) 860-760. Fax: +255 (51) 865 577. URL: (RealAudio only) www.ippmedia.com/Newspapers/radio1.asp. Contact: (general) Abdul Ngarawa, Director of Broadcasting; Mrs. Edda Sanga, Controller of Programs; Abisay Steven, Head of English Service and International Relations Unit; or Ahmed Jongo, Producer, "Your Answer"; (technical) Taha Usi, Chief Engineer; or Emmanuel Mangula, Deputy Chief Engineer. Replies to correspondence in English.
Voice of Tanzania Zanzibar, Department of Broadcasting, P.O. Box 1178, Zanzibar, Tanzania. Phone: +255 (54) 31-088. Fax: + 255 (54) 57 207. Contact: (general) Yusuf Omar Chunda, Director Department of Information and Broadcasting; Ali Bakari Muombwa; Abdulrah'man M. Said; N. Nyamwochd, Director of Broadcasting; or Kassim S. Kassim; (technical) Nassor M. Suleiman, Maintenance Engineer. $1 return postage helpful.

THAILAND World Time +7

BBC World Service—Asia Relay Station, P.O. Box 20, Muang Nakhon, Sawan 60000, Thailand. Contact: Jaruwan Meesaurtong, Personal Assistant.
Mukto Probaho
MAIN ADDRESS: P.O. Box 9406, Calcutta 700016, India. Contact: Sk Abdullah. Correspondence in English and reception reports welcomed. Members' Club. This daily Bengali-language Christian religious program/listener-response show, produced by a studio associated with IBRA Radio (*see* Swe-

den), is aired via transmission facilities of the Voice of Russia. Sometimes verifies via IBRA Radio in Sweden.
BANGKOK ADDRESS: GPO Box 1605, Bangkok 10501, Thailand.
Radio Thailand World Service, 236 Vibhavadi Rangsit Highway, Din Daeng, Huaykhwang, Bangkok 10400, Thailand. Phone: +66 (2) 277-1814, +66 (2) 274-9098. Phone/Fax: +66 (2) 277-6139, +66 (2) 274-9099. E-mail: amporn@usa.net; or amporn@radiothailand.com. URL: www.radiothailand.com/. Contact: Mrs. Amporn Samosorn, Chief of External Services; or Patra Lamjiack. Free pennants. Replies irregularly, especially to those who persist.
Voice of America/IBB—Relay Station Thailand, Udon Thani, Thailand. Phone: +66 (42) 271-490/1. Only matters of urgent importance should be directed to this site. All other correspondence should be directed to the regular VOA address in Washington (*see* USA).

TOGO World Time exactly

Radio Lomé, B.P. 434, Lomé, Togo. Phone: + 228 (21) 2492. Contact: (nontechnical) Batchoudi Malúlaba or Geraldo Isidine. Return postage, $1 or 2 IRCs helpful. French preferred but English accepted.

TONGA World Time +13

Tonga Broadcasting Commission (when operating), A3Z, P.O. Box 36, Nuku'alofa, Tonga, SW Pacific. Phone: +676 23295, +676 23555 or +676 23556. Fax: +676 24417. Contact: (general) Tavake Fusimalohi, General Manager; (technical) Sioeli Maka Tohi, Chief Engineer. Station is currently off the air due to cyclone damage. Plans to return to shortwave if a new transmitter can be obtained from UNESCO.

TUNISIA World Time +1

📻**Radiodiffusion Télévision Tunisienne**, 71 Avenue de la Liberté, TN-1070 Tunis, Tunisia; or try ONT, 13 Rue de Bizerte, TN-1006 Tunis, Tunisia. Phone: +216 (1) 287-300. Fax: +216 (1) 781 058. E-mail: info@radiotunis.com. URL: (includes RealAudio) www.radiotunis.com/news.html. Contact: Mongai Caffai, Director General; Mohamed Abdelkafi, Director; Kamel Cherif, Directeur; Masmoudi Mahmoud; or Smaoui Sadok, Le Sous-Directeur Technique. Replies irregularly and slowly to correspondence in French or Arabic. $1 helpful.

TURKEY World Time +2 (+3 midyear)

Radyo Çinarli, Çinarli Anadolu Teknik ve Endüstri Meslek Lisesi Deneme Radyosu, Çinarli, TR-35.110 İzmir, Turkey. Phone: +90 (232) 486-6434; (technical) +90 (232) 461-7442. Fax: +90 (232) 435 1032. Contact: (general) Ahmet Ayaydin, School Manager; (technical) Göksel Uysal, Technical Manager. Station is run by the local technical institute. Free studio photos and, occasionally, other small souvenirs. Correspondence in English accepted.
Turkish Radio-Television Corporation, Voice of Turkey
MAIN OFFICE, NONTECHNICAL: TRT External Services Department, TRT Sitesi, Turan Gunes Blv., Oran, 06450 Ankara, Turkey; or P.K. 333, Yenisehir, 06443 Ankara, Turkey. Phone: (general) +90 (312) 490-9800/9801; (English Service) +90 (312) 490-9842. Fax: +90 (312) 490 9835/45/46. E-mail: (general) infotsr@tsr.gov.tr; (English Service) englishservice@tsr.gov.tr. URL: http://tsr.gov.tr/ (English: http://tsr.gov.tr/main_en.asp).

Contact: (English & non-technical) Mr. Osman Erkan, Chief, English Service and Host of, "Letterbox"; or Ms. Reshide Morali, Announcer "DX Corner"; (other languages) Mr. Rafet Esit, Director, Foreign Languages Section; (administration) Mr. Danyal Gurdal, Head, External Services Department. Technical correspondence, such as on reception quality should be directed to: Ms. F. Elvan Boratav *see* next entry below. On-air language courses offered in Arabic and German, but no printed course material. Free stickers, pennants, women's embroidery artwork swatches and tourist literature.
MAIN OFFICE, TECHNICAL (FOR EMIRLER AND ÇAKIRLAR TRANSMITTER SITES AND FOR FREQUENCY MANAGEMENT): TRT Teknik Yardimcilik, TRT Sitesi, Kat: 5/C, Oran, 06450 Ankara, Turkey. Phone: +90 (312) 490-1730/2. Fax: +90 (312) 490 1733. E-mail: utis@turnet.net.tr. Contact: Mr. Vural Tekeli, TRT Head of Engineering; F. Elvan Boratav, Chief Engineer, International Technical Relations Service; or Turgay Cakimci, Chief Engineer, International Technical Relations Service.
SAN FRANCISCO OFFICE, SCHEDULES: 2654 17th Avenue, San Francisco CA 94116 USA. Phone: +1 (415) 564-9968. Contact: George Poppin. This address, a volunteer office, only provides TRT schedules to listeners. All other correspondence should be sent directly to Ankara.
Türkiye Polis Radyosu (Turkish Police Radio), T.C. Içişleri Bakanliği, Emniyet Genel Müdürlüğü, Ankara, Turkey. Contact: Fatih Umutlu. Tourist literature for return postage. Replies irregularly.
Meteoroloji Sesi Radyosu (Voice of Meteorology), T.C. Tarim Bakanliği, Devlet Meteoroloji İşleri, Genel Müdürlüğü, P.K. 401, Ankara, Turkey. Phone: +90 (312) 359-7545, X-281. Fax: +90 (312) 314 1196. Contact: (nontechnical) Gühekin Takinalp; Recep Yilmaz, Head of Forecasting Department; or Abdullah Gölpinar; (technical) Mehmet Örmeci, Director General. Free tourist literature. Return postage helpful.

TURKMENISTAN   World Time +5

Radio Turkmenistan, National TV & Radio Broadcasting Company, Mollanepes St. 3, 744000 Ashgabat, Turkmenistan. Phone: +7 (3632) 251-515."Turkmen Milliyet"—*see* Turkmen Radio, below.
Fax: +7 (3632) 251 421. Contact: K. Karayev; or Yu M. Pashaev, Deputy Chairman of State Television and Radio Company; (technical) G. Khanmamedov, Chief of Technical Department; or A.A Armanklichev, Deputy Chief, Technical Department. This country is currently under strict censorship and media people are closely watched. A lot of foreign mail addressed to a particular person may attract the attention of the secret service. Best bet is not to address your mail to particular individuals but to the station itself.

UGANDA   World Time +3

Radio Uganda
GENERAL OFFICE: P.O. Box 7142, Kampala, Uganda. Phone: +256 (41) 257-256. Fax: +256 (41) 256 888. Contact: Charles Byekwaso, Controller of Programmes; Rachel Nakibuuka; or Mrs. Florence Sewanyana, Head of Public Relations. $1 or return postage required. Replies infrequently and slowly.
ENGINEERING DIVISION: P.O. Box 2038, Kampala, Uganda. Contact: Leopold B. Lubega, Principal Broadcasting Engineer; or Rachel Nakibuuka. Four IRCs or $2 required. Enclosing a self addressed envelope may also help to get a reply.

UKRAINE   World Time +2 (+3 midyear)

WARNING-MAIL THEFT: For the time being, letters to Ukrainian stations, especially containing funds or IRCs, are more likely to arrive safely if sent by registered mail.
For Those at Sea, (Dly Tech v More), Krymskoye Radio, ul. Krymskaya d. 6, 333000 Simferopol, Ukraine. Contact: Konstantin Lepin, who collects stamps and is a fan of American jazz. Via the Russian service of Voice of Russia (Golos Rossii), Russia *(see).*
Government Transmission Authority: RRT/Concern of Broadcasting, Radiocommunication & Television, 10 Dorogajtshaya St., 254112 Kiev, Ukraine. Phone: +380 (44) 226-2262 or +380 (44) 440-8688. Fax: +380 (44) 440 8722. Contact: Alexey Karpenko; Nikolai P. Kiriliuk, Head of Operative Management Service; or Mrs. Liudmila Deretskaya, Interpreter.
Radio Ukraine International, Kreshchatik str., 26, 252001 Kiev, Ukraine. Phone: +380 (44) 228-7356, +380 (44) 228-2534 or +380 (44) 229-1757. Fax: +380 (44) 229 4585. Contact: (administration) Inna Chichinadze, Vice-Director of RUI; (technical) *see* Ukrainian Radio, below. Free stickers, calendars and Ukrainian stamps.
Radio Lugansk, ul. Dem'ochina 25, 348000 Lugansk, Ukraine. Contact: A.N. Mospanova.
Ukrainian Radio, Kreshchatik str., 26, 252001 Kiev, Ukraine. Phone: +380 (44) 226-2253. Fax: (administration) +380 (44) 229 4226 or +380 (44) 229 4585. (technical) +380 (44) 220 6733. E-mail: mo@ukrradio.ru.kiev. Contact: (administration) Volodimyr Reznikov, President of National Radio Company of Ukraine; or Victor Nabrusko, First Vice-President of National Radio Company of Ukraine; (technical) Anatoly Ivanov, Frequency Coordination, Engineering Services.

UNITED ARAB EMIRATES   World Time +4

UAE Radio from Abu Dhabi, Ministry of Information & Culture, P.O. Box 63, Abu Dhabi, United Arab Emirates. Phone: +971 (2) 451-000. Fax: (station) +971 (2) 451 155; (Ministry of Information & Culture) +971 (2) 452 504. Contact: (general) Aïda Hamza, Director, Foreign Language Services; or Abdul Hadi Mubarak, Producer, "Live Program"; (technical) Ibrahim Rashid, Director General, Technical Department; or Fauzi Saleh, Chief Engineer. Free stickers, postcards and stamps. Do not enclose money with correspondence.
UAE Radio in Dubai, P.O. Box 1695, Dubai, United Arab Emirates. Phone: +971 (4) 370-255. Fax: +971 (4) 374 111 +971 (4) 370 283 or +971 (4) 371 079. Contact: Ms. Khulud Halaby; or Sameer Aga, Producer, "Cassette Club Cinarabic"; (technical) K.F. Fenner, Chief Engineer—Radio; or Ahmed Al Muhaideb, Assistant Controller, Engineering. Free pennants. Replies irregularly.

UNITED KINGDOM   World Time exactly (+1 midyear)

Adventist World Radio, the Voice of Hope, AWR Branch Administrative Office, Newbold College, Binfield, Bracknell, Berks. RG42 4AN, United Kingdom. Phone: +44 (1344) 401-401. Fax: +44 (1344) 401 409. E-mail: 74617.2230@ compuserve.com. Contact: Andrea Steele, Director Public Relations & Development. Also, *see* AWR listings under Costa Rica, Guam, Guatemala, Italy, Kenya, Russia and USA.
BBC Monitoring, Caversham Park, Reading RG4 8TZ, United Kingdom. Phone: (general) +44 (118) 947-2742; (Customer Service) +44 (118) 946-9338; (Foreign Media Unit—Broadcast

Schedules/monitoring) +44 (118) 946-9261; (Marketing Department) +44 (118) 946-9204. Fax: (Customer Service) +44 (118) 946 1020; (Foreign Media Unit) +44 (118) 946 1993; (Marketing Department) +44 (118) 946 3828. E-mail: (Customer Service) csu@mon.bbc.co.uk; (Marketing Department) stephen_innes@mon.bbc.co.uk; (Foreign Media Unit/World Media) fmu@mon.bbc.co.uk; (Kenny) dave_kenny@mon.bbc.co.uk; (publications and real time services) marketing@mon.bbc.co.uk. URL: www.monitor.bbc.co.uk/Welcome.html. Contact: (administration) Andrew Hills, Director of Monitoring; (World Media) Chris McWhinnie, Editor "World Media"; (World Media Schedules) Dave Kenny, Sub Editor, "World Media"; (Publication Sales) Stephen Innes, Marketing. BBC Monitoring produces the weekly publication *World Media.* Available on yearly subscription, costing £390.00. Price excludes postage overseas. *World Media* is also available online through the Internet or via a direct dial-in bulletin board at an annual cost of £425.00. Broadcasting Schedules, issued weekly by e-mail at an annual cost of £99.00. VISA/MC/AX. The Technical Operations Unit provides detailed observations of broadcasts on the long, medium and short wave bands. This unit provides tailored channel occupancy observations, reception reports, *Broadcast Schedules Database* (constantly updated on over 100 countries) and the *Broadcast Research Log* (a record of broadcasting developments compiled daily). BBC Monitoring works in conjunction with the Foreign Broadcast Information Service (*see* USA).

▣ BBC World Service

MAIN OFFICE, NONTECHNICAL: Bush House, Strand, London WC2B 4PH, United Kingdom. Phone: (general) +44 (171) 240-3456; (Press Office) +44 (171) 557-2947/1; (International Marketing) +44 (171) 557-1179; (administration) +44 (171) 557-2057. Fax: (Audience Relations) +44 (171) 557-1258; ("Write On" listeners' letters program) +44 (171) 436 2800; (International Broadcasting & Audience Research) +44 (171) 557-1254; (International Marketing) +44(171) 257 8254. E-mail: (general listener correspondence) worldservice.letters@bbc.co.uk; (general BBC inquiries concerning domestic and external services) correspondence@bbc.co.uk; ("Write On") writeon@bbc.co.uk. URLs: (general, including RealAudio) www.bbc.co.uk/worldservice/; (entertainment and information) www.beeb.com. Contact: Penny Long, Presenter, or Nick Baker, Executive Producer of "Write On"; Alan Booth, International Marketing Manager; Victoria Briggs, International Marketing Officer; or Sam Younger, Managing Director. Offers *BBC On Air* magazine (*see* below). Also, *see* Antigua, Ascension, Oman, Seychelles, Singapore and Thailand, which are where technical correspondence concerning these BBC relay transmissions should be sent if you seek a reply with full verification data, as no such data are provided via the London address. The present facility at Masirah, Oman, is scheduled to be replaced in 2001 by a new site at Al-Ashkharah, also in Oman, which is to include four 300 kW shortwave transmitters.

SAN FRANCISCO OFFICE, SCHEDULES: 2654 17th Avenue, San Francisco CA 94116 USA. Phone: +1 (415) 564-9968. Contact: George Poppin. This address, a volunteer office, only provides BBC World Service schedules to listeners. All other correspondence should be sent directly to the main office in London.

TECHNICAL: See Merlin Communications International, below. BBC World Service—Publication and Product Sales

BBC ENGLISH magazine, Bush House, Strand, London WC2B 4PH, United Kingdom. Phone: (editorial office) +44 (171) 557-1110. Fax: +44 (171) 557 1316.

BBC WORLD SERVICE SHOP, Bush House Arcade, Strand, London WC2B 4PH, United Kingdom. Phone: +44 (171) 557-2576. Fax: +44 (171) 240 4811. Sells numerous audio/video (video PAL/VHS only) cassettes, publications (including PASSPORT TO WORLD BAND RADIO), portable world band radios, T-shirts, sweatshirts and other BBC souvenirs available from BBC World Service Shop.

BBC ON AIR monthly program guide, Room 227 NW, Bush House, Strand, London WC2B 4PH, United Kingdom. Phone: (editorial office) +44 (171) 557-2211; (Circulation Manager) +44 (171) 557-2855; (advertising) +44 (171) 557-2873; (subscription voice mail) +44 (171) 557-2211. Fax: +44 (171) 240 4899. E-mail: on.air.magazine@bbc.co.uk. Contact: (editorial) Vicky Payne, Editor; (subscriptions) Rosemarie Reid, Circulation Manager; (advertising) Paul Cosgrove. Subscription $30 or £18 per year. VISA/MC/AX/Barclay/EURO/Access, Postal Order, International Money Draft or cheque in pounds sterling. *GERMAN BUREAU:* Am-Taubertsberg4, D-55122 Mainz, Germany.

Commonwealth Broadcasting Association, CBA Secretariat, Room 312, Yalding House, 152-156 Great Portland Street, London W1N 6AJ, United Kingdom. Phone: +44 (171) 765-5144 or +44 (171) 765-5151. Fax: +44 (171) 765 5152. E-mail: cba@cba.org.uk. URL: www.oneworld.org/cba/. Contact: Elizabeth Smith, Secretary-General; Colin Lloyd, Manager—Training & Development. Publishes the annual *Who's Who in Commonwealth Broadcasting* and the quarterly *Combroad.*

Far East Broadcasting Association (FEBA), Ivy Arch Road, Worthing, West Sussex BN14 8BX, United Kingdom. Phone: +44 (1903) 237-281. Fax: +44 (1903) 205 294. E-mail: reception@febaradio.org.uk; or (Richard Whittington) dwhittington@febaradio.org.uk. URL: www.feba.org.uk. Contact: Tony Ford or Richard Whittington. This office is the headquarters for FEBA worldwide.

High Adventure Radio (Voice of Hope), *see* KVOH—High Adventure Radio, USA.

IBC Tamil, IBC-Tamil, P.O. Box 1505, London SW8 2ZH, United Kingdom. Phone: +44 (171) 787-8000. Fax: +44 (171) 787 8010. E-mail: ibc@fastaccess.co.uk. URL: (includes RealAudio) www.fastaccess.co.uk/~ibc/home.html.

Merlin Communications International Limited, 20 Lincoln's Inn Fields, London WC2A 3ES, United Kingdom. Phone: +44 (171) 969-0000. Fax: +44 (171) 396 6221. URL: www.merlincommunications.com. Contact: Nicola Wallbridge, Business Development Assistant; Fiona Lowry, Chief Executive; or Michelle Franks, Scheduling and Frequency Management. Merlin has a ten year contract with the BBC World Service requiring it to provide a full range of complex programme transmission and distribution services from Bush House in London to audiences worldwide. As part of this contract Merlin schedules, operates and maintains the BBC World Service's international network of major shortwave and mediumwave transmitter sites. Merlin also schedules, owns and operates three shortwave and one mediumwave site in the UK and provides design and project management services to establish new BBC broadcasting facilities. As well as serving the BBC World Service, Merlin offers its wide range of broadcast engineering skills and expertise to the individual marketplace.

Merlin Network One, 20 Lincoln's Inn Fields, London WC2A 3ES, United Kingdom. Phone: +44 (171) 396-6220. Fax: +44 (171) 396 6221. To contact the programs between 1800 and 0200 UK Time, call +44 (171) 419-1035 or fax +44 (171) 419

1024. E-mail: mno@cix.co.uk. URLs: www.mno.co.uk/; www.mediazoo.co.uk/mno/. A shortwave and satellite service for international specialist broadcasters provided by Merlin Communications International (*see*, above).

Sunrise Radio, Sunrise House, Sunrise Road, Southall, Middlesex UB2 4AU, United Kingdom. Phone: +44 (181) 574 6666. Fax: +44 (181) 813 9800. Transmits via the facilities of Deutsche Telekom, Germany (*see*).

UCB Europe—*see* Ireland.

World Radio Network Ltd, Wyvil Court, 10 Wyvil Road, London SW8 2TY, United Kingdom. Phone: +44 (171) 896-9000. Fax: +44 (171) 896 9007. E-mail: (general) online@wrn.org or wrn@cityscape.co.uk; (Cohen) jeffc@wrn.org. URLs: (general and Web radio) www.wrn.org; (sound files) http://town.org/radio/wrn.html. Contact: Karl Miosga, Managing Director; Jeffrey Cohen, Director of Development; or Simon Spanswick. Provides Web RealAudio and StreamWorks, plus program placement via satellite in various countries for nearly two dozen international broadcasters.

UNITED NATIONS World Time –5 (–4 midyear)

United Nations Radio, R/S-850, United Nations, New York NY 10017 USA; or write the station over which UN Radio was heard (Radio Myanmar, Radio Cairo, China Radio International, Sierra Leone Broadcasting Service, Radio Zambia, Radio Tanzania, Polish Radio Warsaw, HCJB/Ecuador, /Italy, All India Radio, RFPI/Costa Rica). Fax: +1 (212) 963 1307. E-mail: audio-visual@un.org. URLs: (RealAudio) www.wrn.org/stations/un.html; or www.internetbroadcast.com/un.htm. Contact: (general) Sylvester E. Rowe, Chief, Radio and Video Service; or Ayman El-Amir, Chief, Radio Section, Department of Public Information; (technical and nontechnical) Sandra Guy, Secretary. Free stamps and *UN Frequency* publication. *GENEVA OFFICE: see* Switzerland.

PARIS OFFICE: UNESCO Radio, 7 Pl.de Fontenoy, F-75018 Paris, France. Fax: +33 (1) 45 67 30 72. Contact: Erin Faherty, Executive Radio Producer.

URUGUAY World Time –3

Emisora Ciudad de Montevideo, Canelones 2061, 11200 Montevideo, Uruguay. Fax: +598 (2) 420 700. Contact: Aramazd Yizmeyian, Director General. Free stickers. Return postage helpful.

La Voz de Artigas (when active), Av. Lecueder 483, 55000 Artigas, Uruguay. Phone: +598 (642) 2447 or +598 (642) 3445. Fax: +598 (642) 4744. Contact: (general) Sra. Solange Murillo Ricciardi, Co-Propietario; or Luis Murillo; (technical) Roberto Murillo Ricciardi. Free stickers and pennants. Replies to correspondence in English, Spanish, French, Italian and Portuguese.

Radiodifusion Nacional—*see* SODRE, below.

Radio Monte Carlo, Av. 18 de Julio 1224 piso 1, 11100 Montevideo, Uruguay. Phone:+598 (2) 905-423, +598 (2) 905-612, +598 (2) 914-433 or +598 (2) 983-987. Fax: +598 (2) 917 762. E-mail: cx20@netgate.comintur.com.uy. URL: (includes RealAudio) http://netgate.comintur.com.uy/cx20/. Contact: Ana Ferreira de Errázquin, Secretaria, Departamento de Prensa de la Cooperativa de Radioemisoras; Alexi Haysaniuk, Jefe Técnico; Déborah Ibarra, Secretaria; Emilia Sánchez Vega, Secretaria; or Ulises Graceras. Correspondence in Spanish preferred.

Radio Oriental—Same mailing address and phone/fax numbers as Radio Monte Carlo, above. E-mail: cx12@netgate.comintur.com.uy. URL: (includes RealAudio) http://netgate.comintur.com.uy/cx12/. Correspondence in Spanish preferred.

SODRE

PUBLICITY AND TECHNICAL: Radiodifusión Nacional, Casilla 1412, 11000 Montevideo, Uruguay. E-mail: radioact@chasque.apc.org. URL: (Radioactividades) www.chasque.apc.org/radioact. Contact: (general) Roberto Belo, Radioactividades Producer; (publicity) Daniel Ayala González, Publicidad; (technical) Francisco Escobar, Depto. Técnico. Reception reports may also be sent to: Casilla 7011, Montevideo, Uruguay.

OTHER: "Radioactividades," Casilla 801 (or Casilla 6541), 11000 Montevideo, Uruguay. Fax: +598 (2) 48 71 27. Contact: Daniel Muñoz Faccioli.

USA World Time –4 Atlantic, including Puerto Rico and Virgin Islands; –5 (–4 midyear) Eastern, excluding Indiana; –5 Indiana, except northwest and southwest portions; –6 (–5 midyear) Central, including northwest and southwest Indiana; –7 (–6 midyear) Mountain, except Arizona; –7 Arizona; –8 (–7 midyear) Pacific; –9 (–8 midyear) Alaska, except Aleutian Islands; –10 (–9 midyear) Aleutian Islands; –10 Hawaii; –11 Samoa

Note on Disestablishmentarian Programs: Contact and related information for many American politically oriented shows that are of an anti-establishment bent are listed separately earlier in this chapter, under Disestablishmentarian, following the entries for Denmark.

Adventist World Radio, the Voice of Hope

WORLD HEADQUARTERS: 12501 Old Columbia Pike, Silver Spring MD 20904-6600 USA. Phone: +1 (301) 680-6304. Fax: +1 (301) 680 6303. E-mail: 74617.1621@compuserve.com. URL: (World Wide Website includes RealAudio in English and Japanese) www.awr.org/. Contact: (general) Don Jacobsen, President. Most correspondence and all reception reports are best sent to the station from which the transmission you heard actually emanated (*see* Costa Rica, Guam, Guatemala, Italy (Italy also for Armenia, Germany and Slovakia transmissions) and Russia, rather than to the World Headquarters. Free religious printed matter, stickers, program schedules and other small souvenirs. IRC or $1 appreciated.

INTERNATIONAL RELATIONS: 903 Tanninger Drive, Indianapolis IN 46239 USA. Phone/fax: +1 (317) 891-8540. Contact: Dr. Adrian M. Peterson, International Relations. Provides publications with regular news releases and technical information. Annual DX contest in association with "Wavescan" program, *see* below. Issues some special verification cards. QSL stamps and certificates also available from this address in return for reception reports.

DX PROGRAM: "Wavescan," prepared by Adrian Peterson (*see* preceding); aired on all AWR facilities and also available via RealAudio at www.awr.org/online_programs.html.

LISTENER NEWSLETTER: Current, published quarterly by AWR, is available through AWR stations: Costa Rica, Guam and Italy. Free, but IRCs appreciated.

PUBLIC RELATIONS & DEVELOPMENT—*see* United Kingdom.

FREQUENCY MANAGEMENT OFFICE: AWR-Europe, Postfach 100252, D-64202 Darmstadt, Germany. Phone: +49 (6151) 953-151. Fax: +49 (6151) 953 152. E-mail: 102555.257@compuserve.com. Contact: Claudius Dedio, Frequency Manager. Implied by various reports is that this office will shortly

be merged into the Public Relations & Development Office in the United Kingdom (*see*) or AWR's Italian facility *(see)*.
Also, *see* AWR listings under Costa Rica, Guam, Guatemala, Kenya and Russia.

BBC World Service via WYFR—Family Radio. For verification direct from WYFR's transmitters, contact WYFR—Family Radio (*see* below). Nontechnical correspondence should be sent to the BBC World Service in London (*see*).

Broadcasting Board of Governors (BBG), 330 Independence Avenue SW, Room 3360, Washington DC 20547 USA. Phone: +1 (202) 401-3736. Fax: +1 (202) 401 3376. Contact: (general) Kathleen Harrington, Public Relations; (administration) David Burke, Chairman. The BBG, created in 1994 and headed by nine members nominated by the President, is the overseeing agency for all official non-military United States international broadcasting operations, including the VOA, RFE-RL, Radio Martí and Radio Free Asia.

Central Intelligence Agency, Washington DC 20505 USA. Phone: (press liason) +1 (703) 482-7668; (general) +1 (703) 482-1100. URLs: (general) www.odci.gov/cia/; (Public Affairs) www.odci.gov/cia/public_affairs/pas.html. Contact: (general) Dennis Boxx, Director, Public Affairs; Kent Harrington, Press Liason; (administration) Nora Slatkin, Executive Director. Although the CIA is not believed to be operating any broadcasting stations at present, it is known to have done so in the past, usually in the form of "black" clandestine stations, and could do so again in the future. Additionally, the Agency is reliably reported to have funded a variety of organizations over the years, and may still be funding a relatively small number of organizations today, which operate, control or influence world band programs and stations. Also, *see* Foreign Broadcast Information Service, below.

Disestablishmentarian Programs—*see* Disestablishmentarian listing earlier in this chapter, following the entries for "Denmark."

FEBC Radio International
INTERNATIONAL HEADQUARTERS: Far East Broadcasting Company, Inc., P.O. Box 1, La Mirada CA 90637 USA. Phone: +1 (310) 947-4651. Fax: +1 (310) 943 0160. E-mail: 3350911@ mcimail.com; febc-usa@xc.org. URL: http://febc.org. Operates world band stations in the Northern Mariana Islands, the Philippines and the Seychelles. Does not verify reception reports from this address.
UNITED KINGDOM OFFICE: FEBA Radio, Ivy Arch Road, Worthing, West Sussex BN14 8BX, United Kingdom. Phone: +44 (903) 237-281. Fax: +44 (903) 205 294.

Federal Communications Commission
ORGANIZATION: 1919 M Street NW, Washington DC 20554 USA. Phone: (toll-free for licensed or prospective private broadcasters within the United States) (888) 225-5322 or (888) 322-8255; (general) +1 (202) 418-0200; (public affairs) +1 (202) 418-0500; (public affairs, recorded listing of releases and texts) +1 (202) 418-2222; (international bureau, technical) + 1 (202) 739-0509; (international bureau, administration) +1 (202) 418-0420; (international bureau, legal) +1 (202) 739-0415; (international bureau, notifications and WARC) +1 (202) 418-2156. Fax: (general) +1 (202) 418 0232; (public affairs) +1 (202) 418 2809; (international bureau, technical) +1 (202) 887 6124 or +1 (202) 418 0398; (international bureau, administration) +1 (202) 418 2818; (international bureau, legal) +1 (202) 887 0175. E-mail: (general) fccinfo@fcc.gov; (specific individuals) format is initiallastname@fcc.gov, so to reach, say, Tom Polzin it would be tpolzin@fcc.gov. URLs: (general) http://fcc.gov/; (FTP) ftp://ftp.fcc.gov (shortwave broadcasting files can be downloaded from /pub/Bureaus/International/). Contact: (public affairs) Patricia Chew or Sharon Hurd; (international bureau, technical) Thomas E. Polzin.

Foreign Broadcast Information Service, P.O. Box 2604, Washington DC 20013 USA. Phone: +1 (202) 338-6735. Parented by the CIA (*see*, above) and working in concert with BBC Monitoring (*see* United Kingdom) and selected other organizations, the F.B.I.S., with listening posts in various countries outside the United States, monitors broadcasts worldwide for intelligence-gathering purposes. However, it never engages in broadcasting or jamming of any sort, directly or indirectly.

Fundamental Broadcasting Network, Grace Missionary Baptist Church, Newport NC 28570 USA. Phone: +1 (919) 223-6088. URL: (includes RealAudio) www.clis.com/fbn/. E-mail: fbn@bmd.clis.com. Alternative address: Morehead City NC 28557 USA. Phone: +1 (919) 240-1600. Fax: + (919) 726 2251. Contact: Pastor Clyde Eborn. Provides programming for WGTG, USA.

George Jacobs and Associates, Inc., 8701 Georgia Avenue, Suite 410, Silver Spring MD 20910 USA. Phone: +1 (301) 587-8800. Fax: +1 (301) 587 8801. E-mail: gja@gjainc.com; or gjacobs@clark.net. URL: www.gjainc.com/. Contact: (technical) Bob German or Mrs. Anne Case; (administration) George Jacobs, P.E. This firm provides frequency management and other engineering services for a variety of private U.S. and other world band stations, but does not correspond with the general public.

Herald Broadcasting Syndicate—Shortwave Broadcasts (all locations), Shortwave Broadcasts, P.O. Box 1524, Boston MA 02117-1524 USA. Phone: (general, toll-free within U.S.) 1-800-288-7090 or (general elsewhere) +1 (617) 450-2929 [with either number, extension 2060 to hear recorded frequency information, or 2929 for Shortwave Helpline and request printed schedules and information]. Fax: +1 (617) 450

2283. E-mail: (letters and reception reports) letterbox@csps.com; or (religious questions) sentinel@csps.com. URL: (*The Christian Science Monitor* newspaper) www.csmonitor.com;or (information about The Christian Science Church in Boston) www.tfccs.com. Contact: Catherine Aitken-Smith, Director of International Broadcasting, Herald Broadcasting Syndicate (representative for station activity in Boston); or Tina Hammers, Frequency and Production Coordinator. Free schedules and information about Christian Science. *The Christian Science Monitor* newspaper and a full line of Christian Science books are available from: 1 Norway Street, Boston MA 02115 USA. *Science and Health with Key to the Scriptures* by Mary Baker Eddy is available in English $14.95 paperback ($16.95 in French, German, Portuguese or Spanish paperback; $24.95 in Czech or Russian hardcover) from Science and Health, P.O. Box 1875, Boston MA 02117 USA. Also, *see* Northern Mariana Islands.

Herald Broadcasting Syndicate—WSHB Cypress Creek, Rt. 2, Box 107A, Pineland SC 29934 USA. Phone: (general) +1 (803) 625-5555; (station manager) +1 (803) 625-5551; (engineer) +1 (803) 625-5554. Fax: +1 (803) 625 5559. E-mail: (station manager) cee@csms.com, or cee@hargray.com; (engineer) damian@csms.com; (QSL coordinator) judy@csms.com. URL: www.tfccs.com. Contact: (technical) Damian Centgraf, Chief Engineer; C. Ed Evans, Senior Station Manager; or Judy P. Cooke, QSL Coordinator. Visitors welcome from 9 to 4 Monday through Friday; for other times, contact transmitter site beforehand to make arrangements. This address for technical feedback on South Carolina transmissions only; other inquiries should be directed to the P.O. Box 1524, Boston address.

International Broadcasting Bureau (IBB)—Reports to the Broadcasting Board of Governors (*see*), and includes, among others, the Voice of America, RFE-RL, Radio Martí and Radio Free Asia. IBB Engineering (Office of Engineering and Technical Operations) provides broadcast services for these stations. URL: www.ibb.gov/.

FREQUENCY AND MONITORING OFFICE, TECHNICAL: USIA/IBB/EOF: Spectrum Management Division, International Broadcasting Bureau (IBB), United States Information Agency (USIA), Room 4611 Cohen Bldg., 330 Independence Avenue SW, Washington DC 20547 USA. Phone: +1 (202) 619-1669. Fax: +1 (202) 619 1680. E-mail: (scheduling) dferguson@ibb.gov; (monitoring) bw@his.com. URL: (general) http://voa.his.com/; (monitoring results database) http://fmds.ibb.his.com/; (remote monitoring system) http://voa.his.com/rms2.html. Contact: Dan Ferguson (dferguson@ibb.gov); or Bill Whitacre (bw@his.com).

KAIJ
ADMINISTRATION OFFICE: Two-if-by-Sea Broadcasting Co., 22720 SE 410th St., Enumclaw WA 89022 USA. Phone/fax: (Mike Parker, California) +1 (818) 606-1254; (Washington State office, if and when operating) +1 (206) 825 4517. Contact: Mike Parker (mark envelope, "please forward"). Relays programs of Dr. Gene Scott. Replies occasionally.
STUDIO: Faith Center, 1615 S. Glendale Avenue, Glendale CA 91025 USA. Phone: +1 (818) 246-8121. Contact: Dr. Gene Scott, President.
TRANSMITTER: RR#3 Box 120, Frisco TX 75034 USA (physical location: Highway 380, 3.6 miles west of State Rt. 289, near Denton TX). Phone: +1 (214) 346-2758. Contact: Walt Green or Fred Bithel. Station encourages mail to be sent to administration office, which seldom replies, or the studio (*see* above).

KJES—King Jesus Eternal Savior
STATION: The Lord's Ranch, 230 High Valley Road, Vado NM 88072 USA. Phone: +1 (505) 233-2090. Fax: +1 (505) 233 3019. E-mail: KJES@aol.com. Contact: Michael Reuter, Manager. $1 or return postage appreciated.
SPONSORING ORGANIZATION: Our Lady's Youth Center, P.O. Box 1422, El Paso TX 79948 USA. Phone: +1 (915) 533-9122.

KNLS—New Life Station
OPERATIONS CENTER: 605 Bradley Ct., Franklin TN 37067 USA (letters sent to the Alaska transmitter site are usually forwarded to Franklin). Phone: +1 (615) 371-8707 ext.107. Fax: +1 (615) 371 8791. E-mail: knls@aol.com. URL: www.knls.org. Contact: (general) Wesley Jones, Director, Follow-Up Teaching; or Steven Towell, Senior Producer, English Language Service; (technical) Mike Osborne, Production Manager and Webeditor. Free *Alaska Calling!* newsletter, pennants, stickers, English-language and Russian-language religious tapes and literature, and English-language learning course materials for Russian speakers. Free information about Alaska. Radio-related publications and bibles available; 2 IRCs appreciated for each book. Special, individually numbered, limited edition, verification cards issued for each new transmission period to the first 200 listeners providing confirmed reception reports. Swaps canceled stamps from different countries to help listeners round out their stamp collections. Accepts faxed reports. Return postage appreciated.
TRANSMITTER SITE: P.O. Box 473, Anchor Point AK 99556 USA. Phone: +1 (907) 235-8262. Fax: +1 (907) 235 2326. Contact: (technical) Kevin Chambers, Engineer.

⊞KTBN—Trinity Broadcasting Network:
GENERAL CORRESPONDENCE: P.O. Box A, Santa Ana CA 92711 USA. Phone: +1 (714) 832-2950. Fax: +1 (714) 730 0661, +1 (714) 731 4196 or +1 (714) 665 2101. E-mail: tbntalk@tbn.org. URLs: (Trinity Broadcasting Network, including RealAudio) www.tbn.org; (KTBN) www.tbn.org/ktbn.html. Contact: Dr. Paul F. Crouch, Managing Director; Jay Jones, Producer, "Music of Praise"; or Programming Department. Monthly TBN newsletter. Free booklets, stickers and small souvenirs sometimes available. Return postage (IRC or SASE) helpful.
TECHNICAL CORRESPONDENCE: Engineering/QSL Department, 2442 Michelle Drive, Tustin CA 92780-7015 USA. Phone: +1 (714) 665-2145. Fax: +1 (714) 730 0661. E-mail: bmiller@tbn.org. Contact: Chris Hiser, QSL Manager; or W. Ben Miller, Vice President of Engineering.

KVOH—High Adventure Radio
MAIN OFFICE: P.O. Box 100, Simi Valley CA 93062 USA. Phone: +1 (805) 520-9460; toll-free (within USA) 1-800-517-HOPE. Fax: +1 (805) 520 7823. E-mail: kvoh@highadventure.net. URL: www.highadventure.org. Contact: (listeners' correspondence) Pat Kowalick, "Listeners' Letterbox"; (administration, High Adventure Ministries) George Otis, President and Chairman; (administration, KVOH) Paul Johnson, General Manager, KVOH; (technical) Paul Hunter, Network Chief Engineer. Free program schedules and *Voice of Hope* book. Sells books, audio and video cassettes, T-shirts and world band radios. Booklist available on request. VISA/MC. Also, *see* Lebanon, Palau. Return postage (IRCs) required. Replies as time permits.
CORRESPONDENCE RELATING TO BROADCASTS TO SOUTH ASIA: P.O. Box 93937, Los Angeles CA 90093 USA
VICTORIA, AUSTRALIA OFFICE, NONTECHNICAL: P.O. Box 295, Vermont, Victoria 3133, Australia. Phone: +61 (3) 9801-4648. Fax: +61 (3) 9887 1145. Contact: Roger Pearce, Director; or Helen Pearce.
WESTERN AUSTRALIA OFFICE, NONTECHNICAL: 79 Sycamore Drive, Duncraig WA 6023, Australia. Phone: +61 (9) 9345-1777.

Fax: +61 (9) 9345 5407. Contact: Caron or Peter Hedgeland.
CANADA OFFICE, NONTECHNICAL: Box 425, Station "E",
Toronto, M6H 4E3 Canada. Phone/fax: +1 (416) 898-5447.
Contact: Don McLaughlin, Director.
PALAU OFFICE, NONTECHNICAL: P.O. Box 66, Koror, Palau
96940, Pacific Islands. Phone: +680 488-2162. Fax: +680 488
2163. Contact: Regina Subris.
SINGAPORE OFFICE, NONTECHNICAL: 105 Cairhill Circle, Hill-
tops #13-107, Singapore 0922, Singapore. Phone/fax: + 65
737-1682. Contact: Cyril Seah.
U.K. OFFICE: P.O. Box 109, Hereford HR4 9XR, United King-
dom. Phone: +44 (1432) 359-099 or (mobile) +44 (0589) 078-
444. Fax: +44 (1432) 263 408. E-mail: mail@highadventure.net.
URL: www.highadventure.org/europe1.html. Contact: Peter
Darg, Director; or Helen Darg. This office verifies reports of
Voice of Hope ("European Beacon") broadcasts via Jülich,
Germany and (when in use) Tbilisi, Georgia.

KWHR-World Harvest Radio:

ADMINISTRATION OFFICE: see WHRI, USA, below.
TRANSMITTER: Although located 6½ miles southwest of
Naalehu, 8 miles north of South Cape, and 2000 feet west of
South Point (Ka La) Road (the antennas are easily visible from
this road) on friendly Big Island, Hawaii, the folks at this rural
transmitter site maintain no post office box in or near Naalehu,
and their telephone number is unlisted, Best bet is to contact
them via their administration office (*see* WHRI, below), or to
drive in unannounced (it's just off South Point Road) the next
time you vacation on Big Island.

Leinwoll (Stanley)—Telecommunication Consultant,
305 E. 86th Street, Suite 21S-W, New York NY 10028 USA. Phone:
+1 (212) 987-0456. Fax: +1 (212) 987 3532. E-mail:
stanL00011@aol.com. Contact: Stanley Leinwoll, President.
This firm provides frequency management and other engineering services for a variety of private U.S. world band stations, but does not correspond with the general public.

National Association of Shortwave Broadcasters
HEADQUARTERS: 11185 Columbia Pike, Silver Spring MD
20901 USA. Phone: +1 (301) 593-5409. Fax: +1 (301) 681 0099.
Contact: Tulio R. Haylock, Secretary-Treasurer. Association
of most private U.S. world band stations, as well as a group
of other international broadcasters, equipment manufacturers and organizations related to shortwave broadcasting. Includes committees on various subjects, such as digital
shortwave radio. Interfaces with the Federal Communications
Commission's International Bureau and other broadcasting-
related organizations to advance the interests of its members. Publishes *NASB Newsletter* for members and associate
members; free sample upon request on letterhead of an appropriate organization. Annual one-day convention held near
Washington DC's National Airport early each spring; non-
members wishing to attend should contact the Secretary-Treasurer in advance; convention fee typically $50 per person.
MEMBERSHIP OFFICE: 276 N. Bobwhite, Orange CA 92669
USA. Phone/fax: (membership information) +1 (714) 771-
1843. Contact: William E. "Ted" Haney, Membership Chairman, NASB. Full Membership (only for private U.S. shortwave
broadcasters) $500 or more/year; Associate Membership
(other organizations, subject to approval): $500/year.

Radio Free Asia, Suite 300, 2025 M Street NW, Washington
DC 20036 USA. Phone: (general) +1 (202) 530-4900 or +1 (202)
457-6975; (programming) +1 (202) 530-4907; (president) +1
(202) 457-6948; (vice-president) +1 (202) 536 4402; (technical) +1 (202) 822-6234. Fax: +1 (202) 457 6996 or +1 (202) 530
7794/95. E-mail: the format is lastnameinitial@rfa.org; so to

reach, say, David Baden, it would be badend@rfa.org. URL:
www.rfa.org. Contact: (administration) Richard Richter, President; Craig Perry, Vice President; Daniel Southerland, Executive Editor; (listener contact) Ms. Arin Basu, Secretary;
(technical) David Baden, Director of Technical Operations. Free
stickers. RFA, originally created in 1996 as the Asia Pacific
Network, is funded as a private nonprofit U.S. corporation by
a grant from the Broadcasting Board of Governors, a politically bipartisan body appointed by the President (*see*).

Radio Free Europe-Radio Liberty/RFE-RL

PRAGUE HEADQUARTERS: Vinohradská 1, 110 00 Prague 1,
Czech Republic. Phone: +420 (2) 2112-1111; (president) +420
(2) 2112-3000; (news & current affairs) +420 (2) 2112-6950;
(engineering & technical operations) +420 (2) 2112-3700;
(broadcast operations) +420 (2) 2112-3550. Fax: +420 (2) 2112
3013; (president) +420 (2) 2112 3002; (news & current affairs)
+420 (2) 2112 3613; (engineering & technical operations) +420
(2) 2112 3702; (broadcast operations) +420 (2) 2112 3540. E-
mail: the format is lastnameinitial@rferl.org; so to reach, say,
David Walcutt, it would be walcuttd@rferl.org. URL: (general,
including RealAudio) www.rferl.org/; (broadcast services)
www.rferl.org/bd. Contact: Thomas A. Dine, President; Robert McMahon, Director of News & Current Affairs; Luke
Springer, Acting Director of Engineering & Technical Services;
or Christopher Carzoli, Director of Broadcast Operations.
WASHINGTON OFFICE: 1201 Connecticut Avenue NW, Washington DC 20036 USA. Phone: +1 (202) 457-6900; (news) +1
(202) 457-6950; (technical) +1 (202) 457-6963. Fax: +1 (202)
457 6992; (technical) +1 (202) 457 6913. E-mail and URL: *see*
above. Contact: Jane Lester, Secretary of the Corporation; or
Paul Globe, Director of Communications; (news) Oleh
Zwadiuk, Washington Bureau Chief; (technical) David Walcutt,
Broadcast Operations Liaison. A private non-profit corporation funded by a grant from the Broadcasting Board of Governors, RFE/RL broadcasts in 21 languages (but not English)
from transmission facilities now part of the International
Broadcasting Bureau (IBB), *see*.

Radio Martí, Office of Cuba Broadcasting, 4201 N.W. 77th
Avenue, Miami FL 33166 USA. Phone: +1 (305) 437-7000. E-
mail: ocb@usia.gov. URL: (Gopher) gopher://
gopher.voa.gov:70/11/marti. Contact: (general) Herminio San
Ramón, Director, Office of Cuba Broadcasting; Roberto
Rodríguez-Tejera, Director, Radio Martí; Martha Yedra, Director of Programs; or William Valdez, Director, News; (technical) Michael Pallone, Director of Technical Operations.

Trans World Radio, International Headquarters, P.O. Box
8700, Cary NC 27512-8700 USA. Phone: +1 (919) 460-3700.
Fax: +1 (919) 460 3702. E-mail: info2@twr.org. Contact: (general)
www.gospelcom.net/twr/twr_index.htm. Contact: (general)
Jon Vaught, Public Relations; Richard Greene, Director, Public Relations; Joe Fort, Director, Broadcaster Relations; or Bill
Danick; (technical) Glenn W. Sink, Assistant Vice President,
International Operations. Free "Towers to Eternity" publication for those living in the U.S. Technical correspondence
should be sent to the office nearest the country where the
transmitter is located—Guam, Monaco or Swaziland.
AUSTRALIAN ADDRESS: Box 390, Box Hill Business Centre,
3128 Victoria, Australia. URL: www.citysearch.com.au/mel/
transworldradio.

University Network, P.O. Box 1, Los Angeles CA 90053

USA. Phone: (toll-free within U.S.) 1-800-338-3030; (elsewhere, call collect) +1 (818) 240-8151. E-mail:
drgenescott@drgenescott.org. URLs (including RealAudio):
www.drgenescott.org/; http://207.155.78.66/. Contact: Dr.

Gene Scott. Sells audio and video tapes and books relating to Dr. Scott's teaching. Free copies of *The Truth About* and *The University Cathedral Pulpit* publications. Transmits via its own facilities (KAIJ, USA and Caribbean Beacon, Anguilla) as well as those of WWCR (USA) and Voice of Russia.

USA Radio Network, 2290 Springlake #107, Dallas TX 75234 USA. E-mail: newsroom@usaradio.com. URL: www.usaradio.com/. Does not broadcast on shortwave, but some of its news and other programs are heard via WHRI and WWCR, USA.

⊡Voice of America—All Transmitter Locations

MAIN OFFICE, NONTECHNICAL: United States Information Agency (USIA), International Broadcasting Bureau (IBB), 330 Independence Avenue SW, Washington DC 20547 USA. If contacting the VOA directly is impractical, write c/o the American Embassy or USIS Center in your country. Phone: (to hear VOA-English live) +1 (202) 619-1979; (Office of External Affairs) +1 (202) 619-2358 or +1 (202) 619-2039; (Audience Mail Division) +1 (202) 619-2770; (Africa Division) +1 (202) 619-1666 or +1 (202) 619-2879; ("Communications World") +1 (202) 619-3047; (Office of Research) +1 (202) 619-4965; (administration) +1 (202) 619-1088. Fax: (general information for listeners outside the United States) +1 (202) 376 1066; (Public Liaison for listeners within the United States) +1 (202) 619 1241; (Office of External Affairs) +1 (202) 205 0634 or +1 (202) 205 2875; (Africa Division) +1 (202) 619 1664; ("Communications World," Audience Mail Division and Office of Research) +1 (202) 619 0211; (administration) +1 (202) 619 0085; ("Communications World") +1 (202) 619 2543. E-mail: (general inquiries outside the United States) letters@voa.gov; (reception reports from outside the United States) qsl@voa.gov; (reception reports from within the United States) qsl-usa@voa.gov; ("Communications World") cw@voa.gov; (Office of Research) gmackenz@usia.gov; ("VOA News Now") newsnow@voa.gov; (VOA Special English) special@voa.gov. URL: (includes RealAudio) www.voa.gov/voahome/index.html. Contact: Mrs. Betty Lacy Thompson, Chief, Audience Mail Division, B/K. G759A Cohen; Leo Sarkisian; Rita Rochelle, Africa Division; Kim Andrew Elliott, Producer, "Communications World"; or George Mackenzie, Audience Research Officer. Free stickers and calendars. Free "Music Time in Africa" calendar, to non-U.S. addresses only, from Mrs. Rita Rochelle, Africa Division, Room 1622. If you're an American and miffed because you can't receive these goodies from the VOA, don't blame the station—they're only following the law. The VOA occasionally hosts international broadcasting conventions, and as of 1996 has been accepting limited supplemental funding from the U.S. Agency for International Development (AID).

MAIN OFFICE, TECHNICAL: United States Information Agency (USIA), International Broadcasting Bureau (IBB), 330 Independence Avenue SW, Washington DC 20547 USA. Contact: Mrs. Irene Greene, QSL Desk, Audience Mail Division, Room G-759-C; (administration) George Woodard, Director, Office of Engineering and Technical Operations. E-mail: qsl@voa.gov. Also, *see* Ascension, Botswana, Greece, Morocco, Philippines, São Tomé e Príncipe, Sri Lanka and Thailand.

Voice of America/IBB—Delano Relay Station, Rt. 1, Box 1350, Delano CA 93215 USA. Phone: +1 (805) 725-0150 or +1 (805) 861-4136. Fax: +1 (805) 725 6511. Contact: (technical) Brent Boyd, Manager. Nontechnical correspondence should be sent to the VOA address in Washington.

Voice of America/IBB—Greenville Relay Station, P.O. Box 1826, Greenville NC 27834 USA. Phone: +1 (919) 758-2171 or +1 (919) 752-7115. Fax: +1 (919) 752 5959. Contact:

(technical) Bruce Hunter, Manager. Nontechnical correspondence should be sent to the VOA address in Washington.

WBCQ—"The Planet", 97 High Street, Kennebunk ME 04043 USA. E-mail: (Weiner) allanhw@cybertours.com; (Becker) Director@pcaudio.com. URL: www.wbcq.com. Contact: Allan Weiner; or Scott Becker.

⊡WEWN—EWTN Worldwide Catholic Radio

STATION OFFICE: Eternal Word Radio Network (EWTN), Catholic Radio Service, P.O. Box 100234, Birmingham AL 35210 USA; WEWN Catholic Shortwave Radio, 5817 Old Leeds Rd., Birmingham AL 35210 USA. Phone: (toll-free within U.S. during live shows only) 1-800-585-9396; (elsewhere) +1 (205) 672-7200; (Frequency Manager) +1 (205) 271-2900 ext. 2017. Fax: +1 (205) 672 9988. E-mail: (station & technical) wewn@ewtn.com; (programming) radio@ewtn.com; (Spanish) darcher@ewtn.com. URLs: (EWTN) www.ewtn.com/; (WEWN) www.ewtn.com/WEWN/radio1.htm; (RealAudio streaming, library of programs on demand) www.ewtn.com. Contact: (general) Thom Price, Director of Programming; Mrs. Gwen Carr, Office Manager; Doug Archer, Spanish Program Coordinator; or W. Glen Tapley, Director of Network Radio Operations; (marketing) Scott Hults, Host of "Live Wire" and Director of Radio Marketing and Program Development; (administration) William Steltemeier, President; or Frank Leurck, Station Manager; (technical) Frank Phillips, Vice President of Radio; Joseph A. Dentici, Frequency Manager; or Dennis Dempsey, Chief Engineer. Listener correspondence welcomed; responds to correspondence on-air and by mail. Free *Gabriel's Horn* newsletter and bumper stickers; also, free *At Mary's Knee* quarterly newsletter for children. Sells numerous religious publications ranging from $2 to $20, as well as T-shirts ($10-12), sweatshirts ($15 donation) and world band radios ($50 to $225); list available upon request (VISA/MC). IRC or return postage appreciated for correspondence. Although a Catholic entity, WEWN is not an official station of the Vatican, which operates its own Vatican Radio (*see*). Rather, WEWN reflects the activities of Mother M. Angelica and the Eternal Word Foundation, Inc. Donations and bequests accepted by the Eternal Word Foundation.

ENGINEERING OFFICE: P.O. Box 176, Vandiver AL 35176 USA. Phone and fax: *see* Station Office, above. Contact: Bernard Lockhart, Marketing Manager; or Norman Williams, Manager, Planning & Installation.

RELIGIOUS ORDER and EWTN ORGANIZATIONAL HEADQUARTERS: Our Lady of The Angels Monastery, 5817 Old Leeds Road, Birmingham AL 35210 USA. Phone: +1 (205) 271-2900. Fax: +1 (205) 271 2920.

TRANSMISSION FACILITY: 1500 High Road, Vandiver AL 35176 USA.

WGTG—With Glory To God, Box 1131, Copperhill TN 37317-1131 USA. Phone/fax: +1 (706) 492-5944. E-mail: wgtg@wgtg.com. URL: www.wgtg.com. Contact: (general) Roseanne Frantz, Program Director; or "Mail Bag"; (technical) Dave Frantz, Chief Engineer. $1 or 3 IRCs for verification response. WGTG is a family-run Christian station partly supported by listener donations. Comments on reception quality, and especially audio quality, are welcomed. SASE appreciated. Hopes to add more AM/SSB transmitters, nominally of 50 kW apiece.

PROGRAM PROVIDER: Fundamental Broadcasting Network (*see*). A nonprofit organization, FBN feeds program material to WGTG via satellite.

⊡WHRA-World Harvest Radio:

TRANSMITTER: Located in Greenbush, Maine, but all technical and other correspondence should be sent to WHRI (*see* the next item).

WHRI—World Harvest Radio, WHRI/WHRA/KWHR, LeSEA Broadcasting, P.O. Box 12, South Bend IN 46624 USA. Phone: +1 (219) 291-8200. Fax: (station) +1 (219) 291 9043. E-mail: whr@lesea.com; (Joe Brashier) jbrashier@lesea.com; (Joe Hill) jhill@lesea.com. URLs (including RealAudio): www.whr.org/; (LeSEA Broadcasting parent organization) www.lesea.com/. Contact: (listener contact) Loren Holycross; (general) Pete Sumrall, Vice President; or Joe Hill, Operations Manager; (programming or sales) Joe Hill or Joe Brashier; (technical) Douglas Garlinger, Chief Engineer. World Harvest Radio T-shirts available from 61300 S. Ironwood Road, South Bend IN 46614 USA. Return postage appreciated.

WINB—World International Broadcasters, World International Broadcast Network, P.O. Box 88, Red Lion PA 17356 USA. Phone: (general) +1 (717) 244-5360; (administration) +1 (717) 246-1681; (studio) +1 (717) 244-3145. Fax: +1 (717) 244 9316. Contact: (general) Mrs. Sally Spyker, Correspondence Secretary; John Stockdale, Manager; Clyde H. Campbell, C.F.O.; or John H. Norris, Owner; (technical) Fred W. Wise, Technical Director. Return postage helpful outside United States. No giveaways or items for sale.

WJCR—Jesus Christ Radio, P.O. Box 91, Upton KY 42784 USA. Phone: +1 (502) 369-8614. E-mail: email@wjcr.com. URL: www.wjcr.com. Contact: (general) Pastor Don Powell, President; Gerri Powell; Trish Powell; or A.L. Burile; (technical) Louis Tate, Chief Engineer. Free religious printed matter. Return postage or $1 appreciated. Actively solicits listener contributions.

WMLK—Assemblies of Yahweh, P.O. Box C, Bethel PA 19507 USA. Toll free telephone (U.S only) 1-800-523 3827; (elsewhere) +1 (717) 933-4518 or +1 (717) 933-4880. E-mail: AOY@avana.net. URL: www.assembliesof yahweh.com/ Log.htm. Contact: (general) Elder Jacob O. Meyer, Manager & Producer of "The Open Door to the Living World"; (technical) Gary McAvin, Engineer. Free *Yahweh* magazine, stickers and religious material. Bibles, audio and video (VHS) tapes and religious paperback books offered. Enclosing return postage ($1 or IRCs) helps speed things up. Plans to increase transmitter power to 100 kW in the future.

WRMI—Radio Miami Internacional

MAIN OFFICE: P.O. Box 526852, Miami FL 33152 USA. Phone: +1 (305) 267-1728. Fax: +1 (305) 267 9253. E-mail: wrmi@compuserve.com. URL: http://home.nexus.org/ WRMI/. Contact: (general & technical) Jeff White, General Manager & Producer "Viva Miami"; (technical) Indalecio "Kiko" Espinosa, Chief Engineer. Free station stickers and tourist brochures. Sells PASSPORT TO WORLD BAND RADIO $23-33 (Depending where in the world it is sent), T-shirts $15 (worldwide), baseball-style hats $10 (worldwide)—all postpaid by airmail. No cards. Sells "public access" airtime to nearly anyone to say virtually anything for $1 or more per minute. Radio Miami Internacional also acts as a broker for Cuban exile programs aired via U.S. stations WHRI and KWHR. Technical correspondence may be sent to either WRMI or the station over which the program was heard. Hopes to add one new antenna and an additional 50 kW transmitter in the foreseeable future. Return postage appreciated.

VENEZUELA OFFICE: Apartado 2122, Valencia 2001, Venezuela. Phone:/fax: + 58 (45) 810-362. Contact: Yoslen Silva.

WRNO, Box 100, New Orleans LA 70181 USA; or 4539 I-10 Service Road North, Metairie LA 70006 USA. Phone: +1 (504) 889-2424. Fax: +1 (504) 889 0602. URL: www.wrnoworldwide.com/. Contact: Paul Heingarten, Operations Manager. Single copy of program guide for 2 IRCs or an SASE. Stickers available for SASE. T-shirts available for $10. Sells World Band radios. Carries programs from various organizations; these may be contacted either directly (*see* Disestablishmentarian, earlier in this section) or via WRNO. Correct reception reports verified for 2 IRCs or an SASE.

WSHB—see Herald Broadcasting Syndicate, above.

WWBS, P.O. Box 18174. Macon GA 31209 USA. Phone: +1 (912) 745-1485. E-mail: charlesK4LNL@june.com. Contact: Charles C. Josey; or Joanne Josey.

WWCR—World Wide Christian Radio, F.W. Robbert Broadcasting Co., 1300 WWCR Avenue, Nashville TN 37218 USA. Phone: (general) +1 (615) 255-1300. E-mail: (general) wwcr@aol.com; (head of operations) wwcrl@aol.com; ("Ask WWCR" program) askwwcr@aol.com. URL: www.wwcr.com. Contact: (general) Chuck Adair, Sales Representative; (administration) George McClintock, K4BTY, General Manager; Adam W. Lock, Sr., WA2JAL, Head of Operations; or Dawn Parton, Program Director; (technical) D. Reming, Chief Engineer. Free program guide, updated monthly. Free stickers and small souvenirs sometimes available. Return postage helpful. For items sold on the air, contact the producers of the programs, and *not* WWCR. Replies as time permits. Carries programs from various political organizations; these may be contacted directly (*see* Disestablishmentarian, earlier in this chapter).

WWV/WWVB (official time and frequency stations), Frequency-Time Broadcast Services Section, Time and Frequency Division, NIST, Mail Station 847, 325 Broadway, Boulder CO 80303 USA. Phone: (tape recording of latest shortwave technical propagation data and forecast) +1 (303) 497-3235; (live

WWV audio) +1 (303) 499-7111; (Broadcast Manager) +1 (303) 497-3281; (Public Affairs) +1 (303) 497-3246; (Institute for Tele-communications Sciences) +1 (303) 497-3484. Phone/fax: (technical, call first before trying to fax) +1 (303) 497-3914. Fax: (Public Affairs) +1 (303) 497 3371. Contact: (general) Fred P. McGehan, Public Affairs Officer; (administration) Roger Beehler, Broadcast Manager; (technical) John B. Milton, Engineer-in-Charge; or Matt Deutsch, Engineer. Along with branch sister station WWVH in Hawaii (see below), WWV and WWVB are the official time and frequency stations of the United States, operating over longwave (WWVB) on 60 kHz, and over shortwave (WWV) on 2500, 5000, 10000, 15000 and 20000 kHz. Free Special Publication 432 "NIST Time & Frequency Services" pamphlet. Don't enclose return postage, money or IRCs, as they will only have to be returned by station. Plans to increase power of WWVB, currently 13 kW, before end of decade.

WWVH (official time and frequency station), NIST—Hawaii, P.O. Box 417, Kekaha, Kauai HI 96752 USA. Phone: +1 (808) 335-4361; (live audio) +1 (808) 335-4363. Fax: +1 (808) 335 4747. Contact: (technical) Dean T. Okayama, Engineer-in-Charge. E-mail: None planned. Along with headquarters sister stations WWV and WWVB (see preceding), WWVH is the official time and frequency station of the United States, operating on 2500, 5000, 10000 and 15000 kHz. Free Special Publication 432 "NIST Time & Frequency Services" pamphlet.

WYFR—Family Radio
NONTECHNICAL: Family Stations, Inc., 290 Hegenberger Road, Oakland CA 94621 USA; or P.O. Box 2140 Oakland CA 94621-9985 USA. Phone: (toll-free, U.S. only) 1-800-543-1495; (elsewhere) +1 (510) 568-6200; (engineering) +1 (510) 568-6200 ext. 240. Fax: (main office) +1 (510) 568-6200; (engineering) +1 (510) 562 1023. E-mail: (general) famradio@familyradio.com; (shortwave department) shortwave@familyradio.com. URLs: (Family Radio Network, includes RealAudio) www.familyradio.com; (WYFR) www.familyradio.com/wyfr.htm. Contact: (general) Harold Camping, General Manager; or Thomas Schaff, Shortwave Program Manager; (technical) Dan Elyea, Station Manager; or Shortwave Department. Free gospel tracts (33 languages), books, booklets, quarterly Family Radio News magazine and frequency schedule. 2 IRCs helpful.
BELARUS OFFICE: B.A International, Chapaeva Street #5, 220600 Minsk, Belarus.
INDIA OFFICE: Family Radio, c/o Rev. Alexander, Tekkali 532201 Andra Pradesh India.
TECHNICAL: WYFR—Family Radio, 10400 NW 240th Street, Okeechobee FL 34972 USA. Phone: +1 (941) 763-0281. Fax: +1 (941) 763 1034. Contact: Dan Elyea, Engineering Manager; or Edward F. Dearborn, Assistant Engineer Manager.

UZBEKISTAN   World Time +5

WARNING—MAIL THEFT: Due to increasing local mail theft, Radio Tashkent suggests that those wishing to correspond should try using one of the drop-mailing addresses listed below.

Radio Tashkent
STATION: 49 Khorezm Street, 740047 Tashkent, Uzbekistan. Phone: +7 (3712) 441-210 or +7 (3712) 440 021. Contact: V. Danchev, Correspondence Section; Lenora Hannanowa; Zulfiya Ibragimova; Mrs. G. Babadjanova, Chief Director of Programs; or Mrs. Florida Perevertailo, Producer, "At Listeners' Request." Free pennants, badges, wallet calendars and

postcards. Books in English by Uzbek writers are apparently available for purchase. Station offers free membership to two clubs: The "Salum Aleikum Listeners' Club" is open to anyone who asks to join, whereas "Radio Tashkent DX Club" is open to listeners who send in ten reception reports that are verified by the station.
LONDON OFFICE: 72 Wigmore Street, London W18 9L, United Kingdom.
FRANKFURT OFFICE: Radio Taschkent, c/o Uzbekistan Airways, Merkurhaus, Raum 215, Hauptbahnhof 10, D-60329 Frankfurt, Germany.
BANGKOK OFFICE: 848-850 Ramapur Road, Bangkok 10050, Thailand.
Uzbek Radio—see Radio Tashkent for details.

VANUATU   World Time +12 (+11 midyear)

Radio Vanuatu, Information & Public Relations, P.M.B. 049, Port Vila, Vanuatu. Phone: +678 22999 or +678 23026. Fax: +678 22026. Contact: Jonas Cullwick, General Manager; Ambong Thompson, Head of Programmes; or Allan Kalfabun, Sales & Marketing Consultant, who is interested in exchanging letters and souvenirs from other countries; (technical) K.J. Page, Principal Engineer; or Marianne Berukilkilu, Technical Manager.

VATICAN CITY STATE   World Time +1 (+2 midyear)

Radio Vaticana
MAIN AND PROMOTION OFFICES: I-00120 Città del Vaticano, Vatican City State. Phone: (general) +39 (6) 698-83551; (Promotion Office and schedules) +39 (6) 698-83045 or +39 (6) 698-83463; (technical) +39 (6) 698-85258 or +39 (6) 988-3995. Fax: (general) +39 (6) 698 84565 or +39 (6) 698 83237; (technical) +39 (6) 698 85125 or +39 (6) 698 85062. E-mail: sedoc@vatiradio.va; (general direction) dirgen@vatiradio.va; (technical) mc6790@mclink.it; (technical direction, general) segtec@vatiradio.va; (technical direction, broadcasting) segrsmg@vatiradio.va; (promotion office) promo@vatiradio.va. URLs: (general, including RealAudio) www.vatican.va/news_services/radio/radio_en.htm; (RealAudio in English, German and French, plus text) www.wrn.org/vatican-radio/. Contact: (general) Elisabetta Vitalini Sacconi, Promotion Office and schedules; Eileen O'Neill, Head of Program Development, English Service; Fr. Lech Rynkiewicz S.I., Head of Promotion Office; Fr. Federico Lombardi, S.I., Program Director; P. Moreau, Ufficio Promozione; Solange de Maillardoz, Head of International Relations; or Veronica Scarisbrick, Producer, "On the Air;" (administration) Fr. Pasquale Borgomeo, S.I., Direttore Generale; (technical) Umberto Tolaini, Frequency Manager, Direzione Tecnica; Sergio Salvatori, Assistant Frequency Manager, Direzione Tecnica; Eugenio Matis S.I., Technical Director; or Giovanni Serra, Frequency Management Department. Correspondence sought on religious and programming matters, rather than the technical minutiae of radio. Free station stickers and paper pennants. Music CDs $13; Pope John Paul II: The Pope of the Rosary double CD/cassette $19.98 plus shipping; "Sixty Years . . . a Single Day" PAL video on Vatican Radio for 15,000 lire, including postage, from the Promotion Office. Vatican Radio's annual budget is $10 million.
TOKYO OFFICE: 2-10-10 Shiomi, Koto-ku, Tokyo 135, Japan. Fax: +81 (3) 5632 4457.
INDIAN OFFICE: Loyola College, P.B. No 3301, Chennai-600 03,

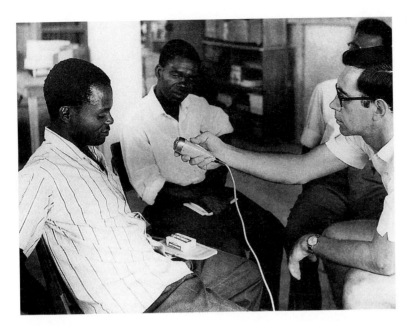

ELWA's news was once considered the most credible in Liberia. For now, though, the station's future is uncertain.   SIM

India. Fax: +91 (44) 825 7340. E-mail: (Tamil) tamil@vatiradio.va; (Hindi) hindi@vatiradio.va; (English) india@vatiradio.va.
REGIONAL OFFICE, INDIA: Pastoral Orientation Centre, P.B. No 2251, Palarivattom, India. Fax: +91 (484) 336 227. E-mail: (Malayalam) malayalam@vatiradio.va.
WARSAW OFFICE: Warszawskie Biuro Sekcji Polskiej Radia Watykanskiego, ul. Skwer Ks. Kard. S, Warsaw, Poland. Phone: +48 (22) 838-8796.

VENEZUELA   World Time –4

Ecos del Torbes, Apartado 152, San Cristóbal 5001-A, Táchira, Venezuela. Phone: +58 (76) 438-244 or (studio): +58 (76) 421-949. Contact: (general) Daphne González Zerpa, Directora; or Dr. Simón Zardman, Program Producer; (technical) Ing. Iván Escobar S., Jefe Técnico.
Observatorio Cagigal—YVTO, Apartado 6745, Armada 84-DHN, Caracas 103, Venezuela. Phone: +58 (2) 481—2761. E-mail: armdhn@ven.net. Contact: Jesús Alberto Escalona, Director Técnico;Gregorio Perez Moreno, Director; or Colonel José Fuentes Goitia, Director. $1 or return postage helpful.
Radio Amazonas, Av. Simón Bolívar 4, Puerto Ayacucho 7101, Amazonas, Venezuela; or if no reply try Francisco José Ocaña at: Urb. 23 de Enero, Calle Nicolás Briceño, No. 18-266, Barinas 5201-A, Venezuela. Contact: Luis Jairo, Director; or Santiago Sangil Gonzales, Gerente. Francisco José Ocaña is a keen collector of U.S. radio station stickers. Sending a few stickers with your letter as well as enclosing $2 may help.
Radio Frontera (when active), Edificio Radio, San Antonio del Táchira, Táchira, Venezuela. Phone: +58 (76) 782-92. Fax: +58 (76) 785 08. Contact: Modesto Marchena, Gerente General. May reply to correspondence in Spanish. $1 or return postage suggested. If no reply, try sending your reports to Venezuelan DXer Antonio J. Contín, Calle Los Lirios #1219, Urbanización Miraflores 4013, Cabimas, Estado Zulia, Venezuela. In return for this service he requests you send $2-3

and would like any spare Latin American pennants and stickers you might have.
Radio Mundial Los Andes (Radio Los Andes 1040) (if reactivated), Calle 44 No. 3-57, Mérida, Venezuela. Phone: +58 (74) 639-286. Contact: Celso Pacheco, Director. May reply to correspondence in Spanish. $1 or return postage suggested.
Radio Nacional de Venezuela (when operating), Final Calle Las Marías, El Pedregal de Chapellín, 1050 Caracas, Venezuela. If this fails, try: Director de la Onda Corta, Sr. Miguel Angel Cariel, Apartado Postal 3979, Caracas 1010-A, Venezuela. The transmitter site is actually located at Campo Carabobo near Valencia, some three hours drive from Caracas. Phone: +58 (2) 745-166. Contact: Miguel Angel Cariel, Director de la Onda Corta.
Radio Occidente, Carrera 4a. No. 6-46, Tovar 5143, Mérida, Venezuela.
Radio Rumbos (if reactivated)
MAIN ADDRESS: Apartado 2618, Caracas 1010A, Venezuela. Phone: +58 (43) 333-734, +58 (43) 335-179, +58 (43) 336-776 or +58 (43) 337-757. Fax: +58 (2) 335 164. E-mail: rumbos@tycom.com.ve. URL: (includes RealAudio) www.tycom.com.ve/rumbos/. Contact: (general) Andrés Felipe Serrano, Vice-Presidente; (technical) Ing. José Corrales; or Jaime L. Ferguson, Departamento Técnico. Free pamphlets, keychains and stickers. $1 or IRC required. Replies occasionally to correspondence in Spanish.
MIAMI ADDRESS: P.O. Box 020010, Miami FL 33102 USA.
Radio Táchira, Apartado 152, San Cristóbal 5001-A, Táchira, Venezuela. Phone: +58 (76) 430-009. Contact: Desirée González Zerpa, Directora; Sra. Albertina, Secretaria; or Eleázar Silva Malavé, Gerente.
Radio Valera, Av. 10 No. 9-31, Valera 3102, Trujillo, Venezuela. Phone: +58 (71) 53-744. Contact: Gladys Barroeta; or Mariela Leal. Replies to correspondence in Spanish. Return postage required. This station has been on the same world band frequency for almost 50 years, which is a record for Latin America. If no response try via Antonio J. Contín. *(see Radio Frontera, above).*

VIETNAM   World Time +7

Bac Thai Broadcasting Service—contact via Voice of Vietnam—Overseas Service, below.

Lai Chau Broadcasting Service—contact via Voice of Vietnam—Overseas Service, below.

Lam Dong Broadcasting Service, Da Lat, Vietnam. Contact: Hoang Van Trung. Replies slowly to correspondence in Vietnamese, but French may also suffice.

Son La Broadcasting Service, Son La, Vietnam. Contact: Nguyen Hang, Director. Replies slowly to correspondence in Vietnamese, but French may also suffice.

Voice of Vietnam—Domestic Service (Đài Tiếng Nói Việt Nam, TNVN)—Addresses and contact numbers as for all sections of Voice of Vietnam—Overseas Service, below. Contact: Phan Quang, Director General.

Voice of Vietnam—Overseas Service

TRANSMISSION FACILITY (MAIN ADDRESS FOR NONTECHNICAL CORRESPONDENCE AND GENERAL VERIFICATIONS): 58 Quán Sú, Hànôi, Vietnam. Phone: +84 (4) 825-7870 or +84 (4) 825-2535. Fax: +84 (4) 825 5765 or +84 (4) 826 1122. Contact: Dao Dinh Tuan, Director of External Broadcasting; or Tran Mai Hanh, Director General. Free paper pennant and, occasionally upon request, Vietnamese stamps. $1 helpful, but IRCs apparently of no use. Replies slowly. Don't send stamps on letters to Vietnam. They're often cut off the letters and the station doesn't receive them. Frankings printed by machines stand a better chance of getting through.

STUDIOS (NONTECHNICAL CORRESPONDENCE AND GENERAL VERIFICATIONS): 45 Ba Trieu Street, Hànôi, Vietnam. Phone: +84 (4) 825-5669 or +84 (4) 825-7870. Fax: +84 (4) 826 1122 or +84 (4) 826 6707. Contact Dinh The Loc, Director.

TECHNICAL CORRESPONDENCE: Office of Radio Reception Quality, Central Department of Radio and Television Broadcast Engineering, Vietnam General Corporation of Posts and Telecommunications, Hànôi, Vietnam.

Yen Bai Broadcasting Station—contact via Voice of Vietnam, Overseas Service, above.

YEMEN   World Time +3

Republic of Yemen Radio, Ministry of Information, P.O. Box 2371, San'a, Yemen; or P.O. Box 2182, San'a, Yemen. Phone: +967 (1) 231-181. Fax: +967 (1) 230 761. Contact: (general) English Service; (technical) Abdullah Farhan, Technical Director.

YUGOSLAVIA   World Time +1 (+2 midyear)

Radiotelevizija Srbije, Hilendarska 2/IV, 11000 Belgrade, Serbia, Yugoslavia. Fax: +381 (11) 332 014. Contact: (technical) B. Miletic, Operations Manager of HF Broadcasting.

Radio Yugoslavia, Hilendarska 2, P.O. Box 200, 11000 Belgrade, Serbia, Yugoslavia. Phone: +381 (11) 346-884 or +381 (11) 346-801; (listener voice mail) +381 (11) 344-455. Fax: +381 (11) 332 014. Contact: (general) Nikola Ivanovic, Director; Aleksandar Georgiev; Aleksandar Popovic, Head of Public Relations; Pance Zafirovski, Head of Programs; or Slobodan Topović, Producer, "Post Office Box 200/Radio Hams' Corner"; (technical) B. Miletic, Operations Manager of HF Broadcasting; Technical Department; or Rodoljub Medan, Chief Engineer. Free pennants, stickers, pins and tourist information. $1 helpful.

ZAMBIA   World Time +2

Radio Christian Voice

STATION: Private Bag E606, Lusaka, Zambia. Phone: +260 (1) 274-251. Fax: +260 (1) 274 526. E-mail: cvoice@zamnet.zm. Contact: Andrew Flynn, Head of Transmission; Philip Haggar, Station Manager; B. Phiri; or Lenganji Nanyangwe, Assistant to Station Manager. Free calendars and stickers pens, as available. Free religious books and items under selected circumstances. Sells T-shirts and sundry other items. $1 or 2 IRCs appreciated for reply. This station broadcasts Christian teachings and music, as well as news and programs on farming, sport, education, health, business and children's affairs.

U. K. OFFICE: Christian Vision, Ryder Street, West Bromwich, West Midlands, B70 0EJ, United Kingdom. Phone:+44 (121) 522-6087. Fax: +44 (121) 522 6083. E-mail: 100131.3711@ compuserve.com. URL: www.christianvision.org/.

Radio Zambia, ZNBC Broadcasting House, P.O. Box 50015, Lusaka, Zambia. Phone: (general) +260 (1) 254-989; (Public Relations) +260 (1) 254-989, X-216; (engineering) +260 (1) 250-380. Fax: +260 (1) 254 317 or +260 (1) 250 5424. Contact: (general) Keith Nalumango, Public Relations Manager; Luke L. Chikani; or Frank Mutubila, Director of Programmes and Producer of "Tell the Nation" listeners' letters program; (administration) Duncan H. Mbazima, Director-General; (technical) Edward H. Mwanza, Principal Engineer, Planning & Development; or Patrick Nkula, Director of Engineering. Free *Zamwaves* newsletter. Sometimes gives away stickers and small publications. $1 required, and postal correspondence should be sent via registered mail. Tours given of the station Tuesdays to Fridays between 9:00 AM and noon local time; inquire in advance. Used to reply slowly and irregularly, but seems to be better now.

ZIMBABWE   World Time +2

Zimbabwe Broadcasting Corporation, P.O. Box HG444, Highlands, Harare, Zimbabwe; or P.O. Box 2271, Harare, Zimbabwe. Phone: +263 (4) 498-610, or +263 (4) 498-630. Fax: (general) +263 (4) 498 613; (technical) +263 (4) 498 608. Contact: (general) Charles Warikandwa; or Luke Z. Chikani; (administration) Edward Moyo, Director General; or Thomas Mandigora, Director of Programmes; (technical) I. Magoryo, Engineer. $1 helpful.

CREDITS: Craig Tyson (Australia), Editor. Also, Tony Jones (Paraguay), Henrik Klemetz (Colombia), Marie Lamb (USA) and Lawrence Magne (USA). Special thanks to Cumbre DX/ *Hans Johnson (USA), Gabriel Iván Barrera (Argentina), Gary Neal (USA), George Poppin (USA), Graeme Dixon (New Zealand),* India Broadbase/*Manosij Guha (India),* Jembatan DX/*Juichi Yamada (Japan),* Número Uno *(USA),* Radio Nuevo Mundo/*Tetsuya Hirahara (Japan),* Relámpago DX/*Takayuki Inoue Nozaki (Japan/Latin America) and* RUS-DX/*Anatoly Klepov (Russia).*

THE MOST POWERFUL COMPACT RADIO!

A masterpiece!
German look! German sound!
German quality!

Grundig is to radio what BMW and Mercedes are to cars.

(measures 7 3/4" X 4 5/8" X 1 3/8")

THE GRUNDIG 400PE
AM/FM Shortwave Receiver

THE BIG BREAKTHROUGH!
Power, performance, and design have reached new heights! The Grundig 400 Professional Edition with its sleek titanium look is packed with features like no other compact radio in the world.

PINPOINT ACCURACY!
The Grundig 400PE does it all: pulls in AM, FM, FM-Stereo, every shortwave band (even aviation and ship-to-shore)—all with lock-on digital precision.

ULTIMATE FEATURES!
Auto tuning! The Grundig 400PE has auto tuning on shortwave and stops at every signal and lets you

listen. With the exceptional sensitivity of the 400PE, you can use the auto tune to catch even the weakest of signals.

INCREDIBLE TIMING FEATURES!
The Grundig 400PE can send you to sleep listening to your favorite music. You can set the alarm to wake up to music or the morning traffic report, then switch to BBC shortwave for the world news. The choice is yours!

POWERFUL MEMORY!
Described as a smart radio with 40 memory positions, the Grundig 400PE remembers your favorites—even if you don't!

NEVER BEFORE VALUE!
The Grundig 400PE includes a deluxe travel pouch, stereo earphones, owner's manual, external antenna and a Grundig AC adaptor.

One Year Warranty

Worldwide Broadcasts in English—1999

Country-by-Country Guide to Best-Heard Stations

Dozens of countries reach out to us in English, and this section covers the times and frequencies where you're likely to hear them. If you want to know which shows are on hour-by-hour, check out the "What's On Tonight" section.

Some tips so you don't waste your time:

• **Best times and frequencies:** "Best Times and Frequencies," ear-

lier in this book, tells where each world band segment is found. It also gives helpful specifics as to when and where to tune.

In general, it is best to listen during the late afternoon and evening, when most programs are beamed your way; in your local winter, tune the world band segments within the 5730-10000 kHz range (5730-15800 kHz local summer). Around breakfast, you can also explore segments within the 5730-17900 kHz range for a smaller, but interesting, number of selections.

• **Strongest (and weakest) frequencies:** Frequencies shown in italics—say, *6175* kHz—tend to be the best, as they are from transmitters that may be located near you. Frequencies with no target zones are typically from transmitters designed for domestic coverage, so these are the least likely to be heard well unless you're in or near that country.

Programs Change Times Midyear

Some stations shift broadcast times by one hour midyear, typically April through October. These are indicated by ◧ (one hour earlier) and ▣ (one hour later). Stations may also extend their hours of transmission, or air special programs, for national holidays or sports events.

Eavesdropping on World Music

Broadcasts in other than English? Turn to the next section, "Voices from Home," or the Blue Pages. Keep in mind that stations for kinsfolk abroad sometimes carry delightful chunks of indigenous music. They make for exceptional listening, regardless of language.

Schedules Prepared for Entire Year

To be as helpful as possible throughout the year, PASSPORT includes not just observed activity and factual schedules, but also activity which we have creatively opined will take place. This predictive information is original from us, and although it's of real value when tuning the airwaves, it is inherently not so exact as real-time data.

Most frequencies are aired year round. Those that are only used seasonally are labeled ⑤ for summer (midyear, typically April through October), and ⑪ for winter.

Times and days of the week are in World Time, explained in "Setting Your World Time Clock" earlier in the book, as well as in the glossary.

> In general, it is best to listen during the late afternoon and evening, when most programs are beamed your way.

HCJB's Curt Cole is Director of English Language Service and Co-producer of "Studio 9." HCJB

ALBANIA
RADIO TIRANA
0145-0200 ▭	6115, 7160 (E North Am)
0130-0200	▣ 6220 (E North Am)
0230-0300 ▭	7160 (E North Am)
0230-0300	w 6140 (E North Am)

ARGENTINA
RADIO ARGENTINA AL EXTERIOR-RAE
0200-0300	Tu-Sa 11710 (Americas)
1800-1900	M-F 15345 (Europe & N Africa)

ARMENIA
VOICE OF ARMENIA
0400-0430 ▭	Sa/Su 4810 (E Europe, Mideast & W Asia)
1000-1030 ▭	Su 4810 (E Europe, Mideast & W Asia), Su 15270 (Europe)
2115-2145 ▭	M-Sa 4810 (E Europe, Mideast & W Asia), M-Sa 9965 (Europe)

AUSTRALIA
ABC/CAAMA RADIO—(Australasia)
0000-0830	4835 & 4910
0830-2130	2310 & 2325
2130-2400	4835 & 4910

ABC/R RUM JUNGLE—(Australasia)
0830-2130	2485
2130-0830	5025

RADIO AUSTRALIA
0000-0200	17795 & 21740 (Pacific & W North Am)
0000-0500	17750 (E Asia & SE Asia)
0000-0800	9660 (Pacific), 15240 (Pacific & E Asia)
0000-0900	12080 (S Pacific)
0100-0500	15415 (E Asia & SE Asia)
0200-0900	15510 (S Pacific)
0600-0900	15415 (E Asia & SE Asia)
0800-0900	5995 & 9710 (Pacific)
0800-2100	9580 (Pacific & N America)
0900-1200	6080 (Pacific & E Asia)
1400-1800	5995 (Pacific & W North Am)
1430-1700	11660 (E Asia & SE Asia)
1800-2000	6080 (Pacific & E Asia)
2000-2200	12080 (S Pacific)
2100-2200	9660 (Pacific)
2100-2400	21740 (Pacific & W North Am)
2200-2400	17795 (Pacific & W North Am)
2300-2400	9660 (Pacific), 12080 (S Pacific)

AUSTRIA
RADIO AUSTRIA INTERNATIONAL
0130-0200	▣ 9495 (S America), ▣ 9655 (E North Am)
0230-0300	▣ 9870 (C America), ▣ 13730 (S America)
0430-0500	▣ 13730 (E Europe)
0530-0600	6015 (N America), ▣ 6155 (Europe), ▣ 13730 (E Europe), ▣ 15410 & ▣ 17870 (Mideast)
0630-0700	▣ 6015 (N America)
0730-0800	▣ 6155 (Europe), ▣ 13730 (E Europe), ▣ 15410 & ▣ 17870 (Mideast)
0830-0900	▣ 6155 (Europe), ▣ 13730 (N Europe), ▣ 17870 (Australasia)
0930-1000	▣ M-Sa 15455 (E Asia), ▣ M-Sa 17870 & ▣ 17870 (Australasia)
1030-1100	▣ Su 15455 (E Asia), ▣ Su 17870 (Australasia)
1230-1300	▣ 6155 (Europe), ▣ 13730 (W Europe & E North Am)
1330-1400	▣ 6155 (Europe), ▣ 13730 (W Europe & E North Am)
1630-1700	▣ 6155 (Europe), ▣ 13710 (S Asia & SE Asia), ▣ 13730 (S Europe & W Africa)
1730-1800	▣ 9655 (Mideast)
2130-2200	▣ 5945 & ▣ 6155 (Europe), ▣ 13730 (S Africa)
2230-2300	▣ 5945 & ▣ 6155 (Europe)

BANGLADESH
BANGLADESH BETAR
1230-1300	7185 & 9550 (SE Asia)
1530-1540 &	
1700-1710	15520 (Mideast & Europe)
1745-1815 &	
1815-1900	7185, 9550 & 15520 (Irr) (Europe)

BRAZIL
RADIO NACIONAL DO BRASIL-RADIOBRAS
1200-1320	15445 (N America & C America)
1800-1920	15265 (Europe & Mideast)

BULGARIA
RADIO BULGARIA
0000-0100 ▭	9485 (E North Am & C America)
0000-0100	▣ 7375 (E North Am)
0200-0300	▣ 11720 (E North Am)
0300-0400 ▭	9485 (E North Am & C America)
0300-0400	▣ 7375 (E North Am)
1900-2000	▣ 11720 (Europe)
2000-2100 ▭	9700 (Europe)
2000-2100	▣ 7530 (Europe)
2100-2200	▣ 11720 (Europe)
2200-2300 ▭	9700 (Europe)
2200-2300	▣ 7530 (Europe)

Manoranjan Das of Radio Bangladesh prepares for the coming radio season.

M. Guha

CAMBODIA

NATIONAL VOICE OF CAMBODIA—(SE Asia)
0000-0015 &	
1200-1215	11940

CANADA

CANADIAN BROADCASTING CORP—(E North Am)
0000-0300	▣	Su 9625
0200-0300	▣	Tu-Sa 9625
0300-0310 &		
0330-0609	▣	M 9625
0400-0609	▣	Su 9625
0500-0609	▣	Tu-Sa 9625
1200-1255	▣	M-F 9625
1200-1505	▣	Sa 9625
1200-1700	▣	Su 9625
1600-1615 &		
1700-1805	▣	Sa 9625
1800-2400	▣	Su 9625
1945-2015,		
2200-2225 &		
2240-2330	▣	M-F 9625

CFRX-CFRB—(E North Am)
24 Hr	6070

CFVP-CKMX—(W North Am)
24 Hr	6030

CHNX-CHNS—(E North Am)
24 Hr	6130

CKZN-CBN—(E North Am)
0930-0500 ▣	6160

CKZU-CBU—(W North Am)
24 Hr	6160

RADIO CANADA INTERNATIONAL
0000-0030		▣ Tu-Sa 6040 (C America)
0000-0100	▣	9755 (E North Am & C America)
0000-0100		▣ 5960 (E North Am)
0100-0130		▣ 9535, ▣ 11715 & ▣ 13670 (C America & S America)
0130-0200		▣ Su/M 9535, ▣ Su/M 11715 & ▣ Su/M 13670 (C America & S America)
0200-0230		9535, ▣ 11715 & ▣ 13670 (C America & S America)
0200-0300	▣	9755 (E North Am & C America)
0200-0300		▣ 11865 (C America & S America)
0200-0330		▣ 6155 (E North Am & C America), ▣ 9780 (C America & S America)
0230-0300		▣ Su/M 9535, ▣ 9535 & ▣ Su/M 11715 (C America & S America)
0300-0330	▣	9755 (E North Am & C America)
0330-0400	▣	Su/M 9755 (E North Am & C America)
0330-0400		▣ Su/M 6155 (E North Am & C America)
0400-0430		▣ 6150, ▣ 9505, ▣ 9645, ▣ 9715, ▣ 11835 & ▣ 11975 (Mideast)
0500-0530		▣ M-F 7295 (W Europe & N Africa), ▣ M-F 15430 (Africa)
0600-0630		▣ M-F 6050 (Europe), ▣ M-F 6150 (Europe & Mideast), ▣ M-F 9740 (N Africa & W Africa), ▣ M-F 9760 (Europe & N Africa), ▣ M-F 11905 (Mideast)

1200-1230	**W** *6150* & **S** *9660* (E Asia), **W** *11730* & **S** *15195* (SE Asia)
1200-1300	**S** 13650 (E North Am & C America)
1300-1400 **◻**	9640 (E North Am), 11855 (E North Am & C America)
1300-1400	**S** Su-F 13650 (E North Am & C America)
1330-1357	*9535* (E Asia)
1330-1400	**W** *6150* & **S** *11795* (E Asia), **S** *15325* & **S** M-Sa 17820 (Europe)
1400-1500 **◻**	M-F 9640 (E North Am), Su-F 11855 (E North Am & C America)
1400-1600	**S** Su 13650 (E North Am & C America)
1400-1700	**W** Su 9640 (E North Am)
1430-1500 **◻**	*11935* (Europe & Mideast)
1430-1500	**W** *9555* (Europe & Mideast), **W** *11915* & **W** *15325* (Europe)
1500-1700 **◻**	Su 11855 (E North Am & C America)
1630-1657	*6140* & *7150* (S Asia)
1630-1700	*6550* (E Asia)
2000-2100	**S** 13650 (Europe & N Africa), **S** 17820 (Africa), **S** 17870 (Europe & N Africa)
2000-2130	**S** 11690 (Europe), **S** 13670 (Africa), **S** 15325 (Europe)
2100-2130	13650 (Europe & N Africa), 17820 (Africa)
2100-2200 **◻**	*5995* (Europe)
2100-2230 **◻**	15150 (Africa)
2100-2230	**W** 7235 (S Europe & N Africa), **W** 9805 (W Europe & N Africa), **W** 11945 (W Africa), **W** 13690 (Africa)
2130-2200	**W** 13650 (Europe & N Africa), **W** 17820 (Africa)
2200-2230	*11705* (SE Asia), **S** 15305 (C America & S America)
2200-2300	**S** 5960 (E North Am)
2200-2400	**S** 13670 (C America & S America)
2300-2330	**W** 6040 (C America), **W** 9535, **W** 11865 & **S** 15305 (C America & S America)
2300-2400 **◻**	9755 (E North Am & C America)
2300-2400	5960 (E North Am)
2330-2400	**W** Sa/Su 6040 (C America), **W** Sa/Su 9535, **W** Sa/Su 11865 & **S** Sa/Su 15305 (C America & S America)

CHINA

CHINA RADIO INTERNATIONAL

0300-0400	*9690* (N America & C America)
0400-0500	*9730* (W North Am)
0500-0600 **◻**	*9560* (N America)
0900-1100	9785, 9890 & 11755 (Australasia)
1140-1155	**W** 6995, **S** 11700 (SE Asia)
1200-1300	9715 (SE Asia), 6950 (Australasia)

1200-1400	11660 & 11980 (SE Asia), 9945 & 11675 (Australasia)
1210-1225	**W** 6995, **S** 11700 & 12110 (SE Asia)
1400-1500	7260, 9535, 9700 & 11825 (S Asia)
1400-1600 **◻**	7405 (W North Am)
1400-1600	7160 & 9785 (S Asia)
1440-1455	**W** 6995, **S** 9880 (SE Asia)
1700-1800	7405 (Africa), 9570 and 9745 (E Africa & S Africa), **S** 11910 (E Africa)
1900-2000	**W** 6955 (N Africa & W Africa), **S** 11515 (Mideast & N Africa)
1900-2100	9440 (N Africa & W Africa)
2000-2100	**S** 7160 (Africa)
2000-2200	6950 & 9920 (Europe)
2100-2130	*7170* (W Africa & N Africa)
2200-2300	**W** *7170* (Europe) **S** *9880* (Europe)

CHINA (TAIWAN)

RADIO TAIPEI INTERNATIONAL

0200-0300	*5950* (E North Am), *11740* (C America)
0200-0400	*9680* (W North Am), 11825 & 15345 (SE Asia)
0300-0400	*5950* (N America & C America), 11745 (E Asia)
0700-0800	*5950* (W North Am & C America)
1200-1300	7130 (E Asia), 9610 (Australasia)
2200-2300	**W** *5810*, **W** *9985*, **S** *15600* & **S** *17750* (Europe)

VOICE OF ASIA—(SE Asia)

| 1100-1200 | 7445 |

COSTA RICA

RADIO FOR PEACE INTERNATIONAL

0100-0200	21460 (N America & Europe)
0100-0530	6975 (N America)
0530-0630	F-W 6975 (N America)
0630-0800	6975 (N America)
1800-2130	15050 (N America), 21460 (N America & Europe)
2130-2230	Th-Tu 15050 (N America), Th-Tu 21460 (N America & Europe)
2230-2330	15050 (N America)
2230-2400	21460 (N America & Europe)

CUBA

RADIO HABANA CUBA

0100-0500	6000 (E North Am), 9820 (N America)
0100-0700	9830 USB (E North Am & Europe)
0500-0700	9820 (W North Am)
2030-2130	**W** 9585 USB, **W** 9620, **S** 13715/13720 & **S** 13750 USB (Europe & E North Am)
2230-2330	6180 (C America)

Ecuador's Presidential Palace and Independence Plaza in Quito. HCJB

CZECH REPUBLIC

RADIO PRAGUE
0000-0030	5930 & 7345 (E North Am)
0100-0130	6200 & 7345 (E North Am)
0300-0330	🆆 5930 (N America), 7345 (E North Am)
0330-0400	9480/7350 (Mideast)
0700-0730	🆂 7345 (W Europe)
1000-1030 ▣	17485 (W Africa)
1130-1200 ▣	7345 (N Europe)
1130-1200	🆆 9505 (W Europe)
1300-1330	🆂 13580 (S Asia & SE Asia)
1400-1430	🆆 13580 (E North Am, S Asia & Australasia), 🆆 21700 (E Africa)
1600-1630	🆂 17485 (E Africa)
1700-1730 ▣	5930 (W Europe)
1700-1730	🆆 9430 (E Africa), 🆂 17485 (C Africa)
1800-1830	🆆 9430 (S Asia & Australasia)
2000-2030	🆂 5930 (W Europe), 🆂 11600 (SE Asia & Australasia)
2100-2130	🆆 5930 (W Europe & E North Am), 🆆 7345 (W Africa)
2230-2300	🆆 5930, 🆆 7345 & 🆂 11600 (E North Am)

ECUADOR

HCJB-VOICE OF THE ANDES
0000-0400	9745 (E North Am)

0000-1600	21455 USB (Europe & Australasia)
0400-0700	9745 (W North Am)
0700-0900	🆂 9765 (Europe)
0700-1100	9640 (Australasia)
1100-1600	12005 (C America), 15115 (N America & S America)
1900-2200	🆆 11960/12015 & 🆂 15115 (Europe), 21455 USB (Europe & Australasia)

EGYPT

RADIO CAIRO
0000-0030	9900 (E North Am)
0200-0330	9475 (N America)
1215-1330	17595 (S Asia)
1630-1830	15255 (C Africa & S Africa)
2030-2200	15375 (W Africa)
2115-2245	9900 (Europe)
2300-2400	9900 (E North Am)

ETHIOPIA

RADIO ETHIOPIA
1030-1100	M-F 7110 (East Africa)
1600-1700	7165 & 9560 (E Africa)

FINLAND

YLE RADIO FINLAND
0200-0230	🆂 9780 & 🆂 11900 (N America)

The Parthenon, symbol of Greece's historic greatness. Today's Greece beams tomorrow's history, today, through world band radio.

N. Grace

1230-1300	**S** Su 11900 (N America)
1330-1400 ▭	Su 15400 (N America)
1330-1400	**W** Su 11735 (N America)
2130-2200 ▭	6135 (Europe)

FRANCE

RADIO FRANCE INTERNATIONALE

1200-1300	9805 (E Europe), *11600* (SE Asia), **W** *13625* (C America & N America), 15155 & 15195 (E Europe), *15540* (W Africa)
1400-1500	**W** *7110* (S Asia), **W** 12030 & **S** 15405 (S Asia & SE Asia), *17560* (Mideast)
1600-1700	**W** 9485 (N Africa, E Africa & Mideast), 11615 (Irr) (N Africa & Mideast), *11700/11705* (W Africa), *12015* & **W** 15530 (S Africa)
1600-1730	**S** 15210 & **S** 15460 (E Africa)

GERMANY

DEUTSCHE WELLE

0100-0150	**W** *5960, 6040* & *6085* (N America), 6145, *9640* & **S** *11810* (N America & C America)
0200-0250	**W** 6035, **W** *7265,* 7285, **W** *7355,* **W** 9515, *9615,* **S** 9690, **S** *11965* & **S** *12045* (S Asia)
0300-0350	**W** 6045, *6085* & *6185* (N America), 9535 & *9640* (N America & C America)
0400-0450	**S** *5990* & 6015 (S Africa), **W** 6065, 7225, **W** *7265,* 9565 & **S** 11765 (Africa)
0500-0550	*5960* (N America), **S** *6045* (N

America & C America), **W** 6100 & **W** *6120* (N America), *6185* (W North Am), **S** 9615 (N America)

0600-0650	**W** 7225, **W** 9565, **W** 11765, **S** 11915, **S** *13790* & **S** 15185 (W Africa), *17820* (E Asia), **S** 17860 (W Africa), **S** *21680* & **W** *21705* (Mideast)
0900-0950	*6160* (Australasia), **W** *7380* (E Asia), *9565* (Africa), **W** *11715* (SE Asia & Australasia), **W** *15145* (E Africa), *15410* (S Africa), **S** *17715* (SE Asia & Australasia), *17800* (W Africa), 21600 (Africa), **S** 21680 (SE Asia & Australasia)
1100-1150	**W** *15410* (W Africa), **W** 17780 (Africa), *17800* (W Africa)
1600-1650	*6170* (S Asia), **W** *7120* & **S** *7130* (S Africa), 7225 & **W** *7305* (S Asia), *9735* (Africa), **S** *9875* (S Asia), *11810* (S Africa), **W** 13610 (C Africa & S Africa), **S** 13690 (S Asia), **W** 15145 (E Africa & S Africa), **S** 17800 (Africa)
1900-1950	**S** *7250,* 9640 & **S** *9670* (Africa), **S** *9735,* **W** 9765 & **S** 11785 (W Africa), **W** 11785 (Africa), *11810* (W Africa), **W** 13690 (E Africa), **S** 13790, *15135* & **W** *15425* (W Africa)
2000-2050	**W** 7285 & **S** *9615* (Europe)
2100-2150	**S** 7115 & *9670* (SE Asia & Australasia), **W** 9690 (Africa), **S** *9735* (W Africa), 9765 & *11785* (SE Asia & Australasia), 11865 (W Africa), **W** *15275* (W Africa & Americas)
2300-2350	**S** *5975* (S Asia & SE Asia), **W** 6045 (SE Asia), **W** *6130,* 7235, **S** 9690 (S Asia & SE Asia)

GHANA

GHANA BROADCASTING CORPORATION

0530-0915	3366, 4915
1200-1700	M-F 6130
1200-2400	4915
1700-2400	3366

GREECE

FONI TIS HELLADAS

0130-0200	[W] 7448, [W] 9420 & 9935/6260 (N America)
0330-0345	[W] 7448 & [W] 9420 (N America)
0745-0755	7450, [S] 9425 & 11645 (Europe & Australasia)
1235-1245	[S] 15175 (Europe & N America)
1335-1345 ⇦	15650 (Europe & N America)
1335-1345	[W] 9420 (Europe & N America)
1840-1855	11645 & 15150 (Africa)
1900-1910	[W] 9375/9380 (Europe)
2000-2010	[S] 7430/9420 (Europe)
2235-2245	9425 (Australasia)
2335-2350	[S] 9395 (C America & S America), [S] 9425 (C America & Australasia), [W] 9425 (C America), 11595 & [W] 11640 (S America)

GUAM

KTWR-TRANS WORLD RADIO

0740-0915	15200 (SE Asia)
0800-0930	15330 (Australasia)
0930-1100	9865 (E Asia)
1500-1630	15330/15105 (S Asia)

GUYANA

VOICE OF GUYANA

24 Hr	5950/3290

HOLLAND

RADIO NETHERLANDS

0000-0125	6020 (E North Am), *6165* (N America), [S] *9845* (E North Am)
0030-0125	[W] *5905* & [W] *7305* (S Asia)
0030-0225	[S] *12090* (S Asia)
0030-0325	[W] *9860* (S Asia)
0430-0525	*6165* & *9590* (W North Am)
0730-0825	[W] *11895* (Australasia)
0730-0925	[W] *9830* (Australasia)
0830-0925	[W] *13700* (Australasia)
0930-1125	[W] *7260* (E Asia), [W] *9810* (SE Asia), [S] *12065* (E Asia), [S] *13710* (E Asia & SE Asia)
1030-1225	[S] *9860* (W Europe)
1130-1325 ⇦	*6045* (W Europe)
1130-1325	[W] *5975/7190* (W Europe)
1330-1525	[S] *9890*, [W] *9895* & [W] 13700 (S Asia)
1730-2025	*6020* (S Africa), [S] *7120* & [W] *9605* (E Africa), [S] 11655 (W Africa)
1830-2025	9895, *15315* & [S] *17605* (W Africa)
2330-2400	6020 (E North Am), *6165* (N America), [S] *9845* (E North Am)

HUNGARY

RADIO BUDAPEST

0100-0130	[S] 9580 (N America)
0230-0300	[S] 11910 (N America)
0330-0400	[W] 6010 (N America)
1900-1930	[S] 7170 (W Europe)
2000-2030 ⇦	3975 (Europe)
2000-2030	[W] 9835 (W Europe)
2100-2130	[S] 11700 (W Europe)
2200-2230 ⇦	3975 (Europe)

INDIA

ALL INDIA RADIO

0000-0045	7150 & 9705 (SE Asia), 9950 (E Asia), 11620 (E Asia & SE Asia)
1000-1100	11585 (E Asia), 13700, 15050 & 17387 (Australasia), 17840 (E Asia)
1330-1500	9545, 11620 & 13710 (SE Asia)
1745-1945	7410 (N Europe), 9950 & 11620 (W Europe), 11935, 13780 & 15075 (E Africa)
2045-2230	7150 (Australasia), 7410 (W Europe), 9910 (Australasia), 9950 (W Europe), 11620 (W Europe & Australasia), 11715 (Australasia)
2245-2400	7150 & 9705 (SE Asia), 9950 (E Asia), 11620 (E Asia & SE Asia)

INDONESIA

VOICE OF INDONESIA

0100-0200 & 0800-0900	9525 (Asia & Pacific)
2000-2100	9525/15150 (Europe)

IRAN

VOICE OF THE ISLAMIC REPUBLIC

0030-0130	[W] 6150/6015 (Europe & C America), [S] 6175 (C America), [W] 7100 (N America), [S] 7180 (C America), [S] 7260 (E North Am), 9022 (N America), [W] 9670 (E North Am)
1100-1230	11745 (Mideast), [S] 11790 (W Asia), [W] 11790 (S Asia & SE Asia), [S] 11875 (S Asia), 11930 (Mideast), 15260 (S Asia & SE Asia)
1530-1630	[W] 9575 (S Asia), [W] 11790 (S Asia & SE Asia), [S] 11875 (S Asia), 15260 & 17750 (S Asia & SE Asia)
1930-2030	7260 & 9022 (Europe)
2130-2230	6175 (Australasia)

ISRAEL

KOL ISRAEL

0400-0415	**S** 11605 (W Europe & E North Am)
0500-0515 **◨**	9435 (W Europe & E North Am), 17545 (Australasia)
0500-0515	**W** 7465 (W Europe & E North Am)
1400-1430	**S** 15650 & **S** 17535 (W Europe & E North Am)
1500-1530	**W** 9365 & **W** 12080 (W Europe & E North Am)
1900-1925	**S** 11605 & **S** 15650 (W Europe & E North Am), **S** 15640 (C America & S America)
2000-2025 **◨**	9435 (W Europe & E North Am)
2000-2025	**W** 7465 (W Europe & E North Am), **W** 9365 & **W** 15640 (Australasia)

ITALY

RADIO ROMA-RAI INTERNATIONAL

0050-0110	6010 (E North Am), 9675 (E North Am & C America), 11800 (N America & C America)
0425-0440	5975 & 7275 (S Europe & N Africa)
1935-1955	**W** 6030, 7235, **S** 9670 & **S** 11905 (N Europe)
2025-2045	**W** 6035, 7110, 9710 & **S** 11840 (Mideast)
2200-2225	6150, 9565 & 11815 (E Asia)

JAPAN

RADIO JAPAN/NHK

0000-0015	11815 & 13650 (SE Asia)
0000-0100	*6155* (W Europe), *6180* (Europe)
0100-0200	*11860* (SE Asia), **W** *11890* (S Asia), 13630 (W North Am), 15570 (E Asia), 15590 (S Asia), 17810 (SE Asia)
0500-0600	*6110* (W North Am & C America), 11715 & **W** 11910 (E Asia), **S** 15230 (Pacific & W North Am)
0500-0700	11840 (E Asia)
0600-0700	*5975* (Europe), *11740* & 17810 (SE Asia)
0700-0800	**W** 11850 (Australasia), **W** *15230* (Mideast)
1000-1200	9695 (SE Asia)
1100-1200	*6120* (E North Am)
1100-1300	7125 (E Asia), **W** 11815 (SE Asia)
1200-1300	**W** *6120* (E North Am)
1500-1600	7240 (S Asia), 9750 (E Asia), 11730 (S Asia), **W** *15355* (S Africa)
1700-1800	**W** 6035 (E Asia), 7110 (Europe), 9535 (W North Am), **S** 9825 (SE Asia)
2100-2200	*6035* (SE Asia), **S** 11850 (Australasia), 13630 (W North Am)

KOREA (DPR)

RADIO PYONGYANG

0000-0100	11845 (SE Asia & C America), 13650 (N America & C America), 15230 (Americas)
1100-1200	9975 & 11335 (SE Asia & C America)
1500-1600	9640 (Mideast & Africa), 9975 (Africa), 13650 (N America & C America)
1800-1900	6575 & 9335 (Europe), 11700 & 13760 (N America)
1900-2000	6520 & 9600 (Mideast & N Africa), 9975 (Africa)
2100-2200	6575 & 9335 (Europe)
2300-2400	11335, 11700, 13760 & 15130 (N America)

KOREA (REPUBLIC)

RADIO KOREA INTERNATIONAL

0200-0300	11725 & 11810 (S America), 15575 (N America)
0800-0900	13670 (Europe)
1030-1100	**S** *11715* (E North Am)
1130-1200	**W** *9650* (E North Am)
1200-1300	7285 (E Asia)
1230-1300	9570 (SE Asia), 9640 (E Asia), 13670 (SE Asia)
1600-1700	5975 (E Asia), 9515 & 9870 (Mideast & Africa)
1900-2000	5975 & 7275 (E Asia)
2100-2130	**S** *3970* (Europe)
2100-2200	15575 (Europe)
2200-2230	**W** *3970* (Europe)

KUWAIT

RADIO KUWAIT—(Europe & E North Am)

1800-2100	11990

LATVIA

RADIO LATVIA

2000-2030 **◨**	Sa 5935 (N Europe)
2130-2135 **◨**	M-F 5935

LEBANON

VOICE OF HOPE

1300-1630 &	
1700-1730	11530 (E Europe, Mideast & W Asia)

VOICE OF LEBANON

0900-0915,	
1315-1330 &	
1800-1815 **◨**	6550

LIBERIA

LIBERIAN COMMUNICATIONS NETWORK
0800-1800   6100
1800-2400   5100

LITHUANIA

RADIO VILNIUS
0030-0100 ⬜   5905 & 🅂 *9855* (E North Am)
0930-1000 ⬛   9710 (Europe)

MALAWI

MALAWI BROADCASTING CORPORATION
0250-2210   3380, 5993

MALAYSIA

VOICE OF MALAYSIA
0500-0830   6175 (SE Asia), 9750 (SE Asia &
              Australasia), 15295 (Australasia)

MONACO

TRANS WORLD RADIO—(W Europe)
0745-0755 ⬛   Sa/Su 9755
0755-0920 ⬛   9755
0920-0935 ⬛   Sa/Su *9755*
0935-0950 ⬛   Su *9755*

MONGOLIA

VOICE OF MONGOLIA
1210-1240   12085 (Australasia)
1430-1500   9720 & 12085 (S Asia & SE Asia)
1830-1900   9720 & 12085 (Europe)

NAMIBIA

NAMIBIAN BROADCASTING CORPORATION
0000-0615 ➡   3270, 3290
0615-1600 ➡   4930, 4965
1600-2400 ➡   3270, 3290

NEPAL

RADIO NEPAL
0215-0225 &
1415-1425   5005, 7164/3230

NEW ZEALAND

RADIO NEW ZEALAND INTERNATIONAL—
(Pacific)
0459-0707   🅂 11690
0500-0706   ⬜ 11905
0707-1015   🅂 6100 & ⬜ 9700
1206-1650   🅂 6100 (Irr)
1650-1850   🅂 M-F 6145
1752-1951   ⬜ M-F 11675

1952-2051   🅂 11735
1952-2052   ⬜ 17675

NIGERIA

VOICE OF NIGERIA
0500-0700,
1000-1100,
1500-1700 &
1900-2100   7255 (Africa), 15120 (Europe & N
              America)

NORWAY

RADIO NORWAY INTERNATIONAL
0100-0130   ⬜ M 7465 (E North Am & C
              America), 🅂 M 9560 (N America)
0300-0330   ⬜ M 7465 (W North Am)
0400-0430   🅂 M 7520 (W North Am)
0600-0630   🅂 Su 7295 (Australasia), 🅂 Su 9590
              (W Africa & Australasia)
0700-0730   ⬜ Su 7180 (W Europe &
              Australasia)
0800-0830   🅂 Su 17855 (Australasia)
1200-1230   🅂 Su 9590 (Europe), 🅂 Su 13800 &
              🅂 Su 15305 (E Asia)
1300-1330   ⬜ Su 9590 (Europe), ⬜ Su 9795 (E
              Asia), 🅂 Su 13800 (SE Asia &
              Australasia), 🅂 Su 15340 (N
              America), ⬜ Su 15605 (SE Asia &
              Australasia)
1400-1430   ⬜ Su 11840 (N America)
1500-1530   ⬜ Su 9520 & ⬜ Su 11730 (Mideast)
1600-1630   🅂 Su 11860 (S Asia), 🅂 Su 13805 (E
              Africa)
1800-1830   🅂 Su 7485 (Europe), 🅂 Su 9590
              (Mideast), 🅂 Su 13805 (W Africa), 🅂
              Su 15220 (C Africa)
1900-1930   ⬜ Su 5930 (Australasia), ⬜ Su 5960
              (Europe), ⬜ Su 7485 (W Africa), ⬜
              Su 9590 (C Africa)
2000-2030   🅂 Su 9590 (Australasia)
2200-2230   ⬜ Su 6200 (E North Am), ⬜ Su 7115
              (E Asia), 🅂 Su 9485 (Australasia)

PAPUA NEW GUINEA

NBC
0730-0900   9675/4890
1200-1930   M-Sa 4890
2200-0730   9675

PHILIPPINES

FEBC RADIO INTERNATIONAL
0100-0300   15450 (S Asia & SE Asia)
0930-1100   11635 (E Asia & Australasia)
1400-1600   11995 (S Asia & SE Asia)
RADYO PILIPINAS—(Mideast)
0230-0330   ⬜ 11805, 🅂 11885 & 15120

POLAND

POLISH RADIO WARSAW

1300-1355 🔲	6095, 7270 & 9525 (W Europe), 11820/11815 (W Europe & E North Am)	
1300-1355	🅦 7145 (W Europe)	
1800-1855 🔲	6095 & 7285 (W Europe)	
1800-1855	🅦 6000 (W Europe)	
2030-2125 🔲	6035, 6095 & 7285 (W Europe)	

ROMANIA

RADIO ROMANIA INTERNATIONAL

0200-0300 &	
0400-0500	5990, 6155, 9510, 9570 & 11940 (E North Am)
0530-0600	11940 (C Africa), 🅦 15250 (C Africa & S Africa), 🆂 15270 (E Asia), 🆂 15340, 🅦 15365, 🅦 17720 & 🅦 17745 (C Africa & S Africa), 17790 (S Africa)
0632-0641	🅦 7105, 🆂 9550, 9665, 🅦 11775 & 🆂 11810 (Europe)
0645-0745	🆂 11740 (E Asia), 🆂 11840 & 15250 (Australasia), 🆂 15270 & 🅦 15405 (E Asia), 17720 & 🅦 17805 (Australasia)
1300-1400	🆂 9690 & 11940 (Europe), 🆂 15365, 🅦 15390 & 🆂 17720 (W Europe)
1430-1530	🅦 11740 & 🆂 11775 (S Asia), 🅦 11810 (Mideast & S Asia), 15335 (S Asia)
1730-1800	🆂 9550, 9750 & 🅦 11740 (S Africa), 🆂 11830 & 11940 (C Africa & S Africa)
1900-2000	🅦 6105, 🅦 7105, 🅦 7195, 🅦 9510, 🆂 9550, 🆂 9690, 🆂 11810 & 🆂 11940 (Europe)
2100-2200	5990, 7105, 7195, 🅦 9510 & 🆂 9690 (Europe)
2300-2400	7135 (Europe), 9570 (E North Am), 9625 (Europe), 11940 (E North Am)

SEYCHELLES

FEBA RADIO—(W Asia & S Asia)

1500-1600	11600

SIERRA LEONE

SIERRA LEONE BROADCASTING SERVICE

0600-0830	3316

SINGAPORE

RADIO SINGAPORE INTERNATIONAL—(SE Asia)

1100-1400	6015 & 6150

RADIO CORPORATION OF SINGAPORE

1400-1600 &	
2300-1100	6150

SLOVAKIA

RADIO SLOVAKIA INTERNATIONAL

0100-0130	5930 (E North Am & C America), 7300 (Africa), 9440 (S America)
0700-0730	🆂 15460 & 🆂 17550 (Australasia)
0830-0900	🅦 11990, 🅦 17485 & 🅦 21705 (Australasia)
1730-1800 🔲	6055 & 7345 (W Europe)
1730-1800	🅦 5915 (W Europe)
1930-2000 🔲	6055 & 7345 (W Europe)
1930-2000	🅦 5915 (W Europe)

SOLOMON ISLANDS

SOLOMON ISLANDS BROADCASTING CORP

0000-0030	M-F 5020
0000-0230	Sa 5020
0030-0230	Su 5020
0100-0800	M-F 5020
0500-0800	Sa/Su 5020
0815-1130	Su 5020
0830-0900	M-F 5020
0845-1130	Sa 5020
0915-0930 &	
0945-1130	M-F 5020
1900-1930	Sa 5020
1900-2030	M-F 5020
1945-2400	Sa 5020
2000-2015 &	
2030-2330	Su 5020
2045-2400	M-F 5020

SOUTH AFRICA

CHANNEL AFRICA

0300-0330	5955 (E Africa & C Africa)
0400-0430	5955 (S Africa)
0500-0530	🅦 9675 (W Africa)
0600-0630	11900 (W Africa)
1300-1455	Sa/Su 9440/9445 (S Africa), Sa/Su 17675 (W Africa), Sa/Su 17870 (E Africa)
1600-1625	🆂 6000 (S Africa)
1700-1730 &	
1800-1830	15240 (W Africa)

TRANS WORLD RADIO—(W Africa)

0600-0630	11730

SPAIN

RADIO EXTERIOR DE ESPANA

0000-0200 &	
0500-0600	6055 (N America & C America)

2000-2100	M-F 6125/9590 (Europe), M-F 11775/11830 (Africa)
2100-2200	Sa/Su 6125/9590 (Europe), Sa/Su 11775/11830 (Africa)

SRI LANKA

SRI LANKA BROADCASTING CORPORATION

0030-0430	9730 & 15425 (S Asia)
1030-1130	11835 (SE Asia & Australasia), 17850 (E Asia)
1230-1630	9730 & 15425 (S Asia)
1900-2000	Sa *6010* (Europe)

SUDAN

RADIO OMDURMAN—(Europe, Mideast & Africa)

1800-1900	9200

SWAZILAND

TRANS WORLD RADIO

0430-0500	3200 (S Africa)
0430-0605	▪ 6100 (S Africa)
0430-0700	4775 (S Africa)
0505-0735	9500 (E Africa)
0605-0735	▪ 9650 (S Africa)
0735-0805	Sa/Su 6100 (S Africa), Sa/Su 9500 (E Africa), ▪ Sa/Su 9650 (S Africa)
1600-1830	9500 (E Africa)
1730-1745	M-Th 3200 (S Africa)
1745-2015	3200 (S Africa)

SWEDEN

RADIO SWEDEN

0230-0300 ▪	7280 (N America)
0330-0400	7115 (N America)
1230-1300 ▪	15240/15235 (N America)
1230-1300	▪ 13740/11650 (N America)
1430-1500 ▪	15240 (N America)
1430-1500	▪ 13740/11650 (N America)
2030-2100 ▪	6065 (Europe)
2130-2200 ▪	Sa/Su 6065 (Europe)
2230-2300 ▪	6065 (Europe)

SWITZERLAND

SWISS RADIO INTERNATIONAL

0100-0130 &	
0400-0500	9885 (N America), *9905* (N America & C America)
0500-0530 &	
0630-0700 ▪	*5840* (E Europe), 6165 (Europe & N Africa)
0730-0800	*9885 & 11860* (W Africa), 13635 (S Africa)
0830-0900	*9885* & 13685 (Australasia)
1100-1130 ▪	6165 (Europe & N Africa), *9535* (W Europe)
1100-1200	*9810/9885* (E Asia), ▪ 17515 (SE Asia)
1300-1330 ▪	6165 (Europe & N Africa), *9535* (W Europe)
1300-1400	*7230* (SE Asia), *7480* (E Asia)
1400-1500	▪ 13635 (W Asia & S Asia)
1900-1930	▪ *9905* (N Europe)
2000-2030 ▪	6165 (Europe & N Africa)

SYRIA

RADIO DAMASCUS

2005-2105	13610/15095 (Europe)
2110-2210	12085 (N America), 13610/15095 (Australasia)

TANZANIA

RADIO TANZANIA—(E Africa)

0330-0430 &	
0900-1030	5050
1030-1530	Sa/Su 5050
1530-1915	5050

THAILAND

RADIO THAILAND

0000-0030	▪ 9680 & ▪ 9690 (S Asia & E Africa)
0000-0100	9655 & 11905 (Asia)
0030-0100	▪ 13695 & ▪ 15395 (N America)
0300-0330	9655 & 11905 (Asia), ▪ 15395 & ▪ 15460 (W North Am)
0530-0600	11905 (Asia), 15115 (Europe)
1230-1300	▪ 9810 & ▪ 9885 (SE Asia & Australasia), 11905 (Asia)
1400-1430	▪ 9530 & ▪ 9830 (SE Asia & Australasia)
1900-2000	▪ 7210 & ▪ 9535 (N Europe), 9655 & 11905 (Asia)
2030-2045	▪ 9535 (Europe), 9655 (Asia), ▪ 9680 (Europe), 11905 (Asia)

TURKEY

VOICE OF TURKEY

0300-0350	▪ 17705 (S Asia, SE Asia & Australasia)
0400-0450 ▪	9655 (Europe & E North Am), 9685 (Mideast & W Asia)
0400-0450	▪ 9560 (W Asia, S Asia & Australasia)
1330-1420 ▪	9445 (Europe), 9630 (W Asia & S Asia)
1830-1850	▪ 9535 (Europe)
1930-2020 ▪	9445 (Europe)
2300-2350 ▪	7280 (Europe), 9560 (W Asia, S Asia & Australasia), 9655 (Europe & E North Am)

UGANDA—(E Africa)

RADIO UGANDA

0300-0545	4976, 5026
0600-1230	7110, 7196
1300-2100	4976, 5026

UKRAINE

RADIO UKRAINE

0000-0100	[S] 5915 & [S] 7240 (Europe), [S] 9550 (E North Am)
0100-0200 [→]	5905 (Europe)
0100-0200	[W] 5915 (W Europe & E North Am), [W] 6050 (W Africa & S America), [W] 7150 (E North Am)
0300-0400	[S] 9550 (E North Am)
0400-0500	[W] 5915 (W Europe & E North Am), [W] 7205 (W Europe, W Africa & S America)
2100-2200	[S] 7380 (Australasia), [S] 9560 (Europe), [S] 12040 (E North Am)
2200-2300 [→]	5905 (Europe), 6080 (W Asia)
2200-2300	[W] 5940 (Europe), [W] 7205 (W Europe, W Africa & S America)

UNITED ARAB EMIRATES

UAE RADIO IN DUBAI

0330-0350	12005, 13675 & 15400 (E North Am & C America)
0530-0550	15435 (Australasia), 17830 (E Asia), 21700 (Australasia)
1030-1050	13675 (Europe), 15370 (N Africa), 15395 & 21605 (Europe)
1330-1350 & 1600-1640	13630 (N Africa), 13675, 15395 & 21605 (Europe)

UNITED KINGDOM

BBC WORLD SERVICE

0000-0030	3915 (SE Asia), 11945 (E Asia)
0000-0045	7110 (SE Asia)
0000-0200	5965 (S Asia), 6195 (SE Asia), 9410 (S Asia), 9590 (C America & S America), 12095 (S America)
0000-0300	9915 (S America), 11955 (S Asia), 15280 (E Asia)
0000-0330	5970 (S America), 6175 (N America), 15360 (SE Asia)
0000-0700	5975 (N America & C America)
0100-0200	[S] 9605 (S Asia)
0200-0300	[S] 6135 (E Africa), [S] 6195 (N Europe), [S] 9410 (Europe), [W] 9410 & 9605 (S Asia)
0230-0330	9895 (C America & S America)
0300-0400	6005 (W Africa & S Africa), 11730 (E Africa)
0300-0430	[S] 9605 (S Asia)
0300-0530	17790 (S Asia), 21660 (E Asia)
0300-0600	3255 (S Africa)
0300-0730	6195 (Europe)
0300-0800	[S] 9600 (S Africa), 11760 (Mideast)
0300-0815	15310 (S Asia)
0300-2200	6190 (S Africa), 9410 (Europe)
0330-0400	[S] 9610 (E Africa)
0330-0500	[W] 6175 (N America), [W] 11955 (E Asia)
0400-0500	[S] 12095 (Europe), [W] 12095 (E Africa)
0400-0600	3955 (Europe)
0400-0630	15420 (E Africa)
0400-0700	7160 (W Africa & C Africa)
0400-0730 [→]	6180 (Europe)
0400-0730	6005 (W Africa)
0430-0800 [→]	6175 (C America)
0500-0630	17885 (E Africa)
0500-0700	17640 (E Africa)
0500-0900	11955 (Australasia)
0500-0915	15360 (SE Asia & Australasia)
0500-1100	9740 (SE Asia)
0500-2000	12095 (Europe)
0530-1030	21660 (SE Asia)
0600-0800	17790 (S Asia)
0600-0810	7145 (Australasia)
0600-0815	7325 (Europe)
0600-1500	15565 (Europe & Mideast)
0600-1600	11940 (S Africa)
0630-0700	15420 (E Africa)
0700-0730	17830 (W Africa)
0700-0800	[W] 5975 (N America & C America)
0700-1500	17640 (E Europe & C Asia)
0700-1800	15485 (W Europe & N Africa)
0715-1000	15400 (W Africa & S Africa)
0730-1000	17830 (W Africa & C Africa)
0900-1000	6065, 9580 & 11955 (E Asia), 15190 (S America)
0900-1100	11765 (Australasia), 15310 (S Asia)
0900-1400	11760 (Mideast)
0900-1500	15575 (Mideast & W Asia)
0900-1530	17705 (N Africa)
0900-1615	6195 (SE Asia)
0915-1030	[W] 15360 (Australasia), 17760 (E Asia & SE Asia)
1000-1100	[S] 5965 (E North Am), Sa/Su 15400 (W Africa), Sa/Su 17830 (W Africa & C Africa)
1000-1130	Sa/Su 15190 (S America)
1000-1400	6195 (C America & N America)
1100-1130	15400 (W Africa), 17790 (S America)
1100-1200	5965 (E North Am)
1100-1300	9580 & 11955 (E Asia)
1100-1400	15220 (Americas)
1100-1600	9740 (SE Asia & Australasia)
1100-1700	21660 (S Africa)
1100-2100	17830 (W Africa & C Africa)
1200-1215	7135, 9605 & 11920 (SE Asia)

1200-1400	🅦 *5965* (E North Am)
1200-1615	*9515* (N America)
1300-1415	*15420* (E Africa)
1300-1600	🅦 *9590* (N America), 🆂 *11865* (W North Am)
1300-1615	*5990* (E Asia)
1300-1700	*11750* (S Asia)
1400-1600	*15220* (N America)
1400-1700	*17840* (Americas), *21470* (E Africa)
1500-1530	*11860, 15420* & *21490* (E Africa)
1500-1700	*15400* (W Africa)
1500-1830	*5975* (S Asia)
1600-1700	🆂 *3255* & 🅦 *11940* (S Africa)
1600-1745	*3915* & *7160* (SE Asia)
1600-1800	🅦 6195 (Europe), *9740* (S Asia)
1615-1700	Sa *9515* (N America), *15420* (E Africa)
1700-1745	🆂 *6005* & *9630* (E Africa)
1700-1830	*9510* (S Asia)
1700-1900	🆂 *11860* (E Africa), *15400* (W Africa & S Africa), 🅦 *15420* (E Africa), 🅦 *17840* (W North Am)
1700-2200	*3255* (S Africa)
1700-2330	🅦 3955 (Europe)
1730-1800	🅦 9685 (E Europe)
1800-2100	*6180* (Europe)
1800-2230	6195 (Europe)
1830-2100	*9630* (E Africa)
1830-2200	*6005* (E Africa), *9740* (Australasia)
1900-2000	🆂 *5975* (Mideast & W Asia)
1900-2100	🅦 *15400* (S Africa)
1900-2300	15400 (W Africa)
1930-2000	🆂 *11835* (W Africa & S Africa)
2000-2200	7325 (Europe)
2000-2300	11835 (W Africa)
2000-2400	*12095* (S America)
2100-2200	*3915* (SE Asia), 🅦 *6110* (E Asia)
2100-2400	*5965* (E Asia), *5975* (N America & C America), *6195* (SE Asia)
2115-2130	M-F *15390* & M-F *17715* (C America)
2130-2145	Tu/F 11680 (Atlantic & S America)
2200-2215	🅦 M-F 7105 (E Europe)
2200-2300	🅦 *7385* (E Asia), *9660* (SE Asia), 🆂 *9890* (E Asia), *12080* (S Pacific)
2200-2400	*6175* (N America), *7110* (SE Asia), *9590* (N America), 9915 (S America), *11955* (SE Asia & Australasia)
2230-2330	🅦 6195 (Europe)
2300-2400	*3915* (SE Asia), *6035* & *11945* (E Asia)

USA

HERALD BROADCASTING SYNDICATE

0000-0057	W/F-M 7535 (E North Am), M/W/F 9430 (C America & S America)
0100-0157	7535 (N America), M 9430 (C America & S America)

David Njoku, past winner of the BBC's "Short Story."

BBC World Service

0200-0257	Su/M 5850 (W North Am), M/Th 7535 (W North Am & C America)
0300-0357	5850 (W North Am), M/W 7535 (E Africa)
0400-0457	M/W 9840 (C Africa & S Africa)
0500-0557	W 7535 (Europe)
0600-0657	Tu/F 7535 (W Europe)
0800-0857	Sa/Su 7535 (Europe), Sa-Th 9845 (Australasia)
0900-0957	Tu/Th 7535 (Europe), 🅦 Su/M/W/F *9430, 11660* & 🆂 Su/M/W/F *15665* (E Asia)
1000-1057	M/W/Th 6095 (E North Am), Su 7395 (S America), 🅦 Th/Sa-Tu *9355, 11660* & 🆂 Th/Sa-Tu *15665* (E Asia)
1100-1157	Tu/F-Su 6095 (E North Am), W/F 7395 (C America & S America), *9355* (SE Asia)
1200-1257	M/W/Th 6095 (E North Am), M/W/F *9355* (SE Asia), Sa 9455 (C America & S America)

1300-1357	Sa-Th 6095 (N America), *9355* (S Asia), Tu/F 9455 (W North Am & C America)
1600-1657	Sa 18930 (E Africa)
1700-1800	Tu/Th/Sa 18930 (C Africa)
1800-1857	⬛W Su 11550 (E Europe), *13820* (S Asia), ⬛S Su 15665 (E Europe), Su/W 18930 (S Africa)
1900-1957	⬛W Su/Tu/Th 11550 & ⬛S Su/Tu/Th 15665 (E Europe)
2000-2057	⬛W W/Su 5850 & ⬛S Su/W 13770 (Europe)
2100-2157	⬛W Su 5850 (E North Am & Europe), ⬛W W/Sa-M 7510 & ⬛S Su 13770 (Europe), ⬛S W/Sa-M 15665 (W Europe)
2200-2257	Su/Th 7510 (Europe), ⬛S Su/Th 13770 (W Europe), ⬛S Su/W 13770 (S Europe & W Africa), ⬛W Su/W 13770 & ⬛S W/Su 15280 (S America)
2300-2357	Su/W 7510 (S Europe & W Africa), ⬛W Su/M 13770 & ⬛S Su/M 15280 (S America)

KAIJ—(N America)

0000-1400	5810
1400-2400	13815

KJES

0100-0230	7555 (W North Am)
1300-1400	11715 (N America)
1400-1500	11715 (W North Am)
1800-1900	15385 (Australasia)

KNLS-NEW LIFE STATION—(E Asia)

0800-0900	⬛W 6150 & ⬛S 9615
1300-1400	7365

KTBN—(E North Am)

0000-0100	⬛W 7510 & ⬛S 15590
0100-1500	7510
1500-1600	⬛W 7510 & ⬛S 15590
1600-2400	15590

KVOH-VOICE OF HOPE—(C America)

0500-0600	9975

KWHR-WORLD HARVEST RADIO

0000-0100	Tu-Su 17510 (E Asia)
0000-0700	17555 (Australasia)
0100-0400	17510 (E Asia)
0400-0500	⬛W 17510 (E Asia)
0400-0800	⬛S 17880 (E Asia)
0700-1600	11565 (Australasia)
1000-1200, 1300-1400 & 1500-1800	9930 (E Asia & SE Asia)
1800-2000	13625 (E Asia & Australasia)
2300-2330	M-F 17510 (E Asia)
2330-2400	Su-F 17510 (E Asia)

UNIVERSITY NETWORK—(S Asia)

0800-1200	*17570*

VOA-VOICE OF AMERICA

0000-0100	7215 & ⬛S *9770* (SE Asia), ⬛W *9770* (SE Asia & Australasia), ⬛W *9890* (SE Asia), Tu-Sa 11695 (C America & S America), *11760* (SE Asia), *15185* (SE Asia & S Pacific), *15290* (E Asia), *17735* (E Asia & Australasia), *17820* (E Asia)
0000-0200	Tu-Sa 5995, Tu-Sa 6130, Tu-Sa 7405, Tu-Sa 9455, Tu-Sa 9775 & Tu-Sa 13740 (C America & S America)
0100-0300	*7115*, *7205*, ⬛S *9635*, ⬛W *9740*, ⬛W *9850*, *11705*, ⬛S *11725*, ⬛S *11820*, *15250*, ⬛W *15300*, *17740* & *17820* (S Asia)
0300-0330	7340 (C Africa & E Africa)
0300-0400	⬛W 6035 & ⬛S *6115* (E Africa & S Africa), 7105 (S Africa)
0300-0430	*9885* (Africa)
0300-0500	6080 (S Africa), ⬛S *7280* (Africa), 7290 (C Africa & E Africa), ⬛W *7415* (Africa), 9575 (W Africa & S Africa)
0400-0500	⬛W 6035 (W Africa & S Africa), ⬛S *7265* (S Africa & E Africa), ⬛S *15205* (Mideast & S Asia)
0400-0600	⬛W *9775* (C Africa & E Africa)
0400-0700	*7170* (N Africa), ⬛S *11965* (Mideast)
0500-0600	⬛W *7295* (W Africa), ⬛W *9700* (N Africa & W Africa)
0500-0630	*5970* (W Africa & C Africa), 6035 (W Africa & S Africa), *6080* & ⬛S *7195* (W Africa), ⬛S *9630* & *12080* (Africa)
0500-0700	⬛W *11825* (Mideast), *15205* (Mideast & S Asia)
0600-0630	⬛W *7285* (W Africa), *11950* (N Africa & E Africa), ⬛W *15600* (C Africa & E Africa)
0600-0700	⬛W *5995* & ⬛S *9680* (N Africa), *11805* (N Africa & W Africa)
0630-0700	Sa/Su *5970* (W Africa & C Africa), Sa/Su 6035 (W Africa & S Africa), Sa/Su *6080*, ⬛S Sa/Su *7195* & ⬛W Sa/Su *7285* (W Africa), ⬛S Sa/Su *9630* (Africa), Sa/Su *11950* (N Africa & E Africa), Sa/Su *12080* (Africa), ⬛W Sa/Su *15600* (C Africa & E Africa)
1000-1100	6165, 7405 & 9590 (C America)
1000-1200	5985/9770 (Pacific & Australasia), *11720* (E Asia & Australasia)
1000-1500	*15425* (SE Asia & Pacific)
1100-1300	⬛W *6110* & ⬛S *6160* (SE Asia)
1100-1400	*9645* (SE Asia & Australasia)
1100-1500	*9760* (E Asia, S Asia & SE Asia), ⬛W *11705* & ⬛S *15160* (E Asia)
1200-1330	*11715* (E Asia & Australasia)
1230-1300	Sa 7769 USB (E North Am)
1300-1800	⬛W *6110* & ⬛S *6160* (S Asia & SE Asia)

1400-1800	7125, 7215 & 9645 (S Asia), **W** 15205 (Mideast & S Asia), **S** 15255 (Mideast), 15395 (S Asia)
1500-1700	**W** 9575 (Mideast & S Asia), 9760 (S Asia & SE Asia), **S** 15205 (Europe, N Africa & Mideast)
1500-1800	**S** 6110 (SE Asia), **S** 9700 (Mideast)
1600-1700	6035 (W Africa), 13600 (C Africa & E Africa), 13710 (Africa), 15225 (S Africa)
1600-1800	**W** 12040 & 15445 (E Africa), 17895 (Africa)
1600-2000	**W** 11920 (E Africa)
1600-2130	15410 (Africa)
1700-1800	M-F 5990 & M-F 6045 (E Asia), **S** M-F 7150 (SE Asia & S Pacific), **S** M-F 7170 (E Asia & Australasia), **W** M-F 9525 (E Asia, SE Asia & S Pacific), **S** M-F 9550 & **W** M-F 9670 (E Asia & SE Asia), **S** M-F 9770 (S Asia & SE Asia), M-F 9770 (E Asia), **W** M-F 9795 (S Asia & SE Asia), **W** M-F 11945 (E Asia & Australasia), **W** 15120 & **S** 15135 (Europe), **W** M-F 15255 (E Asia & Australasia)
1700-1900	**W** 6040 (N Africa & Mideast)
1700-2100	**S** 9760 (N Africa & Mideast), **W** 9760 (Mideast & S Asia)
1800-1900	**S** 7415 & **S** 17895 (Africa)
1800-2000	**W** 12025 (E Africa)
1800-2130	6035 (W Africa), **W** 13710 (Africa), 15580 (W Africa)
1830-1900	**W** Sa/Su 7150, **S** Sa/Su 7170, **S** Sa/Su 7330, **W** Sa/Su 9845, **S** Sa/Su 9860 & **W** Sa/Su 15445 (E Africa)
1900-2000	9525 & 11870 (Australasia), 15180 (Pacific)
1900-2100	**S** 9770 (N Africa & Mideast)
1900-2130	**S** 7375, 7415 & **S** 15445 (Africa)
2000-2030	11855 (W Africa)
2000-2100	17755 (W Africa & C Africa)
2000-2130	17725 (W Africa)
2000-2200	**W** 15205 (Mideast & S Asia)
2100-2200	**S** 6040 & **W** 6070 (Mideast), **S** 9535 (N Africa & Mideast), **W** 9595 (Mideast), 9760 (E Europe & Mideast), 11870 (Australasia)
2100-2400	15185 (SE Asia & S Pacific), 17735 (E Asia & Australasia)
2130-2200	Su-F 6035 (W Africa), **S** Su-F 7375 & Su-F 7415 (Africa), Su-F 11975 (C Africa), **W** Su-F 13710, Su-F 15410 & **S** Su-F 15445 (Africa), Su-F 15580 & Su-F 17725 (W Africa)
2200-2230	M-F 6035 (W Africa), **S** M-F 7340, **S** M-F 7375, M-F 7415, **W** M-F 12080 & **W** M-F 13710 (Africa)

2200-2400	7215 (SE Asia), **S** 9705 (SE Asia & Australasia), **S** 9770 (SE Asia), **W** 9770 (SE Asia & Australasia), **W** 9890 & 11760 (SE Asia), 15290 (E Asia), 15305 (E Asia & Australasia), 17820 (E Asia)

WEWN-ETERNAL WORD RADIO NETWORK

0000-0400	5825 (Europe & E North Am)
0400-0500	**S** Tu-Su 5825 & **W** 5825 (Europe & E North Am)
0500-0600	**W** Tu-Su 5825 (Europe & E North Am)
0600-0700	**S** 5825 (Europe & E North Am)
0700-1000	5825 (Europe & E North Am)
1000-1400	7425 (N America & C America), 15745 (Europe)
1400-1600	11875 (W North Am & C America)
1600-1700	**S** M-Sa 11875 & **W** 11875 (E North Am), **S** M-Sa 13615, **S** Su 13615 & **W** 13615 (W North Am & C America), **S** M-Sa 15665 & **W** 15745 (Europe)
1700-1800	**W** M-Sa 11875 (E North Am), **W** M-Sa 13615 (W North Am & C America), **W** M-Sa 15745 (Europe)
1800-1900	**S** 11875 (E North Am), **S** 13615 (W North Am & C America), **S** 15745 (Europe)
1900-2200	11875 (E North Am), **W** 17695 & **S** 15745 (Europe)
1900-2400	13615 (W North Am & C America)
2000-2200	7425 (E North Am), **S** 13695 (Europe)
2000-2400	5825 (Europe & E North Am)
2200-2400	**W** 13695 & **S** 9975 (Europe)

WGTG—(W North Am & C America)

0000-0600	5085
1000-2155	9400
2155-2255	**S** 9400
2200-2300	**W** 5085
2300-2400	5085

WHRA-WORLD HARVEST RADIO

0300-0500	9400 (Mideast)
0500-0800	11565 (Africa)
1800-2000	17655 (Africa)
2000-2200	15460 (Africa)
2200-2400	13760 (Africa)

WINB-WORLD INTERNATIONAL BROADCASTERS

0000-0600	11950 (C America)
2000-2200	13790 (W Europe)

WJCR

24 Hr	7490 (E North Am), 13595 (W North Am)

WMLK—(Europe, Mideast & N America)

0400-0900 &	
1700-2200	Su-F 9465

WHRI-WORLD HARVEST RADIO

0000-0300	5745 (E North Am)

0145-0200	M 7315 (C America)
0200-0230	Tu-Su 7315 (C America)
0230-0400	7315 (C America)
0300-1000	5760/5745 (E North Am)
0400-0600	Tu-Su 7315 (C America)
0600-0800	7315 (C America)
0800-0900	Sa/Su 7315 (C America)
0900-1000	7315 (C America)
1000-1300	6040 (E North Am & C America)
1300-1500	6040 (E North Am)
1300-1800	15105 (C America)
1500-2100	13760 (E North Am & W Europe)
1800-2400	9495 (N America & C America)
2100-2400	5745 (E North Am)

WRMI-R MIAMI INTERNATIONAL—(N America & C America)

0000-0100 ◻	Tu-Su 9955
0100-0115 ◻	Su-F 9955
0115-0145 ◻	M 9955
0145-0300 ◻	M-Sa 9955
0300-0400 ◻	Su 9955
0400-0430 ◻	Su/Tu/Sa 9955
0430-0445 ◻	Tu-Sa 9955
0445-0500 ◻	M-Su 9955
0500-1100 ◻	M-Sa 9955
1300-1400 ◻	Su 9955
1400-1445 ◻	Sa/Su 9955
1445-1500 ◻	9955
1500-1700 ◻	M-Sa 9955
1700-1715 ◻	M-F 9955
1715-1730 &	
1730-1900 ◻	Su-F 9955
1900-2000 ◻	9955
2000-2115 ◻	Su-F 9955
2115-2200 ◻	9955
2200-2230 &	
2230-2400 ◻	M-Sa 9955

WRNO WORLDWIDE—(E North Am)

0000-0300	**S** 7355
0400-0700 ◻	7395
1400-1500	**S** 7395
1500-1600	7395
1600-2300	7355/15420
2300-2400	**S** 7355

WWCR

0000-0100	7435 (E North Am), 13845 (W North Am)
0000-0300	5070 (E North Am & Europe)
0000-0400	3215 (E North Am)
0100-1000	2390 (E North Am)
0100-1200	5935 (E North Am & Europe)
0200-0300	**W** M 5070 (E North Am & Europe)
0200-0400	Tu-Su 5070 (E North Am & Europe)
0300-0400	**S** M 5070 (E North Am & Europe)
0400-0900	3210 (E North Am)
0400-1100	5070 (E North Am & Europe)
0900-1000	**S** 3210 (E North Am)
0900-1100	**W** 7435 (E North Am)
1000-1100	**S** 15685 (E North Am & Europe)
1000-2200	9475 (E North Am)
1100-1200	**W** 5070 (E North Am & Europe)
1100-1300	7435 (E North Am)
1100-2100	15685 (E North Am & Europe)
1200-1400	**W** 5935 (E North Am & Europe), **S** 13845 (W North Am)
1200-1500	**S** 12160 (E North Am & Europe)
1300-1500	**W** 7435 (E North Am)
1400-2400	13845 (W North Am)
1500-2300	12160 (E North Am & Europe)
2100-2200	**S** 15685 (E North Am & Europe)
2200-2300	**S** 9475 & **W** 9475 (E North Am)
2200-2400	7435 (E North Am)
2215-2245 ◻	F-Tu 15685 (E North Am & Europe)
2245-2400 ◻	Sa/Su 15685 (E North Am & Europe)
2300-2400	5070 (E North Am & Europe), 9475 (E North Am)

WYFR-FAMILY RADIO

0000-0100	6085 (E North Am), **S** 9505 (W North Am)
0100-0445	6065 (E North Am), 9505 (W North Am)
0400-0600	9985 (Europe)
0500-0600	**S** 11580 & **W** 11695 (Europe)
0500-0700	5985 (W North Am)
0600-0745	7355 (Europe)
0700-0800	**W** 9455 & **S** 13695 (W Africa)
1000-1500	5950 (E North Am)
1100-1200	**S** 11830 (W North Am)
1100-1245	**W** 7355 (W North Am)
1200-1245	**S** 6015 (W North Am)
1200-1345	**W** 11970 (C America)
1200-1700	11830 (W North Am), **S** 17750 (C America)
1300-1400	13695 (E North Am)
1400-1700	**W** 17760 (C America)
1600-1700	21525 (C Africa & S Africa)
1600-1745	**S** 21745 (Europe)
1600-1800	**W** 17555 (Europe)
1600-1845	15695 (Europe)
1604-1700	**S** 11705 & **W** 15215 (W North Am)
1800-1900	**W** *9825* & **W** *9835* (N Africa)
1800-1945	17555 (Europe)
1845-1900	**S** 15695 (Europe)
1945-2145	**S** 17555 (Europe)
2000-2045	21525 (C Africa & S Africa)
2000-2100	**S** 5810 (Europe)
2000-2200	**W** 7355 (Europe)
2000-2245	**W** 15565 & **S** 17845 (W Africa)
2045-2245	**S** 21525 (C Africa & S Africa)
2100-2245	**W** 11580 (C Africa & S Africa)
2200-2400	11855 (W North Am)

UZBEKISTAN
RADIO TASHKENT
0100-0130   🔳 5955 (S Asia), 🔳 5975 & 🔳 7190 (Mideast & W Asia), 🔳 7205 (Mideast), 🔳 9715 (Mideast & S Asia)

1200-1230 &
1330-1400   🔳 5060 (S Asia), 🔳 6025 & 🔳 7285 (W Asia & S Asia), 9715 & 🔳 15295 (S Asia)

VATICAN STATE
VATICAN RADIO
0140-0200	5980, 7335 & 🔳 9650 (S Asia)
0250-0310	🔳 6095 & 7305 (E North Am), 🔳 9605 (E North Am & C America)
0310-0340	7360 & 9660 (E Africa)
0500-0530	🔳 7360 (E Africa), 9660 (Africa), 11625 & 🔳 15570 (E Africa)
0600-0620 🔳	4010/4005 (Europe), 5880 (W Europe)
0630-0700	🔳 7360 (W Africa), 🔳 9660 (Africa), 🔳 11625 (W Africa), 🔳 11625 (Africa), 🔳 13765 (W Africa), 🔳 15570 (Africa)
0730-0745 🔳	M-Sa 4010/4005 (Europe), M-Sa 5880 (W Europe), M-Sa 7250 & M-Sa 9645 (Europe), M-Sa 11740 (W Europe & N Africa), M-Sa 15210/15215 (Mideast)
1020-1030	M-Sa 17550 (Africa)
1120-1130 🔳	M-Sa 5880 & M-Sa 7250 (Europe), M-Sa 11740 (W Europe), M-Sa 15210 (Mideast)
1345-1405	13765 (Australasia), 15540 (SE Asia)
1550-1610	🔳 9875, 🔳 11640, 🔳 13765 & 🔳 15500 (S Asia)
1615-1630	🔳 7250 (N Europe), 🔳 11810 (Mideast)
1715-1730 🔳	5880 (Europe), 9645 (W Europe)
1715-1730	🔳 7250 (Mideast)
1730-1800	🔳 7305 & 🔳 9660 (E Africa), 🔳 11625 (E Africa & S Africa), 🔳 13765 (E Africa), 🔳 15570 & 🔳 17750 (Africa)
2000-2030	🔳 7355 & 9645 (Africa), 11625 & 🔳 13765 (W Africa)
2050-2110 🔳	3945/4005 (Europe), 5882/5885 (W Europe)
2245-2305	7305 (E Asia), 9600 & 11830 (Australasia)

VIETNAM
VOICE OF VIETNAM
0100-0130 &
0230-0300   🔳 *5940* & 🔳 *7250* (E North Am)
0330-0400   🔳 *7260* (C America)

1000-1030	9840 & 12020/15010 (SE Asia)
1100-1130	7285 & 9730 (SE Asia)
1230-1300	9840 & 12020/15010 (E Asia & Americas)
1330-1400	9840 & 12020/15010 (SE Asia)
1600-1630	9840 & 12020/15010 (Africa)
1800-1830, 1900-1930 & 2030-2100	9840 & 12020/15010 (Europe)
2330-2400	9840 & 12020/15010 (E Asia & Americas)

YEMEN
REP OF YEMEN RADIO—(Mideast & E Africa)
0600-0700 &
1800-1900   9780

YUGOSLAVIA
RADIO YUGOSLAVIA
0000-0030	🔳 M-Sa *9580* & 🔳 M-Sa 11870 (E North Am)
0100-0130	🔳 M-Sa *6195* & 🔳 M-Sa *7115* (E North Am)
0200-0230	🔳 *6195* & 🔳 *7130* (W North Am)
0430-0500	🔳 *9580* & 🔳 *11870* (W North Am)
1330-1400	🔳 *11835* (Australasia)
1900-1930	🔳 *7230* (Australasia)
1930-2000 🔳	*6100* (W Europe), *9720* (S Africa)
2200-2230 🔳	*6100* (Europe), *6185* (W Europe)

RRI Semarang records a popular program on health issues for its Indonesian audience.   N. Grace

Voices from Home—1999

Country-by-Country Guide to Native Broadcasts

For some listeners, English offerings are merely icing on the cake. Their real interest is in eavesdropping on broadcasts for *nativos*—the home folks. These can be enjoyable regardless of language, especially when they offer traditional music from other cultures.

Some you'll hear, many you won't—depending on your location and receiving equipment. Keep in mind that native-language broadcasts are sometimes weaker than those in English, so you may need more patience and better hardware. PASSPORT REPORTS tests for which radios are best.

When to Tune

Some broadcasts come in best during the day within world band segments from 9300 to 21850 kHz.

However, signals from Latin America and Africa peak near or during darkness, especially from 4700 to 5100 kHz. See "Best Times and Frequencies" earlier in this book for solid guidance.

Times and days of the week are in World Time, explained in "Setting Your World Time Clock" earlier in the book, as well as in the glossary; for local times, see "Addresses PLUS." Midyear, some stations are an hour earlier (■) or later (■) because of daylight saving time, typically April through October. Stations may also extend their hours for holidays or sports events.

Frequencies in *italics* may be best, as they come from relay transmitters that might be near you. Frequencies with no target zones are typically from transmitters designed for domestic coverage, so these are the least likely to be heard well unless you're in or near that country.

> **Broadcasts for *nativos* sometimes come in best during the day. Try segments between 9300 and 21850 kHz.**

Schedules Prepared for Entire Year

To be as helpful as possible throughout the year, Passport includes not just observed activity and factual schedules, but also activity which we have creatively opined will take place. This predictive information is original from us, and although it's of real value when tuning the airwaves, it is inherently not so exact as real-time data.

Most frequencies are aired year round. Those used only seasonally are labeled ■ for summer (midyear), and ■ for winter.

Radio musician Peter Naigow demonstrates a country marimba, made from cow horns, leather, vines and and resonant wooden bars. SIM

ALBANIA—Albanian

RADIO TIRANA

0000-0500 ▣	6090, 7270 (E North Am)	
0800-1100 ▣	7270 (Europe)	
1500-1800 ▣	5985 (S Europe), 7270 (Europe)	
2000-2300 ▣	6170 & 7270 (Europe)	
2300-2400 ▣	6090, 7270 (E North Am)	

RTV SHQIPTAR—(Europe)

0400-2300 ▣	6100
1000-1500 ▣	7150

ARGENTINA—Spanish

RADIO ARGENTINA AL EXTERIOR-RAE

1200-1400	M-F 11710 (S America)
2200-2400	M-F 15345 (Europe & N Africa)

RADIO NACIONAL

0000-0200	Su/M 15345 (N America)
0000-0400	Su/M 6060 (S America)
0900-1100	M-F 15345 (Americas)
0900-1200	6060 (S America)
1200-2400	Sa/Su 6060 (S America)
1800-2400	Sa/Su 15345 (Europe & N Africa)

ARMENIA—Armenian

VOICE OF ARMENIA

0200-0245	9965 (S America)
0815-0900 ▣	Su 4810 (E Europe, Mideast & W Asia), Su 15270 (Europe)
1645-1715 ▣	Sa/Su 4810 (E Europe, Mideast & W Asia)
1930-2015 ▣	M-Sa 4810 (E Europe, Mideast & W Asia), M-Sa 9965 (Europe)

AUSTRIA—German

RADIO AUSTRIA INTERNATIONAL

0000-0030	**W** Tu-Su 9495, **S** 9870 & **S** 13730 (S America)
0100-0130	9870 (S America)
0100-0230	**S** 13730 (S America)
0200-0230	9870 (C America)
0200-0330	**W** 9495 (S America)
0300-0330	9870 (C America), **S** 13730 (S America)
0400-0430	M-Sa 6155 (Europe), M-Sa 13730 (E Europe)
0430-0500	**W** 6155 (Europe), **W** 13730 (E Europe)
0500-0510	**W** 17870 (Mideast)
0500-0530	*6015* (N America), 6155 (Europe), 13730 (E Europe), **S** 15410 (Mideast)
0510-0530	**W** M-Sa 17870 (Mideast)
0530-0600	**S** 6155 (Europe), **S** 13730 (E Europe), **S** 15410 & **S** 17870 (Mideast)
0600-0610	**S** 15410 (Mideast)
0600-0630	*6015* (N America), 6155 (Europe), 13730 (E Europe), **W** 17870 (Mideast)
0610-0630	**S** M-Sa 15410 (Mideast)
0630-0700	**W** 6155 (Europe), **W** 13730 (E Europe), **W** 15410 & **W** 17870 (Mideast)
0700-0730	6155 (Europe), 13730 (E Europe), 15410 & 17870 (Mideast)
0800-0830	6155 (Europe), 13730 (N Europe), 17870 (Australasia)
0830-0900	**S** 6155 (Europe), **S** 13730 (N Europe), **S** 17870 (Australasia)
0900-0930	**W** 15455 (E Asia), 17870 (Australasia)
0900-1100	13730 (N Europe)
0900-1130	6155 (Europe)
0930-1000	**S** Su 15455 (E Asia), **S** Su 17870 (Australasia)
1000-1030	**S** 15455 (E Asia), 17870 (Australasia)
1030-1100	**S** M-Sa 15455 & **W** 15455 (E Asia), **W** 17870 (Australasia)
1100-1130	13730 (W Europe & E North Am), 15455 (E Asia)
1200-1230 & 1300-1330	6155 (Europe), 13730 (W Europe & E North Am)
1400-1430	**S** M-Sa 6155 (Europe), **S** M-Sa 13730 (S Europe & W Africa)
1430-1500	**S** 6155 (Europe)
1430-1530	**S** 13730 (S Europe & W Africa)
1500-1530	**S** 6155 (Europe)
1500-1630	**S** 11855 (Mideast), 13710 (S Asia & SE Asia)
1500-1730	**W** 9655 (Mideast)
1530-1630	6155 (Europe), 13730 (S Europe & W Africa)
1630-1700	**W** 6155 (Europe), **W** 13730 (S Europe & W Africa)
1700-1730	6155 (Europe), **S** 13710 (S Asia & SE Asia), 13730 (S Europe & W Africa)
1800-1810	**S** 11855 & 13730 (Mideast)
1800-1830	5945 & 6155 (Europe)
1810-1830	M-Sa 13730 (Mideast)
1830-1900	**S** 5945 & **S** 6155 (Europe), **S** 13730 (Mideast)
1900-2030	5945 & 6155 (Europe), 13730 (S Africa)
2030-2100	**W** 5945 & **W** 6155 (Europe)
2100-2130	5945 & 6155 (Europe)
2200-2230	5945 & 6155 (Europe), 13730 (S Africa)
2300-2330	**S** M-Sa 9870 (S America)

BANGLADESH—Bangla

BANGLADESH BETAR

1200-1530	15520 (Mideast & Europe)
1540-1700	15520 (Mideast & Europe)

1630-1730	7185 & 9550 (Mideast)
1710-1740	15520 (Mideast & Europe)
1915-2000	7185, 9550 & 15520 (Irr) (Europe)

BELGIUM—Dutch

RADIO VLAANDEREN INTERNATIONAAL

0430-0500	[W] 6120 & [S] *11750* (W North Am)
0600-0725	[S] 5985 & 9925 (S Europe)
0630-0655 [→]	9940 (S Europe & Australasia)
0700-0825	[W] 6130 (S Europe)
0730-0825	[W] 9925 (S Europe)
1000-1025	[W] *15145* & [S] *15535* (S Africa)
1130-1155 [←]	9925 (N Europe)
1200-1230	[W] *6170* (Australasia), [S] *9865* (E Asia & Australasia), [W] *13795* & [S] *15450* (SE Asia), *15250* (S America), [S] 15590 (Atlantic & N Africa)
1200-1255 [←]	9925 (S Europe)
1400-1700 [←]	Su 9925 (S Europe), Su 17680 (Africa)
1600-1630	[S] *12080* (E Europe)
1630-1655	[S] 7290 (E Europe)
1700-1725 [←]	9925 (S Europe)
1700-1725	[W] *11680* (Mideast)
1700-1730	[S] *7415* (N Europe), [S] 17655 (Africa)
1800-1830	[W] 13745 (Africa)
1800-1855	[S] Su-F *13685* (Africa)
1800-1900	[S] *6110* (Europe)
1800-2015	[S] Sa 13685 (Africa)
1900-1955 [←]	M-F 13745 (Africa)
1900-1955	[W] M-F *5960* (E Europe)
1900-2000	[W] *5910* (Europe)
2230-2300	[S] *13655* (E North Am)
2330-2400	[W] *9555* (E North Am)

BRAZIL—Portuguese

RADIO BRASIL CENTRAL

0600-0200 [→]	4985, 11815

RADIO NACIONAL DA AMAZONIA

0700-0800 [→]	M-F 6180, M-F 11780
0800-2400 [→]	6180, 11780

RADIO BANDEIRANTES

24 Hr	6090, 9645, 11925

RADIO CULTURA SAO PAULO

0000-0200 [→]	6170, 9615, 17815
0700-2400 [→]	6170, 9615, 17815

RADIO NACIONAL DO BRASIL-RADIOBRAS

0115-0215	Tu-Sa 11780 (N America)
0415-0515	Tu-Sa 11765 (N America)
1630-1750	15265 (Europe & Mideast)

BULGARIA—Bulgarian

RADIO BULGARIA

0000-0100	[S] 11720 (E North Am), [S] 11660 (S America)
0100-0200 [←]	9485 (E North Am), 9415 (S America)

0100-0200	[W] 7170 (C America & S America), [W] 7375 (E North Am)
0300-0400	[S] 9700 (E Europe), [S] 7380 (W Asia)
0400-0500	[W] 5890 & [W] 5890 (E Europe)
1200-1500	[S] 13770 (Europe)
1300-1600	[W] 9850 (Europe)
1500-1600	[S] 17650 (S Africa)
1500-1800	[S] 9775 (W Asia)
1600-1900	[W] 5935 & [W] 7425 (E Europe)
1800-1900	[S] 7375 (Mideast)
1800-2100	[S] 7465 (Mideast), [S] 7495 (Europe)
1900-2200	[W] 7515 (Mideast)

CANADA—French

CANADIAN BROADCASTING CORP—(E North Am)

0100-0300 [←]	M 9625
0300-0400 [←]	Su 9625 & Tu-Sa 9625
1300-1310 &	
1500-1555 [←]	M-F 9625
1700-1715 [←]	Su 9625
1900-1945 [←]	M-F 9625
1900-2310 [←]	Sa 9625

RADIO CANADA INTERNATIONAL

0000-0030	[S] Tu-Sa 9535, [S] Tu-Sa 11895 & [S] Tu-Sa 13670 (C America & S America)
0000-0100	[S] 5960 (E North Am)
0100-0130	[W] 9535 & [W] 11865 (C America & S America)
0100-0200 [←]	9755 (E North Am & C America)
0130-0200	[W] Su/M 9535 & [W] Su/M 11865 (C America & S America)
0230-0300	[S] Tu-Sa 9535 & [S] Tu-Sa 11715 (C America & S America)
0300-0330	[W] *6025*, [W] *9505*, [S] *9760* & [S] *11835* (Mideast)
0330-0400 [←]	Tu-Sa 9755 (E North Am & C America)
0330-0400	[W] Tu-Sa 6155 (E North Am & C America)
0530-0600	[S] M-F *7295* (W Europe & N Africa), [S] M-F *15430* (Africa)
0630-0700	[W] M-F 6050 (Europe), [W] M-F *6150* (Europe & Mideast), [W] M-F *9740* (N Africa & W Africa), [W] M-F 9760 (Europe & N Africa), [W] M-F *11905* (Mideast)
1200-1300	[S] 15305 (E North Am & C America)
1230-1300	[W] *6150* & [S] *9660* (E Asia), [W] *11730* & [S] *15195* (SE Asia)
1300-1400 [←]	9650 (E North Am & C America)
1300-1400	[W] 15425 (C America)
1300-1600	[S] Su 15305 (E North Am & C America)

Transmitter is adjusted at the Sri Lanka Broadcasting Corporation. M. Guha

1400-1500	**S** M-Sa 15305, **S** *15325* & **S** M-Sa 17820 (Europe), **S** M-Sa 17895 (W Europe & Africa)
1400-1700	**W** Su 15325 (C America)
1500-1600 ▭	*11935* (Europe & Mideast)
1500-1600	**W** *9555* (Europe & Mideast), **W** *11915* & **W** M-Sa 15325 (Europe), **W** 17820 (W Europe & Africa)
1900-2000	**S** 11700 (Europe), **S** 13650 (Europe & N Africa), **S** 13670 (Africa), **S** 15325 (Europe), **S** 17820 (Africa), **S** 17870 (Europe & N Africa)
2000-2100 ▭	*5995* (Europe), 15150 (Africa)
2000-2100	**W** *7235* (S Europe & N Africa), **W** 9805 (W Europe & N Africa), **W** 11945 (W Africa), **W** 13650 (Europe & N Africa), **W** 13690 & **W** 17820 (Africa)
2130-2200	**S** 11690 (Europe), **S** 13650 (Europe & N Africa), **S** 13670 (Africa), **S** 13740 (C America), **S** 15305 (C America & S America), **S** 17820 (Africa)
2230-2300 ▭	9755 (E North Am & C America)
2230-2300	**W** 5960 (E North Am), **W** 5995 (W Europe & N Africa), **W** *7235* (S Europe & N Africa), *11705* (SE Asia), **W** 11945 (W Africa), **W** 13690 (Africa), **S** 15305 (C America & S America)

CHINA

CENTRAL PEOPLE'S BROADCASTING STATION
Chinese

0000-0030	9080, 10260, **S** 12120
0000-0100	**W** 5320, 5880, 5915, 5955, 6125, 6750, **W** 6790, 9170, 9775, **S** 11000, **S** 15500, **S** 15550

0000-0130	7935, 11630
0000-0200	**W** 6890, 9755, **S** 11040, **S** 15390, **S** 17605
0000-0500	7504
0000-0600	9064, 11610, 11800
0000-1600	7770
0030-0200	**W** 9080
0030-0600	12120
0055-0612	11100, 11935, 15710
0100-0200	**S** 17700
0100-0600	15500, 15550
0200-0600	11040, 15390, 17605, 17700
0355-0604	11000, 15880
0600-0855	W-M 9290, W-M 12120, W-M 15390, W-M 15550, W-M 17605
0600-0900	Th/Sa-M 7504, Th/Sa-Tu 11040, Th/Sa-Tu 17700
0600-0955	Th/Sa-Tu 9064, Th/Sa-Tu 11610, Th/Sa-Tu 11800, Th/Sa-Tu 15500
0604-0930	W-M 15880
0604-0955	W-M 11000
0855-0930	17605
0855-1000	15390
0855-1030	15550
0855-1100	11630, 12120
0855-1200	9290
0900-0955	**W** Th/Sa-Tu 6890, **S** Th/Sa-Tu 11040
0900-1730	7504
0930-0955	**W** W-M 5090, **S** W-M 15880
0930-1100	**W** 9080, **S** 17605
0955-1100	11000, **S** 15880, **S** 17700
0955-1130	11800
0955-1200	**W** 6890, **S** 11040
0955-1400	**W** 7620, **S** 11935
0955-1600	9064
0955-1700	**W** 6015, **S** 11100
0955-1804	**W** 5090
0955-2400	**W** 5125, **S** 9380
1000-1200	**S** 15500
1000-1230	**S** 15390
1000-1600	**W** 5163
1000-1730	7935
1030-1230	**S** 15550
1030-1330	**W** 5320
1045-1500	**S** 13610
1100-1330	**S** 12120
1100-1600	7440, 9775
1100-1730	5880, 6125, 6750, 9080, 9800
1100-1804	**W** 6790, **S** 9170, **S** 11000
1130-1600	**W** 3220, 11610, **S** 11800
1200-1330	**W** 4460, 10260, 11630
1200-1600	6890
1330-1730	4460, 5320
1400-2300	7620
1700-2230	6015
2000-2200	4460, 5320, 9290

2000-2400	5880, 5915, 5955, 6110, 6125, 6750, 7504, 7935, 9080, 10260, 11630, 🅂 11800
2055-2200	🅂 11000/6790
2055-2300	🅦 5090, 🅂 9170
2055-2400	🅦 6790
2100-2230	5163
2100-2300	7140
2100-2400	🅦 3220, 6890, 7770, 9064, 9755, 9775
2200-2300	🅦 4460
2200-2400	🅦 5320, 🅂 11000, 🅂 12120
2230-2400	🅦 6015, 🅂 11100
2300-2400	🅦 7620, 9170, 🅂 11935
2330-2400	🅂 15390, 🅂 15500, 🅂 15550

CHINA RADIO INTERNATIONAL

Chinese

0200-0300	*9690* (N America & C America), 15435 (S America)
0300-0400	*9730* (W North Am)
0900-1000	9480 (E Asia), 9945 & 11500 (Australasia), 15180 (E Asia)
0900-1100	11840, 11945 & 12015 (SE Asia)
1200-1400	11945 & 15260 (SE Asia)
1300-1400	9440 (SE Asia)
1500-1600	🅂 7110, 9457 (S Asia), 🅂 11980 (S Asia & E Africa)
1730-1830	🅦 4020 & 5250 (E Asia), 7110, 7335 & 7800 (Europe & N Africa), 9820 (N Africa & W Africa)
2000-2100	🅦 6955 (N Africa & W Africa), 7185, 🅦 7435 & 7660 (E Europe), 🅦 7780 (W Africa), 🅦 9710 (E Africa), 🅂 11650 (E Europe)
2100-2130 🔲	*6165* (Europe)
2230-2300	*7170* (W Africa & N Africa), 9535 (E Asia)
2230-2330	6140 (SE Asia), 🅦 7110 (Australasia), 7190, 🅦 7230 (SE Asia), 7335, 🅂 8260 (E Asia), 9440, 9870, 🅂 11685 & 12015 (SE Asia), 12065, 15400 (SE Asia)

Cantonese

1000-1100	11915 (Australasia)
1100-1200	7335, 11945 (SE Asia)
1700-1800	🅦 6920, 9900 & 🅂 11575 (S Asia & E Africa)
1900-2000	🅦 7780 (W Africa)

CHINA (TAIWAN)

CBS
Chinese

0000-0200	7105/7108 (E Asia)
0000-0300	15125
0000-0500	9280 (E Asia), 11725 (SE Asia)
0000-0600	9610 (E Asia)
0200-1000	11970 (E Asia)
0400-0700	15320 (E Asia)

Radio Nepal daytime personality greets his listeners.

M. Guha

0400-0800	11775 (E Asia)
0400-1000	6180 (E Asia)
0900-1800	15125
0900-2400	3335 (E Asia)
1000-1900	6085, 6180, 7105, 7250 & 9630 (E Asia)
1100-1200 & 1300-1500	9610
1400-1900	6040 & 9690 (E Asia)
2200-2400	*5950* (E North Am), 6040, 7105/7108, 7250, 9610 & 9690 (E Asia), 11725 (SE Asia), 15125, *15440* (W North Am & C America)

RADIO TAIPEI INTERNATIONAL

Amoy

0000-0100	11550 (E Asia), *15440* (W North Am & C America)
0200-0300	11550 (SE Asia)
0200-0400	11915 (E Asia)
0300-0400	7130 (SE Asia)
0500-0600	11745 (SE Asia)
0800-0900	11745 (E Asia)
1000-1100	7130 (E Asia), 11550 (SE Asia), 11745 (E Asia), 15345 (SE Asia)
1300-1400	7130 & 11745 (E Asia), 11860 (SE Asia)

Chinese

0100-0200	🅦 *11825, 15215* & 🅂 *17845* (S America)
0400-0500	*5950* (N America & C America), 7130 (SE Asia), *9680* (W North Am), 11825, 15270 & 15345 (SE Asia)
0700-0800	7130 (SE Asia)

0900-1000	7445 (SE Asia), 9610 (Australasia), 11550 (SE Asia), 11745 (E Asia), 11915 (SE Asia)
1200-1300	11745 (E Asia), 15270 (SE Asia)
1900-2000	9955 (Mideast & N Africa), 🆆 *9985*, 🆂 *15600*, 🆂 *17750* & 🆆 *17760* (Europe)

Cantonese

0000-0500	6040 & 9690 (E Asia)
0100-0200	*5950* (E North Am), *7520* (Europe), *15440* (W North Am & C America)
0300-0400	*11740* (C America)
0500-0600	*5950* (N America & C America), *9680* (W North Am), 11825 (SE Asia), 11915 (E Asia), 15270 & 15345 (SE Asia)
0800-0900	7445 (E Asia)
1000-1100	7285 (SE Asia), 9610 (Australasia), 11915 (SE Asia)
1000-1200	15270 (SE Asia)
1300-1400	9765 (SE Asia)

VOICE OF ASIA
Chinese

0500-0700	7285 (E Asia)
0700-1100	9280 (E Asia)
1300-1500	7445 (SE Asia)

COLOMBIA—Spanish

CARACOL COLOMBIA
24 Hr	5077

RADIODIFUSORA NACIONAL DE COLOMBIA
1100-0445	4955

CUBA—Spanish

RADIO HABANA CUBA

0000-0100	6000 & 9820 (E North Am)
0000-0300	9550 & 11970 (S America)
0000-0500	5965 (C America), 6070 (C America & W North Am), 9505 (S America), 11760 (Americas), 15230 (S America)
0200-0500	6180 (E North Am)
1100-1400	9550 (C America & S America)
1100-1500	6000 & 11760 (C America)
1200-1400	15340 (S America)
1200-1500	6070 (C America & W North Am)
2100-2300	🆆 9820 (Europe & N Africa), 9830 USB (E North Am & Europe), 11760 & 🆂 13680 (Europe & N Africa)

RADIO REBELDE
24 Hr	5025

CYPRUS

CYPRUS BROADCASTING CORP—(Europe)
Greek
2215-2245	F-Su 6180, F-Su 7205 & F-Su 9760 (W Europe)

RADIO MONTE CARLO—(N America)
Arabic
0300-0320	🆂 *6040* & *9755* (N America)
0400-0420	🆆 *5960* & *9755* (N America)

CZECH REPUBLIC—Czech

RADIO PRAGUE

0130-0200	6200 (E North Am), 7345 (S America)
0230-0300	🆆 5930 & 7345 (E North Am)
0930-1000	🆆 21705 (E Africa)
1030-1100 🔲	17485 (W Africa)
1330-1400 🔲	6055 (Europe), 7345 (N Europe)
1430-1500	🆆 13580 (E North Am, S Asia & Australasia), 🆆 21700 (E Africa)
1530-1600	🆂 17485 (E Africa)
1630-1700 🔲	5930 (Europe)
1630-1700	🆆 9430 (E Africa)
1730-1800	🆂 17485 (C Africa)
1830-1900	🆆 9430 (C Africa)
1930-2000	🆂 5930 (W Europe), 🆂 11640 (SE Asia & Australasia)
2030-2100	🆆 5930 (S Europe & W Africa), 🆆 9430 (S Asia & Australasia)
2330-2400	🆆 5930 (E North Am), 🆆 7345 & 🆂 9485 (S America)

DENMARK—Danish

RADIO DANMARK

0030-0055	🆆 *5905* (S America), *7275* (SE Asia & Australasia), *7465* (E North Am & C America), 🆂 *9525* (S America)
0130-0155	🆆 *6120* (N America), *7465* (E North Am & C America), 🆂 *9560* (N America)
0230-0255	🆆 *6120* (N America), 🆂 *7465* (E North Am), 🆆 *7465* (S America), 🆂 *9560* (N America)
0330-0355	🆆 *5965* & *7165* (Mideast), *7465* (W North Am), 🆂 *9565* (Mideast)
0430-0455	🆆 *5965* (E Europe), 🆆 *6040* (Mideast & E Africa), 🆆 *7305* (Mideast), 🆂 *7520* (W North Am), 🆂 *9565* & 🆂 *13805* (Mideast)
0530-0555	🆆 *5965* (E Europe), 🆆 *6195* (W North Am), 🆆 *7180* (E Africa), 🆂 *7465* (E Europe), 🆂 *13805* (E Africa)
0630-0655	🆆 *5965* & 🆂 *7180* (Europe), 🆆 *7180* (W Europe), 🆂 *7295* (Australasia), 🆂 *9590* (W Africa & Australasia), 🆆 *9590* (W Africa), 🆆 *11735* & 🆂 *13805* (E Africa)
0730-0755	🆆 *5965* (Europe), 🆂 *7180* (W Europe), 🆆 *7180* (W Europe & Australasia), 🆂 *7295* (Australasia), *9590* (Europe), 🆂 *13805* (W Africa)

0830-0855   ▣ *9590* & ▣ *13800* (Australasia), ⬛ *15220* (Mideast), ⬛ *17855* (Australasia)

0930-0955   ⬛ *13800* (E Asia), ▣ *15175* (Australasia), ▣ *15230* (Mideast), ⬛ *17855* (Australasia)

1030-1055   ▣ *7295* (Atlantic), ⬛ *9480* (Europe), ▣ *11830* (W Europe), ⬛ *15220* (S America)

1130-1155   *7295* (Europe), ▣ *15270* (S America), ⬛ *17740* (C Africa)

1230-1255   *9590* (Europe), ▣ *9795* (E Asia), ▣ *11850* (E North Am), ⬛ *13800* & ⬛ *15305* (E Asia), ⬛ *15480* (S America), ▣ *15605* (SE Asia)

1330-1355   *9590* (Europe), ▣ *9795* (E Asia), ▣ *11840* (N America), ⬛ *13800* (SE Asia & Australasia), ⬛ *15305* (E Asia), ⬛ *15340* (N America), ▣ *15605* (SE Asia & Australasia)

1430-1455   ▣ *11720* (S Asia), ▣ *11840* (N America), *11850* (SE Asia), ⬛ *13800* (S Asia & SE Asia), ⬛ *15340* (N America)

1530-1555   ▣ *9485* (W North Am), ▣ *9520* & ▣ *11730* (Mideast), ⬛ *11840* (W North Am), ⬛ *13805* & ⬛ *15230* (Mideast)

1630-1655   ▣ *9590* (E Europe), ▣ *11840* (E Africa & W North Am), ⬛ *11860* (S Asia), ⬛ *13805* (E Africa)

1630-1700   ⬛ *15340* (W North Am)

1730-1755   *7485* & ⬛ *7485* (E Europe), ▣ *7525* (W Europe), ▣ *9590* (E Africa), ⬛ *11860* (S Asia), ⬛ *15220* (E Africa)

1830-1855   ▣ *5960* (W Europe), ⬛ *7485* (Europe), ▣ *7485* (W Africa), ⬛ *9590* (Mideast), ▣ *9590* (C Africa), ⬛ *13805* (W Africa), ⬛ *15220* (C Africa)

1930-1955   ▣ *5930* (Australasia), ▣ *5960* & ⬛ *7485* (Europe), ▣ *7485* (W Africa), ▣ *9590* (C Africa), ⬛ *11860* (Australasia), ⬛ *13805* (C Africa), ⬛ *15220* (W Africa)

2030-2055   ⬛ *7485* (Europe & Mideast), ▣ *7520* (Europe), ▣ *9480* (W North Am), ⬛ *9590* (Australasia)

2100-2130   ▣ *7315* (Australasia)

2130-2155   ▣ *5960* (Atlantic), ⬛ *7205* & ▣ *7315* (Australasia), ▣ *9480* (E Asia), ⬛ *9495* (Australasia), ⬛ *9590* (Atlantic)

2230-2255   ▣ *5960* (Australasia), ▣ *6200* (E North Am), ▣ *7115* (E Asia), ⬛ *9485* (Australasia), ⬛ *11840* (E North Am)

2330-2355   ▣ *5905* (S America), *7275* (SE Asia & Australasia), ▣ *7465* & ⬛ *9485* (E North Am)

2330-2400   ⬛ *7490* (S America)

Chief Engineer Elvin Vence and assistant Norman Hansen carry out transmitter maintenance at Adventist World Radio, Guam.   AWR

ECUADOR—Spanish

HCJB-VOICE OF THE ANDES

0000-0100	15140 (Americas)
0100-0500	15140 (C America & W North Am)
0000-0500	6050 (S America)
0700-0730	9765 (Europe)
0900-1100	9765 (S America)
1030-2400	6050 (S America)
1100-1300	11960 (C America)
1100-1700	15140 (S America)
1700-1900	15140 (Americas)
1900-2300	15140 (S America)
2130-2230	▣ *12025* & ⬛ *17795* (Europe)
2300-2400	15140 (Americas)

EGYPT—Arabic

EGYPTIAN RADIO

0000-0030	◧	9700 (N Africa), 11665 (C Africa & E Africa), 15285 (Mideast)
0150-0700	◧	12050 (Europe & E North Am)
0200-2200	◧	9755 (N Africa & Mideast)
0300-0600	◧	9850 (N Africa & Mideast)
0300-2400	◧	15285 (Mideast)

0350-0700 [←]	9620 & 9770 (N Africa)
0350-2400 [←]	9800 (Mideast)
0600-1400 [←]	11980 (N Africa & Mideast)
0700-1100 [←]	15115 (W Africa)
0700-1400 [←]	15475
0700-1500 [←]	11785 (N Africa)
0700-1530 [←]	12050 (Europe, E North Am & E Africa)
1100-2400 [←]	9850 (N Africa)
1245-1900 [←]	17670 (N Africa)
1530-2400 [←]	12050 (Europe & N America)
1800-2400 [←]	9700 (N Africa)
1900-2400 [←]	11665 (C Africa & E Africa)

RADIO CAIRO

0000-0045	15220 (C America & S America), 17770 (S America)
0030-0330	9900 (E North Am)
0330-0430	9900 (W North Am)
1015-1215	17745 (Mideast & S Asia)
1100-1130	17800 (C Africa & S Africa)
1245-1600	15220 (C Africa)
2000-2200	11990 (Australasia)
2345-2400	15220 (C America & S America), 17770 (S America)

FRANCE—French

RADIO FRANCE INTERNATIONALE

0000-0030	[S] *15440* (SE Asia)
0000-0100	[W] 5920 (C America), [W] 7120 (S Asia & SE Asia), 9800 (S America), [S] 9805 (S Asia & SE Asia), [S] 11670 (C America), [W] *12025* (SE Asia)
0000-0200	*9715* (S America)
0000-0300	9790 (C America)
0100-0200	[W] *11600* & [S] *15440* (S Asia)
0130-0500	*9800* (C America)
0200-0300	5920 (C America & N America), 9715 (S America)
0300-0400	7315 & [S] *9805* (Mideast), [S] 11700 (E Africa)
0300-0500	[W] 5945 (E Africa & Mideast), [S] 9550 (Mideast), [S] 9805 (E Africa)
0300-0600	[W] 7280 & [S] 11685 (Mideast)
0300-0700	9790 (Africa)
0300-0800	7135 (Africa)
0330-0445	5990 (E Europe)
0330-0600	6045 (E Europe)
0400-0500	*5920* (C America & N America), [S] *6175* (S Africa)
0400-0600	*4890* (C Africa), 5925 (N Africa), [W] 7315 (Mideast), [S] 9745 (E Europe), [S] 15155 (E Africa)
0400-0700	7280 (E Europe)
0500-0600	11700 (E Africa)
0500-0700 [←]	11995 (E Africa)
0500-0700	[W] 9550 & [S] 15605 (Mideast)
0500-1200	9805 (E Europe)

0600-0700	[W] 5925 (N Africa), [W] 6045 (E Europe), 7305 (Irr) (N Africa), [W] *9845* (W Africa), [W] 15155 & [S] 17620 (E Africa)
0600-0800 [←]	17800 (E Africa)
0600-0800	[W] 11685 (Mideast), 11700 (Africa), [S] 17650 (Mideast)
0600-0900 [←]	9790 (N Africa)
0700-0800	[W] 7305 (N Africa), [S] 17850 (C Africa & S Africa)
0700-0900	11975 (E Europe)
0700-1100	15605 (Mideast & S Asia)
0700-1300	11670 (E Europe)
0700-1500	21620 (E Africa)
0700-1700	15300 & 17620 (Africa)
0800-1200	15155 & 15195 (E Europe)
0800-1600	11845 (N Africa), 17850 (C Africa & S Africa)
0900-1100	[W] 21580 (C Africa & S Africa)
0900-1500	[W] 21685 (W Africa)
0900-1600	15315 (N Africa & W Africa)
1030-1100	[W] *9790* (C America), *11670* (S America)
1030-1125	*5220* (E Asia)
1030-1130	[S] 17575 (C America & E North Am)
1030-1200	[W] *7140* (E Asia), 9830 & [S] *11710* (SE Asia), 15435 (S America)
1100-1200	6175 (W Europe & Atlantic), *11670* (C America & S America), [W] 11700 (E North Am), *11890* (SE Asia), *13640* (C America), [S] 15365 (E North Am), *17605* (S Africa)
1100-1500	21580 (C Africa & S Africa)
1130-1200	17575 (C America & E North Am)
1200-1400	*9790* (C Africa)
1230-1300	*13640* (C America), [S] *17560* (S America)
1230-1400	*15435* (S America)
1300-1330	[W] 11670 (E Europe), *17860* (C America)
1300-1400	[S] 11615, [W] 15155 & 15195 (E Europe), *17560* (S America)
1330-1400	9805 (E Europe), M-Sa *15515* & M-Sa *17860* (C America)
1400-1500	11615 (E Europe)
1400-1600	[S] 15155 & [S] 15195 (E Europe), [W] 15460 (E Africa)
1430-1500	[W] 9805 (E Europe)
1430-1600	[S] *15515*, *17860* & [W] *21645* (C America), [S] *21765* (S America)
1500-1600	[W] 9605, [S] 11615 & [W] 11670 (E Europe), [S] 21580 (C Africa & S Africa), [S] 21620 (E Africa)
1500-1700	[W] 9790 (N Africa)
1700-1800	[S] 9805 & [S] 11670 (E Europe)
1700-1900	[W] 11965 (W Africa)
1700-2000	[W] 7160 (N Africa & W Africa)
1700-2200	15300 (Africa)

1730-1800	**W** 9485 (E Africa & Mideast), **S** 15210 (E Africa)
1730-1900	**S** 15460 (E Africa)
1800-1900	**W** 5900 (E Europe)
1800-2000	11705 (N Africa & E Africa)
1800-2100	**W** 7135 & **S** 9495 (E Europe)
1800-2200	*7160* (C Africa), 9790 (Africa)
1900-2100	**S** 11995 (E Africa)
1900-2200	9485 (E Africa)
2000-2100	5915 (E Europe), **S** 11705 (N Africa & E Africa)
2000-2200	7160 (N Africa & W Africa), **S** 11965 (W Africa)
2100-2200	**S** 5900 & **W** 5915 (E Europe), **W** 5945 (E Africa & Mideast), 6175 (N Africa), 7315 (E Africa & S Africa), **S** 9805 (E Europe)
2130-2200	17630 & 21765 (South America)
2200-2300	**W** 5920 (C America), 9715 (S America), **S** 11670 (C America)
2200-2400	9790 (C America)
2300-2400	**W** 7120 (S Asia & SE Asia), **W** *9570* (SE Asia), *9715* (S America), **S** 9805 (S Asia & SE Asia), **W** *12025* & **S** *15440* (SE Asia)
2330-2400	9800 (S America)

FRENCH GUIANA—French

RFO-GUYANE

24 Hr	5055

FRENCH POLYNESIA—French

RFO POLYNESIE FRANCAISE—(Pacific)

24 Hr	15170

GABON—French

AFRIQUE NUMERO UN

0500-2300	9580 (C Africa)
0700-1600	17630 (W Africa)
1600-1900	15475 (W Africa & E North Am)

RTV GABONAISE

0500-0800	7270/4777
0800-1600	7270
1600-2300	4777

GERMANY—German

BAYERISCHER RUNDFUNK

24 Hr	6085

DEUTSCHE WELLE

0000-0150	**S** 9730 (C America), **W** *11795* & **S** *15410* (S America)
0000-0155	**S** 9545 (N America & C America), **S** *9680* (S Asia & SE Asia), *9765* (C America), *13780* (S America)
0000-0200	6075 (Europe), 9545 (S America), **W** *9690* (S Asia & SE Asia)
0000-0300	**W** *7225* & **S** *9795* (S Asia)
0000-0355	**W** *11785* (W Africa & Americas)
0000-0400	**W** 7130 (S Europe & S America)
0000-0600	3995 (Europe), 6100 (N America & C America)
0200-0400	**W** 6145 (C America), **S** 7130 (N Africa & S America)
0200-0555	**S** 9735 (N America)
0200-0600	6075 (Europe & N America), 9545 (E Africa & S Africa)
0400-0555	**S** 11795 (Africa)
0400-0600	*6085* (N America), **W** *7195* (S Africa), **W** *7235* (W Africa), **S** *9535* (N America & C America), **S** *9700* (S Africa), **W** 9735 (Mideast & Africa)
0500-0600	**S** 9735 (Australasia)
0600-0800	*6185* (Australasia)
0600-0955	**W** 9670 (E Europe & W Asia), *9690*, 9735 & 11795 (Australasia), **S** 11865 (E Europe & W Asia), **S** *21640* (SE Asia & Australasia)
0600-1000	15275 (Africa), 17845 (SE Asia & Australasia)
0600-1800	13780 (S Europe)
0600-2000	6075 (Europe), 9545 (S Europe)
0800-0955	**W** 11865 (E Asia)
0900-1355	*15135* (Africa)
1000-1355	**W** *11865* (E Asia), **W** 12080 (E Europe & W Asia), **S** 13780 (C Asia & E Asia), **S** 15275 (Mideast), **S** 15640 (E Asia), 17845 (S Asia & SE Asia), **S** *17845* (E Asia)
1000-1400	**W** *7340* (E Asia), **W** *9480* (S Asia & SE Asia), **S** *12000* (E Asia), **S** *15490* (SE Asia & Australasia), **S** 17560 (W Africa)
1000-1600	**W** 15275 (S Europe)
1100-1300	**S** *11765* (Europe)
1200-1350	**S** *15285* (S America)
1200-1355	*15285* (N America & C America)
1200-1400	**W** *11805* (Europe), **W** *17765* (S America)
1300-1900	6140 (N Europe)
1400-1600	**W** 9595 & **S** *9655* (S Asia)
1400-1700	**W** *13790* (N America & C America), *17715* (N America), *17765* (S America)
1400-1755	**W** 9620 (S Asia), **W** *15135* (Mideast & Africa), **S** *21560* (Mideast)
1400-1800	**W** 7315 (S Asia), **S** 11795 (Mideast), **S** *12055* & **S** 15275 (S Asia)
1600-1755	**S** *9655* (S Asia)
1600-2000	**W** *7445* (Mideast & E Africa), **S** *9835* (Mideast)
1800-2000	**W** 11795 (W Africa & S America)

HCJB News Director Ralph Kurtenbach. HCJB

1800-2155	**W** *7125* (SE Asia & Australasia), **W** 7215 (Africa), **S** *9655* (SE Asia & Australasia), **W** *9735* (S Africa)
1800-2200	**S** 7185 (Africa), **S** 15275 (W Africa & S America), *17860* (W Africa & Americas)
2000-2200	6075 (Europe & Africa), 9545 & 11795 (W Africa & S America), *17810* (N America & S America)
2000-2400	3995 (Europe)
2200-2355	*9715* (E Asia), **S** *17860* (C America)
2200-2400	**W** *5925* & **W** 6010 (E Asia), 6075 (Europe), 6100 (N America & C America), **S** 7315 (S Asia & SE Asia), 9545 (S America), **S** 9545 (N America & C America), **W** *9690* (S Asia & SE Asia), **S** 9730 & *9765* (C America), **W** *11785* (W Africa & Americas), **S** *11795* (E Asia), **W** *11795* & *13780* (S America), **W** *15275* (C America), **S** *15410* (S America)

DEUTSCHLANDRADIO—(Europe)
24 Hr   6005
SUDWESTRUNDFUNK—(Europe)
24 Hr   7265
0455-2305 ▭ 6030

GREECE—Greek

FONI TIS HELLADAS

0000-0130 &	
0200-0330	**W** 7448, **W** 9420 & 9935/6260 (N America)
0330-0345	9935/6260 (N America)
0400-0525	**W** 7450, 9425/9420, **W** 11645 & 15650 (Mideast)
0600-0745	7450, **S** 9425 & 11645 (Europe & Australasia)
0900-0950	15415/15630 (E Asia), 15650 (Australasia)
1000-1135	9425 & 9915 (Mideast)
1200-1230	**W** 9420 (Mideast), **W** 11645 & **W** 15650 (Africa)
1200-1235 &	
1245-1350	**S** 15175 (Europe & N America)
1300-1335 ▭	15650 (Europe & N America)
1300-1335	**W** 9420 (Europe & N America), 11645 (C Asia)
1345-1450 ▭	15650 (Europe & N America)
1345-1450	**W** 9420 (Europe & N America)
1400-1430	**S** 9420, 11645 & **S** 15630 (Mideast)
1500-1600	**W** 7450 (Europe), **S** 9375, 9420 & 11645 (E Europe)
1710-1725	**W** 7450, **S** 9375, 9425/9420 & **S** 11645 (E Europe)
1800-1840	11645 & 15150 (Africa)
1800-1900	**W** 7450, **W** 9395, **W** 9425 & **W** 11595 (Europe)
1900-2100	**W** 9420 (Europe)
1900-2150	7450 (Europe), **S** 9420/7430 (Europe, N America & Australasia)
2100-2235	9425 (Australasia)
2100-2250	**W** 6260 (Europe)
2200-2300	**W** 6260 (N America)
2200-2305	**S** 9395 (C America & S America), 11595 (S America)
2300-2335	**S** 9425 (C America & Australasia)

RADIOFONIKOS STATHMOS MAKEDONIAS

0500-1700	**S** 9935 (Europe)
0500-1730	**S** 11595 (Mideast)
0600-0800 ▭	7430/6245 (Europe)
0600-1730	**W** 9935 (Mideast)
0600-1900	**W** 11595 (Europe)
1400-2200	7430 (Europe)
1500-2200	**S** 6260 (Europe)
1730-2200	9935 (Mideast)
1900-2300	**W** 6245 (Europe)
2200-2300	**W** 7430 (Europe), **W** 9935 (Mideast)

HOLLAND—Dutch

RADIO NEDERLAND WERELDOMROEP

0000-0025	*7280, 9590,* ☒ *12090* & ☒ *17580* (SE Asia)
0130-0225	6020 (C America), *6165* (N America), ☒ 9895 (E North Am), *15315* (S America)
0330-0425	☒ *9855* & ☒ *9860* (E Africa), *11655* (Mideast)
0500-0600	7130 (Europe)
0500-1700	5955 (W Europe)
0530-0625	*6165* & *9715* (W North Am)
0600-0655	☒ 7130 (Europe)
0600-0800	☒ 11935 (S Europe)
0600-0900	☒ 6020 (S Europe)
0630-0725	*9720* & ☒ *11660* (Australasia)
0800-1700	☒ 13700 (S Europe)
0930-1015	*6020* (C America)
1000-1200	☒ 11895 (S Europe)
1030-1125	*9720* & *9820* (Australasia), *17580* (SE Asia), *21480* (E Asia)
1330-1425	*5930* (E Asia), ☒ *7375* (E Asia & SE Asia), ☒ *12065* (S Asia & E Asia), ☒ *13755* (SE Asia)
1500-1800	☒ 6015 (S Europe)
1530-1625	☒ *12090* (S Asia)
1600-1700	☒ *7310* (W Europe)
1630-1725	*6020* (S Africa), *11655* (E Africa)
1730-1825	☒ 9895 & ☒ 13700 (Mideast), ☒ *17605* (W Africa)
1830-1925	☒ Su 13700 & ☒ *21590* (W Africa)
2030-2125	*6015* (S Africa), 6020 (S Europe & N Africa), ☒ *7120* (C Africa & W Africa), ☒ 11655 & *15315* (W Africa), Su *15525* (S America), *17605* (W Africa)
2130-2225	☒ *6030* & 9895 (C America), ☒ *11730* (E North Am), ☒ 13700 (S America), ☒ *15155* (E North Am), *15315* (S America)
2330-2400	*7280, 9590,* ☒ *12090* & ☒ *17580* (SE Asia)

HUNGARY—Hungarian

RADIO BUDAPEST

0000-0100	☒ M 6165 & ☒ M 9835 (S America), ☒ 11910 (N America)
0100-0200	☒ 6030 (N America)
0130-0230	☒ 11685 (N America)
0230-0330	☒ 6030 (N America)
1000-1100	☒ 15395 & ☒ 17790 (Australasia)
1100-1200	☒ Su 5970 (W Europe), ☒ Su 15395 & ☒ Su 17790 (Australasia)
1200-1300	☒ Su 7220 (W Europe), ☒ Su 9840 (Europe)
1300-1400	☒ Su 5980 (W Europe)
1800-1900	☒ 5990 (W Europe)
1900-2000 & 2100-2200 ▭	3975 (Europe)
2200-2300	☒ 9840 & ☒ 11905 (S America)
2300-2400	☒ 6165, ☒ 9835, ☒ Su 9840, ☒ 11660 & ☒ Su 11905 (S America)

IRAN—Persian

VOICE OF THE ISLAMIC REPUBLIC

0000-0030	☒ 7130 (Mideast & Europe)
0000-1230	15084
0130-1330	15365 (W Asia & S Asia)
1300-2400	15084
1630-1730	7230 (Europe)
1630-1930	*6175/6005* & ☒ 7180 (W Asia)
1630-2400	☒ 7130 (Mideast & Europe)

ISRAEL

KOL ISRAEL

Arabic

0400-2220 ▭	5915 & 15480/15430 (Mideast)
0400-0630 & 1300-2220 ▭	9815 (Mideast)

Yiddish

1600-1625	☒ 11605 (Europe & N America), ☒ 15640 (E Europe), ☒ 15650 (W Europe & E North Am)
1700-1725 ▭	9435 (Europe & N America)
1700-1725	☒ 7395 (W Europe), ☒ 7465 (W Europe & E North Am), ☒ 9365 (E Europe), ☒ 11605 (Europe & N America), ☒ 15650 (W Europe & E North Am)
1800-1825 ▭	9435 (E Europe)
1800-1825	☒ 7465 (W Europe & E North Am), ☒ 9365 (E Europe)

RESHET BET

Hebrew

0000-0530	☒ 11585 (W Europe & E North Am)
0000-0700	☒ 7495 (W Europe & E North Am)
0100-2055	☒ 15615 (W Europe & E North Am)
0400-0700	☒ 9390 (W Europe & E North Am)
0445-2200	☒ 13750 (Europe)
0500-1855	☒ 17545 (W Europe & E North Am)
0700-1455	☒ 17545 (W Europe & E North Am)
0700-1555	☒ 15615 (W Europe & E North Am)
1400-1600	☒ 11585 (W Europe & E North Am)
1500-1600	☒ 12077 (W Europe & E North Am)
1500-1655	☒ 11590 (W Europe & E North Am)
1700-2300	☒ 9390 (W Europe & E North Am)
1730-2400	☒ 7495 & ☒ 9388 (W Europe & E North Am)
1800-2100	☒ 11585 (W Europe & E North Am)
1900-2200	☒ 11585 (W Europe & E North Am)

Archway of the Colosseum in Rome. R. Crane

ITALY—Italian

RADIO ROMA-RAI INTERNATIONAL

0000-0050	6010 (E North Am), 9575 (S America), 9675 (E North Am & C America), 11800 (N America & C America), 11755/11880 (S America)
0130-0230	*6110* & *11765* (S America)
0130-0305	6010 (E North Am), 9575 (S America), 9675 (N America & C America), 11800 (E North Am & C America), 11755/11880 (S America)
0415-0425	5975 & 7275 (S Europe & N Africa)
0435-0510	[W] 9670, [W] 11800, [S] 11880 & [S] 15400 (E Africa)
1000-1100	*11925* (Australasia)
1320-1650	Su 21535 (S America), Su 21710 (C Africa & S Africa)
1400-1430	15245/15250 & 17780 (E North Am)
1500-1525	5990, 7290 & [S] 9670 (S Europe & N Africa)
1555-1625	5990, 7290 & 9755 (Europe)
1700-1800	7235, [S] 9535 & [W] 9710 (N Africa), 11840 & 15230 (Africa), *15320* (S Africa), 17870 (E Africa)
1830-1905	15245/15250 & 17780 (E North Am)
2230-2400	6010 (E North Am), 9575 (S America), 9675 (E North Am & C America), 11800 (N America & C America), 11755/11880 (S America)

RAI-RTV ITALIANA

0000-0500 ⬅	6060 (Europe, Mideast & N Africa)
0500-2300 ⬅	6060 & 9515 (Europe, N Africa & Mideast)
0500-2300	7175 (Europe, Mideast & N Africa)
0600-1300	15240 & 21520 (E Africa)
1320-1650	Su 9855 (Europe), Su 17780 (E North Am), Su 21520 (E Africa), Su 21535 (S America), Su 21710 (C Af & S Africa)
2300-2400 ⬅	6060 (Europe, Mideast & N Africa)

JAPAN—Japanese

RADIO JAPAN/NHK

0200-0300	*11860* (SE Asia), *11890* (S Asia), 15570 (E Asia)
0200-0400	*5960* (E North Am), 13630 (W North Am)
0200-0500	11840 (E Asia)
0300-0330	[W] 13700 (E Africa)
0300-0400	*9515* (Mideast), [W] *11895* (C America), [W] 15230 (Pacific & W North Am)
0300-0500	17810 (SE Asia)
0400-0500	[W] *6110* (W North Am & C America)
0600-0700	*7230* (Europe)
0700-1000	*11920* (Australasia)
0800-1000	*9530* & [W] 9685 (S America), *11740* (SE Asia), 11850 (Australasia), *15220* (W Africa)
0800-1100	[W] 7125 (E Asia)
0900-1100	11815 (SE Asia)
0900-1500	[W] 9855 (SE Asia)
1000-1100	[W] *17780* (S Africa)
1300-1400	[W] *21490* (C Africa)
1300-1500	[S] *11705* (E North Am), [W] *11705* (W North Am), [W] *12045* (S Asia)
1500-1600	*17885* (C Africa)
1600-1700	6035 (E Asia), 9535 (W North Am)
1600-1800	[S] *11880* (Mideast)
1700-1800	[W] 7225 (S Asia)
1800-1900	6035 (E Asia), [W] 7140 (Australasia), [W] *11880* (Mideast)
1800-2000	[W] 9535 (W North Am)
1900-2100	[W] 7110 (Europe)
2000-2100	[W] 6090 (E Asia), [W] 13630 (W North Am)
2100-2400	11665 (SE Asia)

2200-2300	*6115* (Europe), 11850 (Australasia), *15220* (S America)

RADIO TAMPA

0000-0800	3925, 9760
0000-1000	6115
0000-1300	3945
0000-1730	6055, 9595
0800-1730 &	
2020-2300	3925
2030-2400	6055, 9595
2300-2400	3925, 3945, 6115, 9760

JORDAN—Arabic

RADIO JORDAN

0000-0208 ▭	11935 (W Europe & E North Am), 15435 (S America)
0400-0600 ▭	9630 (N Africa & E Africa)
0400-0810	11810 (Mideast, SE Asia & Australasia)
0400-0815 ▭	15435 (W Europe)
0600-0900 ▭	11835 (E Europe)
0830-1515	11810 (Mideast, SE Asia & Australasia)
1100-1300 ▭	15355 (N Africa & C America)
1633-2155 ▭	13630/7155 (N Africa & E Africa)
1800-2155 ▭	9830 (W Europe)
2200-2400 ▭	11935 (W Europe & E North Am), 15435 (S America)

KOREA (DPR)—Korean

PYONGYANG BROADCASTING STATION—(E Asia)

2100-1800	6398
2100-1900	3320

RADIO PYONGYANG

0000-0925	6250 (E Asia)
0800-0900	7200 (E Asia), 9345 (Asia)
1200-1300	6125 & 7200 (E Asia), 9345 (Asia)
1400-1450	9640 (SE Asia), 9975 (SE Asia & C America)
1500-1900	6250 (E Asia)
1600-1650	6520 (Mideast & N Africa), 6575 & 9335 (Europe), 9600 (Mideast & N Africa), 9640 (Mideast & Africa), 9975 (Africa)
1700-1800	6520 (Mideast & N Africa)
2100-2400	6250 (E Asia)

KOREA (REPUBLIC)—Korean

RADIO KOREA INTERNATIONAL

0000-0100	5975 (E Asia), 15575 (N America)
0300-0400	11725 & 11810 (S America), 15575 (N America)
0700-0800	7550 (Europe)
0900-1000	7550 (S America)

0900-1100	5975 & 7275 (E Asia), 9570 (Australasia), 13670 (Europe)
1000-1100	6135 (E Asia)
1100-1130	*6145* (E North Am), 9640 (E Asia), *9650* (E North Am), 11725/9580 (S America)
1300-1400	9640 (E Asia), 13670 (SE Asia)
1700-1900	5975 (E Asia), 7550 & 15575 (Europe)
2100-2200	5975 & 7275 (E Asia), 9640 (SE Asia)
2300-2400	5975 (E Asia), 15575 (N America)

KUWAIT—Arabic

RADIO KUWAIT

0000-0530	11675 (W North Am)
0200-1305	6055 & 15495 (Mideast)
0400-0805	15505 (E Europe)
0445-0930	15110 (S Asia & SE Asia)
0815-1740	15505 (W Africa & C Africa)
0900-1505	17885 (E Asia)
0930-1605	13620 (Europe & E North Am)
1315-1730	15110 (S Asia & SE Asia)
1315-2130	9880 (Mideast)
1615-1800	11990 (Europe & E North Am)
1745-2300	15505 (Europe & E North Am)
1800-2400	9855 (Europe & E North Am), 15495 (W Africa & C Africa)

LEBANON

VOICE OF LEBANON
Arabic

0355-0800,	
0808-0900,	
0915-1300,	
1330-1615,	
1630-1800 &	
1830-2225 ▭	6550

French

0800-0808,	
1300-1315,	
1615-1630 &	
1815-1830 ▭	6550

LIBYA—Arabic

RADIO JAMAHIRIYA

0000-0445 ▭	15235 (W Africa & S America), 15415 (Europe), 15435 (N Africa & Mideast)
1115-1730 ▭	15235 (W Africa & S America), 15415 (Europe), 15435 (N Africa & Mideast)
1800-2400 ▭	15235 (W Africa & S America), 15435 (N Africa & Mideast)
1900-2400 ▭	15415 (Europe)

Flag-raising ceremony at Adventist World Radio, Peru. AWR

LITHUANIA—Lithuanian

LITHUANIAN RADIO—(Europe)
1000-1100 &
1100-1200 ▣ 9710
RADIO VILNIUS
0000-0030 ▣ 5905 & ▣ *9855* (E North Am)
0900-0930 ▣ 9710 (Europe)

MEXICO—Spanish

RADIO EDUCACION
0000-1200 ▣ 6185
RADIO MEXICO INTERNATIONAL—(W North Am & C America)
0000-0400 ▣ 9705
0400-0500 ▣ M 9705
1300-1500 ▣ 5985 & 9705
1900-2000 ▣ 5985 & 9705
2200-2400 ▣ 5985 & 9705

MOROCCO

RADIO MEDI UN—(Europe & N Africa)
French & Arabic
0500-0100 9575
RTV MAROCAINE
Arabic
0000-0500 11920 (N Africa & Mideast)
0900-2100 15345 (N Africa & Mideast)
1100-1500 &
2200-2400 15335 (Europe)

NORWAY—Norwegian

RADIO NORWAY INTERNATIONAL
0000-0030 ▣ 5905 (S America), 7275 (SE Asia

& Australasia), 7465 (E North Am & C America), ▣ 9525 (S America)

0100-0130 ▣ 6120 (N America), ▣ 7465 & ▣ Tu-Su 7465 (E North Am & C America), ▣ Tu-Su 9560 (N America)

0200-0230 ▣ 6120 (N America), ▣ 7465 (E North Am), ▣ 7465 (S America), ▣ 9560 (N America)

0300-0330 ▣ 5965 & 7165 (Mideast), ▣ 7465 & ▣ Tu-Su 7465 (W North Am), ▣ 9565 (Mideast)

0400-0430 ▣ 5965 (E Europe), ▣ 6040 (Mideast & E Africa), ▣ 7305 (Mideast), ▣ Tu-Su 7520 (W North Am), ▣ 9565 & ▣ 13805 (Mideast)

0500-0530 ▣ 5965 (E Europe), ▣ 6195 (W North Am), ▣ 7180 (E Africa), ▣ 7465 (E Europe), ▣ 13805 (E Africa)

0600-0630 ▣ 5965 & ▣ 7180 (Europe), ▣ 7180 (W Europe), ▣ M-Sa 7295 (Australasia), ▣ M-Sa 9590 (W Africa & Australasia), ▣ 9590 (W Africa), ▣ 11735 & ▣ 13805 (E Africa)

0700-0730 ▣ 5965 (Europe), ▣ 7180 (W Europe), ▣ M-Sa 7180 (W Europe & Australasia), ▣ 7295 (Australasia), ▣ 9590 (Europe), ▣ 9590 & ▣ 13805 (W Africa)

0800-0830 ▣ 9590 & ▣ 13800 (Australasia), ▣ 15220 (Mideast), ▣ M-Sa 17855 (Australasia)

0900-0930 ▣ 13800 (E Asia), ▣ 15175 (Australasia), ▣ 15230 (Mideast), ▣ 17855 (Australasia)

1000-1030	⬜ 7295 (Atlantic), 🅂 9480 (Europe), ⬜ 11830 (W Europe), 🅂 15220 (S America)
1100-1130	🅂 7295 (Europe), ⬜ 15270 (S America), 🅂 17740 (C Africa)
1200-1230	🅂 M-Sa 9590 & ⬜ 9590 (Europe), ⬜ 9795 (E Asia), ⬜ 11850 (E North Am), 🅂 M-Sa 13800 & 🅂 M-Sa 15305 (E Asia), 🅂 15480 (S America), ⬜ 15605 (SE Asia)
1300-1330	🅂 9590 & ⬜ M-Sa 9590 (Europe), ⬜ M-Sa 9795 (E Asia), ⬜ 11840 (N America), 🅂 M-Sa 13800 (SE Asia & Australasia), 🅂 15305 (E Asia), 🅂 M-Sa 15340 (N America), ⬜ M-Sa 15605 (SE Asia & Australasia)
1400-1430	⬜ 11720 (S Asia), ⬜ M-Sa 11840 (N America), 11850 (SE Asia), 🅂 13800 (S Asia & SE Asia), 🅂 15340 (N America)
1500-1530	⬜ 9485 (W North Am), ⬜ M-Sa 9520 & ⬜ M-Sa 11730 (Mideast), 🅂 11840 (W North Am), 🅂 13805 & 🅂 15230 (Mideast)
1600-1630	⬜ 9590 (E Europe), ⬜ 11840 (E Africa), ⬜ 11840 (W North Am), 🅂 M-Sa 11860 (S Asia), 🅂 M-Sa 13805 (E Africa), 🅂 15340 (W North Am)
1700-1730	7485 (E Europe), ⬜ 7525 (W Europe), ⬜ 9590 (E Africa), 🅂 11860 (S Asia), 🅂 15220 (E Africa)
1800-1830	⬜ 5960 (W Europe), 🅂 M-Sa 7485 (Europe), ⬜ 7485 (W Africa), 🅂 M-Sa 9590 (Mideast), ⬜ 9590 (C Africa), 🅂 M-Sa 13805 (W Africa), 🅂 M-Sa 15220 (C Africa)
1900-1930	⬜ M-Sa 5930 (Australasia), ⬜ M-Sa 5960 & 🅂 7485 (Europe), ⬜ M-Sa 7485 (W Africa), ⬜ M-Sa 9590 (C Africa), 🅂 11860 (Australasia), 🅂 13805 (C Africa), 🅂 15220 (W Africa)
2000-2030	🅂 7485 (Europe & Mideast), ⬜ 7520 (Europe), ⬜ 9480 (W North Am), 🅂 M-Sa 9590 (Australasia)
2100-2130	⬜ 5960 (Atlantic & E North Am), 🅂 7205 (Australasia), ⬜ 9480 (E Asia), 🅂 9495 (Australasia), 🅂 9590 (Atlantic)
2200-2230	⬜ 5960 (Australasia), ⬜ M-Sa 6200 (E North Am), ⬜ M-Sa 7115 (E Asia), 🅂 M-Sa 9485 (Australasia), 🅂 11840 (E North Am)
2300-2330	⬜ 5905 (S America), 7275 (SE Asia & Australasia), ⬜ 7465 (E North Am), 🅂 7490 (S America), 🅂 9485 (E North Am)

PARAGUAY—Spanish

RADIO ENCARNACION
0700-0300 ➡ 11939

RADIO NACIONAL DEL PARAGUAY
0700-1700 ➡ 9735 (S America & E North Am)
1700-2000 ➡ 9735 (Irr) (S America)
2000-0300 ➡ 9735 (S America & E North Am)

POLAND—Polish

POLISH RADIO WARSAW
1130-1155 ▭ 5995 & 7285 (Europe)
1200-1225 ▭ 7270 (W Europe), 7285 (E Europe)
1630-1725 ▭ 6000 (W Europe), 7285 (E Europe)
1630-1725 ⬜ 9690 (W Europe)
2100-2200 🅂 7270 (E Europe)
2200-2255 ▭ 6035 (E Europe), 6095 (W Europe)

PORTUGAL—Portuguese

RDP INTERNATIONAL-RADIO PORTUGAL
0000-0430 ▭ 9520/9570 (E North Am), 9600/13640 (S America), 11770 (W North Am), 9635/13700 (C America & S America), 11840 (S America)
0600-0800 ▭ M-F 7110/9780 (Europe)
0745-0900 ▭ M-F 9630/11780 (Europe)
0800-1000 ▭ Sa/Su 15555 (E Africa & S Africa), Sa/Su 17725 (SE Asia), Sa/Su 21655 (W Africa & S America)
0800-1400 ▭ 7110/9780 (Europe)
1000-1200 ▭ 17680/15515 (E Africa & S Africa), 21655 (W Africa & S America), M-F 21720 (E Africa & S Africa)
1200-1300 ▭ M-F 17740 (SE Asia)
1200-1800 ▭ Sa/Su 17680/15515 (E Africa & S Africa), Sa/Su 21655 (W Africa & S America)
1300-1430 ▭ M-F 21515 (Mideast & S Asia)
1300-2100 ▭ Sa/Su//Holidays 15200 (E North Am), Sa/Su//Holidays 17745 (C America)
1400-2100 ▭ Sa/Su 9780 (Europe)
1500-1900 ▭ Sa/Su 21515 (Mideast & S Asia)
1800-2400 ▭ 21655 (W Africa & S America)

ROMANIA—Romanian

RADIO ROMANIA
0000-0300 🅂 6105 (W Europe)
0300-0700 9570 (W Europe)
0500-0800 ⬜ 11970 (Europe)
0600-0800 ⬜ 15105 (Europe, N Africa & Mideast)
0700-1200 🅂 11940 (Europe)
0800-1430 15105 (Europe, N Africa & Mideast)

0800-1500	[W] 17720 (Europe)
1200-2100	[S] 11790 (Europe)
1430-2100	[S] 15105 (Europe, N Africa & Mideast)
2100-2400	[S] 6105 (W Europe)

RADIO ROMANIA INTERNATIONAL

0000-0100	9510 & 11940 (E North Am)
0100-0200	9570 (S America)
0600-0614	[W]7105, [S]9550, 9665, [W]11775 & [S] 11810 (Europe)
0715-0815	[S] Su 11740 & Su 15335 (W Asia), Su 15370 & Su 17790 (SE Asia)
0815-0915	[S] Su 11810 (C Africa), Su 15335 (S Africa), Su 15380 (C Africa), [S] Su 17745 (S Africa), [W] Su 17790 (W Africa)
0915-1015	Su 9570 (Europe), [W] Su 9590 (W Europe), Su 9665, Su 11775 & Su 11810 (N Africa), [S] Su 11970 (Europe & Atlantic)
1130-1200	[S] 11790 (Europe)
1300-1330	[S] 11775 (Europe), [W] 15365 & [W] 17790 (Australasia)
1630-1700	[W] 7105, [S] 9510, [W] 9665 & [S] 11775 (Mideast)
1730-1800	[W] 5990, [W] 6105, [W] 7195 & [S] 9510 (Europe)
2000-2030	[W] 7175 (Europe), [S] 9625 (W Europe), [W] 9690 (Europe), [S] 11790 (W Europe)
2230-2300	[W] 9530 (W Europe), 9570 & [S] 11830 (E North Am), [W] 11830 (S America)
2300-2400	[W] 5990 (C America), 7105 & [W] 9550 (Australasia), [W] 11940 (S America)

SAUDI ARABIA—Arabic

BROADCASTING SERVICE OF THE KINGDOM

0300-0600	7150, 9555 (Mideast), 9620/9885 (N Africa), 9720 (W Asia), 11740/11935 (C Asia), [W] 11785, [S] 11870, [S] 17745/17780 & [W] 17745/17720 (C Asia)
0300-1700	9580 (Mideast & E Africa)
0300-2100	10990 (Irr) ISL & 10990 (Irr) ISU (Mideast)
0600-0700	7150
0600-0900	11710 (N Africa), 11950 (W Asia)
0600-1200	11820 (Mideast)
0900-1200	17880/17895 (SE Asia), 21495/21530 (E Asia & SE Asia)
0900-1500	15060 (N Africa)
1200-1500	15230/15175 (W Europe), 15380 (W Asia)
1200-1600	15165 (N Africa), 15280 (Mideast)
1500-1800	11780 (N Africa), 11910/11965 (W Europe), 11950 (W Asia)
1600-1800	9730 (C Africa), 11710 (N Africa), 11835 (Mideast)
1700-2100	6020 (Mideast & E Africa)
1800-2100	9705/9775 (W Asia)
1800-2300	9555 (N Africa), 9870 (W Europe), 11935 (N Africa)
2100-2300	3868 (Irr) USB (Mideast)

SINGAPORE—Chinese

RADIO SINGAPORE INTERNATIONAL—(SE Asia)

1100-1400	6000 & 6120

RADIO CORPORATION OF SINGAPORE

1400-1600 & 2300-1100	6000

SLOVAKIA—Slovak

RADIO SLOVAKIA INTERNATIONAL

0130-0200	5930 (E North Am & C America), 7300 (Africa), 9440 (S America)
0730-0800	[S] 15460 & [S] 17550 (Australasia)
0900-0930	[W] 11990, [W] 17485 & [W] 21705 (Australasia)
1530-1630	[S] 5920 (W Europe)
1630-1730 [✉]	6055 & 7345 (W Europe)
1630-1730	[W] 5915 & [W] 5940 (W Europe)
2000-2030 [✉]	6055 & 7345 (W Europe)
2000-2030	[W] 5915 (W Europe)

SPAIN—Spanish

RADIO EXTERIOR DE ESPANA

0000-0100	Su/M 5970 (C America), Su/M 11815 (N America), Su/M 17870 (S America)
0000-0200	11945 (S America)
0000-0500	6125 (S America), 9540 (N America & C America), 9620 (S America)
0100-0400	Tu-Sa 3210 (C America), Tu-Sa 5970 (N America), Tu-Sa 5990 (S America)
0200-0500	6055 (N America & C America)
0500-0700	9650 (Australasia), 9685 (Europe), 9760 (Australasia), [W] 11890 (Mideast), 11920 (Europe), [S] 15125 (Mideast)
0600-0910	12035 (Europe)
0900-0910	17715 (S America)
0900-1200	Su 9620 (W Europe)
0900-1700	[W] 15110 & [S] 17890 (Mideast)
0900-1900	17755 (W Africa & S Africa)
0910-0940	Su-F 12035 (Europe), Su-F 17715 (S America)
0940-1515	12035 (Europe)
0940-1900	17715 (S America)
1000-1200	9620 (E Asia)
1100-1400	M-F 3210 (C America), M-F 9630 (N America), M-F 11815 (S America)

1200-1400	*5220* (E Asia), *11910* (SE Asia)
1200-1515	9620 (W Europe)
1200-1800	17845/21570 (C America & S America)
1300-1800	Sa/Su *11815* (N America)
1400-1800	Sa/Su *5970* (C America), Sa/Su *17870/11880* (S America)
1515-1600	Sa/Su 9620 (W Europe), Sa/Su 12035 (Europe)
1600-1700	Su 9620 (W Europe), 12035 (Europe), M-Sa 15210 (W Africa & C Africa)
1700-2000	Sa/Su 6125 (W Europe)
1700-2235	7275 (Europe)
1800-1900	**S** Sa/Su 17845/21570 (C America & S America)
1800-2235	*5970* (C America), *11815* (N America), *17870* (S America)
1900-2000	**S** Sa/Su 17845/15125 (C America & S America)
1900-2200	**W** 11880 & **S** 17870 (E North Am & C America)
2000-2100	Sa 6125/9590 (W Europe), **S** Sa 17845/15125 (C America & S America)
2200-2235	11880 (E North Am & C America)
2200-2300	6130 (N Africa), **W** 9580 & **S** 15110 (Mideast)
2235-2255	Su *5970* (C America), Su *11815* (N America), Su 11880 (E North Am & C America), Su *17870* (S America)
2235-2300	Su 7275 (Europe)
2255-2400	*5970* (C America), *11815* (N America), 11880 (E North Am & C America), *17870* (S America)
2300-2400	6125 (S America), 9540 (N America & C America), 9620 & 11945 (S America)

SUDAN—Arabic

REPUBLIC OF SUDAN RADIO

0300-0830	7200
0300-1500	9200
1200-2300	7200
1900-2300	9200

SWEDEN—Swedish

RADIO SWEDEN

0000-0030	9440 (S America)
0100-0130	**W** 7265 (E Asia & Australasia)
0200-0230	**W** 7280 (N America)
0300-0330	7115 (N America)
0500-0705 ▣	M-F 6065 (Europe), M-F 13625 (Europe, N Africa & Mideast)
0700-0900 ▣	Sa 6065 (Europe), Sa 13625 (Europe & N Africa)
0800-1000 ▣	Su 6065 (Europe), Su 13625 (Europe & N Africa)
1110-1130 ▣	Sa/Su 6065 (Europe)
1130-1200	**W** 13740/11650 (E North Am)
1500-1530 ▣	15240 (N America)
1500-1530	**W** 13740/11650 (N America)
1545-1600 ▣	6000 (E Europe)
1545-1600	**S** 17515/21810 (Mideast)
1545-1700 ▣	6065 (Europe)
1700-1710 ▣	M-F 6065 (Europe)
1900-1930 ▣	6065 (Europe & Mideast)
2100-2130 &	
2200-2230 ▣	6065 (Europe)

SWITZERLAND

SWISS RADIO INTERNATIONAL
French

0200-0230	9885 (N America), *9905* (N America & C America)
0500-0530	9885 (N America)
0530-0600 ▣	*5840* (E Europe), 6165 (Europe & N Africa)
0600-0700	*9885 & 11860* (W Africa), 13635 (S Africa)
0615-0630 ▣	*5840* (E Europe), 6165 (Europe & N Africa)
0730-1100 ▣	6165 (Europe & N Africa)
1000-1030	*9885 & 13685* (Australasia)
1200-1230 ▣	6165 (Europe & N Africa), *9535* (W Europe)
1530-1600	*9575* (C Asia & S Asia), **W** 13635 (W Asia & S Asia)
1800-1815	**W** *5850*, **S** 9905 & **S** *12075* (Mideast)
1930-2000 ▣	6165 (Europe & N Africa)
1930-2000	**W** *7410* (N Europe)
2100-2130	9905 (E Africa)
2200-2230	*9885/9905 & 11650* (S America)

German

0030-0100 &	
0330-0400	9885 (N America), *9905* (N America & C America)
0600-0615 ▣	*5840* (E Europe), 6165 (Europe & N Africa)
0800-0815	*9885* (W Africa), 13635 (S Africa)
0930-1000	*9885 & 13685* (Australasia)
1130-1200 ▣	6165 (Europe & N Africa), *9535* (W Europe)
1400-1430	*7230* (SE Asia), *7480* (E Asia)
1600-1900 ▣	6165 (Europe & N Africa)
1730-1800	**S** *9905* (N Europe)
1830-1900	**W** *7410* (N Europe)
2030-2100	*9840/9620* (Africa), 9905 (E Africa)
2230-2300	*11650* (S America)

Italian

0300-0330	9885 (N America), *9905* (N America & C America)
0530-0545	9885 (N America)

0700-0730 ■	5840 (E Europe), 6165 (Europe & N Africa)
0700-0730	9885 & 11860 (W Africa), 13635 (S Africa)
0900-0930 ■	9885 & 13685 (Australasia)
1230-1300 ■	6165 (Europe & N Africa), 9535 (W Europe)
1330-1600 ■	6165 (Europe & N Africa)
1430-1445	7230 (SE Asia), 7480 (E Asia)
1600-1615	W 13635 (W Asia & S Asia)
1630-1700	W 5850 & S 9905 (Mideast)
1800-1830	S 9905 (N Europe)
1900-1930 ■	6165 (Europe & N Africa)
1900-1930	W 7410 (N Europe)
2300-2330	11650 (S America)

SYRIA—Arabic

RADIO DAMASCUS—(S America)

2215-2315	12085 & 13610/15095

SYRIAN BROADCASTING SERVICE

0600-1600 ■	15095/13610
0600-1700 ■	12085

THAILAND—Thai

RADIO THAILAND

0000-1700	6070, 7115
0100-0200	9655 & 11905 (Asia), W 13695 & S 15395 (N America)
0330-0430	9655 & 11905 (Asia), S 15395 & W 15460 (W North Am)
1330-1400	W 7145 (E Asia), 9655 & 11905 (Asia), S 11955 (E Asia)
1800-1900	9655 & 11905 (Asia), S 9690 & W 11855 (Mideast), 11905 (Asia)
2045-2115	W 9535 (Europe), 9655 (Asia), S 9680 (Europe), 11905 (Asia)
2200-2400	6070, 7115

TUNISIA—Arabic

RTV TUNISIENNE

0400-0700	7225/7475 (Europe)
0400-2330	12005 (N Africa & Mideast)
0600-1500	15535 (N Africa & Mideast)
0700-1600	11730 (Europe)
0800-1400	17735 (N Africa & Mideast)
1600-2330	7280 (Europe)
1900-2330	7225/7475 (Europe)

TURKEY—Turkish

VOICE OF TURKEY

0000-0400	S 11725 (Europe & N America)
0000-0800 ■	9445 (Europe & E North Am), 9460 (Europe)
0000-0800	W 11710 (Europe & E North Am)
0000-1000 ■	15385 (Europe)

24 Hr	11955 (Mideast)
0400-0700	S 9505 (Europe, N America & C America)
0400-0900	S 21715 (W Asia, S Asia & Australasia)
0500-1000 ■	11925 & 15145 (W Asia)
0500-1000	W 9560 (W Asia, S Asia & Australasia)
0700-0900	S 13670 (Europe)
0800-2200 ■	9460 (Europe & E North Am)
1000-1500	S F 15625 (N Africa & E Africa)
1000-1700 ■	15350 (Europe)
1000-2300 ■	9560 (W Asia, S Asia & Australasia)
1100-1600	W F 7150 (N Africa)
1300-1500	S 13670 (Europe)
1600-2200	S 7115 (N Africa & Mideast)
1600-2300 ■	5980 (Europe)
1700-2300	W 7255 (Mideast & Africa)
1700-2400 ■	15385 (Europe)
2100-2400	S 11725 (Europe & N America)
2200-2400 ■	9445 (Europe & E North Am), 9460 (Europe)
2200-2400	W 11710 (Europe & E North Am)
2300-2350	S 11810 (Europe & E North Am)

UKRAINE—Ukrainian

RADIO UKRAINE

0000-0300	S 9945 (W Africa & S America)
0100-0300	S 9550 (E North Am)
0200-0400 ■	6080 (W Asia)
0200-0400	W 5915 (W Europe & E North Am), W 7205 (W Europe, W Africa & S America)
0400-1700	S 7320 (W Asia), S 7410 (Europe)
0500-0600	W 5915 (W Europe & E North Am)
0500-0700 ■	6080 (W Asia)
0500-0700	W 7205 (W Europe)
0600-1200 ■	17725 (Australasia)
0600-1300	W 9610 (W Asia)
0600-1600	W 7285 (Arctic)
0630-1400	W 11825 (W Asia)
0700-1000	W 11720 (W Europe)
0700-1600 ■	13590 (Europe)
0800-1500	W 17680 (Europe)
0900-1700	W 9600 (W Asia)
1100-1600	W 9870 (W Europe & E North Am)
1200-1700	S 21510 (W Africa & S America)
1600-1800	W 5905 (Europe)
1900-2000	W 7205 (W Europe)
1900-2100	W 5905 & W 7420 (Europe)
2200-2300	S 5915 (Europe), S 7380 (Australasia), S 9560 (Europe)
2200-2400	S 9550 (E North Am)
2300-2400 ■	5905 (Europe), 6080 (W Asia)
2300-2400	W 5940 (Europe), W 7205 (W Europe, W Africa & S America)

UNITED ARAB EMIRATES—Arabic

UAE RADIO FROM ABU DHABI

0000-0200	9605 (Irr) (Mideast)
0200-0400	6180 (Mideast), **W** 15315 (E Asia)
0200-0500	**S** 17855 (Australasia)
0200-0700	**W** 9605 (Mideast)
0200-0900	**W** 11970 (Mideast)
0500-0700	**S** 21735 (Australasia)
0600-0800	**S** 15265 (Europe)
0600-0900	**W** 13605 (Europe)
0700-1100	**S** 17760 (N Africa)
0700-1400	**W** 17760 (Australasia)
0900-1100	**S** 17825 & **S** 21735 (E Asia)
0900-1400	**W** 15280 & **W** 15380 (Mideast), **W** 17885 (Europe)
1100-1300	**S** 15315 & **W** 21735 (E Asia)
1300-1600	**W** 9605 (Australasia)
1400-1800	**W** 9695 (N Africa)
1400-2200	9770 (Europe)
1500-1700	**S** 13605 (Mideast)
1500-1800	**S** 15265 (N Africa)
1500-2200	**S** 9605 (Mideast)
1600-2200	6180 (Irr) (N Africa & Mideast), 11710 (Europe)

UAE RADIO IN DUBAI

0000-0200	11950/11795 (Irr), 13675 (Irr) (E North Am & C America)
0230-0330	12005, 13675 & 15400 (E North Am & C America)
0400-0530	15435 (Australasia), 17830 (E Asia), 21700 (Australasia)
0600-1030	13675, 15395 & 21605 (Europe)
1050-1200	15370 (N Africa)
1050-1330	13675, 15395 & 21605 (Europe)
1200-1330	13630 (N Africa)
1350-1600	13630 (N Africa), 13675, 15395 & 21605 (Europe)
1640-2055	11950/11795 (Europe), 13630 (N Africa), 13675 & 15395 (Europe)
2055-2400	11950/11795 (Irr), 13675 (Irr) (E North Am & C America)

VENEZUELA—Spanish

ECOS DEL TORBES

0900-1300	4980
1300-1900	9640
2000-0400	4980

RADIO TACHIRA

0130-0400	4830 (Irr)
1000-1300 &	
2000-0130	4830

RADIO VALERA

0300-0330	Tu-Su 4840
1000-0300	4840

VIETNAM—Vietnamese

VOICE OF VIETNAM

0000-0100	9840 & 12020/15010 (E Asia & Americas)
0000-1600	5924, 10059, 12035
0130-0230	**W** *5940* & **S** *7250* (E North Am)
1700-1800	9840 & 12020/15010 (Europe)
2200-2400	5924, 10059, 12035

YEMEN—Arabic

REPUBLIC OF YEMEN RADIO—(Mideast & E Africa)

0300-0600,	
0700-1800 &	
1900-2208	9780
2208-2308	9780 (Irr)

YUGOSLAVIA—Serbian

RADIO YUGOSLAVIA

0000-0030	**S** Su *9580* & **S** Su 11870 (E North Am)
0030-0100	**W** *6195*, **W** *7115*, **S** *9580* & **S** 11870 (E North Am)
0100-0130	**W** Su *6195* & **W** Su *7115* (E North Am)
0130-0200	**W** *6195* & **W** *7115* (E North Am)
1400-1430	**W** *11835* (Australasia)
2030-2100	▬ *7230* (Australasia)
2100-2130	▬ Sa *6100* (W Europe), Sa *7230* (Australasia)
2330-2400	**S** *9580* & **S** 11870 (E North Am)

ELWA spoke to Liberians in their own languages. Here, a local deejay entertains listeners. SIM

Weird Words

PASSPORT's Ultimate Glossary of World Band Terms and Abbreviations

All sorts of terms and abbreviations are used in world band radio. Some are specialized and benefit from explanation; several are foreign words that need translation; and yet others are simply adaptations of everyday usage.

Here, then, is PASSPORT's A-Z guide to what's what in world band buzzwords—including what each one means. For a thorough writeup on nomenclature used in evaluating how well a world band radio performs, see the Radio Database International White Paper, *How to Interpret Receiver Specifications and Lab Tests*.

Active Antenna. An antenna that electronically amplifies signals. Active antennas are typically mounted indoors, but some models can also be mounted outdoors. Active antennas take up relatively little space, but their amplification circuits may introduce certain types of problems that can result in unwanted sounds being heard. *See* Passive Antenna.

Adjacent-Channel Rejection. *See* Selectivity.

AGC. *See* Automatic Gain Control.

Alt. Freq. Alternative frequency or channel. Frequency or channel that may be used in place of the regularly scheduled one.

Amateur Radio. *See* Hams.

AM Band. The local radio band, which currently runs from 520 to 1611 kHz (530–1705 kHz in the Western Hemisphere), within the Medium Frequency (MF) range of the radio spectrum. Outside North America, it is usually called the mediumwave (MW) band. However, in parts of Latin America it is sometimes called, by the general public and a few stations, *onda larga*—longwave—strictly speaking, a misnomer.

Amplified Antenna. *See* Active Antenna.

Analog Frequency Readout. Needle-and-dial or "slide-rule" tuning, greatly inferior to synthesized tuning for scanning the world band airwaves. *See* Synthesizer.

Audio Quality. At PASSPORT, audio quality refers to what in computer testing is called "benchmark" quality. This means, primarily, the freedom from distortion of a signal fed through a receiver's entire circuitry—*not* just the audio stage—from the antenna input through to the speaker terminals. A lesser characteristic of audio quality is the audio bandwidth needed for pleasant world band reception of music. Also, *see* Enhanced Fidelity.

Automatic Gain Control (AGC). Smooths out fluctuations in signal strength brought about by fading, a regular occurrence with world band signals.

AV. A Voz—Portuguese for "The Voice." In PASSPORT, this term is also used to represent "The Voice of."

Bandwidth. A key variable that determines selectivity (*see*), bandwidth is the amount of radio signal at –6 dB a radio's circuitry will let pass, and thus be heard. With world band channel spacing at 5 kHz, the best single bandwidths are usually in the vicinity of 5 to 6 kHz. Better radios offer two or more selectable bandwidths: at least one of 5 to 7 kHz or so for when a station is in the clear, and one or more others between 2 to 4 kHz for when a station is hemmed in by other signals next to it. Proper selectivity is a key determinant of the aural quality of what you hear, and some newer models of tabletop receivers have dozens of bandwidths.

Baud. Measurement of the speed by which radioteletype (*see*), radiofax (*see*) and other digital data are transmitted. Baud is properly written entirely in lower case, and thus is abbreviated as b (baud), kb (kilobaud) or Mb (Megabaud). Baud rate standards are usually set by the international CCITT regulatory body.

BC. Broadcasting, Broadcasting Company, Broadcasting Corporation.

Broadcast. A radio or television transmission meant for the general public. *Compare* Utility Stations, Hams.

BS. Broadcasting Station, Broadcasting Service.

Cd. Ciudad—Spanish for "City."

Channel. An everyday term to indicate where a station is supposed to be located on the dial. World band channels are spaced exactly 5 kHz apart. Stations operating outside this norm are "off-channel" (for these, PASSPORT provides resolution to better than 1 kHz to aid in station identification).

Chugging, Chuffing. The sound made by some synthesized tuning systems when the tuning knob is turned. Called "chugging" or "chuffing," as it is suggestive of the rhythmic "chug, chug" sound of a steam engine or "chugalug" gulping.

Cl. Club, Clube.

Cult. Cultura, Cultural.

Default. The setting at which a control of a digitally operated electronic device, including many world band radios, normally operates, and to which it will eventually return (e.g., when the radio is next switched on).

Digital Frequency Display, Digital Tuning. *See* Synthesizer.

Digital Signal Processing. Technique in which computer-type circuitry is used to enhance the readability or other characteristics of an analog audio signal. Used on certain world band supersets; also, available as an add-on accessory.

Dipole Antenna. *See* Passive Antenna.

Domestic Service. *See* DS.

DS. Domestic Service—Broadcasting intended primarily for audiences in the broadcaster's home country. However, some domestic programs are beamed on world band to expatriates and other kinfolk abroad, as well as interested foreigners. *Compare* ES.

DSP. *See* Digital Signal Processing.

DX, DXers, DXing. From an old telegraph term "to DX"; that is, to communicate over a great distance. Thus, DXers are those who specialize in finding distant or exotic stations that are considered to be rare catches. Few world band listeners are considered to be regular DXers, but many others seek out DX stations every now and then—usually by bandscanning, which is greatly facilitated by PASSPORT's Blue Pages.

Dynamic Range. The ability of a receiver to handle weak signals in the presence of strong competing signals within or near the same world band segment (*see* World Band Spectrum). Sets with inferior dynamic range sometimes "overload," especially with external antennas, causing a mishmash of false signals up and down—and even beyond—the segment being received.

Earliest Heard (or Latest Heard). See key at the bottom of each Blue Page. If the PASSPORT monitoring team cannot establish the definite sign-on (or sign-off) time of a station, the earliest (or latest) time that the station could be traced is indicated by a left-facing or right-facing "arrowhead flag." This means that the station almost certainly operates beyond the time shown by that "flag." It also means that, unless you live relatively close to the station, you're unlikely to be able to hear it beyond that "flagged" time.

EBS. Economic Broadcasting Station, a type of station found in China.

ECSS. Exalted-carrier selectable sideband, a term no longer in general use, yet sometimes mis-used when it does appear. Properly used, it refers to the manual tuning of a conventional AM-mode signal using the receiver's single-sideband circuitry to zero-beat the receiver's BFO with the transmitted signal's carrier. *See* Synchronous Detector.

Ed, Educ. Educational, Educação, Educadora.

Electrical Noise. *See* Noise.

Em. Emissora, Emisora, Emissor, Emetteur—in effect, "station" in various languages.

Enhanced Fidelity. Radios with good audio performance and certain types of high-tech circuitry can improve the fidelity of world band signals. Among the newer fidelity-enhancing techniques is synchronous detection (*see*), especially when coupled with selectable sideband. Another potential technological advance to improve fidelity is digital world band transmission, which is actively being researched and tested.

EP. Emissor Provincial—Portuguese for "Provincial Station."

ER. Emissor Regional—Portuguese for "Regional Station."

Ergonomics. How handy and comfortable—intuitive—a set is to operate, especially hour after hour.

ES. External Service—Broadcasting intended primarily for audiences abroad. *Compare* DS.

External Service. *See* ES.

F. Friday.

Fax. *See* Radiofax.

Feeder, Shortwave. A utility transmission from the broadcaster's home country to a relay site or placement facility some distance away. Although these specialized transmissions carry world band programming, they are not intended to be received by the general public. Many world band radios can process these quasi-broadcasts anyway. Feeders operate in lower sideband (LSB), upper sideband (USB) or independent sideband (termed ISL if heard on the lower side, ISU if heard on the upper side) modes. Nearly all shortwave feeders have now been replaced by satellite and Internet audio feeders. *See* Single Sideband, Utility Stations.

Frequency. The standard term to indicate where a station is located on the dial—regardless of whether it is "on-channel" or "off-channel" (*see* Channel). Measured in kilohertz (kHz) or Megahertz

The Greek islands are a favorite destination for vacationers with world band radios. Swift hydroplanes connect the islands with each other and the mainland.   R. Crane

(MHz), which differ only in the placement of a decimal; e.g., 5975 kHz is the same as 5.975 MHz. Either measurement is equally valid, but to minimize confusion PASSPORT and most stations designate frequencies only in kHz.

Frequency Synthesizer. *See* Synthesizer, Frequency.

Front-End Selectivity. The ability of the initial stage of receiving circuitry to admit only limited frequency ranges into succeeding stages of circuitry. Good front-end selectivity keeps signals from other, powerful bands or segments from being superimposed upon the frequency range you're tuning. For example, a receiver with good front-end selectivity will receive only shortwave signals within the range 3200-3400 kHz. However, a receiver with mediocre front-end selectivity might allow powerful local mediumwave AM stations from 520-1700 kHz to be heard "ghosting in" between 3200 and 3400 kHz, along with the desired shortwave signals. Obviously, mediumwave AM signals don't belong on shortwave. Receivers with inadequate front-end selectivity can benefit from the addition of a preselector (*see*).

GMT. Greenwich Mean Time—*See* World Time.

Hams. Government-licensed amateur radio hobbyists who *transmit* to each other by radio, often by single sideband (*see*), within special amateur bands. Many of these bands are within the shortwave spectrum (*see*). This is the same spectrum used by world band radio, but world band and ham radio, which laymen sometimes confuse with each other, are two very separate entities. The easiest way to think of hams as making something like phone calls, whereas world band stations are like long-distance versions of ordinary FM or mediumwave AM stations.

Harmonic, Harmonic Radiation, Harmonic Signal. Usually, an unwanted weak spurious repeat of a signal in multiple(s) of the fundamental, or "real," frequency. Thus, the third harmonic of a mediumwave AM station on 1120 kHz might be heard faintly on 4480 kHz within the world band spectrum. Stations almost always try to minimize harmonic radiation, as it wastes energy and spectrum space. However, in rare cases stations have been known to amplify a harmonic signal so they can operate inexpensively on a second frequency. Also, *see* Subharmonic.

Hash. Electrical noise. *See* Noise.

High Fidelity. *See* Enhanced Fidelity.

IBS. International Broadcasting Services, Ltd., publishers of *PASSPORT TO WORLD BAND RADIO* and other international broadcasting publications.

Image Rejection. A key type of spurious-signal rejection (*see*).

Independent Sideband. *See* Single Sideband.

Interference. Sounds from other signals, notably on the same ("co-channel") frequency or nearby channels, that are disturbing the one you are trying to hear. Worthy radios reduce interference by having good selectivity (*see*). Nearby television sets and cable television wiring may also generate a special type of radio interference called TVI, a "growl" usually heard every 15 kHz or so.

International Reply Coupon (IRC). Sold by many post offices worldwide, IRCs amount to official international "scrip" that may be exchanged for postage in most countries of the world. Because they amount to an international form of postage repayment, they are handy for listeners trying to encourage foreign stations to write them back. However, IRCs are very costly for the amount in stamps that is provided in return. Too, some countries are not forthcoming about "cashing in" IRCs. Specifics are provided in the Addresses PLUS section of this book.

International Telecommunication Union (ITU). The regulatory body, headquartered in Geneva, for all international telecommunications, including world band radio. Sometimes incorrectly referred to as the "International Telecommunications Union." In recent years, the ITU has become increasingly ineffective as a regulatory body for world band, with much of its former role having been taken up by groups of affiliated international broadcasters voluntarily coordinating their schedules a number of times each year.

Internet Radio. *See* Web radio.

Inverted-L Antenna. *See* Passive Antenna.

Ionosphere. *See* Propagation.

IRC. *See* International Reply Coupon.

Irr. Irregular operation or hours of operation; i.e., schedule tends to be unpredictable.

ISB. Independent sideband. *See* Single Sideband.

ISL. Independent sideband, lower. *See* Feeder.

ISU. Independent sideband, upper. *See* Feeder.

ITU. *See* International Telecommunication Union.

Jamming. Deliberate interference to a transmission with the intent of discouraging listening. Jamming is practiced much less now than it was during the Cold War.

Keypad. On a world band radio, like a computer, a keypad can be used to control many variables. However, unlike a computer, the keypad on most world band radios consists of ten numeric or multifunction keys, usually supplemented by two more keys, as on a telephone keypad. Keypads are used primarily so you can enter a station's frequency for reception, and the best keypads have real keys (not a membrane) in the standard telephone format of 3x4 with "zero" under the "8" key. Many keypads are also used for presets, but this means you have to remember code numbers for stations (e.g., BBC 5975 kHz is "07"); handier radios either have separate keys for presets, or use LCD-displayed "pages" to access presets.

kHz. Kilohertz, the most common unit for measuring where a station is on the world band dial. Formerly known as "kilocycles per second," or kc/s. 1,000 kilohertz equals one Megahertz.

Kilohertz. *See* kHz.

kW. Kilowatt(s), the most common unit of measurement for transmitter power (*see*).

LCD. Liquid-crystal display. LCDs, if properly designed, are fairly easily seen in bright light, but require illumination under darker conditions. LCDs, typically gray on gray, also tend to have mediocre contrast, and sometimes can be read from only a certain angle or angles, but they consume nearly no battery power.

LED. Light-emitting diode. LEDs are very easily read in the dark or in normal room light, but consume battery power and are hard to read in bright light.

Location. The physical location of a station's transmitter, which may be different from the studio location. Transmitter location is useful as a guide to reception quality. For example, if you're in eastern North America and wish to listen to the Voice of Russia, a transmitter located in St. Petersburg will almost certainly provide better reception than one located in Siberia.

Longwave Band. The 148.5–283.5 kHz portion of the low-frequency (LF) radio spectrum used in Europe, the Near East, North Africa, Russia and Mongolia for domestic broadcasting. As a practical matter, these longwave signals, which have nothing to do with world band or other shortwave signals, are not usually audible in other parts of the world.

Longwire Antenna. See Passive Antenna.

LSB. Lower Sideband. See Feeder, Single Sideband.

LV. La Voix, La Voz—French and Spanish for "The Voice." In PASSPORT, this term is also used to represent "The Voice of."

M. Monday.

Mediumwave Band, Mediumwave AM Band. See AM Band.

Megahertz. See MHz.

Memory, Memories. See Preset.

Meters. An outdated unit of measurement used for individual world band segments of the shortwave spectrum. The frequency range covered by a given meters designation—also known as "wavelength"—can be gleaned from the following formula: *frequency (kHz) = 299,792 ÷ meters*. Thus, 49 meters comes out to a frequency of 6118 kHz—well within the range of frequencies included in that segment (see World Band Spectrum). Inversely, meters can be derived from the following: *meters = 299,792 ÷ frequency (kHz)*.

MHz. Megahertz, a common unit to measure where a station is on the dial. Formerly known as "Megacycles per second," or Mc/s. One Megahertz equals 1,000 kilohertz.

Mode. Method of transmission of radio signals. World band radio broadcasts are almost always in the analog AM mode, the same mode used in the mediumwave AM band (see). The AM mode consists of three components: two "sidebands" and one "carrier." Each sideband contains the same programming as the other, and the carrier carries no programming, so a few stations have experimented with the single-sideband (SSB) mode. SSB contains only one sideband, either the lower sideband (LSB) or upper sideband (USB), and a reduced carrier. It requires special radio circuitry to be demodulated, or made intelligible, which is the main reason SSB has not succeeded, and is not expected to succeed, as a world band mode. There are yet other modes used on shortwave, but not for world band. These include CW (Morse-type code), radiofax, RTTY (radioteletype) and narrow-band FM used by utility and ham stations. Narrow-band FM is not used for music, and is different from usual FM. See Single Sideband, ISB, ISL, ISU, LSB and USB.

N. New, Nueva, Nouvelle, Nacional, National, Nationale. *Nac. Nacional.* Spanish and Portuguese for "National."

Nat, Natl, Nat'l. National, Nationale.

Noise. Static, buzzes, pops and the like caused by the earth's atmosphere (typically lightning), and to a lesser extent by galactic noise. Also, electrical noise emanates from such man-made sources as electric blankets, fish-tank heaters, heating pads, electrical and gasoline motors, light dimmers, flickering light bulbs, non-incandescent lights, computers and computer peripherals, office machines, electrical fences, and faulty electrical utility wiring and related components.

Other. Programs are in a language other than one of the world's primary languages.

Overloading. See Dynamic Range.

Passive Antenna. An antenna that is not electronically amplified. Typically, these are mounted outdoors, although the "tape-measure" type that comes as an accessory with some portables is usually strung indoors. For world band reception, virtually all outboard models for consumers are made from wire, rather than rod-type or tubular elements. The two most common designs are the inverted-L (so-called "longwire") and trapped dipole (either horizontal or sloper). These antennas are preferable to active antennas (see), and are reviewed in detail in the Radio Database International White Paper, PASSPORT *Evaluation of Popular Outdoor Antennas (Unamplified).*

PBS. People's Broadcasting Station.

PLL (Phase-Locked Loop). With world band receivers, a PLL circuit means that the radio can be tuned digitally, often using a number of handy tuning techniques, such as a keypad and presets (see).

Power. Transmitter power *before* amplification by the antenna, expressed in kilowatts (kW). The present range of world band powers is 0.01 to 1,000 kW.

Power Lock. See Travel Power Lock.

PR. People's Republic.

Preselector. A device—typically outboard, but sometimes inboard—that effectively limits the range of frequencies which can enter a receiver's circuitry or the circuitry of an active antenna (see); that is, which improves front-end selectivity (see). For example, a preselector may let in the range 15000-16000 kHz, thus helping ensure that your receiver or active antenna will encounter no problems within that range caused by signals from, say, 5800-6200 kHz or local mediumwave AM signals (520-1705 kHz). This range usually can be varied, manually or automatically, according to the frequency to which the receiver is being tuned. A preselector may be passive (unamplified) or active (amplified).

Preset. Allows you to select a station pre-stored in a radio's memory. The handiest presets require only one push of a button, as on a car radio.

Propagation. World band signals travel, like a basketball, up and down from the station to your radio. The "floor" below is the earth's surface, whereas the "player's hand" on high is the *ionosphere*, a gaseous layer that envelops the planet. While the earth's surface remains pretty much the same from day to day, the ionosphere—nature's own passive "satellite"—varies in how it propagates radio signals, depending on how much sunlight hits the "bounce points." Thus, some world band segments do well mainly by day, whereas others are best by night. During winter there's less sunlight, so the "night bands" become unusually active, whereas the "day bands" become correspondingly less useful (see World Band Spectrum). Day-to-day changes in the sun's weather also cause short-term changes in world band radio reception; this explains why some days you can hear rare signals.

Additionally, the 11-year sunspot cycle has a long-term effect on propagation. Currently, the sunspot cycle is at a vigorous phase. This means that the upper world band segments will remain unusually lively over the coming years.

PS. Provincial Station, Pangsong.

Pto. Puerto, Porto.

QSL. See Verification.

R. Radio, Radiodiffusion, Radiodifusora, Radiodifusão, Radiophonikos, Radiostantsiya, Radyo, Radyosu, and so forth.

Radiofax, Radio Facsimile. Like ordinary telefax (facsimile by telephone lines), but by radio.

Radioteletype (RTTY). Characters, but not illustrations, transmitted by radio. See Baud.

RDI. Radio Database International, a registered trademark of International Broadcasting Services, Ltd.

Receiver. Synonym for a radio, but sometimes—especially when called a "communications receiver"—implying a radio with superior tough-signal performance.

Reduced Carrier. See Single Sideband.

Reg. Regional.

Relay. A retransmission facility, often highlighted in "Worldwide Broadcasts in English" and "Voices from Home" in PASSPORT's WorldScan® section. Relay facilities are generally considered to be located outside the broadcaster's country. Being closer to the target audience, they usually provide superior reception. See Feeder.

Rep. Republic, République, República.

RN. See R and N.

RS. Radio Station, Radiostantsiya, Radiostudiya, Radiophonikos Stathmos.

RT, RTV. Radiodiffusion Télévision, Radio Télévision, and so forth.

RTTY. See Radioteletype.

S. As an icon ▫: aired summer (midyear) only. As an ordinary letter: San, Santa, Santo, São, Saint, Sainte. Also, South.

Sa. Saturday.

Scan, Scanning. Circuitry within a radio that allows it to bandscan or memory-scan automatically.

Segments. See Shortwave Spectrum.

Taiwan's historical treasures were spared the vandalism of the Cultural Revolution. Here, the Tse Nan Taoist temple continues to stand as a monument to Chinese architectural glory. R. Crane

Selectivity. The ability of a radio to reject interference (*see*) from signals on adjacent channels. Thus, also known as adjacent-channel rejection, a key variable in radio quality. Also, *see* "Bandwidth" and "Synchronous Detector".

Sensitivity. The ability of a radio to receive weak signals; thus, also known as weak-signal sensitivity. Of special importance if you're listening during the day, or if you're located in such parts of the world as Western North America, Hawaii and Australasia, where signals tend to be relatively weak.

Shortwave Spectrum. The shortwave spectrum—also known as the High Frequency (HF) spectrum—is, strictly speaking, that portion of the radio spectrum from 3-30 MHz (3,000-30,000 kHz). However, common usage places it from 2.3-30 MHz (2,300-30,000 kHz). World band operates on shortwave within 14 discrete segments between 2.3-26.1 MHz, with the rest of the shortwave spectrum being occupied by hams (*see*) and utility stations (*see*). Also, *see* the detailed "Best Times and Frequencies" article elsewhere in this edition.

Sideband. *See* Mode.

Single Sideband, Independent Sideband. Spectrum- and power-conserving modes of transmission commonly used by utility stations and hams. Very few broadcasters use, or are expected ever to use, these modes. Many world band radios are already capable of demodulating single-sideband transmissions, and some can even process independent-sideband signals. Certain single-sideband transmissions operate with a minimum of carrier reduction, which allows them to be listened to, albeit with some distortion, on ordinary radios not equipped to demodulate single sideband. Properly designed synchronous detectors (*see*) may prevent such distortion. *See* Feeder, Mode.

Site. *See* Location.

Slew Controls. Elevator-button-type up and down controls to tune a radio. On many radios with synthesized tuning, slewing is used in lieu of tuning by knob. Better is when slew controls are complemented by a tuning knob, which is more versatile.

Sloper Antenna. *See* Passive Antenna.

SPR. Spurious (false) extra signal from a transmitter actually operating on another frequency. One such type is harmonic (*see*).

Spurious-Signal Rejection. The ability of a radio receiver not to produce false, or "ghost," signals that might otherwise interfere with the clarity of the station you're trying to hear. *See* Image Rejection.

St, Sta, Sto. Abbreviations for words that mean "Saint."

Static. *See* Noise.

Su. Sunday.

Subharmonic. A harmonic heard at 1.5 or 0.5 times the operating frequency. This anomaly is caused by the way signals are generated within vintage-model transmitters, and thus cannot take place with modern transmitters. For example, the subharmonic of a station on 3360 kHz might be heard faintly on 5040 or 1680 kHz. Also, *see* Harmonic.

Sunspot Cycle. *See* Propagation.

Synchronous Detector. World band radios are increasingly coming equipped with this high-tech circuit that greatly reduces fading distortion. Better synchronous detectors also allow for selectable sideband; that is, the ability to select the clearer of the two sidebands of a world band or other AM-mode signal. *See* Mode.

Synchronous Selectable Sideband. *See* Synchronous Detector.

Synthesizer, Frequency. Simple radios often use archaic needle-and-dial tuning that makes it difficult to find a desired channel or to tell which station you are hearing, except by ear. Other models utilize a digital frequency synthesizer to tune to signals without your having to hunt and peck. Among other things, such synthesizers allow for push-button tuning and presets, and display the exact frequency digitally—pluses that make tuning to the world considerably easier. Virtually a "must" feature.

Target. Where a transmission is beamed.

Th. Thursday.

Travel Power Lock. Control to disable the on/off switch to prevent a radio from switching on accidentally.

Transmitter Power. *See* Power.

Trapped Dipole Antenna. *See* Passive Antenna.

Tu. Tuesday.

Universal Day. *See* World Time.

Universal Time. *See* World Time.

URL. Universal Resource Locator; i.e., the Internet address for a given Webpage.

USB. Upper Sideband. *See* Feeder, Single Sideband.

UTC. *See* World Time.

Utility Stations. Most signals within the shortwave spectrum are not world band stations. Rather, they are utility stations—radio telephones, ships at sea, aircraft and the like—that transmit strange sounds (growls, gurgles, dih-dah sounds, etc.) point-to-point and are not intended to be heard by the general public. *Compare* Broadcast, Hams and Feeders.

v. Variable frequency; i.e., one that is unstable or drifting because of a transmitter malfunction or, less often, to avoid jamming or other interference.

Verification. A "QSL" card or letter from a station verifying that a listener indeed heard that particular station. In order to stand a chance of qualifying for a verification card or letter, you need to provide the station heard with, at a minimum, the following information in a three-number "SIO" code, in which "SIO 555" is best and "SIO 111" is worst:

- **S**ignal strength, with 5 being of excellent quality, comparable to that of a local mediumwave AM station, and 1 being inaudible or at least so weak as to be virtually unintelligible. 2 (faint, but somewhat intelligible), 3 (moderate strength) and 4 (good strength) represent the signal-strength levels usually encountered with world band stations.
- **I**nterference from other stations, with 5 indicating no interference whatsoever, and 1 indicating such extreme interference that the desired signal is virtually drowned out. 2 (heavy interference), 3 (moderate interference) and 4 (slight interference) represent the differing degrees of interference more typically en-

countered with world band signals. If possible, indicate the names of the interfering station(s) and the channel(s) they are on. Otherwise, at least describe what the interference sounds like.

- **O**verall quality of the signal, with 5 being best, 1 worst.
- In addition to providing SIO findings, you should indicate which programs you've heard, as well as comments on how you liked or disliked those programs. Refer to the "Addresses PLUS" section of this edition for information on where and to whom your report should be sent, and whether return postage should be included.
- Because of the time involved in listening, few stations wish to receive tape recordings of their transmissions.

Vo. Voice of.

W. As an icon ▣: aired winter only. As a regular letter: Wednesday.

Wavelength. *See* Meters.

Weak-Signal Sensitivity. *See* Sensitivity.

Webcasting. *See* Web Radio.

Web Radio. Broadcasts aired to the public over the World Wide Web. These hundreds of stations worldwide include existing FM, mediumwave AM and world band stations simulcasting over the Web ("Webcasting"), or Web-only "stations." This field is completely explained and documented in the current edition of *Passport to World Band Radio*, available from bookstores and world band dealers, or at www.passport.com.

World Band Radio. Similar to regular mediumwave AM band and FM band radio, except that world band stations can be heard over enormous distances and thus often carry news, music and entertainment programs created especially for audiences abroad. Some world band stations have audiences of up to 120 million each day. Some 600 million people worldwide are believed to listen to world band radio.

World Band Spectrum. *See* "Best Times and Frequencies" elsewhere in this edition.

World Day. *See* World Time.

World Time. Also known as Coordinated Universal Time (UTC), Greenwich Mean Time (GMT) and Zulu time (Z). With nearly 170 countries on world band radio, if each announced its own local time you would need a calculator to figure it all out. To get around this, a single international time—World Time—is used. The difference between World Time and local time is detailed in the "Addresses PLUS" section of this edition, the "Compleat Idiot's Guide to Getting Started" and especially in the last page of this edition. It is also determined simply by listening to World Time announcements given on the hour by world band stations—or minute by minute by WWV and WWVH in the United States on such frequencies as 5000, 10000 and 15000 kHz, or CHU in Canada on 3330, 7335 and 14670 kHz. A 24-hour clock format is used, so "1800 World Time" means 6:00 PM World Time. If you're in, say, North America, Eastern Time is five hours behind World Time winters and four hours behind World Time summers, so 1800 World Time would be 1:00 PM EST or 2:00 PM EDT. The easiest solution is to use a 24-hour clock set to World Time. Many radios already have these built in, and World Time clocks are also available as accessories. World Time also applies to the days of the week. So if it's 9:00 PM (21:00) Wednesday in New York during the winter, it's 0200 *Thursday* World Time.

WS. World Service.

Printed in USA

PASSPORT's Blue Pages— 1999

Channel-by-Channel Guide to World Band Schedules

If you scan the world band airwaves, you'll discover lots more stations than those aimed your way. That's because shortwave signals are capriciously scattered by the heavens, so you can often hear stations not targeted to your area.

PASSPORT's Blue Pages Help Identify Stations

But just dialing around can be frustrating if you don't have a "map"—PASSPORT's Blue Pages. Let's say that you've stumbled across something Asian-sounding on 7410 kHz at 2035 World Time. PASSPORT's Blue Pages show All India Radio in a distinctive tongue beamed to Western Europe, with a hefty 250 kW of power. These clues suggest this is probably what you're hearing, even if you're not in Europe. The Blue Pages also show that English from India will commence on that same channel in about ten minutes.

Schedules for Entire Year

Times and days of the week are in World Time; for local times, see Addresses PLUS. Some stations are shown as one hour earlier (◨) or later (◧) midyear—typically April through October. Stations may also extend their hours for holidays or sports events.

To be as helpful as possible throughout the year, PASSPORT's Blue Pages include not just observed activity and factual schedules, but also those which we have creatively opined will take place. This predictive information is original from us, and although it's of real value when tuning the airwaves, it is inherently not so exact as real-time data.

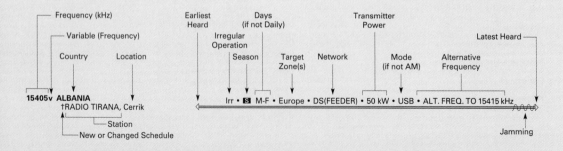

FREQUENCY   COUNTRY, STATION, LOCATION

TARGET • NETWORK • POWER (kW)

World Time
0 1 2 3 4 5 6 7 8 9 10 11 12 13 14 15 16 17 18 19 20 21 22 23 24

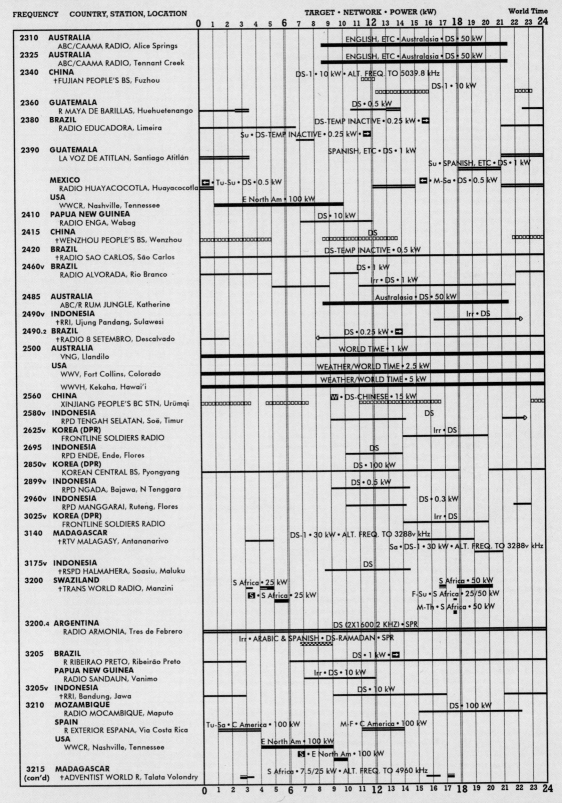

Frequency	Country, Station, Location	Details
2310	**AUSTRALIA** ABC/CAAMA RADIO, Alice Springs	ENGLISH, ETC • Australasia • DS • 50 kW
2325	**AUSTRALIA** ABC/CAAMA RADIO, Tennant Creek	ENGLISH, ETC • Australasia • DS • 50 kW
2340	**CHINA** †FUJIAN PEOPLE'S BS, Fuzhou	DS-1 • 10 kW • ALT. FREQ. TO 5039.8 kHz / DS-1 • 10 kW
2360	**GUATEMALA** R MAYA DE BARILLAS, Huehuetenango	DS • 0.5 kW
2380	**BRAZIL** RADIO EDUCADORA, Limeira	DS-TEMP INACTIVE • 0.25 kW • / Su • DS-TEMP INACTIVE • 0.25 kW •
2390	**GUATEMALA** LA VOZ DE ATITLAN, Santiago Atitlán	SPANISH, ETC • DS • 1 kW / Su • SPANISH, ETC • DS • 1 kW
	MEXICO RADIO HUAYACOCOTLA, Huayacocotla	• Tu-Su • DS • 0.5 kW / • M-Sa • DS • 0.5 kW
	USA WWCR, Nashville, Tennessee	E North Am • 100 kW
2410	**PAPUA NEW GUINEA** RADIO ENGA, Wabag	DS • 10 kW
2415	**CHINA** †WENZHOU PEOPLE'S BS, Wenzhou	DS
2420	**BRAZIL** †RADIO SAO CARLOS, São Carlos	DS-TEMP INACTIVE • 0.5 kW
2460v	**BRAZIL** RADIO ALVORADA, Rio Branco	DS • 1 kW / Irr • DS • 1 kW
2485	**AUSTRALIA** ABC/R RUM JUNGLE, Katherine	Australasia • DS • 50 kW
2490v	**INDONESIA** †RRI, Ujung Pandang, Sulawesi	Irr • DS
2490.2	**BRAZIL** †RADIO 8 SETEMBRO, Descalvado	DS • 0.25 kW •
2500	**AUSTRALIA** VNG, Llandilo	WORLD TIME • 1 kW
	USA WWV, Fort Collins, Colorado	WEATHER/WORLD TIME • 2.5 kW
	WWVH, Kekaha, Hawai'i	WEATHER/WORLD TIME • 5 kW
2560	**CHINA** XINJIANG PEOPLE'S BC STN, Urümqi	W • DS-CHINESE • 15 kW
2580v	**INDONESIA** RPD TENGAH SELATAN, Soë, Timur	DS
2625v	**KOREA (DPR)** FRONTLINE SOLDIERS RADIO	Irr • DS
2695	**INDONESIA** RPD ENDE, Ende, Flores	DS
2850v	**KOREA (DPR)** KOREAN CENTRAL BS, Pyongyang	DS • 100 kW
2899v	**INDONESIA** RPD NGADA, Bajawa, N Tenggara	DS • 0.5 kW
2960v	**INDONESIA** RPD MANGGARAI, Ruteng, Flores	DS • 0.3 kW
3025v	**KOREA (DPR)** FRONTLINE SOLDIERS RADIO	Irr • DS
3140	**MADAGASCAR** †RTV MALAGASY, Antananarivo	DS-1 • 30 kW • ALT. FREQ. TO 3288v kHz / Sa • DS-1 • 30 kW • ALT. FREQ. TO 3288v kHz
3175v	**INDONESIA** †RSPD HALMAHERA, Soasiu, Maluku	DS
3200	**SWAZILAND** †TRANS WORLD RADIO, Manzini	S Africa • 25 kW / S • S Africa • 25 kW / S Africa • 50 kW / F-Su • S Africa • 25/50 kW / M-Th • S Africa • 50 kW
3200.4	**ARGENTINA** RADIO ARMONIA, Tres de Febrero	DS (2X1600 2 KHZ) • SPR / Irr • ARABIC & SPANISH • DS-RAMADAN • SPR
3205	**BRAZIL** R RIBEIRAO PRETO, Ribeirão Preto	DS • 1 kW •
	PAPUA NEW GUINEA RADIO SANDAUN, Vanimo	Irr • DS • 10 kW
3205v	**INDONESIA** †RRI, Bandung, Jawa	DS • 10 kW
3210	**MOZAMBIQUE** RADIO MOCAMBIQUE, Maputo	DS • 100 kW
	SPAIN R EXTERIOR ESPANA, Via Costa Rica	Tu-Sa • C America • 100 kW / M-F • C America • 100 kW
	USA WWCR, Nashville, Tennessee	E North Am • 100 kW / S • E North Am • 100 kW
3215 (con'd)	**MADAGASCAR** †ADVENTIST WORLD R, Talata Volondry	S Africa • 7.5/25 kW • ALT. FREQ. TO 4960 kHz

0 1 2 3 4 5 6 7 8 9 10 11 12 13 14 15 16 17 18 19 20 21 22 23 24

SEASONAL S OR W   1-HR TIMESHIFT MIDYEAR ◧ OR ◨   JAMMING / OR ∧   EARLIEST HEARD ◁   LATEST HEARD ▷   NEW FOR 1999 †

FREQUENCY   COUNTRY, STATION, LOCATION

TARGET • NETWORK • POWER (kW)

World Time

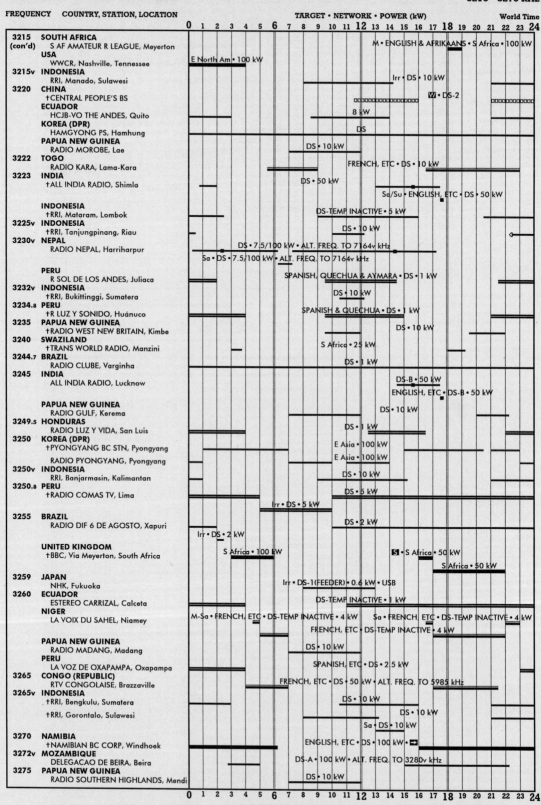

FREQUENCY	COUNTRY, STATION, LOCATION	TARGET • NETWORK • POWER (kW)
3215 (con'd)	**SOUTH AFRICA** S AF AMATEUR R LEAGUE, Meyerton	M • ENGLISH & AFRIKAANS • S Africa • 100 kW
	USA WWCR, Nashville, Tennessee	E North Am • 100 kW
3215v	**INDONESIA** RRI, Manado, Sulawesi	Irr • DS • 10 kW
3220	**CHINA** †CENTRAL PEOPLE'S BS	W • DS-2
	ECUADOR HCJB-VO THE ANDES, Quito	8 kW
	KOREA (DPR) HAMGYONG PS, Hamhung	DS
	PAPUA NEW GUINEA RADIO MOROBE, Lae	DS • 10 kW
3222	**TOGO** RADIO KARA, Lama-Kara	FRENCH, ETC • DS • 10 kW
3223	**INDIA** †ALL INDIA RADIO, Shimla	DS • 50 kW Sa/Su • ENGLISH, ETC • DS • 50 kW
	INDONESIA †RRI, Mataram, Lombok	DS-TEMP INACTIVE • 5 kW
3225v	**INDONESIA** †RRI, Tanjungpinang, Riau	DS • 10 kW
3230v	**NEPAL** RADIO NEPAL, Harriharpur	DS • 7.5/100 kW • ALT. FREQ. TO 7164v kHz Sa • DS • 7.5/100 kW • ALT. FREQ. TO 7164v kHz
	PERU R SOL DE LOS ANDES, Juliaca	SPANISH, QUECHUA & AYMARA • DS • 1 kW
3232v	**INDONESIA** †RRI, Bukittinggi, Sumatera	DS • 10 kW
3234.8	**PERU** †R LUZ Y SONIDO, Huánuco	SPANISH & QUECHUA • DS • 1 kW
3235	**PAPUA NEW GUINEA** †RADIO WEST NEW BRITAIN, Kimbe	DS • 10 kW
3240	**SWAZILAND** †TRANS WORLD RADIO, Manzini	S Africa • 25 kW
3244.7	**BRAZIL** RADIO CLUBE, Varginha	DS • 1 kW
3245	**INDIA** ALL INDIA RADIO, Lucknow	DS-B • 50 kW ENGLISH, ETC • DS-B • 50 kW
	PAPUA NEW GUINEA RADIO GULF, Kerema	DS • 10 kW
3249.5	**HONDURAS** RADIO LUZ Y VIDA, San Luis	DS • 1 kW
3250	**KOREA (DPR)** †PYONGYANG BC STN, Pyongyang	E Asia • 100 kW
	RADIO PYONGYANG, Pyongyang	E Asia • 100 kW
3250v	**INDONESIA** RRI, Banjarmasin, Kalimantan	DS • 10 kW
3250.8	**PERU** †RADIO COMAS TV, Lima	DS • 5 kW Irr • DS • 5 kW
3255	**BRAZIL** RADIO DIF 6 DE AGOSTO, Xapuri	DS • 2 kW Irr • DS • 2 kW
	UNITED KINGDOM †BBC, Via Meyerton, South Africa	S Africa • 100 kW S • S Africa • 50 kW S Africa • 50 kW
3259	**JAPAN** NHK, Fukuoka	Irr • DS-1 (FEEDER) • 0.6 kW • USB
3260	**ECUADOR** ESTEREO CARRIZAL, Calceta	DS-TEMP INACTIVE • 1 kW
	NIGER LA VOIX DU SAHEL, Niamey	M-Sa • FRENCH, ETC • DS-TEMP INACTIVE • 4 kW Sa • FRENCH, ETC • DS-TEMP INACTIVE • 4 kW FRENCH, ETC • DS-TEMP INACTIVE • 4 kW
	PAPUA NEW GUINEA RADIO MADANG, Madang	DS • 10 kW
	PERU LA VOZ DE OXAPAMPA, Oxapampa	SPANISH, ETC • DS • 2.5 kW
3265	**CONGO (REPUBLIC)** RTV CONGOLAISE, Brazzaville	FRENCH, ETC • DS • 50 kW • ALT. FREQ. TO 5985 kHz
3265v	**INDONESIA** †RRI, Bengkulu, Sumatera	DS • 10 kW
	†RRI, Gorontalo, Sulawesi	DS • 10 kW Sa • DS • 10 kW
3270	**NAMIBIA** †NAMIBIAN BC CORP, Windhoek	ENGLISH, ETC • DS • 100 kW • ➡
3272v	**MOZAMBIQUE** DELEGACAO DE BEIRA, Beira	DS-A • 100 kW • ALT. FREQ. TO 3280v kHz
3275	**PAPUA NEW GUINEA** RADIO SOUTHERN HIGHLANDS, Mendi	DS • 10 kW

ENGLISH ▬   ARABIC ∾∾∾   CHINESE □□□   FRENCH ▬▬   GERMAN ▬▬   RUSSIAN ══   SPANISH ▬▬   OTHER ▬

FREQUENCY   COUNTRY, STATION, LOCATION   TARGET • NETWORK • POWER (kW)   World Time

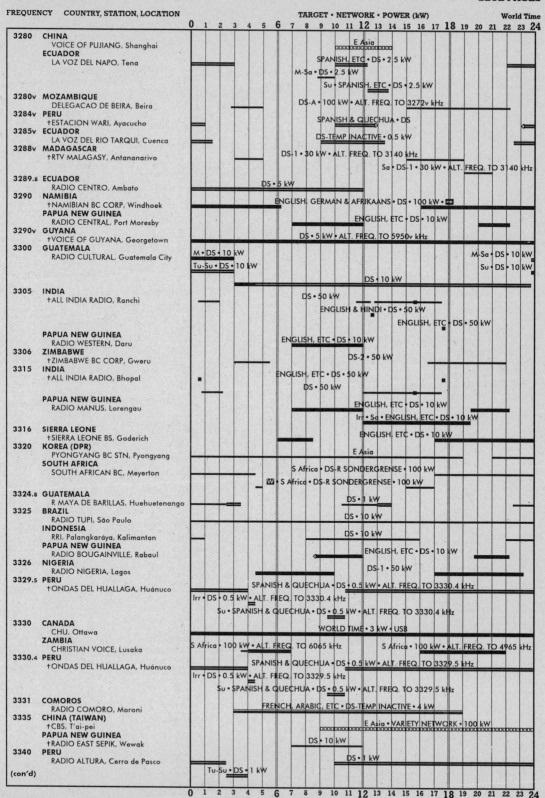

Freq	Country / Station / Location	Notes
3280	**CHINA** VOICE OF PUJIANG, Shanghai	E Asia
	ECUADOR LA VOZ DEL NAPO, Tena	SPANISH, ETC • DS • 2.5 kW / M-Sa • DS • 2.5 kW / Su • SPANISH, ETC • DS • 2.5 kW
3280v	**MOZAMBIQUE** DELEGACAO DE BEIRA, Beira	DS-A • 100 kW • ALT. FREQ. TO 3272v kHz
3284v	**PERU** †ESTACION WARI, Ayacucho	SPANISH & QUECHUA • DS
3285v	**ECUADOR** LA VOZ DEL RIO TARQUI, Cuenca	DS-TEMP INACTIVE • 0.5 kW
3288v	**MADAGASCAR** †RTV MALAGASY, Antananarivo	DS-1 • 30 kW • ALT. FREQ. TO 3140 kHz / Sa • DS-1 • 30 kW • ALT. FREQ. TO 3140 kHz
3289.8	**ECUADOR** RADIO CENTRO, Ambato	DS • 5 kW
3290	**NAMIBIA** †NAMIBIAN BC CORP, Windhoek	ENGLISH, GERMAN & AFRIKAANS • DS • 100 kW •
	PAPUA NEW GUINEA RADIO CENTRAL, Port Moresby	ENGLISH, ETC • DS • 10 kW
3290v	**GUYANA** †VOICE OF GUYANA, Georgetown	DS • 5 kW • ALT. FREQ. TO 5950v kHz
3300	**GUATEMALA** RADIO CULTURAL, Guatemala City	M • DS • 10 kW / Tu-Su • DS • 10 kW / M-Sa • DS • 10 kW / Su • DS • 10 kW / DS • 10 kW
3305	**INDIA** †ALL INDIA RADIO, Ranchi	DS • 50 kW / ENGLISH & HINDI • DS • 50 kW / ENGLISH, ETC • DS • 50 kW
	PAPUA NEW GUINEA RADIO WESTERN, Daru	ENGLISH, ETC • DS • 10 kW
3306	**ZIMBABWE** †ZIMBABWE BC CORP, Gweru	DS-2 • 50 kW
3315	**INDIA** †ALL INDIA RADIO, Bhopal	ENGLISH, ETC • DS • 50 kW / DS • 50 kW
	PAPUA NEW GUINEA RADIO MANUS, Lorengau	ENGLISH, ETC • DS • 10 kW / Irr • Sa • ENGLISH, ETC • DS • 10 kW
3316	**SIERRA LEONE** †SIERRA LEONE BS, Goderich	ENGLISH, ETC • DS • 10 kW
3320	**KOREA (DPR)** PYONGYANG BC STN, Pyongyang	E Asia
	SOUTH AFRICA SOUTH AFRICAN BC, Meyerton	S Africa • DS-R SONDERGRENSE • 100 kW / W • S Africa • DS-R SONDERGRENSE • 100 kW
3324.8	**GUATEMALA** R MAYA DE BARILLAS, Huehuetenango	DS • 1 kW
3325	**BRAZIL** RADIO TUPI, São Paulo	DS • 10 kW
	INDONESIA RRI, Palangkaráya, Kalimantan	DS • 10 kW
	PAPUA NEW GUINEA RADIO BOUGAINVILLE, Rabaul	ENGLISH, ETC • DS • 10 kW
3326	**NIGERIA** RADIO NIGERIA, Lagos	DS-1 • 50 kW
3329.5	**PERU** †ONDAS DEL HUALLAGA, Huánuco	SPANISH & QUECHUA • DS • 0.5 kW • ALT. FREQ. TO 3330.4 kHz / Irr • DS • 0.5 kW • ALT. FREQ. TO 3330.4 kHz / Su • SPANISH & QUECHUA • DS • 0.5 kW • ALT. FREQ. TO 3330.4 kHz
3330	**CANADA** CHU, Ottawa	WORLD TIME • 3 kW • USB
	ZAMBIA CHRISTIAN VOICE, Lusaka	S Africa • 100 kW • ALT. FREQ. TO 6065 kHz / S Africa • 100 kW • ALT. FREQ. TO 4965 kHz
3330.4	**PERU** †ONDAS DEL HUALLAGA, Huánuco	SPANISH & QUECHUA • DS • 0.5 kW • ALT. FREQ. TO 3329.5 kHz / Irr • DS • 0.5 kW • ALT. FREQ. TO 3329.5 kHz / Su • SPANISH & QUECHUA • DS • 0.5 kW • ALT. FREQ. TO 3329.5 kHz
3331	**COMOROS** RADIO COMORO, Moroni	FRENCH, ARABIC, ETC • DS-TEMP INACTIVE • 4 kW
3335	**CHINA (TAIWAN)** †CBS, T'ai-pei	E Asia • VARIETY NETWORK • 100 kW
	PAPUA NEW GUINEA †RADIO EAST SEPIK, Wewak	DS • 10 kW
3340	**PERU** RADIO ALTURA, Cerro de Pasco	DS • 1 kW / Tu-Su • DS • 1 kW

(con'd)

FREQUENCY	COUNTRY, STATION, LOCATION	TARGET • NETWORK • POWER (kW)	World Time

0 1 2 3 4 5 6 7 8 9 10 11 12 13 14 15 16 17 18 19 20 21 22 23 24

3340 (con'd)	UGANDA †RADIO UGANDA, Kampala	ENGLISH, ETC • DS-TEMP INACTIVE • 10 kW
3345	INDIA †ALL INDIA RADIO, Jaipur	DS • 50 kW
		ENGLISH, ETC • DS • 50 kW
	PAPUA NEW GUINEA RADIO NORTHERN, Popondetta	ENGLISH, ETC • DS • 10 kW
	SOUTH AFRICA †CHANNEL AFRICA, Meyerton	S Africa • 100 kW
	USA †ADVENTIST WORLD R, Via South Africa	S Africa • 100 kW
3345v	INDONESIA RRI, Ternate, Maluku	DS • 10 kW
	PHILIPPINES RADYO MINDORO, Baco, Mindoro	Su • DS • 1 kW DS • 1 kW
3350	KOREA (DPR) SOUTH PYONGYANG PS, Pyŏngsong	DS
3354v	ANGOLA RADIO NACIONAL, Luanda	DS-ANTENNA 2 • 10 kW S Africa • 10 kW
3355	PAPUA NEW GUINEA RADIO SIMBU, Kundiawa	DS • 10 kW
3355v	INDONESIA †RRI, Jambi, Sumatera	DS • 7.5 kW
	†RRI, Sumenep, Jawa	DS-TEMP INACTIVE • 0.6 kW
3356	BOTSWANA RADIO BOTSWANA, Gaborone	ENGLISH, ETC • DS-TEMP INACTIVE • 50 kW
3360	ECUADOR LA VOZ DEL UPANO, Macas	DS-VERY IRREGULAR • 10 kW
	GUATEMALA LA VOZ DE NAHUALA, Nahualá	SPANISH, ETC • DS • 0.5/1 kW Su • SPANISH, ETC • DS • 0.5/1 kW
3365	BRAZIL RADIO CULTURA, Araraquara	DS • 1 kW
	INDIA †ALL INDIA RADIO, Delhi	DS • 50 kW
	PAPUA NEW GUINEA RADIO MILNE BAY, Alotau	ENGLISH, ETC • DS • 10 kW
3366	GHANA GHANA BC CORP, Accra	Sa/Su//Holidays • DS-2 • 50 kW DS-2 • 50 kW
3370	GUATEMALA RADIO TEZULUTLAN, Cobán	DS • 1 kW
		Tu-Su • SPANISH, ETC • DS • 1 kW SPANISH, ETC • DS • 1 kW
		M-Sa • SPANISH, ETC • DS • 1 kW Su • SPANISH, ETC • DS • 1 kW
		M-Sa • DS • 1 kW
3370v	MOZAMBIQUE DELEGACAO DE BEIRA, Beira	DS • 10 kW
3373.5	JAPAN NHK, Osaka	Irr • DS-2(FEEDER) • 0.3 kW • USB
3375	ANGOLA RADIO NACIONAL, Luanda	DS-NATIONAL • 10 kW
	BRAZIL RADIO CLUBE, Dourados	DS • 3.5 kW •
	RADIO EDUCADORA, Guajará Mirim	M-Sa • DS • 5 kW DS • 5 kW
	PAPUA NEW GUINEA R WESTERN HIGHLANDS, Mount Hagen	DS • 10 kW
3375v	BRAZIL RADIO NACIONAL, S Gab Cachoeira	DS • 2.5/10 kW
	INDONESIA †RRI, Medan, Sumatera	DS
3380	GUATEMALA RADIO CHORTIS, Jocotán	DS-SPANISH, CHORTI • 1 kW
		Tu-Su • DS • 1 kW M-Sa • DS-SPANISH, CHORTI • 1 kW
	MALAWI MALAWI BC CORP, Limbe	ENGLISH, ETC • DS • 100 kW
3385	BRAZIL R EDUCACAO RURAL, Tefé	DS • 1 kW
		Tu-Su • DS • 1 kW
	INDONESIA †RRI, Kupang, Timur	DS • 10 kW
	MALAYSIA R MALAYSIA SARAWAK, Miri	DS-IBAN • 10 kW
	PAPUA NEW GUINEA RADIO EAST NEW BRITAIN, Rabaul	DS • 10 kW
3390	INDIA †ALL INDIA RADIO, Gangtok	DS • 50 kW
(con'd)	UNITED KINGDOM BBC, Via Meyerton, South Africa	S Africa • 100 kW

0 1 2 3 4 5 6 7 8 9 10 11 12 13 14 15 16 17 18 19 20 21 22 23 24

ENGLISH ▬   ARABIC ≶≶≶   CHINESE ▫▫▫   FRENCH ══   GERMAN ▬▬   RUSSIAN ══   SPANISH ▬▬   OTHER ▬

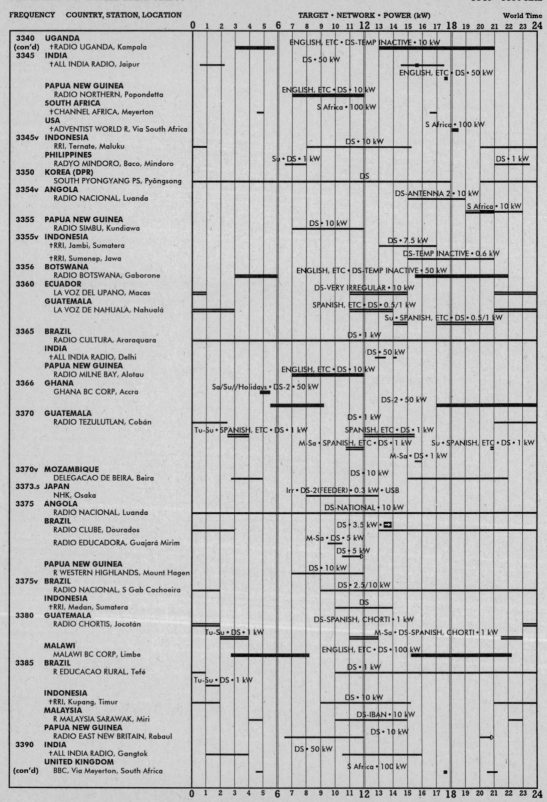

FREQUENCY   COUNTRY, STATION, LOCATION   TARGET • NETWORK • POWER (kW)   World Time

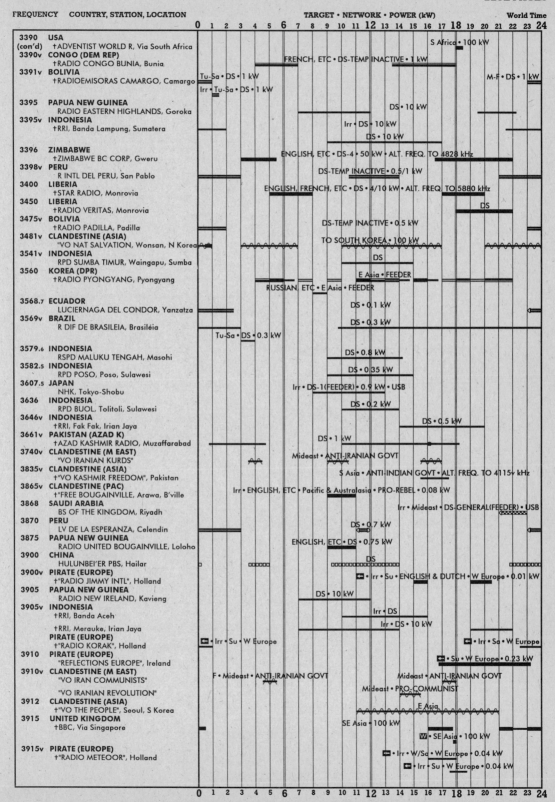

Frequency	Country, Station, Location	Target • Network • Power (kW)
3390 (con'd)	USA †ADVENTIST WORLD R, Via South Africa	S Africa • 100 kW
3390v	CONGO (DEM REP) †RADIO CONGO BUNIA, Bunia	FRENCH, ETC • DS-TEMP INACTIVE • 1 kW
3391v	BOLIVIA †RADIOEMISORAS CAMARGO, Camargo	Tu-Sa • DS • 1 kW M-F • DS • 1 kW; Irr • Tu-Sa • DS • 1 kW
3395	PAPUA NEW GUINEA RADIO EASTERN HIGHLANDS, Goroka	DS • 10 kW
3395v	INDONESIA †RRI, Banda Lampung, Sumatera	Irr • DS • 10 kW; DS • 10 kW
3396	ZIMBABWE †ZIMBABWE BC CORP, Gweru	ENGLISH, ETC • DS-4 • 50 kW • ALT. FREQ. TO 4828 kHz
3398v	PERU R INTL DEL PERU, San Pablo	DS-TEMP INACTIVE • 0.5/1 kW
3400	LIBERIA †STAR RADIO, Monrovia	ENGLISH, FRENCH, ETC • DS • 4/10 kW • ALT. FREQ. TO 5880 kHz
3450	LIBERIA †RADIO VERITAS, Monrovia	DS
3475v	BOLIVIA †RADIO PADILLA, Padilla	DS-TEMP INACTIVE • 0.5 kW
3481v	CLANDESTINE (ASIA) "VO NAT SALVATION, Wonsan, N Korea	TO SOUTH KOREA • 100 kW
3541v	INDONESIA RPD SUMBA TIMUR, Waingapu, Sumba	DS
3560	KOREA (DPR) †RADIO PYONGYANG, Pyongyang	E Asia • FEEDER; RUSSIAN, ETC • E Asia • FEEDER
3568.7	ECUADOR LUCIERNAGA DEL CONDOR, Yanzatza	DS • 0.1 kW
3569v	BRAZIL R DIF DE BRASILEIA, Brasiléia	DS • 0.3 kW; Tu-Sa • DS • 0.3 kW
3579.6	INDONESIA RSPD MALUKU TENGAH, Masohi	DS • 0.8 kW
3582.5	INDONESIA RPD POSO, Poso, Sulawesi	DS • 0.35 kW
3607.5	JAPAN NHK, Tokyo-Shobu	Irr • DS-1(FEEDER) • 0.9 kW • USB
3636	INDONESIA RPD BUOL, Tolitoli, Sulawesi	DS • 0.2 kW
3646v	INDONESIA †RRI, Fak Fak, Irian Jaya	DS • 0.5 kW
3661v	PAKISTAN (AZAD K) †AZAD KASHMIR RADIO, Muzaffarabad	DS • 1 kW
3740v	CLANDESTINE (M EAST) "VO IRANIAN KURDS"	Mideast • ANTI-IRANIAN GOVT
3835v	CLANDESTINE (ASIA) †"VO KASHMIR FREEDOM", Pakistan	S Asia • ANTI-INDIAN GOVT • ALT. FREQ. TO 4115v kHz
3865v	CLANDESTINE (PAC) †"FREE BOUGAINVILLE, Arawa, B'ville	Irr • ENGLISH, ETC • Pacific & Australasia • PRO-REBEL • 0.08 kW
3868	SAUDI ARABIA BS OF THE KINGDOM, Riyadh	Irr • Mideast • DS-GENERAL(FEEDER) • USB
3870	PERU LV DE LA ESPERANZA, Celendin	DS • 0.7 kW
3875	PAPUA NEW GUINEA RADIO UNITED BOUGAINVILLE, Loloho	ENGLISH, ETC • DS • 0.75 kW
3900	CHINA HULUNBEI'ER PBS, Hailar	DS
3900v	PIRATE (EUROPE) †"RADIO JIMMY INTL", Holland	Irr • Su • ENGLISH & DUTCH • W Europe • 0.01 kW
3905	PAPUA NEW GUINEA RADIO NEW IRELAND, Kavieng	DS • 10 kW
3905v	INDONESIA †RRI, Banda Aceh	Irr • DS
	†RRI, Merauke, Irian Jaya	Irr • DS • 10 kW
	PIRATE (EUROPE) †"RADIO KORAK", Holland	Irr • Su • W Europe; Irr • Sa • W Europe
3910	PIRATE (EUROPE) "REFLECTIONS EUROPE", Ireland	Su • W Europe • 0.23 kW
3910v	CLANDESTINE (M EAST) "VO IRAN COMMUNISTS"	F • Mideast • ANTI-IRANIAN GOVT; Mideast • ANTI-IRANIAN GOVT
	"VO IRANIAN REVOLUTION"	Mideast • PRO-COMMUNIST
3912	CLANDESTINE (ASIA) †"VO THE PEOPLE", Seoul, S Korea	E Asia
3915	UNITED KINGDOM †BBC, Via Singapore	SE Asia • 100 kW; W • SE Asia • 100 kW
3915v	PIRATE (EUROPE) †"RADIO METEOOR", Holland	Irr • W/Sa • W Europe • 0.04 kW; Irr • Su • W Europe • 0.04 kW

FREQUENCY   COUNTRY, STATION, LOCATION

TARGET • NETWORK • POWER (kW)

World Time

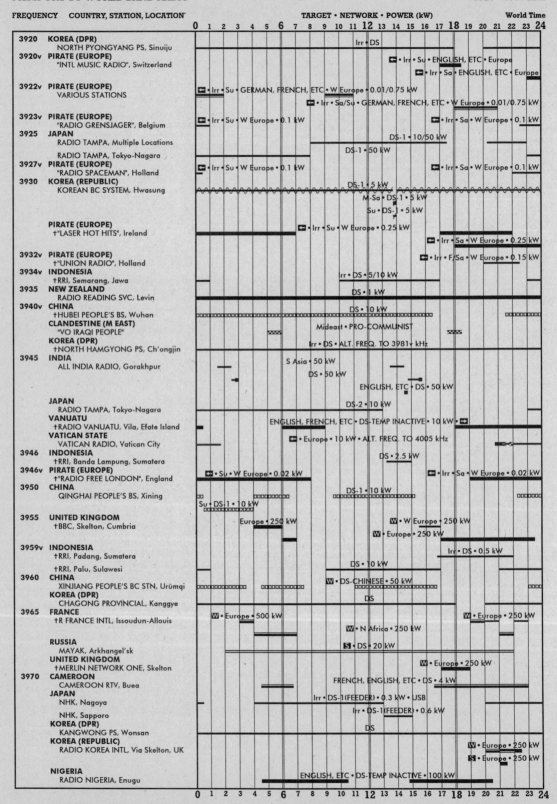

FREQUENCY	COUNTRY, STATION, LOCATION	Notes
3920	KOREA (DPR) — NORTH PYONGYANG PS, Sinuiju	Irr • DS
3920v	PIRATE (EUROPE) — "INTL MUSIC RADIO", Switzerland	Irr • Su • ENGLISH, ETC • Europe / Irr • Sa • ENGLISH, ETC • Europe
3922v	PIRATE (EUROPE) — VARIOUS STATIONS	Irr • Su • GERMAN, FRENCH, ETC • W Europe • 0.01/0.75 kW / Irr • Sa/Su • GERMAN, FRENCH, ETC • W Europe • 0.01/0.75 kW
3923v	PIRATE (EUROPE) — "RADIO GRENSJAGER", Belgium	Irr • Su • W Europe • 0.1 kW / Irr • Sa • W Europe • 0.1 kW
3925	JAPAN — RADIO TAMPA, Multiple Locations	DS-1 • 10/50 kW
	RADIO TAMPA, Tokyo-Nagara	DS-1 • 50 kW
3927v	PIRATE (EUROPE) — "RADIO SPACEMAN", Holland	Irr • Su • W Europe • 0.1 kW / Irr • Sa • W Europe • 0.1 kW
3930	KOREA (REPUBLIC) — KOREAN BC SYSTEM, Hwasung	DS-1 • 5 kW / M-Sa • DS-1 • 5 kW / Su • DS-1 • 5 kW
	PIRATE (EUROPE) — †"LASER HOT HITS", Ireland	Irr • Su • W Europe • 0.25 kW / Irr • Sa • W Europe • 0.25 kW
3932v	PIRATE (EUROPE) — †"UNION RADIO", Holland	Irr • F/Sa • W Europe • 0.15 kW
3934v	INDONESIA — †RRI, Semarang, Jawa	Irr • DS • 5/10 kW
3935	NEW ZEALAND — RADIO READING SVC, Levin	DS • 1 kW
3940v	CHINA — †HUBEI PEOPLE'S BS, Wuhan	DS • 10 kW
	CLANDESTINE (M EAST) — "VO IRAQI PEOPLE"	Mideast • PRO-COMMUNIST
	KOREA (DPR) — †NORTH HAMGYONG PS, Ch'ongjin	Irr • DS • ALT. FREQ. TO 3981v kHz
3945	INDIA — ALL INDIA RADIO, Gorakhpur	S Asia • 50 kW / DS • 50 kW / ENGLISH, ETC • DS • 50 kW
	JAPAN — RADIO TAMPA, Tokyo-Nagara	DS-2 • 10 kW
	VANUATU — †RADIO VANUATU, Vila, Efate Island	ENGLISH, FRENCH, ETC • DS-TEMP INACTIVE • 10 kW
	VATICAN STATE — VATICAN RADIO, Vatican City	Europe • 10 kW • ALT. FREQ. TO 4005 kHz
3946	INDONESIA — †RRI, Banda Lampung, Sumatera	DS • 2.5 kW
3946v	PIRATE (EUROPE) — †"RADIO FREE LONDON", England	Su • W Europe • 0.02 kW / Irr • Sa • W Europe • 0.02 kW
3950	CHINA — QINGHAI PEOPLE'S BS, Xining	DS-1 • 10 kW / Su • DS-1 • 10 kW
3955	UNITED KINGDOM — †BBC, Skelton, Cumbria	Europe • 250 kW / W • W Europe • 250 kW / W • Europe • 250 kW
3959v	INDONESIA — †RRI, Padang, Sumatera	Irr • DS • 0.5 kW
	†RRI, Palu, Sulawesi	DS • 10 kW
3960	CHINA — XINJIANG PEOPLE'S BC STN, Urümqi	W • DS-CHINESE • 50 kW
	KOREA (DPR) — CHAGONG PROVINCIAL, Kanggye	DS
3965	FRANCE — †R FRANCE INTL, Issoudun-Allouis	W • Europe • 500 kW / W • N Africa • 250 kW / W • Europe • 250 kW
	RUSSIA — MAYAK, Arkhangel'sk	S • DS • 20 kW
	UNITED KINGDOM — †MERLIN NETWORK ONE, Skelton	W • Europe • 250 kW
3970	CAMEROON — CAMEROON RTV, Buea	FRENCH, ENGLISH, ETC • DS • 4 kW
	JAPAN — NHK, Nagoya	Irr • DS-1(FEEDER) • 0.3 kW • USB
	NHK, Sapporo	Irr • DS-1(FEEDER) • 0.6 kW
	KOREA (DPR) — KANGWONG PS, Wonsan	DS
	KOREA (REPUBLIC) — RADIO KOREA INTL, Via Skelton, UK	W • Europe • 250 kW / S • Europe • 250 kW
	NIGERIA — RADIO NIGERIA, Enugu	ENGLISH, ETC • DS-TEMP INACTIVE • 100 kW

0 1 2 3 4 5 6 7 8 9 10 11 12 13 14 15 16 17 18 19 20 21 22 23 24

ENGLISH ▬   ARABIC ⌇⌇   CHINESE ▫▫▫   FRENCH ▭   GERMAN ▭   RUSSIAN ═   SPANISH ▭   OTHER ▭

FREQUENCY   COUNTRY, STATION, LOCATION

TARGET • NETWORK • POWER (kW)

World Time

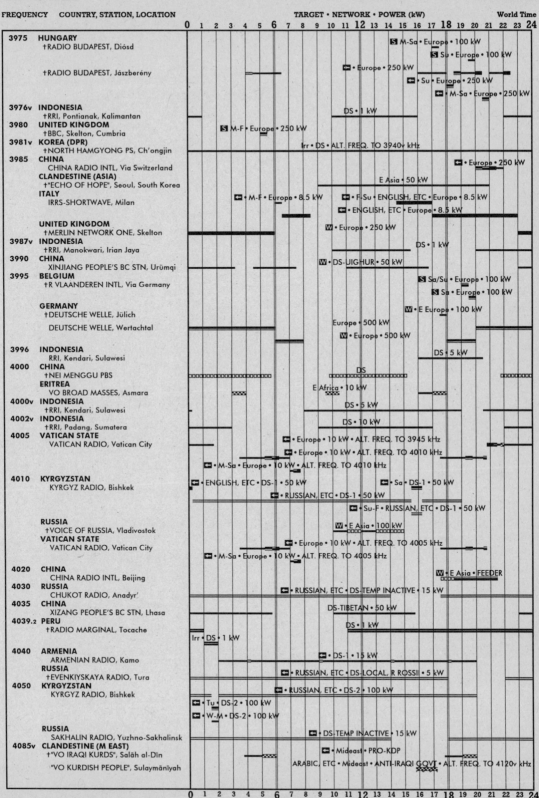

Freq	Country / Station / Location	Schedule
3975	**HUNGARY** †RADIO BUDAPEST, Diósd	S M-Sa • Europe • 100 kW
		S Su • Europe • 100 kW
	†RADIO BUDAPEST, Jászberény	• Europe • 250 kW
		• Su • Europe • 250 kW
		• M-Sa • Europe • 250 kW
3976v	**INDONESIA** †RRI, Pontianak, Kalimantan	DS • 1 kW
3980	**UNITED KINGDOM** †BBC, Skelton, Cumbria	S M-F • Europe • 250 kW
3981v	**KOREA (DPR)** †NORTH HAMGYONG PS, Ch'ongjin	Irr • DS • ALT. FREQ. TO 3940v kHz
3985	**CHINA** CHINA RADIO INTL, Via Switzerland	• Europe • 250 kW
	CLANDESTINE (ASIA) †"ECHO OF HOPE", Seoul, South Korea	E Asia • 50 kW
	ITALY IRRS-SHORTWAVE, Milan	• M-F • Europe • 8.5 kW • F-Su • ENGLISH, ETC • Europe • 8.5 kW
		• ENGLISH, ETC • Europe • 8.5 kW
	UNITED KINGDOM †MERLIN NETWORK ONE, Skelton	W • Europe • 250 kW
3987v	**INDONESIA** †RRI, Manokwari, Irian Jaya	DS • 1 kW
3990	**CHINA** XINJIANG PEOPLE'S BC STN, Urümqi	W • DS-UIGHUR • 50 kW
3995	**BELGIUM** †R VLAANDEREN INTL, Via Germany	S Sa/Su • Europe • 100 kW
		S Sa • Europe • 100 kW
	GERMANY †DEUTSCHE WELLE, Jülich	W • E Europe • 100 kW
	DEUTSCHE WELLE, Wertachtal	Europe • 500 kW
		W • Europe • 500 kW
3996	**INDONESIA** RRI, Kendari, Sulawesi	DS • 5 kW
4000	**CHINA** †NEI MENGGU PBS	DS
	ERITREA VO BROAD MASSES, Asmara	E Africa • 10 kW
4000v	**INDONESIA** †RRI, Kendari, Sulawesi	DS • 5 kW
4002v	**INDONESIA** †RRI, Padang, Sumatera	DS • 10 kW
4005	**VATICAN STATE** VATICAN RADIO, Vatican City	• Europe • 10 kW • ALT. FREQ. TO 3945 kHz
		• Europe • 10 kW • ALT. FREQ. TO 4010 kHz
		• M-Sa • Europe • 10 kW • ALT. FREQ. TO 4010 kHz
4010	**KYRGYZSTAN** KYRGYZ RADIO, Bishkek	• ENGLISH, ETC • DS-1 • 50 kW • Sa • DS-1 • 50 kW
		• RUSSIAN, ETC • DS-1 • 50 kW
		• Su-F • RUSSIAN, ETC • DS-1 • 50 kW
	RUSSIA †VOICE OF RUSSIA, Vladivostok	W • E Asia • 100 kW
	VATICAN STATE VATICAN RADIO, Vatican City	• Europe • 10 kW • ALT. FREQ. TO 4005 kHz
		• M-Sa • Europe • 10 kW • ALT. FREQ. TO 4005 kHz
4020	**CHINA** CHINA RADIO INTL, Beijing	W • E Asia • FEEDER
4030	**RUSSIA** CHUKOT RADIO, Anadyr'	• RUSSIAN, ETC • DS-TEMP INACTIVE • 15 kW
4035	**CHINA** XIZANG PEOPLE'S BC STN, Lhasa	DS-TIBETAN • 50 kW
4039.2	**PERU** †RADIO MARGINAL, Tocache	DS • 1 kW
		Irr • DS • 1 kW
4040	**ARMENIA** ARMENIAN RADIO, Kamo	• DS-1 • 15 kW
	RUSSIA †EVENKIYSKAYA RADIO, Tura	• RUSSIAN, ETC • DS-LOCAL, R ROSSII • 5 kW
4050	**KYRGYZSTAN** KYRGYZ RADIO, Bishkek	• RUSSIAN, ETC • DS-2 • 100 kW
		• Tu • DS-2 • 100 kW
		• W-M • DS-2 • 100 kW
	RUSSIA SAKHALIN RADIO, Yuzhno-Sakhalinsk	• DS-TEMP INACTIVE • 15 kW
4085v	**CLANDESTINE (M EAST)** †"VO IRAQI KURDS", Salāh al-Dīn	• Mideast • PRO-KDP
	"VO KURDISH PEOPLE", Sulaymānīyah	ARABIC, ETC • Mideast • ANTI-IRAQI GOVT • ALT. FREQ. TO 4120v kHz

FREQUENCY   COUNTRY, STATION, LOCATION

TARGET • NETWORK • POWER (kW)

World Time

0 1 2 3 4 5 6 7 8 9 10 11 12 13 14 15 16 17 18 19 20 21 22 23 24

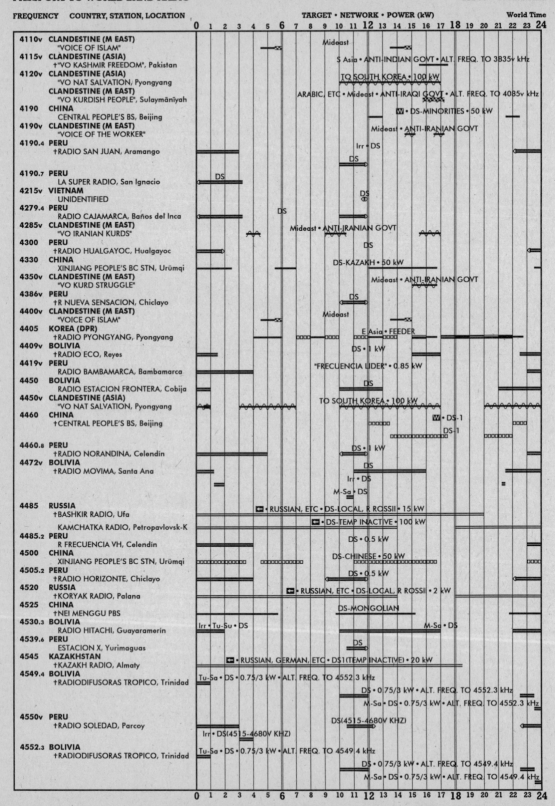

Frequency	Country, Station, Location	Notes
4110v	**CLANDESTINE (M EAST)** "VOICE OF ISLAM"	Mideast
4115v	**CLANDESTINE (ASIA)** †"VO KASHMIR FREEDOM", Pakistan	S Asia • ANTI-INDIAN GOVT • ALT. FREQ. TO 3B35v kHz
4120v	**CLANDESTINE (ASIA)** "VO NAT SALVATION, Pyongyang	TO SOUTH KOREA • 100 kW
	CLANDESTINE (M EAST) "VO KURDISH PEOPLE", Sulaymānīyah	ARABIC, ETC • Mideast • ANTI-IRAQI GOVT • ALT. FREQ. TO 4085v kHz
4190	**CHINA** CENTRAL PEOPLE'S BS, Beijing	W • DS-MINORITIES • 50 kW
4190v	**CLANDESTINE (M EAST)** "VOICE OF THE WORKER"	Mideast • ANTI-IRANIAN GOVT
4190.4	**PERU** †RADIO SAN JUAN, Aramango	Irr • DS / DS
4190.7	**PERU** LA SUPER RADIO, San Ignacio	DS
4215v	**VIETNAM** UNIDENTIFIED	DS
4279.4	**PERU** RADIO CAJAMARCA, Baños del Inca	DS
4285v	**CLANDESTINE (M EAST)** "VO IRANIAN KURDS"	Mideast • ANTI-IRANIAN GOVT
4300	**PERU** †RADIO HUALGAYOC, Hualgayoc	DS
4330	**CHINA** XINJIANG PEOPLE'S BC STN, Urümqi	DS-KAZAKH • 50 kW
4350v	**CLANDESTINE (M EAST)** "VO KURD STRUGGLE"	Mideast • ANTI-IRANIAN GOVT
4386v	**PERU** †R NUEVA SENSACION, Chiclayo	DS
4400v	**CLANDESTINE (M EAST)** "VOICE OF ISLAM"	Mideast
4405	**KOREA (DPR)** †RADIO PYONGYANG, Pyongyang	E Asia • FEEDER
4409v	**BOLIVIA** †RADIO ECO, Reyes	DS • 1 kW
4419v	**PERU** RADIO BAMBAMARCA, Bambamarca	"FRECUENCIA LIDER" • 0.85 kW
4450	**BOLIVIA** RADIO ESTACION FRONTERA, Cobija	
4450v	**CLANDESTINE (ASIA)** "VO NAT SALVATION, Pyongyang	TO SOUTH KOREA • 100 kW
4460	**CHINA** †CENTRAL PEOPLE'S BS, Beijing	W • DS-1 / DS-1
4460.8	**PERU** †RADIO NORANDINA, Celendin	DS • 1 kW
4472v	**BOLIVIA** †RADIO MOVIMA, Santa Ana	DS / Irr • DS / M-Sa • DS
4485	**RUSSIA** †BASHKIR RADIO, Ufa	RUSSIAN, ETC • DS-LOCAL, R ROSSII • 15 kW
	KAMCHATKA RADIO, Petropavlovsk-K	DS-TEMP INACTIVE • 100 kW
4485.2	**PERU** R FRECUENCIA VH, Celendin	DS • 0.5 kW
4500	**CHINA** XINJIANG PEOPLE'S BC STN, Urümqi	DS-CHINESE • 50 kW
4505.2	**PERU** †RADIO HORIZONTE, Chiclayo	DS • 0.5 kW
4520	**RUSSIA** †KORYAK RADIO, Palana	RUSSIAN, ETC • DS-LOCAL, R ROSSII • 2 kW
4525	**CHINA** †NEI MENGGU PBS	DS-MONGOLIAN
4530.3	**BOLIVIA** RADIO HITACHI, Guayaramerín	Irr • Tu-Su • DS / M-Sa • DS
4539.6	**PERU** ESTACION X, Yurimaguas	DS
4545	**KAZAKHSTAN** †KAZAKH RADIO, Almaty	RUSSIAN, GERMAN, ETC • DS1(TEMP INACTIVE) • 20 kW
4549.4	**BOLIVIA** †RADIODIFUSORAS TROPICO, Trinidad	Tu-Sa • DS • 0.75/3 kW • ALT. FREQ. TO 4552.3 kHz / DS • 0.75/3 kW • ALT. FREQ. TO 4552.3 kHz / M-Sa • DS • 0.75/3 kW • ALT. FREQ. TO 4552.3 kHz
4550v	**PERU** †RADIO SOLEDAD, Parcoy	DS(4515-4680V KHZ) / Irr • DS(4515-4680V KHZ)
4552.3	**BOLIVIA** †RADIODIFUSORAS TROPICO, Trinidad	Tu-Sa • DS • 0.75/3 kW • ALT. FREQ. TO 4549.4 kHz / DS • 0.75/3 kW • ALT. FREQ. TO 4549.4 kHz / M-Sa • DS • 0.75/3 kW • ALT. FREQ. TO 4549.4 kHz

0 1 2 3 4 5 6 7 8 9 10 11 12 13 14 15 16 17 18 19 20 21 22 23 24

ENGLISH ▬   ARABIC ⨝⨝   CHINESE □□□   FRENCH ▬▬   GERMAN ▬▬   RUSSIAN ══   SPANISH ▬▬   OTHER ▬▬

FREQUENCY   COUNTRY, STATION, LOCATION

TARGET • NETWORK • POWER (kW)

World Time

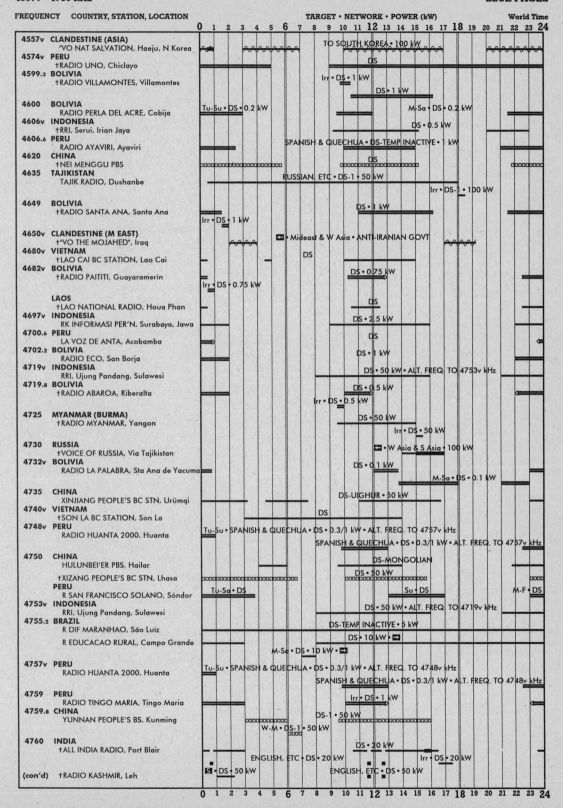

FREQUENCY	COUNTRY, STATION, LOCATION	Notes
4557v	CLANDESTINE (ASIA)	TO SOUTH KOREA • 100 kW
	"VO NAT SALVATION, Haeju, N Korea	
4574v	PERU	DS
	†RADIO UNO, Chiclayo	
4599.3	BOLIVIA	Irr • DS • 1 kW
	†RADIO VILLAMONTES, Villamontes	DS • 1 kW
4600	BOLIVIA	Tu-Su • DS • 0.2 kW M-Sa • DS • 0.2 kW
	RADIO PERLA DEL ACRE, Cobija	
4606v	INDONESIA	DS • 0.5 kW
	†RRI, Serui, Irian Jaya	
4606.6	PERU	SPANISH & QUECHUA • DS-TEMP INACTIVE • 1 kW
	RADIO AYAVIRI, Ayaviri	
4620	CHINA	DS
	†NEI MENGGU PBS	
4635	TAJIKISTAN	RUSSIAN, ETC • DS-1 • 50 kW
	TAJIK RADIO, Dushanbe	Irr • DS-1 • 100 kW
4649	BOLIVIA	DS • 1 kW
	†RADIO SANTA ANA, Santa Ana	Irr • DS • 1 kW
4650v	CLANDESTINE (M EAST)	• Mideast & W Asia • ANTI-IRANIAN GOVT
	†"VO THE MOJAHED", Iraq	
4680v	VIETNAM	DS
	†LAO CAI BC STATION, Lao Cai	
4682v	BOLIVIA	DS • 0.75 kW
	†RADIO PAITITI, Guayaramerin	Irr • DS • 0.75 kW
	LAOS	DS
	†LAO NATIONAL RADIO, Houa Phan	
4697v	INDONESIA	DS • 2.5 kW
	RK INFORMASI PER'N, Surabaya, Jawa	
4700.6	PERU	DS
	LA VOZ DE ANTA, Acobamba	
4702.2	BOLIVIA	DS • 1 kW
	RADIO ECO, San Borja	
4719v	INDONESIA	DS • 50 kW • ALT. FREQ. TO 4753v kHz
	RRI, Ujung Pandang, Sulawesi	
4719.8	BOLIVIA	DS • 0.5 kW
	†RADIO ABAROA, Riberalta	Irr • DS • 0.5 kW
4725	MYANMAR (BURMA)	DS • 50 kW
	†RADIO MYANMAR, Yangon	Irr • DS • 50 kW
4730	RUSSIA	• W Asia & S Asia • 100 kW
	†VOICE OF RUSSIA, Via Tajikistan	
4732v	BOLIVIA	DS • 0.1 kW
	RADIO LA PALABRA, Sta Ana de Yacuma	M-Sa • DS • 0.1 kW
4735	CHINA	DS-UIGHUR • 50 kW
	XINJIANG PEOPLE'S BC STN, Ürümqi	
4740v	VIETNAM	DS
	†SON LA BC STATION, Son La	
4748v	PERU	Tu-Su • SPANISH & QUECHUA • DS • 0.3/1 kW • ALT. FREQ. TO 4757v kHz
	RADIO HUANTA 2000, Huanta	SPANISH & QUECHUA • DS • 0.3/1 kW • ALT. FREQ. TO 4757v kHz
4750	CHINA	DS-MONGOLIAN
	HULUNBEI'ER PBS, Hailar	
	†XIZANG PEOPLE'S BC STN, Lhasa	DS • 50 kW
	PERU	Tu-Sa • DS Su • DS M-F • DS
	R SAN FRANCISCO SOLANO, Sóndor	
4753v	INDONESIA	DS • 50 kW • ALT. FREQ. TO 4719v kHz
	RRI, Ujung Pandang, Sulawesi	
4755.2	BRAZIL	DS-TEMP INACTIVE • 5 kW
	R DIF MARANHAO, São Luiz	DS • 10 kW •
	R EDUCACAO RURAL, Campo Grande	M-Sa • DS • 10 kW •
4757v	PERU	Tu-Su • SPANISH & QUECHUA • DS • 0.3/1 kW • ALT. FREQ. TO 4748v kHz
	RADIO HUANTA 2000, Huanta	SPANISH & QUECHUA • DS • 0.3/1 kW • ALT. FREQ. TO 4748v kHz
4759	PERU	Irr • DS • 1 kW
	RADIO TINGO MARIA, Tingo Maria	
4759.8	CHINA	DS-1 • 50 kW
	YUNNAN PEOPLE'S BS, Kunming	W-M • DS-1 • 50 kW
4760	INDIA	DS • 20 kW
	†ALL INDIA RADIO, Port Blair	ENGLISH, ETC • DS • 20 kW Irr • DS • 20 kW
(con'd)	†RADIO KASHMIR, Leh	S • DS • 50 kW ENGLISH, ETC • DS • 50 kW

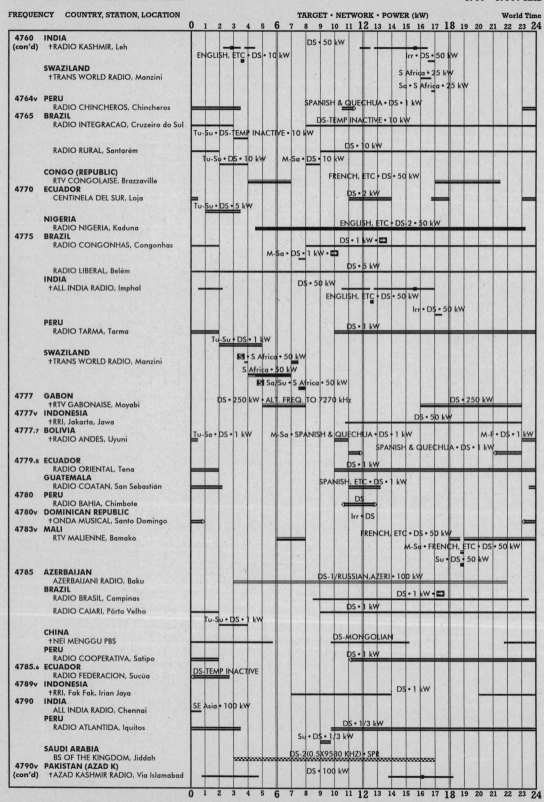

FREQUENCY   COUNTRY, STATION, LOCATION

TARGET • NETWORK • POWER (kW)   World Time

4760 **INDIA**	
(con'd) †RADIO KASHMIR, Leh	DS • 50 kW
	ENGLISH, ETC • DS • 10 kW Irr • DS • 50 kW
SWAZILAND	
†TRANS WORLD RADIO, Manzini	S Africa • 25 kW
	Sa • S Africa • 25 kW
4764v PERU	
RADIO CHINCHEROS, Chincheros	SPANISH & QUECHUA • DS • 1 kW
4765 BRAZIL	
RADIO INTEGRACAO, Cruzeiro do Sul	DS-TEMP INACTIVE • 10 kW
	Tu-Su • DS-TEMP INACTIVE • 10 kW
RADIO RURAL, Santarém	DS • 10 kW
	Tu-Su • DS • 10 kW M-Sa • DS • 10 kW
CONGO (REPUBLIC)	
RTV CONGOLAISE, Brazzaville	FRENCH, ETC • DS • 50 kW
4770 ECUADOR	
CENTINELA DEL SUR, Loja	DS • 2 kW
	Tu-Su • DS • 5 kW
NIGERIA	
RADIO NIGERIA, Kaduna	ENGLISH, ETC • DS-2 • 50 kW
4775 BRAZIL	
RADIO CONGONHAS, Congonhas	DS • 1 kW • ▣
	M-Sa • DS • 1 kW • ▣
RADIO LIBERAL, Belém	DS • 5 kW
INDIA	
†ALL INDIA RADIO, Imphal	DS • 50 kW
	ENGLISH, ETC • DS • 50 kW
	Irr • DS • 50 kW
PERU	
RADIO TARMA, Tarma	DS • 1 kW
	Tu-Su • DS • 1 kW
SWAZILAND	
†TRANS WORLD RADIO, Manzini	⑤ • S Africa • 50 kW
	S Africa • 50 kW
	⑤ Sa/Su • S Africa • 50 kW
4777 GABON	
†RTV GABONAISE, Moyabi	DS • 250 kW • ALT. FREQ. TO 7270 kHz DS • 250 kW
4777v INDONESIA	
†RRI, Jakarta, Jawa	DS • 50 kW
4777.7 BOLIVIA	
†RADIO ANDES, Uyuni	Tu-Sa • DS • 1 kW M-Sa • SPANISH & QUECHUA • DS • 1 kW M-F • DS • 1 kW
	SPANISH & QUECHUA • DS • 1 kW
4779.8 ECUADOR	
RADIO ORIENTAL, Tena	DS • 1 kW
GUATEMALA	
RADIO COATAN, San Sebastián	SPANISH, ETC • DS • 1 kW
4780 PERU	
RADIO BAHIA, Chimbote	DS
4780v DOMINICAN REPUBLIC	
†ONDA MUSICAL, Santo Domingo	Irr • DS
4783v MALI	
RTV MALIENNE, Bamako	FRENCH, ETC • DS • 50 kW
	M-Sa • FRENCH, ETC • DS • 50 kW
	Su • DS • 50 kW
4785 AZERBAIJAN	
AZERBAIJANI RADIO, Baku	DS-1/RUSSIAN, AZERI • 100 kW
BRAZIL	
RADIO BRASIL, Campinas	DS • 1 kW • ▣
RADIO CAIARI, Pôrto Velho	DS • 1 kW
	Tu-Su • DS • 1 kW
CHINA	
†NEI MENGGU PBS	DS-MONGOLIAN
PERU	
RADIO COOPERATIVA, Satipo	DS • 1 kW
4785.6 ECUADOR	
RADIO FEDERACION, Sucúa	DS-TEMP INACTIVE
4789v INDONESIA	
†RRI, Fak Fak, Irian Jaya	DS • 1 kW
4790 INDIA	
ALL INDIA RADIO, Chennai	SE Asia • 100 kW
PERU	
RADIO ATLANTIDA, Iquitos	DS • 1/3 kW
	Su • DS • 1/3 kW
SAUDI ARABIA	
BS OF THE KINGDOM, Jiddah	DS-2(0.5X9580 KHZ) • SPR
4790v PAKISTAN (AZAD K)	
(con'd) †AZAD KASHMIR RADIO, Via Islamabad	DS • 100 kW

ENGLISH ▬ ARABIC ⋙ CHINESE ▭▭ FRENCH ▭▬ GERMAN ▬▬ RUSSIAN ▭▭ SPANISH ▬▬ OTHER ▬

FREQUENCY   COUNTRY, STATION, LOCATION   TARGET • NETWORK • POWER (kW)   World Time

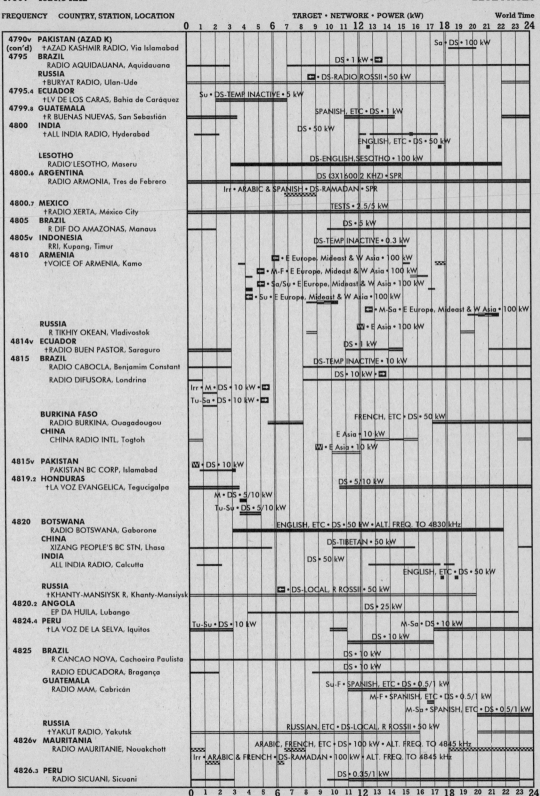

0 1 2 3 4 5 6 7 8 9 10 11 12 13 14 15 16 17 18 19 20 21 22 23 24

Frequency	Country, Station, Location	Target • Network • Power
4790v (con'd)	PAKISTAN (AZAD K) †AZAD KASHMIR RADIO, Via Islamabad	Sa • DS • 100 kW
4795	BRAZIL RADIO AQUIDAUANA, Aquidauana	DS • 1 kW •
	RUSSIA †BURYAT RADIO, Ulan-Ude	DS-RADIO ROSSII • 50 kW
4795.4	ECUADOR †LV DE LOS CARAS, Bahía de Caráquez	Su • DS-TEMP INACTIVE • 5 kW
4799.8	GUATEMALA †R BUENAS NUEVAS, San Sebastián	SPANISH, ETC • DS • 1 kW
4800	INDIA †ALL INDIA RADIO, Hyderabad	DS • 50 kW / ENGLISH, ETC • DS • 50 kW
	LESOTHO RADIO LESOTHO, Maseru	DS-ENGLISH, SESOTHO • 100 kW
4800.6	ARGENTINA RADIO ARMONIA, Tres de Febrero	DS (3X1600 2 KHZ) • SPR / Irr • ARABIC & SPANISH • DS-RAMADAN • SPR
4800.7	MEXICO †RADIO XERTA, México City	TESTS • 2.5/5 kW
4805	BRAZIL R DIF DO AMAZONAS, Manaus	DS • 5 kW
4805v	INDONESIA RRI, Kupang, Timur	DS-TEMP INACTIVE • 0.3 kW
4810	ARMENIA †VOICE OF ARMENIA, Kamo	• E Europe, Mideast & W Asia • 100 kW / M-F • E Europe, Mideast & W Asia • 100 kW / Sa/Su • E Europe, Mideast & W Asia • 100 kW / Su • E Europe, Mideast & W Asia • 100 kW / M-Sa • E Europe, Mideast & W Asia • 100 kW / W • E Asia • 100 kW
	RUSSIA R TIKHIY OKEAN, Vladivostok	
4814v	ECUADOR †RADIO BUEN PASTOR, Saraguro	DS • 1 kW
4815	BRAZIL RADIO CABOCLA, Benjamim Constant	DS-TEMP INACTIVE • 10 kW
	RADIO DIFUSORA, Londrina	DS • 10 kW • / Irr • M • DS • 10 kW • / Tu-Sa • DS • 10 kW •
	BURKINA FASO RADIO BURKINA, Ouagadougou	FRENCH, ETC • DS • 50 kW
	CHINA CHINA RADIO INTL, Togtoh	E Asia • 10 kW / W • E Asia • 10 kW
4815v	PAKISTAN PAKISTAN BC CORP, Islamabad	W • DS • 10 kW
4819.2	HONDURAS †LA VOZ EVANGELICA, Tegucigalpa	DS • 5/10 kW / M • DS • 5/10 kW / Tu-Su • DS • 5/10 kW
4820	BOTSWANA RADIO BOTSWANA, Gaborone	ENGLISH, ETC • DS • 50 kW • ALT. FREQ. TO 4830 kHz
	CHINA XIZANG PEOPLE'S BC STN, Lhasa	DS-TIBETAN • 50 kW
	INDIA ALL INDIA RADIO, Calcutta	DS • 50 kW / ENGLISH, ETC • DS • 50 kW
	RUSSIA †KHANTY-MANSIYSK R, Khanty-Mansiysk	DS-LOCAL, R ROSSII • 50 kW
4820.2	ANGOLA EP DA HUILA, Lubango	DS • 25 kW
4824.4	PERU †LA VOZ DE LA SELVA, Iquitos	Tu-Su • DS • 10 kW / M-Sa • DS • 10 kW / DS • 10 kW
4825	BRAZIL R CANCAO NOVA, Cachoeira Paulista	DS • 10 kW
	RADIO EDUCADORA, Bragança	DS • 10 kW
	GUATEMALA RADIO MAM, Cabricán	Su-F • SPANISH, ETC • DS • 0.5/1 kW / M-F • SPANISH, ETC • DS • 0.5/1 kW / M-Sa • SPANISH, ETC • DS • 0.5/1 kW
	RUSSIA †YAKUT RADIO, Yakutsk	RUSSIAN, ETC • DS-LOCAL, R ROSSII • 50 kW
4826v	MAURITANIA RADIO MAURITANIE, Nouakchott	ARABIC, FRENCH, ETC • DS • 100 kW • ALT. FREQ. TO 4845 kHz / Irr • ARABIC & FRENCH • DS-RAMADAN • 100 kW • ALT. FREQ. TO 4845 kHz
4826.3	PERU RADIO SICUANI, Sicuani	DS • 0.35/1 kW

0 1 2 3 4 5 6 7 8 9 10 11 12 13 14 15 16 17 18 19 20 21 22 23 24

FREQUENCY   COUNTRY, STATION, LOCATION

TARGET • NETWORK • POWER (kW)

World Time

0 1 2 3 4 5 6 7 8 9 10 11 12 13 14 15 16 17 18 19 20 21 22 23 24

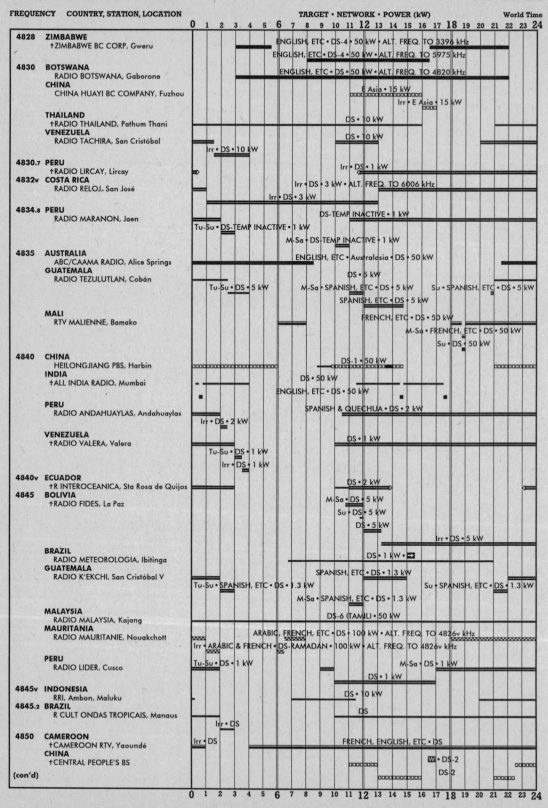

Frequency	Country, Station, Location	Details
4828	**ZIMBABWE** †ZIMBABWE BC CORP, Gweru	ENGLISH, ETC • DS-4 • 50 kW • ALT. FREQ. TO 3396 kHz / ENGLISH, ETC • DS-4 • 50 kW • ALT. FREQ. TO 5975 kHz
4830	**BOTSWANA** RADIO BOTSWANA, Gaborone	ENGLISH, ETC • DS • 50 kW • ALT. FREQ. TO 4820 kHz
	CHINA CHINA HUAYI BC COMPANY, Fuzhou	E Asia • 15 kW / Irr • E Asia • 15 kW
	THAILAND †RADIO THAILAND, Pathum Thani	DS • 10 kW
	VENEZUELA RADIO TACHIRA, San Cristóbal	DS • 10 kW / Irr • DS • 10 kW
4830.7	**PERU** †RADIO LIRCAY, Lircay	Irr • DS • 1 kW
4832v	**COSTA RICA** RADIO RELOJ, San José	Irr • DS • 3 kW • ALT. FREQ. TO 6006 kHz / Irr • DS • 3 kW
4834.8	**PERU** RADIO MARANON, Jaen	DS-TEMP INACTIVE • 1 kW / Tu-Su • DS-TEMP INACTIVE • 1 kW / M-Sa • DS-TEMP INACTIVE • 1 kW
4835	**AUSTRALIA** ABC/CAAMA RADIO, Alice Springs	ENGLISH, ETC • Australasia • DS • 50 kW
	GUATEMALA RADIO TEZULUTLAN, Cobán	DS • 5 kW / Tu-Su • DS • 5 kW / M-Sa • SPANISH, ETC • DS • 5 kW / Su • SPANISH, ETC • DS • 5 kW / SPANISH, ETC • DS • 5 kW
	MALI RTV MALIENNE, Bamako	FRENCH, ETC • DS • 50 kW / M-Sa • FRENCH, ETC • DS • 50 kW / Su • DS • 50 kW
4840	**CHINA** HEILONGJIANG PBS, Harbin	DS-1 • 50 kW
	INDIA †ALL INDIA RADIO, Mumbai	DS • 50 kW / ENGLISH, ETC • DS • 50 kW
	PERU RADIO ANDAHUAYLAS, Andahuaylas	SPANISH & QUECHUA • DS • 2 kW / Irr • DS • 2 kW
	VENEZUELA †RADIO VALERA, Valera	DS • 1 kW / Tu-Su • DS • 1 kW / Irr • DS • 1 kW
4840v	**ECUADOR** †R INTEROCEANICA, Sta Rosa de Quijos	DS • 2 kW
4845	**BOLIVIA** †RADIO FIDES, La Paz	M-Sa • DS • 5 kW / Su • DS • 5 kW / DS • 5 kW / Irr • DS • 5 kW
	BRAZIL RADIO METEOROLOGIA, Ibitinga	DS • 1 kW
	GUATEMALA RADIO K'EKCHI, San Cristóbal V	SPANISH, ETC • DS • 1.3 kW / Tu-Su • SPANISH, ETC • DS • 1.3 kW / Su • SPANISH, ETC • DS • 1.3 kW / M-Sa • SPANISH, ETC • DS • 1.3 kW
	MALAYSIA RADIO MALAYSIA, Kajang	DS-6 (TAMIL) • 50 kW
	MAURITANIA RADIO MAURITANIE, Nouakchott	ARABIC, FRENCH, ETC • DS • 100 kW • ALT. FREQ. TO 4826v kHz / Irr • ARABIC & FRENCH • DS-RAMADAN • 100 kW • ALT. FREQ. TO 4826v kHz
	PERU RADIO LIDER, Cusco	Tu-Su • DS • 1 kW / M-Sa • DS • 1 kW / DS • 1 kW
4845v	**INDONESIA** RRI, Ambon, Maluku	DS • 10 kW
4845.2	**BRAZIL** R CULT ONDAS TROPICAIS, Manaus	DS / Irr • DS
4850	**CAMEROON** †CAMEROON RTV, Yaoundé	Irr • DS / FRENCH, ENGLISH, ETC • DS
	CHINA †CENTRAL PEOPLE'S BS	W • DS-2 / DS-2

(con'd)

0 1 2 3 4 5 6 7 8 9 10 11 12 13 14 15 16 17 18 19 20 21 22 23 24

ENGLISH ▬   ARABIC ⬚⬚⬚   CHINESE □□□   FRENCH ▬   GERMAN ▬   RUSSIAN ═══   SPANISH ▬   OTHER ▬

FREQUENCY   COUNTRY, STATION, LOCATION

TARGET • NETWORK • POWER (kW)

World Time

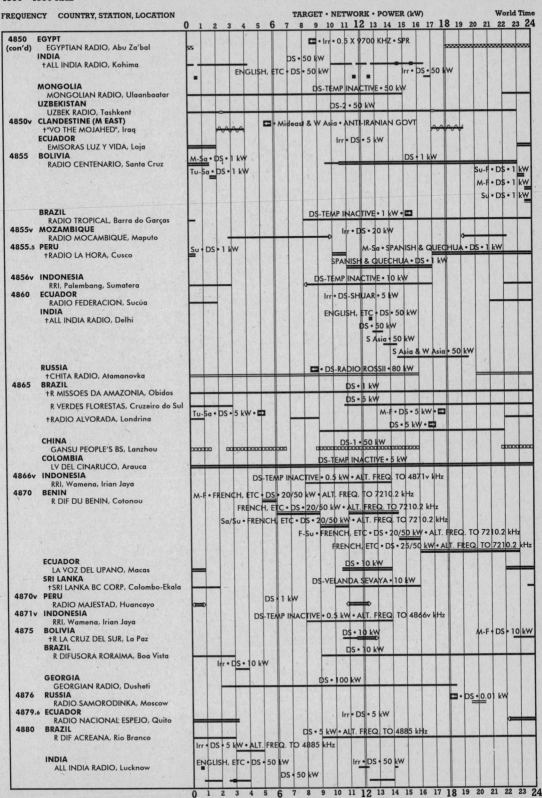

Frequency	Country, Station, Location	Listing
4850 (con'd)	EGYPT — EGYPTIAN RADIO, Abu Za'bal	Irr • 0.5 X 9700 KHZ • SPR
	INDIA — †ALL INDIA RADIO, Kohima	DS • 50 kW / ENGLISH, ETC • DS • 50 kW / Irr • DS • 50 kW
	MONGOLIA — MONGOLIAN RADIO, Ulaanbaatar	DS-TEMP INACTIVE • 50 kW
	UZBEKISTAN — UZBEK RADIO, Tashkent	DS-2 • 50 kW
4850v	CLANDESTINE (M EAST) — †"VO THE MOJAHED", Iraq	Mideast & W Asia • ANTI-IRANIAN GOVT
	ECUADOR — EMISORAS LUZ Y VIDA, Loja	Irr • DS • 5 kW
4855	BOLIVIA — RADIO CENTENARIO, Santa Cruz	M-Sa • DS • 1 kW / Tu-Sa • DS • 1 kW / DS • 1 kW / Su-F • DS • 1 kW / M-F • DS • 1 kW / Su • DS • 1 kW
	BRAZIL — RADIO TROPICAL, Barra do Garças	DS-TEMP INACTIVE • 1 kW •
4855v	MOZAMBIQUE — RADIO MOCAMBIQUE, Maputo	Irr • DS • 20 kW
4855.5	PERU — †RADIO LA HORA, Cusco	Su • DS • 1 kW / M-Sa • SPANISH & QUECHUA • DS • 1 kW / SPANISH & QUECHUA • DS • 1 kW
4856v	INDONESIA — RRI, Palembang, Sumatera	DS-TEMP INACTIVE • 10 kW
4860	ECUADOR — RADIO FEDERACION, Sucúa	Irr • DS-SHUAR • 5 kW
	INDIA — †ALL INDIA RADIO, Delhi	ENGLISH, ETC • DS • 50 kW / DS • 50 kW / S Asia • 50 kW / S Asia & W Asia • 50 kW
	RUSSIA — †CHITA RADIO, Atamanovka	DS-RADIO ROSSII • 80 kW
4865	BRAZIL — †R MISSOES DA AMAZONIA, Obidos	DS • 1 kW
	R VERDES FLORESTAS, Cruzeiro do Sul	DS • 5 kW
	†RADIO ALVORADA, Londrina	Tu-Sa • DS • 5 kW • / M-F • DS • 5 kW • / DS • 5 kW •
	CHINA — GANSU PEOPLE'S BS, Lanzhou	DS-1 • 50 kW
	COLOMBIA — LV DEL CINARUCO, Arauca	DS-TEMP INACTIVE • 5 kW
4866v	INDONESIA — RRI, Wamena, Irian Jaya	DS-TEMP INACTIVE • 0.5 kW • ALT. FREQ. TO 4871v kHz
4870	BENIN — R DIF DU BENIN, Cotonou	M-F • FRENCH, ETC • DS • 20/50 kW • ALT. FREQ. TO 7210.2 kHz / FRENCH, ETC • DS • 20/50 kW • ALT. FREQ. TO 7210.2 kHz / Sa/Su • FRENCH, ETC • DS • 20/50 kW • ALT. FREQ. TO 7210.2 kHz / F-Su • FRENCH, ETC • DS • 20/50 kW • ALT. FREQ. TO 7210.2 kHz / FRENCH, ETC • DS • 25/50 kW • ALT. FREQ. TO 7210.2 kHz
	ECUADOR — LA VOZ DEL UPANO, Macas	DS • 10 kW
	SRI LANKA — †SRI LANKA BC CORP, Colombo-Ekala	DS-VELANDA SEVAYA • 10 kW
4870v	PERU — RADIO MAJESTAD, Huancayo	DS • 1 kW
4871v	INDONESIA — RRI, Wamena, Irian Jaya	DS-TEMP INACTIVE • 0.5 kW • ALT. FREQ. TO 4866v kHz
4875	BOLIVIA — †R LA CRUZ DEL SUR, La Paz	DS • 10 kW / M-F • DS • 10 kW
	BRAZIL — R DIFUSORA RORAIMA, Boa Vista	DS • 10 kW / Irr • DS • 10 kW
	GEORGIA — GEORGIAN RADIO, Dusheti	DS • 100 kW
4876	RUSSIA — RADIO SAMORODINKA, Moscow	DS • 0.01 kW
4879.6	ECUADOR — RADIO NACIONAL ESPEJO, Quito	Irr • DS • 5 kW
4880	BRAZIL — R DIF ACREANA, Rio Branco	DS • 5 kW • ALT. FREQ. TO 4885 kHz / Irr • DS • 5 kW • ALT. FREQ. TO 4885 kHz
	INDIA — ALL INDIA RADIO, Lucknow	ENGLISH, ETC • DS • 50 kW / Irr • DS • 50 kW / DS • 50 kW

FREQUENCY   COUNTRY, STATION, LOCATION

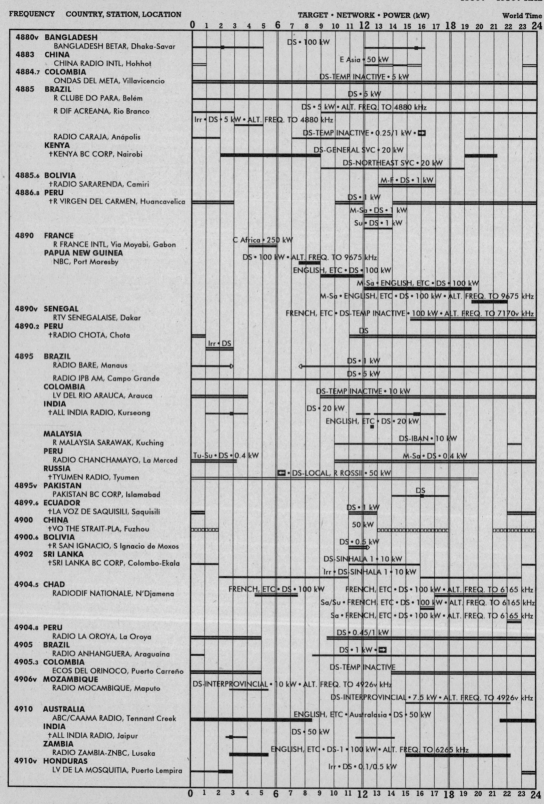

FREQUENCY	COUNTRY, STATION, LOCATION	TARGET • NETWORK • POWER (kW)
4880v	**BANGLADESH**	
	BANGLADESH BETAR, Dhaka-Savar	DS • 100 kW
4883	**CHINA**	
	CHINA RADIO INTL, Hohhot	E Asia • 50 kW
4884.7	**COLOMBIA**	
	ONDAS DEL META, Villavicencio	DS-TEMP INACTIVE • 5 kW
4885	**BRAZIL**	
	R CLUBE DO PARA, Belém	DS • 5 kW
	R DIF ACREANA, Rio Branco	DS • 5 kW • ALT. FREQ. TO 4880 kHz
		Irr • DS • 5 kW • ALT. FREQ. TO 4880 kHz
	RADIO CARAJA, Anápolis	DS-TEMP INACTIVE • 0.25/1 kW •
	KENYA	
	†KENYA BC CORP, Nairobi	DS-GENERAL SVC • 20 kW
		DS-NORTHEAST SVC • 20 kW
4885.6	**BOLIVIA**	
	†RADIO SARARENDA, Camiri	M-F • DS • 1 kW
4886.8	**PERU**	
	†R VIRGEN DEL CARMEN, Huancavelica	DS • 1 kW
		M-Sa • DS • 1 kW
		Su • DS • 1 kW
4890	**FRANCE**	
	R FRANCE INTL, Via Moyabi, Gabon	C Africa • 250 kW
	PAPUA NEW GUINEA	
	NBC, Port Moresby	DS • 100 kW • ALT. FREQ. TO 9675 kHz
		ENGLISH, ETC • DS • 100 kW
		M-Sa • ENGLISH, ETC • DS • 100 kW
		M-Sa • ENGLISH, ETC • DS • 100 kW • ALT. FREQ. TO 9675 kHz
4890v	**SENEGAL**	
	RTV SENEGALAISE, Dakar	FRENCH, ETC • DS-TEMP INACTIVE • 100 kW • ALT. FREQ. TO 7170v kHz
4890.2	**PERU**	
	†RADIO CHOTA, Chota	DS
		Irr • DS
4895	**BRAZIL**	
	RADIO BARE, Manaus	DS • 1 kW
	RADIO IPB AM, Campo Grande	DS • 5 kW
	COLOMBIA	
	LV DEL RIO ARAUCA, Arauca	DS-TEMP INACTIVE • 10 kW
	INDIA	
	†ALL INDIA RADIO, Kurseong	DS • 20 kW
		ENGLISH, ETC • DS • 20 kW
	MALAYSIA	
	R MALAYSIA SARAWAK, Kuching	DS-IBAN • 10 kW
	PERU	
	RADIO CHANCHAMAYO, La Merced	Tu-Su • DS • 0.4 kW M-Sa • DS • 0.4 kW
	RUSSIA	
	†TYUMEN RADIO, Tyumen	• DS-LOCAL, R ROSSII • 50 kW
4895v	**PAKISTAN**	
	PAKISTAN BC CORP, Islamabad	DS
4899.6	**ECUADOR**	
	†LA VOZ DE SAQUISILI, Saquisili	DS • 1 kW
4900	**CHINA**	
	†VO THE STRAIT-PLA, Fuzhou	50 kW
4900.6	**BOLIVIA**	
	†R SAN IGNACIO, S Ignacio de Moxos	DS • 0.5 kW
4902	**SRI LANKA**	
	†SRI LANKA BC CORP, Colombo-Ekala	DS-SINHALA 1 • 10 kW
		Irr • DS-SINHALA 1 • 10 kW
4904.5	**CHAD**	
	RADIODIF NATIONALE, N'Djamena	FRENCH, ETC • DS • 100 kW FRENCH, ETC • DS • 100 kW • ALT. FREQ. TO 6165 kHz
		Sa/Su • FRENCH, ETC • DS • 100 kW • ALT. FREQ. TO 6165 kHz
		Sa • FRENCH, ETC • DS • 100 kW • ALT. FREQ. TO 6165 kHz
4904.8	**PERU**	
	RADIO LA OROYA, La Oroya	DS • 0.45/1 kW
4905	**BRAZIL**	
	RADIO ANHANGUERA, Araguaína	DS • 1 kW •
4905.3	**COLOMBIA**	
	ECOS DEL ORINOCO, Puerto Carreño	DS-TEMP INACTIVE
4906v	**MOZAMBIQUE**	
	RADIO MOCAMBIQUE, Maputo	DS-INTERPROVINCIAL • 10 kW • ALT. FREQ. TO 4926v kHz
		DS-INTERPROVINCIAL • 7.5 kW • ALT. FREQ. TO 4926v kHz
4910	**AUSTRALIA**	
	ABC/CAAMA RADIO, Tennant Creek	ENGLISH, ETC • Australasia • DS • 50 kW
	INDIA	
	†ALL INDIA RADIO, Jaipur	DS • 50 kW
	ZAMBIA	
	RADIO ZAMBIA-ZNBC, Lusaka	ENGLISH, ETC • DS-1 • 100 kW • ALT. FREQ. TO 6265 kHz
4910v	**HONDURAS**	
	LV DE LA MOSQUITIA, Puerto Lempira	Irr • DS • 0.1/0.5 kW

ENGLISH ▬   ARABIC ≈≈≈   CHINESE □□□   FRENCH ══   GERMAN ▬▬   RUSSIAN ══   SPANISH ▬▬   OTHER ──

FREQUENCY   COUNTRY, STATION, LOCATION

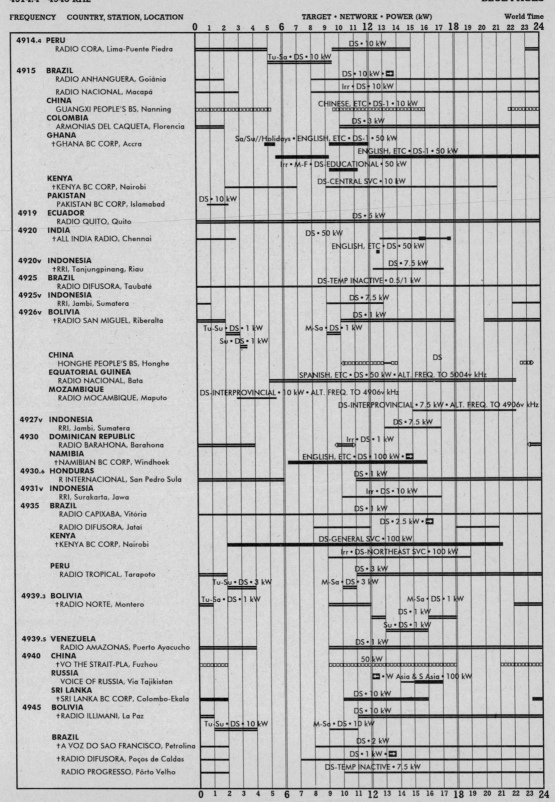

TARGET • NETWORK • POWER (kW)

World Time

FREQUENCY	COUNTRY, STATION, LOCATION	TARGET • NETWORK • POWER (kW)
4914.4	**PERU**	
	RADIO CORA, Lima-Puente Piedra	DS • 10 kW
		Tu-Sa • DS • 10 kW
4915	**BRAZIL**	
	RADIO ANHANGUERA, Goiânia	DS • 10 kW • ⊟
	RADIO NACIONAL, Macapá	Irr • DS • 10 kW
	CHINA	
	GUANGXI PEOPLE'S BS, Nanning	CHINESE, ETC • DS-1 • 10 kW
	COLOMBIA	
	ARMONIAS DEL CAQUETA, Florencia	DS • 3 kW
	GHANA	
	†GHANA BC CORP, Accra	Sa/Su//Holidays • ENGLISH, ETC • DS-1 • 50 kW
		ENGLISH, ETC • DS-1 • 50 kW
		Irr • M-F • DS-EDUCATIONAL • 50 kW
	KENYA	DS-CENTRAL SVC • 10 kW
	†KENYA BC CORP, Nairobi	
	PAKISTAN	
	PAKISTAN BC CORP, Islamabad	DS • 10 kW
4919	**ECUADOR**	
	RADIO QUITO, Quito	DS • 5 kW
4920	**INDIA**	
	†ALL INDIA RADIO, Chennai	DS • 50 kW
		ENGLISH, ETC • DS • 50 kW
4920v	**INDONESIA**	
	†RRI, Tanjungpinang, Riau	DS • 7.5 kW
4925	**BRAZIL**	
	RADIO DIFUSORA, Taubaté	DS-TEMP INACTIVE • 0.5/1 kW
4925v	**INDONESIA**	
	RRI, Jambi, Sumatera	DS • 7.5 kW
4926v	**BOLIVIA**	
	†RADIO SAN MIGUEL, Riberalta	DS • 1 kW
		Tu-Su • DS • 1 kW M-Sa • DS • 1 kW
		Su • DS • 1 kW
	CHINA	
	HONGHE PEOPLE'S BS, Honghe	DS
	EQUATORIAL GUINEA	
	RADIO NACIONAL, Bata	SPANISH, ETC • DS • 50 kW • ALT. FREQ. TO 5004v kHz
	MOZAMBIQUE	
	RADIO MOCAMBIQUE, Maputo	DS-INTERPROVINCIAL • 10 kW • ALT. FREQ. TO 4906v kHz
		DS-INTERPROVINCIAL • 7.5 kW • ALT. FREQ. TO 4906v kHz
4927v	**INDONESIA**	
	RRI, Jambi, Sumatera	DS • 7.5 kW
4930	**DOMINICAN REPUBLIC**	
	RADIO BARAHONA, Barahona	Irr • DS • 1 kW
	NAMIBIA	
	†NAMIBIAN BC CORP, Windhoek	ENGLISH, ETC • DS • 100 kW • ⊟
4930.6	**HONDURAS**	
	R INTERNACIONAL, San Pedro Sula	DS • 1 kW
4931v	**INDONESIA**	
	RRI, Surakarta, Jawa	Irr • DS • 10 kW
4935	**BRAZIL**	
	RADIO CAPIXABA, Vitória	DS • 1 kW
	RADIO DIFUSORA, Jatai	DS • 2.5 kW • ⊟
	KENYA	
	†KENYA BC CORP, Nairobi	DS-GENERAL SVC • 100 kW
		Irr • DS-NORTHEAST SVC • 100 kW
	PERU	
	RADIO TROPICAL, Tarapoto	DS • 3 kW
		Tu-Su • DS • 3 kW M-Sa • DS • 3 kW
4939.3	**BOLIVIA**	
	†RADIO NORTE, Montero	Tu-Sa • DS • 1 kW M-Sa • DS • 1 kW
		DS • 1 kW
		Su • DS • 1 kW
4939.5	**VENEZUELA**	
	RADIO AMAZONAS, Puerto Ayacucho	DS • 1 kW
4940	**CHINA**	
	†VO THE STRAIT-PLA, Fuzhou	50 kW
	RUSSIA	
	VOICE OF RUSSIA, Via Tajikistan	⊟ • W Asia & S Asia • 100 kW
	SRI LANKA	
	†SRI LANKA BC CORP, Colombo-Ekala	DS • 10 kW
4945	**BOLIVIA**	
	†RADIO ILLIMANI, La Paz	DS • 10 kW
		Tu-Su • DS • 10 kW M-Sa • DS • 10 kW
	BRAZIL	
	†A VOZ DO SAO FRANCISCO, Petrolina	DS • 2 kW
	†RADIO DIFUSORA, Poços de Caldas	DS • 1 kW • ⊟
	RADIO PROGRESSO, Pôrto Velho	DS-TEMP INACTIVE • 7.5 kW

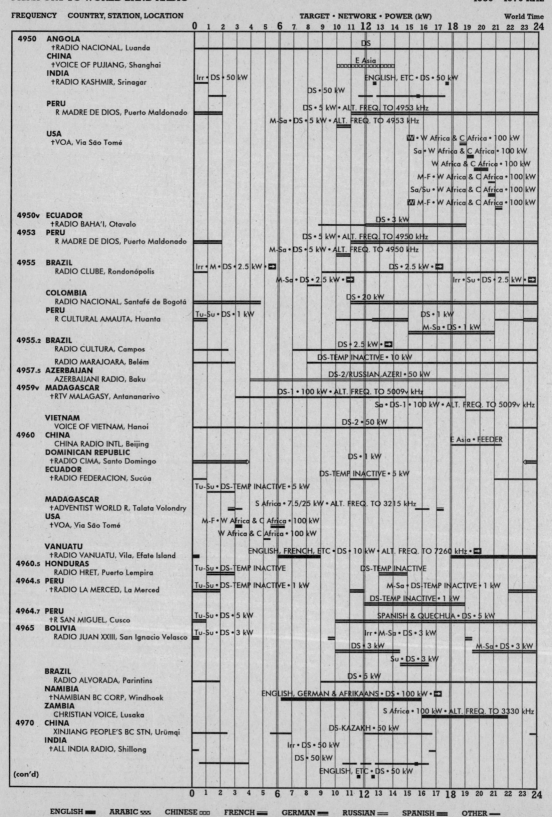

4950   ANGOLA
    †RADIO NACIONAL, Luanda
CHINA
    †VOICE OF PUJIANG, Shanghai
INDIA
    †RADIO KASHMIR, Srinagar

PERU
    R MADRE DE DIOS, Puerto Maldonado

USA
    †VOA, Via São Tomé

4950v ECUADOR
    †RADIO BAHA'I, Otavalo
4953   PERU
    R MADRE DE DIOS, Puerto Maldonado

4955   BRAZIL
    RADIO CLUBE, Rondonópolis

COLOMBIA
    RADIO NACIONAL, Santafé de Bogotá
PERU
    R CULTURAL AMAUTA, Huanta

4955.2 BRAZIL
    RADIO CULTURA, Campos
    RADIO MARAJOARA, Belém
4957.5 AZERBAIJAN
    AZERBAIJANI RADIO, Baku
4959v MADAGASCAR
    †RTV MALAGASY, Antananarivo

VIETNAM
    VOICE OF VIETNAM, Hanoi
4960   CHINA
    CHINA RADIO INTL, Beijing
DOMINICAN REPUBLIC
    †RADIO CIMA, Santo Domingo
ECUADOR
    †RADIO FEDERACION, Sucúa

MADAGASCAR
    †ADVENTIST WORLD R, Talata Volondry
USA
    †VOA, Via São Tomé

VANUATU
    †RADIO VANUATU, Vila, Efate Island
4960.5 HONDURAS
    RADIO HRET, Puerto Lempira
4964.5 PERU
    †RADIO LA MERCED, La Merced

4964.7 PERU
    †R SAN MIGUEL, Cusco
4965   BOLIVIA
    RADIO JUAN XXIII, San Ignacio Velasco

BRAZIL
    RADIO ALVORADA, Parintins
NAMIBIA
    †NAMIBIAN BC CORP, Windhoek
ZAMBIA
    CHRISTIAN VOICE, Lusaka
4970   CHINA
    XINJIANG PEOPLE'S BC STN, Urümqi
INDIA
    †ALL INDIA RADIO, Shillong

(con'd)

ENGLISH ▬   ARABIC ≋   CHINESE ▭▭▭   FRENCH ▬   GERMAN ▬   RUSSIAN ═   SPANISH ▬   OTHER ▬

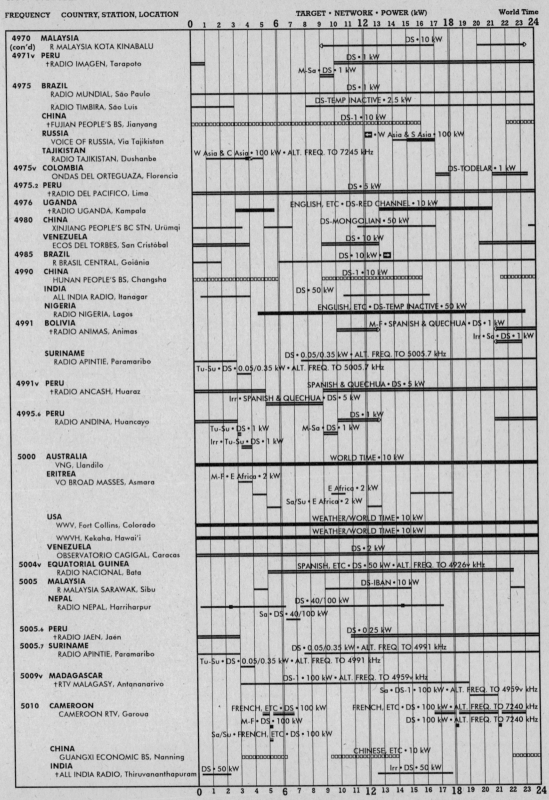

Frequency	Country, Station, Location	Target • Network • Power
4970 (con'd)	**MALAYSIA** R MALAYSIA KOTA KINABALU	DS • 10 kW
4971v	**PERU** †RADIO IMAGEN, Tarapoto	DS • 1 kW / M-Sa • DS • 1 kW
4975	**BRAZIL** RADIO MUNDIAL, São Paulo	DS • 1 kW
	RADIO TIMBIRA, São Luís	DS-TEMP INACTIVE • 2.5 kW
	CHINA †FUJIAN PEOPLE'S BS, Jianyang	DS-1 • 10 kW
	RUSSIA VOICE OF RUSSIA, Via Tajikistan	• W Asia & S Asia • 100 kW
	TAJIKISTAN RADIO TAJIKISTAN, Dushanbe	W Asia & C Asia • 100 kW • ALT. FREQ. TO 7245 kHz
4975v	**COLOMBIA** ONDAS DEL ORTEGUAZA, Florencia	DS-TODELAR • 1 kW
4975.2	**PERU** †RADIO DEL PACIFICO, Lima	DS • 5 kW
4976	**UGANDA** †RADIO UGANDA, Kampala	ENGLISH, ETC • DS-RED CHANNEL • 10 kW
4980	**CHINA** XINJIANG PEOPLE'S BC STN, Urümqi	DS-MONGOLIAN • 50 kW
	VENEZUELA ECOS DEL TORBES, San Cristóbal	DS • 10 kW
4985	**BRAZIL** R BRASIL CENTRAL, Goiânia	DS • 10 kW •
4990	**CHINA** HUNAN PEOPLE'S BS, Changsha	DS-1 • 10 kW
	INDIA ALL INDIA RADIO, Itanagar	DS • 50 kW
	NIGERIA RADIO NIGERIA, Lagos	ENGLISH, ETC • DS-TEMP INACTIVE • 50 kW
4991	**BOLIVIA** †RADIO ANIMAS, Animas	M-F • SPANISH & QUECHUA • DS • 1 kW / Irr • Sa • DS • 1 kW
	SURINAME RADIO APINTIE, Paramaribo	DS • 0.05/0.35 kW • ALT. FREQ. TO 5005.7 kHz / Tu-Su • DS • 0.05/0.35 kW • ALT. FREQ. TO 5005.7 kHz
4991v	**PERU** †RADIO ANCASH, Huaraz	SPANISH & QUECHUA • DS • 5 kW / Irr • SPANISH & QUECHUA • DS • 5 kW
4995.6	**PERU** RADIO ANDINA, Huancayo	DS • 1 kW / Tu-Su • DS • 1 kW / M-Sa • DS • 1 kW / Irr • Tu-Su • DS • 1 kW
5000	**AUSTRALIA** VNG, Llandilo	WORLD TIME • 10 kW
	ERITREA VO BROAD MASSES, Asmara	M-F • E Africa • 2 kW / E Africa • 2 kW / Sa/Su • E Africa • 2 kW
	USA WWV, Fort Collins, Colorado	WEATHER/WORLD TIME • 10 kW
	WWVH, Kekaha, Hawai'i	WEATHER/WORLD TIME • 10 kW
	VENEZUELA OBSERVATORIO CAGIGAL, Caracas	DS • 2 kW
5004v	**EQUATORIAL GUINEA** RADIO NACIONAL, Bata	SPANISH, ETC • DS • 50 kW • ALT. FREQ. TO 4926v kHz
5005	**MALAYSIA** R MALAYSIA SARAWAK, Sibu	DS-IBAN • 10 kW
	NEPAL RADIO NEPAL, Harriharpur	DS • 40/100 kW / Sa • DS • 40/100 kW
5005.6	**PERU** †RADIO JAEN, Jaén	DS • 0.25 kW
5005.7	**SURINAME** RADIO APINTIE, Paramaribo	DS • 0.05/0.35 kW • ALT. FREQ. TO 4991 kHz / Tu-Su • DS • 0.05/0.35 kW • ALT. FREQ. TO 4991 kHz
5009v	**MADAGASCAR** †RTV MALAGASY, Antananarivo	DS-1 • 100 kW • ALT. FREQ. TO 4959v kHz / Sa • DS-1 • 100 kW • ALT. FREQ. TO 4959v kHz
5010	**CAMEROON** CAMEROON RTV, Garoua	FRENCH, ETC • DS • 100 kW / FRENCH, ETC • DS • 100 kW • ALT. FREQ. TO 7240 kHz / M-F • DS • 100 kW / DS • 100 kW • ALT. FREQ. TO 7240 kHz / Sa/Su • FRENCH, ETC • DS • 100 kW
	CHINA GUANGXI ECONOMIC BS, Nanning	CHINESE, ETC • 10 kW
	INDIA †ALL INDIA RADIO, Thiruvananthapuram	DS • 50 kW / Irr • DS • 50 kW

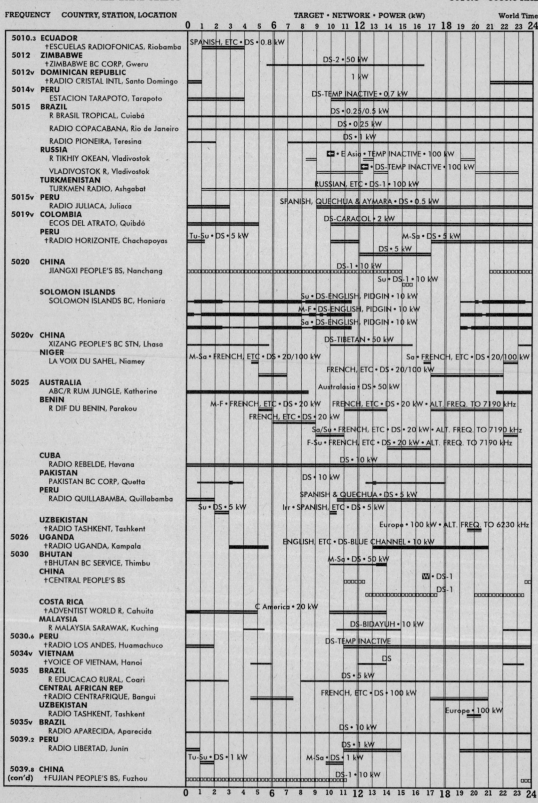

FREQUENCY   COUNTRY, STATION, LOCATION   TARGET • NETWORK • POWER (kW)   World Time

Frequency	Country / Station	Notes
5010.3	**ECUADOR** †ESCUELAS RADIOFONICAS, Riobamba	SPANISH, ETC • DS • 0.8 kW
5012	**ZIMBABWE** †ZIMBABWE BC CORP, Gweru	DS-2 • 50 kW
5012v	**DOMINICAN REPUBLIC** †RADIO CRISTAL INTL, Santo Domingo	1 kW
5014v	**PERU** ESTACION TARAPOTO, Tarapoto	DS-TEMP INACTIVE • 0.7 kW
5015	**BRAZIL** R BRASIL TROPICAL, Cuiabá	DS • 0.25/0.5 kW
	RADIO COPACABANA, Rio de Janeiro	DS • 0.25 kW
	RADIO PIONEIRA, Teresina	DS • 1 kW
	RUSSIA R TIKHIY OKEAN, Vladivostok	E Asia • TEMP INACTIVE • 100 kW
	VLADIVOSTOK R, Vladivostok	DS-TEMP INACTIVE • 100 kW
	TURKMENISTAN TURKMEN RADIO, Ashgabat	RUSSIAN, ETC • DS-1 • 100 kW
5015v	**PERU** RADIO JULIACA, Juliaca	SPANISH, QUECHUA & AYMARA • DS • 0.5 kW
5019v	**COLOMBIA** ECOS DEL ATRATO, Quibdó	DS-CARACOL • 2 kW
	PERU †RADIO HORIZONTE, Chachapoyas	Tu-Su • DS • 5 kW M-Sa • DS • 5 kW DS • 5 kW
5020	**CHINA** JIANGXI PEOPLE'S BS, Nanchang	DS-1 • 10 kW Su • DS-1 • 10 kW
	SOLOMON ISLANDS SOLOMON ISLANDS BC, Honiara	Su • DS-ENGLISH, PIDGIN • 10 kW M-F • DS-ENGLISH, PIDGIN • 10 kW Sa • DS-ENGLISH, PIDGIN • 10 kW
5020v	**CHINA** XIZANG PEOPLE'S BC STN, Lhasa	DS-TIBETAN • 50 kW
	NIGER LA VOIX DU SAHEL, Niamey	M-Sa • FRENCH, ETC • DS • 20/100 kW Sa • FRENCH, ETC • DS • 20/100 kW FRENCH, ETC • DS • 20/100 kW
5025	**AUSTRALIA** ABC/R RUM JUNGLE, Katherine	Australasia • DS • 50 kW
	BENIN R DIF DU BENIN, Parakou	M-F • FRENCH, ETC • DS • 20 kW FRENCH, ETC • DS • 20 kW • ALT. FREQ. TO 7190 kHz FRENCH, ETC • DS • 20 kW Sa/Su • FRENCH, ETC • DS • 20 kW • ALT. FREQ. TO 7190 kHz F-Su • FRENCH, ETC • DS • 20 kW • ALT. FREQ. TO 7190 kHz
	CUBA RADIO REBELDE, Havana	DS • 10 kW
	PAKISTAN PAKISTAN BC CORP, Quetta	DS • 10 kW
	PERU RADIO QUILLABAMBA, Quillabamba	SPANISH & QUECHUA • DS • 5 kW Su • DS • 5 kW Irr • SPANISH, ETC • DS • 5 kW
	UZBEKISTAN †RADIO TASHKENT, Tashkent	Europe • 100 kW • ALT. FREQ. TO 6230 kHz
5026	**UGANDA** †RADIO UGANDA, Kampala	ENGLISH, ETC • DS-BLUE CHANNEL • 10 kW
5030	**BHUTAN** †BHUTAN BC SERVICE, Thimbu	M-Sa • DS • 50 kW
	CHINA †CENTRAL PEOPLE'S BS	W • DS-1 DS-1
	COSTA RICA †ADVENTIST WORLD R, Cahuita	C America • 20 kW
	MALAYSIA R MALAYSIA SARAWAK, Kuching	DS-BIDAYUH • 10 kW
5030.6	**PERU** †RADIO LOS ANDES, Huamachuco	DS-TEMP INACTIVE
5034v	**VIETNAM** †VOICE OF VIETNAM, Hanoi	DS
5035	**BRAZIL** R EDUCACAO RURAL, Coari	DS • 5 kW
	CENTRAL AFRICAN REP †RADIO CENTRAFRIQUE, Bangui	FRENCH, ETC • DS • 100 kW
	UZBEKISTAN RADIO TASHKENT, Tashkent	Europe • 100 kW
5035v	**BRAZIL** RADIO APARECIDA, Aparecida	DS • 10 kW
5039.2	**PERU** RADIO LIBERTAD, Junín	DS • 1 kW Tu-Su • DS • 1 kW M-Sa • DS • 1 kW
5039.8 (con'd)	**CHINA** †FUJIAN PEOPLE'S BS, Fuzhou	DS-1 • 10 kW

ENGLISH ▬▬   ARABIC ≋≋≋   CHINESE □□□   FRENCH ══   GERMAN ▬▬   RUSSIAN ══   SPANISH ══   OTHER ▬

FREQUENCY   COUNTRY, STATION, LOCATION   TARGET • NETWORK • POWER (kW)   World Time

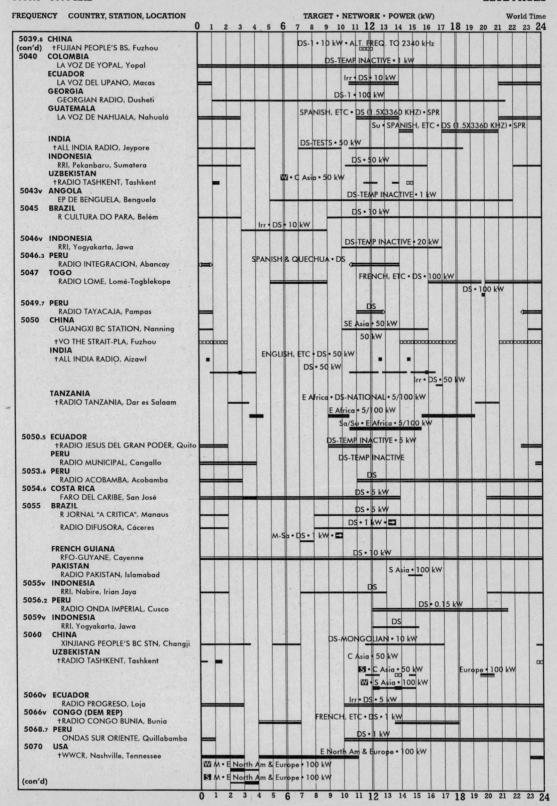

5039.8 **CHINA**	
(con'd) †FUJIAN PEOPLE'S BS, Fuzhou	DS-1 • 10 kW • ALT. FREQ. TO 2340 kHz
5040 **COLOMBIA**	
LA VOZ DE YOPAL, Yopal	DS-TEMP INACTIVE • 1 kW
ECUADOR	
LA VOZ DEL UPANO, Macas	Irr • DS • 10 kW
GEORGIA	
GEORGIAN RADIO, Dusheti	DS-1 • 100 kW
GUATEMALA	
LA VOZ DE NAHUALA, Nahualá	SPANISH, ETC • DS (1.5X3360 KHZ) • SPR
	Su • SPANISH, ETC • DS (1.5X3360 KHZ) • SPR
INDIA	
†ALL INDIA RADIO, Jeypore	DS-TESTS • 50 kW
INDONESIA	
RRI, Pekanbaru, Sumatera	DS • 50 kW
UZBEKISTAN	
†RADIO TASHKENT, Tashkent	W • C Asia • 50 kW
5043v **ANGOLA**	
EP DE BENGUELA, Benguela	DS-TEMP INACTIVE • 1 kW
5045 **BRAZIL**	
R CULTURA DO PARA, Belém	DS • 10 kW
	Irr • DS • 10 kW
5046v **INDONESIA**	
RRI, Yogyakarta, Jawa	DS-TEMP INACTIVE • 20 kW
5046.3 **PERU**	
RADIO INTEGRACION, Abancay	SPANISH & QUECHUA • DS
5047 **TOGO**	
RADIO LOME, Lomé-Togblekope	FRENCH, ETC • DS • 100 kW
	DS • 100 kW
5049.7 **PERU**	
RADIO TAYACAJA, Pampas	DS
5050 **CHINA**	
GUANGXI BC STATION, Nanning	SE Asia • 50 kW
†VO THE STRAIT-PLA, Fuzhou	50 kW
INDIA	
†ALL INDIA RADIO, Aizawl	ENGLISH, ETC • DS • 50 kW
	DS • 50 kW
	Irr • DS • 50 kW
TANZANIA	
†RADIO TANZANIA, Dar es Salaam	E Africa • DS-NATIONAL • 5/100 kW
	E Africa • 5/100 kW
	Sa/Su • E Africa • 5/100 kW
5050.5 **ECUADOR**	
†RADIO JESUS DEL GRAN PODER, Quito	DS-TEMP INACTIVE • 5 kW
PERU	
RADIO MUNICIPAL, Cangallo	DS-TEMP INACTIVE
5053.6 **PERU**	
RADIO ACOBAMBA, Acobamba	DS
5054.6 **COSTA RICA**	
FARO DEL CARIBE, San José	DS • 5 kW
5055 **BRAZIL**	
R JORNAL "A CRITICA", Manaus	DS • 5 kW
RADIO DIFUSORA, Cáceres	DS • 1 kW • ➡
	M-Sa • DS • 1 kW • ➡
FRENCH GUIANA	
RFO-GUYANE, Cayenne	DS • 10 kW
PAKISTAN	
RADIO PAKISTAN, Islamabad	S Asia • 100 kW
5055v **INDONESIA**	
RRI, Nabire, Irian Jaya	DS
5056.2 **PERU**	
RADIO ONDA IMPERIAL, Cusco	DS • 0.15 kW
5059v **INDONESIA**	
RRI, Yogyakarta, Jawa	DS
5060 **CHINA**	
XINJIANG PEOPLE'S BC STN, Changji	DS-MONGOLIAN • 10 kW
UZBEKISTAN	
†RADIO TASHKENT, Tashkent	C Asia • 50 kW
	S • C Asia • 50 kW Europe • 100 kW
	W • S Asia • 100 kW
5060v **ECUADOR**	
RADIO PROGRESO, Loja	Irr • DS • 5 kW
5066v **CONGO (DEM REP)**	
†RADIO CONGO BUNIA, Bunia	FRENCH, ETC • DS • 1 kW
5068.7 **PERU**	
ONDAS SUR ORIENTE, Quillabamba	DS • 1 kW
5070 **USA**	
†WWCR, Nashville, Tennessee	E North Am & Europe • 100 kW
	W M • E North Am & Europe • 100 kW
(con'd)	S M • E North Am & Europe • 100 kW

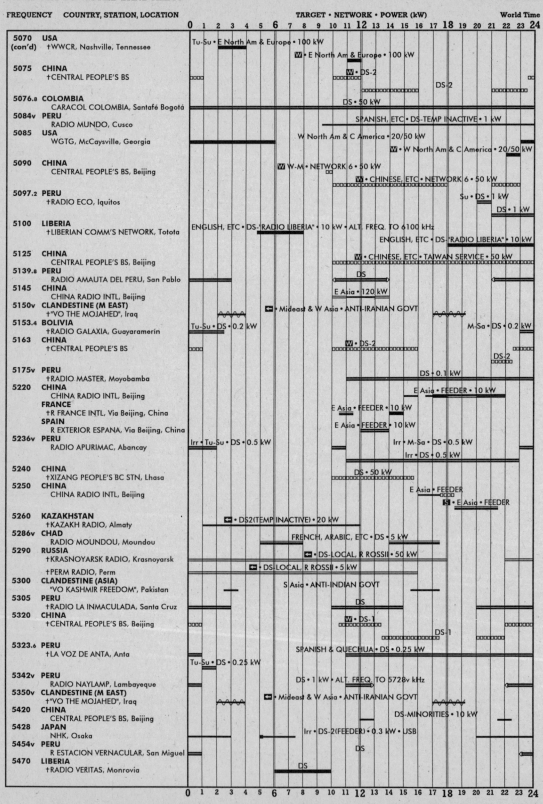

FREQUENCY   COUNTRY, STATION, LOCATION

TARGET • NETWORK • POWER (kW)   World Time

0 1 2 3 4 5 6 7 8 9 10 11 12 13 14 15 16 17 18 19 20 21 22 23 24

Freq	Country / Station
5070 (con'd)	**USA** †WWCR, Nashville, Tennessee — Tu-Su • E North Am & Europe • 100 kW / W • E North Am & Europe • 100 kW
5075	**CHINA** †CENTRAL PEOPLE'S BS — W • DS-2 / DS-2
5076.8	**COLOMBIA** CARACOL COLOMBIA, Santafé Bogotá — DS • 50 kW
5084v	**PERU** RADIO MUNDO, Cusco — SPANISH, ETC • DS-TEMP INACTIVE • 1 kW
5085	**USA** WGTG, McCaysville, Georgia — W North Am & C America • 20/50 kW / W • W North Am & C America • 20/50 kW
5090	**CHINA** CENTRAL PEOPLE'S BS, Beijing — W W-M • NETWORK 6 • 50 kW / W • CHINESE, ETC • NETWORK 6 • 50 kW
5097.2	**PERU** †RADIO ECO, Iquitos — Su • DS • 1 kW / DS • 1 kW
5100	**LIBERIA** †LIBERIAN COMM'S NETWORK, Totota — ENGLISH, ETC • DS-"RADIO LIBERIA" • 10 kW • ALT. FREQ. TO 6100 kHz / ENGLISH, ETC • DS-"RADIO LIBERIA" • 10 kW
5125	**CHINA** CENTRAL PEOPLE'S BS, Beijing — W • CHINESE, ETC • TAIWAN SERVICE • 50 kW
5139.8	**PERU** RADIO AMAUTA DEL PERU, San Pablo — DS
5145	**CHINA** CHINA RADIO INTL, Beijing — E Asia • 120 kW
5150v	**CLANDESTINE (M EAST)** †"VO THE MOJAHED", Iraq — Mideast & W Asia • ANTI-IRANIAN GOVT
5153.4	**BOLIVIA** †RADIO GALAXIA, Guayaramerin — Tu-Su • DS • 0.2 kW / M-Sa • DS • 0.2 kW
5163	**CHINA** †CENTRAL PEOPLE'S BS — W • DS-2 / DS-2
5175v	**PERU** †RADIO MASTER, Moyobamba — DS • 0.1 kW
5220	**CHINA** CHINA RADIO INTL, Beijing — E Asia • FEEDER • 10 kW
	FRANCE †R FRANCE INTL, Via Beijing, China — E Asia • FEEDER • 10 kW
	SPAIN R EXTERIOR ESPANA, Via Beijing, China — E Asia • FEEDER • 10 kW
5236v	**PERU** RADIO APURIMAC, Abancay — Irr • Tu-Su • DS • 0.5 kW / Irr • M-Sa • DS • 0.5 kW / Irr • DS • 0.5 kW
5240	**CHINA** †XIZANG PEOPLE'S BC STN, Lhasa — DS • 50 kW
5250	**CHINA** CHINA RADIO INTL, Beijing — E Asia • FEEDER / S • E Asia • FEEDER
5260	**KAZAKHSTAN** †KAZAKH RADIO, Almaty — DS2 (TEMP INACTIVE) • 20 kW
5286v	**CHAD** RADIO MOUNDOU, Moundou — FRENCH, ARABIC, ETC • DS • 5 kW
5290	**RUSSIA** †KRASNOYARSK RADIO, Krasnoyarsk — DS-LOCAL, R ROSSII • 50 kW
	†PERM RADIO, Perm — DS-LOCAL, R ROSSII • 5 kW
5300	**CLANDESTINE (ASIA)** "VO KASHMIR FREEDOM", Pakistan — S Asia • ANTI-INDIAN GOVT
5305	**PERU** †RADIO LA INMACULADA, Santa Cruz — DS
5320	**CHINA** †CENTRAL PEOPLE'S BS, Beijing — W • DS-1 / DS-1
5323.6	**PERU** †LA VOZ DE ANTA, Anta — SPANISH & QUECHUA • DS • 0.25 kW / Tu-Su • DS • 0.25 kW
5342v	**PERU** RADIO NAYLAMP, Lambayeque — DS • 1 kW • ALT. FREQ. TO 5728v kHz
5350v	**CLANDESTINE (M EAST)** †"VO THE MOJAHED", Iraq — Mideast & W Asia • ANTI-IRANIAN GOVT
5420	**CHINA** CENTRAL PEOPLE'S BS, Beijing — DS-MINORITIES • 10 kW
5428	**JAPAN** NHK, Osaka — Irr • DS-2 (FEEDER) • 0.3 kW • USB
5454v	**PERU** R ESTACION VERNACULAR, San Miguel — DS
5470	**LIBERIA** †RADIO VERITAS, Monrovia — DS

0 1 2 3 4 5 6 7 8 9 10 11 12 13 14 15 16 17 18 19 20 21 22 23 24

ENGLISH ▬ **ARABIC** ∾∾∾ **CHINESE** □□□ **FRENCH** ▬▬ **GERMAN** ▬▬ **RUSSIAN** ══ **SPANISH** ▬▬ **OTHER** ▬

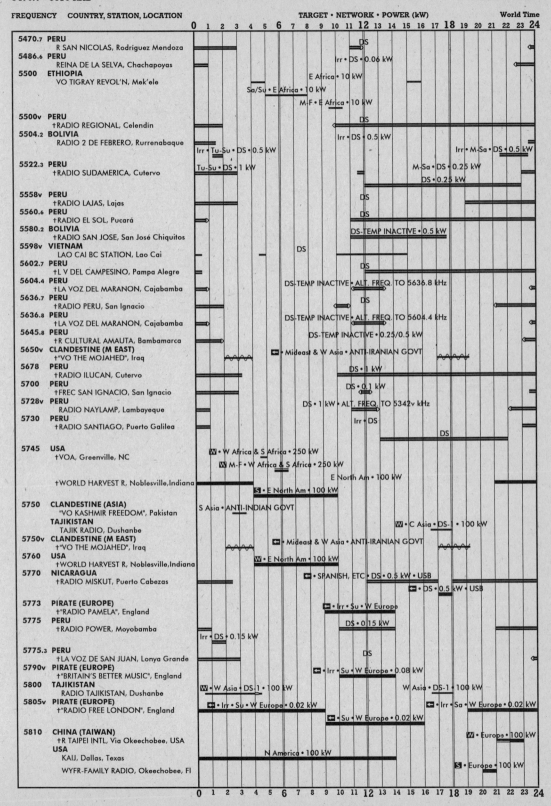

FREQUENCY   COUNTRY, STATION, LOCATION

TARGET • NETWORK • POWER (kW)   World Time

Frequency	Country, Station, Location	Notes
5470.7	**PERU** R SAN NICOLAS, Rodriguez Mendoza	DS
5486.6	**PERU** REINA DE LA SELVA, Chachapoyas	Irr • DS • 0.06 kW
5500	**ETHIOPIA** VO TIGRAY REVOL'N, Mek'ele	E Africa • 10 kW / Sa/Su • E Africa • 10 kW / M-F • E Africa • 10 kW
5500v	**PERU** †RADIO REGIONAL, Celendin	DS
5504.2	**BOLIVIA** RADIO 2 DE FEBRERO, Rurrenabaque	Irr • DS • 0.5 kW / Irr • Tu-Su • DS • 0.5 kW / Irr • M-Sa • DS • 0.5 kW
5522.3	**PERU** †RADIO SUDAMERICA, Cutervo	Tu-Su • DS • 1 kW / M-Sa • DS • 0.25 kW / DS • 0.25 kW
5558v	**PERU** †RADIO LAJAS, Lajas	DS
5560.6	**PERU** †RADIO EL SOL, Pucará	DS
5580.2	**BOLIVIA** †RADIO SAN JOSE, San José Chiquitos	DS-TEMP INACTIVE • 0.5 kW
5598v	**VIETNAM** LAO CAI BC STATION, Lao Cai	DS
5602.7	**PERU** †L V DEL CAMPESINO, Pampa Alegre	DS
5604.4	**PERU** †LA VOZ DEL MARANON, Cajabamba	DS-TEMP INACTIVE • ALT. FREQ. TO 5636.8 kHz
5636.7	**PERU** †RADIO PERU, San Ignacio	DS
5636.8	**PERU** †LA VOZ DEL MARANON, Cajabamba	DS-TEMP INACTIVE • ALT. FREQ. TO 5604.4 kHz
5645.8	**PERU** †R CULTURAL AMAUTA, Bambamarca	DS-TEMP INACTIVE • 0.25/0.5 kW
5650v	**CLANDESTINE (M EAST)** †"VO THE MOJAHED", Iraq	Mideast & W Asia • ANTI-IRANIAN GOVT
5678	**PERU** †RADIO ILUCAN, Cutervo	DS • 1 kW
5700	**PERU** †FREC SAN IGNACIO, San Ignacio	DS • 0.1 kW
5728v	**PERU** RADIO NAYLAMP, Lambayeque	DS • 1 kW • ALT. FREQ. TO 5342v kHz
5730	**PERU** †RADIO SANTIAGO, Puerto Galilea	Irr • DS / DS
5745	**USA** †VOA, Greenville, NC	W • W Africa & S Africa • 250 kW / M-F • W Africa & S Africa • 250 kW
	†WORLD HARVEST R, Noblesville, Indiana	E North Am • 100 kW / S • E North Am • 100 kW
5750	**CLANDESTINE (ASIA)** "VO KASHMIR FREEDOM", Pakistan	S Asia • ANTI-INDIAN GOVT
	TAJIKISTAN TAJIK RADIO, Dushanbe	W • C Asia • DS-1 • 100 kW
5750v	**CLANDESTINE (M EAST)** †"VO THE MOJAHED", Iraq	Mideast & W Asia • ANTI-IRANIAN GOVT
5760	**USA** †WORLD HARVEST R, Noblesville, Indiana	W • E North Am • 100 kW
5770	**NICARAGUA** †RADIO MISKUT, Puerto Cabezas	SPANISH, ETC • DS • 0.5 kW • USB / DS • 0.5 kW • USB
5773	**PIRATE (EUROPE)** †"RADIO PAMELA", England	Irr • Su • W Europa
5775	**PERU** †RADIO POWER, Moyobamba	DS • 0.15 kW / Irr • DS • 0.15 kW
5775.3	**PERU** †LA VOZ DE SAN JUAN, Lonya Grande	DS
5790v	**PIRATE (EUROPE)** †"BRITAIN'S BETTER MUSIC", England	Irr • Su • W Europe • 0.08 kW
5800	**TAJIKISTAN** RADIO TAJIKISTAN, Dushanbe	W • W Asia • DS-1 • 100 kW / W Asia • DS-1 • 100 kW
5805v	**PIRATE (EUROPE)** †"RADIO FREE LONDON", England	Irr • Su • W Europe • 0.02 kW / Irr • Sa • W Europe • 0.02 kW / Su • W Europe • 0.02 kW
5810	**CHINA (TAIWAN)** †R TAIPEI INTL, Via Okeechobee, USA	W • Europe • 100 kW
	USA KAIJ, Dallas, Texas	N America • 100 kW
	WYFR-FAMILY RADIO, Okeechobee, Fl	S • Europe • 100 kW

FREQUENCY   COUNTRY, STATION, LOCATION

TARGET • NETWORK • POWER (kW)

World Time

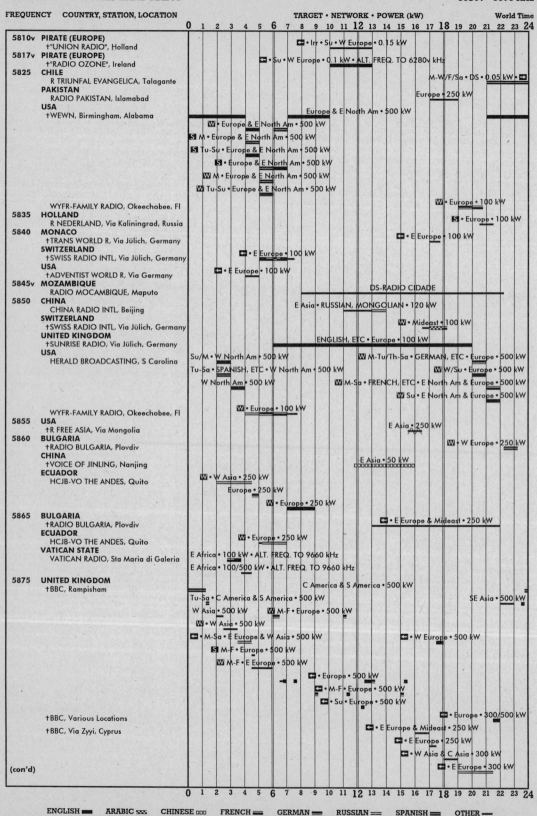

Frequency	Country, Station, Location	Target • Network • Power
5810v	**PIRATE (EUROPE)**	
	†"UNION RADIO", Holland	▭ • Irr • Su • W Europe • 0.15 kW
5817v	**PIRATE (EUROPE)**	
	†"RADIO OZONE", Ireland	▭ • Su • W Europe • 0.1 kW • ALT. FREQ. TO 6280v kHz
5825	**CHILE**	
	R TRIUNFAL EVANGELICA, Talagante	M-W/F/Sa • DS • 0.05 kW • ▭
	PAKISTAN	
	RADIO PAKISTAN, Islamabad	Europe • 250 kW
	USA	
	†WEWN, Birmingham, Alabama	Europe & E North Am • 500 kW
		W • Europe & E North Am • 500 kW
		S M • Europe & E North Am • 500 kW
		S Tu-Su • Europe & E North Am • 500 kW
		S • Europe & E North Am • 500 kW
		W M • Europe & E North Am • 500 kW
		W Tu-Su • Europe & E North Am • 500 kW
	WYFR-FAMILY RADIO, Okeechobee, Fl	W • Europe • 100 kW
5835	**HOLLAND**	
	R NEDERLAND, Via Kaliningrad, Russia	S • Europe • 100 kW
5840	**MONACO**	
	†TRANS WORLD R, Via Jülich, Germany	▭ • E Europe • 100 kW
	SWITZERLAND	
	†SWISS RADIO INTL, Via Jülich, Germany	▭ • E Europe • 100 kW
	USA	
	†ADVENTIST WORLD R, Via Germany	▭ • E Europe • 100 kW
5845v	**MOZAMBIQUE**	
	RADIO MOCAMBIQUE, Maputo	DS-RADIO CIDADE
5850	**CHINA**	
	CHINA RADIO INTL, Beijing	E Asia • RUSSIAN, MONGOLIAN • 120 kW
	SWITZERLAND	
	†SWISS RADIO INTL, Via Jülich, Germany	W • Mideast • 100 kW
	UNITED KINGDOM	
	†SUNRISE RADIO, Via Jülich, Germany	ENGLISH, ETC • Europe • 100 kW
	USA	
	HERALD BROADCASTING, S Carolina	Su/M • W North Am • 500 kW W M-Tu/Th-Sa • GERMAN, ETC • Europe • 500 kW
		Tu-Sa • SPANISH, ETC • W North Am • 500 kW W W/Su • Europe • 500 kW
		W North Am • 500 kW W M-Sa • FRENCH, ETC • E North Am & Europe • 500 kW
		W Su • E North Am & Europe • 500 kW
	WYFR-FAMILY RADIO, Okeechobee, Fl	W • Europe • 100 kW
5855	**USA**	
	†R FREE ASIA, Via Mongolia	E Asia • 250 kW
5860	**BULGARIA**	
	†RADIO BULGARIA, Plovdiv	W • W Europe • 250 kW
	CHINA	
	†VOICE OF JINLING, Nanjing	E Asia • 50 kW
	ECUADOR	
	HCJB-VO THE ANDES, Quito	W • W Asia • 250 kW
		Europe • 250 kW
		W • Europe • 250 kW
5865	**BULGARIA**	
	†RADIO BULGARIA, Plovdiv	▭ • E Europe & Mideast • 250 kW
	ECUADOR	
	HCJB-VO THE ANDES, Quito	W • Europe • 250 kW
	VATICAN STATE	
	VATICAN RADIO, Sta Maria di Galeria	E Africa • 100 kW • ALT. FREQ. TO 9660 kHz
		E Africa • 100/500 kW • ALT. FREQ. TO 9660 kHz
5875	**UNITED KINGDOM**	
	†BBC, Rampisham	C America & S America • 500 kW
		Tu-Sa • C America & S America • 500 kW SE Asia • 500 kW
		W Asia • 500 kW W M-F • Europe • 500 kW
		W • W Asia • 500 kW
		▭ • M-Sa • E Europe & W Asia • 500 kW ▭ • W Europe • 500 kW
		S M-F • Europe • 500 kW
		W M-F • E Europe • 500 kW
		▭ • Europe • 500 kW
		▭ • M-F • Europe • 500 kW
		▭ • Su • Europe • 500 kW
	†BBC, Various Locations	▭ • Europe • 300/500 kW
	†BBC, Via Zyyi, Cyprus	▭ • E Europe & Mideast • 250 kW
		▭ • E Europe • 250 kW
		▭ • W Asia & C Asia • 300 kW
(con'd)		▭ • E Europe • 300 kW

ENGLISH ▬ ARABIC ⸚ CHINESE ⸬ FRENCH ═ GERMAN ▬ RUSSIAN ═ SPANISH ═ OTHER ▬

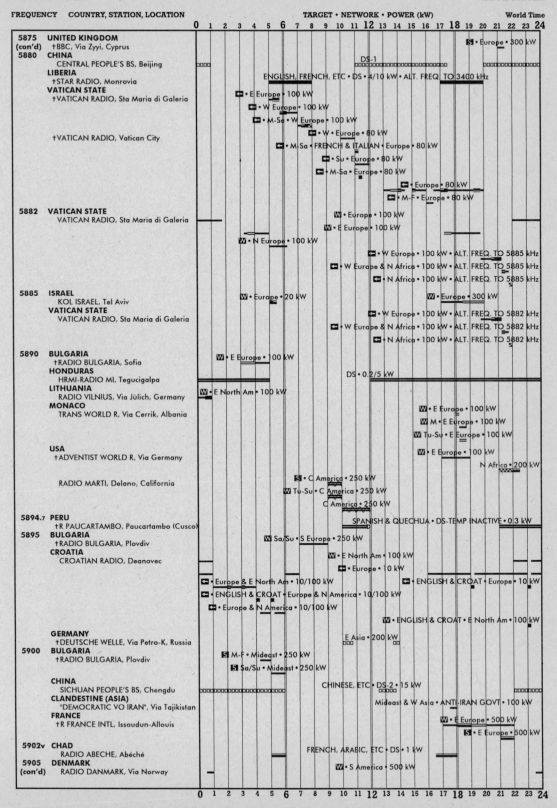

FREQUENCY   COUNTRY, STATION, LOCATION   TARGET • NETWORK • POWER (kW)   World Time

5875   **UNITED KINGDOM**
(con'd)   †BBC, Via Zyyi, Cyprus   S • Europe • 300 kW
5880   **CHINA**   DS-1
         CENTRAL PEOPLE'S BS, Beijing
       LIBERIA   ENGLISH, FRENCH, ETC • DS • 4/10 kW • ALT. FREQ. TO 3400 kHz
         †STAR RADIO, Monrovia
       VATICAN STATE
         †VATICAN RADIO, Sta Maria di Galeria   • E Europe • 100 kW
                                • W Europe • 100 kW
                            • M-Sa • W Europe • 100 kW
         †VATICAN RADIO, Vatican City   • W Europe • 80 kW
                        • M-Sa • FRENCH & ITALIAN • Europe • 80 kW
                           • Su • Europe • 80 kW
                        • M-Sa • Europe • 80 kW
                                • Europe • 80 kW
                              • M-F • Europe • 80 kW

5882   **VATICAN STATE**
         VATICAN RADIO, Sta Maria di Galeria   W • Europe • 100 kW
                              W • E Europe • 100 kW
              W • N Europe • 100 kW
                              • W Europe • 100 kW • ALT. FREQ. TO 5885 kHz
                          • W Europe & N Africa • 100 kW • ALT. FREQ. TO 5885 kHz
                             • N Africa • 100 kW • ALT. FREQ. TO 5885 kHz

5885   **ISRAEL**
         KOL ISRAEL, Tel Aviv   W • Europe • 20 kW   W • Europe • 300 kW
       VATICAN STATE
         VATICAN RADIO, Sta Maria di Galeria   • W Europe • 100 kW • ALT. FREQ. TO 5882 kHz
                              • W Europe & N Africa • 100 kW • ALT. FREQ. TO 5882 kHz
                              • N Africa • 100 kW • ALT. FREQ. TO 5882 kHz

5890   **BULGARIA**
         †RADIO BULGARIA, Sofia   W • E Europe • 100 kW
       HONDURAS   DS • 0.2/5 kW
         HRMI-RADIO MI, Tegucigalpa
       LITHUANIA
         RADIO VILNIUS, Via Jülich, Germany   W • E North Am • 100 kW
       MONACO
         TRANS WORLD R, Via Cerrik, Albania   W • E Europe • 100 kW
                                  W M • E Europe • 100 kW
                                  W Tu-Su • E Europe • 100 kW
       USA   W • E Europe • 100 kW
         †ADVENTIST WORLD R, Via Germany   N Africa • 200 kW
                        S • C America • 250 kW
         RADIO MARTI, Delano, California   W Tu-Su • C America • 250 kW
                            C America • 250 kW

5894.7   **PERU**
         †R PAUCARTAMBO, Paucartambo (Cusco)   SPANISH & QUECHUA • DS-TEMP INACTIVE • 0.3 kW
5895   **BULGARIA**
         †RADIO BULGARIA, Plovdiv   W Sa/Su • S Europe • 250 kW
       CROATIA
         CROATIAN RADIO, Deanovec   W • E North Am • 100 kW
                             • Europe • 10 kW
               • Europe & E North Am • 10/100 kW   • ENGLISH & CROAT • Europe • 10 kW
              • ENGLISH & CROAT • Europe & N America • 10/100 kW
              • Europe & N America • 10/100 kW
                            W • ENGLISH & CROAT • E North Am • 100 kW
       GERMANY   E Asia • 200 kW
         †DEUTSCHE WELLE, Via Petro-K, Russia
5900   **BULGARIA**
         †RADIO BULGARIA, Plovdiv   S M-F • Mideast • 250 kW
                     S Sa/Su • Mideast • 250 kW
       CHINA
         SICHUAN PEOPLE'S BS, Chengdu   CHINESE, ETC • DS-2 • 15 kW
       CLANDESTINE (ASIA)
         "DEMOCRATIC VO IRAN", Via Tajikistan   Mideast & W Asia • ANTI-IRAN GOVT • 100 kW
       FRANCE
         †R FRANCE INTL, Issoudun-Allouis   W • E Europe • 500 kW
                                  S • E Europe • 500 kW

5902v   **CHAD**
         RADIO ABECHE, Abéché   FRENCH, ARABIC, ETC • DS • 1 kW
5905   **DENMARK**
(con'd)   RADIO DANMARK, Via Norway   W • S America • 500 kW

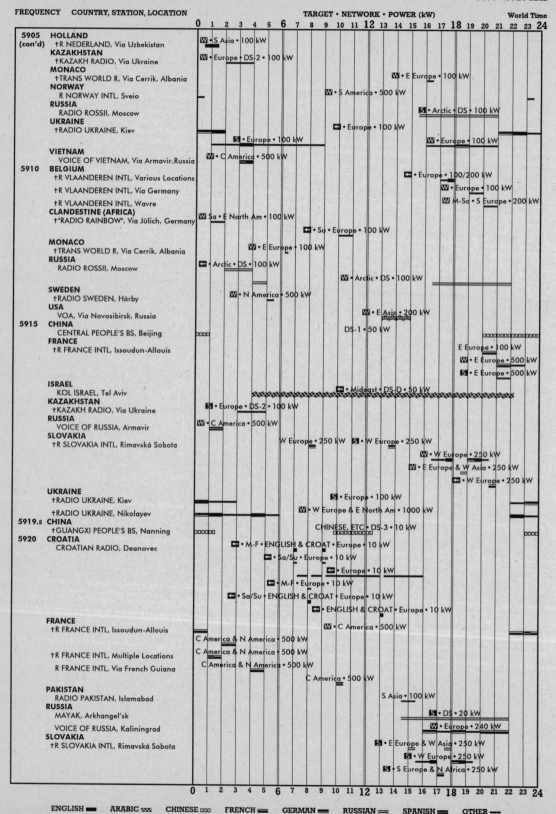

FREQUENCY   COUNTRY, STATION, LOCATION

TARGET • NETWORK • POWER (kW)

World Time

5905 (con'd)	**HOLLAND** †R NEDERLAND, Via Uzbekistan
	KAZAKHSTAN †KAZAKH RADIO, Via Ukraine
	MONACO †TRANS WORLD R, Via Cerrik, Albania
	NORWAY R NORWAY INTL, Sveio
	RUSSIA RADIO ROSSII, Moscow
	UKRAINE †RADIO UKRAINE, Kiev
	VIETNAM VOICE OF VIETNAM, Via Armavir, Russia
5910	**BELGIUM** †R VLAANDEREN INTL, Various Locations †R VLAANDEREN INTL, Via Germany †R VLAANDEREN INTL, Wavre
	CLANDESTINE (AFRICA) †"RADIO RAINBOW", Via Jülich, Germany
	MONACO †TRANS WORLD R, Via Cerrik, Albania
	RUSSIA RADIO ROSSII, Moscow
	SWEDEN †RADIO SWEDEN, Hörby
	USA VOA, Via Novosibirsk, Russia
5915	**CHINA** CENTRAL PEOPLE'S BS, Beijing
	FRANCE †R FRANCE INTL, Issoudun-Allouis
	ISRAEL KOL ISRAEL, Tel Aviv
	KAZAKHSTAN †KAZAKH RADIO, Via Ukraine
	RUSSIA VOICE OF RUSSIA, Armavir
	SLOVAKIA †R SLOVAKIA INTL, Rimavská Sobota
	UKRAINE †RADIO UKRAINE, Kiev †RADIO UKRAINE, Nikolayev
5919.5	**CHINA** †GUANGXI PEOPLE'S BS, Nanning
5920	**CROATIA** CROATIAN RADIO, Deanovec
	FRANCE †R FRANCE INTL, Issoudun-Allouis †R FRANCE INTL, Multiple Locations R FRANCE INTL, Via French Guiana
	PAKISTAN RADIO PAKISTAN, Islamabad
	RUSSIA MAYAK, Arkhangel'sk VOICE OF RUSSIA, Kaliningrad
	SLOVAKIA †R SLOVAKIA INTL, Rimavská Sobota

Chart data (target • network • power):

- R NEDERLAND: W • S Asia • 100 kW
- KAZAKH RADIO: W • Europe • DS-2 • 100 kW
- TRANS WORLD R: W • E Europe • 100 kW
- R NORWAY INTL: W • S America • 500 kW
- RADIO ROSSII: S • Arctic • DS • 100 kW
- RADIO UKRAINE: • Europe • 100 kW; S • Europe • 100 kW; W • Europe • 100 kW
- VOICE OF VIETNAM: W • C America • 500 kW
- R VLAANDEREN INTL (Various): • Europe • 100/200 kW
- R VLAANDEREN INTL (Via Germany): W • Europe • 100 kW
- R VLAANDEREN INTL (Wavre): W M-Sa • S Europe • 200 kW
- "RADIO RAINBOW": W Sa • E North Am • 100 kW
- (Rainbow second): • Su • Europe • 100 kW
- TRANS WORLD R: W • E Europe • 100 kW
- RADIO ROSSII: • Arctic • DS • 100 kW; W • Arctic • DS • 100 kW
- RADIO SWEDEN: W • N America • 500 kW
- VOA: W • E Asia • 200 kW
- CENTRAL PEOPLE'S BS: DS-1 • 50 kW
- R FRANCE INTL: E Europe • 100 kW; W • E Europe • 500 kW; S • E Europe • 500 kW
- KOL ISRAEL: • Mideast • DS-D • 50 kW
- KAZAKH RADIO: S • Europe • DS-2 • 100 kW
- VOICE OF RUSSIA: W • C America • 500 kW
- R SLOVAKIA INTL: W Europe • 250 kW; S • W Europe • 250 kW; W • W Europe • 250 kW; W • E Europe & W Asia • 250 kW; • W Europe • 250 kW
- RADIO UKRAINE (Kiev): S • Europe • 100 kW
- RADIO UKRAINE (Nikolayev): W • W Europe & E North Am • 1000 kW
- GUANGXI PEOPLE'S BS: CHINESE, ETC • DS-3 • 10 kW
- CROATIAN RADIO: • M-F • ENGLISH & CROAT • Europe • 10 kW; • Sa/Su • Europe • 10 kW; • Europe • 10 kW; • M-F • Europe • 10 kW; • Sa/Su • ENGLISH & CROAT • Europe • 10 kW; • ENGLISH & CROAT • Europe • 10 kW
- R FRANCE INTL: W • C America • 500 kW; C America & N America • 500 kW; C America & N America • 500 kW; C America & N America • 500 kW; C America • 500 kW
- RADIO PAKISTAN: S Asia • 100 kW
- MAYAK: S • DS • 20 kW
- VOICE OF RUSSIA: W • Europe • 240 kW
- R SLOVAKIA INTL: S • E Europe & W Asia • 250 kW; S • W Europe • 250 kW; S • S Europe & N Africa • 250 kW

ENGLISH ▬   ARABIC ≋   CHINESE ▫▫▫   FRENCH ▬   GERMAN ▬   RUSSIAN ═   SPANISH ▬   OTHER ▬

FREQUENCY COUNTRY, STATION, LOCATION — TARGET • NETWORK • POWER (kW) — World Time

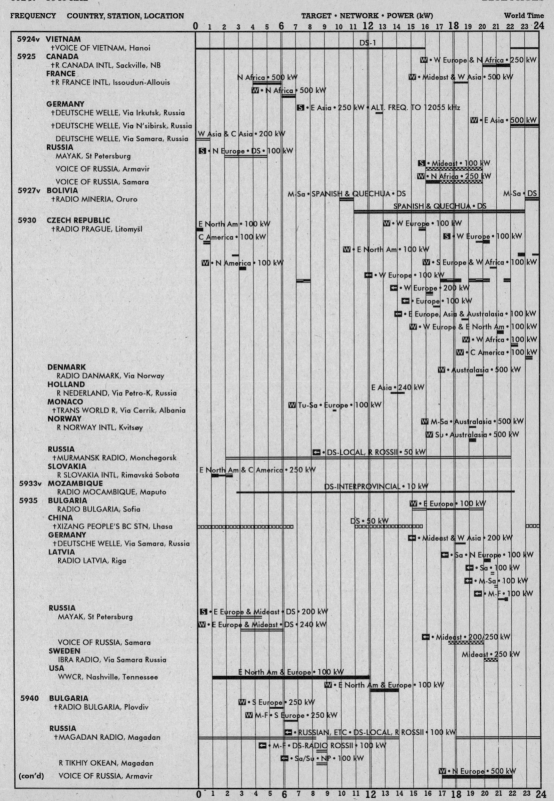

FREQUENCY	COUNTRY, STATION, LOCATION	TARGET • NETWORK • POWER (kW)
5924v	**VIETNAM** †VOICE OF VIETNAM, Hanoi	DS-1
5925	**CANADA** †R CANADA INTL, Sackville, NB	W • W Europe & N Africa • 250 kW
	FRANCE †R FRANCE INTL, Issoudun-Allouis	N Africa • 500 kW; W • Mideast & W Asia • 500 kW; W • N Africa • 500 kW
	GERMANY †DEUTSCHE WELLE, Via Irkutsk, Russia	S • E Asia • 250 kW • ALT. FREQ. TO 12055 kHz
	†DEUTSCHE WELLE, Via N'sibirsk, Russia	W • E Asia • 500 kW
	DEUTSCHE WELLE, Via Samara, Russia	W Asia & C Asia • 200 kW
	RUSSIA MAYAK, St Petersburg	S • N Europe • DS • 100 kW
	VOICE OF RUSSIA, Armavir	S • Mideast • 100 kW
	VOICE OF RUSSIA, Samara	W • N Africa • 250 kW
5927v	**BOLIVIA** †RADIO MINERIA, Oruro	M-Sa • SPANISH & QUECHUA • DS; M-Sa • DS; SPANISH & QUECHUA • DS
5930	**CZECH REPUBLIC** †RADIO PRAGUE, Litomyšl	E North Am • 100 kW; C America • 100 kW; W • W Europe • 100 kW; S • W Europe • 100 kW; W • E North Am • 100 kW; W • N America • 100 kW; W • S Europe & W Africa • 100 kW; ⊡ • W Europe • 100 kW; ⊡ • W Europe • 200 kW; ⊡ • Europe • 100 kW; ⊡ • E Europe, Asia & Australasia • 100 kW; W • W Europe & E North Am • 100 kW; W • W Africa • 100 kW; W • C America • 100 kW
	DENMARK RADIO DANMARK, Via Norway	W • Australasia • 500 kW
	HOLLAND R NEDERLAND, Via Petro-K, Russia	E Asia • 240 kW
	MONACO †TRANS WORLD R, Via Cerrik, Albania	W Tu-Sa • Europe • 100 kW
	NORWAY R NORWAY INTL, Kvitsøy	W M-Sa • Australasia • 500 kW; W Su • Australasia • 500 kW
	RUSSIA †MURMANSK RADIO, Monchegorsk	⊡ • DS-LOCAL, R ROSSII • 50 kW
	SLOVAKIA R SLOVAKIA INTL, Rimavská Sobota	E North Am & C America • 250 kW
5933v	**MOZAMBIQUE** RADIO MOCAMBIQUE, Maputo	DS-INTERPROVINCIAL • 10 kW
5935	**BULGARIA** RADIO BULGARIA, Sofia	W • E Europe • 100 kW
	CHINA †XIZANG PEOPLE'S BC STN, Lhasa	DS • 50 kW
	GERMANY †DEUTSCHE WELLE, Via Samara, Russia	⊡ • Mideast & W Asia • 200 kW
	LATVIA RADIO LATVIA, Riga	⊡ • Sa • N Europe • 100 kW; ⊡ • Sa • 100 kW; ⊡ • M-Sa • 100 kW; ⊡ • M-F • 100 kW
	RUSSIA MAYAK, St Petersburg	S • E Europe & Mideast • DS • 200 kW; W • E Europe & Mideast • DS • 240 kW
	VOICE OF RUSSIA, Samara	⊡ • Mideast • 200/250 kW
	SWEDEN IBRA RADIO, Via Samara Russia	Mideast • 250 kW
	USA WWCR, Nashville, Tennessee	E North Am & Europe • 100 kW; W • E North Am & Europe • 100 kW
5940	**BULGARIA** †RADIO BULGARIA, Plovdiv	W • S Europe • 250 kW; W M-F • S Europe • 250 kW
	RUSSIA †MAGADAN RADIO, Magadan	⊡ • RUSSIAN, ETC • DS-LOCAL, R ROSSII • 100 kW; ⊡ • M-F • DS-RADIO ROSSII • 100 kW; ⊡ • Sa/Su • NP • 100 kW
	R TIKHIY OKEAN, Magadan	
(con'd)	VOICE OF RUSSIA, Armavir	W • N Europe • 500 kW

FREQUENCY   COUNTRY, STATION, LOCATION

TARGET • NETWORK • POWER (kW)

World Time

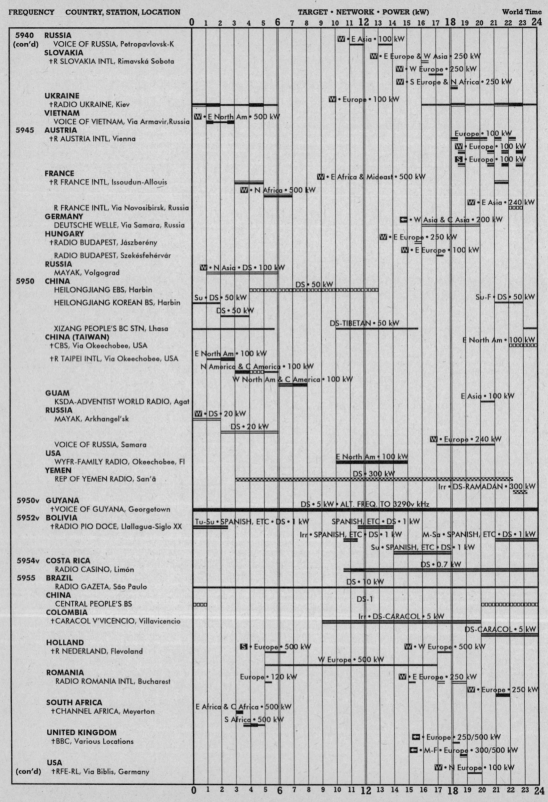

Frequency	Country, Station, Location	Target • Network • Power (kW)
5940 (con'd)	RUSSIA — VOICE OF RUSSIA, Petropavlovsk-K	W • E Asia • 100 kW
	SLOVAKIA — †R SLOVAKIA INTL, Rimavská Sobota	W • E Europe & W Asia • 250 kW; W • W Europe • 250 kW; W • S Europe & N Africa • 250 kW
	UKRAINE — †RADIO UKRAINE, Kiev	W • Europe • 100 kW
	VIETNAM — VOICE OF VIETNAM, Via Armavir, Russia	W • E North Am • 500 kW
5945	AUSTRIA — †R AUSTRIA INTL, Vienna	Europe • 100 kW; W • Europe • 100 kW; S • Europe • 100 kW
	FRANCE — †R FRANCE INTL, Issoudun-Allouis	W • E Africa & Mideast • 500 kW; W • N Africa • 500 kW
	R FRANCE INTL, Via Novosibirsk, Russia	W • E Asia • 240 kW
	GERMANY — DEUTSCHE WELLE, Via Samara, Russia	W Asia & C Asia • 200 kW
	HUNGARY — †RADIO BUDAPEST, Jászberény	W • E Europe • 250 kW
	RADIO BUDAPEST, Székesfehérvár	W • E Europe • 100 kW
	RUSSIA — MAYAK, Volgograd	W • N Asia • DS • 100 kW
5950	CHINA — HEILONGJIANG EBS, Harbin	DS • 50 kW
	HEILONGJIANG KOREAN BS, Harbin	Su • DS • 50 kW; Su-F • DS • 50 kW; DS • 50 kW
	XIZANG PEOPLE'S BC STN, Lhasa	DS-TIBETAN • 50 kW
	CHINA (TAIWAN) — †CBS, Via Okeechobee, USA	E North Am • 100 kW; E North Am • 100 kW
	†R TAIPEI INTL, Via Okeechobee, USA	N America & C America • 100 kW; W North Am & C America • 100 kW
	GUAM — KSDA-ADVENTIST WORLD RADIO, Agat	E Asia • 100 kW
	RUSSIA — MAYAK, Arkhangel'sk	W • DS • 20 kW; DS • 20 kW
	VOICE OF RUSSIA, Samara	W • Europe • 240 kW
	USA — WYFR-FAMILY RADIO, Okeechobee, Fl	E North Am • 100 kW
	YEMEN — REP OF YEMEN RADIO, San'ā	DS • 300 kW; Irr • DS-RAMADAN • 300 kW
5950v	GUYANA — †VOICE OF GUYANA, Georgetown	DS • 5 kW • ALT. FREQ. TO 3290v kHz
5952v	BOLIVIA — †RADIO PIO DOCE, Llallagua-Siglo XX	Tu-Su • SPANISH, ETC • DS • 1 kW; SPANISH, ETC • DS • 1 kW; Irr • SPANISH, ETC • DS • 1 kW; M-Sa • SPANISH, ETC • DS • 1 kW; Su • SPANISH, ETC • DS • 1 kW
5954v	COSTA RICA — RADIO CASINO, Limón	DS • 0.7 kW
5955	BRAZIL — RADIO GAZETA, São Paulo	DS • 10 kW
	CHINA — CENTRAL PEOPLE'S BS	DS-1
	COLOMBIA — †CARACOL V'VICENCIO, Villavicencio	Irr • DS-CARACOL • 5 kW; DS-CARACOL • 5 kW
	HOLLAND — †R NEDERLAND, Flevoland	S • Europe • 500 kW; W Europe • 500 kW; W • W Europe • 500 kW
	ROMANIA — RADIO ROMANIA INTL, Bucharest	Europe • 120 kW; W • E Europe • 250 kW; W • Europe • 250 kW
	SOUTH AFRICA — †CHANNEL AFRICA, Meyerton	E Africa & C Africa • 500 kW; S Africa • 500 kW
	UNITED KINGDOM — †BBC, Various Locations	Europe • 250/500 kW; M-F • Europe • 300/500 kW
(con'd)	USA — †RFE-RL, Via Biblis, Germany	W • N Europe • 100 kW

FREQUENCY   COUNTRY, STATION, LOCATION   TARGET • NETWORK • POWER (kW)   World Time

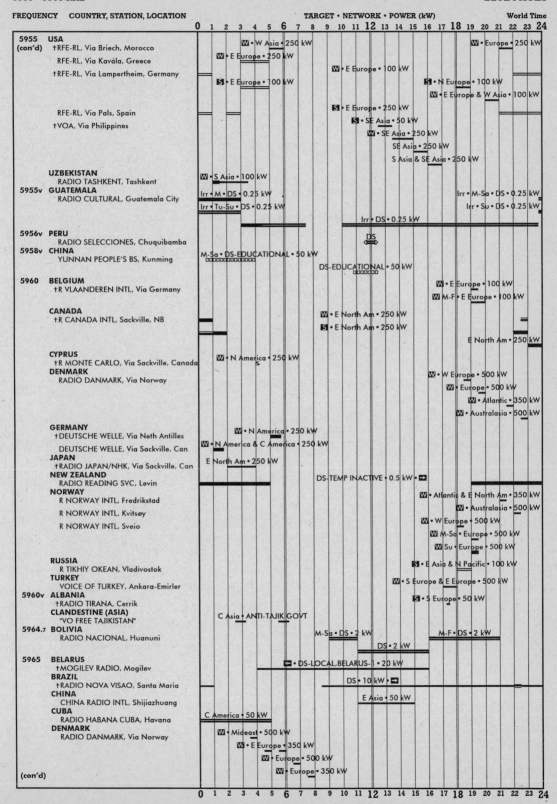

FREQUENCY	COUNTRY, STATION, LOCATION	TARGET • NETWORK • POWER
5955 (con'd)	USA	
	†RFE-RL, Via Briech, Morocco	W • W Asia • 250 kW / W • Europe • 250 kW
	RFE-RL, Via Kavála, Greece	W • E Europe • 250 kW
	†RFE-RL, Via Lampertheim, Germany	W • E Europe • 100 kW / S • E Europe • 100 kW / S • N Europe • 100 kW / W • E Europe & W Asia • 100 kW
	RFE-RL, Via Pals, Spain	S • E Europe • 250 kW
	†VOA, Via Philippines	S • SE Asia • 50 kW / W • SE Asia • 250 kW / SE Asia • 250 kW / S Asia & SE Asia • 250 kW
	UZBEKISTAN	
	RADIO TASHKENT, Tashkent	W • S Asia • 100 kW
5955v	GUATEMALA	
	RADIO CULTURAL, Guatemala City	Irr • M • DS • 0.25 kW / Irr • M-Sa • DS • 0.25 kW / Irr • Tu-Su • DS • 0.25 kW / Irr • Su • DS • 0.25 kW / Irr • DS • 0.25 kW
5956v	PERU	
	RADIO SELECCIONES, Chuquibamba	DS
5958v	CHINA	
	YUNNAN PEOPLE'S BS, Kunming	M-Sa • DS-EDUCATIONAL • 50 kW / DS-EDUCATIONAL • 50 kW
5960	BELGIUM	
	†R VLAANDEREN INTL, Via Germany	W • E Europe • 100 kW / W M-F • E Europe • 100 kW
	CANADA	
	†R CANADA INTL, Sackville, NB	W • E North Am • 250 kW / S • E North Am • 250 kW / E North Am • 250 kW
	CYPRUS	
	†R MONTE CARLO, Via Sackville, Canada	W • N America • 250 kW
	DENMARK	
	RADIO DANMARK, Via Norway	W • W Europe • 500 kW / W • Europe • 500 kW / W • Atlantic • 350 kW / W • Australasia • 500 kW
	GERMANY	
	†DEUTSCHE WELLE, Via Neth Antilles	W • N America • 250 kW
	DEUTSCHE WELLE, Via Sackville, Can	W • N America & C America • 250 kW
	JAPAN	
	†RADIO JAPAN/NHK, Via Sackville, Can	E North Am • 250 kW
	NEW ZEALAND	
	RADIO READING SVC, Levin	DS-TEMP INACTIVE • 0.5 kW • ▢
	NORWAY	
	R NORWAY INTL, Fredrikstad	W • Atlantic & E North Am • 350 kW / W • Australasia • 500 kW
	R NORWAY INTL, Kvitsøy	W • W Europe • 500 kW / W M-Sa • Europe • 500 kW / W Su • Europe • 500 kW
	R NORWAY INTL, Sveio	
	RUSSIA	
	R TIKHIY OKEAN, Vladivostok	S • E Asia & N Pacific • 100 kW
	TURKEY	
	VOICE OF TURKEY, Ankara-Emirler	W • S Europe & E Europe • 500 kW
5960v	ALBANIA	
	†RADIO TIRANA, Cerrik	S • S Europe • 50 kW
	CLANDESTINE (ASIA)	
	"VO FREE TAJIKISTAN"	C Asia • ANTI-TAJIK GOVT
5964.7	BOLIVIA	
	RADIO NACIONAL, Huanuni	M-Sa • DS • 2 kW / DS • 2 kW / M-F • DS • 2 kW
5965	BELARUS	
	†MOGILEV RADIO, Mogilev	▢ • DS-LOCAL, BELARUS-1 • 20 kW
	BRAZIL	
	†RADIO NOVA VISAO, Santa Maria	DS • 10 kW • ▢
	CHINA	
	CHINA RADIO INTL, Shijiazhuang	E Asia • 50 kW
	CUBA	
	RADIO HABANA CUBA, Havana	C America • 50 kW
	DENMARK	
	RADIO DANMARK, Via Norway	W • Mideast • 500 kW / W • E Europe • 350 kW / W • Europe • 500 kW / W • Europe • 350 kW

(con'd)

FREQUENCY   COUNTRY, STATION, LOCATION   TARGET • NETWORK • POWER (kW)   World Time

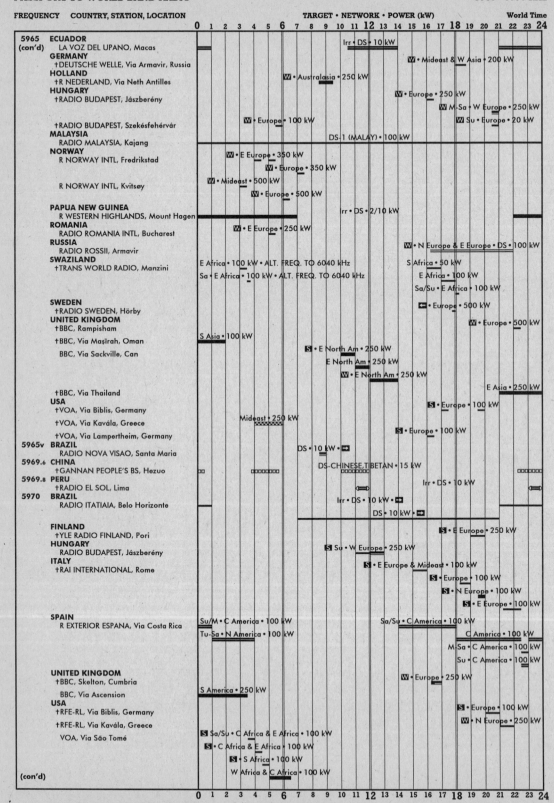

FREQUENCY	COUNTRY, STATION, LOCATION	TARGET • NETWORK • POWER (kW)
5965 (con'd)	**ECUADOR** LA VOZ DEL UPANO, Macas	Irr • DS • 10 kW
	GERMANY †DEUTSCHE WELLE, Via Armavir, Russia	W • Mideast & W Asia • 200 kW
	HOLLAND †R NEDERLAND, Via Neth Antilles	W • Australasia • 250 kW
	HUNGARY †RADIO BUDAPEST, Jászberény	W • Europe • 250 kW; W • M-Sa • W Europe • 250 kW; W • Su • Europe • 20 kW
	†RADIO BUDAPEST, Székésfehérvár	W • Europe • 100 kW
	MALAYSIA RADIO MALAYSIA, Kajang	DS-1 (MALAY) • 100 kW
	NORWAY R NORWAY INTL, Fredrikstad	W • E Europe • 350 kW; W • Europe • 350 kW
	R NORWAY INTL, Kvitsøy	W • Mideast • 500 kW; W • Europe • 500 kW
	PAPUA NEW GUINEA R WESTERN HIGHLANDS, Mount Hagen	Irr • DS • 2/10 kW
	ROMANIA RADIO ROMANIA INTL, Bucharest	W • E Europe • 250 kW
	RUSSIA RADIO ROSSII, Armavir	W • N Europe & E Europe • DS • 100 kW
	SWAZILAND †TRANS WORLD RADIO, Manzini	E Africa • 100 kW • ALT. FREQ. TO 6040 kHz; S Africa • 50 kW; Sa • E Africa • 100 kW • ALT. FREQ. TO 6040 kHz; E Africa • 100 kW; Sa/Su • E Africa • 100 kW
	SWEDEN †RADIO SWEDEN, Hörby	☐ • Europe • 500 kW
	UNITED KINGDOM †BBC, Rampisham	W • Europe • 500 kW
	†BBC, Via Maşīrah, Oman	S Asia • 100 kW
	BBC, Via Sackville, Can	S • E North Am • 250 kW; E North Am • 250 kW; W • E North Am • 250 kW
	†BBC, Via Thailand	E Asia • 250 kW
	USA †VOA, Via Biblis, Germany	S • Europe • 100 kW
	†VOA, Via Kavála, Greece	Mideast • 250 kW
	†VOA, Via Lampertheim, Germany	S • Europe • 100 kW
5965v	**BRAZIL** RADIO NOVA VISAO, Santa Maria	DS • 10 kW • ☐
5969.6	**CHINA** †GANNAN PEOPLE'S BS, Hezuo	DS-CHINESE, TIBETAN • 15 kW
5969.8	**PERU** †RADIO EL SOL, Lima	Irr • DS • 10 kW
5970	**BRAZIL** RADIO ITATIAIA, Belo Horizonte	Irr • DS • 10 kW • ☐; DS • 10 kW • ☐
	FINLAND †YLE RADIO FINLAND, Pori	S • E Europe • 250 kW
	HUNGARY RADIO BUDAPEST, Jászberény	S • Su • W Europe • 250 kW
	ITALY †RAI INTERNATIONAL, Rome	S • E Europe & Mideast • 100 kW; S • Europe • 100 kW; S • N Europe • 100 kW; S • E Europe • 100 kW
	SPAIN R EXTERIOR ESPANA, Via Costa Rica	Su/M • C America • 100 kW; Sa/Su • C America • 100 kW; Tu-Sa • N America • 100 kW; C America • 100 kW; M-Sa • C America • 100 kW; Su • C America • 100 kW
	UNITED KINGDOM †BBC, Skelton, Cumbria	W • Europe • 250 kW
	BBC, Via Ascension	S America • 250 kW
	USA †RFE-RL, Via Biblis, Germany	S • Europe • 100 kW
	†RFE-RL, Via Kavála, Greece	W • N Europe • 250 kW
	VOA, Via São Tomé	S • Sa/Su • C Africa & E Africa • 100 kW; S • C Africa & E Africa • 100 kW; S • S Africa • 100 kW; W Africa & C Africa • 100 kW
(con'd)		

ENGLISH ▬   ARABIC ⋙   CHINESE ▭▭▭   FRENCH ▬   GERMAN ▬   RUSSIAN ═   SPANISH ▬   OTHER ▬

FREQUENCY	COUNTRY, STATION, LOCATION	TARGET • NETWORK • POWER (kW)	World Time

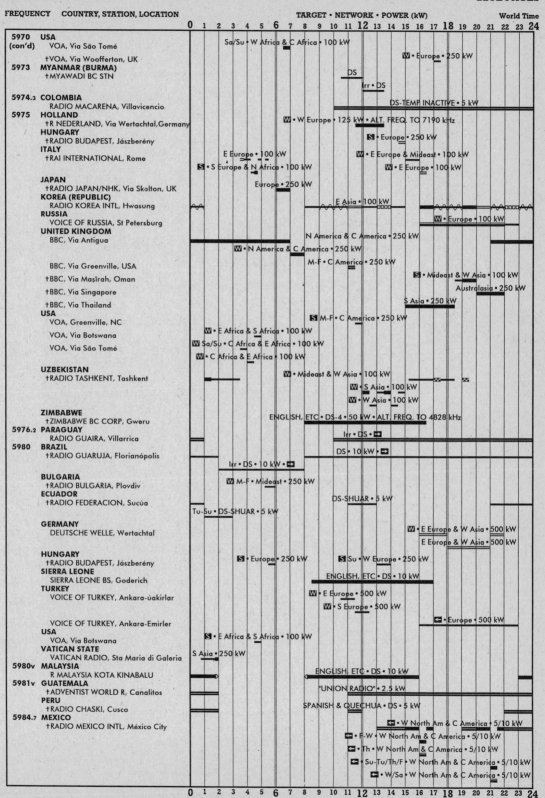

Frequency	Country, Station, Location	Target • Network • Power
5970 (con'd)	USA — VOA, Via São Tomé	Sa/Su • W Africa & C Africa • 100 kW
	†VOA, Via Woofferton, UK	W • Europe • 250 kW
5973	MYANMAR (BURMA) — †MYAWADI BC STN	DS / Irr • DS
5974.3	COLOMBIA — RADIO MACARENA, Villavicencio	DS-TEMP INACTIVE • 5 kW
5975	HOLLAND — †R NEDERLAND, Via Wertachtal, Germany	W • W Europe • 125 kW • ALT. FREQ. TO 7190 kHz
	HUNGARY — †RADIO BUDAPEST, Jászberény	S • Europe • 250 kW
	ITALY — †RAI INTERNATIONAL, Rome	E Europe • 100 kW / W • E Europe & Mideast • 100 kW / S • S Europe & N Africa • 100 kW / W • E Europe • 100 kW
	JAPAN — †RADIO JAPAN/NHK, Via Skelton, UK	Europe • 250 kW
	KOREA (REPUBLIC) — RADIO KOREA INTL, Hwasung	E Asia • 100 kW
	RUSSIA — VOICE OF RUSSIA, St Petersburg	W • Europe • 100 kW
	UNITED KINGDOM — BBC, Via Antigua	N America & C America • 250 kW / W • N America & C America • 250 kW
	BBC, Via Greenville, USA	M-F • C America • 250 kW
	†BBC, Via Maşīrah, Oman	S • Mideast & W Asia • 100 kW
	†BBC, Via Singapore	Australasia • 250 kW
	†BBC, Via Thailand	S Asia • 250 kW
	USA — VOA, Greenville, NC	S • M-F • C America • 250 kW
	VOA, Via Botswana	W • E Africa & S Africa • 100 kW / W Sa/Su • C Africa & E Africa • 100 kW
	VOA, Via São Tomé	W • C Africa & E Africa • 100 kW
	UZBEKISTAN — †RADIO TASHKENT, Tashkent	W • Mideast & W Asia • 100 kW / W • S Asia • 100 kW / W • W Asia • 100 kW
	ZIMBABWE — †ZIMBABWE BC CORP, Gweru	ENGLISH, ETC • DS-4 • 50 kW • ALT. FREQ. TO 4828 kHz
5976.2	PARAGUAY — RADIO GUAIRA, Villarrica	Irr • DS
5980	BRAZIL — †RADIO GUARUJA, Florianópolis	DS • 10 kW / Irr • DS • 10 kW
	BULGARIA — †RADIO BULGARIA, Plovdiv	W M-F • Mideast • 250 kW
	ECUADOR — †RADIO FEDERACION, Sucúa	DS-SHUAR • 5 kW / Tu-Su • DS-SHUAR • 5 kW
	GERMANY — DEUTSCHE WELLE, Wertachtal	W • E Europe & W Asia • 500 kW / E Europe & W Asia • 500 kW
	HUNGARY — †RADIO BUDAPEST, Jászberény	S • Europe • 250 kW / S Su • W Europe • 250 kW
	SIERRA LEONE — SIERRA LEONE BS, Goderich	ENGLISH, ETC • DS • 10 kW
	TURKEY — VOICE OF TURKEY, Ankara-úakirlar	W • E Europe • 500 kW / W • S Europe • 500 kW
	VOICE OF TURKEY, Ankara-Emirler	Europe • 500 kW
	USA — VOA, Via Botswana	S • E Africa & S Africa • 100 kW
	VATICAN STATE — VATICAN RADIO, Sta Maria di Galeria	S Asia • 250 kW
5980v	MALAYSIA — R MALAYSIA KOTA KINABALU	ENGLISH, ETC • DS • 10 kW
5981v	GUATEMALA — †ADVENTIST WORLD R, Canalitos	"UNION RADIO" • 2.5 kW
	PERU — †RADIO CHASKI, Cusco	SPANISH & QUECHUA • DS • 5 kW
5984.7	MEXICO — †RADIO MEXICO INTL, México City	W North Am & C America • 5/10 kW / F-W • W North Am & C America • 5/10 kW / Th • W North Am & C America • 5/10 kW / Su-Tu/Th/F • W North Am & C America • 5/10 kW / W/Sa • W North Am & C America • 5/10 kW

FREQUENCY   COUNTRY, STATION, LOCATION

TARGET • NETWORK • POWER (kW)

World Time

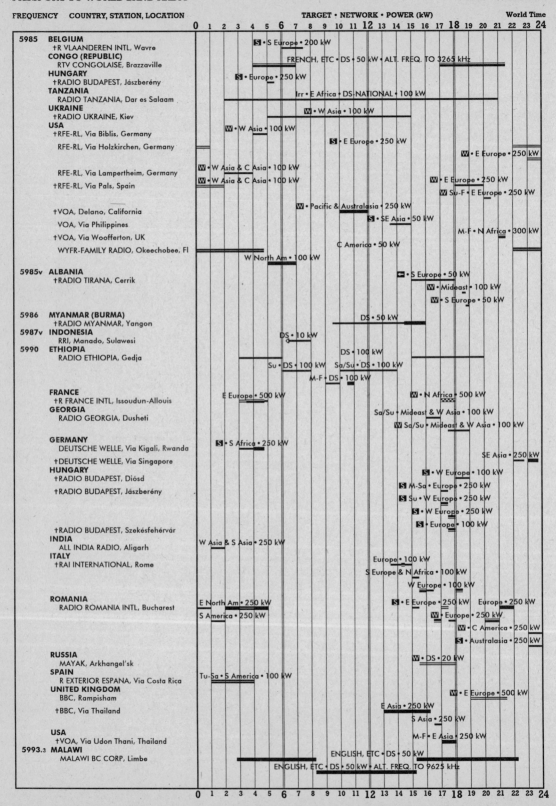

5985	**BELGIUM**
	†R VLAANDEREN INTL, Wavre
	CONGO (REPUBLIC)
	RTV CONGOLAISE, Brazzaville
	HUNGARY
	†RADIO BUDAPEST, Jászberény
	TANZANIA
	RADIO TANZANIA, Dar es Salaam
	UKRAINE
	†RADIO UKRAINE, Kiev
	USA
	†RFE-RL, Via Biblis, Germany
	RFE-RL, Via Holzkirchen, Germany
	RFE-RL, Via Lampertheim, Germany
	†RFE-RL, Via Pals, Spain
	†VOA, Delano, California
	VOA, Via Philippines
	†VOA, Via Woofferton, UK
	WYFR-FAMILY RADIO, Okeechobee, Fl
5985v	**ALBANIA**
	†RADIO TIRANA, Cerrik
5986	**MYANMAR (BURMA)**
	†RADIO MYANMAR, Yangon
5987v	**INDONESIA**
	RRI, Manado, Sulawesi
5990	**ETHIOPIA**
	RADIO ETHIOPIA, Gedja
	FRANCE
	†R FRANCE INTL, Issoudun-Allouis
	GEORGIA
	RADIO GEORGIA, Dusheti
	GERMANY
	DEUTSCHE WELLE, Via Kigali, Rwanda
	†DEUTSCHE WELLE, Via Singapore
	HUNGARY
	†RADIO BUDAPEST, Diósd
	†RADIO BUDAPEST, Jászberény
	†RADIO BUDAPEST, Székesfehérvár
	INDIA
	ALL INDIA RADIO, Aligarh
	ITALY
	†RAI INTERNATIONAL, Rome
	ROMANIA
	RADIO ROMANIA INTL, Bucharest
	RUSSIA
	MAYAK, Arkhangel'sk
	SPAIN
	R EXTERIOR ESPANA, Via Costa Rica
	UNITED KINGDOM
	BBC, Rampisham
	†BBC, Via Thailand
	USA
	†VOA, Via Udon Thani, Thailand
5993.3	**MALAWI**
	MALAWI BC CORP, Limbe

S • S Europe • 200 kW

FRENCH, ETC • DS • 50 kW • ALT. FREQ. TO 3265 kHz

S • Europe • 250 kW

Irr • E Africa • DS • NATIONAL • 100 kW

W • W Asia • 100 kW

W • W Asia • 100 kW

S • E Europe • 250 kW

W • E Europe • 250 kW

W • W Asia & C Asia • 100 kW

W • W Asia & C Asia • 100 kW

W • E Europe • 250 kW

W Su-F • E Europe • 250 kW

W • Pacific & Australasia • 250 kW

S • SE Asia • 50 kW

M-F • N Africa • 300 kW

C America • 50 kW

W North Am • 100 kW

◄ • S Europe • 50 kW

W • Mideast • 100 kW

W • S Europe • 50 kW

DS • 50 kW

DS • 10 kW

DS • 100 kW

Su • DS • 100 kW   Sa/Su • DS • 100 kW

M-F • DS • 100 kW

E Europe • 500 kW

W • N Africa • 500 kW

Sa/Su • Mideast & W Asia • 100 kW

W Sa/Su • Mideast & W Asia • 100 kW

S • S Africa • 250 kW

SE Asia • 250 kW

S • W Europe • 100 kW

S M-Sa • Europe • 250 kW

S Su • W Europe • 250 kW

S • W Europe • 250 kW

S • Europe • 100 kW

W Asia & S Asia • 250 kW

Europe • 100 kW

S Europe & N Africa • 100 kW

W Europe • 100 kW

E North Am • 250 kW

S • E Europe • 250 kW   Europe • 250 kW

S America • 250 kW

W • Europe • 250 kW

W • C America • 250 kW

S • Australasia • 250 kW

W • DS • 20 kW

Tu-Sa • S America • 100 kW

W • E Europe • 500 kW

E Asia • 250 kW

S Asia • 250 kW

M-F • E Asia • 250 kW

ENGLISH, ETC • DS • 50 kW

ENGLISH, ETC • DS • 50 kW • ALT. FREQ. TO 9625 kHz

FREQUENCY   COUNTRY, STATION, LOCATION

TARGET • NETWORK • POWER (kW)

World Time

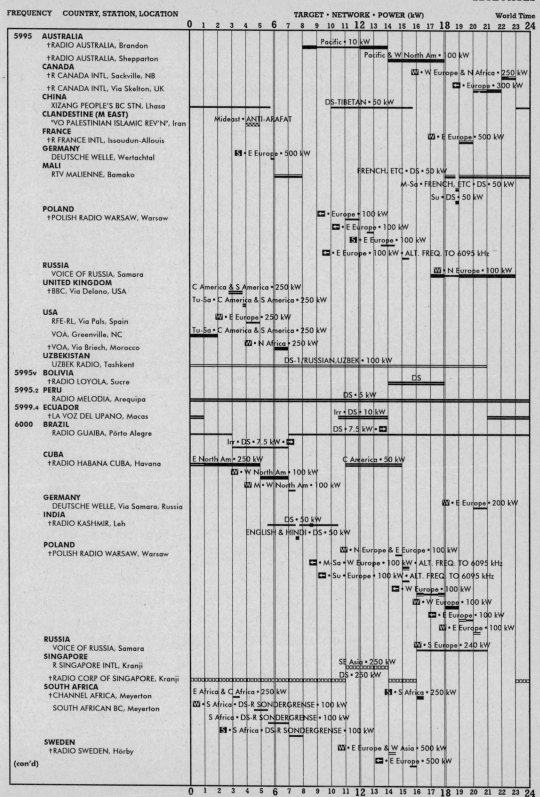

FREQUENCY	COUNTRY, STATION, LOCATION	TARGET • NETWORK • POWER (kW)
5995	**AUSTRALIA**	
	†RADIO AUSTRALIA, Brandon	Pacific • 10 kW
	†RADIO AUSTRALIA, Shepparton	Pacific & W North Am • 100 kW
	CANADA	
	†R CANADA INTL, Sackville, NB	W • W Europe & N Africa • 250 kW
	†R CANADA INTL, Via Skelton, UK	➡ • Europe • 300 kW
	CHINA	
	XIZANG PEOPLE'S BC STN, Lhasa	DS-TIBETAN • 50 kW
	CLANDESTINE (M EAST)	
	"VO PALESTINIAN ISLAMIC REV'N", Iran	Mideast • ANTI-ARAFAT
	FRANCE	
	†R FRANCE INTL, Issoudun-Allouis	W • E Europe • 500 kW
	GERMANY	
	DEUTSCHE WELLE, Wertachtal	S • E Europe • 500 kW
	MALI	
	RTV MALIENNE, Bamako	FRENCH, ETC • DS • 50 kW
		M-Sa • FRENCH, ETC • DS • 50 kW
		Su • DS • 50 kW
	POLAND	
	†POLISH RADIO WARSAW, Warsaw	➡ • Europe • 100 kW
		➡ • E Europe • 100 kW
		S • E Europe • 100 kW
		➡ • E Europe • 100 kW • ALT. FREQ. TO 6095 kHz
	RUSSIA	
	VOICE OF RUSSIA, Samara	W • N Europe • 100 kW
	UNITED KINGDOM	
	†BBC, Via Delano, USA	C America & S America • 250 kW
		Tu-Sa • C America & S America • 250 kW
	USA	
	RFE-RL, Via Pals, Spain	W • E Europe • 250 kW
	VOA, Greenville, NC	Tu-Sa • C America & S America • 250 kW
	†VOA, Via Briech, Morocco	W • N Africa • 250 kW
	UZBEKISTAN	
	UZBEK RADIO, Tashkent	DS-1/RUSSIAN, UZBEK • 100 kW
5995v	**BOLIVIA**	
	†RADIO LOYOLA, Sucre	DS
5995.2	**PERU**	
	RADIO MELODIA, Arequipa	DS • 5 kW
5999.4	**ECUADOR**	
	†LA VOZ DEL UPANO, Macas	Irr • DS • 10 kW
6000	**BRAZIL**	
	RADIO GUAIBA, Pôrto Alegre	DS • 7.5 kW • ➡
		Irr • DS • 7.5 kW • ➡
	CUBA	
	†RADIO HABANA CUBA, Havana	E North Am • 250 kW
		C America • 50 kW
		W • W North Am • 100 kW
		W M • W North Am • 100 kW
	GERMANY	
	DEUTSCHE WELLE, Via Samara, Russia	W • E Europe • 200 kW
	INDIA	
	†RADIO KASHMIR, Leh	DS • 50 kW
		ENGLISH & HINDI • DS • 50 kW
	POLAND	
	†POLISH RADIO WARSAW, Warsaw	W • N Europe & E Europe • 100 kW
		➡ • M-Sa • W Europe • 100 kW • ALT. FREQ. TO 6095 kHz
		➡ • Su • Europe • 100 kW • ALT. FREQ. TO 6095 kHz
		➡ • W Europe • 100 kW
		W • W Europe • 100 kW
		➡ • E Europe • 100 kW
		W • E Europe • 100 kW
	RUSSIA	
	VOICE OF RUSSIA, Samara	W • S Europe • 240 kW
	SINGAPORE	
	R SINGAPORE INTL, Kranji	SE Asia • 250 kW
		DS • 250 kW
	†RADIO CORP OF SINGAPORE, Kranji	
	SOUTH AFRICA	
	†CHANNEL AFRICA, Meyerton	E Africa & C Africa • 250 kW
		S • S Africa • 250 kW
	SOUTH AFRICAN BC, Meyerton	W • S Africa • DS-R SONDERGRENSE • 100 kW
		S Africa • DS-R SONDERGRENSE • 100 kW
		S • S Africa • DS-R SONDERGRENSE • 100 kW
	SWEDEN	
	†RADIO SWEDEN, Hörby	W • E Europe & W Asia • 500 kW
		➡ • E Europe • 500 kW
(con'd)		

FREQUENCY	COUNTRY, STATION, LOCATION	TARGET • NETWORK • POWER (kW)	World Time

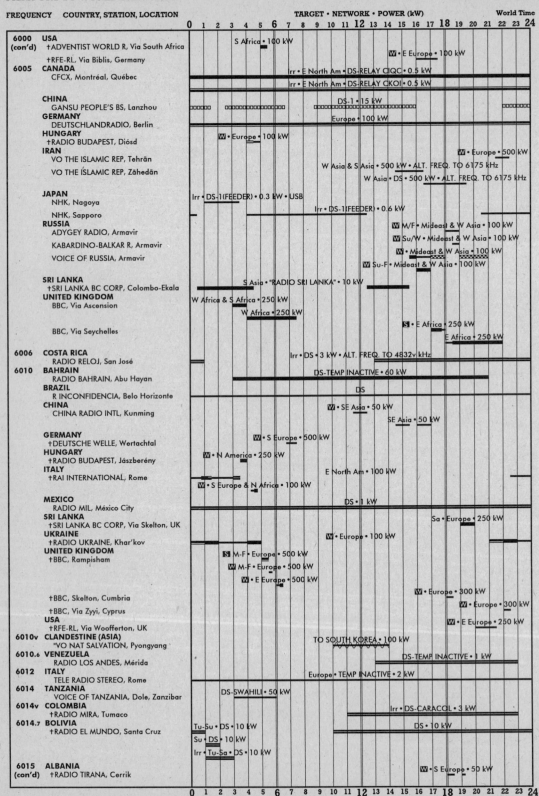

6000	**USA**	
(con'd)	†ADVENTIST WORLD R, Via South Africa	S Africa • 100 kW
	†RFE-RL, Via Biblis, Germany	W • E Europe • 100 kW
6005	**CANADA**	
	CFCX, Montréal, Québec	Irr • E North Am • DS-RELAY CIQC • 0.5 kW
		Irr • E North Am • DS-RELAY CKOI • 0.5 kW
	CHINA	
	GANSU PEOPLE'S BS, Lanzhou	DS-1 • 15 kW
	GERMANY	
	DEUTSCHLANDRADIO, Berlin	Europe • 100 kW
	HUNGARY	
	†RADIO BUDAPEST, Diósd	W • Europe • 100 kW
	IRAN	
	VO THE ISLAMIC REP, Tehrān	W • Europe • 500 kW
		W Asia & S Asia • 500 kW • ALT. FREQ. TO 6175 kHz
	VO THE ÍSLAMIC REP, Zāhedān	W Asia • DS • 500 kW • ALT. FREQ. TO 6175 kHz
	JAPAN	
	NHK, Nagoya	Irr • DS-1(FEEDER) • 0.3 kW • USB
	NHK, Sapporo	Irr • DS-1(FEEDER) • 0.6 kW
	RUSSIA	
	ADYGEY RADIO, Armavir	W M/F • Mideast & W Asia • 100 kW
	KABARDINO-BALKAR R, Armavir	W Su/W • Mideast & W Asia • 100 kW
	VOICE OF RUSSIA, Armavir	W • Mideast & W Asia • 100 kW
		W Su-F • Mideast & W Asia • 100 kW
	SRI LANKA	
	†SRI LANKA BC CORP, Colombo-Ekala	S Asia • "RADIO SRI LANKA" • 10 kW
	UNITED KINGDOM	
	BBC, Via Ascension	W Africa & S Africa • 250 kW
		W Africa • 250 kW
	BBC, Via Seychelles	S • E Africa • 250 kW
		E Africa • 250 kW
6006	**COSTA RICA**	
	RADIO RELOJ, San José	Irr • DS • 3 kW • ALT. FREQ. TO 4832v kHz
6010	**BAHRAIN**	
	RADIO BAHRAIN, Abu Hayan	DS-TEMP INACTIVE • 60 kW
	BRAZIL	
	R INCONFIDENCIA, Belo Horizonte	DS
	CHINA	
	CHINA RADIO INTL, Kunming	W • SE Asia • 50 kW
		SE Asia • 50 kW
	GERMANY	
	†DEUTSCHE WELLE, Wertachtal	W • S Europe • 500 kW
	HUNGARY	
	†RADIO BUDAPEST, Jászberény	W • N America • 250 kW
	ITALY	
	†RAI INTERNATIONAL, Rome	E North Am • 100 kW
		W • S Europe & N Africa • 100 kW
	MEXICO	
	RADIO MIL, México City	DS • 1 kW
	SRI LANKA	
	†SRI LANKA BC CORP, Via Skelton, UK	Sa • Europe • 250 kW
	UKRAINE	
	†RADIO UKRAINE, Khar'kov	W • Europe • 100 kW
	UNITED KINGDOM	
	†BBC, Rampisham	S M-F • Europe • 500 kW
		W M-F • Europe • 500 kW
		W • E Europe • 500 kW
	†BBC, Skelton, Cumbria	W • Europe • 300 kW
	†BBC, Via Zyyi, Cyprus	W • Europe • 300 kW
	USA	
	†RFE-RL, Via Woofferton, UK	W • E Europe • 250 kW
6010v	**CLANDESTINE (ASIA)**	
	"VO NAT SALVATION, Pyongyang	TO SOUTH KOREA • 100 kW
6010.6	**VENEZUELA**	
	RADIO LOS ANDES, Mérida	DS-TEMP INACTIVE • 1 kW
6012	**ITALY**	
	TELE RADIO STEREO, Rome	Europe • TEMP INACTIVE • 2 kW
6014	**TANZANIA**	
	VOICE OF TANZANIA, Dole, Zanzibar	DS-SWAHILI • 50 kW
6014v	**COLOMBIA**	
	†RADIO MIRA, Tumaco	Irr • DS-CARACOL • 3 kW
6014.7	**BOLIVIA**	
	†RADIO EL MUNDO, Santa Cruz	Tu-Su • DS • 10 kW
		DS • 10 kW
		Su • DS • 10 kW
		Irr • Tu-Sa • DS • 10 kW
6015	**ALBANIA**	
(con'd)	†RADIO TIRANA, Cerrik	W • S Europe • 50 kW

ENGLISH ▬▬ ARABIC ⌇⌇⌇ CHINESE ▫▫▫ FRENCH ▬▬ GERMAN ▬▬ RUSSIAN ══ SPANISH ▬▬ OTHER ▬▬

FREQUENCY   COUNTRY, STATION, LOCATION   TARGET • NETWORK • POWER (kW)   World Time

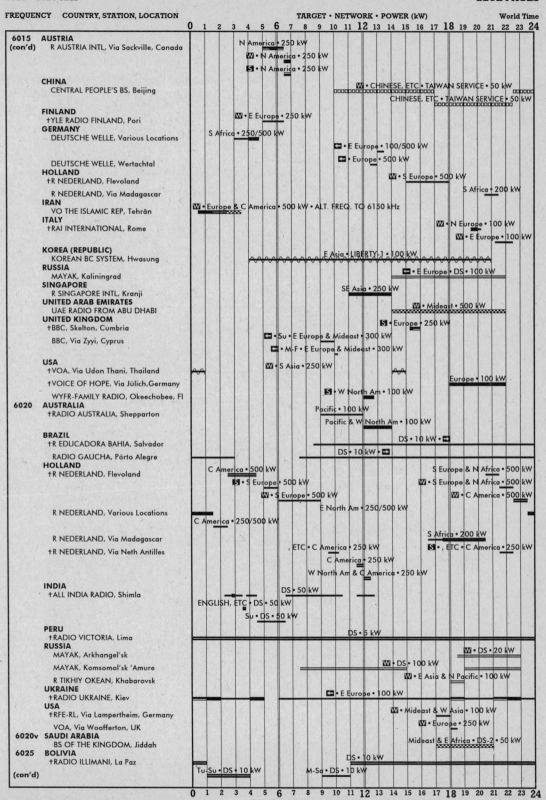

Frequency	Country, Station, Location	Target • Network • Power
6015 (con'd)	AUSTRIA	
	R AUSTRIA INTL, Via Sackville, Canada	N America • 250 kW / W • N America • 250 kW / S • N America • 250 kW
	CHINA	
	CENTRAL PEOPLE'S BS, Beijing	W • CHINESE, ETC • TAIWAN SERVICE • 50 kW / CHINESE, ETC • TAIWAN SERVICE • 50 kW
	FINLAND	
	†YLE RADIO FINLAND, Pori	W • E Europe • 250 kW
	GERMANY	
	DEUTSCHE WELLE, Various Locations	S Africa • 250/500 kW / E Europe • 100/500 kW / Europe • 500 kW
	DEUTSCHE WELLE, Wertachtal	
	HOLLAND	
	†R NEDERLAND, Flevoland	W • S Europe • 500 kW
	R NEDERLAND, Via Madagascar	S Africa • 200 kW
	IRAN	
	VO THE ISLAMIC REP, Tehrān	W • Europe & C America • 500 kW • ALT. FREQ. TO 6150 kHz
	ITALY	
	†RAI INTERNATIONAL, Rome	W • N Europe • 100 kW / W • E Europe • 100 kW
	KOREA (REPUBLIC)	
	KOREAN BC SYSTEM, Hwasung	E Asia • LIBERTY-1 • 100 kW
	RUSSIA	
	MAYAK, Kaliningrad	E Europe • DS • 100 kW
	SINGAPORE	
	R SINGAPORE INTL, Kranji	SE Asia • 250 kW
	UNITED ARAB EMIRATES	
	UAE RADIO FROM ABU DHABI	W • Mideast • 500 kW
	UNITED KINGDOM	
	†BBC, Skelton, Cumbria	S • Europe • 250 kW
	BBC, Via Zyyi, Cyprus	Su • E Europe & Mideast • 300 kW / M-F • E Europe & Mideast • 300 kW
	USA	
	†VOA, Via Udon Thani, Thailand	W • S Asia • 250 kW
	†VOICE OF HOPE, Via Jülich, Germany	Europe • 100 kW
	WYFR-FAMILY RADIO, Okeechobee, Fl	S • W North Am • 100 kW
6020	AUSTRALIA	
	†RADIO AUSTRALIA, Shepparton	Pacific • 100 kW / Pacific & W North Am • 100 kW
	BRAZIL	
	†R EDUCADORA BAHIA, Salvador	DS • 10 kW
	RADIO GAUCHA, Pôrto Alegre	DS • 10 kW
	HOLLAND	
	†R NEDERLAND, Flevoland	C America • 500 kW / S Europe & N Africa • 500 kW / S • S Europe • 500 kW / W • S Europe & N Africa • 500 kW / W • S Europe • 500 kW / W • C America • 500 kW
		E North Am • 250/500 kW
	R NEDERLAND, Various Locations	C America • 250/500 kW
	R NEDERLAND, Via Madagascar	S Africa • 200 kW
	†R NEDERLAND, Via Neth Antilles	, ETC • C America • 250 kW / S • , ETC • C America • 250 kW / C America • 250 kW / W North Am & C America • 250 kW
	INDIA	
	†ALL INDIA RADIO, Shimla	DS • 50 kW / ENGLISH, ETC • DS • 50 kW / Su • DS • 50 kW
	PERU	
	†RADIO VICTORIA, Lima	DS • 5 kW
	RUSSIA	
	MAYAK, Arkhangel'sk	W • DS • 20 kW
	MAYAK, Komsomol'sk 'Amure	W • DS • 100 kW
	R TIKHIY OKEAN, Khabarovsk	W • E Asia & N Pacific • 100 kW
	UKRAINE	
	†RADIO UKRAINE, Kiev	E Europe • 100 kW
	USA	
	†RFE-RL, Via Lampertheim, Germany	W • Mideast & W Asia • 100 kW
	VOA, Via Woofferton, UK	W • Europe • 250 kW
6020v	SAUDI ARABIA	
	BS OF THE KINGDOM, Jiddah	Mideast & E Africa • DS-2 • 50 kW
6025	BOLIVIA	
	†RADIO ILLIMANI, La Paz	DS • 10 kW / Tu-Su • DS • 10 kW / M-Sa • DS • 10 kW
(con'd)		

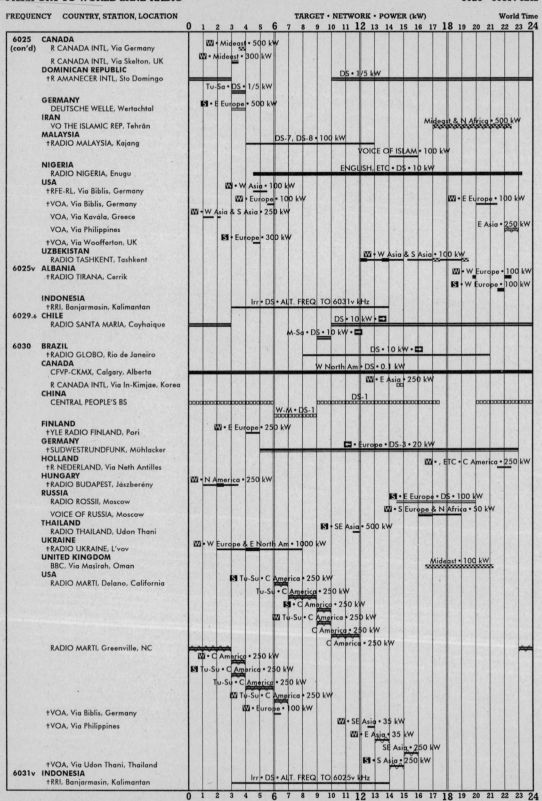

FREQUENCY	COUNTRY, STATION, LOCATION	TARGET • NETWORK • POWER (kW)	World Time

6025 **CANADA**
(con'd) R CANADA INTL, Via Germany — W • Mideast • 500 kW
R CANADA INTL, Via Skelton, UK — W • Mideast • 300 kW
DOMINICAN REPUBLIC
†R AMANECER INTL, Sto Domingo — DS • 1/5 kW
Tu-Sa • DS • 1/5 kW
GERMANY
DEUTSCHE WELLE, Wertachtal — S • E Europe • 500 kW
IRAN
VO THE ISLAMIC REP, Tehrān — Mideast & N Africa • 500 kW
MALAYSIA
†RADIO MALAYSIA, Kajang — DS-7, DS-8 • 100 kW
VOICE OF ISLAM • 100 kW
NIGERIA
RADIO NIGERIA, Enugu — ENGLISH, ETC • DS • 10 kW
USA
†RFE-RL, Via Biblis, Germany — W • W Asia • 100 kW
W • Europe • 100 kW — W • E Europe • 100 kW
†VOA, Via Biblis, Germany — W • W Asia & S Asia • 250 kW
VOA, Via Kavála, Greece — E Asia • 250 kW
VOA, Via Philippines
†VOA, Via Woofferton, UK — S • Europe • 300 kW
UZBEKISTAN
RADIO TASHKENT, Tashkent — W • W Asia & S Asia • 100 kW
6025v **ALBANIA**
†RADIO TIRANA, Cerrik — W • W Europe • 100 kW
S • W Europe • 100 kW
INDONESIA
†RRI, Banjarmasin, Kalimantan — Irr • DS • ALT. FREQ TO 6031v kHz
6029.6 **CHILE**
RADIO SANTA MARIA, Coyhaique — DS • 10 kW
M-Sa • DS • 10 kW
6030 **BRAZIL**
†RADIO GLOBO, Rio de Janeiro — DS • 10 kW
CANADA
CFVP-CKMX, Calgary, Alberta — W North Am • DS • 0.1 kW
R CANADA INTL, Via In-Kimjae, Korea — W • E Asia • 250 kW
CHINA
CENTRAL PEOPLE'S BS — DS-1
W-M • DS-1
FINLAND
†YLE RADIO FINLAND, Pori — W • E Europe • 250 kW
GERMANY
†SUDWESTRUNDFUNK, Mühlacker — • Europe • DS-3 • 20 kW
HOLLAND
†R NEDERLAND, Via Neth Antilles — W • , ETC • C America • 250 kW
HUNGARY
†RADIO BUDAPEST, Jászberény — W • N America • 250 kW
RUSSIA
RADIO ROSSII, Moscow — S • E Europe • DS • 100 kW
VOICE OF RUSSIA, Moscow — W • S Europe & N Africa • 50 kW
THAILAND
RADIO THAILAND, Udon Thani — S • SE Asia • 500 kW
UKRAINE
†RADIO UKRAINE, L'vov — W • W Europe & E North Am • 1000 kW
UNITED KINGDOM
BBC, Via Maṣirah, Oman — Mideast • 100 kW
USA
RADIO MARTI, Delano, California — S Tu-Su • C America • 250 kW
Tu-Su • C America • 250 kW
S • C America • 250 kW
W Tu-Su • C America • 250 kW
C America • 250 kW
C America • 250 kW
RADIO MARTI, Greenville, NC — W • C America • 250 kW
S Tu-Su • C America • 250 kW
Tu-Su • C America • 250 kW
W Tu-Su • C America • 250 kW
W • Europe • 100 kW
†VOA, Via Biblis, Germany — W • SE Asia • 35 kW
†VOA, Via Philippines — W • E Asia • 35 kW
SE Asia • 250 kW
S • S Asia • 250 kW
†VOA, Via Udon Thani, Thailand
6031v **INDONESIA**
†RRI, Banjarmasin, Kalimantan — Irr • DS • ALT. FREQ TO 6025v kHz

ENGLISH ▬ ARABIC ∽∽∽ CHINESE □□□ FRENCH ▬ GERMAN ▬ RUSSIAN ═ SPANISH ▬ OTHER ▬

| FREQUENCY | COUNTRY, STATION, LOCATION | TARGET • NETWORK • POWER (kW) | World Time |

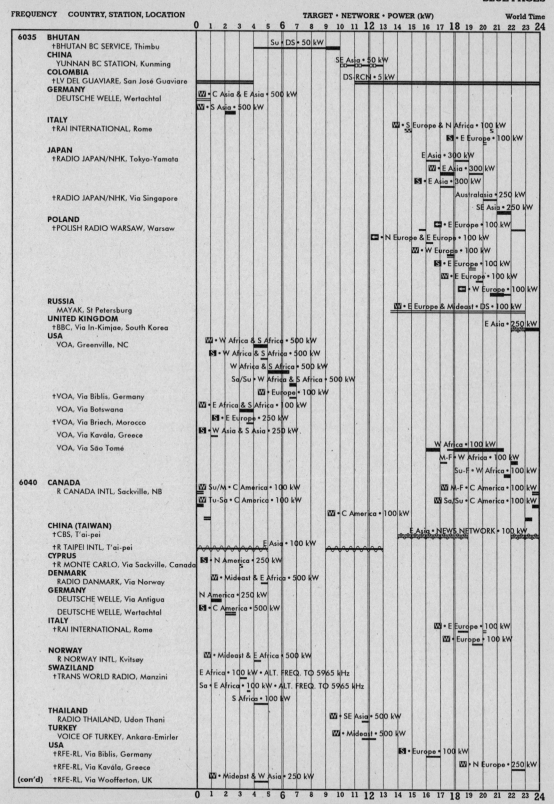

6035 BHUTAN
  †BHUTAN BC SERVICE, Thimbu — Su • DS • 50 kW
CHINA
  YUNNAN BC STATION, Kunming — SE Asia • 50 kW
COLOMBIA
  †LV DEL GUAVIARE, San José Guaviare — DS-RCN • 5 kW
GERMANY
  DEUTSCHE WELLE, Wertachtal — W • C Asia & E Asia • 500 kW; W • S Asia • 500 kW
ITALY
  †RAI INTERNATIONAL, Rome — W • S Europe & N Africa • 100 kW; S • E Europe • 100 kW
JAPAN
  †RADIO JAPAN/NHK, Tokyo-Yamata — E Asia • 300 kW; W • E Asia • 300 kW; S • E Asia • 300 kW
  †RADIO JAPAN/NHK, Via Singapore — Australasia • 250 kW; SE Asia • 250 kW
POLAND
  †POLISH RADIO WARSAW, Warsaw — E Europe • 100 kW; N Europe & E Europe • 100 kW; W • W Europe • 100 kW; S • E Europe • 100 kW; W • E Europe • 100 kW; W Europe • 100 kW
RUSSIA
  MAYAK, St Petersburg — W • E Europe & Mideast • DS • 100 kW
UNITED KINGDOM
  †BBC, Via In-Kimjae, South Korea — E Asia • 250 kW
USA
  VOA, Greenville, NC — W • W Africa & S Africa • 500 kW; S • W Africa & S Africa • 500 kW; W Africa & S Africa • 500 kW; Sa/Su • W Africa & S Africa • 500 kW; W • Europe • 100 kW
  †VOA, Via Biblis, Germany — W • E Africa & S Africa • 100 kW
  VOA, Via Botswana — S • E Europe • 250 kW
  †VOA, Via Briech, Morocco — S • W Asia & S Asia • 250 kW
  VOA, Via Kavála, Greece
  VOA, Via São Tomé — W Africa • 100 kW; M-F • W Africa • 100 kW; Su-F • W Africa • 100 kW

6040 CANADA
  R CANADA INTL, Sackville, NB — W Su/M • C America • 100 kW; W Tu-Sa • C America • 100 kW; W • C America • 100 kW; W M-F • C America • 100 kW; W Sa/Su • C America • 100 kW
CHINA (TAIWAN)
  †CBS, T'ai-pei — E Asia • NEWS NETWORK • 100 kW
  †R TAIPEI INTL, T'ai-pei — E Asia • 100 kW
CYPRUS
  †R MONTE CARLO, Via Sackville, Canada — S • N America • 250 kW
DENMARK
  RADIO DANMARK, Via Norway — W • Mideast & E Africa • 500 kW
GERMANY
  DEUTSCHE WELLE, Via Antigua — N America • 250 kW
  DEUTSCHE WELLE, Wertachtal — S • C America • 500 kW
ITALY
  †RAI INTERNATIONAL, Rome — W • E Europe • 100 kW; W • Europe • 100 kW
NORWAY
  R NORWAY INTL, Kvitsøy — W • Mideast & E Africa • 500 kW
SWAZILAND
  †TRANS WORLD RADIO, Manzini — E Africa • 100 kW • ALT. FREQ. TO 5965 kHz; Sa • E Africa • 100 kW • ALT. FREQ. TO 5965 kHz; S Africa • 100 kW
THAILAND
  RADIO THAILAND, Udon Thani — W • SE Asia • 500 kW
TURKEY
  VOICE OF TURKEY, Ankara-Emirler — W • Mideast • 500 kW
USA
  †RFE-RL, Via Biblis, Germany — S • Europe • 100 kW
  †RFE-RL, Via Kavála, Greece — W • N Europe • 250 kW
(con'd) †RFE-RL, Via Woofferton, UK — W • Mideast & W Asia • 250 kW

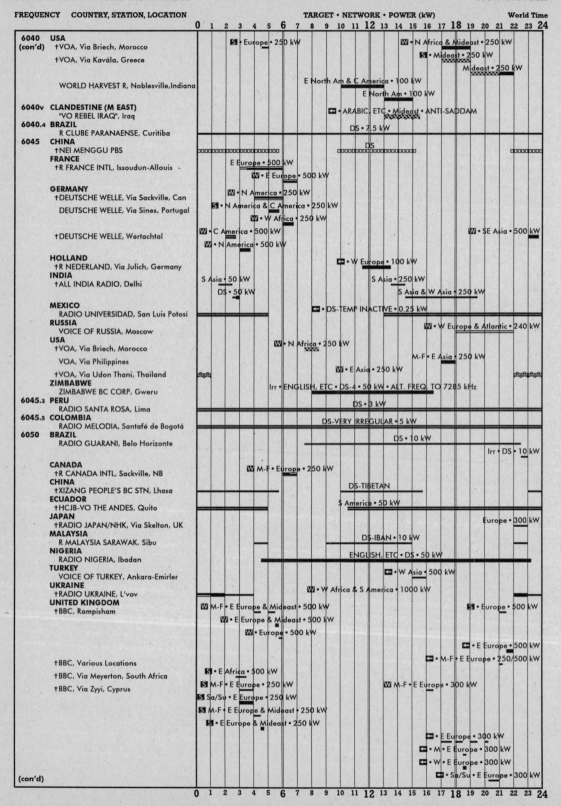

FREQUENCY   COUNTRY, STATION, LOCATION   TARGET • NETWORK • POWER (kW)   World Time

6040	**USA**	
(con'd)	†VOA, Via Briech, Morocco	S • Europe • 250 kW / W • N Africa & Mideast • 250 kW
	†VOA, Via Kavála, Greece	S • Mideast • 250 kW / Mideast • 250 kW
	WORLD HARVEST R, Noblesville, Indiana	E North Am & C America • 100 kW / E North Am • 100 kW
6040v	**CLANDESTINE (M EAST)**	
	"VO REBEL IRAQ", Iraq	ARABIC, ETC • Mideast • ANTI-SADDAM
6040.4	**BRAZIL**	
	R CLUBE PARANAENSE, Curitiba	DS • 7.5 kW
6045	**CHINA**	
	†NEI MENGGU PBS	DS
	FRANCE	
	†R FRANCE INTL, Issoudun-Allouis	E Europe • 500 kW / W • E Europe • 500 kW
	GERMANY	
	†DEUTSCHE WELLE, Via Sackville, Can	W • N America • 250 kW
	DEUTSCHE WELLE, Via Sines, Portugal	S • N America & C America • 250 kW / W • W Africa • 250 kW
	†DEUTSCHE WELLE, Wertachtal	W • C America • 500 kW / W • SE Asia • 500 kW / W • N America • 500 kW
	HOLLAND	
	†R NEDERLAND, Via Julich, Germany	W • W Europe • 100 kW
	INDIA	
	†ALL INDIA RADIO, Delhi	S Asia • 50 kW / S Asia • 250 kW / DS • 50 kW / S Asia & W Asia • 250 kW
	MEXICO	
	RADIO UNIVERSIDAD, San Luis Potosí	DS-TEMP INACTIVE • 0.25 kW
	RUSSIA	
	VOICE OF RUSSIA, Moscow	W • W Europe & Atlantic • 240 kW
	USA	
	†VOA, Via Briech, Morocco	W • N Africa • 250 kW
	VOA, Via Philippines	M-F • E Asia • 250 kW
	†VOA, Via Udon Thani, Thailand	W • E Asia • 250 kW
	ZIMBABWE	
	ZIMBABWE BC CORP, Gweru	Irr • ENGLISH, ETC • DS-4 • 50 kW • ALT. FREQ. TO 7285 kHz
6045.3	**PERU**	
	RADIO SANTA ROSA, Lima	DS • 3 kW
6045.5	**COLOMBIA**	
	RADIO MELODIA, Santafé de Bogotá	DS-VERY IRREGULAR • 5 kW
6050	**BRAZIL**	
	RADIO GUARANI, Belo Horizonte	DS • 10 kW / Irr • DS • 10 kW
	CANADA	
	†R CANADA INTL, Sackville, NB	W • M-F • Europe • 250 kW
	CHINA	
	†XIZANG PEOPLE'S BC STN, Lhasa	DS-TIBETAN
	ECUADOR	
	†HCJB-VO THE ANDES, Quito	S America • 50 kW
	JAPAN	
	†RADIO JAPAN/NHK, Via Skelton, UK	Europe • 300 kW
	MALAYSIA	
	R MALAYSIA SARAWAK, Sibu	DS-IBAN • 10 kW
	NIGERIA	
	RADIO NIGERIA, Ibadan	ENGLISH, ETC • DS • 50 kW
	TURKEY	
	VOICE OF TURKEY, Ankara-Emirler	W Asia • 500 kW
	UKRAINE	
	†RADIO UKRAINE, L'vov	W • W Africa & S America • 1000 kW
	UNITED KINGDOM	
	†BBC, Rampisham	W • M-F • E Europe & Mideast • 500 kW / S • Europe • 500 kW / W • E Europe & Mideast • 500 kW / W • Europe • 500 kW / E Europe • 500 kW / M-F • E Europe • 250/500 kW
	†BBC, Various Locations	S • E Africa • 500 kW
	†BBC, Via Meyerton, South Africa	S • M-F • E Europe • 250 kW / W • M-F • E Europe • 300 kW
	†BBC, Via Zyyi, Cyprus	S • Sa/Su • E Europe • 250 kW / S • M-F • E Europe & Mideast • 250 kW / S • E Europe & Mideast • 250 kW / E Europe • 300 kW / M • E Europe • 300 kW / W • E Europe • 300 kW / Sa/Su • E Europe • 300 kW
(con'd)		

FREQUENCY   COUNTRY, STATION, LOCATION

TARGET • NETWORK • POWER (kW)

World Time

0 1 2 3 4 5 6 7 8 9 10 11 12 13 14 15 16 17 18 19 20 21 22 23 24

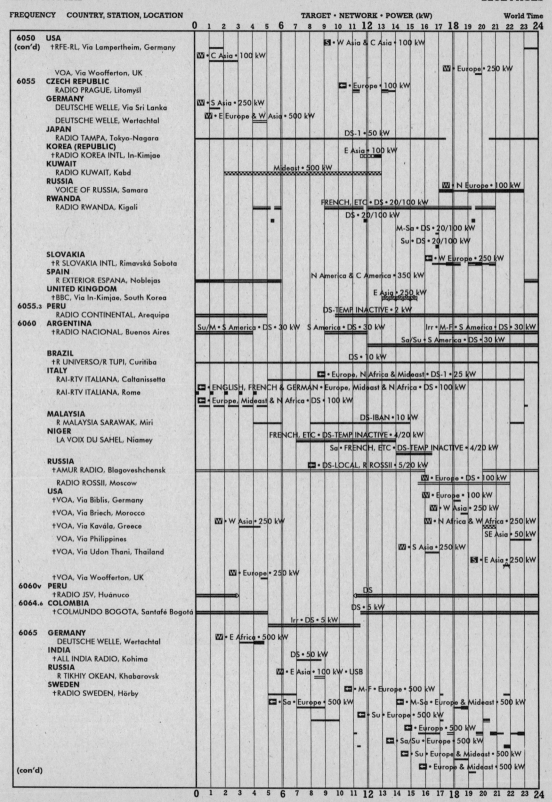

6050	USA	
(con'd)	†RFE-RL, Via Lampertheim, Germany	S • W Asia & C Asia • 100 kW / W • C Asia • 100 kW
	VOA, Via Woofferton, UK	W • Europe • 250 kW
6055	CZECH REPUBLIC	
	RADIO PRAGUE, Litomyšl	⇆ • Europe • 100 kW
	GERMANY	
	DEUTSCHE WELLE, Via Sri Lanka	W • S Asia • 250 kW
	DEUTSCHE WELLE, Wertachtal	W • E Europe & W Asia • 500 kW
	JAPAN	
	RADIO TAMPA, Tokyo-Nagara	DS-1 • 50 kW
	KOREA (REPUBLIC)	
	†RADIO KOREA INTL, In-Kimjae	E Asia • 100 kW
	KUWAIT	
	RADIO KUWAIT, Kabd	Mideast • 500 kW
	RUSSIA	
	VOICE OF RUSSIA, Samara	W • N Europe • 100 kW
	RWANDA	
	RADIO RWANDA, Kigali	FRENCH, ETC • DS • 20/100 kW / DS • 20/100 kW / M-Sa • DS • 20/100 kW / Su • DS • 20/100 kW
	SLOVAKIA	
	†R SLOVAKIA INTL, Rimavská Sobota	⇆ • W Europe • 250 kW
	SPAIN	
	R EXTERIOR ESPANA, Noblejas	N America & C America • 350 kW
	UNITED KINGDOM	
	†BBC, Via In-Kimjae, South Korea	E Asia • 250 kW
6055.3	PERU	
	RADIO CONTINENTAL, Arequipa	DS-TEMP INACTIVE • 2 kW
6060	ARGENTINA	
	†RADIO NACIONAL, Buenos Aires	Su/M • S America • DS • 30 kW / S America • DS • 30 kW / Irr • M-F • S America • DS • 30 kW / Sa/Su • S America • DS • 30 kW
	BRAZIL	
	†R UNIVERSO/R TUPI, Curitiba	DS • 10 kW
	ITALY	
	RAI-RTV ITALIANA, Caltanissetta	⇆ • Europe, N Africa & Mideast • DS-1 • 25 kW
	RAI-RTV ITALIANA, Rome	⇆ • ENGLISH, FRENCH & GERMAN • Europe, Mideast & N Africa • DS • 100 kW / ⇆ • Europe, Mideast & N Africa • DS • 100 kW
	MALAYSIA	
	R MALAYSIA SARAWAK, Miri	DS-IBAN • 10 kW
	NIGER	
	LA VOIX DU SAHEL, Niamey	FRENCH, ETC • DS-TEMP INACTIVE • 4/20 kW / Sa • FRENCH, ETC • DS-TEMP INACTIVE • 4/20 kW
	RUSSIA	
	†AMUR RADIO, Blagoveshchensk	⇆ • DS-LOCAL, R ROSSII • 5/20 kW
	RADIO ROSSII, Moscow	W • Europe • DS • 100 kW
	USA	
	†VOA, Via Biblis, Germany	W • Europe • 100 kW
	†VOA, Via Briech, Morocco	W • W Asia • 250 kW
	†VOA, Via Kavála, Greece	W • W Asia • 250 kW / W • N Africa & W Africa • 250 kW / SE Asia • 50 kW
	VOA, Via Philippines	W • S Asia • 250 kW
	†VOA, Via Udon Thani, Thailand	S • E Asia • 250 kW
	†VOA, Via Woofferton, UK	W • Europe • 250 kW
6060v	PERU	
	†RADIO JSV, Huánuco	DS
6064.6	COLOMBIA	
	†COLMUNDO BOGOTA, Santafé Bogotá	DS • 5 kW / Irr • DS • 5 kW
6065	GERMANY	
	DEUTSCHE WELLE, Wertachtal	W • E Africa • 500 kW
	INDIA	
	†ALL INDIA RADIO, Kohima	DS • 50 kW
	RUSSIA	
	R TIKHIY OKEAN, Khabarovsk	W • E Asia • 100 kW • USB
	SWEDEN	
	†RADIO SWEDEN, Hörby	⇆ • M-F • Europe • 500 kW / ⇆ • M-Sa • Europe & Mideast • 500 kW / ⇆ • Sa • Europe • 500 kW / ⇆ • Su • Europe • 500 kW / ⇆ • Europe • 500 kW / ⇆ • Sa/Su • Europe • 500 kW / ⇆ • Su • Europe & Mideast • 500 kW / ⇆ • Europe & Mideast • 500 kW
(con'd)		

0 1 2 3 4 5 6 7 8 9 10 11 12 13 14 15 16 17 18 19 20 21 22 23 24

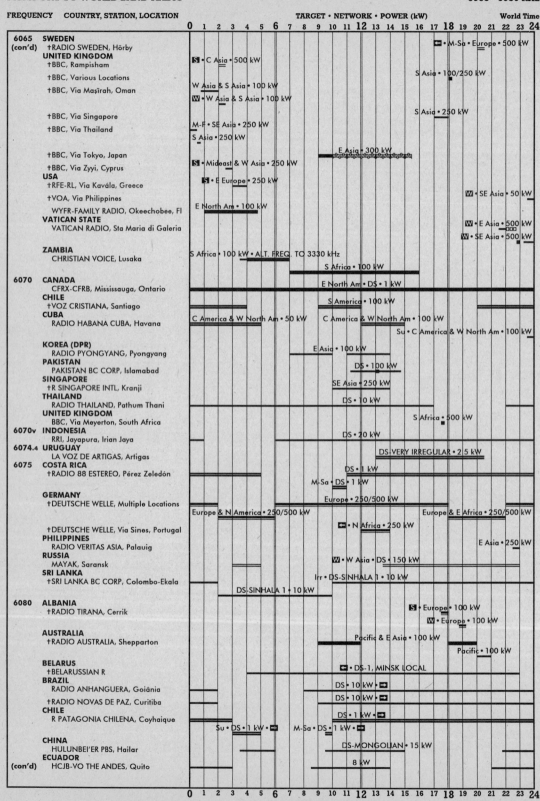

FREQUENCY   COUNTRY, STATION, LOCATION   TARGET • NETWORK • POWER (kW)   World Time

6065	SWEDEN	
(con'd)	†RADIO SWEDEN, Hörby	M-Sa • Europe • 500 kW
	UNITED KINGDOM	
	†BBC, Rampisham	S • C Asia • 500 kW
	†BBC, Various Locations	S Asia • 100/250 kW
	†BBC, Via Maşīrah, Oman	W Asia & S Asia • 100 kW / W • W Asia & S Asia • 100 kW
	†BBC, Via Singapore	S Asia • 250 kW
	†BBC, Via Thailand	M-F • SE Asia • 250 kW / S Asia • 250 kW
	†BBC, Via Tokyo, Japan	E Asia • 300 kW
	†BBC, Via Zyyi, Cyprus	S • Mideast & W Asia • 250 kW
	USA	
	†RFE-RL, Via Kavála, Greece	S • E Europe • 250 kW
	†VOA, Via Philippines	W • SE Asia • 50 kW
	WYFR-FAMILY RADIO, Okeechobee, Fl	E North Am • 100 kW
	VATICAN STATE	
	VATICAN RADIO, Sta Maria di Galeria	W • E Asia • 500 kW / W • SE Asia • 500 kW
	ZAMBIA	
	CHRISTIAN VOICE, Lusaka	S Africa • 100 kW • ALT. FREQ. TO 3330 kHz / S Africa • 100 kW
6070	CANADA	
	CFRX-CFRB, Mississauga, Ontario	E North Am • DS • 1 kW
	CHILE	
	†VOZ CRISTIANA, Santiago	S America • 100 kW
	CUBA	
	RADIO HABANA CUBA, Havana	C America & W North Am • 50 kW / C America & W North Am • 100 kW / Su • C America & W North Am • 100 kW
	KOREA (DPR)	
	RADIO PYONGYANG, Pyongyang	E Asia • 100 kW
	PAKISTAN	
	PAKISTAN BC CORP, Islamabad	DS • 100 kW
	SINGAPORE	
	†R SINGAPORE INTL, Kranji	SE Asia • 250 kW
	THAILAND	
	RADIO THAILAND, Pathum Thani	DS • 10 kW
	UNITED KINGDOM	
	BBC, Via Meyerton, South Africa	S Africa • 500 kW
6070v	INDONESIA	
	RRI, Jayapura, Irian Jaya	DS • 20 kW
6074.4	URUGUAY	
	LA VOZ DE ARTIGAS, Artigas	DS • VERY IRREGULAR • 2.5 kW
6075	COSTA RICA	
	†RADIO 88 ESTEREO, Pérez Zeledón	DS • 1 kW / M-Sa • DS • 1 kW
	GERMANY	
	†DEUTSCHE WELLE, Multiple Locations	Europe • 250/500 kW / Europe & N America • 250/500 kW / Europe & E Africa • 250/500 kW
	†DEUTSCHE WELLE, Via Sines, Portugal	N Africa • 250 kW
	PHILIPPINES	
	RADIO VERITAS ASIA, Palauig	E Asia • 250 kW
	RUSSIA	
	MAYAK, Saransk	W • W Asia • DS • 150 kW
	SRI LANKA	
	†SRI LANKA BC CORP, Colombo-Ekala	Irr • DS-SINHALA 1 • 10 kW / DS-SINHALA 1 • 10 kW
6080	ALBANIA	
	†RADIO TIRANA, Cerrik	S • Europe • 100 kW / W • Europe • 100 kW
	AUSTRALIA	
	†RADIO AUSTRALIA, Shepparton	Pacific & E Asia • 100 kW / Pacific • 100 kW
	BELARUS	
	†BELARUSSIAN R	DS-1, MINSK LOCAL
	BRAZIL	
	RADIO ANHANGUERA, Goiânia	DS • 10 kW •
	†RADIO NOVAS DE PAZ, Curitiba	DS • 10 kW •
	CHILE	
	R PATAGONIA CHILENA, Coyhaique	DS • 1 kW • / Su • DS • 1 kW • / M-Sa • DS • 1 kW •
	CHINA	
	HULUNBEI'ER PBS, Hailar	DS-MONGOLIAN • 15 kW
	ECUADOR	
(con'd)	HCJB-VO THE ANDES, Quito	8 kW

FREQUENCY	COUNTRY, STATION, LOCATION	TARGET • NETWORK • POWER (kW)	World Time

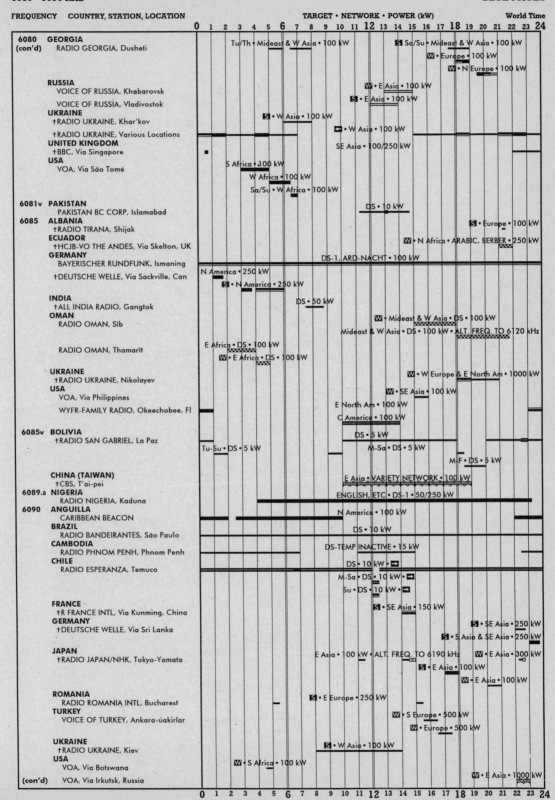

0 1 2 3 4 5 6 7 8 9 10 11 12 13 14 15 16 17 18 19 20 21 22 23 24

6080   **GEORGIA**
(con'd)   RADIO GEORGIA, Dusheti
- Tu/Th • Mideast & W Asia • 100 kW
- S Sa/Su • Mideast & W Asia • 100 kW
- W • Europe • 100 kW
- W • N Europe • 100 kW

RUSSIA
   VOICE OF RUSSIA, Khabarovsk
- W • E Asia • 100 kW

   VOICE OF RUSSIA, Vladivostok
- S • E Asia • 100 kW

UKRAINE
   †RADIO UKRAINE, Khar'kov
- S • W Asia • 100 kW

   †RADIO UKRAINE, Various Locations
- W Asia • 100 kW

UNITED KINGDOM
   †BBC, Via Singapore
- SE Asia • 100/250 kW

USA
   VOA, Via São Tomé
- S Africa • 100 kW
- W Africa • 100 kW
- Sa/Su • W Africa • 100 kW

6081v   **PAKISTAN**
   PAKISTAN BC CORP, Islamabad
- DS • 10 kW

6085   **ALBANIA**
   †RADIO TIRANA, Shijak
- S • Europe • 100 kW

ECUADOR
   †HCJB-VO THE ANDES, Via Skelton, UK
- W • N Africa • ARABIC, BERBER • 250 kW

GERMANY
   BAYERISCHER RUNDFUNK, Ismaning
- DS-1, ARD-NACHT • 100 kW

   †DEUTSCHE WELLE, Via Sackville, Can
- N America • 250 kW
- S • N America • 250 kW

INDIA
   †ALL INDIA RADIO, Gangtok
- DS • 50 kW

OMAN
   RADIO OMAN, Sïb
- W • Mideast & W Asia • DS • 100 kW
- Mideast & W Asia • DS • 100 kW • ALT. FREQ. TO 6120 kHz

   RADIO OMAN, Thamarït
- E Africa • DS • 100 kW
- W • E Africa • DS • 100 kW

UKRAINE
   †RADIO UKRAINE, Nikolayev
- W • W Europe & E North Am • 1000 kW

USA
   VOA, Via Philippines
- W • SE Asia • 100 kW

   WYFR-FAMILY RADIO, Okeechobee, Fl
- E North Am • 100 kW
- C America • 100 kW

6085v   **BOLIVIA**
   †RADIO SAN GABRIEL, La Paz
- DS • 5 kW
- Tu-Su • DS • 5 kW
- M-Sa • DS • 5 kW
- M-F • DS • 5 kW

CHINA (TAIWAN)
   †CBS, T'ai-pei
- E Asia • VARIETY NETWORK • 100 kW

6089.8   **NIGERIA**
   RADIO NIGERIA, Kaduna
- ENGLISH, ETC • DS-1 • 50/250 kW

6090   **ANGUILLA**
   CARIBBEAN BEACON
- N America • 100 kW

BRAZIL
   RADIO BANDEIRANTES, São Paulo
- DS • 10 kW

CAMBODIA
   RADIO PHNOM PENH, Phnom Penh
- DS-TEMP INACTIVE • 15 kW

CHILE
   RADIO ESPERANZA, Temuco
- DS • 10 kW
- M-Sa • DS • 10 kW
- Su • DS • 10 kW

FRANCE
   †R FRANCE INTL, Via Kunming, China
- S • SE Asia • 150 kW

GERMANY
   †DEUTSCHE WELLE, Via Sri Lanka
- S • SE Asia • 250 kW
- S • S Asia & SE Asia • 250 kW

JAPAN
   †RADIO JAPAN/NHK, Tokyo-Yamata
- E Asia • 100 kW • ALT. FREQ. TO 6190 kHz
- W • E Asia • 300 kW
- S • E Asia • 100 kW
- W • E Asia • 100 kW

ROMANIA
   RADIO ROMANIA INTL, Bucharest
- S • E Europe • 250 kW

TURKEY
   VOICE OF TURKEY, Ankara-úakirlar
- W • S Europe • 500 kW
- W • Europe • 500 kW

UKRAINE
   †RADIO UKRAINE, Kiev
- S • W Asia • 100 kW

USA
   VOA, Via Botswana
- W • S Africa • 100 kW

(con'd)   VOA, Via Irkutsk, Russia
- W • E Asia • 1000 kW

0 1 2 3 4 5 6 7 8 9 10 11 12 13 14 15 16 17 18 19 20 21 22 23 24

SEASONAL S OR W   1-HR TIMESHIFT MIDYEAR ⇦ OR ⇨   JAMMING / OR /\   EARLIEST HEARD ◁   LATEST HEARD ▷   NEW FOR 1999 †

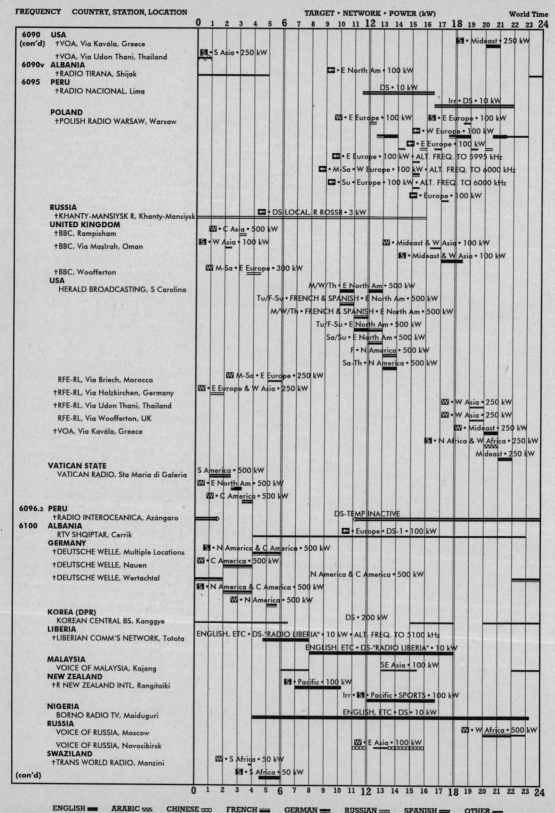

FREQUENCY   COUNTRY, STATION, LOCATION   TARGET • NETWORK • POWER (kW)   World Time

6090   **USA**
(con'd)   †VOA, Via Kavála, Greece — S • Mideast • 250 kW
       †VOA, Via Udon Thani, Thailand — S • S Asia • 250 kW
6090v   **ALBANIA**
       †RADIO TIRANA, Shijak — • E North Am • 100 kW
6095   **PERU**
       †RADIO NACIONAL, Lima — DS • 10 kW / Irr • DS • 10 kW

       POLAND
       †POLISH RADIO WARSAW, Warsaw — W • E Europe • 100 kW / S • E Europe • 100 kW
       • W Europe • 100 kW
       • E Europe • 100 kW
       • E Europe • 100 kW • ALT. FREQ. TO 5995 kHz
       • M-Sa • W Europe • 100 kW • ALT. FREQ. TO 6000 kHz
       • Su • Europe • 100 kW • ALT. FREQ. TO 6000 kHz
       • Europe • 100 kW

       RUSSIA
       †KHANTY-MANSIYSK R, Khanty-Mansiysk — • DS-LOCAL, R ROSSII • 3 kW
       UNITED KINGDOM
       †BBC, Rampisham — W • C Asia • 500 kW
       †BBC, Via Maṣīrah, Oman — S • W Asia • 100 kW / W • Mideast & W Asia • 100 kW / S • Mideast & W Asia • 100 kW

       †BBC, Woofferton — W • M-Sa • E Europe • 300 kW
       USA
       HERALD BROADCASTING, S Carolina — M/W/Th • E North Am • 500 kW
       Tu/F-Su • FRENCH & SPANISH • E North Am • 500 kW
       M/W/Th • FRENCH & SPANISH • E North Am • 500 kW
       Tu/F-Su • E North Am • 500 kW
       Sa/Su • E North Am • 500 kW
       F • N America • 500 kW
       Sa-Th • N America • 500 kW

       RFE-RL, Via Briech, Morocco — W • M-Sa • E Europe • 250 kW
       †RFE-RL, Via Holzkirchen, Germany — W • E Europe & W Asia • 250 kW
       †RFE-RL, Via Udon Thani, Thailand — W • W Asia • 250 kW
       RFE-RL, Via Woofferton, UK — W • W Asia • 250 kW
       †VOA, Via Kavála, Greece — W • Mideast • 250 kW / S • N Africa & W Africa • 250 kW / Mideast • 250 kW

       VATICAN STATE
       VATICAN RADIO, Sta Maria di Galeria — S America • 500 kW
       W • E North Am • 500 kW
       W • C America • 500 kW

6096.3 **PERU**
       †RADIO INTEROCEANICA, Azángaro — DS-TEMP INACTIVE
6100   **ALBANIA**
       RTV SHQIPTAR, Cerrik — • Europe • DS-1 • 100 kW
       GERMANY
       †DEUTSCHE WELLE, Multiple Locations — S • N America & C America • 500 kW
       †DEUTSCHE WELLE, Nauen — W • C America • 500 kW
       †DEUTSCHE WELLE, Wertachtal — N America & C America • 500 kW
       S • N America & C America • 500 kW
       W • N America • 500 kW

       KOREA (DPR)
       KOREAN CENTRAL BS, Kanggye — DS • 200 kW
       LIBERIA
       †LIBERIAN COMM'S NETWORK, Totota — ENGLISH, ETC • DS-"RADIO LIBERIA" • 10 kW • ALT. FREQ. TO 5100 kHz / ENGLISH ETC • DS-"RADIO LIBERIA" • 10 kW

       MALAYSIA
       VOICE OF MALAYSIA, Kajang — SE Asia • 100 kW
       NEW ZEALAND
       †R NEW ZEALAND INTL, Rangitaiki — S • Pacific • 100 kW / Irr • S • Pacific • SPORTS • 100 kW

       NIGERIA
       BORNO RADIO TV, Maiduguri — ENGLISH, ETC • DS • 10 kW
       RUSSIA
       VOICE OF RUSSIA, Moscow — W • W Africa • 500 kW
       VOICE OF RUSSIA, Novosibirsk — W • E Asia • 100 kW
       SWAZILAND
       †TRANS WORLD RADIO, Manzini — W • S Africa • 50 kW / S • S Africa • 50 kW

(con'd)

0 1 2 3 4 5 6 7 8 9 10 11 12 13 14 15 16 17 18 19 20 21 22 23 24

ENGLISH ▬   ARABIC ≈≈≈   CHINESE □□□   FRENCH ▬▬   GERMAN ▬   RUSSIAN ═══   SPANISH ▬▬   OTHER ▭

FREQUENCY   COUNTRY, STATION, LOCATION   TARGET • NETWORK • POWER (kW)   World Time

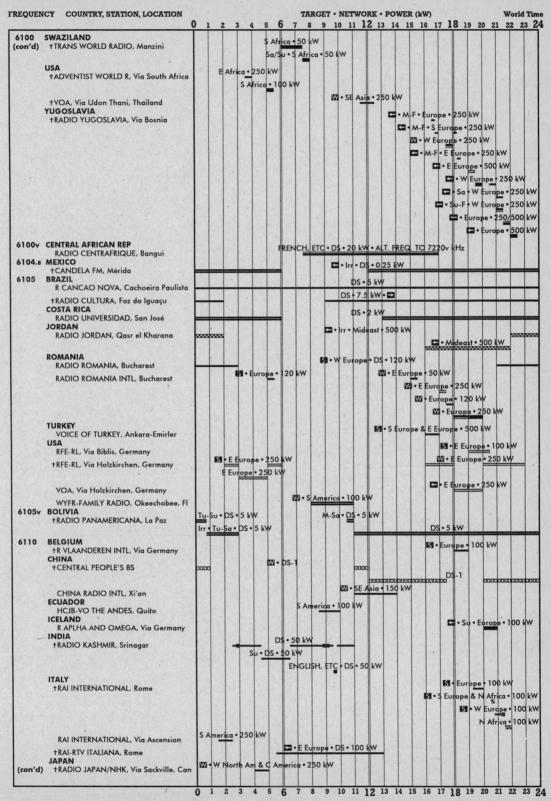

Frequency	Country, Station, Location	Target • Network • Power
6100 (con'd)	**SWAZILAND** †TRANS WORLD RADIO, Manzini	S Africa • 50 kW; Sa/Su • S Africa • 50 kW
	USA †ADVENTIST WORLD R, Via South Africa	E Africa • 250 kW; S Africa • 100 kW
	†VOA, Via Udon Thani, Thailand	W • SE Asia • 250 kW
	YUGOSLAVIA †RADIO YUGOSLAVIA, Via Bosnia	M-F • Europe • 250 kW; M-F • S Europe • 250 kW; W • W Europe • 250 kW; M-F • E Europe • 250 kW; E Europe • 500 kW; W Europe • 250 kW; Sa • W Europe • 250 kW; Su-F • W Europe • 250 kW; Europe • 250/500 kW; Europe • 500 kW
6100v	**CENTRAL AFRICAN REP** RADIO CENTRAFRIQUE, Bangui	FRENCH, ETC • DS • 20 kW • ALT. FREQ. TO 7220v kHz
6104.8	**MEXICO** †CANDELA FM, Mérida	Irr • DS • 0.25 kW
6105	**BRAZIL** R CANCAO NOVA, Cachoeira Paulista	DS • 5 kW
	†RADIO CULTURA, Foz do Iguaçu	DS • 7.5 kW
	COSTA RICA RADIO UNIVERSIDAD, San José	DS • 2 kW
	JORDAN RADIO JORDAN, Qasr el Kharana	Irr • Mideast • 500 kW; Mideast • 500 kW
	ROMANIA RADIO ROMANIA, Bucharest	S • W Europe • DS • 120 kW
	RADIO ROMANIA INTL, Bucharest	S • Europe • 120 kW; W • E Europe • 50 kW; W • E Europe • 250 kW; W • Europe • 120 kW; W • Europe • 250 kW
	TURKEY VOICE OF TURKEY, Ankara-Emirler	S • S Europe & E Europe • 500 kW
	USA RFE-RL, Via Biblis, Germany	S • E Europe • 100 kW
	†RFE-RL, Via Holzkirchen, Germany	S • E Europe • 250 kW; E Europe • 250 kW; W • E Europe • 250 kW
	VOA, Via Holzkirchen, Germany	E Europe • 250 kW
	WYFR-FAMILY RADIO, Okeechobee, Fl	W • S America • 100 kW
6105v	**BOLIVIA** †RADIO PANAMERICANA, La Paz	Tu-Su • DS • 5 kW; M-Sa • DS • 5 kW; Irr • Tu-Sa • DS • 5 kW; DS • 5 kW
6110	**BELGIUM** †R VLAANDEREN INTL, Via Germany	S • Europe • 100 kW
	CHINA †CENTRAL PEOPLE'S BS	W • DS-1; DS-1
	CHINA RADIO INTL, Xi'an	W • SE Asia • 150 kW
	ECUADOR HCJB-VO THE ANDES, Quito	S America • 100 kW
	ICELAND R APLHA AND OMEGA, Via Germany	Su • Europe • 100 kW
	INDIA †RADIO KASHMIR, Srinagar	DS • 50 kW; Su • DS • 50 kW; ENGLISH, ETC • DS • 50 kW
	ITALY †RAI INTERNATIONAL, Rome	S • Europe • 100 kW; S • S Europe & N Africa • 100 kW; S • W Europe • 100 kW; N Africa • 100 kW
	RAI INTERNATIONAL, Via Ascension	S America • 250 kW
	†RAI-RTV ITALIANA, Rome	E Europe • DS • 100 kW
(con'd)	**JAPAN** †RADIO JAPAN/NHK, Via Sackville, Can	W • W North Am & C America • 250 kW

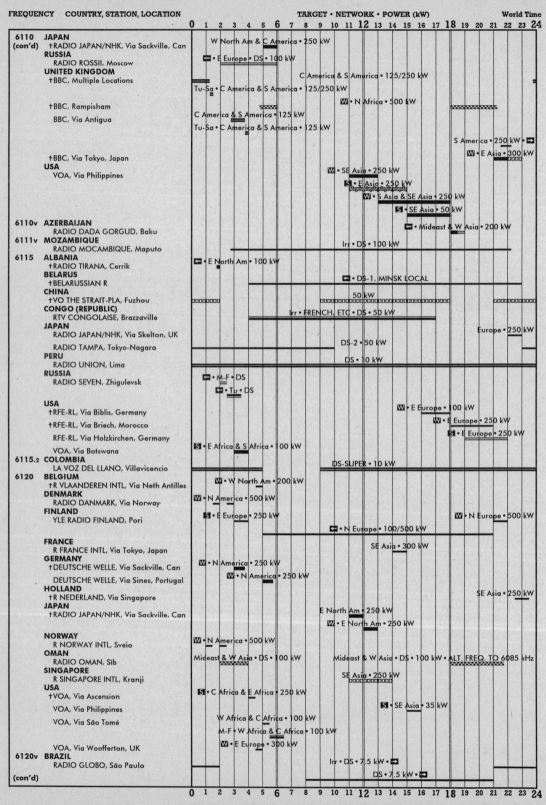

FREQUENCY   COUNTRY, STATION, LOCATION

TARGET • NETWORK • POWER (kW)

World Time

6110	JAPAN
(con'd)	†RADIO JAPAN/NHK, Via Sackville, Can — W North Am & C America • 250 kW
	RUSSIA
	RADIO ROSSII, Moscow — E Europe • DS • 100 kW
	UNITED KINGDOM
	†BBC, Multiple Locations — C America & S America • 125/250 kW; Tu-Sa • C America & S America • 125/250 kW
	W • N Africa • 500 kW
	†BBC, Rampisham
	BBC, Via Antigua — C America & S America • 125 kW; Tu-Sa • C America & S America • 125 kW
	S America • 250 kW; W • E Asia • 300 kW
	†BBC, Via Tokyo, Japan
	USA
	VOA, Via Philippines — W • SE Asia • 250 kW; S • E Asia • 250 kW; W • S Asia & SE Asia • 250 kW; S • SE Asia • 50 kW
6110v	AZERBAIJAN
	RADIO DADA GORGUD, Baku — Mideast & W Asia • 200 kW
6111v	MOZAMBIQUE
	RADIO MOCAMBIQUE, Maputo — Irr • DS • 100 kW
6115	ALBANIA
	†RADIO TIRANA, Cerrik — E North Am • 100 kW
	BELARUS
	†BELARUSSIAN R — DS-1, MINSK LOCAL
	CHINA
	†VO THE STRAIT-PLA, Fuzhou — 50 kW
	CONGO (REPUBLIC)
	RTV CONGOLAISE, Brazzaville — Irr • FRENCH, ETC • DS • 50 kW
	JAPAN
	RADIO JAPAN/NHK, Via Skelton, UK — Europe • 250 kW
	RADIO TAMPA, Tokyo-Nagara — DS-2 • 50 kW
	PERU
	RADIO UNION, Lima — DS • 10 kW
	RUSSIA
	RADIO SEVEN, Zhigulevsk — M-F • DS; Tu • DS
	USA
	†RFE-RL, Via Biblis, Germany — W • E Europe • 100 kW
	†RFE-RL, Via Briech, Morocco — W • E Europe • 250 kW
	RFE-RL, Via Holzkirchen, Germany — S • E Europe • 250 kW
	VOA, Via Botswana — S • E Africa & S Africa • 100 kW
6115.2	COLOMBIA
	LA VOZ DEL LLANO, Villavicencio — DS-SUPER • 10 kW
6120	BELGIUM
	†R VLAANDEREN INTL, Via Neth Antilles — W • W North Am • 200 kW
	DENMARK
	RADIO DANMARK, Via Norway — W • N America • 500 kW
	FINLAND
	YLE RADIO FINLAND, Pori — S • E Europe • 250 kW; W • N Europe • 500 kW; N Europe • 100/500 kW
	FRANCE
	R FRANCE INTL, Via Tokyo, Japan — SE Asia • 300 kW
	GERMANY
	†DEUTSCHE WELLE, Via Sackville, Can — W • N America • 250 kW
	DEUTSCHE WELLE, Via Sines, Portugal — W • N America • 250 kW
	HOLLAND
	†R NEDERLAND, Via Singapore — SE Asia • 250 kW
	JAPAN
	†RADIO JAPAN/NHK, Via Sackville, Can — E North Am • 250 kW; W • E North Am • 250 kW
	NORWAY
	R NORWAY INTL, Sveio — W • N America • 500 kW
	OMAN
	RADIO OMAN, Sib — Mideast & W Asia • DS • 100 kW; Mideast & W Asia • DS • 100 kW • ALT. FREQ. TO 6085 kHz
	SINGAPORE
	R SINGAPORE INTL, Kranji — SE Asia • 250 kW
	USA
	†VOA, Via Ascension — S • C Africa & E Africa • 250 kW
	VOA, Via Philippines — S • SE Asia • 35 kW
	VOA, Via São Tomé — W Africa & C Africa • 100 kW; M-F • W Africa & C Africa • 100 kW
	VOA, Via Woofferton, UK — W • E Europe • 300 kW
6120v	BRAZIL
	RADIO GLOBO, São Paulo — Irr • DS • 7.5 kW; DS • 7.5 kW
(con'd)	

ENGLISH ▬   ARABIC ⋙   CHINESE ▭▭   FRENCH ▬   GERMAN ▬   RUSSIAN ═   SPANISH ▬   OTHER ▬

FREQUENCY   COUNTRY, STATION, LOCATION

TARGET • NETWORK • POWER (kW)

World Time

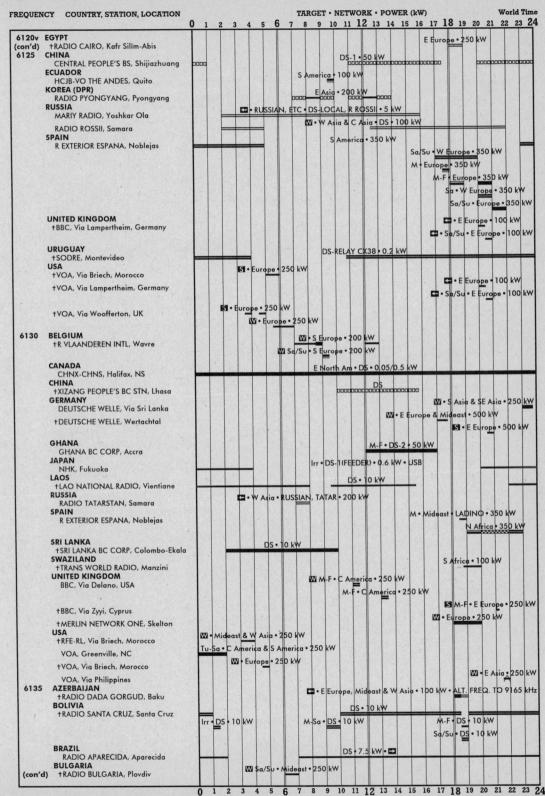

FREQUENCY	COUNTRY, STATION, LOCATION	TARGET • NETWORK • POWER (kW)
6120v (con'd)	EGYPT †RADIO CAIRO, Kafr Silim-Abis	E Europe • 250 kW
6125	CHINA CENTRAL PEOPLE'S BS, Shijiazhuang	DS-1 • 50 kW
	ECUADOR HCJB-VO THE ANDES, Quito	S America • 100 kW
	KOREA (DPR) RADIO PYONGYANG, Pyongyang	E Asia • 200 kW
	RUSSIA MARIY RADIO, Yoshkar Ola	RUSSIAN, ETC DS-LOCAL, R ROSSII • 5 kW
	RADIO ROSSII, Samara	W • W Asia & C Asia • DS • 100 kW
	SPAIN R EXTERIOR ESPANA, Noblejas	S America • 350 kW
		Sa/Su • W Europe • 350 kW
		M • Europe • 350 kW
		M-F • Europe • 350 kW
		Sa • W Europe • 350 kW
		Sa/Su • Europe • 350 kW
	UNITED KINGDOM †BBC, Via Lampertheim, Germany	E Europe • 100 kW
		Sa/Su • E Europe • 100 kW
	URUGUAY †SODRE, Montevideo	DS-RELAY CX38 • 0.2 kW
	USA †VOA, Via Briech, Morocco	S • Europe • 250 kW
	†VOA, Via Lampertheim, Germany	E Europe • 100 kW
		Sa/Su • E Europe • 100 kW
	†VOA, Via Woofferton, UK	S • Europe • 250 kW
		W • Europe • 250 kW
6130	BELGIUM †R VLAANDEREN INTL, Wavre	W • S Europe • 200 kW
		W Sa/Su • S Europe • 200 kW
	CANADA CHNX-CHNS, Halifax, NS	E North Am • DS • 0.05/0.5 kW
	CHINA †XIZANG PEOPLE'S BC STN, Lhasa	DS
	GERMANY DEUTSCHE WELLE, Via Sri Lanka	W • S Asia & SE Asia • 250 kW
	†DEUTSCHE WELLE, Wertachtal	W • E Europe & Mideast • 500 kW
		S • E Europe • 500 kW
	GHANA GHANA BC CORP, Accra	M-F • DS-2 • 50 kW
	JAPAN NHK, Fukuoka	Irr • DS-1 (FEEDER) • 0.6 kW • USB
	LAOS †LAO NATIONAL RADIO, Vientiane	DS • 10 kW
	RUSSIA RADIO TATARSTAN, Samara	W Asia • RUSSIAN, TATAR • 200 kW
	SPAIN R EXTERIOR ESPANA, Noblejas	M • Mideast • LADINO • 350 kW
		N Africa • 350 kW
	SRI LANKA †SRI LANKA BC CORP, Colombo-Ekala	DS • 10 kW
	SWAZILAND †TRANS WORLD RADIO, Manzini	S Africa • 100 kW
	UNITED KINGDOM BBC, Via Delano, USA	W M-F • C America • 250 kW
		M-F • C America • 250 kW
	†BBC, Via Zyyi, Cyprus	S M-F • E Europe • 250 kW
	†MERLIN NETWORK ONE, Skelton	W • Europe • 250 kW
	USA †RFE-RL, Via Briech, Morocco	W • Mideast & W Asia • 250 kW
	VOA, Greenville, NC	Tu-Sa • C America & S America • 250 kW
	†VOA, Via Briech, Morocco	W • Europe • 250 kW
	VOA, Via Philippines	W • E Asia • 250 kW
6135	AZERBAIJAN †RADIO DADA GORGUD, Baku	E Europe, Mideast & W Asia • 100 kW • ALT. FREQ. TO 9165 kHz
	BOLIVIA †RADIO SANTA CRUZ, Santa Cruz	DS • 10 kW
		Irr • DS • 10 kW
		M-Sa • DS • 10 kW
		M-F • DS • 10 kW
		Sa/Su • DS • 10 kW
	BRAZIL RADIO APARECIDA, Aparecida	DS • 7.5 kW
	BULGARIA	W Sa/Su • Mideast • 250 kW
(con'd)	†RADIO BULGARIA, Plovdiv	

FREQUENCY   COUNTRY, STATION, LOCATION

TARGET • NETWORK • POWER (kW)

World Time

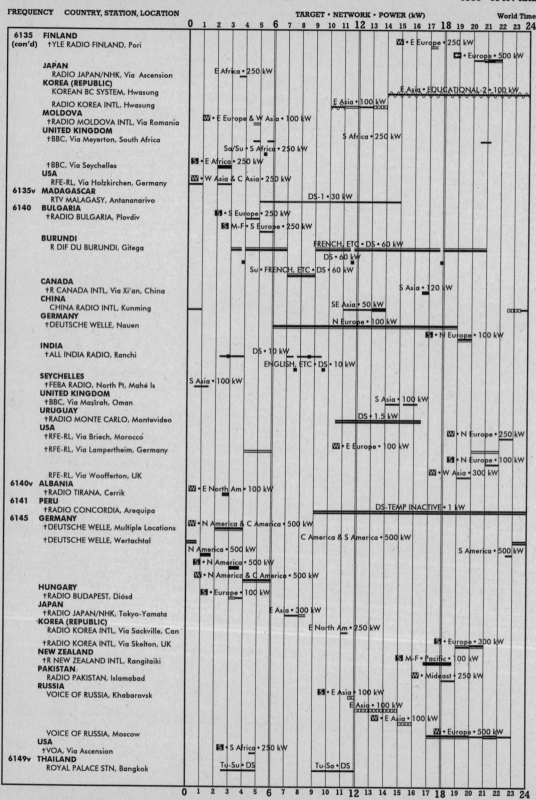

FREQUENCY	COUNTRY, STATION, LOCATION	TARGET • NETWORK • POWER (kW)
6135 (con'd)	FINLAND †YLE RADIO FINLAND, Pori	W • E Europe • 250 kW / • Europe • 500 kW
	JAPAN RADIO JAPAN/NHK, Via Ascension	E Africa • 250 kW
	KOREA (REPUBLIC) KOREAN BC SYSTEM, Hwasung	E Asia • EDUCATIONAL-2 • 100 kW
	RADIO KOREA INTL, Hwasung	E Asia • 100 kW
	MOLDOVA †RADIO MOLDOVA INTL, Via Romania	W • E Europe & W Asia • 100 kW
	UNITED KINGDOM †BBC, Via Meyerton, South Africa	S Africa • 250 kW / Sa/Su • S Africa • 250 kW
	†BBC, Via Seychelles	S • E Africa • 250 kW
	USA RFE-RL, Via Holzkirchen, Germany	W • W Asia & C Asia • 250 kW
6135v	MADAGASCAR RTV MALAGASY, Antananarivo	DS-1 • 30 kW
6140	BULGARIA †RADIO BULGARIA, Plovdiv	S • S Europe • 250 kW / S M-F • S Europe • 250 kW
	BURUNDI R DIF DU BURUNDI, Gitega	FRENCH, ETC • DS • 60 kW / DS • 60 kW / Su • FRENCH, ETC • DS • 60 kW
	CANADA †R CANADA INTL, Via Xi'an, China	S Asia • 120 kW
	CHINA CHINA RADIO INTL, Kunming	SE Asia • 50 kW
	GERMANY †DEUTSCHE WELLE, Nauen	N Europe • 100 kW / S • N Europe • 100 kW
	INDIA †ALL INDIA RADIO, Ranchi	DS • 10 kW / ENGLISH, ETC • DS • 10 kW
	SEYCHELLES †FEBA RADIO, North Pt, Mahé Is	S Asia • 100 kW
	UNITED KINGDOM †BBC, Via Maṣīrah, Oman	S Asia • 100 kW
	URUGUAY †RADIO MONTE CARLO, Montevideo	DS • 1.5 kW
	USA †RFE-RL, Via Briech, Morocco	W • N Europe • 250 kW
	†RFE-RL, Via Lampertheim, Germany	W • E Europe • 100 kW / S • N Europe • 100 kW
	RFE-RL, Via Woofferton, UK	W • W Asia • 300 kW
6140v	ALBANIA †RADIO TIRANA, Cerrik	W • E North Am • 100 kW
6141	PERU †RADIO CONCORDIA, Arequipa	DS-TEMP INACTIVE • 1 kW
6145	GERMANY †DEUTSCHE WELLE, Multiple Locations	W • N America & C America • 500 kW / C America & S America • 500 kW
	†DEUTSCHE WELLE, Wertachtal	N America • 500 kW / S America • 500 kW / S • N America • 500 kW / W • N America & C America • 500 kW
	HUNGARY †RADIO BUDAPEST, Diósd	S • Europe • 100 kW
	JAPAN †RADIO JAPAN/NHK, Tokyo-Yamata	E Asia • 300 kW
	KOREA (REPUBLIC) RADIO KOREA INTL, Via Sackville, Can	E North Am • 250 kW
	†RADIO KOREA INTL, Via Skelton, UK	S • Europe • 300 kW
	NEW ZEALAND †R NEW ZEALAND INTL, Rangitaiki	S M-F • Pacific • 100 kW
	PAKISTAN RADIO PAKISTAN, Islamabad	W • Mideast • 250 kW
	RUSSIA VOICE OF RUSSIA, Khabarovsk	S • E Asia • 100 kW / E Asia • 100 kW / W • E Asia • 100 kW
	VOICE OF RUSSIA, Moscow	W • Europe • 500 kW
	USA †VOA, Via Ascension	S • S Africa • 250 kW
6149v	THAILAND ROYAL PALACE STN, Bangkok	Tu-Su • DS / Tu-Sa • DS

ENGLISH ▬ ARABIC ▨ CHINESE ▢▢▢ FRENCH ▬ GERMAN ▬ RUSSIAN ═ SPANISH ▬ OTHER ▬

FREQUENCY   COUNTRY, STATION, LOCATION

TARGET • NETWORK • POWER (kW)

World Time

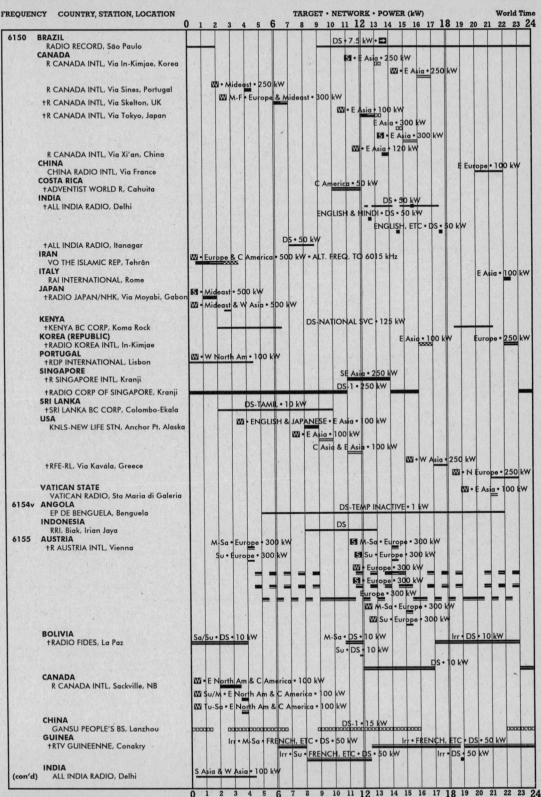

FREQUENCY	COUNTRY, STATION, LOCATION	TARGET • NETWORK • POWER (kW)
6150	**BRAZIL**	
	RADIO RECORD, São Paulo	DS • 7.5 kW • ▣
	CANADA	
	R CANADA INTL, Via In-Kimjae, Korea	S • E Asia • 250 kW / W • E Asia • 250 kW
	R CANADA INTL, Via Sines, Portugal	W • Mideast • 250 kW
	†R CANADA INTL, Via Skelton, UK	W • M-F • Europe & Mideast • 300 kW
	†R CANADA INTL, Via Tokyo, Japan	W • E Asia • 100 kW / E Asia • 300 kW / S • E Asia • 300 kW
	R CANADA INTL, Via Xi'an, China	W • E Asia • 120 kW
	CHINA	
	CHINA RADIO INTL, Via France	E Europe • 100 kW
	COSTA RICA	
	†ADVENTIST WORLD R, Cahuita	C America • 50 kW
	INDIA	
	†ALL INDIA RADIO, Delhi	DS • 50 kW / ENGLISH & HINDI • DS • 50 kW / ENGLISH, ETC • DS • 50 kW
	†ALL INDIA RADIO, Itanagar	DS • 50 kW
	IRAN	
	VO THE ISLAMIC REP, Tehrān	W • Europe & C America • 500 kW • ALT. FREQ. TO 6015 kHz
	ITALY	
	RAI INTERNATIONAL, Rome	E Asia • 100 kW
	JAPAN	
	†RADIO JAPAN/NHK, Via Moyabi, Gabon	S • Mideast • 500 kW / W • Mideast & W Asia • 500 kW
	KENYA	
	†KENYA BC CORP, Koma Rock	DS-NATIONAL SVC • 125 kW
	KOREA (REPUBLIC)	
	†RADIO KOREA INTL, In-Kimjae	E Asia • 100 kW / Europe • 250 kW
	PORTUGAL	
	†RDP INTERNATIONAL, Lisbon	W • W North Am • 100 kW
	SINGAPORE	
	†R SINGAPORE INTL, Kranji	SE Asia • 250 kW
	†RADIO CORP OF SINGAPORE, Kranji	DS-1 • 250 kW
	SRI LANKA	
	†SRI LANKA BC CORP, Colombo-Ekala	DS-TAMIL • 10 kW
	USA	
	KNLS-NEW LIFE STN, Anchor Pt, Alaska	W • ENGLISH & JAPANESE • E Asia • 100 kW / W • E Asia • 100 kW / C Asia & E Asia • 100 kW
	†RFE-RL, Via Kavála, Greece	W • W Asia • 250 kW / W • N Europe • 250 kW
	VATICAN STATE	
	VATICAN RADIO, Sta Maria di Galeria	W • E Asia • 100 kW
6154v	**ANGOLA**	
	EP DE BENGUELA, Benguela	DS-TEMP INACTIVE • 1 kW
	INDONESIA	
	RRI, Biak, Irian Jaya	DS
6155	**AUSTRIA**	
	†R AUSTRIA INTL, Vienna	M-Sa • Europe • 300 kW / S M-Sa • Europe • 300 kW / Su • Europe • 300 kW / S Su • Europe • 300 kW / W • Europe • 300 kW / S • Europe • 300 kW / Europe • 300 kW / W M-Sa • Europe • 300 kW / W Su • Europe • 300 kW
	BOLIVIA	
	†RADIO FIDES, La Paz	Sa/Su • DS • 10 kW / M-Sa • DS • 10 kW / Su • DS • 10 kW / Irr • DS • 10 kW / DS • 10 kW
	CANADA	
	R CANADA INTL, Sackville, NB	W • E North Am & C America • 100 kW / W Su/M • E North Am & C America • 100 kW / W Tu-Sa • E North Am & C America • 100 kW
	CHINA	
	GANSU PEOPLE'S BS, Lanzhou	DS-1 • 15 kW
	GUINEA	
	†RTV GUINEENNE, Conakry	Irr • M-Sa • FRENCH, ETC • DS • 50 kW / Irr • FRENCH, ETC • DS • 50 kW / Irr • Su • FRENCH, ETC • DS • 50 kW / Irr • DS • 50 kW
(con'd)	**INDIA** ALL INDIA RADIO, Delhi	S Asia & W Asia • 100 kW

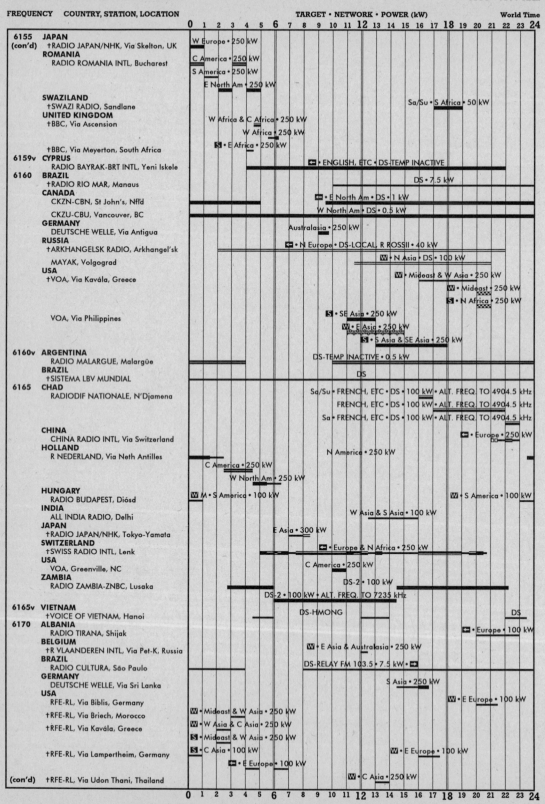

FREQUENCY   COUNTRY, STATION, LOCATION

TARGET • NETWORK • POWER (kW)

World Time

FREQUENCY	COUNTRY, STATION, LOCATION	TARGET • NETWORK • POWER (kW)
6155 (con'd)	JAPAN †RADIO JAPAN/NHK, Via Skelton, UK	W Europe • 250 kW
	ROMANIA RADIO ROMANIA INTL, Bucharest	C America • 250 kW / S America • 250 kW / E North Am • 250 kW
	SWAZILAND †SWAZI RADIO, Sandlane	Sa/Su • S Africa • 50 kW
	UNITED KINGDOM †BBC, Via Ascension	W Africa & C Africa • 250 kW / W Africa • 250 kW
	†BBC, Via Meyerton, South Africa	⊠ E Africa • 250 kW
6159v	CYPRUS RADIO BAYRAK-BRT INTL, Yeni Iskele	⊡ • ENGLISH, ETC • DS-TEMP INACTIVE
6160	BRAZIL †RADIO RIO MAR, Manaus	DS • 7.5 kW
	CANADA CKZN-CBN, St John's, Nfld	⊡ • E North Am • DS • 1 kW
	CKZU-CBU, Vancouver, BC	W North Am • DS • 0.5 kW
	GERMANY DEUTSCHE WELLE, Via Antigua	Australasia • 250 kW
	RUSSIA †ARKHANGELSK RADIO, Arkhangel'sk	⊡ • N Europe • DS-LOCAL, R ROSSII • 40 kW
	MAYAK, Volgograd	W • N Asia • DS • 100 kW
	USA †VOA, Via Kavála, Greece	W • Mideast & W Asia • 250 kW / W • Mideast • 250 kW / ⊠ • N Africa • 250 kW
	VOA, Via Philippines	⊠ • SE Asia • 250 kW / W • E Asia • 250 kW / ⊠ • S Asia & SE Asia • 250 kW
6160v	ARGENTINA RADIO MALARGÜE, Malargüe	DS-TEMP INACTIVE • 0.5 kW
	BRAZIL †SISTEMA LBV MUNDIAL	DS
6165	CHAD RADIODIF NATIONALE, N'Djamena	Sa/Su • FRENCH, ETC • DS • 100 kW • ALT. FREQ. TO 4904.5 kHz / FRENCH, ETC • DS • 100 kW • ALT. FREQ. TO 4904.5 kHz / Sa • FRENCH, ETC • DS • 100 kW • ALT. FREQ. TO 4904.5 kHz
	CHINA CHINA RADIO INTL, Via Switzerland	⊡ • Europe • 250 kW
	HOLLAND R NEDERLAND, Via Neth Antilles	N America • 250 kW / C America • 250 kW / W North Am • 250 kW
	HUNGARY RADIO BUDAPEST, Diósd	W • M • S America • 100 kW / W • S America • 100 kW
	INDIA ALL INDIA RADIO, Delhi	W Asia & S Asia • 100 kW
	JAPAN †RADIO JAPAN/NHK, Tokyo-Yamata	E Asia • 300 kW
	SWITZERLAND †SWISS RADIO INTL, Lenk	⊡ • Europe & N Africa • 250 kW
	USA VOA, Greenville, NC	C America • 250 kW
	ZAMBIA RADIO ZAMBIA-ZNBC, Lusaka	DS-2 • 100 kW / DS-2 • 100 kW • ALT. FREQ. TO 7235 kHz
6165v	VIETNAM †VOICE OF VIETNAM, Hanoi	DS-HMONG / DS
6170	ALBANIA RADIO TIRANA, Shijak	⊡ • Europe • 100 kW
	BELGIUM †R VLAANDEREN INTL, Via Pet-K, Russia	W • E Asia & Australasia • 250 kW
	BRAZIL RADIO CULTURA, São Paulo	DS-RELAY FM 103.5 • 7.5 kW • ⊡
	GERMANY DEUTSCHE WELLE, Via Sri Lanka	S Asia • 250 kW
	USA RFE-RL, Via Biblis, Germany	W • E Europe • 100 kW
	†RFE-RL, Via Briech, Morocco	W • Mideast & W Asia • 250 kW
	†RFE-RL, Via Kavála, Greece	W • W Asia & C Asia • 250 kW / ⊠ • Mideast & W Asia • 250 kW
	†RFE-RL, Via Lampertheim, Germany	⊠ • C Asia • 100 kW / W • E Europe • 100 kW / ⊡ • E Europe • 100 kW
(con'd)	†RFE-RL, Via Udon Thani, Thailand	W • C Asia • 250 kW

ENGLISH ▬ ARABIC ⧩ CHINESE ⊡⊡⊡ FRENCH ═ GERMAN ▬ RUSSIAN ═ SPANISH ▬ OTHER ▬

FREQUENCY   COUNTRY, STATION, LOCATION

TARGET • NETWORK • POWER (kW)

World Time

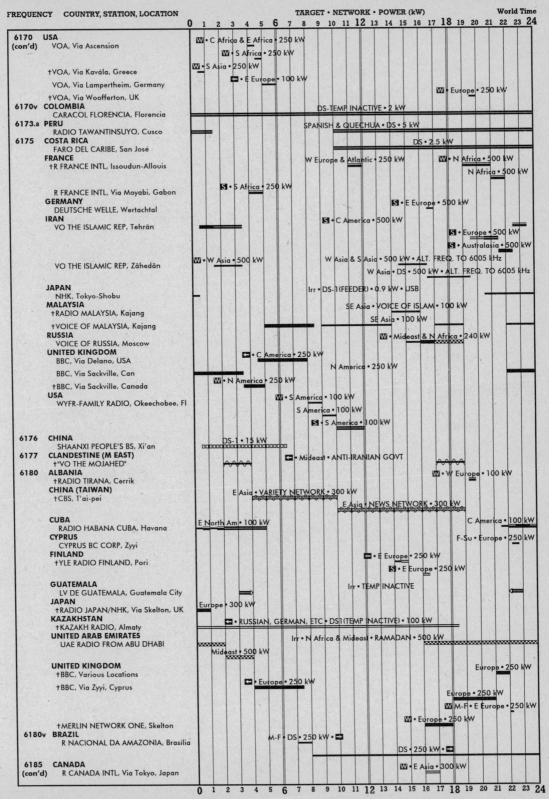

FREQUENCY	COUNTRY, STATION, LOCATION	TARGET • NETWORK • POWER
6170 (con'd)	USA VOA, Via Ascension	W • C Africa & E Africa • 250 kW
		W • S Africa • 250 kW
		W • S Asia • 250 kW
	†VOA, Via Kavála, Greece	
	VOA, Via Lampertheim, Germany	E Europe • 100 kW
	†VOA, Via Woofferton, UK	W • Europe • 250 kW
6170v	COLOMBIA CARACOL FLORENCIA, Florencia	DS-TEMP INACTIVE • 2 kW
6173.8	PERU RADIO TAWANTINSUYO, Cusco	SPANISH & QUECHUA • DS • 5 kW
6175	COSTA RICA FARO DEL CARIBE, San José	DS • 2.5 kW
	FRANCE †R FRANCE INTL, Issoudun-Allouis	W Europe & Atlantic • 250 kW W • N Africa • 500 kW
		N Africa • 500 kW
	R FRANCE INTL, Via Moyabi, Gabon	S • S Africa • 250 kW
	GERMANY DEUTSCHE WELLE, Wertachtal	S • E Europe • 500 kW
	IRAN VO THE ISLAMIC REP, Tehrān	S • C America • 500 kW
		S • Europe • 500 kW
		S • Australasia • 500 kW
	VO THE ISLAMIC REP, Zāhedān	W • W Asia • 500 kW W Asia & S Asia • 500 kW • ALT. FREQ. TO 6005 kHz
		W Asia • DS • 500 kW • ALT. FREQ. TO 6005 kHz
	JAPAN NHK, Tokyo-Shobu	Irr • DS-1 (FEEDER) • 0.9 kW • USB
	MALAYSIA †RADIO MALAYSIA, Kajang	SE Asia • VOICE OF ISLAM • 100 kW
	†VOICE OF MALAYSIA, Kajang	SE Asia • 100 kW
	RUSSIA VOICE OF RUSSIA, Moscow	W • Mideast & N Africa • 240 kW
	UNITED KINGDOM BBC, Via Delano, USA	C America • 250 kW
	BBC, Via Sackville, Can	N America • 250 kW
	†BBC, Via Sackville, Canada	W • N America • 250 kW
	USA WYFR-FAMILY RADIO, Okeechobee, Fl	W • S America • 100 kW
		S America • 100 kW
		S • S America • 100 kW
6176	CHINA SHAANXI PEOPLE'S BS, Xi'an	DS-1 • 15 kW
6177	CLANDESTINE (M EAST) †"VO THE MOJAHED"	Mideast • ANTI-IRANIAN GOVT
6180	ALBANIA †RADIO TIRANA, Cerrik	W • W Europe • 100 kW
	CHINA (TAIWAN) †CBS, T'ai-pei	E Asia • VARIETY NETWORK • 300 kW
		E Asia • NEWS NETWORK • 300 kW
	CUBA RADIO HABANA CUBA, Havana	E North Am • 100 kW C America • 100 kW
	CYPRUS CYPRUS BC CORP, Zyyi	F-Su • Europe • 250 kW
	FINLAND †YLE RADIO FINLAND, Pori	E Europe • 250 kW
		S • E Europe • 250 kW
	GUATEMALA LV DE GUATEMALA, Guatemala City	Irr • TEMP INACTIVE
	JAPAN †RADIO JAPAN/NHK, Via Skelton, UK	Europe • 300 kW
	KAZAKHSTAN †KAZAKH RADIO, Almaty	RUSSIAN, GERMAN, ETC • DS1 (TEMP INACTIVE) • 100 kW
	UNITED ARAB EMIRATES UAE RADIO FROM ABU DHABI	Irr • N Africa & Mideast • RAMADAN • 500 kW
		Mideast • 500 kW
	UNITED KINGDOM †BBC, Various Locations	Europe • 250 kW
	†BBC, Via Zyyi, Cyprus	Europe • 250 kW
		Europe • 250 kW
		W M-F • E Europe • 250 kW
	†MERLIN NETWORK ONE, Skelton	W • Europe • 250 kW
6180v	BRAZIL R NACIONAL DA AMAZONIA, Brasilia	M-F • DS • 250 kW •
		DS • 250 kW •
6185 (con'd)	CANADA R CANADA INTL, Via Tokyo, Japan	W • E Asia • 300 kW

SEASONAL S OR W   1-HR TIMESHIFT MIDYEAR ← OR →   JAMMING / OR ∧   EARLIEST HEARD ◁   LATEST HEARD ▷   NEW FOR 1999 †

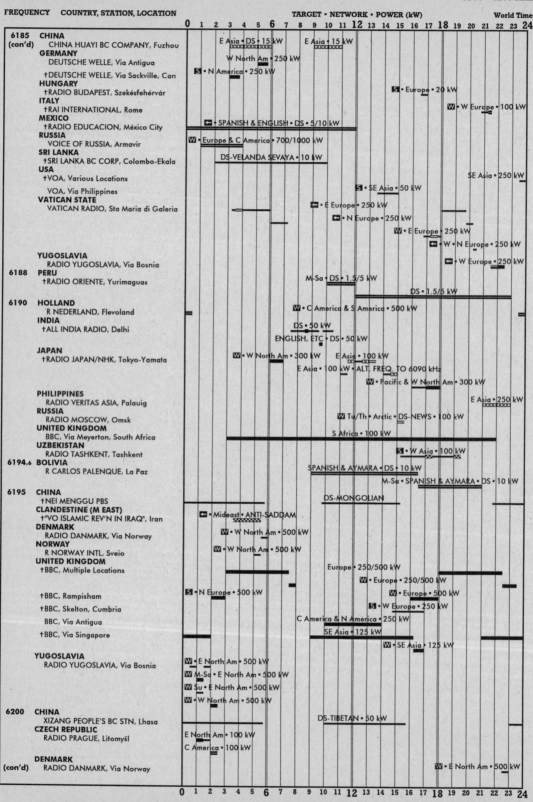

FREQUENCY	COUNTRY, STATION, LOCATION	TARGET • NETWORK • POWER (kW)
6185 (con'd)	CHINA	
	CHINA HUAYI BC COMPANY, Fuzhou	E Asia • DS • 15 kW E Asia • 15 kW
	GERMANY	
	DEUTSCHE WELLE, Via Antigua	W North Am • 250 kW
	†DEUTSCHE WELLE, Via Sackville, Can	S • N America • 250 kW
	HUNGARY	
	†RADIO BUDAPEST, Székesfehérvár	S • Europe • 20 kW
	ITALY	
	†RAI INTERNATIONAL, Rome	W • W Europe • 100 kW
	MEXICO	
	†RADIO EDUCACION, México City	SPANISH & ENGLISH • DS • 5/10 kW
	RUSSIA	
	VOICE OF RUSSIA, Armavir	W • Europe & C America • 700/1000 kW
	SRI LANKA	
	†SRI LANKA BC CORP, Colombo-Ekala	DS-VELANDA SEVAYA • 10 kW
	USA	
	†VOA, Various Locations	SE Asia • 250 kW
	VOA, Via Philippines	S • SE Asia • 50 kW
	VATICAN STATE	
	VATICAN RADIO, Sta Maria di Galeria	E Europe • 250 kW
		N Europe • 250 kW
		W • E Europe • 250 kW
		W • N Europe • 250 kW
	YUGOSLAVIA	
	RADIO YUGOSLAVIA, Via Bosnia	W • W Europe • 250 kW
6188	PERU	
	†RADIO ORIENTE, Yurimaguas	M-Sa • DS • 1.5/5 kW
		DS • 1.5/5 kW
6190	HOLLAND	
	R NEDERLAND, Flevoland	W • C America & S America • 500 kW
	INDIA	
	†ALL INDIA RADIO, Delhi	DS • 50 kW
		ENGLISH, ETC • DS • 50 kW
	JAPAN	
	†RADIO JAPAN/NHK, Tokyo-Yamata	W • W North Am • 300 kW E Asia • 100 kW
		E Asia • 100 kW • ALT. FREQ. TO 6090 kHz
		W • Pacific & W North Am • 300 kW
	PHILIPPINES	
	RADIO VERITAS ASIA, Palauig	E Asia • 250 kW
	RUSSIA	
	RADIO MOSCOW, Omsk	W Tu/Th • Arctic • DS-NEWS • 100 kW
	UNITED KINGDOM	
	BBC, Via Meyerton, South Africa	S Africa • 100 kW
	UZBEKISTAN	
	RADIO TASHKENT, Tashkent	S • W Asia • 100 kW
6194.6	BOLIVIA	
	R CARLOS PALENQUE, La Paz	SPANISH & AYMARA • DS • 10 kW
		M-Sa • SPANISH & AYMARA • DS • 10 kW
6195	CHINA	
	†NEI MENGGU PBS	DS-MONGOLIAN
	CLANDESTINE (M EAST)	
	†"VO ISLAMIC REV'N IN IRAQ", Iran	Mideast • ANTI-SADDAM
	DENMARK	
	RADIO DANMARK, Via Norway	W • W North Am • 500 kW
	NORWAY	
	R NORWAY INTL, Sveio	W • W North Am • 500 kW
	UNITED KINGDOM	
	†BBC, Multiple Locations	Europe • 250/500 kW
		W • Europe • 250/500 kW
	†BBC, Rampisham	S • N Europe • 500 kW W • Europe • 500 kW
	†BBC, Skelton, Cumbria	S • W Europe • 250 kW
	BBC, Via Antigua	C America & N America • 250 kW
	†BBC, Via Singapore	SE Asia • 125 kW
		W • SE Asia • 125 kW
	YUGOSLAVIA	
	RADIO YUGOSLAVIA, Via Bosnia	W • E North Am • 500 kW
		W M-Sa • E North Am • 500 kW
		W Su • E North Am • 500 kW
		W • W North Am • 500 kW
6200	CHINA	
	XIZANG PEOPLE'S BC STN, Lhasa	DS-TIBETAN • 50 kW
	CZECH REPUBLIC	
	RADIO PRAGUE, Litomyšl	E North Am • 100 kW
		C America • 100 kW
	DENMARK	
(con'd)	RADIO DANMARK, Via Norway	W • E North Am • 500 kW

ENGLISH ▬   ARABIC ▧   CHINESE ▢▢▢   FRENCH ▬   GERMAN ▬   RUSSIAN ══   SPANISH ▭   OTHER ▬

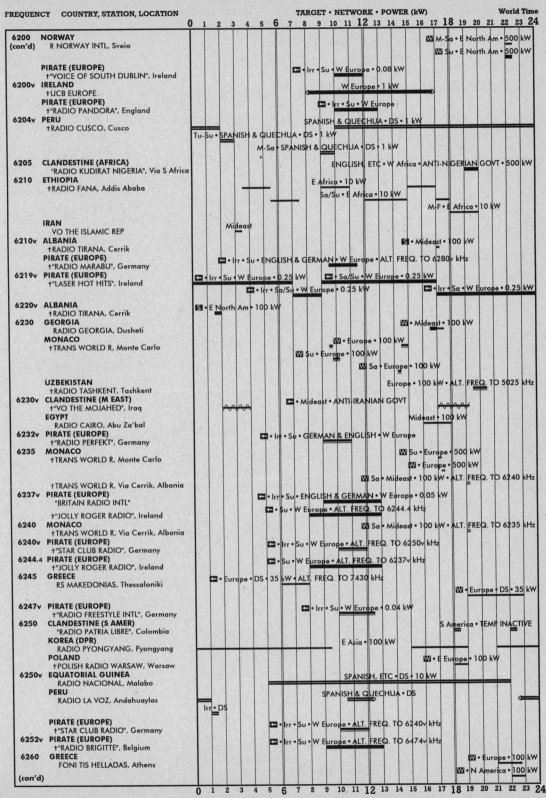

FREQUENCY	COUNTRY, STATION, LOCATION	TARGET • NETWORK • POWER (kW)	World Time

6200 **NORWAY**
(con'd)   R NORWAY INTL, Sveio
— W • M-Sa • E North Am • 500 kW
— W • Su • E North Am • 500 kW

PIRATE (EUROPE)
†"VOICE OF SOUTH DUBLIN", Ireland — • Irr • Su • W Europe • 0.08 kW

6200v **IRELAND**
†UCB EUROPE — W Europe • 1 kW

PIRATE (EUROPE)
†"RADIO PANDORA", England — • Irr • Su • W Europe

6204v **PERU**
†RADIO CUSCO, Cusco — SPANISH & QUECHUA • DS • 1 kW
— Tu-Su • SPANISH & QUECHUA • DS • 1 kW
— M-Sa • SPANISH & QUECHUA • DS • 1 kW

6205 **CLANDESTINE (AFRICA)**
"RADIO KUDIRAT NIGERIA", Via S Africa — ENGLISH, ETC • W Africa • ANTI-NIGERIAN GOVT • 500 kW

6210 **ETHIOPIA**
†RADIO FANA, Addis Ababa — E Africa • 10 kW
— Sa/Su • E Africa • 10 kW
— M-F • E Africa • 10 kW

IRAN
VO THE ISLAMIC REP — Mideast

6210v **ALBANIA**
†RADIO TIRANA, Cerrik — S • Mideast • 100 kW

PIRATE (EUROPE)
†"RADIO MARABU", Germany — • Irr • Su • ENGLISH & GERMAN • W Europe • ALT. FREQ. TO 6280v kHz

6219v **PIRATE (EUROPE)**
†"LASER HOT HITS", Ireland — • Irr • Su • W Europe • 0.25 kW   — • Sa/Su • W Europe • 0.25 kW
— • Irr • Sa/Su • W Europe • 0.25 kW   — • Irr • Sa • W Europe • 0.25 kW

6220v **ALBANIA**
†RADIO TIRANA, Cerrik — S • E North Am • 100 kW

6230 **GEORGIA**
RADIO GEORGIA, Dusheti — W • Mideast • 100 kW

MONACO
†TRANS WORLD R, Monte Carlo — W • Europe • 100 kW
— W • Su • Europe • 100 kW
— W • Sa • Europe • 100 kW

UZBEKISTAN
†RADIO TASHKENT, Tashkent — Europe • 100 kW • ALT. FREQ. TO 5025 kHz

6230v **CLANDESTINE (M EAST)**
†"VO THE MOJAHED", Iraq — • Mideast • ANTI-IRANIAN GOVT

EGYPT
RADIO CAIRO, Abu Za'bal — Mideast • 100 kW

6232v **PIRATE (EUROPE)**
†"RADIO PERFEKT", Germany — • Irr • Su • GERMAN & ENGLISH • W Europe

6235 **MONACO**
†TRANS WORLD R, Monte Carlo — W • Su • Europe • 500 kW
— W • Europe • 500 kW

†TRANS WORLD R, Via Cerrik, Albania — W • Sa • Mideast • 100 kW • ALT. FREQ. TO 6240 kHz

6237v **PIRATE (EUROPE)**
"BRITAIN RADIO INTL" — • Irr • Su • ENGLISH & GERMAN • W Europe • 0.05 kW
— • Su • W Europe • ALT. FREQ. TO 6244.4 kHz

†"JOLLY ROGER RADIO", Ireland

6240 **MONACO**
†TRANS WORLD R, Via Cerrik, Albania — W • Sa • Mideast • 100 kW • ALT. FREQ. TO 6235 kHz

6240v **PIRATE (EUROPE)**
†"STAR CLUB RADIO", Germany — • Irr • Su • W Europe • ALT. FREQ. TO 6250v kHz

6244.4 **PIRATE (EUROPE)**
†"JOLLY ROGER RADIO", Ireland — • Su • W Europe • ALT. FREQ. TO 6237v kHz

6245 **GREECE**
RS MAKEDONIAS, Thessaloniki — • Europe • DS • 35 kW • ALT. FREQ. TO 7430 kHz
— W • Europe • DS • 35 kW

6247v **PIRATE (EUROPE)**
†"RADIO FREESTYLE INTL", Germany — • Irr • Su • W Europe • 0.04 kW

6250 **CLANDESTINE (S AMER)**
"RADIO PATRIA LIBRE", Colombia — S America • TEMP INACTIVE

KOREA (DPR)
RADIO PYONGYANG, Pyongyang — E Asia • 100 kW

POLAND
†POLISH RADIO WARSAW, Warsaw — W • E Europe • 100 kW

6250v **EQUATORIAL GUINEA**
RADIO NACIONAL, Malabo — SPANISH, ETC • DS • 10 kW

PERU
RADIO LA VOZ, Andahuaylas — SPANISH & QUECHUA • DS
— Irr • DS

PIRATE (EUROPE)
†"STAR CLUB RADIO", Germany — • Irr • Su • W Europe • ALT. FREQ. TO 6240v kHz

6252v **PIRATE (EUROPE)**
†"RADIO BRIGITTE", Belgium — • Irr • Su • W Europe • ALT. FREQ. TO 6474v kHz

6260 **GREECE**
FONI TIS HELLADAS, Athens — W • Europe • 100 kW
— W • N America • 100 kW

(con'd)

FREQUENCY   COUNTRY, STATION, LOCATION

TARGET • NETWORK • POWER (kW)

World Time

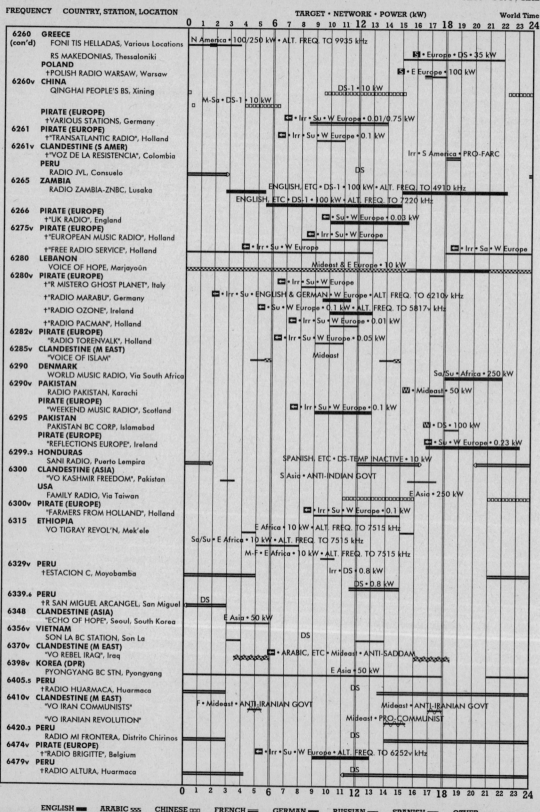

Frequency	Country / Station / Location	Notes
6260 (con'd)	**GREECE** FONI TIS HELLADAS, Various Locations	N America • 100/250 kW • ALT. FREQ. TO 9935 kHz
	RS MAKEDONIAS, Thessaloniki	S • Europe • DS • 35 kW
	POLAND †POLISH RADIO WARSAW, Warsaw	S • E Europe • 100 kW
6260v	**CHINA** QINGHAI PEOPLE'S BS, Xining	DS-1 • 10 kW; M-Sa • DS-1 • 10 kW
6261	**PIRATE (EUROPE)** †VARIOUS STATIONS, Germany	• Irr • Su • W Europe • 0.01/0.75 kW
	PIRATE (EUROPE) †"TRANSATLANTIC RADIO", Holland	Irr • Su • W Europe • 0.1 kW
6261v	**CLANDESTINE (S AMER)** †"VOZ DE LA RESISTENCIA", Colombia	Irr • S America • PRO-FARC
	PERU RADIO JVL, Consuelo	DS
6265	**ZAMBIA** RADIO ZAMBIA-ZNBC, Lusaka	ENGLISH, ETC • DS-1 • 100 kW • ALT. FREQ. TO 4910 kHz; ENGLISH, ETC • DS-1 • 100 kW • ALT. FREQ. TO 7220 kHz
6266	**PIRATE (EUROPE)** †"UK RADIO", England	Su • W Europe • 0.03 kW
6275v	**PIRATE (EUROPE)** †"EUROPEAN MUSIC RADIO", Holland	Irr • Su • W Europe
	†"FREE RADIO SERVICE", Holland	Irr • Su • W Europe; Irr • Sa • W Europe
6280	**LEBANON** VOICE OF HOPE, Marjayoûn	Mideast & E Europe • 10 kW
6280v	**PIRATE (EUROPE)** †"R MISTERO GHOST PLANET", Italy	Irr • Su • W Europe
	†"RADIO MARABU", Germany	Irr • Su • ENGLISH & GERMAN • W Europe • ALT. FREQ. TO 6210v kHz
	†"RADIO OZONE", Ireland	Su • W Europe • 0.1 kW • ALT. FREQ. TO 5817v kHz
	†"RADIO PACMAN", Holland	Irr • Su • W Europe • 0.01 kW
6282v	**PIRATE (EUROPE)** †"RADIO TORENVALK", Holland	Irr • Su • W Europe • 0.05 kW
6285v	**CLANDESTINE (M EAST)** "VOICE OF ISLAM"	Mideast
6290	**DENMARK** WORLD MUSIC RADIO, Via South Africa	Sa/Su • Africa • 250 kW
6290v	**PAKISTAN** RADIO PAKISTAN, Karachi	W • Mideast • 50 kW
	PIRATE (EUROPE) "WEEKEND MUSIC RADIO", Scotland	Irr • Su • W Europe • 0.1 kW
6295	**PAKISTAN** PAKISTAN BC CORP, Islamabad	W • DS • 100 kW
	PIRATE (EUROPE) "REFLECTIONS EUROPE", Ireland	Su • W Europe • 0.23 kW
6299.3	**HONDURAS** SANI RADIO, Puerto Lempira	SPANISH, ETC • DS-TEMP INACTIVE • 10 kW
6300	**CLANDESTINE (ASIA)** "VO KASHMIR FREEDOM", Pakistan	S Asia • ANTI-INDIAN GOVT
	USA FAMILY RADIO, Via Taiwan	E Asia • 250 kW
6300v	**PIRATE (EUROPE)** "FARMERS FROM HOLLAND", Holland	Irr • Su • W Europe • 0.1 kW
6315	**ETHIOPIA** VO TIGRAY REVOL'N, Mek'ele	E Africa • 10 kW • ALT. FREQ. TO 7515 kHz; Sa/Su • E Africa • 10 kW • ALT. FREQ. TO 7515 kHz; M-F • E Africa • 10 kW • ALT. FREQ. TO 7515 kHz
6329v	**PERU** †ESTACION C, Moyobamba	Irr • DS • 0.8 kW; DS • 0.8 kW
6339.6	**PERU** †R SAN MIGUEL ARCANGEL, San Miguel	DS
6348	**CLANDESTINE (ASIA)** "ECHO OF HOPE", Seoul, South Korea	E Asia • 50 kW
6356v	**VIETNAM** SON LA BC STATION, Son La	DS
6370v	**CLANDESTINE (M EAST)** "VO REBEL IRAQ", Iraq	ARABIC, ETC • Mideast • ANTI-SADDAM
6398v	**KOREA (DPR)** PYONGYANG BC STN, Pyongyang	E Asia • 50 kW
6405.5	**PERU** †RADIO HUARMACA, Huarmaca	DS
6410v	**CLANDESTINE (M EAST)** "VO IRAN COMMUNISTS"	F • Mideast • ANTI-IRANIAN GOVT; Mideast • ANTI-IRANIAN GOVT
	"VO IRANIAN REVOLUTION"	Mideast • PRO-COMMUNIST
6420.3	**PERU** RADIO MI FRONTERA, Distrito Chirinos	DS
6474v	**PIRATE (EUROPE)** †"RADIO BRIGITTE", Belgium	Irr • Su • W Europe • ALT. FREQ. TO 6252v kHz
6479v	**PERU** †RADIO ALTURA, Huarmaca	DS

FREQUENCY　　COUNTRY, STATION, LOCATION　　　　　　TARGET • NETWORK • POWER (kW)　　　World Time

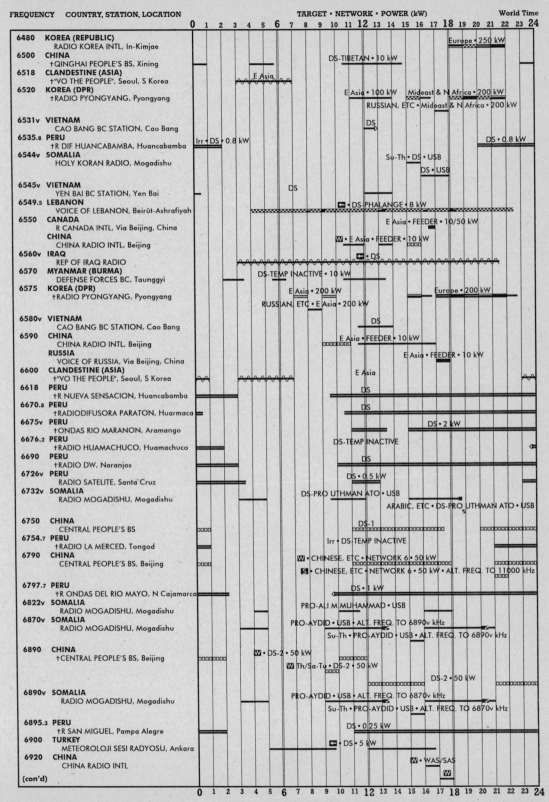

0 1 2 3 4 5 6 7 8 9 10 11 12 13 14 15 16 17 18 19 20 21 22 23 24

Frequency	Country, Station, Location	Notes
6480	KOREA (REPUBLIC)	
	RADIO KOREA INTL, In-Kimjae	Europe • 250 kW
6500	CHINA	
	†QINGHAI PEOPLE'S BS, Xining	DS-TIBETAN • 10 kW
6518	CLANDESTINE (ASIA)	
	†"VO THE PEOPLE", Seoul, S Korea	E Asia
6520	KOREA (DPR)	
	†RADIO PYONGYANG, Pyongyang	E Asia • 100 kW ／ Mideast & N Africa • 200 kW ／ RUSSIAN, ETC • Mideast & N Africa • 200 kW
6531v	VIETNAM	
	CAO BANG BC STATION, Cao Bang	DS
6535.8	PERU	
	†R DIF HUANCABAMBA, Huancabamba	Irr • DS • 0.8 kW ／ DS • 0.8 kW
6544v	SOMALIA	
	HOLY KORAN RADIO, Mogadishu	Su-Th • DS • USB ／ DS • USB
6545v	VIETNAM	
	YEN BAI BC STATION, Yen Bai	DS
6549.5	LEBANON	
	VOICE OF LEBANON, Beirūt-Ashrafiyah	DS-PHALANGE • 8 kW
6550	CANADA	
	R CANADA INTL, Via Beijing, China	E Asia • FEEDER • 10/50 kW
	CHINA	
	CHINA RADIO INTL, Beijing	W • E Asia • FEEDER • 10 kW
6560v	IRAQ	
	REP OF IRAQ RADIO	DS
6570	MYANMAR (BURMA)	
	DEFENSE FORCES BC, Taunggyi	DS-TEMP INACTIVE • 10 kW
6575	KOREA (DPR)	
	†RADIO PYONGYANG, Pyongyang	E Asia • 200 kW ／ Europe • 200 kW ／ RUSSIAN, ETC • E Asia • 200 kW
6580v	VIETNAM	
	CAO BANG BC STATION, Cao Bang	DS
6590	CHINA	
	CHINA RADIO INTL, Beijing	E Asia • FEEDER • 10 kW
	RUSSIA	
	VOICE OF RUSSIA, Via Beijing, China	E Asia • FEEDER • 10 kW
6600	CLANDESTINE (ASIA)	
	†"VO THE PEOPLE", Seoul, S Korea	E Asia
6618	PERU	
	†R NUEVA SENSACION, Huancabamba	DS
6670.8	PERU	
	†RADIODIFUSORA PARATON, Huarmaca	DS
6675v	PERU	
	†ONDAS RIO MARANON, Aramango	DS • 2 kW
6676.2	PERU	
	†RADIO HUAMACHUCO, Huamachuco	DS-TEMP INACTIVE
6690	PERU	
	†RADIO DW, Naranjos	DS
6726v	PERU	
	RADIO SATELITE, Santa Cruz	DS • 0.5 kW
6732v	SOMALIA	
	RADIO MOGADISHU, Mogadishu	DS-PRO UTHMAN ATO • USB ／ ARABIC, ETC • DS-PRO UTHMAN ATO • USB
6750	CHINA	
	CENTRAL PEOPLE'S BS	DS-1
6754.7	PERU	
	†RADIO LA MERCED, Tongod	Irr • DS-TEMP INACTIVE
6790	CHINA	
	CENTRAL PEOPLE'S BS, Beijing	W • CHINESE, ETC • NETWORK 6 • 50 kW ／ S • CHINESE, ETC • NETWORK 6 • 50 kW • ALT. FREQ. TO 11000 kHz
6797.7	PERU	
	†R ONDAS DEL RIO MAYO, N Cajamarca	DS • 1 kW
6822v	SOMALIA	
	RADIO MOGADISHU, Mogadishu	PRO-ALI M MUHAMMAD • USB
6870v	SOMALIA	
	RADIO MOGADISHU, Mogadishu	PRO-AYDID • USB • ALT. FREQ. TO 6890v kHz ／ Su-Th • PRO-AYDID • USB • ALT. FREQ. TO 6890v kHz
6890	CHINA	
	†CENTRAL PEOPLE'S BS, Beijing	W • DS-2 • 50 kW ／ W Th/Sa-Tu • DS-2 • 50 kW ／ DS-2 • 50 kW
6890v	SOMALIA	
	RADIO MOGADISHU, Mogadishu	PRO-AYDID • USB • ALT. FREQ. TO 6870v kHz ／ Su-Th • PRO-AYDID • USB • ALT. FREQ. TO 6870v kHz
6895.3	PERU	
	†R SAN MIGUEL, Pampa Alegre	DS • 0.25 kW
6900	TURKEY	
	METEOROLOJI SESI RADYOSU, Ankara	DS • 5 kW
6920	CHINA	
	CHINA RADIO INTL	W • WAS/SAS

(con'd)

0 1 2 3 4 5 6 7 8 9 10 11 12 13 14 15 16 17 18 19 20 21 22 23 24

SEASONAL S OR W　　1-HR TIMESHIFT MIDYEAR ⊟ OR ⊞　　JAMMING / OR ∧　　EARLIEST HEARD ◁　　LATEST HEARD ▷　　NEW FOR 1999 †

FREQUENCY   COUNTRY, STATION, LOCATION

TARGET • NETWORK • POWER (kW)

World Time

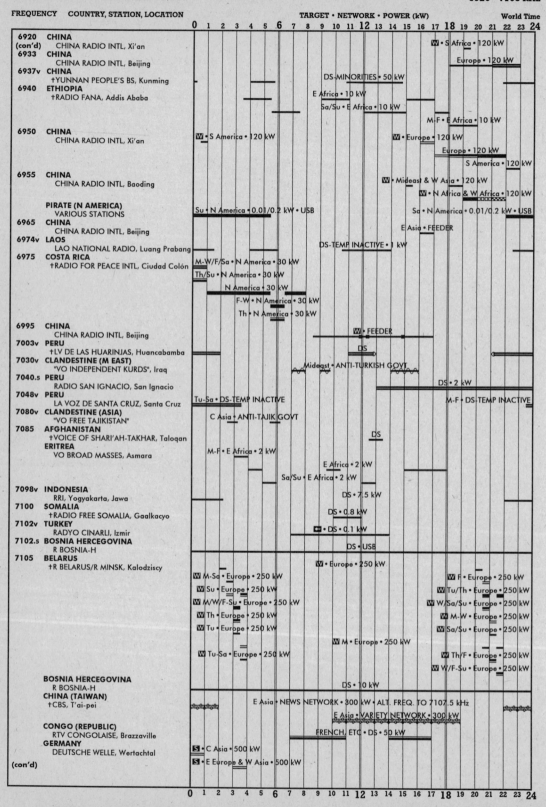

Frequency	Country, Station, Location	Details
6920 (con'd)	**CHINA** CHINA RADIO INTL, Xi'an	W • S Africa • 120 kW
6933	**CHINA** CHINA RADIO INTL, Beijing	Europe • 120 kW
6937v	**CHINA** †YUNNAN PEOPLE'S BS, Kunming	DS-MINORITIES • 50 kW
6940	**ETHIOPIA** †RADIO FANA, Addis Ababa	E Africa • 10 kW; Sa/Su • E Africa • 10 kW; M-F • E Africa • 10 kW
6950	**CHINA** CHINA RADIO INTL, Xi'an	W • S America • 120 kW; W • Europe • 120 kW; Europe • 120 kW; S America • 120 kW
6955	**CHINA** CHINA RADIO INTL, Baoding	W • Mideast & W Asia • 120 kW; W • N Africa & W Africa • 120 kW
	PIRATE (N AMERICA) VARIOUS STATIONS	Su • N America • 0.01/0.2 kW • USB; Sa • N America • 0.01/0.2 kW • USB
6965	**CHINA** CHINA RADIO INTL, Beijing	E Asia • FEEDER
6974v	**LAOS** LAO NATIONAL RADIO, Luang Prabang	DS-TEMP INACTIVE • 1 kW
6975	**COSTA RICA** †RADIO FOR PEACE INTL, Ciudad Colón	M-W/F/Sa • N America • 30 kW; Th/Su • N America • 30 kW; N America • 30 kW; F-W • N America • 30 kW; Th • N America • 30 kW
6995	**CHINA** CHINA RADIO INTL, Beijing	W • FEEDER
7003v	**PERU** †LV DE LAS HUARINJAS, Huancabamba	DS
7030v	**CLANDESTINE (M EAST)** "VO INDEPENDENT KURDS", Iraq	Mideast • ANTI-TURKISH GOVT
7040.5	**PERU** RADIO SAN IGNACIO, San Ignacio	DS • 2 kW
7048v	**PERU** LA VOZ DE SANTA CRUZ, Santa Cruz	Tu-Sa • DS-TEMP INACTIVE; M-F • DS-TEMP INACTIVE
7080v	**CLANDESTINE (ASIA)** "VO FREE TAJIKISTAN"	C Asia • ANTI-TAJIK GOVT
7085	**AFGHANISTAN** †VOICE OF SHARI'AH-TAKHAR, Taloqan	DS
	ERITREA VO BROAD MASSES, Asmara	M-F • E Africa • 2 kW; E Africa • 2 kW; Sa/Su • E Africa • 2 kW
7098v	**INDONESIA** RRI, Yogyakarta, Jawa	DS • 7.5 kW
7100	**SOMALIA** †RADIO FREE SOMALIA, Gaalkacyo	DS • 0.8 kW
7102v	**TURKEY** RADYO CINARLI, Izmir	• DS • 0.1 kW
7102.5	**BOSNIA HERCEGOVINA** R BOSNIA-H	DS • USB
7105	**BELARUS** †R BELARUS/R MINSK, Kalodziscy	W • Europe • 250 kW; W M-Sa • Europe • 250 kW; W Su • Europe • 250 kW; W M/W/F-Su • Europe • 250 kW; W Th • Europe • 250 kW; W Tu • Europe • 250 kW; W Tu-Sa • Europe • 250 kW; W M • Europe • 250 kW; W F • Europe • 250 kW; W Tu/Th • Europe • 250 kW; W W/Sa/Su • Europe • 250 kW; W M-W • Europe • 250 kW; W Sa/Su • Europe • 250 kW; W Th/F • Europe • 250 kW; W W/F-Su • Europe • 250 kW
	BOSNIA HERCEGOVINA R BOSNIA-H	DS • 10 kW
	CHINA (TAIWAN) †CBS, T'ai-pei	E Asia • NEWS NETWORK • 300 kW • ALT. FREQ. TO 7107.5 kHz; E Asia • VARIETY NETWORK • 300 kW
	CONGO (REPUBLIC) RTV CONGOLAISE, Brazzaville	FRENCH, ETC • DS • 50 kW
	GERMANY DEUTSCHE WELLE, Wertachtal	S • C Asia • 500 kW; S • E Europe & W Asia • 500 kW
(con'd)		

ENGLISH ▬   ARABIC ≋   CHINESE □□□   FRENCH ═   GERMAN ▬   RUSSIAN ═   SPANISH ▬   OTHER ▬

FREQUENCY   COUNTRY, STATION, LOCATION   TARGET • NETWORK • POWER (kW)   World Time

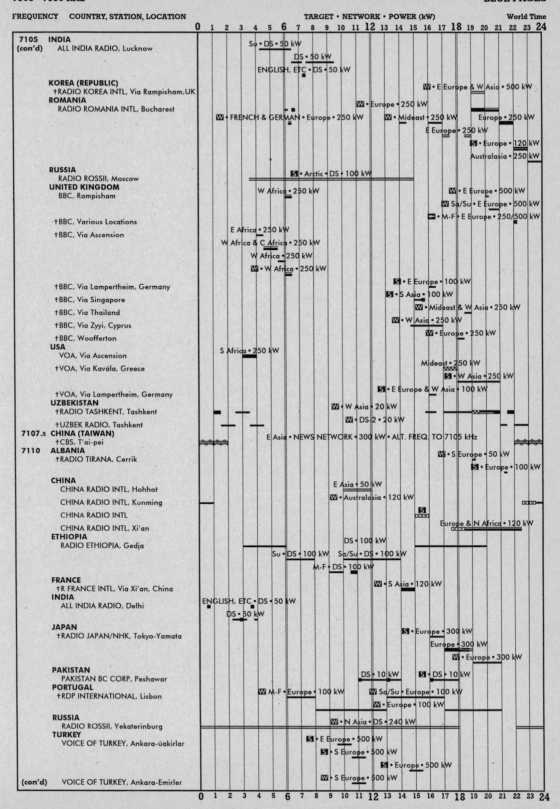

7105   INDIA
(con'd)   ALL INDIA RADIO, Lucknow

        KOREA (REPUBLIC)
        †RADIO KOREA INTL, Via Rampisham, UK
        ROMANIA
        RADIO ROMANIA INTL, Bucharest

        RUSSIA
        RADIO ROSSII, Moscow
        UNITED KINGDOM
        BBC, Rampisham

        †BBC, Various Locations
        †BBC, Via Ascension

        †BBC, Via Lampertheim, Germany
        †BBC, Via Singapore
        †BBC, Via Thailand
        †BBC, Via Zyyi, Cyprus
        †BBC, Woofferton
        USA
        VOA, Via Ascension
        †VOA, Via Kavála, Greece

        †VOA, Via Lampertheim, Germany
        UZBEKISTAN
        †RADIO TASHKENT, Tashkent

        †UZBEK RADIO, Tashkent
7107.5 CHINA (TAIWAN)
        †CBS, T'ai-pei
7110   ALBANIA
        †RADIO TIRANA, Cerrik

        CHINA
        CHINA RADIO INTL, Hohhot
        CHINA RADIO INTL, Kunming
        CHINA RADIO INTL
        CHINA RADIO INTL, Xi'an
        ETHIOPIA
        RADIO ETHIOPIA, Gedja

        FRANCE
        †R FRANCE INTL, Via Xi'an, China
        INDIA
        ALL INDIA RADIO, Delhi

        JAPAN
        †RADIO JAPAN/NHK, Tokyo-Yamata

        PAKISTAN
        PAKISTAN BC CORP, Peshawar
        PORTUGAL
        †RDP INTERNATIONAL, Lisbon

        RUSSIA
        RADIO ROSSII, Yekaterinburg
        TURKEY
        VOICE OF TURKEY, Ankara-üakirlar

(con'd)   VOICE OF TURKEY, Ankara-Emirler

| FREQUENCY | COUNTRY, STATION, LOCATION | TARGET • NETWORK • POWER (kW) | World Time |

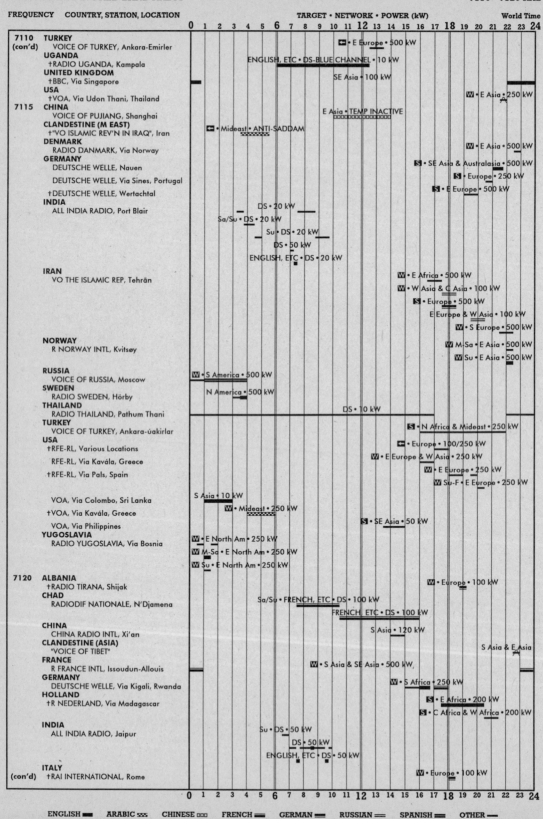

7110
(con'd) **TURKEY**
VOICE OF TURKEY, Ankara-Emirler — ▭ • E Europe • 500 kW
UGANDA
†RADIO UGANDA, Kampala — ENGLISH, ETC • DS-BLUE CHANNEL • 10 kW
UNITED KINGDOM
†BBC, Via Singapore — SE Asia • 100 kW
USA
†VOA, Via Udon Thani, Thailand — W • E Asia • 250 kW

7115 **CHINA**
VOICE OF PUJIANG, Shanghai — E Asia • TEMP INACTIVE
CLANDESTINE (M EAST)
†"VO ISLAMIC REV'N IN IRAQ", Iran — ▭ • Mideast • ANTI-SADDAM
DENMARK
RADIO DANMARK, Via Norway — W • E Asia • 500 kW
GERMANY
DEUTSCHE WELLE, Nauen — S • SE Asia & Australasia • 500 kW

DEUTSCHE WELLE, Via Sines, Portugal — S • Europe • 250 kW

†DEUTSCHE WELLE, Wertachtal — S • E Europe • 500 kW
INDIA
ALL INDIA RADIO, Port Blair — DS • 20 kW
Sa/Su • DS • 20 kW
Su • DS • 20 kW
DS • 50 kW
ENGLISH, ETC • DS • 20 kW

IRAN
VO THE ISLAMIC REP, Tehrān — W • E Africa • 500 kW
W • W Asia & C Asia • 100 kW
S • Europe • 500 kW
E Europe & W Asia • 100 kW
W • S Europe • 500 kW

NORWAY
R NORWAY INTL, Kvitsøy — W M-Sa • E Asia • 500 kW
W Su • E Asia • 500 kW

RUSSIA
VOICE OF RUSSIA, Moscow — W • S America • 500 kW
SWEDEN
RADIO SWEDEN, Hörby — N America • 500 kW
THAILAND
RADIO THAILAND, Pathum Thani — DS • 10 kW
TURKEY
VOICE OF TURKEY, Ankara-úakirlar — S • N Africa & Mideast • 250 kW
USA
†RFE-RL, Various Locations — ▭ • Europe • 100/250 kW
RFE-RL, Via Kavála, Greece — W • E Europe & W Asia • 250 kW
†RFE-RL, Via Pals, Spain — W • E Europe • 250 kW
W Su-F • E Europe • 250 kW

VOA, Via Colombo, Sri Lanka — S Asia • 10 kW
†VOA, Via Kavála, Greece — W • Mideast • 250 kW
VOA, Via Philippines — S • SE Asia • 50 kW
YUGOSLAVIA
RADIO YUGOSLAVIA, Via Bosnia — W • E North Am • 250 kW
W M-Sa • E North Am • 250 kW
W Su • E North Am • 250 kW

7120 **ALBANIA**
†RADIO TIRANA, Shijak — W • Europe • 100 kW
CHAD
RADIODIF NATIONALE, N'Djamena — Sa/Su • FRENCH, ETC • DS • 100 kW
FRENCH, ETC • DS • 100 kW

CHINA
CHINA RADIO INTL, Xi'an — S Asia • 120 kW
CLANDESTINE (ASIA)
"VOICE OF TIBET" — S Asia & E Asia
FRANCE
R FRANCE INTL, Issoudun-Allouis — W • S Asia & SE Asia • 500 kW
GERMANY
DEUTSCHE WELLE, Via Kigali, Rwanda — W • S Africa • 250 kW
HOLLAND
†R NEDERLAND, Via Madagascar — S • E Africa • 200 kW
S • C Africa & W Africa • 200 kW

INDIA
ALL INDIA RADIO, Jaipur — Su • DS • 50 kW
DS • 50 kW
ENGLISH, ETC • DS • 50 kW

ITALY
(con'd) †RAI INTERNATIONAL, Rome — W • Europe • 100 kW

ENGLISH ▬ ARABIC ∞∞ CHINESE □□□ FRENCH ══ GERMAN ▬▬ RUSSIAN ══ SPANISH ═══ OTHER ▬

FREQUENCY   COUNTRY, STATION, LOCATION   TARGET • NETWORK • POWER (kW)   World Time

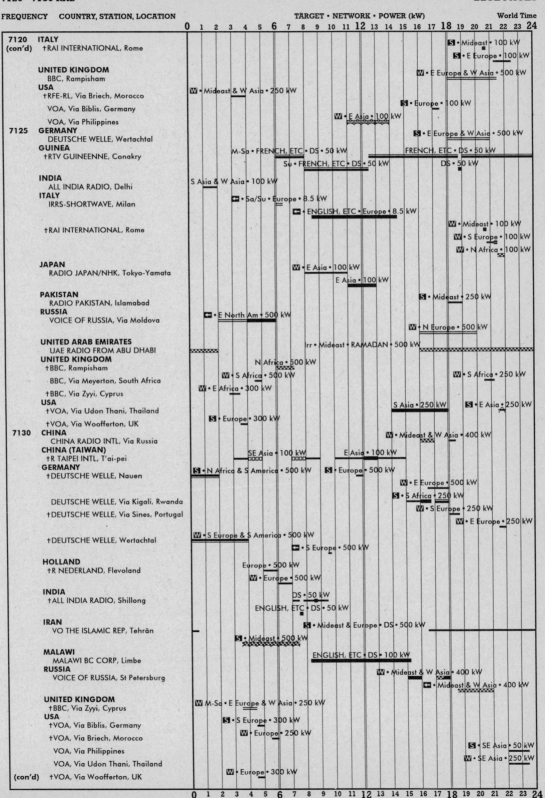

0 1 2 3 4 5 6 7 8 9 10 11 12 13 14 15 16 17 18 19 20 21 22 23 24

7120 ITALY
(con'd)   †RAI INTERNATIONAL, Rome
          S • Mideast • 100 kW
          S • E Europe • 100 kW

      UNITED KINGDOM
          BBC, Rampisham
          W • E Europe & W Asia • 500 kW
      USA
          †RFE-RL, Via Briech, Morocco
          W • Mideast & W Asia • 250 kW

          VOA, Via Biblis, Germany
          S • Europe • 100 kW

          VOA, Via Philippines
          W • E Asia • 100 kW
7125 GERMANY
          DEUTSCHE WELLE, Wertachtal
          S • E Europe & W Asia • 500 kW
      GUINEA
          †RTV GUINEENNE, Conakry
          M-Sa • FRENCH, ETC • DS • 50 kW   FRENCH, ETC • DS • 50 kW
          Su • FRENCH, ETC • DS • 50 kW   DS • 50 kW

      INDIA
          ALL INDIA RADIO, Delhi
          S Asia & W Asia • 100 kW
      ITALY
          IRRS-SHORTWAVE, Milan
          Sa/Su • Europe • 8.5 kW
          ENGLISH, ETC • Europe • 8.5 kW

          †RAI INTERNATIONAL, Rome
          W • Mideast • 100 kW
          W • S Europe • 100 kW
          W • N Africa • 100 kW

      JAPAN
          RADIO JAPAN/NHK, Tokyo-Yamata
          W • E Asia • 100 kW
          E Asia • 100 kW

      PAKISTAN
          RADIO PAKISTAN, Islamabad
          S • Mideast • 250 kW
      RUSSIA
          VOICE OF RUSSIA, Via Moldova
          • E North Am • 500 kW
          W • N Europe • 500 kW

      UNITED ARAB EMIRATES
          UAE RADIO FROM ABU DHABI
          Irr • Mideast • RAMADAN • 500 kW
      UNITED KINGDOM
          †BBC, Rampisham
          N Africa • 500 kW
          BBC, Via Meyerton, South Africa
          W • S Africa • 500 kW   W • S Africa • 250 kW
          †BBC, Via Zyyi, Cyprus
          W • E Africa • 300 kW
      USA
          †VOA, Via Udon Thani, Thailand
          S Asia • 250 kW   S • E Asia • 250 kW
          †VOA, Via Woofferton, UK
          S • Europe • 300 kW
7130 CHINA
          CHINA RADIO INTL, Via Russia
          W • Mideast & W Asia • 400 kW
      CHINA (TAIWAN)
          †R TAIPEI INTL, T'ai-pei
          SE Asia • 100 kW   E Asia • 100 kW
      GERMANY
          †DEUTSCHE WELLE, Nauen
          S • N Africa & S America • 500 kW   S • Europe • 500 kW
          W • E Europe • 500 kW
          DEUTSCHE WELLE, Via Kigali, Rwanda
          S • S Africa • 250 kW
          †DEUTSCHE WELLE, Via Sines, Portugal
          W • S Europe • 250 kW
          W • E Europe • 250 kW
          †DEUTSCHE WELLE, Wertachtal
          W • S Europe & S America • 500 kW
          • S Europe • 500 kW

      HOLLAND
          †R NEDERLAND, Flevoland
          Europe • 500 kW
          W • Europe • 500 kW

      INDIA
          †ALL INDIA RADIO, Shillong
          DS • 50 kW
          ENGLISH, ETC • DS • 50 kW

      IRAN
          VO THE ISLAMIC REP, Tehrān
          S • Mideast & Europe • DS • 500 kW
          S • Mideast • 500 kW

      MALAWI
          MALAWI BC CORP, Limbe
          ENGLISH, ETC • DS • 100 kW
      RUSSIA
          VOICE OF RUSSIA, St Petersburg
          W • Mideast & W Asia • 400 kW
          • Mideast & W Asia • 400 kW

      UNITED KINGDOM
          †BBC, Via Zyyi, Cyprus
          W • M-Sa • E Europe & W Asia • 250 kW
      USA
          †VOA, Via Biblis, Germany
          S • S Europe • 300 kW
          †VOA, Via Briech, Morocco
          W • Europe • 250 kW

          VOA, Via Philippines
          S • SE Asia • 50 kW

          VOA, Via Udon Thani, Thailand
          W • SE Asia • 250 kW

(con'd)   †VOA, Via Woofferton, UK
          W • Europe • 300 kW

0 1 2 3 4 5 6 7 8 9 10 11 12 13 14 15 16 17 18 19 20 21 22 23 24

SEASONAL S OR W   1-HR TIMESHIFT MIDYEAR ◩ OR ◪   JAMMING / OR /\   EARLIEST HEARD ◁   LATEST HEARD ▷   NEW FOR 1999 †

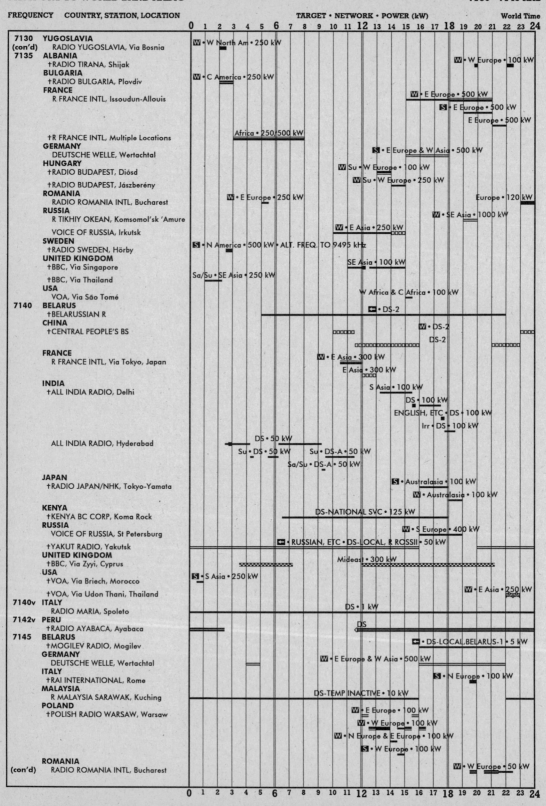

FREQUENCY   COUNTRY, STATION, LOCATION   TARGET • NETWORK • POWER (kW)   World Time

Frequency	Country, Station, Location	Details
7130 (con'd)	YUGOSLAVIA — RADIO YUGOSLAVIA, Via Bosnia	W • W North Am • 250 kW
7135	ALBANIA — †RADIO TIRANA, Shijak	W • W Europe • 100 kW
	BULGARIA — †RADIO BULGARIA, Plovdiv	W • C America • 250 kW
	FRANCE — R FRANCE INTL, Issoudun-Allouis	W • E Europe • 500 kW; S • E Europe • 500 kW; E Europe • 500 kW
	†R FRANCE INTL, Multiple Locations	Africa • 250/500 kW
	GERMANY — DEUTSCHE WELLE, Wertachtal	S • E Europe & W Asia • 500 kW
	HUNGARY — †RADIO BUDAPEST, Diósd	W Su • W Europe • 100 kW
	†RADIO BUDAPEST, Jászberény	W Su • W Europe • 250 kW
	ROMANIA — RADIO ROMANIA INTL, Bucharest	W • E Europe • 250 kW; Europe • 120 kW
	RUSSIA — R TIKHIY OKEAN, Komsomol'sk 'Amure	W • SE Asia • 1000 kW
	VOICE OF RUSSIA, Irkutsk	W • E Asia • 250 kW
	SWEDEN — †RADIO SWEDEN, Hörby	S • N America • 500 kW • ALT. FREQ. TO 9495 kHz
	UNITED KINGDOM — †BBC, Via Singapore	SE Asia • 100 kW
	†BBC, Via Thailand	Sa/Su • SE Asia • 250 kW
	USA — VOA, Via São Tomé	W Africa & C Africa • 100 kW
7140	BELARUS — †BELARUSSIAN R	• DS-2
	CHINA — †CENTRAL PEOPLE'S BS	W • DS-2; DS-2
	FRANCE — R FRANCE INTL, Via Tokyo, Japan	W • E Asia • 300 kW; E Asia • 300 kW
	INDIA — †ALL INDIA RADIO, Delhi	S Asia • 100 kW; DS • 100 kW; ENGLISH, ETC • DS • 100 kW; Irr • DS • 100 kW
	ALL INDIA RADIO, Hyderabad	DS • 50 kW; Su • DS • 50 kW; Su • DS-A • 50 kW; Sa/Su • DS-A • 50 kW
	JAPAN — †RADIO JAPAN/NHK, Tokyo-Yamata	S • Australasia • 100 kW; W • Australasia • 100 kW
	KENYA — †KENYA BC CORP, Koma Rock	DS-NATIONAL SVC • 125 kW
	RUSSIA — VOICE OF RUSSIA, St Petersburg	W • S Europe • 400 kW
	†YAKUT RADIO, Yakutsk	• RUSSIAN, ETC • DS-LOCAL, R ROSSII • 50 kW
	UNITED KINGDOM — †BBC, Via Zyyi, Cyprus	Mideast • 300 kW
	USA — †VOA, Via Briech, Morocco	S • S Asia • 250 kW
	†VOA, Via Udon Thani, Thailand	W • E Asia • 250 kW
7140v	ITALY — RADIO MARIA, Spoleto	DS • 1 kW
7142v	PERU — †RADIO AYABACA, Ayabaca	DS
7145	BELARUS — †MOGILEV RADIO, Mogilev	• DS-LOCAL, BELARUS-1 • 5 kW
	GERMANY — DEUTSCHE WELLE, Wertachtal	W • E Europe & W Asia • 500 kW
	ITALY — †RAI INTERNATIONAL, Rome	S • N Europe • 100 kW
	MALAYSIA — R MALAYSIA SARAWAK, Kuching	DS-TEMP INACTIVE • 10 kW
	POLAND — †POLISH RADIO WARSAW, Warsaw	W • E Europe • 100 kW; W • W Europe • 100 kW; W • N Europe & E Europe • 100 kW; S • W Europe • 100 kW
(con'd)	ROMANIA — RADIO ROMANIA INTL, Bucharest	W • W Europe • 50 kW

ENGLISH ▪▪   ARABIC ⌇⌇⌇   CHINESE □□□   FRENCH ▬▬   GERMAN ▬▬   RUSSIAN ══   SPANISH ▬▬   OTHER ▬▬

FREQUENCY   COUNTRY, STATION, LOCATION   TARGET • NETWORK • POWER (kW)   World Time

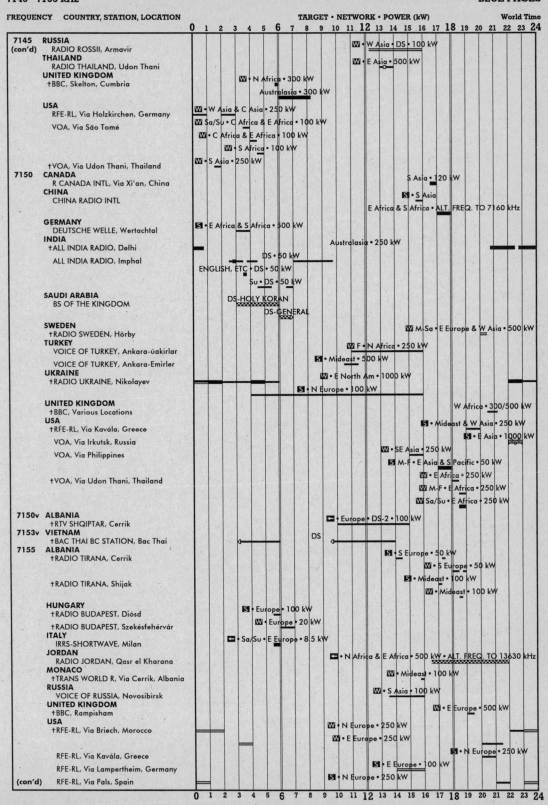

Frequency	Country, Station, Location	Target • Network • Power (kW)
7145 (con'd)	**RUSSIA**	
	RADIO ROSSII, Armavir	W • W Asia • DS • 100 kW
	THAILAND	
	RADIO THAILAND, Udon Thani	W • E Asia • 500 kW
	UNITED KINGDOM	
	†BBC, Skelton, Cumbria	W • N Africa • 300 kW
		Australasia • 300 kW
	USA	
	RFE-RL, Via Holzkirchen, Germany	W • W Asia & C Asia • 250 kW
	VOA, Via São Tomé	W Sa/Su • C Africa & E Africa • 100 kW
		W • C Africa & E Africa • 100 kW
		W • S Africa • 100 kW
	†VOA, Via Udon Thani, Thailand	W • S Asia • 250 kW
7150	**CANADA**	
	R CANADA INTL, Via Xi'an, China	S Asia • 120 kW
	CHINA	
	CHINA RADIO INTL	S • S Asia
		E Africa & S Africa • ALT. FREQ. TO 7160 kHz
	GERMANY	
	DEUTSCHE WELLE, Wertachtal	S • E Africa & S Africa • 500 kW
	INDIA	
	†ALL INDIA RADIO, Delhi	Australasia • 250 kW
	ALL INDIA RADIO, Imphal	DS • 50 kW
		ENGLISH, ETC • DS • 50 kW
		Su • DS • 50 kW
	SAUDI ARABIA	
	BS OF THE KINGDOM	DS-HOLY KORAN
		DS-GENERAL
	SWEDEN	
	†RADIO SWEDEN, Hörby	W M-Sa • E Europe & W Asia • 500 kW
	TURKEY	
	VOICE OF TURKEY, Ankara-úakirlar	W F • N Africa • 250 kW
	VOICE OF TURKEY, Ankara-Emirler	S • Mideast • 500 kW
	UKRAINE	
	†RADIO UKRAINE, Nikolayev	W • E North Am • 1000 kW
		S • N Europe • 100 kW
	UNITED KINGDOM	
	†BBC, Various Locations	W Africa • 300/500 kW
	USA	
	†RFE-RL, Via Kavála, Greece	S • Mideast & W Asia • 250 kW
	VOA, Via Irkutsk, Russia	S • E Asia • 1000 kW
	VOA, Via Philippines	W • SE Asia • 250 kW
		S M-F • E Asia & S Pacific • 50 kW
	†VOA, Via Udon Thani, Thailand	W • E Africa • 250 kW
		W M-F • E Africa • 250 kW
		W Sa/Su • E Africa • 250 kW
7150v	**ALBANIA**	
	†RTV SHQIPTAR, Cerrik	▱ • Europe • DS-2 • 100 kW
7153v	**VIETNAM**	
	†BAC THAI BC STATION, Bac Thai	DS
7155	**ALBANIA**	
	†RADIO TIRANA, Cerrik	S • S Europe • 50 kW
		W • S Europe • 50 kW
	†RADIO TIRANA, Shijak	S • Mideast • 100 kW
		W • Mideast • 100 kW
	HUNGARY	
	†RADIO BUDAPEST, Diósd	S • Europe • 100 kW
		W • Europe • 20 kW
	†RADIO BUDAPEST, Székésfehérvár	
	ITALY	
	IRRS-SHORTWAVE, Milan	▱ • Sa/Su • E Europe • 8.5 kW
	JORDAN	
	RADIO JORDAN, Qasr el Kharana	▱ • N Africa & E Africa • 500 kW • ALT. FREQ. TO 13630 kHz
	MONACO	
	†TRANS WORLD R, Via Cerrik, Albania	W • Mideast • 100 kW
	RUSSIA	
	VOICE OF RUSSIA, Novosibirsk	W • S Asia • 100 kW
	UNITED KINGDOM	
	†BBC, Rampisham	W • E Europe • 500 kW
	USA	
	†RFE-RL, Via Briech, Morocco	W • N Europe • 250 kW
		W • E Europe • 250 kW
	RFE-RL, Via Kavála, Greece	S • N Europe • 250 kW
	RFE-RL, Via Lampertheim, Germany	S • E Europe • 100 kW
(con'd)	RFE-RL, Via Pals, Spain	S • N Europe • 250 kW

FREQUENCY   COUNTRY, STATION, LOCATION

TARGET • NETWORK • POWER (kW)

World Time

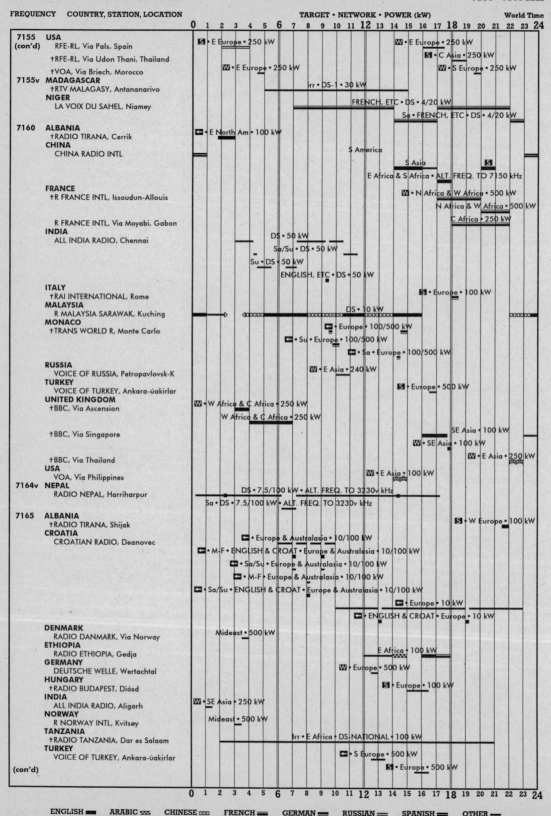

FREQUENCY	COUNTRY, STATION, LOCATION	Schedule
7155 (con'd)	**USA** RFE-RL, Via Pals, Spain	W • E Europe • 250 kW
	†RFE-RL, Via Udon Thani, Thailand	S • C Asia • 250 kW
	†VOA, Via Briech, Morocco	W • E Europe • 250 kW / W • S Europe • 250 kW
7155v	**MADAGASCAR** †RTV MALAGASY, Antananarivo	Irr • DS-1 • 30 kW
	NIGER LA VOIX DU SAHEL, Niamey	FRENCH, ETC • DS • 4/20 kW / Sa • FRENCH, ETC • DS • 4/20 kW
7160	**ALBANIA** †RADIO TIRANA, Cerrik	E North Am • 100 kW
	CHINA CHINA RADIO INTL	S America / S Asia / E Africa & S Africa • ALT. FREQ. TO 7150 kHz
	FRANCE †R FRANCE INTL, Issoudun-Allouis	W • N Africa & W Africa • 500 kW / N Africa & W Africa • 500 kW
	R FRANCE INTL, Via Moyabi, Gabon	C Africa • 250 kW
	INDIA ALL INDIA RADIO, Chennai	DS • 50 kW / Sa/Su • DS • 50 kW / Su • DS • 50 kW / ENGLISH, ETC • DS • 50 kW
	ITALY †RAI INTERNATIONAL, Rome	S • Europe • 100 kW
	MALAYSIA R MALAYSIA SARAWAK, Kuching	DS • 10 kW
	MONACO †TRANS WORLD R, Monte Carlo	Europe • 100/500 kW / Su • Europe • 100/500 kW / Sa • Europe • 100/500 kW
	RUSSIA VOICE OF RUSSIA, Petropavlovsk-K	W • E Asia • 240 kW
	TURKEY VOICE OF TURKEY, Ankara-úakirlar	S • Europe • 500 kW
	UNITED KINGDOM †BBC, Via Ascension	W • W Africa & C Africa • 250 kW / W Africa & C Africa • 250 kW
	†BBC, Via Singapore	SE Asia • 100 kW / W • SE Asia • 100 kW
	†BBC, Via Thailand	W • E Asia • 250 kW
	USA VOA, Via Philippines	W • E Asia • 100 kW
7164v	**NEPAL** RADIO NEPAL, Harriharpur	DS • 7.5/100 kW • ALT. FREQ. TO 3230v kHz / Sa • DS • 7.5/100 kW • ALT. FREQ. TO 3230v kHz
7165	**ALBANIA** †RADIO TIRANA, Shijak	S • W Europe • 100 kW
	CROATIA CROATIAN RADIO, Deanovec	Europe & Australasia • 10/100 kW / M-F • ENGLISH & CROAT • Europe & Australasia • 10/100 kW / Sa/Su • Europe & Australasia • 10/100 kW / M-F • Europe & Australasia • 10/100 kW / Sa/Su • ENGLISH & CROAT • Europe & Australasia • 10/100 kW / Europe • 10 kW / ENGLISH & CROAT • Europe • 10 kW
	DENMARK RADIO DANMARK, Via Norway	Mideast • 500 kW
	ETHIOPIA RADIO ETHIOPIA, Gedja	E Africa • 100 kW
	GERMANY DEUTSCHE WELLE, Wertachtal	W • Europe • 500 kW
	HUNGARY †RADIO BUDAPEST, Diósd	S • Europe • 100 kW
	INDIA ALL INDIA RADIO, Aligarh	W • SE Asia • 250 kW
	NORWAY R NORWAY INTL, Kvitsøy	Mideast • 500 kW
	TANZANIA †RADIO TANZANIA, Dar es Salaam	Irr • E Africa • DS-NATIONAL • 100 kW
	TURKEY VOICE OF TURKEY, Ankara-úakirlar	S Europe • 500 kW / S • Europe • 500 kW
(con'd)		

ENGLISH ▬   ARABIC ⁓⁓⁓   CHINESE □□□   FRENCH ══   GERMAN ▬▬   RUSSIAN ══   SPANISH ══   OTHER ▬

FREQUENCY   COUNTRY, STATION, LOCATION

TARGET • NETWORK • POWER (kW)

World Time

0 1 2 3 4 5 6 7 8 9 10 11 12 13 14 15 16 17 18 19 20 21 22 23 24

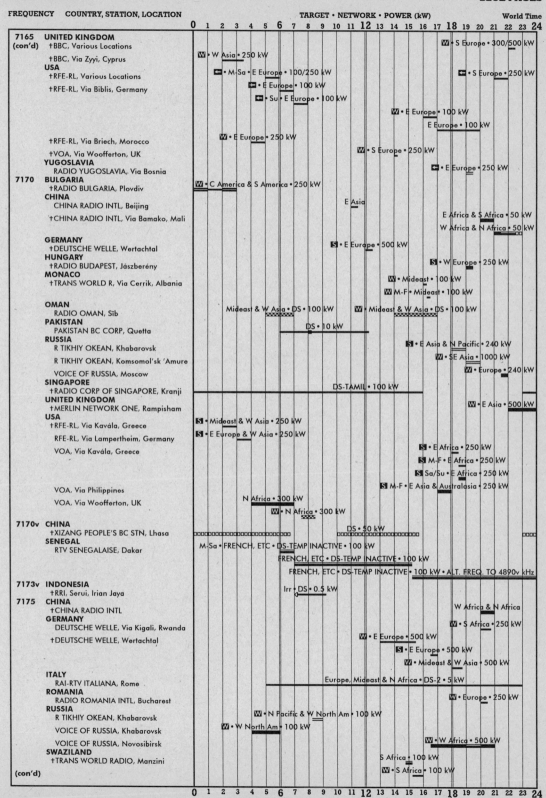

Frequency	Country, Station, Location	Target • Network • Power
7165 (con'd)	**UNITED KINGDOM**	
	†BBC, Various Locations	W • W Asia • 250 kW W • S Europe • 300/500 kW
	†BBC, Via Zyyi, Cyprus	
	USA	
	†RFE-RL, Various Locations	M-Sa • E Europe • 100/250 kW S Europe • 250 kW
	†RFE-RL, Via Biblis, Germany	E Europe • 100 kW
		Su • E Europe • 100 kW
		W • E Europe • 100 kW
		E Europe • 100 kW
	†RFE-RL, Via Briech, Morocco	W • E Europe • 250 kW
	†VOA, Via Woofferton, UK	W • S Europe • 250 kW
	YUGOSLAVIA	
	RADIO YUGOSLAVIA, Via Bosnia	E Europe • 250 kW
7170	**BULGARIA**	
	†RADIO BULGARIA, Plovdiv	W • C America & S America • 250 kW
	CHINA	
	CHINA RADIO INTL, Beijing	E Asia
	†CHINA RADIO INTL, Via Bamako, Mali	E Africa & S Africa • 50 kW
		W Africa & N Africa • 50 kW
	GERMANY	
	†DEUTSCHE WELLE, Wertachtal	S • E Europe • 500 kW
	HUNGARY	
	†RADIO BUDAPEST, Jászberény	S • W Europe • 250 kW
	MONACO	
	†TRANS WORLD R, Via Cerrik, Albania	W • Mideast • 100 kW
		W M-F • Mideast • 100 kW
	OMAN	
	RADIO OMAN, Sīb	Mideast & W Asia • DS • 100 kW W • Mideast & W Asia • DS • 100 kW
	PAKISTAN	
	PAKISTAN BC CORP, Quetta	DS • 10 kW
	RUSSIA	
	R TIKHIY OKEAN, Khabarovsk	S • E Asia & N Pacific • 240 kW
	R TIKHIY OKEAN, Komsomol'sk 'Amure	W • SE Asia • 1000 kW
	VOICE OF RUSSIA, Moscow	W • Europe • 240 kW
	SINGAPORE	
	†RADIO CORP OF SINGAPORE, Kranji	DS-TAMIL • 100 kW
	UNITED KINGDOM	
	†MERLIN NETWORK ONE, Rampisham	W • E Asia • 500 kW
	USA	
	†RFE-RL, Via Kavála, Greece	S • Mideast & W Asia • 250 kW
	RFE-RL, Via Lampertheim, Germany	S • E Europe & W Asia • 250 kW
	VOA, Via Kavála, Greece	S • E Africa • 250 kW
		S M-F • E Africa • 250 kW
		S Sa/Su • E Africa • 250 kW
		S M-F • E Asia & Australasia • 250 kW
	VOA, Via Philippines	N Africa • 300 kW
	VOA, Via Woofferton, UK	W • N Africa • 300 kW
7170v	**CHINA**	
	†XIZANG PEOPLE'S BC STN, Lhasa	DS • 50 kW
	SENEGAL	
	RTV SENEGALAISE, Dakar	M-Sa • FRENCH, ETC • DS-TEMP INACTIVE • 100 kW
		FRENCH, ETC • DS-TEMP INACTIVE • 100 kW
		FRENCH, ETC • DS-TEMP INACTIVE • 100 kW • ALT. FREQ. TO 4890v kHz
7173v	**INDONESIA**	
	†RRI, Serui, Irian Jaya	Irr • DS • 0.5 kW
7175	**CHINA**	
	†CHINA RADIO INTL	W Africa & N Africa
	GERMANY	
	DEUTSCHE WELLE, Via Kigali, Rwanda	W • S Africa • 250 kW
	†DEUTSCHE WELLE, Wertachtal	W • E Europe • 500 kW
		S • E Europe • 500 kW
		W • Mideast & W Asia • 500 kW
	ITALY	
	RAI-RTV ITALIANA, Rome	Europe, Mideast & N Africa • DS-2 • 5 kW
	ROMANIA	
	RADIO ROMANIA INTL, Bucharest	W • Europe • 250 kW
	RUSSIA	
	R TIKHIY OKEAN, Khabarovsk	W • N Pacific & W North Am • 100 kW
	VOICE OF RUSSIA, Khabarovsk	W • W North Am • 100 kW
	VOICE OF RUSSIA, Novosibirsk	W • W Africa • 500 kW
	SWAZILAND	
	†TRANS WORLD RADIO, Manzini	S Africa • 100 kW
		W • S Africa • 100 kW
(con'd)		

0 1 2 3 4 5 6 7 8 9 10 11 12 13 14 15 16 17 18 19 20 21 22 23 24

| FREQUENCY | COUNTRY, STATION, LOCATION | TARGET • NETWORK • POWER (kW) | World Time |

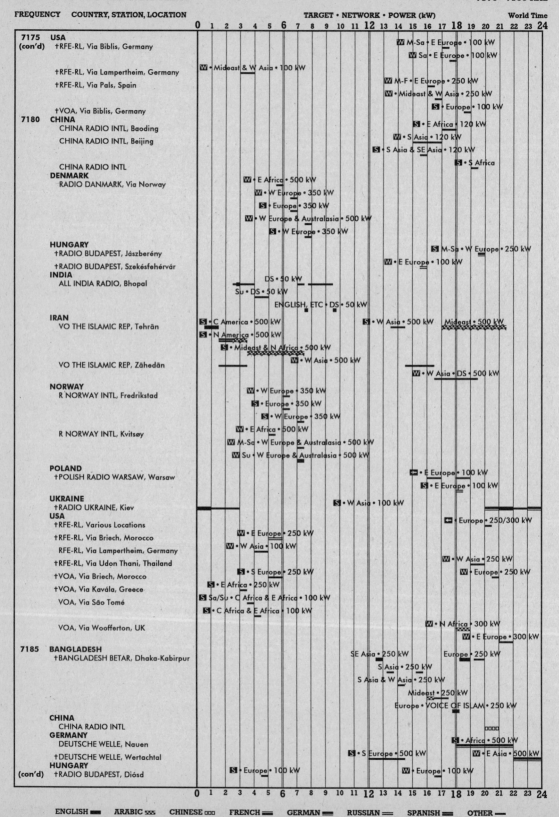

FREQUENCY / COUNTRY, STATION, LOCATION:

7175 **USA**
(con'd) †RFE-RL, Via Biblis, Germany — ⓦ M-Sa • E Europe • 100 kW / ⓦ Sa • E Europe • 100 kW

†RFE-RL, Via Lampertheim, Germany — ⓦ • Mideast & W Asia • 100 kW

†RFE-RL, Via Pals, Spain — ⓦ M-F • E Europe • 250 kW / ⓦ • Mideast & W Asia • 250 kW

†VOA, Via Biblis, Germany — Ⓢ • Europe • 100 kW

7180 **CHINA**
CHINA RADIO INTL, Baoding — Ⓢ • E Africa • 120 kW
CHINA RADIO INTL, Beijing — ⓦ • S Asia • 120 kW / Ⓢ • S Asia & SE Asia • 120 kW

CHINA RADIO INTL — Ⓢ • S Africa

DENMARK
RADIO DANMARK, Via Norway — ⓦ • E Africa • 500 kW / ⓦ • W Europe • 350 kW / Ⓢ • Europe • 350 kW / ⓦ • W Europe & Australasia • 500 kW / Ⓢ • W Europe • 350 kW

HUNGARY
†RADIO BUDAPEST, Jászberény — Ⓢ M-Sa • W Europe • 250 kW
†RADIO BUDAPEST, Szekésfehérvár — ⓦ • E Europe • 100 kW

INDIA
ALL INDIA RADIO, Bhopal — DS • 50 kW / Su • DS • 50 kW / ENGLISH, ETC • DS • 50 kW

IRAN
VO THE ISLAMIC REP, Tehrān — Ⓢ • C America • 500 kW / Ⓢ • W Asia • 500 kW / Mideast • 500 kW / Ⓢ • N America • 500 kW / Ⓢ • Mideast & N Africa • 500 kW / ⓦ • W Asia • 500 kW

VO THE ISLAMIC REP, Zāhedān — ⓦ • W Asia • DS • 500 kW

NORWAY
R NORWAY INTL, Fredrikstad — ⓦ • W Europe • 350 kW / Ⓢ • Europe • 350 kW / Ⓢ • W Europe • 350 kW

R NORWAY INTL, Kvitsøy — ⓦ • E Africa • 500 kW / ⓦ M-Sa • W Europe & Australasia • 500 kW / ⓦ Su • W Europe & Australasia • 500 kW

POLAND
†POLISH RADIO WARSAW, Warsaw — ▣ • E Europe • 100 kW / Ⓢ • E Europe • 100 kW

UKRAINE
†RADIO UKRAINE, Kiev — Ⓢ • W Asia • 100 kW

USA
†RFE-RL, Various Locations — ▣ • Europe • 250/300 kW
†RFE-RL, Via Briech, Morocco — ⓦ • E Europe • 250 kW
RFE-RL, Via Lampertheim, Germany — ⓦ • W Asia • 100 kW
†RFE-RL, Via Udon Thani, Thailand — ⓦ • W Asia • 250 kW
†VOA, Via Briech, Morocco — Ⓢ • S Europe • 250 kW / ⓦ • Europe • 250 kW
†VOA, Via Kavála, Greece — Ⓢ • E Africa • 250 kW
VOA, Via São Tomé — Ⓢ Sa/Su • C Africa & E Africa • 100 kW / Ⓢ • C Africa & E Africa • 100 kW

VOA, Via Woofferton, UK — ⓦ • N Africa • 300 kW / ⓦ • E Europe • 300 kW

7185 **BANGLADESH**
†BANGLADESH BETAR, Dhaka-Kabirpur — SE Asia • 250 kW / Europe • 250 kW / S Asia • 250 kW / S Asia & W Asia • 250 kW / Mideast • 250 kW / Europe • VOICE OF ISLAM • 250 kW

CHINA
CHINA RADIO INTL

GERMANY
DEUTSCHE WELLE, Nauen — Ⓢ • Africa • 500 kW
†DEUTSCHE WELLE, Wertachtal — Ⓢ • S Europe • 500 kW / ⓦ • E Asia • 500 kW

HUNGARY
(con'd) †RADIO BUDAPEST, Diósd — Ⓢ • Europe • 100 kW / ⓦ • Europe • 100 kW

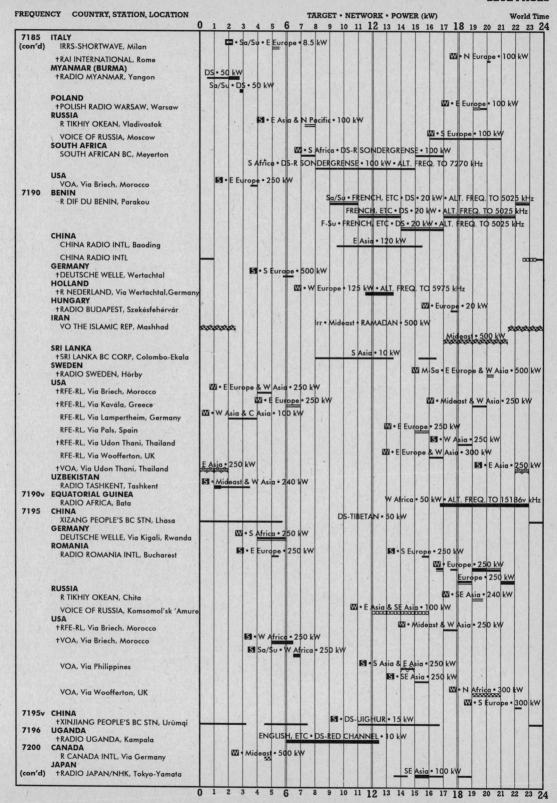

FREQUENCY   COUNTRY, STATION, LOCATION   TARGET • NETWORK • POWER (kW)   World Time

FREQUENCY	COUNTRY, STATION, LOCATION	TARGET • NETWORK • POWER (kW)
7185 (con'd)	ITALY IRRS-SHORTWAVE, Milan	⊡ • Sa/Su • E Europe • 8.5 kW
	†RAI INTERNATIONAL, Rome	W • N Europe • 100 kW
	MYANMAR (BURMA) †RADIO MYANMAR, Yangon	DS • 50 kW Sa/Su • DS • 50 kW
	POLAND †POLISH RADIO WARSAW, Warsaw	W • E Europe • 100 kW
	RUSSIA R TIKHIY OKEAN, Vladivostok	S • E Asia & N Pacific • 100 kW
	VOICE OF RUSSIA, Moscow	W • S Europe • 100 kW
	SOUTH AFRICA SOUTH AFRICAN BC, Meyerton	W • S Africa • DS-R SONDERGRENSE • 100 kW S Africa • DS-R SONDERGRENSE • 100 kW • ALT. FREQ. TO 7270 kHz
	USA VOA, Via Briech, Morocco	S • E Europe • 250 kW
7190	BENIN R DIF DU BENIN, Parakou	Sa/Su • FRENCH, ETC • DS • 20 kW • ALT. FREQ. TO 5025 kHz FRENCH, ETC • DS • 20 kW • ALT. FREQ. TO 5025 kHz F-Su • FRENCH, ETC • DS • 20 kW • ALT. FREQ. TO 5025 kHz
	CHINA CHINA RADIO INTL, Baoding	E Asia • 120 kW
	CHINA RADIO INTL	
	GERMANY †DEUTSCHE WELLE, Wertachtal	S • S Europe • 500 kW
	HOLLAND †R NEDERLAND, Via Wertachtal, Germany	W • W Europe • 125 kW • ALT. FREQ. TO 5975 kHz
	HUNGARY †RADIO BUDAPEST, Szekésfehérvár	W • Europe • 20 kW
	IRAN VO THE ISLAMIC REP, Mashhad	Irr • Mideast • RAMADAN • 500 kW Mideast • 500 kW
	SRI LANKA †SRI LANKA BC CORP, Colombo-Ekala	S Asia • 10 kW
	SWEDEN †RADIO SWEDEN, Hörby	W • M-Sa • E Europe & W Asia • 500 kW
	USA †RFE-RL, Via Briech, Morocco	W • E Europe & W Asia • 250 kW
	†RFE-RL, Via Kavála, Greece	W • E Europe • 250 kW W • Mideast & W Asia • 250 kW
	RFE-RL, Via Lampertheim, Germany	W • W Asia & C Asia • 100 kW
	RFE-RL, Via Pals, Spain	W • E Europe • 250 kW
	†RFE-RL, Via Udon Thani, Thailand	S • W Asia • 250 kW
	RFE-RL, Via Woofferton, UK	W • E Europe & W Asia • 300 kW
	†VOA, Via Udon Thani, Thailand	E Asia • 250 kW S • E Asia • 250 kW
	UZBEKISTAN RADIO TASHKENT, Tashkent	S • Mideast & W Asia • 240 kW
7190v	EQUATORIAL GUINEA RADIO AFRICA, Bata	W Africa • 50 kW • ALT. FREQ. TO 15186v kHz
7195	CHINA XIZANG PEOPLE'S BC STN, Lhasa	DS-TIBETAN • 50 kW
	GERMANY DEUTSCHE WELLE, Via Kigali, Rwanda	W • S Africa • 250 kW
	ROMANIA RADIO ROMANIA INTL, Bucharest	S • E Europe • 250 kW S • S Europe • 250 kW W • Europe • 250 kW Europe • 250 kW
	RUSSIA R TIKHIY OKEAN, Chita	W • SE Asia • 240 kW
	VOICE OF RUSSIA, Komsomol'sk 'Amure	W • E Asia & SE Asia • 100 kW
	USA †RFE-RL, Via Briech, Morocco	W • Mideast & W Asia • 250 kW
	†VOA, Via Briech, Morocco	S • W Africa • 250 kW S • Sa/Su • W Africa • 250 kW
	VOA, Via Philippines	S • S Asia & E Asia • 250 kW S • SE Asia • 250 kW
	VOA, Via Woofferton, UK	W • N Africa • 300 kW W • S Europe • 300 kW
7195v	CHINA †XINJIANG PEOPLE'S BC STN, Urümqi	S • DS-UIGHUR • 15 kW
7196	UGANDA †RADIO UGANDA, Kampala	ENGLISH, ETC • DS-RED CHANNEL • 10 kW
7200	CANADA R CANADA INTL, Via Germany	W • Mideast • 500 kW
(con'd)	JAPAN †RADIO JAPAN/NHK, Tokyo-Yamata	SE Asia • 100 kW

FREQUENCY   COUNTRY, STATION, LOCATION

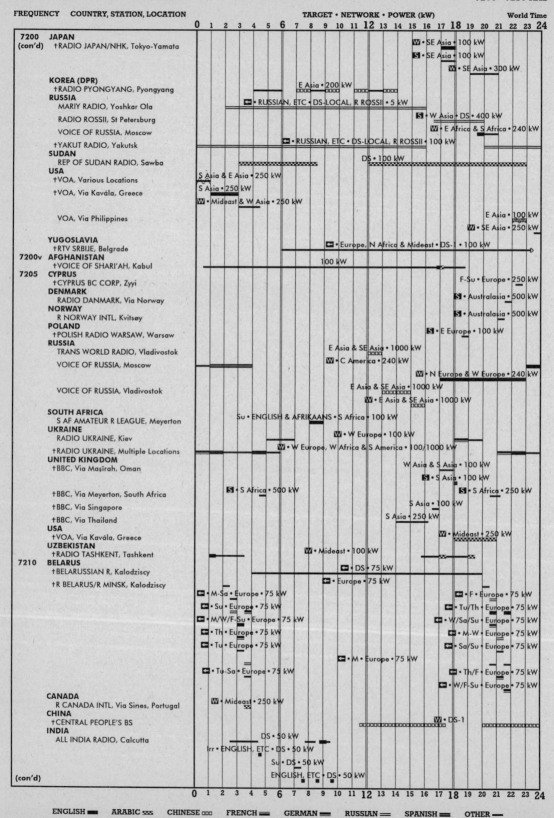

TARGET • NETWORK • POWER (kW)   World Time

7200	JAPAN	
(con'd)	†RADIO JAPAN/NHK, Tokyo-Yamata	W • SE Asia • 100 kW
		S • SE Asia • 100 kW
		W • SE Asia • 300 kW
	KOREA (DPR)	
	†RADIO PYONGYANG, Pyongyang	E Asia • 200 kW
	RUSSIA	
	MARIY RADIO, Yoshkar Ola	⬛ • RUSSIAN, ETC • DS-LOCAL, R ROSSII • 5 kW
	RADIO ROSSII, St Petersburg	S • W Asia • DS • 400 kW
	VOICE OF RUSSIA, Moscow	W • E Africa & S Africa • 240 kW
	†YAKUT RADIO, Yakutsk	⬛ • RUSSIAN, ETC • DS-LOCAL, R ROSSII • 100 kW
	SUDAN	
	REP OF SUDAN RADIO, Sawba	DS • 100 kW
	USA	
	†VOA, Various Locations	S Asia & E Asia • 250 kW
	†VOA, Via Kavála, Greece	S Asia • 250 kW
		W • Mideast & W Asia • 250 kW
	VOA, Via Philippines	E Asia • 100 kW
		W • SE Asia • 250 kW
	YUGOSLAVIA	
	†RTV SRBIJE, Belgrade	⬛ • Europe, N Africa & Mideast • DS-1 • 100 kW
7200v	AFGHANISTAN	
	†VOICE OF SHARI'AH, Kabul	100 kW
7205	CYPRUS	
	†CYPRUS BC CORP, Zyyi	F-Su • Europe • 250 kW
	DENMARK	
	RADIO DANMARK, Via Norway	S • Australasia • 500 kW
	NORWAY	
	R NORWAY INTL, Kvitsøy	S • Australasia • 500 kW
	POLAND	
	†POLISH RADIO WARSAW, Warsaw	S • E Europe • 100 kW
	RUSSIA	
	TRANS WORLD RADIO, Vladivostok	E Asia & SE Asia • 1000 kW
	VOICE OF RUSSIA, Moscow	W • C America • 240 kW
		W • N Europe & W Europe • 240 kW
	VOICE OF RUSSIA, Vladivostok	E Asia & SE Asia • 1000 kW
		W • E Asia & SE Asia • 1000 kW
	SOUTH AFRICA	
	S AF AMATEUR R LEAGUE, Meyerton	Su • ENGLISH & AFRIKAANS • S Africa • 100 kW
	UKRAINE	
	RADIO UKRAINE, Kiev	W • W Europe • 100 kW
	†RADIO UKRAINE, Multiple Locations	W • W Europe, W Africa & S America • 100/1000 kW
	UNITED KINGDOM	
	†BBC, Via Maṣīrah, Oman	W Asia & S Asia • 100 kW
		S • S Asia • 100 kW
	†BBC, Via Meyerton, South Africa	S • S Africa • 500 kW
		S • S Africa • 250 kW
	†BBC, Via Singapore	S Asia • 100 kW
	†BBC, Via Thailand	S Asia • 250 kW
	USA	
	†VOA, Via Kavála, Greece	W • Mideast • 250 kW
	UZBEKISTAN	
	†RADIO TASHKENT, Tashkent	W • Mideast • 100 kW
7210	BELARUS	
	†BELARUSSIAN R, Kalodziscy	⬛ • DS • 75 kW
	†R BELARUS/R MINSK, Kalodziscy	⬛ • Europe • 75 kW
		⬛ • M-Sa • Europe • 75 kW
		⬛ • F • Europe • 75 kW
		⬛ • Su • Europe • 75 kW
		⬛ • Tu/Th • Europe • 75 kW
		⬛ • M/W/F-Su • Europe • 75 kW
		⬛ • W/Sa/Su • Europe • 75 kW
		⬛ • Th • Europe • 75 kW
		⬛ • M-W • Europe • 75 kW
		⬛ • Tu • Europe • 75 kW
		⬛ • Sa/Su • Europe • 75 kW
		⬛ • M • Europe • 75 kW
		⬛ • Tu-Sa • Europe • 75 kW
		⬛ • Th/F • Europe • 75 kW
		⬛ • W/F-Su • Europe • 75 kW
	CANADA	
	R CANADA INTL, Via Sines, Portugal	W • Mideast • 250 kW
	CHINA	
	†CENTRAL PEOPLE'S BS	W • DS-1
	INDIA	
	ALL INDIA RADIO, Calcutta	DS • 50 kW
		Irr • ENGLISH, ETC • DS • 50 kW
		Su • DS • 50 kW
		ENGLISH, ETC • DS • 50 kW
(con'd)		

FREQUENCY   COUNTRY, STATION, LOCATION   TARGET • NETWORK • POWER (kW)   World Time

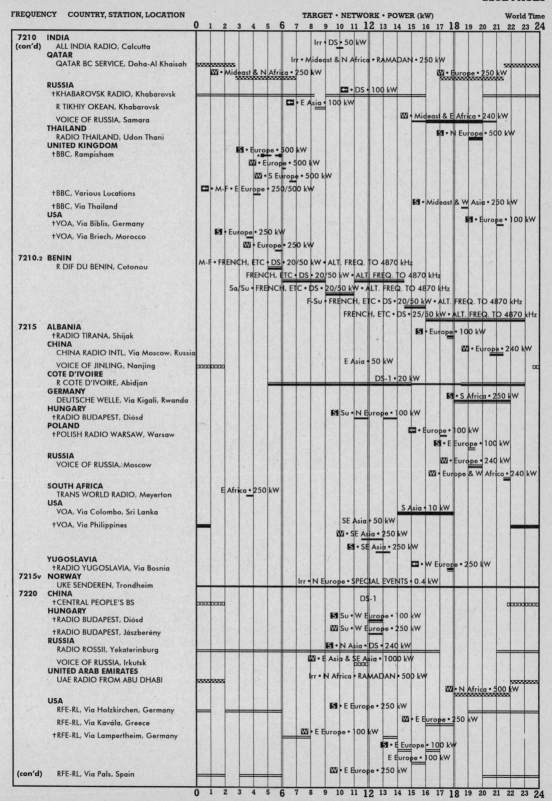

7210	**INDIA**
(con'd)	ALL INDIA RADIO, Calcutta
	QATAR
	QATAR BC SERVICE, Doha-Al Khaisah
	RUSSIA
	†KHABAROVSK RADIO, Khabarovsk
	R TIKHIY OKEAN, Khabarovsk
	VOICE OF RUSSIA, Samara
	THAILAND
	RADIO THAILAND, Udon Thani
	UNITED KINGDOM
	†BBC, Rampisham
	†BBC, Various Locations
	†BBC, Via Thailand
	USA
	†VOA, Via Biblis, Germany
	†VOA, Via Briech, Morocco
7210.2	**BENIN**
	R DIF DU BENIN, Cotonou
7215	**ALBANIA**
	†RADIO TIRANA, Shijak
	CHINA
	CHINA RADIO INTL, Via Moscow, Russia
	VOICE OF JINLING, Nanjing
	COTE D'IVOIRE
	R COTE D'IVOIRE, Abidjan
	GERMANY
	DEUTSCHE WELLE, Via Kigali, Rwanda
	HUNGARY
	†RADIO BUDAPEST, Diósd
	POLAND
	†POLISH RADIO WARSAW, Warsaw
	RUSSIA
	VOICE OF RUSSIA, Moscow
	SOUTH AFRICA
	TRANS WORLD RADIO, Meyerton
	USA
	VOA, Via Colombo, Sri Lanka
	†VOA, Via Philippines
	YUGOSLAVIA
	†RADIO YUGOSLAVIA, Via Bosnia
7215v	**NORWAY**
	UKE SENDEREN, Trondheim
7220	**CHINA**
	†CENTRAL PEOPLE'S BS
	HUNGARY
	†RADIO BUDAPEST, Diósd
	†RADIO BUDAPEST, Jászberény
	RUSSIA
	RADIO ROSSII, Yekaterinburg
	VOICE OF RUSSIA, Irkutsk
	UNITED ARAB EMIRATES
	UAE RADIO FROM ABU DHABI
	USA
	RFE-RL, Via Holzkirchen, Germany
	RFE-RL, Via Kavála, Greece
	†RFE-RL, Via Lampertheim, Germany
(con'd)	RFE-RL, Via Pals, Spain

Schedule entries (TARGET • NETWORK • POWER):

- ALL INDIA RADIO, Calcutta — Irr • DS • 50 kW
- QATAR BC SERVICE — Irr • Mideast & N Africa • RAMADAN • 250 kW
- QATAR BC SERVICE — **W** • Mideast & N Africa • 250 kW
- QATAR BC SERVICE — **W** • Europe • 250 kW
- KHABAROVSK RADIO — ⊡ • DS • 100 kW
- R TIKHIY OKEAN — ⊡ • E Asia • 100 kW
- VOICE OF RUSSIA, Samara — **W** • Mideast & E Africa • 240 kW
- RADIO THAILAND — **S** • N Europe • 500 kW
- †BBC, Rampisham — **S** • Europe • 500 kW
- †BBC, Rampisham — **W** • Europe • 500 kW
- †BBC, Rampisham — **W** • S Europe • 500 kW
- †BBC, Various Locations — ⊡ • M-F • E Europe • 250/500 kW
- †BBC, Via Thailand — **S** • Mideast & W Asia • 250 kW
- †VOA, Via Biblis — **S** • Europe • 100 kW
- †VOA, Via Biblis — **S** • Europe • 250 kW
- †VOA, Via Briech — **W** • Europe • 250 kW
- R DIF DU BENIN — M-F • FRENCH, ETC • DS • 20/50 kW • ALT. FREQ. TO 4870 kHz
- R DIF DU BENIN — FRENCH, ETC • DS • 20/50 kW • ALT. FREQ. TO 4870 kHz
- R DIF DU BENIN — Sa/Su • FRENCH, ETC • DS • 20/50 kW • ALT. FREQ. TO 4870 kHz
- R DIF DU BENIN — F-Su • FRENCH, ETC • DS • 20/50 kW • ALT. FREQ. TO 4870 kHz
- R DIF DU BENIN — FRENCH, ETC • DS • 25/50 kW • ALT. FREQ. TO 4870 kHz
- RADIO TIRANA — **S** • Europe • 100 kW
- CHINA RADIO INTL — **W** • Europe • 240 kW
- VOICE OF JINLING — E Asia • 50 kW
- R COTE D'IVOIRE — DS-1 • 20 kW
- DEUTSCHE WELLE — **S** • S Africa • 250 kW
- RADIO BUDAPEST, Diósd — **S** • Su • N Europe • 100 kW
- POLISH RADIO WARSAW — ⊡ • Europe • 100 kW
- POLISH RADIO WARSAW — **S** • E Europe • 100 kW
- VOICE OF RUSSIA, Moscow — **W** • Europe • 240 kW
- VOICE OF RUSSIA, Moscow — **W** • Europe & W Africa • 240 kW
- TRANS WORLD RADIO — E Africa • 250 kW
- VOA, Via Colombo — S Asia • 10 kW
- †VOA, Via Philippines — SE Asia • 50 kW
- †VOA, Via Philippines — **W** • SE Asia • 250 kW
- †VOA, Via Philippines — **S** • SE Asia • 250 kW
- RADIO YUGOSLAVIA — ⊡ • W Europe • 250 kW
- UKE SENDEREN — Irr • N Europe • SPECIAL EVENTS • 0.4 kW
- CENTRAL PEOPLE'S BS — DS-1
- RADIO BUDAPEST, Diósd — **S** • Su • W Europe • 100 kW
- RADIO BUDAPEST, Jászberény — **W** • Su • W Europe • 250 kW
- RADIO ROSSII — **S** • N Asia • DS • 240 kW
- VOICE OF RUSSIA, Irkutsk — **W** • E Asia & SE Asia • 1000 kW
- UAE RADIO FROM ABU DHABI — Irr • N Africa • RAMADAN • 500 kW
- UAE RADIO FROM ABU DHABI — **W** • N Africa • 500 kW
- RFE-RL, Via Holzkirchen — **S** • E Europe • 250 kW
- RFE-RL, Via Kavála — **W** • E Europe • 250 kW
- RFE-RL, Via Lampertheim — **W** • E Europe • 100 kW
- RFE-RL, Via Lampertheim — **S** • E Europe • 100 kW
- RFE-RL, Via Lampertheim — E Europe • 100 kW
- RFE-RL, Via Pals — **W** • E Europe • 250 kW

FREQUENCY   COUNTRY, STATION, LOCATION   TARGET • NETWORK • POWER (kW)   World Time

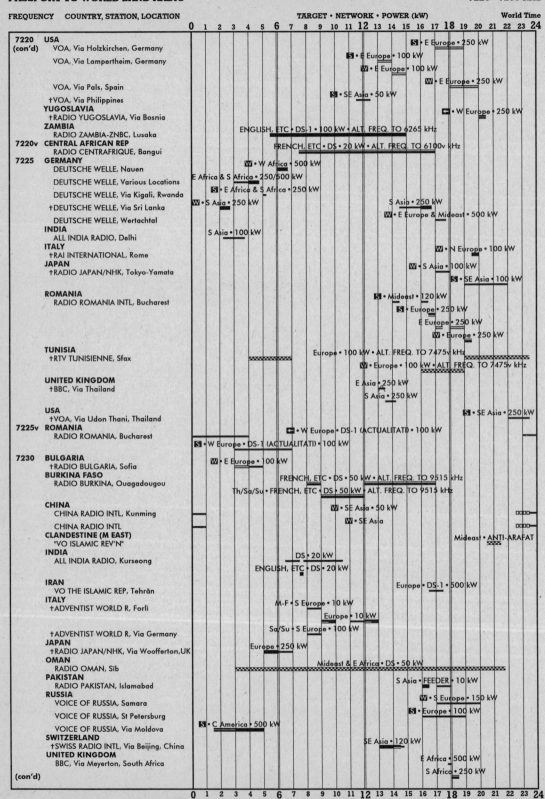

7220	**USA**	
(con'd)	VOA, Via Holzkirchen, Germany	S • E Europe • 250 kW
	VOA, Via Lampertheim, Germany	S • E Europe • 100 kW
		W • E Europe • 100 kW
	VOA, Via Pals, Spain	W • E Europe • 250 kW
	†VOA, Via Philippines	S • SE Asia • 50 kW
	YUGOSLAVIA	
	†RADIO YUGOSLAVIA, Via Bosnia	▭ • W Europe • 250 kW
	ZAMBIA	
	RADIO ZAMBIA-ZNBC, Lusaka	ENGLISH, ETC • DS-1 • 100 kW • ALT. FREQ. TO 6265 kHz
7220v	**CENTRAL AFRICAN REP**	
	RADIO CENTRAFRIQUE, Bangui	FRENCH, ETC • DS • 20 kW • ALT. FREQ. TO 6100v kHz
7225	**GERMANY**	
	DEUTSCHE WELLE, Nauen	W • W Africa • 500 kW
	DEUTSCHE WELLE, Various Locations	E Africa & S Africa • 250/500 kW
	DEUTSCHE WELLE, Via Kigali, Rwanda	S • E Africa & S Africa • 250 kW
	†DEUTSCHE WELLE, Via Sri Lanka	W • S Asia • 250 kW S Asia • 250 kW
	DEUTSCHE WELLE, Wertachtal	W • E Europe & Mideast • 500 kW
	INDIA	
	ALL INDIA RADIO, Delhi	S Asia • 100 kW
	ITALY	
	†RAI INTERNATIONAL, Rome	W • N Europe • 100 kW
	JAPAN	
	†RADIO JAPAN/NHK, Tokyo-Yamata	W • S Asia • 100 kW
		S • SE Asia • 100 kW
	ROMANIA	
	RADIO ROMANIA INTL, Bucharest	S • Mideast • 120 kW
		S • Europe • 250 kW
		E Europe • 250 kW
		W • Europe • 250 kW
	TUNISIA	
	†RTV TUNISIENNE, Sfax	Europe • 100 kW • ALT. FREQ. TO 7475v kHz
		W • Europe • 100 kW • ALT. FREQ. TO 7475v kHz
	UNITED KINGDOM	
	†BBC, Via Thailand	E Asia • 250 kW
		S Asia • 250 kW
	USA	
	†VOA, Via Udon Thani, Thailand	S • SE Asia • 250 kW
7225v	**ROMANIA**	
	RADIO ROMANIA, Bucharest	▭ • W Europe • DS-1 (ACTUALITATI) • 100 kW
		S • W Europe • DS-1 (ACTUALITATI) • 100 kW
7230	**BULGARIA**	
	†RADIO BULGARIA, Sofia	W • E Europe • 100 kW
	BURKINA FASO	
	RADIO BURKINA, Ouagadougou	FRENCH, ETC • DS • 50 kW • ALT. FREQ. TO 9515 kHz
		Th/Sa/Su • FRENCH, ETC • DS • 50 kW • ALT. FREQ. TO 9515 kHz
	CHINA	
	CHINA RADIO INTL, Kunming	W • SE Asia • 50 kW
	CHINA RADIO INTL	W • SE Asia
	CLANDESTINE (M EAST)	
	"VO ISLAMIC REV'N"	Mideast • ANTI-ARAFAT
	INDIA	
	ALL INDIA RADIO, Kurseong	DS • 20 kW
		ENGLISH, ETC • DS • 20 kW
	IRAN	
	VO THE ISLAMIC REP, Tehrān	Europe • DS-1 • 500 kW
	ITALY	
	†ADVENTIST WORLD R, Forlì	M-F • S Europe • 10 kW
		Europe • 10 kW
		Sa/Su • S Europe • 100 kW
	†ADVENTIST WORLD R, Via Germany	
	JAPAN	
	†RADIO JAPAN/NHK, Via Woofferton,UK	Europe • 250 kW
	OMAN	
	RADIO OMAN, Sīb	Mideast & E Africa • DS • 50 kW
	PAKISTAN	
	RADIO PAKISTAN, Islamabad	S Asia • FEEDER • 10 kW
	RUSSIA	
	VOICE OF RUSSIA, Samara	W • S Europe • 150 kW
	VOICE OF RUSSIA, St Petersburg	S • Europe • 100 kW
	VOICE OF RUSSIA, Via Moldova	S • C America • 500 kW
	SWITZERLAND	
	†SWISS RADIO INTL, Via Beijing, China	SE Asia • 120 kW
	UNITED KINGDOM	
	BBC, Via Meyerton, South Africa	E Africa • 500 kW
		S Africa • 250 kW
(con'd)		

ENGLISH ▬   **ARABIC** ⋙   **CHINESE** ⛉   **FRENCH** ▬   **GERMAN** ▬   **RUSSIAN** ═   **SPANISH** ▬   **OTHER** ▬

FREQUENCY	COUNTRY, STATION, LOCATION	TARGET • NETWORK • POWER (kW)	World Time

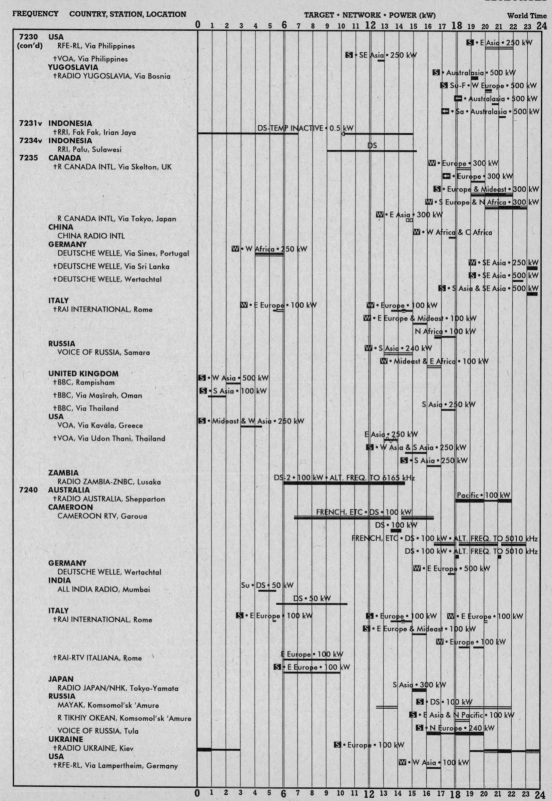

7230 USA
(con'd) RFE-RL, Via Philippines — S • E Asia • 250 kW
  †VOA, Via Philippines — S • SE Asia • 250 kW
YUGOSLAVIA
  †RADIO YUGOSLAVIA, Via Bosnia — S • Australasia • 500 kW
    Su-F • W Europe • 500 kW
    • Australasia • 500 kW
    • Sa • Australasia • 500 kW

7231v INDONESIA
  †RRI, Fak Fak, Irian Jaya — DS-TEMP INACTIVE • 0.5 kW
7234v INDONESIA
  RRI, Palu, Sulawesi — DS
7235 CANADA
  †R CANADA INTL, Via Skelton, UK — W • Europe • 300 kW
    • Europe • 300 kW
    S • Europe & Mideast • 300 kW
    W • S Europe & N Africa • 300 kW
  R CANADA INTL, Via Tokyo, Japan — W • E Asia • 300 kW
CHINA
  CHINA RADIO INTL — W • W Africa & C Africa
GERMANY
  DEUTSCHE WELLE, Via Sines, Portugal — W • W Africa • 250 kW
  †DEUTSCHE WELLE, Via Sri Lanka — W • SE Asia • 250 kW
  †DEUTSCHE WELLE, Wertachtal — S • SE Asia • 500 kW
    S • S Asia & SE Asia • 500 kW
ITALY
  †RAI INTERNATIONAL, Rome — W • E Europe • 100 kW
    W • Europe • 100 kW
    W • E Europe & Mideast • 100 kW
    N Africa • 100 kW
RUSSIA
  VOICE OF RUSSIA, Samara — W • S Asia • 240 kW
    W • Mideast & E Africa • 100 kW
UNITED KINGDOM
  †BBC, Rampisham — S • W Asia • 500 kW
  †BBC, Via Maşirah, Oman — S • S Asia • 100 kW
  †BBC, Via Thailand — S Asia • 250 kW
USA
  VOA, Via Kavála, Greece — S • Mideast & W Asia • 250 kW
  †VOA, Via Udon Thani, Thailand — E Asia • 250 kW
    S • W Asia & S Asia • 250 kW
    S • S Asia • 250 kW
ZAMBIA
  RADIO ZAMBIA-ZNBC, Lusaka — DS-2 • 100 kW • ALT. FREQ. TO 6165 kHz
7240 AUSTRALIA
  †RADIO AUSTRALIA, Shepparton — Pacific • 100 kW
CAMEROON
  CAMEROON RTV, Garoua — FRENCH, ETC • DS • 100 kW
    DS • 100 kW
    FRENCH, ETC • DS • 100 kW • ALT. FREQ. TO 5010 kHz
    DS • 100 kW • ALT. FREQ. TO 5010 kHz
GERMANY
  DEUTSCHE WELLE, Wertachtal — W • E Europe • 500 kW
INDIA
  ALL INDIA RADIO, Mumbai — Su • DS • 50 kW
    DS • 50 kW
ITALY
  †RAI INTERNATIONAL, Rome — S • E Europe • 100 kW
    S • Europe • 100 kW   W • E Europe • 100 kW
    S • E Europe & Mideast • 100 kW
    W • Europe • 100 kW
  †RAI-RTV ITALIANA, Rome — E Europe • 100 kW
    S • E Europe • 100 kW
JAPAN
  RADIO JAPAN/NHK, Tokyo-Yamata — S Asia • 300 kW
RUSSIA
  MAYAK, Komsomol'sk 'Amure — S • DS • 100 kW
  R TIKHIY OKEAN, Komsomol'sk 'Amure — S • E Asia & N Pacific • 100 kW
  VOICE OF RUSSIA, Tula — S • N Europe • 240 kW
UKRAINE
  †RADIO UKRAINE, Kiev — S • Europe • 100 kW
USA
  †RFE-RL, Via Lampertheim, Germany — W • W Asia • 100 kW

World Time scale: 0 1 2 3 4 5 6 7 8 9 10 11 12 13 14 15 16 17 18 19 20 21 22 23 24

FREQUENCY   COUNTRY, STATION, LOCATION   TARGET • NETWORK • POWER (kW)   World Time

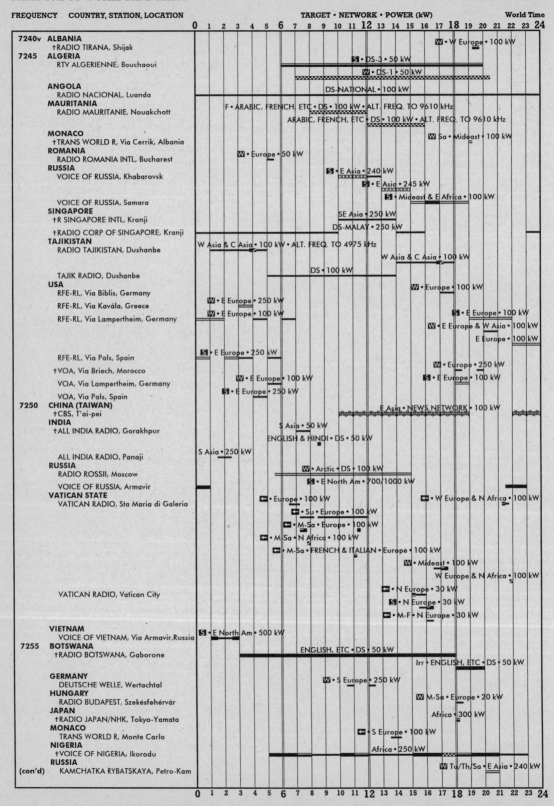

FREQUENCY	COUNTRY, STATION, LOCATION	TARGET • NETWORK • POWER (kW)
7240v	**ALBANIA**	
	†RADIO TIRANA, Shijak	W • W Europe • 100 kW
7245	**ALGERIA**	
	RTV ALGERIENNE, Bouchaoui	S • DS-3 • 50 kW
		W • DS-1 • 50 kW
	ANGOLA	
	RADIO NACIONAL, Luanda	DS-NATIONAL • 100 kW
	MAURITANIA	
	RADIO MAURITANIE, Nouakchott	F • ARABIC, FRENCH, ETC • DS • 100 kW • ALT. FREQ. TO 9610 kHz
		ARABIC, FRENCH, ETC • DS • 100 kW • ALT. FREQ. TO 9610 kHz
	MONACO	
	†TRANS WORLD R, Via Cerrik, Albania	W • Sa • Mideast • 100 kW
	ROMANIA	
	RADIO ROMANIA INTL, Bucharest	W • Europe • 50 kW
	RUSSIA	
	VOICE OF RUSSIA, Khabarovsk	S • E Asia • 240 kW
		S • E Asia • 245 kW
	VOICE OF RUSSIA, Samara	S • Mideast & E Africa • 100 kW
	SINGAPORE	
	†R SINGAPORE INTL, Kranji	SE Asia • 250 kW
	†RADIO CORP OF SINGAPORE, Kranji	DS-MALAY • 250 kW
	TAJIKISTAN	
	RADIO TAJIKISTAN, Dushanbe	W Asia & C Asia • 100 kW • ALT. FREQ. TO 4975 kHz
		W Asia & C Asia • 100 kW
	TAJIK RADIO, Dushanbe	DS • 100 kW
	USA	
	RFE-RL, Via Biblis, Germany	W • Europe • 100 kW
	RFE-RL, Via Kavála, Greece	W • E Europe • 250 kW
	RFE-RL, Via Lampertheim, Germany	W • E Europe • 100 kW
		S • E Europe • 100 kW
		W • E Europe & W Asia • 100 kW
		E Europe • 100 kW
	RFE-RL, Via Pals, Spain	S • E Europe • 250 kW
	†VOA, Via Briech, Morocco	W • Europe • 250 kW
	VOA, Via Lampertheim, Germany	W • E Europe • 100 kW
		S • E Europe • 100 kW
	VOA, Via Pals, Spain	S • E Europe • 250 kW
7250	**CHINA (TAIWAN)**	
	†CBS, T'ai-pei	E Asia • NEWS NETWORK • 100 kW
	INDIA	
	†ALL INDIA RADIO, Gorakhpur	S Asia • 50 kW
		ENGLISH & HINDI • DS • 50 kW
	ALL INDIA RADIO, Panaji	S Asia • 250 kW
	RUSSIA	
	RADIO ROSSII, Moscow	W • Arctic • DS • 100 kW
	VOICE OF RUSSIA, Armavir	S • E North Am • 700/1000 kW
	VATICAN STATE	
	VATICAN RADIO, Sta Maria di Galeria	• Europe • 100 kW
		• W Europe & N Africa • 100 kW
		• Su • Europe • 100 kW
		• M-Sa • Europe • 100 kW
		• M-Sa • N Africa • 100 kW
		• M-Sa • FRENCH & ITALIAN • Europe • 100 kW
		W • Mideast • 100 kW
		W Europe & N Africa • 100 kW
	VATICAN RADIO, Vatican City	• N Europe • 30 kW
		S • N Europe • 30 kW
		• M-F • N Europe • 30 kW
	VIETNAM	
	VOICE OF VIETNAM, Via Armavir, Russia	S • E North Am • 500 kW
7255	**BOTSWANA**	
	†RADIO BOTSWANA, Gaborone	ENGLISH, ETC • DS • 50 kW
		Irr • ENGLISH, ETC • DS • 50 kW
	GERMANY	
	DEUTSCHE WELLE, Wertachtal	W • S Europe • 250 kW
	HUNGARY	
	RADIO BUDAPEST, Szekésfehérvár	W • M-Sa • Europe • 20 kW
	JAPAN	
	†RADIO JAPAN/NHK, Tokyo-Yamata	Africa • 300 kW
	MONACO	
	TRANS WORLD R, Monte Carlo	• S Europe • 100 kW
	NIGERIA	
	†VOICE OF NIGERIA, Ikorodu	Africa • 250 kW
	RUSSIA	
(con'd)	KAMCHATKA RYBATSKAYA, Petro-Kam	W • Tu/Th/Sa • E Asia • 240 kW

FREQUENCY   COUNTRY, STATION, LOCATION   TARGET • NETWORK • POWER (kW)   World Time

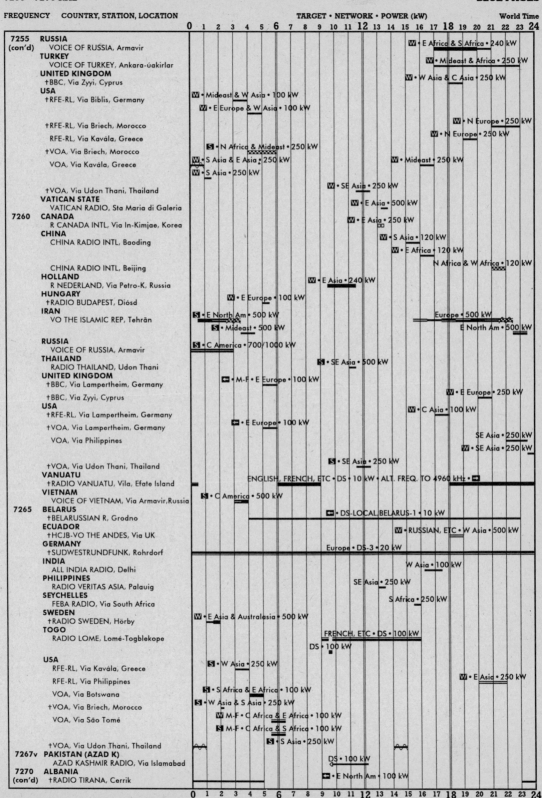

7255 **RUSSIA**
(con'd)   VOICE OF RUSSIA, Armavir   W • E Africa & S Africa • 240 kW
    TURKEY
        VOICE OF TURKEY, Ankara-úakirlar   W • Mideast & Africa • 250 kW
    UNITED KINGDOM
        †BBC, Via Zyyi, Cyprus   W • W Asia & C Asia • 250 kW
    USA
        †RFE-RL, Via Biblis, Germany   W • Mideast & W Asia • 100 kW
                W • E Europe & W Asia • 100 kW

        †RFE-RL, Via Briech, Morocco   W • N Europe • 250 kW
        RFE-RL, Via Kavála, Greece   W • N Europe • 250 kW
        †VOA, Via Briech, Morocco   S • N Africa & Mideast • 250 kW
        VOA, Via Kavála, Greece   W • S Asia & E Asia • 250 kW   W • Mideast • 250 kW
                W • S Asia • 250 kW

        †VOA, Via Udon Thani, Thailand   W • SE Asia • 250 kW
    VATICAN STATE
        VATICAN RADIO, Sta Maria di Galeria   W • E Asia • 500 kW
7260 **CANADA**
        R CANADA INTL, Via In-Kimjae, Korea   W • E Asia • 250 kW
    CHINA
        CHINA RADIO INTL, Baoding   W • S Asia • 120 kW
                W • E Africa • 120 kW

        CHINA RADIO INTL, Beijing   N Africa & W Africa • 120 kW
    HOLLAND
        R NEDERLAND, Via Petro-K, Russia   W • E Asia • 240 kW
    HUNGARY
        †RADIO BUDAPEST, Diósd   W • E Europe • 100 kW
    IRAN
        VO THE ISLAMIC REP, Tehrän   S • E North Am • 500 kW   Europe • 500 kW
                S • Mideast • 500 kW   E North Am • 500 kW

    RUSSIA
        VOICE OF RUSSIA, Armavir   S • C America • 700/1000 kW
    THAILAND
        RADIO THAILAND, Udon Thani   S • SE Asia • 500 kW
    UNITED KINGDOM
        †BBC, Via Lampertheim, Germany   • M-F • E Europe • 100 kW
        †BBC, Via Zyyi, Cyprus   W • E Europe • 250 kW
    USA
        †RFE-RL, Via Lampertheim, Germany   W • C Asia • 100 kW
        †VOA, Via Lampertheim, Germany   • E Europe • 100 kW
        VOA, Via Philippines   SE Asia • 250 kW
                W • SE Asia • 250 kW

        †VOA, Via Udon Thani, Thailand   S • SE Asia • 250 kW
    VANUATU
        †RADIO VANUATU, Vila, Efate Island   ENGLISH, FRENCH, ETC • DS • 10 kW • ALT. FREQ. TO 4960 kHz •
    VIETNAM
        VOICE OF VIETNAM, Via Armavir, Russia   S • C America • 500 kW
7265 **BELARUS**
        †BELARUSSIAN R, Grodno   • DS-LOCAL BELARUS-1 • 10 kW
    ECUADOR
        †HCJB-VO THE ANDES, Via UK   W • RUSSIAN, ETC • W Asia • 500 kW
    GERMANY
        †SUDWESTRUNDFUNK, Rohrdorf   Europe • DS-3 • 20 kW
    INDIA
        ALL INDIA RADIO, Delhi   W Asia • 100 kW
    PHILIPPINES
        RADIO VERITAS ASIA, Palauig   SE Asia • 250 kW
    SEYCHELLES
        FEBA RADIO, Via South Africa   S Africa • 250 kW
    SWEDEN
        †RADIO SWEDEN, Hörby   W • E Asia & Australasia • 500 kW
    TOGO
        RADIO LOME, Lomé-Togblekope   FRENCH, ETC • DS • 100 kW
                DS • 100 kW

    USA
        RFE-RL, Via Kavála, Greece   S • W Asia • 250 kW
        RFE-RL, Via Philippines   W • E Asia • 250 kW
        VOA, Via Botswana   S • S Africa & E Africa • 100 kW
        †VOA, Via Briech, Morocco   S • W Asia & S Asia • 250 kW
        VOA, Via São Tomé   W • M-F • C Africa & E Africa • 100 kW
                S • M-F • C Africa & S Africa • 100 kW

        †VOA, Via Udon Thani, Thailand   S • S Asia • 250 kW
7267v **PAKISTAN (AZAD K)**
        AZAD KASHMIR RADIO, Via Islamabad   DS • 100 kW
7270 **ALBANIA**
(con'd) †RADIO TIRANA, Cerrik   • E North Am • 100 kW

FREQUENCY   COUNTRY, STATION, LOCATION   TARGET • NETWORK • POWER (kW)   World Time

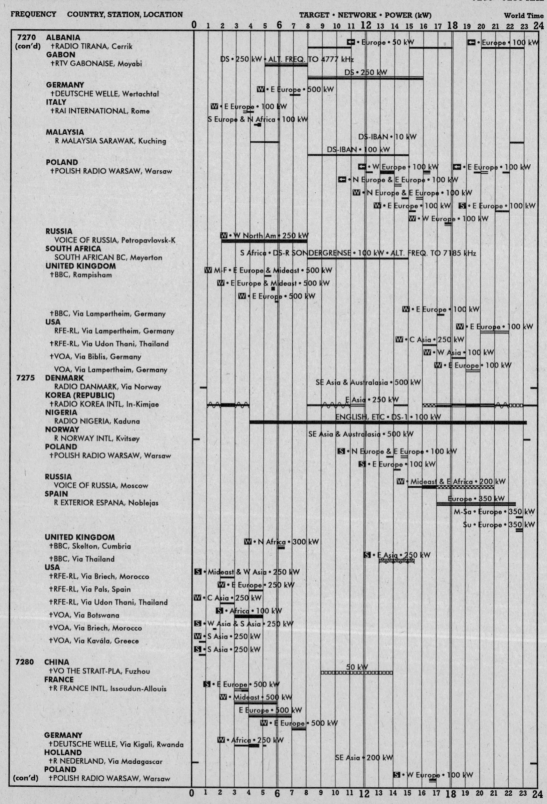

FREQUENCY	COUNTRY, STATION, LOCATION	TARGET • NETWORK • POWER (kW)
7270 (con'd)	ALBANIA †RADIO TIRANA, Cerrik	• Europe • 50 kW / • Europe • 100 kW
	GABON †RTV GABONAISE, Moyabi	DS • 250 kW • ALT. FREQ. TO 4777 kHz / DS • 250 kW
	GERMANY †DEUTSCHE WELLE, Wertachtal	W • E Europe • 500 kW
	ITALY †RAI INTERNATIONAL, Rome	W • E Europe • 100 kW / S Europe & N Africa • 100 kW
	MALAYSIA R MALAYSIA SARAWAK, Kuching	DS-IBAN • 10 kW / DS-IBAN • 100 kW
	POLAND †POLISH RADIO WARSAW, Warsaw	• W Europe • 100 kW / • E Europe • 100 kW / • N Europe & E Europe • 100 kW / W • N Europe & E Europe • 100 kW / W • E Europe • 100 kW / S • E Europe • 100 kW / W • W Europe • 100 kW
	RUSSIA VOICE OF RUSSIA, Petropavlovsk-K	W • W North Am • 250 kW
	SOUTH AFRICA SOUTH AFRICAN BC, Meyerton	S Africa • DS-R SONDERGRENSE • 100 kW • ALT. FREQ. TO 7185 kHz
	UNITED KINGDOM †BBC, Rampisham	W • M-F • E Europe & Mideast • 500 kW / W • E Europe & Mideast • 500 kW / W • E Europe • 500 kW
	†BBC, Via Lampertheim, Germany	W • E Europe • 100 kW
	USA RFE-RL, Via Lampertheim, Germany	W • E Europe • 100 kW
	†RFE-RL, Via Udon Thani, Thailand	W • C Asia • 250 kW
	†VOA, Via Biblis, Germany	W • W Asia • 100 kW
	VOA, Via Lampertheim, Germany	W • E Europe • 100 kW
7275	DENMARK RADIO DANMARK, Via Norway	SE Asia & Australasia • 500 kW
	KOREA (REPUBLIC) †RADIO KOREA INTL, In-Kimjae	E Asia • 250 kW
	NIGERIA RADIO NIGERIA, Kaduna	ENGLISH, ETC • DS-1 • 100 kW
	NORWAY R NORWAY INTL, Kvitsøy	SE Asia & Australasia • 500 kW
	POLAND †POLISH RADIO WARSAW, Warsaw	S • N Europe & E Europe • 100 kW / S • E Europe • 100 kW
	RUSSIA VOICE OF RUSSIA, Moscow	W • Mideast & E Africa • 200 kW
	SPAIN R EXTERIOR ESPANA, Noblejas	Europe • 350 kW / M-Sa • Europe • 350 kW / Su • Europe • 350 kW
	UNITED KINGDOM †BBC, Skelton, Cumbria	W • N Africa • 300 kW
	†BBC, Via Thailand	S • E Asia • 250 kW
	USA †RFE-RL, Via Briech, Morocco	S • Mideast & W Asia • 250 kW
	†RFE-RL, Via Pals, Spain	W • E Europe • 250 kW
	†RFE-RL, Via Udon Thani, Thailand	W • C Asia • 250 kW
	†VOA, Via Botswana	S • Africa • 100 kW
	†VOA, Via Briech, Morocco	S • W Asia & S Asia • 250 kW
	†VOA, Via Kavála, Greece	W • S Asia • 250 kW / S • S Asia • 250 kW
7280	CHINA †VO THE STRAIT-PLA, Fuzhou	50 kW
	FRANCE †R FRANCE INTL, Issoudun-Allouis	S • E Europe • 500 kW / W • Mideast • 500 kW / E Europe • 500 kW / W • E Europe • 500 kW
	GERMANY †DEUTSCHE WELLE, Via Kigali, Rwanda	W • Africa • 250 kW
	HOLLAND †R NEDERLAND, Via Madagascar	SE Asia • 200 kW
	POLAND (con'd) †POLISH RADIO WARSAW, Warsaw	S • W Europe • 100 kW

0 1 2 3 4 5 6 7 8 9 10 11 12 13 14 15 16 17 18 19 20 21 22 23 24

ENGLISH ▬   ARABIC ∾∾∾   CHINESE ▫▫▫   FRENCH ▬▬   GERMAN ▬▬   RUSSIAN ══   SPANISH ▬   OTHER ▬

FREQUENCY   COUNTRY, STATION, LOCATION

TARGET • NETWORK • POWER (kW)

World Time

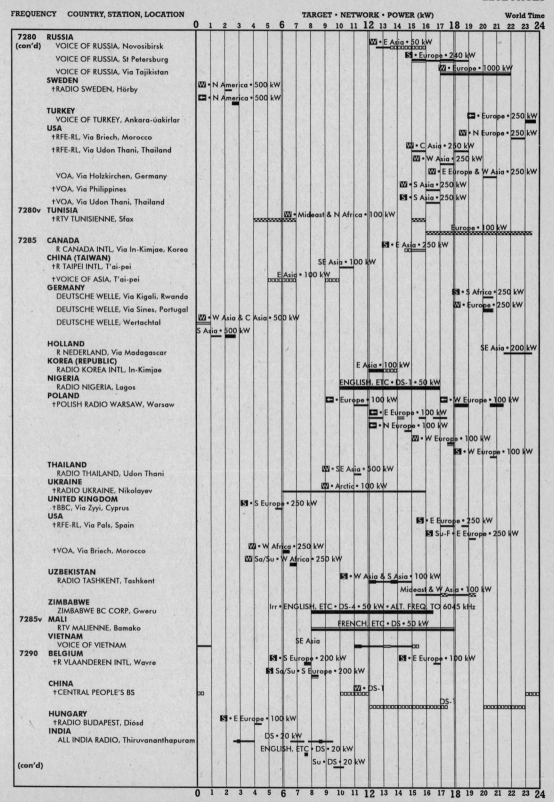

FREQUENCY	COUNTRY, STATION, LOCATION	TARGET • NETWORK • POWER (kW)
7280 (con'd)	**RUSSIA**	
	VOICE OF RUSSIA, Novosibirsk	W • E Asia • 50 kW
	VOICE OF RUSSIA, St Petersburg	S • Europe • 240 kW
	VOICE OF RUSSIA, Via Tajikistan	W • Europe • 1000 kW
	SWEDEN	
	†RADIO SWEDEN, Hörby	W • N America • 500 kW
		• N America • 500 kW
	TURKEY	
	VOICE OF TURKEY, Ankara-úakirlar	• Europe • 250 kW
	USA	
	†RFE-RL, Via Briech, Morocco	W • N Europe • 250 kW
	†RFE-RL, Via Udon Thani, Thailand	W • C Asia • 250 kW
		W • W Asia • 250 kW
	VOA, Via Holzkirchen, Germany	W • E Europe & W Asia • 250 kW
	†VOA, Via Philippines	W • S Asia • 250 kW
	†VOA, Via Udon Thani, Thailand	S • S Asia • 250 kW
7280v	**TUNISIA**	
	†RTV TUNISIENNE, Sfax	W • Mideast & N Africa • 100 kW
		Europe • 100 kW
7285	**CANADA**	
	R CANADA INTL, Via In-Kimjae, Korea	S • E Asia • 250 kW
	CHINA (TAIWAN)	
	†R TAIPEI INTL, T'ai-pei	SE Asia • 100 kW
	†VOICE OF ASIA, T'ai-pei	E Asia • 100 kW
	GERMANY	
	DEUTSCHE WELLE, Via Kigali, Rwanda	S • S Africa • 250 kW
	DEUTSCHE WELLE, Via Sines, Portugal	W • Europe • 250 kW
		W • W Asia & C Asia • 500 kW
	DEUTSCHE WELLE, Wertachtal	S Asia • 500 kW
	HOLLAND	
	R NEDERLAND, Via Madagascar	SE Asia • 200 kW
	KOREA (REPUBLIC)	
	RADIO KOREA INTL, In-Kimjae	E Asia • 100 kW
	NIGERIA	
	RADIO NIGERIA, Lagos	ENGLISH, ETC • DS-1 • 50 kW
	POLAND	
	†POLISH RADIO WARSAW, Warsaw	• Europe • 100 kW • W Europe • 100 kW
		• E Europe • 100 kW
		• N Europe • 100 kW
		W • W Europe • 100 kW
		S • W Europe • 100 kW
	THAILAND	
	RADIO THAILAND, Udon Thani	W • SE Asia • 500 kW
	UKRAINE	
	†RADIO UKRAINE, Nikolayev	W • Arctic • 100 kW
	UNITED KINGDOM	
	†BBC, Via Zyyi, Cyprus	S • S Europe • 250 kW
	USA	
	†RFE-RL, Via Pals, Spain	S • E Europe • 250 kW
		S • Su-F • E Europe • 250 kW
	†VOA, Via Briech, Morocco	W • W Africa • 250 kW
		W • Sa/Su • W Africa • 250 kW
	UZBEKISTAN	
	RADIO TASHKENT, Tashkent	S • W Asia & S Asia • 100 kW
		Mideast & W Asia • 100 kW
	ZIMBABWE	
	ZIMBABWE BC CORP, Gweru	Irr • ENGLISH, ETC • DS-4 • 50 kW • ALT. FREQ. TO 6045 kHz
7285v	**MALI**	
	RTV MALIENNE, Bamako	FRENCH, ETC • DS • 50 kW
	VIETNAM	
	VOICE OF VIETNAM	SE Asia
7290	**BELGIUM**	
	†R VLAANDEREN INTL, Wavre	S • S Europe • 200 kW S • E Europe • 100 kW
		S • Sa/Su • S Europe • 200 kW
	CHINA	
	†CENTRAL PEOPLE'S BS	W • DS-1
		DS-1
	HUNGARY	
	†RADIO BUDAPEST, Diósd	S • E Europe • 100 kW
	INDIA	
	ALL INDIA RADIO, Thiruvananthapuram	DS • 20 kW
		ENGLISH, ETC • DS • 20 kW
		Su • DS • 20 kW
(con'd)		

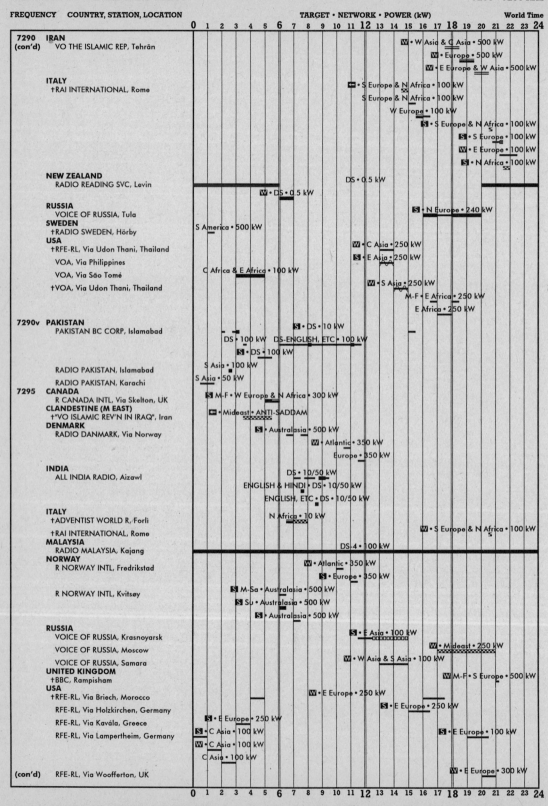

FREQUENCY   COUNTRY, STATION, LOCATION

TARGET • NETWORK • POWER (kW)

World Time

7290
(con'd)   **IRAN**
        VO THE ISLAMIC REP, Tehrān — W · W Asia & C Asia · 500 kW / W · Europe · 500 kW / W · E Europe & W Asia · 500 kW

        ITALY
        †RAI INTERNATIONAL, Rome — S Europe & N Africa · 100 kW / S Europe & N Africa · 100 kW / W Europe · 100 kW / S · S Europe & N Africa · 100 kW / S · S Europe · 100 kW / W · E Europe · 100 kW / S · N Africa · 100 kW

        NEW ZEALAND
        RADIO READING SVC, Levin — DS · 0.5 kW / W · DS · 0.5 kW

        RUSSIA
        VOICE OF RUSSIA, Tula — S · N Europe · 240 kW
        SWEDEN
        †RADIO SWEDEN, Hörby — S America · 500 kW
        USA
        †RFE-RL, Via Udon Thani, Thailand — W · C Asia · 250 kW / S · E Asia · 250 kW

        VOA, Via Philippines

        VOA, Via São Tomé — C Africa & E Africa · 100 kW

        †VOA, Via Udon Thani, Thailand — W · S Asia · 250 kW / M-F · E Africa · 250 kW / E Africa · 250 kW

7290v PAKISTAN
        PAKISTAN BC CORP, Islamabad — S · DS · 10 kW / DS · 100 kW / DS-ENGLISH, ETC · 100 kW / S · DS · 100 kW

        RADIO PAKISTAN, Islamabad — S Asia · 100 kW

        RADIO PAKISTAN, Karachi — S Asia · 50 kW
7295   CANADA
        R CANADA INTL, Via Skelton, UK — S · M-F · W Europe & N Africa · 300 kW
        CLANDESTINE (M EAST)
        †"VO ISLAMIC REV'N IN IRAQ", Iran — Mideast · ANTI-SADDAM
        DENMARK
        RADIO DANMARK, Via Norway — S · Australasia · 500 kW / W · Atlantic · 350 kW / Europe · 350 kW

        INDIA
        ALL INDIA RADIO, Aizawl — DS · 10/50 kW / ENGLISH & HINDI · DS · 10/50 kW / ENGLISH, ETC · DS · 10/50 kW

        ITALY
        †ADVENTIST WORLD R, Forlì — N Africa · 10 kW

        †RAI INTERNATIONAL, Rome — W · S Europe & N Africa · 100 kW
        MALAYSIA
        RADIO MALAYSIA, Kajang — DS-4 · 100 kW
        NORWAY
        R NORWAY INTL, Fredrikstad — W · Atlantic · 350 kW / S · Europe · 350 kW

        R NORWAY INTL, Kvitsøy — S · M-Sa · Australasia · 500 kW / S · Su · Australasia · 500 kW / S · Australasia · 500 kW

        RUSSIA
        VOICE OF RUSSIA, Krasnoyarsk — S · E Asia · 100 kW / W · Mideast · 250 kW
        VOICE OF RUSSIA, Moscow

        VOICE OF RUSSIA, Samara — W · W Asia & S Asia · 100 kW
        UNITED KINGDOM
        †BBC, Rampisham — W · M-F · S Europe · 500 kW
        USA
        †RFE-RL, Via Briech, Morocco — W · E Europe · 250 kW / S · E Europe · 250 kW

        RFE-RL, Via Holzkirchen, Germany

        RFE-RL, Via Kavála, Greece — S · E Europe · 250 kW

        RFE-RL, Via Lampertheim, Germany — S · C Asia · 100 kW / S · E Europe · 100 kW / W · C Asia · 100 kW / C Asia · 100 kW

(con'd)   RFE-RL, Via Woofferton, UK — W · E Europe · 300 kW

FREQUENCY	COUNTRY, STATION, LOCATION	TARGET • NETWORK • POWER (kW)	World Time

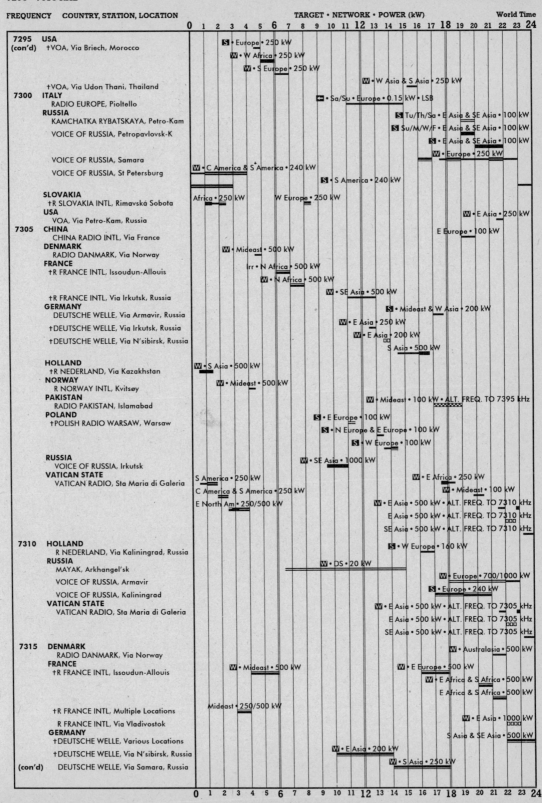

7295 USA
(con'd) †VOA, Via Briech, Morocco
S • Europe • 250 kW
W • W Africa • 250 kW
W • S Europe • 250 kW

†VOA, Via Udon Thani, Thailand
W • W Asia & S Asia • 250 kW

7300 ITALY
RADIO EUROPE, Pioltello
Sa/Su • Europe • 0.15 kW • LSB

RUSSIA
KAMCHATKA RYBATSKAYA, Petro-Kam
S • Tu/Th/Sa • E Asia & SE Asia • 100 kW

VOICE OF RUSSIA, Petropavlovsk-K
S • Su/M/W/F • E Asia & SE Asia • 100 kW
S • E Asia & SE Asia • 100 kW

VOICE OF RUSSIA, Samara
W • Europe • 250 kW

VOICE OF RUSSIA, St Petersburg
W • C America & S America • 240 kW
S • S America • 240 kW

SLOVAKIA
†R SLOVAKIA INTL, Rimavská Sobota
Africa • 250 kW   W Europe • 250 kW

USA
VOA, Via Petro-Kam, Russia
W • E Asia • 250 kW

7305 CHINA
CHINA RADIO INTL, Via France
E Europe • 100 kW

DENMARK
RADIO DANMARK, Via Norway
W • Mideast • 500 kW

FRANCE
†R FRANCE INTL, Issoudun-Allouis
Irr • N Africa • 500 kW
W • N Africa • 500 kW

†R FRANCE INTL, Via Irkutsk, Russia
W • SE Asia • 500 kW

GERMANY
DEUTSCHE WELLE, Via Armavir, Russia
S • Mideast & W Asia • 200 kW

†DEUTSCHE WELLE, Via Irkutsk, Russia
W • E Asia • 250 kW

†DEUTSCHE WELLE, Via N'sibirsk, Russia
W • E Asia • 200 kW
S Asia • 500 kW

HOLLAND
†R NEDERLAND, Via Kazakhstan
W • S Asia • 500 kW

NORWAY
R NORWAY INTL, Kvitsøy
W • Mideast • 500 kW

PAKISTAN
RADIO PAKISTAN, Islamabad
W • Mideast • 100 kW • ALT. FREQ. TO 7395 kHz

POLAND
†POLISH RADIO WARSAW, Warsaw
S • E Europe • 100 kW
S • N Europe & E Europe • 100 kW
S • W Europe • 100 kW

RUSSIA
VOICE OF RUSSIA, Irkutsk
W • SE Asia • 1000 kW

VATICAN STATE
VATICAN RADIO, Sta Maria di Galeria
S America • 250 kW
W • E Africa • 250 kW
C America & S America • 250 kW
W • Mideast • 100 kW
E North Am • 250/500 kW
W • E Asia • 500 kW • ALT. FREQ. TO 7310 kHz
E Asia • 500 kW • ALT. FREQ. TO 7310 kHz
SE Asia • 500 kW • ALT. FREQ. TO 7310 kHz

7310 HOLLAND
R NEDERLAND, Via Kaliningrad, Russia
S • W Europe • 160 kW

RUSSIA
MAYAK, Arkhangel'sk
W • DS • 20 kW

VOICE OF RUSSIA, Armavir
W • Europe • 700/1000 kW

VOICE OF RUSSIA, Kaliningrad
S • Europe • 240 kW

VATICAN STATE
VATICAN RADIO, Sta Maria di Galeria
W • E Asia • 500 kW • ALT. FREQ. TO 7305 kHz
E Asia • 500 kW • ALT. FREQ. TO 7305 kHz
SE Asia • 500 kW • ALT. FREQ. TO 7305 kHz

7315 DENMARK
RADIO DANMARK, Via Norway
W • Australasia • 500 kW

FRANCE
†R FRANCE INTL, Issoudun-Allouis
W • Mideast • 500 kW
W • E Europe • 500 kW
W • E Africa & S Africa • 500 kW
E Africa & S Africa • 500 kW

†R FRANCE INTL, Multiple Locations
Mideast • 250/500 kW

R FRANCE INTL, Via Vladivostok
W • E Asia • 1000 kW

GERMANY
†DEUTSCHE WELLE, Various Locations
S Asia & SE Asia • 500 kW

†DEUTSCHE WELLE, Via N'sibirsk, Russia
W • E Asia • 200 kW

(con'd) DEUTSCHE WELLE, Via Samara, Russia
S • S Asia • 250 kW

FREQUENCY   COUNTRY, STATION, LOCATION

TARGET • NETWORK • POWER (kW)

World Time

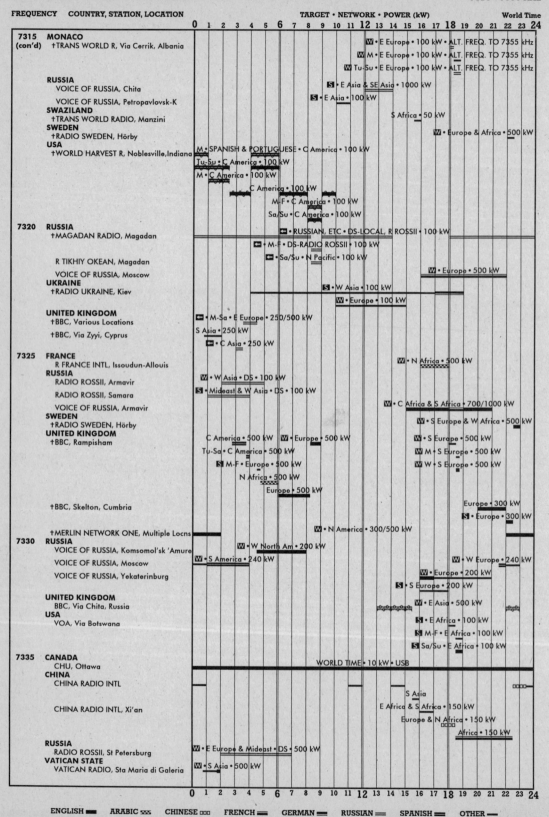

7315	MONACO
(con'd)	†TRANS WORLD R, Via Cerrik, Albania

W • E Europe • 100 kW • ALT. FREQ. TO 7355 kHz
W M • E Europe • 100 kW • ALT. FREQ. TO 7355 kHz
W Tu-Su • E Europe • 100 kW • ALT. FREQ. TO 7355 kHz

RUSSIA
VOICE OF RUSSIA, Chita — S E Asia & SE Asia • 1000 kW
VOICE OF RUSSIA, Petropavlovsk-K — S E Asia • 100 kW
SWAZILAND
†TRANS WORLD RADIO, Manzini — S Africa • 50 kW
SWEDEN
†RADIO SWEDEN, Hörby — W • Europe & Africa • 500 kW
USA
†WORLD HARVEST R, Noblesville,Indiana — M • SPANISH & PORTUGUESE • C America • 100 kW
Tu-Su • C America • 100 kW
M • C America • 100 kW
C America • 100 kW
M–F • C America • 100 kW
Sa/Su • C America • 100 kW

7320	RUSSIA
	†MAGADAN RADIO, Magadan

□ • RUSSIAN, ETC • DS-LOCAL, R ROSSII • 100 kW
□ • M–F • DS-RADIO ROSSII • 100 kW
R TIKHIY OKEAN, Magadan — □ • Sa/Su • N Pacific • 100 kW
VOICE OF RUSSIA, Moscow — W • Europe • 500 kW
UKRAINE
†RADIO UKRAINE, Kiev — S • W Asia • 100 kW
W • Europe • 100 kW

UNITED KINGDOM
†BBC, Various Locations — □ • M-Sa • E Europe • 250/500 kW
†BBC, Via Zyyi, Cyprus — S Asia • 250 kW
□ • C Asia • 250 kW

7325	FRANCE
	R FRANCE INTL, Issoudun-Allouis

W • N Africa • 500 kW
RUSSIA
RADIO ROSSII, Armavir — W • W Asia • DS • 100 kW
RADIO ROSSII, Samara — S • Mideast & W Asia • DS • 100 kW
VOICE OF RUSSIA, Armavir — W • C Africa & S Africa • 700/1000 kW
SWEDEN
†RADIO SWEDEN, Hörby — W • S Europe & W Africa • 500 kW
UNITED KINGDOM
†BBC, Rampisham — C America • 500 kW   W • Europe • 500 kW   W • S Europe • 500 kW
Tu-Sa • C America • 500 kW   W M • S Europe • 500 kW
S M–F • Europe • 500 kW   W W • S Europe • 500 kW
N Africa • 500 kW
Europe • 500 kW

†BBC, Skelton, Cumbria — Europe • 300 kW
S • Europe • 300 kW

†MERLIN NETWORK ONE, Multiple Locns — W • N America • 300/500 kW

7330	RUSSIA
	VOICE OF RUSSIA, Komsomol'sk 'Amure

W • W North Am • 200 kW
VOICE OF RUSSIA, Moscow — W • S America • 240 kW   W • W Europe • 240 kW
VOICE OF RUSSIA, Yekaterinburg — W • Europe • 200 kW
S • S Europe • 200 kW

UNITED KINGDOM
BBC, Via Chita, Russia — W • E Asia • 500 kW
USA
VOA, Via Botswana — S • E Africa • 100 kW
S M–F • E Africa • 100 kW
S Sa/Su • E Africa • 100 kW

7335	CANADA
	CHU, Ottawa

WORLD TIME • 10 kW • USB
CHINA
CHINA RADIO INTL — S Asia
E Africa & S Africa • 150 kW
CHINA RADIO INTL, Xi'an — Europe & N Africa • 150 kW
Africa • 150 kW

RUSSIA
RADIO ROSSII, St Petersburg — W • E Europe & Mideast • DS • 500 kW
VATICAN STATE
VATICAN RADIO, Sta Maria di Galeria — W • S Asia • 500 kW

FREQUENCY   COUNTRY, STATION, LOCATION   TARGET • NETWORK • POWER (kW)   World Time

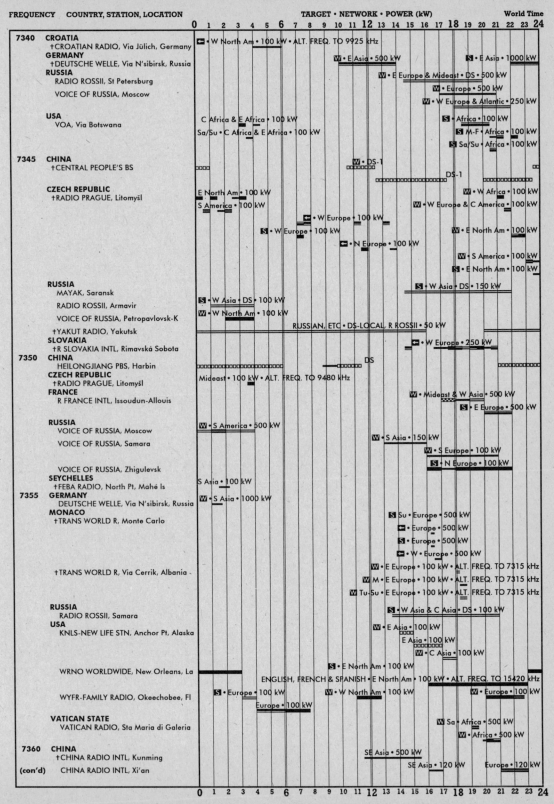

		0 1 2 3 4 5 6 7 8 9 10 11 12 13 14 15 16 17 18 19 20 21 22 23 24

7340   **CROATIA**
           †CROATIAN RADIO, Via Jülich, Germany — W North Am • 100 kW • ALT. FREQ. TO 9925 kHz
           GERMANY
           †DEUTSCHE WELLE, Via N'sibirsk, Russia — W • E Asia • 500 kW   S • E Asia • 1000 kW
           RUSSIA
           RADIO ROSSII, St Petersburg — W • E Europe & Mideast • DS • 500 kW
           VOICE OF RUSSIA, Moscow — W • Europe • 500 kW / W • W Europe & Atlantic • 250 kW

           USA
           VOA, Via Botswana — C Africa & E Africa • 100 kW
                               Sa/Su • C Africa & E Africa • 100 kW
                               S • Africa • 100 kW
                               S M-F • Africa • 100 kW
                               S Sa/Su • Africa • 100 kW

7345   **CHINA**
           †CENTRAL PEOPLE'S BS — W • DS-1 / DS-1

           CZECH REPUBLIC
           †RADIO PRAGUE, Litomyšl — E North Am • 100 kW   W • W Africa • 100 kW
                                     S America • 100 kW   W • W Europe & C America • 100 kW
                                     • W Europe • 100 kW
                                     S • W Europe • 100 kW   W • E North Am • 100 kW
                                     • N Europe • 100 kW
                                     W • S America • 100 kW
                                     S • E North Am • 100 kW

           RUSSIA
           MAYAK, Saransk — S • W Asia • DS • 150 kW
           RADIO ROSSII, Armavir — S • W Asia • DS • 100 kW
           VOICE OF RUSSIA, Petropavlovsk-K — W • W North Am • 100 kW
           †YAKUT RADIO, Yakutsk — RUSSIAN, ETC • DS-LOCAL, R ROSSII • 50 kW
           SLOVAKIA
           †R SLOVAKIA INTL, Rimavská Sobota — • W Europe • 250 kW
7350   **CHINA**
           HEILONGJIANG PBS, Harbin — DS
           CZECH REPUBLIC
           †RADIO PRAGUE, Litomyšl — Mideast • 100 kW • ALT. FREQ. TO 9480 kHz
           FRANCE
           R FRANCE INTL, Issoudun-Allouis — W • Mideast & W Asia • 500 kW
                                              S • E Europe • 500 kW
           RUSSIA
           VOICE OF RUSSIA, Moscow — W • S America • 500 kW
           VOICE OF RUSSIA, Samara — W • S Asia • 150 kW
                                      W • S Europe • 100 kW
           VOICE OF RUSSIA, Zhigulevsk — S • N Europe • 100 kW
           SEYCHELLES
           †FEBA RADIO, North Pt, Mahé Is — S Asia • 100 kW
7355   **GERMANY**
           DEUTSCHE WELLE, Via N'sibirsk, Russia — W • S Asia • 1000 kW
           MONACO
           †TRANS WORLD R, Monte Carlo — S • Su • Europe • 500 kW
                                          • Europe • 500 kW
                                          S • Europe • 500 kW
                                          • W • Europe • 500 kW

           †TRANS WORLD R, Via Cerrik, Albania — W • E Europe • 100 kW • ALT. FREQ. TO 7315 kHz
                                                 W M • E Europe • 100 kW • ALT. FREQ. TO 7315 kHz
                                                 W Tu-Su • E Europe • 100 kW • ALT. FREQ. TO 7315 kHz
           RUSSIA
           RADIO ROSSII, Samara — S • W Asia & C Asia • DS • 100 kW
           USA
           KNLS-NEW LIFE STN, Anchor Pt, Alaska — W • E Asia • 100 kW
                                                   E Asia • 100 kW
                                                   W • C Asia • 100 kW

           WRNO WORLDWIDE, New Orleans, La — S • E North Am • 100 kW
                                             ENGLISH, FRENCH & SPANISH • E North Am • 100 kW • ALT. FREQ. TO 15420 kHz
           WYFR-FAMILY RADIO, Okeechobee, Fl — S • Europe • 100 kW   W • W North Am • 100 kW   W • Europe • 100 kW
                                               Europe • 100 kW

           VATICAN STATE
           VATICAN RADIO, Sta Maria di Galeria — W Sa • Africa • 500 kW
                                                 W • Africa • 500 kW

7360   **CHINA**
           †CHINA RADIO INTL, Kunming — SE Asia • 500 kW
(con'd) CHINA RADIO INTL, Xi'an — SE Asia • 120 kW   Europe • 120 kW

		0 1 2 3 4 5 6 7 8 9 10 11 12 13 14 15 16 17 18 19 20 21 22 23 24

SEASONAL S OR W   1-HR TIMESHIFT MIDYEAR ◩ OR ◪   JAMMING / OR ∧   EARLIEST HEARD ◁   LATEST HEARD ▷   NEW FOR 1999 †

FREQUENCY   COUNTRY, STATION, LOCATION   TARGET • NETWORK • POWER (kW)   World Time

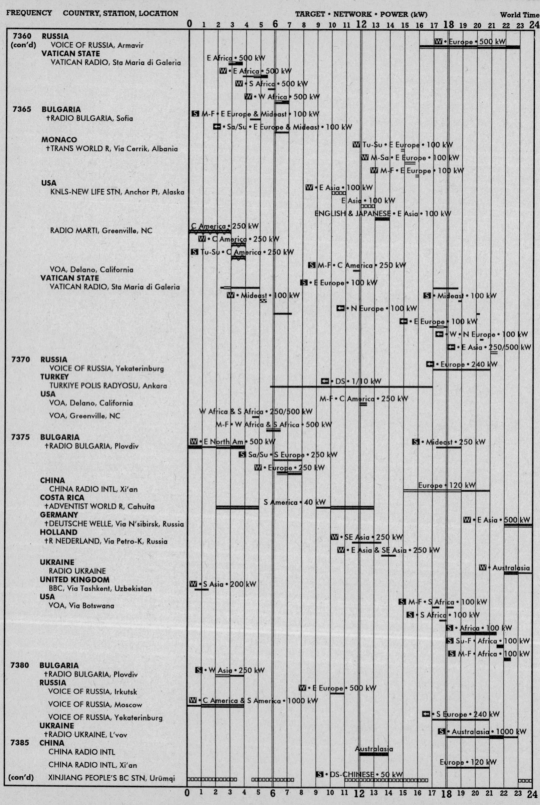

7360	RUSSIA
(con'd)	VOICE OF RUSSIA, Armavir
	VATICAN STATE
	VATICAN RADIO, Sta Maria di Galeria
7365	BULGARIA
	†RADIO BULGARIA, Sofia
	MONACO
	†TRANS WORLD R, Via Cerrik, Albania
	USA
	KNLS-NEW LIFE STN, Anchor Pt, Alaska
	RADIO MARTI, Greenville, NC
	VOA, Delano, California
	VATICAN STATE
	VATICAN RADIO, Sta Maria di Galeria
7370	RUSSIA
	VOICE OF RUSSIA, Yekaterinburg
	TURKEY
	TURKIYE POLIS RADYOSU, Ankara
	USA
	VOA, Delano, California
	VOA, Greenville, NC
7375	BULGARIA
	†RADIO BULGARIA, Plovdiv
	CHINA
	CHINA RADIO INTL, Xi'an
	COSTA RICA
	†ADVENTIST WORLD R, Cahuita
	GERMANY
	†DEUTSCHE WELLE, Via N'sibirsk, Russia
	HOLLAND
	†R NEDERLAND, Via Petro-K, Russia
	UKRAINE
	RADIO UKRAINE
	UNITED KINGDOM
	BBC, Via Tashkent, Uzbekistan
	USA
	VOA, Via Botswana
7380	BULGARIA
	†RADIO BULGARIA, Plovdiv
	RUSSIA
	VOICE OF RUSSIA, Irkutsk
	VOICE OF RUSSIA, Moscow
	VOICE OF RUSSIA, Yekaterinburg
	UKRAINE
	†RADIO UKRAINE, L'vov
7385	CHINA
	CHINA RADIO INTL
	CHINA RADIO INTL, Xi'an
(con'd)	XINJIANG PEOPLE'S BC STN, Urümqi

Chart data (target • network • power):

- VOICE OF RUSSIA, Armavir: W • Europe • 500 kW
- VATICAN RADIO, Sta Maria di Galeria: E Africa • 500 kW
- W • E Africa • 500 kW
- W • S Africa • 500 kW
- W • W Africa • 500 kW
- †RADIO BULGARIA, Sofia: S M-F • E Europe & Mideast • 100 kW
- S Sa/Su • E Europe & Mideast • 100 kW
- †TRANS WORLD R: W Tu-Su • E Europe • 100 kW
- W M-Sa • E Europe • 100 kW
- W M-F • E Europe • 100 kW
- KNLS-NEW LIFE STN: W • E Asia • 100 kW
- E Asia • 100 kW
- ENGLISH & JAPANESE • E Asia • 100 kW
- RADIO MARTI: C America • 250 kW
- W • C America • 250 kW
- S Tu-Su • C America • 250 kW
- VOA, Delano: S M-F • C America • 250 kW
- VATICAN RADIO: S • E Europe • 100 kW
- W • Mideast • 100 kW
- S • Mideast • 100 kW
- S • N Europe • 100 kW
- S • E Europe • 100 kW
- S • W • N Europe • 100 kW
- S • E Asia • 250/500 kW
- VOICE OF RUSSIA, Yekaterinburg: S • Europe • 240 kW
- TURKIYE POLIS RADYOSU: S • DS • 1/10 kW
- VOA, Delano: M-F • C America • 250 kW
- VOA, Greenville: W Africa & S Africa • 250/500 kW
- M-F • W Africa & S Africa • 500 kW
- †RADIO BULGARIA, Plovdiv: W • E North Am • 500 kW
- S • Mideast • 250 kW
- S Sa/Su • S Europe • 250 kW
- W • Europe • 250 kW
- CHINA RADIO INTL, Xi'an: Europe • 120 kW
- †ADVENTIST WORLD R: S America • 40 kW
- †DEUTSCHE WELLE: W • E Asia • 500 kW
- †R NEDERLAND: W • SE Asia • 250 kW
- W • E Asia & SE Asia • 250 kW
- RADIO UKRAINE: W • Australasia
- BBC, Via Tashkent: W • S Asia • 200 kW
- VOA, Via Botswana: S M-F • S Africa • 100 kW
- S • S Africa • 100 kW
- S • Africa • 100 kW
- S Su-F • Africa • 100 kW
- S M-F • Africa • 100 kW
- †RADIO BULGARIA, Plovdiv: S • W Asia • 250 kW
- VOICE OF RUSSIA, Irkutsk: W • E Europe • 500 kW
- VOICE OF RUSSIA, Moscow: W • C America & S America • 1000 kW
- VOICE OF RUSSIA, Yekaterinburg: S • S Europe • 240 kW
- †RADIO UKRAINE, L'vov: S • Australasia • 1000 kW
- CHINA RADIO INTL: Australasia
- CHINA RADIO INTL, Xi'an: Europe • 120 kW
- XINJIANG PEOPLE'S BC STN, Urümqi: S • DS-CHINESE • 50 kW

ENGLISH ▬   ARABIC ░░   CHINESE □□□   FRENCH ▭   GERMAN ▬   RUSSIAN ═   SPANISH ▬   OTHER ▬

FREQUENCY　　COUNTRY, STATION, LOCATION　　　　　　TARGET • NETWORK • POWER (kW)　　　World Time

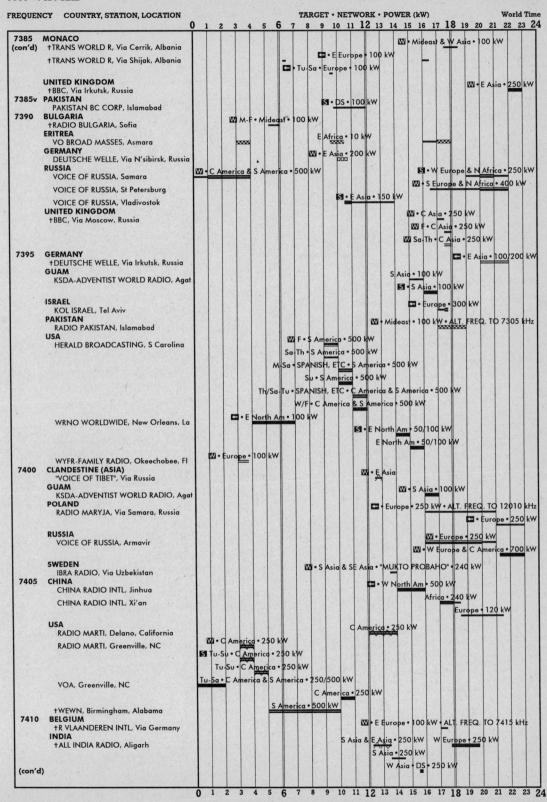

FREQUENCY	COUNTRY, STATION, LOCATION	Target • Network • Power
7385 (con'd)	**MONACO**	
	†TRANS WORLD R, Via Cerrik, Albania	W • Mideast & W Asia • 100 kW
	†TRANS WORLD R, Via Shijak, Albania	• E Europe • 100 kW
		Tu-Sa • Europe • 100 kW
	UNITED KINGDOM	
	†BBC, Via Irkutsk, Russia	W • E Asia • 250 kW
7385v	**PAKISTAN**	
	PAKISTAN BC CORP, Islamabad	S • DS • 100 kW
7390	**BULGARIA**	
	†RADIO BULGARIA, Sofia	W M-F • Mideast • 100 kW
	ERITREA	
	VO BROAD MASSES, Asmara	E Africa • 10 kW
	GERMANY	
	DEUTSCHE WELLE, Via N'sibirsk, Russia	W • E Asia • 200 kW
	RUSSIA	
	VOICE OF RUSSIA, Samara	W • C America & S America • 500 kW
		S • W Europe & N Africa • 250 kW
	VOICE OF RUSSIA, St Petersburg	W • S Europe & N Africa • 400 kW
	VOICE OF RUSSIA, Vladivostok	S • E Asia • 150 kW
	UNITED KINGDOM	
	†BBC, Via Moscow, Russia	W • C Asia • 250 kW
		W F • C Asia • 250 kW
		W Sa-Th • C Asia • 250 kW
7395	**GERMANY**	
	†DEUTSCHE WELLE, Via Irkutsk, Russia	• E Asia • 100/200 kW
	GUAM	
	KSDA-ADVENTIST WORLD RADIO, Agat	S Asia • 100 kW
		S • S Asia • 100 kW
	ISRAEL	
	KOL ISRAEL, Tel Aviv	• Europe • 300 kW
	PAKISTAN	
	RADIO PAKISTAN, Islamabad	W • Mideast • 100 kW • ALT. FREQ. TO 7305 kHz
	USA	
	HERALD BROADCASTING, S Carolina	W F • S America • 500 kW
		Sa-Th • S America • 500 kW
		M-Sa • SPANISH, ETC • S America • 500 kW
		Su • S America • 500 kW
		Th/Sa-Tu • SPANISH, ETC • C America & S America • 500 kW
		W/F • C America & S America • 500 kW
	WRNO WORLDWIDE, New Orleans, La	• E North Am • 100 kW
		S • E North Am • 50/100 kW
		E North Am • 50/100 kW
	WYFR-FAMILY RADIO, Okeechobee, Fl	W • Europe • 100 kW
7400	**CLANDESTINE (ASIA)**	
	"VOICE OF TIBET", Via Russia	W • E Asia
	GUAM	
	KSDA-ADVENTIST WORLD RADIO, Agat	W • S Asia • 100 kW
	POLAND	
	RADIO MARYJA, Via Samara, Russia	• Europe • 250 kW • ALT. FREQ. TO 12010 kHz
		• Europe • 250 kW
	RUSSIA	
	VOICE OF RUSSIA, Armavir	W • Europe • 250 kW
		W • W Europe & C America • 700 kW
	SWEDEN	
	IBRA RADIO, Via Uzbekistan	W • S Asia & SE Asia • "MUKTO PROBAHO" • 240 kW
7405	**CHINA**	
	CHINA RADIO INTL, Jinhua	• W North Am • 500 kW
	CHINA RADIO INTL, Xi'an	Africa • 240 kW
		Europe • 120 kW
	USA	
	RADIO MARTI, Delano, California	C America • 250 kW
	RADIO MARTI, Greenville, NC	W • C America • 250 kW
		S Tu-Su • C America • 250 kW
		Tu-Su • C America • 250 kW
	VOA, Greenville, NC	Tu-Sa • C America & S America • 250/500 kW
		C America • 250 kW
	†WEWN, Birmingham, Alabama	S America • 500 kW
7410	**BELGIUM**	
	†R VLAANDEREN INTL, Via Germany	W • E Europe • 100 kW • ALT. FREQ. TO 7415 kHz
	INDIA	
	†ALL INDIA RADIO, Aligarh	S Asia & E Asia • 250 kW　W Europe • 250 kW
		S Asia • 250 kW
		W Asia • DS • 250 kW
(con'd)		

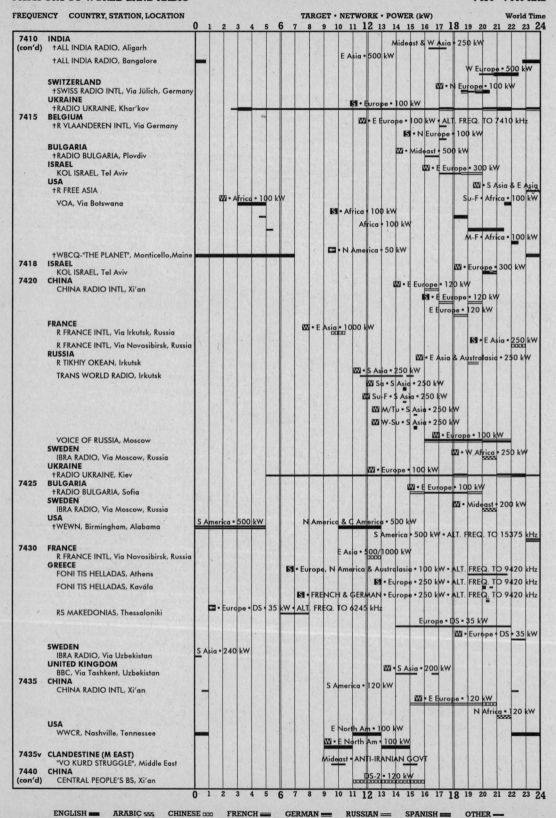

FREQUENCY   COUNTRY, STATION, LOCATION

TARGET • NETWORK • POWER (kW)

World Time

FREQUENCY	COUNTRY, STATION, LOCATION	TARGET • NETWORK • POWER (kW)
7410 (con'd)	**INDIA** †ALL INDIA RADIO, Aligarh	Mideast & W Asia • 250 kW
	†ALL INDIA RADIO, Bangalore	E Asia • 500 kW
	SWITZERLAND †SWISS RADIO INTL, Via Jülich, Germany	W Europe • 500 kW W • N Europe • 100 kW
	UKRAINE †RADIO UKRAINE, Khar'kov	S • Europe • 100 kW
7415	**BELGIUM** †R VLAANDEREN INTL, Via Germany	W • E Europe • 100 kW • ALT. FREQ. TO 7410 kHz S • N Europe • 100 kW
	BULGARIA †RADIO BULGARIA, Plovdiv	W • Mideast • 500 kW
	ISRAEL KOL ISRAEL, Tel Aviv	W • E Europe • 300 kW
	USA †R FREE ASIA	S Asia & E Asia
	VOA, Via Botswana	W • Africa • 100 kW Su-F • Africa • 100 kW
		S • Africa • 100 kW
		Africa • 100 kW
		M-F • Africa • 100 kW
	†WBCQ-"THE PLANET", Monticello, Maine	• N America • 50 kW
7418	**ISRAEL** KOL ISRAEL, Tel Aviv	W • Europe • 300 kW
7420	**CHINA** CHINA RADIO INTL, Xi'an	W • E Europe • 120 kW S • E Europe • 120 kW E Europe • 120 kW
	FRANCE R FRANCE INTL, Via Irkutsk, Russia	W • E Asia • 1000 kW
	R FRANCE INTL, Via Novosibirsk, Russia	S • E Asia • 250 kW
	RUSSIA R TIKHIY OKEAN, Irkutsk	W • E Asia & Australasia • 250 kW
	TRANS WORLD RADIO, Irkutsk	W • S Asia • 250 kW
		W Sa • S Asia • 250 kW
		W Su-F • S Asia • 250 kW
		W M/Tu • S Asia • 250 kW
		W W-Su • S Asia • 250 kW
	VOICE OF RUSSIA, Moscow	W • Europe • 100 kW
	SWEDEN IBRA RADIO, Via Moscow, Russia	W • W Africa • 250 kW
	UKRAINE †RADIO UKRAINE, Kiev	W • Europe • 100 kW
7425	**BULGARIA** †RADIO BULGARIA, Sofia	W • E Europe • 100 kW
	SWEDEN IBRA RADIO, Via Moscow, Russia	W • Mideast • 200 kW
	USA †WEWN, Birmingham, Alabama	S America • 500 kW N America & C America • 500 kW S America • 500 kW • ALT. FREQ. TO 15375 kHz
7430	**FRANCE** R FRANCE INTL, Via Novosibirsk, Russia	E Asia • 500/1000 kW
	GREECE FONI TIS HELLADAS, Athens	S • Europe, N America & Australasia • 100 kW • ALT. FREQ. TO 9420 kHz
	FONI TIS HELLADAS, Kavála	S • Europe • 250 kW • ALT. FREQ. TO 9420 kHz
		S • FRENCH & GERMAN • Europe • 250 kW • ALT. FREQ. TO 9420 kHz
	RS MAKEDONIAS, Thessaloniki	• Europe • DS • 35 kW • ALT. FREQ. TO 6245 kHz
		Europe • DS • 35 kW
		W • Europe • DS • 35 kW
	SWEDEN IBRA RADIO, Via Uzbekistan	S Asia • 240 kW
	UNITED KINGDOM BBC, Via Tashkent, Uzbekistan	W • S Asia • 200 kW
7435	**CHINA** CHINA RADIO INTL, Xi'an	S America • 120 kW W • E Europe • 120 kW N Africa • 120 kW
	USA WWCR, Nashville, Tennessee	E North Am • 100 kW W • E North Am • 100 kW
7435v	**CLANDESTINE (M EAST)** "VO KURD STRUGGLE", Middle East	Mideast • ANTI-IRANIAN GOVT
7440 (con'd)	**CHINA** CENTRAL PEOPLE'S BS, Xi'an	DS-2 • 120 kW

FREQUENCY   COUNTRY, STATION, LOCATION

TARGET • NETWORK • POWER (kW)

World Time

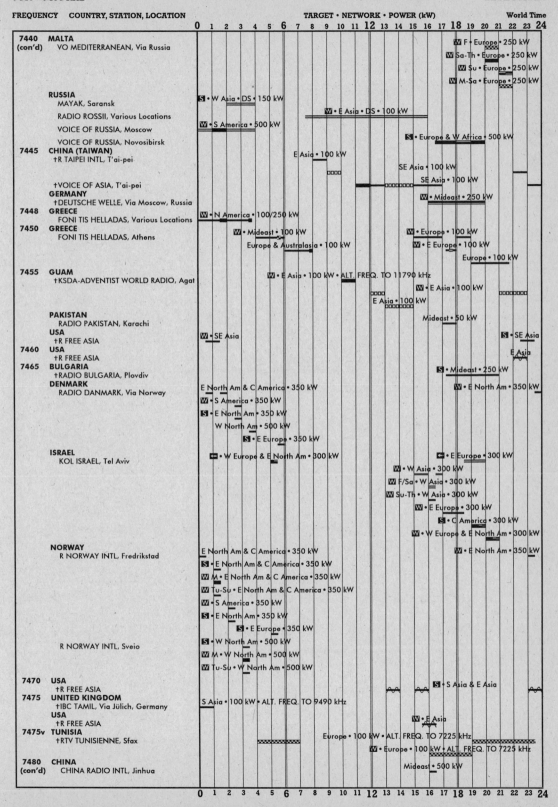

7440 (con'd)	**MALTA** VO MEDITERRANEAN, Via Russia	**W** F • Europe • 250 kW; **W** Sa-Th • Europe • 250 kW; **W** Su • Europe • 250 kW; **W** M-Sa • Europe • 250 kW
	RUSSIA MAYAK, Saransk	**S** • W Asia • DS • 150 kW
	RADIO ROSSII, Various Locations	**W** • E Asia • DS • 100 kW
	VOICE OF RUSSIA, Moscow	**W** • S America • 500 kW
	VOICE OF RUSSIA, Novosibirsk	**S** • Europe & W Africa • 500 kW
7445	**CHINA (TAIWAN)** †R TAIPEI INTL, T'ai-pei	E Asia • 100 kW; SE Asia • 100 kW; SE Asia • 100 kW
	†VOICE OF ASIA, T'ai-pei	
	GERMANY †DEUTSCHE WELLE, Via Moscow, Russia	**W** • Mideast • 250 kW
7448	**GREECE** FONI TIS HELLADAS, Various Locations	**W** • N America • 100/250 kW
7450	**GREECE** FONI TIS HELLADAS, Athens	**W** • Mideast • 100 kW; Europe & Australasia • 100 kW; **W** • Europe • 100 kW; **W** • E Europe • 100 kW; Europe • 100 kW
7455	**GUAM** †KSDA-ADVENTIST WORLD RADIO, Agat	**W** • E Asia • 100 kW • ALT. FREQ. TO 11790 kHz; **W** • E Asia • 100 kW; E Asia • 100 kW
	PAKISTAN RADIO PAKISTAN, Karachi	Mideast • 50 kW
	USA †R FREE ASIA	**W** • SE Asia; **S** • SE Asia
7460	**USA** †R FREE ASIA	E Asia
7465	**BULGARIA** †RADIO BULGARIA, Plovdiv	**S** • Mideast • 250 kW
	DENMARK RADIO DANMARK, Via Norway	E North Am & C America • 350 kW; **W** • E North Am • 350 kW; **W** • S America • 350 kW; **S** • E North Am • 350 kW; W North Am • 500 kW; **S** • E Europe • 350 kW
	ISRAEL KOL ISRAEL, Tel Aviv	⇔ • W Europe & E North Am • 300 kW; ⇔ • E Europe • 300 kW; **W** • W Asia • 300 kW; **W** F/Sa • W Asia • 300 kW; **W** Su-Th • W Asia • 300 kW; **W** • E Europe • 300 kW; **S** • C America • 300 kW; **W** • W Europe & E North Am • 300 kW
	NORWAY R NORWAY INTL, Fredrikstad	E North Am & C America • 350 kW; **S** • E North Am & C America • 350 kW; **W** M • E North Am & C America • 350 kW; **W** Tu-Su • E North Am & C America • 350 kW; **W** • S America • 350 kW; **S** • E North Am • 350 kW; **S** • E Europe • 350 kW; **W** • E North Am • 350 kW
	R NORWAY INTL, Sveio	**S** • W North Am • 500 kW; **W** M • W North Am • 500 kW; **W** Tu-Su • W North Am • 500 kW
7470	**USA** †R FREE ASIA	**S** • S Asia & E Asia
7475	**UNITED KINGDOM** †IBC TAMIL, Via Jülich, Germany	S Asia • 100 kW • ALT. FREQ. TO 9490 kHz
	USA †R FREE ASIA	**W** • E Asia
7475v	**TUNISIA** †RTV TUNISIENNE, Sfax	Europe • 100 kW • ALT. FREQ. TO 7225 kHz; **W** • Europe • 100 kW • ALT. FREQ. TO 7225 kHz
7480 (con'd)	**CHINA** CHINA RADIO INTL, Jinhua	Mideast • 500 kW

FREQUENCY   COUNTRY, STATION, LOCATION   TARGET • NETWORK • POWER (kW)   World Time

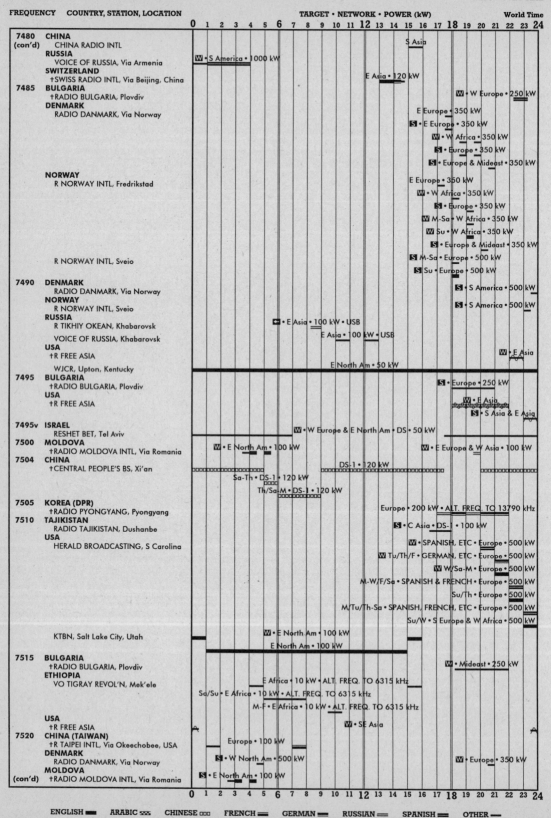

Frequency	Country / Station / Location	Target • Network • Power
7480 (con'd)	**CHINA** CHINA RADIO INTL	S Asia
	RUSSIA VOICE OF RUSSIA, Via Armenia	W • S America • 1000 kW
	SWITZERLAND †SWISS RADIO INTL, Via Beijing, China	E Asia • 120 kW
7485	**BULGARIA** †RADIO BULGARIA, Plovdiv	W • W Europe • 250 kW
	DENMARK RADIO DANMARK, Via Norway	E Europe • 350 kW; S • E Europe • 350 kW; W • W Africa • 350 kW; S • Europe • 350 kW; S • Europe & Mideast • 350 kW
	NORWAY R NORWAY INTL, Fredrikstad	E Europe • 350 kW; W • W Africa • 350 kW; S • Europe • 350 kW; W M-Sa • W Africa • 350 kW; W Su • W Africa • 350 kW; S • Europe & Mideast • 350 kW
	R NORWAY INTL, Sveio	S M-Sa • Europe • 500 kW; S Su • Europe • 500 kW
7490	**DENMARK** RADIO DANMARK, Via Norway	S • S America • 500 kW
	NORWAY R NORWAY INTL, Sveio	S • S America • 500 kW
	RUSSIA R TIKHIY OKEAN, Khabarovsk	• E Asia • 100 kW • USB
	VOICE OF RUSSIA, Khabarovsk	E Asia • 100 kW • USB
	USA †R FREE ASIA	W • E Asia
	WJCR, Upton, Kentucky	E North Am • 50 kW
7495	**BULGARIA** †RADIO BULGARIA, Plovdiv	S • Europe • 250 kW
	USA †R FREE ASIA	W • E Asia; S • S Asia & E Asia
7495v	**ISRAEL** RESHET BET, Tel Aviv	W • W Europe & E North Am • DS • 50 kW
7500	**MOLDOVA** †RADIO MOLDOVA INTL, Via Romania	W • E North Am • 100 kW; W • E Europe & W Asia • 100 kW
7504	**CHINA** †CENTRAL PEOPLE'S BS, Xi'an	DS-1 • 120 kW; Sa-Th • DS-1 • 120 kW; Th/Sa-M • DS-1 • 120 kW
7505	**KOREA (DPR)** †RADIO PYONGYANG, Pyongyang	Europe • 200 kW • ALT. FREQ. TO 13790 kHz
7510	**TAJIKISTAN** RADIO TAJIKISTAN, Dushanbe	S • C Asia • DS-1 • 100 kW
	USA HERALD BROADCASTING, S Carolina	W • SPANISH, ETC • Europe • 500 kW; W Tu/Th/F • GERMAN, ETC • Europe • 500 kW; W W/Sa-M • Europe • 500 kW; M-W/F/Sa • SPANISH & FRENCH • Europe • 500 kW; Su/Th • Europe • 500 kW; M/Tu/Th-Sa • SPANISH, FRENCH, ETC • Europe • 500 kW; Su/W • S Europe & W Africa • 500 kW
	KTBN, Salt Lake City, Utah	W • E North Am • 100 kW; E North Am • 100 kW
7515	**BULGARIA** †RADIO BULGARIA, Plovdiv	W • Mideast • 250 kW
	ETHIOPIA VO TIGRAY REVOL'N, Mek'ele	E Africa • 10 kW • ALT. FREQ. TO 6315 kHz; Sa/Su • E Africa • 10 kW • ALT. FREQ. TO 6315 kHz; M-F • E Africa • 10 kW • ALT. FREQ. TO 6315 kHz
	USA †R FREE ASIA	W • SE Asia
7520	**CHINA (TAIWAN)** †R TAIPEI INTL, Via Okeechobee, USA	Europe • 100 kW
	DENMARK RADIO DANMARK, Via Norway	S • W North Am • 500 kW; W • Europe • 350 kW
(con'd)	**MOLDOVA** †RADIO MOLDOVA INTL, Via Romania	S • E North Am • 100 kW

ENGLISH ▬ ARABIC ⌇⌇⌇ CHINESE □□□ FRENCH ▭▭ GERMAN ▬ RUSSIAN ═══ SPANISH ▬▬ OTHER ▬

FREQUENCY	COUNTRY, STATION, LOCATION	TARGET • NETWORK • POWER (kW)
7520 (con'd)	**MOLDOVA** †RADIO MOLDOVA INTL, Via Romania	S • E Europe & W Asia • 100 kW
		← • Europe • 100 kW
	NORWAY R NORWAY INTL, Fredrikstad	W • Europe • 350 kW
	R NORWAY INTL, Sveio	S M • W North Am • 500 kW
		S Tu-Su • W North Am • 500 kW
	USA †R FREE ASIA	W • SE Asia
		SE Asia
	WYFR-FAMILY RADIO, Okeechobee, Fl	Europe • 100 kW
7525	**DENMARK** RADIO DANMARK, Via Norway	W • W Europe • 500 kW
	NORWAY R NORWAY INTL, Sveio	W • W Europe • 500 kW
7530	**BULGARIA** †RADIO BULGARIA, Plovdiv	W • Europe • 500 kW
		W • W Europe • 500 kW
	USA †R FREE ASIA	S • SE Asia
		W • E Asia
		W • SE Asia
7535	**USA** HERALD BROADCASTING, S Carolina	Th • E North Am • 500 kW
		Tu • E North Am • 500 kW
		W/F-M • E North Am • 500 kW
		N America • 500 kW
		Sa/Su • Europe • 500 kW
		M/Th • W North Am & C America • 500 kW
		Tu/F-Su • W North Am & C America • 500 kW
		M/W • E Africa • 500 kW
		Tu/Th-Su • FRENCH & SPANISH • E Africa • 500 kW
		F • Europe • 500 kW
		Sa-Th • Europe • 500 kW
		Th-M • Europe • 500 kW
		Tu • Europe • 500 kW
		W • Europe • 500 kW
		M/W/Sa • W Europe • 500 kW
		Su/Th • W Europe • 500 kW
		Tu/F • W Europe • 500 kW
		GERMAN, ETC • W Europe • 500 kW
		M-F • RUSSIAN, ETC • Europe • 500 kW
		Tu/Th • Europe • 500 kW
		W/F-M • GERMAN, ETC • Europe • 500 kW
7537v	**SOMALIA** RADIO HARGEISA, Hargeisa	DS • 25 kW • USB
		Irr • DS • 25 kW • USB
7540	**GUAM** KSDA-ADVENTIST WORLD RADIO, Agat	W • Mideast • 100 kW
	USA †R FREE ASIA	W • SE Asia
7550	**KOREA (REPUBLIC)** RADIO KOREA INTL, In-Kimjae	Europe • 250 kW
		S America • 250 kW
	USA †R FREE ASIA	W • SE Asia
		W • S Asia & E Asia
7555v	**USA** KJES, Vado, New Mexico	W North Am • 50 kW
7570	**CLANDESTINE (AFRICA)** †"VO UNITED FREE ETHIOPIA"	Su/W • E Africa • ALT. FREQ. TO 12105 kHz
7580	**KOREA (DPR)** RADIO PYONGYANG, Pyongyang	E Asia • 100 kW
7590	**CHINA** CHINA RADIO INTL, Beijing	S Asia • 120 kW
7620	**CHINA** CENTRAL PEOPLE'S BS, Beijing	W • CHINESE, ETC • TAIWAN SERVICE • 50 kW
		CHINESE, ETC • TAIWAN SERVICE • 50 kW
7660	**CHINA** CHINA RADIO INTL, Xi'an	W • E Europe • 120 kW
		E Europe • 120 kW
7670	**BULGARIA** BULGARIAN RADIO, Stolnik	← • E Europe, Mideast & N Africa • DS-TEMP INACTIVE • 15 kW
7735	**ICELAND** RIKISUTVARPID, Reykjavik	Atlantic & Europe • DS-1 • 10 kW • ALT. FREQ. TO 11402 kHz

World Time 0 1 2 3 4 5 6 7 8 9 10 11 12 13 14 15 16 17 18 19 20 21 22 23 24

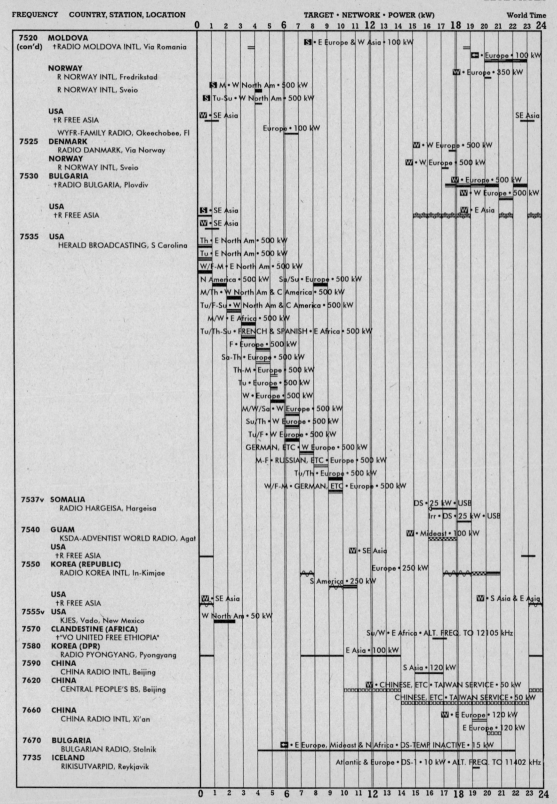

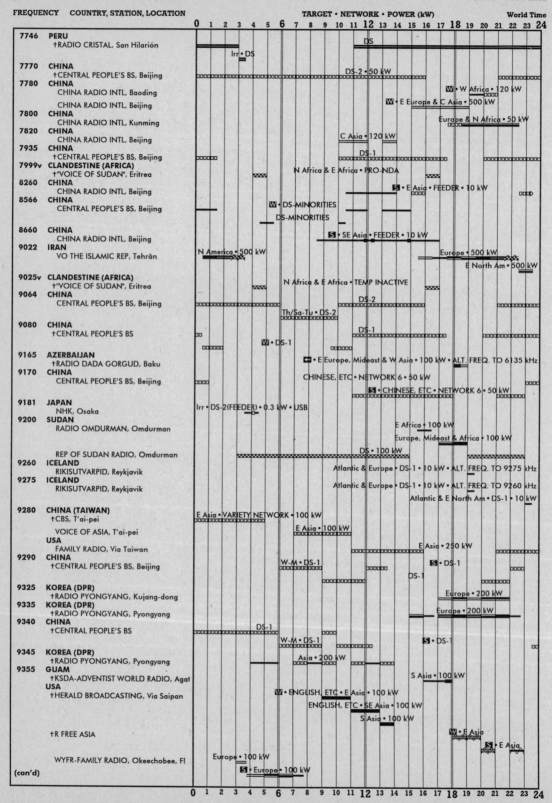

FREQUENCY   COUNTRY, STATION, LOCATION

Frequency	Country, Station, Location
7746	**PERU** — †RADIO CRISTAL, San Hilarión
7770	**CHINA** — †CENTRAL PEOPLE'S BS, Beijing
7780	**CHINA** — CHINA RADIO INTL, Baoding / CHINA RADIO INTL, Beijing
7800	**CHINA** — CHINA RADIO INTL, Kunming
7820	**CHINA** — CHINA RADIO INTL, Beijing
7935	**CHINA** — †CENTRAL PEOPLE'S BS, Beijing
7999v	**CLANDESTINE (AFRICA)** — †"VOICE OF SUDAN", Eritrea
8260	**CHINA** — CHINA RADIO INTL, Beijing
8566	**CHINA** — CENTRAL PEOPLE'S BS, Beijing
8660	**CHINA** — CHINA RADIO INTL, Beijing
9022	**IRAN** — VO THE ISLAMIC REP, Tehrān
9025v	**CLANDESTINE (AFRICA)** — †"VOICE OF SUDAN", Eritrea
9064	**CHINA** — CENTRAL PEOPLE'S BS, Beijing
9080	**CHINA** — †CENTRAL PEOPLE'S BS
9165	**AZERBAIJAN** — †RADIO DADA GORGUD, Baku
9170	**CHINA** — CENTRAL PEOPLE'S BS, Beijing
9181	**JAPAN** — NHK, Osaka
9200	**SUDAN** — RADIO OMDURMAN, Omdurman / REP OF SUDAN RADIO, Omdurman
9260	**ICELAND** — RIKISUTVARPID, Reykjavik
9275	**ICELAND** — RIKISUTVARPID, Reykjavik
9280	**CHINA (TAIWAN)** — †CBS, T'ai-pei / VOICE OF ASIA, T'ai-pei / **USA** FAMILY RADIO, Via Taiwan
9290	**CHINA** — †CENTRAL PEOPLE'S BS, Beijing
9325	**KOREA (DPR)** — †RADIO PYONGYANG, Kujang-dong
9335	**KOREA (DPR)** — †RADIO PYONGYANG, Pyongyang
9340	**CHINA** — †CENTRAL PEOPLE'S BS
9345	**KOREA (DPR)** — †RADIO PYONGYANG, Pyongyang
9355	**GUAM** — †KSDA-ADVENTIST WORLD RADIO, Agat / **USA** †HERALD BROADCASTING, Via Saipan / †R FREE ASIA / WYFR-FAMILY RADIO, Okeechobee, Fl

(con'd)

ENGLISH ▪▪▪   ARABIC ≋≋≋   CHINESE □□□   FRENCH ══   GERMAN ▬▬   RUSSIAN ══   SPANISH ══   OTHER ──

FREQUENCY   COUNTRY, STATION, LOCATION   TARGET • NETWORK • POWER (kW)   World Time

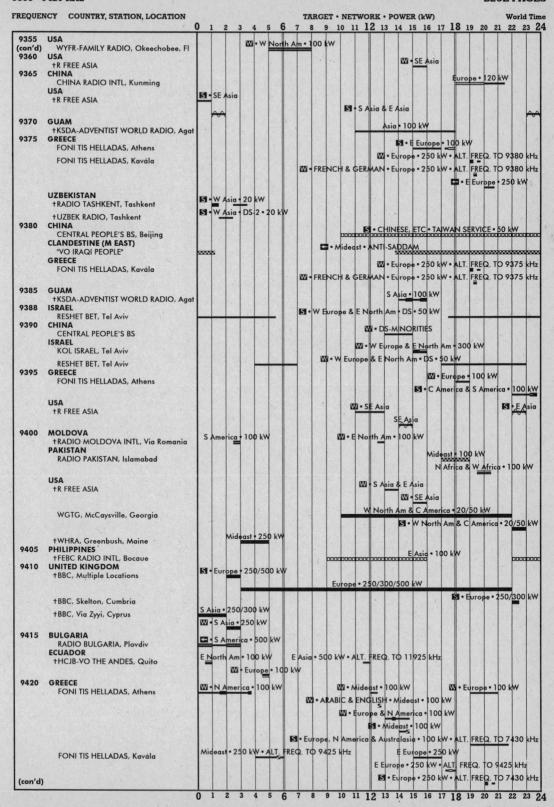

Freq	Country / Station / Location	Target • Network • Power
9355 (con'd)	USA — WYFR-FAMILY RADIO, Okeechobee, Fl	W • W North Am • 100 kW
9360	USA — †R FREE ASIA	W • SE Asia
9365	CHINA — CHINA RADIO INTL, Kunming	Europe • 120 kW
	USA — †R FREE ASIA	S • SE Asia; S • S Asia & E Asia
9370	GUAM — †KSDA-ADVENTIST WORLD RADIO, Agat	Asia • 100 kW
9375	GREECE — FONI TIS HELLADAS, Athens	S • E Europe • 100 kW; W • Europe • 250 kW • ALT. FREQ. TO 9380 kHz
	FONI TIS HELLADAS, Kavála	W • FRENCH & GERMAN • Europe • 250 kW • ALT. FREQ. TO 9380 kHz; ⇦ • E Europe • 250 kW
	UZBEKISTAN — †RADIO TASHKENT, Tashkent	S • W Asia • 20 kW
	†UZBEK RADIO, Tashkent	S • W Asia • DS-2 • 20 kW
9380	CHINA — CENTRAL PEOPLE'S BS, Beijing	S • CHINESE, ETC • TAIWAN SERVICE • 50 kW
	CLANDESTINE (M EAST) — "VO IRAQI PEOPLE"	⇦ • Mideast • ANTI-SADDAM
	GREECE — FONI TIS HELLADAS, Kavála	W • Europe • 250 kW • ALT. FREQ. TO 9375 kHz; W • FRENCH & GERMAN • Europe • 250 kW • ALT. FREQ. TO 9375 kHz
9385	GUAM — †KSDA-ADVENTIST WORLD RADIO, Agat	S Asia • 100 kW
9388	ISRAEL — RESHET BET, Tel Aviv	S • W Europe & E North Am • DS • 50 kW
9390	CHINA — CENTRAL PEOPLE'S BS	W • DS-MINORITIES
	ISRAEL — KOL ISRAEL, Tel Aviv	W • W Europe & E North Am • 300 kW
	RESHET BET, Tel Aviv	W • W Europe & E North Am • DS • 50 kW
9395	GREECE — FONI TIS HELLADAS, Athens	W • Europe • 100 kW; S • C America & S America • 100 kW
	USA — †R FREE ASIA	W • SE Asia; S • E Asia; SE Asia
9400	MOLDOVA — †RADIO MOLDOVA INTL, Via Romania	S America • 100 kW; W • E North Am • 100 kW
	PAKISTAN — RADIO PAKISTAN, Islamabad	Mideast • 100 kW; N Africa & W Africa • 100 kW
	USA — †R FREE ASIA	W • S Asia & E Asia; W • SE Asia
	WGTG, McCaysville, Georgia	W North Am & C America • 20/50 kW; S • W North Am & C America • 20/50 kW
	†WHRA, Greenbush, Maine	Mideast • 250 kW
9405	PHILIPPINES — †FEBC RADIO INTL, Bocaue	E Asia • 100 kW
9410	UNITED KINGDOM — †BBC, Multiple Locations	S • Europe • 250/500 kW; Europe • 250/300/500 kW; S • Europe • 250/300 kW
	†BBC, Skelton, Cumbria	S Asia • 250/300 kW
	†BBC, Via Zyyi, Cyprus	W • S Asia • 250 kW
9415	BULGARIA — RADIO BULGARIA, Plovdiv	⇦ • S America • 500 kW
	ECUADOR — †HCJB-VO THE ANDES, Quito	E North Am • 100 kW; E Asia • 500 kW • ALT. FREQ. TO 11925 kHz; W • Europe • 100 kW
9420	GREECE — FONI TIS HELLADAS, Athens	W • N America • 100 kW; W • Mideast • 100 kW; W • Europe • 100 kW; W • ARABIC & ENGLISH • Mideast • 100 kW; W • Europe & N America • 100 kW; S • Mideast • 100 kW; S • Europe, N America & Australasia • 100 kW • ALT. FREQ. TO 7430 kHz
	FONI TIS HELLADAS, Kavála	Mideast • 250 kW • ALT. FREQ. TO 9425 kHz; E Europe • 250 kW; E Europe • 250 kW • ALT. FREQ. TO 9425 kHz; S • Europe • 250 kW • ALT. FREQ. TO 7430 kHz

(con'd)

FREQUENCY   COUNTRY, STATION, LOCATION

TARGET • NETWORK • POWER (kW)

World Time

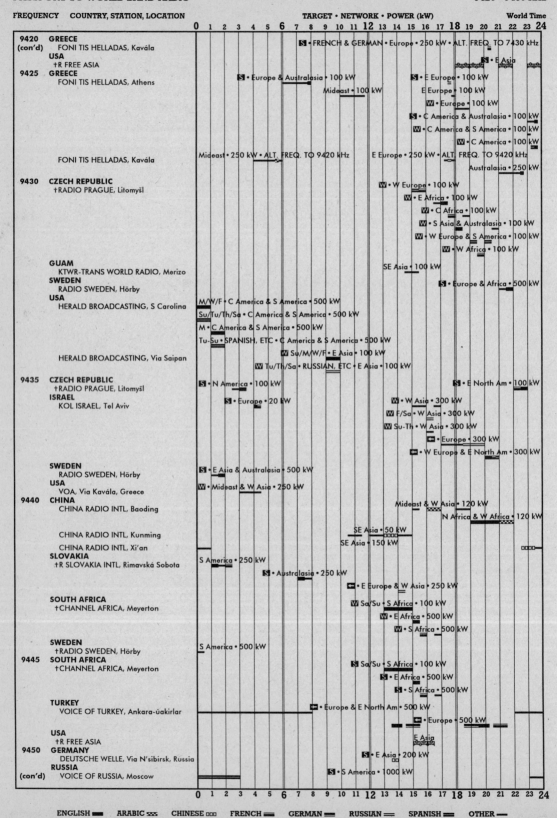

Frequency	Country / Station / Location	Details
9420 (con'd)	**GREECE** FONI TIS HELLADAS, Kavála	🅂 • FRENCH & GERMAN • Europe • 250 kW • ALT. FREQ. TO 7430 kHz
	USA †R FREE ASIA	🅂 • E Asia
9425	**GREECE** FONI TIS HELLADAS, Athens	🅂 • Europe & Australasia • 100 kW / 🅂 • E Europe • 100 kW
		Mideast • 100 kW / E Europe • 100 kW
		🅆 • Europe • 100 kW
		🅂 • C America & Australasia • 100 kW
		🅆 • C America & S America • 100 kW
		🅆 • C America • 100 kW
	FONI TIS HELLADAS, Kavála	Mideast • 250 kW • ALT. FREQ. TO 9420 kHz / E Europe • 250 kW • ALT. FREQ. TO 9420 kHz
		Australasia • 250 kW
9430	**CZECH REPUBLIC** †RADIO PRAGUE, Litomyšl	🅆 • W Europe • 100 kW
		🅆 • E Africa • 100 kW
		🅆 • C Africa • 100 kW
		🅆 • S Asia & Australasia • 100 kW
		🅆 • W Europe & S America • 100 kW
		🅆 • W Africa • 100 kW
	GUAM KTWR-TRANS WORLD RADIO, Merizo	SE Asia • 100 kW
	SWEDEN RADIO SWEDEN, Hörby	🅂 • Europe & Africa • 500 kW
	USA HERALD BROADCASTING, S Carolina	M/W/F • C America & S America • 500 kW
		Su/Tu/Th/Sa • C America & S America • 500 kW
		M • C America & S America • 500 kW
		Tu-Su • SPANISH, ETC • C America & S America • 500 kW
	HERALD BROADCASTING, Via Saipan	🅆 Su/M/W/F • E Asia • 100 kW
		🅆 Tu/Th/Sa • RUSSIAN, ETC • E Asia • 100 kW
9435	**CZECH REPUBLIC** †RADIO PRAGUE, Litomyšl	🅂 • N America • 100 kW / 🅂 • E North Am • 100 kW
	ISRAEL KOL ISRAEL, Tel Aviv	🅂 • Europe • 20 kW
		🅆 • W Asia • 300 kW
		🅆 F/Sa • W Asia • 300 kW
		🅆 Su-Th • W Asia • 300 kW
		• Europe • 300 kW
		• W Europe & E North Am • 300 kW
	SWEDEN RADIO SWEDEN, Hörby	🅂 • E Asia & Australasia • 500 kW
	USA VOA, Via Kavála, Greece	🅆 • Mideast & W Asia • 250 kW
9440	**CHINA** CHINA RADIO INTL, Baoding	Mideast & W Asia • 120 kW
		N Africa & W Africa • 120 kW
	CHINA RADIO INTL, Kunming	SE Asia • 50 kW
	CHINA RADIO INTL, Xi'an	SE Asia • 150 kW
	SLOVAKIA †R SLOVAKIA INTL, Rimavská Sobota	S America • 250 kW
		🅂 • Australasia • 250 kW
		• E Europe & W Asia • 250 kW
	SOUTH AFRICA †CHANNEL AFRICA, Meyerton	🅆 Sa/Su • S Africa • 100 kW
		🅆 • E Africa • 500 kW
		🅆 • S Africa • 500 kW
	SWEDEN †RADIO SWEDEN, Hörby	S America • 500 kW
9445	**SOUTH AFRICA** †CHANNEL AFRICA, Meyerton	🅂 Sa/Su • S Africa • 100 kW
		🅂 • E Africa • 500 kW
		🅂 • S Africa • 500 kW
	TURKEY VOICE OF TURKEY, Ankara-úakirlar	• Europe & E North Am • 500 kW
		• Europe • 500 kW
	USA †R FREE ASIA	E Asia
9450	**GERMANY** DEUTSCHE WELLE, Via N'sibirsk, Russia	🅂 • E Asia • 200 kW
	RUSSIA	🅂 • S America • 1000 kW
(con'd)	VOICE OF RUSSIA, Moscow	

FREQUENCY	COUNTRY, STATION, LOCATION	TARGET • NETWORK • POWER (kW)	World Time

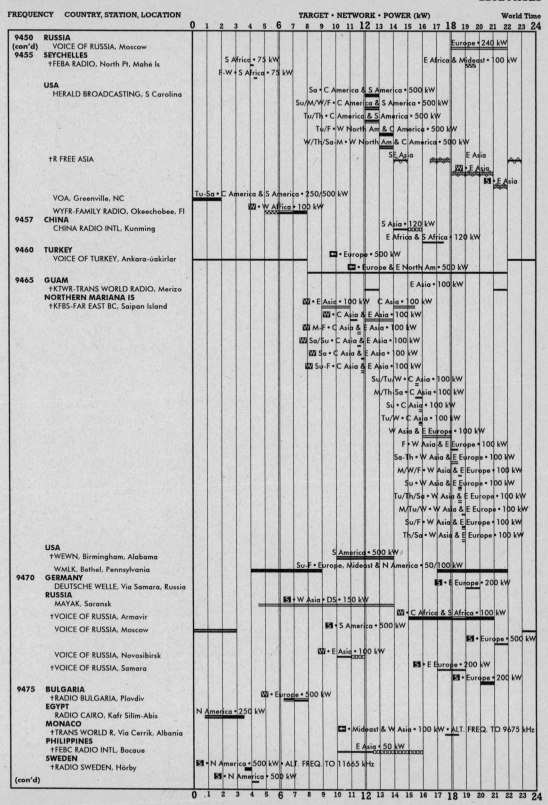

9450 **RUSSIA**
(con'd) VOICE OF RUSSIA, Moscow — Europe • 240 kW

9455 **SEYCHELLES**
†FEBA RADIO, North Pt, Mahé Is — S Africa • 75 kW / F-W • S Africa • 75 kW / E Africa & Mideast • 100 kW

USA
HERALD BROADCASTING, S Carolina
- Sa • C America & S America • 500 kW
- Su/M/W/F • C America & S America • 500 kW
- Tu/Th • C America & S America • 500 kW
- Tu/F • W North Am & C America • 500 kW
- W/Th/Sa-M • W North Am & C America • 500 kW

†R FREE ASIA
- SE Asia
- E Asia
- W • E Asia
- S • E Asia

VOA, Greenville, NC — Tu-Sa • C America & S America • 250/500 kW

WYFR-FAMILY RADIO, Okeechobee, Fl — W • W Africa • 100 kW

9457 **CHINA**
CHINA RADIO INTL, Kunming
- S Asia • 120 kW
- E Africa & S Africa • 120 kW

9460 **TURKEY**
VOICE OF TURKEY, Ankara-úakirlar
- Europe • 500 kW
- Europe & E North Am • 500 kW

9465 **GUAM**
†KTWR-TRANS WORLD RADIO, Merizo — E Asia • 100 kW
NORTHERN MARIANA IS
†KFBS-FAR EAST BC, Saipan Island
- W • E Asia • 100 kW   C Asia • 100 kW
- W • C Asia & E Asia • 100 kW
- W M-F • C Asia & E Asia • 100 kW
- W Sa/Su • C Asia & E Asia • 100 kW
- W Sa • C Asia & E Asia • 100 kW
- W Su-F • C Asia & E Asia • 100 kW
- Su/Tu/W • C Asia • 100 kW
- M/Th-Sa • C Asia • 100 kW
- Su • C Asia • 100 kW
- Tu/W • C Asia • 100 kW
- W Asia & E Europe • 100 kW
- F • W Asia & E Europe • 100 kW
- Sa-Th • W Asia & E Europe • 100 kW
- M/W/F • W Asia & E Europe • 100 kW
- Su • W Asia & E Europe • 100 kW
- Tu/Th/Sa • W Asia & E Europe • 100 kW
- M/Tu/W • W Asia & E Europe • 100 kW
- Su/F • W Asia & E Europe • 100 kW
- Th/Sa • W Asia & E Europe • 100 kW

USA
†WEWN, Birmingham, Alabama — S America • 500 kW

WMLK, Bethel, Pennsylvania — Su-F • Europe, Mideast & N America • 50/100 kW

9470 **GERMANY**
DEUTSCHE WELLE, Via Samara, Russia — S • E Europe • 200 kW
RUSSIA
MAYAK, Saransk — S • W Asia • DS • 150 kW

†VOICE OF RUSSIA, Armavir — W • C Africa & S Africa • 100 kW

VOICE OF RUSSIA, Moscow — S • S America • 500 kW / S • Europe • 500 kW

VOICE OF RUSSIA, Novosibirsk — W • E Asia • 100 kW

†VOICE OF RUSSIA, Samara — S • E Europe • 200 kW / S • Europe • 200 kW

9475 **BULGARIA**
†RADIO BULGARIA, Plovdiv — W • Europe • 500 kW
EGYPT
RADIO CAIRO, Kafr Silim-Abis — N America • 250 kW
MONACO
†TRANS WORLD R, Via Cerrik, Albania — Mideast & W Asia • 100 kW • ALT. FREQ. TO 9675 kHz
PHILIPPINES
†FEBC RADIO INTL, Bocaue — E Asia • 50 kW
SWEDEN
†RADIO SWEDEN, Hörby — S • N America • 500 kW • ALT. FREQ. TO 11665 kHz / S • N America • 500 kW

(con'd)

FREQUENCY   COUNTRY, STATION, LOCATION

TARGET • NETWORK • POWER (kW)   World Time

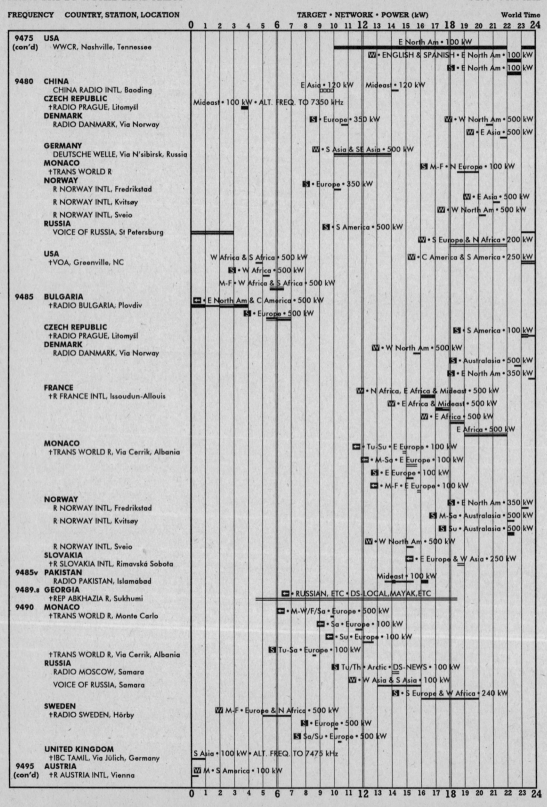

FREQUENCY	COUNTRY, STATION, LOCATION	TARGET • NETWORK • POWER (kW)
9475 (con'd)	**USA** WWCR, Nashville, Tennessee	E North Am • 100 kW W • ENGLISH & SPANISH • E North Am • 100 kW S • E North Am • 100 kW
9480	**CHINA** CHINA RADIO INTL, Baoding	E Asia • 120 kW Mideast • 120 kW
	CZECH REPUBLIC †RADIO PRAGUE, Litomyšl	Mideast • 100 kW • ALT. FREQ. TO 7350 kHz
	DENMARK RADIO DANMARK, Via Norway	S • Europe • 350 kW W • W North Am • 500 kW W • E Asia • 500 kW
	GERMANY DEUTSCHE WELLE, Via N'sibirsk, Russia	W • S Asia & SE Asia • 500 kW
	MONACO †TRANS WORLD R	S • M-F • N Europe • 100 kW
	NORWAY R NORWAY INTL, Fredrikstad	S • Europe • 350 kW
	R NORWAY INTL, Kvitsøy	W • E Asia • 500 kW
	R NORWAY INTL, Sveio	W • W North Am • 500 kW
	RUSSIA VOICE OF RUSSIA, St Petersburg	S • S America • 500 kW W • S Europe & N Africa • 200 kW
	USA †VOA, Greenville, NC	W Africa & S Africa • 500 kW W • C America & S America • 250 kW S • W Africa • 500 kW M-F • W Africa & S Africa • 500 kW
9485	**BULGARIA** †RADIO BULGARIA, Plovdiv	E North Am & C America • 500 kW S • Europe • 500 kW
	CZECH REPUBLIC †RADIO PRAGUE, Litomyšl	S • S America • 100 kW
	DENMARK RADIO DANMARK, Via Norway	W • W North Am • 500 kW S • Australasia • 500 kW S • E North Am • 350 kW
	FRANCE †R FRANCE INTL, Issoudun-Allouis	W • N Africa, E Africa & Mideast • 500 kW W • E Africa & Mideast • 500 kW W • E Africa • 500 kW E Africa • 500 kW
	MONACO †TRANS WORLD R, Via Cerrik, Albania	Tu-Su • E Europe • 100 kW M-Sa • E Europe • 100 kW S • E Europe • 100 kW M-F • E Europe • 100 kW
	NORWAY R NORWAY INTL, Fredrikstad	S • E North Am • 350 kW S M-Sa • Australasia • 500 kW S Su • Australasia • 500 kW
	R NORWAY INTL, Kvitsøy	
	R NORWAY INTL, Sveio	W • W North Am • 500 kW
	SLOVAKIA †R SLOVAKIA INTL, Rimavská Sobota	E Europe & W Asia • 250 kW
9485v	**PAKISTAN** RADIO PAKISTAN, Islamabad	Mideast • 100 kW
9489.8	**GEORGIA** †REP ABKHAZIA R, Sukhumi	RUSSIAN, ETC • DS-LOCAL, MAYAK, ETC
9490	**MONACO** †TRANS WORLD R, Monte Carlo	M-W/F/Sa • Europe • 500 kW Sa • Europe • 100 kW Su • Europe • 100 kW
	†TRANS WORLD R, Via Cerrik, Albania	S Tu-Sa • Europe • 100 kW
	RUSSIA RADIO MOSCOW, Samara	S Tu/Th • Arctic • DS-NEWS • 100 kW
	VOICE OF RUSSIA, Samara	W • W Asia & S Asia • 100 kW S • S Europe & W Africa • 240 kW
	SWEDEN †RADIO SWEDEN, Hörby	W M-F • Europe & N Africa • 500 kW S • Europe • 500 kW S Sa/Su • Europe • 500 kW
	UNITED KINGDOM †IBC TAMIL, Via Jülich, Germany	S Asia • 100 kW • ALT. FREQ. TO 7475 kHz
9495 (con'd)	**AUSTRIA** †R AUSTRIA INTL, Vienna	W M • S America • 100 kW

FREQUENCY	COUNTRY, STATION, LOCATION	TARGET • NETWORK • POWER (kW)	World Time

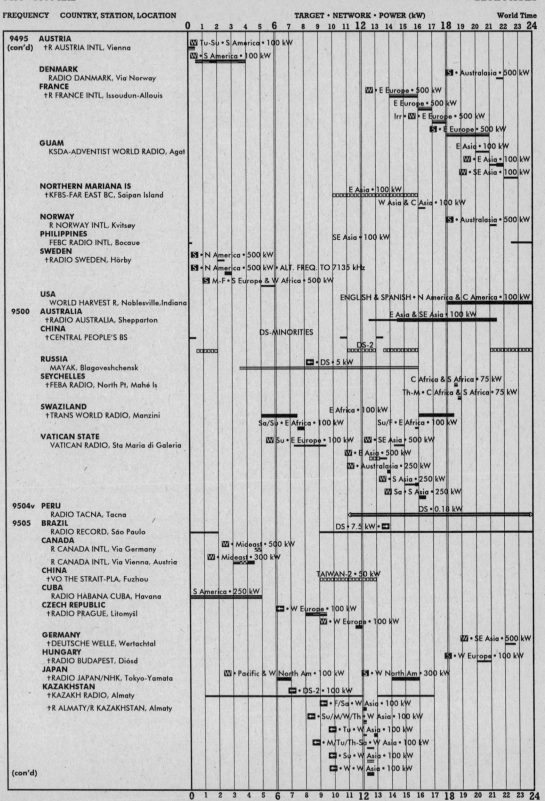

0 1 2 3 4 5 6 7 8 9 10 11 12 13 14 15 16 17 18 19 20 21 22 23 24

9495 **AUSTRIA**
(con'd) †R AUSTRIA INTL, Vienna
- W • Tu-Su • S America • 100 kW
- W • S America • 100 kW

DENMARK
 RADIO DANMARK, Via Norway
- S • Australasia • 500 kW

FRANCE
 †R FRANCE INTL, Issoudun-Allouis
- W • E Europe • 500 kW
- E Europe • 500 kW
- Irr • W • E Europe • 500 kW
- S • E Europe • 500 kW

GUAM
 KSDA-ADVENTIST WORLD RADIO, Agat
- E Asia • 100 kW
- W • E Asia • 100 kW
- W • SE Asia • 100 kW

NORTHERN MARIANA IS
 †KFBS-FAR EAST BC, Saipan Island
- E Asia • 100 kW
- W Asia & C Asia • 100 kW

NORWAY
 R NORWAY INTL, Kvitsøy
- S • Australasia • 500 kW

PHILIPPINES
 FEBC RADIO INTL, Bocaue
- SE Asia • 100 kW

SWEDEN
 †RADIO SWEDEN, Hörby
- S • N America • 500 kW
- S • N America • 500 kW • ALT. FREQ. TO 7135 kHz
- S • M-F • S Europe & W Africa • 500 kW

USA
 WORLD HARVEST R, Noblesville, Indiana
- ENGLISH & SPANISH • N America & C America • 100 kW

9500 **AUSTRALIA**
 †RADIO AUSTRALIA, Shepparton
- E Asia & SE Asia • 100 kW

CHINA
 †CENTRAL PEOPLE'S BS
- DS-MINORITIES
- DS-2
- (DS)

RUSSIA
 MAYAK, Blagoveshchensk
- DS • 5 kW

SEYCHELLES
 †FEBA RADIO, North Pt, Mahé Is
- C Africa & S Africa • 75 kW
- Th-M • C Africa & S Africa • 75 kW

SWAZILAND
 †TRANS WORLD RADIO, Manzini
- E Africa • 100 kW
- Sa/Su • E Africa • 100 kW
- Su/F • E Africa • 100 kW

VATICAN STATE
 VATICAN RADIO, Sta Maria di Galeria
- W • Su • E Europe • 100 kW
- W • SE Asia • 500 kW
- W • E Asia • 500 kW
- W • Australasia • 250 kW
- W • S Asia • 250 kW
- W • Sa • S Asia • 250 kW

9504v **PERU**
 RADIO TACNA, Tacna
- DS • 0.18 kW

9505 **BRAZIL**
 RADIO RECORD, São Paulo
- DS • 7.5 kW •

CANADA
 R CANADA INTL, Via Germany
- W • Mideast • 500 kW
 R CANADA INTL, Via Vienna, Austria
- W • Mideast • 300 kW

CHINA
 †VO THE STRAIT-PLA, Fuzhou
- TAIWAN-2 • 50 kW

CUBA
 RADIO HABANA CUBA, Havana
- S America • 250 kW

CZECH REPUBLIC
 †RADIO PRAGUE, Litomyšl
- W Europe • 100 kW
- W • W Europe • 100 kW

GERMANY
 †DEUTSCHE WELLE, Wertachtal
- W • SE Asia • 500 kW

HUNGARY
 †RADIO BUDAPEST, Diósd
- S • W Europe • 100 kW

JAPAN
 †RADIO JAPAN/NHK, Tokyo-Yamata
- W • Pacific & W North Am • 100 kW
- S • W North Am • 300 kW

KAZAKHSTAN
 †KAZAKH RADIO, Almaty
- DS-2 • 100 kW
 †R ALMATY/R KAZAKHSTAN, Almaty
- F/Sa • W Asia • 100 kW
- Su/M/W/Th • W Asia • 100 kW
- Tu • W Asia • 100 kW
- M/Tu/Th-Sa • W Asia • 100 kW
- Su • W Asia • 100 kW
- W • W Asia • 100 kW

(con'd)

0 1 2 3 4 5 6 7 8 9 10 11 12 13 14 15 16 17 18 19 20 21 22 23 24

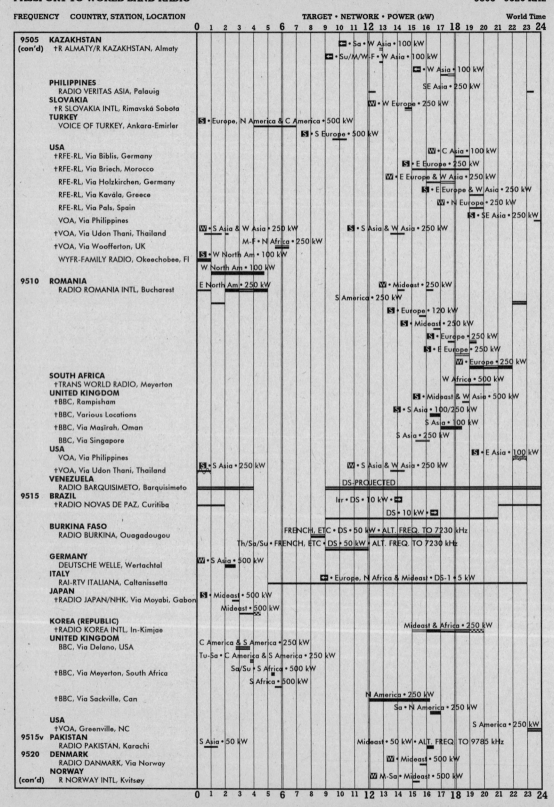

9505 KAZAKHSTAN
(con'd)   †R ALMATY/R KAZAKHSTAN, Almaty

PHILIPPINES
  RADIO VERITAS ASIA, Palauig
SLOVAKIA
  †R SLOVAKIA INTL, Rimavská Sobota
TURKEY
  VOICE OF TURKEY, Ankara-Emirler

USA
  †RFE-RL, Via Biblis, Germany
  †RFE-RL, Via Briech, Morocco
  RFE-RL, Via Holzkirchen, Germany
  RFE-RL, Via Kavála, Greece
  RFE-RL, Via Pals, Spain
  VOA, Via Philippines
  †VOA, Via Udon Thani, Thailand
  †VOA, Via Woofferton, UK
  WYFR-FAMILY RADIO, Okeechobee, Fl

9510 ROMANIA
  RADIO ROMANIA INTL, Bucharest

SOUTH AFRICA
  †TRANS WORLD RADIO, Meyerton
UNITED KINGDOM
  †BBC, Rampisham
  †BBC, Various Locations
  †BBC, Via Maşīrah, Oman
  BBC, Via Singapore
USA
  VOA, Via Philippines
  †VOA, Via Udon Thani, Thailand
VENEZUELA
  RADIO BARQUISIMETO, Barquisimeto
9515 BRAZIL
  †RADIO NOVAS DE PAZ, Curitiba

BURKINA FASO
  RADIO BURKINA, Ouagadougou

GERMANY
  DEUTSCHE WELLE, Wertachtal
ITALY
  RAI-RTV ITALIANA, Caltanissetta
JAPAN
  †RADIO JAPAN/NHK, Via Moyabi, Gabon

KOREA (REPUBLIC)
  †RADIO KOREA INTL, In-Kimjae
UNITED KINGDOM
  BBC, Via Delano, USA
  †BBC, Via Meyerton, South Africa
  †BBC, Via Sackville, Can

USA
  †VOA, Greenville, NC
9515v PAKISTAN
  RADIO PAKISTAN, Karachi
9520 DENMARK
  RADIO DANMARK, Via Norway
NORWAY
(con'd)   R NORWAY INTL, Kvitsøy

FREQUENCY	COUNTRY, STATION, LOCATION	TARGET • NETWORK • POWER (kW)	World Time

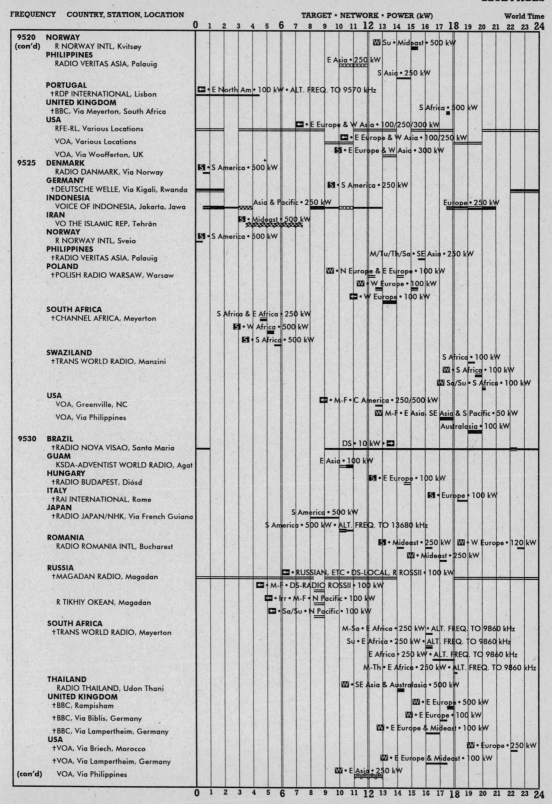

FREQUENCY   COUNTRY, STATION, LOCATION

TARGET • NETWORK • POWER (kW)

World Time

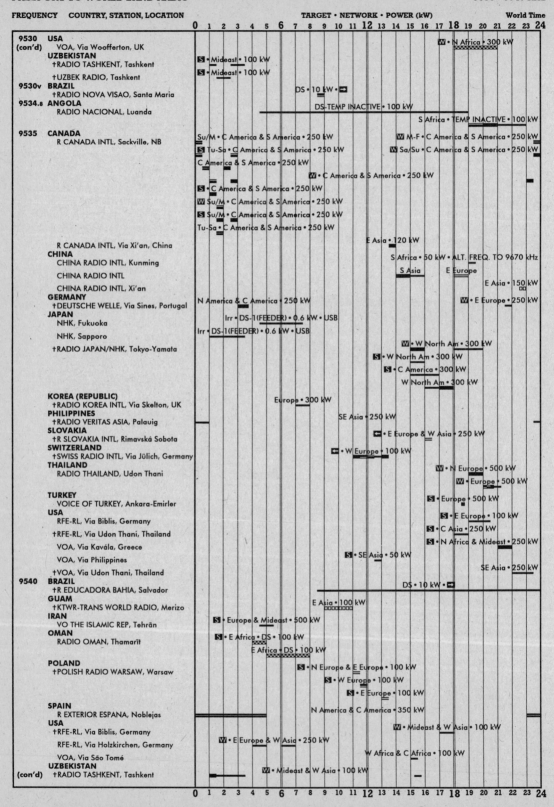

FREQUENCY	COUNTRY, STATION, LOCATION	TARGET • NETWORK • POWER (kW)
9530 (con'd)	**USA**	
	VOA, Via Woofferton, UK	W • N Africa • 300 kW
	UZBEKISTAN	
	†RADIO TASHKENT, Tashkent	S • Mideast • 100 kW
	†UZBEK RADIO, Tashkent	S • Mideast • 100 kW
9530v	**BRAZIL**	
	†RADIO NOVA VISAO, Santa Maria	DS • 10 kW • →
9534.8	**ANGOLA**	
	RADIO NACIONAL, Luanda	DS-TEMP INACTIVE • 100 kW / S Africa • TEMP INACTIVE • 100 kW
9535	**CANADA**	
	R CANADA INTL, Sackville, NB	Su/M • C America & S America • 250 kW / W • M-F • C America & S America • 250 kW
		S • Tu-Sa • C America & S America • 250 kW / W • Sa/Su • C America & S America • 250 kW
		C America & S America • 250 kW
		W • C America & S America • 250 kW
		S • C America & S America • 250 kW
		W • Su/M • C America & S America • 250 kW
		S • Su/M • C America & S America • 250 kW
		Tu-Sa • C America & S America • 250 kW
	R CANADA INTL, Via Xi'an, China	E Asia • 120 kW
	CHINA	
	CHINA RADIO INTL, Kunming	S Africa • 50 kW • ALT. FREQ. TO 9670 kHz
	CHINA RADIO INTL	S Asia E Europe
	CHINA RADIO INTL, Xi'an	E Asia • 150 kW
	GERMANY	
	†DEUTSCHE WELLE, Via Sines, Portugal	N America & C America • 250 kW / W • E Europe • 250 kW
	JAPAN	
	NHK, Fukuoka	Irr • DS-1 (FEEDER) • 0.6 kW • USB
	NHK, Sapporo	Irr • DS-1 (FEEDER) • 0.6 kW • USB
	†RADIO JAPAN/NHK, Tokyo-Yamata	W • W North Am • 300 kW
		S • W North Am • 300 kW
		S • C America • 300 kW
		W North Am • 300 kW
	KOREA (REPUBLIC)	
	†RADIO KOREA INTL, Via Skelton, UK	Europe • 300 kW
	PHILIPPINES	
	†RADIO VERITAS ASIA, Palauig	SE Asia • 250 kW
	SLOVAKIA	
	†R SLOVAKIA INTL, Rimavská Sobota	← • E Europe & W Asia • 250 kW
	SWITZERLAND	
	†SWISS RADIO INTL, Via Jülich, Germany	← • W Europe • 100 kW
	THAILAND	
	RADIO THAILAND, Udon Thani	W • N Europe • 500 kW
		W • Europe • 500 kW
	TURKEY	
	VOICE OF TURKEY, Ankara-Emirler	S • Europe • 500 kW
	USA	
	RFE-RL, Via Biblis, Germany	S • E Europe • 100 kW
	†RFE-RL, Via Udon Thani, Thailand	S • C Asia • 250 kW
	VOA, Via Kavála, Greece	S • N Africa & Mideast • 250 kW
	VOA, Via Philippines	S • SE Asia • 50 kW
	†VOA, Via Udon Thani, Thailand	SE Asia • 250 kW
9540	**BRAZIL**	
	†R EDUCADORA BAHIA, Salvador	DS • 10 kW • →
	GUAM	
	†KTWR-TRANS WORLD RADIO, Merizo	E Asia • 100 kW
	IRAN	
	VO THE ISLAMIC REP, Tehrān	S • Europe & Mideast • 500 kW
	OMAN	
	RADIO OMAN, Thamarīt	S • E Africa • DS • 100 kW / E Africa • DS • 100 kW
	POLAND	
	†POLISH RADIO WARSAW, Warsaw	S • N Europe & E Europe • 100 kW
		S • W Europe • 100 kW
		S • E Europe • 100 kW
	SPAIN	
	R EXTERIOR ESPANA, Noblejas	N America & C America • 350 kW
	USA	
	†RFE-RL, Via Biblis, Germany	W • Mideast & W Asia • 100 kW
	RFE-RL, Via Holzkirchen, Germany	W • E Europe & W Asia • 250 kW
	VOA, Via São Tomé	W Africa & C Africa • 100 kW
	UZBEKISTAN	
(con'd)	†RADIO TASHKENT, Tashkent	W • Mideast & W Asia • 100 kW

ENGLISH ▬   ARABIC ▨   CHINESE ▫▫▫   FRENCH ▬   GERMAN ▬   RUSSIAN ═   SPANISH ▬   OTHER ▬

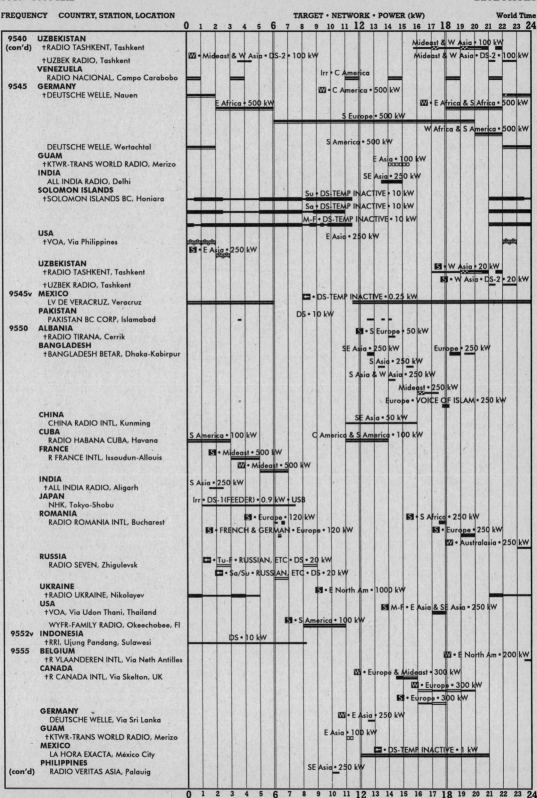

FREQUENCY   COUNTRY, STATION, LOCATION

TARGET • NETWORK • POWER (kW)

World Time

9540	UZBEKISTAN
(con'd)	†RADIO TASHKENT, Tashkent
	†UZBEK RADIO, Tashkent
	VENEZUELA
	RADIO NACIONAL, Campo Carabobo
9545	GERMANY
	†DEUTSCHE WELLE, Nauen

Mideast & W Asia • 100 kW
W • Mideast & W Asia • DS-2 • 100 kW
Mideast & W Asia • DS-2 • 100 kW

Irr • C America
W • C America • 500 kW
E Africa • 500 kW
W • E Africa & S Africa • 500 kW
S Europe • 500 kW
W Africa & S America • 500 kW

DEUTSCHE WELLE, Wertachtal
S America • 500 kW

GUAM
†KTWR-TRANS WORLD RADIO, Merizo
E Asia • 100 kW

INDIA
ALL INDIA RADIO, Delhi
SE Asia • 250 kW

SOLOMON ISLANDS
†SOLOMON ISLANDS BC, Honiara
Su • DS-TEMP INACTIVE • 10 kW
Sa • DS-TEMP INACTIVE • 10 kW
M-F • DS-TEMP INACTIVE • 10 kW

USA
†VOA, Via Philippines
E Asia • 250 kW
S • E Asia • 250 kW

UZBEKISTAN
†RADIO TASHKENT, Tashkent
S • W Asia • 20 kW

†UZBEK RADIO, Tashkent
S • W Asia • DS-2 • 20 kW

9545v	MEXICO
	LV DE VERACRUZ, Veracruz
	PAKISTAN
	PAKISTAN BC CORP, Islamabad
9550	ALBANIA
	†RADIO TIRANA, Cerrik
	BANGLADESH
	†BANGLADESH BETAR, Dhaka-Kabirpur

• DS-TEMP INACTIVE • 0.25 kW
DS • 10 kW
S • S Europe • 50 kW
SE Asia • 250 kW   Europe • 250 kW
S Asia • 250 kW
S Asia & W Asia • 250 kW
Mideast • 250 kW
Europe • VOICE OF ISLAM • 250 kW

CHINA
CHINA RADIO INTL, Kunming
SE Asia • 50 kW

CUBA
RADIO HABANA CUBA, Havana
S America • 100 kW   C America & S America • 100 kW

FRANCE
R FRANCE INTL, Issoudun-Allouis
S • Mideast • 500 kW
W • Mideast • 500 kW

INDIA
†ALL INDIA RADIO, Aligarh
S Asia • 250 kW

JAPAN
NHK, Tokyo-Shobu
Irr • DS-1 (FEEDER) • 0.9 kW • USB

ROMANIA
RADIO ROMANIA INTL, Bucharest
S • Europe • 120 kW   S • S Africa • 250 kW
S • FRENCH & GERMAN • Europe • 120 kW   S • Europe • 250 kW
W • Australasia • 250 kW

RUSSIA
RADIO SEVEN, Zhigulevsk
• Tu-F • RUSSIAN, ETC • DS • 20 kW
• Sa/Su • RUSSIAN, ETC • DS • 20 kW

UKRAINE
†RADIO UKRAINE, Nikolayev
S • E North Am • 1000 kW

USA
†VOA, Via Udon Thani, Thailand
S M-F • E Asia & SE Asia • 250 kW

WYFR-FAMILY RADIO, Okeechobee, Fl
S • S America • 100 kW

9552v	INDONESIA
	†RRI, Ujung Pandang, Sulawesi
9555	BELGIUM
	†R VLAANDEREN INTL, Via Neth Antilles
	CANADA
	†R CANADA INTL, Via Skelton, UK

DS • 10 kW
W • E North Am • 200 kW
W • Europe & Mideast • 300 kW
W • Europe • 300 kW
S • Europe • 300 kW

GERMANY
DEUTSCHE WELLE, Via Sri Lanka
W • E Asia • 250 kW

GUAM
†KTWR-TRANS WORLD RADIO, Merizo
E Asia • 100 kW

MEXICO
LA HORA EXACTA, México City
• DS-TEMP INACTIVE • 1 kW

PHILIPPINES
(con'd)   RADIO VERITAS ASIA, Palauig
SE Asia • 250 kW

FREQUENCY   COUNTRY, STATION, LOCATION

TARGET • NETWORK • POWER (kW)

World Time

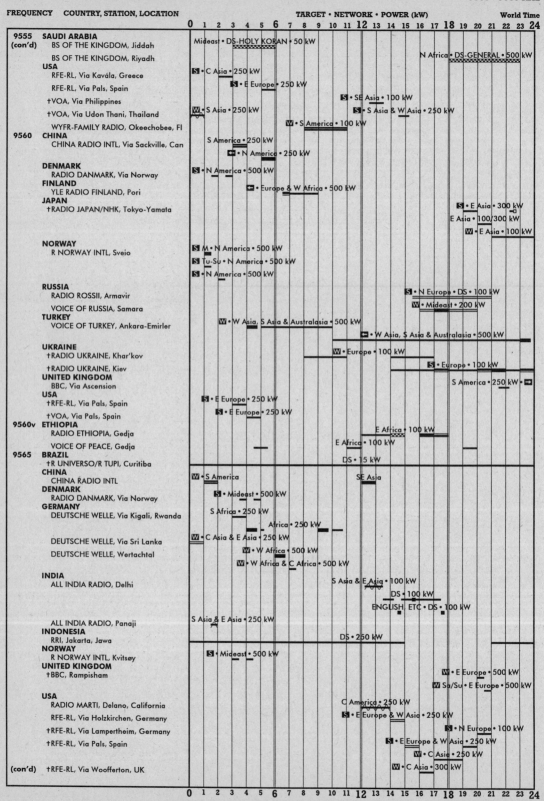

FREQUENCY	COUNTRY, STATION, LOCATION	TARGET • NETWORK • POWER (kW)
9555 (con'd)	**SAUDI ARABIA**	
	BS OF THE KINGDOM, Jiddah	Mideast • DS-HOLY KORAN • 50 kW
	BS OF THE KINGDOM, Riyadh	N Africa • DS-GENERAL • 500 kW
	USA	
	RFE-RL, Via Kavála, Greece	S • C Asia • 250 kW
	RFE-RL, Via Pals, Spain	S • E Europe • 250 kW
	†VOA, Via Philippines	S • SE Asia • 100 kW
	†VOA, Via Udon Thani, Thailand	W • S Asia • 250 kW S • S Asia & W Asia • 250 kW
	WYFR-FAMILY RADIO, Okeechobee, Fl	W • S America • 100 kW
9560	**CHINA**	
	CHINA RADIO INTL, Via Sackville, Can	S America • 250 kW • N America • 250 kW
	DENMARK	
	RADIO DANMARK, Via Norway	S • N America • 500 kW
	FINLAND	
	YLE RADIO FINLAND, Pori	• Europe & W Africa • 500 kW
	JAPAN	
	†RADIO JAPAN/NHK, Tokyo-Yamata	S • E Asia • 300 kW E Asia • 100/300 kW W • E Asia • 100 kW
	NORWAY	
	R NORWAY INTL, Sveio	S • M • N America • 500 kW S • Tu-Su • N America • 500 kW S • N America • 500 kW
	RUSSIA	
	RADIO ROSSII, Armavir	S • N Europe • DS • 100 kW
	VOICE OF RUSSIA, Samara	W • Mideast • 200 kW
	TURKEY	
	VOICE OF TURKEY, Ankara-Emirler	W • W Asia, S Asia & Australasia • 500 kW • W Asia, S Asia & Australasia • 500 kW
	UKRAINE	
	†RADIO UKRAINE, Khar'kov	W • Europe • 100 kW
	†RADIO UKRAINE, Kiev	S • Europe • 100 kW
	UNITED KINGDOM	
	BBC, Via Ascension	S America • 250 kW •
	USA	
	†RFE-RL, Via Pals, Spain	S • E Europe • 250 kW
	†VOA, Via Pals, Spain	S • E Europe • 250 kW
9560v	**ETHIOPIA**	
	RADIO ETHIOPIA, Gedja	E Africa • 100 kW
	VOICE OF PEACE, Gedja	E Africa • 100 kW
9565	**BRAZIL**	
	†R UNIVERSO/R TUPI, Curitiba	DS • 15 kW
	CHINA	
	CHINA RADIO INTL	W • S America SE Asia
	DENMARK	
	RADIO DANMARK, Via Norway	S • Mideast • 500 kW
	GERMANY	
	DEUTSCHE WELLE, Via Kigali, Rwanda	S Africa • 250 kW Africa • 250 kW
	DEUTSCHE WELLE, Via Sri Lanka	W • C Asia & E Asia • 250 kW
	DEUTSCHE WELLE, Wertachtal	W • W Africa • 500 kW W • W Africa & C Africa • 500 kW
	INDIA	
	ALL INDIA RADIO, Delhi	S Asia & E Asia • 100 kW DS • 100 kW ENGLISH ETC • DS • 100 kW
	ALL INDIA RADIO, Panaji	S Asia & E Asia • 250 kW
	INDONESIA	
	RRI, Jakarta, Jawa	DS • 250 kW
	NORWAY	
	R NORWAY INTL, Kvitsøy	S • Mideast • 500 kW
	UNITED KINGDOM	
	†BBC, Rampisham	W • E Europe • 500 kW W • Sa/Su • E Europe • 500 kW
	USA	
	RADIO MARTI, Delano, California	C America • 250 kW
	RFE-RL, Via Holzkirchen, Germany	S • E Europe & W Asia • 250 kW
	†RFE-RL, Via Lampertheim, Germany	S • N Europe • 100 kW
	†RFE-RL, Via Pals, Spain	S • E Europe & W Asia • 250 kW
		W • C Asia • 250 kW
(con'd)	†RFE-RL, Via Woofferton, UK	W • C Asia • 300 kW

FREQUENCY	COUNTRY, STATION, LOCATION	TARGET • NETWORK • POWER (kW)	World Time

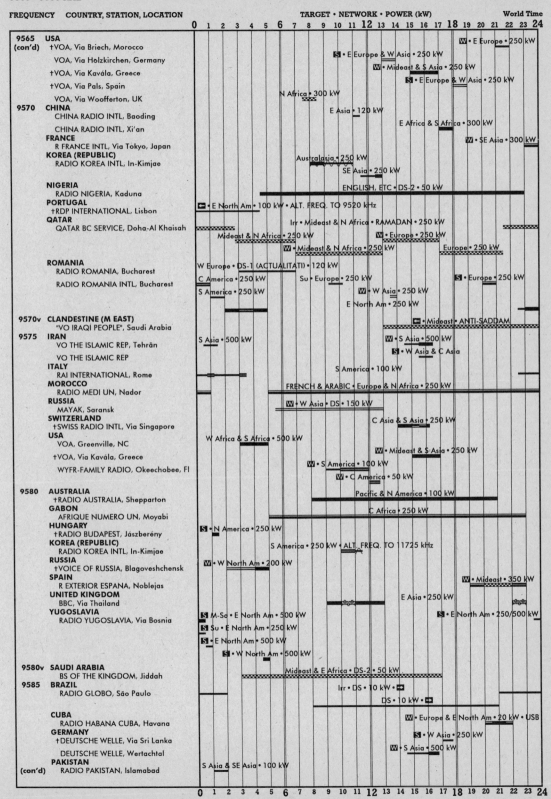

9565 USA
(con'd) †VOA, Via Briech, Morocco
         VOA, Via Holzkirchen, Germany
         †VOA, Via Kavála, Greece
         †VOA, Via Pals, Spain
         VOA, Via Woofferton, UK
9570 CHINA
         CHINA RADIO INTL, Baoding
         CHINA RADIO INTL, Xi'an
         FRANCE
         R FRANCE INTL, Via Tokyo, Japan
         KOREA (REPUBLIC)
         RADIO KOREA INTL, In-Kimjae

         NIGERIA
         RADIO NIGERIA, Kaduna
         PORTUGAL
         †RDP INTERNATIONAL, Lisbon
         QATAR
         QATAR BC SERVICE, Doha-Al Khaisah

         ROMANIA
         RADIO ROMANIA, Bucharest
         RADIO ROMANIA INTL, Bucharest

9570v CLANDESTINE (M EAST)
         "VO IRAQI PEOPLE", Saudi Arabia
9575 IRAN
         VO THE ISLAMIC REP, Tehrān
         VO THE ISLAMIC REP
         ITALY
         RAI INTERNATIONAL, Rome
         MOROCCO
         RADIO MEDI UN, Nador
         RUSSIA
         MAYAK, Saransk
         SWITZERLAND
         †SWISS RADIO INTL, Via Singapore
         USA
         VOA, Greenville, NC
         †VOA, Via Kavála, Greece
         WYFR-FAMILY RADIO, Okeechobee, Fl

9580 AUSTRALIA
         †RADIO AUSTRALIA, Shepparton
         GABON
         AFRIQUE NUMERO UN, Moyabi
         HUNGARY
         †RADIO BUDAPEST, Jászberény
         KOREA (REPUBLIC)
         RADIO KOREA INTL, In-Kimjae
         RUSSIA
         †VOICE OF RUSSIA, Blagoveshchensk
         SPAIN
         R EXTERIOR ESPANA, Noblejas
         UNITED KINGDOM
         BBC, Via Thailand
         YUGOSLAVIA
         RADIO YUGOSLAVIA, Via Bosnia

9580v SAUDI ARABIA
         BS OF THE KINGDOM, Jiddah
9585 BRAZIL
         RADIO GLOBO, São Paulo

         CUBA
         RADIO HABANA CUBA, Havana
         GERMANY
         †DEUTSCHE WELLE, Via Sri Lanka
         DEUTSCHE WELLE, Wertachtal
         PAKISTAN
(con'd) RADIO PAKISTAN, Islamabad

FREQUENCY   COUNTRY, STATION, LOCATION   TARGET • NETWORK • POWER (kW)   World Time

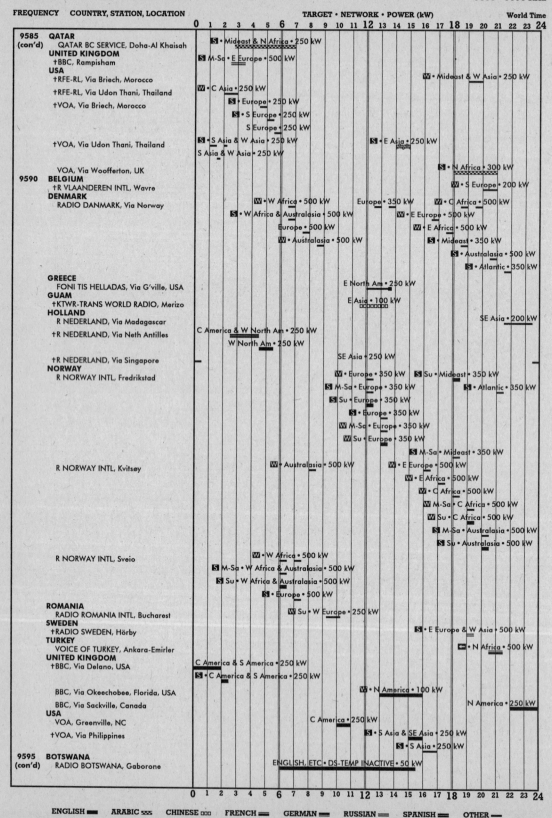

Frequency	Country, Station, Location	Target • Network • Power
9585 (con'd)	**QATAR** QATAR BC SERVICE, Doha-Al Khaisah	S • Mideast & N Africa • 250 kW
	UNITED KINGDOM †BBC, Rampisham	S M-Sa • E Europe • 500 kW
	USA †RFE-RL, Via Briech, Morocco	W • Mideast & W Asia • 250 kW
	†RFE-RL, Via Udon Thani, Thailand	W • C Asia • 250 kW
	†VOA, Via Briech, Morocco	S • Europe • 250 kW / S • S Europe • 250 kW / S Europe • 250 kW
	†VOA, Via Udon Thani, Thailand	S • S Asia & W Asia • 250 kW / S Asia & W Asia • 250 kW / S • E Asia • 250 kW
	VOA, Via Woofferton, UK	S • N Africa • 300 kW
9590	**BELGIUM** †R VLAANDEREN INTL, Wavre	W • S Europe • 200 kW
	DENMARK RADIO DANMARK, Via Norway	W • W Africa • 500 kW / S • W Africa & Australasia • 500 kW / Europe • 500 kW / W • Australasia • 500 kW / Europe • 350 kW / W • E Europe • 500 kW / W • C Africa • 500 kW / W • E Africa • 500 kW / S • Mideast • 350 kW / S • Australasia • 500 kW / S • Atlantic • 350 kW
	GREECE FONI TIS HELLADAS, Via G'ville, USA	E North Am • 250 kW
	GUAM †KTWR-TRANS WORLD RADIO, Merizo	E Asia • 100 kW
	HOLLAND R NEDERLAND, Via Madagascar	SE Asia • 200 kW
	†R NEDERLAND, Via Neth Antilles	C America & W North Am • 250 kW / W North Am • 250 kW
	†R NEDERLAND, Via Singapore	SE Asia • 250 kW
	NORWAY R NORWAY INTL, Fredrikstad	W • Europe • 350 kW / S M-Sa • Europe • 350 kW / S Su • Europe • 350 kW / S • Europe • 350 kW / W M-Sa • Europe • 350 kW / W Su • Europe • 350 kW / S Su • Mideast • 350 kW
	R NORWAY INTL, Kvitsøy	W • Australasia • 500 kW / S M-Sa • Mideast • 350 kW / W • E Europe • 500 kW / S • Atlantic • 350 kW / W • E Africa • 500 kW / W • C Africa • 500 kW / W M-Sa • C Africa • 500 kW / W Su • C Africa • 500 kW / S M-Sa • Australasia • 500 kW / S Su • Australasia • 500 kW
	R NORWAY INTL, Sveio	W • W Africa • 500 kW / S M-Sa • W Africa & Australasia • 500 kW / S Su • W Africa & Australasia • 500 kW / S • Europe • 500 kW
	ROMANIA RADIO ROMANIA INTL, Bucharest	W Su • W Europe • 250 kW
	SWEDEN †RADIO SWEDEN, Hörby	S • E Europe & W Asia • 500 kW
	TURKEY VOICE OF TURKEY, Ankara-Emirler	• N Africa • 500 kW
	UNITED KINGDOM †BBC, Via Delano, USA	C America & S America • 250 kW / S • C America & S America • 250 kW
	BBC, Via Okeechobee, Florida, USA	W • N America • 100 kW
	BBC, Via Sackville, Canada	N America • 250 kW
	USA VOA, Greenville, NC	C America • 250 kW
	†VOA, Via Philippines	S • S Asia & SE Asia • 250 kW / S • S Asia • 250 kW
9595 (con'd)	**BOTSWANA** RADIO BOTSWANA, Gaborone	ENGLISH, ETC • DS-TEMP INACTIVE • 50 kW

ENGLISH ▬   ARABIC ≋   CHINESE ▫▫▫   FRENCH ▬   GERMAN ▬   RUSSIAN ═   SPANISH ▬   OTHER ▬

FREQUENCY   COUNTRY, STATION, LOCATION   TARGET • NETWORK • POWER (kW)   World Time

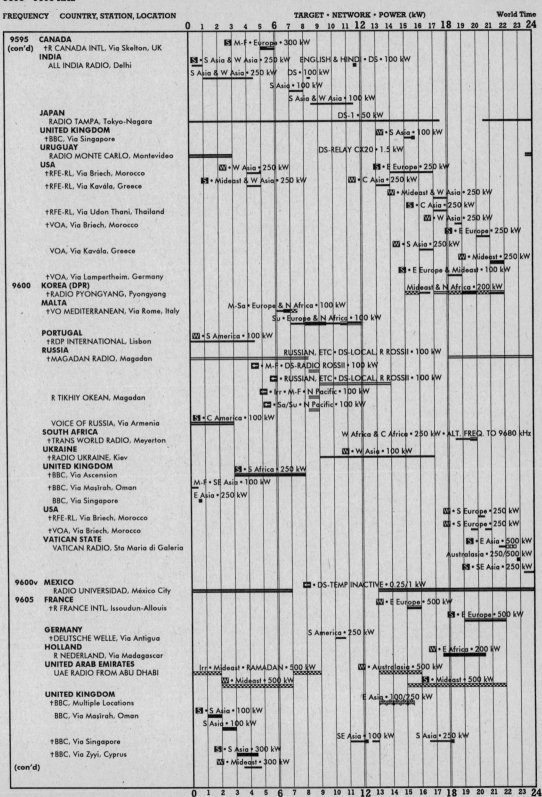

9595	**CANADA**
(con'd)	†R CANADA INTL, Via Skelton, UK
	INDIA
	ALL INDIA RADIO, Delhi
	JAPAN
	RADIO TAMPA, Tokyo-Nagara
	UNITED KINGDOM
	†BBC, Via Singapore
	URUGUAY
	RADIO MONTE CARLO, Montevideo
	USA
	†RFE-RL, Via Briech, Morocco
	†RFE-RL, Via Kavála, Greece
	†RFE-RL, Via Udon Thani, Thailand
	†VOA, Via Briech, Morocco
	VOA, Via Kavála, Greece
	†VOA, Via Lampertheim, Germany
9600	**KOREA (DPR)**
	†RADIO PYONGYANG, Pyongyang
	MALTA
	†VO MEDITERRANEAN, Via Rome, Italy
	PORTUGAL
	†RDP INTERNATIONAL, Lisbon
	RUSSIA
	†MAGADAN RADIO, Magadan
	R TIKHIY OKEAN, Magadan
	VOICE OF RUSSIA, Via Armenia
	SOUTH AFRICA
	†TRANS WORLD RADIO, Meyerton
	UKRAINE
	†RADIO UKRAINE, Kiev
	UNITED KINGDOM
	†BBC, Via Ascension
	†BBC, Via Maşīrah, Oman
	BBC, Via Singapore
	USA
	†RFE-RL, Via Briech, Morocco
	†VOA, Via Briech, Morocco
	VATICAN STATE
	VATICAN RADIO, Sta Maria di Galeria
9600v	**MEXICO**
	RADIO UNIVERSIDAD, México City
9605	**FRANCE**
	†R FRANCE INTL, Issoudun-Allouis
	GERMANY
	†DEUTSCHE WELLE, Via Antigua
	HOLLAND
	R NEDERLAND, Via Madagascar
	UNITED ARAB EMIRATES
	UAE RADIO FROM ABU DHABI
	UNITED KINGDOM
	†BBC, Multiple Locations
	BBC, Via Maşīrah, Oman
	†BBC, Via Singapore
	†BBC, Via Zyyi, Cyprus
(con'd)	

FREQUENCY   COUNTRY, STATION, LOCATION

TARGET • NETWORK • POWER (kW)   World Time

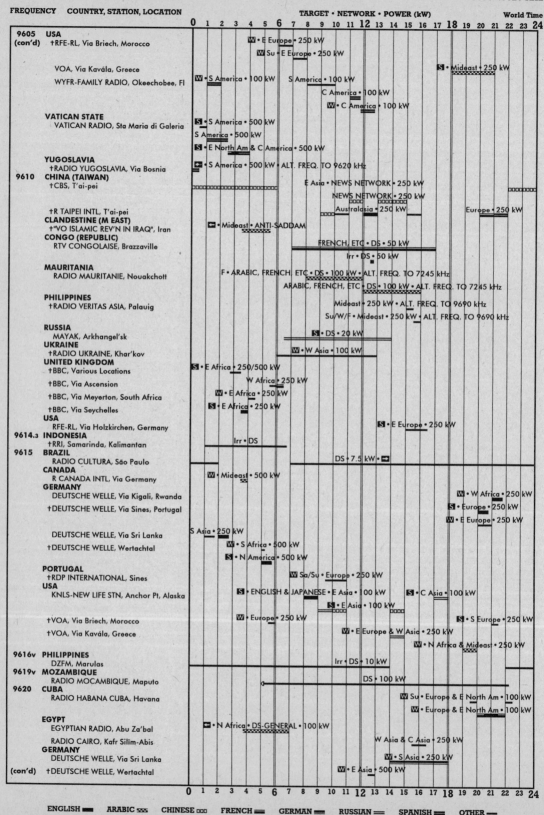

FREQUENCY	COUNTRY, STATION, LOCATION	Schedule
9605 (con'd)	USA †RFE-RL, Via Briech, Morocco	W • E Europe • 250 kW; W Su • E Europe • 250 kW
	VOA, Via Kavála, Greece	S • Mideast • 250 kW
	WYFR-FAMILY RADIO, Okeechobee, Fl	W • S America • 100 kW; S America • 100 kW; C America • 100 kW; W • C America • 100 kW
	VATICAN STATE VATICAN RADIO, Sta Maria di Galeria	S • S America • 500 kW; S America • 500 kW; S • E North Am & C America • 500 kW
	YUGOSLAVIA †RADIO YUGOSLAVIA, Via Bosnia	S America • 500 kW • ALT. FREQ. TO 9620 kHz
9610	CHINA (TAIWAN) †CBS, T'ai-pei	E Asia • NEWS NETWORK • 250 kW; NEWS NETWORK • 250 kW
	†R TAIPEI INTL, T'ai-pei	Australasia • 250 kW; Europe • 250 kW
	CLANDESTINE (M EAST) †"VO ISLAMIC REV'N IN IRAQ", Iran	• Mideast • ANTI-SADDAM
	CONGO (REPUBLIC) RTV CONGOLAISE, Brazzaville	FRENCH, ETC • DS • 50 kW; Irr • DS • 50 kW
	MAURITANIA RADIO MAURITANIE, Nouakchott	F • ARABIC, FRENCH, ETC • DS • 100 kW • ALT. FREQ. TO 7245 kHz; ARABIC, FRENCH, ETC • DS • 100 kW • ALT. FREQ. TO 7245 kHz
	PHILIPPINES †RADIO VERITAS ASIA, Palauig	Mideast • 250 kW • ALT. FREQ. TO 9690 kHz; Su/W/F • Mideast • 250 kW • ALT. FREQ. TO 9690 kHz
	RUSSIA MAYAK, Arkhangel'sk	S • DS • 20 kW
	UKRAINE †RADIO UKRAINE, Khar'kov	W • W Asia • 100 kW
	UNITED KINGDOM †BBC, Various Locations	S • E Africa • 250/500 kW
	†BBC, Via Ascension	W Africa • 250 kW
	†BBC, Via Meyerton, South Africa	W • E Africa • 250 kW
	†BBC, Via Seychelles	S • E Africa • 250 kW
	USA RFE-RL, Via Holzkirchen, Germany	S • E Europe • 250 kW
9614.3	INDONESIA †RRI, Samarinda, Kalimantan	Irr • DS
9615	BRAZIL RADIO CULTURA, São Paulo	DS • 7.5 kW •
	CANADA R CANADA INTL, Via Germany	W • Mideast • 500 kW
	GERMANY DEUTSCHE WELLE, Via Kigali, Rwanda	W • W Africa • 250 kW
	†DEUTSCHE WELLE, Via Sines, Portugal	S • Europe • 250 kW; W • E Europe • 250 kW
	DEUTSCHE WELLE, Via Sri Lanka	S Asia • 250 kW
	†DEUTSCHE WELLE, Wertachtal	W • S Africa • 500 kW; S • N America • 500 kW
	PORTUGAL †RDP INTERNATIONAL, Sines	W Sa/Su • Europe • 250 kW
	USA KNLS-NEW LIFE STN, Anchor Pt, Alaska	S • ENGLISH & JAPANESE • E Asia • 100 kW; S • E Asia • 100 kW; S • C Asia • 100 kW
	†VOA, Via Briech, Morocco	W • Europe • 250 kW; S • S Europe • 250 kW
	†VOA, Via Kavála, Greece	W • E Europe & W Asia • 250 kW; W • N Africa & Mideast • 250 kW
9616v	PHILIPPINES DZFM, Marulas	Irr • DS • 10 kW
9619v	MOZAMBIQUE RADIO MOCAMBIQUE, Maputo	DS • 100 kW
9620	CUBA RADIO HABANA CUBA, Havana	W Su • Europe & E North Am • 100 kW; W • Europe & E North Am • 100 kW
	EGYPT EGYPTIAN RADIO, Abu Za'bal	• N Africa • DS-GENERAL • 100 kW
	RADIO CAIRO, Kafr Silim-Abis	W Asia & C Asia • 250 kW
	GERMANY DEUTSCHE WELLE, Via Sri Lanka	W • S Asia • 250 kW
(con'd)	†DEUTSCHE WELLE, Wertachtal	W • E Asia • 500 kW

FREQUENCY   COUNTRY, STATION, LOCATION

TARGET • NETWORK • POWER (kW)   World Time

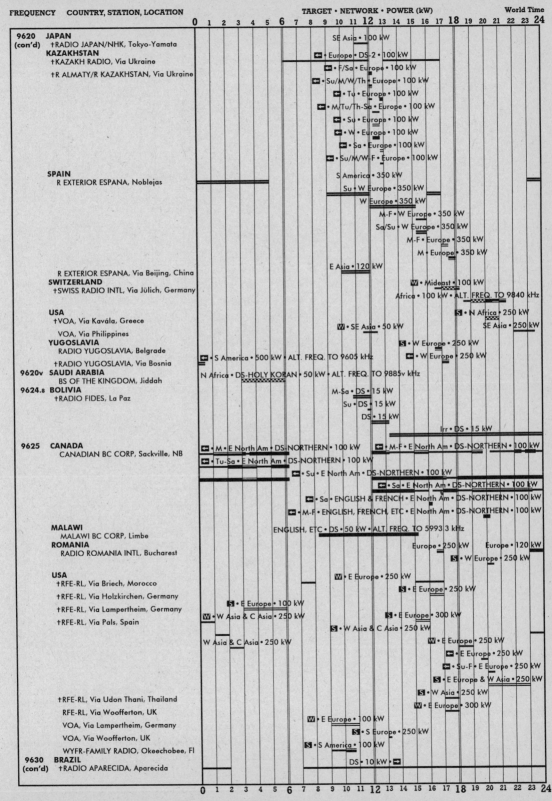

Freq	Country / Station / Location	Listing
9620 (con'd)	**JAPAN** †RADIO JAPAN/NHK, Tokyo-Yamata	SE Asia • 100 kW
	KAZAKHSTAN †KAZAKH RADIO, Via Ukraine	Europe • DS-2 • 100 kW
	†R ALMATY/R KAZAKHSTAN, Via Ukraine	F/Sa • Europe • 100 kW
		Su/M/W/Th • Europe • 100 kW
		Tu • Europe • 100 kW
		M/Tu/Th-Sa • Europe • 100 kW
		Su • Europe • 100 kW
		W • Europe • 100 kW
		Sa • Europe • 100 kW
		Su/M/W/F • Europe • 100 kW
	SPAIN R EXTERIOR ESPANA, Noblejas	S America • 350 kW
		Su • W Europe • 350 kW
		W Europe • 350 kW
		M-F • W Europe • 350 kW
		Sa/Su • W Europe • 350 kW
		M-F • Europe • 350 kW
		M • Europe • 350 kW
	R EXTERIOR ESPANA, Via Beijing, China	E Asia • 120 kW
	SWITZERLAND †SWISS RADIO INTL, Via Jülich, Germany	W • Mideast • 100 kW
		Africa • 100 kW • ALT. FREQ. TO 9840 kHz
	USA †VOA, Via Kavála, Greece	S • N Africa • 250 kW
	VOA, Via Philippines	W • SE Asia • 50 kW SE Asia • 250 kW
	YUGOSLAVIA RADIO YUGOSLAVIA, Belgrade	S • W Europe • 250 kW
	†RADIO YUGOSLAVIA, Via Bosnia	S America • 500 kW • ALT. FREQ. TO 9605 kHz W • Europe • 250 kW
9620v	**SAUDI ARABIA** BS OF THE KINGDOM, Jiddah	N Africa • DS-HOLY KORAN • 50 kW • ALT. FREQ. TO 9885v kHz
9624.8	**BOLIVIA** †RADIO FIDES, La Paz	M-Sa • DS • 15 kW
		Su • DS • 15 kW
		DS • 15 kW
		Irr • DS • 15 kW
9625	**CANADA** CANADIAN BC CORP, Sackville, NB	M • E North Am • DS-NORTHERN • 100 kW M-F • E North Am • DS-NORTHERN • 100 kW
		Tu-Sa • E North Am • DS-NORTHERN • 100 kW
		Su • E North Am • DS-NORTHERN • 100 kW
		Sa • E North Am • DS-NORTHERN • 100 kW
		Sa • ENGLISH & FRENCH • E North Am • DS-NORTHERN • 100 kW
		M-F • ENGLISH, FRENCH, ETC • E North Am • DS-NORTHERN • 100 kW
	MALAWI MALAWI BC CORP, Limbe	ENGLISH, ETC • DS • 50 kW • ALT. FREQ. TO 5993.3 kHz
	ROMANIA RADIO ROMANIA INTL, Bucharest	Europe • 250 kW Europe • 120 kW
		S • W Europe • 250 kW
	USA †RFE-RL, Via Briech, Morocco	W • E Europe • 250 kW
	†RFE-RL, Via Holzkirchen, Germany	S • E Europe • 250 kW
	†RFE-RL, Via Lampertheim, Germany	S • E Europe • 100 kW S • E Europe • 300 kW
	†RFE-RL, Via Pals, Spain	W • W Asia & C Asia • 250 kW S • W Asia & C Asia • 250 kW
		W Asia & C Asia • 250 kW W • E Europe • 250 kW
		E Europe • 250 kW
		Su-F • E Europe • 250 kW
		S • E Europe & W Asia • 250 kW
	†RFE-RL, Via Udon Thani, Thailand	S • W Asia • 250 kW
	RFE-RL, Via Woofferton, UK	W • E Europe • 300 kW
	VOA, Via Lampertheim, Germany	W • E Europe • 100 kW
	VOA, Via Woofferton, UK	S • S Europe • 250 kW
	WYFR-FAMILY RADIO, Okeechobee, Fl	S • S America • 100 kW
9630 (con'd)	**BRAZIL** †RADIO APARECIDA, Aparecida	DS • 10 kW

FREQUENCY   COUNTRY, STATION, LOCATION

TARGET • NETWORK • POWER (kW)

World Time

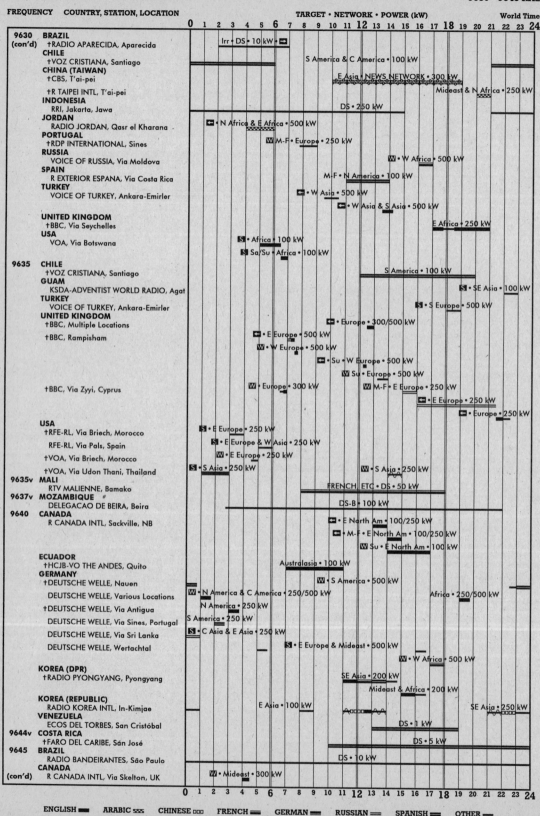

Freq	Country / Station / Location	Target · Network · Power
9630 (con'd)	BRAZIL	
	†RADIO APARECIDA, Aparecida	Irr • DS • 10 kW
	CHILE	
	†VOZ CRISTIANA, Santiago	S America & C America • 100 kW
	CHINA (TAIWAN)	
	†CBS, T'ai-pei	E Asia • NEWS NETWORK • 300 kW
	†R TAIPEI INTL, T'ai-pei	Mideast & N Africa • 250 kW
	INDONESIA	
	RRI, Jakarta, Jawa	DS • 250 kW
	JORDAN	
	RADIO JORDAN, Qasr el Kharana	N Africa & E Africa • 500 kW
	PORTUGAL	
	†RDP INTERNATIONAL, Sines	W M-F • Europe • 250 kW
	RUSSIA	
	VOICE OF RUSSIA, Via Moldova	W • W Africa • 500 kW
	SPAIN	
	R EXTERIOR ESPANA, Via Costa Rica	M-F • N America • 100 kW
	TURKEY	
	VOICE OF TURKEY, Ankara-Emirler	W Asia • 500 kW
		W Asia & S Asia • 500 kW
	UNITED KINGDOM	
	†BBC, Via Seychelles	E Africa • 250 kW
	USA	
	VOA, Via Botswana	S • Africa • 100 kW
		Sa/Su • Africa • 100 kW
9635	CHILE	
	†VOZ CRISTIANA, Santiago	S America • 100 kW
	GUAM	
	KSDA-ADVENTIST WORLD RADIO, Agat	S • SE Asia • 100 kW
	TURKEY	
	VOICE OF TURKEY, Ankara-Emirler	S • S Europe • 500 kW
	UNITED KINGDOM	
	†BBC, Multiple Locations	• Europe • 300/500 kW
	†BBC, Rampisham	• E Europe • 500 kW
		W • W Europe • 500 kW
		• Su • W Europe • 500 kW
		W Su • Europe • 500 kW
	†BBC, Via Zyyi, Cyprus	W • Europe • 300 kW / W M-F • E Europe • 250 kW
		• E Europe • 250 kW
		• Europe • 250 kW
	USA	
	†RFE-RL, Via Briech, Morocco	S • E Europe • 250 kW
	RFE-RL, Via Pals, Spain	S • E Europe & W Asia • 250 kW
	†VOA, Via Briech, Morocco	W • E Europe • 250 kW
	†VOA, Via Udon Thani, Thailand	S • S Asia • 250 kW / W • S Asia • 250 kW
9635v	MALI	
	RTV MALIENNE, Bamako	FRENCH, ETC • DS • 50 kW
9637v	MOZAMBIQUE	
	DELEGACAO DE BEIRA, Beira	DS-B • 100 kW
9640	CANADA	
	R CANADA INTL, Sackville, NB	• E North Am • 100/250 kW
		• M-F • E North Am • 100/250 kW
		W Su • E North Am • 100 kW
	ECUADOR	
	†HCJB-VO THE ANDES, Quito	Australasia • 100 kW
	GERMANY	
	†DEUTSCHE WELLE, Nauen	W • S America • 500 kW
	DEUTSCHE WELLE, Various Locations	W • N America & C America • 250/500 kW / Africa • 250/500 kW
	†DEUTSCHE WELLE, Via Antigua	N America • 250 kW
	DEUTSCHE WELLE, Via Sines, Portugal	S America • 250 kW
	DEUTSCHE WELLE, Via Sri Lanka	S • C Asia & E Asia • 250 kW
	DEUTSCHE WELLE, Wertachtal	S • E Europe & Mideast • 500 kW / W • W Africa • 500 kW
	KOREA (DPR)	
	†RADIO PYONGYANG, Pyongyang	SE Asia • 200 kW
		Mideast & Africa • 200 kW
	KOREA (REPUBLIC)	
	RADIO KOREA INTL, In-Kimjae	E Asia • 100 kW / SE Asia • 250 kW
	VENEZUELA	
	ECOS DEL TORBES, San Cristóbal	DS • 1 kW
9644v	COSTA RICA	
	†FARO DEL CARIBE, Sán José	DS • 5 kW
9645	BRAZIL	
	RADIO BANDEIRANTES, São Paulo	DS • 10 kW
	CANADA	
(con'd)	R CANADA INTL, Via Skelton, UK	W • Mideast • 300 kW

0 1 2 3 4 5 6 7 8 9 10 11 12 13 14 15 16 17 18 19 20 21 22 23 24

ENGLISH ▬ ARABIC ≈≈≈ CHINESE □□□ FRENCH ══ GERMAN ▬▬ RUSSIAN ══ SPANISH ▬▬ OTHER ▬

FREQUENCY   COUNTRY, STATION, LOCATION   TARGET • NETWORK • POWER (kW)   World Time

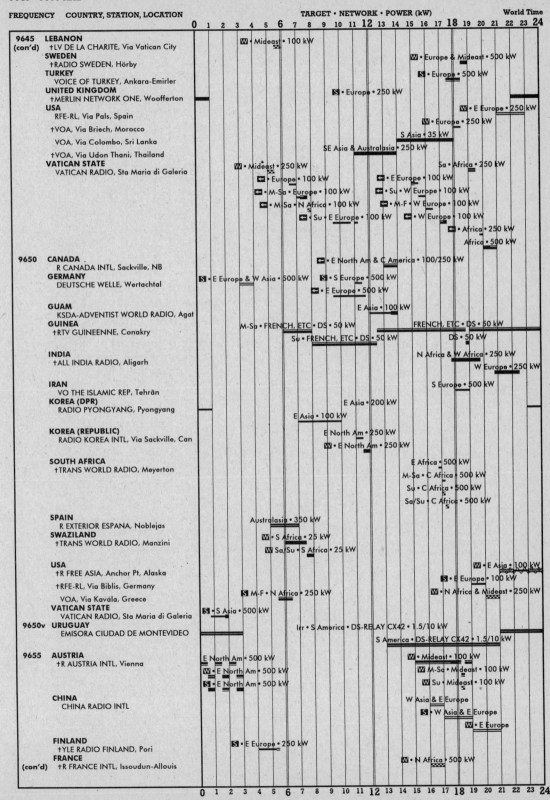

Frequency	Country, Station, Location	Target • Network • Power
9645 (con'd)	**LEBANON** †LV DE LA CHARITE, Via Vatican City	W • Mideast • 100 kW
	SWEDEN †RADIO SWEDEN, Hörby	W • Europe & Mideast • 500 kW
	TURKEY VOICE OF TURKEY, Ankara-Emirler	S • Europe • 500 kW
	UNITED KINGDOM †MERLIN NETWORK ONE, Woofferton	S • Europe • 250 kW
	USA RFE-RL, Via Pals, Spain	W • E Europe • 250 kW
	†VOA, Via Briech, Morocco	W • Europe • 250 kW
	VOA, Via Colombo, Sri Lanka	S Asia • 35 kW
	†VOA, Via Udon Thani, Thailand	SE Asia & Australasia • 250 kW
	VATICAN STATE VATICAN RADIO, Sta Maria di Galeria	W • Mideast • 250 kW Sa • Africa • 250 kW • Europe • 100 kW • E Europe • 100 kW M-Sa • Europe • 100 kW Su • W Europe • 100 kW M-Sa • N Africa • 100 kW M-F • W Europe • 100 kW Su • E Europe • 100 kW • W Europe • 100 kW • Africa • 250 kW Africa • 500 kW
9650	**CANADA** R CANADA INTL, Sackville, NB	• E North Am & C America • 100/250 kW
	GERMANY DEUTSCHE WELLE, Wertachtal	S • E Europe & W Asia • 500 kW S • S Europe • 500 kW • E Europe • 500 kW
	GUAM KSDA-ADVENTIST WORLD RADIO, Agat	E Asia • 100 kW
	GUINEA †RTV GUINEENNE, Conakry	M-Sa • FRENCH, ETC • DS • 50 kW FRENCH, ETC • DS • 50 kW Su • FRENCH, ETC • DS • 50 kW DS • 50 kW
	INDIA †ALL INDIA RADIO, Aligarh	N Africa & W Africa • 250 kW W Europe • 250 kW
	IRAN VO THE ISLAMIC REP, Tehrãn	S Europe • 500 kW
	KOREA (DPR) RADIO PYONGYANG, Pyongyang	E Asia • 200 kW E Asia • 100 kW
	KOREA (REPUBLIC) RADIO KOREA INTL, Via Sackville, Can	E North Am • 250 kW W • E North Am • 250 kW
	SOUTH AFRICA †TRANS WORLD RADIO, Meyerton	E Africa • 500 kW M-Sa • C Africa • 500 kW Su • C Africa • 500 kW Sa/Su • C Africa • 500 kW
	SPAIN R EXTERIOR ESPANA, Noblejas	Australasia • 350 kW
	SWAZILAND †TRANS WORLD RADIO, Manzini	W • S Africa • 25 kW W Sa/Su • S Africa • 25 kW
	USA †R FREE ASIA, Anchor Pt, Alaska	W • E Asia • 100 kW
	†RFE-RL, Via Biblis, Germany	S • E Europe • 100 kW
	VOA, Via Kavála, Greece	S M-F • N Africa • 250 kW W • N Africa & Mideast • 250 kW
	VATICAN STATE VATICAN RADIO, Sta Maria di Galeria	S • S Asia • 500 kW
9650v	**URUGUAY** EMISORA CIUDAD DE MONTEVIDEO	Irr • S America • DS-RELAY CX42 • 1.5/10 kW S America • DS-RELAY CX42 • 1.5/10 kW
9655	**AUSTRIA** †R AUSTRIA INTL, Vienna	E North Am • 500 kW W • Mideast • 100 kW W • E North Am • 500 kW W M-Sa • Mideast • 100 kW S • E North Am • 500 kW W Su • Mideast • 100 kW
	CHINA CHINA RADIO INTL	W Asia & E Europe S • W Asia & E Europe W • E Europe
	FINLAND †YLE RADIO FINLAND, Pori	S • E Europe • 250 kW
(con'd)	**FRANCE** †R FRANCE INTL, Issoudun-Allouis	W • N Africa • 500 kW

SEASONAL S OR W   1-HR TIMESHIFT MIDYEAR ⊟ OR ⊞   JAMMING / OR /\   EARLIEST HEARD ◁   LATEST HEARD ▷   NEW FOR 1999 †

FREQUENCY   COUNTRY, STATION, LOCATION   TARGET • NETWORK • POWER (kW)   World Time

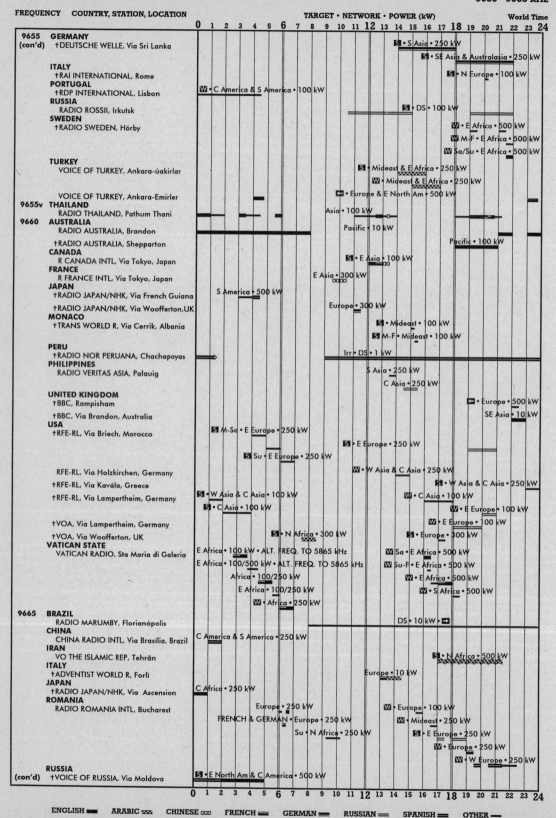

FREQUENCY	COUNTRY, STATION, LOCATION	TARGET • NETWORK • POWER (kW)
9655 (con'd)	**GERMANY** †DEUTSCHE WELLE, Via Sri Lanka	S • S Asia • 250 kW; S • SE Asia & Australasia • 250 kW; S • N Europe • 100 kW
	ITALY †RAI INTERNATIONAL, Rome	
	PORTUGAL †RDP INTERNATIONAL, Lisbon	W • C America & S America • 100 kW
	RUSSIA RADIO ROSSII, Irkutsk	S • DS • 100 kW
	SWEDEN †RADIO SWEDEN, Hörby	W • E Africa • 500 kW; W • M-F • E Africa • 500 kW; W • Sa/Su • E Africa • 500 kW
	TURKEY VOICE OF TURKEY, Ankara-úakirlar	S • Mideast & E Africa • 250 kW; W • Mideast & E Africa • 250 kW
	VOICE OF TURKEY, Ankara-Emirler	• Europe & E North Am • 500 kW
9655v	**THAILAND** RADIO THAILAND, Pathum Thani	Asia • 100 kW
9660	**AUSTRALIA** RADIO AUSTRALIA, Brandon	Pacific • 10 kW
	†RADIO AUSTRALIA, Shepparton	Pacific • 100 kW
	CANADA R CANADA INTL, Via Tokyo, Japan	S • E Asia • 100 kW
	FRANCE R FRANCE INTL, Via Tokyo, Japan	E Asia • 300 kW
	JAPAN †RADIO JAPAN/NHK, Via French Guiana	S America • 500 kW
	†RADIO JAPAN/NHK, Via Woofferton, UK	Europe • 300 kW
	MONACO †TRANS WORLD R, Via Cerrik, Albania	S • Mideast • 100 kW; S • M-F • Mideast • 100 kW
	PERU †RADIO NOR PERUANA, Chachapoyas	Irr • DS • 1 kW
	PHILIPPINES RADIO VERITAS ASIA, Palauig	S Asia • 250 kW; C Asia • 250 kW
	UNITED KINGDOM †BBC, Rampisham	• Europe • 500 kW
	†BBC, Via Brandon, Australia	SE Asia • 10 kW
	USA †RFE-RL, Via Briech, Morocco	S • M-Sa • E Europe • 250 kW; S • E Europe • 250 kW; S • Su • E Europe • 250 kW
	RFE-RL, Via Holzkirchen, Germany	W • W Asia & C Asia • 250 kW; S • W Asia & C Asia • 250 kW
	†RFE-RL, Via Kavála, Greece	S • W Asia & C Asia • 100 kW; W • C Asia • 100 kW
	†RFE-RL, Via Lampertheim, Germany	S • C Asia • 100 kW; W • E Europe • 100 kW; W • E Europe • 100 kW
	†VOA, Via Lampertheim, Germany	S • N Africa • 300 kW; S • Europe • 300 kW
	†VOA, Via Woofferton, UK	
	VATICAN STATE VATICAN RADIO, Sta Maria di Galeria	E Africa • 100 kW • ALT. FREQ. TO 5865 kHz; W • Sa • E Africa • 500 kW; E Africa • 100/500 kW • ALT. FREQ. TO 5865 kHz; W • Su-F • E Africa • 500 kW; Africa • 100/250 kW; W • E Africa • 500 kW; E Africa • 100/250 kW; W • S Africa • 500 kW; W • Africa • 250 kW
9665	**BRAZIL** RADIO MARUMBY, Florianópolis	DS • 10 kW •
	CHINA CHINA RADIO INTL, Via Brasília, Brazil	C America & S America • 250 kW
	IRAN VO THE ISLAMIC REP, Tehrän	S • N Africa • 500 kW
	ITALY †ADVENTIST WORLD R, Forlì	Europe • 10 kW
	JAPAN †RADIO JAPAN/NHK, Via Ascension	C Africa • 250 kW
	ROMANIA RADIO ROMANIA INTL, Bucharest	Europe • 250 kW; W • Europe • 100 kW; FRENCH & GERMAN • Europe • 250 kW; W • Mideast • 250 kW; Su • N Africa • 250 kW; S • E Europe • 250 kW; W • Europe • 250 kW; W • W Europe • 250 kW
9665 (con'd)	**RUSSIA** †VOICE OF RUSSIA, Via Moldova	S • E North Am & C America • 500 kW

ENGLISH ▬   ARABIC ⌇⌇⌇   CHINESE □□□   FRENCH ═   GERMAN ▬   RUSSIAN ═   SPANISH ═   OTHER ▬

| FREQUENCY | COUNTRY, STATION, LOCATION | TARGET • NETWORK • POWER (kW) | World Time |

World Time scale: 0 1 2 3 4 5 6 7 8 9 10 11 12 13 14 15 16 17 18 19 20 21 22 23 24

9665 **USA**
(con'd)   RFE-RL, Via Lampertheim, Germany — S • E Europe & W Asia • 100 kW
          †VOA, Via Briech, Morocco — W • N Africa & Mideast • 250 kW

9665v **KOREA (DPR)**
          KOREAN CENTRAL BS, Pyongyang — DS • 200 kW

9670 **CHINA**
          CHINA RADIO INTL, Kunming — S Africa • 50 kW • ALT. FREQ. TO 9535 kHz
          CLANDESTINE (M EAST)
          "VO PALESTINIAN ISLAMIC REV'N", Iran — Mideast • ANTI-ARAFAT
          GERMANY
          †DEUTSCHE WELLE, Various Locations — S Europe • 100/500 kW — S Africa • 250 kW

          DEUTSCHE WELLE, Via Sri Lanka — S • Africa • 250 kW
                                          SE Asia & Australasia • 250 kW

          IRAN
          VO THE ISLAMIC REP, Tehrān — W • E North Am • 500 kW
                                       W • C America • 500 kW
                                       S • Australasia • 500 kW

          ITALY
          †RAI INTERNATIONAL, Rome — E Europe • 100 kW
                                     S • S Europe & N Africa • 100 kW
                                     N Africa • 100 kW
                                     Europe • 100 kW
                                     S • Europe • 100 kW

          MONACO
          †TRANS WORLD R, Via Cerrik, Albania — S • E Europe • 100 kW
          NORTHERN MARIANA IS
          KFBS-FAR EAST BC, Saipan Island — SE Asia • 100 kW
          PHILIPPINES
          †RADIO VERITAS ASIA, Palauig — S Asia • 250 kW • ALT. FREQ. TO 11805 kHz
                                         SE Asia • 250 kW
                                         S Asia • 250 kW

          RUSSIA
          MAYAK, Komsomol'sk 'Amure — DS • 100 kW
                                      S • DS • 100 kW

          R TIKHIY OKEAN, Komsomol'sk 'Amure — S • E Asia & N Pacific • 100 kW
          UNITED KINGDOM
          BBC, Via Delano, USA — M-F • C America • 250 kW
          †BBC, Via Zyyi, Cyprus — M-Sa • E Europe • 250/300 kW
          USA
          †R FREE ASIA — S • S Asia & E Asia

          RFE-RL, Via Biblis, Germany — W • W Asia • 100 kW
          VOA, Delano, California — W • M-F • C America • 250 kW
          †VOA, Greenville, NC — W • C America • 250 kW
                                 S • S America • 250 kW

          VOA, Via Holzkirchen, Germany — W • E Europe • 250 kW
          VOA, Via Kavála, Greece — W • W Asia & S Asia • 250 kW
          VOA, Via Udon Thani, Thailand — W • M-F • E Asia & SE Asia • 250 kW
          VOA, Via Woofferton, UK — S • Europe • 300 kW

9674.8 **PERU**
          RADIO DEL PACIFICO, Lima — DS • 5 kW

9675 **BRAZIL**
          R CANCAO NOVA, Cachoeira Paulista — DS • 10 kW
          CHINA
          CHINA RADIO INTL — W • S Asia & W Asia
          ITALY
          RAI INTERNATIONAL, Rome — E North Am & C America • 100 kW
                                    N America & C America • 100 kW
                                    E Asia • 100 kW

          MONACO
          †TRANS WORLD R, Via Cerrik, Albania — S • Mideast & W Asia • 100 kW • ALT. FREQ. TO 9475 kHz
          PAPUA NEW GUINEA
          NBC, Port Moresby — DS • 100 kW
                              DS • 100 kW • ALT. FREQ. TO 4890 kHz
                              M-Sa • ENGLISH, ETC • DS • 100 kW • ALT. FREQ. TO 4890 kHz

          SOUTH AFRICA
          †CHANNEL AFRICA, Meyerton — W • W Africa • 500 kW
                                      S • S Africa & W Africa • 500 kW

          TURKEY
          VOICE OF TURKEY, Ankara-úakirlar — S • Mideast • 250 kW
          VOICE OF TURKEY, Ankara-Emirler — S • E Europe & W Asia • 500 kW
                                            S • Europe • 500 kW

          USA
          †RFE-RL, Via Pals, Spain — W • C Asia • 250 kW
          VOA, Via São Tomé — E Africa • 100 kW

World Time scale: 0 1 2 3 4 5 6 7 8 9 10 11 12 13 14 15 16 17 18 19 20 21 22 23 24

SEASONAL **S** OR **W**   1-HR TIMESHIFT MIDYEAR **⊐** OR **⊏**   JAMMING / OR ∧   EARLIEST HEARD ◁   LATEST HEARD ▷   NEW FOR 1999 †

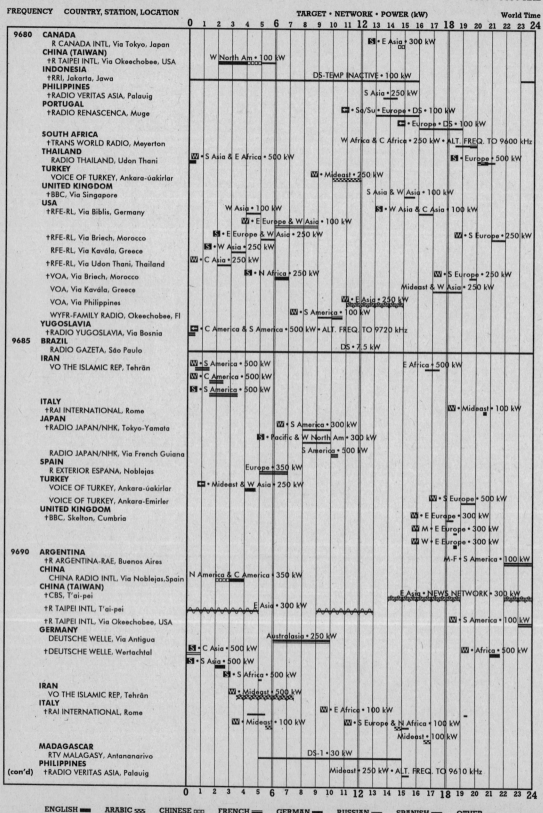

FREQUENCY	COUNTRY, STATION, LOCATION	TARGET • NETWORK • POWER (kW) / World Time

9680
- **CANADA** — R CANADA INTL, Via Tokyo, Japan — S • E Asia • 300 kW
- **CHINA (TAIWAN)** — †R TAIPEI INTL, Via Okeechobee, USA — W North Am • 100 kW
- **INDONESIA** — †RRI, Jakarta, Jawa — DS-TEMP INACTIVE • 100 kW
- **PHILIPPINES** — †RADIO VERITAS ASIA, Palauig — S Asia • 250 kW
- **PORTUGAL** — †RADIO RENASCENCA, Muge — Sa/Su • Europe • DS • 100 kW / • Europe • DS • 100 kW
- **SOUTH AFRICA** — †TRANS WORLD RADIO, Meyerton — W Africa & C Africa • 250 kW • ALT. FREQ. TO 9600 kHz
- **THAILAND** — RADIO THAILAND, Udon Thani — W • S Asia & E Africa • 500 kW / S • Europe • 500 kW
- **TURKEY** — VOICE OF TURKEY, Ankara-úakirlar — W • Mideast • 250 kW
- **UNITED KINGDOM** — †BBC, Via Singapore — S Asia & W Asia • 100 kW
- **USA** — †RFE-RL, Via Biblis, Germany — W Asia • 100 kW / S • W Asia & C Asia • 100 kW
  - †RFE-RL, Via Briech, Morocco — W • E Europe & W Asia • 100 kW / W • S Europe • 250 kW
  - †RFE-RL — S • E Europe & W Asia • 250 kW
  - RFE-RL, Via Kavála, Greece — S • W Asia • 250 kW
  - †RFE-RL, Via Udon Thani, Thailand — W • C Asia • 250 kW
  - †VOA, Via Briech, Morocco — S • N Africa • 250 kW
  - VOA, Via Kavála, Greece — W • S Europe • 250 kW / Mideast & W Asia • 250 kW
  - VOA, Via Philippines — W • E Asia • 250 kW
  - WYFR-FAMILY RADIO, Okeechobee, Fl — W • S America • 100 kW
- **YUGOSLAVIA** — †RADIO YUGOSLAVIA, Via Bosnia — C America & S America • 500 kW • ALT. FREQ. TO 9720 kHz

9685
- **BRAZIL** — RADIO GAZETA, São Paulo — DS • 7.5 kW
- **IRAN** — VO THE ISLAMIC REP, Tehrãn — W • S America • 500 kW / E Africa • 500 kW / W • C America • 500 kW / S • S America • 500 kW
- **ITALY** — †RAI INTERNATIONAL, Rome — W • Mideast • 100 kW
- **JAPAN** — †RADIO JAPAN/NHK, Tokyo-Yamata — W • S America • 300 kW / S • Pacific & W North Am • 300 kW
  - RADIO JAPAN/NHK, Via French Guiana — S America • 500 kW
- **SPAIN** — R EXTERIOR ESPANA, Noblejas — Europe • 350 kW
- **TURKEY** — VOICE OF TURKEY, Ankara-úakirlar — Mideast & W Asia • 250 kW
  - VOICE OF TURKEY, Ankara-Emirler — W • S Europe • 500 kW
- **UNITED KINGDOM** — †BBC, Skelton, Cumbria — W • E Europe • 300 kW / W M • E Europe • 300 kW / W W • E Europe • 300 kW

9690
- **ARGENTINA** — †R ARGENTINA-RAE, Buenos Aires — M-F • S America • 100 kW
- **CHINA** — CHINA RADIO INTL, Via Noblejas, Spain — N America & C America • 350 kW
- **CHINA (TAIWAN)** — †CBS, T'ai-pei — E Asia • NEWS NETWORK • 300 kW
  - †R TAIPEI INTL, T'ai-pei — E Asia • 300 kW
  - †R TAIPEI INTL, Via Okeechobee, USA — W • S America • 100 kW
- **GERMANY** — DEUTSCHE WELLE, Via Antigua — Australasia • 250 kW
  - †DEUTSCHE WELLE, Wertachtal — S • C Asia • 500 kW / W • Africa • 500 kW / S • S Asia • 500 kW / S • S Africa • 500 kW
- **IRAN** — VO THE ISLAMIC REP, Tehrãn — W • Mideast • 500 kW
- **ITALY** — †RAI INTERNATIONAL, Rome — W • E Africa • 100 kW / W • Mideast • 100 kW / W • S Europe & N Africa • 100 kW / Mideast • 100 kW
- **MADAGASCAR** — RTV MALAGASY, Antananarivo — DS-1 • 30 kW
- **PHILIPPINES** (con'd) — †RADIO VERITAS ASIA, Palauig — Mideast • 250 kW • ALT. FREQ. TO 9610 kHz

ENGLISH ▬ ARABIC ▨ CHINESE ▫▫▫ FRENCH ═ GERMAN ▬ RUSSIAN ═ SPANISH ▬ OTHER ▬

FREQUENCY   COUNTRY, STATION, LOCATION   TARGET • NETWORK • POWER (kW)   World Time

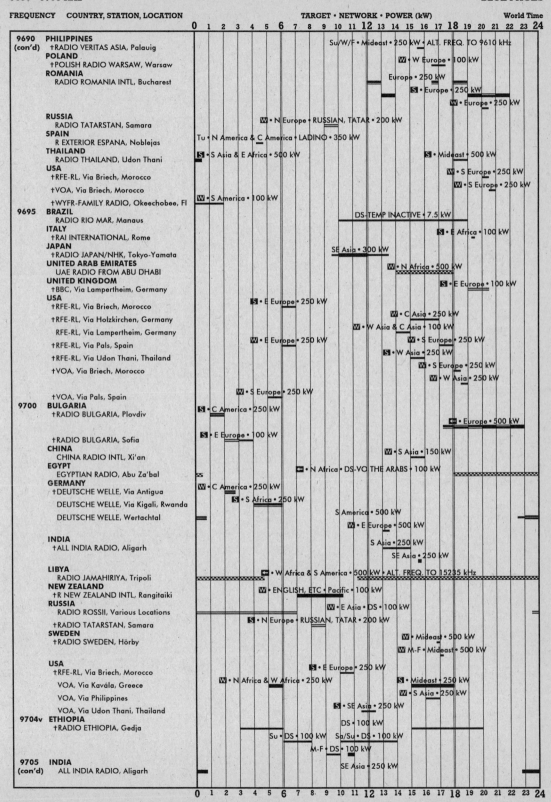

FREQUENCY	COUNTRY, STATION, LOCATION	TARGET • NETWORK • POWER (kW)
9690 (con'd)	PHILIPPINES	
	†RADIO VERITAS ASIA, Palauig	Su/W/F • Mideast • 250 kW • ALT. FREQ. TO 9610 kHz
	POLAND	
	†POLISH RADIO WARSAW, Warsaw	W • W Europe • 100 kW
	ROMANIA	
	RADIO ROMANIA INTL, Bucharest	Europe • 250 kW / S • Europe • 250 kW / W • Europe • 250 kW
	RUSSIA	
	RADIO TATARSTAN, Samara	W • N Europe • RUSSIAN, TATAR • 200 kW
	SPAIN	
	R EXTERIOR ESPANA, Noblejas	Tu • N America & C America • LADINO • 350 kW
	THAILAND	
	RADIO THAILAND, Udon Thani	S • S Asia & E Africa • 500 kW / S • Mideast • 500 kW
	USA	
	†RFE-RL, Via Briech, Morocco	W • S Europe • 250 kW
	†VOA, Via Briech, Morocco	W • S Europe • 250 kW
	†WYFR-FAMILY RADIO, Okeechobee, Fl	W • S America • 100 kW
9695	BRAZIL	
	RADIO RIO MAR, Manaus	DS-TEMP INACTIVE • 7.5 kW
	ITALY	
	†RAI INTERNATIONAL, Rome	S • E Africa • 100 kW
	JAPAN	
	†RADIO JAPAN/NHK, Tokyo-Yamata	SE Asia • 300 kW
	UNITED ARAB EMIRATES	
	UAE RADIO FROM ABU DHABI	W • N Africa • 500 kW
	UNITED KINGDOM	
	†BBC, Via Lampertheim, Germany	S • E Europe • 100 kW
	USA	
	†RFE-RL, Via Briech, Morocco	S • E Europe • 250 kW
	†RFE-RL, Via Holzkirchen, Germany	W • C Asia • 250 kW
	RFE-RL, Via Lampertheim, Germany	W • W Asia & C Asia • 100 kW
	†RFE-RL, Via Pals, Spain	W • E Europe • 250 kW / W • S Europe • 250 kW
	†RFE-RL, Via Udon Thani, Thailand	S • W Asia • 250 kW
	†VOA, Via Briech, Morocco	W • S Europe • 250 kW / W • W Asia • 250 kW
	†VOA, Via Pals, Spain	W • S Europe • 250 kW
9700	BULGARIA	
	†RADIO BULGARIA, Plovdiv	S • C America • 250 kW / • Europe • 500 kW
	†RADIO BULGARIA, Sofia	S • E Europe • 100 kW
	CHINA	
	CHINA RADIO INTL, Xi'an	W • S Asia • 150 kW
	EGYPT	
	EGYPTIAN RADIO, Abu Za'bal	• N Africa • DS-VO THE ARABS • 100 kW
	GERMANY	
	†DEUTSCHE WELLE, Via Antigua	W • C America • 250 kW
	DEUTSCHE WELLE, Via Kigali, Rwanda	S • S Africa • 250 kW
	DEUTSCHE WELLE, Wertachtal	S America • 500 kW / W • E Europe • 500 kW
	INDIA	
	†ALL INDIA RADIO, Aligarh	S Asia • 250 kW / SE Asia • 250 kW
	LIBYA	
	RADIO JAMAHIRIYA, Tripoli	• W Africa & S America • 500 kW • ALT. FREQ. TO 15235 kHz
	NEW ZEALAND	
	†R NEW ZEALAND INTL, Rangitaiki	W • ENGLISH, ETC • Pacific • 100 kW
	RUSSIA	
	RADIO ROSSII, Various Locations	W • E Asia • DS • 100 kW
	†RADIO TATARSTAN, Samara	S • N Europe • RUSSIAN, TATAR • 200 kW
	SWEDEN	
	†RADIO SWEDEN, Hörby	W • Mideast • 500 kW / W • M-F • Mideast • 500 kW
	USA	
	†RFE-RL, Via Briech, Morocco	S • E Europe • 250 kW
	VOA, Via Kavála, Greece	W • N Africa & W Africa • 250 kW / S • Mideast • 250 kW
	VOA, Via Philippines	W • S Asia • 250 kW
	VOA, Via Udon Thani, Thailand	S • SE Asia • 250 kW
9704v	ETHIOPIA	
	†RADIO ETHIOPIA, Gedja	DS • 100 kW / Su • DS • 100 kW / Sa/Su • DS • 100 kW / M-F • DS • 100 kW
9705 (con'd)	INDIA	
	ALL INDIA RADIO, Aligarh	SE Asia • 250 kW

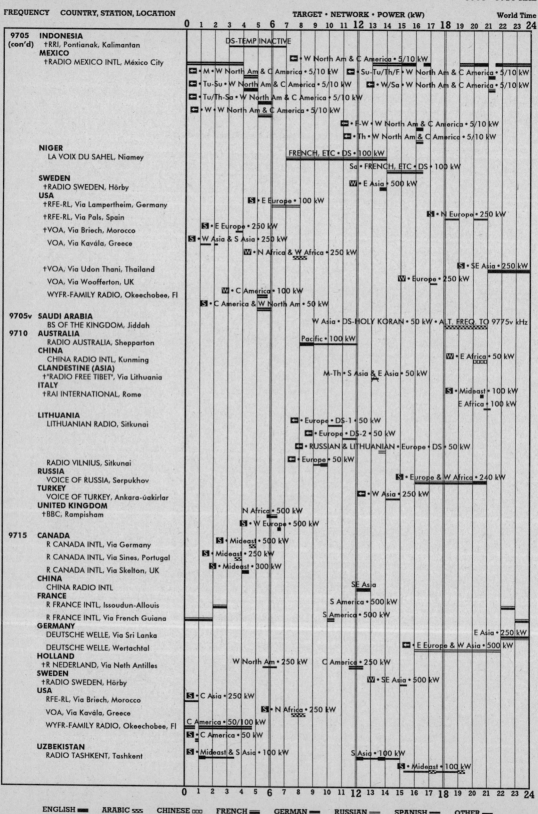

FREQUENCY	COUNTRY, STATION, LOCATION	TARGET • NETWORK • POWER (kW)
9705 (con'd)	**INDONESIA**	
	†RRI, Pontianak, Kalimantan	DS-TEMP INACTIVE
	MEXICO	
	†RADIO MEXICO INTL, México City	W North Am & C America • 5/10 kW
		M • W North Am & C America • 5/10 kW · Su-Tu/Th/F • W North Am & C America • 5/10 kW
		Tu-Su • W North Am & C America • 5/10 kW · W/Sa • W North Am & C America • 5/10 kW
		Tu/Th-Sa • W North Am & C America • 5/10 kW
		W • W North Am & C America • 5/10 kW
		F-W • W North Am & C America • 5/10 kW
		Th • W North Am & C America • 5/10 kW
	NIGER	
	LA VOIX DU SAHEL, Niamey	FRENCH, ETC • DS • 100 kW
		Sa • FRENCH, ETC • DS • 100 kW
	SWEDEN	
	†RADIO SWEDEN, Hörby	W • E Asia • 500 kW
	USA	
	†RFE-RL, Via Lampertheim, Germany	S • E Europe • 100 kW
	†RFE-RL, Via Pals, Spain	S • N Europe • 250 kW
	†VOA, Via Briech, Morocco	S • E Europe • 250 kW
	VOA, Via Kavála, Greece	S • W Asia & S Asia • 250 kW
		W • N Africa & W Africa • 250 kW
	†VOA, Via Udon Thani, Thailand	S • SE Asia • 250 kW
	VOA, Via Woofferton, UK	W • Europe • 250 kW
	WYFR-FAMILY RADIO, Okeechobee, Fl	W • C America • 100 kW
		S • C America & W North Am • 50 kW
9705v	**SAUDI ARABIA**	
	BS OF THE KINGDOM, Jiddah	W Asia • DS-HOLY KORAN • 50 kW • ALT. FREQ. TO 9775v kHz
9710	**AUSTRALIA**	
	RADIO AUSTRALIA, Shepparton	Pacific • 100 kW
	CHINA	
	CHINA RADIO INTL, Kunming	W • E Africa • 50 kW
	CLANDESTINE (ASIA)	
	†"RADIO FREE TIBET", Via Lithuania	M-Th • S Asia & E Asia • 50 kW
	ITALY	
	†RAI INTERNATIONAL, Rome	S • Mideast • 100 kW
		E Africa • 100 kW
	LITHUANIA	
	LITHUANIAN RADIO, Sitkunai	• Europe • DS-1 • 50 kW
		• Europe • DS-2 • 50 kW
		• RUSSIAN & LITHUANIAN • Europe • DS • 50 kW
	RADIO VILNIUS, Sitkunai	• Europe • 50 kW
	RUSSIA	
	VOICE OF RUSSIA, Serpukhov	S • Europe & W Africa • 240 kW
	TURKEY	
	VOICE OF TURKEY, Ankara-úakirlar	• W Asia • 250 kW
	UNITED KINGDOM	
	†BBC, Rampisham	N Africa • 500 kW
		S • W Europe • 500 kW
9715	**CANADA**	
	R CANADA INTL, Via Germany	S • Mideast • 500 kW
	R CANADA INTL, Via Sines, Portugal	S • Mideast • 250 kW
	R CANADA INTL, Via Skelton, UK	S • Mideast • 300 kW
	CHINA	
	CHINA RADIO INTL	SE Asia
	FRANCE	
	R FRANCE INTL, Issoudun-Allouis	S America • 500 kW
	R FRANCE INTL, Via French Guiana	S America • 500 kW
	GERMANY	
	DEUTSCHE WELLE, Via Sri Lanka	E Asia • 250 kW
	DEUTSCHE WELLE, Wertachtal	• E Europe & W Asia • 500 kW
	HOLLAND	
	†R NEDERLAND, Via Neth Antilles	W North Am • 250 kW · C America • 250 kW
	SWEDEN	
	†RADIO SWEDEN, Hörby	W • SE Asia • 500 kW
	USA	
	RFE-RL, Via Briech, Morocco	S • C Asia • 250 kW
	VOA, Via Kavála, Greece	S • N Africa • 250 kW
	WYFR-FAMILY RADIO, Okeechobee, Fl	C America • 50/100 kW
		S • C America • 50 kW
	UZBEKISTAN	
	RADIO TASHKENT, Tashkent	S • Mideast & S Asia • 100 kW · S Asia • 100 kW
		S • Mideast • 100 kW

ENGLISH ▬   ARABIC ⌇⌇⌇   CHINESE □□□   FRENCH ═══   GERMAN ▬▬   RUSSIAN ══   SPANISH ▬▬   OTHER ▬

FREQUENCY   COUNTRY, STATION, LOCATION   TARGET • NETWORK • POWER (kW)   World Time

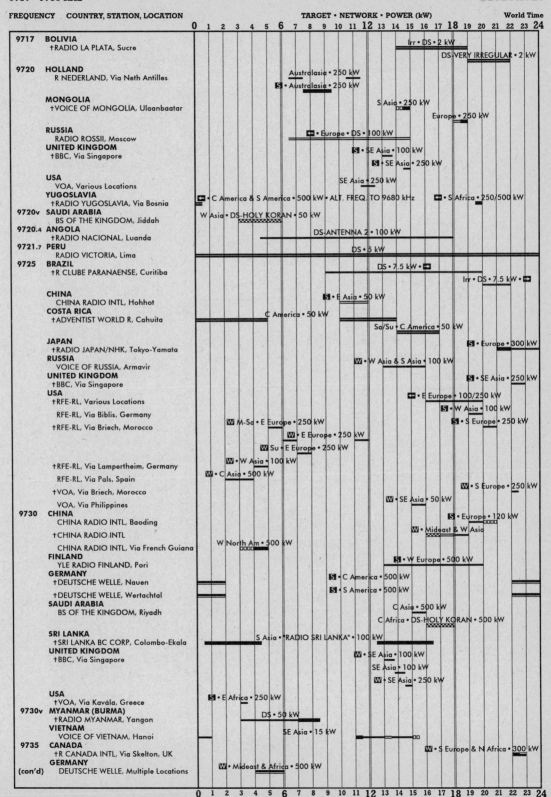

Frequency	Country / Station / Location	Target • Network • Power
9717	**BOLIVIA**	
	†RADIO LA PLATA, Sucre	Irr • DS • 2 kW
		DS • VERY IRREGULAR • 2 kW
9720	**HOLLAND**	
	R NEDERLAND, Via Neth Antilles	Australasia • 250 kW
		[S] • Australasia • 250 kW
	MONGOLIA	
	†VOICE OF MONGOLIA, Ulaanbaatar	S Asia • 250 kW
		Europe • 250 kW
	RUSSIA	
	RADIO ROSSII, Moscow	⬌ • Europe • DS • 100 kW
	UNITED KINGDOM	
	†BBC, Via Singapore	[S] • SE Asia • 100 kW
		[S] • SE Asia • 250 kW
	USA	
	VOA, Various Locations	SE Asia • 250 kW
	YUGOSLAVIA	
	†RADIO YUGOSLAVIA, Via Bosnia	◀ • C America & S America • 500 kW • ALT. FREQ. TO 9680 kHz ◀ • S Africa • 250/500 kW
9720v	**SAUDI ARABIA**	
	BS OF THE KINGDOM, Jiddah	W Asia • DS-HOLY KORAN • 50 kW
9720.4	**ANGOLA**	
	†RADIO NACIONAL, Luanda	DS-ANTENNA 2 • 100 kW
9721.7	**PERU**	
	RADIO VICTORIA, Lima	DS • 5 kW
9725	**BRAZIL**	
	†R CLUBE PARANAENSE, Curitiba	DS • 7.5 kW • ⬌
		Irr • DS • 7.5 kW • ⬌
	CHINA	
	CHINA RADIO INTL, Hohhot	[S] • E Asia • 50 kW
	COSTA RICA	
	†ADVENTIST WORLD R, Cahuita	C America • 50 kW
		Sa/Su • C America • 50 kW
	JAPAN	
	†RADIO JAPAN/NHK, Tokyo-Yamata	[S] • Europe • 300 kW
	RUSSIA	
	VOICE OF RUSSIA, Armavir	[W] • W Asia & S Asia • 100 kW
	UNITED KINGDOM	
	†BBC, Via Singapore	[S] • SE Asia • 250 kW
	USA	
	†RFE-RL, Various Locations	⬌ • E Europe • 100/250 kW
	RFE-RL, Via Biblis, Germany	[S] • W Asia • 100 kW
	†RFE-RL, Via Briech, Morocco	[W] M-Sa • E Europe • 250 kW [S] • S Europe • 250 kW
		[W] • E Europe • 250 kW
		[W] Su • E Europe • 250 kW
	†RFE-RL, Via Lampertheim, Germany	[W] • W Asia • 100 kW
	RFE-RL, Via Pals, Spain	[W] • C Asia • 500 kW
		[W] • S Europe • 250 kW
	†VOA, Via Briech, Morocco	[W] • SE Asia • 50 kW
	VOA, Via Philippines	
9730	**CHINA**	
	CHINA RADIO INTL, Baoding	[S] • Europe • 120 kW
	†CHINA RADIO INTL	[W] • Mideast & W Asia
	CHINA RADIO INTL, Via French Guiana	W North Am • 500 kW
	FINLAND	
	YLE RADIO FINLAND, Pori	[S] • W Europe • 500 kW
	GERMANY	
	†DEUTSCHE WELLE, Nauen	[S] • C America • 500 kW
	†DEUTSCHE WELLE, Wertachtal	[S] • S America • 500 kW
	SAUDI ARABIA	
	BS OF THE KINGDOM, Riyadh	C Asia • 500 kW
		C Africa • DS-HOLY KORAN • 500 kW
	SRI LANKA	
	†SRI LANKA BC CORP, Colombo-Ekala	S Asia • "RADIO SRI LANKA" • 100 kW
	UNITED KINGDOM	
	†BBC, Via Singapore	[W] • SE Asia • 100 kW
		SE Asia • 100 kW
		[W] • SE Asia • 250 kW
	USA	
	†VOA, Via Kavála, Greece	[S] • E Africa • 250 kW
9730v	**MYANMAR (BURMA)**	
	†RADIO MYANMAR, Yangon	DS • 50 kW
	VIETNAM	
	VOICE OF VIETNAM, Hanoi	SE Asia • 15 kW
9735	**CANADA**	
	†R CANADA INTL, Via Skelton, UK	[W] • S Europe & N Africa • 300 kW
	GERMANY	
(con'd)	DEUTSCHE WELLE, Multiple Locations	[W] • Mideast & Africa • 500 kW

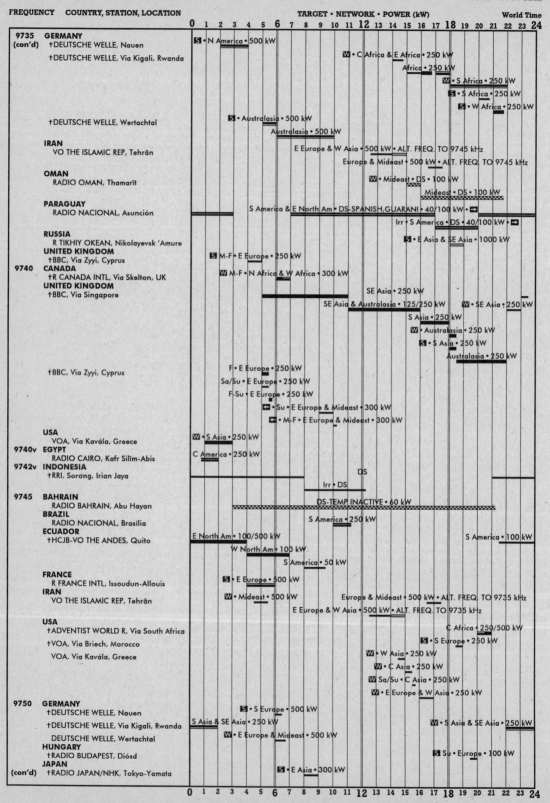

FREQUENCY   COUNTRY, STATION, LOCATION   TARGET • NETWORK • POWER (kW)   World Time

9735 (con'd)	GERMANY	
	†DEUTSCHE WELLE, Nauen	S • N America • 500 kW
	†DEUTSCHE WELLE, Via Kigali, Rwanda	W • C Africa & E Africa • 250 kW / Africa • 250 kW / W • S Africa • 250 kW / S • S Africa • 250 kW / S • W Africa • 250 kW
	†DEUTSCHE WELLE, Wertachtal	S • Australasia • 500 kW / Australasia • 500 kW
	IRAN	
	VO THE ISLAMIC REP, Tehrān	E Europe & W Asia • 500 kW • ALT. FREQ. TO 9745 kHz / Europe & Mideast • 500 kW • ALT. FREQ. TO 9745 kHz
	OMAN	
	RADIO OMAN, Thamarīt	W • Mideast • DS • 100 kW / Mideast • DS • 100 kW
	PARAGUAY	
	RADIO NACIONAL, Asunción	S America & E North Am • DS-SPANISH, GUARANI • 40/100 kW • ⇨ / Irr • S America • DS • 40/100 kW • ⇨
	RUSSIA	
	R TIKHIY OKEAN, Nikolayevsk 'Amure	S • E Asia & SE Asia • 1000 kW
	UNITED KINGDOM	
	†BBC, Via Zyyi, Cyprus	S • M-F • E Europe • 250 kW
9740	CANADA	
	†R CANADA INTL, Via Skelton, UK	W • M-F • N Africa & W Africa • 300 kW
	UNITED KINGDOM	
	†BBC, Via Singapore	SE Asia • 250 kW / SE Asia & Australasia • 125/250 kW / W • SE Asia • 250 kW / S Asia • 250 kW / W • Australasia • 250 kW / S • S Asia • 250 kW / Australasia • 250 kW
	†BBC, Via Zyyi, Cyprus	F • E Europe • 250 kW / Sa/Su • E Europe • 250 kW / F-Su • E Europe • 250 kW / ⇨ • Su • E Europe & Mideast • 300 kW / ⇨ • M-F • E Europe & Mideast • 300 kW
	USA	
	VOA, Via Kavála, Greece	W • S Asia • 250 kW
9740v	EGYPT	
	RADIO CAIRO, Kafr Silīm-Abis	C America • 250 kW
9742v	INDONESIA	
	†RRI, Sorong, Irian Jaya	DS / Irr • DS
9745	BAHRAIN	
	RADIO BAHRAIN, Abu Hayan	DS-TEMP INACTIVE • 60 kW
	BRAZIL	
	RADIO NACIONAL, Brasília	S America • 250 kW
	ECUADOR	
	†HCJB-VO THE ANDES, Quito	E North Am • 100/500 kW / S America • 100 kW / W North Am • 100 kW / S America • 50 kW
	FRANCE	
	R FRANCE INTL, Issoudun-Allouis	S • E Europe • 500 kW
	IRAN	
	VO THE ISLAMIC REP, Tehrān	W • Mideast • 500 kW / Europe & Mideast • 500 kW • ALT. FREQ. TO 9735 kHz / E Europe & W Asia • 500 kW • ALT. FREQ. TO 9735 kHz
	USA	
	†ADVENTIST WORLD R, Via South Africa	C Africa • 250/500 kW
	†VOA, Via Briech, Morocco	S • S Europe • 250 kW
	VOA, Via Kavála, Greece	W • W Asia • 250 kW / W • C Asia • 250 kW / W • Sa/Su • C Asia • 250 kW / S • E Europe & W Asia • 250 kW
9750	GERMANY	
	†DEUTSCHE WELLE, Nauen	S • S Europe • 500 kW
	†DEUTSCHE WELLE, Via Kigali, Rwanda	S Asia & SE Asia • 250 kW / W • S Asia & SE Asia • 250 kW
	DEUTSCHE WELLE, Wertachtal	W • E Europe & Mideast • 500 kW
	HUNGARY	
	†RADIO BUDAPEST, Diósd	S • Su • Europe • 100 kW
	JAPAN	
(con'd)	†RADIO JAPAN/NHK, Tokyo-Yamata	S • E Asia • 300 kW

FREQUENCY   COUNTRY, STATION, LOCATION

TARGET • NETWORK • POWER (kW)

World Time

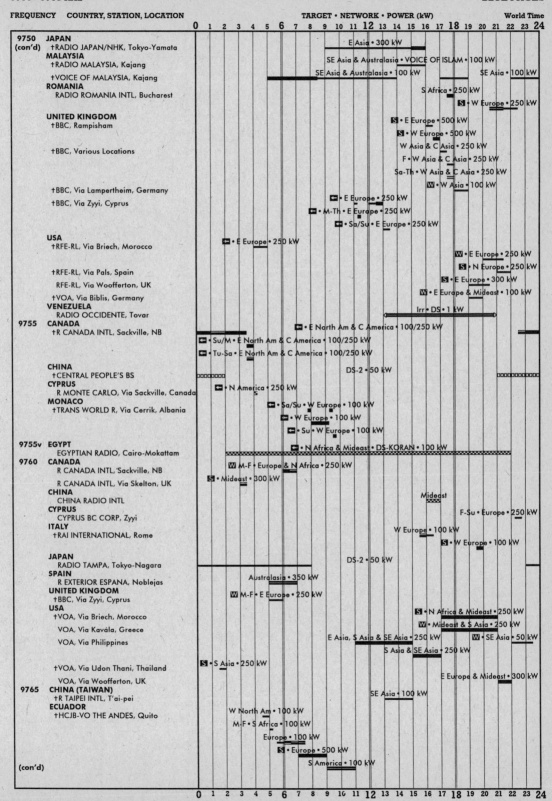

FREQUENCY	COUNTRY, STATION, LOCATION	TARGET • NETWORK • POWER (kW)
9750 (con'd)	**JAPAN** †RADIO JAPAN/NHK, Tokyo-Yamata	E Asia • 300 kW
	MALAYSIA †RADIO MALAYSIA, Kajang	SE Asia & Australasia • VOICE OF ISLAM • 100 kW
	†VOICE OF MALAYSIA, Kajang	SE Asia & Australasia • 100 kW / SE Asia • 100 kW
	ROMANIA RADIO ROMANIA INTL, Bucharest	S Africa • 250 kW / S • W Europe • 250 kW
	UNITED KINGDOM †BBC, Rampisham	S • E Europe • 500 kW / S • W Europe • 500 kW
	†BBC, Various Locations	W Asia & C Asia • 250 kW / F • W Asia & C Asia • 250 kW / Sa-Th • W Asia & C Asia • 250 kW / W • W Asia • 100 kW
	†BBC, Via Lampertheim, Germany	E Europe • 250 kW
	†BBC, Via Zyyi, Cyprus	M-Th • E Europe • 250 kW / Sa/Su • E Europe • 250 kW
	USA †RFE-RL, Via Briech, Morocco	E Europe • 250 kW
	†RFE-RL, Via Pals, Spain	W • E Europe • 250 kW / S • N Europe • 250 kW / S • E Europe • 300 kW
	RFE-RL, Via Woofferton, UK	
	†VOA, Via Biblis, Germany	W • E Europe & Mideast • 100 kW
	VENEZUELA RADIO OCCIDENTE, Tovar	Irr • DS • 1 kW
9755	**CANADA** †R CANADA INTL, Sackville, NB	E North Am & C America • 100/250 kW / Su/M • E North Am & C America • 100/250 kW / Tu-Sa • E North Am & C America • 100/250 kW
	CHINA †CENTRAL PEOPLE'S BS	DS-2 • 50 kW
	CYPRUS R MONTE CARLO, Via Sackville, Canada	N America • 250 kW
	MONACO †TRANS WORLD R, Via Cerrik, Albania	Sa/Su • W Europe • 100 kW / W Europe • 100 kW / Su • W Europe • 100 kW
9755v	**EGYPT** EGYPTIAN RADIO, Cairo-Mokattam	N Africa & Mideast • DS-KORAN • 100 kW
9760	**CANADA** R CANADA INTL, Sackville, NB	W • M-F • Europe & N Africa • 250 kW / S • Mideast • 300 kW
	R CANADA INTL, Via Skelton, UK	
	CHINA CHINA RADIO INTL	Mideast
	CYPRUS CYPRUS BC CORP, Zyyi	F-Su • Europe • 250 kW
	ITALY †RAI INTERNATIONAL, Rome	W Europe • 100 kW / S • W Europe • 100 kW
	JAPAN RADIO TAMPA, Tokyo-Nagara	DS-2 • 50 kW
	SPAIN R EXTERIOR ESPANA, Noblejas	Australasia • 350 kW
	UNITED KINGDOM †BBC, Via Zyyi, Cyprus	W • M-F • E Europe • 250 kW
	USA †VOA, Via Briech, Morocco	S • N Africa & Mideast • 250 kW / W • Mideast & S Asia • 250 kW
	VOA, Via Kavála, Greece	E Asia, S Asia & SE Asia • 250 kW / W • SE Asia • 50 kW
	VOA, Via Philippines	S Asia & SE Asia • 250 kW
	†VOA, Via Udon Thani, Thailand	S • S Asia • 250 kW
	VOA, Via Woofferton, UK	E Europe & Mideast • 300 kW
9765	**CHINA (TAIWAN)** †R TAIPEI INTL, T'ai-pei	SE Asia • 100 kW
	ECUADOR †HCJB-VO THE ANDES, Quito	W North Am • 100 kW / M-F • S Africa • 100 kW / Europe • 100 kW / S • Europe • 500 kW / S America • 100 kW
(con'd)		

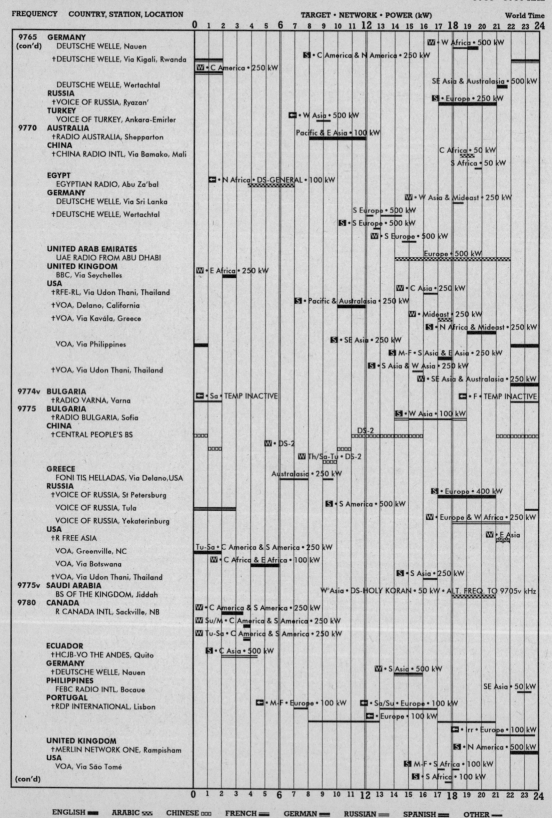

FREQUENCY	COUNTRY, STATION, LOCATION	TARGET • NETWORK • POWER (kW) — World Time
9765 (con'd)	GERMANY	
	DEUTSCHE WELLE, Nauen	W • W Africa • 500 kW
	†DEUTSCHE WELLE, Via Kigali, Rwanda	S • C America & N America • 250 kW W • C America • 250 kW
	DEUTSCHE WELLE, Wertachtal	SE Asia & Australasia • 500 kW
	RUSSIA	
	†VOICE OF RUSSIA, Ryazan'	S • Europe • 250 kW
	TURKEY	
	VOICE OF TURKEY, Ankara-Emirler	▭ • W Asia • 500 kW
9770	AUSTRALIA	
	†RADIO AUSTRALIA, Shepparton	Pacific & E Asia • 100 kW
	CHINA	
	†CHINA RADIO INTL, Via Bamako, Mali	C Africa • 50 kW S Africa • 50 kW
	EGYPT	
	EGYPTIAN RADIO, Abu Za'bal	▭ • N Africa • DS-GENERAL • 100 kW
	GERMANY	
	DEUTSCHE WELLE, Via Sri Lanka	W • W Asia & Mideast • 250 kW
	†DEUTSCHE WELLE, Wertachtal	S Europe • 500 kW S • S Europe • 500 kW W • S Europe • 500 kW
	UNITED ARAB EMIRATES	
	UAE RADIO FROM ABU DHABI	Europe • 500 kW
	UNITED KINGDOM	
	BBC, Via Seychelles	W • E Africa • 250 kW
	USA	
	†RFE-RL, Via Udon Thani, Thailand	W • C Asia • 250 kW
	†VOA, Delano, California	S • Pacific & Australasia • 250 kW
	†VOA, Via Kavála, Greece	W • Mideast • 250 kW S • N Africa & Mideast • 250 kW
	VOA, Via Philippines	S • SE Asia • 250 kW S • M-F • S Asia & E Asia • 250 kW
	†VOA, Via Udon Thani, Thailand	S • S Asia & W Asia • 250 kW W • SE Asia & Australasia • 250 kW
9774v	BULGARIA	
	†RADIO VARNA, Varna	▭ • Sa • TEMP INACTIVE ▭ • F • TEMP INACTIVE
9775	BULGARIA	
	†RADIO BULGARIA, Sofia	S • W Asia • 100 kW
	CHINA	
	†CENTRAL PEOPLE'S BS	DS-2 W • DS-2 W • Th/Sa-Tu • DS-2
	GREECE	
	FONI TIS HELLADAS, Via Delano, USA	Australasia • 250 kW
	RUSSIA	
	†VOICE OF RUSSIA, St Petersburg	S • Europe • 400 kW
	VOICE OF RUSSIA, Tula	S • S America • 500 kW
	VOICE OF RUSSIA, Yekaterinburg	W • Europe & W Africa • 250 kW
	USA	
	†R FREE ASIA	W • E Asia
	VOA, Greenville, NC	Tu-Sa • C America & S America • 250 kW
	VOA, Via Botswana	W • C Africa & E Africa • 100 kW
	†VOA, Via Udon Thani, Thailand	S • S Asia • 250 kW
9775v	SAUDI ARABIA	
	BS OF THE KINGDOM, Jiddah	W Asia • DS-HOLY KORAN • 50 kW • ALT. FREQ. TO 9705v kHz
9780	CANADA	
	R CANADA INTL, Sackville, NB	W • C America & S America • 250 kW W Su/M • C America & S America • 250 kW W Tu-Sa • C America & S America • 250 kW
	ECUADOR	
	†HCJB-VO THE ANDES, Quito	S • C Asia • 500 kW
	GERMANY	
	†DEUTSCHE WELLE, Nauen	W • S Asia • 500 kW
	PHILIPPINES	
	FEBC RADIO INTL, Bocaue	SE Asia • 50 kW
	PORTUGAL	
	†RDP INTERNATIONAL, Lisbon	▭ • M-F • Europe • 100 kW ▭ • Sa/Su • Europe • 100 kW ▭ • Europe • 100 kW ▭ • Irr • Europe • 100 kW
	UNITED KINGDOM	
	†MERLIN NETWORK ONE, Rampisham	S • N America • 500 kW
	USA	
	VOA, Via São Tomé	S • M-F • S Africa • 100 kW S • S Africa • 100 kW
(con'd)		

FREQUENCY   COUNTRY, STATION, LOCATION

TARGET • NETWORK • POWER (kW)

World Time

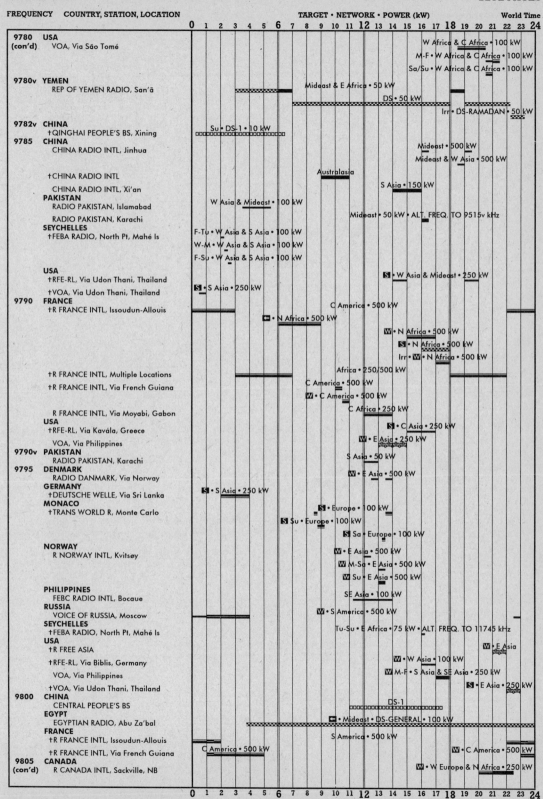

FREQUENCY	COUNTRY, STATION, LOCATION	TARGET • NETWORK • POWER (kW)
9780 (con'd)	USA VOA, Via São Tomé	W Africa & C Africa • 100 kW / M-F • W Africa & C Africa • 100 kW / Sa/Su • W Africa & C Africa • 100 kW
9780v	YEMEN REP OF YEMEN RADIO, San'ā	Mideast & E Africa • 50 kW / DS • 50 kW / Irr • DS-RAMADAN • 50 kW
9782v	CHINA †QINGHAI PEOPLE'S BS, Xining	Su • DS-1 • 10 kW
9785	CHINA CHINA RADIO INTL, Jinhua	Mideast • 500 kW / Mideast & W Asia • 500 kW
	†CHINA RADIO INTL	Australasia
	CHINA RADIO INTL, Xi'an	S Asia • 150 kW
	PAKISTAN RADIO PAKISTAN, Islamabad	W Asia & Mideast • 100 kW
	RADIO PAKISTAN, Karachi	Mideast • 50 kW • ALT. FREQ. TO 9515v kHz
	SEYCHELLES †FEBA RADIO, North Pt, Mahé Is	F-Tu • W Asia & S Asia • 100 kW / W-M • W Asia & S Asia • 100 kW / F-Su • W Asia & S Asia • 100 kW
	USA †RFE-RL, Via Udon Thani, Thailand	S • W Asia & Mideast • 250 kW
	†VOA, Via Udon Thani, Thailand	S • S Asia • 250 kW
9790	FRANCE †R FRANCE INTL, Issoudun-Allouis	C America • 500 kW / N Africa • 500 kW / W • N Africa • 500 kW / S • N Africa • 500 kW / Irr • W • N Africa • 500 kW
	†R FRANCE INTL, Multiple Locations	Africa • 250/500 kW
	†R FRANCE INTL, Via French Guiana	C America • 500 kW / W • C America • 500 kW
	R FRANCE INTL, Via Moyabi, Gabon	C Africa • 250 kW
	USA †RFE-RL, Via Kavála, Greece	S • C Asia • 250 kW
	VOA, Via Philippines	W • E Asia • 250 kW
9790v	PAKISTAN RADIO PAKISTAN, Karachi	S Asia • 50 kW
9795	DENMARK RADIO DANMARK, Via Norway	W • E Asia • 500 kW
	GERMANY †DEUTSCHE WELLE, Via Sri Lanka	S • S Asia • 250 kW
	MONACO †TRANS WORLD R, Monte Carlo	S • Europe • 100 kW / Su • Europe • 100 kW / Sa • Europe • 100 kW
	NORWAY R NORWAY INTL, Kvitsøy	W • E Asia • 500 kW / W M-Sa • E Asia • 500 kW / W Su • E Asia • 500 kW
	PHILIPPINES FEBC RADIO INTL, Bocaue	SE Asia • 100 kW
	RUSSIA VOICE OF RUSSIA, Moscow	W • S America • 500 kW
	SEYCHELLES †FEBA RADIO, North Pt, Mahé Is	Tu-Su • E Africa • 75 kW • ALT. FREQ. TO 11745 kHz
	USA †R FREE ASIA	W • E Asia
	†RFE-RL, Via Biblis, Germany	W • W Asia • 100 kW
	VOA, Via Philippines	W M-F • S Asia & SE Asia • 250 kW
	†VOA, Via Udon Thani, Thailand	S • E Asia • 250 kW
9800	CHINA CENTRAL PEOPLE'S BS	DS-1
	EGYPT EGYPTIAN RADIO, Abu Za'bal	Mideast • DS-GENERAL • 100 kW
	FRANCE †R FRANCE INTL, Issoudun-Allouis	S America • 500 kW
	†R FRANCE INTL, Via French Guiana	C America • 500 kW / W • C America • 500 kW
9805 (con'd)	CANADA R CANADA INTL, Sackville, NB	W • W Europe & N Africa • 250 kW

FREQUENCY   COUNTRY, STATION, LOCATION

TARGET • NETWORK • POWER (kW)   World Time

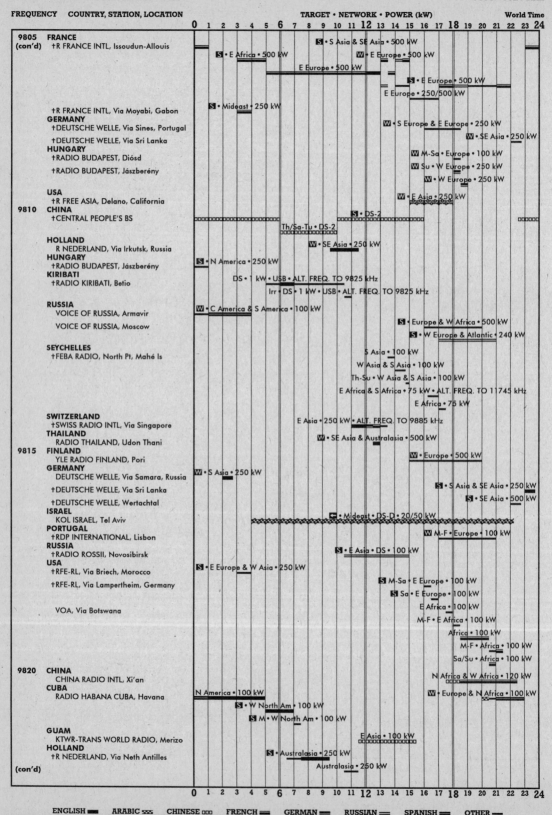

9805	FRANCE
(con'd)	†R FRANCE INTL, Issoudun-Allouis
	†R FRANCE INTL, Via Moyabi, Gabon
	GERMANY
	†DEUTSCHE WELLE, Via Sines, Portugal
	†DEUTSCHE WELLE, Via Sri Lanka
	HUNGARY
	†RADIO BUDAPEST, Diósd
	†RADIO BUDAPEST, Jászberény
	USA
	†R FREE ASIA, Delano, California
9810	CHINA
	†CENTRAL PEOPLE'S BS
	HOLLAND
	R NEDERLAND, Via Irkutsk, Russia
	HUNGARY
	†RADIO BUDAPEST, Jászberény
	KIRIBATI
	†RADIO KIRIBATI, Betio
	RUSSIA
	VOICE OF RUSSIA, Armavir
	VOICE OF RUSSIA, Moscow
	SEYCHELLES
	†FEBA RADIO, North Pt, Mahé Is
	SWITZERLAND
	†SWISS RADIO INTL, Via Singapore
	THAILAND
	RADIO THAILAND, Udon Thani
9815	FINLAND
	YLE RADIO FINLAND, Pori
	GERMANY
	DEUTSCHE WELLE, Via Samara, Russia
	†DEUTSCHE WELLE, Via Sri Lanka
	†DEUTSCHE WELLE, Wertachtal
	ISRAEL
	KOL ISRAEL, Tel Aviv
	PORTUGAL
	†RDP INTERNATIONAL, Lisbon
	RUSSIA
	†RADIO ROSSII, Novosibirsk
	USA
	†RFE-RL, Via Briech, Morocco
	†RFE-RL, Via Lampertheim, Germany
	VOA, Via Botswana
9820	CHINA
	CHINA RADIO INTL, Xi'an
	CUBA
	RADIO HABANA CUBA, Havana
	GUAM
	KTWR-TRANS WORLD RADIO, Merizo
	HOLLAND
	†R NEDERLAND, Via Neth Antilles
(con'd)	

ENGLISH ▬▬   ARABIC ⧢⧢⧢   CHINESE □□□   FRENCH ▬▬   GERMAN ▬▬   RUSSIAN ══   SPANISH ▬▬   OTHER ▬

FREQUENCY   COUNTRY, STATION, LOCATION

TARGET • NETWORK • POWER (kW)   World Time

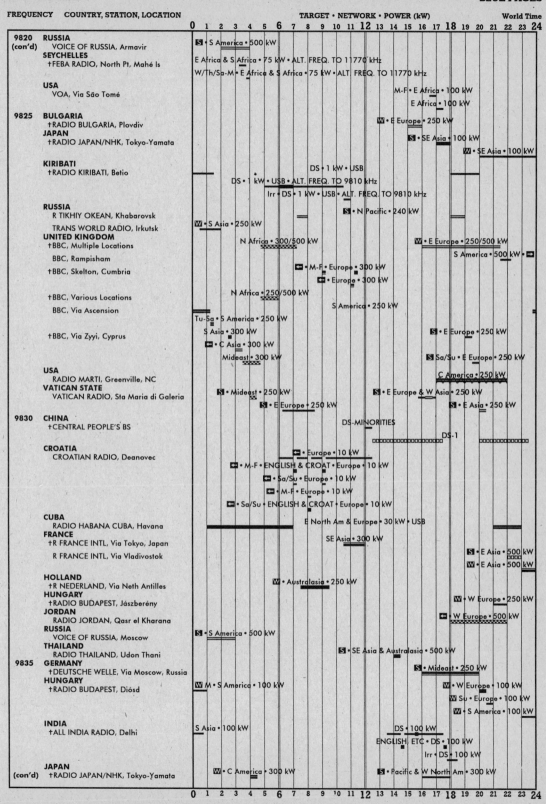

FREQUENCY	COUNTRY, STATION, LOCATION	TARGET • NETWORK • POWER (kW)
9820 (con'd)	**RUSSIA** VOICE OF RUSSIA, Armavir	S • S America • 500 kW
	SEYCHELLES †FEBA RADIO, North Pt, Mahé Is	E Africa & S Africa • 75 kW • ALT. FREQ. TO 11770 kHz / W/Th/Sa–M • E Africa & S Africa • 75 kW • ALT. FREQ. TO 11770 kHz
	USA VOA, Via São Tomé	M–F • E Africa • 100 kW / E Africa • 100 kW
9825	**BULGARIA** †RADIO BULGARIA, Plovdiv	W • E Europe • 250 kW
	JAPAN †RADIO JAPAN/NHK, Tokyo-Yamata	S • SE Asia • 100 kW / W • SE Asia • 100 kW
	KIRIBATI †RADIO KIRIBATI, Betio	DS • 1 kW • USB / DS • 1 kW • USB • ALT. FREQ. TO 9810 kHz / Irr • DS • 1 kW • USB • ALT. FREQ. TO 9810 kHz
	RUSSIA R TIKHIY OKEAN, Khabarovsk	S • N Pacific • 240 kW
	TRANS WORLD RADIO, Irkutsk	W • S Asia • 250 kW
	UNITED KINGDOM †BBC, Multiple Locations	N Africa • 300/500 kW / W • E Europe • 250/500 kW
	BBC, Rampisham	S America • 500 kW • →
	†BBC, Skelton, Cumbria	M–F • Europe • 300 kW / Europe • 300 kW
	†BBC, Various Locations	N Africa • 250/500 kW
	BBC, Via Ascension	S America • 250 kW / Tu–Sa • S America • 250 kW
	†BBC, Via Zyyi, Cyprus	S Asia • 300 kW / S • E Europe • 250 kW / C Asia • 300 kW / Sa/Su • E Europe • 250 kW / Mideast • 300 kW
	USA RADIO MARTI, Greenville, NC	C America • 250 kW
	VATICAN STATE VATICAN RADIO, Sta Maria di Galeria	S • Mideast • 250 kW / S • E Europe & W Asia • 250 kW / S • E Europe • 250 kW / S • E Asia • 250 kW
9830	**CHINA** †CENTRAL PEOPLE'S BS	DS-MINORITIES / DS-1
	CROATIA CROATIAN RADIO, Deanovec	• Europe • 10 kW / M–F • ENGLISH & CROAT • Europe • 10 kW / • Sa/Su • Europe • 10 kW / M–F • Europe • 10 kW / • Sa/Su • ENGLISH & CROAT • Europe • 10 kW
	CUBA RADIO HABANA CUBA, Havana	E North Am & Europe • 30 kW • USB
	FRANCE †R FRANCE INTL, Via Tokyo, Japan	SE Asia • 300 kW
	R FRANCE INTL, Via Vladivostok	S • E Asia • 500 kW / W • E Asia • 500 kW
	HOLLAND †R NEDERLAND, Via Neth Antilles	W • Australasia • 250 kW
	HUNGARY †RADIO BUDAPEST, Jászberény	W • W Europe • 250 kW
	JORDAN RADIO JORDAN, Qasr el Kharana	W Europe • 500 kW
	RUSSIA VOICE OF RUSSIA, Moscow	S • S America • 500 kW
	THAILAND RADIO THAILAND, Udon Thani	S • SE Asia & Australasia • 500 kW
9835	**GERMANY** †DEUTSCHE WELLE, Via Moscow, Russia	S • Mideast • 250 kW
	HUNGARY †RADIO BUDAPEST, Diósd	W M • S America • 100 kW / W • W Europe • 100 kW / W Su • Europe • 100 kW / W • S America • 100 kW
	INDIA †ALL INDIA RADIO, Delhi	S Asia • 100 kW / DS • 100 kW / ENGLISH, ETC • DS • 100 kW / Irr • DS • 100 kW
	JAPAN (con'd) †RADIO JAPAN/NHK, Tokyo-Yamata	W • C America • 300 kW / S • Pacific & W North Am • 300 kW

FREQUENCY	COUNTRY, STATION, LOCATION	TARGET • NETWORK • POWER (kW)	World Time

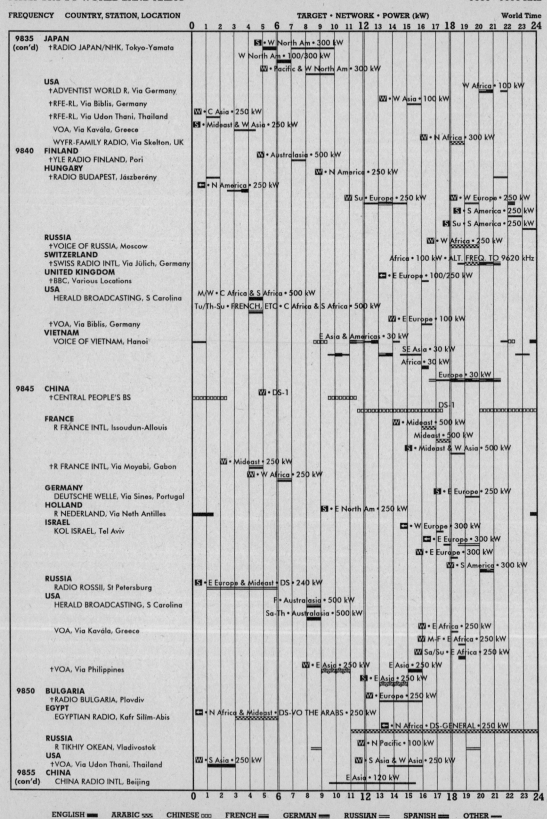

9835 JAPAN
(con'd) †RADIO JAPAN/NHK, Tokyo-Yamata
- S • W North Am • 300 kW
- W North Am • 100/300 kW
- W • Pacific & W North Am • 300 kW

USA
- †ADVENTIST WORLD R, Via Germany — W Africa • 100 kW
- †RFE-RL, Via Biblis, Germany — W • W Asia • 100 kW
- †RFE-RL, Via Udon Thani, Thailand — W • C Asia • 250 kW
- VOA, Via Kavála, Greece — S • Mideast & W Asia • 250 kW
- WYFR-FAMILY RADIO, Via Skelton, UK — W • N Africa • 300 kW

9840 FINLAND
- †YLE RADIO FINLAND, Pori — W • Australasia • 500 kW

HUNGARY
- †RADIO BUDAPEST, Jászberény
- W • N America • 250 kW
- N America • 250 kW
- W Su • Europe • 250 kW / W • W Europe • 250 kW
- S • S America • 250 kW
- S Su • S America • 250 kW

RUSSIA
- †VOICE OF RUSSIA, Moscow — W • W Africa • 250 kW

SWITZERLAND
- †SWISS RADIO INTL, Via Jülich, Germany — Africa • 100 kW • ALT. FREQ. TO 9620 kHz

UNITED KINGDOM
- †BBC, Various Locations — E Europe • 100/250 kW

USA
- HERALD BROADCASTING, S Carolina — M/W • C Africa & S Africa • 500 kW
- Tu/Th-Su • FRENCH, ETC • C Africa & S Africa • 500 kW
- †VOA, Via Biblis, Germany — W • E Europe • 100 kW

VIETNAM
- VOICE OF VIETNAM, Hanoi
- E Asia & Americas • 30 kW
- SE Asia • 30 kW
- Africa • 30 kW
- Europe • 30 kW

9845 CHINA
- †CENTRAL PEOPLE'S BS
- W • DS-1
- DS-1

FRANCE
- R FRANCE INTL, Issoudun-Allouis
- W • Mideast • 500 kW
- Mideast • 500 kW
- S • Mideast & W Asia • 500 kW
- †R FRANCE INTL, Via Moyabi, Gabon
- W • Mideast • 250 kW
- W • W Africa • 250 kW

GERMANY
- DEUTSCHE WELLE, Via Sines, Portugal — S • E Europe • 250 kW

HOLLAND
- R NEDERLAND, Via Neth Antilles — S • E North Am • 250 kW

ISRAEL
- KOL ISRAEL, Tel Aviv
- W Europe • 300 kW
- E Europe • 300 kW
- W • E Europe • 300 kW
- W • S America • 300 kW

RUSSIA
- RADIO ROSSII, St Petersburg — S • E Europe & Mideast • DS • 240 kW

USA
- HERALD BROADCASTING, S Carolina
- F • Australasia • 500 kW
- Sa-Th • Australasia • 500 kW
- VOA, Via Kavála, Greece
- W • E Africa • 250 kW
- W M-F • E Africa • 250 kW
- W Sa/Su • E Africa • 250 kW
- †VOA, Via Philippines
- W • E Asia • 250 kW / E Asia • 250 kW
- S • E Asia • 250 kW

9850 BULGARIA
- †RADIO BULGARIA, Plovdiv — W • Europe • 250 kW

EGYPT
- EGYPTIAN RADIO, Kafr Silim-Abis
- N Africa & Mideast • DS-VO THE ARABS • 250 kW
- N Africa • DS-GENERAL • 250 kW

RUSSIA
- R TIKHIY OKEAN, Vladivostok — W • N Pacific • 100 kW

USA
- †VOA, Via Udon Thani, Thailand
- W • S Asia • 250 kW
- W • S Asia & W Asia • 250 kW

9855 CHINA
(con'd) CHINA RADIO INTL, Beijing — E Asia • 120 kW

ENGLISH ▬▬ ARABIC ≈≈≈ CHINESE □□□ FRENCH ▬▬ GERMAN ▬▬ RUSSIAN ══ SPANISH ▬▬ OTHER ▬

FREQUENCY   COUNTRY, STATION, LOCATION   TARGET • NETWORK • POWER (kW)   World Time

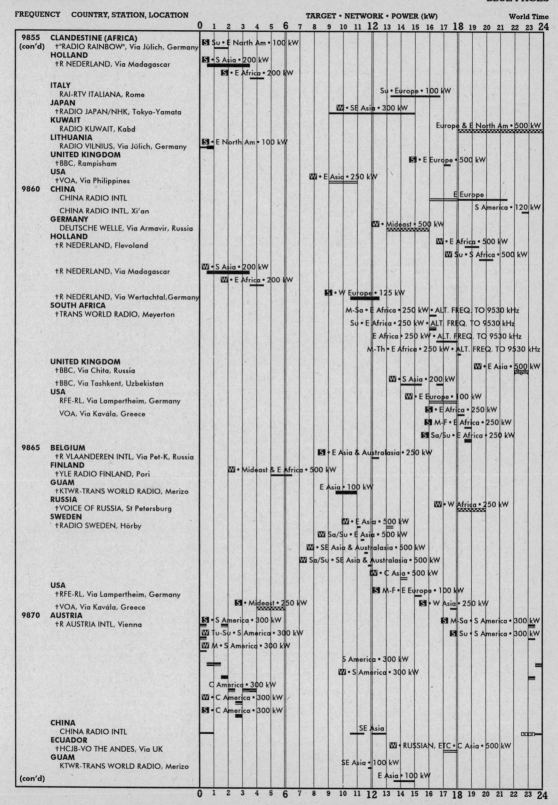

FREQUENCY	COUNTRY, STATION, LOCATION	TARGET • NETWORK • POWER (kW)
9855 (con'd)	CLANDESTINE (AFRICA)	
	†"RADIO RAINBOW", Via Jülich, Germany	⑤ Su • E North Am • 100 kW
	HOLLAND	
	†R NEDERLAND, Via Madagascar	⑤ • S Asia • 200 kW
		⑤ • E Africa • 200 kW
	ITALY	
	RAI-RTV ITALIANA, Rome	Su • Europe • 100 kW
	JAPAN	
	†RADIO JAPAN/NHK, Tokyo-Yamata	Ⓦ • SE Asia • 300 kW
	KUWAIT	
	RADIO KUWAIT, Kabd	Europe & E North Am • 500 kW
	LITHUANIA	
	RADIO VILNIUS, Via Jülich, Germany	⑤ • E North Am • 100 kW
	UNITED KINGDOM	
	†BBC, Rampisham	⑤ • E Europe • 500 kW
	USA	
	†VOA, Via Philippines	Ⓦ • E Asia • 250 kW
9860	CHINA	
	CHINA RADIO INTL	E Europe
	CHINA RADIO INTL, Xi'an	S America • 120 kW
	GERMANY	
	DEUTSCHE WELLE, Via Armavir, Russia	Ⓦ • Mideast • 500 kW
	HOLLAND	
	†R NEDERLAND, Flevoland	Ⓦ • E Africa • 500 kW
		Ⓦ Su • S Africa • 500 kW
	†R NEDERLAND, Via Madagascar	Ⓦ • S Asia • 200 kW
		Ⓦ • E Africa • 200 kW
	†R NEDERLAND, Via Wertachtal, Germany	⑤ • W Europe • 125 kW
	SOUTH AFRICA	
	†TRANS WORLD RADIO, Meyerton	M-Sa • E Africa • 250 kW • ALT. FREQ. TO 9530 kHz
		Su • E Africa • 250 kW • ALT. FREQ. TO 9530 kHz
		E Africa • 250 kW • ALT. FREQ. TO 9530 kHz
		M-Th • E Africa • 250 kW • ALT. FREQ. TO 9530 kHz
	UNITED KINGDOM	
	†BBC, Via Chita, Russia	Ⓦ • E Asia • 500 kW
	†BBC, Via Tashkent, Uzbekistan	Ⓦ • S Asia • 200 kW
	USA	
	RFE-RL, Via Lampertheim, Germany	Ⓦ • E Europe • 100 kW
	VOA, Via Kavála, Greece	⑤ • E Africa • 250 kW
		⑤ M-F • E Africa • 250 kW
		⑤ Sa/Su • E Africa • 250 kW
9865	BELGIUM	
	†R VLAANDEREN INTL, Via Pet-K, Russia	⑤ • E Asia & Australasia • 250 kW
	FINLAND	
	†YLE RADIO FINLAND, Pori	Ⓦ • Mideast & E Africa • 500 kW
	GUAM	
	†KTWR-TRANS WORLD RADIO, Merizo	E Asia • 100 kW
	RUSSIA	
	†VOICE OF RUSSIA, St Petersburg	Ⓦ • W Africa • 250 kW
	SWEDEN	
	†RADIO SWEDEN, Hörby	Ⓦ • E Asia • 500 kW
		Ⓦ Sa/Su • E Asia • 500 kW
		Ⓦ • SE Asia & Australasia • 500 kW
		Ⓦ Sa/Su • SE Asia & Australasia • 500 kW
		Ⓦ • C Asia • 500 kW
	USA	
	†RFE-RL, Via Lampertheim, Germany	⑤ M-F • E Europe • 100 kW
	†VOA, Via Kavála, Greece	⑤ • W Asia • 250 kW
9870	AUSTRIA	
	†R AUSTRIA INTL, Vienna	⑤ • Mideast • 250 kW
		⑤ • S America • 300 kW
		Ⓦ Tu-Su • S America • 300 kW
		Ⓦ M • S America • 300 kW
		⑤ M-Sa • S America • 300 kW
		⑤ Su • S America • 300 kW
		S America • 300 kW
		Ⓦ • S America • 300 kW
		C America • 300 kW
		Ⓦ • C America • 300 kW
		⑤ • C America • 300 kW
	CHINA	
	CHINA RADIO INTL	SE Asia
	ECUADOR	
	†HCJB-VO THE ANDES, Via UK	Ⓦ • RUSSIAN, ETC • C Asia • 500 kW
	GUAM	
	KTWR-TRANS WORLD RADIO, Merizo	SE Asia • 100 kW
(con'd)		E Asia • 100 kW

SEASONAL ⑤ OR Ⓦ   1-HR TIMESHIFT MIDYEAR ⊡ OR ⊡   JAMMING / OR ∧   EARLIEST HEARD ◁   LATEST HEARD ▷   NEW FOR 1999 †

FREQUENCY   COUNTRY, STATION, LOCATION

TARGET • NETWORK • POWER (kW)

World Time

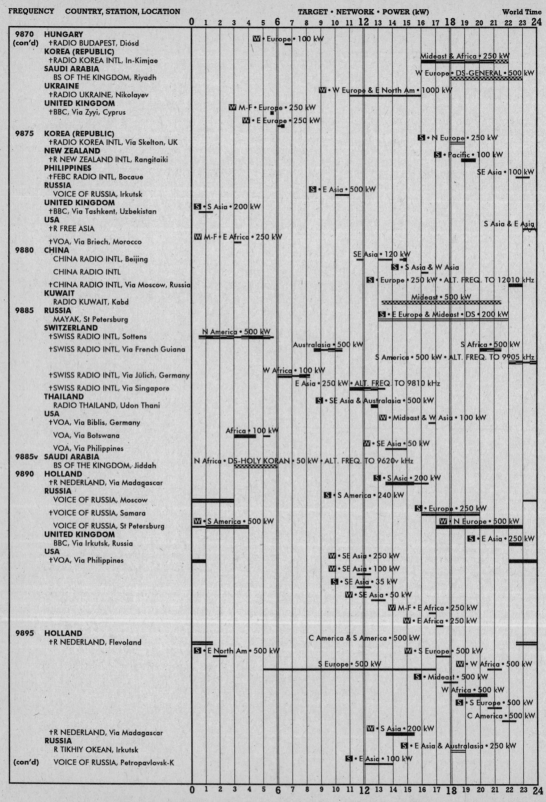

FREQUENCY	COUNTRY, STATION, LOCATION	TARGET • NETWORK • POWER (kW)
9870 (con'd)	**HUNGARY** †RADIO BUDAPEST, Diósd	W • Europe • 100 kW
	KOREA (REPUBLIC) †RADIO KOREA INTL, In-Kimjae	Mideast & Africa • 250 kW
	SAUDI ARABIA BS OF THE KINGDOM, Riyadh	W Europe • DS-GENERAL • 500 kW
	UKRAINE †RADIO UKRAINE, Nikolayev	W • W Europe & E North Am • 1000 kW
	UNITED KINGDOM †BBC, Via Zyyi, Cyprus	W • M-F • Europe • 250 kW
		W • E Europe • 250 kW
9875	**KOREA (REPUBLIC)** †RADIO KOREA INTL, Via Skelton, UK	S • N Europe • 250 kW
	NEW ZEALAND †R NEW ZEALAND INTL, Rangitaiki	S • Pacific • 100 kW
	PHILIPPINES †FEBC RADIO INTL, Bocaue	SE Asia • 100 kW
	RUSSIA VOICE OF RUSSIA, Irkutsk	S • E Asia • 500 kW
	UNITED KINGDOM †BBC, Via Tashkent, Uzbekistan	S • S Asia • 200 kW
	USA †R FREE ASIA	S Asia & E Asia
	†VOA, Via Briech, Morocco	W • M-F • E Africa • 250 kW
9880	**CHINA** CHINA RADIO INTL, Beijing	SE Asia • 120 kW
	CHINA RADIO INTL	S • S Asia & W Asia
	†CHINA RADIO INTL, Via Moscow, Russia	S • Europe • 250 kW • ALT. FREQ. TO 12010 kHz
	KUWAIT RADIO KUWAIT, Kabd	Mideast • 500 kW
9885	**RUSSIA** MAYAK, St Petersburg	S • E Europe & Mideast • DS • 200 kW
	SWITZERLAND †SWISS RADIO INTL, Sottens	N America • 500 kW
	†SWISS RADIO INTL, Via French Guiana	Australasia • 500 kW S Africa • 500 kW
		S America • 500 kW • ALT. FREQ. TO 9905 kHz
	†SWISS RADIO INTL, Via Jülich, Germany	W Africa • 100 kW
	†SWISS RADIO INTL, Via Singapore	E Asia • 250 kW • ALT. FREQ. TO 9810 kHz
	THAILAND RADIO THAILAND, Udon Thani	S • SE Asia & Australasia • 500 kW
	USA †VOA, Via Biblis, Germany	W • Mideast & W Asia • 100 kW
	VOA, Via Botswana	Africa • 100 kW
	VOA, Via Philippines	W • SE Asia • 50 kW
9885v	**SAUDI ARABIA** BS OF THE KINGDOM, Jiddah	N Africa • DS-HOLY KORAN • 50 kW • ALT. FREQ. TO 9620v kHz
9890	**HOLLAND** †R NEDERLAND, Via Madagascar	S • S Asia • 200 kW
	RUSSIA VOICE OF RUSSIA, Moscow	S • S America • 240 kW
	†VOICE OF RUSSIA, Samara	S • Europe • 250 kW
	VOICE OF RUSSIA, St Petersburg	W • S America • 500 kW W • N Europe • 500 kW
	UNITED KINGDOM BBC, Via Irkutsk, Russia	S • E Asia • 250 kW
	USA †VOA, Via Philippines	W • SE Asia • 250 kW
		W • SE Asia • 100 kW
		S • SE Asia • 35 kW
		W • SE Asia • 50 kW
		W • M-F • E Africa • 250 kW
		W • E Africa • 250 kW
9895	**HOLLAND** †R NEDERLAND, Flevoland	C America & S America • 500 kW
		S • E North Am • 500 kW W • S Europe • 500 kW
		S Europe • 500 kW W • W Africa • 500 kW
		S • Mideast • 500 kW
		W Africa • 500 kW
		S • S Europe • 500 kW
		C America • 500 kW
	†R NEDERLAND, Via Madagascar	W • S Asia • 200 kW
	RUSSIA R TIKHIY OKEAN, Irkutsk	S • E Asia & Australasia • 250 kW
(con'd)	VOICE OF RUSSIA, Petropavlovsk-K	S • E Asia • 100 kW

FREQUENCY	COUNTRY, STATION, LOCATION	TARGET • NETWORK • POWER (kW)	World Time

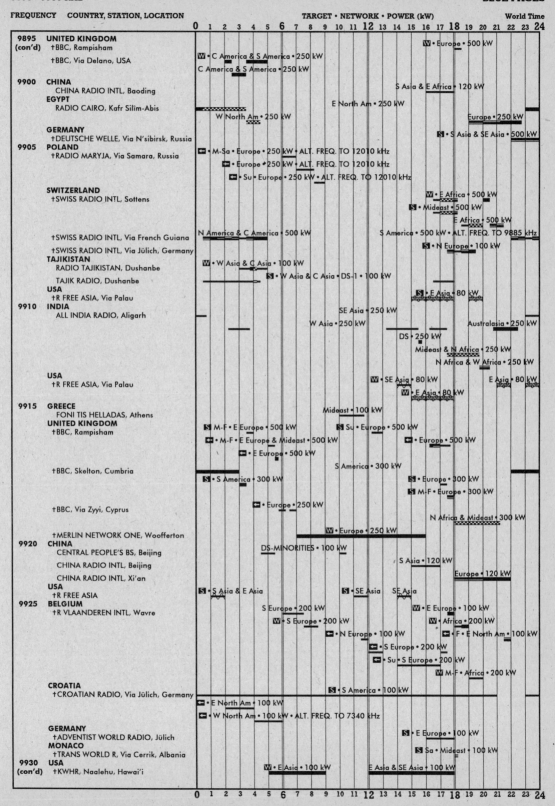

9895
(con'd) UNITED KINGDOM
         †BBC, Rampisham — W • Europe • 500 kW
         †BBC, Via Delano, USA — W • C America & S America • 250 kW
                                 C America & S America • 250 kW

9900   CHINA
         CHINA RADIO INTL, Baoding — S Asia & E Africa • 120 kW
         EGYPT
         RADIO CAIRO, Kafr Silim-Abis — E North Am • 250 kW
                                        W North Am • 250 kW
                                        Europe • 250 kW

         GERMANY
         †DEUTSCHE WELLE, Via N'sibirsk, Russia — S • S Asia & SE Asia • 500 kW
9905   POLAND
         †RADIO MARYJA, Via Samara, Russia — • M-Sa • Europe • 250 kW • ALT. FREQ. TO 12010 kHz
                                             • Europe • 250 kW • ALT. FREQ. TO 12010 kHz
                                             • Su • Europe • 250 kW • ALT. FREQ. TO 12010 kHz

         SWITZERLAND
         †SWISS RADIO INTL, Sottens — W • E Africa • 500 kW
                                       S • Mideast • 500 kW
                                       E Africa • 500 kW

         †SWISS RADIO INTL, Via French Guiana — N America & C America • 500 kW   S America • 500 kW • ALT. FREQ. TO 9885 kHz
         †SWISS RADIO INTL, Via Jülich, Germany — S • N Europe • 100 kW
         TAJIKISTAN
         RADIO TAJIKISTAN, Dushanbe — W • W Asia & C Asia • 100 kW
         TAJIK RADIO, Dushanbe — S • W Asia & C Asia • DS-1 • 100 kW
         USA
         †R FREE ASIA, Via Palau — S • E Asia • 80 kW
9910   INDIA
         ALL INDIA RADIO, Aligarh — SE Asia • 250 kW
                                    W Asia • 250 kW   Australasia • 250 kW
                                    DS • 250 kW
                                    Mideast & N Africa • 250 kW
                                    N Africa & W Africa • 250 kW

         USA
         †R FREE ASIA, Via Palau — W • SE Asia • 80 kW   E Asia • 80 kW
                                    W • E Asia • 80 kW

9915   GREECE
         FONI TIS HELLADAS, Athens — Mideast • 100 kW
         UNITED KINGDOM
         †BBC, Rampisham — S • M-F • E Europe • 500 kW   S • Su • Europe • 500 kW
                            • M-F • E Europe & Mideast • 500 kW   • Europe • 500 kW
                            • E Europe • 500 kW

         †BBC, Skelton, Cumbria — S America • 300 kW
                                  S • S America • 300 kW   S • Europe • 300 kW
                                                            M • M-F • Europe • 300 kW

         †BBC, Via Zyyi, Cyprus — • Europe • 250 kW
                                  N Africa & Mideast • 300 kW
         †MERLIN NETWORK ONE, Woofferton — W • Europe • 250 kW
9920   CHINA
         CENTRAL PEOPLE'S BS, Beijing — DS-MINORITIES • 100 kW
         CHINA RADIO INTL, Beijing — S Asia • 120 kW
         CHINA RADIO INTL, Xi'an — Europe • 120 kW
         USA
         †R FREE ASIA — S • S Asia & E Asia   S • SE Asia   SE Asia
9925   BELGIUM
         †R VLAANDEREN INTL, Wavre — S Europe • 200 kW   W • E Europe • 100 kW
                                     W • S Europe • 200 kW   W • Africa • 200 kW
                                     • N Europe • 100 kW   • F • E North Am • 100 kW
                                     • S Europe • 200 kW
                                     • Su • S Europe • 200 kW
                                     W M-F • Africa • 200 kW

         CROATIA
         †CROATIAN RADIO, Via Jülich, Germany — S • S America • 100 kW
                                                • E North Am • 100 kW
                                                • W North Am • 100 kW • ALT. FREQ. TO 7340 kHz

         GERMANY
         †ADVENTIST WORLD RADIO, Jülich — S • E Europe • 100 kW
         MONACO
         †TRANS WORLD R, Via Cerrik, Albania — S Sa • Mideast • 100 kW
9930   USA
(con'd) †KWHR, Naalehu, Hawai'i — W • E Asia • 100 kW   E Asia & SE Asia • 100 kW

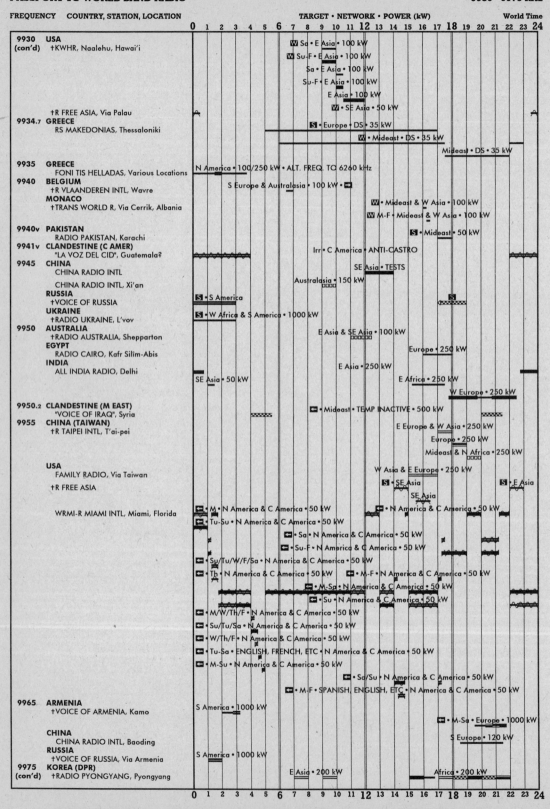

FREQUENCY   COUNTRY, STATION, LOCATION   TARGET • NETWORK • POWER (kW)   World Time

Frequency	Country, Station, Location	Details
9930 (con'd)	USA †KWHR, Naalehu, Hawai'i	W Sa • E Asia • 100 kW; W Su-F • E Asia • 100 kW; Sa • E Asia • 100 kW; Su-F • E Asia • 100 kW; E Asia • 100 kW; W • SE Asia • 50 kW
	†R FREE ASIA, Via Palau	
9934.7	GREECE RS MAKEDONIAS, Thessaloniki	S • Europe • DS • 35 kW; W • Mideast • DS • 35 kW; Mideast • DS • 35 kW
9935	GREECE FONI TIS HELLADAS, Various Locations	N America • 100/250 kW • ALT. FREQ. TO 6260 kHz
9940	BELGIUM †R VLAANDEREN INTL, Wavre	S Europe & Australasia • 100 kW •
	MONACO †TRANS WORLD R, Via Cerrik, Albania	W • Mideast & W Asia • 100 kW; W M-F • Mideast & W Asia • 100 kW
9940v	PAKISTAN RADIO PAKISTAN, Karachi	S • Mideast • 50 kW
9941v	CLANDESTINE (C AMER) "LA VOZ DEL CID", Guatemala?	Irr • C America • ANTI-CASTRO
9945	CHINA CHINA RADIO INTL	SE Asia • TESTS
	CHINA RADIO INTL, Xi'an	Australasia • 150 kW
	RUSSIA †VOICE OF RUSSIA	S • S America
	UKRAINE †RADIO UKRAINE, L'vov	S • W Africa & S America • 1000 kW
9950	AUSTRALIA †RADIO AUSTRALIA, Shepparton	E Asia & SE Asia • 100 kW
	EGYPT RADIO CAIRO, Kafr Silim-Abis	Europe • 250 kW
	INDIA ALL INDIA RADIO, Delhi	E Asia • 250 kW; SE Asia • 50 kW; E Africa • 250 kW; W Europe • 250 kW
9950.2	CLANDESTINE (M EAST) "VOICE OF IRAQ", Syria	• Mideast • TEMP INACTIVE • 500 kW
9955	CHINA (TAIWAN) †R TAIPEI INTL, T'ai-pei	E Europe & W Asia • 250 kW; Europe • 250 kW; Mideast & N Africa • 250 kW; W Asia & E Europe • 250 kW
	USA FAMILY RADIO, Via Taiwan	
	†R FREE ASIA	S • SE Asia; SE Asia; S • E Asia
	WRMI-R MIAMI INTL, Miami, Florida	• M • N America & C America • 50 kW; • Tu-Su • N America & C America • 50 kW; • Sa • N America & C America • 50 kW; • Su-F • N America & C America • 50 kW; • Su/Tu/W/F/Sa • N America & C America • 50 kW; • Th • N America & C America • 50 kW; • M-F • N America & C America • 50 kW; • M-Sa • N America & C America • 50 kW; • Su • N America & C America • 50 kW; • M/W/Th/F • N America & C America • 50 kW; • Su/Tu/Sa • N America & C America • 50 kW; • W/Th/F • N America & C America • 50 kW; • Tu-Sa • ENGLISH, FRENCH, ETC • N America & C America • 50 kW; • M-Su • N America & C America • 50 kW; • Sa/Su • N America & C America • 50 kW; • M-F • SPANISH, ENGLISH, ETC • N America & C America • 50 kW
9965	ARMENIA †VOICE OF ARMENIA, Kamo	S America • 1000 kW; • M-Sa • Europe • 1000 kW
	CHINA CHINA RADIO INTL, Baoding	S Europe • 120 kW
	RUSSIA †VOICE OF RUSSIA, Via Armenia	S America • 1000 kW
9975 (con'd)	KOREA (DPR) †RADIO PYONGYANG, Pyongyang	E Asia • 200 kW; Africa • 200 kW

ENGLISH ▬   ARABIC ⧆   CHINESE ▫▫▫   FRENCH ▭   GERMAN ═   RUSSIAN ≡   SPANISH ▭   OTHER ▬

FREQUENCY   COUNTRY, STATION, LOCATION   TARGET • NETWORK • POWER (kW)   World Time

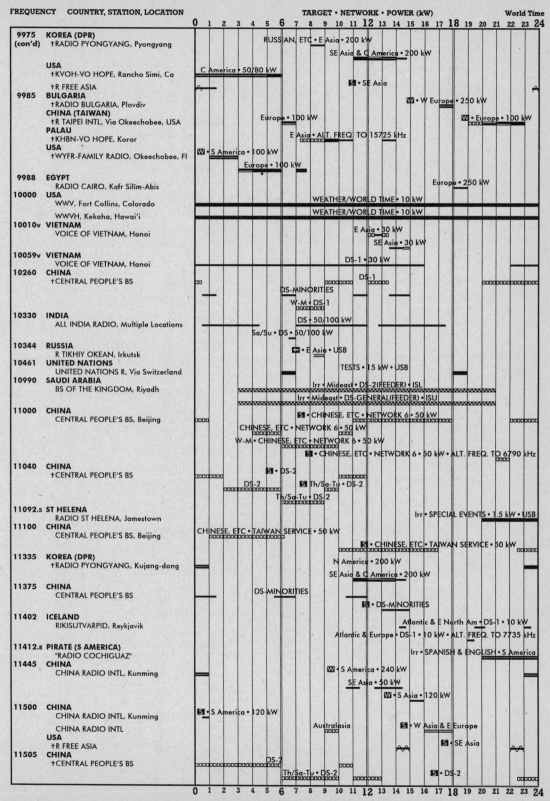

FREQUENCY	COUNTRY, STATION, LOCATION	TARGET • NETWORK • POWER (kW)
9975 (con'd)	KOREA (DPR) †RADIO PYONGYANG, Pyongyang	RUSSIAN, ETC • E Asia • 200 kW / SE Asia & C America • 200 kW
	USA †KVOH-VO HOPE, Rancho Simi, Ca	C America • 50/80 kW
	†R FREE ASIA	S • SE Asia
9985	BULGARIA †RADIO BULGARIA, Plovdiv	W • W Europe • 250 kW
	CHINA (TAIWAN) †R TAIPEI INTL, Via Okeechobee, USA	Europe • 100 kW / W • Europe • 100 kW
	PALAU †KHBN-VO HOPE, Koror	E Asia • ALT. FREQ. TO 15725 kHz
	USA †WYFR-FAMILY RADIO, Okeechobee, Fl	W • S America • 100 kW / Europe • 100 kW
9988	EGYPT RADIO CAIRO, Kafr Silim-Abis	Europe • 250 kW
10000	USA WWV, Fort Collins, Colorado	WEATHER/WORLD TIME • 10 kW
	WWVH, Kekaha, Hawai'i	WEATHER/WORLD TIME • 10 kW
10010v	VIETNAM VOICE OF VIETNAM, Hanoi	E Asia • 30 kW / SE Asia • 30 kW
10059v	VIETNAM VOICE OF VIETNAM, Hanoi	DS-1 • 30 kW
10260	CHINA †CENTRAL PEOPLE'S BS	DS-1 / DS-MINORITIES / W-M • DS-1
10330	INDIA ALL INDIA RADIO, Multiple Locations	DS • 50/100 kW / Sa/Su • DS • 50/100 kW
10344	RUSSIA R TIKHIY OKEAN, Irkutsk	• E Asia • USB
10461	UNITED NATIONS UNITED NATIONS R, Via Switzerland	TESTS • 15 kW • USB
10990	SAUDI ARABIA BS OF THE KINGDOM, Riyadh	Irr • Mideast • DS-2(FEEDER) • ISL / Irr • Mideast • DS-GENERAL(FEEDER) • ISU
11000	CHINA CENTRAL PEOPLE'S BS, Beijing	S • CHINESE, ETC • NETWORK 6 • 50 kW / CHINESE, ETC • NETWORK 6 • 50 kW / W-M • CHINESE, ETC • NETWORK 6 • 50 kW / S • CHINESE, ETC • NETWORK 6 • 50 kW • ALT. FREQ. TO 6790 kHz
11040	CHINA †CENTRAL PEOPLE'S BS	S • DS-2 / DS-2 / S • Th/Sa-Tu • DS-2 / Th/Sa-Tu • DS-2
11092.5	ST HELENA RADIO ST HELENA, Jamestown	Irr • SPECIAL EVENTS • 1.5 kW • USB
11100	CHINA CENTRAL PEOPLE'S BS, Beijing	CHINESE, ETC • TAIWAN SERVICE • 50 kW / S • CHINESE, ETC • TAIWAN SERVICE • 50 kW
11335	KOREA (DPR) †RADIO PYONGYANG, Kujang-dong	N America • 200 kW / SE Asia & C America • 200 kW
11375	CHINA CENTRAL PEOPLE'S BS	DS-MINORITIES / S • DS-MINORITIES
11402	ICELAND RIKISUTVARPID, Reykjavik	Atlantic & E North Am • DS-1 • 10 kW / Atlantic & Europe • DS-1 • 10 kW • ALT. FREQ. TO 7735 kHz
11412.8	PIRATE (S AMERICA) "RADIO COCHIGUAZ"	Irr • SPANISH & ENGLISH • S America
11445	CHINA CHINA RADIO INTL, Kunming	W • S America • 240 kW / SE Asia • 50 kW / W • S Asia • 120 kW
11500	CHINA CHINA RADIO INTL, Kunming	S • S America • 120 kW
	CHINA RADIO INTL	Australasia / S • W Asia & E Europe
	USA †R FREE ASIA	S • SE Asia
11505	CHINA †CENTRAL PEOPLE'S BS	DS-2 / Th/Sa-Tu • DS-2 / S • DS-2

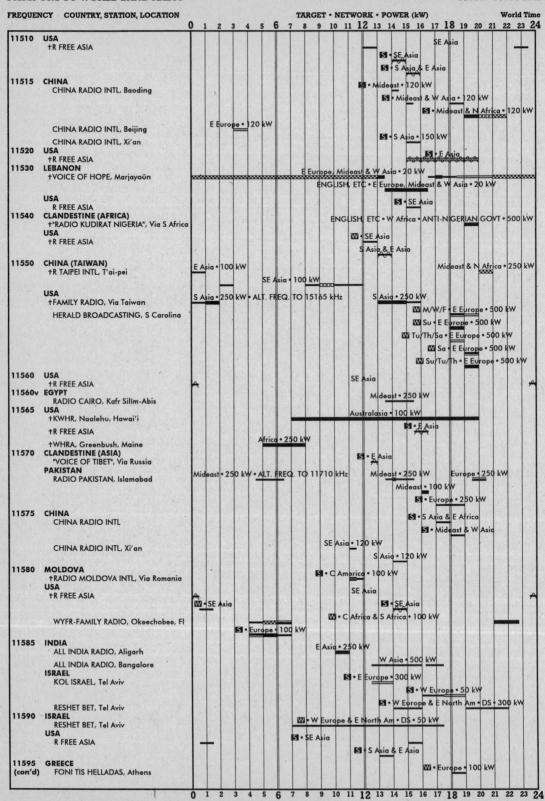

FREQUENCY COUNTRY, STATION, LOCATION

TARGET • NETWORK • POWER (kW)

World Time

FREQUENCY	COUNTRY, STATION, LOCATION
11510	USA †R FREE ASIA
11515	CHINA CHINA RADIO INTL, Baoding CHINA RADIO INTL, Beijing CHINA RADIO INTL, Xi'an
11520	USA †R FREE ASIA
11530	LEBANON †VOICE OF HOPE, Marjayoûn USA R FREE ASIA
11540	CLANDESTINE (AFRICA) †"RADIO KUDIRAT NIGERIA", Via S Africa USA †R FREE ASIA
11550	CHINA (TAIWAN) †R TAIPEI INTL, T'ai-pei USA †FAMILY RADIO, Via Taiwan HERALD BROADCASTING, S Carolina
11560	USA †R FREE ASIA
11560v	EGYPT RADIO CAIRO, Kafr Silîm-Abis
11565	USA †KWHR, Naalehu, Hawai'i †R FREE ASIA †WHRA, Greenbush, Maine
11570	CLANDESTINE (ASIA) "VOICE OF TIBET", Via Russia PAKISTAN RADIO PAKISTAN, Islamabad
11575	CHINA CHINA RADIO INTL CHINA RADIO INTL, Xi'an
11580	MOLDOVA †RADIO MOLDOVA INTL, Via Romania USA †R FREE ASIA WYFR-FAMILY RADIO, Okeechobee, Fl
11585	INDIA ALL INDIA RADIO, Aligarh ALL INDIA RADIO, Bangalore ISRAEL KOL ISRAEL, Tel Aviv RESHET BET, Tel Aviv
11590	ISRAEL RESHET BET, Tel Aviv USA R FREE ASIA
11595 (con'd)	GREECE FONI TIS HELLADAS, Athens

Target/network annotations:
- 11510 USA †R FREE ASIA: SE Asia; S • SE Asia; S • S Asia & E Asia
- 11515 CHINA RADIO INTL, Baoding: S • Mideast • 120 kW; S • Mideast & W Asia • 120 kW; S • Mideast & N Africa • 120 kW
- CHINA RADIO INTL, Beijing: E Europe • 120 kW
- CHINA RADIO INTL, Xi'an: S • S Asia • 150 kW
- 11520 USA †R FREE ASIA: S • E Asia
- 11530 LEBANON †VOICE OF HOPE, Marjayoûn: E Europe, Mideast & W Asia • 20 kW; ENGLISH, ETC • E Europe, Mideast & W Asia • 20 kW
- USA R FREE ASIA: S • SE Asia
- 11540 CLANDESTINE (AFRICA) †"RADIO KUDIRAT NIGERIA", Via S Africa: ENGLISH, ETC • W Africa • ANTI-NIGERIAN GOVT • 500 kW
- USA †R FREE ASIA: W • SE Asia; S Asia & E Asia
- 11550 CHINA (TAIWAN) †R TAIPEI INTL, T'ai-pei: E Asia • 100 kW; SE Asia • 100 kW; Mideast & N Africa • 250 kW
- USA †FAMILY RADIO, Via Taiwan: S Asia • 250 kW • ALT. FREQ. TO 15165 kHz; S Asia • 250 kW
- HERALD BROADCASTING, S Carolina: W M/W/F • E Europe • 500 kW; W Su • E Europe • 500 kW; W Tu/Th/Sa • E Europe • 500 kW; W Sa • E Europe • 500 kW; W Su/Tu/Th • E Europe • 500 kW
- 11560 USA †R FREE ASIA: SE Asia
- 11560v EGYPT RADIO CAIRO, Kafr Silîm-Abis: Mideast • 250 kW
- 11565 USA †KWHR, Naalehu, Hawai'i: Australasia • 100 kW; S • E Asia
- †WHRA, Greenbush, Maine: Africa • 250 kW
- 11570 CLANDESTINE (ASIA) "VOICE OF TIBET", Via Russia: S • E Asia
- PAKISTAN RADIO PAKISTAN, Islamabad: Mideast • 250 kW • ALT. FREQ. TO 11710 kHz; Mideast • 250 kW; Europe • 250 kW; Mideast • 100 kW; S • Europe • 250 kW
- 11575 CHINA RADIO INTL: S • S Asia & E Africa; S • Mideast & W Asia
- CHINA RADIO INTL, Xi'an: SE Asia • 120 kW; S Asia • 120 kW
- 11580 MOLDOVA †RADIO MOLDOVA INTL, Via Romania: S • C America • 100 kW
- USA †R FREE ASIA: SE Asia; W • SE Asia; S • SE Asia
- WYFR-FAMILY RADIO, Okeechobee, Fl: W • C Africa & S Africa • 100 kW; S • Europe • 100 kW
- 11585 INDIA ALL INDIA RADIO, Aligarh: E Asia • 250 kW
- ALL INDIA RADIO, Bangalore: W Asia • 500 kW
- ISRAEL KOL ISRAEL, Tel Aviv: S • E Europe • 300 kW; S • W Europe • 50 kW; S • W Europe & E North Am • DS • 300 kW
- 11590 ISRAEL RESHET BET, Tel Aviv: W • W Europe & E North Am • DS • 50 kW
- USA R FREE ASIA: S • SE Asia; S • S Asia & E Asia
- 11595 GREECE FONI TIS HELLADAS, Athens: W • Europe • 100 kW

World Time scale: 0 1 2 3 4 5 6 7 8 9 10 11 12 13 14 15 16 17 18 19 20 21 22 23 24

ENGLISH ▬ ARABIC ⬚ CHINESE ⬚ FRENCH ▬ GERMAN ▬ RUSSIAN ═ SPANISH ▬ OTHER ▬

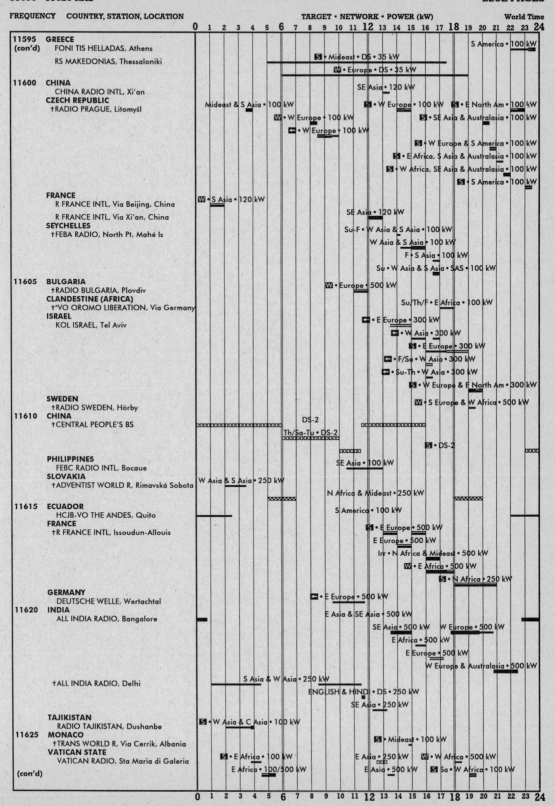

11595 **GREECE**
(con'd)   FONI TIS HELLADAS, Athens — S America • 100 kW
          RS MAKEDONIAS, Thessaloniki — S • Mideast • DS • 35 kW; W • Europe • DS • 35 kW

11600 **CHINA**
          CHINA RADIO INTL, Xi'an — SE Asia • 120 kW
          CZECH REPUBLIC
          †RADIO PRAGUE, Litomyšl — Mideast & S Asia • 100 kW; S • W Europe • 100 kW; S • E North Am • 100 kW; W • W Europe • 100 kW; ⇦ • W Europe • 100 kW; S • SE Asia & Australasia • 100 kW; S • W Europe & S America • 100 kW; S • E Africa, S Asia & Australasia • 100 kW; S • W Africa, SE Asia & Australasia • 100 kW; S • S America • 100 kW

          FRANCE
          R FRANCE INTL, Via Beijing, China — W • S Asia • 120 kW
          R FRANCE INTL, Via Xi'an, China — SE Asia • 120 kW
          SEYCHELLES
          †FEBA RADIO, North Pt, Mahé Is — Su-F • W Asia & S Asia • 100 kW; W Asia & S Asia • 100 kW; F • S Asia • 100 kW; Su • W Asia & S Asia • SAS • 100 kW

11605 **BULGARIA**
          †RADIO BULGARIA, Plovdiv — W • Europe • 500 kW
          CLANDESTINE (AFRICA)
          †"VO OROMO LIBERATION, Via Germany — Su/Th/F • E Africa • 100 kW
          ISRAEL
          KOL ISRAEL, Tel Aviv — ⇦ • E Europe • 300 kW; S • W Asia • 300 kW; S • E Europe • 300 kW; ⇦ • F/Sa • W Asia • 300 kW; ⇦ • Su-Th • W Asia • 300 kW; S • W Europe & E North Am • 300 kW; W • S Europe & W Africa • 500 kW

          SWEDEN
          †RADIO SWEDEN, Hörby
11610 **CHINA**
          †CENTRAL PEOPLE'S BS — DS-2; Th/Sa-Tu • DS-2; S • DS-2

          PHILIPPINES
          FEBC RADIO INTL, Bocaue — SE Asia • 100 kW
          SLOVAKIA
          †ADVENTIST WORLD R, Rimavská Sobota — W Asia & S Asia • 250 kW; N Africa & Mideast • 250 kW

11615 **ECUADOR**
          HCJB-VO THE ANDES, Quito — S America • 100 kW
          FRANCE
          †R FRANCE INTL, Issoudun-Allouis — S • E Europe • 500 kW; E Europe • 500 kW; Irr • N Africa & Mideast • 500 kW; W • E Africa • 500 kW; S • N Africa • 250 kW

          GERMANY
          DEUTSCHE WELLE, Wertachtal — ⇦ • E Europe • 500 kW
11620 **INDIA**
          ALL INDIA RADIO, Bangalore — E Asia & SE Asia • 500 kW; SE Asia • 500 kW; W Europe • 500 kW; E Africa • 500 kW; E Europe • 500 kW; W Europe & Australasia • 500 kW

          †ALL INDIA RADIO, Delhi — S Asia & W Asia • 250 kW; ENGLISH & HINDI • DS • 250 kW; SE Asia • 250 kW

          TAJIKISTAN
          RADIO TAJIKISTAN, Dushanbe — S • W Asia & C Asia • 100 kW
11625 **MONACO**
          †TRANS WORLD R, Via Cerrik, Albania — S • Mideast • 100 kW
          VATICAN STATE
          VATICAN RADIO, Sta Maria di Galeria — S • E Africa • 100 kW; E Asia • 250 kW; W • W Africa • 500 kW; E Africa • 100/500 kW; E Asia • 500 kW; S • Sa • W Africa • 100 kW

(con'd)

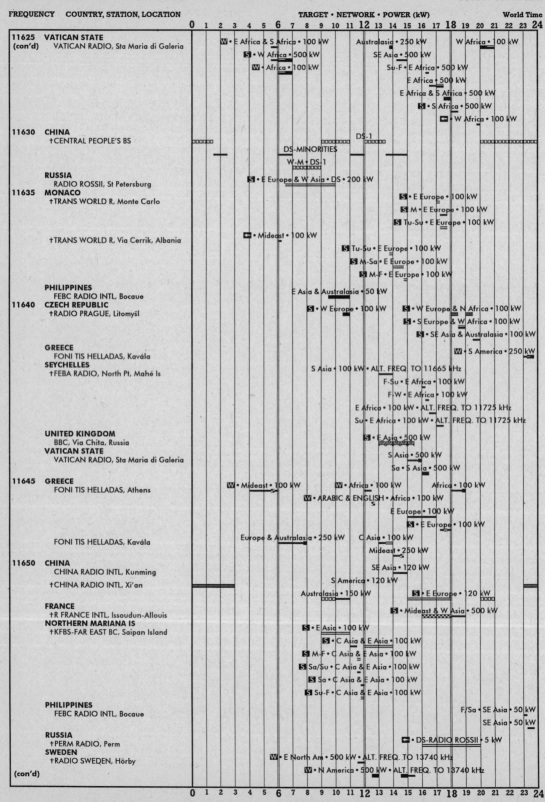

FREQUENCY   COUNTRY, STATION, LOCATION

TARGET • NETWORK • POWER (kW)   World Time

Freq	Country / Station	Details
11625 (con'd)	**VATICAN STATE** VATICAN RADIO, Sta Maria di Galeria	W • E Africa & S Africa • 100 kW; Australasia • 250 kW; W Africa • 100 kW; S • W Africa • 500 kW; SE Asia • 500 kW; W • Africa • 100 kW; Su-F • E Africa • 500 kW; E Africa • 500 kW; E Africa & S Africa • 500 kW; S • S Africa • 500 kW; W Africa • 100 kW
11630	**CHINA** †CENTRAL PEOPLE'S BS	DS-1; DS-MINORITIES; W-M • DS-1
	RUSSIA RADIO ROSSII, St Petersburg	S • E Europe & W Asia • DS • 200 kW
11635	**MONACO** †TRANS WORLD R, Monte Carlo	S • E Europe • 100 kW; S M • E Europe • 100 kW; S Tu-Su • E Europe • 100 kW
	†TRANS WORLD R, Via Cerrik, Albania	• Mideast • 100 kW; S Tu-Su • E Europe • 100 kW; S M-Sa • E Europe • 100 kW; S M-F • E Europe • 100 kW
	PHILIPPINES FEBC RADIO INTL, Bocaue	E Asia & Australasia • 50 kW
11640	**CZECH REPUBLIC** †RADIO PRAGUE, Litomyšl	S • W Europe • 100 kW; S • W Europe & N Africa • 100 kW; S • S Europe & W Africa • 100 kW; S • SE Asia & Australasia • 100 kW
	GREECE FONI TIS HELLADAS, Kavála	W • S America • 250 kW
	SEYCHELLES †FEBA RADIO, North Pt, Mahé Is	S Asia • 100 kW • ALT. FREQ. TO 11665 kHz; F-Su • E Africa • 100 kW; F-W • E Africa • 100 kW; E Africa • 100 kW • ALT. FREQ. TO 11725 kHz; Su • E Africa • 100 kW • ALT. FREQ. TO 11725 kHz
	UNITED KINGDOM BBC, Via Chita, Russia	S • E Asia • 500 kW
	VATICAN STATE VATICAN RADIO, Sta Maria di Galeria	S Asia • 500 kW; Sa • S Asia • 500 kW
11645	**GREECE** FONI TIS HELLADAS, Athens	W • Mideast • 100 kW; W • Africa • 100 kW; Africa • 100 kW; W • ARABIC & ENGLISH • Africa • 100 kW; E Europe • 100 kW; S • E Europe • 100 kW
	FONI TIS HELLADAS, Kavála	Europe & Australasia • 250 kW; C Asia • 100 kW; Mideast • 250 kW
11650	**CHINA** CHINA RADIO INTL, Kunming	SE Asia • 120 kW
	†CHINA RADIO INTL, Xi'an	S America • 120 kW; Australasia • 150 kW; S • E Europe • 120 kW
	FRANCE †R FRANCE INTL, Issoudun-Allouis	S • Mideast & W Asia • 500 kW
	NORTHERN MARIANA IS †KFBS-FAR EAST BC, Saipan Island	S • E Asia • 100 kW; S • C Asia & E Asia • 100 kW; S M-F • C Asia & E Asia • 100 kW; S Sa/Su • C Asia & E Asia • 100 kW; S Sa • C Asia & E Asia • 100 kW; S Su-F • C Asia & E Asia • 100 kW
	PHILIPPINES FEBC RADIO INTL, Bocaue	F/Sa • SE Asia • 50 kW; SE Asia • 50 kW
	RUSSIA †PERM RADIO, Perm	• DS-RADIO ROSSII • 5 kW
	SWEDEN †RADIO SWEDEN, Hörby	W • E North Am • 500 kW • ALT. FREQ. TO 13740 kHz; W • N America • 500 kW • ALT. FREQ. TO 13740 kHz
(con'd)		

ENGLISH ▬ ARABIC ⌇⌇⌇ CHINESE □□□ FRENCH ▬▬ GERMAN ▬▬ RUSSIAN ══ SPANISH ▬▬ OTHER ──

FREQUENCY   COUNTRY, STATION, LOCATION

TARGET • NETWORK • POWER (kW)

World Time

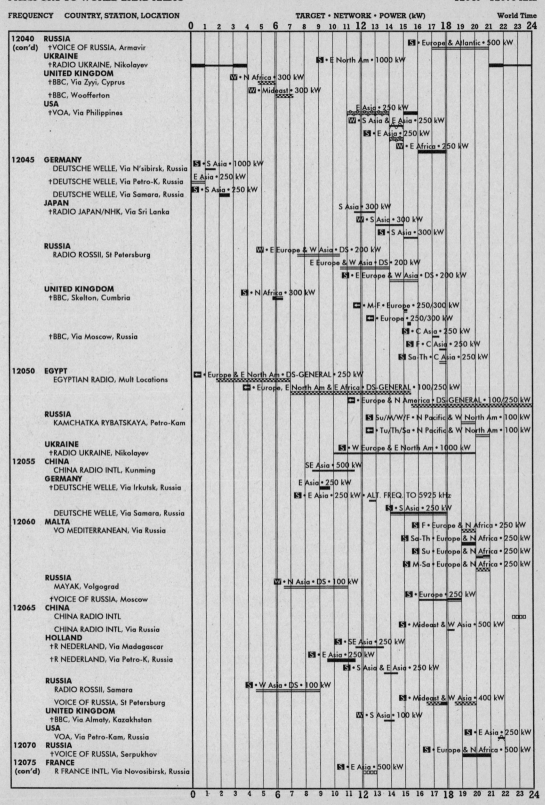

Frequency	Country, Station, Location
12040 (con'd)	**RUSSIA** †VOICE OF RUSSIA, Armavir
	UKRAINE †RADIO UKRAINE, Nikolayev
	UNITED KINGDOM †BBC, Via Zyyi, Cyprus
	†BBC, Woofferton
	USA †VOA, Via Philippines
12045	**GERMANY** DEUTSCHE WELLE, Via N'sibirsk, Russia
	†DEUTSCHE WELLE, Via Petro-K, Russia
	DEUTSCHE WELLE, Via Samara, Russia
	JAPAN †RADIO JAPAN/NHK, Via Sri Lanka
	RUSSIA RADIO ROSSII, St Petersburg
	UNITED KINGDOM †BBC, Skelton, Cumbria
	†BBC, Via Moscow, Russia
12050	**EGYPT** EGYPTIAN RADIO, Mult Locations
	RUSSIA KAMCHATKA RYBATSKAYA, Petro-Kam
	UKRAINE †RADIO UKRAINE, Nikolayev
12055	**CHINA** CHINA RADIO INTL, Kunming
	GERMANY †DEUTSCHE WELLE, Via Irkutsk, Russia
	DEUTSCHE WELLE, Via Samara, Russia
12060	**MALTA** VO MEDITERRANEAN, Via Russia
	RUSSIA MAYAK, Volgograd
	†VOICE OF RUSSIA, Moscow
12065	**CHINA** CHINA RADIO INTL
	CHINA RADIO INTL, Via Russia
	HOLLAND †R NEDERLAND, Via Madagascar
	†R NEDERLAND, Via Petro-K, Russia
	RUSSIA RADIO ROSSII, Samara
	VOICE OF RUSSIA, St Petersburg
	UNITED KINGDOM †BBC, Via Almaty, Kazakhstan
	USA VOA, Via Petro-Kam, Russia
12070	**RUSSIA** †VOICE OF RUSSIA, Serpukhov
12075 (con'd)	**FRANCE** R FRANCE INTL, Via Novosibirsk, Russia

Program listings (target • network • power):

- **12040 RUSSIA** †VOICE OF RUSSIA, Armavir: S • Europe & Atlantic • 500 kW
- **UKRAINE** †RADIO UKRAINE, Nikolayev: S • E North Am • 1000 kW
- **UNITED KINGDOM** †BBC, Via Zyyi, Cyprus: W • N Africa • 300 kW
- †BBC, Woofferton: W • Mideast • 300 kW
- **USA** †VOA, Via Philippines: E Asia • 250 kW; W • S Asia & E Asia • 250 kW; S • E Asia • 250 kW; W • E Africa • 250 kW
- **12045 GERMANY** DEUTSCHE WELLE, Via N'sibirsk: S • S Asia • 1000 kW
- †DEUTSCHE WELLE, Via Petro-K: E Asia • 250 kW
- DEUTSCHE WELLE, Via Samara: S • S Asia • 250 kW
- **JAPAN** †RADIO JAPAN/NHK: S Asia • 300 kW; W • S Asia • 300 kW; S • S Asia • 300 kW
- **RUSSIA** RADIO ROSSII, St Petersburg: W • E Europe & W Asia • DS • 200 kW; E Europe & W Asia • DS • 200 kW; S • E Europe & W Asia • DS • 200 kW
- **UNITED KINGDOM** †BBC, Skelton: S • N Africa • 300 kW
- M-F • Europe • 250/300 kW; Europe • 250/300 kW
- †BBC, Via Moscow: S • C Asia • 250 kW; F • C Asia • 250 kW; Sa-Th • C Asia • 250 kW
- **12050 EGYPT** EGYPTIAN RADIO: Europe & E North Am • DS-GENERAL • 250 kW; Europe, E North Am & E Africa • DS-GENERAL • 100/250 kW; Europe & N America • DS-GENERAL • 100/250 kW
- **RUSSIA** KAMCHATKA RYBATSKAYA: Su/M/W/F • N Pacific & W North Am • 100 kW; Tu/Th/Sa • N Pacific & W North Am • 100 kW
- **UKRAINE** †RADIO UKRAINE: S • W Europe & E North Am • 1000 kW
- **12055 CHINA** CHINA RADIO INTL, Kunming: SE Asia • 500 kW
- **GERMANY** †DEUTSCHE WELLE, Via Irkutsk: E Asia • 250 kW; S • E Asia • 250 kW • ALT. FREQ. TO 5925 kHz
- DEUTSCHE WELLE, Via Samara: S • S Asia • 250 kW
- **12060 MALTA** VO MEDITERRANEAN: S • F • Europe & N Africa • 250 kW; S • Sa-Th • Europe & N Africa • 250 kW; S • Su • Europe & N Africa • 250 kW; S • M-Sa • Europe & N Africa • 250 kW
- **RUSSIA** MAYAK, Volgograd: W • N Asia • DS • 100 kW
- †VOICE OF RUSSIA, Moscow: S • Europe • 250 kW
- **12065 CHINA** CHINA RADIO INTL
- CHINA RADIO INTL, Via Russia: S • Mideast & W Asia • 500 kW
- **HOLLAND** †R NEDERLAND, Via Madagascar: S • SE Asia • 250 kW
- †R NEDERLAND, Via Petro-K: S • E Asia • 250 kW; S • S Asia & E Asia • 250 kW
- **RUSSIA** RADIO ROSSII, Samara: S • W Asia • DS • 100 kW
- VOICE OF RUSSIA, St Petersburg: S • Mideast & W Asia • 400 kW
- **UNITED KINGDOM** †BBC, Via Almaty: W • S Asia • 100 kW
- **USA** VOA, Via Petro-Kam: S • E Asia • 250 kW
- **12070 RUSSIA** †VOICE OF RUSSIA, Serpukhov: S • Europe & N Africa • 500 kW
- **12075 FRANCE** R FRANCE INTL, Via Novosibirsk: S • E Asia • 500 kW

ENGLISH ■   ARABIC ▨   CHINESE ▫▫▫   FRENCH ═══   GERMAN ▬▬   RUSSIAN ══   SPANISH ▬▬   OTHER ▬

FREQUENCY	COUNTRY, STATION, LOCATION	TARGET • NETWORK • POWER (kW) — World Time

11670
(con'd) FRANCE
†R FRANCE INTL, Issoudun-Allouis
- S • C America • 500 kW
- E Europe • 500 kW
- C America • 500 kW
- W • E Europe • 500 kW
- S • E Europe • 500 kW

†R FRANCE INTL, Via French Guiana
- S • C America • 500 kW
- S America • 500 kW
- C America & S America • 500 kW
- W • C America • 500 kW

GUAM
†KTWR-TRANS WORLD RADIO, Merizo
- E Asia • 100 kW

USA
VOA, Via Kavála, Greece
- W • Mideast • 250 kW
- S • Mideast & N Africa • 250 kW

11675 CHINA
CHINA RADIO INTL, Xi'an
- S • S Asia • 120 kW

KUWAIT
RADIO KUWAIT, Kabd
- W North Am • 500 kW

NEW ZEALAND
†R NEW ZEALAND INTL, Rangitaiki
- W • M-F • Pacific • 100 kW

RUSSIA
VOICE OF RUSSIA, Via Moldova
- S • N Europe • 1000 kW

VOICE OF RUSSIA, Yekaterinburg
- S • E Asia • 240 kW

SEYCHELLES
FEBA RADIO, North Pt, Mahé Is
- FRENCH & CREOLE • S Africa • 75 kW

11680 BELGIUM
†R VLAANDEREN INTL, Via Germany
- W • Mideast • 100 kW

CROATIA
†CROATIAN RADIO, Via Jülich, Germany
- W • S America • 100 kW

HOLLAND
R NEDERLAND, Flevoland
- S • S America • 500 kW

UNITED KINGDOM
†BBC, Rampisham
- ⊡ • E Europe • 500 kW
- ⊡ • Su • Europe • 500 kW
- ⊡ • E Europe • 5 kW

†BBC, Various Locations
- ⊡ • E Europe • 250/500 kW
- N Africa • 300/500 kW
- Tu/F • Atlantic & S America • FALKLANDS SVC • 250/500 kW

†BBC, Via Biblis, Germany
- ⊡ • E Europe • 100 kW
- ⊡ • Sa/Su • E Europe • 100 kW

†BBC, Via Lampertheim, Germany
- S • E Europe & Mideast • 100 kW

†BBC, Via Zyyi, Cyprus
- ⊡ • M-F • S Europe • 250 kW

USA
†VOA, Via Biblis, Germany
- ⊡ • E Europe • 100 kW
- S • E Europe • 100 kW

†VOA, Via Lampertheim, Germany
- S • E Europe & Mideast • 100 kW

11680v KOREA (DPR)
KOREAN CENTRAL BS, Pyongyang
- DS • 100/200 kW

11685 CHINA
CHINA RADIO INTL, Kunming
- S • SE Asia • 120 kW
- SE Asia • 120 kW

CHINA RADIO INTL, Xi'an
- S • E Europe • 120 kW

FRANCE
R FRANCE INTL, Issoudun-Allouis
- S • Mideast • 500 kW
- W • Mideast • 500 kW

HUNGARY
†RADIO BUDAPEST, Jászberény
- S • N America • 250 kW

ISRAEL
KOL ISRAEL, Tel Aviv
- S • E Europe • 300 kW
- W • W Europe & E North Am • 300 kW

UNITED KINGDOM
†BBC, Via Singapore
- W • S Asia • 250 kW
- S Asia • 250 kW

†BBC, Via Thailand
- S Asia • 250 kW

†BBC, Via Zyyi, Cyprus
- Sa/Su • SE Asia • 250 kW

11690 CANADA
R CANADA INTL, Sackville, NB
- S • Europe • 250 kW

CHILE
†VOZ CRISTIANA, Santiago
- C America & W North Am • 100 kW

GUAM
†KTWR-TRANS WORLD RADIO, Merizo
- E Asia • 100 kW

HOLLAND
(con'd) †R NEDERLAND, Via Singapore
- SE Asia • 250 kW

ENGLISH ▬▬ ARABIC ≈≈≈ CHINESE □□□ FRENCH ▬▬ GERMAN ▬▬ RUSSIAN ══ SPANISH ▬▬ OTHER ▬▬

FREQUENCY   COUNTRY, STATION, LOCATION

TARGET • NETWORK • POWER (kW)

World Time

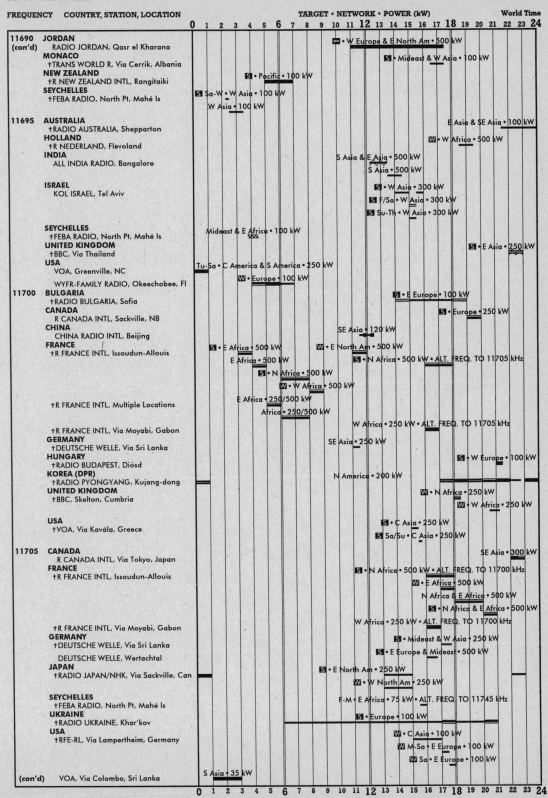

0 1 2 3 4 5 6 7 8 9 10 11 12 13 14 15 16 17 18 19 20 21 22 23 24

Frequency	Station	Target • Network • Power
11690	**JORDAN**	
(con'd)	RADIO JORDAN, Qasr el Kharana	• W Europe & E North Am • 500 kW
	MONACO	
	†TRANS WORLD R, Via Cerrik, Albania	S • Mideast & W Asia • 100 kW
	NEW ZEALAND	
	†R NEW ZEALAND INTL, Rangitaiki	S • Pacific • 100 kW
	SEYCHELLES	
	†FEBA RADIO, North Pt, Mahé Is	S • Sa-W • W Asia • 100 kW
		W Asia • 100 kW
11695	**AUSTRALIA**	
	†RADIO AUSTRALIA, Shepparton	E Asia & SE Asia • 100 kW
	HOLLAND	
	†R NEDERLAND, Flevoland	W • W Africa • 500 kW
	INDIA	
	ALL INDIA RADIO, Bangalore	S Asia & E Asia • 500 kW
		S Asia • 500 kW
	ISRAEL	
	KOL ISRAEL, Tel Aviv	S • W Asia • 300 kW
		S • F/Sa • W Asia • 300 kW
		S • Su-Th • W Asia • 300 kW
	SEYCHELLES	
	†FEBA RADIO, North Pt, Mahé Is	Mideast & E Africa • 100 kW
	UNITED KINGDOM	
	†BBC, Via Thailand	S • E Asia • 250 kW
	USA	
	VOA, Greenville, NC	Tu-Sa • C America & S America • 250 kW
	WYFR-FAMILY RADIO, Okeechobee, Fl	W • Europe • 100 kW
11700	**BULGARIA**	
	†RADIO BULGARIA, Sofia	S • E Europe • 100 kW
	CANADA	
	R CANADA INTL, Sackville, NB	S • Europe • 250 kW
	CHINA	
	CHINA RADIO INTL, Beijing	SE Asia • 120 kW
	FRANCE	
	†R FRANCE INTL, Issoudun-Allouis	S • E Africa • 500 kW
		W • E North Am • 500 kW
		E Africa • 500 kW
		S • N Africa • 500 kW • ALT. FREQ. TO 11705 kHz
		S • N Africa • 500 kW
		W • W Africa • 500 kW
	†R FRANCE INTL, Multiple Locations	E Africa • 250/500 kW
		Africa • 250/500 kW
	†R FRANCE INTL, Via Moyabi, Gabon	W Africa • 250 kW • ALT. FREQ. TO 11705 kHz
	GERMANY	
	†DEUTSCHE WELLE, Via Sri Lanka	SE Asia • 250 kW
	HUNGARY	
	†RADIO BUDAPEST, Diósd	S • W Europe • 100 kW
	KOREA (DPR)	
	†RADIO PYONGYANG, Kujang-dong	N America • 200 kW
	UNITED KINGDOM	
	†BBC, Skelton, Cumbria	W • N Africa • 250 kW
		W • W Africa • 250 kW
	USA	
	†VOA, Via Kavála, Greece	S • C Asia • 250 kW
		S • Sa/Su • C Asia • 250 kW
11705	**CANADA**	
	R CANADA INTL, Via Tokyo, Japan	SE Asia • 300 kW
	FRANCE	
	†R FRANCE INTL, Issoudun-Allouis	S • N Africa • 500 kW • ALT. FREQ. TO 11700 kHz
		W • E Africa • 500 kW
		N Africa & E Africa • 500 kW
		S • N Africa & E Africa • 500 kW
	†R FRANCE INTL, Via Moyabi, Gabon	W Africa • 250 kW • ALT. FREQ. TO 11700 kHz
	GERMANY	
	†DEUTSCHE WELLE, Via Sri Lanka	S • Mideast & W Asia • 250 kW
	DEUTSCHE WELLE, Wertachtal	S • E Europe & Mideast • 500 kW
	JAPAN	
	†RADIO JAPAN/NHK, Via Sackville, Can	S • E North Am • 250 kW
		W • W North Am • 250 kW
	SEYCHELLES	
	†FEBA RADIO, North Pt, Mahé Is	F-M • E Africa • 75 kW • ALT. FREQ. TO 11745 kHz
	UKRAINE	
	†RADIO UKRAINE, Khar'kov	S • Europe • 100 kW
	USA	
	†RFE-RL, Via Lampertheim, Germany	W • C Asia • 100 kW
		W • M-Sa • E Europe • 100 kW
		W • Sa • E Europe • 100 kW
(con'd)	VOA, Via Colombo, Sri Lanka	S Asia • 35 kW

0 1 2 3 4 5 6 7 8 9 10 11 12 13 14 15 16 17 18 19 20 21 22 23 24

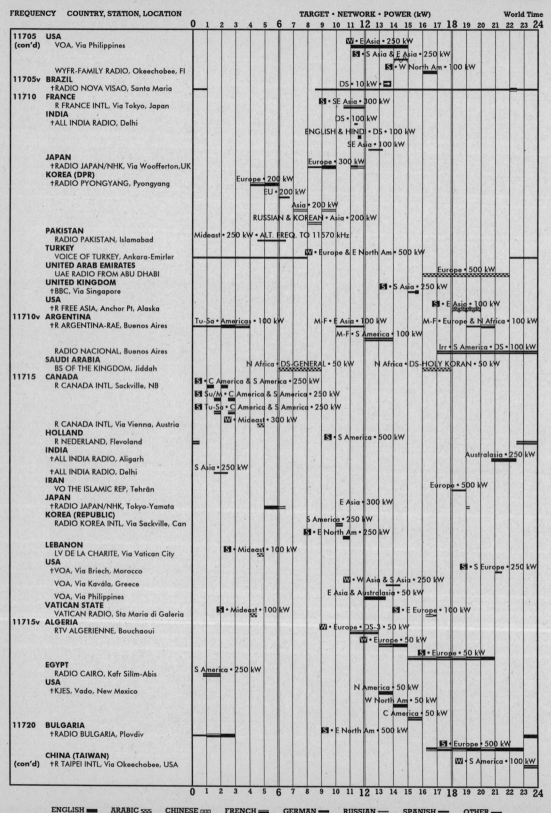

FREQUENCY   COUNTRY, STATION, LOCATION   TARGET • NETWORK • POWER (kW)   World Time

11705 (con'd) **USA**	VOA, Via Philippines — W • E Asia • 250 kW; S • S Asia & E Asia • 250 kW; S • W North Am • 100 kW
	WYFR-FAMILY RADIO, Okeechobee, Fl
11705v BRAZIL	†RADIO NOVA VISAO, Santa Maria — DS • 10 kW • →
11710 FRANCE	R FRANCE INTL, Via Tokyo, Japan — S • SE Asia • 300 kW
INDIA	†ALL INDIA RADIO, Delhi — DS • 100 kW; ENGLISH & HINDI • DS • 100 kW; SE Asia • 100 kW
JAPAN	†RADIO JAPAN/NHK, Via Woofferton, UK — Europe • 300 kW
KOREA (DPR)	†RADIO PYONGYANG, Pyongyang — Europe • 200 kW; EU • 200 kW; Asia • 200 kW; RUSSIAN & KOREAN • Asia • 200 kW
PAKISTAN	RADIO PAKISTAN, Islamabad — Mideast • 250 kW • ALT. FREQ. TO 11570 kHz
TURKEY	VOICE OF TURKEY, Ankara-Emirler — W • Europe & E North Am • 500 kW
UNITED ARAB EMIRATES	UAE RADIO FROM ABU DHABI — Europe • 500 kW
UNITED KINGDOM	†BBC, Via Singapore — S • S Asia • 250 kW
USA	†R FREE ASIA, Anchor Pt, Alaska — S • E Asia • 100 kW
11710v ARGENTINA	†R ARGENTINA-RAE, Buenos Aires — Tu-Sa • Americas • 100 kW; M-F • E Asia • 100 kW; M-F • S America • 100 kW; M-F • Europe & N Africa • 100 kW
	RADIO NACIONAL, Buenos Aires — Irr • S America • DS • 100 kW
SAUDI ARABIA	BS OF THE KINGDOM, Jiddah — N Africa • DS-GENERAL • 50 kW; N Africa • DS-HOLY KORAN • 50 kW
11715 CANADA	R CANADA INTL, Sackville, NB — S • C America & S America • 250 kW; S Su/M • C America & S America • 250 kW; S Tu-Sa • C America & S America • 250 kW; W • Mideast • 300 kW
	R CANADA INTL, Via Vienna, Austria
HOLLAND	R NEDERLAND, Flevoland — S • S America • 500 kW
INDIA	†ALL INDIA RADIO, Aligarh — Australasia • 250 kW
	†ALL INDIA RADIO, Delhi — S Asia • 250 kW
IRAN	VO THE ISLAMIC REP, Tehrān — Europe • 500 kW
JAPAN	†RADIO JAPAN/NHK, Tokyo-Yamata — E Asia • 300 kW
KOREA (REPUBLIC)	RADIO KOREA INTL, Via Sackville, Can — S America • 250 kW; S • E North Am • 250 kW
LEBANON	LV DE LA CHARITE, Via Vatican City — S • Mideast • 100 kW
USA	†VOA, Via Briech, Morocco — S • S Europe • 250 kW
	VOA, Via Kavála, Greece — W • W Asia & S Asia • 250 kW
	VOA, Via Philippines — E Asia & Australasia • 50 kW
VATICAN STATE	VATICAN RADIO, Sta Maria di Galeria — S • Mideast • 100 kW; S • E Europe • 100 kW
11715v ALGERIA	RTV ALGERIENNE, Bouchaoui — W • Europe • DS-3 • 50 kW; W • Europe • 50 kW; S • Europe • 50 kW
EGYPT	RADIO CAIRO, Kafr Silīm-Abis — S America • 250 kW
USA	†KJES, Vado, New Mexico — N America • 50 kW; W North Am • 50 kW; C America • 50 kW
11720 BULGARIA	†RADIO BULGARIA, Plovdiv — S • E North Am • 500 kW; S • Europe • 500 kW
CHINA (TAIWAN) (con'd)	†R TAIPEI INTL, Via Okeechobee, USA — W • S America • 100 kW

ENGLISH ■■ ARABIC ⋙ CHINESE □□□ FRENCH ▬▬ GERMAN ▬▬ RUSSIAN ══ SPANISH ▬▬ OTHER ▬

FREQUENCY   COUNTRY, STATION, LOCATION

TARGET • NETWORK • POWER (kW)

World Time

0 1 2 3 4 5 6 7 8 9 10 11 12 13 14 15 16 17 18 19 20 21 22 23 24

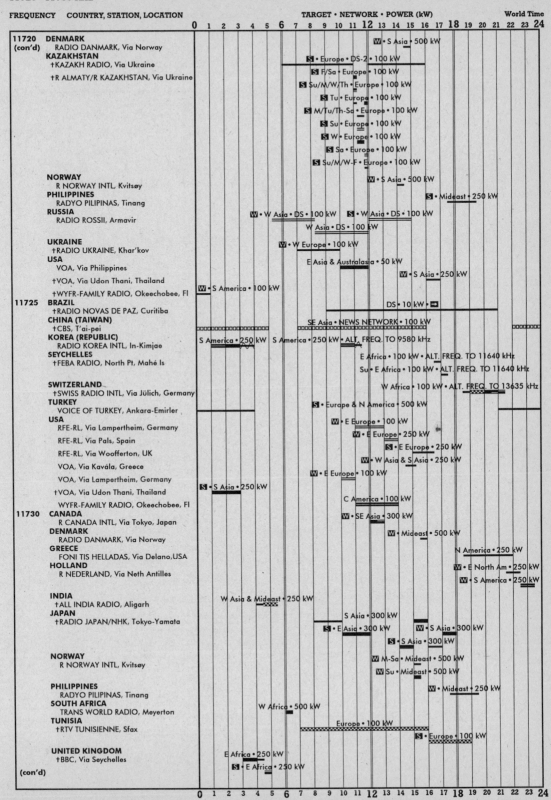

FREQUENCY	COUNTRY, STATION, LOCATION	TARGET • NETWORK • POWER (kW)
11720 (con'd)	DENMARK	
	RADIO DANMARK, Via Norway	W • S Asia • 500 kW
	KAZAKHSTAN	
	†KAZAKH RADIO, Via Ukraine	S • Europe • DS-2 • 100 kW
	†R ALMATY/R KAZAKHSTAN, Via Ukraine	S F/Sa • Europe • 100 kW
		S Su/M/W/Th • Europe • 100 kW
		S Tu • Europe • 100 kW
		S M/Tu/Th-Sa • Europe • 100 kW
		S Su • Europe • 100 kW
		S W • Europe • 100 kW
		S Sa • Europe • 100 kW
		S Su/M/W-F • Europe • 100 kW
	NORWAY	
	R NORWAY INTL, Kvitsøy	W • S Asia • 500 kW
	PHILIPPINES	
	RADYO PILIPINAS, Tinang	S • Mideast • 250 kW
	RUSSIA	
	RADIO ROSSII, Armavir	W • W Asia • DS • 100 kW S • W Asia • DS • 100 kW
		W Asia • DS • 100 kW
	UKRAINE	
	†RADIO UKRAINE, Khar'kov	W • W Europe • 100 kW
	USA	
	VOA, Via Philippines	E Asia & Australasia • 50 kW
	†VOA, Via Udon Thani, Thailand	W • S Asia • 250 kW
	†WYFR-FAMILY RADIO, Okeechobee, Fl	W • S America • 100 kW
11725	BRAZIL	
	†RADIO NOVAS DE PAZ, Curitiba	DS • 10 kW • ⇥
	CHINA (TAIWAN)	
	†CBS, T'ai-pei	SE Asia • NEWS NETWORK • 100 kW
	KOREA (REPUBLIC)	
	RADIO KOREA INTL, In-Kimjae	S America • 250 kW S America • 250 kW • ALT. FREQ. TO 9580 kHz
	SEYCHELLES	
	†FEBA RADIO, North Pt, Mahé Is	E Africa • 100 kW • ALT. FREQ. TO 11640 kHz
		Su • E Africa • 100 kW • ALT. FREQ. TO 11640 kHz
	SWITZERLAND	
	†SWISS RADIO INTL, Via Jülich, Germany	W Africa • 100 kW • ALT. FREQ. TO 13635 kHz
	TURKEY	
	VOICE OF TURKEY, Ankara-Emirler	S • Europe & N America • 500 kW
	USA	
	RFE-RL, Via Lampertheim, Germany	W • E Europe • 100 kW
	RFE-RL, Via Pals, Spain	W • E Europe • 250 kW
	RFE-RL, Via Woofferton, UK	S • E Europe • 250 kW
	VOA, Via Kavála, Greece	W • W Asia & S Asia • 250 kW
	VOA, Via Lampertheim, Germany	W • E Europe • 100 kW
	†VOA, Via Udon Thani, Thailand	S • S Asia • 250 kW
	WYFR-FAMILY RADIO, Okeechobee, Fl	C America • 100 kW
11730	CANADA	
	R CANADA INTL, Via Tokyo, Japan	W • SE Asia • 300 kW
	DENMARK	
	RADIO DANMARK, Via Norway	W • Mideast • 500 kW
	GREECE	
	FONI TIS HELLADAS, Via Delano, USA	N America • 250 kW
	HOLLAND	
	R NEDERLAND, Via Neth Antilles	W • E North Am • 250 kW
		W • S America • 250 kW
	INDIA	
	†ALL INDIA RADIO, Aligarh	W Asia & Mideast • 250 kW
	JAPAN	
	†RADIO JAPAN/NHK, Tokyo-Yamata	S Asia • 300 kW
		S • E Asia • 300 kW W • S Asia • 300 kW
		S • S Asia • 300 kW
	NORWAY	
	R NORWAY INTL, Kvitsøy	W M-Sa • Mideast • 500 kW
		W Su • Mideast • 500 kW
	PHILIPPINES	
	RADYO PILIPINAS, Tinang	W • Mideast • 250 kW
	SOUTH AFRICA	
	TRANS WORLD RADIO, Meyerton	W Africa • 500 kW
	TUNISIA	
	†RTV TUNISIENNE, Sfax	Europe • 100 kW
		S • Europe • 100 kW
	UNITED KINGDOM	
	†BBC, Via Seychelles	E Africa • 250 kW
		S • E Africa • 250 kW
(con'd)		

0 1 2 3 4 5 6 7 8 9 10 11 12 13 14 15 16 17 18 19 20 21 22 23 24

SEASONAL S OR W   1-HR TIMESHIFT MIDYEAR ⇥ OR ⇤   JAMMING / OR ∧   EARLIEST HEARD ◁   LATEST HEARD ▷   NEW FOR 1999 †

FREQUENCY   COUNTRY, STATION, LOCATION

TARGET • NETWORK • POWER (kW)

World Time

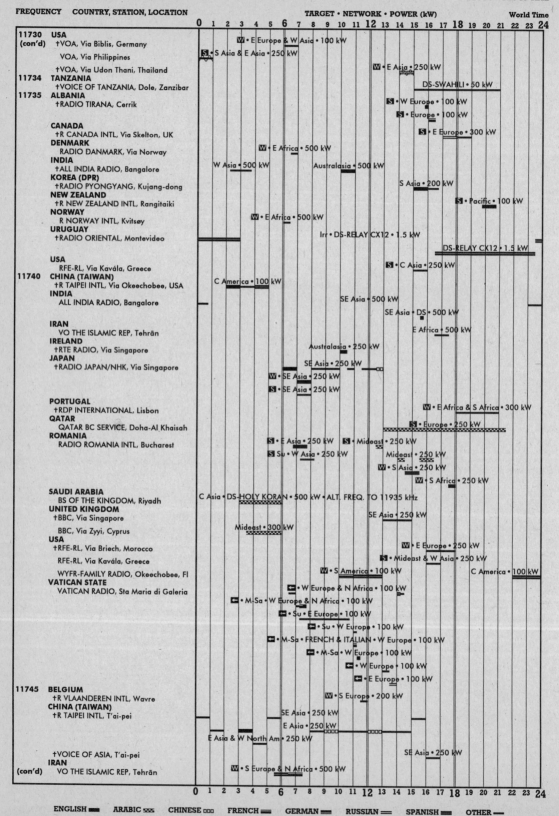

11730	**USA**
(con'd)	†VOA, Via Biblis, Germany
	VOA, Via Philippines
	†VOA, Via Udon Thani, Thailand
11734	**TANZANIA**
	†VOICE OF TANZANIA, Dole, Zanzibar
11735	**ALBANIA**
	†RADIO TIRANA, Cerrik
	CANADA
	†R CANADA INTL, Via Skelton, UK
	DENMARK
	RADIO DANMARK, Via Norway
	INDIA
	†ALL INDIA RADIO, Bangalore
	KOREA (DPR)
	†RADIO PYONGYANG, Kujang-dong
	NEW ZEALAND
	†R NEW ZEALAND INTL, Rangitaiki
	NORWAY
	R NORWAY INTL, Kvitsøy
	URUGUAY
	†RADIO ORIENTAL, Montevideo
	USA
	RFE-RL, Via Kavála, Greece
11740	**CHINA (TAIWAN)**
	†R TAIPEI INTL, Via Okeechobee, USA
	INDIA
	ALL INDIA RADIO, Bangalore
	IRAN
	VO THE ISLAMIC REP, Tehrān
	IRELAND
	†RTE RADIO, Via Singapore
	JAPAN
	†RADIO JAPAN/NHK, Via Singapore
	PORTUGAL
	†RDP INTERNATIONAL, Lisbon
	QATAR
	QATAR BC SERVICE, Doha-Al Khaisah
	ROMANIA
	RADIO ROMANIA INTL, Bucharest
	SAUDI ARABIA
	BS OF THE KINGDOM, Riyadh
	UNITED KINGDOM
	†BBC, Via Singapore
	BBC, Via Zyyi, Cyprus
	USA
	†RFE-RL, Via Briech, Morocco
	RFE-RL, Via Kavála, Greece
	WYFR-FAMILY RADIO, Okeechobee, Fl
	VATICAN STATE
	VATICAN RADIO, Sta Maria di Galeria
11745	**BELGIUM**
	†R VLAANDEREN INTL, Wavre
	CHINA (TAIWAN)
	†R TAIPEI INTL, T'ai-pei
	†VOICE OF ASIA, T'ai-pei
	IRAN
(con'd)	VO THE ISLAMIC REP, Tehrān

Chart annotations:

- W • E Europe & W Asia • 100 kW
- S • S Asia & E Asia • 250 kW
- W • E Asia • 250 kW
- DS-SWAHILI • 50 kW
- S • W Europe • 100 kW
- S • Europe • 100 kW
- S • E Europe • 300 kW
- W • E Africa • 500 kW
- W Asia • 500 kW
- Australasia • 500 kW
- S Asia • 200 kW
- S • Pacific • 100 kW
- W • E Africa • 500 kW
- Irr • DS-RELAY CX12 • 1.5 kW
- DS-RELAY CX12 • 1.5 kW
- S • C Asia • 250 kW
- C America • 100 kW
- SE Asia • 500 kW
- SE Asia • DS • 500 kW
- E Africa • 500 kW
- Australasia • 250 kW
- SE Asia • 250 kW
- W • SE Asia • 250 kW
- S • SE Asia • 250 kW
- W • E Africa & S Africa • 300 kW
- S • Europe • 250 kW
- S • E Asia • 250 kW
- S • Mideast • 250 kW
- S Su • W Asia • 250 kW
- Mideast • 250 kW
- W • S Asia • 250 kW
- W • S Africa • 250 kW
- C Asia • DS-HOLY KORAN • 500 kW • ALT. FREQ. TO 11935 kHz
- SE Asia • 250 kW
- Mideast • 300 kW
- W • E Europe • 250 kW
- S • Mideast & W Asia • 250 kW
- W • S America • 100 kW
- C America • 100 kW
- ⇦ • W Europe & N Africa • 100 kW
- ⇦ • M-Sa • W Europe & N Africa • 100 kW
- ⇦ • Su • E Europe • 100 kW
- ⇦ • Su • W Europe • 100 kW
- ⇦ • M-Sa • FRENCH & ITALIAN • W Europe • 100 kW
- ⇦ • M-Sa • W Europe • 100 kW
- ⇦ • W Europe • 100 kW
- ⇦ • E Europe • 100 kW
- W • S Europe • 200 kW
- SE Asia • 250 kW
- E Asia • 250 kW
- E Asia & W North Am • 250 kW
- SE Asia • 250 kW
- W • S Europe & N Africa • 500 kW

FREQUENCY   COUNTRY, STATION, LOCATION

TARGET • NETWORK • POWER (kW)

World Time

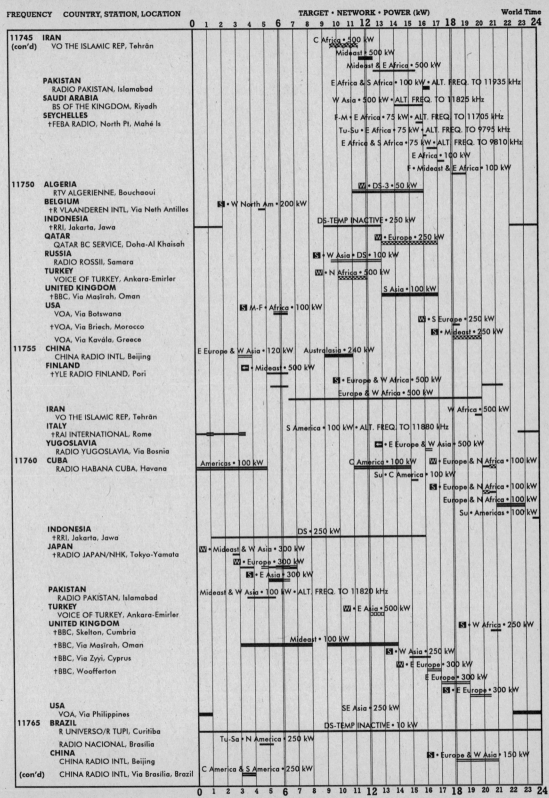

11745	**IRAN**
(con'd)	VO THE ISLAMIC REP, Tehrän
	PAKISTAN
	RADIO PAKISTAN, Islamabad
	SAUDI ARABIA
	BS OF THE KINGDOM, Riyadh
	SEYCHELLES
	†FEBA RADIO, North Pt, Mahé Is
11750	**ALGERIA**
	RTV ALGERIENNE, Bouchaoui
	BELGIUM
	†R VLAANDEREN INTL, Via Neth Antilles
	INDONESIA
	†RRI, Jakarta, Jawa
	QATAR
	QATAR BC SERVICE, Doha-Al Khaisah
	RUSSIA
	RADIO ROSSII, Samara
	TURKEY
	VOICE OF TURKEY, Ankara-Emirler
	UNITED KINGDOM
	†BBC, Via Maşīrah, Oman
	USA
	VOA, Via Botswana
	†VOA, Via Briech, Morocco
	VOA, Via Kavála, Greece
11755	**CHINA**
	CHINA RADIO INTL, Beijing
	FINLAND
	†YLE RADIO FINLAND, Pori
	IRAN
	VO THE ISLAMIC REP, Tehrän
	ITALY
	†RAI INTERNATIONAL, Rome
	YUGOSLAVIA
	RADIO YUGOSLAVIA, Via Bosnia
11760	**CUBA**
	RADIO HABANA CUBA, Havana
	INDONESIA
	†RRI, Jakarta, Jawa
	JAPAN
	†RADIO JAPAN/NHK, Tokyo-Yamata
	PAKISTAN
	RADIO PAKISTAN, Islamabad
	TURKEY
	VOICE OF TURKEY, Ankara-Emirler
	UNITED KINGDOM
	†BBC, Skelton, Cumbria
	†BBC, Via Maşīrah, Oman
	†BBC, Via Zyyi, Cyprus
	†BBC, Woofferton
	USA
	VOA, Via Philippines
11765	**BRAZIL**
	R UNIVERSO/R TUPI, Curitiba
	RADIO NACIONAL, Brasília
	CHINA
	CHINA RADIO INTL, Beijing
(con'd)	CHINA RADIO INTL, Via Brasília, Brazil

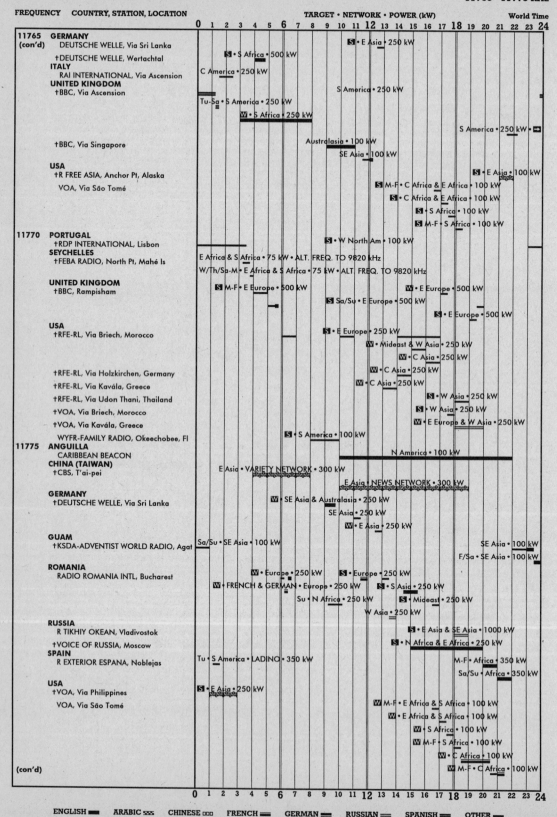

FREQUENCY   COUNTRY, STATION, LOCATION   TARGET • NETWORK • POWER (kW)   World Time

0 1 2 3 4 5 6 7 8 9 10 11 12 13 14 15 16 17 18 19 20 21 22 23 24

11765 GERMANY
(con'd) DEUTSCHE WELLE, Via Sri Lanka — Ⓢ • E Asia • 250 kW
  †DEUTSCHE WELLE, Wertachtal — Ⓢ • S Africa • 500 kW
ITALY
  RAI INTERNATIONAL, Via Ascension — C America • 250 kW
UNITED KINGDOM
  †BBC, Via Ascension — S America • 250 kW
    Tu-Sa • S America • 250 kW
    Ⓦ • S Africa • 250 kW
    S America • 250 kW • ➡
  †BBC, Via Singapore — Australasia • 100 kW
    SE Asia • 100 kW
USA
  †R FREE ASIA, Anchor Pt, Alaska — Ⓢ • E Asia • 100 kW
  VOA, Via São Tomé — Ⓢ M-F • C Africa & E Africa • 100 kW
    Ⓢ • C Africa & E Africa • 100 kW
    Ⓢ • S Africa • 100 kW
    Ⓢ M-F • S Africa • 100 kW

11770 PORTUGAL
  †RDP INTERNATIONAL, Lisbon — Ⓢ • W North Am • 100 kW
SEYCHELLES
  †FEBA RADIO, North Pt, Mahé Is — E Africa & S Africa • 75 kW • ALT. FREQ. TO 9820 kHz
    W/Th/Sa-M • E Africa & S Africa • 75 kW • ALT. FREQ. TO 9820 kHz
UNITED KINGDOM
  †BBC, Rampisham — Ⓢ M-F • E Europe • 500 kW
    Ⓦ • E Europe • 500 kW
    Ⓢ Sa/Su • E Europe • 500 kW
    Ⓢ • E Europe • 500 kW
USA
  †RFE-RL, Via Briech, Morocco — Ⓢ • E Europe • 250 kW
    Ⓦ • Mideast & W Asia • 250 kW
    Ⓦ • C Asia • 250 kW
  †RFE-RL, Via Holzkirchen, Germany — Ⓦ • C Asia • 250 kW
  †RFE-RL, Via Kavála, Greece — Ⓦ • C Asia • 250 kW
  †RFE-RL, Via Udon Thani, Thailand — Ⓢ • W Asia • 250 kW
  †VOA, Via Briech, Morocco — Ⓢ • W Asia • 250 kW
  †VOA, Via Kavála, Greece — Ⓦ • E Europe & W Asia • 250 kW
  WYFR-FAMILY RADIO, Okeechobee, Fl — Ⓢ • S America • 100 kW
11775 ANGUILLA
  CARIBBEAN BEACON — N America • 100 kW
CHINA (TAIWAN)
  †CBS, T'ai-pei — E Asia • VARIETY NETWORK • 300 kW
    E Asia • NEWS NETWORK • 300 kW
GERMANY
  †DEUTSCHE WELLE, Via Sri Lanka — Ⓦ • SE Asia & Australasia • 250 kW
    SE Asia • 250 kW
    Ⓦ • E Asia • 250 kW
GUAM
  †KSDA-ADVENTIST WORLD RADIO, Agat — Sa/Su • SE Asia • 100 kW
    SE Asia • 100 kW
    F/Sa • SE Asia • 100 kW
ROMANIA
  RADIO ROMANIA INTL, Bucharest — Ⓦ • Europe • 250 kW
    Ⓢ • Europe • 250 kW
    Ⓦ • FRENCH & GERMAN • Europe • 250 kW
    Ⓢ • S Asia • 250 kW
    Su • N Africa • 250 kW
    Ⓢ • Mideast • 250 kW
    W Asia • 250 kW
RUSSIA
  R TIKHIY OKEAN, Vladivostok — Ⓢ • E Asia & SE Asia • 1000 kW
  †VOICE OF RUSSIA, Moscow — Ⓢ • N Africa & E Africa • 250 kW
SPAIN
  R EXTERIOR ESPANA, Noblejas — Tu • S America • LADINO • 350 kW
    M-F • Africa • 350 kW
    Sa/Su • Africa • 350 kW
USA
  †VOA, Via Philippines — Ⓢ • E Asia • 250 kW
  VOA, Via São Tomé — Ⓦ M-F • E Africa & S Africa • 100 kW
    Ⓦ • E Africa & S Africa • 100 kW
    Ⓦ • S Africa • 100 kW
    Ⓦ M-F • S Africa • 100 kW
    Ⓦ • C Africa • 100 kW
    Ⓦ M-F • C Africa • 100 kW

(con'd)

0 1 2 3 4 5 6 7 8 9 10 11 12 13 14 15 16 17 18 19 20 21 22 23 24

ENGLISH ▬   ARABIC ⨯⨯⨯   CHINESE □□□   FRENCH ▬   GERMAN ▬   RUSSIAN ▬   SPANISH ▬   OTHER ▬

FREQUENCY   COUNTRY, STATION, LOCATION

TARGET • NETWORK • POWER (kW)

World Time

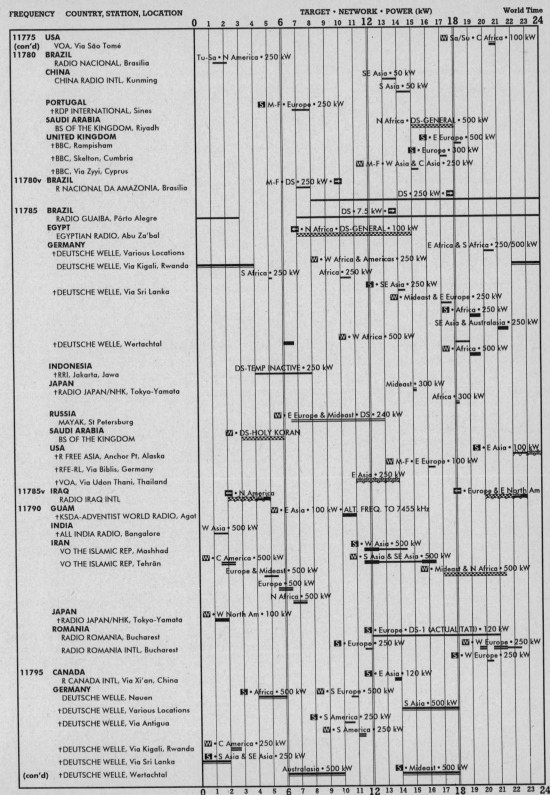

FREQUENCY	COUNTRY, STATION, LOCATION	TARGET • NETWORK • POWER (kW)
11775 (con'd)	USA — VOA, Via São Tomé	W Sa/Su • C Africa • 100 kW
11780	BRAZIL — RADIO NACIONAL, Brasilia	Tu-Sa • N America • 250 kW
	CHINA — CHINA RADIO INTL, Kunming	SE Asia • 50 kW; S Asia • 50 kW
	PORTUGAL — †RDP INTERNATIONAL, Sines	S M-F • Europe • 250 kW
	SAUDI ARABIA — BS OF THE KINGDOM, Riyadh	N Africa • DS-GENERAL • 500 kW
	UNITED KINGDOM — †BBC, Rampisham	S • E Europe • 500 kW
	†BBC, Skelton, Cumbria	S • Europe • 300 kW
	†BBC, Via Zyyi, Cyprus	W M-F • W Asia & C Asia • 250 kW
11780v	BRAZIL — R NACIONAL DA AMAZONIA, Brasilia	M-F • DS • 250 kW • ; DS • 250 kW •
11785	BRAZIL — RADIO GUAIBA, Pôrto Alegre	DS • 7.5 kW •
	EGYPT — EGYPTIAN RADIO, Abu Za'bal	• N Africa • DS-GENERAL • 100 kW
	GERMANY — †DEUTSCHE WELLE, Various Locations	E Africa & S Africa • 250/500 kW
	DEUTSCHE WELLE, Via Kigali, Rwanda	W • W Africa & Americas • 250 kW; S Africa • 250 kW; Africa • 250 kW
	†DEUTSCHE WELLE, Via Sri Lanka	S • SE Asia • 250 kW; W • Mideast & E Europe • 250 kW; S • Africa • 250 kW; SE Asia & Australasia • 250 kW
	†DEUTSCHE WELLE, Wertachtal	W • W Africa • 500 kW; W • Africa • 500 kW
	INDONESIA — †RRI, Jakarta, Jawa	DS-TEMP INACTIVE • 250 kW
	JAPAN — †RADIO JAPAN/NHK, Tokyo-Yamata	Mideast • 300 kW; Africa • 300 kW
	RUSSIA — MAYAK, St Petersburg	W • E Europe & Mideast • DS • 240 kW
	SAUDI ARABIA — BS OF THE KINGDOM	W • DS-HOLY KORAN
	USA — †R FREE ASIA, Anchor Pt, Alaska	S • E Asia • 100 kW
	†RFE-RL, Via Biblis, Germany	W M-F • E Europe • 100 kW
	†VOA, Via Udon Thani, Thailand	E Asia • 250 kW
11785v	IRAQ — RADIO IRAQ INTL	• N America; • Europe & E North Am
11790	GUAM — †KSDA-ADVENTIST WORLD RADIO, Agat	W • E Asia • 100 kW • ALT. FREQ. TO 7455 kHz
	INDIA — †ALL INDIA RADIO, Bangalore	W Asia • 500 kW
	IRAN — VO THE ISLAMIC REP, Mashhad	S • W Asia • 500 kW
	VO THE ISLAMIC REP, Tehrān	W • C America • 500 kW; W • S Asia & SE Asia • 500 kW; W • Mideast & N Africa • 500 kW; Europe & Mideast • 500 kW; Europe • 500 kW; N Africa • 500 kW
	JAPAN — †RADIO JAPAN/NHK, Tokyo-Yamata	W • W North Am • 100 kW
	ROMANIA — RADIO ROMANIA, Bucharest	S • Europe • DS-1 (ACTUALITATI) • 120 kW
	RADIO ROMANIA INTL, Bucharest	S • Europe • 250 kW; W • W Europe • 250 kW; S • W Europe • 250 kW
11795	CANADA — R CANADA INTL, Via Xi'an, China	S • E Asia • 120 kW
	GERMANY — DEUTSCHE WELLE, Nauen	S • Africa • 500 kW; W • S Europe • 500 kW; S Asia • 500 kW
	†DEUTSCHE WELLE, Various Locations	S • S America • 250 kW
	†DEUTSCHE WELLE, Via Antigua	W • S America • 250 kW
	†DEUTSCHE WELLE, Via Kigali, Rwanda	W • C America • 250 kW
	†DEUTSCHE WELLE, Via Sri Lanka	S • S Asia & SE Asia • 250 kW
(con'd)	†DEUTSCHE WELLE, Wertachtal	Australasia • 500 kW; S • Mideast • 500 kW

FREQUENCY   COUNTRY, STATION, LOCATION

TARGET • NETWORK • POWER (kW)   World Time

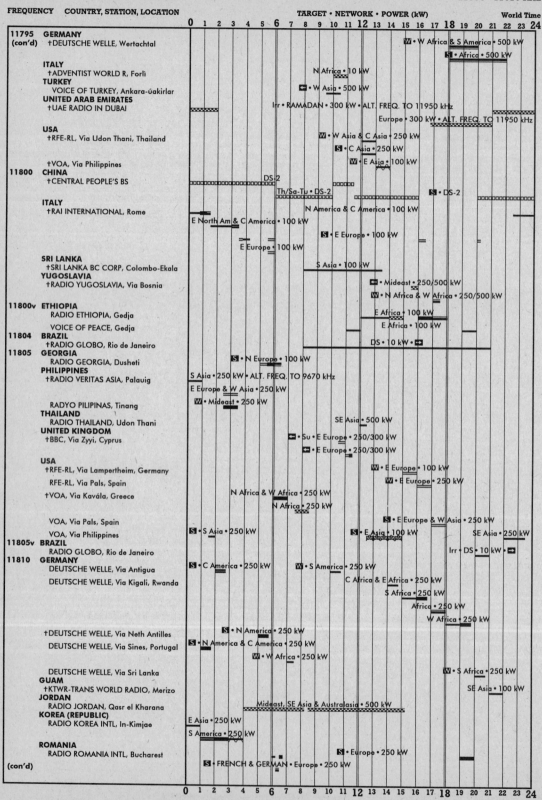

Frequency	Country, Station, Location	Details
11795 (con'd)	**GERMANY** †DEUTSCHE WELLE, Wertachtal	W • W Africa & S America • 500 kW / S • Africa • 500 kW
	ITALY †ADVENTIST WORLD R, Forli	N Africa • 10 kW
	TURKEY VOICE OF TURKEY, Ankara-úakirlar	• W Asia • 500 kW
	UNITED ARAB EMIRATES †UAE RADIO IN DUBAI	Irr • RAMADAN • 300 kW • ALT. FREQ. TO 11950 kHz / Europe • 300 kW • ALT. FREQ. TO 11950 kHz
	USA †RFE-RL, Via Udon Thani, Thailand	W • W Asia & C Asia • 250 kW / S • C Asia • 250 kW
	†VOA, Via Philippines	W • E Asia • 100 kW
11800	**CHINA** †CENTRAL PEOPLE'S BS	DS-2 / Th/Sa-Tu • DS-2 / S • DS-2
	ITALY †RAI INTERNATIONAL, Rome	N America & C America • 100 kW / E North Am & C America • 100 kW / S • E Europe • 100 kW / E Europe • 100 kW
	SRI LANKA †SRI LANKA BC CORP, Colombo-Ekala	S Asia • 100 kW
	YUGOSLAVIA †RADIO YUGOSLAVIA, Via Bosnia	• Mideast • 250/500 kW / W • N Africa & W Africa • 250/500 kW
11800v	**ETHIOPIA** RADIO ETHIOPIA, Gedja	E Africa • 100 kW
	VOICE OF PEACE, Gedja	E Africa • 100 kW
11804	**BRAZIL** †RADIO GLOBO, Rio de Janeiro	DS • 10 kW •
11805	**GEORGIA** RADIO GEORGIA, Dusheti	S • N Europe • 100 kW
	PHILIPPINES †RADIO VERITAS ASIA, Palauig	S Asia • 250 kW • ALT. FREQ. TO 9670 kHz / E Europe & W Asia • 250 kW / W • Mideast • 250 kW
	RADYO PILIPINAS, Tinang	
	THAILAND RADIO THAILAND, Udon Thani	SE Asia • 500 kW
	UNITED KINGDOM †BBC, Via Zyyi, Cyprus	• Su • E Europe • 250/300 kW / • E Europe • 250/300 kW
	USA †RFE-RL, Via Lampertheim, Germany	W • E Europe • 100 kW
	RFE-RL, Via Pals, Spain	W • E Europe • 250 kW
	†VOA, Via Kavála, Greece	N Africa & W Africa • 250 kW / N Africa • 250 kW
	VOA, Via Pals, Spain	S • E Europe & W Asia • 250 kW
	VOA, Via Philippines	S • S Asia • 250 kW / S • E Asia • 100 kW / SE Asia • 250 kW
11805v	**BRAZIL** RADIO GLOBO, Rio de Janeiro	Irr • DS • 10 kW •
11810	**GERMANY** DEUTSCHE WELLE, Via Antigua	S • C America • 250 kW / W • S America • 250 kW
	DEUTSCHE WELLE, Via Kigali, Rwanda	C Africa & E Africa • 250 kW / S Africa • 250 kW / Africa • 250 kW / W Africa • 250 kW
	†DEUTSCHE WELLE, Via Neth Antilles	S • N America • 250 kW
	DEUTSCHE WELLE, Via Sines, Portugal	S • N America & C America • 250 kW / W • W Africa • 250 kW
	DEUTSCHE WELLE, Via Sri Lanka	W • S Africa • 250 kW / SE Asia • 100 kW
	GUAM †KTWR-TRANS WORLD RADIO, Merizo	
	JORDAN RADIO JORDAN, Qasr el Kharana	Mideast, SE Asia & Australasia • 500 kW
	KOREA (REPUBLIC) RADIO KOREA INTL, In-Kimjae	E Asia • 250 kW / S America • 250 kW
	ROMANIA RADIO ROMANIA INTL, Bucharest	S • Europe • 250 kW / S • FRENCH & GERMAN • Europe • 250 kW
(con'd)		

ENGLISH ▬ ARABIC ∾∾ CHINESE ▢▢▢ FRENCH ▬▬ GERMAN ▬▬ RUSSIAN ═══ SPANISH ▬▬ OTHER ▬

FREQUENCY   COUNTRY, STATION, LOCATION

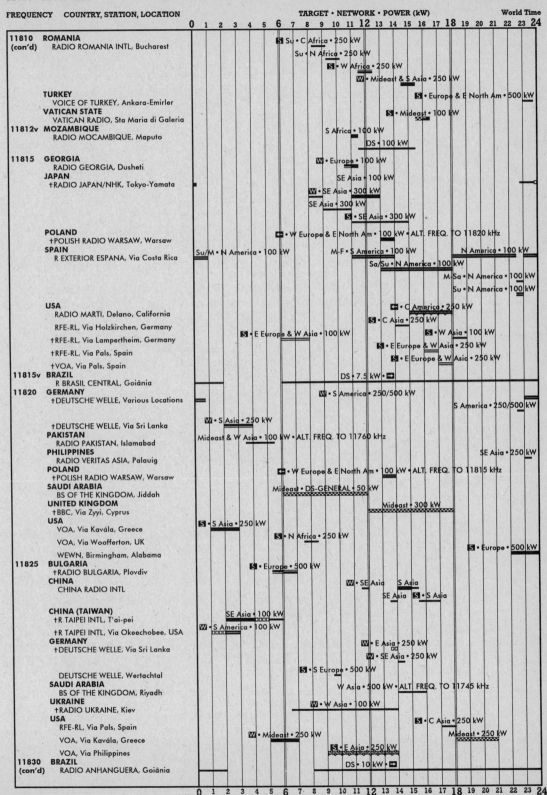

0 1 2 3 4 5 6 7 8 9 10 11 12 13 14 15 16 17 18 19 20 21 22 23 24

11810 **ROMANIA**
(con'd) RADIO ROMANIA INTL, Bucharest
- Su • C Africa • 250 kW
- Su • N Africa • 250 kW
- S • W Africa • 250 kW
- W • Mideast & S Asia • 250 kW

TURKEY
VOICE OF TURKEY, Ankara-Emirler
- S • Europe & E North Am • 500 kW
VATICAN STATE
VATICAN RADIO, Sta Maria di Galeria
- S • Mideast • 100 kW

11812v **MOZAMBIQUE**
RADIO MOCAMBIQUE, Maputo
- S Africa • 100 kW
- DS • 100 kW

11815 **GEORGIA**
RADIO GEORGIA, Dusheti
- W • Europe • 100 kW
JAPAN
†RADIO JAPAN/NHK, Tokyo-Yamata
- SE Asia • 100 kW
- W • SE Asia • 300 kW
- SE Asia • 300 kW
- S • SE Asia • 300 kW

POLAND
†POLISH RADIO WARSAW, Warsaw
- • W Europe & E North Am • 100 kW • ALT. FREQ. TO 11820 kHz
SPAIN
R EXTERIOR ESPANA, Via Costa Rica
- Su/M • N America • 100 kW
- M-F • S America • 100 kW
- N America • 100 kW
- Sa/Su • N America • 100 kW
- M-Sa • N America • 100 kW
- Su • N America • 100 kW

USA
RADIO MARTI, Delano, California
- • C America • 250 kW
RFE-RL, Via Holzkirchen, Germany
- S • C Asia • 250 kW
- W Asia • 100 kW
†RFE-RL, Via Lampertheim, Germany
- S • E Europe & W Asia • 100 kW
†RFE-RL, Via Pals, Spain
- S • E Europe & W Asia • 250 kW
†VOA, Via Pals, Spain
- S • E Europe & W Asia • 250 kW

11815v **BRAZIL**
R BRASIL CENTRAL, Goiânia
- DS • 7.5 kW •

11820 **GERMANY**
†DEUTSCHE WELLE, Various Locations
- W • S America • 250/500 kW
- S America • 250/500 kW

†DEUTSCHE WELLE, Via Sri Lanka
- W • S Asia • 250 kW
PAKISTAN
RADIO PAKISTAN, Islamabad
- Mideast & W Asia • 100 kW • ALT. FREQ. TO 11760 kHz
PHILIPPINES
RADIO VERITAS ASIA, Palauig
- SE Asia • 250 kW
POLAND
†POLISH RADIO WARSAW, Warsaw
- • W Europe & E North Am • 100 kW • ALT. FREQ. TO 11815 kHz
SAUDI ARABIA
BS OF THE KINGDOM, Jiddah
- Mideast • DS-GENERAL • 50 kW
UNITED KINGDOM
†BBC, Via Zyyi, Cyprus
- Mideast • 300 kW
USA
VOA, Via Kavála, Greece
- S • S Asia • 250 kW
VOA, Via Woofferton, UK
- S • N Africa • 250 kW
WEWN, Birmingham, Alabama
- S • Europe • 500 kW

11825 **BULGARIA**
†RADIO BULGARIA, Plovdiv
- S • Europe • 500 kW
CHINA
CHINA RADIO INTL
- W • SE Asia
- S Asia
- SE Asia
- S • S Asia

CHINA (TAIWAN)
†R TAIPEI INTL, T'ai-pei
- SE Asia • 100 kW
†R TAIPEI INTL, Via Okeechobee, USA
- W • S America • 100 kW
GERMANY
†DEUTSCHE WELLE, Via Sri Lanka
- W • E Asia • 250 kW
- W • SE Asia • 250 kW

DEUTSCHE WELLE, Wertachtal
- S • S Europe • 500 kW
SAUDI ARABIA
BS OF THE KINGDOM, Riyadh
- W Asia • 500 kW • ALT. FREQ. TO 11745 kHz
UKRAINE
†RADIO UKRAINE, Kiev
- W • W Asia • 100 kW
USA
RFE-RL, Via Pals, Spain
- S • C Asia • 250 kW
VOA, Via Kavála, Greece
- W • Mideast • 250 kW
- Mideast • 250 kW
VOA, Via Philippines
- S • E Asia • 250 kW

11830 **BRAZIL**
(con'd) RADIO ANHANGUERA, Goiânia
- DS • 10 kW •

0 1 2 3 4 5 6 7 8 9 10 11 12 13 14 15 16 17 18 19 20 21 22 23 24

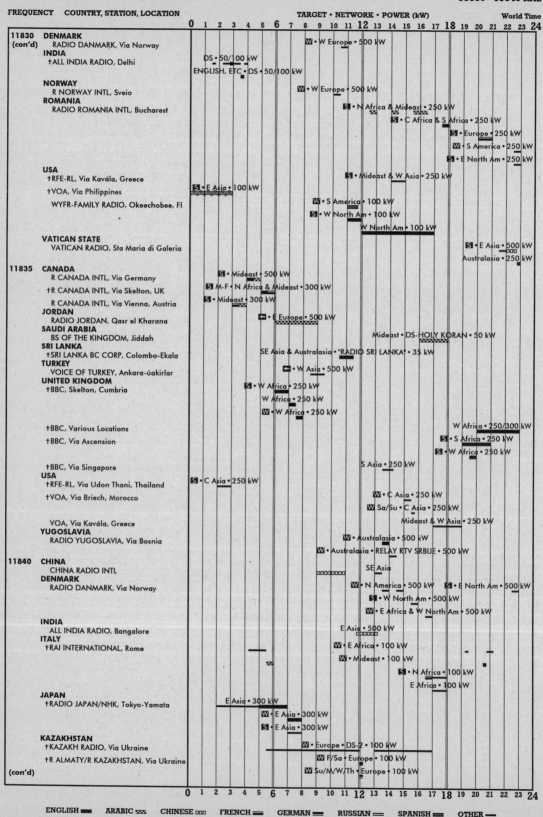

FREQUENCY   COUNTRY, STATION, LOCATION

TARGET • NETWORK • POWER (kW)   World Time

11830	DENMARK	
(con'd)	RADIO DANMARK, Via Norway	W • W Europe • 500 kW
	INDIA	
	†ALL INDIA RADIO, Delhi	DS • 50/100 kW
		ENGLISH, ETC • DS • 50/100 kW
	NORWAY	
	R NORWAY INTL, Sveio	W • W Europe • 500 kW
	ROMANIA	
	RADIO ROMANIA INTL, Bucharest	S • N Africa & Mideast • 250 kW
		S • C Africa & S Africa • 250 kW
		S • Europe • 250 kW
		W • S America • 250 kW
		S • E North Am • 250 kW
	USA	
	†RFE-RL, Via Kavála, Greece	S • Mideast & W Asia • 250 kW
	†VOA, Via Philippines	S • E Asia • 100 kW
	WYFR-FAMILY RADIO, Okeechobee, Fl	W • S America • 100 kW
		S • W North Am • 100 kW
		W North Am • 100 kW
	VATICAN STATE	
	VATICAN RADIO, Sta Maria di Galeria	S • E Asia • 500 kW
		Australasia • 250 kW

11835	CANADA	
	R CANADA INTL, Via Germany	S • Mideast • 500 kW
	†R CANADA INTL, Via Skelton, UK	S M-F • N Africa & Mideast • 300 kW
	R CANADA INTL, Via Vienna, Austria	S • Mideast • 300 kW
	JORDAN	
	RADIO JORDAN, Qasr el Kharana	• E Europe • 500 kW
	SAUDI ARABIA	
	BS OF THE KINGDOM, Jiddah	Mideast • DS-HOLY KORAN • 50 kW
	SRI LANKA	
	†SRI LANKA BC CORP, Colombo-Ekala	SE Asia & Australasia • "RADIO SRI LANKA" • 35 kW
	TURKEY	
	VOICE OF TURKEY, Ankara-úakirlar	• W Asia • 500 kW
	UNITED KINGDOM	
	†BBC, Skelton, Cumbria	S • W Africa • 250 kW
		W Africa • 250 kW
		W • W Africa • 250 kW
	†BBC, Various Locations	W Africa • 250/300 kW
	†BBC, Via Ascension	S • S Africa • 250 kW
		S • W Africa • 250 kW
	†BBC, Via Singapore	S Asia • 250 kW
	USA	
	†RFE-RL, Via Udon Thani, Thailand	S • C Asia • 250 kW
	†VOA, Via Briech, Morocco	W • C Asia • 250 kW
		W Sa/Su • C Asia • 250 kW
	VOA, Via Kavála, Greece	Mideast & W Asia • 250 kW
	YUGOSLAVIA	
	RADIO YUGOSLAVIA, Via Bosnia	W • Australasia • 500 kW
		W • Australasia • RELAY RTV SRBIJE • 500 kW

11840	CHINA	
	CHINA RADIO INTL	SE Asia
	DENMARK	
	RADIO DANMARK, Via Norway	W • N America • 500 kW	S • E North Am • 500 kW
		S • W North Am • 500 kW
		W • E Africa & W North Am • 500 kW
	INDIA	
	ALL INDIA RADIO, Bangalore	E Asia • 500 kW
	ITALY	
	†RAI INTERNATIONAL, Rome	W • E Africa • 100 kW
		W • Mideast • 100 kW
		S • N Africa • 100 kW
		E Africa • 100 kW
	JAPAN	
	†RADIO JAPAN/NHK, Tokyo-Yamata	E Asia • 300 kW
		W • E Asia • 300 kW
		S • E Asia • 300 kW
	KAZAKHSTAN	
	†KAZAKH RADIO, Via Ukraine	W • Europe • DS-2 • 100 kW
	†R ALMATY/R KAZAKHSTAN, Via Ukraine	W F/Sa • Europe • 100 kW
(con'd)		W Su/M/W/Th • Europe • 100 kW

ENGLISH ▬ ARABIC ▨ CHINESE ▢▢ FRENCH ▬▬ GERMAN ▬ RUSSIAN ═ SPANISH ▬ OTHER ▬

FREQUENCY   COUNTRY, STATION, LOCATION

TARGET • NETWORK • POWER (kW)   World Time

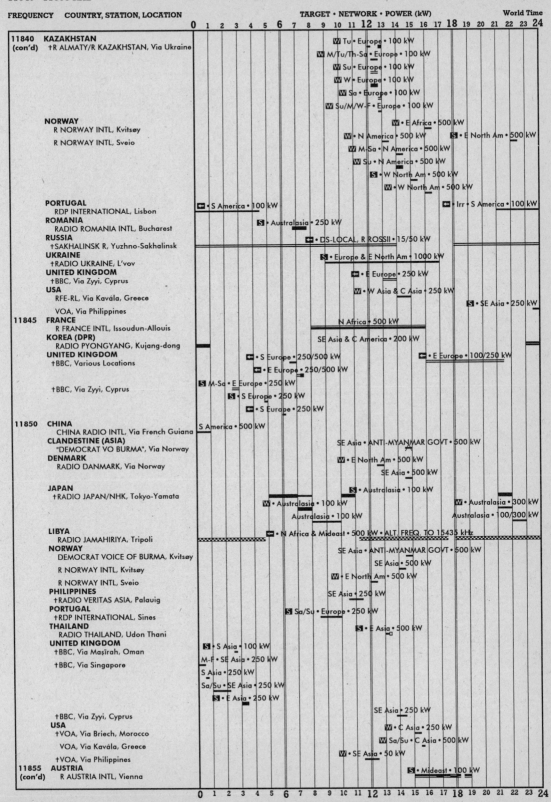

11840 KAZAKHSTAN
(con'd) †R ALMATY/R KAZAKHSTAN, Via Ukraine
W Tu • Europe • 100 kW
W M/Tu/Th-Sa • Europe • 100 kW
W Su • Europe • 100 kW
W W • Europe • 100 kW
W Sa • Europe • 100 kW
W Su/M/W-F • Europe • 100 kW

NORWAY
R NORWAY INTL, Kvitsøy
W • E Africa • 500 kW
R NORWAY INTL, Sveio
W • N America • 500 kW   S • E North Am • 500 kW
W M-Sa • N America • 500 kW
W Su • N America • 500 kW
S • W North Am • 500 kW
W • W North Am • 500 kW

PORTUGAL
RDP INTERNATIONAL, Lisbon
• S America • 100 kW   Irr • S America • 100 kW
ROMANIA
RADIO ROMANIA INTL, Bucharest
S • Australasia • 250 kW
RUSSIA
†SAKHALINSK R, Yuzhno-Sakhalinsk
• DS-LOCAL, R ROSSII • 15/50 kW
UKRAINE
†RADIO UKRAINE, L'vov
S • Europe & E North Am • 1000 kW
UNITED KINGDOM
†BBC, Via Zyyi, Cyprus
• E Europe • 250 kW
USA
RFE-RL, Via Kavála, Greece
W • W Asia & C Asia • 250 kW
VOA, Via Philippines
S • SE Asia • 250 kW

11845 FRANCE
R FRANCE INTL, Issoudun-Allouis
N Africa • 500 kW
KOREA (DPR)
RADIO PYONGYANG, Kujang-dong
SE Asia & C America • 200 kW
UNITED KINGDOM
†BBC, Various Locations
• S Europe • 250/500 kW   • E Europe • 100/250 kW
• E Europe • 250/500 kW

†BBC, Via Zyyi, Cyprus
S M-Sa • E Europe • 250 kW
S • S Europe • 250 kW
• S Europe • 250 kW

11850 CHINA
CHINA RADIO INTL, Via French Guiana
S America • 500 kW
CLANDESTINE (ASIA)
"DEMOCRAT VO BURMA", Via Norway
SE Asia • ANTI-MYANMAR GOVT • 500 kW
DENMARK
RADIO DANMARK, Via Norway
W • E North Am • 500 kW
SE Asia • 500 kW

JAPAN
†RADIO JAPAN/NHK, Tokyo-Yamata
S • Australasia • 100 kW
W • Australasia • 100 kW   W • Australasia • 300 kW
Australasia • 100 kW   Australasia • 100/300 kW

LIBYA
RADIO JAMAHIRIYA, Tripoli
• N Africa & Mideast • 500 kW • ALT. FREQ. TO 15435 kHz
NORWAY
DEMOCRAT VOICE OF BURMA, Kvitsøy
SE Asia • ANTI-MYANMAR GOVT • 500 kW
R NORWAY INTL, Kvitsøy
SE Asia • 500 kW
R NORWAY INTL, Sveio
W • E North Am • 500 kW
PHILIPPINES
†RADIO VERITAS ASIA, Palauig
SE Asia • 250 kW
PORTUGAL
†RDP INTERNATIONAL, Sines
S Sa/Su • Europe • 250 kW
THAILAND
RADIO THAILAND, Udon Thani
S • E Asia • 500 kW
UNITED KINGDOM
†BBC, Via Maşirah, Oman
S • S Asia • 100 kW
†BBC, Via Singapore
M-F • SE Asia • 250 kW
S Asia • 250 kW
Sa/Su • SE Asia • 250 kW
S • E Asia • 250 kW

†BBC, Via Zyyi, Cyprus
SE Asia • 250 kW
USA
†VOA, Via Briech, Morocco
W • C Asia • 250 kW
VOA, Via Kavála, Greece
W Sa/Su • C Asia • 500 kW
†VOA, Via Philippines
W • SE Asia • 50 kW
11855 AUSTRIA
(con'd) R AUSTRIA INTL, Vienna
S • Mideast • 100 kW

FREQUENCY   COUNTRY, STATION, LOCATION   TARGET • NETWORK • POWER (kW)   World Time

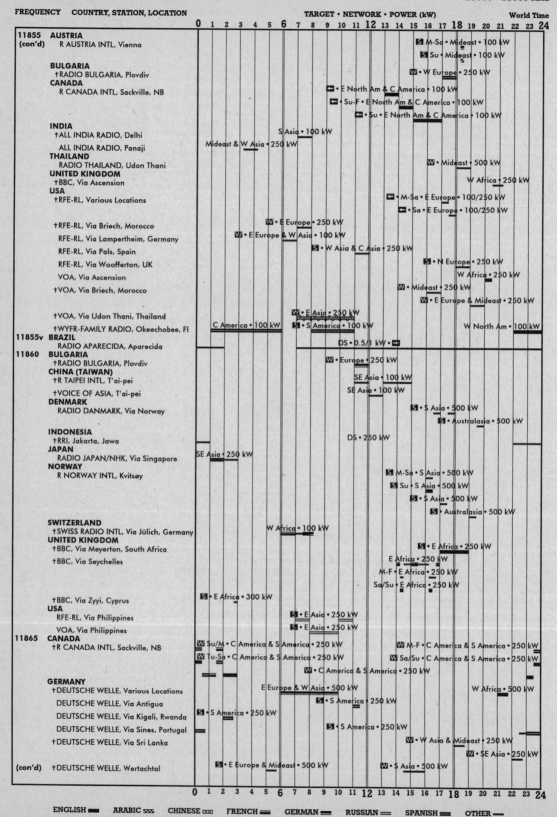

FREQUENCY	COUNTRY, STATION, LOCATION	TARGET • NETWORK • POWER (kW)
11855 (con'd)	**AUSTRIA** R AUSTRIA INTL, Vienna	S M-Sa • Mideast • 100 kW / S Su • Mideast • 100 kW
	BULGARIA †RADIO BULGARIA, Plovdiv	W • W Europe • 250 kW
	CANADA R CANADA INTL, Sackville, NB	▣ • E North Am & C America • 100 kW / ▣ • Su-F • E North Am & C America • 100 kW / ▣ • Su • E North Am & C America • 100 kW
	INDIA †ALL INDIA RADIO, Delhi	S Asia • 100 kW
	ALL INDIA RADIO, Panaji	Mideast & W Asia • 250 kW
	THAILAND RADIO THAILAND, Udon Thani	W • Mideast • 500 kW
	UNITED KINGDOM †BBC, Via Ascension	W Africa • 250 kW
	USA †RFE-RL, Various Locations	▣ • M-Sa • E Europe • 100/250 kW / ▣ • Sa • E Europe • 100/250 kW
	†RFE-RL, Via Briech, Morocco	W • E Europe • 250 kW
	RFE-RL, Via Lampertheim, Germany	W • E Europe & W Asia • 100 kW
	RFE-RL, Via Pals, Spain	S • W Asia & C Asia • 250 kW
	RFE-RL, Via Woofferton, UK	S • N Europe • 250 kW
	VOA, Via Ascension	W Africa • 250 kW
	†VOA, Via Briech, Morocco	W • Mideast • 250 kW
		W • E Europe & Mideast • 250 kW
	†VOA, Via Udon Thani, Thailand	W • E Asia • 250 kW
	†WYFR-FAMILY RADIO, Okeechobee, Fl	C America • 100 kW / S • S America • 100 kW / W North Am • 100 kW
11855v	**BRAZIL** RADIO APARECIDA, Aparecida	DS • 0.5/1 kW • ▣
11860	**BULGARIA** †RADIO BULGARIA, Plovdiv	W • Europe • 250 kW
	CHINA (TAIWAN) †R TAIPEI INTL, T'ai-pei	SE Asia • 100 kW
	†VOICE OF ASIA, T'ai-pei	SE Asia • 100 kW
	DENMARK RADIO DANMARK, Via Norway	S • S Asia • 500 kW / S • Australasia • 500 kW
	INDONESIA †RRI, Jakarta, Jawa	DS • 250 kW
	JAPAN RADIO JAPAN/NHK, Via Singapore	SE Asia • 250 kW
	NORWAY R NORWAY INTL, Kvitsøy	S M-Sa • S Asia • 500 kW / S Su • S Asia • 500 kW / S • S Asia • 500 kW / S • Australasia • 500 kW
	SWITZERLAND †SWISS RADIO INTL, Via Jülich, Germany	W Africa • 100 kW
	UNITED KINGDOM †BBC, Via Meyerton, South Africa	S • E Africa • 250 kW
	†BBC, Via Seychelles	E Africa • 250 kW / M-F • E Africa • 250 kW / Sa/Su • E Africa • 250 kW
	†BBC, Via Zyyi, Cyprus	S • E Africa • 300 kW
	USA RFE-RL, Via Philippines	S • E Asia • 250 kW
	VOA, Via Philippines	S • E Asia • 250 kW
11865	**CANADA** †R CANADA INTL, Sackville, NB	W Su/M • C America & S America • 250 kW / W M-F • C America & S America • 250 kW / W Tu-Sa • C America & S America • 250 kW / W Sa/Su • C America & S America • 250 kW / W • C America & S America • 250 kW
	GERMANY †DEUTSCHE WELLE, Various Locations	E Europe & W Asia • 500 kW / W Africa • 500 kW
	DEUTSCHE WELLE, Via Antigua	S • S America • 250 kW
	DEUTSCHE WELLE, Via Kigali, Rwanda	S • S America • 250 kW
	DEUTSCHE WELLE, Via Sines, Portugal	S • S America • 250 kW
	†DEUTSCHE WELLE, Via Sri Lanka	W • W Asia & Mideast • 250 kW / W • SE Asia • 250 kW
(con'd)	†DEUTSCHE WELLE, Wertachtal	S • E Europe & Mideast • 500 kW / W • S Asia • 500 kW

ENGLISH ▬   ARABIC ≋   CHINESE □□□   FRENCH ▬▬   GERMAN ▭▭   RUSSIAN ══   SPANISH ▬▬   OTHER ──

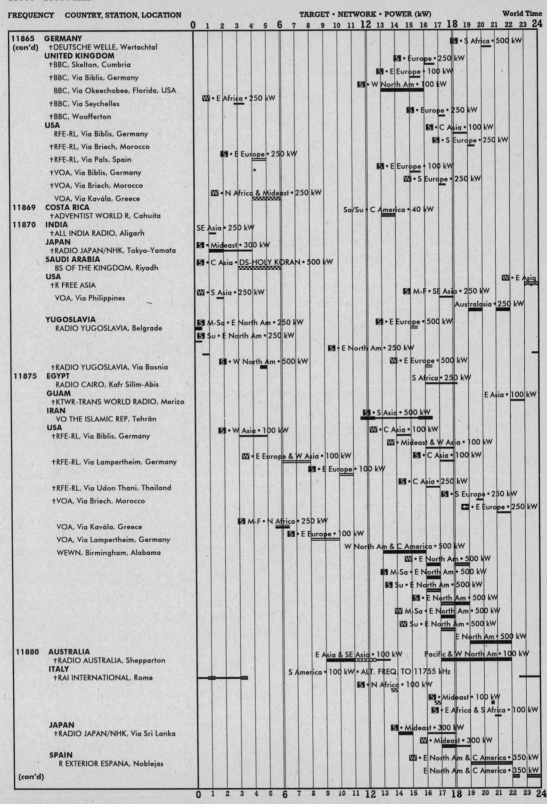

FREQUENCY   COUNTRY, STATION, LOCATION

TARGET • NETWORK • POWER (kW)   World Time

FREQUENCY	COUNTRY, STATION, LOCATION	Schedule
11865 (con'd)	**GERMANY**	
	†DEUTSCHE WELLE, Wertachtal	S • S Africa • 500 kW
	UNITED KINGDOM	
	†BBC, Skelton, Cumbria	S • Europe • 250 kW
	†BBC, Via Biblis, Germany	S • E Europe • 100 kW
	BBC, Via Okeechobee, Florida, USA	S • W North Am • 100 kW
	†BBC, Via Seychelles	W • E Africa • 250 kW
	†BBC, Woofferton	S • Europe • 250 kW
	USA	
	RFE-RL, Via Biblis, Germany	S • C Asia • 100 kW
	†RFE-RL, Via Briech, Morocco	S • S Europe • 250 kW
	†RFE-RL, Via Pals, Spain	S • E Europe • 250 kW
	†VOA, Via Biblis, Germany	S • E Europe • 100 kW
	†VOA, Via Briech, Morocco	W • S Europe • 250 kW
	VOA, Via Kavála, Greece	W • N Africa & Mideast • 250 kW
11869	**COSTA RICA**	
	†ADVENTIST WORLD R, Cahuita	Sa/Su • C America • 40 kW
11870	**INDIA**	
	†ALL INDIA RADIO, Aligarh	SE Asia • 250 kW
	JAPAN	
	†RADIO JAPAN/NHK, Tokyo-Yamata	S • Mideast • 300 kW
	SAUDI ARABIA	
	BS OF THE KINGDOM, Riyadh	S • C Asia • DS-HOLY KORAN • 500 kW
	USA	
	†R FREE ASIA	W • E Asia
	VOA, Via Philippines	W • S Asia • 250 kW S M-F • SE Asia • 250 kW
		Australasia • 250 kW
	YUGOSLAVIA	
	RADIO YUGOSLAVIA, Belgrade	S M-Sa • E North Am • 250 kW S • E Europe • 500 kW
		S Su • E North Am • 250 kW
		S • E North Am • 250 kW
	†RADIO YUGOSLAVIA, Via Bosnia	S • W North Am • 500 kW W • E Europe • 500 kW
11875	**EGYPT**	
	RADIO CAIRO, Kafr Silim-Abis	S Africa • 250 kW
	GUAM	
	†KTWR-TRANS WORLD RADIO, Merizo	E Asia • 100 kW
	IRAN	
	VO THE ISLAMIC REP, Tehrān	S • S Asia • 500 kW
	USA	
	†RFE-RL, Via Biblis, Germany	S • W Asia • 100 kW W • C Asia • 100 kW
		W • Mideast & W Asia • 100 kW
	†RFE-RL, Via Lampertheim, Germany	W • E Europe & W Asia • 100 kW S • C Asia • 100 kW
		S • E Europe • 100 kW
	†RFE-RL, Via Udon Thani, Thailand	S • C Asia • 250 kW
	†VOA, Via Briech, Morocco	S • S Europe • 250 kW
		⇆ • E Europe • 250 kW
	VOA, Via Kavála, Greece	S M-F • N Africa • 250 kW
	VOA, Via Lampertheim, Germany	S • E Europe • 100 kW
	WEWN, Birmingham, Alabama	W North Am & C America • 500 kW
		W • E North Am • 500 kW
		S M-Sa • E North Am • 500 kW
		S Su • E North Am • 500 kW
		S • E North Am • 500 kW
		W M-Sa • E North Am • 500 kW
		W Su • E North Am • 500 kW
		E North Am • 500 kW
11880	**AUSTRALIA**	
	†RADIO AUSTRALIA, Shepparton	E Asia & SE Asia • 100 kW Pacific & W North Am • 100 kW
	ITALY	
	†RAI INTERNATIONAL, Rome	S America • 100 kW • ALT. FREQ. TO 11755 kHz
		S • N Africa • 100 kW
		S • Mideast • 100 kW
		S • E Africa & S Africa • 100 kW
	JAPAN	
	†RADIO JAPAN/NHK, Via Sri Lanka	S • Mideast • 300 kW
		W • Mideast • 300 kW
	SPAIN	
	R EXTERIOR ESPANA, Noblejas	W • E North Am & C America • 350 kW
		E North Am & C America • 350 kW
(con'd)		

FREQUENCY   COUNTRY, STATION, LOCATION

TARGET • NETWORK • POWER (kW)   World Time

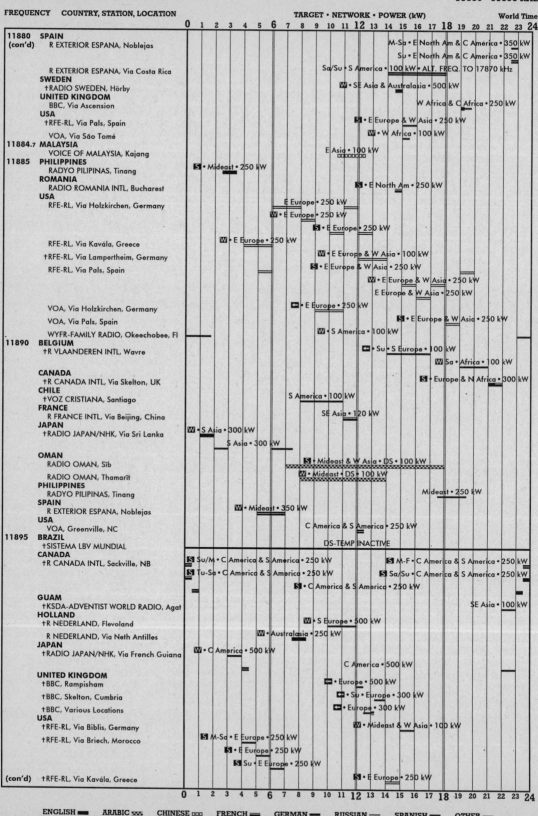

FREQUENCY	COUNTRY, STATION, LOCATION	TARGET • NETWORK • POWER (kW)
11880 (con'd)	**SPAIN** R EXTERIOR ESPANA, Noblejas	M-Sa • E North Am & C América • 350 kW
		Su • E North Am & C América • 350 kW
	R EXTERIOR ESPANA, Via Costa Rica	Sa/Su • S America • 100 kW • ALT. FREQ. TO 17870 kHz
	SWEDEN †RADIO SWEDEN, Hörby	W • SE Asia & Australasia • 500 kW
	UNITED KINGDOM BBC, Via Ascension	W Africa & C Africa • 250 kW
	USA †RFE-RL, Via Pals, Spain	S • E Europe & W Asia • 250 kW
	VOA, Via São Tomé	W • W Africa • 100 kW
11884.7	**MALAYSIA** VOICE OF MALAYSIA, Kajang	E Asia • 100 kW
11885	**PHILIPPINES** RADYO PILIPINAS, Tinang	S • Mideast • 250 kW
	ROMANIA RADIO ROMANIA INTL, Bucharest	S • E North Am • 250 kW
	USA RFE-RL, Via Holzkirchen, Germany	E Europe • 250 kW
		W • E Europe • 250 kW
		S • E Europe • 250 kW
	RFE-RL, Via Kavála, Greece	W • E Europe • 250 kW
	†RFE-RL, Via Lampertheim, Germany	W • E Europe & W Asia • 100 kW
	RFE-RL, Via Pals, Spain	S • E Europe & W Asia • 250 kW
		W • E Europe & W Asia • 250 kW
		E Europe & W Asia • 250 kW
	VOA, Via Holzkirchen, Germany	⊏⊐ • E Europe • 250 kW
	VOA, Via Pals, Spain	S • E Europe & W Asia • 250 kW
	WYFR-FAMILY RADIO, Okeechobee, Fl	W • S America • 100 kW
11890	**BELGIUM** †R VLAANDEREN INTL, Wavre	⊏⊐ • Su • S Europe • 100 kW
	CANADA †R CANADA INTL, Via Skelton, UK	W • Sa • Africa • 100 kW
	CHILE †VOZ CRISTIANA, Santiago	S • Europe & N Africa • 300 kW
	FRANCE R FRANCE INTL, Via Beijing, China	S America • 100 kW
	JAPAN †RADIO JAPAN/NHK, Via Sri Lanka	SE Asia • 120 kW
		W • S Asia • 300 kW
		S Asia • 300 kW
	OMAN RADIO OMAN, Sīb	S • Mideast & W Asia • DS • 100 kW
	RADIO OMAN, Thamarīt	W • Mideast • DS • 100 kW
	PHILIPPINES RADYO PILIPINAS, Tinang	Mideast • 250 kW
	SPAIN R EXTERIOR ESPANA, Noblejas	W • Mideast • 350 kW
	USA VOA, Greenville, NC	C America & S America • 250 kW
11895	**BRAZIL** †SISTEMA LBV MUNDIAL	DS-TEMP INACTIVE
	CANADA †R CANADA INTL, Sackville, NB	S • Su/M • C America & S America • 250 kW S • M-F • C America & S America • 250 kW
		S • Tu-Sa • C America & S America • 250 kW S • Sa/Su • C America & S America • 250 kW
		S • C America & S America • 250 kW
	GUAM †KSDA-ADVENTIST WORLD RADIO, Agat	SE Asia • 100 kW
	HOLLAND †R NEDERLAND, Flevoland	W • S Europe • 500 kW
	R NEDERLAND, Via Neth Antilles	W • Australasia • 250 kW
	JAPAN †RADIO JAPAN/NHK, Via French Guiana	W • C America • 500 kW
		C America • 500 kW
	UNITED KINGDOM †BBC, Rampisham	⊏⊐ • Europe • 500 kW
	†BBC, Skelton, Cumbria	⊏⊐ • Su • Europe • 300 kW
	†BBC, Various Locations	⊏⊐ • Europe • 300 kW
	USA †RFE-RL, Via Biblis, Germany	W • Mideast & W Asia • 100 kW
	†RFE-RL, Via Briech, Morocco	S • M-Sa • E Europe • 250 kW
		S • E Europe • 250 kW
		S • Su • E Europe • 250 kW
(con'd)	†RFE-RL, Via Kavála, Greece	S • E Europe • 250 kW

FREQUENCY   COUNTRY, STATION, LOCATION

TARGET • NETWORK • POWER (kW)

World Time

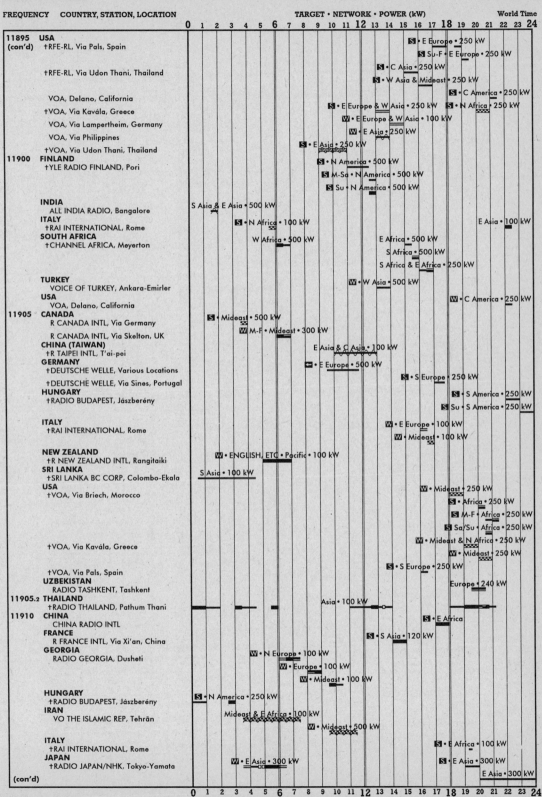

FREQUENCY	COUNTRY, STATION, LOCATION	TARGET • NETWORK • POWER (kW)
11895 (con'd)	**USA** †RFE-RL, Via Pals, Spain	S • E Europe • 250 kW / S Su-F • E Europe • 250 kW
	†RFE-RL, Via Udon Thani, Thailand	S • C Asia • 250 kW / S • W Asia & Mideast • 250 kW
	VOA, Delano, California	S • C America • 250 kW
	†VOA, Via Kavála, Greece	S • E Europe & W Asia • 250 kW / S • N Africa • 250 kW
	VOA, Via Lampertheim, Germany	W • E Europe & W Asia • 100 kW
	VOA, Via Philippines	W • E Asia • 250 kW
	†VOA, Via Udon Thani, Thailand	S • E Asia • 250 kW
11900	**FINLAND** †YLE RADIO FINLAND, Pori	S • N America • 500 kW / S M-Sa • N America • 500 kW / S Su • N America • 500 kW
	INDIA ALL INDIA RADIO, Bangalore	S Asia & E Asia • 500 kW
	ITALY †RAI INTERNATIONAL, Rome	S • N Africa • 100 kW / E Asia • 100 kW
	SOUTH AFRICA †CHANNEL AFRICA, Meyerton	W Africa • 500 kW / E Africa • 500 kW / S Africa • 500 kW / S Africa & E Africa • 250 kW
	TURKEY VOICE OF TURKEY, Ankara-Emirler	W • W Asia • 500 kW
	USA VOA, Delano, California	W • C America • 250 kW
11905	**CANADA** R CANADA INTL, Via Germany	S • Mideast • 500 kW / W M-F • Mideast • 300 kW
	R CANADA INTL, Via Skelton, UK	
	CHINA (TAIWAN) †R TAIPEI INTL, T'ai-pei	E Asia & C Asia • 100 kW
	GERMANY †DEUTSCHE WELLE, Various Locations	• E Europe • 500 kW
	†DEUTSCHE WELLE, Via Sines, Portugal	S • S Europe • 250 kW
	HUNGARY †RADIO BUDAPEST, Jászberény	S • S America • 250 kW / S Su • S America • 250 kW
	ITALY †RAI INTERNATIONAL, Rome	W • E Europe • 100 kW / W • Mideast • 100 kW
	NEW ZEALAND †R NEW ZEALAND INTL, Rangitaiki	W • ENGLISH, ETC • Pacific • 100 kW
	SRI LANKA †SRI LANKA BC CORP, Colombo-Ekala	S Asia • 100 kW
	USA †VOA, Via Briech, Morocco	W • Mideast • 250 kW / S • Africa • 250 kW / S M-F • Africa • 250 kW / S Sa/Su • Africa • 250 kW
	†VOA, Via Kavála, Greece	W • Mideast & N Africa • 250 kW / W • Mideast • 250 kW
	†VOA, Via Pals, Spain	S • S Europe • 250 kW
	UZBEKISTAN RADIO TASHKENT, Tashkent	Europe • 240 kW
11905.2	**THAILAND** †RADIO THAILAND, Pathum Thani	Asia • 100 kW
11910	**CHINA** CHINA RADIO INTL	S • E Africa
	FRANCE R FRANCE INTL, Via Xi'an, China	S • S Asia • 120 kW
	GEORGIA RADIO GEORGIA, Dusheti	W • N Europe • 100 kW / W • Europe • 100 kW / W • Mideast • 100 kW
	HUNGARY †RADIO BUDAPEST, Jászberény	S • N America • 250 kW
	IRAN VO THE ISLAMIC REP, Tehrān	Mideast & E Africa • 100 kW / W • Mideast • 500 kW
	ITALY †RAI INTERNATIONAL, Rome	S • E Africa • 100 kW
	JAPAN †RADIO JAPAN/NHK, Tokyo-Yamata	W • E Asia • 300 kW / S • E Asia • 300 kW / E Asia • 300 kW
(con'd)		

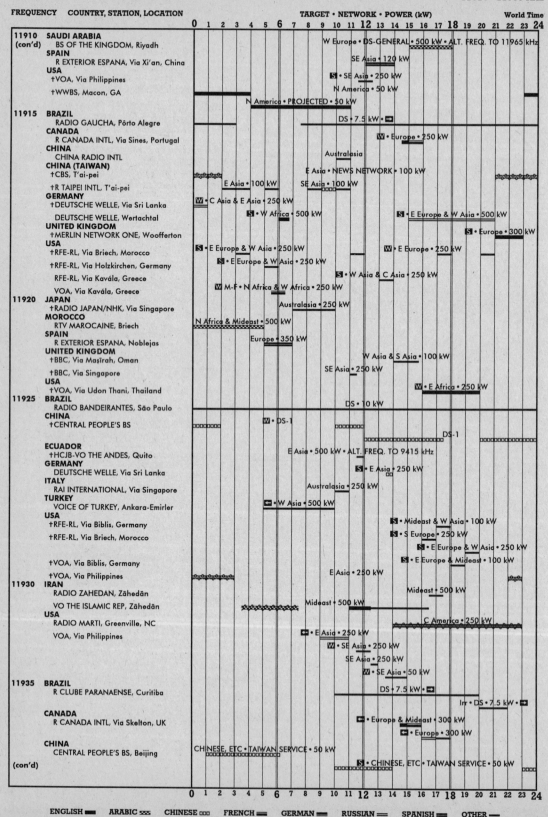

FREQUENCY	COUNTRY, STATION, LOCATION	TARGET • NETWORK • POWER (kW)

11910
(con'd) SAUDI ARABIA — BS OF THE KINGDOM, Riyadh — W Europe • DS-GENERAL • 500 kW • ALT. FREQ. TO 11965 kHz
SPAIN — R EXTERIOR ESPANA, Via Xi'an, China — SE Asia • 120 kW
USA — †VOA, Via Philippines — S • SE Asia • 250 kW
†WWBS, Macon, GA — N America • 50 kW / N America • PROJECTED • 50 kW

11915 BRAZIL — RADIO GAUCHA, Pôrto Alegre — DS • 7.5 kW •
CANADA — R CANADA INTL, Via Sines, Portugal — W • Europe • 250 kW
CHINA — CHINA RADIO INTL — Australasia
CHINA (TAIWAN) — †CBS, T'ai-pei — E Asia • NEWS NETWORK • 100 kW
†R TAIPEI INTL, T'ai-pei — E Asia • 100 kW / SE Asia • 100 kW
GERMANY — †DEUTSCHE WELLE, Via Sri Lanka — W • C Asia & E Asia • 250 kW
DEUTSCHE WELLE, Wertachtal — S • W Africa • 500 kW / S • E Europe & W Asia • 500 kW
UNITED KINGDOM — †MERLIN NETWORK ONE, Woofferton — S • Europe • 300 kW
USA — †RFE-RL, Via Briech, Morocco — S • E Europe & W Asia • 250 kW / W • E Europe • 250 kW
†RFE-RL, Via Holzkirchen, Germany — S • E Europe & W Asia • 250 kW
RFE-RL, Via Kavála, Greece — S • W Asia & C Asia • 250 kW
VOA, Via Kavála, Greece — W M-F • N Africa & W Africa • 250 kW

11920 JAPAN — †RADIO JAPAN/NHK, Via Singapore — Australasia • 250 kW
MOROCCO — RTV MAROCAINE, Briech — N Africa & Mideast • 500 kW
SPAIN — R EXTERIOR ESPANA, Noblejas — Europe • 350 kW
UNITED KINGDOM — †BBC, Via Maşīrah, Oman — W Asia & S Asia • 100 kW
†BBC, Via Singapore — SE Asia • 250 kW
USA — †VOA, Via Udon Thani, Thailand — W • E Africa • 250 kW

11925 BRAZIL — RADIO BANDEIRANTES, São Paulo — DS • 10 kW
CHINA — †CENTRAL PEOPLE'S BS — W • DS-1 / DS-1
ECUADOR — †HCJB-VO THE ANDES, Quito — E Asia • 500 kW • ALT. FREQ. TO 9415 kHz
GERMANY — DEUTSCHE WELLE, Via Sri Lanka — S • E Asia • 250 kW
ITALY — RAI INTERNATIONAL, Via Singapore — Australasia • 250 kW
TURKEY — VOICE OF TURKEY, Ankara-Emirler — • W Asia • 500 kW
USA — †RFE-RL, Via Biblis, Germany — S • Mideast & W Asia • 100 kW
†RFE-RL, Via Briech, Morocco — S • S Europe • 250 kW / S • E Europe & W Asia • 250 kW
†VOA, Via Biblis, Germany — S • E Europe & Mideast • 100 kW
†VOA, Via Philippines — E Asia • 250 kW

11930 IRAN — RADIO ZAHEDAN, Zāhedān — Mideast • 500 kW
VO THE ISLAMIC REP, Zāhedān — Mideast • 500 kW
USA — RADIO MARTI, Greenville, NC — C America • 250 kW
VOA, Via Philippines — • E Asia • 250 kW / W • SE Asia • 250 kW / SE Asia • 250 kW / W • SE Asia • 50 kW

11935 BRAZIL — R CLUBE PARANAENSE, Curitiba — DS • 7.5 kW • / Irr • DS • 7.5 kW •
CANADA — R CANADA INTL, Via Skelton, UK — • Europe & Mideast • 300 kW / • Europe • 300 kW
CHINA — CENTRAL PEOPLE'S BS, Beijing — CHINESE, ETC • TAIWAN SERVICE • 50 kW / S • CHINESE, ETC • TAIWAN SERVICE • 50 kW
(con'd)

FREQUENCY   COUNTRY, STATION, LOCATION   TARGET • NETWORK • POWER (kW)   World Time

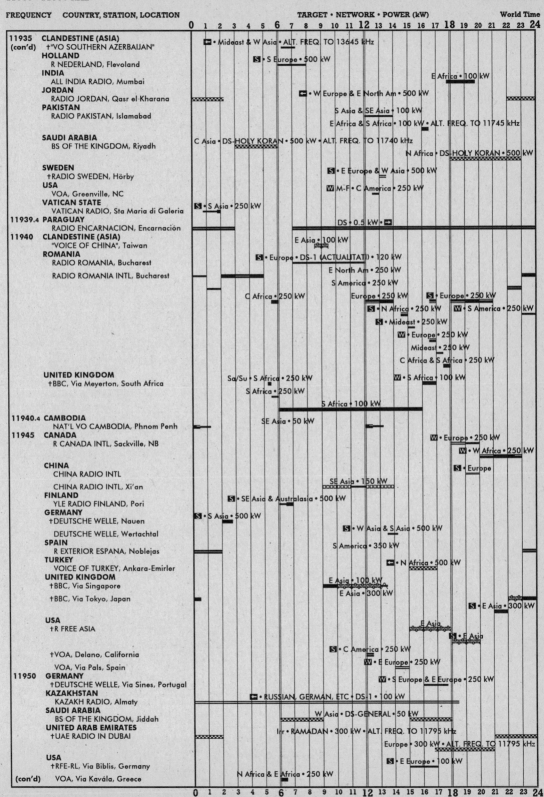

FREQUENCY	COUNTRY, STATION, LOCATION	TARGET • NETWORK • POWER (kW)
11935 (con'd)	CLANDESTINE (ASIA) †"VO SOUTHERN AZERBAIJAN"	• Mideast & W Asia • ALT. FREQ. TO 13645 kHz
	HOLLAND R NEDERLAND, Flevoland	S • S Europe • 500 kW
	INDIA ALL INDIA RADIO, Mumbai	E Africa • 100 kW
	JORDAN RADIO JORDAN, Qasr el Kharana	• W Europe & E North Am • 500 kW
	PAKISTAN RADIO PAKISTAN, Islamabad	S Asia & SE Asia • 100 kW / E Africa & S Africa • 100 kW • ALT. FREQ. TO 11745 kHz
	SAUDI ARABIA BS OF THE KINGDOM, Riyadh	C Asia • DS-HOLY KORAN • 500 kW • ALT. FREQ. TO 11740 kHz / N Africa • DS-HOLY KORAN • 500 kW
	SWEDEN †RADIO SWEDEN, Hörby	S • E Europe & W Asia • 500 kW
	USA VOA, Greenville, NC	W • M-F • C America • 250 kW
	VATICAN STATE VATICAN RADIO, Sta Maria di Galeria	S • S Asia • 250 kW
11939.4	PARAGUAY RADIO ENCARNACION, Encarnación	DS • 0.5 kW •
11940	CLANDESTINE (ASIA) "VOICE OF CHINA", Taiwan	E Asia • 100 kW
	ROMANIA RADIO ROMANIA, Bucharest	S • Europe • DS-1 (ACTUALITATI) • 120 kW
	RADIO ROMANIA INTL, Bucharest	E North Am • 250 kW / S America • 250 kW / C Africa • 250 kW / Europe • 250 kW / S • Europe • 250 kW / S • N Africa • 250 kW / W • S America • 250 kW / S • Mideast • 250 kW / W • Europe • 250 kW / Mideast • 250 kW / C Africa & S Africa • 250 kW
	UNITED KINGDOM †BBC, Via Meyerton, South Africa	Sa/Su • S Africa • 250 kW / W • S Africa • 100 kW / S Africa • 250 kW / S Africa • 100 kW
11940.4	CAMBODIA NAT'L VO CAMBODIA, Phnom Penh	SE Asia • 50 kW
11945	CANADA R CANADA INTL, Sackville, NB	W • Europe • 250 kW / W • W Africa • 250 kW
	CHINA CHINA RADIO INTL	S • Europe
	CHINA RADIO INTL, Xi'an	SE Asia • 150 kW
	FINLAND YLE RADIO FINLAND, Pori	S • SE Asia & Australasia • 500 kW
	GERMANY †DEUTSCHE WELLE, Nauen	S • S Asia • 500 kW
	DEUTSCHE WELLE, Wertachtal	S • W Asia & S Asia • 500 kW
	SPAIN R EXTERIOR ESPANA, Noblejas	S America • 350 kW
	TURKEY VOICE OF TURKEY, Ankara-Emirler	• N Africa • 500 kW
	UNITED KINGDOM †BBC, Via Singapore	E Asia • 100 kW
	†BBC, Via Tokyo, Japan	E Asia • 300 kW / S • E Asia • 300 kW
	USA †R FREE ASIA	E Asia / S • E Asia
	†VOA, Delano, California	S • C America • 250 kW
	VOA, Via Pals, Spain	W • E Europe • 250 kW
11950	GERMANY †DEUTSCHE WELLE, Via Sines, Portugal	W • S Europe & E Europe • 250 kW
	KAZAKHSTAN KAZAKH RADIO, Almaty	• RUSSIAN, GERMAN, ETC • DS-1 • 100 kW
	SAUDI ARABIA BS OF THE KINGDOM, Jiddah	W Asia • DS-GENERAL • 50 kW
	UNITED ARAB EMIRATES †UAE RADIO IN DUBAI	Irr • RAMADAN • 300 kW • ALT. FREQ. TO 11795 kHz / Europe • 300 kW • ALT. FREQ. TO 11795 kHz
	USA †RFE-RL, Via Biblis, Germany	S • E Europe • 100 kW
(con'd)	VOA, Via Kavála, Greece	N Africa & E Africa • 250 kW

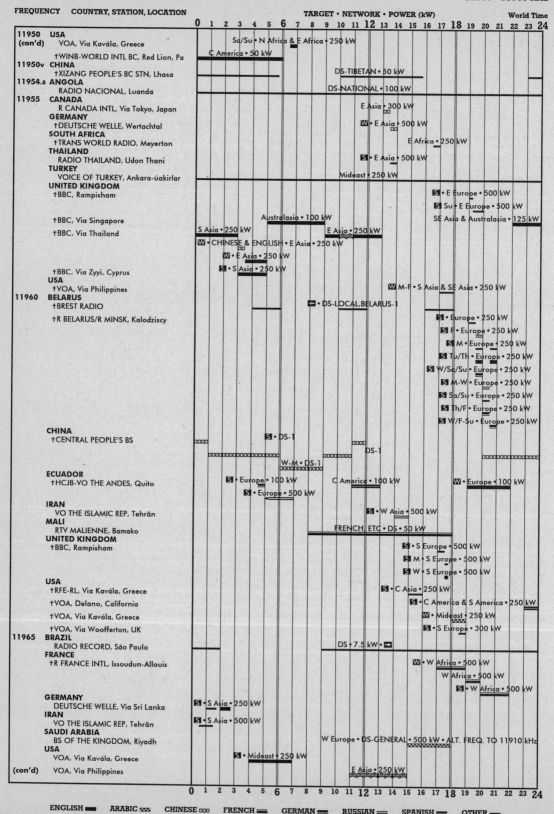

FREQUENCY   COUNTRY, STATION, LOCATION

TARGET • NETWORK • POWER (kW)

World Time

FREQUENCY	COUNTRY, STATION, LOCATION	TARGET • NETWORK • POWER (kW)
11950 (con'd)	**USA** — VOA, Via Kavála, Greece	Sa/Su • N Africa & E Africa • 250 kW
	†WINB-WORLD INTL BC, Red Lion, Pa	C America • 50 kW
11950v	**CHINA** — †XIZANG PEOPLE'S BC STN, Lhasa	DS-TIBETAN • 50 kW
11954.8	**ANGOLA** — RADIO NACIONAL, Luanda	DS-NATIONAL • 100 kW
11955	**CANADA** — R CANADA INTL, Via Tokyo, Japan	E Asia • 300 kW
	GERMANY — †DEUTSCHE WELLE, Wertachtal	W • E Asia • 500 kW
	SOUTH AFRICA — †TRANS WORLD RADIO, Meyerton	E Africa • 250 kW
	THAILAND — RADIO THAILAND, Udon Thani	S • E Asia • 500 kW
	TURKEY — VOICE OF TURKEY, Ankara-úakirlar	Mideast • 250 kW
	UNITED KINGDOM — †BBC, Rampisham	S • E Europe • 500 kW; S Su • E Europe • 500 kW
	†BBC, Via Singapore	Australasia • 100 kW; SE Asia & Australasia • 125 kW
	†BBC, Via Thailand	S Asia • 250 kW; E Asia • 250 kW
		W • CHINESE & ENGLISH • E Asia • 250 kW
		W • E Asia • 250 kW
	†BBC, Via Zyyi, Cyprus	S • S Asia • 250 kW
	USA — †VOA, Via Philippines	W M-F • S Asia & SE Asia • 250 kW
11960	**BELARUS** — †BREST RADIO	DS-LOCAL, BELARUS-1
	†R BELARUS/R MINSK, Kalodziscy	S • Europe • 250 kW; S F • Europe • 250 kW; S M • Europe • 250 kW; S Tu/Th • Europe • 250 kW; S W/Sa/Su • Europe • 250 kW; S M-W • Europe • 250 kW; S Sa/Su • Europe • 250 kW; S Th/F • Europe • 250 kW; S W/F-Su • Europe • 250 kW
	CHINA — †CENTRAL PEOPLE'S BS	S • DS-1; DS-1; W-M • DS-1
	ECUADOR — †HCJB-VO THE ANDES, Quito	S • Europe • 100 kW; C America • 100 kW; W • Europe • 100 kW; S • Europe • 500 kW
	IRAN — VO THE ISLAMIC REP, Tehrān	S • W Asia • 500 kW
	MALI — RTV MALIENNE, Bamako	FRENCH, ETC • DS • 50 kW
	UNITED KINGDOM — †BBC, Rampisham	S • S Europe • 500 kW; S M • S Europe • 500 kW; S W • S Europe • 500 kW
	USA — †RFE-RL, Via Kavála, Greece	S • C Asia • 250 kW
	†VOA, Delano, California	S • C America & S America • 250 kW
	†VOA, Via Kavála, Greece	W • Mideast • 250 kW
	†VOA, Via Woofferton, UK	S • S Europe • 300 kW
11965	**BRAZIL** — RADIO RECORD, São Paulo	DS • 7.5 kW • →
	FRANCE — †R FRANCE INTL, Issoudun-Allouis	W • W Africa • 500 kW; W Africa • 500 kW; S • W Africa • 500 kW
	GERMANY — DEUTSCHE WELLE, Via Sri Lanka	S • S Asia • 250 kW
	IRAN — VO THE ISLAMIC REP, Tehrān	S • S Asia • 500 kW
	SAUDI ARABIA — BS OF THE KINGDOM, Riyadh	W Europe • DS-GENERAL • 500 kW • ALT. FREQ. TO 11910 kHz
	USA — VOA, Via Kavála, Greece	S • Mideast • 250 kW
(con'd)	VOA, Via Philippines	E Asia • 250 kW

ENGLISH ▬   ARABIC ▨   CHINESE ▫▫   FRENCH ▬   GERMAN ▬   RUSSIAN ═   SPANISH ▬   OTHER ▬

FREQUENCY   COUNTRY, STATION, LOCATION   TARGET • NETWORK • POWER (kW)   World Time

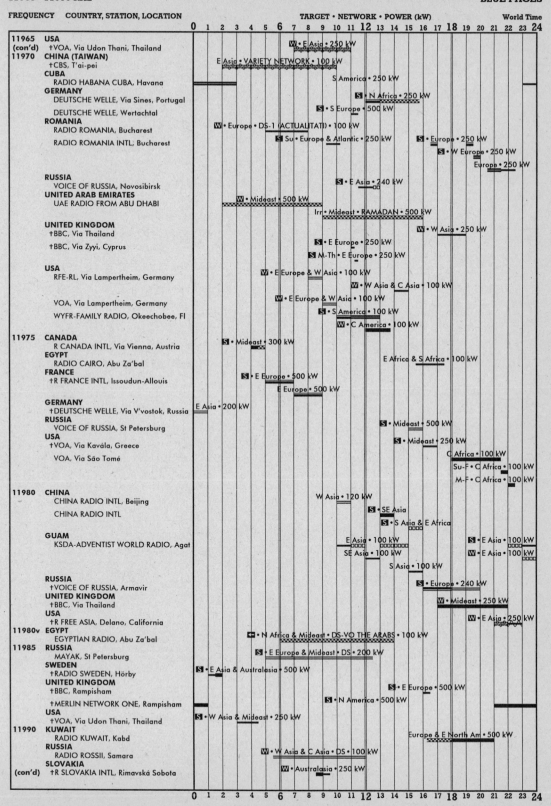

FREQUENCY	COUNTRY, STATION, LOCATION	TARGET • NETWORK • POWER (kW)
11965 (con'd)	**USA** †VOA, Via Udon Thani, Thailand	W • E Asia • 250 kW
11970	**CHINA (TAIWAN)** †CBS, T'ai-pei	E Asia • VARIETY NETWORK • 100 kW
	CUBA RADIO HABANA CUBA, Havana	S America • 250 kW
	GERMANY DEUTSCHE WELLE, Via Sines, Portugal	S • N Africa • 250 kW
	DEUTSCHE WELLE, Wertachtal	S • S Europe • 500 kW
	ROMANIA RADIO ROMANIA, Bucharest	W • Europe • DS-1 (ACTUALITATI) • 100 kW
	RADIO ROMANIA INTL, Bucharest	S • Su • Europe & Atlantic • 250 kW / S • Europe • 250 kW
		S • W Europe • 250 kW
		Europe • 250 kW
	RUSSIA VOICE OF RUSSIA, Novosibirsk	S • E Asia • 240 kW
	UNITED ARAB EMIRATES UAE RADIO FROM ABU DHABI	W • Mideast • 500 kW
		Irr • Mideast • RAMADAN • 500 kW
	UNITED KINGDOM †BBC, Via Thailand	W • W Asia • 250 kW
	†BBC, Via Zyyi, Cyprus	S • E Europe • 250 kW
		S M-Th • E Europe • 250 kW
	USA RFE-RL, Via Lampertheim, Germany	W • E Europe & W Asia • 100 kW
		W • W Asia & C Asia • 100 kW
	VOA, Via Lampertheim, Germany	W • E Europe & W Asia • 100 kW
	WYFR-FAMILY RADIO, Okeechobee, Fl	S • S America • 100 kW
		W • C America • 100 kW
11975	**CANADA** R CANADA INTL, Via Vienna, Austria	S • Mideast • 300 kW
	EGYPT RADIO CAIRO, Abu Za'bal	E Africa & S Africa • 100 kW
	FRANCE †R FRANCE INTL, Issoudun-Allouis	S • E Europe • 500 kW
		E Europe • 500 kW
	GERMANY †DEUTSCHE WELLE, Via V'vostok, Russia	E Asia • 200 kW
	RUSSIA VOICE OF RUSSIA, St Petersburg	S • Mideast • 500 kW
	USA †VOA, Via Kavála, Greece	S • Mideast • 250 kW
	VOA, Via São Tomé	C Africa • 100 kW
		Su-F • C Africa • 100 kW
		M-F • C Africa • 100 kW
11980	**CHINA** CHINA RADIO INTL, Beijing	W Asia • 120 kW
	CHINA RADIO INTL	S • SE Asia
		S • S Asia & E Africa
	GUAM KSDA-ADVENTIST WORLD RADIO, Agat	E Asia • 100 kW
		S • E Asia • 100 kW
		SE Asia • 100 kW
		W • E Asia • 100 kW
		S Asia • 100 kW
	RUSSIA †VOICE OF RUSSIA, Armavir	S • Europe • 240 kW
	UNITED KINGDOM †BBC, Via Thailand	W • Mideast • 250 kW
	USA †R FREE ASIA, Delano, California	W • E Asia • 250 kW
11980v	**EGYPT** EGYPTIAN RADIO, Abu Za'bal	• N Africa & Mideast • DS-VO THE ARABS • 100 kW
11985	**RUSSIA** MAYAK, St Petersburg	S • E Europe & Mideast • DS • 200 kW
	SWEDEN †RADIO SWEDEN, Hörby	S • E Asia & Australasia • 500 kW
	UNITED KINGDOM †BBC, Rampisham	S • E Europe • 500 kW
	†MERLIN NETWORK ONE, Rampisham	S • N America • 500 kW
	USA †VOA, Via Udon Thani, Thailand	S • W Asia & Mideast • 250 kW
11990	**KUWAIT** RADIO KUWAIT, Kabd	Europe & E North Am • 500 kW
	RUSSIA RADIO ROSSII, Samara	W • W Asia & C Asia • DS • 100 kW
(con'd)	**SLOVAKIA** †R SLOVAKIA INTL, Rimavská Sobota	W • Australasia • 250 kW

FREQUENCY   COUNTRY, STATION, LOCATION   TARGET • NETWORK • POWER (kW)   World Time

0 1 2 3 4 5 6 7 8 9 10 11 12 13 14 15 16 17 18 19 20 21 22 23 24

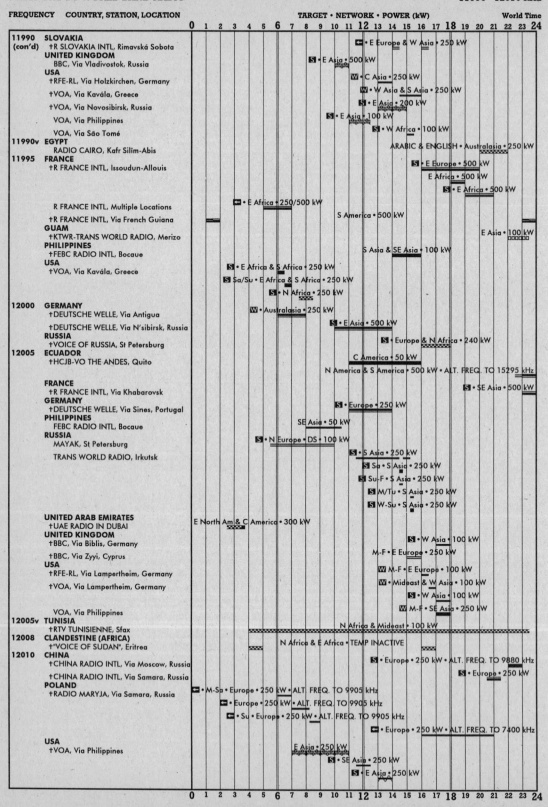

Frequency	Country, Station, Location	Target • Network • Power
11990 (con'd)	**SLOVAKIA** †R SLOVAKIA INTL, Rimavská Sobota	E Europe & W Asia • 250 kW
	UNITED KINGDOM BBC, Via Vladivostok, Russia	S • E Asia • 500 kW
	USA †RFE-RL, Via Holzkirchen, Germany	W • C Asia • 250 kW
	†VOA, Via Kavála, Greece	W • W Asia & S Asia • 250 kW
	†VOA, Via Novosibirsk, Russia	S • E Asia • 200 kW
	VOA, Via Philippines	S • E Asia • 100 kW
	VOA, Via São Tomé	S • W Africa • 100 kW
11990v	**EGYPT** RADIO CAIRO, Kafr Silim-Abis	ARABIC & ENGLISH • Australasia • 250 kW
11995	**FRANCE** †R FRANCE INTL, Issoudun-Allouis	S • E Europe • 500 kW / E Africa • 500 kW / S • E Africa • 500 kW
	R FRANCE INTL, Multiple Locations	E Africa • 250/500 kW
	†R FRANCE INTL, Via French Guiana	S America • 500 kW
	GUAM †KTWR-TRANS WORLD RADIO, Merizo	E Asia • 100 kW
	PHILIPPINES †FEBC RADIO INTL, Bocaue	S Asia & SE Asia • 100 kW
	USA †VOA, Via Kavála, Greece	S • E Africa & S Africa • 250 kW / Sa/Su • E Africa & S Africa • 250 kW / S • N Africa • 250 kW
12000	**GERMANY** †DEUTSCHE WELLE, Via Antigua	W • Australasia • 250 kW
	†DEUTSCHE WELLE, Via N'sibirsk, Russia	S • E Asia • 500 kW
	RUSSIA †VOICE OF RUSSIA, St Petersburg	S • Europe & N Africa • 240 kW
12005	**ECUADOR** †HCJB-VO THE ANDES, Quito	C America • 50 kW / N America & S America • 500 kW • ALT. FREQ. TO 15295 kHz
	FRANCE †R FRANCE INTL, Via Khabarovsk	S • SE Asia • 500 kW
	GERMANY †DEUTSCHE WELLE, Via Sines, Portugal	S • Europe • 250 kW
	PHILIPPINES FEBC RADIO INTL, Bocaue	SE Asia • 50 kW
	RUSSIA MAYAK, St Petersburg	S • N Europe • DS • 100 kW
	TRANS WORLD RADIO, Irkutsk	S • S Asia • 250 kW / S • Sa • S Asia • 250 kW / S • Su-F • S Asia • 250 kW / S • M/Tu • S Asia • 250 kW / S • W-Su • S Asia • 250 kW
	UNITED ARAB EMIRATES †UAE RADIO IN DUBAI	E North Am & C America • 300 kW
	UNITED KINGDOM †BBC, Via Biblis, Germany	S • W Asia • 100 kW
	†BBC, Via Zyyi, Cyprus	M-F • E Europe • 250 kW
	USA †RFE-RL, Via Lampertheim, Germany	W M-F • E Europe • 100 kW
	†VOA, Via Lampertheim, Germany	W • Mideast & W Asia • 100 kW / S • W Asia • 100 kW / W M-F • SE Asia • 250 kW
	VOA, Via Philippines	
12005v	**TUNISIA** †RTV TUNISIENNE, Sfax	N Africa & Mideast • 100 kW
12008	**CLANDESTINE (AFRICA)** †"VOICE OF SUDAN", Eritrea	N Africa & E Africa • TEMP INACTIVE
12010	**CHINA** †CHINA RADIO INTL, Via Moscow, Russia	S • Europe • 250 kW • ALT. FREQ. TO 9880 kHz
	†CHINA RADIO INTL, Via Samara, Russia	S • Europe • 250 kW
	POLAND †RADIO MARYJA, Via Samara, Russia	• M-Sa • Europe • 250 kW • ALT. FREQ. TO 9905 kHz / • Europe • 250 kW • ALT. FREQ. TO 9905 kHz / • Su • Europe • 250 kW • ALT. FREQ. TO 9905 kHz / • Europe • 250 kW • ALT. FREQ. TO 7400 kHz
	USA †VOA, Via Philippines	E Asia • 250 kW / S • SE Asia • 250 kW / S • E Asia • 250 kW

0 1 2 3 4 5 6 7 8 9 10 11 12 13 14 15 16 17 18 19 20 21 22 23 24

ENGLISH ▬   ARABIC ∾∾   CHINESE □□□   FRENCH ▬   GERMAN ▬   RUSSIAN ▭   SPANISH ▬   OTHER ▬

FREQUENCY	COUNTRY, STATION, LOCATION	TARGET • NETWORK • POWER (kW) / World Time
		0 1 2 3 4 5 6 7 8 9 10 11 12 13 14 15 16 17 18 19 20 21 22 23 24

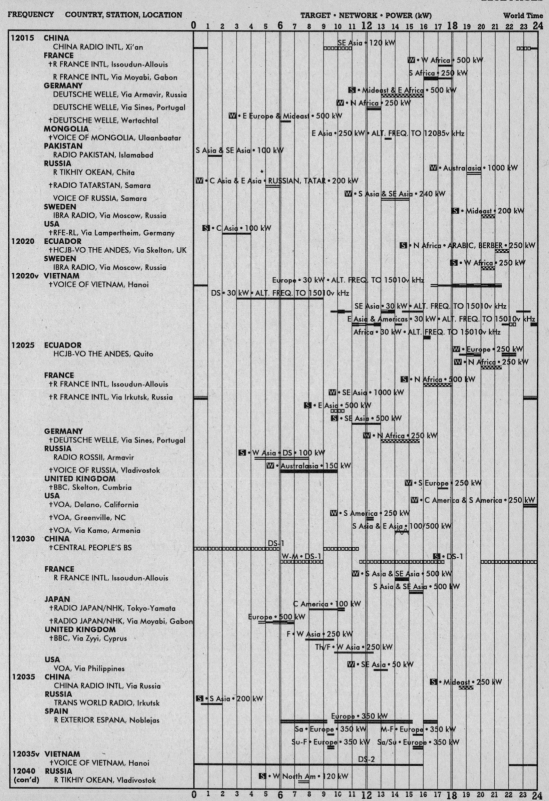

12015 CHINA
CHINA RADIO INTL, Xi'an — SE Asia • 120 kW

FRANCE
†R FRANCE INTL, Issoudun-Allouis — W • W Africa • 500 kW
R FRANCE INTL, Via Moyabi, Gabon — S Africa • 250 kW

GERMANY
DEUTSCHE WELLE, Via Armavir, Russia — S • Mideast & E Africa • 500 kW
DEUTSCHE WELLE, Via Sines, Portugal — W • N Africa • 250 kW
†DEUTSCHE WELLE, Wertachtal — W • E Europe & Mideast • 500 kW

MONGOLIA
†VOICE OF MONGOLIA, Ulaanbaatar — E Asia • 250 kW • ALT. FREQ. TO 12085v kHz

PAKISTAN
RADIO PAKISTAN, Islamabad — S Asia & SE Asia • 100 kW

RUSSIA
R TIKHIY OKEAN, Chita — W • Australasia • 1000 kW
†RADIO TATARSTAN, Samara — W • C Asia & E Asia • RUSSIAN, TATAR • 200 kW
VOICE OF RUSSIA, Samara — W • S Asia & SE Asia • 240 kW

SWEDEN
IBRA RADIO, Via Moscow, Russia — S • Mideast • 200 kW

USA
†RFE-RL, Via Lampertheim, Germany — S • C Asia • 100 kW

12020 ECUADOR
†HCJB-VO THE ANDES, Via Skelton, UK — S • N Africa • ARABIC, BERBER • 250 kW

SWEDEN
IBRA RADIO, Via Moscow, Russia — S • W Africa • 250 kW

12020v VIETNAM
†VOICE OF VIETNAM, Hanoi — Europe • 30 kW • ALT. FREQ. TO 15010v kHz
— DS • 30 kW • ALT. FREQ. TO 15010v kHz
— SE Asia • 30 kW • ALT. FREQ. TO 15010v kHz
— E Asia & Americas • 30 kW • ALT. FREQ. TO 15010v kHz
— Africa • 30 kW • ALT. FREQ. TO 15010v kHz

12025 ECUADOR
HCJB-VO THE ANDES, Quito — W • Europe • 250 kW
— W • N Africa • 250 kW

FRANCE
†R FRANCE INTL, Issoudun-Allouis — S • N Africa • 500 kW
†R FRANCE INTL, Via Irkutsk, Russia — W • SE Asia • 1000 kW
— S • E Asia • 500 kW
— S • SE Asia • 500 kW

GERMANY
†DEUTSCHE WELLE, Via Sines, Portugal — W • N Africa • 250 kW

RUSSIA
RADIO ROSSII, Armavir — S • W Asia • DS • 100 kW
†VOICE OF RUSSIA, Vladivostok — W • Australasia • 150 kW

UNITED KINGDOM
†BBC, Skelton, Cumbria — W • S Europe • 250 kW

USA
†VOA, Delano, California — W • C America & S America • 250 kW
†VOA, Greenville, NC — W • S America • 250 kW
†VOA, Via Kamo, Armenia — S Asia & E Asia • 100/500 kW

12030 CHINA
†CENTRAL PEOPLE'S BS — DS-1
— W-M • DS-1
— S • DS-1

FRANCE
R FRANCE INTL, Issoudun-Allouis — W • S Asia & SE Asia • 500 kW
— S Asia & SE Asia • 500 kW

JAPAN
†RADIO JAPAN/NHK, Tokyo-Yamata — C America • 100 kW
†RADIO JAPAN/NHK, Via Moyabi, Gabon — Europe • 500 kW

UNITED KINGDOM
†BBC, Via Zyyi, Cyprus — F • W Asia • 250 kW
— Th/F • W Asia • 250 kW

USA
VOA, Via Philippines — W • SE Asia • 50 kW

12035 CHINA
CHINA RADIO INTL, Via Russia — S • Mideast • 250 kW

RUSSIA
TRANS WORLD RADIO, Irkutsk — S • S Asia • 200 kW

SPAIN
R EXTERIOR ESPANA, Noblejas — Europe • 350 kW
— Sa • Europe • 350 kW   M-F • Europe • 350 kW
— Su-F • Europe • 350 kW   Sa/Su • Europe • 350 kW

12035v VIETNAM
†VOICE OF VIETNAM, Hanoi — DS-2

12040 RUSSIA
(con'd) R TIKHIY OKEAN, Vladivostok — S • W North Am • 120 kW

| 0 1 2 3 4 5 6 7 8 9 10 11 12 13 14 15 16 17 18 19 20 21 22 23 24 |

FREQUENCY   COUNTRY, STATION, LOCATION

TARGET • NETWORK • POWER (kW)   World Time

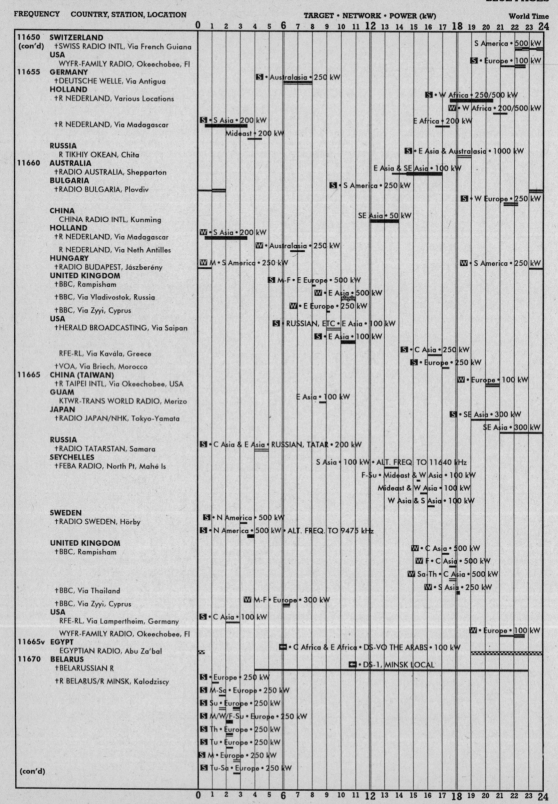

FREQUENCY	COUNTRY, STATION, LOCATION	TARGET • NETWORK • POWER (kW)
11650 (con'd)	**SWITZERLAND** †SWISS RADIO INTL, Via French Guiana	S America • 500 kW (21–23)
	USA WYFR-FAMILY RADIO, Okeechobee, Fl	S • Europe • 100 kW (21–23)
11655	**GERMANY** †DEUTSCHE WELLE, Via Antigua	S • Australasia • 250 kW (6–8)
	HOLLAND †R NEDERLAND, Various Locations	S • W Africa • 250/500 kW (18–19)
		W • W Africa • 200/500 kW (19–20)
	†R NEDERLAND, Via Madagascar	S • S Asia • 200 kW (0–2) / E Africa • 200 kW (16–18)
		Mideast • 200 kW (4–6)
	RUSSIA R TIKHIY OKEAN, Chita	S • E Asia & Australasia • 1000 kW (18)
11660	**AUSTRALIA** †RADIO AUSTRALIA, Shepparton	E Asia & SE Asia • 100 kW (13–16)
	BULGARIA †RADIO BULGARIA, Plovdiv	S • S America • 250 kW (12–14)
		S • W Europe • 250 kW (21–23)
	CHINA CHINA RADIO INTL, Kunming	SE Asia • 50 kW (13–15)
	HOLLAND †R NEDERLAND, Via Madagascar	W • S Asia • 200 kW (0–2)
	R NEDERLAND, Via Neth Antilles	W • Australasia • 250 kW (6–8)
	HUNGARY †RADIO BUDAPEST, Jászberény	W M • S America • 250 kW (0–2) / W • S America • 250 kW (21–23)
	UNITED KINGDOM †BBC, Rampisham	S M-F • E Europe • 500 kW (6–8)
	†BBC, Via Vladivostok, Russia	W • E Asia • 500 kW (8–10)
	†BBC, Via Zyyi, Cyprus	W • E Europe • 250 kW (7–9)
	USA †HERALD BROADCASTING, Via Saipan	S • RUSSIAN, ETC • E Asia • 100 kW (6–9)
		S • E Asia • 100 kW (8–10)
	RFE-RL, Via Kavála, Greece	S • C Asia • 250 kW (15–18)
	†VOA, Via Briech, Morocco	S • Europe • 250 kW (16–18)
11665	**CHINA (TAIWAN)** †R TAIPEI INTL, Via Okeechobee, USA	W • Europe • 100 kW (19–21)
	GUAM KTWR-TRANS WORLD RADIO, Merizo	E Asia • 100 kW (8–11)
	JAPAN †RADIO JAPAN/NHK, Tokyo-Yamata	S • SE Asia • 300 kW (17–19)
		SE Asia • 300 kW (18–20)
	RUSSIA †RADIO TATARSTAN, Samara	S • C Asia & E Asia • RUSSIAN, TATAR • 200 kW (0–3)
	SEYCHELLES †FEBA RADIO, North Pt, Mahé Is	S Asia • 100 kW • ALT. FREQ. TO 11640 kHz (13–15)
		F-Su • Mideast & W Asia • 100 kW (13–15)
		Mideast & W Asia • 100 kW (14–16)
		W Asia & S Asia • 100 kW (15–17)
	SWEDEN †RADIO SWEDEN, Hörby	S • N America • 500 kW (0–2)
		S • N America • 500 kW • ALT. FREQ. TO 9475 kHz (0–3)
	UNITED KINGDOM †BBC, Rampisham	W • C Asia • 500 kW (15–17)
		W F • C Asia • 500 kW (15–17)
		W Sa-Th • C Asia • 500 kW (15–17)
		W • S Asia • 250 kW (16–18)
	†BBC, Via Thailand	W M-F • Europe • 300 kW (5–7)
	†BBC, Via Zyyi, Cyprus	
	USA RFE-RL, Via Lampertheim, Germany	S • C Asia • 100 kW (0–2)
	WYFR-FAMILY RADIO, Okeechobee, Fl	W • Europe • 100 kW (21–23)
11665v	**EGYPT** EGYPTIAN RADIO, Abu Za'bal	• C Africa & E Africa • DS-VO THE ARABS • 100 kW (6–14 / 22–24)
11670	**BELARUS** †BELARUSSIAN R	• DS-1, MINSK LOCAL (12–14)
	†R BELARUS/R MINSK, Kalodziscy	S • Europe • 250 kW (0–2)
		S M-Sa • Europe • 250 kW (0–2)
		S Su • Europe • 250 kW (0–2)
		S M/W/F-Su • Europe • 250 kW (0–2)
		S Th • Europe • 250 kW (0–2)
		S Tu • Europe • 250 kW (0–2)
		S M • Europe • 250 kW (0–2)
(con'd)		S Tu-Sa • Europe • 250 kW (0–2)

| FREQUENCY | COUNTRY, STATION, LOCATION | TARGET • NETWORK • POWER (kW) | World Time |

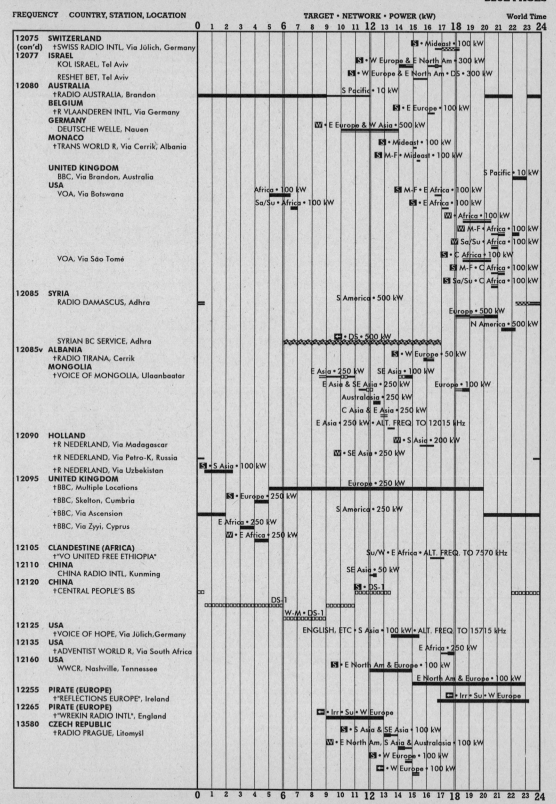

12075 **SWITZERLAND**
(con'd) †SWISS RADIO INTL, Via Jülich, Germany — S • Mideast • 100 kW
12077 **ISRAEL**
    KOL ISRAEL, Tel Aviv — S • W Europe & E North Am • 300 kW
    RESHET BET, Tel Aviv — S • W Europe & E North Am • DS • 300 kW
12080 **AUSTRALIA**
    †RADIO AUSTRALIA, Brandon — S Pacific • 10 kW
    BELGIUM
    †R VLAANDEREN INTL, Via Germany — S • E Europe • 100 kW
    GERMANY
    DEUTSCHE WELLE, Nauen — W • E Europe & W Asia • 500 kW
    MONACO
    †TRANS WORLD R, Via Cerrik, Albania — S • Mideast • 100 kW
    S M-F • Mideast • 100 kW

    UNITED KINGDOM
    BBC, Via Brandon, Australia — S Pacific • 10 kW
    USA
    VOA, Via Botswana — Africa • 100 kW
    S M-F • E Africa • 100 kW
    Sa/Su • Africa • 100 kW
    S • E Africa • 100 kW
    W • Africa • 100 kW
    W M-F • Africa • 100 kW
    W Sa/Su • Africa • 100 kW
    VOA, Via São Tomé — S • C Africa • 100 kW
    S M-F • C Africa • 100 kW
    S Sa/Su • C Africa • 100 kW

12085 **SYRIA**
    RADIO DAMASCUS, Adhra — S America • 500 kW
    Europe • 500 kW
    N America • 500 kW

    SYRIAN BC SERVICE, Adhra — DS • 500 kW
12085v **ALBANIA**
    †RADIO TIRANA, Cerrik — S • W Europe • 50 kW
    MONGOLIA
    †VOICE OF MONGOLIA, Ulaanbaatar — E Asia • 250 kW   SE Asia • 100 kW
    E Asia & SE Asia • 250 kW   Europe • 100 kW
    Australasia • 250 kW
    C Asia & E Asia • 250 kW
    E Asia • 250 kW • ALT. FREQ. TO 12015 kHz

12090 **HOLLAND**
    †R NEDERLAND, Via Madagascar — W • S Asia • 200 kW
    †R NEDERLAND, Via Petro-K, Russia — W • SE Asia • 250 kW
    †R NEDERLAND, Via Uzbekistan — S • S Asia • 100 kW
12095 **UNITED KINGDOM**
    †BBC, Multiple Locations — Europe • 250 kW
    †BBC, Skelton, Cumbria — S • Europe • 250 kW
    †BBC, Via Ascension — S America • 250 kW
    †BBC, Via Zyyi, Cyprus — E Africa • 250 kW
    W • E Africa • 250 kW
12105 **CLANDESTINE (AFRICA)**
    †"VO UNITED FREE ETHIOPIA" — Su/W • E Africa • ALT. FREQ. TO 7570 kHz
12110 **CHINA**
    CHINA RADIO INTL, Kunming — SE Asia • 50 kW
12120 **CHINA**
    †CENTRAL PEOPLE'S BS — S • DS-1
    DS-1
    W-M • DS-1
12125 **USA**
    †VOICE OF HOPE, Via Jülich, Germany — ENGLISH, ETC • S Asia • 100 kW • ALT. FREQ. TO 15715 kHz
12135 **USA**
    †ADVENTIST WORLD R, Via South Africa — E Africa • 250 kW
12160 **USA**
    WWCR, Nashville, Tennessee — S • E North Am & Europe • 100 kW
    E North Am & Europe • 100 kW
12255 **PIRATE (EUROPE)**
    †"REFLECTIONS EUROPE", Ireland — Irr • Su • W Europe
12265 **PIRATE (EUROPE)**
    †"WREKIN RADIO INTL", England — Irr • Su • W Europe
13580 **CZECH REPUBLIC**
    †RADIO PRAGUE, Litomyšl — S • S Asia & SE Asia • 100 kW
    W • E North Am, S Asia & Australasia • 100 kW
    S • W Europe • 100 kW
    • W Europe • 100 kW

FREQUENCY　　COUNTRY, STATION, LOCATION　　　　　　　　TARGET • NETWORK • POWER (kW)　　　　World Time

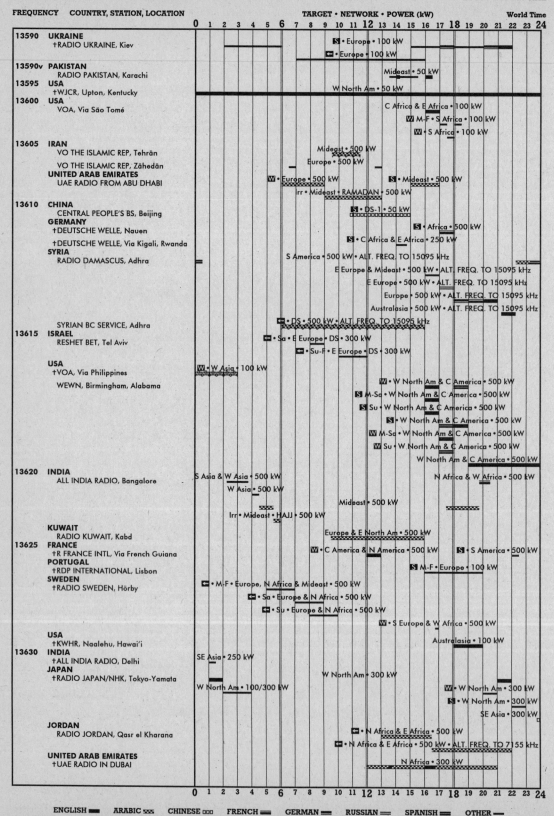

0 1 2 3 4 5 6 7 8 9 10 11 12 13 14 15 16 17 18 19 20 21 22 23 24

13590	**UKRAINE**	
	†RADIO UKRAINE, Kiev	S • Europe • 100 kW
		⊡ • Europe • 100 kW
13590v	**PAKISTAN**	
	RADIO PAKISTAN, Karachi	Mideast • 50 kW
13595	**USA**	
	†WJCR, Upton, Kentucky	W North Am • 50 kW
13600	**USA**	
	VOA, Via São Tomé	C Africa & E Africa • 100 kW
		W M-F • S Africa • 100 kW
		W • S Africa • 100 kW
13605	**IRAN**	
	VO THE ISLAMIC REP, Tehrān	Mideast • 500 kW
	VO THE ISLAMIC REP, Zāhedān	Europe • 500 kW
	UNITED ARAB EMIRATES	
	UAE RADIO FROM ABU DHABI	W • Europe • 500 kW ・ S • Mideast • 500 kW
		Irr • Mideast • RAMADAN • 500 kW
13610	**CHINA**	
	CENTRAL PEOPLE'S BS, Beijing	S • DS-1 • 50 kW
	GERMANY	
	†DEUTSCHE WELLE, Nauen	S • Africa • 500 kW
	†DEUTSCHE WELLE, Via Kigali, Rwanda	S • C Africa & E Africa • 250 kW
	SYRIA	
	RADIO DAMASCUS, Adhra	S America • 500 kW • ALT. FREQ. TO 15095 kHz
		E Europe & Mideast • 500 kW • ALT. FREQ. TO 15095 kHz
		E Europe • 500 kW • ALT. FREQ. TO 15095 kHz
		Europe • 500 kW • ALT. FREQ. TO 15095 kHz
		Australasia • 500 kW • ALT. FREQ. TO 15095 kHz
	SYRIAN BC SERVICE, Adhra	⊡ • DS • 500 kW • ALT. FREQ. TO 15095 kHz
13615	**ISRAEL**	
	RESHET BET, Tel Aviv	⊡ • Sa • E Europe • DS • 300 kW
		⊡ • Su-F • E Europe • DS • 300 kW
	USA	
	†VOA, Via Philippines	W • W Asia • 100 kW
	WEWN, Birmingham, Alabama	W • W North Am & C America • 500 kW
		S M-Sa • W North Am & C America • 500 kW
		S Su • W North Am & C America • 500 kW
		S • W North Am & C America • 500 kW
		W M-Sa • W North Am & C America • 500 kW
		W Su • W North Am & C America • 500 kW
		W North Am & C America • 500 kW
13620	**INDIA**	
	ALL INDIA RADIO, Bangalore	S Asia & W Asia • 500 kW ・ N Africa & W Africa • 500 kW
		W Asia • 500 kW
		Mideast • 500 kW
		Irr • Mideast • HAJJ • 500 kW
	KUWAIT	
	RADIO KUWAIT, Kabd	Europe & E North Am • 500 kW
13625	**FRANCE**	
	†R FRANCE INTL, Via French Guiana	W • C America & N America • 500 kW ・ S • S America • 500 kW
	PORTUGAL	
	†RDP INTERNATIONAL, Lisbon	S M-F • Europe • 100 kW
	SWEDEN	
	†RADIO SWEDEN, Hörby	⊡ • M-F • Europe, N Africa & Mideast • 500 kW
		⊡ • Sa • Europe & N Africa • 500 kW
		⊡ • Su • Europe & N Africa • 500 kW
		W • S Europe & W Africa • 500 kW
	USA	
	†KWHR, Naalehu, Hawai'i	Australasia • 100 kW
13630	**INDIA**	
	†ALL INDIA RADIO, Delhi	SE Asia • 250 kW
	JAPAN	
	†RADIO JAPAN/NHK, Tokyo-Yamata	W North Am • 300 kW
		W North Am • 100/300 kW
		W • W North Am • 300 kW
		S • W North Am • 300 kW
		SE Asia • 300 kW
	JORDAN	
	RADIO JORDAN, Qasr el Kharana	⊡ • N Africa & E Africa • 500 kW
		⊡ • N Africa & E Africa • 500 kW • ALT. FREQ. TO 7155 kHz
	UNITED ARAB EMIRATES	
	†UAE RADIO IN DUBAI	N Africa • 300 kW

0 1 2 3 4 5 6 7 8 9 10 11 12 13 14 15 16 17 18 19 20 21 22 23 24

ENGLISH ▬　**ARABIC** ▨　**CHINESE** ▫▫▫　**FRENCH** ▭▭　**GERMAN** ▬　**RUSSIAN** ＝　**SPANISH** ▭　**OTHER** ▬

FREQUENCY   COUNTRY, STATION, LOCATION   TARGET • NETWORK • POWER (kW)   World Time

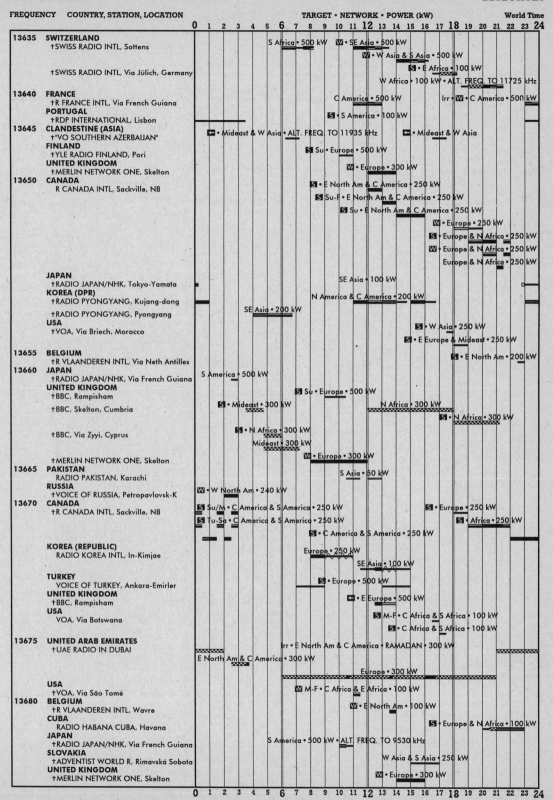

0 1 2 3 4 5 6 7 8 9 10 11 12 13 14 15 16 17 18 19 20 21 22 23 24

13635   SWITZERLAND
          †SWISS RADIO INTL, Sottens
          S Africa • 500 kW   W • SE Asia • 500 kW
          W • W Asia & S Asia • 500 kW
          †SWISS RADIO INTL, Via Jülich, Germany
          S • E Africa • 100 kW
          W Africa • 100 kW • ALT. FREQ. TO 11725 kHz

13640   FRANCE
          †R FRANCE INTL, Via French Guiana
          C America • 500 kW   Irr • W • C America • 500 kW
          PORTUGAL
          †RDP INTERNATIONAL, Lisbon
          S • S America • 100 kW

13645   CLANDESTINE (ASIA)
          †"VO SOUTHERN AZERBAIJAN"
          ▣ • Mideast & W Asia • ALT. FREQ. TO 11935 kHz   ▣ • Mideast & W Asia
          FINLAND
          †YLE RADIO FINLAND, Pori
          S • Su • Europe • 500 kW
          UNITED KINGDOM
          †MERLIN NETWORK ONE, Skelton
          W • Europe • 300 kW

13650   CANADA
          R CANADA INTL, Sackville, NB
          S • E North Am & C America • 250 kW
          S • Su-F • E North Am & C America • 250 kW
          S • Su • E North Am & C America • 250 kW
          W • Europe • 250 kW
          S • Europe & N Africa • 250 kW
          W • Europe & N Africa • 250 kW
          Europe & N Africa • 250 kW

          JAPAN
          †RADIO JAPAN/NHK, Tokyo-Yamata
          SE Asia • 100 kW
          KOREA (DPR)
          †RADIO PYONGYANG, Kujang-dong
          N America & C America • 200 kW
          †RADIO PYONGYANG, Pyongyang
          SE Asia • 200 kW
          USA
          †VOA, Via Briech, Morocco
          S • W Asia • 250 kW
          S • E Europe & Mideast • 250 kW

13655   BELGIUM
          †R VLAANDEREN INTL, Via Neth Antilles
          S • E North Am • 200 kW
13660   JAPAN
          †RADIO JAPAN/NHK, Via French Guiana
          S America • 500 kW
          UNITED KINGDOM
          †BBC, Rampisham
          S • Su • Europe • 500 kW
          †BBC, Skelton, Cumbria
          S • Mideast • 300 kW   N Africa • 300 kW
          S • N Africa • 300 kW
          †BBC, Via Zyyi, Cyprus
          S • N Africa • 300 kW
          Mideast • 300 kW
          †MERLIN NETWORK ONE, Skelton
          W • Europe • 300 kW

13665   PAKISTAN
          RADIO PAKISTAN, Karachi
          S Asia • 50 kW
          RUSSIA
          †VOICE OF RUSSIA, Petropavlovsk-K
          W • W North Am • 240 kW
13670   CANADA
          †R CANADA INTL, Sackville, NB
          S • Su/M • C America & S America • 250 kW   S • Europe • 250 kW
          S • Tu-Sa • C America & S America • 250 kW   S • Africa • 250 kW
          S • C America & S America • 250 kW

          KOREA (REPUBLIC)
          RADIO KOREA INTL, In-Kimjae
          Europe • 250 kW
          SE Asia • 100 kW
          TURKEY
          VOICE OF TURKEY, Ankara-Emirler
          S • Europe • 500 kW
          UNITED KINGDOM
          †BBC, Rampisham
          ▣ • E Europe • 500 kW
          USA
          VOA, Via Botswana
          S • M-F • C Africa & S Africa • 100 kW
          S • C Africa & S Africa • 100 kW

13675   UNITED ARAB EMIRATES
          †UAE RADIO IN DUBAI
          Irr • E North Am & C America • RAMADAN • 300 kW
          E North Am & C America • 300 kW
          Europe • 300 kW

          USA
          †VOA, Via São Tomé
          W • M-F • C Africa & E Africa • 100 kW
13680   BELGIUM
          †R VLAANDEREN INTL, Wavre
          W • E North Am • 100 kW
          CUBA
          RADIO HABANA CUBA, Havana
          S • Europe & N Africa • 100 kW
          JAPAN
          †RADIO JAPAN/NHK, Via French Guiana
          S America • 500 kW • ALT. FREQ. TO 9530 kHz
          SLOVAKIA
          †ADVENTIST WORLD R, Rimavská Sobota
          W Asia & S Asia • 250 kW
          UNITED KINGDOM
          †MERLIN NETWORK ONE, Skelton
          W • Europe • 300 kW

0 1 2 3 4 5 6 7 8 9 10 11 12 13 14 15 16 17 18 19 20 21 22 23 24

FREQUENCY   COUNTRY, STATION, LOCATION   TARGET • NETWORK • POWER (kW)   World Time

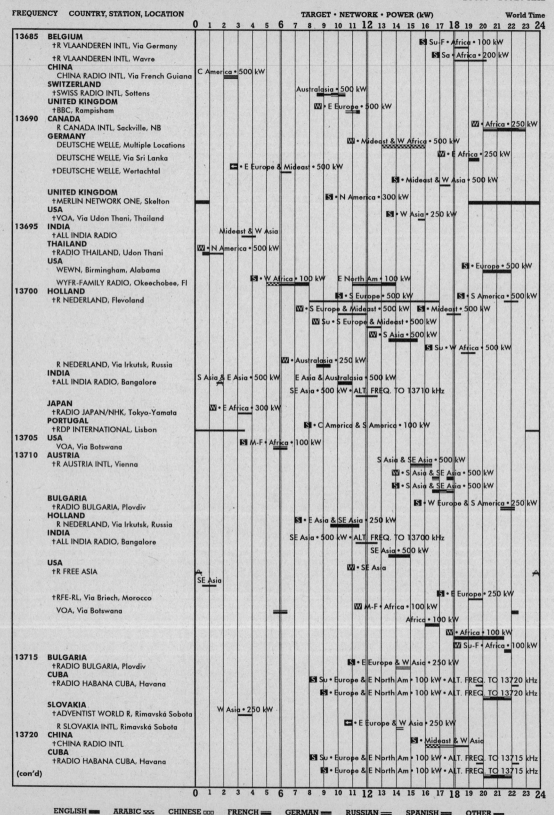

13685	BELGIUM
	†R VLAANDEREN INTL, Via Germany	S Su-F • Africa • 100 kW
	†R VLAANDEREN INTL, Wavre	Sa • Africa • 200 kW
	CHINA
	CHINA RADIO INTL, Via French Guiana	C America • 500 kW
	SWITZERLAND
	†SWISS RADIO INTL, Sottens	Australasia • 500 kW
	UNITED KINGDOM
	†BBC, Rampisham	W • E Europe • 500 kW
13690	CANADA
	R CANADA INTL, Sackville, NB	W • Africa • 250 kW
	GERMANY
	DEUTSCHE WELLE, Multiple Locations	W • Mideast & W Africa • 500 kW
	DEUTSCHE WELLE, Via Sri Lanka	W • E Africa • 250 kW
	†DEUTSCHE WELLE, Wertachtal	E Europe & Mideast • 500 kW
		S • Mideast & W Asia • 500 kW
	UNITED KINGDOM
	†MERLIN NETWORK ONE, Skelton	S • N America • 300 kW
	USA
	†VOA, Via Udon Thani, Thailand	S • W Asia • 250 kW
13695	INDIA
	†ALL INDIA RADIO	Mideast & W Asia
	THAILAND
	†RADIO THAILAND, Udon Thani	W • N America • 500 kW
	USA
	WEWN, Birmingham, Alabama	S • Europe • 500 kW
	WYFR-FAMILY RADIO, Okeechobee, Fl	S • W Africa • 100 kW E North Am • 100 kW
13700	HOLLAND
	†R NEDERLAND, Flevoland	S • S Europe • 500 kW S • S America • 500 kW
		W • S Europe & Mideast • 500 kW S • Mideast • 500 kW
		W Su • S Europe & Mideast • 500 kW
		W • S Asia • 500 kW
		S Su • W Africa • 500 kW
	R NEDERLAND, Via Irkutsk, Russia	W • Australasia • 250 kW
	INDIA
	†ALL INDIA RADIO, Bangalore	S Asia & E Asia • 500 kW E Asia & Australasia • 500 kW
		SE Asia • 500 kW • ALT. FREQ. TO 13710 kHz
	JAPAN
	†RADIO JAPAN/NHK, Tokyo-Yamata	W • E Africa • 300 kW
	PORTUGAL
	†RDP INTERNATIONAL, Lisbon	S • C America & S America • 100 kW
13705	USA
	VOA, Via Botswana	S • M-F • Africa • 100 kW
13710	AUSTRIA
	†R AUSTRIA INTL, Vienna	S Asia & SE Asia • 500 kW
		W • S Asia & SE Asia • 500 kW
		S • S Asia & SE Asia • 500 kW
	BULGARIA
	†RADIO BULGARIA, Plovdiv	S • W Europe & S America • 250 kW
	HOLLAND
	R NEDERLAND, Via Irkutsk, Russia	S • E Asia & SE Asia • 250 kW
	INDIA
	†ALL INDIA RADIO, Bangalore	SE Asia • 500 kW • ALT. FREQ. TO 13700 kHz
		SE Asia • 500 kW
	USA
	†R FREE ASIA	W • SE Asia
		SE Asia
	†RFE-RL, Via Briech, Morocco	S • E Europe • 250 kW
	VOA, Via Botswana	W • M-F • Africa • 100 kW
		Africa • 100 kW
		W • Africa • 100 kW
		W Su-F • Africa • 100 kW
13715	BULGARIA
	†RADIO BULGARIA, Plovdiv	S • E Europe & W Asia • 250 kW
	CUBA
	†RADIO HABANA CUBA, Havana	S Su • Europe & E North Am • 100 kW • ALT. FREQ. TO 13720 kHz
		S • Europe & E North Am • 100 kW • ALT. FREQ. TO 13720 kHz
	SLOVAKIA
	†ADVENTIST WORLD R, Rimavská Sobota	W Asia • 250 kW
	R SLOVAKIA INTL, Rimavská Sobota	E Europe & W Asia • 250 kW
13720	CHINA
	†CHINA RADIO INTL	S • Mideast & W Asia
	CUBA
	†RADIO HABANA CUBA, Havana	S Su • Europe & E North Am • 100 kW • ALT. FREQ. TO 13715 kHz
		S • Europe & E North Am • 100 kW • ALT. FREQ. TO 13715 kHz

(con'd)

FREQUENCY   COUNTRY, STATION, LOCATION

TARGET • NETWORK • POWER (kW)

World Time

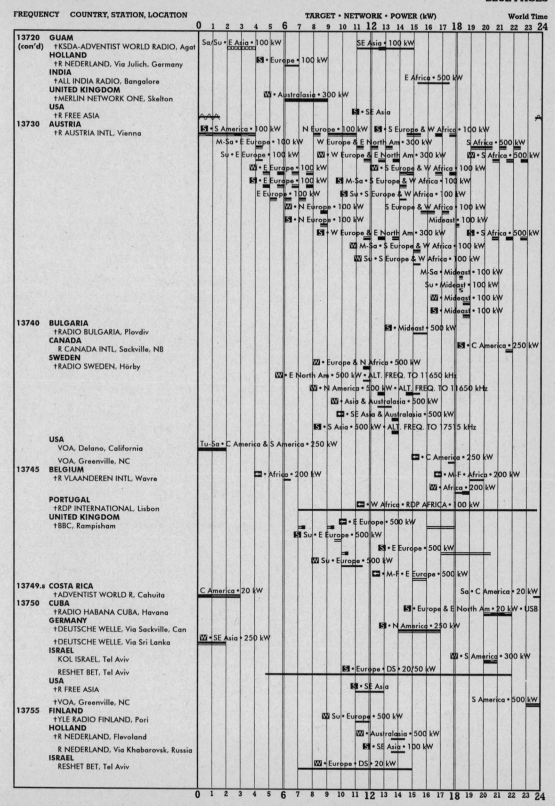

13720 GUAM
(con'd) †KSDA-ADVENTIST WORLD RADIO, Agat — Sa/Su • E Asia • 100 kW / SE Asia • 100 kW
HOLLAND
  †R NEDERLAND, Via Julich, Germany — S • Europe • 100 kW
INDIA
  †ALL INDIA RADIO, Bangalore — E Africa • 500 kW
UNITED KINGDOM
  †MERLIN NETWORK ONE, Skelton — W • Australasia • 300 kW
USA
  †R FREE ASIA — S • SE Asia
13730 AUSTRIA
  †R AUSTRIA INTL, Vienna
    S • S America • 100 kW / N Europe • 100 kW / S • S Europe & W Africa • 100 kW
    M-Sa • E Europe • 100 kW / W Europe & E North Am • 300 kW / S Africa • 500 kW
    Su • E Europe • 100 kW / W • W Europe & E North Am • 300 kW / W • S Africa • 500 kW
    W • E Europe • 100 kW / W • S Europe & W Africa • 100 kW
    S • E Europe • 100 kW / S M-Sa • S Europe & W Africa • 100 kW
    E Europe • 100 kW / Su • S Europe & W Africa • 100 kW
    W • N Europe • 100 kW / S Europe & W Africa • 100 kW
    S • N Europe • 100 kW / Mideast • 100 kW
    S • W Europe & E North Am • 300 kW / S • S Africa • 500 kW
    W M-Sa • S Europe & W Africa • 100 kW
    W Su • S Europe & W Africa • 100 kW
    M-Sa • Mideast • 100 kW
    Su • Mideast • 100 kW
    W • Mideast • 100 kW
    S • Mideast • 100 kW
13740 BULGARIA
  †RADIO BULGARIA, Plovdiv — S • Mideast • 500 kW
CANADA
  R CANADA INTL, Sackville, NB — S • C America • 250 kW
SWEDEN
  †RADIO SWEDEN, Hörby
    W • Europe & N Africa • 500 kW
    W • E North Am • 500 kW • ALT. FREQ. TO 11650 kHz
    W • N America • 500 kW • ALT. FREQ. TO 11650 kHz
    W • Asia & Australasia • 500 kW
    ⊡ • SE Asia & Australasia • 500 kW
    S • S Asia • 500 kW • ALT. FREQ. TO 17515 kHz
USA
  VOA, Delano, California — Tu-Sa • C America & S America • 250 kW

  VOA, Greenville, NC — W • C America • 250 kW
13745 BELGIUM
  †R VLAANDEREN INTL, Wavre
    ⊡ • Africa • 200 kW
    ⊡ • M-F • Africa • 200 kW
    W • Africa • 200 kW
PORTUGAL
  †RDP INTERNATIONAL, Lisbon — ⊡ • W Africa • RDP AFRICA • 100 kW
UNITED KINGDOM
  †BBC, Rampisham
    ⊡ • E Europe • 500 kW
    S Su • E Europe • 500 kW
    S • E Europe • 500 kW
    W Su • Europe • 500 kW
    ⊡ • M-F • E Europe • 500 kW
13749.8 COSTA RICA
  †ADVENTIST WORLD R, Cahuita — C America • 20 kW / Sa • C America • 20 kW
13750 CUBA
  †RADIO HABANA CUBA, Havana — S • Europe & E North Am • 20 kW • USB
GERMANY
  †DEUTSCHE WELLE, Via Sackville, Can — S • N America • 250 kW

  †DEUTSCHE WELLE, Via Sri Lanka — W • SE Asia • 250 kW
ISRAEL
  KOL ISRAEL, Tel Aviv — W • S America • 300 kW

  RESHET BET, Tel Aviv — S • Europe • DS • 20/50 kW
USA
  †R FREE ASIA — S • SE Asia

  †VOA, Greenville, NC — S America • 500 kW
13755 FINLAND
  †YLE RADIO FINLAND, Pori — W Su • Europe • 500 kW
HOLLAND
  †R NEDERLAND, Flevoland — W • Australasia • 500 kW

  R NEDERLAND, Via Khabarovsk, Russia — S • SE Asia • 100 kW
ISRAEL
  RESHET BET, Tel Aviv — W • Europe • DS • 20 kW

SEASONAL S OR W   1-HR TIMESHIFT MIDYEAR ⊡ OR ⊡   JAMMING / OR ∧   EARLIEST HEARD ◁   LATEST HEARD ▷   NEW FOR 1999 †

FREQUENCY   COUNTRY, STATION, LOCATION   TARGET • NETWORK • POWER (kW)   World Time

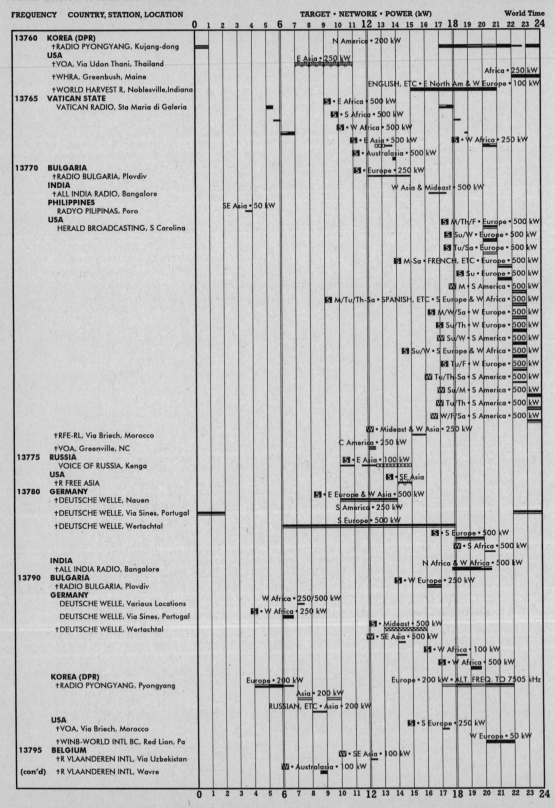

FREQUENCY	COUNTRY, STATION, LOCATION	TARGET • NETWORK • POWER (kW)
13760	KOREA (DPR)	
	†RADIO PYONGYANG, Kujang-dong	N America • 200 kW
	USA	
	†VOA, Via Udon Thani, Thailand	E Asia • 250 kW
	†WHRA, Greenbush, Maine	Africa • 250 kW
	†WORLD HARVEST R, Noblesville, Indiana	ENGLISH, ETC • E North Am & W Europe • 100 kW
13765	VATICAN STATE	
	VATICAN RADIO, Sta Maria di Galeria	S • E Africa • 500 kW
		S • S Africa • 500 kW
		S • W Africa • 500 kW
		S • E Asia • 500 kW / S • W Africa • 250 kW
		S • Australasia • 500 kW
13770	BULGARIA	
	†RADIO BULGARIA, Plovdiv	S • Europe • 250 kW
	INDIA	
	†ALL INDIA RADIO, Bangalore	W Asia & Mideast • 500 kW
	PHILPPINES	
	RADYO PILIPINAS, Poro	SE Asia • 50 kW
	USA	
	HERALD BROADCASTING, S Carolina	S • M/Th/F • Europe • 500 kW
		S • Su/W • Europe • 500 kW
		S • Tu/Sa • Europe • 500 kW
		S • M-Sa • FRENCH, ETC • Europe • 500 kW
		S • Su • Europe • 500 kW
		W • M • S America • 500 kW
		S • M/Tu/Th-Sa • SPANISH, ETC • S Europe & W Africa • 500 kW
		S • M/W/Sa • W Europe • 500 kW
		S • Su/Th • W Europe • 500 kW
		W • Su/W • S America • 500 kW
		S • Su/W • S Europe & W Africa • 500 kW
		S • Tu/F • W Europe • 500 kW
		W • Tu/Th-Sa • S America • 500 kW
		W • Su/M • S America • 500 kW
		W • Tu/Th • S America • 500 kW
		W • W/F/Sa • S America • 500 kW
	†RFE-RL, Via Briech, Morocco	W • Mideast & W Asia • 250 kW
	†VOA, Greenville, NC	C America • 250 kW
13775	RUSSIA	
	VOICE OF RUSSIA, Kenga	S • E Asia • 100 kW
	USA	
	†R FREE ASIA	S • SE Asia
13780	GERMANY	
	†DEUTSCHE WELLE, Nauen	S • E Europe & W Asia • 500 kW
	†DEUTSCHE WELLE, Via Sines, Portugal	S America • 250 kW
	†DEUTSCHE WELLE, Wertachtal	S Europe • 500 kW
		S • S Europe • 500 kW
		W • S Africa • 500 kW
	INDIA	
	†ALL INDIA RADIO, Bangalore	N Africa & W Africa • 500 kW
13790	BULGARIA	
	†RADIO BULGARIA, Plovdiv	S • W Europe • 250 kW
	GERMANY	
	DEUTSCHE WELLE, Various Locations	W Africa • 250/500 kW
	DEUTSCHE WELLE, Via Sines, Portugal	S • W Africa • 250 kW
	†DEUTSCHE WELLE, Wertachtal	S • Mideast • 500 kW
		W • SE Asia • 500 kW
		S • W Africa • 100 kW
		S • W Africa • 500 kW
	KOREA (DPR)	
	†RADIO PYONGYANG, Pyongyang	Europe • 200 kW / Europe • 200 kW • ALT. FREQ. TO 7505 kHz
		Asia • 200 kW
		RUSSIAN, ETC • Asia • 200 kW
	USA	
	†VOA, Via Briech, Morocco	S • S Europe • 250 kW
	†WINB-WORLD INTL BC, Red Lion, Pa	W Europe • 50 kW
13795	BELGIUM	
	†R VLAANDEREN INTL, Via Uzbekistan	W • SE Asia • 100 kW
(con'd)	†R VLAANDEREN INTL, Wavre	W • Australasia • 100 kW

ENGLISH ▬ ARABIC ≋ CHINESE ▫▫▫ FRENCH ══ GERMAN ▬▬ RUSSIAN ══ SPANISH ▬▬ OTHER ──

FREQUENCY   COUNTRY, STATION, LOCATION

TARGET • NETWORK • POWER (kW)

World Time

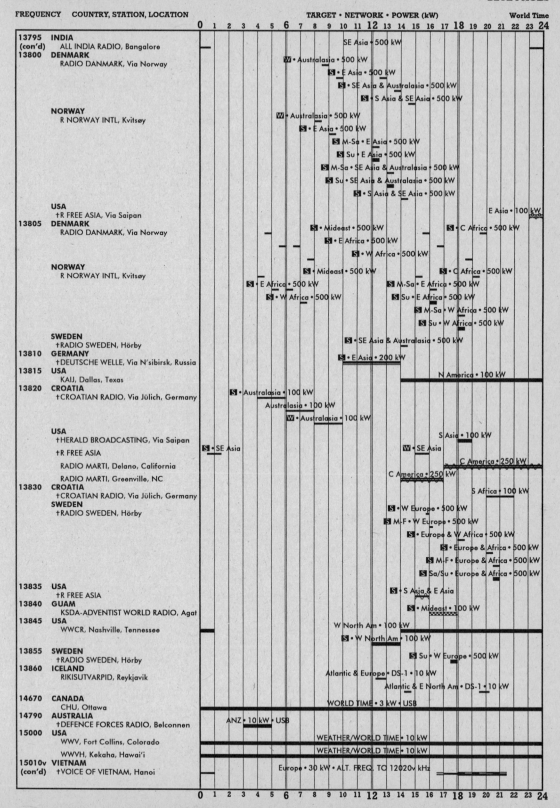

FREQUENCY	COUNTRY, STATION, LOCATION	TARGET • NETWORK • POWER (kW)
13795 (con'd)	**INDIA** ALL INDIA RADIO, Bangalore	SE Asia • 500 kW
13800	**DENMARK** RADIO DANMARK, Via Norway	W • Australasia • 500 kW / S • E Asia • 500 kW / S • SE Asia & Australasia • 500 kW / S • S Asia & SE Asia • 500 kW
	NORWAY R NORWAY INTL, Kvitsøy	W • Australasia • 500 kW / S • E Asia • 500 kW / S M-Sa • E Asia • 500 kW / S Su • E Asia • 500 kW / S M-Sa • SE Asia & Australasia • 500 kW / S Su • SE Asia & Australasia • 500 kW / S • S Asia & SE Asia • 500 kW
	USA †R FREE ASIA, Via Saipan	E Asia • 100 kW
13805	**DENMARK** RADIO DANMARK, Via Norway	S • Mideast • 500 kW / S • E Africa • 500 kW / S • W Africa • 500 kW / S • C Africa • 500 kW
	NORWAY R NORWAY INTL, Kvitsøy	S • E Africa • 500 kW / S • W Africa • 500 kW / S • Mideast • 500 kW / S M-Sa • E Africa • 500 kW / S Su • E Africa • 500 kW / S • C Africa • 500 kW / S M-Sa • W Africa • 500 kW / S Su • W Africa • 500 kW
	SWEDEN †RADIO SWEDEN, Hörby	S • SE Asia & Australasia • 500 kW
13810	**GERMANY** †DEUTSCHE WELLE, Via N'sibirsk, Russia	S • E Asia • 200 kW
13815	**USA** KAIJ, Dallas, Texas	N America • 100 kW
13820	**CROATIA** †CROATIAN RADIO, Via Jülich, Germany	S • Australasia • 100 kW / Australasia • 100 kW / W • Australasia • 100 kW
	USA †HERALD BROADCASTING, Via Saipan	S • SE Asia / W • SE Asia / S Asia • 100 kW
	†R FREE ASIA	
	RADIO MARTI, Delano, California	C America • 250 kW
	RADIO MARTI, Greenville, NC	C America • 250 kW / S Africa • 100 kW
13830	**CROATIA** †CROATIAN RADIO, Via Jülich, Germany	
	SWEDEN †RADIO SWEDEN, Hörby	S • W Europe • 500 kW / S M-F • W Europe • 500 kW / S • Europe & W Africa • 500 kW / S • Europe & Africa • 500 kW / S M-F • Europe & Africa • 500 kW / S Sa/Su • Europe & Africa • 500 kW
13835	**USA** †R FREE ASIA	S • S Asia & E Asia
13840	**GUAM** KSDA-ADVENTIST WORLD RADIO, Agat	S • Mideast • 100 kW
13845	**USA** WWCR, Nashville, Tennessee	W North Am • 100 kW / S • W North Am • 100 kW
13855	**SWEDEN** †RADIO SWEDEN, Hörby	S Su • W Europe • 500 kW
13860	**ICELAND** RIKISUTVARPID, Reykjavik	Atlantic & Europe • DS-1 • 10 kW / Atlantic & E North Am • DS-1 • 10 kW
14670	**CANADA** CHU, Ottawa	WORLD TIME • 3 kW • USB
14790	**AUSTRALIA** †DEFENCE FORCES RADIO, Belconnen	ANZ • 10 kW • USB
15000	**USA** WWV, Fort Collins, Colorado	WEATHER/WORLD TIME • 10 kW
	WWVH, Kekaha, Hawai'i	WEATHER/WORLD TIME • 10 kW
15010v (con'd)	**VIETNAM** †VOICE OF VIETNAM, Hanoi	Europe • 30 kW • ALT. FREQ. TO 12020v kHz

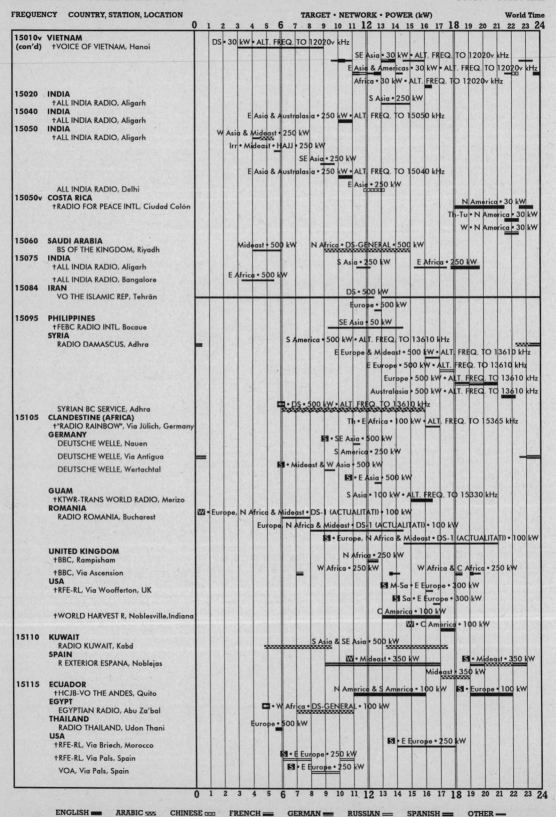

FREQUENCY   COUNTRY, STATION, LOCATION

TARGET • NETWORK • POWER (kW)

World Time

Frequency	Country, Station, Location	Details
15010v (con'd)	VIETNAM †VOICE OF VIETNAM, Hanoi	DS • 30 kW • ALT. FREQ. TO 12020v kHz; SE Asia • 30 kW • ALT. FREQ. TO 12020v kHz; E Asia & Americas • 30 kW • ALT. FREQ. TO 12020v kHz; Africa • 30 kW • ALT. FREQ. TO 12020v kHz
15020	INDIA †ALL INDIA RADIO, Aligarh	S Asia • 250 kW
15040	INDIA †ALL INDIA RADIO, Aligarh	E Asia & Australasia • 250 kW • ALT. FREQ. TO 15050 kHz
15050	INDIA †ALL INDIA RADIO, Aligarh	W Asia & Mideast • 250 kW; Irr • Mideast • HAJJ • 250 kW; SE Asia • 250 kW; E Asia & Australasia • 250 kW • ALT. FREQ. TO 15040 kHz
	ALL INDIA RADIO, Delhi	E Asia • 250 kW
15050v	COSTA RICA †RADIO FOR PEACE INTL, Ciudad Colón	N America • 30 kW; Th-Tu • N America • 30 kW; W • N America • 30 kW
15060	SAUDI ARABIA BS OF THE KINGDOM, Riyadh	Mideast • 500 kW; N Africa • DS-GENERAL • 500 kW
15075	INDIA †ALL INDIA RADIO, Aligarh	S Asia • 250 kW; E Africa • 250 kW
	†ALL INDIA RADIO, Bangalore	E Africa • 500 kW
15084	IRAN VO THE ISLAMIC REP, Tehrān	DS • 500 kW
15095	PHILIPPINES †FEBC RADIO INTL, Bocaue	Europe • 500 kW; SE Asia • 50 kW
	SYRIA RADIO DAMASCUS, Adhra	S America • 500 kW • ALT. FREQ. TO 13610 kHz; E Europe & Mideast • 500 kW • ALT. FREQ. TO 13610 kHz; E Europe • 500 kW • ALT. FREQ. TO 13610 kHz; Europe • 500 kW • ALT. FREQ. TO 13610 kHz; Australasia • 500 kW • ALT. FREQ. TO 13610 kHz
	SYRIAN BC SERVICE, Adhra	DS • 500 kW • ALT. FREQ. TO 13610 kHz
15105	CLANDESTINE (AFRICA) †"RADIO RAINBOW", Via Jülich, Germany	Th • E Africa • 100 kW • ALT. FREQ. TO 15365 kHz
	GERMANY DEUTSCHE WELLE, Nauen	SE Asia • 500 kW
	DEUTSCHE WELLE, Via Antigua	S America • 250 kW
	DEUTSCHE WELLE, Wertachtal	Mideast & W Asia • 500 kW
		E Asia • 500 kW
	GUAM †KTWR-TRANS WORLD RADIO, Merizo	S Asia • 100 kW • ALT. FREQ. TO 15330 kHz
	ROMANIA RADIO ROMANIA, Bucharest	W • Europe, N Africa & Mideast • DS-1 (ACTUALITATI) • 100 kW; Europe, N Africa & Mideast • DS-1 (ACTUALITATI) • 100 kW; S • Europe, N Africa & Mideast • DS-1 (ACTUALITATI) • 100 kW
	UNITED KINGDOM †BBC, Rampisham	N Africa • 250 kW
	†BBC, Via Ascension	W Africa • 250 kW; W Africa & C Africa • 250 kW
	USA †RFE-RL, Via Woofferton, UK	M-Sa • E Europe • 300 kW; Sa • E Europe • 300 kW
	†WORLD HARVEST R, Noblesville, Indiana	C America • 100 kW; W • C America • 100 kW
15110	KUWAIT RADIO KUWAIT, Kabd	S Asia & SE Asia • 500 kW
	SPAIN R EXTERIOR ESPANA, Noblejas	W • Mideast • 350 kW; Mideast • 350 kW; Mideast • 350 kW
15115	ECUADOR †HCJB-VO THE ANDES, Quito	N America & S America • 100 kW; Europe • 100 kW
	EGYPT EGYPTIAN RADIO, Abu Za'bal	W Africa • DS-GENERAL • 100 kW
	THAILAND RADIO THAILAND, Udon Thani	Europe • 500 kW
	USA †RFE-RL, Via Briech, Morocco	E Europe • 250 kW
	†RFE-RL, Via Pals, Spain	E Europe • 250 kW
	VOA, Via Pals, Spain	E Europe • 250 kW

ENGLISH ▬   ARABIC ∼∼∼   CHINESE □□□   FRENCH ═══   GERMAN ▬▬   RUSSIAN ══   SPANISH ▬▬   OTHER ──

FREQUENCY   COUNTRY, STATION, LOCATION

TARGET • NETWORK • POWER (kW)

World Time

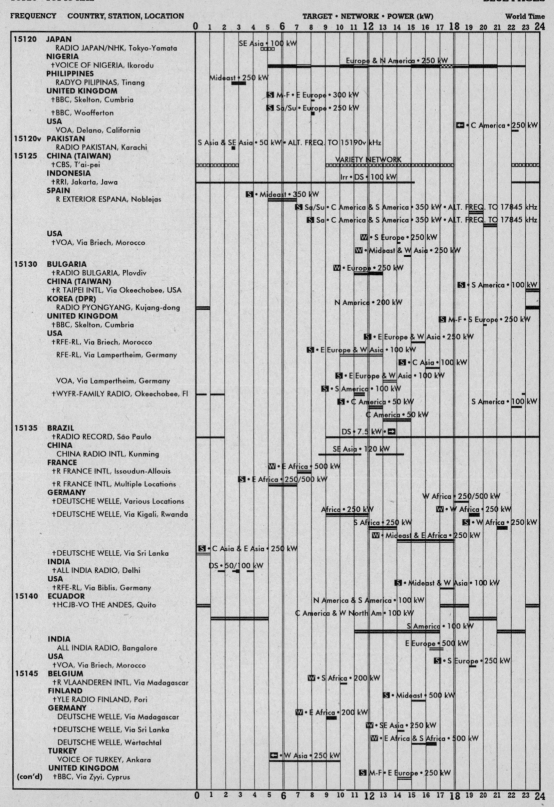

FREQUENCY	COUNTRY, STATION, LOCATION	Notes
15120	**JAPAN** RADIO JAPAN/NHK, Tokyo-Yamata	SE Asia • 100 kW
	NIGERIA †VOICE OF NIGERIA, Ikorodu	Europe & N America • 250 kW
	PHILIPPINES RADYO PILIPINAS, Tinang	Mideast • 250 kW
	UNITED KINGDOM †BBC, Skelton, Cumbria	S M-F • E Europe • 300 kW
	†BBC, Woofferton	S Sa/Su • Europe • 250 kW
	USA VOA, Delano, California	C America • 250 kW
15120v	**PAKISTAN** RADIO PAKISTAN, Karachi	S Asia & SE Asia • 50 kW • ALT. FREQ. TO 15190v kHz
15125	**CHINA (TAIWAN)** †CBS, T'ai-pei	VARIETY NETWORK
	INDONESIA †RRI, Jakarta, Jawa	Irr • DS • 100 kW
	SPAIN R EXTERIOR ESPANA, Noblejas	S • Mideast • 350 kW
		S Sa/Su • C America & S America • 350 kW • ALT. FREQ. TO 17845 kHz
		S Sa • C America & S America • 350 kW • ALT. FREQ. TO 17845 kHz
	USA †VOA, Via Briech, Morocco	W • S Europe • 250 kW
		W • Mideast & W Asia • 250 kW
15130	**BULGARIA** †RADIO BULGARIA, Plovdiv	W • Europe • 250 kW
	CHINA (TAIWAN) †R TAIPEI INTL, Via Okeechobee, USA	S • S America • 100 kW
	KOREA (DPR) RADIO PYONGYANG, Kujang-dong	N America • 200 kW
	UNITED KINGDOM †BBC, Skelton, Cumbria	S M-F • S Europe • 250 kW
	USA †RFE-RL, Via Briech, Morocco	S • E Europe & W Asia • 250 kW
	RFE-RL, Via Lampertheim, Germany	S • E Europe & W Asia • 100 kW
		S • C Asia • 100 kW
	VOA, Via Lampertheim, Germany	S • E Europe & W Asia • 100 kW
	†WYFR-FAMILY RADIO, Okeechobee, Fl	S • S America • 100 kW
		S • C America • 50 kW
		C America • 50 kW / S America • 100 kW
15135	**BRAZIL** †RADIO RECORD, São Paulo	DS • 7.5 kW •
	CHINA CHINA RADIO INTL, Kunming	SE Asia • 120 kW
	FRANCE †R FRANCE INTL, Issoudun-Allouis	W • E Africa • 500 kW
	†R FRANCE INTL, Multiple Locations	S • E Africa • 250/500 kW
	GERMANY †DEUTSCHE WELLE, Various Locations	W Africa • 250/500 kW
	†DEUTSCHE WELLE, Via Kigali, Rwanda	Africa • 250 kW / W • W Africa • 250 kW
		S Africa • 250 kW / S • W Africa • 250 kW
		W • Mideast & E Africa • 250 kW
	†DEUTSCHE WELLE, Via Sri Lanka	S • C Asia & E Asia • 250 kW
	INDIA †ALL INDIA RADIO, Delhi	DS • 50/100 kW
	USA †RFE-RL, Via Biblis, Germany	S • Mideast & W Asia • 100 kW
15140	**ECUADOR** †HCJB-VO THE ANDES, Quito	N America & S America • 100 kW
		C America & W North Am • 100 kW
		S America • 100 kW
	INDIA ALL INDIA RADIO, Bangalore	E Europe • 500 kW
	USA †VOA, Via Briech, Morocco	S • S Europe • 250 kW
15145	**BELGIUM** †R VLAANDEREN INTL, Via Madagascar	W • S Africa • 200 kW
	FINLAND †YLE RADIO FINLAND, Pori	S • Mideast • 500 kW
	GERMANY DEUTSCHE WELLE, Via Madagascar	W • E Africa • 200 kW
	†DEUTSCHE WELLE, Via Sri Lanka	W • SE Asia • 250 kW
	DEUTSCHE WELLE, Wertachtal	W • E Africa & S Africa • 500 kW
	TURKEY VOICE OF TURKEY, Ankara	W Asia • 250 kW
	UNITED KINGDOM	
(con'd)	†BBC, Via Zyyi, Cyprus	S M-F • E Europe • 250 kW

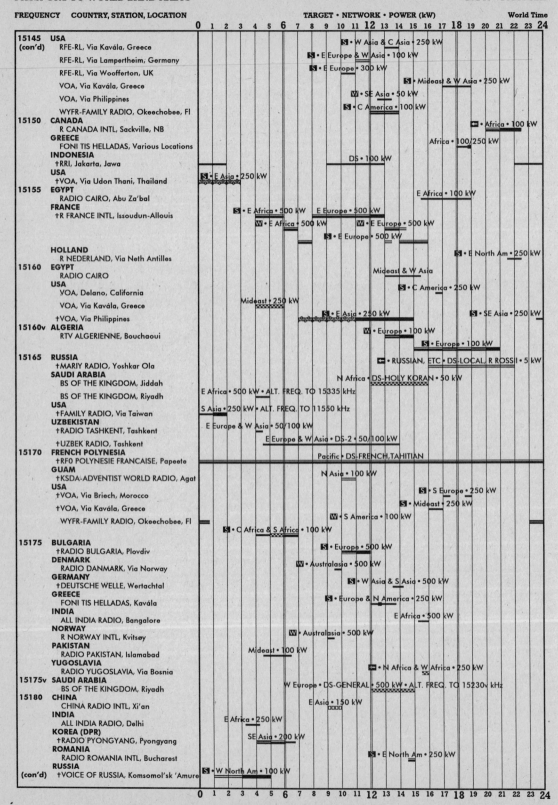

FREQUENCY	COUNTRY, STATION, LOCATION	TARGET • NETWORK • POWER (kW)
15145 (con'd)	USA	
	RFE-RL, Via Kavála, Greece	S • W Asia & C Asia • 250 kW
	RFE-RL, Via Lampertheim, Germany	S • E Europe & W Asia • 100 kW
	RFE-RL, Via Woofferton, UK	S • E Europe • 300 kW
	VOA, Via Kavála, Greece	S • Mideast & W Asia • 250 kW
	VOA, Via Philippines	W • SE Asia • 50 kW
	WYFR-FAMILY RADIO, Okeechobee, Fl	S • C America • 100 kW
15150	CANADA	
	R CANADA INTL, Sackville, NB	▣ • Africa • 100 kW
	GREECE	
	FONI TIS HELLADAS, Various Locations	Africa • 100/250 kW
	INDONESIA	
	†RRI, Jakarta, Jawa	DS • 100 kW
	USA	
	†VOA, Via Udon Thani, Thailand	S • E Asia • 250 kW
15155	EGYPT	
	RADIO CAIRO, Abu Za'bal	E Africa • 100 kW
	FRANCE	
	†R FRANCE INTL, Issoudun-Allouis	S • E Africa • 500 kW E Europe • 500 kW
		W • E Africa • 500 kW W • E Europe • 500 kW
		S • E Europe • 500 kW
	HOLLAND	
	R NEDERLAND, Via Neth Antilles	S • E North Am • 250 kW
15160	EGYPT	
	RADIO CAIRO	Mideast & W Asia
	USA	
	VOA, Delano, California	S • C America • 250 kW
	VOA, Via Kavála, Greece	Mideast • 250 kW
	†VOA, Via Philippines	S • E Asia • 250 kW S • SE Asia • 250 kW
15160v	ALGERIA	
	RTV ALGERIENNE, Bouchaoui	W • Europe • 100 kW
		S • Europe • 100 kW
15165	RUSSIA	
	†MARIY RADIO, Yoshkar Ola	▣ • RUSSIAN, ETC • DS-LOCAL, R ROSSII • 5 kW
	SAUDI ARABIA	
	BS OF THE KINGDOM, Jiddah	N Africa • DS-HOLY KORAN • 50 kW
	BS OF THE KINGDOM, Riyadh	E Africa • 500 kW • ALT. FREQ. TO 15335 kHz
	USA	
	†FAMILY RADIO, Via Taiwan	S Asia • 250 kW • ALT. FREQ. TO 11550 kHz
	UZBEKISTAN	
	†RADIO TASHKENT, Tashkent	E Europe & W Asia • 50/100 kW
	†UZBEK RADIO, Tashkent	E Europe & W Asia • DS-2 • 50/100 kW
15170	FRENCH POLYNESIA	
	†RFO POLYNESIE FRANCAISE, Papeete	Pacific • DS-FRENCH, TAHITIAN
	GUAM	
	†KSDA-ADVENTIST WORLD RADIO, Agat	N Asia • 100 kW
	USA	
	†VOA, Via Briech, Morocco	S • S Europe • 250 kW
	†VOA, Via Kavála, Greece	S • Mideast • 250 kW
	WYFR-FAMILY RADIO, Okeechobee, Fl	W • S America • 100 kW
		S • C Africa & S Africa • 100 kW
15175	BULGARIA	
	†RADIO BULGARIA, Plovdiv	S • Europe • 500 kW
	DENMARK	
	RADIO DANMARK, Via Norway	W • Australasia • 500 kW
	GERMANY	
	†DEUTSCHE WELLE, Wertachtal	S • W Asia & S Asia • 500 kW
	GREECE	
	FONI TIS HELLADAS, Kavála	S • Europe & N America • 250 kW
	INDIA	
	ALL INDIA RADIO, Bangalore	E Africa • 500 kW
	NORWAY	
	R NORWAY INTL, Kvitsøy	W • Australasia • 500 kW
	PAKISTAN	
	RADIO PAKISTAN, Islamabad	Mideast • 100 kW
	YUGOSLAVIA	
	RADIO YUGOSLAVIA, Via Bosnia	▣ • N Africa & W Africa • 250 kW
15175v	SAUDI ARABIA	
	BS OF THE KINGDOM, Riyadh	W Europe • DS-GENERAL • 500 kW • ALT. FREQ. TO 15230v kHz
15180	CHINA	
	CHINA RADIO INTL, Xi'an	E Asia • 150 kW
	INDIA	
	ALL INDIA RADIO, Delhi	E Africa • 250 kW
	KOREA (DPR)	
	†RADIO PYONGYANG, Pyongyang	SE Asia • 200 kW
	ROMANIA	
	RADIO ROMANIA INTL, Bucharest	S • E North Am • 250 kW
	RUSSIA	
(con'd)	†VOICE OF RUSSIA, Komsomol'sk 'Amure	S • W North Am • 100 kW

World Time

0 1 2 3 4 5 6 7 8 9 10 11 12 13 14 15 16 17 18 19 20 21 22 23 24

ENGLISH ▬   ARABIC ⧓   CHINESE ▭▭▭   FRENCH ▬   GERMAN ▬   RUSSIAN ═   SPANISH ▬   OTHER ▬

FREQUENCY   COUNTRY, STATION, LOCATION   TARGET • NETWORK • POWER (kW)   World Time
                                                    0 1 2 3 4 5 6 7 8 9 10 11 12 13 14 15 16 17 18 19 20 21 22 23 24

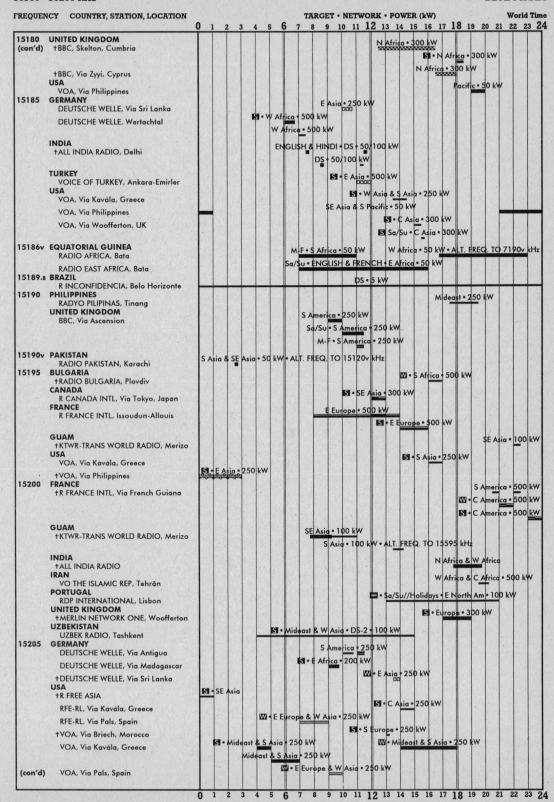

15180 **UNITED KINGDOM**
(con'd)   †BBC, Skelton, Cumbria — N Africa • 300 kW; S • N Africa • 300 kW; N Africa • 300 kW

          †BBC, Via Zyyi, Cyprus — Pacific • 50 kW
          USA
          VOA, Via Philippines
15185 **GERMANY**
          DEUTSCHE WELLE, Via Sri Lanka — E Asia • 250 kW
          DEUTSCHE WELLE, Wertachtal — S • W Africa • 500 kW; W Africa • 500 kW

          INDIA
          †ALL INDIA RADIO, Delhi — ENGLISH & HINDI • DS • 50/100 kW; DS • 50/100 kW

          TURKEY
          VOICE OF TURKEY, Ankara-Emirler — S • E Asia • 500 kW
          USA
          VOA, Via Kavála, Greece — S • W Asia & S Asia • 250 kW
          VOA, Via Philippines — SE Asia & S Pacific • 50 kW
          VOA, Via Woofferton, UK — S • C Asia • 300 kW; S • Sa/Su • C Asia • 300 kW

15186v **EQUATORIAL GUINEA**
          RADIO AFRICA, Bata — M-F • S Africa • 50 kW; W Africa • 50 kW • ALT. FREQ. TO 7190v kHz
          RADIO EAST AFRICA, Bata — Sa/Su • ENGLISH & FRENCH • E Africa • 50 kW
15189.8 **BRAZIL**
          R INCONFIDENCIA, Belo Horizonte — DS • 5 kW
15190 **PHILIPPINES**
          RADYO PILIPINAS, Tinang — Mideast • 250 kW
          UNITED KINGDOM
          BBC, Via Ascension — S America • 250 kW; Sa/Su • S America • 250 kW; M-F • S America • 250 kW

15190v **PAKISTAN**
          RADIO PAKISTAN, Karachi — S Asia & SE Asia • 50 kW • ALT. FREQ. TO 15120v kHz
15195 **BULGARIA**
          †RADIO BULGARIA, Plovdiv — W • S Africa • 500 kW
          CANADA
          R CANADA INTL, Via Tokyo, Japan — S • SE Asia • 300 kW
          FRANCE
          R FRANCE INTL, Issoudun-Allouis — E Europe • 500 kW; S • E Europe • 500 kW

          GUAM
          †KTWR-TRANS WORLD RADIO, Merizo — SE Asia • 100 kW
          USA
          VOA, Via Kavála, Greece — S • S Asia • 250 kW
          †VOA, Via Philippines — S • E Asia • 250 kW
15200 **FRANCE**
          †R FRANCE INTL, Via French Guiana — S America • 500 kW; W • C America • 500 kW; S • C America • 500 kW

          GUAM
          †KTWR-TRANS WORLD RADIO, Merizo — SE Asia • 100 kW; S Asia • 100 kW • ALT. FREQ. TO 15595 kHz

          INDIA
          †ALL INDIA RADIO — N Africa & W Africa
          IRAN
          VO THE ISLAMIC REP, Tehrān — W Africa & C Africa • 500 kW
          PORTUGAL
          RDP INTERNATIONAL, Lisbon — Sa/Su//Holidays • E North Am • 100 kW
          UNITED KINGDOM
          †MERLIN NETWORK ONE, Woofferton — S • Europe • 300 kW
          UZBEKISTAN
          UZBEK RADIO, Tashkent — S • Mideast & W Asia • DS-2 • 100 kW
15205 **GERMANY**
          DEUTSCHE WELLE, Via Antigua — S America • 250 kW
          DEUTSCHE WELLE, Via Madagascar — S • E Africa • 200 kW
          †DEUTSCHE WELLE, Via Sri Lanka — W • E Asia • 250 kW
          USA
          †R FREE ASIA — S • SE Asia
          RFE-RL, Via Kavála, Greece — S • C Asia • 250 kW
          RFE-RL, Via Pals, Spain — W • E Europe & W Asia • 250 kW; S • S Europe • 250 kW
          †VOA, Via Briech, Morocco — S • Mideast & S Asia • 250 kW; W • Mideast & S Asia • 250 kW
          VOA, Via Kavála, Greece — Mideast & S Asia • 250 kW

(con'd)   VOA, Via Pals, Spain — W • E Europe & W Asia • 250 kW

                                                    0 1 2 3 4 5 6 7 8 9 10 11 12 13 14 15 16 17 18 19 20 21 22 23 24

FREQUENCY   COUNTRY, STATION, LOCATION   TARGET • NETWORK • POWER (kW)   World Time

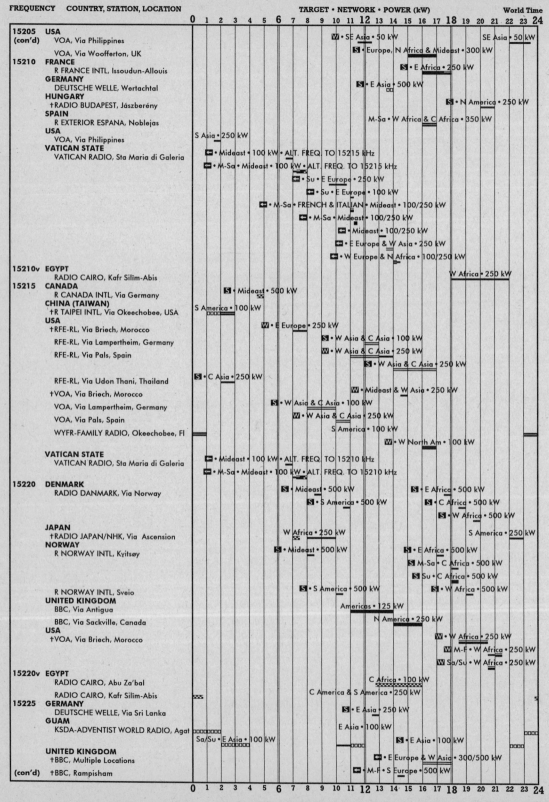

FREQUENCY	COUNTRY, STATION, LOCATION	TARGET • NETWORK • POWER (kW)
15205 (con'd)	USA	
	VOA, Via Philippines	W • SE Asia • 50 kW / SE Asia • 50 kW
	VOA, Via Woofferton, UK	S • Europe, N Africa & Mideast • 300 kW
15210	FRANCE	
	R FRANCE INTL, Issoudun-Allouis	S • E Africa • 250 kW
	GERMANY	
	DEUTSCHE WELLE, Wertachtal	S • E Asia • 500 kW
	HUNGARY	
	†RADIO BUDAPEST, Jászberény	S • N America • 250 kW
	SPAIN	
	R EXTERIOR ESPANA, Noblejas	M-Sa • W Africa & C Africa • 350 kW
	USA	
	VOA, Via Philippines	S Asia • 250 kW
	VATICAN STATE	
	VATICAN RADIO, Sta Maria di Galeria	• Mideast • 100 kW • ALT. FREQ. TO 15215 kHz
		• M-Sa • Mideast • 100 kW • ALT. FREQ. TO 15215 kHz
		• Su • E Europe • 250 kW
		• Su • E Europe • 100 kW
		• M-Sa • FRENCH & ITALIAN • Mideast • 100/250 kW
		• M-Sa • Mideast • 100/250 kW
		• Mideast • 100/250 kW
		• E Europe & W Asia • 250 kW
		• W Europe & N Africa • 100/250 kW
15210v	EGYPT	
	RADIO CAIRO, Kafr Silim-Abis	W Africa • 250 kW
15215	CANADA	
	R CANADA INTL, Via Germany	S • Mideast • 500 kW
	CHINA (TAIWAN)	
	†R TAIPEI INTL, Via Okeechobee, USA	S America • 100 kW
	USA	
	†RFE-RL, Via Briech, Morocco	W • E Europe • 250 kW
	RFE-RL, Via Lampertheim, Germany	S • W Asia & C Asia • 100 kW
	RFE-RL, Via Pals, Spain	W • W Asia & C Asia • 250 kW
		S • W Asia & C Asia • 250 kW
	RFE-RL, Via Udon Thani, Thailand	S • C Asia • 250 kW
	†VOA, Via Briech, Morocco	W • Mideast & W Asia • 250 kW
	VOA, Via Lampertheim, Germany	S • W Asia & C Asia • 100 kW
	VOA, Via Pals, Spain	W • W Asia & C Asia • 250 kW
	WYFR-FAMILY RADIO, Okeechobee, Fl	S America • 100 kW
		W • W North Am • 100 kW
	VATICAN STATE	
	VATICAN RADIO, Sta Maria di Galeria	• Mideast • 100 kW • ALT. FREQ. TO 15210 kHz
		• M-Sa • Mideast • 100 kW • ALT. FREQ. TO 15210 kHz
15220	DENMARK	
	RADIO DANMARK, Via Norway	S • Mideast • 500 kW / S • E Africa • 500 kW
		S • S America • 500 kW / S • C Africa • 500 kW
		S • W Africa • 500 kW
	JAPAN	
	†RADIO JAPAN/NHK, Via Ascension	W Africa • 250 kW / S America • 250 kW
	NORWAY	
	R NORWAY INTL, Kvitsøy	S • Mideast • 500 kW / S • E Africa • 500 kW
		S M-Sa • C Africa • 500 kW
		S Su • C Africa • 500 kW
	R NORWAY INTL, Sveio	S • S America • 500 kW / S • W Africa • 500 kW
	UNITED KINGDOM	
	BBC, Via Antigua	Americas • 125 kW
	BBC, Via Sackville, Canada	N America • 250 kW
	USA	
	†VOA, Via Briech, Morocco	W • W Africa • 250 kW
		W M-F • W Africa • 250 kW
		W Sa/Su • W Africa • 250 kW
15220v	EGYPT	
	RADIO CAIRO, Abu Za'bal	C Africa • 100 kW
	RADIO CAIRO, Kafr Silim-Abis	C America & S America • 250 kW
15225	GERMANY	
	DEUTSCHE WELLE, Via Sri Lanka	S • E Asia • 250 kW
	GUAM	
	KSDA-ADVENTIST WORLD RADIO, Agat	E Asia • 100 kW
		Sa/Su • E Asia • 100 kW / S • E Asia • 100 kW
	UNITED KINGDOM	
	†BBC, Multiple Locations	• E Europe & W Asia • 300/500 kW
(con'd)	†BBC, Rampisham	• M-F • S Europe • 500 kW

ENGLISH ▬▬   ARABIC ⋙   CHINESE ▫▫▫   FRENCH ▭▭   GERMAN ▬▬   RUSSIAN ══   SPANISH ▬▬   OTHER ▬▬

FREQUENCY   COUNTRY, STATION, LOCATION   TARGET • NETWORK • POWER (kW)   World Time

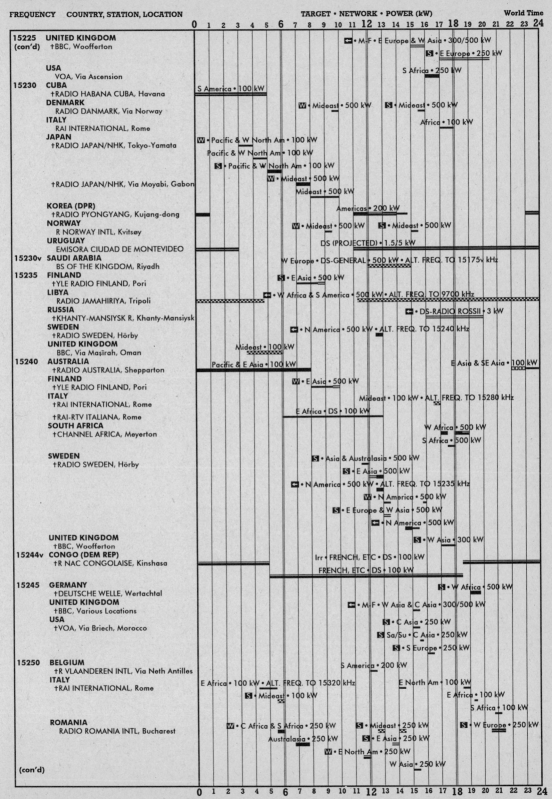

Frequency	Country, Station, Location	Target • Network • Power
15225 (con'd)	**UNITED KINGDOM** †BBC, Woofferton	M-F • E Europe & W Asia • 300/500 kW; E Europe • 250 kW
	USA VOA, Via Ascension	S Africa • 250 kW
15230	**CUBA** †RADIO HABANA CUBA, Havana	S America • 100 kW
	DENMARK RADIO DANMARK, Via Norway	Mideast • 500 kW; Mideast • 500 kW
	ITALY RAI INTERNATIONAL, Rome	Africa • 100 kW
	JAPAN †RADIO JAPAN/NHK, Tokyo-Yamata	Pacific & W North Am • 100 kW; Pacific & W North Am • 100 kW; Pacific & W North Am • 100 kW
	†RADIO JAPAN/NHK, Via Moyabi, Gabon	Mideast • 500 kW; Mideast • 500 kW
	KOREA (DPR) †RADIO PYONGYANG, Kujang-dong	Americas • 200 kW
	NORWAY R NORWAY INTL, Kvitsøy	Mideast • 500 kW; Mideast • 500 kW
	URUGUAY EMISORA CIUDAD DE MONTEVIDEO	DS (PROJECTED) • 1.5/5 kW
15230v	**SAUDI ARABIA** BS OF THE KINGDOM, Riyadh	W Europe • DS-GENERAL • 500 kW • ALT. FREQ. TO 15175v kHz
15235	**FINLAND** †YLE RADIO FINLAND, Pori	E Asia • 500 kW
	LIBYA RADIO JAMAHIRIYA, Tripoli	W Africa & S America • 500 kW • ALT. FREQ. TO 9700 kHz
	RUSSIA †KHANTY-MANSIYSK R, Khanty-Mansiysk	DS-RADIO ROSSII • 3 kW
	SWEDEN †RADIO SWEDEN, Hörby	N America • 500 kW • ALT. FREQ. TO 15240 kHz
	UNITED KINGDOM BBC, Via Maşīrah, Oman	Mideast • 100 kW
15240	**AUSTRALIA** †RADIO AUSTRALIA, Shepparton	Pacific & E Asia • 100 kW; E Asia & SE Asia • 100 kW
	FINLAND †YLE RADIO FINLAND, Pori	E Asia • 500 kW
	ITALY †RAI INTERNATIONAL, Rome	Mideast • 100 kW • ALT. FREQ. TO 15280 kHz
	†RAI-RTV ITALIANA, Rome	E Africa • DS • 100 kW
	SOUTH AFRICA †CHANNEL AFRICA, Meyerton	W Africa • 500 kW; S Africa • 500 kW
	SWEDEN †RADIO SWEDEN, Hörby	Asia & Australasia • 500 kW; E Asia • 500 kW; N America • 500 kW • ALT. FREQ. TO 15235 kHz; N America • 500 kW; E Europe & W Asia • 500 kW; N America • 500 kW
	UNITED KINGDOM †BBC, Woofferton	W Asia • 300 kW
15244v	**CONGO (DEM REP)** †R NAC CONGOLAISE, Kinshasa	Irr • FRENCH, ETC • DS • 100 kW; FRENCH, ETC • DS • 100 kW
15245	**GERMANY** †DEUTSCHE WELLE, Wertachtal	W Africa • 500 kW
	UNITED KINGDOM †BBC, Various Locations	M-F • W Asia & C Asia • 300/500 kW
	USA †VOA, Via Briech, Morocco	C Asia • 250 kW; Sa/Su • C Asia • 250 kW; S Europe • 250 kW
15250	**BELGIUM** †R VLAANDEREN INTL, Via Neth Antilles	S America • 200 kW
	ITALY †RAI INTERNATIONAL, Rome	E Africa • 100 kW • ALT. FREQ. TO 15320 kHz; Mideast • 100 kW; E North Am • 100 kW; E Africa • 100 kW; S Africa • 100 kW
	ROMANIA RADIO ROMANIA INTL, Bucharest	C Africa & S Africa • 250 kW; Mideast • 250 kW; W Europe • 250 kW; Australasia • 250 kW; E Asia • 250 kW; E North Am • 250 kW; W Asia • 250 kW

(con'd)

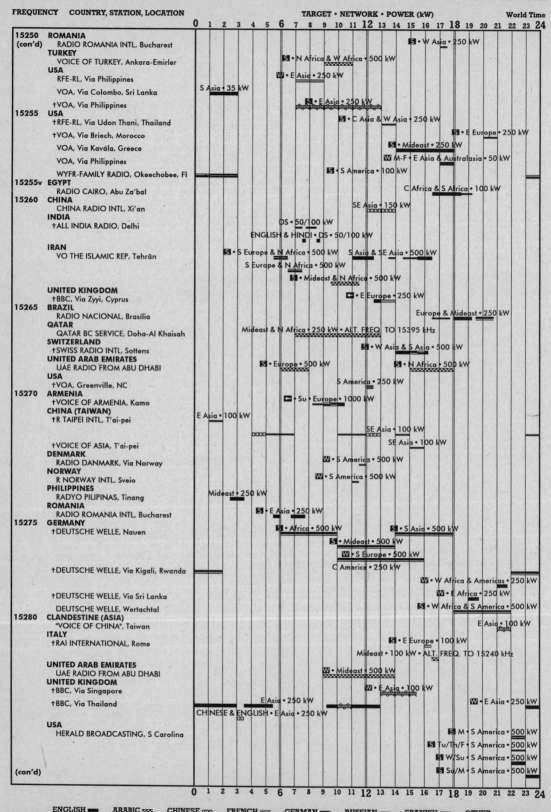

FREQUENCY   COUNTRY, STATION, LOCATION

TARGET • NETWORK • POWER (kW)   World Time

15250	ROMANIA	
(con'd)	RADIO ROMANIA INTL, Bucharest	S • W Asia • 250 kW
	TURKEY	
	VOICE OF TURKEY, Ankara-Emirler	S • N Africa & W Africa • 500 kW
	USA	
	RFE-RL, Via Philippines	W • E Asia • 250 kW
	VOA, Via Colombo, Sri Lanka	S Asia • 35 kW
	†VOA, Via Philippines	S • E Asia • 250 kW
15255	USA	
	†RFE-RL, Via Udon Thani, Thailand	S • C Asia & W Asia • 250 kW
	†VOA, Via Briech, Morocco	S • E Europe • 250 kW
	VOA, Via Kavála, Greece	S • Mideast • 250 kW
	VOA, Via Philippines	W M-F • E Asia & Australasia • 50 kW
	WYFR-FAMILY RADIO, Okeechobee, Fl	S • S America • 100 kW
15255v	EGYPT	
	RADIO CAIRO, Abu Za'bal	C Africa & S Africa • 100 kW
15260	CHINA	
	CHINA RADIO INTL, Xi'an	SE Asia • 150 kW
	INDIA	
	†ALL INDIA RADIO, Delhi	DS • 50/100 kW
		ENGLISH & HINDI • DS • 50/100 kW
	IRAN	
	VO THE ISLAMIC REP, Tehrān	S • S Europe & N Africa • 500 kW S Asia & SE Asia • 500 kW
		S Europe & N Africa • 500 kW
		S • Mideast & N Africa • 500 kW
	UNITED KINGDOM	
	†BBC, Via Zyyi, Cyprus	⊡ • E Europe • 250 kW
15265	BRAZIL	
	RADIO NACIONAL, Brasília	Europe & Mideast • 250 kW
	QATAR	
	QATAR BC SERVICE, Doha-Al Khaisah	Mideast & N Africa • 250 kW • ALT. FREQ. TO 15395 kHz
	SWITZERLAND	
	†SWISS RADIO INTL, Sottens	S • W Asia & S Asia • 500 kW
	UNITED ARAB EMIRATES	
	UAE RADIO FROM ABU DHABI	S • Europe • 500 kW S • N Africa • 500 kW
	USA	
	†VOA, Greenville, NC	S America • 250 kW
15270	ARMENIA	
	†VOICE OF ARMENIA, Kamo	⊡ • Su • Europe • 1000 kW
	CHINA (TAIWAN)	
	†R TAIPEI INTL, T'ai-pei	E Asia • 100 kW
		SE Asia • 100 kW
	†VOICE OF ASIA, T'ai-pei	SE Asia • 100 kW
	DENMARK	
	RADIO DANMARK, Via Norway	W • S America • 500 kW
	NORWAY	
	R NORWAY INTL, Sveio	W • S America • 500 kW
	PHILIPPINES	
	RADYO PILIPINAS, Tinang	Mideast • 250 kW
	ROMANIA	
	RADIO ROMANIA INTL, Bucharest	S • E Asia • 250 kW
15275	GERMANY	
	†DEUTSCHE WELLE, Nauen	S • Africa • 500 kW S • S Asia • 500 kW
		S • Mideast • 500 kW
		W • S Europe • 500 kW
	†DEUTSCHE WELLE, Via Kigali, Rwanda	C America • 250 kW
		W • W Africa & Americas • 250 kW
	†DEUTSCHE WELLE, Via Sri Lanka	W • E Africa • 250 kW
	DEUTSCHE WELLE, Wertachtal	S • W Africa & S America • 500 kW
15280	CLANDESTINE (ASIA)	
	"VOICE OF CHINA", Taiwan	E Asia • 100 kW
	ITALY	
	†RAI INTERNATIONAL, Rome	S • E Europe • 100 kW
		Mideast • 100 kW • ALT. FREQ. TO 15240 kHz
	UNITED ARAB EMIRATES	
	UAE RADIO FROM ABU DHABI	W • Mideast • 500 kW
	UNITED KINGDOM	
	†BBC, Via Singapore	W • E Asia • 100 kW
	†BBC, Via Thailand	E Asia • 250 kW W • E Asia • 250 kW
		CHINESE & ENGLISH • E Asia • 250 kW
	USA	
	HERALD BROADCASTING, S Carolina	S M • S America • 500 kW
		S Tu/Th/F • S America • 500 kW
		S W/Su • S America • 500 kW
		S Su/M • S America • 500 kW
(con'd)		

ENGLISH ▬ ARABIC ⧨ CHINESE □□□ FRENCH ▭ GERMAN ▬ RUSSIAN ═ SPANISH ▬ OTHER ▬

FREQUENCY   COUNTRY, STATION, LOCATION   TARGET • NETWORK • POWER (kW)   World Time

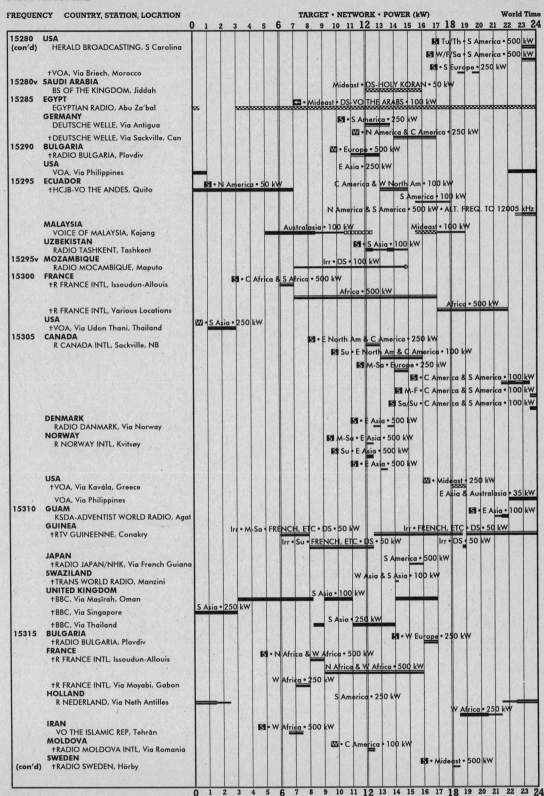

Frequency	Country, Station, Location	Target • Network • Power
15280 (con'd)	USA — HERALD BROADCASTING, S Carolina	S Tu/Th • S America • 500 kW; S W/F/Sa • S America • 500 kW; S • S Europe • 250 kW
	†VOA, Via Briech, Morocco	
15280v	SAUDI ARABIA — BS OF THE KINGDOM, Jiddah	Mideast • DS-HOLY KORAN • 50 kW
15285	EGYPT — EGYPTIAN RADIO, Abu Za'bal	Mideast • DS-VO THE ARABS • 100 kW
	GERMANY — DEUTSCHE WELLE, Via Antigua	S • S America • 250 kW; W • N America & C America • 250 kW
	†DEUTSCHE WELLE, Via Sackville, Can	
15290	BULGARIA — †RADIO BULGARIA, Plovdiv	W • Europe • 500 kW
	USA — VOA, Via Philippines	E Asia • 250 kW
15295	ECUADOR — †HCJB-VO THE ANDES, Quito	S • N America • 50 kW; C America & W North Am • 100 kW; S America • 100 kW; N America & S America • 500 kW • ALT. FREQ. TO 12005 kHz
	MALAYSIA — VOICE OF MALAYSIA, Kajang	Australasia • 100 kW; Mideast • 100 kW
	UZBEKISTAN — RADIO TASHKENT, Tashkent	S • S Asia • 100 kW
15295v	MOZAMBIQUE — RADIO MOCAMBIQUE, Maputo	Irr • DS • 100 kW
15300	FRANCE — †R FRANCE INTL, Issoudun-Allouis	S • C Africa & S Africa • 500 kW; Africa • 500 kW; Africa • 500 kW
	USA — †VOA, Via Udon Thani, Thailand	W • S Asia • 250 kW
15305	CANADA — R CANADA INTL, Sackville, NB	S • E North Am & C America • 250 kW; S Su • E North Am & C America • 100 kW; S M-Sa • Europe • 250 kW; S • C America & S America • 100 kW; S M-F • C America & S America • 100 kW; S Sa/Su • C America & S America • 100 kW
	DENMARK — RADIO DANMARK, Via Norway	S • E Asia • 500 kW
	NORWAY — R NORWAY INTL, Kvitsøy	S M-Sa • E Asia • 500 kW; S Su • E Asia • 500 kW; S • E Asia • 500 kW
	USA — †VOA, Via Kavála, Greece	W • Mideast • 250 kW
	VOA, Via Philippines	E Asia & Australasia • 35 kW
15310	GUAM — KSDA-ADVENTIST WORLD RADIO, Agat	S • E Asia • 100 kW
	GUINEA — †RTV GUINEENNE, Conakry	Irr • M-Sa • FRENCH, ETC • DS • 50 kW; Irr • FRENCH, ETC • DS • 50 kW; Irr • Su • FRENCH, ETC • DS • 50 kW; Irr • DS • 50 kW
	JAPAN — †RADIO JAPAN/NHK, Via French Guiana	S America • 500 kW
	SWAZILAND — †TRANS WORLD RADIO, Manzini	W Asia & S Asia • 100 kW
	UNITED KINGDOM — †BBC, Via Maşīrah, Oman	S Asia • 100 kW
	†BBC, Via Singapore	S Asia • 250 kW
	†BBC, Via Thailand	S Asia • 250 kW
15315	BULGARIA — †RADIO BULGARIA, Plovdiv	S • W Europe • 250 kW
	FRANCE — †R FRANCE INTL, Issoudun-Allouis	S • N Africa & W Africa • 500 kW; N Africa & W Africa • 500 kW
	†R FRANCE INTL, Via Moyabi, Gabon	W Africa • 250 kW
	HOLLAND — R NEDERLAND, Via Neth Antilles	S America • 250 kW; W Africa • 250 kW
	IRAN — VO THE ISLAMIC REP, Tehrān	S • W Africa • 500 kW
	MOLDOVA — †RADIO MOLDOVA INTL, Via Romania	W • C America • 100 kW
	SWEDEN (con'd) — †RADIO SWEDEN, Hörby	S • Mideast • 500 kW

SEASONAL S OR W   1-HR TIMESHIFT MIDYEAR ⟵ OR ⟶   JAMMING / OR /\   EARLIEST HEARD ◁   LATEST HEARD ▷   NEW FOR 1999 †

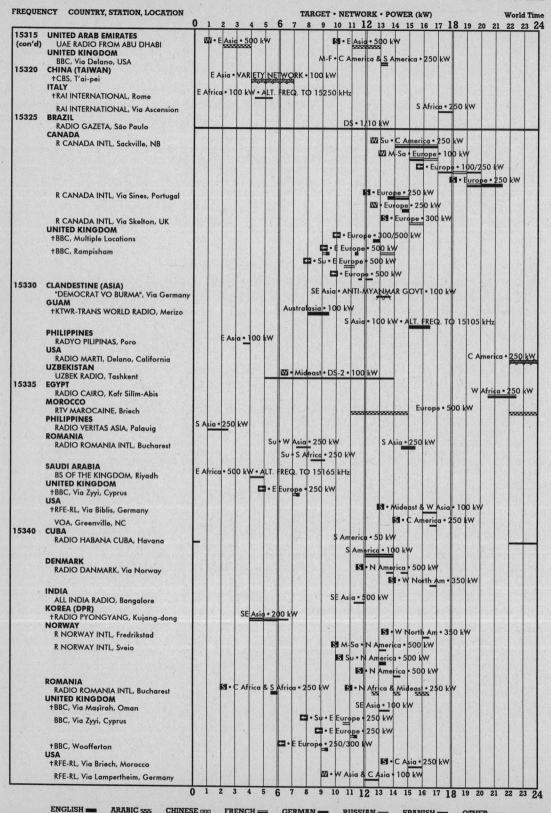

15315 **UNITED ARAB EMIRATES**
(con'd)   UAE RADIO FROM ABU DHABI
        UNITED KINGDOM
        BBC, Via Delano, USA
15320 **CHINA (TAIWAN)**
        †CBS, T'ai-pei
        ITALY
        †RAI INTERNATIONAL, Rome
        RAI INTERNATIONAL, Via Ascension
15325 **BRAZIL**
        RADIO GAZETA, São Paulo
        CANADA
        R CANADA INTL, Sackville, NB

        R CANADA INTL, Via Sines, Portugal

        R CANADA INTL, Via Skelton, UK
        UNITED KINGDOM
        †BBC, Multiple Locations

        †BBC, Rampisham

15330 **CLANDESTINE (ASIA)**
        "DEMOCRAT VO BURMA", Via Germany
        GUAM
        †KTWR-TRANS WORLD RADIO, Merizo

        PHILIPPINES
        RADYO PILIPINAS, Poro
        USA
        RADIO MARTI, Delano, California
        UZBEKISTAN
        UZBEK RADIO, Tashkent
15335 **EGYPT**
        RADIO CAIRO, Kafr Silîm-Abis
        MOROCCO
        RTV MAROCAINE, Briech
        PHILIPPINES
        RADIO VERITAS ASIA, Palauig
        ROMANIA
        RADIO ROMANIA INTL, Bucharest

        SAUDI ARABIA
        BS OF THE KINGDOM, Riyadh
        UNITED KINGDOM
        †BBC, Via Zyyi, Cyprus
        USA
        †RFE-RL, Via Biblis, Germany

        VOA, Greenville, NC
15340 **CUBA**
        RADIO HABANA CUBA, Havana

        DENMARK
        RADIO DANMARK, Via Norway

        INDIA
        ALL INDIA RADIO, Bangalore
        KOREA (DPR)
        †RADIO PYONGYANG, Kujang-dong
        NORWAY
        R NORWAY INTL, Fredrikstad

        R NORWAY INTL, Sveio

        ROMANIA
        RADIO ROMANIA INTL, Bucharest
        UNITED KINGDOM
        †BBC, Via Maşirah, Oman

        BBC, Via Zyyi, Cyprus

        †BBC, Woofferton
        USA
        †RFE-RL, Via Briech, Morocco

        RFE-RL, Via Lampertheim, Germany

ENGLISH ▬   ARABIC ▨   CHINESE ▫▫▫   FRENCH ═   GERMAN ▬   RUSSIAN ═   SPANISH ═   OTHER ▬

FREQUENCY	COUNTRY, STATION, LOCATION	TARGET • NETWORK • POWER (kW)	World Time

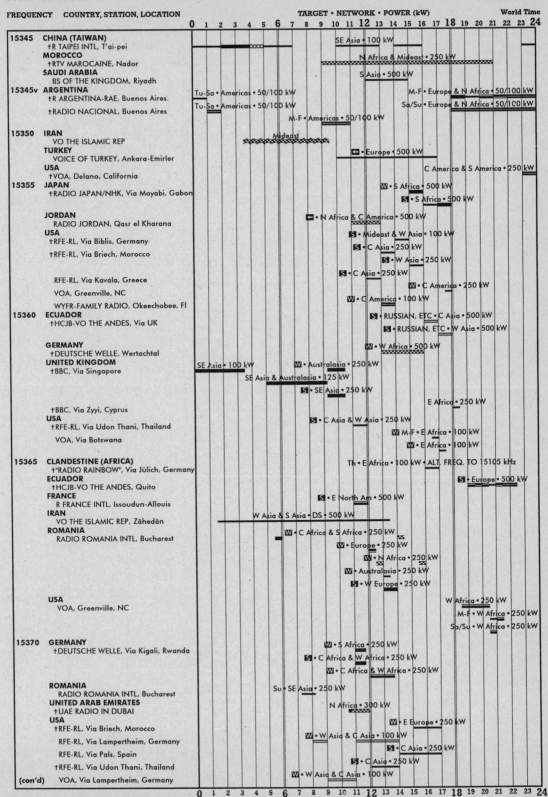

15345 — CHINA (TAIWAN)
  †R TAIPEI INTL, T'ai-pei — SE Asia • 100 kW
  MOROCCO
  †RTV MAROCAINE, Nador — N Africa & Mideast • 250 kW
  SAUDI ARABIA
  BS OF THE KINGDOM, Riyadh — S Asia • 500 kW
15345v ARGENTINA
  †R ARGENTINA-RAE, Buenos Aires — Tu-Sa • Americas • 50/100 kW / M-F • Europe & N Africa • 50/100 kW
  †RADIO NACIONAL, Buenos Aires — Tu-Sa • Americas • 50/100 kW / Sa/Su • Europe & N Africa • 50/100 kW
  M-F • Americas • 50/100 kW
15350 — IRAN
  VO THE ISLAMIC REP — Mideast
  TURKEY
  VOICE OF TURKEY, Ankara-Emirler — Europe • 500 kW
  USA
  †VOA, Delano, California — C America & S America • 250 kW
15355 — JAPAN
  †RADIO JAPAN/NHK, Via Moyabi, Gabon — W • S Africa • 500 kW / S • S Africa • 500 kW
  JORDAN
  RADIO JORDAN, Qasr el Kharana — N Africa & C America • 500 kW
  USA
  †RFE-RL, Via Biblis, Germany — S • Mideast & W Asia • 100 kW
  †RFE-RL, Via Briech, Morocco — S • C Asia • 250 kW / S • W Asia • 250 kW
  RFE-RL, Via Kavála, Greece — S • C Asia • 250 kW
  VOA, Greenville, NC — W • C America • 250 kW
  WYFR-FAMILY RADIO, Okeechobee, Fl — W • C America • 100 kW
15360 — ECUADOR
  †HCJB-VO THE ANDES, Via UK — S • RUSSIAN, ETC • C Asia • 500 kW / S • RUSSIAN, ETC • W Asia • 500 kW
  GERMANY
  †DEUTSCHE WELLE, Wertachtal — W • W Africa • 500 kW
  UNITED KINGDOM
  †BBC, Via Singapore — SE Asia • 100 kW / W • Australasia • 250 kW
  SE Asia & Australasia • 125 kW
  S • SE Asia • 250 kW
  †BBC, Via Zyyi, Cyprus — E Africa • 250 kW
  USA
  †RFE-RL, Via Udon Thani, Thailand — S • C Asia & W Asia • 250 kW
  VOA, Via Botswana — W • M-F • E Africa • 100 kW / W • E Africa • 100 kW
15365 — CLANDESTINE (AFRICA)
  †"RADIO RAINBOW", Via Jülich, Germany — Th • E Africa • 100 kW • ALT. FREQ. TO 15105 kHz
  ECUADOR
  †HCJB-VO THE ANDES, Quito — S • Europe • 500 kW
  FRANCE
  R FRANCE INTL, Issoudun-Allouis — S • E North Am • 500 kW
  IRAN
  VO THE ISLAMIC REP, Zāhedān — W Asia & S Asia • DS • 500 kW
  ROMANIA
  RADIO ROMANIA INTL, Bucharest — W • C Africa & S Africa • 250 kW
  W • Europe • 250 kW
  W • N Africa • 250 kW
  W • Australasia • 250 kW
  S • W Europe • 250 kW
  USA
  VOA, Greenville, NC — W Africa • 250 kW / M-F • W Africa • 250 kW / Sa/Su • W Africa • 250 kW
15370 — GERMANY
  †DEUTSCHE WELLE, Via Kigali, Rwanda — W • S Africa • 250 kW / S • C Africa & W Africa • 250 kW / W • C Africa & W Africa • 250 kW
  ROMANIA
  RADIO ROMANIA INTL, Bucharest — Su • SE Asia • 250 kW
  UNITED ARAB EMIRATES
  †UAE RADIO IN DUBAI — N Africa • 300 kW
  USA
  †RFE-RL, Via Briech, Morocco — W • E Europe • 250 kW
  RFE-RL, Via Lampertheim, Germany — W • W Asia & C Asia • 100 kW / S • C Asia • 250 kW
  RFE-RL, Via Pals, Spain — S • C Asia • 250 kW
  †RFE-RL, Via Udon Thani, Thailand
  (con'd) — VOA, Via Lampertheim, Germany — W • W Asia & C Asia • 100 kW

SEASONAL S OR W   1-HR TIMESHIFT MIDYEAR ⊟ OR ⊞   JAMMING / OR /\   EARLIEST HEARD ◁   LATEST HEARD ▷   NEW FOR 1999 †

FREQUENCY   COUNTRY, STATION, LOCATION

TARGET • NETWORK • POWER (kW)   World Time

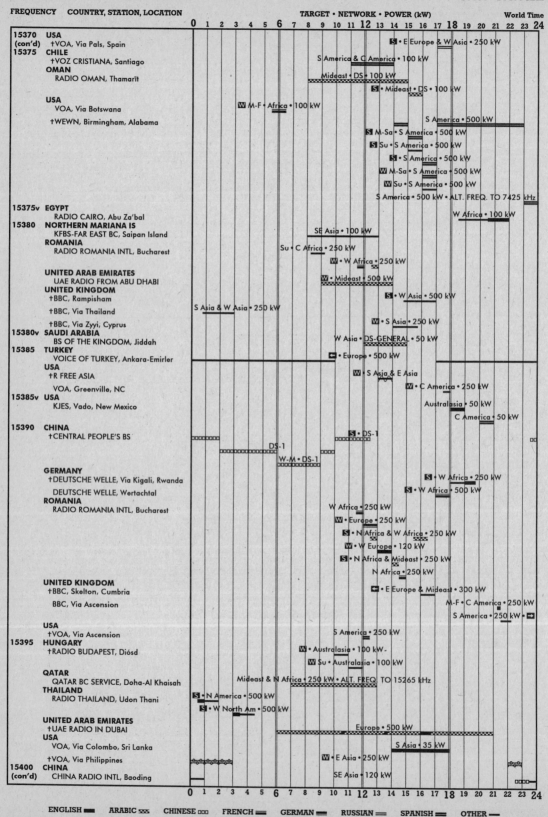

FREQUENCY	COUNTRY, STATION, LOCATION
15370 (con'd)	**USA**
	†VOA, Via Pals, Spain
15375	**CHILE**
	†VOZ CRISTIANA, Santiago
	OMAN
	RADIO OMAN, Thamarīt
	USA
	VOA, Via Botswana
	†WEWN, Birmingham, Alabama
15375v	**EGYPT**
	RADIO CAIRO, Abu Za'bal
15380	**NORTHERN MARIANA IS**
	KFBS-FAR EAST BC, Saipan Island
	ROMANIA
	RADIO ROMANIA INTL, Bucharest
	UNITED ARAB EMIRATES
	UAE RADIO FROM ABU DHABI
	UNITED KINGDOM
	†BBC, Rampisham
	†BBC, Via Thailand
	†BBC, Via Zyyi, Cyprus
15380v	**SAUDI ARABIA**
	BS OF THE KINGDOM, Jiddah
15385	**TURKEY**
	VOICE OF TURKEY, Ankara-Emirler
	USA
	†R FREE ASIA
	VOA, Greenville, NC
15385v	**USA**
	KJES, Vado, New Mexico
15390	**CHINA**
	†CENTRAL PEOPLE'S BS
	GERMANY
	†DEUTSCHE WELLE, Via Kigali, Rwanda
	DEUTSCHE WELLE, Wertachtal
	ROMANIA
	RADIO ROMANIA INTL, Bucharest
	UNITED KINGDOM
	†BBC, Skelton, Cumbria
	BBC, Via Ascension
	USA
	†VOA, Via Ascension
15395	**HUNGARY**
	†RADIO BUDAPEST, Diósd
	QATAR
	QATAR BC SERVICE, Doha-Al Khaisah
	THAILAND
	RADIO THAILAND, Udon Thani
	UNITED ARAB EMIRATES
	†UAE RADIO IN DUBAI
	USA
	VOA, Via Colombo, Sri Lanka
	†VOA, Via Philippines
15400 (con'd)	**CHINA**
	CHINA RADIO INTL, Baoding

Target/Network/Power entries (by station):

- VOA, Via Pals, Spain — E Europe & W Asia • 250 kW
- VOZ CRISTIANA, Santiago — S America & C America • 100 kW
- RADIO OMAN, Thamarīt — Mideast • DS • 100 kW; Mideast • DS • 100 kW
- VOA, Via Botswana — M-F • Africa • 100 kW
- WEWN, Birmingham, Alabama — S America • 500 kW; M-Sa • S America • 500 kW; Su • S America • 500 kW; S America • 500 kW; M-Sa • S America • 500 kW; Su • S America • 500 kW; S America • 500 kW • ALT. FREQ. TO 7425 kHz
- RADIO CAIRO, Abu Za'bal — W Africa • 100 kW
- KFBS-FAR EAST BC, Saipan Island — SE Asia • 100 kW
- RADIO ROMANIA INTL, Bucharest — Su • C Africa • 250 kW; W • W Africa • 250 kW
- UAE RADIO FROM ABU DHABI — W • Mideast • 500 kW
- BBC, Rampisham — W Asia • 500 kW
- BBC, Via Thailand — S Asia & W Asia • 250 kW
- BBC, Via Zyyi, Cyprus — W • S Asia • 250 kW
- BS OF THE KINGDOM, Jiddah — W Asia • DS-GENERAL • 50 kW
- VOICE OF TURKEY, Ankara-Emirler — Europe • 500 kW
- R FREE ASIA — W • S Asia & E Asia
- VOA, Greenville, NC — W • C America • 250 kW
- KJES, Vado, New Mexico — Australasia • 50 kW; C America • 50 kW
- CENTRAL PEOPLE'S BS — S • DS-1; DS-1; W-M • DS-1
- DEUTSCHE WELLE, Via Kigali, Rwanda — W Africa • 250 kW
- DEUTSCHE WELLE, Wertachtal — W Africa • 500 kW; W Africa • 250 kW; W • Europe • 250 kW; S • N Africa & W Africa • 250 kW; W • W Europe • 120 kW; S • N Africa & Mideast • 250 kW; N Africa • 250 kW
- BBC, Skelton, Cumbria — E Europe & Mideast • 300 kW
- BBC, Via Ascension — M-F • C America • 250 kW; S America • 250 kW
- VOA, Via Ascension — S America • 250 kW
- RADIO BUDAPEST, Diósd — W • Australasia • 100 kW; W • Su • Australasia • 100 kW
- QATAR BC SERVICE — Mideast & N Africa • 250 kW • ALT. FREQ. TO 15265 kHz
- RADIO THAILAND, Udon Thani — S • N America • 500 kW; S • W North Am • 500 kW
- UAE RADIO IN DUBAI — Europe • 500 kW
- VOA, Via Colombo, Sri Lanka — S Asia • 35 kW
- VOA, Via Philippines — W • E Asia • 250 kW
- CHINA RADIO INTL, Baoding — SE Asia • 120 kW

FREQUENCY   COUNTRY, STATION, LOCATION

TARGET • NETWORK • POWER (kW)   World Time

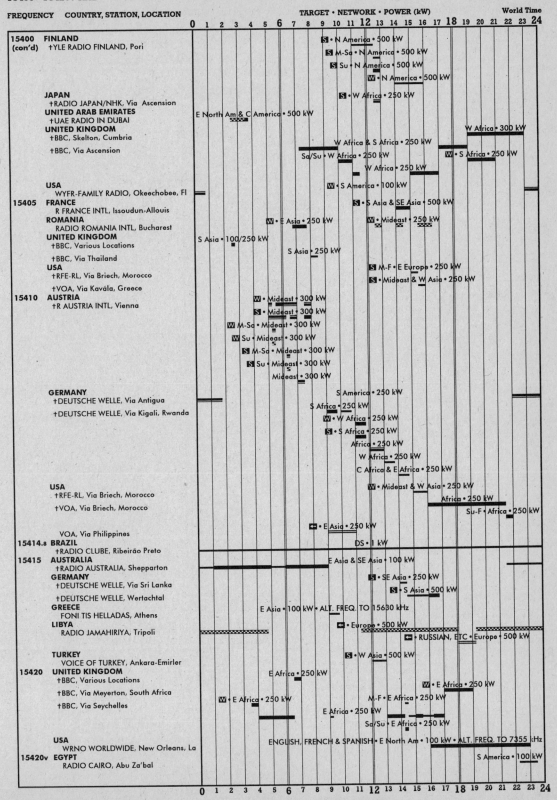

Freq	Country / Station / Location
15400 (con'd)	FINLAND †YLE RADIO FINLAND, Pori
	JAPAN †RADIO JAPAN/NHK, Via Ascension
	UNITED ARAB EMIRATES †UAE RADIO IN DUBAI
	UNITED KINGDOM †BBC, Skelton, Cumbria
	†BBC, Via Ascension
	USA WYFR-FAMILY RADIO, Okeechobee, Fl
15405	FRANCE R FRANCE INTL, Issoudun-Allouis
	ROMANIA RADIO ROMANIA INTL, Bucharest
	UNITED KINGDOM †BBC, Various Locations
	†BBC, Via Thailand
	USA †RFE-RL, Via Briech, Morocco
	†VOA, Via Kavála, Greece
15410	AUSTRIA †R AUSTRIA INTL, Vienna
	GERMANY †DEUTSCHE WELLE, Via Antigua
	†DEUTSCHE WELLE, Via Kigali, Rwanda
	USA †RFE-RL, Via Briech, Morocco
	†VOA, Via Briech, Morocco
	VOA, Via Philippines
15414.8	BRAZIL †RADIO CLUBE, Ribeirão Preto
15415	AUSTRALIA †RADIO AUSTRALIA, Shepparton
	GERMANY †DEUTSCHE WELLE, Via Sri Lanka
	†DEUTSCHE WELLE, Wertachtal
	GREECE FONI TIS HELLADAS, Athens
	LIBYA RADIO JAMAHIRIYA, Tripoli
	TURKEY VOICE OF TURKEY, Ankara-Emirler
15420	UNITED KINGDOM †BBC, Various Locations
	†BBC, Via Meyerton, South Africa
	†BBC, Via Seychelles
	USA WRNO WORLDWIDE, New Orleans, La
15420v	EGYPT RADIO CAIRO, Abu Za'bal

SEASONAL S OR W   1-HR TIMESHIFT MIDYEAR ◨ OR ◧   JAMMING / OR ∧   EARLIEST HEARD ◁   LATEST HEARD ▷   NEW FOR 1999 †

FREQUENCY   COUNTRY, STATION, LOCATION   TARGET • NETWORK • POWER (kW)   World Time

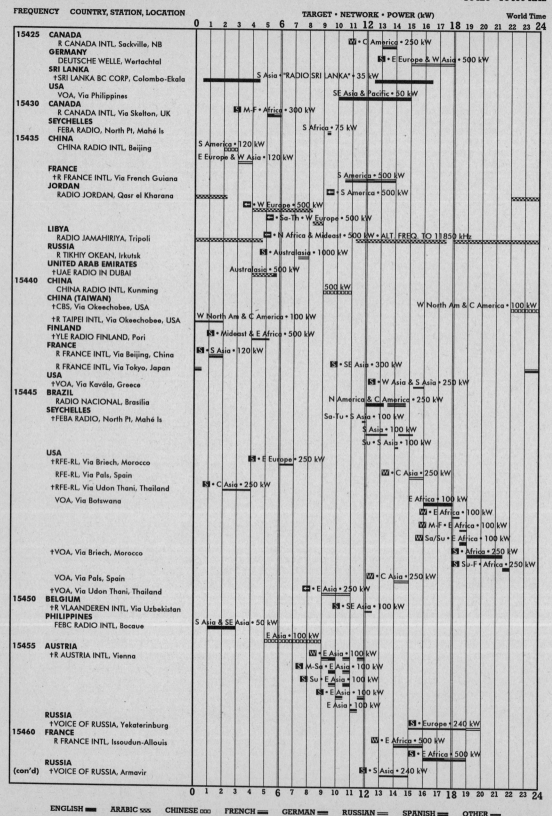

Frequency	Country, Station, Location	Target • Network • Power
15425	**CANADA** R CANADA INTL, Sackville, NB	W • C America • 250 kW
	GERMANY DEUTSCHE WELLE, Wertachtal	S • E Europe & W Asia • 500 kW
	SRI LANKA †SRI LANKA BC CORP, Colombo-Ekala	S Asia • "RADIO SRI LANKA" • 35 kW
	USA VOA, Via Philippines	SE Asia & Pacific • 50 kW
15430	**CANADA** R CANADA INTL, Via Skelton, UK	S • M-F • Africa • 300 kW
	SEYCHELLES FEBA RADIO, North Pt, Mahé Is	S Africa • 75 kW
15435	**CHINA** CHINA RADIO INTL, Beijing	S America • 120 kW / E Europe & W Asia • 120 kW
	FRANCE †R FRANCE INTL, Via French Guiana	S America • 500 kW
	JORDAN RADIO JORDAN, Qasr el Kharana	S America • 500 kW / W Europe • 500 kW / Sa-Th • W Europe • 500 kW
	LIBYA RADIO JAMAHIRIYA, Tripoli	N Africa & Mideast • 500 kW • ALT. FREQ. TO 11850 kHz
	RUSSIA R TIKHIY OKEAN, Irkutsk	S • Australasia • 1000 kW
	UNITED ARAB EMIRATES †UAE RADIO IN DUBAI	Australasia • 500 kW
15440	**CHINA** CHINA RADIO INTL, Kunming	500 kW
	CHINA (TAIWAN) †CBS, Via Okeechobee, USA	W North Am & C America • 100 kW
	†R TAIPEI INTL, Via Okeechobee, USA	W North Am & C America • 100 kW
	FINLAND †YLE RADIO FINLAND, Pori	S • Mideast & E Africa • 500 kW
	FRANCE R FRANCE INTL, Via Beijing, China	S • S Asia • 120 kW
	R FRANCE INTL, Via Tokyo, Japan	S • SE Asia • 300 kW
	USA †VOA, Via Kavála, Greece	S • W Asia & S Asia • 250 kW
15445	**BRAZIL** RADIO NACIONAL, Brasília	N America & C America • 250 kW
	SEYCHELLES †FEBA RADIO, North Pt, Mahé Is	Sa-Tu • S Asia • 100 kW / S Asia • 100 kW / Su • S Asia • 100 kW
	USA †RFE-RL, Via Briech, Morocco	S • E Europe • 250 kW
	RFE-RL, Via Pals, Spain	W • C Asia • 250 kW
	†RFE-RL, Via Udon Thani, Thailand	S • C Asia • 250 kW
	VOA, Via Botswana	E Africa • 100 kW / W • E Africa • 100 kW / W • M-F • E Africa • 100 kW / W • Sa/Su • E Africa • 100 kW
	†VOA, Via Briech, Morocco	S • Africa • 250 kW / S • Su-F • Africa • 250 kW
	VOA, Via Pals, Spain	W • C Asia • 250 kW
	†VOA, Via Udon Thani, Thailand	E Asia • 250 kW
15450	**BELGIUM** †R VLAANDEREN INTL, Via Uzbekistan	S • SE Asia • 100 kW
	PHILIPPINES FEBC RADIO INTL, Bocaue	S Asia & SE Asia • 50 kW
15455	**AUSTRIA** †R AUSTRIA INTL, Vienna	E Asia • 100 kW / W • E Asia • 100 kW / M-Sa • E Asia • 100 kW / Su • E Asia • 100 kW / S • E Asia • 100 kW / E Asia • 100 kW
	RUSSIA †VOICE OF RUSSIA, Yekaterinburg	S • Europe • 240 kW
15460	**FRANCE** R FRANCE INTL, Issoudun-Allouis	W • E Africa • 500 kW / S • E Africa • 500 kW
(con'd)	**RUSSIA** †VOICE OF RUSSIA, Armavir	S • S Asia • 240 kW

ENGLISH ▬   ARABIC ⬚   CHINESE ▫▫▫   FRENCH ▬   GERMAN ▬   RUSSIAN ▬   SPANISH ▬   OTHER ▬

FREQUENCY   COUNTRY, STATION, LOCATION   TARGET • NETWORK • POWER (kW)   World Time

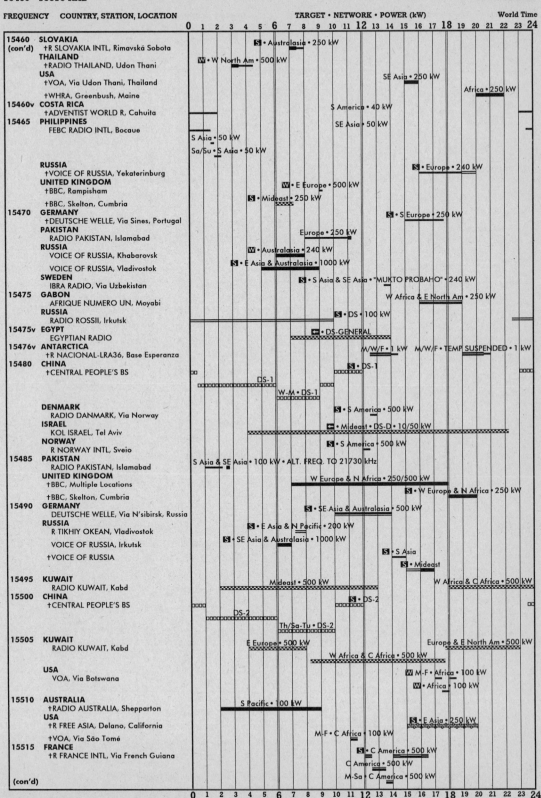

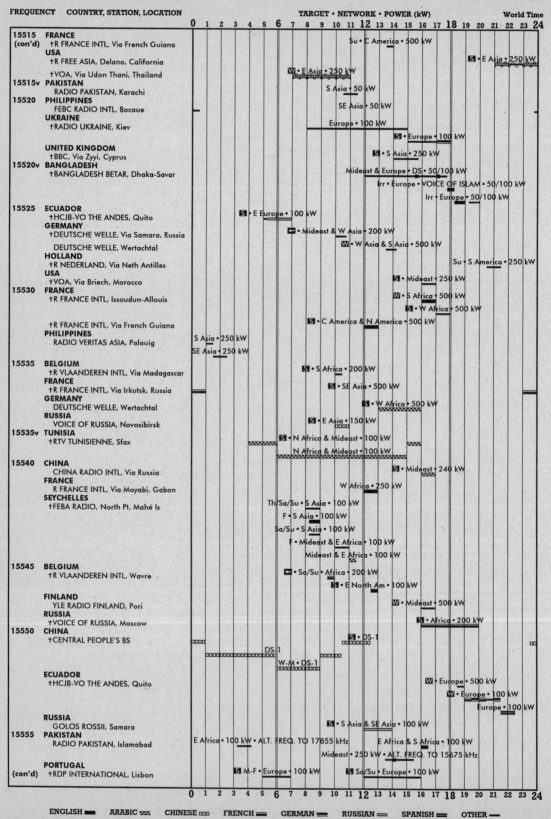

FREQUENCY   COUNTRY, STATION, LOCATION

TARGET • NETWORK • POWER (kW)   World Time

Frequency	Country, Station, Location
15515 (con'd)	**FRANCE** †R FRANCE INTL, Via French Guiana — Su • C America • 500 kW
	USA †R FREE ASIA, Delano, California — S • E Asia • 250 kW
	†VOA, Via Udon Thani, Thailand — W • E Asia • 250 kW
15515v	**PAKISTAN** RADIO PAKISTAN, Karachi — S Asia • 50 kW
15520	**PHILIPPINES** FEBC RADIO INTL, Bocaue — SE Asia • 50 kW
	UKRAINE †RADIO UKRAINE, Kiev — Europe • 100 kW / S • Europe • 100 kW
	UNITED KINGDOM †BBC, Via Zyyi, Cyprus — S • S Asia • 250 kW
15520v	**BANGLADESH** †BANGLADESH BETAR, Dhaka-Savar — Mideast & Europe • DS • 50/100 kW
	Irr • Europe • VOICE OF ISLAM • 50/100 kW
	Irr • Europe • 50/100 kW
15525	**ECUADOR** †HCJB-VO THE ANDES, Quito — S • E Europe • 100 kW
	GERMANY †DEUTSCHE WELLE, Via Samara, Russia — • Mideast & W Asia • 200 kW
	DEUTSCHE WELLE, Wertachtal — W • W Asia & S Asia • 500 kW
	HOLLAND †R NEDERLAND, Via Neth Antilles — Su • S America • 250 kW
	USA †VOA, Via Briech, Morocco — S • Mideast • 250 kW
15530	**FRANCE** †R FRANCE INTL, Issoudun-Allouis — W • S Africa • 500 kW / S • W Africa • 500 kW
	†R FRANCE INTL, Via French Guiana — S • C America & N America • 500 kW
	PHILIPPINES RADIO VERITAS ASIA, Palauig — S Asia • 250 kW / SE Asia • 250 kW
15535	**BELGIUM** †R VLAANDEREN INTL, Via Madagascar — S • S Africa • 200 kW
	FRANCE †R FRANCE INTL, Via Irkutsk, Russia — S • SE Asia • 500 kW
	GERMANY DEUTSCHE WELLE, Wertachtal — S • W Africa • 500 kW
	RUSSIA VOICE OF RUSSIA, Novosibirsk — S • E Asia • 150 kW
15535v	**TUNISIA** †RTV TUNISIENNE, Sfax — S • N Africa & Mideast • 100 kW / N Africa & Mideast • 100 kW
15540	**CHINA** CHINA RADIO INTL, Via Russia — S • Mideast • 240 kW
	FRANCE R FRANCE INTL, Via Moyabi, Gabon — W Africa • 250 kW
	SEYCHELLES †FEBA RADIO, North Pt, Mahé Is — Th/Sa/Su • S Asia • 100 kW
	F • S Asia • 100 kW
	Sa/Su • S Asia • 100 kW
	F • Mideast & E Africa • 100 kW
	Mideast & E Africa • 100 kW
15545	**BELGIUM** †R VLAANDEREN INTL, Wavre — • Sa/Su • Africa • 200 kW
	S • E North Am • 100 kW
	FINLAND YLE RADIO FINLAND, Pori — W • Mideast • 500 kW
	RUSSIA †VOICE OF RUSSIA, Moscow — S • Africa • 200 kW
15550	**CHINA** †CENTRAL PEOPLE'S BS — S • DS-1
	DS-1 / W-M • DS-1
	ECUADOR †HCJB-VO THE ANDES, Quito — W • Europe • 500 kW
	W • Europe • 100 kW / Europe • 100 kW
	RUSSIA GOLOS ROSSII, Samara — S • S Asia & SE Asia • 100 kW
15555	**PAKISTAN** RADIO PAKISTAN, Islamabad — E Africa • 100 kW • ALT. FREQ. TO 17855 kHz / E Africa & S Africa • 100 kW
	Mideast • 250 kW • ALT. FREQ. TO 15675 kHz
(con'd)	**PORTUGAL** †RDP INTERNATIONAL, Lisbon — S • M-F • Europe • 100 kW / S • Sa/Su • Europe • 100 kW

ENGLISH ▬   ARABIC ⟩⟩⟩   CHINESE □□□   FRENCH ▬   GERMAN ▬   RUSSIAN =   SPANISH ▬   OTHER —

FREQUENCY   COUNTRY, STATION, LOCATION   TARGET • NETWORK • POWER (kW)   World Time

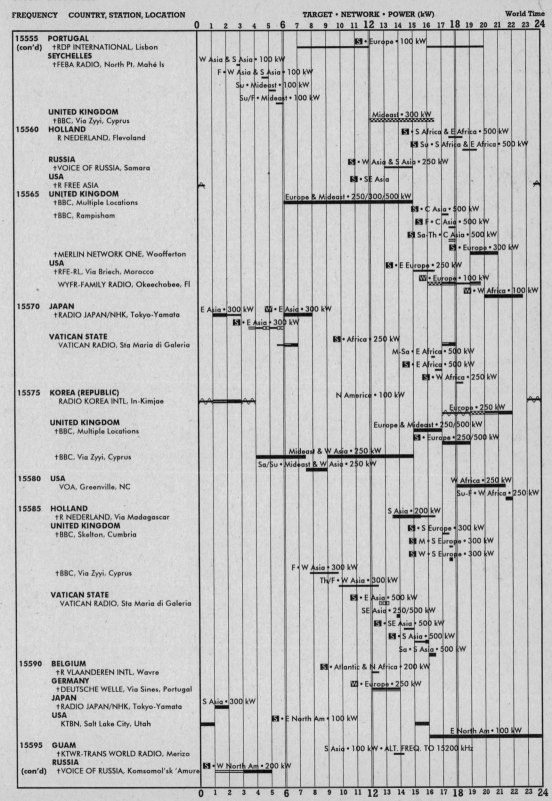

Frequency	Country, Station, Location	Target • Network • Power
15555 (con'd)	**PORTUGAL** †RDP INTERNATIONAL, Lisbon	S • Europe • 100 kW
	SEYCHELLES †FEBA RADIO, North Pt, Mahé Is	W Asia & S Asia • 100 kW; F • W Asia & S Asia • 100 kW; Su • Mideast • 100 kW; Su/F • Mideast • 100 kW
	UNITED KINGDOM †BBC, Via Zyyi, Cyprus	Mideast • 300 kW
15560	**HOLLAND** R NEDERLAND, Flevoland	S • S Africa & E Africa • 500 kW; S Su • S Africa & E Africa • 500 kW
	RUSSIA †VOICE OF RUSSIA, Samara	S • W Asia & S Asia • 250 kW
	USA †R FREE ASIA	S • SE Asia
15565	**UNITED KINGDOM** †BBC, Multiple Locations	Europe & Mideast • 250/300/500 kW
	†BBC, Rampisham	S • C Asia • 500 kW; S F • C Asia • 500 kW; S Sa-Th • C Asia • 500 kW; S • Europe • 300 kW
	†MERLIN NETWORK ONE, Woofferton	
	USA †RFE-RL, Via Briech, Morocco	S • E Europe • 250 kW
	WYFR-FAMILY RADIO, Okeechobee, Fl	W • Europe • 100 kW; W • W Africa • 100 kW
15570	**JAPAN** †RADIO JAPAN/NHK, Tokyo-Yamata	E Asia • 300 kW; W • E Asia • 300 kW; S • E Asia • 300 kW
	VATICAN STATE VATICAN RADIO, Sta Maria di Galeria	S • Africa • 250 kW; M-Sa • E Africa • 500 kW; S • E Africa • 500 kW; S • W Africa • 250 kW
15575	**KOREA (REPUBLIC)** RADIO KOREA INTL, In-Kimjae	N America • 100 kW; Europe • 250 kW
	UNITED KINGDOM †BBC, Multiple Locations	Europe & Mideast • 250/500 kW; S • Europe • 250/500 kW
	†BBC, Via Zyyi, Cyprus	Mideast & W Asia • 250 kW; Sa/Su • Mideast & W Asia • 250 kW
15580	**USA** VOA, Greenville, NC	W Africa • 250 kW; Su-F • W Africa • 250 kW
15585	**HOLLAND** †R NEDERLAND, Via Madagascar	S Asia • 200 kW
	UNITED KINGDOM †BBC, Skelton, Cumbria	S • S Europe • 300 kW; S M • S Europe • 300 kW; S W • S Europe • 300 kW
	†BBC, Via Zyyi, Cyprus	F • W Asia • 300 kW; Th/F • W Asia • 300 kW
	VATICAN STATE VATICAN RADIO, Sta Maria di Galeria	S • E Asia • 500 kW; SE Asia • 250/500 kW; S • SE Asia • 500 kW; S • S Asia • 500 kW; Sa • S Asia • 500 kW
15590	**BELGIUM** †R VLAANDEREN INTL, Wavre	S • Atlantic & N Africa • 200 kW
	GERMANY †DEUTSCHE WELLE, Via Sines, Portugal	W • Europe • 250 kW
	JAPAN †RADIO JAPAN/NHK, Tokyo-Yamata	S Asia • 300 kW
	USA KTBN, Salt Lake City, Utah	S • E North Am • 100 kW; E North Am • 100 kW
15595	**GUAM** †KTWR-TRANS WORLD RADIO, Merizo	S Asia • 100 kW • ALT. FREQ. TO 15200 kHz
(con'd)	**RUSSIA** †VOICE OF RUSSIA, Komsomol'sk 'Amure	S • W North Am • 200 kW

0 1 2 3 4 5 6 7 8 9 10 11 12 13 14 15 16 17 18 19 20 21 22 23 24

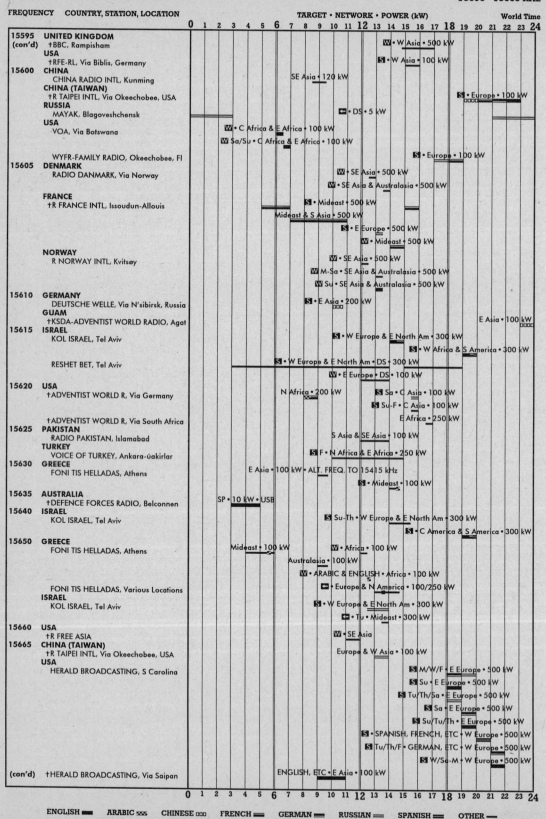

FREQUENCY   COUNTRY, STATION, LOCATION   TARGET • NETWORK • POWER (kW)   World Time

FREQUENCY	COUNTRY, STATION, LOCATION	TARGET • NETWORK • POWER (kW)
15595 (con'd)	**UNITED KINGDOM** †BBC, Rampisham	W • W Asia • 500 kW S • W Asia • 100 kW
	USA †RFE-RL, Via Biblis, Germany	
15600	**CHINA** CHINA RADIO INTL, Kunming	SE Asia • 120 kW
	CHINA (TAIWAN) †R TAIPEI INTL, Via Okeechobee, USA	S • Europe • 100 kW
	RUSSIA MAYAK, Blagoveshchensk	□ • DS • 5 kW
	USA VOA, Via Botswana	W • C Africa & E Africa • 100 kW W Sa/Su • C Africa & E Africa • 100 kW
	WYFR-FAMILY RADIO, Okeechobee, Fl	S • Europe • 100 kW
15605	**DENMARK** RADIO DANMARK, Via Norway	W • SE Asia • 500 kW W • SE Asia & Australasia • 500 kW
	FRANCE †R FRANCE INTL, Issoudun-Allouis	S • Mideast • 500 kW Mideast & S Asia • 500 kW S • E Europe • 500 kW W • Mideast • 500 kW
	NORWAY R NORWAY INTL, Kvitsøy	W • SE Asia • 500 kW W M-Sa • SE Asia & Australasia • 500 kW W Su • SE Asia & Australasia • 500 kW
15610	**GERMANY** DEUTSCHE WELLE, Via N'sibirsk, Russia	S • E Asia • 200 kW
	GUAM †KSDA-ADVENTIST WORLD RADIO, Agat	E Asia • 100 kW
15615	**ISRAEL** KOL ISRAEL, Tel Aviv	S • W Europe & E North Am • 300 kW S • W Africa & S America • 300 kW
	RESHET BET, Tel Aviv	S • W Europe & E North Am • DS • 300 kW W • E Europe • DS • 100 kW
15620	**USA** †ADVENTIST WORLD R, Via Germany	N Africa • 200 kW S Sa • C Asia • 100 kW S Su-F • C Asia • 100 kW E Africa • 250 kW
	†ADVENTIST WORLD R, Via South Africa	
15625	**PAKISTAN** RADIO PAKISTAN, Islamabad	S Asia & SE Asia • 100 kW
	TURKEY VOICE OF TURKEY, Ankara-úakirlar	S F • N Africa & E Africa • 250 kW
15630	**GREECE** FONI TIS HELLADAS, Athens	E Asia • 100 kW • ALT. FREQ. TO 15415 kHz S • Mideast • 100 kW
15635	**AUSTRALIA** †DEFENCE FORCES RADIO, Belconnen	SP • 10 kW • USB
15640	**ISRAEL** KOL ISRAEL, Tel Aviv	S Su-Th • W Europe & E North Am • 300 kW S • C America & S America • 300 kW
15650	**GREECE** FONI TIS HELLADAS, Athens	Mideast • 100 kW W • Africa • 100 kW Australasia • 100 kW W • ARABIC & ENGLISH • Africa • 100 kW □ • Europe & N America • 100/250 kW
	FONI TIS HELLADAS, Various Locations	
	ISRAEL KOL ISRAEL, Tel Aviv	S • W Europe & E North Am • 300 kW □ • Tu • Mideast • 300 kW
15660	**USA** †R FREE ASIA	W • SE Asia
15665	**CHINA (TAIWAN)** †R TAIPEI INTL, Via Okeechobee, USA	Europe & W Asia • 100 kW
	USA HERALD BROADCASTING, S Carolina	S M/W/F • E Europe • 500 kW S Su • E Europe • 500 kW S Tu/Th/Sa • E Europe • 500 kW S Sa • E Europe • 500 kW S Su/Tu/Th • E Europe • 500 kW S • SPANISH, FRENCH, ETC • W Europe • 500 kW S Tu/Th/F • GERMAN, ETC • W Europe • 500 kW S W/Sa-M • W Europe • 500 kW
(con'd)	†HERALD BROADCASTING, Via Saipan	ENGLISH, ETC • E Asia • 100 kW

ENGLISH ▬▬   ARABIC ⋙   CHINESE □□□   FRENCH ══   GERMAN ▬▬   RUSSIAN ══   SPANISH ══   OTHER ▬

FREQUENCY	COUNTRY, STATION, LOCATION

TARGET • NETWORK • POWER (kW)

World Time

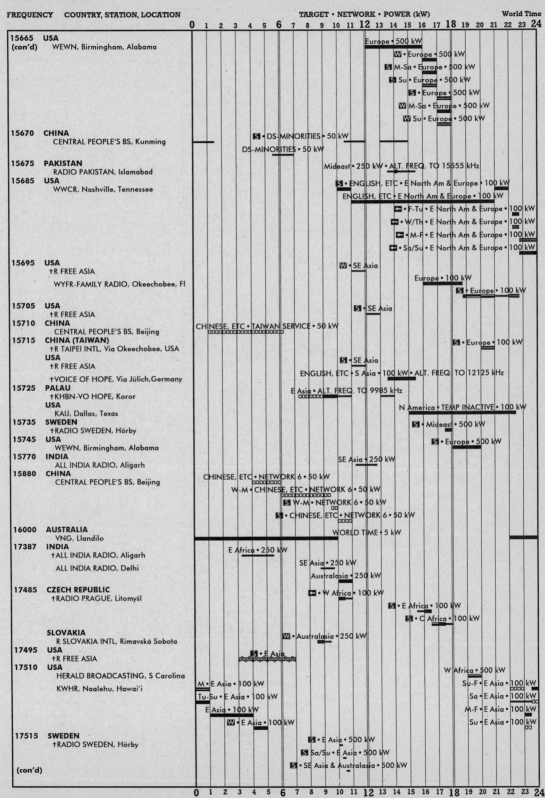

15665	USA
(con'd)	WEWN, Birmingham, Alabama
15670	CHINA
	CENTRAL PEOPLE'S BS, Kunming
15675	PAKISTAN
	RADIO PAKISTAN, Islamabad
15685	USA
	WWCR, Nashville, Tennessee
15695	USA
	†R FREE ASIA
	WYFR-FAMILY RADIO, Okeechobee, Fl
15705	USA
	†R FREE ASIA
15710	CHINA
	CENTRAL PEOPLE'S BS, Beijing
15715	CHINA (TAIWAN)
	†R TAIPEI INTL, Via Okeechobee, USA
	USA
	†R FREE ASIA
	†VOICE OF HOPE, Via Jülich, Germany
15725	PALAU
	†KHBN-VO HOPE, Koror
	USA
	KAIJ, Dallas, Texas
15735	SWEDEN
	†RADIO SWEDEN, Hörby
15745	USA
	WEWN, Birmingham, Alabama
15770	INDIA
	ALL INDIA RADIO, Aligarh
15880	CHINA
	CENTRAL PEOPLE'S BS, Beijing
16000	AUSTRALIA
	VNG, Llandilo
17387	INDIA
	†ALL INDIA RADIO, Aligarh
	ALL INDIA RADIO, Delhi
17485	CZECH REPUBLIC
	†RADIO PRAGUE, Litomyšl
	SLOVAKIA
	R SLOVAKIA INTL, Rimavská Sobota
17495	USA
	†R FREE ASIA
17510	USA
	HERALD BROADCASTING, S Carolina
	KWHR, Naalehu, Hawai'i
17515	SWEDEN
	†RADIO SWEDEN, Hörby
(con'd)	

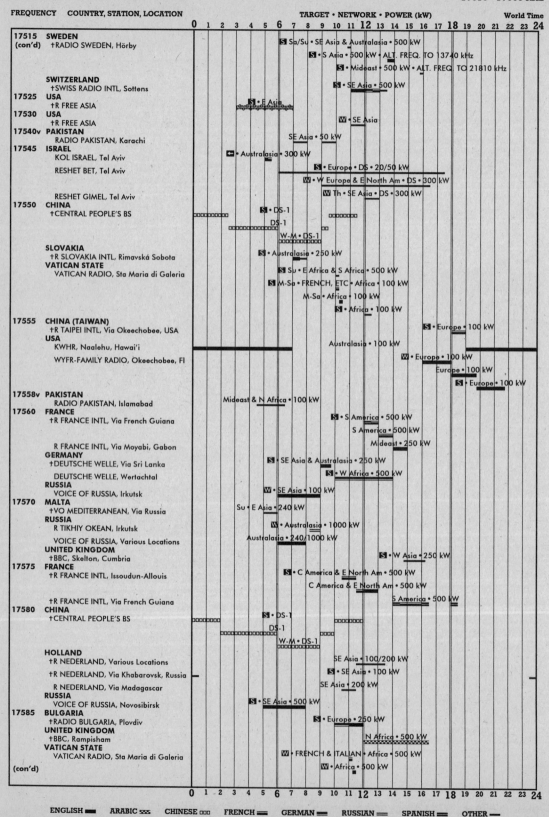

FREQUENCY   COUNTRY, STATION, LOCATION

TARGET • NETWORK • POWER (kW)

World Time

FREQUENCY	COUNTRY, STATION, LOCATION
17515 (con'd)	SWEDEN †RADIO SWEDEN, Hörby
	SWITZERLAND †SWISS RADIO INTL, Sottens
17525	USA †R FREE ASIA
17530	USA †R FREE ASIA
17540v	PAKISTAN RADIO PAKISTAN, Karachi
17545	ISRAEL KOL ISRAEL, Tel Aviv
	RESHET BET, Tel Aviv
	RESHET GIMEL, Tel Aviv
17550	CHINA †CENTRAL PEOPLE'S BS
	SLOVAKIA †R SLOVAKIA INTL, Rimavská Sobota
	VATICAN STATE VATICAN RADIO, Sta Maria di Galeria
17555	CHINA (TAIWAN) †R TAIPEI INTL, Via Okeechobee, USA
	USA KWHR, Naalehu, Hawai'i
	WYFR-FAMILY RADIO, Okeechobee, Fl
17558v	PAKISTAN RADIO PAKISTAN, Islamabad
17560	FRANCE †R FRANCE INTL, Via French Guiana
	R FRANCE INTL, Via Moyabi, Gabon
	GERMANY †DEUTSCHE WELLE, Via Sri Lanka
	DEUTSCHE WELLE, Wertachtal
	RUSSIA VOICE OF RUSSIA, Irkutsk
17570	MALTA †VO MEDITERRANEAN, Via Russia
	RUSSIA R TIKHIY OKEAN, Irkutsk
	VOICE OF RUSSIA, Various Locations
	UNITED KINGDOM †BBC, Skelton, Cumbria
17575	FRANCE †R FRANCE INTL, Issoudun-Allouis
	†R FRANCE INTL, Via French Guiana
17580	CHINA †CENTRAL PEOPLE'S BS
	HOLLAND †R NEDERLAND, Various Locations
	†R NEDERLAND, Via Khabarovsk, Russia
	R NEDERLAND, Via Madagascar
	RUSSIA VOICE OF RUSSIA, Novosibirsk
17585	BULGARIA †RADIO BULGARIA, Plovdiv
	UNITED KINGDOM †BBC, Rampisham
	VATICAN STATE VATICAN RADIO, Sta Maria di Galeria
(con'd)	

Schedule annotations (as shown on chart):

- **S** Sa/Su • SE Asia & Australasia • 500 kW
- **S** S Asia • 500 kW • ALT. FREQ. TO 13740 kHz
- **S** Mideast • 500 kW • ALT. FREQ. TO 21810 kHz
- **S** SE Asia • 500 kW
- **S** E Asia
- **W** SE Asia
- SE Asia • 50 kW
- Australasia • 300 kW
- **S** Europe • DS • 20/50 kW
- **W** W Europe & E North Am • DS • 300 kW
- **W** Th • SE Asia • DS • 300 kW
- **S** DS-1
- DS-1
- W–M • DS-1
- **S** Australasia • 250 kW
- **S** Su • E Africa & S Africa • 500 kW
- **S** M-Sa • FRENCH, ETC • Africa • 100 kW
- M-Sa • Africa • 100 kW
- **S** Africa • 100 kW
- **S** Europe • 100 kW
- Australasia • 100 kW
- **W** Europe • 100 kW
- Europe • 100 kW
- **S** Europe • 100 kW
- Mideast & N Africa • 100 kW
- **S** S America • 500 kW
- S America • 500 kW
- Mideast • 250 kW
- **S** SE Asia & Australasia • 250 kW
- **S** W Africa • 500 kW
- **W** SE Asia • 100 kW
- Su • E Asia • 240 kW
- **W** Australasia • 1000 kW
- Australasia • 240/1000 kW
- **S** W Asia • 250 kW
- **S** C America & E North Am • 500 kW
- C America & E North Am • 500 kW
- S America • 500 kW
- **S** DS-1
- DS-1
- W–M • DS-1
- SE Asia • 100/200 kW
- **S** SE Asia • 100 kW
- SE Asia • 200 kW
- **S** SE Asia • 500 kW
- **S** Europe • 250 kW
- N Africa • 500 kW
- **W** FRENCH & ITALIAN • Africa • 500 kW
- **W** Africa • 500 kW

FREQUENCY   COUNTRY, STATION, LOCATION   TARGET • NETWORK • POWER (kW)   World Time

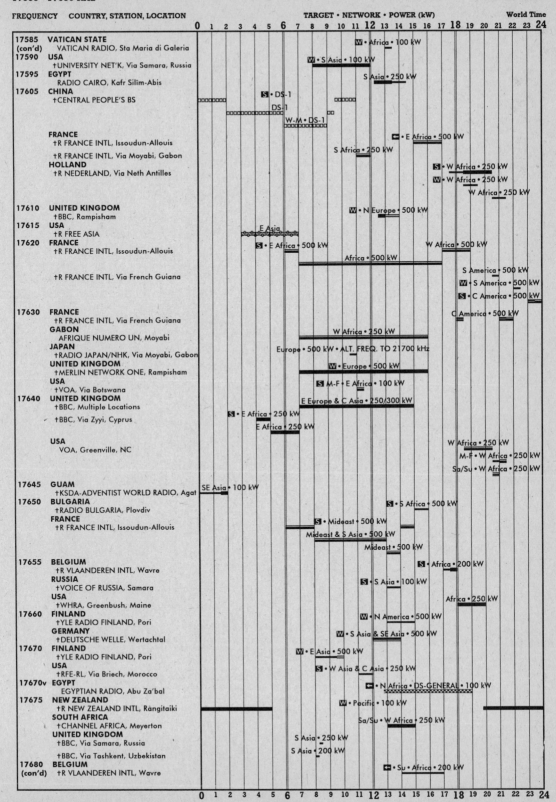

FREQUENCY	COUNTRY, STATION, LOCATION	TARGET • NETWORK • POWER (kW)
17585 (con'd)	**VATICAN STATE** VATICAN RADIO, Sta Maria di Galeria	W • Africa • 100 kW
17590	**USA** †UNIVERSITY NET'K, Via Samara, Russia	W • S Asia • 100 kW
17595	**EGYPT** RADIO CAIRO, Kafr Silim-Abis	S Asia • 250 kW
17605	**CHINA** †CENTRAL PEOPLE'S BS	S • DS-1 / DS-1 / W-M • DS-1
	FRANCE †R FRANCE INTL, Issoudun-Allouis	• E Africa • 500 kW
	†R FRANCE INTL, Via Moyabi, Gabon	S Africa • 250 kW
	HOLLAND †R NEDERLAND, Via Neth Antilles	S • W Africa • 250 kW / W • W Africa • 250 kW / W Africa • 250 kW
17610	**UNITED KINGDOM** †BBC, Rampisham	W • N Europe • 500 kW
17615	**USA** †R FREE ASIA	E Asia
17620	**FRANCE** †R FRANCE INTL, Issoudun-Allouis	S • E Africa • 500 kW / W Africa • 500 kW / Africa • 500 kW
	†R FRANCE INTL, Via French Guiana	S America • 500 kW / W • S America • 500 kW / S • C America • 500 kW
17630	**FRANCE** †R FRANCE INTL, Via French Guiana	C America • 500 kW
	GABON AFRIQUE NUMERO UN, Moyabi	W Africa • 250 kW
	JAPAN †RADIO JAPAN/NHK, Via Moyabi, Gabon	Europe • 500 kW • ALT. FREQ. TO 21700 kHz
	UNITED KINGDOM †MERLIN NETWORK ONE, Rampisham	W • Europe • 500 kW
	USA †VOA, Via Botswana	S M-F • E Africa • 100 kW
17640	**UNITED KINGDOM** †BBC, Multiple Locations	E Europe & C Asia • 250/300 kW
	†BBC, Via Zyyi, Cyprus	S • E Africa • 250 kW / E Africa • 250 kW
	USA VOA, Greenville, NC	W Africa • 250 kW / M-F • W Africa • 250 kW / Sa/Su • W Africa • 250 kW
17645	**GUAM** †KSDA-ADVENTIST WORLD RADIO, Agat	SE Asia • 100 kW
17650	**BULGARIA** †RADIO BULGARIA, Plovdiv	S • S Africa • 500 kW
	FRANCE †R FRANCE INTL, Issoudun-Allouis	S • Mideast • 500 kW / Mideast & S Asia • 500 kW / Mideast • 500 kW
17655	**BELGIUM** †R VLAANDEREN INTL, Wavre	S • Africa • 200 kW
	RUSSIA †VOICE OF RUSSIA, Samara	S • S Asia • 100 kW
	USA †WHRA, Greenbush, Maine	Africa • 250 kW
17660	**FINLAND** †YLE RADIO FINLAND, Pori	W • N America • 500 kW
	GERMANY †DEUTSCHE WELLE, Wertachtal	W • S Asia & SE Asia • 500 kW
17670	**FINLAND** †YLE RADIO FINLAND, Pori	W • E Asia • 500 kW
	USA †RFE-RL, Via Briech, Morocco	S • W Asia & C Asia • 250 kW
17670v	**EGYPT** EGYPTIAN RADIO, Abu Za'bal	• N Africa • DS-GENERAL • 100 kW
17675	**NEW ZEALAND** †R NEW ZEALAND INTL, Rangitaiki	W • Pacific • 100 kW
	SOUTH AFRICA †CHANNEL AFRICA, Meyerton	Sa/Su • W Africa • 250 kW
	UNITED KINGDOM †BBC, Via Samara, Russia	S Asia • 250 kW
	†BBC, Via Tashkent, Uzbekistan	S Asia • 200 kW
17680 (con'd)	**BELGIUM** †R VLAANDEREN INTL, Wavre	• Su • Africa • 200 kW

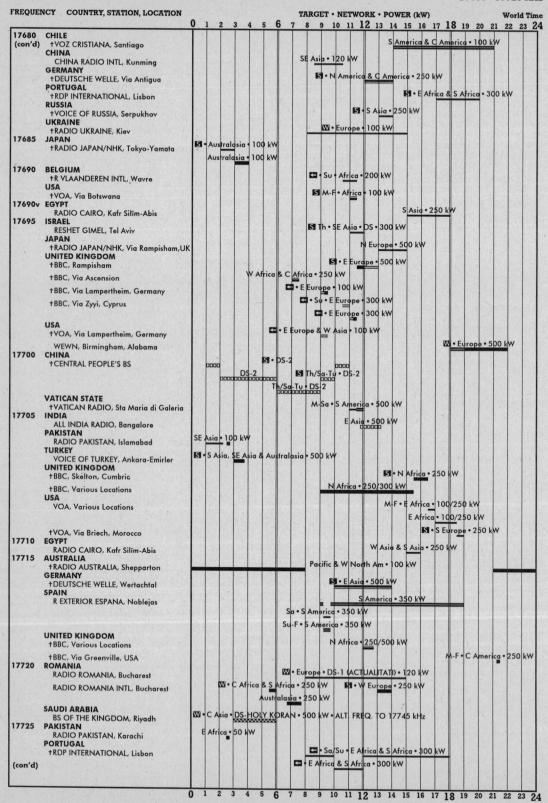

FREQUENCY   COUNTRY, STATION, LOCATION

TARGET • NETWORK • POWER (kW)

Frequency	Country / Station / Location	Notes
17680 (con'd)	**CHILE** †VOZ CRISTIANA, Santiago	S America & C America • 100 kW
	CHINA CHINA RADIO INTL, Kunming	SE Asia • 120 kW
	GERMANY †DEUTSCHE WELLE, Via Antigua	S • N America & C America • 250 kW
	PORTUGAL †RDP INTERNATIONAL, Lisbon	S • E Africa & S Africa • 300 kW
	RUSSIA †VOICE OF RUSSIA, Serpukhov	S • S Asia • 250 kW
	UKRAINE †RADIO UKRAINE, Kiev	W • Europe • 100 kW
17685	**JAPAN** †RADIO JAPAN/NHK, Tokyo-Yamata	S • Australasia • 100 kW / Australasia • 100 kW
17690	**BELGIUM** †R VLAANDEREN INTL, Wavre	Su • Africa • 200 kW
	USA †VOA, Via Botswana	S M-F • Africa • 100 kW
17690v	**EGYPT** RADIO CAIRO, Kafr Silim-Abis	S Asia • 250 kW
17695	**ISRAEL** RESHET GIMEL, Tel Aviv	S Th • SE Asia • DS • 300 kW
	JAPAN †RADIO JAPAN/NHK, Via Rampisham, UK	N Europe • 500 kW
	UNITED KINGDOM †BBC, Rampisham	S • E Europe • 500 kW
	†BBC, Via Ascension	W Africa & C Africa • 250 kW
	†BBC, Via Lampertheim, Germany	E Europe • 100 kW
	†BBC, Via Zyyi, Cyprus	Su • E Europe • 300 kW
	†BBC, Via Zyyi, Cyprus	E Europe • 300 kW
	USA †VOA, Via Lampertheim, Germany	E Europe & W Asia • 100 kW
	WEWN, Birmingham, Alabama	W • Europe • 500 kW
17700	**CHINA** †CENTRAL PEOPLE'S BS	S • DS-2 / DS-2 / Th/Sa-Tu • DS-2 / Th/Sa-Tu • DS-2
	VATICAN STATE †VATICAN RADIO, Sta Maria di Galeria	M-Sa • S America • 500 kW
17705	**INDIA** ALL INDIA RADIO, Bangalore	E Asia • 500 kW
	PAKISTAN RADIO PAKISTAN, Islamabad	SE Asia • 100 kW
	TURKEY VOICE OF TURKEY, Ankara-Emirler	S • S Asia, SE Asia & Australasia • 500 kW
	UNITED KINGDOM †BBC, Skelton, Cumbria	S • N Africa • 250 kW
	†BBC, Various Locations	N Africa • 250/300 kW
	USA VOA, Various Locations	M-F • E Africa • 100/250 kW / E Africa • 100/250 kW
	†VOA, Via Briech, Morocco	S • S Europe • 250 kW
17710	**EGYPT** RADIO CAIRO, Kafr Silim-Abis	W Asia & S Asia • 250 kW
17715	**AUSTRALIA** †RADIO AUSTRALIA, Shepparton	Pacific & W North Am • 100 kW
	GERMANY †DEUTSCHE WELLE, Wertachtal	S • E Asia • 500 kW
	SPAIN R EXTERIOR ESPANA, Noblejas	S America • 350 kW / Sa • S America • 350 kW / Su-F • S America • 350 kW
	UNITED KINGDOM †BBC, Various Locations	N Africa • 250/500 kW
	†BBC, Via Greenville, USA	M-F • C America • 250 kW
17720	**ROMANIA** RADIO ROMANIA, Bucharest	W • Europe • DS-1 (ACTUALITATI) • 120 kW
	RADIO ROMANIA INTL, Bucharest	W • C Africa & S Africa • 250 kW / S • W Europe • 250 kW / Australasia • 250 kW
	SAUDI ARABIA BS OF THE KINGDOM, Riyadh	W • C Asia • DS-HOLY KORAN • 500 kW • ALT FREQ. TO 17745 kHz
17725	**PAKISTAN** RADIO PAKISTAN, Karachi	E Africa • 50 kW
	PORTUGAL †RDP INTERNATIONAL, Lisbon	Sa/Su • E Africa & S Africa • 300 kW
(con'd)		E Africa & S Africa • 300 kW

ENGLISH ▬ ARABIC ≈≈ CHINESE □□□ FRENCH ▬ GERMAN ▬ RUSSIAN ═ SPANISH ▬ OTHER ▬

FREQUENCY   COUNTRY, STATION, LOCATION

TARGET • NETWORK • POWER (kW)

World Time

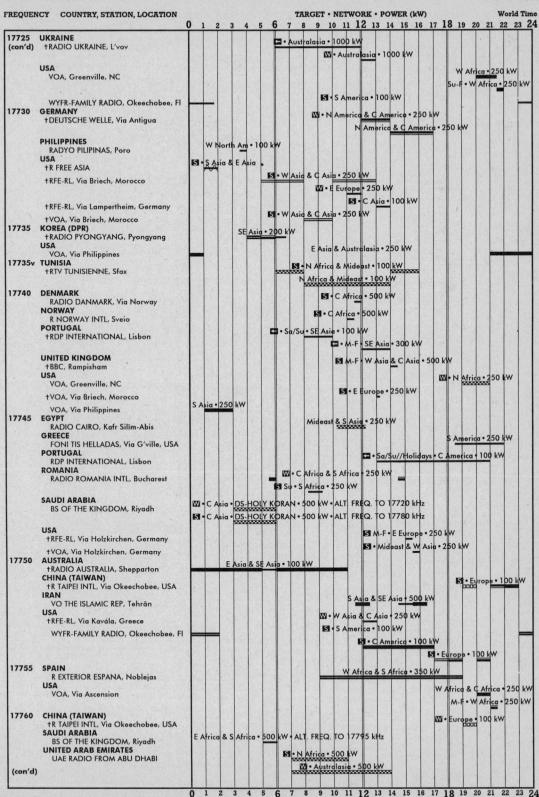

0 1 2 3 4 5 6 7 8 9 10 11 12 13 14 15 16 17 18 19 20 21 22 23 24

| 17725 | UKRAINE |
| (con'd) | †RADIO UKRAINE, L'vov |

- • Australasia • 1000 kW
- W • Australasia • 1000 kW

USA
VOA, Greenville, NC
- W Africa • 250 kW
- Su-F • W Africa • 250 kW

WYFR–FAMILY RADIO, Okeechobee, Fl
- S • S America • 100 kW

| 17730 | GERMANY |
| | †DEUTSCHE WELLE, Via Antigua |

- W • N America & C America • 250 kW
- N America & C America • 250 kW

PHILIPPINES
RADYO PILIPINAS, Poro
- W North Am • 100 kW

USA
†R FREE ASIA
- S • S Asia & E Asia

†RFE-RL, Via Briech, Morocco
- S • W Asia & C Asia • 250 kW
- W • E Europe • 250 kW
- S • C Asia • 100 kW

†RFE-RL, Via Lampertheim, Germany

†VOA, Via Briech, Morocco
- S • W Asia & C Asia • 250 kW

| 17735 | KOREA (DPR) |
| | †RADIO PYONGYANG, Pyongyang |

- SE Asia • 200 kW

USA
VOA, Via Philippines
- E Asia & Australasia • 250 kW

| 17735v | TUNISIA |
| | †RTV TUNISIENNE, Sfax |

- S • N Africa & Mideast • 100 kW
- N Africa & Mideast • 100 kW

| 17740 | DENMARK |
| | RADIO DANMARK, Via Norway |

- S • C Africa • 500 kW

NORWAY
R NORWAY INTL, Sveio
- S • C Africa • 500 kW

PORTUGAL
†RDP INTERNATIONAL, Lisbon
- • Sa/Su • SE Asia • 100 kW
- • M-F • SE Asia • 300 kW

UNITED KINGDOM
†BBC, Rampisham
- S • M-F • W Asia & C Asia • 500 kW

USA
VOA, Greenville, NC
- W • N Africa • 250 kW

†VOA, Via Briech, Morocco
- S • E Europe • 250 kW

VOA, Via Philippines
- S Asia • 250 kW

| 17745 | EGYPT |
| | RADIO CAIRO, Kafr Silim-Abis |

- Mideast & S Asia • 250 kW

GREECE
FONI TIS HELLADAS, Via G'ville, USA
- S America • 250 kW

PORTUGAL
RDP INTERNATIONAL, Lisbon
- • Sa/Su//Holidays • C America • 100 kW

ROMANIA
RADIO ROMANIA INTL, Bucharest
- W • C Africa & S Africa • 250 kW
- S • Su • S Africa • 250 kW

SAUDI ARABIA
BS OF THE KINGDOM, Riyadh
- W • C Asia • DS-HOLY KORAN • 500 kW • ALT. FREQ. TO 17720 kHz
- S • C Asia • DS-HOLY KORAN • 500 kW • ALT. FREQ. TO 17780 kHz

USA
†RFE-RL, Via Holzkirchen, Germany
- S • M-F • E Europe • 250 kW

†VOA, Via Holzkirchen, Germany
- S • Mideast & W Asia • 250 kW

| 17750 | AUSTRALIA |
| | †RADIO AUSTRALIA, Shepparton |

- E Asia & SE Asia • 100 kW

CHINA (TAIWAN)
†R TAIPEI INTL, Via Okeechobee, USA
- S • Europe • 100 kW

IRAN
VO THE ISLAMIC REP, Tehrān
- S Asia & SE Asia • 500 kW

USA
†RFE-RL, Via Kavála, Greece
- W • W Asia & C Asia • 250 kW
- S • S America • 100 kW

WYFR–FAMILY RADIO, Okeechobee, Fl
- S • C America • 100 kW
- S • Europe • 100 kW

| 17755 | SPAIN |
| | R EXTERIOR ESPANA, Noblejas |

- W Africa & S Africa • 350 kW

USA
VOA, Via Ascension
- W Africa & C Africa • 250 kW
- M-F • W Africa • 250 kW

| 17760 | CHINA (TAIWAN) |
| | †R TAIPEI INTL, Via Okeechobee, USA |

- W • Europe • 100 kW

SAUDI ARABIA
BS OF THE KINGDOM, Riyadh
- E Africa & S Africa • 500 kW • ALT. FREQ. TO 17795 kHz

UNITED ARAB EMIRATES
UAE RADIO FROM ABU DHABI
- S • N Africa • 500 kW
- W • Australasia • 500 kW

(con'd)

0 1 2 3 4 5 6 7 8 9 10 11 12 13 14 15 16 17 18 19 20 21 22 23 24

SEASONAL S OR W   1-HR TIMESHIFT MIDYEAR ⊡ OR ⊡   JAMMING / OR ∧   EARLIEST HEARD ◁   LATEST HEARD ▷   NEW FOR 1999 †

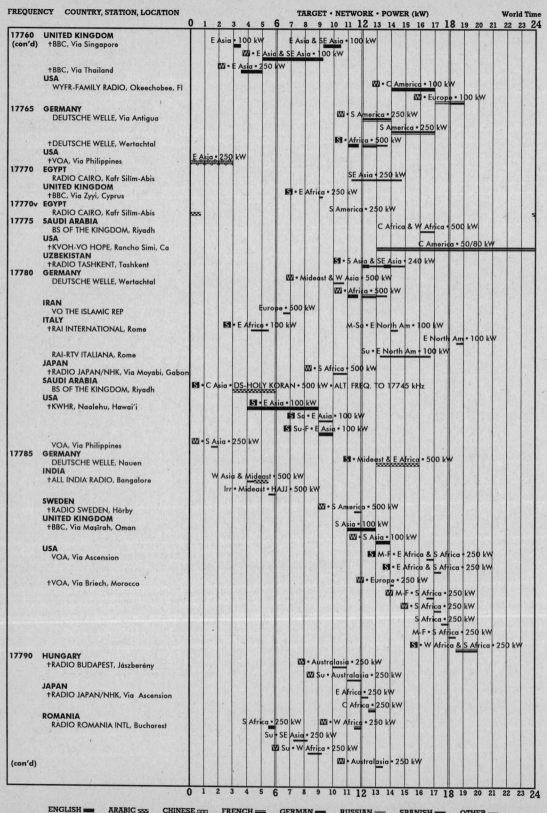

FREQUENCY   COUNTRY, STATION, LOCATION

TARGET • NETWORK • POWER (kW)

World Time

Frequency	Country, Station, Location	Schedule
17760 (con'd)	UNITED KINGDOM †BBC, Via Singapore	E Asia • 100 kW / E Asia & SE Asia • 100 kW / W • E Asia & SE Asia • 100 kW
	†BBC, Via Thailand	W • E Asia • 250 kW
	USA WYFR-FAMILY RADIO, Okeechobee, Fl	W • C America • 100 kW / W • Europe • 100 kW
17765	GERMANY DEUTSCHE WELLE, Via Antigua	W • S America • 250 kW / S America • 250 kW
	†DEUTSCHE WELLE, Wertachtal	S • Africa • 500 kW
	USA †VOA, Via Philippines	E Asia • 250 kW
17770	EGYPT RADIO CAIRO, Kafr Silîm-Abis	SE Asia • 250 kW
	UNITED KINGDOM †BBC, Via Zyyi, Cyprus	S • E Africa • 250 kW
17770v	EGYPT RADIO CAIRO, Kafr Silîm-Abis	S America • 250 kW
17775	SAUDI ARABIA BS OF THE KINGDOM, Riyadh	C Africa & W Africa • 500 kW
	USA †KVOH-VO HOPE, Rancho Simi, Ca	C America • 50/80 kW
	UZBEKISTAN †RADIO TASHKENT, Tashkent	S • S Asia & SE Asia • 240 kW
17780	GERMANY DEUTSCHE WELLE, Wertachtal	W • Mideast & W Asia • 500 kW / W • Africa • 500 kW
	IRAN VO THE ISLAMIC REP	Europe • 500 kW
	ITALY †RAI INTERNATIONAL, Rome	S • E Africa • 100 kW / M-Sa • E North Am • 100 kW / E North Am • 100 kW
	RAI-RTV ITALIANA, Rome	Su • E North Am • 100 kW
	JAPAN †RADIO JAPAN/NHK, Via Moyabi, Gabon	W • S Africa • 500 kW
	SAUDI ARABIA BS OF THE KINGDOM, Riyadh	S • C Asia • DS-HOLY KORAN • 500 kW • ALT. FREQ. TO 17745 kHz
	USA †KWHR, Naalehu, Hawai'i	S • E Asia • 100 kW / Sa • E Asia • 100 kW / Su-F • E Asia • 100 kW
	VOA, Via Philippines	W • S Asia • 250 kW
17785	GERMANY DEUTSCHE WELLE, Nauen	S • Mideast & E Africa • 500 kW
	INDIA †ALL INDIA RADIO, Bangalore	W Asia & Mideast • 500 kW / Irr • Mideast • HAJJ • 500 kW
	SWEDEN †RADIO SWEDEN, Hörby	W • S America • 500 kW
	UNITED KINGDOM †BBC, Via Maṣīrah, Oman	S Asia • 100 kW / W • S Asia • 100 kW
	USA VOA, Via Ascension	S • M-F • E Africa & S Africa • 250 kW / S • E Africa & S Africa • 250 kW
	†VOA, Via Briech, Morocco	W • Europe • 250 kW / W M-F • S Africa • 250 kW / W • S Africa • 250 kW / S Africa • 250 kW / M-F • S Africa • 250 kW / S • W Africa & S Africa • 250 kW
17790	HUNGARY †RADIO BUDAPEST, Jászberény	W • Australasia • 250 kW / W Su • Australasia • 250 kW
	JAPAN †RADIO JAPAN/NHK, Via Ascension	E Africa • 250 kW / C Africa • 250 kW
	ROMANIA RADIO ROMANIA INTL, Bucharest	S Africa • 250 kW / W • W Africa • 250 kW / Su • SE Asia • 250 kW / W Su • W Africa • 250 kW
(con'd)		W • Australasia • 250 kW

FREQUENCY   COUNTRY, STATION, LOCATION

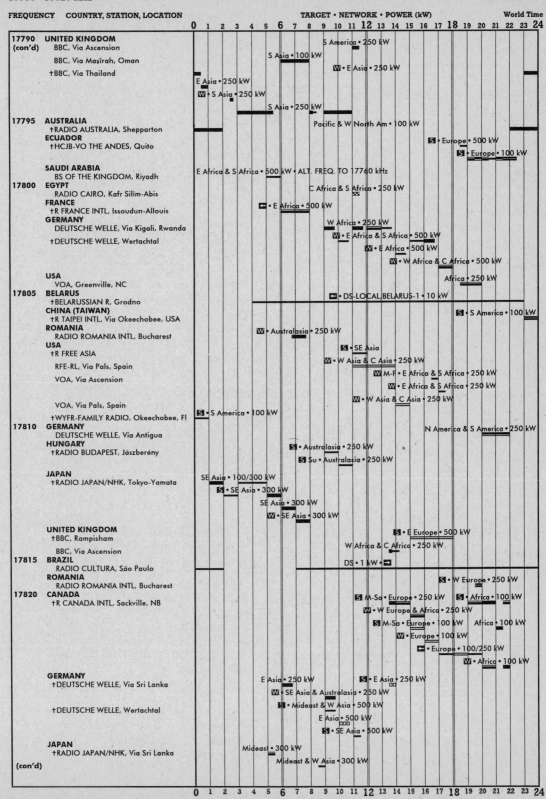

FREQUENCY	COUNTRY, STATION, LOCATION	TARGET • NETWORK • POWER (kW)
17790 (con'd)	UNITED KINGDOM	
	BBC, Via Ascension	S America • 250 kW
	BBC, Via Maṣīrah, Oman	S Asia • 100 kW
	†BBC, Via Thailand	W • E Asia • 250 kW
		E Asia • 250 kW
		W • S Asia • 250 kW
		S Asia • 250 kW
17795	AUSTRALIA	
	†RADIO AUSTRALIA, Shepparton	Pacific & W North Am • 100 kW
	ECUADOR	S • Europe • 500 kW
	†HCJB-VO THE ANDES, Quito	S • Europe • 100 kW
	SAUDI ARABIA	
	BS OF THE KINGDOM, Riyadh	E Africa & S Africa • 500 kW • ALT. FREQ. TO 17760 kHz
17800	EGYPT	
	RADIO CAIRO, Kafr Silim-Abis	C Africa & S Africa • 250 kW
	FRANCE	
	†R FRANCE INTL, Issoudun-Allouis	⇦ • E Africa • 500 kW
	GERMANY	
	DEUTSCHE WELLE, Via Kigali, Rwanda	W Africa • 250 kW
		W • E Africa & S Africa • 500 kW
	†DEUTSCHE WELLE, Wertachtal	W • E Africa • 500 kW
		W • W Africa & C Africa • 500 kW
	USA	
	VOA, Greenville, NC	Africa • 250 kW
17805	BELARUS	
	†BELARUSSIAN R, Grodno	⇦ • DS-LOCAL BELARUS-1 • 10 kW
	CHINA (TAIWAN)	
	†R TAIPEI INTL, Via Okeechobee, USA	S • S America • 100 kW
	ROMANIA	
	RADIO ROMANIA INTL, Bucharest	W • Australasia • 250 kW
	USA	
	†R FREE ASIA	S • SE Asia
	RFE-RL, Via Pals, Spain	W • W Asia & C Asia • 250 kW
	VOA, Via Ascension	W M-F • E Africa & S Africa • 250 kW
		W • E Africa & S Africa • 250 kW
	VOA, Via Pals, Spain	W • W Asia & C Asia • 250 kW
	†WYFR-FAMILY RADIO, Okeechobee, Fl	S • S America • 100 kW
17810	GERMANY	
	DEUTSCHE WELLE, Via Antigua	N America & S America • 250 kW
	HUNGARY	
	†RADIO BUDAPEST, Jászberény	S • Australasia • 250 kW
		S Su • Australasia • 250 kW
	JAPAN	
	†RADIO JAPAN/NHK, Tokyo-Yamata	SE Asia • 100/300 kW
		S • SE Asia • 300 kW
		SE Asia • 300 kW
		W • SE Asia • 300 kW
	UNITED KINGDOM	
	†BBC, Rampisham	S • E Europe • 500 kW
	BBC, Via Ascension	W Africa & C Africa • 250 kW
17815	BRAZIL	
	RADIO CULTURA, São Paulo	DS • 1 kW • ⇨
	ROMANIA	
	RADIO ROMANIA INTL, Bucharest	S • W Europe • 250 kW
17820	CANADA	
	†R CANADA INTL, Sackville, NB	S M-Sa • Europe • 250 kW S • Africa • 100 kW
		W • W Europe & Africa • 250 kW
		S M-Sa • Europe • 100 kW Africa • 100 kW
		W • Europe • 100 kW
		⇦ • Europe • 100/250 kW
		W • Africa • 100 kW
	GERMANY	
	†DEUTSCHE WELLE, Via Sri Lanka	E Asia • 250 kW S • E Asia • 250 kW
		W • SE Asia & Australasia • 250 kW
	†DEUTSCHE WELLE, Wertachtal	S • Mideast & W Asia • 500 kW
		E Asia • 500 kW
		S • SE Asia • 500 kW
	JAPAN	
	†RADIO JAPAN/NHK, Via Sri Lanka	Mideast • 300 kW
		Mideast & W Asia • 300 kW
(con'd)		

FREQUENCY   COUNTRY, STATION, LOCATION

TARGET • NETWORK • POWER (kW)   World Time

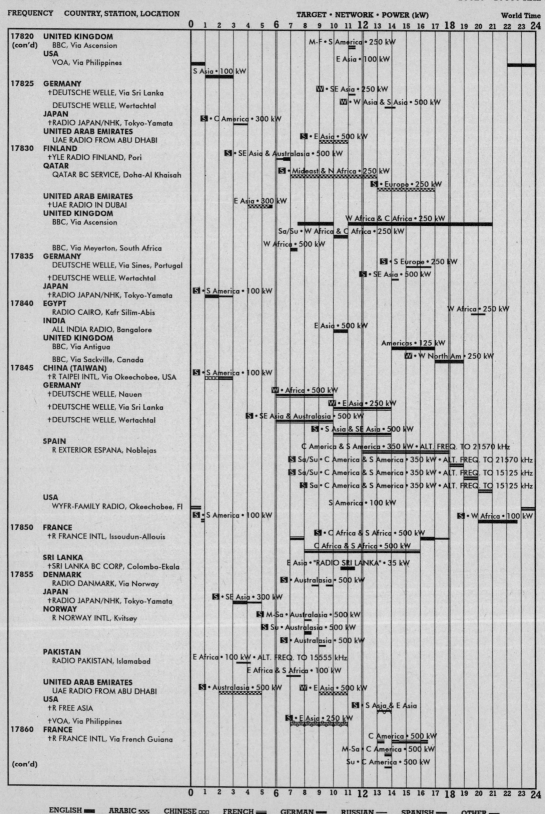

Frequency	Country, Station, Location
17820 (con'd)	**UNITED KINGDOM** — BBC, Via Ascension — M-F • S America • 250 kW
	USA — VOA, Via Philippines — E Asia • 100 kW; S Asia • 100 kW
17825	**GERMANY** — †DEUTSCHE WELLE, Via Sri Lanka — W • SE Asia • 250 kW
	DEUTSCHE WELLE, Wertachtal — W • W Asia & S Asia • 500 kW
	JAPAN — †RADIO JAPAN/NHK, Tokyo-Yamata — S • C America • 300 kW
	UNITED ARAB EMIRATES — UAE RADIO FROM ABU DHABI — S • E Asia • 500 kW
17830	**FINLAND** — †YLE RADIO FINLAND, Pori — S • SE Asia & Australasia • 500 kW
	QATAR — QATAR BC SERVICE, Doha-Al Khaisah — S • Mideast & N Africa • 250 kW; S • Europe • 250 kW
	UNITED ARAB EMIRATES — †UAE RADIO IN DUBAI — E Asia • 300 kW
	UNITED KINGDOM — BBC, Via Ascension — W Africa & C Africa • 250 kW; Sa/Su • W Africa & C Africa • 250 kW
	BBC, Via Meyerton, South Africa — W Africa • 500 kW
17835	**GERMANY** — DEUTSCHE WELLE, Via Sines, Portugal — S • S Europe • 250 kW
	†DEUTSCHE WELLE, Wertachtal — S • SE Asia • 500 kW
	JAPAN — †RADIO JAPAN/NHK, Tokyo-Yamata — S • S America • 100 kW
17840	**EGYPT** — RADIO CAIRO, Kafr Silim-Abis — W Africa • 250 kW
	INDIA — ALL INDIA RADIO, Bangalore — E Asia • 500 kW
	UNITED KINGDOM — BBC, Via Antigua — Americas • 125 kW
	BBC, Via Sackville, Canada — W • W North Am • 250 kW
17845	**CHINA (TAIWAN)** — †R TAIPEI INTL, Via Okeechobee, USA — S • S America • 100 kW
	GERMANY — †DEUTSCHE WELLE, Nauen — W • Africa • 500 kW
	†DEUTSCHE WELLE, Via Sri Lanka — W • E Asia • 250 kW
	†DEUTSCHE WELLE, Wertachtal — S • SE Asia & Australasia • 500 kW; S • S Asia & SE Asia • 500 kW
	SPAIN — R EXTERIOR ESPANA, Noblejas — C America & S America • 350 kW • ALT. FREQ. TO 21570 kHz; S Sa/Su • C America & S America • 350 kW • ALT. FREQ. TO 21570 kHz; S Sa/Su • C America & S America • 350 kW • ALT. FREQ. TO 15125 kHz; S Sa • C America & S America • 350 kW • ALT. FREQ. TO 15125 kHz
	USA — WYFR-FAMILY RADIO, Okeechobee, Fl — S America • 100 kW; S • S America • 100 kW; S • W Africa • 100 kW
17850	**FRANCE** — †R FRANCE INTL, Issoudun-Allouis — S • C Africa & S Africa • 500 kW; C Africa & S Africa • 500 kW
	SRI LANKA — †SRI LANKA BC CORP, Colombo-Ekala — E Asia • "RADIO SRI LANKA" • 35 kW
17855	**DENMARK** — RADIO DANMARK, Via Norway — S • Australasia • 500 kW
	JAPAN — †RADIO JAPAN/NHK, Tokyo-Yamata — S • SE Asia • 300 kW
	NORWAY — R NORWAY INTL, Kvitsøy — S M-Sa • Australasia • 500 kW; S Su • Australasia • 500 kW; S • Australasia • 500 kW
	PAKISTAN — RADIO PAKISTAN, Islamabad — E Africa • 100 kW • ALT. FREQ. TO 15555 kHz; E Africa & S Africa • 100 kW
	UNITED ARAB EMIRATES — UAE RADIO FROM ABU DHABI — S • Australasia • 500 kW; W • E Asia • 500 kW
	USA — †R FREE ASIA — S • S Asia & E Asia
	†VOA, Via Philippines — S • E Asia • 250 kW
17860	**FRANCE** — †R FRANCE INTL, Via French Guiana — C America • 500 kW; M-Sa • C America • 500 kW; Su • C America • 500 kW
(con'd)	

0 1 2 3 4 5 6 7 8 9 10 11 12 13 14 15 16 17 18 19 20 21 22 23 24

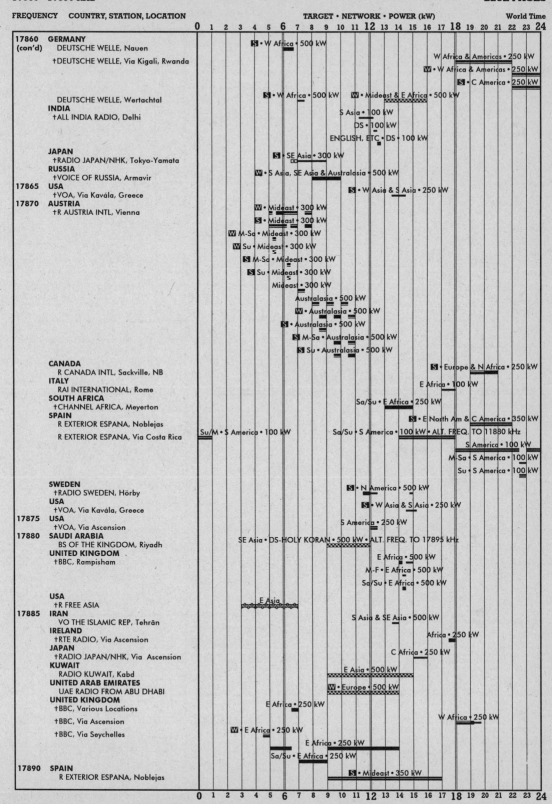

FREQUENCY	COUNTRY, STATION, LOCATION	TARGET • NETWORK • POWER (kW)	World Time

17860 (con'd) **GERMANY**
DEUTSCHE WELLE, Nauen — S • W Africa • 500 kW
†DEUTSCHE WELLE, Via Kigali, Rwanda — W Africa & Americas • 250 kW / W • W Africa & Americas • 250 kW / S • C America • 250 kW
DEUTSCHE WELLE, Wertachtal — S • W Africa • 500 kW / W • Mideast & E Africa • 500 kW

INDIA
†ALL INDIA RADIO, Delhi — S Asia • 100 kW / DS • 100 kW / ENGLISH, ETC • DS • 100 kW

JAPAN
†RADIO JAPAN/NHK, Tokyo-Yamata — S • SE Asia • 300 kW

RUSSIA
†VOICE OF RUSSIA, Armavir — W • S Asia, SE Asia & Australasia • 500 kW

17865 USA
†VOA, Via Kavála, Greece — S • W Asia & S Asia • 250 kW

17870 AUSTRIA
†R AUSTRIA INTL, Vienna — W • Mideast • 300 kW / S • Mideast • 300 kW / W M-Sa • Mideast • 300 kW / W Su • Mideast • 300 kW / S M-Sa • Mideast • 300 kW / S Su • Mideast • 300 kW / Mideast • 300 kW / Australasia • 500 kW / W • Australasia • 500 kW / S • Australasia • 500 kW / S M-Sa • Australasia • 500 kW / S Su • Australasia • 500 kW

CANADA
R CANADA INTL, Sackville, NB — S • Europe & N Africa • 250 kW

ITALY
RAI INTERNATIONAL, Rome — E Africa • 100 kW

SOUTH AFRICA
†CHANNEL AFRICA, Meyerton — Sa/Su • E Africa • 250 kW

SPAIN
R EXTERIOR ESPANA, Noblejas — S • E North Am & C America • 350 kW
R EXTERIOR ESPANA, Via Costa Rica — Su/M • S America • 100 kW / Sa/Su • S America • 100 kW • ALT. FREQ. TO 11880 kHz / S America • 100 kW / M-Sa • S America • 100 kW / Su • S America • 100 kW

SWEDEN
†RADIO SWEDEN, Hörby — S • N America • 500 kW

USA
†VOA, Via Kavála, Greece — S • W Asia & S Asia • 250 kW

17875 USA
†VOA, Via Ascension — S America • 250 kW

17880 SAUDI ARABIA
BS OF THE KINGDOM, Riyadh — SE Asia • DS-HOLY KORAN • 500 kW • ALT. FREQ. TO 17895 kHz

UNITED KINGDOM
†BBC, Rampisham — E Africa • 500 kW / M-F • E Africa • 500 kW / Sa/Su • E Africa • 500 kW

USA
†R FREE ASIA — E Asia

17885 IRAN
VO THE ISLAMIC REP, Tehrān — S Asia & SE Asia • 500 kW

IRELAND
†RTE RADIO, Via Ascension — Africa • 250 kW

JAPAN
†RADIO JAPAN/NHK, Via Ascension — C Africa • 250 kW

KUWAIT
RADIO KUWAIT, Kabd — E Asia • 500 kW

UNITED ARAB EMIRATES
UAE RADIO FROM ABU DHABI — W • Europe • 500 kW

UNITED KINGDOM
†BBC, Various Locations — E Africa • 250 kW
†BBC, Via Ascension — W Africa • 250 kW
†BBC, Via Seychelles — W • E Africa • 250 kW / E Africa • 250 kW / Sa/Su • E Africa • 250 kW

17890 SPAIN
R EXTERIOR ESPANA, Noblejas — S • Mideast • 350 kW

World Time: 0 1 2 3 4 5 6 7 8 9 10 11 12 13 14 15 16 17 18 19 20 21 22 23 24

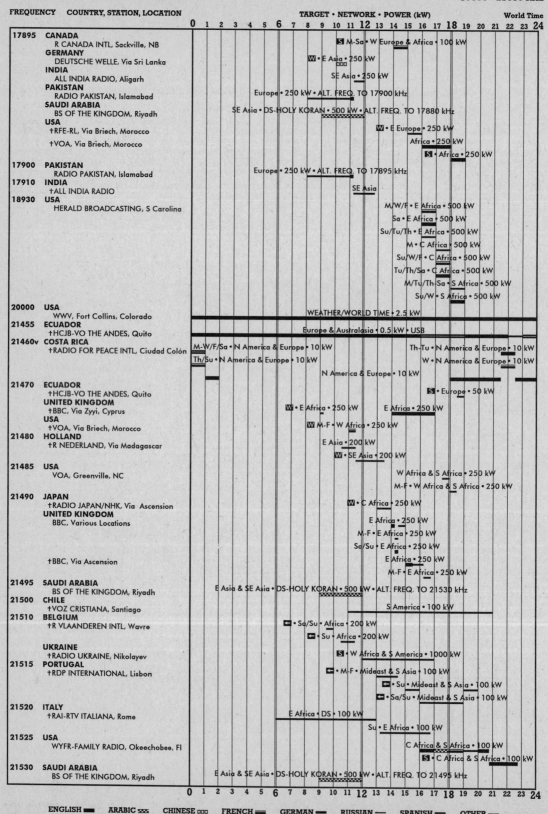

FREQUENCY   COUNTRY, STATION, LOCATION   TARGET • NETWORK • POWER (kW)   World Time

Frequency	Country / Station / Location	Target • Network • Power
17895	**CANADA** R CANADA INTL, Sackville, NB	S • M-Sa • W Europe & Africa • 100 kW
	GERMANY DEUTSCHE WELLE, Via Sri Lanka	W • E Asia • 250 kW
	INDIA ALL INDIA RADIO, Aligarh	SE Asia • 250 kW
	PAKISTAN RADIO PAKISTAN, Islamabad	Europe • 250 kW • ALT. FREQ. TO 17900 kHz
	SAUDI ARABIA BS OF THE KINGDOM, Riyadh	SE Asia • DS-HOLY KORAN • 500 kW • ALT. FREQ. TO 17880 kHz
	USA †RFE-RL, Via Briech, Morocco	W • E Europe • 250 kW
	†VOA, Via Briech, Morocco	Africa • 250 kW
		S • Africa • 250 kW
17900	**PAKISTAN** RADIO PAKISTAN, Islamabad	Europe • 250 kW • ALT. FREQ. TO 17895 kHz
17910	**INDIA** †ALL INDIA RADIO	SE Asia
18930	**USA** HERALD BROADCASTING, S Carolina	M/W/F • E Africa • 500 kW
		Sa • E Africa • 500 kW
		Su/Tu/Th • E Africa • 500 kW
		M • C Africa • 500 kW
		Su/W/F • C Africa • 500 kW
		Tu/Th/Sa • C Africa • 500 kW
		M/Tu/Th/Sa • S Africa • 500 kW
		Su/W • S Africa • 500 kW
20000	**USA** WWV, Fort Collins, Colorado	WEATHER/WORLD TIME • 2.5 kW
21455	**ECUADOR** †HCJB-VO THE ANDES, Quito	Europe & Australasia • 0.5 kW • USB
21460v	**COSTA RICA** †RADIO FOR PEACE INTL, Ciudad Colón	M-W/F/Sa • N America & Europe • 10 kW
		Th/Su • N America & Europe • 10 kW
		Th-Tu • N America & Europe • 10 kW
		W • N America & Europe • 10 kW
		N America & Europe • 10 kW
21470	**ECUADOR** †HCJB-VO THE ANDES, Quito	S • Europe • 50 kW
	UNITED KINGDOM †BBC, Via Zyyi, Cyprus	W • E Africa • 250 kW
		E Africa • 250 kW
	USA †VOA, Via Briech, Morocco	W M-F • W Africa • 250 kW
21480	**HOLLAND** †R NEDERLAND, Via Madagascar	E Asia • 200 kW
		W • SE Asia • 200 kW
21485	**USA** VOA, Greenville, NC	W Africa & S Africa • 250 kW
		M-F • W Africa & S Africa • 250 kW
21490	**JAPAN** †RADIO JAPAN/NHK, Via Ascension	W • C Africa • 250 kW
	UNITED KINGDOM BBC, Various Locations	E Africa • 250 kW
		M-F • E Africa • 250 kW
		Sa/Su • E Africa • 250 kW
	†BBC, Via Ascension	E Africa • 250 kW
		M-F • E Africa • 250 kW
21495	**SAUDI ARABIA** BS OF THE KINGDOM, Riyadh	E Asia & SE Asia • DS-HOLY KORAN • 500 kW • ALT. FREQ. TO 21530 kHz
21500	**CHILE** †VOZ CRISTIANA, Santiago	S America • 100 kW
21510	**BELGIUM** †R VLAANDEREN INTL, Wavre	Sa/Su • Africa • 200 kW
		Su • Africa • 200 kW
	UKRAINE †RADIO UKRAINE, Nikolayev	S • W Africa & S America • 1000 kW
21515	**PORTUGAL** †RDP INTERNATIONAL, Lisbon	M-F • Mideast & S Asia • 100 kW
		Su • Mideast & S Asia • 100 kW
		Sa/Su • Mideast & S Asia • 100 kW
21520	**ITALY** †RAI-RTV ITALIANA, Rome	E Africa • DS • 100 kW
		Su • E Africa • 100 kW
21525	**USA** WYFR-FAMILY RADIO, Okeechobee, Fl	C Africa & S Africa • 100 kW
		S • C Africa & S Africa • 100 kW
21530	**SAUDI ARABIA** BS OF THE KINGDOM, Riyadh	E Asia & SE Asia • DS-HOLY KORAN • 500 kW • ALT. FREQ. TO 21495 kHz

ENGLISH ▬   ARABIC ≈≈≈   CHINESE □□□   FRENCH ▬   GERMAN ▬   RUSSIAN ═   SPANISH ▬   OTHER ▬